MISALIGNMENT: The New Financial Order and the Failure of Financial Regulation

MISALIGNMENT: The New Financial Order and the Failure of Financial Regulation

Joel Seligman

Wolters Kluwer

Published by Wolters Kluwer in New York.

Wolters Kluwer Legal & Regulatory U.S. serves customers worldwide with CCH, Aspen Publishers and Kluwer Law International products.

Printed in the United States of America

ISBN 978-1-5438-2956-3

SUSTAINABLE FORESTRY INITIATIVE
Certified Chain of Custody
Promoting Sustainable Forestry
www.sfiprogram.org

About Wolters Kluwer Legal & Regulatory U.S.

Wolters Kluwer Legal & Regulatory U.S. delivers expert content and solutions in the areas of law, corporate compliance, health compliance, reimbursement, and legal education. Its practical solutions help customers successfully navigate the demands of a changing environment to drive their daily activities, enhance decision quality and inspire confident outcomes.

Serving customers worldwide, its legal and regulatory portfolio includes products under the Aspen Publishers, CCH Incorporated, Kluwer Law International, ftwilliam.com and MediRegs names. They are regarded as exceptional and trusted resources for general legal and practice-specific knowledge, compliance and risk management, dynamic workflow solutions, and expert commentary.

For Mary

The symmetry is now complete

Contents

Preface: In a Time of Crisis

The financial implications of the 2019–2020 coronavirus pandemic (COVID-19) were still fast developing as this volume goes to print. By May 2020, 40 million Americans had filed for unemployment in six weeks, a breathtakingly high figure, one-fourth of the United States workforce.

Years from now historians will have a far greater capacity to fully understand the health crisis, the related financial crisis, the effectiveness of the governmental response and how COVID-19 will alter the United States and global societies.

It is not too soon, however, to recognize how similar critical aspects of the Federal government response to the COVID-19 pandemic were to the 2007–2009 Financial Meltdown and the earlier financial regulatory emergencies that are the topic of this book.

First, we were unprepared. Unprepared, not just in the sense that a planning office in the White House that addressed health emergencies had been closed. But more fundamentally in terms of the alignment of federal and state government agencies to address either the health emergency or the financial crisis. If there was one word that typified the initial months of government response it was improvisation. To be sure, because of the 2007–2009 Financial Meltdown, the federal government toolbox of responses, including massive federal aid programs, was better understood. But in terms of coordination of the White House, the Treasury, Congress, and state governments, there was little crisis planning, too often a confused sense of who is in charge, that led to a series of hastily improvised plans that often equally hastily were soon changed.

Second, we were again painfully reminded how fragile our economy and indeed American democracy in fact are. The fragility of our government is particularly evident during times of crisis. The United States Constitution with its emphasis on separation of branches, checks and balances, and federalism was originally designed to prevent the emergence of tyrants. Our Constitution is not designed for crisis management. This lack of Constitutional emergency mechanisms has been coincident with some of the finest moments in our history such as leadership during the Civil War and World War II, but it also has led to periods of extreme overreaction such as the invasions of civil liberties after World War I and II and the tendency of anxious leaders to stretch the truth, if not fully invent it.

Third, a key mechanism to effectively respond in crises, whether war, health, or financial is for a bipartisan governmental response with all consequential leaders in one way or another "at the table." The most effective emergency response in our nation's history, that of Franklin D. Roosevelt during World War II, began with Roosevelt effectively ending partisan politics for war planning to secure the most talented business, labor, governmental, and academic leaders for the War effort. The failure to rapidly build a bipartisan response during the COVID-19 Pandemic and related financial emergency, no doubt, will be highlighted by historians and policy analysts as a critical shortcoming. Too often rancor and suspicion substituted for what should have been a unified effort to confront an unprecedented emergency.

Fourth, the massive deficits of the federal government as of May 2020, $25 trillion or over 80 percent of our gross domestic product, will grow even more threatening to our way of life in the decades to come. By late April 2020, the 2020 annual deficit was estimated to be another $3.8 billion with little likelihood that this astonishingly high number will soon decline. There either will have to be massive cuts in federal expenditures or massive increases in taxation to cover the ever rising cost of our deficit. Our social safety net with unemployment, Social Security, and healthcare will be threatened at the federal level as will be infrastructure, education, and national and local security at all levels of government.

This is the ultimate consequence of precipitous federal spending for decades without any plan to reduce the overall size of our deficit. It is heuristic to compare current policies with those of Roosevelt and his Secretary of Treasury Henry Morgenthau during World War II.

They sought to fund 50 percent of World War II expenditures with higher taxes to minimize the inevitable large deficits that the War would occasion.

I wrote this book convinced that in studying the past we can better prepare for our future. I retain that hope, but with the awareness that the COVID-19 Pandemic and associated financial emergency underline how much we have yet to learn.

In *The Transformation of Wall Street: A History of the Securities and Exchange Commission and Modern Corporate Finance*, I wrote a history of the Securities and Exchange Commission from 1929–1933 stock market crash until the enactment of the Sarbanes-Oxley Act in 2002.

Misalignment: The New Financial Order and the Failure of Regulation is a broader account of banking, insurance, and securities regulation from the beginning of the United States through the 2007–2009 financial crisis.

The history of our financial system is a vital part of our national history. In crisis, national politics often have been driven by financial emergencies. At all times in our history, without a fundamental understanding of the relationship of money to politics, the United States political system is not fully comprehensible.

Misalignment presents a Tolstoyian narrative to capture the background of why our financial and economic system melted down during the 2007–2009 Meltdown and to explain what should be done now. The fundamental question is why did our $30 trillion financial system prove so unexpectedly fragile? This is a story that reaches back to the formation of our banking, securities, insurance, and housing regulatory systems, a story of well-intended regulation, typically designed to address specific crises, utterly overwhelmed by a national emergency.

Why did the meltdown of 2007–2009 occur?

By 2007–2009, our systems of financial regulation faced challenges caused by growth and complexity that were unimaginable when the systems were designed. The growth alone was breathtaking. On September 1, 1929, the aggregate value of all securities listed on the New York Stock Exchange was approximately $90 billion. At year-end 2006, the total assets of the United States securities sector equaled $12.4 trillion, the banking sector had assets of $12.6 trillion, and the United States insurance industry held assets totaling $6 trillion.

The 2007–2009 Meltdown was the consequence of a regulatory system too balkanized to succeed. The federal system of regulation included five separate federal depository institutions—the Federal Reserve System, the Office of the Comptroller of the Currency, the Federal Deposit Insurance Corporation, the Office of Thrift Supervision, and the National Credit Union Administration—as well as state banking regulation in each state. We were one of the few countries that separately regulated securities and commodities. Securities regulation, like banking, occurs both at the national and state level. Insurance was regulated solely at the state level. Housing finance was provided in substantial part by the Federal National Mortgage Association (*Fannie Mae*) and Federal Home Loan Mortgage Corporation (*Freddie Mac*) subject to a succession of weak federal housing regulatory agencies. Each of these regulatory systems functioned largely in isolation from each another.

In the 1930s and for several subsequent decades, we achieved a period of alignment between commercial banking, securities firms, and insurance and their regulatory agencies. During this period, this alignment was based upon the atomized regulation of commercial banks, securities, and insurance firms.

In 2008–2009, the New Deal financial regulatory model failed. Our economy melted down. By 2008, there was an urgent need for a fundamental restructuring of United States financial regulation, primarily based on three overlapping immediate causes.

First, an ongoing economic emergency initially rooted in housing and related credit markets was succeeded by the collapse or near collapse of several leading banks, securities firms, insurance companies, and ultimately the broader economy with dramatic declines in stock market prices, a seizing up of debt markets, and rapidly elevated levels of unemployment and a protracted recession.

Second, breakdowns in the enforcement of financial regulation, illustrated by the collapse of Bear Stearns in March 2008, the bankruptcy of Lehman Brothers in September 2008, and the termination of the Securities and Exchange Commission's Consolidated Supervised Enterprise Program later in 2008, ending SEC regulation of the five largest investment holding companies. Nearly simultaneously, federal government conservatorships were created for Fannie Mae and Freddie Mac, which at the time owned approximately 50 percent of the $4 trillion in outstanding residential mortgages, and the Bernie Madoff case, the largest financial fraud in our history, occurred with cumulative losses of approximately $65 billion.

Third, a belated recognition that United States banking, securities, insurance, housing, commodities, and unregulated firms in hedge funds were fundamentally misaligned with then existing federal and state regulation. There long was too little focus on systemic risk. There was poor coordination between the White House, the Department of Treasury, the Federal Reserve Board, and federal and state banking, securities, insurance, and commodities regulators. There were serious gaps and omissions in regulation such as those for hedge funds and derivative securities and little effective planning for the internationalization of finance which, by then, was quite advanced.

The structure of financial regulation that was developed during the 1930s did not keep pace with fundamental changes in finance:

- In the New Deal period, most finance was atomized into separate investment banking, commercial banking, or insurance firms. By 2008, finance was dominated by a New Financial Order of bank and financial holding companies that operated in each of these and cognate areas such as commodities.
- In the New Deal period, the challenge of regulating finance primarily was domestic. By 2008, when credit markets were increasingly reliant on trades originating from abroad, major financial institutions traded simultaneously throughout the world, and information technology had made international money transfers virtually instantaneous, the fundamental challenge was increasingly global.
- In 1930, approximately 1.5 percent of the American public directly owned stock on the New York Stock Exchange. During the first quarter of 2008, approximately 47 percent of U.S. households owned equities or bonds. A dramatic deterioration in stock prices affected the retirement plans and the livelihood of millions of Americans.
- In the New Deal period, the choice of financial investments was largely limited to stocks, debt, and bank accounts. By 2008, we lived in an age of increasingly complex derivative instruments, some of which were not well understood by investors and on some occasions by issuers, traders, or counterparties.

The history of financial regulation in the United States is a history of crisis reaction—an uncoordinated series of specialized federal and state laws that responded to specific crises in different financial industries with different objectives and methods. Before the New Deal, uncoordinated regulatory systems were established in banking (beginning with the 1863 creation of the Office of the Comptroller of the Currency and the 1913 Federal Reserve Act), securities (state securities regulation effectively began with Kansas in 1911), and insurance (state law led by New York early in the 20th century). There was little coordination between federal and state financial regulation.

In the New Deal period, we achieved a long-stable model of financial regulation that atomized financial firms and substantially increased investor and depositor protection. For banks, this was largely at the federal level through the Banking Act of 1933, which established the Federal Deposit Insurance Corporation with depository insurance and related legislation that addressed savings and loan institutions. For securities firms, this was through the seven New Deal federal securities law statutes enacted between 1933 and 1940. Insurance regulation remained at the State level through 56 state and territorial insurance laws and the McCarran-Ferguson Act of 1945, which authorized the states to regulate interstate insurance transactions.

A key to atomization was the Glass-Steagall Act of 1933, which divorced commercial banking from securities firms by largely prohibiting financial institutions to be in both domains.

For six decades after World War II, the United States experienced sustained growth and only modest economic perturbations through the combination of overall oversight of fiscal and monetary policy administered by the Executive Branch, Federal Reserve Board, and financial regulation administered by the separate regulatory systems generally aligned with commercial banking and savings and loans, the securities industry, and insurance. Professor David Moss of the Harvard Business School wrote in 2011:

> The simple truth is that New Deal financial regulation worked. In fact, it worked remarkably well. Banking crises essentially disappeared after 1933 . . . without *any* apparent reduction in economic growth. Not only was the period 1933-1980 one of unusually strong growth, but the growth was broad based, associated with stable or *falling* income inequality, rather than with the *rising* inequality that took hold after 1980.

After World War II, the New Deal financial regulatory model deteriorated. In 1956, the Bank Holding Company Act, as subsequently amended and implemented, authorized banks to form holding companies that held securities, insurance, and other nonbank companies. Step by step the separation of commercial banking from investment banking dissolved. For a long time, one generalization was safe— public sale of securities was underwritten by investment banks. National banks and national bank holding companies were prohibited from underwriting the public sale of securities. In 1984, the United States Supreme Court approved the acquisition by a bank holding company of a securities broker. In 1999, the Glass-Steagall Act was repealed by the Gramm- Leach-Bliley Act, ending the historic barrier between commercial and investment banking.

Similar steps were taken to allow insurance corporations to operate in investment fields, illustrated by AIG, the American International Group, the large life and property and casualty insurer, that formed a Financial Products Division that ultimately operated self-destructively in credit default swaps and other derivative securities.

Vast areas of finance evolved outside of regulation, including mortgage originators such as Countrywide, which packaged mortgages, sold them to investment banks that in turn would market them to institutional clients.

The Commodities Futures Modernization Act of 2000 authorized the trading of financial futures in an unregulated environment. Nearly simultaneously, hedge funds and private equity funds, not subject to either banking or securities regulation, became an increasingly prominent force in purchasing private businesses.

Compounding an increasingly byzantine regulatory structure was regulatory arbitrage. By 2008, there were several competing bank regulators. Banks could choose to be regulated by the most accommodating federal or state regulator. Trading in securities could be conducted indirectly through financial futures subject to the Commodities Futures Trading Commission, not the Securities and Exchange Commission (*SEC*). Most retirement investments were regulated by the Department of Labor, not the SEC.

The New Deal financial regulatory structure deteriorated over several decades, largely because of the transformation of the leading financial firms into a New Financial Order that operated simultaneously in banking, securities, and insurance and in unregulated areas such as hedge funds, derivative and swap financial instruments simultaneous with the evisceration of legal restrictions that limited financial firms to a single core industry. Financial regulation became more fragmented, less able to effectively regulate the financial supermarkets that had gathered force during the prior four decades. The countervailing power of federal regulation achieved in the New Deal period was substantially reduced.

No event better crystalized this deterioration than the financial debacle of 2007–2009, during which stock indices fell 55 percent, debt markets did not function for a sustained period, and systemic breakdowns occurred in financial enforcement. To prevent a total meltdown, Congress and the Executive Branch engineered a series of rescue initiatives including the 2008 Troubled Asset Relief Program of $700 billion and Obama administration $787 billion stimulus program that provided support for firms as variegated as leading commercial banks, leading securities firms, insurance giant AIG, and the auto industry. In 2010, the Dodd-Frank Wall Street Reform and Consumer Protection Act was enacted.

There is a myopia in analysis of the 2007–2009 Meltdown. The Meltdown was not primarily caused by banks too big to fail, corporate cupidity, conflicts besetting credit rating agencies, securitization of mortgages resulting in neither mortgage originators nor securities firms having "skin in the game," or incompetence by the Department of Treasury, the White House or the regulatory agencies. To be sure, these were proximate causes that contributed to the crisis.

The principal ultimate cause of the 2008–2009 Meltdown was the misalignment of the leading financial firms with the federal regulatory structure. This misalignment was aggravated by new financial products that could convert into securities financial instruments long outside of financial regulation such as home mortgages, as well as the globalization of finance and a technological revolution that made it possible to electronically trade anywhere with breathtaking speed that undercut the historic significance of self-regulatory institutions such as the New York Stock Exchange.

The legislative response to the 2007–2009 financial meltdown was the enactment of the Dodd-Frank Wall Street Reform and Consumer Protection Act of 2010. Dodd-Frank is long—some 845 pages in its official version. But the length was explicable given its 16 titles addressing banks and bank holding company securities; commodities and mortgage regulation; provisions to prevent banks too big to fail by requiring the adoption of Orderly Liquidation Plans for the banks when they reach specified levels of dysfunction; creation of a new Bureau of Consumer Financial Protection; regulation of previously unregulated areas such as hedge fund investment advisers and derivative securities; strengthening of payment clearance and settlement; and tightening the regulation of credit ratings, asset-backed securities and corporate governance.

Dodd-Frank was notable for a change in the objectives of financial regulation to emphasize systemic risk rather than regulation by industry sector. The Act created the Financial Stability Oversight Council, with members from each relevant federal regulatory agency and empowered the Council to require new capital, liquidity, and risk management standards, for banks and other covered financial institutions.

Dodd-Frank also addressed critical gaps in prior financial regulation by empowering the SEC to regulate investment advisers to hedge funds and other private equity funds, authorizing the SEC and CFTC to regulate swap transactions, and enhancing SEC authority to regulate credit rating agencies.

Dodd-Frank has many laudable features such as those requiring covered institutions to have higher minimum capital ratios. But Dodd-Frank overall is inadequate for the challenges of a financial system dominated by a New Financial Order.

The most consequential neglected imperative was to create a regulatory system that provides countervailing powers to the financial supermarkets it regulates. Dodd-Frank largely builds on the structure of the earlier financial regulatory agencies. The Act strengthens the SEC, the CFTC, the Department of the Treasury, the Office of the Comptroller, the Federal Reserve System, and the FDIC. This is not surprising. Much of the text of the Act appears to have been written by their staffs. Only one agency — the late unlamented Office of Thrift Supervision — was abolished. Only one new agency — the Bureau of Consumer Financial Protection — was established, although within existing agencies and departments, there are a plethora of new required offices as well as broadened jurisdiction.

This then is the paradox of the current federal financial regulatory model: Since the Stock Market Crash of 1929–1933, no set of regulators was so incompetent in predicting a financial catastrophe, so slow in response, so rigid in regulatory approach, so inadequate in enforcing existing law as the financial regulators during the 2007–2009 crisis. Yet the principal winners in the Dodd-Frank Act were the same regulators who so spectacularly failed.

There remain critical gaps and omissions in the new law. Banking and securities regulation today are subject to a concurrent system of federal and state regulation with the largest firms generally subject to federal regulation and intrastate firms generally subject only to state law. Insurance is regulated by 56 states, the District of Columbia, and territorial insurance commissions. The logic by which banks and securities firms are subject to federal regulation — the difficulty of a state enforcing laws across state lines, the likelihood that regulated firms would seek regulation from the most accommodating state, the problems of coordinated regulation — also apply to insurance.

Federal and state regulation remains widely disparate in their objectives. Dodd-Frank emphasizes systemic risk reduction, stability of the overall system, and eliminating expectations of federal intervention to shield shareholders, creditors, and others from losses in the event of catastrophic failures. Bank regulation generally is predicated on protection of the safety and soundness of depository institutions. Securities regulation focuses on investor protection. Dodd-Frank also addresses consumer protection. There is a cacophony of objectives, predictable given the crisis response nature of financial regulation over a 160-year-period.

Dodd-Frank did not change the structure or objectives of the constituent agencies and departments, but attempted to build a superstructure through the Financial Stability Oversight Council (*FSOC*) to apply systemic risk reduction and other Dodd-Frank objectives to all federal financial regulators. The problem with this approach is that the real regulatory power remains in the Department of Treasury and the financial regulatory agencies. FSOC's powers generally are not command and control — but rather the more limited authority to make recommendations to resolve a dispute among two or more members when "a member agency has a dispute with another member agency about the respective jurisdiction over a particular bank holding company, nonbank financial or financial activity or product. . . ." Only once in its first five years did the FSOC use its powers to recommend harmonization of rulemaking at a single regulatory agency and, in that case, it at best achieved partial success. The FSOC is largely a monitor, rather than a control entity or arbitrator.

A related question unresolved is the appropriate model for regulation in each federal regulatory department or agency. Should financial regulation be centralized and expressly made part of the

Executive Branch in an agency such as the Department of Treasury? Or should the emphasis on attempting to have regulation be apolitical be preserved with independent regulatory agencies such as the Federal Reserve System or the SEC? Dodd-Frank did not effectively address the implications of either model other through than the limited Financial Stability Oversight Council coordination.

Several efforts to strengthen the existing regulatory agencies were rebuffed. The Federal Reserve System, for example, is self-funding and can set competitive salary levels for its employees and expand its staff consistent with regulatory needs. The SEC and other financial regulatory agencies are subject to annual appropriations from Congress and go through binge-purge cycles in which they are underfunded and have higher staff turnover than the Federal Reserve System. For former Congressman Barney Frank, a legislative leader in the enactment of Dodd-Frank, the failure to achieve agency self-funding was an important failure.

A separate issue of consequence to federal regulation involves agencies with overlapping or competitive functions. For decades, proposals have been made to combine the SEC and CFTC, both of which regulate financial products that can substitute for each other (securities on the part of the SEC, financial futures and swaps on the part of the CFTC) and often have been bogged down in jurisdictional disputes or litigation brought by covered firms. Similarly, proposals have been made to combine federal banking agencies including the Federal Reserve System, the Office of the Comptroller of the Currency, the Federal Deposit Insurance Commission, and the National Credit Union Administration. Dodd-Frank did end the Office of Thrift Supervision, but this at most was a partial solution to a broader problem of overlapping regulation.

Why has federal financial regulation been so hamstrung? The principal culprit has been the committee system in Congress under which several separate Senate and House Committees have jurisdiction over competitive regulatory agencies and usually have proven unwilling to surrender it. Congressional turf battles have made it virtually impossible to enact a coherent legislative model—why do we have so many federal financial regulators, parallel systems of state banking and securities regulation, exclusive state insurance regulation, additional self-regulatory organizations such as stock exchanges and the Municipal Securities Rulemaking Board? Congress has orchestrated increased limitations on rulemaking and regulatory agency action through more demanding standards of judicial review that further hamstring the regulatory agencies' abilities to respond to crisis.

The Dodd-Frank Act at best is a halfway house that is inadequate to effectively address misalignment. The failure of the Dodd-Frank Act to address the structure of financial regulation was its most conspicuous failure. This volume concludes with a plan for a fundamentally different approach to financial regulation that is more likely to avoid financial meltdowns such as 2007–2009 in the future and minimize financial perturbations over time.

It is particularly urgent that our system of financial regulation be addressed now. As Columbia Law Professor Jack Coffee wrote in a 2018 paper entitled *The Retreat from Systemic Risk Regulation*: "Since 2012 and the passage of the JOBS Act, regulatory and legislative movements in the United States have been almost entirely in the direction of deregulation." In May 2018, Congress enacted the Economic Growth, Regulatory Relief and Consumer Protection Act, which accelerated the Trump Administration efforts to dismantle key protections in Dodd-Frank. The Act, among other things, substantially broadened exemptions from Dodd-Frank, including the Volcker Rule which partially succeeded the Glass-Steagall Act separation of commercial and investment banking.

A decade after the 2007–2009 crisis, former Federal Reserve Chair Ben Bernanke, former New York Federal Reserve President and later Treasury Secretary Tim Geithner, and former Treasury Secretary Hank Paulson, the three leaders in responding to the 2007–2009 debacle, warned in a brief history, *Firefighting*, about the Fire Next Time. They have no doubt that there will be future financial crises. Bernanke, Geithner, and Paulson wrote that the safeguards such as minimum capital requirements in place to avoid a panic are stronger than they were in 2007. These requirements are applied to 88 percent of the financial system in contrast to before the crisis when only the assets of commercial banks, some 42 percent of the assets in the financial system, were subject to significant capital constraints. But Bernanke, Geithner, and Paulson stressed the federal government now has a weaker emergency arsenal than it did before the 2007–2009 crisis. Crisis managers today "lack the power to inject capital, guarantee liabilities, or purchase assets without going to Congress. The Treasury has lost its power to rescue individual firms and faces new constraints on its lending powers, while the Fed has lost its ability to use the Exchange Stabilization Fund for guarantees."

Their basic point: "Crisis managers of tomorrow will have less authority and less flexibility to take action to support the financial crisis than we had."

A future deficit spending crisis already is apparent. Peacetime debt now over 80 percent of our gross domestic product and fast growing is a relatively recent phenomenon. President Franklin Delano Roosevelt in adopting a Keynesian approach to national fiscal policy acted on the belief that deficit spending only would be necessary during war or economic emergency. As late as the beginning of Ronald Reagan's presidency in 1981, national debt was less than $1 trillion. Under Reagan and President George H.W. Bush, debt quadrupled from $997 billion to $3.77 trillion held by the public at the start of the Clinton administration in 2001. Clinton would begin the process of debt reduction with tax increases and budget cuts that led to a $452.7 billion reduction in the national debt between 1998 and 2000, reducing the national debt held by the public to $3.32 billion.

The decision by President George W. Bush to reverse the Clinton administration's glide path towards zero debt by the 2009 fiscal year is one of the most consequential political decisions in our history. The assertion by Bush Vice President Dick Cheney in 2004 that "Reagan proved that deficits don't matter" characterized a mindset of short-term political expediency, and long-term economic folly. As with Reagan, the second President Bush doubled the nation's debt during his eight years in office, largely during a booming economy, the time Keynes had stressed that debt should be reduced.

We have seen this tragedy before. Yale historian Paul Kennedy memorably wrote in the Epilogue of his *The Rise and Fall of the Great Powers: Economic Change and Military Conflict from 1500 to 2000*:

> [I]t has been a common dilemma facing previous "number-one" countries that even as their relative economic strength is ebbing, the growing foreign challenges to their position have compelled them to allocate more and more of their resources into the military sector, which in turn squeezes out productive investment and, over time, leads to the downward spiral of slower growth, heavier taxes, deepening domestic splits over spending priorities, and a weakening capacity to bear the burdens of defense.

To paraphrase Bernanke, Geithner, and Paulson: There will be a Fire Next Time.

We are not ready for it.

J.S.
May 2020

MISALIGNMENT: The New Financial Order and the Failure of Financial Regulation

Wolters Kluwer

1

Meltdown — The Financial Debacle of 2007–2009

The greatest financial crisis of the past century was popularly known as the Stock Market Crash of 1929. Between September 1, 1929, and July 1, 1932, the value of all stocks listed on the New York Stock Exchange shrank from a total of nearly $90 billion to just under $16 billion — a loss of 83 percent. In a comparable period, bonds listed on the New York Stock Exchange declined from a value of $49 billion to $31 billion. "The annals of finance," the Senate Banking Committee would write, "present no counterpart to this enormous decline in security prices." Nor did these figures, staggering as they were, fully gauge the extent of the 1929–1932 stock market crash. During the post-World War I decade, approximately $50 billion of new securities were sold in the United States. Approximately half, or $25 billion, would prove near or totally valueless. Leading "blue chip" securities, including General Electric, Sears, Roebuck, and U.S. Steel common stock, would lose over 90 percent of their value between selected dates in 1929 and 1932.[1]

The response of the federal and state governments, largely developed during the New Deal, was to fashion a comprehensive financial regulatory system with five federal regulatory agencies (the Federal Reserve Board, the Federal Depository Insurance Corporation (*FDIC*), the Office of the Comptroller of the Currency (*OCC*), the Office of Thrift Supervision (*OTS*), and the National Credit Union Administration) and state banking commissions regulating banks, savings and loans, and credit unions; the Securities and Exchange Commission (*SEC*), Financial Industry Regulatory Authority, and state securities commissions regulating securities; the Commodity Futures Trading Commission regulating financial futures; state insurance commissions regulating insurance; and the Federal Housing Financial Agency overseeing housing finance.[2]

Before 1929–1933, major financial crises had occurred frequently in United States history—in 1792, 1797, 1819, 1837, 1857, 1873, 1893, and 1907.[3] After the Great Crash of 1929–1933, between 1934 and 2007, a period over 70 years, there was no comparable financial calamity.[4]

Then in 2007–2009, this financial regulatory model spectacularly failed. Between October 9, 2007 and March 9, 2009, the Dow Jones Industrial Average fell from 14,146.43 to 6547 or 54 percent.[5] Global stock market values declined approximately $35 trillion between selected dates in 2008 and 2009.[6] While there was no Banking Holiday as in 1933, credit markets dried up or froze for many firms and individuals for a sustained period of time. Ford and Chrysler traded at $1 per share, Bank of America at $3, a collapse of 90 percent in six months.[7]

Unemployment grew from approximately 4.5 percent in the summer of 2007 to 10.1 percent in October 2009 and remained above 8 percent for the next three years, the longest stretch of unemployment above 8 percent in the United States since the Great Depression, with total job losses of approximately 8.8 million.[8] During the last four months of 2008, 2.4 million jobs were lost. During the final six months of 2009, 3.8 million jobs were lost, a staggering average job loss of 620,000 jobs per month during these 10 months.[9] When the Final Report of the National Commission on the Causes of the Financial and Economic Crisis in the United States was published in 2011, it reported that there were "... more than 26 million Americans out of work, cannot find full-time work, or have given up looking for work. About four million families have lost their homes to foreclosure and another four and a half million have slipped into the foreclosure process or are seriously behind on their mortgages."[10]

Median household net worth fell by $49,000 per family or by nearly 39 percent between 2007 and 2010.[11] Significantly contributing to the collapse of median net worth was a 32 percent decline in home prices between their peak in 2006 to their low point early in 2009.[12] In aggregate, households collectively were estimated to have lost approximately $17 trillion from the first quarter 2007 to the first quarter of 2009 in household net worth, with about $5.6 trillion due to declining home prices and the remaining due to the declining value of financial assets.[13] In addition, from the 2007–2009 meltdown output losses were estimated to be over $10 trillion.[14]

The annual federal deficit exploded, growing from $459 billion in 2008 to $1.413 trillion in 2009.[15]

For the United States economy, this was a near total meltdown, a dramatic failure of government and private mechanisms to prevent catastrophe or near catastrophe occurring.

As with the Stock Market Crash of 1929–1933, the 2007–2009 meltdown initially moved in slow motion.

The meltdown began in housing.

The Housing Bubble

For a long period, the dominant method of home purchase had involved a bank or savings and loan lending to home purchasers and typically receiving a down payment of 20 percent or more, often for a term of 30 years. The bank would conduct due diligence on each loan and have "skin in the game." The bank would be the ultimate owner of the home in the case of a default.[16]

This approach to home mortgages was largely supplanted in the decades before the 2007–2009 meltdown by a more complex system of mortgage finance. Mortgages often were originated by mortgage originators such as Countrywide and then sold to one of two government-sponsored enterprises (*GSEs*): the Federal National Mortgage Association, popularly known as Fannie Mae, or the Federal Home Loan Mortgage Corporation, popularly known as Freddie Mac, which then resold most mortgages. Alternatively, mortgages could be originated by banks and savings and loans and sold to investment banks who securitized the loans and resold them to investors throughout the world. Pivotal to the process of securitization were positive credit ratings to assure investors of the quality of the mortgaged-backed securities, and derivative securities which in theory reduced the risk of holding tranches of mortgage-backed securities.

Key actors in the transformation to the new system of mortgage finance were Fannie Mae and Freddie Mac. Fannie Mae had initially been chartered in 1938 to purchase mortgages insured by the Federal Housing Administration or later by the Veterans Administration. This was a New Deal effort to address a foreclosure crisis. Through the Great Depression as much as 25 percent of mortgages were in default. Fannie was required to adhere to the Federal Housing Administration's underwriting standards. To purchase mortgages, Fannie Mae borrowed. By 1968, Fannie's debt had grown to $7.2 billion when the Johnson administration and Congress changed its status from a government agency to a for-profit, shareholder-owned, publicly traded *GSE* and removed Fannie's debt from the federal budget.

In 1970, Freddie Mac, a second GSE, was created to purchase mortgages from thrift institutions. The 1970 legislation authorized both Fannie and Freddie to purchase fixed-rate mortgages not backed by the Federal Housing Administration or Veterans Administration.

The two GSEs long had a dual mission: Support the housing market and maximize returns for shareholders. They were, as Ben Bernanke, Chair of the Federal Reserve, Tim Geithner, President of the New York Federal Reserve Bank and Hank Paulson, Treasury Secretary, later wrote: "Strange hybrids. They had federal charters to promote affordable home ownership, but they were also lucrative private firms that dominated the secondary mortgage markets." In the housing market, Congress gave Fannie and Freddie significant advantages: Exemption from state and local taxes and the ability to borrow from the Treasury at below market rates. In addition, Fannie and Freddie were allowed to retain a lower amount of capital than commercial banks — 0.45 percent to back their guarantees of mortgage-backed securities and 2.5 percent for mortgages they retained in their portfolios.[17] The lower borrowing cost for Fannie and Freddie meant that they also were incentivized to retain mortgages for their own portfolios as well as purchasing, guaranteeing, and selling mortgages. By year end 2009, Fannie or Freddie owned or guaranteed $5.39 trillion in mortgages, of which 27 percent or $1.71 trillion was retained in their portfolios as an investment. With their low borrowing costs and related underwriting standards, Fannie and Freddie were highly profitable during the 1990s. In 2000, for example, Fannie had a return on earnings of 26 percent, Freddie, 39 percent.[18]

In 1992, Congress enacted the Federal Housing Enterprise Finance Safety and Soundness Act, which charged the GSEs with an "affirmative obligation to facilitate the financing of affordable housing for low-income and moderate-income families." This was intended to boost home ownership. Between 1993 and 1995, almost 2.8 million households became home owners, nearly doubling the rate of the prior two years. In 1995, President Clinton announced an initiative to boost home ownership from 65.1 to 67.5 percent of families by 2000. By 2004, home ownership would reach 69.2 percent.[19]

Besides encouraging the American dream of home ownership, the affordable housing objective of Fannie Mae and Freddie Mac also was expected to counteract racial discrimination in mortgage lending. Earlier, in 1977, Congress had enacted the Community Reinvestment Act in response to concerns that banks and thrift institutions were refusing to lend in certain neighborhoods or redlining potential borrowers typically on the basis of race or poverty regardless of their creditworthiness. President Clinton in 1993 expressly sought to improve bank compliance with the Community Reinvestment Act. Before 2005, 50 percent or less of GSE loan purchases had to satisfy affordable housing goals. In 2005, the goal was increased above 50 percent.[20]

Fannie Mae Chief Executive Officer James A. Johnson coupled a "moral crusade for justice" and a 1994 $1 trillion commitment to provide housing for 10 million low-to-moderate income families with efforts to reduce underwriting standards. The 1992 Act itself encouraged Fannie and Freddie to buy mortgages with 5 percent or less as a down payment.[21] In 1999, Fannie Mae and Freddie Mac began underwriting subprime mortgages (those with less than 20 percent down payments, good borrower credit histories, and low debt-to-income ratios after a loan was closed).[22]

By the 1990s, Fannie Mae in particular had become legendary for its political influence. Johnson, a former senior advisor to Vice President Walter Mondale, was criticized for Fannie Mae's aggressive lobbying of Congress, spending approximately $100 million between 1989 and 2009 on lobbying and campaign contributions, and the creation of the Fannie Mae Foundation, a charitable organization that in 1979, for example, spent $38.6 million in that year alone on advertising.[23] Secretary of Treasury Hank Paulson in his memoir made a separate point: "The GSEs wielded incredible power on the Hill thanks in no small part to their long history of employing—and enriching—Washington insiders as they cycled in and out of government."[24]

The political influence of Fannie Mae and Freddie Mac long was telling. Paulson elaborated: "Oversight was weak. They had dual regulators: The Department of Housing and Urban Development oversaw their housing mission, while the Office of Federal Housing Enterprise Oversight (*OFHEO*), an overmatched HUD offshoot, created in 1997, kept watch on their finances."[25] Jonathan Koppell, a former OFHEO staff member who became a professor at Yale's School of Management, attributed the weakness of the GSE oversight to their successful lobbying. Koppell wrote in a 2003 book, *The Politics of Quasi-Government*: "Fannie Mae was able to design its regulation. The government sponsored enterprises control their own controller."[26]

This was overstated. In 2003, OFHEO released a Report on an examination of Freddie Mac, stating in part: "Excessive attention and dedication of corporate resources of a government-sponsored enterprise to management of earnings for the purpose of meeting securities market expectations, without an additional, overriding business purpose, is an unsafe and unsound practice." Freddie was required to improve its financial disclosures or to increase its capital up to 30 percent until it remedied its deficiencies.[27] OFHEO subsequently received tacit support from Federal Reserve Chair Alan Greenspan who in 2003 testimony compared the lower levels of capital required at Fannie and Freddie to the higher levels required of commercial banks and savings and loans. The ratio of debt to capital is known as *leverage*. Greenspan opined:

> Without the expectation of government support in a crisis, such leverage would not be possible without a significantly higher case of debt. I should emphasize that Fannie and Freddie, to date, appear to have managed these risks well and we see nothing on the immediate horizon that is likely to create a systemic problem. But to fend off possible future systemic difficulties, which we assess as likely if GSE expansion continues unabated, preventive actions are required sooner rather than later.[28]

When Greenspan testified, the required level of capital for Fannie and Freddie (2.5 percent) translated into a leverage ratio of 40:1. From 2000 to 2007, banks and savings and loans generally had leverage ratios between 16:1 and 22:1.[29]

Later in 2006, OFHEO reported that Fannie Mae had overstated earnings from 1998 through 2002 by $11 billion using accounting misrepresentations. OFHEO required Fannie to improve accounting controls, maintain the same 30 percent capital surplus earlier imposed on Freddie Mac and improve governance. Fannie's Board replaced its CEO, Franklin Raines, and settled SEC and OFHEO enforcement actions by paying $400 million in penalties.[30]

Beginning in 1992, Fannie Mae had increasingly emphasized incentive compensation for its senior executives correlated with earnings growth. Between 1993 and 2000, for example, incentive compensation for its senior executives grew from $8.5 million to $35.1 million. Of the $90 million in executive compensation received by Franklin Raines between 1998 and 2003, $52 million was the result of achieving earnings per share targets.[31]

These aspects of Fannie and Freddie were controversial, often unwise. But the GSEs' most significant roles in the 2007–2008 financial meltdown involved their roles in contributing to a new Mortgage Financial Model, sometimes called the Mortgage Machine.[32]

By 2007, there was a well-established system of shadow banks competing with commercial banks for what earlier had been commercial bank or commercial bank and savings and loan businesses alone. Banks and savings and loans were subject to Federal banking regulation. Shadow banks were not. Shadow banks included Fannie Mae and Freddie Mac, money market funds, insurance companies like AIG, corporate finance companies such as GE Capital or GMAC, mortgage originators, investment banks, and nonbank affiliates of commercial banks. At times during the early 2000s, the total funding of shadow banking exceeded that of traditional banking. In 1970, commercial banks, savings institutions, and credit unions held 54.41 percent of the assets in the financial sector. By 2005, their aggregate share of financial sector assets had declined to 24.22 percent. By 2009, the value of home loans financed by shadow banks was more than twice the value of home loans financed by banks.[33]

There were critical differences between traditional banking and shadow banking, as Tim Geithner, President of the New York Federal Reserve Bank, a banking regulator, in his memoir of the 2007–2009 crisis emphasized: "Huge swaths of the financial system — investment banks, Fannie Mae and Freddie Mac, and many other large firms that behaved like banks without having to obey bank safety and soundness rules—were outside the Fed's jurisdiction as well as the Fed's safety net. These 'nonbanks' or 'shadow banks' were borrowing short and lending long, just like . . . any other bank. But they were not subject to the capital requirements and other safeguards imposed on banks to limit risk, and they did not have deposit insurance to prevent runs, and they would not be able to access the discount window [which provided capital to banks subject to banking law] if they faced runs."[34]

In the brave new world of shadow banking, Fannie Mae and Freddie Mac played a pivotal role in supporting new mortgage origination outside the traditional banking system. Most notorious of the new mortgage originators was Countrywide. Between 1995 and 2007, Countrywide was the largest supplier of loans to Fannie and Freddie, accounting for 29 percent of Fannie's purchases and 16 percent of Freddie's.[35] In 2003, Countrywide sold 72 percent of its loans to Fannie Mae, 45 percent in 2004, and 32 percent in 2005. Countrywide long was rewarded for its aggressive tactics. Between 1994 and 2004, Countrywide's annual earnings increased over tenfold, from $180 million to $2.2 billion.[36]

Underlying Countrywide's growth and that of many similar mortgage originators including New Century Financial, Ameriquest, and American Home Mortgage, and later major commercial and investment banks including Citigroup, Lehman Brothers, and Washington Mutual, were aggressive loan practices including zero down payment loans, and "teaser" adjustable rate mortgages, which initially set low interest rates and after a period of years rates often substantially higher on subprime mortgages.

Alternatively, mortgages with lower quality compared to traditional prime mortgages were denominated Alt-A loans. Alt-A loans might involve reduced documentation, a borrower's obligation to pay interest only, a low down payment or a second mortgage. Initially, Alt-A mortgages, meaning "Alternative to Agencies" could not be sold to GSEs. GSEs eventually became the biggest buyer of Alt-A loans. At its worst, loan practices deteriorated to NINA loans, meaning no income, no assets, or worse, NINJA loans, meaning no income, no job, no assets, and often no documentation.

By 2008, half of all mortgages in the United States, 31 million loans, were subprime or Alt-A. Adjustable rate mortgages whose rates shot up after two years made up 31 percent of all subprime mortgages in 1999 and 69 percent in 2006.[37]

A 2011 study reported that the delinquency rate on Fannie Mae or Freddie Mac prime mortgages (20 percent down, good borrowing credit histories, and low debt-to-income ratios) was 2.0 to 2.6 percent in relevant years. The delinquency rate on Fannie or Freddie subprime, Alt-A or option adjustable rate mortgages was between 13.8 to 45 percent.[38]

On the other hand, the shadow banking system did expand borrower choice, lowered costs, and subjected traditional banks and their regulators to competition. Shadow banking inspired traditional banks to seek new, lower cost or higher yield products. Yale Management and Finance Professor Gary Gorton phrased the advantages of the new system of mortgage finance succinctly as intending "to allow poorer (and disproportionately minority) people and riskier borrowers access to mortgage finance in order to own homes."[39]

Given the high level of profitability of mortgage securities issuance in the period 2000–2007, investment banks including Bear Stearns, Lehman Brothers, Merrill Lynch, and commercial banks including Citigroup and Wachovia were increasingly involved in mortgage securitization. In 2005 and 2006, investment banks were securitizing one-third more mortgage loans than Fannie and Freddie. In total, securitized loans equaled more than 60 percent of total loans in 2005 and 2006. Citigroup's Charles Prince later looked back at this period with regret: "Securitization could be seen as a factory line. As more and more of these subprime mortgages were created as new material for the securitization process, not surprisingly in hindsight, more and more of it was of lower and lower quality. And at the end of that period, the raw material going into it was actually bad quality, it was toxic quality."

As with Fannie Mae and Freddie Mac, incentive compensation was strikingly high in major commercial and investment banks specializing in mortgage-backed securities. Columbia Law School Professor John "Jack" Coffee found that Citigroup, which would lose $27.7 billion in 2008, had a bonus pool of $5.33 billion. Merrill Lynch that year similarly would lose $27.6 billion but had a bonus pool of $3.6 billion. Goldman Sachs, JP Morgan Chase, and Morgan Stanley each would have bonus pools exceeding their 2008 earnings. Bank of America, with $4 billion in earnings, would have a bonus pool equal to $3.3 billion or 83 percent of earnings:

Leading Bank 2008 Bonus Compensation

Institution	Earnings/ (Losses)	Bonus Pool	No. of Employees Receiving Bonus ≥ $3 million	No. of Employees Receiving Bonus ≥ $1 million
Bank of America	$4 billion	$3.3 billion	28	172
Citigroup, Inc.	$(27.7 billion)	$5.33 billion	124	738
Goldman, Sachs Group	$2.322 billion	$4.823 billion	212	953
JP Morgan Chase & Co.	$5.6 billion	$8.693 billion	≥ 200	1626
Merrill Lynch	$(27.6 billion)	$3.6 billion	149	696
Morgan Stanley	$1.707 billion	$4.475 billion	101	428

These numbers, staggeringly high as they were, were dwarfed by the compensation of the leading figures in hedge funds and private equity. Columbia History Professor Adam Tooze calculated that "[i]n 2007, the six top hedge fund managers earned at least a billion dollars each in compensation."

Fannie Mae's response in 2006 to the growing Wall Street competition was to increase its participation in subprime mortgage purchases.[40] To be able to market mortgages with varying levels of risk, Fannie and Freddie popularized securitization. In simple terms, mortgage originators, whether shadow banks such as Countrywide or traditional banks, would assemble a portfolio of mortgages and sell them to Fannie Mae or Freddie Mac or directly to investment banks such as Bear Stearns, Lehman Brothers, or Citigroup. From the point-of-view of the mortgage originator, the sale of the pool of mortgages had advantages: The originator received a fee for the packaging and sale of the mortgages and did not bear the risk of holding loans that might default. If the originator was a commercial bank, the bank also did not need to retain the capital necessary to offset the increased debt.

For investors, mortgage securitization had other advantages. When many mortgages were pooled into one security, a default of a few mortgages in theory would have minimal impact. There was an application of what finance calls *portfolio theory* by which firm specific risk is diversified away in a sufficiently large portfolio of securities.

Tranches of mortgages could be customized for investor preferences. As the National Commission on the Causes of the Financial and Economic Crisis explained: "Structured finance securities could . . . be sliced and sold in portions — known as tranches — which let investors customize their payments. Risk-averse investors would buy tranches that paid off first in the event of default, but had lower yields. Return-oriented investors bought riskier tranches with higher yields." "These securities fetched a higher price than if the underlying loans were sold individually" reported the National Commission, "because the securities were customized to investors' needs, were more diversified and could be easily traded."

Investment banks, in turn, earned fees for issuing mortgage-backed securities, typically to the ultimate buyers of mortgage-backed securities, often pension funds and other institutional investors or overseas sovereign wealth funds or foreign banks. For the investors, tranches of mortgage-backed securities had the advantage over Treasury securities of higher interest rates without much perceived additional risk.[41]

As the demand for mortgage-backed securities increased in the period up to 2007, there often would be an escalating number of tranches in each mortgage pool. In 2006, the National Commission reported $974 million in mortgage-backed securities involving 4499 mortgages were sold by New Century Financial, a California mortgage originator, in a deal labelled *CMLTI 2006-NC²*, to Citigroup. Citigroup then divided the mortgages into 19 tranches, giving each investment a different priority claim on the covered mortgages, a different interest rate and different repayment schedule.[42] Over time, as the number of tranches increased, it became common to characterize the safest tranches as senior securities; the next levels as mezzanine, those that would be paid only if the senior securities had received all of their expected proceeds; and the lowest levels in the paying order as equity tranches, which had the highest interest rates and the highest risk.[43]

The Credit Rating Agencies

To certify the quality of the differentiated tranches of mortgage-backed securities, investment banks relied upon credit ratings agencies, most often Moody's, Standard & Poor (*S&P*) or Fitch, to issue credit ratings. In the S&P classification system, these began with the highest rating AAA, then proceeded through AA, A, BBB and BB and were further denominated by ratings of + or −. Ratings below BBB− were characterized as junk. This did not necessarily mean they could not be sold. Lower ratings meant the issuer would have to pay higher interest payments in the risk adjusted world of modern finance.

In the Citigroup sale of CMLTI 2006-NC^2 mortgages, the three most senior tranches were rated AAA, three were A, three were BBB, the lowest investment grade rating for many institutional investors, and two were BB. Critically, 78 percent of the CMLTI deal, or $737 million, was rated Triple A, which the National Commission on the Causes of the Financial and Economic Crisis reported was typical. "The expectation of safety was important, so the firms structuring securities focused on achieving high ratings."[44] A 2012 article by two University of Toronto School of Management professors calculated for a sample of subprime mortgages between 2000 and 2006, 81 percent initially received AAA− ratings or higher, for resecuritizations, 90 percent did so.[45]

Investment banks in the 2000s popularized new means to compete through financial engineering that could transform low quality mortgages, often graded BBB or A, and repackage them into Collateralized Debt Obligations or CDOs, 80 percent of which would be rated AAA, by selling senior tranches of the mortgage pool that would be given the superior place in the payout order and rely on the size and diversification of the tranche to minimize risk. "Between 2003 and 2007, as housing prices rose 27% nationally and $4 trillion in mortgage-backed securities were created, Wall Street issued nearly $700 billion in CDOs that included mortgage-backed securities as collateral. . . . By 2004, creators of CDOs were the dominant buyers of the BBB-rated tranches of mortgage-backed securities."[46]

The risk of a CDO, in turn, could be reduced, it was believed, by acquiring a credit default swap that could be designed to reimburse a CDO investor for any losses in the CDO in exchange for premium payments. "The credit default swap made the CDOs much more attractive to potential investors because they appeared to be virtually risk free, but it created huge exposure for credit default swap issuers if significant losses did occur," an exposure that would cause grievous harm later to AIG.[47]

Ultimately, financial engineers assembled synthetic CDOs out of credit swaps, effectively transforming a hedging device into an investment gamble. Issuance of synthetic CDOs increased from $15 billion in 2005 to $61 billion in 2006. The National Commission on the Causes of the Financial and Economic Crisis explained:

> Synthetic CDOs were complex paper transactions involving credit default swaps. Unlike the traditional cash CDO, synthetic CDOs contained no actual tranches of mortgage-backed securities, or even tranches of other CDOs. Instead, they simply referenced these mortgage securities and thus were bets on whether borrowers would pay their mortgages. In the place of real mortgage assets, these CDOs contained credit default swaps and did not finance a single home purchase. Investors in these CDOs included "funded" long investors, who paid cash to purchase actual securities issued by the CDO; "unfunded" long investors, who entered into swaps with the CDO, making money if the reference securities performed; and "short" investors, who bought credit default swaps on the reference securities, making money if the securities failed. While funded investors received interest if the reference securities performed, they could lose all of their investment if the reference securities defaulted. . . .
>
> . . . [S]ynthetic CDOs [were] cheaper and easier to create than traditional CDOs at the same time as the supply of mortgages was beginning to dry up. Because there were no mortgage assets to collect and finance, creating synthetic CDOs took a fraction of the time. They also were easier to customize, because CDO managers and underwriters could reference any mortgage-backed security — they were not limited to the universe of securities available for them to buy.[48]

Until it fell apart, the credit rating agency seal of good approval was highly trusted. The AAA rating was considered reassurance that a security was virtually as safe as a Treasury security, which was backed by the full faith and credit of the United States itself. AAA mortgage-backed securities, whether issued by Fannie Mae or Freddie Mac or investment banks, usually were over-collateralized. FDIC Chair Shiela Bair would write in 2012: "'Overcollateralization' was the primary reason the rating agencies routinely gave them Triple-A ratings."[49]

Since 1931, when the Comptroller of the Currency allowed covered banks to report publicly traded bonds with an investment grade rating of BBB or better at book value (the price they paid), credit ratings also had been fortified by a federal government imprimatur of trustworthiness. In 1975, the Securities and Exchange Commission took the first of several similar steps when it specified in its broker-dealer net capital requirements that covered securities had to receive specified credit ratings from a nationally recognized statistical rating organization (*NRSRO*), meaning a credit rating agency such as Moody's, S&P, or Fitch.[50] In 1968, New York City Finance Administrator Roy Goodman characterized the rules applicable to certain credit rating agencies as endowing them with "almost biblical authority." As the Comptroller of the Currency stated in 1977: "Ratings are important because investors generally accept ratings . . . in lieu of consulting a due diligence investigation of the underlying assets."[51]

Many investors such as some pension funds and university endowments relied on the credit ratings because they did not have access to the same data as the rating agencies nor the analytical ability to assess the securities. In the period 1998 to 2004, foreign holdings of GSE securities increased five-fold, from $186 to $875 billion.[52]

The credit rating review process of mortgage-backed securities in retrospect was deeply flawed. Moody's, for example, used three models to rate mortgage-backed securities. The first developed in 1996 applied to residential mortgage-backed securities. A second developed in 2003 applied to prime, jumbo, and Alt-A deals. Only in 2006 did Moody's develop M3 Prime, a model for rating subprime mortgages:

> The models incorporated firm- and security-specific factors, regulatory and legal factors, and macroeconomic trends. The M3 Prime Model let Moody's automate more of the process. Although Moody's did not sample or review individual loans, the company used loan-level information from the issuer. Relying on loan-to-value ratios, borrower creditor scores, originator quality, and loan terms and other information, the model

> simulated the performance of each loan in 1,250 scenarios, including variations in interest rates and state-level unemployment, as well as home price changes.

After the initial quantitative analysis was conducted, the debt issuance would be reviewed by a credit rating committee. But critically, included in the quantitative analysis was a key assumption: "On average, across the scenarios, home prices trended upward at 4% per year. The model put little weight on the possibility prices would fall sharply nationwide." Moody's position at least through 2005 was that there was no national housing bubble. "In June 2005, Moody's updated its approach for estimating default correlation, but it based a new model on trends from the previous 20 years, a period when housing prices were rising and delinquencies were very low. . . ."[53]

In 2008, the SEC would publish harsh conclusions about the credit rating process during this period, criticizing Moody's for failure to verify the accuracy of mortgage information it received from issuers, leaving that work to due diligence firms, failure to retain documentation about how many deals were rated, allowing rating the quality of CDO deals to be compromised by its complexity, having insufficient staff to rate CDOs, as well as rushing some ratings with insufficient review and allowing conflicts of interest to affect rating decisions. Journalist Roger Lowenstein was allowed to review a Countrywide $430 million 2006 debt issuance and found that 43 percent of mortgages were issued to borrowers who did not provide written verification of their incomes.[54] With CDOs, the National Commission on the Causes of the Financial Economic Crisis stated that Moody's "relied almost exclusively on its own ratings of the mortgage-backed securities purchased by the CDOs" rather than looking through the CDOs securities to the underlying subprime mortgages.[55]

In July 2007, during the same month that two Bear Stearns hedge funds involved in mortgage-backed securities failed, S&P, Moody's, and Fitch, in effect, began acknowledging how flawed their credit rating process had been with a massive number of mortgage-backed security downgrades. In 2008, the SEC would report that Moody's had downgraded at least one tranche of 94.2 percent of subprime residential mortgage-backed securities (*RMBS*) it rated in 2006 and 76.9 of all RMBS securities it rated in 2007; S&P had downgraded 44.3 percent of the subprime RMBS tranches it had rated between the first quarter of 2005 and the third quarter of

2007; Fitch had issued downgrades to 1299 of the 3,616 tranches issued in 2006 and the first quarter of 2007.[56]

There were four causes of the disastrous credit rating agency performance. First, the credit rating agencies received high proportions of their revenue from mortgage-backed securities. In 2005, 2006, and 2007, the rating of structured financial products including mortgage-backed securities was responsible for close to one-half of Moody's rating revenues. Second, credit rating agencies were paid by the issuer of securities, which meant built in conflict of interest since issuers sought the highest possible rating for their payments, rather than by the users of ratings. Third, the perceived laxity of the credit rating review process may have contributed to a deterioration of investment bank and GSE underwriting standards. As a Moody team managing director for their CDO unit explained: "The underlying collateral just completely disintegrated below us and we didn't react and we should have.... We had to be looking for a problem. And we weren't looking." They were supposed to be the gatekeeper of the issuance process. They were not.[57] Fourth, in a growing number of cases, the laxity of credit rating agency review contributed to fraud.

Throughout the 2001–2007 period, a real estate boom and housing bubble nonetheless buttressed the mortgage financial model. Between 1995 and 2005, housing starts increased 53 percent from 1.4 million units in 1995 to more than 2 million homes in 2005. As the Federal Reserve Bank cut interest rates early in the new century and mortgage rates fell, home refinancing swelled from $460 billion in 2000 to $2.8 trillion in 2003. Between 2000 and 2003 for credit-worthy home buyers, the interest rate on a 30-year fixed rate mortgage dropped 3 percentage points.[58] Jurist and economist Richard Posner generalized after the 2007–2009 meltdown: "Low interest rates in the early 2000s set the stage for the financial crisis. They caused or more precisely enabled or assisted a housing bubble, a stock market bubble, and a credit bubble. The bursting of the bubbles collapsed the banking system."[59]

Between 2001 and 2007, aggregate mortgage indebtedness increased from $5.3 trillion to $10.5 trillion. Home prices surged increasing, according to the two leading indices, by over 150 and over 200 percent between 2000 and 2006 or 2007. In 2003 to 2005, home prices rose in double digits each year, reaching 15 percent growth in 2005. In 2005, Ben Bernanke, then Chair of President

Bush's Council of Economic Advisers, reported that "house prices have risen by nearly 25 percent over the past two years." A former Lehman Brothers executive believed by 2005: "The U.S. housing market had essentially gone berserk." In hot real estate markets such as San Francisco and Los Angeles, 2005 surveys by Case and Shiller and the *Economist* reported homebuyers expected annual price increases of 14 to 22 percent over the next decade.[60]

The Bubble Bursts

Then, in 2006, accelerating in 2007, the housing bubble burst. Sales of existing homes experienced the sharpest decline in 25 years in 2007. Home prices on average declined 9 percent in 2007, then 17 percent in 2008. Mortgage delinquencies, around 1 percent early in the decade, skyrocketed to 9.7 percent by the end of 2009. In the "sand states" of California, Arizona, Nevada, and Florida, where the housing price surge had been most pronounced, delinquency rates reached 15 percent in late 2009.[61]

As troublesome as the bursting of the housing bubble appeared to be as late as March 2007, Federal Reserve Chair Bernanke testified: "The impact on the broader economy and financial market seemed likely to be contained." Secretary of Treasury Paulson similarly testified: "It looks to me like this housing issue is going to be contained."[62] New York Federal Reserve President Geithner also shared this view. "Subprime was only about one-seventh of the mortgage market, barely $1 trillion of the nation's $55 trillion in financial assets, and it did not appear to be infecting the rest of the credit boom," the Fed Staff reported to him about that time.[63]

By the summer of 2007, the housing bubble was spectacularly bursting. By year's end, the contagion would touch the Nation's leading commercial and investment banks, insurance companies, and hedge funds. The Final Report of the National Commission on the Causes of the Financial and Economic Crisis would generalize:

> Citigroup and Merrill Lynch reported the most spectacular losses, largely because of their extensive collateralized debt obligations (*CDO*) businesses, writing down a total of $23.8 billion and $24.7 billion, respectively, by the end of the year. Billions more in losses were reported by large financial institutions such as Bank of America ($9.7 billion), Morgan Stanley

> ($10.3 billion), JP Morgan ($5.3 billion) and Bear Stearns ($2.6 billion). Insurance companies, hedge funds and other financial institutions collectively had taken mortgage-related losses of about $100 billion.[64]

This was retrospect. The crisis unfolded step-by-step with the Federal Reserve System, among others, largely reacting to events rather than anticipating them. As the Crisis Report put it, "the economy was beginning to show signs of stress. Facing turmoil in the financial markets, declining home prices, and oil prices above $75 a barrel, consumer spending was slowing." Step-by-step, the Fed gradually lowered overnight bank borrowing interest rates in four rate changes to 4.25 percent by December 2007.

Federal Reserve Chair Ben Bernanke, New York Federal Reserve President Tim Geithner, and Treasury Secretary Paulson would generalize about the critical powers that the Fed had in helping to administer our financial system:

> In normal times, the main role of a central bank is to lower or raise interest rates — giving the economy a boost to promote growth or hitting the brakes to avoid inflation. But when confidence erodes and credit markets seize up, central banks can also be the "lender of last resort," providing liquidity to solvent firms when private lenders won't. The Federal Reserve's lender-of-last-resort function, known as the "discount window," offers emergency liquidity to any commercial bank facing a cash crunch. Access to the discount window is intended to allow banks to meet withdrawals by private creditors without having to dump their assets in a destabilizing fire sale.[65]

In June 2007, two hedge funds managed by Bear Stearns, the fifth largest United States investment bank, began to suffer heavy losses. The Bear fund repurchase agreement or repo lenders demanded more collateral or refused to lend. Repo lending originally had involved the sale and repurchase of Treasury Notes. Over time, the collateral for repo loans had become riskier, including mortgage-backed securities. On June 7, Bear froze redemptions by investors in the funds and subsequently propped up the funds with a $1.6 billion loan.

Shortly after Bear Stearns froze redemptions, Merrill Lynch seized more than $850 million of collateral Bear had posted for outstanding repo payments. Ominously "Merrill was able to sell just

$181 million of the seized collateral at auction by July 5 — and at discounts to its face value," reported the Final Report of the National Commission on the Causes of the Financial and Economic Crisis. On July 31, both Bear funds declared bankruptcy and Bear lost most of its loan.[66]

In late July IIKB Deutsche Industriebank discovered that an SIV (an off balance sheet, Structural Investment Vehicle) it ran was having difficulty rolling over its asset-backed commercial paper causing the German government to step in and organize a $4.8 billion rescue.[67] The implications of this failure were far broader. "From its peak of $1.2 trillion on August 8, 2007, the asset-backed commercial paper market would decline by almost $400 billion by the end of 2007."[68]

On August 6, 2007, American Home Mortgage Investment Corporation was bankrupt by its losses on adjustable rate mortgages.[69] Earlier in late July, the AAA portion of the mortgage-related paper had plunged to 45 percent of its face value.[70] On August 3, the Dow Jones Industrial Average fell 300 points after the Chief Financial Officer at Bear Stearns claimed that credit markets were tighter than at any time in 20 years.[71]

On August 9, BNP Paribas, the largest French bank, suspended redemption payments on three investment funds that had fallen 20 percent in fewer than two weeks. Total assets in these funds were $2.2 billion with a third in subprime securities rated AA or higher. BNP Paribas also stated that it was calculating its own fair market value for the funds because "the complete evaporation of liquidity in certain market segments of the U.S. Securitization Market has made it impossible to value certain assets fairly regardless of their quality or credit rating."[72]

"The problem? The market for certain assets, especially those backed by American mortgage loans, had essentially dried up, making it difficult to determine what they were actually worth."[73]

The day after the BNP Paribas suspension of redemption payments, the European Central Bank infused 95 billion in euros (or $130 billion) into overnight lending and reduced interest rates. The Federal Reserve Bank announced that it would "provide liquidity as necessary to facilitate the orderly functioning of markets" and provided $62 billion into the United States financial system.[74]

To Federal Reserve Bank of New York President Timothy Geithner, this was a big deal. As he wrote in *Stress Test*, his memoir of the 2007–2009 financial crisis:

> Wow. My first response to the news was a string of expletives. . . . This wasn't just a little problem on the fringes of the U.S. mortgage market.
>
> I had a sick feeling in my stomach. I knew what financial crises felt like, and they felt like this."[75]

By August 2, 2007, Countrywide, the largest United States mortgage originator, recognized that it would be unable to roll over its commercial paper. To Angelo Mozilo, Countrywide's CEO, "that is our 9/11." On August 6, Mozilo reported to Countrywide's Board, "the secondary market for virtually all classes of mortgage securities . . . had unexpectedly and with almost no warning seized up. . . . The company was unable to sell high-quality mortgage backed securities."[76] On August 14th, Countrywide released its July 2007 Operating Results confirming that foreclosures and delinquencies had increased and loan production fell 14 percent in July. The next day, August 15, Countrywide drew down $11.5 billion from its backup lines of credit, causing investment analysts such as Merrill Lynch's Keith Bruce to switch his "buy" rating issued days before to "sell." He warned that cash pressures could force Countrywide into bankruptcy. Countrywide shares fell 11 percent in one day and had declined 50 percent that year to date. Bank of America provided a short-term fix with a $2 billion investment later in August. Subsequently, in October, Countrywide reported a net quarterly loss of $1.2 billion, its first quarterly loss in 25 years. On January 11, 2008, Bank of America purchased the rest of Countrywide for $4 billion with a press release announcing that it would stop originating subprime loans.[77]

On the morning of August 17, "financial conditions," as Federal Reserve Chairman Ben Bernanke later wrote, "had deteriorated to the point where we're ready to be more aggressive." The Federal Reserve Board announced a one-half percent discount rate cut and opened its Discount Window loans to a broader array of banks. Under applicable law, the Fed could not loan to Countrywide, a holding company and in any event, Bernanke and others at the Fed already feared that Countrywide was insolvent.[78]

While the moves by Bank of America to shore up Countrywide and the Fed's opening up of the Discount Window and lower discount rates provided some stabilization to the markets, the bad news kept coming. On September 19, 2007, the Bank of England announced for the first time it would inject 10 billion pounds (roughly $20 billion) into British money markets, prompted by a bank run on Northern Rock, one of the largest mortgage banks in Great Britain. Soon after the Bank of England's intervention, the British government announced it would guarantee all deposits in Northern Rock. In February 2008, the British government nationalized Northern Rock.[79]

On October 24, Merrill Lynch unexpectedly announced that it would sustain a third quarter loss of $6.9 billion on its CDOs and $1 billion on its subprime mortgages. The $7.9 billion was the largest Wall Street write-down to that date and substantially higher than the $4.5 billion loss that Merrill had warned investors to expect three weeks earlier. Five days later, Merrill Lynch CEO Stanley O'Neal resigned.

Merrill's unexpectedly large losses were the consequence of a strategy articulated in the fall of 2006 to be "bullish on [the subprime] asset class." Merrill Lynch was a leading packager of CDOs. As New York Fed President Timothy Geithner later wrote, "[i]t made billions selling them to investors around the world." Between September 2006 and June 2007, Merrill's retention of super senior CDO tranches had increased three fold from $9.3 billion to $30.4 billion. The net exposure of over $30 billion in CDO positions, that is, the amount of CDO positions left after subtracting of off-setting hedges, was a gamble, Merrill Lynch effectively lost with its October 2007 announcement. The gamble was a calculated one. In 2006, for example, Merrill underwrote $54 billion of CDOs, with $44 billion backed by subprime mortgages, a three fold increase from 2005. When Merrill could not find enough buyers, Merrill kept its CDOs and built up a massive exposure.[80] This occurred over time. Between 2002 and 2007, Merrill Lynch underwrote 100 CDOs, 27 more than runner-up Citigroup. Merrill was aware of the frailty of its position. In August 2007, O'Neal had held merger discussions with Ken Lewis, President of Bank of America, and subsequently Ken Thompson of Wachovia.[81]

A similar story played out at Citigroup within days. In early November, Citigroup announced its total subprime exposure was

$65 billion, some $42 billion more than it had disclosed three weeks earlier. Citigroup further announced that it anticipated taking an $8 to $11 billion loss on its subprime mortgage related holdings. Chuck Prince, Citigroup CEO, resigned, earlier immortalized by his July 2007 *Financial Times* interview in which he stated, "When the music stops, in terms of liquidity, there will be complications. But as long as the music is playing, you've got to get up and dance." As with Stan O'Neal at Merrill, Prince had learned late of Citigroup's CDO related exposures. "Effective communication across businesses was lacking," a Federal regulator later observed.[82]

The 2011 Final Report of the National Commission on the Causes of the Financial and Economic Crisis would conclude: "Citigroup had two key problems: Lack of effective enterprise-wide management to monitor and control risks and a lack of proper infrastructure and internal controls with respect to the creation of CDOs."[83]

There was more to it than that. Tim Geithner explained: "By 2007, Citi's $2 trillion balance sheet was much riskier than it looked.... Citi had stashed another $1.2 trillion in assets off its balance sheet in ways that allowed it to hold virtually no capital in losses in these areas." As with Merrill Lynch, Citi financed some of its off balance sheet securities by issuing commercial paper which it promised to purchase if no outside buyers would do so. In 2007, the market turned against asset-backed commercial paper, shrinking 30 percent in the last six months of that year. Citi had to pay out $25 billion given its earlier assurances.[84]

What was striking in retrospect is how often the financial markets and the federal regulators prematurely concluded that the financial crisis was under control. "Bernanke had made good on his intention to lower interest rates and bankers to think they could muddle through. The stock market rallied in September, and by early October, the Dow reached a new record, just about 14,000."[85] The stock markets had confidence in other steps taken by the Fed. In November 2007, the Fed pumped $47.25 billion in temporary reserves into the banking system. Secretary of Treasury Paulson called this "the biggest injection since 9/11." On November 11, the Fed again cut interest rates by a quarter point. On November 12, the Fed announced that it had established $24 billion in "swap lines" with the European Central Bank and the Swiss Central Bank to increase the supply of dollars to overseas credit markets. On November 13, the Fed announced the creation of the Term Auction Facility (*TAF*) designed to lend funds to depository institutions for terms between 24 and 84 days against a wide array of collateral as an alternative to the Fed discount window. By December 20, the TAF had provided $40 billion in 28- and 35-day credit.[86]

Each of these and other steps addressed symptoms of the crisis. They were not based on a in depth analysis of its causes nor were there steps to that point that addressed such fundamental questions as how systemic financial and economic risk could be materially reduced through more aggressive intervention by financial institution's organization, capital structure, or investments. With the advantage of 20-20 hindsight, the long interval from the Summer of 2007 to September 2008 was the period when inadequate federal regulatory response most consequentially contributed to a near total financial meltdown.

In 2008, the crisis became far more serious. The rat-a-tat-tat of dismal news accelerated. As Federal Reserve Bank President Ben Bernanke wrote in his memoir of the crisis: "A panic was building. And the economy and credit markets were increasingly mired in their own destructive feedback loop — bad economic news, fueled financial turmoil, and the turmoil in turn disrupted the flow of credit that powered economic activity."[87]

Monoline insurers were among the early 2008 victims. The Final Report of the National Commission on the Causes of the Financial and Economic Crisis wrote: "[T]he rating agencies continued to downgrade mortgage-backed securities and CDOs through 2007. By January 2008, as a result of the stress in the mortgage market, S&P had downgraded 3389 tranches of residential mortgage-backed securities and 1383 tranches from 420 CDOs."[88] Many of these tranches were insured by monoline insurers, the two largest of whom, MBIA and Ambank, had a combined $265 billion of guarantees on mortgage securities and other products. On January 18, 2008, Ambank lost its AAA credit rating. MBIA would follow in June 2008. ACA, the smallest monoline, reported a $1.7 billion net loss for 2007. This news was stunning. As its CEO explained: "We never expected losses." Pressured by insurance regulators and the credit rating agencies, MBIA and Ambank raised respectively $1.65 and $1.5 billion in new capital in 2008. Most monolines stopped writing new coverage.[89]

Products insured by the monolines were subject to growing turmoil. Auction-rate securities, issued mostly by state and local governments, student loan authorities, and hospitals, almost always succeeded in placing their securities. On February 14, 2008, an unprecedented 80 percent of the auctions of these securities failed for lack of investor interest. The following week 67 percent of the auctions failed. The Port Authority of New York and New Jersey witnessed its interest rates more than quadruple from 4.3 to 20 percent in a single week in February 2008.[90]

The contagion spread. On February 11, 2008, insurance giant AIG reported in an SEC filing that it had recognized a $3.6 billion write down on holdings of derivatives tied to subprime mortgages. On February 14, Swiss bank UBS reported an $11.3 billion loss for the fourth quarter of 2007, $2 billion of which it attributed to a write-down of its exposure to Alt-A mortgages. On March 3, Thornburgh Mortgage, with $36 billion in assets, was unable to respond to margin calls from anxious creditors demanding additional collateral. The Fed declined to provide emergency relief and Thornburgh failed. On March 6, an investment fund sponsored by the Carlyle Group whose $22 billion portfolio consisted almost entirely of mortgage-backed securities issued and guaranteed by Fannie Mae and Freddie Mac survived by selling nearly $6 billion in assets at fire sale prices.[91]

Bear Stearns

Serious as these events were, they were soon eclipsed by the mid-March near collapse of Bear Stearns, saved by a rescue merger with JP Morgan, which was made possible only because of a $29 billion guarantee from the Federal Reserve Bank. The impact on Bear was devastating. Bear Stearns stock was at $173 per share in January 2007. JP Morgan acquired Bear at $10 per share in March 2008.

Bear was the fifth largest of the United States investment Bank Holding Companies with assets of $395 billion as of November 30, 2007. Bear had made a huge bet on mortgage securities especially the subprime mortgage business with mortgage securitization accounting for 45 percent of the firm's revenues through what economist Alan Blinder termed "a full-service, vertically integrated mortgage machine" that "originated home-mortgage loans, bundled them for securitization, and sold them the resulting securities — profiting on each step in the chain." Between 2000 and 2007, Bear was a top three underwriter of private label mortgage securities.[92]

Repo loans were both the key to Bear Stearn's high level of profitability between 2000 and 2007, and its ultimate demise. Bear used its AAA and AA securities as collateral for repo loans, providing the equivalent to 5 percent capital for each dollar borrowed, achieving 20-to-1 leverage. As the Final Report of the National Commission on the Causes of the Financial and Economic Crisis explained: "With this amount of leverage, a 5% change in the value of the mortgage-backed securities can double the investor's money — or lose all of the initial investment."[93]

Bear Stearns executives were amply rewarded for this level of risk. Its top five executives took home $1.4 billion in cash and stock sales between 2000 and 2008.[94]

In the aftermath of the March 2008 collapse of Bear, there was particular focus on the repo market. "Market participants and regulators now better appreciated how the quality of repo collateral had shifted over time from Treasury notes and securities issued by Fannie Mae and Freddie Mac to highly rated non-GSE mortgage-backed securities and collateralized debt obligations. At its peak before the crisis, the riskier collateral accounted for as much as 30% of the total posted."[95] Among others, JP Morgan's Jamie Dimon stated in an interview that he had not become fully aware of the risks stemming from the bank's tri-party repo clearing business until the Bear crisis in 2008. As Dimon explained: "If [investment banks] defaulted intraday, we own the securities and we have to liquidate them. That's a huge risk for us."[96]

Bear was, as Tim Geithner phrased, "Wall Street's weakest link, badly managed, disproportionately exposed to mortgages," with $33 in borrowing for every $1 of capital in a securities industry in which broker-dealer firms long generally had limited themselves to a 10-to-1 debt-to-equity ratio.[97]

Bear Stearns unraveled in one climatic week in March 2008. As Hank Paulson put it, "when financial institutions die, they die fast."[98] Between March 10 and March 13, Bear Stearns cash reserves dwindled from $18 billion to $2 billion.

It was announced on Tuesday March 11 that the Federal Reserve Bank would create a Term Securities Lending Facility to make available up to $200 billion in Treasury securities, GSE mortgage-backed securities such as those from Fannie Mae and Freddie Mac, and non-GSE mortgage-backed securities including CDOs. The new Term Securities Lending Facility was intended to lend to investment banks and other primary dealers for up to 28 days. "The borrowers would trade higher rated securities, including debt in government-sponsored enterprises, in return for Treasuries. The primary dealers could then use those Treasuries to borrow cash in the repo market."[99] These terms were widely perceived as a means to prop up Bear Stearns. It failed to do so. The Term Securities Lending Facility was scheduled to become operative on March 27, 2008, too late in March to help Bear Stearns, then in *extremis.*

On Friday, March 14, the Fed made an emergency $12.9 billion loan to Bear Stearns through JP Morgan to get Bear Stearns through the weekend.

Climaxing a frantic week, over the weekend, the Treasury, the Federal Reserve Bank of New York, JP Morgan, and Bear Stearns hammered out the initial version of a $30 billion guarantee to Bear under which JP Morgan would acquire Bear initially for $2 per share, later raised to $10 per share, and the Federal Reserve Board, backed by the Treasury would guarantee Bear Stearns losses to $28.82 billion after JP Morgan bore the first $1.15 billion of losses.[100]

To the federal financial regulators, Bear was "too interconnected to fail" with nearly 400 subsidiaries, 5000 trading counterparties and 750,000 open derivatives contracts. Federal Reserve Chairman Ben Bernanke viewed the large risk as the $2.8 trillion tri-party repo market in which a clearing bank serves as an intermediary between repo borrowers, like Bear, and lenders. Bear had borrowed about $80 billion in the tri-party repo market and in 2008, was raising most of its capital in the tri-party repo market with JP Morgan as its clearing bank. If Bear's repo lenders refused to renew their loans, JP Morgan would be on the hook for tens of billions of its own shareholder's dollars and would likely dispose of its Bear Stearns collateral in a fire sale which, in Bernanke's view, shared by Paulson and Geithner, "would drive securities prices further down, leading to a new wave of losses and write-downs. . . . The remaining four major investment banks [Lehman Brothers, Merrill Lynch, Goldman Sachs, and Morgan Stanley] would be particularly vulnerable and the failure of Bear could lead to runs on these firms as well." Bernanke's "own greatest fear, if Bear collapsed, was that the repo market might break down entirely, with disastrous consequences for financial markets and, as credit froze and asset prices plunged, for the entire economy." The belief that Lehman Brothers demise would be next if Bear failed was widespread in March 2008. Lehman's stock dropped 14.6 percent in one day of Bear's climactic week in March.[101]

Because of the overall risk to the financial markets and the economy, Treasury Secretary Paulson stated: "I'm prepared to do anything. If there is any chance of avoiding [Bear Stearns] failure, we need to take it."[102]

These were, however, highly controversial beliefs that posed a fundamental moral hazard. By rewarding failure with what was widely derided as a bailout, the federal regulators risked taking away the incentive for other endangered firms such as Lehman Brothers to save themselves. The critics of the Bear Stearns deal were excoriating. "This is socialism," Senator Jim Bunning [R-KY] thundered. Senator Richard Shelby [R-AL] called it a "bad precedent." Former Federal Reserve President Paul Volcker characterized the Fed as going to "the very edge of its lawful and implied powers." Anna Schwartz, Milton Friedman's coauthor of "A Monetary History of the United States, 1867–1960," termed the Bear Stearns transition as a "rogue operation." Vincent Reinhart, a Federal Reserve bank's top staff member since 2006, characterized the decision to sell Bear Stearns "the worst policy mistake in a generation," predicting that it would set a precedent. From then on, any large financial institution in a similar position could expect to be saved by the Fed.

Bernanke, Geithner, and Paulson disagreed:

> Bear itself didn't get bailed out. The firm ceased to exist. Its senior executives lost their jobs and much of their wealth. Its shareholders did receive more than the zero dollars the firm would have been worth in bankruptcy, but 95 percent less than the firm was worth at its peak in early 2007. All interventions create some moral hazard, but it was hard to see how Bear's fate would have encouraged other firms to emulate its reckless approach....
>
> In any case, we did not squander taxpayer dollars; the Bear loan was ultimately repaid and produced a $2.5 billion return for the government. But the point of the loan was not to make money; it was to prevent the messy collapse of a systemically important firm and the inevitable economic damage that would have followed.[103]

With the Bear Stearns transition, Federal financial regulation crossed a Maginot line.

These were *Ten Days That Changed Capitalism,* as Peter Wallison later recounted, quoting the title of an article by *Wall Street Journal* writer David Wessel. "The past 10 days," Wessel wrote in March 2008, "will be remembered as the time the U.S. government discarded a half-century of rules to save American financial capitalism from collapse."[104]

Wallison then quoted the Shadow Financial Regulatory Committee, conservative scholars sponsored by the American Enterprise Institute, who emphasized the moral hazard consequences of the Bear Stearns rescue:

> After Bear Stearns was revived . . . Merrill Lynch, Morgan Stanley and Goldman Sachs all sat on their hands for six months waiting further positive developments (notably, an improvement in the market environment or a handout from the Federal government). In particular, Lehman did little to raise capital or shore up its position not only because management theorized financial conditions would improve, but also because its Chief Executive Officer thought the government would never let it fail.[105]

The criticism of the Shadow Financial Regulatory Committee was overwrought. As Bernanke recounted:

> The Bear Stearns action brought a period of relative calm to financial markets. . . . In a vote of confidence in the U.S. financial system, big commercial banks and the investment banks were able to raise an impressive $140 billion in new capital by the end of June. . . . The Dow closed at 12,263 on March 30, virtually unchanged from its level before the Bear Stearns crisis. By May, the Dow had climbed to 13,758, within 8 percent of its October peak.[106]

These positive developments may have been in part a consequence of the revival of Bear Stearns and the Federal Reserve Board's new lending program. Nonetheless, there is a substantial element of truth in the moral hazard argument. It is not accurate to write that the four remaining investment banks "all sat on their hands." It is an accurate historical judgment to state they did too little.

Federal financial regulation fundamentally changed in March 2008.

For the first time, the Fed extended emergency credit to a non-commercial bank. To do so, the Fed invoked its authority under § 13(3) of the Federal Reserve Act and determined that there were "unusual and exigent circumstances."[107] This was the first use of the § 13(3) authority to extend funds since 1936. The fact that the Fed invoked its § 13(3) was a long-delayed consequence of the Glass-Steagall Act of 1933, which generally prohibited depository institutions such as commercial banks from engaging in securities underwriting. Banks and other depository institutions were subject to federal and state banking regulations, which meant in many circumstances that they could turn to the Federal Reserve as a lender of last resort. Investment banks such as Bear Stearns were regulated by the Securities and Exchange Commission and had no access to federal loans until the Fed's March 2008 decisions to provide Federal Reserve funds.[108]

The Bear Stearns rescue was not an inevitable decision. In 1990, the Federal Reserve Board had allowed Drexel Burnham Lambert, the leading junk bond securities broker, to collapse without Federal intervention. In 1998, the Fed had judged the financial markets as too fragile in the wake of the Asian crisis and Russian default to withstand the unwinding of the highly interconnected hedge fund Long Term Capital Management. Long Term Capital employed complex mathematical models, developed in part by two Nobel Laureates, to profit from price discrepancies in securities markets. In 1994 and 1995, the firm had made 40 percent profits and investors and lenders had provided substantial funds to expand the firm. By 1998, the model was no longer working. Long Term Capital Management had set off what Princeton economist Alan Blinder called "a worldwide financial crisis, one that seemed monumental until it was dwarfed by the stunning events of 2007–2009." Federal Reserve Chair Alan Greenspan was more succinct: "Hollywood could not have scripted a more dramatic financial train wreck." But the New York Fed had engineered a purely private $3.65 billion private sector fund without using Federal funds to save Long Term Capital Management.[109]

Bear became a precedent for several subsequent interventions. This was predictable at the time of the Bear Stearns rescue. In the course of the Bear Stearns transaction, the Fed created the Term Securities Lending Facility and the Primary Dealer Credit Facility, each of which broadened the Fed lending power beyond commercial banks. The Primary Dealer Credit Facility was broader than the Term Securities Lending Facility and provided cash, not Treasury securities, to investment banks and other primary dealers on terms close to those provided to commercial banks through the Federal Discount Window.[110]

The Primary Dealer Credit Facility offered overnight cash loans in exchange for collateral. It was an alternative to the then stuttering repo market. This program, adopted shortly after the Bear Stearns rescue merger, was rapidly employed, providing over $340 billion in cash in its first week of operations to, among others, Bear Stearns.[111] In May, the Fed broadened the collateral allowed in the Term Securities Lending Facility to include other AAA rated asset-backed securities.[112]

Another consequence for the federal financial regulatory system was particularly consequential. As New York Federal Reserve President Tim Geithner put it: "We couldn't rely on the SEC anymore." In part, Geithner's reaction to the Commission was based on the incompetence and over-optimism of the Securities and Exchange Commission's performance. As late as Wednesday, March 12, "SEC staffers were still assuring us Bear had plenty of liquidity." SEC Chairman Christopher Cox told reporters his agency had "a good deal of comfort with Bear's capital cushion." Geithner was taken aback by a senior SEC official during an emergency call Thursday, March 13th, who concluded "We'll talk in the morning." As Geithner later declaimed: "Really? With a $400 billion investment bank about to default on its obligations, it seemed a bit early to call it a night."[113]

The Final Report of the National Commission on the Causes of the Financial and Economic Crisis echoed this criticism: "In the fourth quarter of 2007, Bear Stearns reported its first quarterly loss, $379 million. Still, the SEC saw no evidence of any deterioration in the firm's liquidity position following the release and related negative press coverage." The SEC concluded, "Bear Stearns liquidity post remains stable." As late as the week of March 3, "when SEC Staff inspected Bear's liquidity post," they identified no "significant issues."[114]

The more serious deficiency with SEC oversight of investment banking holding companies was structural. Since 1956, the Federal Reserve had overseen bank holding companies and over time had established highly regarded staff and examination practices and procedures, in some instances providing a near full time on-site presence at major bank holding companies such as JP Morgan or Citigroup. The SEC Consolidated Supervised Entities (*CSE*) program was established in 2004 as a voluntary system of overseeing investment bank holding companies, but was never comparably staffed or comparably effective. The decision to adopt the CSE program was a regulatory response to the Gramm-Leach-Bliley Act of 1999, which denominated the SEC the principal regulator of broker-dealers and investment advisers with little attention to how holding companies that owned these types of securities firms and affiliated entities would be regulated.

A September 2008 Report from the SEC Office of the Inspector General, *SEC's Oversight of Bear Stearns and Related Entities: The Consolidated Supervised Entity Program*[115] characterized the SEC's dismal performance with respect to Bear Stearns as a failure of the Commission's CSE program, which oversaw investment bank holding companies for which the SEC was the principal regulator:

> [I]t is undisputable that the CSE program failed to carry out its mission in its oversight of Bear Stearns because under the Commission and the CSE program's watch, Bear Stearns suffered significant financial weaknesses and the [Federal Reserve Bank of New York] needed to intervene during the week of March 10, 2008, to prevent significant harm to the broader financial system.

The Inspector General Report criticized CSE program requirements as inadequate, identified several "potential red flags regarding its concentration of mortgage securities, high leverage, shortcomings of risk management in mortgage-backed securities and lack of compliance with the spirit of certain Basel II [that is applicable capital] standards but did not take actions to limit these risk factors."[116]

The National Commission on the Causes of the Financial and Economic Crisis further generalized about the meltdown of Bear Stearns:

> . . . bankers and their regulators were haunted by the speed of Bear Stearn's demise. And they knew that other investment banks shared Bear's weaknesses: leverage, reliance on overnight funding, dependence on securitization markets, and concentration in illiquid mortgage securities and other troubled assets. In

> particular, the run on Bear had exposed the dangers of tri-party repo agreements and the counterparty risk caused by derivative contracts.[117]

Simultaneous with the release of the damning SEC Inspector General Report in September 2008, the Commission terminated the CSE program, with Chairman Christopher Cox stating in part: "[T]he CSE program was fundamentally flawed from the beginning, because investment banks could opt in or opt out of supervision voluntarily." Cox insisted that the major findings of the Inspector General "are ultimately derivative of the lack of specific legal authority for the SEC or any other agency to sit as the regulator of these large investment bank holding companies."

Cox concluded:

> With each of the major investment banks that had been part of the CSE program being reconstituted within a Bank Holding Company, they will be subject to statutory supervision by the Federal Reserve. Under the Bank Holding Company Act, the Federal Reserve has robust statutory authority to impose and enforce supervisory requirements on those entities. Thus there is not currently a regulatory gap in this area.[118]

Three months after Bear's rescue merger in July 2008, the SEC and the Fed had executed a Memorandum of Understanding to better coordinate the sharing of data and analysis.[119]

During this period, the Treasury Department under Treasury Secretary Hank Paulson's leadership had been most attentive to structural issues in the financial system. In March 2008, the Department of the Treasury had published a detailed *Blueprint for a Modernized Financial Regulatory Structure,* which will be discussed later in this book.[120] The nearly simultaneous Bear Stearns crisis meant that the *Blueprint* was dead on arrival. As Paulson subsequently wrote: "Our timing was dreadful. It seemed premature to suggest steps to avoid a future crisis with no end in sight to this one."

Paulson and Federal Reserve Chairman Bernanke proposed legislation to Barney Frank, the Democrat Chairman of the House Financial Services Committee, to enact legislation to give the federal government formal power to wind down failing large noncommercial bank institutions and guarantee their obligations. The FDIC already had these powers for commercial banks. Despite the gerry built comparable effort that had resulted in the Bear Stearns rescue merger, Frank told Paulson and Bernanke this idea they had had no chance unless the Treasury Secretary and Fed Chair trumpeted their fears about Lehman and persuaded Congress that its failure would devastate the American economy. Paulson and Bernanke then were unwilling to do so because of concerns that alarmist rhetoric would rattle the markets and precipitate the failure they were trying to avoid. It is worth noting that this rhetoric might also have been anathema to incumbent Republicans preparing for the 2008 election and wanted to run on the strength of the economy.[121]

Fannie Mae and Freddie Mac

Paulson then focused on Fannie Mae and Freddie Mac. In 2006, Paulson and Frank had negotiated a bipartisan compromise to create a more powerful regulator of Fannie and Freddie and tougher regulatory standards. The Bill was passed by the House but was not adopted by the Senate. "The market's weakness," Paulson believed, "ultimately stemmed from housing trouble."[122]

If the collapse of Bear Stearns was the first signal event of the 2007–2009 financial meltdown, in the next six months two more seismic events occurred.

The first involved the September 7, 2008 takeover of Fannie Mae and Freddie Mac. As soon as Paulson was briefed on these two GSEs in June 2006, he realized that they were "a disaster waiting to happen." But simultaneously, once housing market finance dried up in 2007, Fannie Mae and Freddie Mac had become "the only game in town." By the spring of 2008, Paulson further believed that they were "the engine we needed to get through the problem."[123]

To Geithner, Fannie Mae and Freddie Mac were the most dangerous examples of moral hazard in the financial system. With an implicit guarantee of their debt from the federal government, and a line of credit from the United States Treasury, "Fannie and Freddie borrowed at artificially low rates, because markets assumed the government would never let them default, and poured the cash into mortgages, mortgage guarantees, and other highly leveraged bets on the U.S housing market."[124]

By September 2008, Fannie and Freddie owned and guaranteed $5.3 trillion of mortgages with capital of less than 2 percent. By the fall of 2007, the two GSEs were sinking with mounting losses. But in 2007, Fannie and Freddie were responsible for purchasing

75 percent of new mortgages, roughly double what they purchased in 2006. As Geithner put it, "The housing market was as dependent on the GSEs as the GSEs were dependent on the housing market."[125]

Fannie Mae and Freddie Mac were the only game in town in part because of powerful political support from such Democratic party stalwarts as Senator Chris Dodd [D-CT] and Representative Barney Frank [D-MA]. The response of the Department of Treasury and GSE regulator, the Office of Federal Housing Enterprise Oversight (*OFHEO*), on March 19, 2008, four days after Bear Stearns was rescued, was to reduce Fannie and Freddie's required capital and with the exposure of up to $200 billion in immediate liquidity being provided to the mortgage-backed securities market, enough, as OFHEO reported a month later, to "allow the GSEs to purchase or guarantee about $2 trillion in mortgages this year."[126]

The wheels soon came off the train. In March 2008, White House Economist Jason Thomas e-mailed Robert Steel, who then was overseeing Fannie and Freddie at the Department of Treasury, an alarming analysis. Based on 2007 financial results, Thomas believed that Fannie Mae was masking its insolvency through fraudulent accounting practices. *Barron's* published a similar analysis on March 10th: "Any realistic assessment of Fannie Mae's capital position would show the company is currently insolvent. Accounting fraud has resulted in several asset categories (non-agency securities, deferred tax assets, low-income partnership investment) being overstated, while the guarantee obligation is understated. These accounting shenanigans add up to tens of billions of exaggerated net worth." *Barron's* correctly predicted "a government seizure of the company is inevitable."[127]

By April, Paulson had determined to act on what then was known as the Federal Housing Finance Reform Act of 2008, which was approved by the Senate Banking Committee on May 20th. But before the Bill could morph into the Housing and Economic Recovery Act in July, Indy Mac spectacularly failed. Originally started by Countrywide, Indy Mac was spun off in 1997. IndyMac then was the seventh largest mortgage originator. It provided or guaranteed more than $5 billion of mortgages to home buyers frequently with inadequate income or assets, often through adjustable rate mortgages. When the $32 billion bank went bust, the FDIC and the Office of Thrift Supervision shut down IndyMac.[128] Indy's collapse left the FDIC with $10.7 billion in insurance costs and the second largest bank failure in United States history.[129]

The bad news for Fannie and Freddie kept coming. On July 7, 2008, Lehman Brothers published a report speculating that Fannie and Freddie might need as much as $75 billion in additional capital. Freddie's stock fell by 18 percent on July 7; Fannie's fell 16 percent to $15.74. After President Bush and then Secretary Paulson issued reassuring statements, Fannie's shares fell 22 percent on July 11, to $10.25, Freddie's 3.1 percent to $7.75. "[I]nvestors" Secretary Paulson was concerned, "had lost faith in Fannie and Freddie."[130]

In July 2008, the Housing and Economic Recovery Act[131] was enacted. In Paulson's summary:

> The legislation gave us broad discretion to provide support to the GSEs as we saw fit. The terms and conditions of the support were left almost entirely to the discretion of the Treasury Secretary giving us ample flexibility to structure investments and loans in any way that made sense. The legislation did not impose any limitations on the amount of that support except . . . that we would need the GSEs to approve any equity investment we made in them. All told, it was perhaps the most expansive power to commit funds ever given to a Treasury Secretary.[132]

The Act achieved virtually everything Secretary Paulson had sought — the ability to extend secured lines of credit to Fannie and Freddie, to purchase their mortgage securities, and to inject capital. To replace the minimally effective Office of Federal Housing Enterprise Oversight, the Act created the Federal Housing Finance Agency (*FHFA*) as an independent federal agency as Fannie and Freddie's primary regulator with expanded authority over their portfolios, capital levels, and compensation.[133]

Memorably, in earlier testimony to the Senate Banking Committee, Paulson had stated: "If you've got a squirt gun in your pocket, you may have to take it out. If you've got a bazooka, and people know you've got it, you will not have to take it out." The ultimate bazooka in the Housing and Economic Recovery Act involved the power of the new Federal Housing Finance Agency to take over Fannie and Freddie through a conservatorship or receivership. Within weeks, this bazooka would be fired.[134]

After the Federal Reserve consented in mid-July to furnish emergency loans, the Fed, the Office of Comptroller of the Currency

(*OCC*), and Morgan Stanley, acting as an adviser to the Treasury, initiated a review of Fannie and Freddie:

> The Fed and the OCC discovered that the problems were worse than their suspicions or reports from [the former Federal Housing Finance Agency] had led them to believe. . . . The Fed found that the GSEs were significantly "under-reserved" with huge potential losses, and their operations were "unsafe and unsound."[135]

Among other things, the review rejected the forecasting methodologies employed by Fannie and Freddie, found their loss projection methodology was flawed, and criticized Fannie's failure to charge off delinquent loans for two years — banks then were required to charge off delinquent loans once they are 180 days delinquent. "If the GSEs were not insolvent at the time, they were almost there," the National Commission on the Causes of the Financial and Economic Crisis quoted the OCC as concluding.[136]

On September 6, 2008, Fannie Mae and Freddie Mac were placed in conservatorship. At the time, Fannie and Freddie were responsible for about one-half of the residential mortgages and mortgage-backed securities in the country — some $1.7 trillion issues in debt each year. They were in tatters. Fannie's stock price had declined 90 percent in one year — from $66 to $7.32. "By the end of August," reported Treasury Secretary Paulson, "neither could raise equity capital from private investors or in the public markets."[137] Under conservatorship, the Treasury caused the CEOs of Fannie and Freddie to be replaced and provided $189.5 billion in support. In return, the Treasury received warrants to purchase 79.9 percent of the common stock outstanding. "Existing common and preferred stockholders were effectively wiped out." Fannie and Freddie were obligated to shrink their loan portfolios and to end lobbying of the government.[138]

Through the third quarter in 2010, Fannie and Freddie had lost $229 billion, eliminating the $71 billion in capital they held as of year-end 2007. By 2015, the Treasury had provided $187.5 billion in funding to the GSEs and maintained commitments to fund any issues up to $445.5 billion. Federal Reserve Governor Kevin Warsh characterized the takeover of Fannie and Freddie as "a massive, under-reported underappreciated jolt to the system."[139]

The reason for the under-reporting and underappreciation was simple enough. Within nine days, Lehman Brothers was bankrupt, the most consequential event to that date of the 2007–2009 meltdown.

Lehman Brothers

The Lehman Brothers bankruptcy transformed an accelerating cascade of financial crisis into a global financial and economic meltdown. "There is," Princeton economist Alan Blinder later wrote, "close to universal agreement that the demise of Lehman Brothers was the watershed event of the entire financial crisis and that the decision to allow it to fail was the watershed decision." To Merrill Lynch's John Thain "[a]llowing Lehman to go bankrupt was the single biggest mistake of the whole financial crisis."[140]

On September 15, 2008, Lehman Brothers filed for Chapter 11 bankruptcy protection. Three days later, the Securities Investor Protection Corporation placed Lehman in liquidation. According to leading bankruptcy attorney Harvey Miller, the Lehman bankruptcy represented "the largest, most complex, multifaceted and far-reaching bankruptcy ever filed in the United States."[141] At the time, Lehman Brothers was the fourth largest investment bank in the United States with $639 billion in assets as of May 31, 2008, making Lehman roughly 50 percent larger than Bear Stearns had been on the eve of its acquisition by JP Morgan. Lehman had 26,000 employees, 8000 subsidiaries and affiliates, and over 100,000 creditors. Lehman Brothers, in the view of both Federal Reserve Chair Bernanke and Treasury Secretary Paulson, was even more interconnected than Bear Stearns. As Bernanke wrote later, "its derivative 'book' was twice the size that Bear's had been."[142]

Lehman's business strategy was fundamentally flawed. Lehman had determined to acquire mortgage-related assets in 2006 and 2007, increasing its holdings from $67 billion in 2006 to $111 billion in 2007. In Bernanke's account, "[Lehman CEO Richard] Fuld and his lieutenants had been aggressive even by pre-crisis Wall Street standards, propelling the company into commercial real estate, leveraged lending (lending to already indebted firms to finance takeovers and other speculative activity) and private-label mortgage-backed securities. In the process, they had blown through the company's established guidelines for controlling risk." "[A]s late as May 2007,

[Lehman] led financing for a wildly overpriced $22 billion acquisition of the real estate from Archstone," Tim Geithner recalled. When real estate crashed, Lehman had been slow to mark down the values it assigned to its real estate assets. The lack of urgency of Lehman Brothers was attributed by Paulson to Fuld's reluctance to accept reality. This was debatable.[143]

As Lehman Brothers finances deteriorated after the Bear Stearns rescue merger, there were several efforts to strengthen the firm. In July 2008, Lehman Brothers CEO had suggested that the Federal Reserve Board allow Lehman to become a bank holding company and open its Discount Window to Lehman. Tim Geithner rejected the idea as "gimmicky," although the Fed within days of the Lehman failure would allow two other investment banks, Morgan Stanley and Goldman Sachs, to be transformed into bank holding companies.[144]

Lehman Brothers took some steps to improve its capital position reducing real estate exposures from $71 billion at the end of May 2008 to $54 billion at the end of the Summer and raising $15.5 in new capital through preferred stock and subordinated debt between April and June 2008.[145] These steps proved insufficient.

Lehman Brothers unsuccessfully sought asset infusions or mergers with the Korea Development Bank, Bank of America, and Barclays. "In late August, Fuld floated the idea of dividing Lehman into two pieces," Bernanke recalled, "a 'good bank' that would retain the Company's best assets and its operating business, and a 'bad bank', which would hold the Company's troubled commercial mortgages and other real estate assets." In each of these cases, Paulson and Geithner declined to support using government resources or guarantees to facilitate a rescue transaction.[146]

An effort during the last days of Lehman Brothers to persuade lending financial firms to jointly provide a private sector rescue similar to that which had saved Long Term Capital Management failed on September 12th and 13th, 2008. Paulson later viewed this as decisive. In answer to President Bush's question: "Will we be able to explain why Lehman is different from Bear Stearns?" Paulson explained: "We couldn't find a buyer even with other firms' help."[147]

The death spiral had begun on June 9. Lehman announced a $2.8 billion loss for its second quarter, its first loss since going public in 1994. Its stock price declined to $30; it had been $46.49 on March 18th. On June 12th, Lehman announced it was dismissing its Chief

Operating Officer and Chief Financial Officer. The stock price fell to $22.70. When Lehman reported a $3.9 billion loss because of asset write down on September 4, its days were numbered.[148]

On September 9th, JP Morgan, Lehman's clearing bank, required an additional $3.6 billion of collateral and then on September 12 secured another $5 billion. On September 12, Lehman's stock fell 13.5 percent and closed at $13.65. By September 15, 2008, Lehman's stock price had fallen 95 percent.[149]

Paulson insisted that no federal government money would be available for a Lehman Brothers deal. "We need to do everything we can to fashion a private-sector alternative." Each of the key Federal actors — Paulson, Bernanke, and Geithner — knew a Lehman Brothers collapse would be a disaster.[150] But Paulson was sensitive to the fact that after Bear Stearns, Fannie and Freddie, "the country, Congress and both parties were fed up with bailouts. Obama and McCain, neck and neck in the national polls, each spoke out against them on the campaign trail. . . . McCain and [Vice Presidential candidate] Sarah Palin had published an op-ed in the *Wall Street Journal* entitled, 'We'll Protect Taxpayers from More Bailouts.' " Paulson did not want to be known as "Mr. Bailout."[151]

Geithner in almost every other key decision during the crisis was in concord with Paulson. But he felt the adamance of Paulson's "No Federal Money for Lehman" was unwise. As he wrote in his memoir of the crisis: "Whatever the merits of no-public-money as a bargaining position, I didn't think it made sense as general public policy. The Bear intervention had been a well-deserved solution to a serious problem. I believed that if we could find a buyer to play the JP Morgan role and buy Lehman, and we had to take some risk to close the deal, it would be in the best interest of the country for us to do so, whether we liked it or not. . . . If Lehman failed, and the U.S. government publicly proclaimed that we were done with bailouts, national investors would simply run from other financial institutions."

In their joint 2019 recounting of the 2008–2009 financial crisis, Paulson stated that the "no federal money for Lehman" was meant to be a negotiating tactic, not a policy decision. Paulson "said he would gladly reverse his position if we got an opportunity to save Lehman." Be that as it may, what was publicly understood was Paulson's message of tough love: No federal money for Lehman.

Geithner would be deeply affected by the failure of Lehman: "After Lehman, I lost whatever minimal tolerance I might have had for letting moral hazard or political considerations impede our efforts to attack the crisis. I supported anything that would discourage running and encourages investing; I opposed anything that would weaken confidence or stability." Geithner ultimately pled guilty to suffering "Lehman syndrome, a kind of financial post-traumatic stress disorder... [I]f you weren't traumatized by the fall of Lehman or terrified by the thought of another Lehman, you weren't paying attention."[152]

There were substantive reasons to support a no bailout approach to Lehman. By the time of its bankruptcy, Lehman Brothers had overstated real assets estimated by as much as $65 to $100 billion. The exact amount proved difficult to calculate during the last frantic days of Lehman Brothers. This was different than Bear Stearns, whose assets "were clear enough to secure sufficiently a $29 billion Fed loan."[153]

Bernanke believed that Lehman lacked sufficient collateral to justify Federal Reserve intervention. The emergency power that the Fed had used with Bear Stearns under § 13(3) of the Federal Reserve Act required collateral to be "secured to the satisfaction" of the lending Federal Reserve Bank. "In other words," explained Bernanke, "the borrower's reliance had to be sound enough that the Federal Reserve could reasonably expect full payment."[154]

Whether the § 13(3) argument could be overcome or not, the Lehman failure proved to be far worse than predicted. As economist Alan Blinder wrote: "The consequences of letting Lehman go down turned out to be more severe than probably anyone imagined. The financial system literally started to fall apart." On September 15, 2008, when Lehman filed for bankruptcy, the Dow Jones fell more than 500 points, or 4 percent, the worst single day since the 9/11 terrorist attacks. The National Commission on the Cause of the Financial and Economic Crisis reported, "$700 billion in value from retirement plans, government pension funds, and other investment portfolios disappeared."[155]

John Mack, Morgan Stanley CEO during the crisis, later testified: "In the immediate wake of Lehman's failure on September 15, Morgan Stanley and similar institutions experienced a classic 'run on the bank' as investors lost confidence in financial institutions and the entire investment banking business model came under siege." Ben Bernanke, a leading scholar of the Great Depression "honestly believed that September and October of 2008 was the worst financial crisis in global history, including the Great Depression. If you look at the firms that came under pressure in that period... only one...was not at serious risk of failure. So out of...13 of the most important financial institutions in the United States, 12 were at risk of failure within a week or two."[156] Treasury Secretary Paulson stated shortly later: "The entire economy was on the risk of collapsing."[157]

Crisis Upon Crisis

Events moved with dizzying speed, with crisis upon crisis for several weeks.

On the same day that Lehman Brothers failed, Bank of American acquired Merrill Lynch for $50 billion in an all stock deal.[158] In the general view, as articulated by Paulson, "Merrill was the next weakest bank."[159] Merrill was the largest of the five investment bank holding companies in terms of employment with 15,000 brokers and 700 branch offices. It was the best known brokerage firm in the nation with television commercials celebrating its optimistic "bullish on America" messages. Merrill's enthusiasm for mortgage-backed securities, however, had been misplaced. As Alan Blinder later wrote: "Losses mounted in late 2007 and 2008. By September 2008, it was reported that the firm had cumulatively lost $52 billion on its holdings of mortgage-backed securities — a sum larger than Merrill's remaining net worth."[160] By moving as decisively as Merrill had before the economy further deteriorated, "[Merrill Lynch CEO John] Thain had managed to arrange a sale at $29 per share, a 70 percent premium [that is, payment] over Merrill's market price." Paulson was relieved, "Without this, I knew Merrill would not have lasted the week."[161]

The rescue merger of Merrill inevitably focused attention on the remaining investment bank holding companies. Paulson recalled:

> With Merrill Lynch seemingly secure in the arms of Bank of America, all eyes were on Morgan Stanley and Goldman Sachs. If either remaining investment bank failed, it would almost certainly bring down the other and touch off a worldwide run that would be catastrophic for the American people. And a failure was a very real possibility.[162]

Morgan Stanley, by then following industry custom, had aggressively invested in mortgage securities in 2005 and had begun to write down its subprime holdings in 2007, with a November 7 $3.7 billion write down, increased to $9.4 billion in December.[163]

Goldman was an industry leader in the creation and sale of mortgage securities. "From 2004 to 2006, Goldman issued 318 mortgage securitizations totaling $184 billion (about a quarter were subprime) and 63 CDOs totaling $32 billion.... In total between July 1, 2004 and May 31, 2007, Goldman packaged and sold 47 synthetic CDOs with an aggregate face value of $66 billion."[164]

In retrospect, synthetic CDOs would be criticized for "[multiplying] the effects of the collapse in subprime." and characterized as a "casino." As University of Maryland law Professor Michael Greenberger would testify: "[T]he concept of lawful betting of billions of dollars on the question of whether a homeowner would default on a mortgage that was not owned by either party, has had a profound effect on the American public and taxpayers."[165]

Goldman also would be criticized for conflicts in its mortgage and CDO securities transactions. Journalists Bethany McLean and Joe Nocera explained:

> The Goldman mortgage department...was, by its nature, conflict central. It built CDOs that included its own mortgage-backed securities and those of others. It created synthetic CDOs, allowing clients to take either the long or short side of the bet. Sometimes Goldman itself was on the other side of a client bet. It also actively traded all these instruments for its clients—and itself.[166]

That was retrospect. In September 2008, the pivotal operational issue was the vulnerability of Morgan Stanley and Goldman Sachs to rapid withdrawals of capital when clients or lenders feared their capital might be frozen or lost in bankruptcy proceedings.

Both Morgan Stanley and Goldman Sachs as late as Friday, September 12, had, as the National Commission on the Causes of the Financial and Economic Crisis stated with respect to Morgan Stanley: "[s]ome reason for confidence. On the previous Friday, [Morgan Stanley's] liquidity pool was more than $130 billion—Goldman's was $120 billion—and, like Goldman, [Morgan

Stanley] had passed the regulator's liquidity stress tests months earlier."[167]

The collapse came with breathtaking speed. On Monday, September 15, the annual cost of protection of $10 million in Morgan Stanley debt through credit default swaps soared to $682,000 — double the cost for Goldman. Hedge funds began to pull billions of dollars in cash and other assets out of Morgan Stanley and Goldman in favor of bank holding companies such as JP Morgan, leading foreign banks such as Deutsche Bank and Credit Suisse, and custodian banks such as BNY Mellon and Northern Trust — each believed to be safer. The dollar magnitudes were staggering. Hedge funds requested $10 billion on Monday from Morgan Stanley; $32 billion on Wednesday, a day after Morgan issued its quarterly report, a day early in what was viewed as a sign of weakness. Morgan's stock fell 28 percent in a matter of hours on Tuesday. AIG received a significant bailout on Tuesday, September 16. This precipitated a different kind of hedge fund run. "Many of the hedge funds now sought to exercise their contractual capacity to borrow more from Morgan Stanley's prime brokerage without needing to post collateral. Prime brokerage included hedge funds parking their securities with investment banks such as Morgan which could use the securities to create excess liquidity. Morgan Stanley separately borrowed $13 billion from the Fed's PDCF [Prime Dealer Credit Facility] on Tuesday, $27 billion on Wednesday, and $35.3 billion on Friday."

Within one week, Morgan's liquidity had dropped from $130 billion to $55 billion. Hedge funds had taken out $86 billion from Morgan Stanley's prime brokerage.[168]

Goldman Sachs experienced a similar pummeling. Its capital had fallen from $120 billion on Friday, September 12 to $57 billion on Thursday, September 18. Bernanke "believed the run on Goldman could lead to its failure."[169] Geithner was less delicate: "At that moment, fear was a sign you were awake and intelligent. Anyone who wasn't scared had no idea how close we were to the abyss."[170]

By the weekend of September 20–21, Geithner, Bernanke, and Paulson believed: "Morgan and Goldman needed immediate solutions. As [Goldman CEO] Lloyd Blankfein put it later, this would be their 'existential weekend.'" Paulson, Bernanke, and SEC Chair Chris Cox called Blankfein and Morgan Stanley CEO John Mack to persuade them to seek new partners as Merrill had done with

Bank of America. Geithner "got Blankfein to call Vikram Pandit about merging Goldman with Citi, but they both hated the idea. I urged John Mack to call Jamie Dimon to push them to reunite Morgan Stanley with JP Morgan Chase, remnants of the original House of Morgan. Neither side liked that idea either." An effort was made to merge Goldman and Wachovia, "but Goldman was daunted by what it found in Wachovia's books." Goldman was willing to go forward with a transaction at Wachovia's closing price on Friday, September 19, but only if the federal government guaranteed Wachovia's entire portfolio of ARM option mortgages for approximately $120 billion. That too was a nonstarter. China's sovereign wealth fund explored an investment in Morgan Stanley, but these talks also quickly failed. On Sunday, Geithner and Paulson, according to journalist Roger Lowenstein, directed Morgan Stanley's Mack to sell his company to JP Morgan or Citigroup. Mack protested: "I have had discussions with Vikram. I've had discussions with Jamie. They don't want to do it." Geithner insisted: "You have to. We'll tell them you have to." Reluctantly, Mack called Jamie Dimon who declined. "I did Bear. I can't do this."[171]

On Sunday, both Morgan Stanley and Goldman Sachs applied to the Fed to become bank holding companies. Both companies long had opposed Federal Reserve supervision. The Fed, working in tandem with the Department of Justice, approved both applications with extraordinary speed. In Bernanke's account: "We allowed the changes in status to take effect immediately." The National Commission on the Causes of the Financial and Economic Crisis concluded: "The two companies gained the immediate benefit of emergency access to the discount window for terms up to 90 days." But, more important, John Mack believed "I think the biggest benefit is it would show . . . that you're important to the system and the Fed would not make you a holding company if they thought in a very short period of time you'd be out of business. It sends a signal both companies are going to survive." Subsequently Warren Buffet invested $5 billion in Goldman Sachs and Mitsubishi UFJ invested $9 million in Morgan Stanley. By the end of September, Morgan Stanley's liquidity position had stabilized at $55 billion, Goldman Sachs, at $80 billion. By then Morgan had received $96 billion in loans from two federal credit facilities, Goldman, $96.5 billion.[172]

Breathtakingly, in six months, beginning with Bear Stearns, the five leading investment bank holding companies ceased to be investment banks. Bear Stearns and Merrill Lynch had been acquired through rescue mergers. Lehman Brothers was bankrupt. Goldman Sachs and Morgan Stanley had converted to bank holding companies. On Monday, Bank of America's CEO Ken Lewis declared: "The Golden Age of investment banking is over." The *New York Times* described the conversion of Goldman Sachs and Morgan Stanley as "a move that fundamentally reshapes the era of high finance that defined the Modern Golden Age." The *Times* characterized the conversions as "a blunt acknowledgement that their model of finance and investing had become too risky."[173]

In that period of crisis on top of crisis, there was little time for reflection.

AIG

The day after Lehman Brothers went bankrupt, the Department of Treasury orchestrated what was then an $85 billion rescue package for insurance giant AIG, the American International Group.[174] Subsequently, this would grow to approximately $182 billion with the United States Government receiving 79.9 percent of AIG equity.[175] The U.S. government, in effect, assumed the full cost and full risk of saving AIG. As Representative Barney Frank [D-MA] sarcastically explained on September 16th, the day after Lehman's demise: "The national commitment to the free market lasted one day. It was Monday." President Bush recognized:

> There was nothing appealing about the deal. It was basically a nationalization of America's largest insurance company. Less than forth-eight hours after Lehman filed for bankruptcy, saving AIG would look like a glaring contradiction. But that was a hell of a lot better than a financial collapse.[176]

In 2004, AIG was the largest insurance company in the world in terms of stock market capitalization, with $850 billion in aggregate assets, $74 million individual and corporate customers, 116,000 employees in 130 countries and 223 subsidiaries. AIG provided commercial insurance to 180,000 businesses employing 106 million people — two-thirds of the American workforce. Highly regarded for its core insurance operations, AIG was one of only six private companies in the United States with a AAA or Aaa rating from Moody's and Standard & Poor, which facilitated low interest borrowing.[177] At that time, AIG ranked tenth on the *Fortune* 500 list with almost $100 billion in revenues and more than $11 billion in profits. AIG was roughly twice the size of Lehman and more interconnected with counterparties.

The AAA rating was of particular consequence to AIG Financial Products, a noninsurance subsidiary of AIG. AIG Financial Products became a major player in writing Credit Default Swaps (*CDS*), writing $379 billion by 2007. CDS may have seemed like insurance to banks and other institutions purchasing them, in that they provided an obligation to reimburse the investor in the event of a default on a mortgage-backed or other security. But AIG Financial's CDS sales were not insurance. They were not subject, as much else of AIG was, to state insurance regulation and AIG Financial did not set aside reserves, as is required for insurance products, in the event of its own losses. AIG Financial instead relied on AIG's AAA credit rating and the financial advantages to its bank customers of a product that both appeared to reduce the risk of purchasing tranches of mortgage-backed securities and reducing the capital that the banks would need to hold against the insured securities.[178] By 2007, AIG Financial also was involved in writing Collateralized Debt Obligations (*CDOs*).

AIG had other critical weaknesses, more obvious in retrospect than they were before September 2008. At the federal level, AIG, despite its size and ability to endanger the international financial system, was regulated only by the Office of Thrift Supervision (*OTS*) because of AIG's ownership of a small savings and loan company. The OTS would be the only federal financial regulator abolished by the Dodd-Frank Act, an outcome in part justified by its incompetence in regulating AIG.[179] The OTS was not designed to regulate a global derivatives business. It was badly out of its depth as AIG's crisis intensified, believing during the last few days before federal intervention that AIG's risks were moderate and manageable. The OTS, as Geithner put it, "had been oblivious to [AIG's] troubles." The OTS Acting Director in March 2009 Congressional testimony similarly acknowledged that the OTS failed to recognize the effect of liquidity risk posed by AIG Financial's CDS portfolio. In August 2008, OTS officials represented to the Federal Reserve that it was "generally comfortable with [AIG's] current liquidity and confident that the firm could access the capital markets with no problem if it had to."

Compounding the riskiness of the AIG Financial Products CDS portfolio and incompetence of the OTS oversight was the opacity of AIG's financial reporting and valuation techniques. Senior executives at AIG little understood the collateral triggers by which a counterparty could demand that AIG put up collateral if specific events occurred. A key trigger was a drop in AIG's credit rating to Single A; a second was a downgrade of the super senior securities for which AIG had written CDOs; a third was a decline in the market value of specific securities even if AIG retained its AAA credit rating.[180]

From 1968 until 2005, AIG had been run by Hank Greenberg, a legend in the insurance industry, who ran AIG with an iron fist, and a divide and conquer style that included 30 direct reports. Greenberg believed that AIG's AAA credit rating gave it the ability to take risks virtually none of its competitors could take.

As with many investment firms, AIG sought to enhance its earnings by lending securities it owned to short sellers who provided cash as collateral as the short seller sought to profit from stock price declines. If stock prices rise, the short sellers and securities lenders absorbed the stock loss. To obviate this risk, securities lenders typically invested the cash collateral in low risk, easy to sell securities. AIG Financial, in contrast, instead invested the cash in CDO securities. With $78 billion of its securities lending program invested in mortgage-backed securities, this was a highly reckless strategy.[181]

In the Spring of 2005, AIG lost its AAA rating after AIG agreed to pay $126 million to settle criminal and civil charges for accounting fraud that had allowed PNC Financial Services to shift $762 million in bad loans off its financial statements. AIG in February 2005 received a subpoena from Elliot Spitzer, New York State's Attorney General, about a purported $5 million payment to General Re, a leading reinsurance firm, that allowed AIG to increase its reserves to $500 million. Earlier in 2004, Spitzer had brought a bid rigging case against Marsh & McLennan and several insurance companies including AIG. In March 2005, Greenberg resigned as CEO of AIG. In 2006, AIG Financial stopped writing CDS contracts.[182]

In July 2007, after the Standard & Poor's, Moody's, and the Fitch credit rating firms downgraded hundreds of subprime mortgage backed securities, Goldman Sachs sought $1.8 billion in additional collateral from AIG Financial Products. Goldman Sachs and AIG subsequently engaged in a protracted dispute over the correct model to calculate AIG's increased need to post collateral.

In August 2007, AIG publicly disclosed that it held $79 billion in CDO swaps in super senior CDO tranches, $64 billion of which were backed by subprime mortgages. By November, Goldman Sachs demanded another $3 billion in collateral, and AIG had come to agree with its auditor that its valuation system was inadequate for valuing its super senior CDO book.

In February 2008, AIG disclosed in an SEC filing that its auditor had identified material weaknesses in its accounting resulting in a $3.6 billion valuation loss. AIG's stock price declined 12 percent that day. AIG also reported potential losses stemming from its securities lending program.[183]

First quarter results for AIG in 2008 were dismal. AIG reported a $9.1 billion write down on credit derivatives and a $7.8 billion loss, its largest ever. Standard & Poor cut its credit rating to AA minus (AA–).[184]

In the next few months, AIG spun out of control. By late August as Roger Lowenstein put it: "[T]he casino was running wild. The price of insuring $10 million worth of AIG's senior debt has climbed from $70,000 at the start of the year to $375,000."[185]

By September 12, 2008, AIG was in free fall. In June 2008, credit derivative swap counterparties had demanded $15.7 billion in collateral and AIG had posted $13.2 billion. By September 12, collateral calls had increased to $23.4 billion and AIG had paid $18.9 billion. On September 13, Standard & Poor's and Moody's warned of potential downgrades that would likely trigger $10 billion in new collateral calls or credit derivatives and approximately $4 to $5 billion of commercial paper. Counterparties in addition were demanding $24 billion to offset the shortfall in AIG's securities lending program.

One month earlier, Kevin Coffey, a Federal Reserve analyst, had concluded that AIG would need "to raise substantial longer term funds to address the impact of deteriorating asset values on its capital and available liquidity." Coffey listed six concerns:

> . . . (1) AIG's significant losses on investment, primarily because of securities lending activities; (2) $26.5 billion in mark-to-market losses on AIG Financial Products' credit default swap book and related margin calls, for which AIG had posted $16.5 billion in collateral by mid-August; (3) significant near-term liabilities; (4) commitments to purchase collateralized debt obligations due to outstanding liquidity puts; (5) ratings-based triggers in derivative contracts that could cause significant

> additional collateral calls if AIG were downgraded; and (6) limited standby credit facilities to manage sudden cash needs.[186]

At a September 12 meeting with the Federal Reserve Board, AIG executives reported that the company was "facing serious liquidity issues that threaten[ed] its survival viability." AIG stock, which once traded as high as $145.84, reached an intraday low of $11.49 that day. Insurance on $10 million of AIG debt rocketed to $1.4 million per year.[187]

September 12th to the 14th, 2008 would be popularized as the Lehman weekend. It was also the weekend Merrill Lynch trembled on the brink with the potential for Morgan Stanley and Goldman Sachs to fall next. For Paulson, Bernanke, and Geithner, AIG became the third major crisis that had to be rapidly addressed that weekend, effectively reaching urgent crisis levels near 5:00 p.m. on September 12th when Robert Willumstad, then AIG CEO informed the New York Federal Reserve Bank that AIG had failed to generate an acceptable proposal from private equity investors.

Geithner later wrote of his fear of contagion:

> AIG insured the lives, health, property, vehicles, and retirement accounts of millions of American households. . . . [AIG] also had $2.7 trillion of derivatives contracts, and its credit default swaps provided much of the financial system with protection against disaster. If it collapsed, the world's largest financial institutions would suddenly find themselves without the benefit of that catastrophic risk insurance just when they needed it most. A default could also create uncertainty around AIG's retail insurance businesses, and by extension, damage global confidence in the insurance industry.

Paulson, Bernanke, and Geithner understood "that an AIG bankruptcy would be devastating, leading to the failure of many other institutions."

By September 12th, there realistically were only two paths forward if bankruptcy was precluded as an option for AIG. Either a consortium of investment and commercial banks would provide what became $75 billion to provide AIG emergency liquidity support, or the federal government would have to step in. The state of New York did give AIG permission to use $20 billion from its insurance operations to meet AIG Financial Products collateral calls. "[B]ut the temporary relief," as Geithner reflected, "only highlighted [AIG's] desperation. The company was bleeding to death."

The accelerating collapse of AIG ultimately precluded a private sector solution. On Friday, September 12, AIG shares had plunged 31 percent. In the first hour of trading on September 15, AIG shares plunged nearly half to $6.65 per share. By September 16, AIG stock would be trading below $2 per share. Simultaneously, AIG's liquidity needs were skyrocketing. On Sunday, September 14th, AIG sought $50 billion. By Tuesday, September 16th, AIG needed $85 billion. Unlike with Lehman, Bernanke believed that AIG had enough collateral in its insurance subsidiaries to justify a loan. But AIG's inability to identify its liquidity needs led to the conclusion that no support for AIG would be possible without substantial assistance from the Federal Reserve System.

On Monday, September 15th, the three leading credit rating firms downgraded AIG, prompting an additional $13 billion collateral call on AIG Financial Products credit default swaps. Aggregate collateral calls reached $32 billion and AIG payouts increased to $19.5 billion.

Financial leaders, such as the French Finance Minister Christine Legarde, were calling Paulson with the message, "everyone was exposed to AIG... its failure would be catastrophic." On Monday, September 15th, the Dow Jones Industrial Average plummeted 500 points, the steepest one day decline since the first day of trading after September 11, 2001. There were multiple reasons for the decline, but one point was indelible. The stock market was panicking. After the markets closed on September 15, AIG informed the New York Federal Reserve Bank that it could no longer secure short-term loans in the commercial paper market.

By the end of September 16th, Paulson and Bernanke had informed President Bush that the Federal Reserve would lend AIG $85 billion, charging the company 11.5 percent interest and receive 79.9 percent ownership. The initial plan was to gradually liquidate AIG to pay off the Federal Reserve loan. Paulson and Bernanke informed Robert Willumstad that he would be replaced as AIG CEO. The federal government retained the right to veto dividend payments to AIG shareholders. Geithner took the lead in persuading AIG not to file for bankruptcy and to accept the reality that the federal government terms were non-negotiable.

This was a momentous decision. The same troika of federal government financial regulatory leaders who had so often sought private solutions to financial crises were now orchestrating the takeover of the largest insurance company in the world. And they were doing it all alone. As Senate Majority leader Harry Reid [D-NV] put it after an evening benefit September 16th: "This is your decision and your responsibility."[188]

Bernanke later would write: "No one (including me) felt much sympathy for AIG. It got itself into trouble. Congress, which had shown little ability to agree on any subject, stood united in virulent opposition to this bailout. . . . Congress, of course, was only reflecting American public opinion." In terms of perception of the AIG rescue, it mattered little that the Federal Reserve System and Treasury ultimately realized a gain of $23 billion when the AIG shares later were sold to private investors.[189]

Firefighting

The unrelenting onslaught of crises did not abate. On September 16, 2008, the day after Lehman Brothers announced its bankruptcy, the Reserve Fund, a money market fund, made the stunning announcement that it would break the buck, *i.e.*, price its money market securities at 97 cents for each dollar investors held in its Primary Fund. No money market fund had ever earlier dipped below $1 for $1 invested. The Reserve Fund held $785 million in Lehman Brothers commercial paper. Redemptions in the Primary Fund set in motion redemptions from other money market funds. During the week of September 15, 2008, investors withdrew approximately $300 billion from private money market funds or 14 percent of the assets of those funds. Because money market funds often invested in commercial paper and other short-term corporate debt that turned out to be riskier than earlier assessed, there was a real risk that Reserve Fund's breaking the buck could lead to what Bernanke termed "serious economic damage, not only by adding to the market panic but also because many large corporations depend on money market funds to buy commercial paper."

Within days, the Department of Treasury and the Federal Reserve orchestrated a program to guarantee money market funds and prevent what Paulson feared could be a $3.5 trillion implosion in money market funds. The total in money market funds by September 2008 was roughly half the total in FDIC insured banks at the time. On September 19th, the Federal Reserve announced an

Asset-Backed Commercial Paper Money Market Fund Liquidity Facility to extend nonrecourse loans to United States depository institutions and bank holding companies to enable banks to buy commercial paper from money market funds. "Within two weeks," Bernanke, Geithner, and Paulson wrote, "the program was financing $150 billion worth of securities the market no longer trusted."[190]

The Treasury Department significantly decided on September 19 to use $50 billion from the Exchange Stabilization Fund to guarantee money market funds. The Exchange Stabilization Fund had never been used for such a purpose. It had been created in 1934 to intervene in foreign exchange markets to stabilize the dollar.[191] By using the Exchange Stabilization Fund, the Treasury sought to create a guarantee for money market funds much as the FDIC guaranteed ordinary bank deposits. Paulson agreed with Sheila Bair, then Chair of the FDIC, to limit coverage to individual account balances at the close of the business day. From Bair's point of view: "That had the desired effect: it stabilized money market funds without destabilizing bank accounts."

On September 19, the Securities and Exchange Commission in a separate move invoked its emergency powers to issue an Order prohibiting the short selling of 799 financial firms for up to 30 days. Short sellers profit from stock market declines. SEC Chair Cox urged in a statement that short selling may have contributed to the demise of the IndyMac bank and Bear Stearns. Whether this Order made any real difference in protecting firms from stock market manipulation by short sellers or *pro contra* reduced liquidity is debatable. But the intensity of convictions on the part of John Mack, Morgan Stanley's CEO, and other financial firm leaders was not. Paulson in his memoir described a telephone call in which Mack insisted: "Hank, the SEC needs to act before the short sellers destroy Morgan Stanley." Paulson believed that: "Short selling is a crucial element in price discovery and transparency. . . . I had long compared banning short selling to burning books, but now I recognized short selling as a big problem. I concluded that even though an outright ban would lead to all sorts of unintended consequences, it couldn't be worse than what we were experiencing just then. We needed to do something." Geithner agreed that banning "the short selling of 799 financial firms [was] a heavy-handed effort to stop the stampede of speculation and rumor mongering. . . . [SEC Chair

Christopher] Cox wanted broad political cover before he would take action, so Hank asked Ben and me to encourage Cox to act. I figured it was worth a shot. I basically thought we should throw everything we had at the panic, and I really wanted us to stick together."[192]

The Search for a Comprehensive Solution

In the immediate aftermath of the Lehman and AIG crises, Paulson, Bernanke, and Geithner came to believe, as Bernanke wrote, that they were "weary of putting out fires one by one. We needed a more comprehensive solution to the crisis and that meant asking Congress for tax dollars. . . . As we looked ahead, many financial institutions, and indeed the entire economic and financial system, were at serious risk. To secure the necessary authority, the fiscal fire power, and the democratic legitimacy needed to stop the crisis and avoid unthinkable outcomes, we had to go to Congress."[193]

As Paulson later wrote:

> We had been dealing with these crises one at a time on an *ad hoc* basis. But now we needed to take a more systemic approach before we bled to death. We all knew that the root cause lay in the housing collapse that had clogged bank balance sheets with toxic mortgage assets that made them unwilling to lend. We were going to need to buy those assets where necessary, actions that required new powers from Congress and a massive appropriation of funds. In asking for this, we would be bailing out Wall Street. And that would look just plain bad to everyone from free-market devotees to populist demagogues. But not doing this would be disastrous for Main Street and ordinary citizens.[194]

The legislation popularly known as TARP, the Troubled Assets Relief Program, arose from the impulse to achieve a comprehensive approach to the ever escalating financial and economic crisis. TARP would be the largest relief program of the Bush Administration, legislation that as Alan Blinder put it, "may be among the most successful — but least understood — economic policy innovations in our nation's history."

The path to enactment of TARP was contentious and would have been impossible but for the belief held by many — but not all — that the nation then faced an overwhelming economic crisis.

In April 2008, in the aftermath of the Bear Stearns debacle, within the Treasury and the Federal Reserve Board, there had been discussion of five policy options in the Break the Glass memo, developed in the case that the United States faced a financial meltdown to provide emergency options. By September 2008, the nation clearly did. The options in the memo framed the core of the debate concerning TARP. The Break the Glass Discussion Draft urged that the United States government could:

1. Purchase $500 billion of mortgage-backed securities from financial institutions via an auction mechanism. These, in essence, were the troubled assets that ultimately gave TARP its name.
2. Act as a guarantor of non-agency mortgage-backed securities.
3. Inject capital directly into banks through nonrecourse loans.
4. Refinance home mortgages of higher delinquent loans.
5. Purchase equity in banks to allow the banks to rebuild their capital without requiring the United States government to purchase toxic assets.[195]

The last four options were particularly skeletal in the Break the Glass memo.

In the crisis atmosphere of September 2008, there was no immediate consensus on which one or more of these options to pursue.

Bernanke favored investing capital into the banking system:

> Historically, governments have often ended banking crises by injecting capital into (that is, buying stock in) viable firms, so-called good banks. In some cases, troubled firms were made into good banks by separating their bad assets into newly incorporated vehicles — bad banks. The bad banks would be separately financed and, over time, would sell off their low-quality loans. I was inclined toward that approach, including having the government invest directly in banks in exchange for newly created stock. It seemed the simplest and most direct way to restore the banking system to solvency, to provide reassurance to investors and the public, and to support the flow of credit to households and businesses.[196]

A key advantage of direct investment in banks was leverage. For each dollar invested in a bank, the bank could ultimately lend a multiple of the amount invested, say 20 times as many dollars to support the economy.[197]

The key rival approach within the Bush administration was to buy troubled assets. Paulson was the key initial advocate of this approach. He began with the premise: "This is the economic equivalent of war. The market is ready to collapse." Paulson undoubtedly realized that purchasing troubled assets would have a much smaller impact than direct investment. Geithner illustrated this point with a simple example: "Imagine a bank with $1 trillion in mortgage assets and $25 billion in capital, a 40:1 leverage ratio. To get it to a much safer 20:1 leverage ratio, the government could buy $500 billion of its assets, which would drain most of TARP on one institution. Or it could inject $25 billion in additional capital, achieving the same ratio with one-twentieth of the cash." But to Paulson, direct investment seemed a nonstarter, "even mentioning the possibility of direct capital investment would have been bad politics, raising the specter of nationalization." As Bernanke put it: "Hank feared that potential government ownership of banks would look socialistic, or like more bailouts. . . . He believed, in particular, the House Republicans would never accept a plan that looked like a government takeover of banks."[198]

This was the first of the political complexities of enacting TARP. By September 2008, when Paulson presented Congress with a three page bill to address the accelerating economic turmoil, the Federal Reserve had provided nearly $300 billion to investment and commercial banks through lending facilities to "quell the storms in the repos market," as the National Commission on the Causes of the Financial and Economic Crisis wrote, and a major new guarantee program had been adopted to support money market funds. By the end of September, the Federal Reserve's balance sheet had grown 67 percent to $1.5 trillion.

Nonetheless, the proposal to empower the Treasury to spend as much as $700 billion to purchase toxic assets from financial institutions was breathtaking. With almost surreal brevity, the Treasury legislative proposal provided that:

> The Secretary is authorized to purchase, and to make and fund commitments to purchase, on such terms and conditions as determined by the Secretary, mortgage-related assets from any

financial institution having its headquarters in the United States.

"Decisions by the Secretary pursuant to the authority of this Act are non-reviewable and committed to agency discretion, and may not be reviewed by any court of law or any administrative agency."

Paulson was ridiculed. Senator Chris Dodd [D-CT], Chair of the Senate Banking, Housing & Urban Affairs Committee, which initially received the Treasury proposal, characterized the proposal as "stunning and unprecedented in its scope and lack of detail.... It is not just our economy at risk, but our Constitution as well." Others scorned Paulson as King Henry, arrogant, un-American, a financial socialist. TARP itself was rebranded a "Total Abdication of Responsibility to the Public."

Paulson had attempted to comply with Senator Dodd's request to involve Congress by providing a bare bones bill. He acknowledged that the three page draft turned out to be a "political mistake." "Making no provision for judicial review came across as overreaching."

The errors in the Bill were far worse than that. Paulson and Bernanke were effective in private meetings with the President and Congressional leaders, and at September 23–24, 2008, House and Senate hearings in articulating the urgent need for action: "[W]e are witnessing a financial panic," Bernanke had told the President on September 18. This, Bernanke opined, is the worst crisis since the Great Depression "and it could get worse." Bernanke predicted that if stock prices dropped 20 percent, General Motors would go bankrupt, and unemployment would rise by about 50 percent. Paulson, as recalled by President Bush, was just as emphatic: "America's financial system is at stake."

Neither the Bill nor the testimony by Paulson and Bernanke, however, effectively answered how the $700 billion would be allocated to the Department of Treasury, how asset repurchases would be priced, why the United States government should not profit from the resale of troubled assets if they could be successfully resold, and why ideas popular with the Democrats such as limits on executive compensation were off the table. Members of both political parties were critical. As Bernanke recalled on September 24, the second day's hearings "felt like cruel and unusual punishment."

Further complicating the road to TARP was the reality that September 2008 was fewer than two months before the then hotly contested Presidential Election between Senator John McCain and Barack Obama. With ongoing negotiations between Congressional leaders, Treasury and Federal Reserve starting to make some progress, McCain announced that he was suspending his Presidential campaign to come to Washington to help resolve the crisis. This was an election year gambit that backfired.

McCain insisted on a September 25th meeting at the White House with President Bush, Senator Obama, Congressional leaders, and key actors from the Treasury and Federal Reserve. Obama spoke first, according to Paulson, delivering "a thoughtful, well-prepared presentation, sketching the broad outlines of the problem and stressing the need for immediate action." McCain surprisingly declined President Bush's offer to speak next and only spoke late in the meeting and anticlimactically. Bernanke later criticized McCain: "He certainly did not think through his decision to suspend his campaign to come to Washington. He arrived without clear buy-in or a plan from Republican Congressional leaders." The ineptitude of McCain's performance contributed to Obama's election in November.[199]

Meanwhile, the economic crisis continued to gather force.

WaMu and Wachovia

On September 25th, 2008, Washington Mutual, popularly known as WaMu, the largest thrift in the country with $207 billion in assets as of June 30, 2008 and $190 billion in insured deposits, was taken over with the FDIC appointed as receiver. This was the largest bank failure in United States history. "WaMu," the National Commission on the Causes of the Financial and Economic Crisis reported, "had been the subject of concern for some time because of its poor mortgage underwriting standards and its exposure to payment-option adjustable-rate mortgages (*ARMs*)." Beginning in the final quarter of 2007, WaMu had a series of asset write-downs — $1.9 billion in the last quarter of 2007 and $1.1 billion in the first quarter of 2008 — and quarterly losses — $3.3 billion in the second quarter of 2008. In the days after that report, depositors pulled $10 billion out of WaMu. In eight days after Lehman Brothers failed, depositors pulled $16.7 billion out of WaMu.

On September 11, 2008, Moody's had downgraded WaMu's senior unsecured debt to junk status because of "WaMu's reduced financial flexibility, deteriorating asset quality and franchise erosion." WaMu was the largest insured depository institution to fail. JP Morgan paid $1.9 billion to acquire WaMu's banking operations on September 25th. On September 26, WaMu filed for Chapter 11 bankruptcy reorganization. Sheila Bair, then Chair of the FDIC, was sharply critical of the OTS's regulation of WaMu. "Having lost two of its three major charges (Countrywide and Golden West) that were regulated by the OCC [Office of the Comptroller of the Currency], I feared that OTS would work to prevent an acquisition of WaMu to preserve its one remaining charter. These fears were continued when we were alerted by JP Morgan Chase that WaMu CEO Kerry Killinger had refused to talk about a possible acquisition because of JP Morgan's understandable desire to conduct due diligence on WaMu's loan portfolio before making an offer." In Bair's view, WaMu failed because "[i]ts valuable deposit franchise was eroded through massive withdrawals."[200]

Tim Geithner separately criticized the FDIC orchestrated purchase of WaMu's uninsured and insured deposits by JP Morgan Chase.[201] "In one of the least appreciated episodes of the crisis, the U.S. government made things worse. . . . The FDIC did not require JP Morgan to stand behind WaMu's other obligations, as we had required it to do with Bear Stearns, leaving WaMu's senior debt holders exposed to severe losses. . . . As . . . the entire history of financial crisis makes clear, imposing haircuts [that is, losses] on bank creditors during a systemic panic is a sure way to accelerate the panic."[202] Senior debt holders ultimately received about 55 cents on the dollar. Bernanke, a leading scholar of the financial crisis, as well as Federal Reserve Chair, was milder in his critique of the FDIC. He acknowledged that Bair "was pleased because JP Morgan's acquisition involved no cost to the FDIC and no losses to uninsured depositors, such as corporations and municipalities." But Bernanke continued "that the WaMu decision, while perhaps not catastrophic, hastened the fall of the next domino — Wachovia."[203]

Wachovia, the nation's fourth largest bank holding company indeed was the next domino poised to fall. With 3300 bank branches and $420 billion in deposits, Wachovia was twice as large as WaMu and larger than Lehman Brothers. As with WaMu, the bank's crisis had gathered momentum in 2007 and early 2008, before accelerating out of control in September 2008. Credit losses on adjustable rate mortgages held in Golden West, a subsidiary, contributed to Wachovia's near demise. Payment option adjustable rate mortgages of Golden West particularly would be blamed. These were the same products associated with the failure of Countrywide and WaMu. Wachovia had acquired Golden West for $25 billion in 2006 and acquired also its portfolio of what Bernanke termed "mostly lower-quality residential mortgages." Journalist Andrew Sorkin would report that Wachovia owned $122 billion of pay option adjustable rate mortgages in 2008.

In April 2008, Wachovia announced a loss of $350 million for the first three months of the year, prompting depositors to withdraw $15 billion in the following weeks. In June 2008, Wachovia fired Ken Thompson, its CEO of 32 years. Wachovia stopped originating Golden West's pick-a-pay adjustable rate mortgages later that month.

It was already too late. On July 22, Wachovia reported an $8.9 billion second-quarter loss. That same day, Standard & Poor's downgraded Wachovia and the Federal Reserve Bank projected losses for 2008, likely to consume recently raised capital. The Fed was sharply critical of the board and senior management for creating "an environment with incessant and inadequate identification, escalation and coverage of all risk-taking activities." On August 4, the OCC downgraded Wachovia and characterized its overall risk profile as "high".

Through the Lehman bankruptcy, the Fed had viewed Wachovia as strong enough to withstand a burgeoning liquidity crisis. This belief rapidly transformed after Lehman and then WaMu fell. On September 26, the day after WaMu was taken over by JP Morgan, Wachovia lost $5.7 billion of deposits and saw the value of its ten-year bonds collapse from 73 cents on the dollar to 29 cents. Wachovia's stock price declined 27 percent that day.

There rapidly evolved a consensus among federal finance regulators that Wachovia was too weak to open for business on Monday, September 29. By the weekend of September 27–28, it was anticipated by the FDIC and the OCC that Wachovia, with $17 billion in cash and cash equivalents, could face up to $115 billion of cash outflows the following week, including $42 billion of deposit withdrawals, $42 billion from corporate deposit accounts and $30 billion from retail brokerage accounts. While the FDIC and OCC estimated that Wachovia could raise $86 billion from the Federal Reserve Discount Window, the repo market, and other securities, its ability to continue as a stand-alone bank holding company appeared highly improbable.

The Federal Reserve staff argued that a Wachovia failure "would contribute to weaker economic performance, high unemployment and reduced wealth." The Treasury "vigorously advocated" saving Wachovia. White House Chief of Staff Josh Bolten called Sheila Bair on Sunday, September 28 to express support for the systemic risk provision to provide federal support. After the Treasury took the consequential step of guaranteeing all government losses from the FDIC's Deposit Insurance Fund, the FDIC voted to support government assistance, and the Federal Reserve Board on September 28 voted to approve the systemic risk exception for the first time in 17 years. Both Citicorp, which first signed an agreement in principle with Wachovia, and Wells Fargo, with the ultimate successful bid, pursued Wachovia. On October 3rd, Wells Fargo signed a definitive agreement with Wachovia to purchase its shares at $7 per share without government assistance. The Federal Reserve Board approved the Wells Fargo-Wachovia merger on October 9.[204]

The Bush Administration's initial effort to enact TARP failed on September 29 when the House of Representatives rejected the bill by a vote of 228–205. Two-thirds of the Republicans voted against the TARP bill, 60 percent of Democrats voted for the bill. TARP was wildly unpopular. As Republican Senator Jon Kyl [R-AZ] told Bernanke, his constituents calls were running 50–50: "Fifty percent no, fifty percent hell no."

The stock market's response to the vote was brutal. The Dow Jones Industrial Average fell 778 points, approximately 7 percent. The broader Standard & Poor's 500 Index was hit even harder and fell almost 9 percent. "Overall," as Paulson observed, "more than $1 trillion on stock market value was wiped out — a jarring one-day record."

The precipitousness of the stock market fall saved TARP. Sometimes nothing succeeds like failure. Geithner recalled: "The market crash seemed to focus [the public's] minds. Before Monday [September 29], the public's reaction to TARP had been all anti-bailout anger, but now politicians started hearing from constituents whose life savings were disappearing."

The Act itself was now 168 pages in length, replete with provisions providing alternative minimum tax relief, extension of numerous individual and business tax provisions, and energy production incentives.

The thrust of the Act remained the Secretary of Treasury's authority to purchase troubled assets. This was virtually identical to the earlier three-page proposal. But virtually everything else was new.

Republican Eric Cantor [R-VA], House Majority Leader, had proposed an insurance program as an alternative to direct asset purchases. For a fee, the government would insure institutions holding troubled assets against losses. While both Paulson and Bernanke were skeptical, some House Republicans liked the idea and dutifully TARP included a section to allow the Treasury to develop a program to insure troubled assets through a government guarantee and fee collection program for participating financial institutions. The program would never be implemented.

To secure Democratic party votes, the Act included sections that limited executive compensation of senior executives in any financial institution that sells $300 million or more in troubled assets to the Secretary of Treasury. These limits included a prohibition on golden parachute (or severance payments) to senior executives (the top five highest paid executives of a public company) "during the period that the Secretary holds an equity or debt position in the financial institution and reduced the tax deductibility for corporations paying compensation for such executives from $1 million to $500,000.

This was a reluctantly accepted compromise by Paulson, Bernanke, and Geithner. While each understood the political appeal of compensation limits, they also questioned the relevance of these limits to resolving a financial crisis. Paulson was particularly adamantly opposed to executive compensation provisions in part because he feared if the limits were a price of participating in a troubled asset program, fewer institutions would participate. Paulson, as well as Bernanke and Geithner, came to understand: "To get the votes, we're going to need executive compensation restrictions."

TARP included several other sweeteners and compromises.

The FDIC and Federal Credit Union Administration were authorized to increase deposit insurance from $100,000 to $250,000 for each individual account. The authorization initially only ran until December 31, 2009, in the TARP Act but was later made permanent.

Multiple supervisory boards or audits were established, including a Financial Stability Oversight Board (comprised of the Federal Reserve Chair, the Secretary of Treasury, the Director of the Federal Housing Finance Agency, the SEC Chair, and the Secretary of Housing and Urban Development). The Comptroller General was directed to commence audits of TARP. Separately, a Special Inspector General was established for TARP, as well as a bipartisan and bicameral Congressional Oversight Panel.

The Secretary of Treasury was given graduated authorization to spend up to $700 billion. Initially the authority was limited to $350 billion with authorization of the President to seek up to an additional $350 billion. The Act held back the last $350 billion given the possibility that there would be a new party in the White House within a few weeks.

The Secretary of the Treasury was authorized to engage in foreclosure mitigation efforts at least for acquired residential real estate. Judicial review was expressly established.

On October 1, 2008, the Senate passed the Emergency Economic Stabilization Act of 2008, which included TARP, by a vote of 74–25.

Two days later, the House reversed itself and approved TARP by a vote of 263–171 with 32 Democrats and 26 Republicans flipping their votes to approve the new law.[205]

The enactment of TARP did not slow the rapidly deteriorating economy. In the week immediately following TARP's passage, October 3–10, 2008, the Dow Jones Industrial Average fell 1874 points, 18 percent. "[C]onfidence in financial institutions had nearly evaporated," Bernanke recalled. "The 'fear index' [the volatility index]," Geithner wrote, "a measure of market volatility, hit an all-time high." Geithner continued:

> In the United States, private credit was now virtually unavailable. The financial system was increasingly unable to play its most basic role in the economy: facilitating the flow of money from those who wanted to lend to those who wanted to invest or consume. The run on money market funds after Lehman, followed by the broader run on the banking system that consumed WaMu and Wachovia, had spilled into the unsecured commercial paper market where businesses with strong credit histories could raise money to finance their day-to-day operations.

The National Commission on Causes of the Financial and Economic Crisis adumbrated: "The spread between the interest rate at which banks lend to one another and interest rates on Treasuries — a closely watched indicator of market confidence — hit an all-time high. And the dollar value of outstanding commercial paper issued by both financial and nonfinancial companies had fallen by $264 billion in the month between Lehman's failure and TARP's enactment."[206]

Lawrence McDonald, a former Lehman Brothers Vice President, described the escalating panic:

> On Monday, October 6, the first full trading day since the bill was passed, the Dow crashed down through 10,000 with an intraday low of 9,525. It closed at 9,955 in a day packed with fear-laden trading and volatility, a day in which the Volatility Index (*VXO*) broke 50 for the first time since 1987. This wasn't volatility. This was hysteria.
>
> There were no brakes, and on Tuesday, October 7, there was another collapse of the Dow. It went down more than 500 points on the day, closing at 9,447. No one could remember traders being this scared. But they found out what fear really meant two days later, on Thursday, October 9, when the Dow continued its free fall, losing 682 points on the day. The VXO ripped straight up to an all-time high of 64, and the closing bell sounded out a chilling death knell of 8,579 on the Dow.
>
> No one on Wall Street slept a wink that Thursday night. No one who had ever the remotest concept of the untold damage being inflicted on the economy could possibly have found rest. There were people who stayed in their offices for the whole night, waiting for the dawn, waiting once more for the thunder of the heavy artillery blasting the U.S. economy apart.
>
> October 10 came in with fire and fury. The Dow collapsed, with a difference between the intraday high and low of over 1,000 points. The VXO registered an all-time squeal of terror, closing at 76.94. No one had ever seen anything like it. At the closing bell the Dow stood at 8,451. But it was not the number, it was the nerve-shaking up-down frenzy that got it there.[207]

The crisis was now global. Journalist Roger Lowenstein reported:

> On Monday, October 6, the world experienced a global panic. Foreigners who had breezily invested in American mortgages on the offhand assumption that America was immune to

> financial collapse woke up to the sobering realization that global markets were just as connected on the downside of the cycle. China's stock market fell 5 percent in a day, Japan's and Korea's more than 3 percent, Russia's a devastating 19 percent. . . . The panic rolled on: France fell 9 percent, Britain 8 percent. In America, . . . Jim Cramer, broadcasting's jittery market oracle, told listeners to "sell everything now."[208]

Author and CNBC contributor Lawrence McDonald amplified:

> Europe collapsed first. Germany's DAX, the thirty blue chips, hit 4,308, down from a May high of 7,231. France's CAC-40, the forty top companies listed on the Paris Bourse, plummeted to 3,047 off a May high of 5,142. Spain's IBEX-35 index, the thirty-five most liquid stocks on the Madrid board, had fallen to 9,462 from 14,247. Ireland's ISEQ, the official list of equities on the Dublin exchange, dropped from a high of 6,460 to 2,751. Iceland was on its way to 677 from its May high of 4,942.
>
> London's FTSE closed at 3,873; in May it had been 6,300. Russia's MICEX, their thirty largest companies, was closed on October 10, but the day before it had fallen to 637 from a May high of 1,966. China's CSI-300 had gone from 3,936 in May to 1,881. The Nikkei 225 closed at 8.115, having hit 14,343 on May 19. The Hang Seng Index in Hong Kong was at 14,398, from a May high of 25,822.
>
> Nowhere was immune, no matter the distance from Wall Street. Australia's preeminent benchmark, the S&P/ASX-200 Index, had fallen just over 2,000 points from its May high and now closed at 3,960. Brazil had caved in from 73,440 to 33,230.[209]

On September 29, Ireland had guaranteed all liabilities, including uninsured deposits and debt instruments of its largest banks.

On Monday October 5, 2008, Germany arranged a $68 billion rescue for its second largest commercial property lender, Hypo Real Estate, and Chancellor Angela Merkel stated — but later backed off a commitment — that her country would guarantee all personal savings accounts, calculated by some to be a $1 trillion guarantee. The previous day, Belgium, the Netherlands, and Luxembourg had injected the equivalent to $16 billion into Fortis, a banking and insurance company. Belgium in late September had made a large loan to Depfa, a Hypo Real Estate subsidiary.

Iceland on October 7 took over two of its three largest banks and was negotiating a loan from Russia. This turned, as economist Alan Blinder wrote, "a bank's crisis into a sovereign debt crisis. Ireland's annual government budget deficit in 2010 was a shocking 32 percent of [Gross Domestic Product], likely setting a modern-day world record."

On October 8, the British Government announced a capital investment of $87 billion in eight large banks, receiving in return convertible preferred stock to give British taxpayers some profit if these investments later could be successfully sold.[210]

In a crisis spiraling out of control, Bernanke and Paulson rapidly improvised. The Federal Reserve on October 7 doubled its swap lines to other Central Banks to $620 billion and increased six times scheduled auctions of Discount Window credit to banks in the United States to $900 billion. On October 8, the Federal Reserve Bank in tandem with the European Central Bank, the Bank of England, the Bank of Canada, the Swiss National Bank, and Sweden's Riksbank, each announced interest rate cuts of one half of one percent.

On October 7, the Federal Reserve also created the Commercial Paper Funding Facility to purchase short term debt. The National Commission on the Causes of the Financial and Economic Crisis emphasized: "This program, which allowed firms to roll over their debt, would be widely used by financial and nonfinancial firms. The three financial firms that made the greatest use of the program were foreign institutions: UBS (which borrowed a cumulative $72 billion over time), Dexia ($53 billion), and Barclays ($38 billion)."

Paulson praised the emergency creation of the Commercial Paper Funding Facility:

> Something had to be done. The credit markets remained locked up, endangering businesses — and employment — around the world. On Tuesday, the Fed made another attempt to thaw the markets, unveiling its new Commercial Paper Funding Facility.
>
> ... This new approach created a special purpose vehicle to buy three-month paper from all U.S. issuers, vastly improving the liquidity in the market. The new facility represented a radical move by the Fed, but Ben Bernanke and his board knew that extraordinary measures had to be taken.

Roger Lowenstein went further, characterizing the Facility to buy commercial paper "as revolutionary as paper money or aluminum bats":

> The Fed had always been a banker to *banks.* If it wanted to stimulate auto sales or manufacturing, it lent money to financial intermediaries, confident that the added liquidity would flow toward the rest of the economy. But the banks were moribund — useless. Bernanke was saying that the Fed would lend directly to department stores, computer makers, and airlines by buying their commercial paper. It would be the banker to, if need be, every firm in America.

Bernanke believed that the Commercial Paper Funding Facility "quickly proved its value." By October 29, two days after it began operations, the Facility had purchased $145 billion in three-month commercial paper. By January 2009, the peak of the program, the Facility held $350 billion in short term paper.

But Bernanke acknowledged that in early October 2008, "the financial system was still reeling from the Lehman shock." On Tuesday, October 7, the Dow Jones Industrial Average fell 508 points or 5.1 percent, the Standard & Poor's 500 fell below 1000 for the first time since 2003.[211]

On October 10, the G-7 Group met in Washington D.C. in the Treasury Department's Cash Room with the leaders of the International Monetary Fund and World Bank. There was intense anger among the G-7 members. Bernanke recalled: "Most of the financial ministers and central bank governors assembled blamed the United States for the crisis. Whose financial deregulation had subjected the world to the depredations of 'cowboy capitalism'? Whose subprime mortgages had infected the assets of financial institutions around the world? Who had let Lehman fail?" Despite the initial finger pointing, the meeting did release a five point set of Guidelines:

> The G-7 agrees today that the current situation calls for urgent and exceptional action. We commit to continue working together to stabilize financial markets and restore the flow of credit, to support global economic growth. We agree to:
>
> 1. Take decisive action to use all available tools to support systemically important financial institutions and prevent their failure.

2. Take all necessary steps to unfreeze credit and money markets and ensure that banks and other financial institutions have broad access to liquidity and funding.
3. Ensure that our banks and other major financial intermediaries, as needed, can raise capital from public as well as private sources, in sufficient amounts to re-establish confidence and permit them to continue lending to households and businesses.
4. Ensure that our respective national deposit insurance and guarantee programs are robust and consistent so that our retail depositors will continue to have confidence in the safety of their deposits.
5. Take action, where appropriate, to restart the secondary markets for mortgages and other securitized assets. Accurate valuation and transparent disclosure of assets and consistent implementation of high quality accounting standards are necessary.

These generalizations alone did not assuage the market. October 10th was a day of extraordinary volatility. The Dow Jones Industrial Average was in free fall at the opening, falling 8 percent or 680 points in the first seven minutes of trading. The Dow Jones then rose 631 points in the next 40 minutes. Ultimately, the market closed down 128 points for the day.[212]

At this point, the most decisive steps of the Bush Administration response to the financial crisis occurred.

Repurposing TARP

Even before the October 3 enactment of TARP, Paulson had begun to gravitate towards the preferred strategy of Bernanke and Geithner — investing capital into key financial institutions with the federal government acquiring stock, that is, partial ownership of the banks. For Bernanke, the logic of this approach was self-evident: "Capital injections would strengthen banks directly, by increasing the buffer available to absorb losses. In contrast, purchases of troubled assets would strengthen banks indirectly and only to the extent that they raised the prices of the assets that banks held." Bernanke recalled that Paulson had raised the possibility on October 1 during lunch with President Bush of using TARP funds to provide new capital to banks as well as asset purchases.

By October 10, "Hank had clearly shifted away from asset purchases. Whatever the merits of the strategy in the abstract, it was becoming clear that financial markets and the economy were deteriorating too quickly. There just wasn't time to design and implement an effective asset-purchase program." The Department of Treasury, Geithner wrote, "thought it would take at least forty-five days after passage before the [asset purchase] program could begin."

President Bush agreed:

> I loathed the idea of the government owning pieces of banks. I worried Congress would consider it a bait and switch to spend the money on something other than buying toxic assets. But that was a risk we had to take. The plan for TARP had to change because the financial situation was worsening rapidly.

Coincident with the decision to inject capital into the banks was a second, critical step: Guaranteeing financial firms' debt was first. Geithner stressed: "Capital was necessary to make banks stronger, but creditors were running away from banks regardless of their strength, and capital alone wouldn't stop a run already in progress. We needed to stop the run on liquidity first, and that would require guarantees."[213]

A multiprong plan was presented to nine leading financial institutions. Four were the largest commercial banks then in the nation — Bank of America, Citigroup, JP Morgan, and Wells Fargo; three recently had been key investment banks — Goldman Sachs, Morgan Stanley, and Merrill Lynch; and two were major clearing and settlement banks, critical to the financial infrastructure — BNY Mellon and State Street. Collectively, these nine institutions held more than $11 trillion in assets or about 75 percent of the assets of all United States banks.

At an intense October 13th meeting at the Treasury, Paulson, Bernanke, and Geithner explained that the Treasury would set aside $250 billion from TARP to purchase equity in financial firms under a new Capital Purchase Program in return for nonvoting preferred stock that would receive a 5 percent dividend for five years and then rise to 9 percent after that to encourage the companies to repurchase the government investment. The senior executives of these firms would be subject to the new TARP limits on executive compensation. The terms were intended to be attractive. "We didn't want it to look or be like a nationalization," Paulson later testified.

Specifically, these nine firms would receive one half or $125 billion of the $250 billion in funds: $25 billion each to Citigroup, JP Morgan, and Wells Fargo; $15 billion to Bank of America; $10 billion each to Merrill Lynch, Morgan Stanley, and Goldman Sachs; $3 billion to BNY Mellon; and $2 billion to State Street. These numbers were equal to investments of 3 percent of each institution's risk-weighted assets.

The National Commission on the Causes of the Financial and Economic Crisis further explained:

> Later in the week, Treasury opened TARP to qualifying "healthy" and "viable" banks, thrifts, and holding companies, under the same terms that the first nine firms had received. The appropriate federal regulator — the Fed, FDIC, OCC, or OTS — would review applications and pass them to Treasury for final approval. The program was intended not only to restore confidence in the banking system but also to provide banks with sufficient capital to fulfill their "responsibilities in the areas of lending, dividend and compensation policies, and foreclosure mitigation."

Ultimately, $205 billion would be invested through TARP's Capital Purchase Program in 707 financial institutions.[214]

Simultaneously, the FDIC would guarantee all new senior debt of banks and bank holding companies for more than 30 days up to three years. In return, unless an institution chose to opt out, the bank had to pay a fee for the protection. The guarantee, however, would not cover existing debt or reach broker-dealer subsidiaries. Ultimately, 122 banks and bank holding companies would issue $346 billion in guaranteed debt through a program officially named the Temporary Loan Guarantee Program. Geithner often had sharp differences with FDIC Chair Sheila Bair, but on this issue, he was effusive in his praise: Her "willingness to use the FDIC's guarantee authority was one of the turning points of the crisis."

The FDIC also extended deposit insurance to non-interest-bearing deposits such as checking accounts at all insured depository institutions.

At the October 13th meeting with the nine leading financial institutions, Geithner emphasized that the capital and debt programs were linked: You could not have one without the other.

The reaction in Europe and in the stock markets to the Treasury-Financial Reserve-FDIC plan was enthusiastic. On October 12,

15 eurozone countries agreed to inject billions of euros into their banks through equity stakes and guarantee new bank debt through 2009.

On Monday, October 13, the United Kingdom's FTSE 100 index rose 8.3 percent; German and French markets rose more than 11 percent. Before the results of the October 13th meeting with the United States financial institutions were announced, the Dow Jones Industrial Average achieved its largest single day jump in history — 936 points or 11 percent, followed by 4.1 percent on October 14, a day in which the London FTSE 100 index rose another 3.2 percent and the Japanese Nikkei index rocketed 14.2 percent.

There nonetheless was considerable criticism of the October 13th decision. Just ten days earlier, Congress had enacted TARP with the assumption that the sole or main purpose of the new law with its astonishingly large $700 billion authorization was to repurchase troubled assets. Now, no assets were repurchased or planned to be repurchased and the Treasury had abruptly shifted to a capital injection plan. Significantly, the capital was being invested in the nation's largest financial institutions, not troubled mortgages or Main Street. Whether derided as a bailout, subject to conflicts of interest — Paulson had been CEO of Goldman Sachs — or just protecting the fat cats of the economy, TARP as implemented would prove remarkably unpopular.[215]

History is the study of consequences. And the real measure of a program's success is how well it works over time.

In the short term, TARP did not succeed. It is worth stressing that no program begun when TARP started could have succeeded in the short term to have prevented the shocks that continued throughout 2008 and 2009. The shocks nonetheless were severe.

AIG, by early October, as Paulson later wrote, "had run through most of its $85 billion loan — in barely three weeks." On October 6, the Federal Reserve Bank established another $37.8 billion program for AIG, authorizing the Federal Reserve Bank of New York to extend cash collateral in return for investment grade, fixed-income securities. "During the previous few weeks," Geithner wrote, "we had committed more money to AIG than the federal government had spent on Social Security and Medicare." The new $37.8 billion infusion also did not work.

On October 14, AIG reported what Geithner termed "a devastating $24 billion third-quarter loss. . . . AIG was getting crushed by incessant margin calls, prompting rating agencies to consider new downgrades, which would lead to additional margin calls. The company was once again on the brink of default, even after our twelve-figure assistance package."

Geithner, Paulson, and Bernanke each believed that: "Defunding was not an option, unless we wanted a global stampede that could have made the aftermath of Lehman look relatively mild." On the other hand, none of the three wanted to keep "throwing money into the bottomless pit." "AIG," Geithner wrote, "was starting to look like our Vietnam."

On November 10, AIG became the first TARP recipient that was not part of the Capital Purchase Program, which then essentially was limited to strengthening healthy financial firms. The Treasury purchased from the member Created Commercial Paper Funding Facilities $40 billion in AIG preferred stock, receiving warrants for 2 percent of AIG's stock and imposed dividend and executive compensation restrictions. This $40 billion allowed AIG to repay the supplemental $37.8 billion that it had received from the Federal Reserve Bank and to reduce the original $85 billion credit line to $60 billion. The Treasury and Federal Reserve also substantially lowered the interest rate from 8.5 to 3 percent above the then standard LIBOR (the London Interbank Offered Rate) being charged AIG and extended the time for repayment from three to five years. In 2012, the Treasury would receive $15.1 billion on the sale of its AIG shares.

On November 10th, the Federal Reserve also began implementation of a plan under § 13(3) of the Federal Reserve Act to allow the New York Federal Reserve Bank to create and finance two new facilities called Maiden Lane II and Maiden Lane III to purchase AIG's bad debts. The New York Federal Reserve Bank was authorized to loan $22.5 billion to Maiden Lane II to acquire the residential mortgage securities that, as Bernanke wrote, "had inflicted so many losses on AIG." Maiden Lane III was separately lent $30 billion by the New York Federal Reserve Bank to buy collateralized debt obligations from AIG counterparties that had been created by AIG's Financial Products Division. "By acquiring the CDOs, we effectively closed out the insurance policies that had brought AIG to the brink in September." In addition, "[m]ore than 20 AIG subsidiaries would be sold. "AIG," Paulson reported, "would become a much smaller, more narrowly focused property/casualty insurer."

In the long run, the rescue plan for AIG worked. By January 2011, AIG had fully repaid its $182.3 billion debt.

The political fury caused by the AIG catastrophe was intense. When Paulson and other Treasury officials presented the AIG plan to President Bush, Paulson reported Bush's frustration "with both the incompetence of the company's prior management and the rating agencies that had failed to catch AIG's problems earlier:"

> President Bush's anger quickly echoed across the country when taxpayers learned the government was revamping its September bailout plan and giving AIG easier loan terms along with much-needed capital. To the public, AIG symbolized everything that had gone wrong with the system — incompetence rewarded with big bonuses and lavish spending.

The National Commission on the Causes of the Financial and Economic Crisis emphasized another dimension of the public's outrage over AIG. Goldman Sachs received $14 billion in payments from Maiden Lane III related to the credit default swaps it had purchased from AIG. In all, $43.7 billion would be paid to counterparties by Maiden Lane II and Maiden Lane III. The National Commission summarized the criticism of these and other payments to AIG counterparties:

> That AIG's counterparties did not incur any losses on their investments — because AIG, once it was backed by the government, paid claims to CDS counterparties at 100% of face value — has been widely criticized. In November 2009, SIGTARP [Special Inspector General for TARP] faulted the New York Fed for failing to obtain concessions. The inspector general said that seven of the top eight counterparties had insisted on 100% coverage and that the New York Fed had agreed because efforts to obtain concessions from all counterparties had little hope of success. . . .
>
> In June 2010, TARP's Congressional Oversight Panel criticized the AIG bailout for having a "poisonous" effect on capital markets. The report said the government's failure to require "shared sacrifice" among AIG's creditors effectively altered the relationship between the government and the markets, signaling an implicit "too big to fail" guarantee for certain firms. The report said the New York Fed should have insisted on concessions from counterparties.

Geithner, Bernanke, and Sarah Dahlgren, who supervised the Maiden II transaction of the New York Federal Reserve Bank, controverted this analysis. In the view of Treasury and Federal Reserve Bank officials, an issuance of concessions would have led to an instant ratings downgrade and precipitated a run on AIG. Nor, in Dahlgren's view, could the federal government threaten AIG's bankruptcy to secure concessions. "There was a financial meltdown. The credibility of the United States government was on the line."[216]

Citigroup

In early October 2008, as Bernanke later wrote: "AIG was not the only corporate patient in critical care. Within a few weeks, Citigroup also looked to be on the brink." Citigroup was three times the size of Lehman Brothers and far more integral to the functioning of a global economy, as Geithner emphasized. After Citi's 1998 merger with insurance giant Travelers Insurance Group, Citi had been the nation's largest bank holding company, only eclipsed in the years before 2008 by JP Morgan Chase.

With more than $2 trillion in assets, Citi was a global giant with operations in more than 100 countries, but with an awkward corporate structure having been built through several acquisitions with a modest domestic retail deposit base for a bank of its size. This made Citi more dependent on higher risk commercial mortgages, credit cards, and collateralized debt obligations. By 2008, Citi had more than $1.2 trillion in assets off its balance sheet in structured investment vehicles (*SIVs*), half related to mortgages. Citi was widely regarded as the weakest of the major United States banks.

In 2007, with Citi's leverage ratio in recent years having grown from 18:1 to 32:1, Citi had brought $80 billion of its off balance sheet assets onto its balance sheet. Off balance sheet assets were permitted by federal bank agencies to exist but not be counted in capital requirements. Sheila Bair was particularly critical of Citi's SIV practices:

> A number of large financial institutions, led by Citigroup, started having trouble accessing enough funding to support their mortgages and [mortgage-backed securities] investments. Citi and a few other large banks had set up something called "structured investment vehicles" as a way to invest in mortgages and mortgage-backed securities. For reasons that still today

> remain a mystery to me, they were allowed by their regulators — the Fed and the OCC — to keep the investments off balance sheet, meaning that they were not included in the financial reports insured banks filed with us, and, most important, they were not required to hold capital or reserves against those assets to absorb losses. Indeed, our examiners did not know anything about SIVs until the Federal Reserve Board alerted us to Citi's difficulties.
>
> Here was the problem: Citi's SIVs issued "commercial paper" — extremely short term bonds of usually thirty days or less — to finance the acquisition of mortgages and mortgage-backed securities. It was nothing short of idiotic for Citi and others to be funding such long-term assets with very short term bonds, but they did so because the rate they had to pay investors on short-term commercial paper was much lower than what they would have paid on bonds for multiyear duration.

About 20 percent of Citi's off balance sheet operations were funded through foreign deposits. This reduced the cost of Citi funding itself because foreign deposits were not FDIC-insured and Citi did not have to pay insurance premiums on them. However, when Citi's finances deteriorated, the foreign deposits began to run, adding to Citi's financial deterioration. Citi had a total of approximately $500 billion in foreign deposits.

Citi's internal corporate culture added to the stresses of the firm with notable tensions between its commercial bank senior leaders and investment bankers such as Citi CEO Vikram Pandit. In Bair's view, Citi "had been hijacked by an investment banking culture that made profits through high-stakes betting on the direction of the markets, in contrast to traditional banking, which focused on making loans to people based on their ability to repay."

Beginning in 2007, Citi's quarterly financial results had deteriorated — a $9.8 billion reported loss in the fourth quarter of 2007, a $5.1 billion loss in the first quarter of 2008, a $2.5 billion loss in the second quarter of 2008, a $2.8 billion loss in the third quarter of 2008, and ultimately an $8.3 billion loss in the fourth quarter.

By October 2008, Citi was fragile. Beginning in 2003, Citi had become a national leader in Collateralized Debt Obligations (CDOs), creating $18 billion in 2003 and 2004, using structure earlier pioneered by Goldman Sachs of structuring its CDOs as short-term asset-backed commercial paper. This was risky — commercial paper had to be rolled over when due. Most CDOs had issued long-term debt without this type of liquidity risk. "To mitigate the liquidity risk," the National Commission on the Causes of the Financial and Economic Crisis reported, "and to ensure that the rating agencies would give it their top ratings, Citibank (Citigroup's national bank subsidiary) provided assurances to investors, in the form of liquidity puts. In selling the liquidity put, for an ongoing fee the bank would be on the hook to step in and buy the commercial paper if there were no buyers when it matured or if the cost of funding rose by a predetermined amount."

Between 2003 and 2006, Citi would write liquidity puts on $25 billion of commercial paper issued by CDOs, more than any other company. This created another risk that if triggered saddled Citi with liabilities. Beginning in 2007, when the subprime mortgage market cracked, Citi was required to come up with $25 billion in cash to cover its commercial paper as well as more capital to satisfy its bank regulators. Citi stopped writing liquidity puts in 2006.

When Wachovia decided to abandon its exclusivity agreement with Citi and instead pursue an agreement with Wells Fargo, Geithner was deeply concerned:

> I was worried that scuttling the Citi deal could end up crippling an already vulnerable $2 trillion institution, weakening it at the worst possible time. Citi's stock price, after rising on the news of the Wachovia merger, would fall 18 percent on the news the merger was off, its steepest drop in two decades. Markets now assumed that Citi must have needed Wachovia's domestic deposits to survive.

Geithner added:

> Citi was . . . a mess, choking on mortgages on and off its balance sheet, with a highly vulnerable funding base compared to other major U.S. banks. Its stock price briefly rebounded after its TARP capital injection, but the glow wore off quickly as its losses kept mounting. Its problems intensified on November 12, when Hank announced that the Bush Treasury would not be purchasing any illiquid assets after all. I agreed with Hank's decision, but the announcement seemed unnecessary, sucking hope out of the markets at a fragile time, pushing down asset prices and hurting confidence in financial firms at a moment when Citi looked like the weakest link. A week later, the off-balance-sheet SIVs that got Citi in trouble in the fall of 2007

> faced such daunting losses that the company had to bring the rest of them back onto its balance sheet, spooking the markets yet again. Its stock price dropped below $4, down 93 percent from its 2006 peak.

On October 13th, Citi had been the recipient of $25 billion in the first swath of TARP money provided to nine leading financial institutions. This was a lifeline. Paulson, Bernanke, and Geithner each believed after the G-7 October 10th release that they would not let another major financial institution fail. President Bush had emphasized on November 19: "Just don't let Citi fail." Citi also had received other substantial government support. The National Commission on the Causes of the Financial and Economic Crisis summarized: "In addition to the $25 billion from TARP, . . . [a]s of November 21, [Citi] had $24.3 billion outstanding under the Fed, collateralized liquidity programs and $200 million under the Fed's Commercial Paper Funding Facility. And [Citi] had borrowed $84 billion from the Federal Home Loan banks."

By October 2008, Citi's stock price had become unnervingly volatile. To Citi CEO Pandit, the October crisis was not about capital or funding, but the stock price where, "perception [had become] reality." Citi's stock price had fallen 18 percent on October 3, the day Wachovia announced that it preferred Wells Fargo's offer, following by another 43 percent decline within a week. Citi's stock price had risen 18 percent on October 14, the first trading day after the $25 billion TARP commitment had been announced. Then Citi's stock price fell 17 percent in the week beginning October 16 when its $2.8 billion third quarter loss was announced. By November 12, Citi's stock was selling below $10 for the first time since 1996.

Citi was now in a death spiral. The National Commission on the Causes of the Financial and Economic Crisis summarized:

> The market's unease was heightened by press speculation that the company's board had lost confidence in senior management.
>
> . . . On November 19, the company announced that the value of the SIVs had fallen by $1.1 billion in the month since it had released third-quarter earnings. Citigroup was therefore going to bring the remaining $17.4 billion in off-balance-sheet SIV assets onto its books. Investors clipped almost another 24% off the value of the stock, its largest single-day drop since the October 1987 stock market crash. Two days later, the stock closed at

> $3.77. Credit defaults swaps on Citigroup reached a steep $500,000 annually to protect $10 million in Citigroup debt against default.

On Friday, November 21, the United Kingdom's Financial Services Authority imposed a $6.4 billion cash lockup to protect Citi's London broker-dealer.

With the current expectation of 2 percent outflow of deposits per day by November 2008, Citi anticipated that without a large and immediate injection of funds, Citi would be without funds by that weekend.

On Sunday, November 23, 2008, the Treasury, Federal Reserve, and FDIC entered into a historic agreement with Citigroup to support financial market stability. Under the agreement, the FDIC and Treasury agreed to "ring fence" or help guarantee $306 billion of what Paulson called Citi's toxic assets, including residential and commercial mortgage-related securities and troubled corporate loans. Specifically, Citi was committed to absorbing the first $37 billion of losses in the $306 billion pool and 10 percent of any remainder. The federal government assumed the risk of 90 percent of the losses on the pool. The Treasury and FDIC would absorb the next $15 billion. The first $5 billion would come out of TARP; the FDIC would take the next $10 billion. If losses were still larger, the Treasury would cover the rest through a nonrecourse loan.

The Treasury also provided Citi $20 billion more in TARP funds.

In return, Citi issued $7 billion of preferred stock with an 8 percent dividend to the Treasury and the FDIC, as well as warrants convertible into a 4.5 percent share in Citi's common stock. Citi further agreed to virtually eliminate its stock dividends and stricter limits on executive compensation than those in the Treasury Capital Purchase Program. Citi also had to implement the FDIC's stringent IndyMac protocol on mortgage modification.

Citi, as Princeton economist Alan Blinder recognized, "was now essentially sheltered from the storm." Its stock rose 58 percent the day of the announcement, rising to a close of $5.95.

"Why," Bernanke later wrote, "did we ring-fence Citi assets, rather than just add more capital? The ring fence, modeled on the deal that the FDIC had struck when Citi was trying to acquire Wachovia, was intended to protect Citi from a worst-case scenario. Eliminating the relatively small risk that Citi could suffer extreme losses reassured investors while requiring a relatively smaller commitment of dwindling TARP funds."

There was one more critical political reality to the Treasury-Federal Reserve-FDIC rescue of Citi. The Democrats in Congress now expected the Treasury to help the automakers. Paulson paraphrased their message: "You can't just take care of fat-cat Wall Street bankers and ignore the plight of working Americans."[217]

The Auto Industry

Nearly simultaneously with the gathering AIG debacle had been the deterioration of General Motors and Chrysler. On September 30, President Bush had signed a $25 billion loan package to help the Big Three automakers meet federal fuel economy standards. On October 13, GM reported to Paulson that creditors and suppliers were not being paid on time and without a $10 billion loan, GM feared bankruptcy. Paulson believed that he lacked the authority to make a TARP loan to GM. House Majority Leader Nancy Pelosi [D-CA] declined to change the language of the $25 billion fuel efficiency loan, contending that Paulson could use TARP funds to rescue automobile firms. Bernanke agreed that consistent with the Federal Reserve's original purpose, "we should focus our efforts on the financial panic. We were hardly the right agency to oversee the restructuring of a specific industry, an area in which we had little or no expertise. And unlike the financial emergencies that required quick responses, the threats to the auto industry were unfolding more slowly, giving Congress time to debate options."

On October 27, Moody's downgraded the credit ratings on GM and Chrysler debt contributing to a 203 point decline in the Dow Jones Industrial Average that day.

The November 4th election of Barack Obama was a factor in the subsequent provision of funds for the automobile industry. Five days after the election, General Motors, once the very epitome of United States industrial might, announced it would run out of cash by the middle of 2009 unless it received government assistance, sold assets, or was merged into another company.

Six days after the election, President Bush, who had opposed Jimmy Carter's bailout of Chrysler in 1979, met with President-elect Obama and told him: "I won't let the automakers fail." In his memoir, Bush wrote: "[M]y economic advisers had warned that the immediate bankruptcy of the Big Three would cost more than a million jobs, decrease tax revenues by $150 billion, and set back America's GDP by hundreds of billions of dollars."

At Paulson's last lunch with President Bush in December 2008, Bush informed Paulson that he would support the auto bailout:

> For President Bush, the auto bailout was a bitter pill to swallow, especially as the last major economic decision of his administration. He disliked bailouts, and he distained Detroit for not making cars people wanted to buy. But we were in the midst of a financial crisis and a deepening recession, and he recognized that if the giant companies were to declare bankruptcy, they would be doing so without advance planning or inadequate financing for an orderly restructuring. The consequences for the economy would be devastating. It would create more panic, and it would crush auto suppliers and other carmakers — not just Chrysler and Ford, but also Honda's and Toyota's U.S. operations.

On December 19, President Bush announced initial support for the automobile industry — up to $13.4 billion in loans for General Motors and $4 billion for Chrysler. On December 19, the Treasury announced a $5 billion infusion into General Motors Acceptance Corporation (*GMAC*), long the finance company associated with GM, which by then had become a bank holding company, along with $1 billion for General Motors to invest in GMAC. On January 16, the Treasury committed $1.5 billion of TARP funds to Chrysler Financial. The Bush Administration understood that the incoming Obama Administration was determined to support the auto industry.[218]

Bank of America

The rat-a-tat of bad news continued. In the first two weeks after Obama's November 3rd election, the Dow fell 17 percent. On December 1st, the National Bureau of Economic Research announced that the United States had been in a recession for the past year. The Dow Jones fell 680 points or 7.7 percent.[219]

Bank of America (*BofA*), which earlier had acquired Countrywide and on September 15 announced it would merge with Merrill Lynch, BofA now also was wobbly. The Merrill Lynch merger, scheduled to be completed early in 2009, fortified Bank of America as owning the world's largest broker-dealer. BofA already was the Nation's largest depository institution. On October 13, 2008, the Treasury had committed $25 billion to BofA but only in full after the Merrill Lynch merger was completed.

Merrill Lynch, then reporting financials separately, skidded precipitously in late 2008. On October 16, Merrill reported a third quarter loss of $5.1 billion, in part because of CDO positions. BofA separately reported a 68 percent drop in earnings for the third quarter and announced plans to raise $10 billion in equity.

On November 26th, the Federal Reserve Board approved the BofA merger with Merrill Lynch. Shareholders of both companies separately approved the acquisition on December 5.

However, when Merrill Lynch's projected after tax losses in the fourth quarter of 2008 grew from $5 billion in mid-November to $7 billion on December 3, $9 billion on December 9, and $12 billion on December 14, BofA had second thoughts about the merger. BofA CEO Ken Lewis was surprised by the extent of the deterioration in Merrill Lynch assets. The SEC disagreed and brought an enforcement action against BofA for failing to disclose $9.5 billion of known and expected Merrill losses before the December 5 BofA shareholder vote. In February 2010, BofA paid $150 million to settle the suit. In 2012, BofA settled a related shareholder suit for $2.5 billion.

On December 17, BofA's Lewis telephoned Paulson that the deterioration at Merrill Lynch was so serious that BofA was considering invoking the material adverse change clause to exit the merger agreement.

Paulson recalled that Lewis informed him "that he had recently learned about Merrill Lynch's fourth quarter losses . . . expected to run about $18 billion pretax — way out of line with what he or anyone had expected." Paulson characterized material adverse change clauses as "common in [m]erger agreements . . . [but] I had never heard of a buyer successfully invoking a MAC after a shareholder vote. Moreover, the MAC clause was unusually favorable to Merrill Lynch in that it could not be invoked for a general deterioration in market conditions."

Paulson termed the $18 billion potential loss as shocking and implored Lewis: "You need to come to Washington and meet with the Fed immediately."

Paulson and Bernanke did not believe that an attempt by BofA to invoke the material adverse change clause was a "legally reasonable option." Both Paulson and Bernanke agreed to take a "tough line" on BofA's potential invocation of the material adverse change clause. They anticipated that the invocation of the paragraph would cause a loss of confidence in BofA's management given the three months of due diligence BofA had provided for the deal and "would lead to a broader systemic crisis that would result in further deterioration at the two companies." Bernanke believed that if the merger was not consummated, Merrill Lynch would "face an immediate run by funders, customers and other counterparties, a run that could easily spread to Bank of America as well."

Both Paulson and Bernanke wanted the "shotgun wedding" between BofA and Merrill Lynch. On December 19, Lewis reported to the Federal Reserve that the situation had grown worse. Merrill Lynch's losses in the previous two days had grown from $18 to $22 billion pretax. Paulson "remained adamant that [Lewis] needed to close the Merrill deal." As Paulson wrote in his memoir: "Merrill Lynch's staggering fourth-quarter losses now threatened the viability of two huge institutions with combined assets of $2.7 trillion."

Lewis, no doubt, well understood all of this and worked with the Treasury and Federal Reserve on a rescue package for the BofA-Merrill Lynch merger, similar to Citigroup's ring fence.

Paulson was sympathetic to Lewis:

> Since we had been so clear about our commitment to a government support program, I doubted that Ken was just testing us. Indeed, I concluded from earlier conversations that Ken himself was unsure about what kind of government help was appropriate or needed. He seemed to be having a difficult time with his board.

But Paulson again invoked tough love:

> I got back to Ken later and again emphasized to him that the government would not let any systemically important institution fail; that exercising the MAC would show a colossal lack of judgment of BofA; that such an action would jeopardize his bank, Merrill Lynch, and the entire financial system; and that under such circumstances, the Fed, as BofA regulator, could take extreme measures, including the removal of [BofA] management and the board."

"I understand," Ken said. "Let us de-escalate."

On December 21, the BofA Board decided not to invoke the material adverse change clause but "with the understanding," as the National Commission on the Causes of the Financial and Economic Crisis found, "that the government assistance would be 'fully documented' by the time fourth quarter [2008] earnings were announced in mid January." Paulson declined to provide written assurance before the rescue package was finalized. On New Year's Eve, Lewis called Paulson and agreed to proceed because "he trusted [Paulson] to make sure the government would come up with a program for BofA."

The merger was completed on January 1. The initial $50 billion purchase price had by then declined to $19 billion, correlative with the deterioration of the two companies' stock prices since the September 2008 merger announcement.

There was considerable federal support for the merger. BofA received all $25 billion in capital from TARP funds announced in October including $10 billion allocated to Merrill Lynch.

On January 16, the Treasury, Federal Reserve and FDIC publicly committed to a BofA rescue package. Treasury provided $20 billion in TARP funds to purchase BofA preferred stock with an 8 percent dividend. The three federal regulators designated $118 billion of bad assets, primarily from Merrill Lynch, which were ring fenced. The National Commission reported:

> The pool was analogous to Citigroup's ring fence. In this case, Bank of America would be responsible for the first $10 billion in losses on the pool, and the government would cover 90% of any additional losses. Should the government losses materialize, Treasury would cover 75%, up to a limit of $7.5 billion, and the FDIC 25%, up to a limit of $2.5 billion. Ninety percent of any additional losses would be covered by the Fed.

As with Citi, BofA also agreed to mortgage modifications and more stringent restrictions on executive compensation.

On January 16, BofA also disclosed its own fourth quarter loss of $1.79 billion and a $22 billion pretax loss for its new subsidiary, Merrill Lynch. The Merrill Lynch loss included a $15.3 billion net loss and real estate relaxed writedowns and charges. The stock market initially was not impressed. BofA's stock price fell 14 percent that day. But both BofA and Merrill Lynch survived. Later, on March 6,

BofA began the process of exiting the ring fence arrangement when it determined that its losses would not exceed $10 billion, the amount it would have to entirely cover under the ring fence in any event.[220]

The Collapse of SEC Fraud Enforcement

Paralleling the financial debacle was a breakdown in fraud enforcement, particularly striking at the Securities and Exchange Commission. In December 2008, the *New York Times* reported: "There were 133 [SEC] prosecutions for securities fraud in the first 11 months of this fiscal year. That is down from 437 cases in 2000 and 513 cases in 2002, when Wall Street scandals from Enron to WorldCom led to a crackdown on corporate crime." SEC investigations that led to Justice Department prosecutions for fraud dropped from 69 in 2000 to 9 in 2007, a decline of 87 percent.

The poster child for the deterioration in SEC fraud enforcement was Bernie Madoff.

On December 11, 2008, Madoff, the former NASDAQ stock market Chair, was charged by both the SEC and the United States Attorney with perpetuating a massive fraud on his investors. Losses were estimated by prosecutors to be approximately $65 billion.

The Commission's Office of Inspector General published three Reports related to the Madoff debacle, the first of which stated:

> In May 2000, Harry Markopolos provided the SEC's Boston District Office (*BDO*) with an eight-page complaint questioning the legitimacy of Madoff's report returns. The 2000 complaint posited the following two explanations for Madoff's unusually consistent returns: (1) that "[t]he returns are real, but they are coming from some process other than the one being advertised, in which case an investigation is in order;" or (2) "[t]he entire fund is nothing more than a Ponzi Scheme." Markopolos' complaint stated that Madoff's returns were unachievable using the trading strategy he claimed to employ, noting Madoff's "perfect market-timing ability." Markopolos also referenced the fact that Madoff did not allow outside performance audits. . . .
>
> In March 2001, Markopolos provided the BDO with a second complaint, which supplemented his previous 2000 complaint with updated information and additional analysis. Markopolos' 2001 complaint included an analysis of Madoff's returns versus

> the S&P 500, showing that he had only three down months versus the market's 26 down months during the same period, with a worst down month of only 1.44% versus the market's worst down month of 14.58%. Markopolos concluded that Madoff's "numbers really are too good to be true." . . .
>
> Just one month after NERO [SEC's Northeast Regional Office] decided not to pursue Markopolos' second submission to the SEC, in May 2001, *MARHedge* and *Barron's* both published articles questioning Madoff's unusually consistent returns and secretive operations. The *MARHedge* article, written by Michael Ocrant and entitled "Madoff tops charts; skeptics ask how," stated how many were "baffled by the way [Madoff's] firm has obtained such consistent, nonvolatile returns month after month and year after year," describing the fact Madoff "reported losses of no more than 55 basis points in just four of the past 139 consecutive months, while generating highly consistent gross returns of slightly more than 1.5% a month and net annual returns roughly in the range of 15.0%." . . .
>
> The *Barron's* article, written by Erin Arvelund and entitled "Don't Ask, Don't Tell: Bernie Madoff is so secretive, he even asks his investors to keep mum," discussed how Madoff's operation was among the three largest hedge funds, and has "produced compound average annual returns of 15% for more than a decade" with the largest fund "never [having] a down year." . . .

After an SEC staff investigation was closed in 2005 without seeking to initiate a case against Madoff:

> Markopolos provided the SEC's BDO with a third version of his complaint entitled "The World's Largest Hedge Fund is a Fraud." Markopolos' 2005 complaint detailed approximately 30 red flags indicating Madoff was operating a Ponzi scheme, a scenario Markopolos described as *highly likely*. . . . The red flags identified by Markopolos were similar to the ones previously raised in the Hedge Fund Manager's complaint and the internal e-mails that led to the two cause examinations of Madoff, although somewhat more detailed. They generally fell into one of three categories: (1) Madoff's obsessive secrecy; (2) the impossibility of Madoff's returns, particularly the consistency of those returns; and (3) the unrealistic volume of options Madoff was supposedly trading.
>
> . . .

Why did the subsequent and earlier SEC investigations fail to uncover Madoff's fraud? The Office of Inspector General Report emphasized:

> While the Madoff investigation was assigned within . . . Enforcement, it was assigned to a team with little to no experience conducting Ponzi scheme investigations. The majority of the investigatory work was conducted by a staff attorney who recently graduated from law school and only joined the SEC nineteen months before she was given the Madoff investigation. She had never previously been the lead staff attorney on any investigation, and had been involved in very few investigations overall. The Madoff assignment was also her first real exposure to broker-dealer issues. . . .
>
> The OIG investigation also found the Enforcement staff was skeptical about Markopolos' complaint because Madoff did not fit the *profile* of a Ponzi scheme operator; with the branch chief on the Madoff investigation noting that there was "an inherent bias towards [the] sort of people who are seen as reputable members of society." . . .
>
> Similarly, after Madoff claimed his purported trading activity took place in Europe, the Enforcement staff did not seek help from the SEC's Office of International Affairs (*OIA*). Had they simply sought assistance from OIA on matters within its area of expertise, the Enforcement staff should have discovered that Madoff was not purchasing equities from foreign broker dealers and that he did not have Over-the-Counter (*OTC*) options agreements with European counterparties. . . .
>
> . . . Essentially, Madoff claimed his remarkable returns were due to his personal *feel* for when to get in and out of the market, stating "Some people feel the market. Some people just understand how to analyze the numbers that they're looking at." Because of the Enforcement staff's inexperience and lack of understanding of equity and options trading, they did not appreciate that Madoff was unable to provide a logical explanation for his incredibly consistent returns. Each member of the Enforcement staff accepted as plausible Madoff's claim that his returns were due to his perfect *gut feel* for when the market would go up or down.
>
> During his testimony, Madoff also told the Enforcement investigators that the trades for all of his advisory accounts were cleared through this account at [the Depository Trade Corporation or *DTC*]. He testified further that his advisory account positions were segregated at DTC and gave the Enforcement staff

> his DTC account number. During an interview with the OIG, Madoff stated that he had thought that he was caught after his testimony about the DTC account, noting that when they asked for the DTC account number, "I thought it was the end game, over. Monday morning they'll call DTC and this will be over . . . and it never happened." Madoff further stated that when Enforcement did not follow up with DTC, he "was astonished."
>
> This was perhaps the most egregious failure in the Enforcement investigation of Madoff; that they never verified Madoff's purported trading with any independent third parties. . . .
>
> A simple inquiry to one of several third parties could have immediately revealed the fact that Madoff was not trading in the volume he was claiming.

In August 2006, the SEC Enforcement staff effectively closed the Madoff investigation after Madoff, previously registered as a broker-dealer, agreed also to register with the SEC as an investment adviser.

For federal financial regulators such as Tim Geithner, the Madoff fraud was not a significant cause of the financial crisis, "but . . . more a feature of the mania . . . fueled by the dominant belief that risk-taking was no longer particularly risky."[221]

Geithner's argument is debatable. The breakdown in fraud enforcement arguably encouraged riskier or illegal behavior generally, but in any event, Geithner's argument is not persuasive with respect to the breakdown in deterrence of the financial misconduct that was at the core of the 2007–2009 meltdown. By 2008, for example, several leading investment and commercial banks were subject to SEC and state Attorney General lawsuits concerning Auction Rate Securities. In 2008, the Commission, North American Securities Administrators Association (NASAA), and New York Attorney General Cuomo regulated settlements with Citigroup to redeem $7.3 billion in illiquid ARS and pay a $100 million penalty. There were several other settlements in 2008 and 2009. Wachovia agreed to repay investors more than $8.5 billion and pay a $50 million fine. Citigroup and UBS separately agreed to a $30 billion Auction Rate Security.[222]

Annus Horribilis

For the economy, 2008 would be a frightening and brutal year, an *annus horribilis.* The United States economy lost 3.6 million jobs in

2008. The National Commission on the Causes of the Financial Crisis would characterize this as "the largest annual plunge since record keeping began in 1940." 2009 would be even worse. "By December 2009," the National Commission continued, "the United States had lost another 4.7 million jobs." Only in 2010 would jobs begin to be recovered. By November 2010, the economy had regained nearly one million jobs, the beginning of a slow recovery. Unemployment climbed to 7.3 percent in December 2008.

Gross Domestic Product (*GDP*), the nation's measure of economic output, fell an annual rate of 4 percent in the third quarter of 2008 and 6.8 in the fourth quarter of that year. The GDP continued to fall throughout the first six months of 2009 before modestly growing in the second half. In 2009, the average GDP was 2.6 percent lower than in 2008, the largest decline since 1946. In June 2009, the United States emerged from the recession that began 18 months earlier. United States households lost 16 percent of their wealth in 2008, a decline, Geithner noted, that was "five times higher than the 3 percent loss of wealth during the financial shock that precipitated the Depression in 1929."

The finances of the Nation were ravaged in 2008. Of the $17 trillion lost between 2007 and the first quarter of 2009, $5.6 trillion was attributed to lower housing prices, most of the rest because of loss in the value of financial assets. The Standard & Poor 500 index fell by one-third in 2008, the largest one year decline since 1974. Assets in retirement accounts also lost about one-third of their value between September 2007 and December 2008 or $2.8 trillion.

The National Commission on the Causes of the Financial and Economic Crisis emphasized:

> The recession devastated not only many companies and their workers but also state and local governments that saw their tax revenue fall —just when people who had lost their jobs, or were in bankruptcy or foreclosure proceedings, were demanding more services. Those services included Medicaid, unemployment compensation, and welfare, in addition to local assistance for mental health care, for children, and for the homeless. "At least 46 states struggled to close shortfalls when adopting budgets for the current fiscal year," recently reported the Center on Budget and Policy Priorities, a Washington think tank.

Tim Geithner, who would become President Obama's Secretary of Treasury early in 2009, described 2008 in near apocalyptic terms:

> It had been a brutal year. Of the twenty-five largest financial institutions at the start of 2008, thirteen either failed (Lehman, WaMu), received government help to avoid failure (Fannie, Freddie, AIG, Citi, BofA), merged to avoid failure (Countrywide, Bear, Merrill, Wachovia), or transformed their business structure to avoid failure (Morgan Stanley, Goldman). The stock market dropped more than 40 percent from its 2007 peak.... The contagion had spread far beyond finance to the cars, homes, malls, and factories that made up the everyday American experience. No matter how much money the Fed pumped into the financial system, no matter how low it reduced interest rates, its efforts to strengthen growth were being undermined by the overhang of excessive borrowing that triggered the crisis and by a critically damaged financial system. Low rates didn't matter much when few Americans wanted to borrow and few banks wanted to lend.
>
> ...
>
> The President-elect would be inheriting an economy in absolute free fall, suffering not from a sudden loss of its ability to produce things, but from an acute shortfall of demand. And even though the panic in the markets had subsided a bit, the financial system was still broken. Our credit channels were frozen. Months of zigzags had left the world unsure whether the U.S. government was willing and able to prevent additional defaults by major institutions.... As the recession intensified, the price of securities would keep falling, increasing fears about the solvency of financial institutions.[223]

The financial and economic meltdown accelerated during the initial months of 2009. Stock prices fell 11 percent between January 2 and January 20, President Obama's inauguration. By March 9, they would fall another 16 percent, with the Dow Jones Industrial Average closing at 6547, the lowest level in the crisis.

On January 15, Congress in response to a request from outgoing President Bush voted to release the second half of the TARP funds, $350 billion to President Obama, on a strikingly partisan vote in the Senate with only 52 Senators supporting the release. Of the 34 Republican Senators who supported the Bush Administration's TARP legislation, only six voted to support the same authority in the Obama Administration.

Unemployment throughout 2009 continued to skyrocket. The unemployment rate reached 8.7 percent in March after a month in which 800,000 jobs were lost. January to March 2009 were the three worst months for jobs since the end of World War II when the defense industry closed wartime facilities. An average of about 300,000 jobs a month were lost from May to August 2009, with the jobless rate reaching 10.1 percent in October. "[T]he atmosphere in which Obama took office [was] as frightening an economic landscape as had greeted any new president since FDR in 1933."[224]

The Obama Administration and separately the Federal Reserve Bank pursued several new initiatives in addition to the new TARP funds.

Initially, most dramatic was the $787 billion American Recovery and Reinvestment Act of 2009, the major stimulus package of the Obama Administration. In retrospect, both Bernanke and Geithner would view the package to be too small, but likely the largest number politically possible in the hyper-partisan Washington D.C. of 2009.

In terms of stimulating the economy, the package was heavily compromised. At the insistence of Senate Republicans, some $288 billion was for tax reductions, including a temporary reduction in Social Security payroll taxes. In the Senate, given the need for 60 votes to prevent a filibuster, the Act just barely squeaked by with a 60–38 vote. A separate $144 billion aided state and local governments, largely to support education and Medicaid, both badly stretched by the 2007–2009 recession. Bernanke later wrote that he believed "some of the Medicaid spending and certain tax fixes . . . likely would have occurred anyway." The remaining $355 billion supported several federal spending programs, including $40 billion for infrastructure investment. Bernanke wrote, "much of the effect [of this spending] was offset by spending cuts and tax increases undertaken by state and local governments." Unlike the New Deal 1933–1935 response to the Great Depression, there were no job creation programs such as the Civilian Conservation Corps, which provided work for 300,000 young men by June 1933, and over 2.5 million throughout the life of the program.

From Geithner's perspective, the key aspects of the Obama stimulus package were size and speed:

> I did not have strong convictions about the Recovery Act's exact contents. I was fine with well-targeted tax cuts, which can quickly get money into people's pockets and the broader

> economy. I was also fine with public works projects, which are slower but pack more economic punch. Direct aid to the unemployed and other victims of the recession would be fast and powerful, since they would be likely to spend the money right away. I was leery of the varied demands from Congressional Democrats — as well as some members of the President-elect's staff — who wanted to plus up their favorite programs after eight years in the wilderness. But we didn't have time for protracted negotiations to optimize the package. I thought we should get as much as we could, as quickly as we could.

In February 2008, the Bush Administration had negotiated with Congressional Democrats a $170 billion tax rebate for households and tax incentives for businesses. By Obama's Inauguration, there was broad consensus that this level of stimulus, 1 percent of GDP, was too small. Every major Republican and Democratic Presidential candidate had proposed a stimulus package in 2008.

To Geithner, clarity was also critical:

> The ad hoc, inconsistent crisis response of 2008 — which was mostly but not entirely a result of the limits on the Fed's and Treasury's authority before TARP — had added to the pervasive uncertainty about what remained at risk and what we might do next. Even where we had authority to act, we had not established clear rules of the game. Investors were not only unsure how to evaluate the health of institutions during a financial crisis and an economic collapse; they were also unsure how the U.S. government might handle institutions that started falling into the abyss. Bank shareholders had no idea whether they would face substantial dilution, or a government nationalization that could wipe them out. Creditors were still worried about Lehman-style defaults and WaMu-style haircuts. We hadn't fully committed to removing catastrophic risk from the system, and we had adjusted our approach so often that our commitments wouldn't necessarily be trusted, anyway. There was a general sense that the U.S. government might not have the will or even the ability to do what was necessary to end the crisis.[225]

The combination of the additional TARP funds and the America Recovery and Reinvestment Act empowered the Obama Administration to address several enduring challenges.

The Obama Administration

The Obama Administration was more aggressive than the Bush Administration in addressing the foreclosure crisis. In 2008, there were three million foreclosure filings. By 2010, four million families had lost their homes to foreclosure and four and one-half million were in the foreclosure process or seriously behind on mortgage payments. The mortgage foreclosure rate had soared from less than 1 percent before 2007 to 9 percent of outstanding mortgages in 2009. Between 2006 and 2009, home prices had fallen 32 percent, resulting in 22.5 percent of mortgages being "underwater," that is, more was owed on the home mortgage than the value of the home. The prime culprit in this crisis was not hard to identify. In the spring of 2010, 85 percent of a survey of mayors rated subprime or non-prime mortgages as the first or second cause of foreclosures.

The Bush Administration support for home mortgage relief had been limited. Hope for Homeowners, adopted in July 2008, had authorized the Federal Housing Administration (*FHA*) to refinance up to $300 billion of troubled mortgages after losses were borne by the banks and other private sector holders of the mortgages. The program failed. Bernanke explained: "Only a few hundred [to be precise, 312] borrowers ever applied. Crucially, Congress had been unwilling to spend much on loan modifications. It made the terms for FHA financing and refinancing unattractive for lenders, who mostly refused to participate. Congress's tightfistedness . . . reflected the fact that many people apparently regarded trouble homeowners as 'one more bailout' of irresponsible actions."

On February 18, 2009, within the first month after his Inauguration, President Obama unveiled a three part strategy to reduce mortgage foreclosures. The Home Affordable Refinance Program (*HARP*) applied solely to mortgages owned or guaranteed by Fannie Mae or Freddie Mac and provided homeowners who were current on their payments but underwater in their mortgages to secure better terms, significantly including lower monthly terms.

The Home Affordable Modification Program (*HAMP*) applied to homeowners who had already missed payments. HAMP was financed by TARP and also covered mortgages not owned by Fannie Mae and Freddie Mac, when the homeowner's monthly debt burden exceeded 31 percent of their gross monthly income. To create incentives for private mortgage services to participate in HAMP, the servicers both would be paid a fee for each permanent modification they completed and monthly payments when borrowers remained current on their modified mortgages. As had been the case during the Bush Administration, Fannie Mae, Freddie Mac, and the FHA in 2009 were virtually the only remaining sources of housing finance and were, Geithner believed, "keeping the mortgage market afloat."

Simultaneously, another $200 billion was provided to Fannie Mae and Freddie Mac on top of the $200 billion earlier provided.

The Obama Administration's efforts to reduce mortgage foreclosures would achieve only modest success. The HARP program, designed to help four to five million borrowers refinance their mortgages, would modify about 1.3 million mortgages through 2013, saving the median homeowner more than $500 a month. Banks and other private sector lenders, however, also modified 3.9 million mortgages without government assistance. The FHA mitigated the losses of two million other mortgages.

The HAMP program produced temporary relief for another 360,000 homeowners and facilitated fewer than 2000 permanent loan modifications.

The Obama Administration's housing program, although more determined than that of the Bush Administration, was pilloried by both political progressives and libertarians. Sheila Bair, for example, was particularly critical of the slow start of the program:

> [T]he financial incentives [in HARP] were not enough. By the end of 2010, nearly two years into the program's operation, only about 522,000 successful permanent modifications had been completed. The government had spent about $2 billion on the program. The number of proprietary modifications — those that banks and servicers had done on their own outside of the program — was four times as high. (Of course, many of these provided no meaningful payment relief.)

Even more vociferous was the response on the political right. On cable station CNBC, Rich Santelli in February 2009 blasted the homeowner bailout, a rant widely believed to have helped inspire the libertarian Tea Party movement. "How many of you people," Santelli asked traders on the floor of the Chicago Mercantile Exchange, "want to pay for your neighbor's mortgage that had an extra bathroom and can't pay their bills, raise your hands." Many screamed "No." Santelli asked, "President Obama, are you listening?"[226]

More successful were the Obama Administration's efforts to bail out the auto industry. By late 2008, auto industry sales had fallen 40 percent. Beginning in late March 2009, the Obama Administration built on the December 2008 Bush Administration's $25 billion loans and investments to General Motors, Chrysler, General Motors Acceptance Corporation, and Chrysler Financial to invest $81 billion of TARP funds in the auto industry. The terms were demanding. On March 30, 2009, Obama asserted: "Year after year, decade after decade, we've seen problems papered over and tough choices kicked down the road, even as foreign competitors outpaced us. . . . [W]e have reached the end of that road." "Team Auto" was created to restructure GM and Chrysler. Among other steps, GM CEO Rick Wagoner was fired. By the end of the Spring, both GM and Chrysler would be in bankruptcy reorganization, meaning reduced payments or "haircuts" to creditors, reduced payments to auto workers, retired autoworkers, and auto dealers. Some 2000 dealerships were closed. Plants were closed. Brands, including Hummer, Pontiac, Saturn, and Saab, were ended. This was tough medicine. Greater sacrifices were required of the industry than of the banks.

Geithner defended the tough terms. Banks were vulnerable to contagion:

> The automakers did not rely heavily on runnable short-term financing, and lenders could more easily tell which of them were in trouble. Using the bankruptcy process to reduce their debt obligations would send a message about the dangers only of lending to failing car companies, not car companies in general. By contrast, confidence is the lifeblood of the entire financial industry, and in a crisis, investors have a much harder time distinguishing the strong from the weak among banks than they do in other industries. That's why haircuts for bank creditors or disorderly failures of systemic banks during a panic can trigger runs on the entire financial system, especially when the system is relying on short-term funding that can flee in an instant.

Steven Rattner, who led the Obama Auto Team, believed without saving GM and Chrysler, a couple of million people would have been out of work, GM and Chrysler would have been liquidated, which would have devastated a web of workers, suppliers, and communities, especially in the Midwest. GM, Rattner believed, was "too big, too important" to fail. In 2011, Rattner termed the $10 billion (ultimately $9.3 billion) to save the auto industry "well spent."

As with the foreclosure program, the auto bailout was unpopular — in 2009, according to a CNN/Opinion Research Corporation Poll, only 37 percent of those polled approved the plan. Mitt Romney, the 2012 Republican candidate for President, pointedly wrote in a 2008 *New York Times* opinion piece: "If General Motors, Ford and Chrysler get the bailout that their chief executives asked for — you can kiss the American automobile industry goodbye."

Unpopular or not, the auto industry bailout worked. GM emerged from bankruptcy in 39 days, Chrysler in 42 days. Obama would be re-elected in 2012 in part because he was the President who saved General Motors. In 2012, 56 percent of Americans in one poll then approved the auto bailout. By 2015, 640,000 new auto jobs had been created. GM, Chrysler, and Ford, which did not receive TARP funds, would be profitable.[227]

Meanwhile, Citigroup, which in November 2008 had been revived by the Treasury, Federal Reserve, and FDIC's historic ring fence guarantee, had badly deteriorated. On February 27th, the Treasury increased its investment into Citigroup, converting up to $25 billion of preferred stock for common stock. This meant that the federal government's ownership of Citi increased 8 percent to a total of 36 percent. At first, the markets were not reassured.

On March 5, 2009, Citi's stock traded below $1 per share. By then its leverage ratio had reached $60 assets for even $1 in common stock equity, a stratospheric level. Rumors that the federal government soon would nationalize Citigroup had caused investors to desert Citi's common stock.

But over time, Citi stabilized. On December 23, 2009, Citi repaid $20 billion of trust preferred stock held by the Treasury using TARP funds and exited from the ring fence pool. The Treasury then continued to hold 27 percent of Citi common stock, but with a 2009 loss of $1.6 billion compared to $27.7 billion in 2008, Citi had stabilized.[228]

AIG endured as the single most dysfunctional private company in the crisis. In September 2008, the Department of Treasury had orchestrated $85 billion to AIG dramatically reversing the tough love policy that had led to Lehman Brothers' bankruptcy. Within one month of this bailout, in October, Treasury provided another \$38 billion loan to AIG. In November, the original bailout had been restructured to include a \$40 billion TARP investment, lower interest rates, and a longer term for repayment. None of this worked. As Bernanke wrote:

> But instead of stabilizing, the company lost an astonishing \$62 billion in the fourth quarter, bringing its losses for 2008 to \$99 billion, roughly equal to the annual economic output of Mississippi. To avoid a downgrade in AIG's credit rating, which would have triggered a new — likely bankruptcy-inducing — outflow of cash, the Fed and Treasury restructured the bailout once again in March 2009. We completed the new arrangements on a Sunday, one day before the company's announcement on March 2 of its huge fourth-quarter loss. The new deal included an additional \$30 billion in TARP capital, bringing the total TARP investment to \$70 billion, or 10 percent of the total congressional appropriation. And that figure didn't include the Fed's lending support.

Specifically, in March 2009, the Federal Reserve Board and Treasury restructured AIG's bailout by reducing AIG debt by \$26 billion in exchange for the Federal Reserve Bank of New York receiving convertible equity in two special purpose vehicles that held the outstanding stock of two AIG life insurance companies. The new Federal Reserve Bank also was authorized to extend up to \$8.5 billion to specified AIG life insurance subsidiaries' special purpose vehicles. In April, Treasury established a \$29.835 billion equity capital facility in return for fixed rate perpetual preferred shares and a warrant to purchase 3000 AIG common shares.

The public outcry over AIG went nuclear later in March when newspapers disclosed that AIG would pay \$155 million in bonuses to executives and employees of its Financial Products Division, which more than any other cause, had led to AIG's downfall. Members of Congress denounced AIG's "arrogance, incompetence and greed." Conservative columnist Charles Krauthammer urged "an exemplary hanging or two." Even before the Financial Products bonuses, somebody, Geithner reported, had suggested "Take FP out back and shoot it."

President Obama, Bernanke, and Geithner considered stopping the payments, only to be frustrated by the fact that they were protected by legally binding contracts. The AIG bonuses were an unmitigated public relations disaster. Geithner recalled: "The public was understandably incredulous that major TARP recipients had expressed their appreciation for taxpayer-financed reserves by paying out boom-level bonuses." The House of Representatives passed a confiscatory 90 percent tax on Wall Street bonuses. This was not enacted into law by the Senate but reflected the intense populist fury leveled, particularly at Geithner. "Fire Geithner," an activist banner declared at a March 2009 hearing. On March 27, President Obama informed the CEOs of several major banks that his Administration was the only thing standing between them and the pitchforks. "The politics," Geithner later reflected, "of crisis response were unspeakably awful."[229]

In July 2009, CIT Group, a leading funder of small and medium-sized businesses with $75 billion in assets, which had received $2.3 billion in TARP funds in late 2008, was again experiencing liquidity problems. CIT was less than one-fifth the size of Bear Stearns, and its focus on factoring or lending to businesses and shipping goods was notably different than banks such as Citigroup. The FDIC rejected CIT's request for further relief, forcing CIT into bankruptcy reorganization in October. The FDIC did not regard CIT as viable. "The failure," Sheila Bair write, "was not systemic." CIT reemerged from bankruptcy in December after reducing its debt by $10.5 billion. The bankruptcy would cost the Treasury its $2.3 billion investment in CIT.[230]

The Stress Test

The signature program of the Department of Treasury's efforts to restore financial stability popularly was known as the Stress Test and officially called the Supervisory Capital Assessment Program. Geithner, the new Secretary of Treasury, was its principal architect. The Stress Test was widely believed to have been a decisive step in ending the financial meltdown. Economist Alan Blinder later wrote: "Few people realized it at the time, but the successful Stress Test was a turning point. They marked the end of the actual stage of the financial crisis and the beginning of the return to normalcy — albeit just the beginning. It would not be long before everyone stopped worrying about the survival of the big American banks. Not long after that, the institutions started generating profits again." Bernanke was more crisp: "The Stress Test was a decisive turning point. From then on, the U.S. banking system would strengthen steadily—and, eventually, the economy would follow."

The Financial Stability Program, including the Stress Test, was introduced February 10, 2009, by Geithner, some 20 days into the Obama Administration, in what was widely criticized as the "deer in the headlights" speech. Geithner, later so proud of the Stress Test he would title his memoir *Stress Test*, characterized his remarks as a disaster. "My speech . . . sucked. . . . The consensus view was that my inept delivery and lack of detail had dramatically increased uncertainty in the financial system." "The general reaction was that [the Stress Test] looked like a whitewash, a fraud exam designed to give a clean bill of health to a gravely ill banking system." The next day, the Dow Jones Industrial Average plummeted 382 points. A few days earlier, Geithner had been confirmed by a vote of 60–34, the narrowest margin for a modern Secretary of Treasury, after it had been disclosed that he had not paid payroll taxes during earlier service at the International Monetary Fund. Geithner testified that this was a mistake, prompting late night comedian Jay Leno to quip: "So the guy who's going to be in charge of the IRS is not a criminal. Phew, just incompetent." David Axelrod, earlier Obama's campaign manager, then working as a close associate to Obama, characterized the horrible reception of Geithner's debut as Secretary of Treasury in grim terms: "Geithner, that poor son of a bitch. He was going to be the first human sacrifice of our administration as far as Washington was concerned."

While brief and lacking in detail, Geithner provided three programs to address the crisis. The Stress Test was most significant:

> First, we're going to require banking institutions to go through a carefully designed comprehensive stress test, to use the medical term. We want their balance sheets cleaner, and stronger. And we are going to help this process by providing a new program of capital support for those institutions which need it.
>
> To do this, we are going to bring together the government agencies with authority over our nation's major banks and initiate a more consistent, realistic, and forward looking assessment about the risk on balance sheets, and we're going to introduce new measures to improve disclosure.
>
> Those institutions that need additional capital will be able to access a new funding mechanism that uses funds from the Treasury as a bridge to private capital. The capital will come with conditions to help ensure that every dollar of assistance is used

> to generate a level of lending greater than what would have been possible in the absence of government support. And this assistance will come with terms that should encourage the institutions to replace public assistance with private capital as soon as that is possible.

Dreadful as was this introduction to the Stress Test, it subsequently was effectively developed and implemented.

The Stress Test applied to all domestic bank holding companies with year-end assets in 2008 exceeding $100 billion. There were 19 firms in all, including four that largely were not commercial banks — GMAC, Goldman Sachs, MetLife, and Morgan Stanley, as well as many more traditional banks such as Bank of America, Wells Fargo, Citigroup, and JP Morgan. The 19 firms collectively held two-thirds of the assets and more than one half of the loans in the United States banking system.

The firms were asked to project their credit losses and revenues for 2009 and 2010 including the level of reserve that they would need at year end 2010 to cover losses under two alternate scenarios. The baseline scenario reflected the consensus expectation in February 2009 among professional forecasters on the depth and duration of the recession. The more adverse scenario was designed for a recession that was longer and more severe than the consensus expectation. Under either scenario, the numbers were grim:

Economic Scenarios: Baseline and More Adverse Alternatives (Minus signs indicate negative values)

	2009	2010
Real GDP		
Average Baseline	−2.0	2.1
Consensus Forecasts	−2.1	2.0
Blue Chip	−1.9	2.1
Survey of Professional Forecasters	−2.0	2.2
Alternative More Adverse	−3.3	0.5

(continues)

Economic Scenarios: Baseline and More Adverse Alternatives (Minus signs indicate negative values)		
	2009	2010
Civilian unemployment rate		
Average Baseline	8.4	8.8
Consensus Forecasts	8.4	9.0
Blue Chip	9.3	8.7
Survey of Professional Forecasters	8.4	8.8
Alternative More Adverse	8.9	10.3
House prices		
Baseline	–14	–4
Alternative More Adverse	–22	–7

After the forecasts of the 19 firms were reviewed by 150 supervisors and analysts for the federal financial regulatory agencies, the Stress Test could result in a determination that a bank holding company needed to augment its capital to provide a buffer against negative results under either scenario. By year end 2010, the 19 firms were expected to achieve Tier 1 Capital equal to at least 6 percent under the consensus forecast and at least 4 percent under the worst case scenario.

Those firms that fell below these thresholds were given six months to implement plans to develop sufficient capital to address their capital shortfall. This could be done in a variety of ways, including:

- Issuance of new private capital instruments;
- Restructuring current capital instruments;
- Sales of business lines, legal entities, assets or minority interests through private transactions and through sales to the Public–Private Investment Program (*PPIP*);
- Use of joint ventures, spin-offs, or other capital enhancing transactions; and

- Conservation of internal capital generation, including continued restrictions on dividends and stock repurchases and dividend deferrals, waivers and suspensions on preferred securities including trust preferred securities, with the expectation that plans should not rely on near-term potential increases in revenues to meet the capital buffer it is expected to have.

The Treasury would invest enough TARP money in these firms that failed to achieve minimum levels after six months to make up the difference and receive convertible preferred stock. The preferred could be converted into common stock in such magnitudes as the shortfall warranted.

To address the uncertainty caused by the wait for the results of the Stress Test to be announced and the six month subsequent delay to raise capital, the Treasury, as Geithner wrote in his memoir:

> would pay for stock in a bank just below the stock's price in the run-up to my February 10 speech, even if the market price dipped much lower. It did not eliminate the risk for bank investors, but it eliminated a lot of the uncertainty that was frightening them, and it reduced the risk that they would get totally clobbered.

Contrary to the near sacrosanct concept of supervisory confidentiality at the bank regulatory agencies, each bank was required to make public in considerable detail its test results, including projected losses for each type of asset. This was considered essential by the Treasury and the Federal Reserve "to reduce the ongoing uncertainty about banks' financial health."

The purpose of this valuation exercise was to restore confidence. Bernanke explained:

> If market analysts found the estimate credible, the stress test would increase confidence in the banks that passed. Banks that came up short would get a chance to raise capital privately; if they couldn't, Treasury would fill the hole with TARP funds. Either way, we hoped, customers, counterparties, and potential investors would know the banks were viable.

On May 7, the results of the Stress Test were announced and, as both Geithner and Bernanke stated, "were quite reassuring." In the more adverse scenario, the Federal Reserve projected that the 19 firms would lose another $600 billion in 2009 and 2010 on top of the $400 billion earlier lost. This was, Geithner wrote, "huge by historical standards but not insurmountable." Geithner continued:

> The news about capital was even better. After taking account of some modest future earnings, as well as existing reserves and capital, the stress test found that as of January 1, the nineteen firms needed an additional $185 billion in capital. But those firms — mostly Citi — had already increased their common equity by $110 billion since January 1. That meant the ten firms that still needed capital would have to raise only another $75 billion. We thought they could do most of that without new TARP dollars.
>
> Bank of America had the largest need at $33.9 billion, a significant but manageable problem for such a giant institution, especially after the Citi share conversion of TARP preferred shares into common equity provided a model. Wells Fargo . . . was next with $13.7 billion. Citi needed only another $5.5 billion, because it had already increased its common equity by $87 billion. The only institution that seemed to be in deep trouble was GMAC, which was diagnosed with an $11.5 billion capital shortfall, almost twice the amount of its common equity.

The test did succeed in raising confidence in the banks. By November, six months later, the ten banks required to raise capital had done so, collectively raising capital by $77 billion. Only GMAC could not raise all required capital. The Treasury invested $3.8 billion of TARP money into GMAC, subsequently renamed Ally Financial. "The ultimate text of the stress test," Geithner wrote, "was whether private investors would take the risk of investing new capital in banks, and they would do that on an impressive scale, driving BofA's stock price up 63 percent that week, and Citi's up 35 percent." "The message," economist Alan Blinder wrote, "from the government was clear. Large U.S. banks could now be trusted, you could deal with them with no fear."

Nonetheless questions persisted about the Stress Test. Were Treasury and the Federal Reserve too easy on the banks even if the Stress Test results were credible? Regulators, for example, did not seek to fire any CEO or replace members of any board. Geithner defended the test in terms of its rigor. The requirement that banks have risk-weighted assets of 4 percent was twice the level that some Federal Reserve staff had proposed.

A broader question was more fundamental. The Stress Test was a diagnostic tool that provided the basis for supporting existing banks. It was predicated on the assumptions that the crisis primarily was a financial meltdown where contagion effects had reached the real economy of manufacturing, services and Main Street. The assumption was that if you fixed finance, you indirectly revived the real economy. There were many who were skeptical of this analysis. Nobel Laureate Paul Krugman urged that "we didn't pass the [Stress] Test — we failed badly." As Krugman put it: "Banks and markets recovered, but the real economy, and the job market in particular, didn't.":

> By any plausible accounting, we've lost trillions of dollars' worth of goods and services that we could and should have produced; millions of Americans have lost their jobs, their homes, and their dreams. Call it the Lesser Depression — not as bad as the 1930s, but still a terrible thing.

Krugman viewed Geithner as unenthusiastic about the stimulus and more or less hostile to mortgage debt relief. Krugman and others urged that nationalization of some banks and other more far reaching steps were preferable. Geithner and Bernanke, among others, were reluctant to consider nationalization except under extreme circumstances such as AIG. In Bernanke's view:

> I knew that nationalization might have some political appeal. It would look less like a bailout, and we could implement reforms at nationalized institutions without having to deal with private boards and shareholders. But, based on our recent experiences with the semi-nationalizations of Fannie, Freddie, and AIG, I believed in practice it would be a nightmare. Once nationalized, banks could be wards of the state for many years. Governments do not have the expertise to run banks effectively, and private investors are hardly likely to want to put money in banks that are government-controlled. And politics would almost certainly intrude — for example, nationalized banks might be pressured to extend credit to government-favored groups, irrespective of creditworthiness, which could lead to more losses and bailouts.

Ultimately, as Ryan Lizza wrote in *The New Yorker*: "There was a 'real risk' that seizing control of banks could, in fact, destroy them."

The one thing that was most clear to the Obama Administration was that they did not have the ability to return to Congress for more money. This precluded the "Swedish solution" of creating a government-backed bank to acquire toxic assets from the banks as a means to recapitalize the banks, which Lizza characterized as "essentially a version of nationalization," and what the Swedish government had done during Sweden's financial crisis of the early 1990s.

In the end, Larry Summers, a former Secretary of Treasury and Obama's influential Chair of the President's National Economic Council, concluded there was no better option than the Stress Test. On March 31, Summers had sent Obama a memo outlining the reasons not to nationalize any banks. In Lizza's summary:

> ... First, Summers explained that there was no legal authority to take over large bank-holding companies like Bank of America and Citigroup. Next, he pointed out that full nationalization of a financial institution might trigger systemic shocks, as investors retreated from other banks, creating exactly the kind of panic that nationalization was intended to prevent....
>
> Furthermore, Summers said, there was a medium-term risk that nationalized banks would lose value, in the same way that the act of foreclosure decreases the value of a home. Summers pointed to the example of Sweden, which was regularly cited by economists who favored nationalization. But Summers noted that Sweden didn't nationalize for two and a half years, by which time the situation had become so severe — interest rates had reached a hundred percent — that there were no other options. In addition, Nordbanken, the largest bank nationalized in Sweden, was already eighty percent government-owned. Summers concluded by emphasizing that nationalization was a strategy that governments turn to only after it is very clear that nothing else can work.

In his February 10th Financial Stability Plan, Geithner proposed two other potentially far-reaching reform programs.[231]

First, in March 2009, the Obama Administration and Federal Reserve Board built on a November 2008 Bush Administration program called TALF (Term Asset-Backed Securities Loan Facility), to aid small business and consumers to seek to revise the securitization market.

Regarding the November 2008 Bush initiative, Bernanke wrote:

> Under the TALF, we would lend for terms of up to five years to investors who would buy AAA-rated securities backed by credit card loans, student loans, auto loans, commercial mortgages, and loans guaranteed by the Small Business Administration. Our loans would be without recourse, meaning that the borrower could give us the asset-backed securities they had purchased in lieu of fully repaying the loan. That provided "downside protection" for the borrowers. But turning over the securities to us before maturity would make sense only if the return on the securities dropped below the cost of the loan.

The Bush Administration Treasury provided $20 billion in TARP funds to support Federal Reserve Bank lending of up to $200 billion.

In March 2009, the Obama Administration "vastly expanded the capacity of the Fed's TALF program," increasing the objective to provide up to $1 trillion in support and expanding the types of assets that could be covered such as small business loans and loans to finance business equipment. In Geithner's view:

> TALF wouldn't get much media attention, but it would be remarkably effective, reviving stalled credit markets that were vital to the American Dream. The securitization markets for auto loans, student loans, and other consumer loans that had disappeared after Lehman quickly rebounded after the launch of TALF. It would be one of the least controversial planks of our strategy, because it wasn't about the banks.

Separately, in May 2009, the Obama Administration also championed the Public-Private Investment Program (*PPIP*) to move toxic assets off of the balance sheets of banks. PIPP was intended to combine money from private investment funds with government support. The Treasury proposed making available TARP funds to generate between $500 million and $1 billion in purchases of legacy assets, including the market for unpackaged loans and "private" mortgage securities not backed by Fannie Mae, Freddie Mac, or other government-sponsored institutions. There were two primary PPIP programs — the Legacy Loans Program and Legacy Securities Program. The FDIC would provide up to 85 percent of the purchase price of the troubled assets. The balance was intended to be raised from private investors using TARP funds.

Sheila Bair, FDIC Chair, was critical of the PPIP program, characterizing this as a program "that would allow banks and other financial institutions to sell securities that they held on their balance sheet at market value. Because the PPIP would provide favorable government financing to investors to purchase those securities, they could provide purchase prices above current market values." Bair recalled:

> After a few months of fits and starts, the Treasury and Fed launched the securities purchase program, but it never really took off. It was easier for the banks, if they wanted to sell, to simply do so directly through the Fed. Also, the few banks that did sell securities in the PPIP took losses, suggesting that they were not carrying the securities at true market prices.

In retrospect, Geithner would also agree that PPIP was not "a decisive element of our strategy." Ultimately only $22 billion would be invested in PPIP, "a far cry from the $1 trillion we had initially announced."[232]

Quantitative Easing

Beginning earlier than Geithner's February 10th Financial Stability Plan rollout, the Federal Reserve System purchased hundreds of billions of dollars of securities in what the financial world termed Quantitative Easing or QE. This was, as Bernanke later wrote "definitely the most controversial tool we would employ." Japan earlier had initiated Quantitative Easing. It was not used elsewhere until late in 2008 when the United States and United Kingdom began using QE.

In late November 2008, the Federal Reserve System had announced that it would purchase up to $100 billion of debt issued by Fannie Mae, Freddie Mac and the Federal Home Loan Banks as well as $500 billion of mortgage-backed securities guaranteed by Fannie Mae, Freddie Mac, and Ginnie Mae, the Government National Mortgage Association. The market reaction was favorable and rapid. Interest rates on 30-year mortgages dropped approximately one-half of one percent, and Fannie Mae and Freddie Mac securities increased in value.

In December 2008, the Federal Reserve Open Market Committee set and long held its interest rate at 0 to .25 percent and articulated its expectation that rates would remain low for an extended period. This limited the tools that the Federal Reserve had to stimulate the economy. What became a robust QE policy was the innovation Bernanke championed.

In March 2009, the Federal Reserve announced that it would increase its 2009 purchase of mortgage-backed securities guaranteed by Fannie Mae, Freddie Mac, and Ginnie Mae from $750 billion to $1.25 trillion. The Federal Reserve also doubled its purchases of Fannie Mae and Freddie Mac debt to $200 billion and announced plans to buy $300 billion of Treasury securities over the next six months. By August 2010, the Federal Reserve would hold more than $2 trillion in such securities. QE would become an established Federal Reserve policy with total assets in mortgage-backed securities and Treasury securities increasing from $882 billion to $4.473 trillion between December 2007 and May 2017, that is from 6 percent of GDP in 2007 to 23.5 in 2017. QE would be widely replicated. By December 2016, the Bank of Japan's balance sheet would be 88 percent of GDP; Switzerland, 115 percent; Bank of England, 24 percent; European Central Bank, 34 percent.

In his memoir, Bernanke would characterize QE as an unqualified success:

> A new era of monetary policy activism had arrived, and our announcement had powerful effects. Between the day before the meeting and the end of the year, the Dow would rise more than 3,000 points — more than 40 percent — to 10,428. Longer-term interest rates fell on our announcement, with the yield on ten-year Treasury securities dropping from about 3 percent to about 2.5 percent in one day, a very large move. Over the summer, longer-term yields would reverse and rise to above 4 percent. We would see that increase as a sign of success. Higher yields suggested that investors were expecting both more growth and higher inflation, consistent with our goal of economic revival. Indeed, after four quarters of contraction, revised data would show that the economy would grow at a 1.3 percent rate in the third quarter and a 3.9 percent rate in the fourth.[233]

By 2009, the financial meltdown had ended and the worst consequences of the United States recession had begun to dissipate. In total, the Congress would appropriate $1.657 trillion in three stimulus Acts in 2008 and 2009, including TARP in October 2008 and the American Recovery and Reinvestment Act of 2009. Contrary to initial expectations fueled by an April 2009 International Monetary Fund estimate that TARP would incur nearly $2 trillion in direct costs, the Department of Treasury in 2008 calculated that TARP including proceeds from AIG shares would generate $14.72 billion in positive return.

Within a decade, Jamie Dimon, JP Morgan Chase CEO, would proclaim "a golden age of banking." The six leading investment banks—JP Morgan Chase, Bank of America, Wells Fargo, Citigroup, Goldman Sachs, and Morgan Stanley—would see their aggregate pretax profits nearly double between 2010 and 2017, from $75 billion to $141 billion. By June 2019, a new generation of mortgage originators, largely operating through the Internet, led by Quicken Loans, loanDepot, and Caliber Home Loans, was responsible for 52 percent of annual mortgage originations.

Separately, the Federal Reserve would invest $1.7 trillion in QE between September 2008 and October 2010. There also were several emergency programs including the Federal Reserve System's Term Securities Lending Facility which peaked at $483 billion, the Primary Dealer Credit Facility which was as high as $156 billion, money market funding reached $350 billion in January 2009 and the Commercial Paper Funding Facility that reached $365 billion in January 2009. The FDIC program to guarantee senior debt for all FDIC-insured institutions was prepared to backstop as much as $939 billion in bank debt.

These were huge numbers. There also were large and long enduring other indirect costs of the financial meltdown. Unemployment, which began 2008 at 4.9 percent, would more than double in October 2009 to 10.2 percent, and remain above 9 percent through 2010, only slowly declining to 4.9 percent again in 2016.

The federal deficit, which had been $161 billion in 2007, grew to $1.413 trillion in 2009, $1.294 trillion in 2010, $1.3 trillion in 2011, and $1.087 trillion in 2012. The 2009 deficit equaled a stunning 9.8 percent of GDP, a number only exceeded in World War II.

The backlash to the massive federal programs, the perceived favoritism of large banks over Main Street, the widely believed conflicts of interest fueled the libertarian Tea Party movement, which was widely credited with helping flip control of the House of Representatives in 2010 to the more conservative Republican Party. The Republican Party gained 63 seats in the House of Representatives, the largest change in a midterm election since 1948. In the Senate, the Republicans gained six seats, decreasing the Democratic Party majority from 57 to 51 seats.

The Crisis Becomes International

The financial debacle soon became an international calamity. For Columbia History Professor Adam Tooze:

> What made the collapse of 2008 so severe was its extraordinary global synchronization. Of the 104 countries for which the World Trade Organization collects data, every single one experienced a fall in both imports and exports between the second half of 2008 and the first half of 2009. Every country and every type of traded goods, without exception, experienced a decline.

The financial crisis was global and interdependent. By 2007–2008, 12 of the top 20 broker-dealers in New York were 50 percent or more foreign owned. Adam Tooze generalized: "The upward spiral of asset prices and balance sheets that drove the U.S. boom was even more pronounced in Europe. Between 2001 and 2006, Greece, Finland, Sweden, Belgium, Denmark, the UK, France, Ireland and Spain all experienced real estate booms more severe than those that energized the United States."

The subsequent collapse in the housing markets "slashed personal wealth." In Spain, net worth per person fell by at least 10 percent between 2007 and 2009. Within five years, personal wealth would plunge by 28 percent, or 1.4 million euros, more than a year's worth of output. In the U.K., as the stock market and industry prices slumped, household losses in 2008–2009 were estimated by the IMF to be $1.5 trillion — 50 percent of GDP in a matter of twelve months.

In Europe, a debt crisis, in economist Alan Blinder's view, would be "arguably the biggest aftershock from the 2007–2009 financial earthquake."[234] With 17 nations awkwardly bound together by a common currency and common central bank, but no common government or common national budget, Europe was slower and less competent in its initial response to its financial meltdown.

As with the United States, the crisis began in housing and often purchases of derivative securities, many of which originated in the United States.

But there were critical differences in the European financial crisis. The European Central Bank (*ECB*) was created by the Maastricht Treaty (the Treaty on European Union), which reiterated a reluctance ever to repeat the hyperinflation of Weimar Germany that led to political instability and Nazi Germany. The Treaty strongly discouraged bailouts of individual governments or central bank financing of budget deficits. The overarching goal of the ECB was to keep inflation low.

These concerns were amplified by the distrust of individual European states for each other and by fears of political backlash. Germany, for example, had been conscientious in its central banking and there was wide spread German hostility to steps to bail out Greece, which among other things, had vastly understated its national debt to join the ECB in 2001 by stating that it satisfied the Maastricht Treaty 60 percent debt limit of GDO, when it may have been as high as 120 percent. In 2009, the Greek debt was 13 percent of annual output compared to 3 percent that it had agreed to in the Stability and Economic Growth Pact. As Blinder wrote: "As Europe's largest economy, Germany is destined to bear the largest share of any bailout. Yet tax-paying, orderly Germans want to know why they should pay for the failings of undisciplined Greeks who — they believe — work shorter hours, retire earlier and don't pay taxes." Those beliefs may have been exaggerated. But the critical point is that they were held.

The European debt crisis began late in 2009 when Greece announced its public debt was far higher than previously reported. By 2010, Standard & Poor's cut Greece's sovereign debt rating to BB+ or "junk" level amid fears of default. The response of the ECB was to provide a 110 billion euro loan, which initially was too small, with conditions that Greece raise taxes, lower its minimum wage by 22 percent, and end specified public services. This approach led to a succession of governments in Greece and helped spread the European debt crisis over time to Portugal, Ireland, Spain, and Italy.

Ultimately, the ECB provided 110 billion euros (or $145 billion) to Greece in May 2010. Two-thirds came from individual European countries, one-third from the International Monetary Fund. This also proved too little too late. In October 2011, Greece received a second 130 billion conditional euro bailout package, which prompted the resignation of Greek Prime Minister George Papandreou. By October 20th, unemployment had reached 19.7 percent, up from 8 percent in 2008.

Subsequent ECB initiatives were more effective. In December 2011 and February 2012, the ECB authorized 1 trillion euros in its Longer-Term Refinancing Operations Facility to lend money for terms up to three years. This was similar to steps the United States had taken in 2008 and 2009. In September 2012, the ECB implemented the Outright Monetary Transactions Facility, which supported all 17 eurozone countries by reducing the costs of debt. Mario Draghi summarized the view of the ECB then: "[The ECB] would do whatever it takes to preserve the Euro." Given fears that some member states would default and resume direct control over their currencies, this was a decisive commitment and soon helped calm the markets.

In 2012, after a 67.5 billion euro bailout package in 2010, Ireland was able to return to financial markets selling 5 billion euros in government debt. In 2013, Ireland ended its bailout program as scheduled.

Portugal similarly received a 78 billion euro bailout package in 2011. This helped stabilize its economy. Unemployment rose to 17 percent by year end 2012 but subsequently decreased. In 2014, Portugal left its European Union bailout.

Spain received a 59 billion euro bailout in 2012 to help address real estate losses. By 2013, Spain had a 27 percent unemployment rate which declined to 16 percent in 2018. In January 2014, Spain left the European Union/IMF bailout mechanism.

The costs of the European financial meltdown were severe. Unemployment, for example, in Greece reached 27 percent with youth unemployment reaching 62 percent on selected dates between 2008 and 2013. Seasonal adjusted output in Greece declined 28 percent between 2005 and 2011. Poverty levels in Greece were calculated to be as high as 33 percent. Overall political shifts, in part or large part influenced by the crisis, occurred in 10 eurozone countries — Greece, Ireland, France, Italy, Portugal, Spain, Slovenia, Slovakia, Belgium, and the Netherlands as well as the United Kingdom.[235]

Nobel Laureate in Economics Robert Shiller described global political instability:

> Public street protests against both government and the financial establishment were front-page news in 2011. . . . The protests apparently took their inspiration from those of the Arab Spring against dictatorial governments in the Middle East. They began to be directed against the financial establishment with the Movimiento 15-M in Madrid, then with Occupy Wall Street in New York, along with Occupy Boston, Occupy Los Angeles, Occupy London, Occupy Melbourne, Occupy Rome, and other variants.

The December 2011 election protests in Russia reflected dissatisfaction with the cozy situation of rich "business oligarchs."[236]

What Happened?

How was it possible for the most successful economy that ever existed with the most sophisticated financial regulatory system ever designed to be reduced within a matter of months to frantic fire-fighting and the most expensive bailout in United States history?

The Majority Report of the National Commission on the Causes of the Financial and Economic Crisis in 2011 concluded:

- Widespread failure in financial regulation and supervision proved devastating to the stability of the nation's financial markets.
- Dramatic failures of corporate governance and risk management at many systematically important financial institutions were a key cause of this crisis.
- A combination of excessive borrowing, risky investments, and lack of transparency put the financial system on a collision course with crisis.
- The Government was ill prepared for the crisis, and its inconsistent response added to the uncertainty and panic in the financial markets.
- There was a systemic breakdown in accountability and ethics.
- Collapsing mortgage-lending standards and the mortgage securitization pipeline lit and spread the flame of contagion and crisis.
- Over-the-counter derivatives contributed significantly to this crisis.
- The failure of credit rating agencies were essential cogs in the wheel of financial destruction.

Dissenting members of the National Commission emphasized different causes, including:

- The credit bubble and Federal Reserve policy
- The housing bubble

- Leverage and liquidity risk
- Fannie Mae and Freddie Mac emphasis on nontraditional mortgages

Others have focused on counterfactuals to urge that the financial meltdown was avoidable. Most frequently, the decision to allow the Lehman Brothers bankruptcy has been widely criticized.[237]

These can be characterized as immediate or proximate causes of the Crisis. More significant are what Aristotle termed ultimate causes.

Above all others, there are two ultimate causes underlying the 2007–2009 financial meltdown.

The first involves the ideology or belief structure of the principal decisionmakers. What was striking in the 2007–2009 crisis is that the two most relevant strands of ideological conviction played out in quite different ways.

The commitment to homeownership was bipartisan, shared by Presidents Clinton and George W. Bush alike, as well as Congress, which in 1992 enacted the Federal Housing Enterprise Finance Safety and Soundness Act to authorize Fannie Mae and Freddie Mac "to facilitate the financing of affordable housing for low-income and moderate-income families." The objective was commendable, but it was taken too far. The weakness of oversight of the housing agencies, the deterioration of mortgage standards, and the encouragement of mortgages that at their most extreme did not require corroboration of income, assets or jobs were consequences of a bipartisan enthusiasm that turned a blind eye to accountability. George W. Bush in retrospect articulated thoughts that were shared by many:

> At the height of the housing boom, homeownership hit an all-time high of almost 70 percent. I had supported policies to expand homeownership, including down-payment assistance for low-income and first-time buyers. I was pleased to see the ownership society grow. But the exuberance of the moment masked the underlying risk. Together, the global pool of cash, easy monetary policy, booming housing market, insatiable appetite for mortgage-backed assets, complexity of Wall Street financial engineering, and leverage of financial institutions created a house of cards. This precarious structure was fated to collapse as soon as the underlying card — the nonstop growth of housing

> prices — was pulled out. That was clear in retrospect. But very few saw it at the time, including me.[238]

There were pernicious consequences of the bipartisan enthusiasm for housing. Regulatory agencies, for example, such as the FDIC, saw its staff reduced by 63 percent between 1995 and 2006 (from 12,000 to 4,500).

Ideological divisions were most evident in the period preceding the financial meltdown. President George W. Bush, for example, emphasized in his economic message the primacy of tax cuts. As he wrote in his President memoir, *Decision Points*: "The centerpiece of my [initial economic] plan was an across-the-board tax cut." He was proud that in June 2001, he signed the first tax cut since President Reagan's first term. In 2003, he called on Congress to accelerate the 2001 tax cuts. He began his final year in office "the same way I had started my first . . . pushing for tax relief."

Bush characterized himself "as a wartime President," who emphasized two non-economic priorities, "protecting the homeland and supporting our troops." He was committed to free market principles, including allowing unsuccessful companies to fail.

In his memoir and in the accounts of others, Bush's leadership was notable for his delegation during the 2007–2009 crisis of decision-making to Hank Paulson and to a lesser degree Ben Bernanke and Tim Geithner. He paid a price for the extent of his delegation. He repeatedly explained in his memoir that he was "surprised" or "blindsided" by the financial crisis.

At critical moments, Bush was a pragmatist. He was willing to compromise core principles to avoid a catastrophe. Repeatedly, he would observe that his first instinct with Bear Stearns, Lehman Brothers, AIG, TARP, and the auto industry was to allow unsuccessful companies to fail, but he ultimately would support "a breathtaking intervention in the free market," even when "[i]t flew against all my instincts." When Paulson or Bernanke convinced him "it was necessary to pull the country out of the panic. . . . I . . . made up my mind: The U.S. Government was going all in." As he stated to a Republican House member in seeking support for the initial version of TARP: "Do you think I like the idea of doing this? Believe me, I'd be fine if the companies fail. But the whole economy is on the line. The son of a bitch is going to go down if we don't step in."

Underlying Bush's sense of pragmatism was his awareness of his legacy. "If we're really looking at another Great Depression," he stated in September 2008, "you can be damn sure I'm going to be Roosevelt, not Hoover."[239]

Secretary of Treasury Hank Paulson was the point man for the Bush Administration's response to the financial meltdown. Bush viewed him as the "Rough Rider of my financial team, Secretary of the Treasury Hank Paulson, a natural leader with decades of experience in international finance." As long time CEO of Goldman Sachs, Paulson was recruited in 2006 as a "hard charger — smart, energetic and credible with the financial markets." Paulson took some persuading, but agreed to join the Administration when President Bush "assured him he would be my prime economic adviser and have unlimited access." Both Bernanke and Geithner stressed that Paulson was "imposing and action-oriented." Geithner recalled: "[Paulson] used to say his general approach to life was that if you see a problem, run at it, not away from it." Bernanke recalled. "We hit [it] off well, notwithstanding the sharp differences in our background and personality. It was academic rigor meeting street smarts, which Hank possessed in abundance."

Paulson did possess street smarts, but they were Wall Street smarts. Paulson understood finance and knew most of the key actors in finance, both in the United States and abroad, notably in China. As with Bush, Paulson was committed to free markets, but pragmatic in his willingness to support aggressive approaches, including the conservatorship of Fannie Mae and Freddie Mac and the nationalization of AIG. Nonetheless, Paulson could be stubborn. His tough love approach to Lehman Brothers backfired. He was reluctant to compromise with the Democrats on executive compensation, and reluctant to support the auto bailout. He would be hypersensitive to news stories accusing him of being "Mr. Bailout" and with TARP fearful that investments in banks, while a wise use of TARP funds, would expose him to criticism for supporting partial nationalization or subsidiaries to Wall Street. Paulson would prove to be an effective crisis leader, but one whose diplomatic skills were uneven.[240]

Complementing Paulson's leadership in the 2007–2009 financial meltdown was Federal Reserve Chair Ben Bernanke. A leading scholar of the Great Depression, he prided himself on *The Courage to Act,* as he titled his crisis memoir. Tim Geithner would characterize Bernanke as believing that:

> [C]entral bankers who fail to act in a crisis could make it exponentially worse. In his academic life, Bernanke had been a

> leading scholar of the Great Depression. His research at Princeton had demonstrated how central bankers of the 1930s were too timid, too reluctant to provide liquidity, too faithful to the tight-money orthodoxies of their day, allowing widespread bank failures and clogged credit channels to turn a financial crisis into an economic disaster. Ben is a low-key guy, not prone to hysteria or exaggeration — I called him the Buddha of central banking — but he was determined not to repeat their mistakes.

Unlike his predecessor, Alan Greenspan, as Fed Chair, "who expected the Fed to follow his lead," "Ben's instincts ran toward deference and consensus building." As the financial crisis deepened, Ben became less deferential to the hawks on the policymaking Federal Reserve Open Market Committee: "If I'm going to be hung, I want to be hung for my own judgments, not theirs."

Bernanke would acknowledge in his memoir that he "failed to imagine" in the years running up to the 2008 near collapse, how the pieces of the economic puzzle "fit together to produce a financial crisis that compared to, and arguably surpassed, the financial crisis that occurred in the Great Depression." Bernanke characterized himself as a moderate Republican — liberal on social issues, more conservative on fiscal and defense, with the standard economist's preference for relying on market forecasts where possible."

At Princeton, Bernanke was an economist's economist, Chair of the Princeton Economics Department, with a research specialty in macroeconomics and almost a reverence for the Federal Reserve System. In 2002, Bernanke had begun at the Federal Reserve Board "with the goal of increasing the Fed's transparency and accountability — and, in particular, of instituting a numerical target for inflation by which the Fed's performance could be judged." Bernanke was persistent. He became Chair of the Fed in 2006. In 2012, the Federal Reserve began using inflation targets.

Economist Alan Blinder, who served as Vice Chair of the Federal Reserve Bank between 1994 and 1996 and a colleague of Bernanke at Princeton, characterized Bernanke's views in historical terms:

> The Federal Reserve is the *primus inter pares* [first among equals] of the four federal banking regulators. It was led for more than eighteen years by Alan Greenspan, a self-described disciple of the libertarian philosopher Ayn Rand, and proud of it. Greenspan was, shall we say, a less-than-enthusiastic regulator. He was also, as he later confessed, unduly enamored of

banks' mathematical risk models and their abilities to use them with both skill and integrity.

Blinder added: "Bernanke also characterized himself as a libertarian — before the crisis." In financial journalist Roger Lowenstein's view, "Bernanke was too quick to believe that Greenspan succeeded — that central bankers had truly muted the economic cycle."

Bernanke would characterize the differences between Greenspan and himself in his memoir:

> On substance, Greenspan and I agreed on many things. He was passionate, as was I, about maintaining the Fed's independence from short-term political pressures. The chairman made policy decisions in an apolitical, nonpartisan way. Like me, he also believed that monetary policy is a powerful tool, and he was prepared to act forcefully when warranted. We agreed on the benefits of low and stable inflation, and we largely agreed that monetary policy could remain effective even if short-term interest rates reached zero. Greenspan also shared my views that monetary policymakers could not reliably identify asset-price bubbles or safety "pop" them by raising interest rates.
>
> Our thinking diverged in several areas. I championed, and he distrusted, formal policy frameworks like inflation targeting, which were intended to improve the Fed's transparency. . . . Also, he did not put much stock in the ability of bank regulation and supervision to keep banks out of trouble. He believed that, so long as banks had enough of their own money at stake, in the form of capital, market forces would deter them from unnecessarily risky lending. And, while I had argued that regulation and supervision should be the first line of defense against asset-price bubbles, he was more inclined to keep hands off and use after-the-fact interest rate cuts to cushion the economic consequences of a burst bubble.

Bernanke added: "Chairman Greenspan did not put a high priority on consumer protection. He distrusted what he saw as heavy-handed interventions in the financial services marketplace."

Bernanke, powerfully aided and abetted by New York Federal Reserve President Tim Geithner and many in the Federal Reserve Board staff, would prove imaginative in policy innovations such as techniques to support nonbanking institutions during the crisis and Quantitative Easing. As Bernanke stated during the meltdown: "There are no atheists in foxholes and no ideologues in financial crises." Bernanke would end his tenure as Federal Reserve Chair in 2014 with the judgment:

> The Federal Reserve changed substantially during my time as chairman. We became more transparent and more focused on financial stability. At the same time, new threats emerged that could hamper future Fed policymakers' ability to act forcefully to preserve financial stability and support the economy. Our inability to foresee or prevent the crisis, and some of our responses, especially our rescues of AIG and Bear Stearns, hurt the Fed politically and created new risks for its independence.[241]

Geithner was the junior member of the Bush Administration's economic troika. Geithner was 42 when he became President of the New York Federal Reserve Bank, which as Geithner aptly put it was "the government's main outpost in America's financial center,...The largest and most influential of the Federal Reserve's twelve regional banks." The President of the New York Fed long had been regarded as the second most important position in the Federal Reserve system, a position that legendary predecessors such as Benjamin Strong, Jerry Corrigan, and Paul Volcker had held.

Geithner not only was young for such a responsibility, but looked younger. Investment banker Pete Peterson, who led the search for the President of the New York Fed, supposedly declaimed: "He's twelve years old!" Geithner was unusual in terms of Federal Reserve senior leaders in neither having earned a Ph.D. or served as a senior executive of a leading business.

What he had, an initially unimpressed Ben Bernanke would come to recognize, was "the equivalent of a Ph.D. in financial crisis management:"

> After working at Henry Kissinger's global consulting firm, he had joined the staff of the Treasury Department in 1988. He rose quickly, impressing Rubin and Summers with his intelligence and savvy and playing an important role in the Treasury's efforts to put out financial fires around the world, most notably the Asian financial crisis in 1997.

When Geithner was named the first Secretary of Treasury in the Obama Administration, Bernanke realized how grateful he was for Geithner's raw intelligence, obsessive discipline, and political courage. Bernanke thanked him for his service at the New York Fed: "You have been just the sort of person anyone would want alongside them in the financial crisis foxhole." Bernanke "would miss the profanity-laced intensity that he brought to our deliberations and his distinctive aphorisms: 'Plan beats no plan', 'foam on the runway', 'Old Testament thinking,' and more."

A quite different view of Geithner was held by FDIC Chair Sheila Bair who not only stressed philosophical differences with Geithner in her memoir, *Bull by the Horns,* but questioned Geithner's aggressive efforts to use the FDIC for Fed purposes as well as Geithner's good faith.

Geithner brought to the New York Fed a zeal to reduce what he regarded as the systemic risk of the nation's banking system. He was not doctrinaire:

> I don't think I'm hawkish or dovish by nature. I've always been pretty pragmatic, suspicious of ideology in any form, and I took both halves of the Fed's dual mandate seriously. But I found the more hawkish obsessions with moral hazard and inflation during a credit crunch bizarre and frustrating. Recession seemed like a more plausible threat than inflation. The notion that a slight tweak in the discount rate was too aggressive during an incipient panic just baffled me; in fact, it ended up being largely ineffectual at overcoming the stigma of the [Discount] window, since only a handful of banks actually came and borrowed.[242]

The core beliefs that Paulson, Bernanke, and Geithner shared were shaped by their experience leading or regulating financial institutions. They shared a commitment to the protection, and when possible strengthening, of our financial and economic system by addressing systemic risk at systemically important banks and cognate institutions, a distrust of regulation to promote other social goals, such as consumerism, a concern that moral hazards could drain the discipline out of the private sector, a faith in free markets and business innovation, and a deep loyalty to the Department of Treasury and Federal Reserve as the key financial and economic actors in our economy.

In these views, they often were sharply at odds with leading Democrats, who in the financial and economic realm were more concerned with social goals such as income distribution, job protection and growth, protection of the auto industry, foreclosure mitigation and affordable mortgages, helping Main Street, that is, small business, and stronger regulation of finance and corporate governance. The Democrats were more willing to consider nationalization as a solution to the banking crisis and bridled at the low levels of criminal prosecution of those they believed responsible for the financial meltdown.

To be sure, neither Republicans nor Democrats wanted to be responsible for a total financial and economic meltdown. Republicans and Democrats generally wanted to avoid bailouts and ensure that no company was too big to fail.

The inevitable partisan differences in national politics is a powerful constraint on the ability to effectively act. This should come as no surprise. Our Constitution established a political system that seeks to avoid the absolute power of a King with checks and balances such as federalism preserving state power, a bicameral Congress, a President subject to Congressional power to enact legislation and budgets, and judicial review empowering a third branch of the government with the power to declare laws or actions of either Congress or the President unconstitutional.

The Failure of Structure

The second ultimate cause of the 2007–2009 financial meltdown was the persistence of a dysfunctional, obsolete, and too often ineffectual structure of financial regulation.

In 2016, the structure of federal and state financial regulation was depicted in the following Chart printed in a GAO Report:

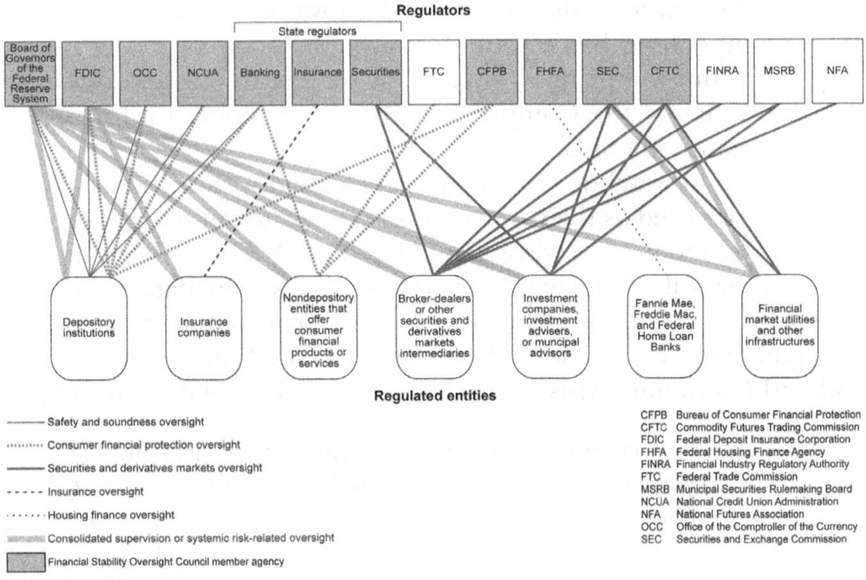

Source: GAO. | GAO-16-175

This structure is rife with overlapping regulations, competitive regulatory agencies, and frequent uncertainty as to responsibility. Historically the model has been slow to predict crises, slow to resolve jurisdictional conflict and too often forced into crisis response when financial debacle is well advanced.

In retrospect, weaknesses in this structure were glaringly apparent. As Geithner generalized in his 2014 memoir criticizing "American balkanized regulatory system": "It was riddled with gaps and turf battles. It was full of real and perceived sources of capture. And nobody was accountable for the scalability of the entire system."

The "byzantine mess" began with the traditional banking system:

> with responsibilities for supervising thousands of commercial banks divided among the Fed, the Federal Deposit Insurance Corporation (*FDIC*), as well as state banking regulators working from fifty different sets of rules. The Office of Thrift Supervision (*OTS*) regulated "thrifts," which were essentially banks focused on mortgage markets; their deposit-taking subsidiaries were subject to capital requirements and eligible for the Fed's discount window, but the riskier affiliates and parent companies generally operated without adult supervision. There were also geographic divisions within the Fed. The New York Fed oversaw Citigroup and JP Morgan Chase, while the Richmond Fed supervised Bank of America and Wachovia, and the San Francisco Fed handled Wells Fargo.

Regulation of a single company often was divided. The Federal Reserve supervised bank holding companies such as JP Morgan or Citigroup, but the primary supervisor for their commercial banks was the Office of the Comptroller of the Currency and for investment banking, the SEC.

The "glut of watchdogs" encouraged regulatory arbitrage. "Banks often reorganized as thrifts," Geithner wrote, "to get the notoriously weak OTS as their supervisor. The OTS and OCC were both funded by fees they collected from their member banks which gave them an incentive to try to woo banks into their orbit by offering lighter enforcement." The National Committee on the Causes of the Financial and Economic Crisis similarly highlighted regulatory arbitrage:

> The patchwork quilt of regulators created opportunities for banks to shop for the most lenient regulator, and the presence of more than one supervisor at an organization. For example,

> a large firm like Citigroup could have the Fed supervising the Bank Holding Company, the OCC supervising the national bank subsidiary, the SEC supervising the securities firm, and the OTS supervising the thrift subsidiary — creating the potential for both gaps in coverage and problematic overlap.

Divisions among bank regulators were acute. FDIC Chair Bair complained in her 2012 memoir: "It was not uncommon for the OCC and the Fed to team up against the FDIC." She was particularly incensed that the OCC and Fed took so long to alert the FDIC to Wachovia's problems and that the New York Fed was "in discussions with Citi about a Wachovia acquisition, based on the understanding — not shared by others — that the FDIC would help cover its losses." In 2003, the Comptroller and OTS blocked state efforts to regulate predatory mortgages in the subprime market invoking the doctrine of preemption.

Bank regulation was only part of a much broader system of financial regulation. In Geithner's view:

> But if the scrutiny of commercial banking was problematic, the rest of the financial system was under even less scrutiny, with none of the constraints of bank regulations and virtually no safety and soundness oversight. Investment banks were monitored by the SEC, which was much better equipped to focus on investor protection issues than on the financial health of the investment banks, and imposed few constraints on leverage. Money market funds, which functioned much like traditional banks, offering deposit-like instruments to their customers, were also under the SEC umbrella, but without the capital requirements or constraints on risk taking faced by banks. Hedge funds were growing fast without any meaningful oversight or leverage limits. The same was true of large finance companies such as GE Capital and the General Motors Acceptance Corporation (*GMAC*). Fannie and Freddie had their own compliant Washington regulator, which allowed them to build up a huge portfolio of mortgage assets without requiring them to hold much capital. The CFTC [Commodity Futures Trading Commission] was supposed to monitor futures traders. State insurance departments were largely responsible for insurance companies, even though AIG and other insurance firms had evolved into multinational financial conglomerates.

Compounding the complexity of federal and state financial regulation were gaps and omissions in the overall regulatory structure. During the 2007–2009 period, most acute were difficulties in regulation of mortgage origination, hedge funds, and new products including collateralized debt obligations.

The breakdown in regulation was notoriously deficient in the housing industry. Subprime mortgages received too little attention from the Department of Treasury and the Federal Reserve System, the two regulators most responsible for a systematic view of the overall economy. As economist Alan Blinder explained:

> ... [N]one of the banking regulators, not even the quartet as a whole, saw the complete sorry picture for what it was. A large and growing share of the worst subprime mortgages were not issued by banks at all, but rather by nonbank lenders who would originate dodgy mortgages, perhaps hold them for only a matter of days, and then sell them off to securitizers.... For example, only one of the top ten subprime mortgage originators in 2005 was a regulated commercial bank (Wells Fargo). By 2007 more than half of all subprime loans were being originated by mortgage brokers rather than by banks. Indeed,... only 20 percent of subprime loans granted in 2005 came from regularly supervised banks and thrifts.

Paulson continued:

> Why were we so off? We missed the dreadful quality of the most recent mortgages, and we believed the problem was largely confined to subprime loans. Default rates on subprime adjustable-rate mortgage loans (*ARMs*) from 2005 to 2007 were far higher than ever; ARMs made up half of subprime loans, or about 6.5 percent of all mortgages, but they accounted for 50 percent of all foreclosures. Even worse, the problems were coming far more quickly. In some cases, borrowers were missing their very first payments.

To National Commissioner dissenter Peter Wallison, subsequently author of *Hidden in Plain Sight*, the breakdown was data driven. There was a paucity of authentic information about the extent to which Fannie Mae and Freddie Mac increasingly were holding nontraditional mortgages (subprime mortgages and those where borrowers had FICO scores below 600), and misstating their exposure to subprime mortgages.

In these circumstances, mortgages and securities grew increasingly opaque, regulatory response often was uncertain or delayed. In 2007, former Federal Reserve Chair Alan Greenspan would bemoan the collapse of financial regulation:

> Markets have become too huge, complex, and fast-moving to be subject to twentieth-century supervision and regulation. No wonder this globalized financial behemoth stretches beyond the full comprehension of even the most sophisticated market participants. Financial regulators are required to oversee a system far more complex than what existed when the regulations still governing financial markets were originally written. Today, oversight of these transactions is essentially by means of individual-market-participant counterparty surveillance. Each lender, to protect its shareholders, keeps a tab on its customers' investment positions. Regulators can still pretend to provide oversight, but their capabilities are much diminished and declining.

The National Commission on the Causes of the Financial and Economic Crisis was more brutal in its assessment:

> . . . [K]ey policy makers — the Treasury Department, the Federal Reserve Board, and the Federal Reserve Bank of New York — who were best positioned to watch over our markets were ill prepared for the events of 2007 and 2008. Other agencies were also behind the curve. They were hampered because they did not have a clear grasp of the financial system they were charged with overseeing, particularly as it had evolved in the years leading up to the crisis. This was in no small measure due to the lack of transparency in key markets. They thought risk had been diversified when, in fact, it had been concentrated. Time and again, from the spring of 2007 on, policy makers and regulators were caught off guard as the contagion spread, responding on an ad hoc basis with specific programs to put fingers in the dike. There was no comprehensive and strategic plan for containment, because they lacked a full understanding of the risks and interconnections in the financial markets.

The ability before the 2007–2009 crisis to effectively take a comprehensive view of our financial system did not exist. Legislation created this awkward structure. One hundred and fifty years of legislative response to specific industry crises led to a system that was fragmented and complex, uneven in enforcement, too often burdened in jurisdictional litigation or failures in coordination and collaboration.[243]

The remainder of this book focuses on three fundamental questions:

How did this system evolve?

Why is the Dodd-Frank Act and other legislation and regulation not adequate to address a system of dysfunctional regulation?

How can we design a financial regulatory system more likely to prevent future crises?

ENDNOTES:

1. Joel Seligman, The Transformation of Wall Street 1–2 (3d ed. 2003).
2. See, e.g., GAO, Financial Regulation (GAO-16-175 Feb. 2016). As of October 2008, state banking regulators oversaw 6,107 state chartered banks; state insurance commissioners regulated 7,000 insurance entities; state securities regulators regulated 19,291 investment advisory and brokerage firms; the SEC oversaw 34,285 financial firms and public companies; the Federal Reserve Board supervised 597 financial holding companies and 878 state member banks; the FDIC regulated 5,151 banks; the Office of the Comptroller of the Currency oversaw 1,576 national banks; the Office of Thrift Supervision regulated 1,308 thrifts and thrift holding companies; the Commodity Futures Trading Commission regulated 3,753 firms and individuals; and the Financial Industry Regulation Authority, a self-regulatory organization subject to SEC oversight, oversaw 5,000 brokerage firms. Nina Easton, Main Street against Wall Street 100–101 (Fortune Oct. 20, 2008).
3. David Moss, An Ounce of Prevention: Financial Regulation, Moral Hazard, and the End of "Too Big to Fail" in New Directions in Financial Services Regulation 99 (Roger Porter, Robert Glauber & Thomas Healey eds. MIT Press 2011).
4. Gary Gorton, Slapped by the Invisible Hand: The Panic of 2007 13 (Oxford Univ. Press 2010); Gary Gorton, Misunderstanding Financial Crises (Oxford Univ. Press 2012).
5. Kimberly Amaded, Dow Highest Closing Records (updated Feb. 18, 2017).
6. Arthur Milmarth, The Dark Side of Universal Banking: Financial Conglomerates and the Origins of the Subprime Financial Crisis, 41 Conn. L. Rev. 963, 967 (2009).
7. Final Report of the National Commission on the Causes of the Financial and Economic Crisis in the United States 394–397 (2011) (Crisis Report).

8. GAO, Financial Regulatory Reform: Financial Crisis Losses and Potential Impact of the Dodd-Frank Act 17–18 (GAO 13-180 Jan. 2013); Alan Blinder, After the Music Stopped: The Financial Crisis, the Response and the Work Ahead 11 (Penguin Books 2014).
9. Ben Bernanke, The Courage to Act: A Memoir of a Crisis and its Aftermath 405 (2015). In some Midwestern factory towns, unemployment rose to 20 percent by March 2009. Timothy Geithner, Stress Test: Reflections on Financial Crises 336–337 (Crown Pub. 2014).
10. Id. at xv.
11. GAO, supra n. 8, at 20.
12. Crisis Report, supra n. 7, at 391–392 (2011).
13. Ibid.
14. GAO, supra n. 8, at 5.
15. Blinder, supra n. 8, at 235.
16. Bernanke, supra n. 9 at 85; Blinder, supra n. 8, at 47; Crisis Report, supra n. 7, at 109.
17. Crisis Report, supra n. 7, at 38–40; Laurie Goodson, A Realistic Assessment of Housing Finance Reform, Urban Inst. 1 (2014); Blinder, supra n. 8, at 323–324; Ben Bernanke, Tim Geithner & Henry Paulson, Firefighting: The Financial Crisis and Its Lessons 54-60 (Penguin 2019). See generally Bethany McLean, Shaking Ground: The Strange Saga of the U.S. Mortgage Giants (2015).
18. Viral Acharya, et al., Guaranteed to Fail: Fannie Mae, Freddie Mac and the Debacle of Mortgage Finance, 136 (2011); Crisis Report, supra n. 7, at 42.
19. Goodson, supra n. 17; Crisis Report, supra n. 7, at 41, 86; Blinder, supra n. 8, at 18. Cf. Peter Wallison, Hidden in Plain Sight: Who Really Cursed the World's Worst Financial Crisis and Why It Could Happen Again 5–6 (2015).
20. Crisis Report, supra n. 7, at 72–74, 123. See also Wallison, supra n. 19, at 115–122; Gretchen Morgenson & Joshua Rosner, Reckless Endangerment 31–39, 59–60.
21. Morgenson & Rosner, supra n., 20, at 26–28.
22. Aaron Ross Sorkin, Too Big To Fail: The Inside Story of How Wall Street and Washington Fought to Save the Finance System and Themselves 184 (2009); Wallison, supra n. 19, at 114–117, 161–162.
23. Morgenson & Rosner, supra n. 20, at 8–12, 71–72.
24. Henry Paulson, On the Brink: Inside the Race to Stop the Collapse of the Global Financial System 57 (2010). See also Morgenson & Rosner, supra n. 20, at 24, 172.
25. Paulson, supra n. 24, at 56; Morgenson & Rosner, supra n. 20, at 78–81 (describing successful Fannie Mae and Freddie Mac efforts between 1994 and 1996 to dissuade the Department of Treasury to

not conclude in a required report tht the GSEs should lose their government sponsorship).

26. Koppell quoted in Morgenson, & Rosner supra n. 20, at 249. See generally at 27–30.
27. Morgenson & Rosner, supra n. 20, at 249–250.
28. Greenspan quoted in Morgenson & Rosner, supra n. 20, at 252.
29. Crisis Report, supra n. 7, at 65.
30. Crisis Report, supra n. 7, at 122.
31. Crisis Report, supra n. 7, at 122; Morgenson & Rosner, supra n. 20, at 23, 30, 78–81, 254–257.
32. See, e.g., Crisis Report, supra n. 7, Chapter 7.
33. Crisis Report, supra n. 7 at 27–34; Int'l Monetary Fund, Global Financial Stability Report: Risk Taking, Liquidity and Shadow Banking Ch. 2 (Oct. 2014); Kathryn Judge, Information Gaps and Shadow Banking, 103 Va. L. Rev. 411 (2017); Tobias Adrian & Adam Ashcraft, Shadow Banking: A Review of the Literature, Fed. Res. Bank of N.Y. Staff Report No. 580 (Oct. 2012); Bernanke, supra n. 9, at 137; Blinder, supra n. 8, at 58–64; Gorton, supra n. 4 at 38–53.
34. Geithner, supra n. 9, at 81.
35. Crisis Report, supra n. 7, at 20; Wallison, supra n. 19, at 163–164; Roger Lowenstein, The End of Wall Street 28-32 (2010).
36. Crisis Report, supra n. 7, at 16–17, 22–23, 88, 104–111, 118; Morgenson & Rosner, supra n. 20, at 183; Wallison, supra n. 19, at 174.
37. Wallison, supra n. 19, at 7–10, 27–29, 178; Lowenstein, supra n. 35, at 13; Bethany McLean & Joe Nocera, All the Devils Are Here: The Hidden History of the Financial Crises 211 (2010).
38. Edward J. Pinto, Government Housing Policies in the Lead-Up to the Financial Crisis: A Forensic Study Chart 53 (Draft Manuscript Feb. 5, 2011), summarized in Wallison, supra n. 19, at 202.
39. Gorton, supra n. 4, at 63. See also Erik Gerding, Law, Bubbles and Financial Regulation ch. 1 (Routledge 2014).
40. Crisis Report, supra n. 7, at 102–105, 180–181; John Coffee, The Retreat from Systemic Risk Regulation: What Explained It? (and Why It Was Predictable), at 11 (Columbia L.S. Sept. 2018); Adam Tooze, Crashed: How a Decade of Financial Crises Changed the World 65 (Viking 2018); Bernanke, supra n. 9, at 401–403; Gorton, Misunderstanding Financial Crises, supra n. 4, at 130.
41. Crisis Report, supra n. 7, at 42–45; Lowell Bryan, Structured Securitized Credit: A Superior Technology for Lending, 1 J. Applied Corp. Fin. 6 (1988).
42. Crisis Report, supra n. 7, at 71–72.
43. Ibid; Sheila Bair, Bull by the Horns 51–53 (Free Press 2012); Gorton, supra n. 4, at 21–23.

44. Crisis Report, supra n. 7, at 71–72; John Hull & Alan White, Ratings, Mortgage Securitizations, and the Apparent Creation of Value in Rethinking the Financial Crisis (Alan Blinder, Andrew Lo & Robert Solon Eds. 2012) at 192. There were modest differences in debt rating classification systems. Moody's uses Aaa, Aa, A, Baa, Caa, Ca, and C. Fitch divides all categories except AAA into three subcategories. For example, AA, is divided into AA+, AA and AA–.
45. Hull & White, supra n. 44, at 205. On the design of subprime mortgages see generally Gorton, supra n. 4, at 74–97.
46. Crisis Report, supra n. 7, at 127–132, 188–190; Gorton, supra n. 4, at 97–107; Wallison, supra n. 19, at 89–107 (summarizing a Federal Reserve Bank of Philadelphia Staff Study that found a total of 727 CDO pools were issued between 1999 and 2007 with a total value of $641 billion. Almost two-thirds of the CDOs were issued in 2006 and 2007); McLean & Nocera, supra n. 37, at 267–273, 311–314.
47. Crisis Report, supra n. 7, at 132; Nicholas Varchaver & Katie Benner, The $55 Trillion Question, Fortune (Oct. 20, 2008) at 134.
48. Crisis Report, supra n. 7, at 142–143, 191. See generally id. at 190–195; Blinder, supra n. 8, at 65–68.
49. Bair, supra n. 43, at 52.
50. Crisis Report, supra n. 7, at 118–120; see generally 2 Louis Loss, Joel Seligman & Troy Paredes, Securities Regulation 118–155 (5th ed. 2014).
51. Goodman & Comptroller quoted in McLean & Nocera, supra n. 37, at 113.
52. Crisis Report supra n. 7, at 104, 119.
53. Crisis Report, supra n. 7, at 120, 147. See generally id. at 120–122.
54. Crisis Report, supra n. 7, at 211–212; Lowenstein, supra n. 35, at 42.
55. Crisis Report, supra n. 7, at 146–150.
56. Sec. Ex. Act Rel. 57,967, 93 SEC Dock. 1266, 1267–1275 (2008).
57. Crisis Report, supra n. 7, at 105, 118, 146–147, 160–169; Hull & White, supra n. 44, at 193; Blinder, supra n. 8, at 79–81.
58. Crisis Report, supra n. 7, at 5, 85, 103.
59. Richard Posner, Underlying Causes of the Financial Crisis of 2008-2009; Porter, et al., supra n. 3, at 24. At the beginning of 2000, the federal funds rate was 5.45 percent and the average interest rate for a 30-year fixed rate mortgage was 8.21 percent. By December 2003, in the aftermath of the collapse of the dotcom stock market bubble, 30-year mortgage interest rates were 5.80 percent. Id. at 29.
60. Crisis Report, supra n. 7, at 7, 214; Blinder, supra n. 8, at 17–18, 34–37; Wallison, supra n. 19, at 13–18; Lawrence McDonald & Patrick Robinson, A Colossal Failure of Common Sense 120–121 (Crown Business 2009).

61. Crisis Report, supra n. 7, at 215. See generally id. at 213–230; Bernanke, supra n. 9, at 407–409; R. Shiller, Finance and the Good Society ix–x (2012) (U.S. home prices fell 40 percent between 2006 and 2011).
62. Bernanke and Paulson quoted in Morgenson & Rosner, supra n. 20, at 296.
63. Geithner, supra n. 9, at 112–113.
64. Crisis Report, supra n. 7, at 256.
65. Crisis Report, supra n. 7, at 256; Bernanke, Geithner & Paulson, supra n. 17, at 34.
66. Crisis Report, supra n. 7, at 238–242, 281; Bernanke, supra n. 9, at 140; Lowenstein, supra n. 35, at 90; McClean & Nocera, supra n. 37, at 285–295; 3 Jerry Markham, A Financial History of the United States 103–104 (Routledge 2015).
67. Crisis Report, supra n. 7, at 246–248; Paulson, supra n. 24, at 71.
68. Crisis Report, supra n. 7, at 248.
69. Bernanke, supra n. 9, at 141; Paulson, supra n. 24, at 71–72; Lowenstein, supra n. 35, at 95.
70. Paulson, supra n. 24, at 72.
71. Lowenstein, supra n. 35, at 95.
72. Crisis Report, supra n. 7, at 250–251; Bernanke, supra n. 9, at 133–134, 144–145; Sorkin, supra n. 22, at 87–90.
73. Sorkin, supra n. 22, at 88.
74. Crisis Report, supra n. 7, at 252; Geithner, supra n. 9, at 117–120; Paulson, supra n. 24, at 61–64.
75. Geithner, supra n. 9, at 117. Geithner was not alone in these sentiments. Jim Cramer, a hedge fund trader, who had become a television personality on CNBC, prone to hyperbole, ranted "We have Armageddon . . . Bernanke is being an academic." Cramer quoted in Lowenstein, supra n. 35, at 95.
76. Crisis Report, supra n. 7, at 248.
77. Crisis Report, supra n. 7, at 249–250; Bernanke, supra n. 9, at 134; Geithner, supra n. 9, at 122–127; McDonald, supra n. 60, at 257 (reporting that as early as June 20, 2007, one in four of Countrywide's subprime loans was delinquent); Keoun, Countrywide Taps $11.5 Billion Credit Line from Banks, *www.bloomberg.com* (Aug. 16, 2007); El Boghdady, No. 1 Home Lender Taps $11.5 Billion Line of Credit, *www.washingtonpost.com* (Aug. 17, 2007). See also Lowenstein, supra n. 35, at 117 ("In Countrywide's portfolio an incredible 27 percent of subprime mortgages were delinquent; 5-1/2 percent were in foreclosure").
78. Bernanke, supra n. 9, at 147–153; Paulson, supra n. 24, at 73.
79. Bernanke, supra n. 9, at 164–165; Paulson, supra n. 24, at 77–78; Lowenstein, supra n. 35, at 102. See generally Wallison, supra n.

19, at 291–292 (After August 2007: "The market was a mess."). With respect to Northern Rock, see especially HM Treasury, the Nationalisation of Northern Rock (20 Mar. 2009).

80. Crisis Report, supra n. 7, at 202–204, 256–259; Geithner, supra n. 9, at 133–134; Sorkin, supra n. 22, at 73, 94.
81. Lowenstein, supra n. 35, at 99–100; McLean & Nocera, supra n. 37, at 163, 318–321.
82. Crisis Report, supra n. 7, at 260–265; Geithner, supra n. 9, at 134–135; Lowenstein, supra n. 35, at 99; Siew, Citi Losses Expose Tip of Billion-Dollar Iceberg, *www.reuters.com* (Nov. 5, 2007); Embattled Citigroup CEO Resigns, *www.cbsnews.com* (Nov. 5, 2007).
83. Crisis Report, supra n. 7, at 303.
84. Geithner, supra n. 9, at 136; Bernanke, supra n. 9, at 176–178 (describing the structured investment vehicles or SIVs in which Citi held on more than a third of its assets); Bair, supra n. 43, at 73.
85. Lowenstein, supra n. 35, at 100.
86. Paulson, supra n. 24, at 83–84.
87. Bernanke, supra n. 9, at 200–201.
88. Crisis Report, supra n. 7, at 276.
89. Crisis Report, supra n. 7, at 276–277; Bernanke, supra n. 9, at 201–202.
90. Bernanke, supra n. 9, at 201–202; Crisis Report, supra n. 7, at 271–278.
91. Bernanke, supra n. 9, at 202–204; Crisis Report, supra n. 7, at 273.
92. Blinder, supra n. 8, at 101–102, 111; Crisis Report, supra n. 7, at 280–281. See generally Kate Kelly, Street Fighters: The Last 72 Hours of Bear Stearns, the Toughest Firm on Wall Street (2009).
93. Crisis Report, supra n. 7, at 135; Gorton, Misunderstanding Financial Crises, supra n. 4, at 39–41.
94. Crisis Report, supra n. 7, at 285; Blinder, supra n. 8, at 101.
95. Crisis Report, supra n. 7, at 293.
96. Crisis Report, supra n. 7, at 295.
97. Geithner, supra n. 9, at 148. See also Lowenstein, supra n. 35, at 125.
98. Paulson, supra n. 24, at 93.
99. Crisis Report, supra n. 7, at 294.
100. Crisis Report, supra n. 7, at 286–291; Bernanke, supra n. 9, at 208–211; Paulson, supra n. 24, at 91–92, 106–121; Geithner, supra n. 9, at 151–161.
101. Bernanke, supra n. 9, at 215–216; Geithner, supra n. 9, at 150–151, 164–167; Sorkin, supra n. 22, at 11; McLean & Nocera, supra n. 37, at 349–351; Blinder, supra n. 8, at 112–113.
102. Paulson, supra n. 24, at 101. This was a very powerful statement from a lifelong proponent of free markets who initially had caused JP Morgan to lower its per share bid for Bear Stearns to avoid the

appearance of a bailout of Bear's stockholders. Id. at 120; Lowenstein, supra n. 35, at 128.

103. Bernanke, supra n. 9, at 224; Paulson, supra n. 24, at 117; Geithner, supra n. 9, at 160; Blinder, supra n. 8, at 110–111; Bernanke, Geithner & Paulson, supra n. 17, at 52.
104. Wallison, supra n. 19, at 310; see generally id. at 310–315.
105. Id. at 325.
106. Bernanke, supra n. 9, at 223. Geithner notes that the four investment bank holding companies raised $140 billion in capital in the spring of 2008. Geithner, supra n. 9, at 165.
107. Crisis Report, supra n. 7, at 287; Bernanke, supra n. 9, at 205, 217 ("From 1932 to 1936, [the Fed] used its § 13(3) authority to [make] 123 loans, mostly very small."); Paulson, supra n. 24, at 114–115.
108. Paulson, supra n. 24, at 94–95.
109. Paulson, supra n. 24, at 102; Bernanke, supra n. 9, at 215. Regarding Long Term Capital Management, see generally Roger Lowenstein, When Genius Failed: The Rise and Fall of Long Term Capital Management (Random House 2000); Blinder, supra n. 8, at 62; Sorkin, supra n. 22, at 62; Crisis Report, supra n. 7, at 47–48, 56–59; Morgenson & Rosner, supra n. 20, at 124–125; Alan Greenspan, The Age of Turbulence 193–195 (Penguin Press 2007); Robert Rubin, In an Uncertain World 284–286 (Random House 2003); Bob Woodward, Maestro: Greenspan's Fed and the American Boom 198–206 (Simon & Schuster 2000).
110. Lowenstein, supra n. 35, at 130–131; Crisis Report, supra n. 7, at 294; Bernanke, supra n. 9, at 220–221; Paulson, supra n. 24, at 120, 128.
111. Crisis Report, supra n. 7, at 294.
112. Crisis Report, supra n. 7, at 295.
113. Geithner, supra n. 9, at 148–149, 162.
114. Crisis Report, supra n. 7, at 284, 286. See also SEC Press Rel. 2008-48 (Mar. 20, 2008), quoting Chairman Cox letter to the Chair of the Basel Committee on Banking Supervision: "[T]he conclusion to which these data point is that the fate of Bear Stearns was the result of a lack of confidence, not a lack of capital." Few agreed with Chairman Cox. In late June 2008, a *Wall Street Journal* article summarized criticism of Chairman Cox for his low key leadership of the Commission during the Bear Stearns crisis. Scannell & Craig, SEC Chief under Fire as Fed Seeks a Bigger Wall Street Role, Wall St. J., June 23, 2008, at A1.
115. Report No. 446-A 2008. See also Crisis Report, supra n. 7, at 296–297.
116. The SEC Inspector General Report and related statements are quoted at length in 6 Louis Loss, Joel Seligman & Troy Paredes, Securities Regulation 406–479 (5th ed. 2016).

117. Crisis Report, supra n. 7, at 292.
118. See Chairman Cox Announces End of Consolidated Supervised Entities Program, SEC Press Rel. 2008-230 (Sept. 26, 2008). See also Crisis Report, supra n. 7, at 150–154; McLean & Nocera, supra n. 37, at 243–245; Bair, supra n. 43, at 36–37; Labaton, Agency's '04 Rule Let Banks Pile up New Debt, and Risk, *N.Y. Times*, Oct. 3, 2008, at A1; SEC Ends Voluntary Program for Supervising Major Wall Street Firms' Capital and Liquidity, 40 Sec. Reg. & L. Rep. (BNA) 1532 (2008); Markey Demands Answers from SEC over Failures Cited in Recent IG Report, 40 id. 1587.
119. Crisis Report, supra n. 7, at 298.
120. See summary in 6 Loss, Seligman & Paredes, supra n. 116, at 463–468 and Paulson, supra n. 24, at 90–91. Cf. Fear of Regulating, *N.Y. Times*, Apr. 3, 2008, at A26: "[T]he blueprint was mostly developed before the current financial crisis and accordingly came across as outdated."
121. Bernanke, Geithner & Paulson, supra n. 17, at 54; Geithner, supra n. 9, at 164.
122. Paulson, supra n. 24, at 112. Lowenstein recounts a plan by Paulson during the Bear Stearns crisis week to use Fannie Mae and Freddie Mac to buy more mortgage-backed securities to help the hard pressed banks. Given the weaknesses then of Fannie and Freddie — each was close to insolvency — Lowenstein characterizes this as a "fantastic scheme, which Paulson must have realized." Lowenstein, supra n. 35, at 129–130.
123. Crisis Report, supra n. 7, at 309, 312; Bernanke, Geithner & Paulson, supra n. 17, at 54–60.
124. Geithner, supra n. 9, at 169; see also Crisis Report, supra n. 7, at 316; Blinder, supra n. 8, at 115; Testimony of Federal Reserve Chair Alan Greenspan, Government-Sponsored Enterprises, before Senate Comm. on Banking, Housing & Urban Affairs at 4 (Feb. 24, 2004).
125. Geithner, supra n. 9, at 170; Crisis Report, supra n. 7, at 310–316.
126. McLean & Nocera, supra n. 37, at 348; Crisis Report, supra n. 7, at 312; Blinder, supra n. 8, at 117–118. On this issue, the Republican party was more in favor of regulation than the Democrats. President Bush spoke in favor of stronger regulation of Fannie Mae and Freddie Mac 17 times between 2003 and the summer of 2008. G. Bush, Decision Points, 454–455 (2010).
127. Crisis Report, supra n. 7, at 314.
128. Paulson, supra n. 24, at 130–135; Blinder, supra n. 8, at 330-332; Geithner, supra n. 9, at 168–169; Bernanke, Geithner & Paulson, supra n. 17, at 55; Bair, supra n. 43, at 79–81; Sorkin, supra n. 22, at 190.

129. Lowenstein, supra n. 35, at 144–145; McDonald & Robinson, supra n. 60, at 308.
130. Paulson, supra n. 24, at 142–144, 147.
131. Pub. L. No. 110-289, 122 Stat. 2653.
132. Paulson, supra n. 24, at 155.
133. Crisis Report, supra n. 7, at 316–317.
134. Paulson, supra n. 24, at 151; Blinder, supra n. 8, at 118.
135. Crisis Report, supra n. 7, at 317.
136. Crisis Report, supra n. 7, at 317–318, 322; Paulson, supra n. 24, at 162; Lowenstein, supra n. 35, at 152–155.
137. Paulson, supra n. 24, at 3. See generally id. at 1–18.
138. Paulson, supra n. 24, at 161–170; Lowenstein, supra n. 35, at 160–163; McLean & Nocera, supra n. 37, at 356; Crisis Report, supra n. 7, at 320.
139. Crisis Report, supra n. 7, at 321–322; Michael Barr, Howell Jackson & Margaret Tahyar, Financial Regulation: Law and Policy 1176 (2016).
140. Blinder, supra n. 8, at 128; Crisis Report, supra n. 7, at 342 (*quoting* Thain). President Bush disagreed that the Lehman bankruptcy was a mistake. "I felt we had done the best we could." Bush, supra n. 126, at 457. Bernanke, Geithner & Paulson agreed. See supra n. 17, at 61–71.
141. Lehman Brothers Holdings Files Ch. 11 Petition after Gov't Denies Funding, 40 Sec. Reg. & L. Rep. (BNA) 1476 (2008); To East Accounts Transfer to Barclays, SIPC to Place Lehman in SIPA Liquidation, 40 id. 1477. See generally McDonald & Robinson, supra n. 60 (a book length account of the collapse of Lehman Brothers); Sorkin, supra n. 22, *inter alia*; Paulson, supra n. 24, at 170–221; Bernanke, supra n. 9, at 248–269; Geithner, supra n. 9, at 162–210; Blinder, supra n. 8, at 119–128; Lowenstein, supra n. 35, *inter alia*; Stewart & Equis, Lehman Revisited: The Bailout that Never Was, *N.Y. Times*, Sept. 30, 2014, at A1; Gorton, Misunderstanding Financial Crises, supra n. 4, at 147–149.
142. Crisis Report, supra n. 7, at 339–340; Blinder, supra n. 8, at 121; Bernanke, supra n. 9, at 259; Paulson, supra n. 24, at 181.
143. Crisis Report, supra n. 7, at 177; Bernanke, supra n. 9, at 249–250; Geithner, supra n. 9, at 207; Paulson, supra n. 24, at 80, 138; Lowenstein, supra n. 35, at 92.
144. Crisis Report, supra n. 7, at 328; Bernanke was more blunt: "If Lehman had been a midsize commercial bank, forcing Fuld to raise more capital would have been straightforward. Either the company met the supervisors' expectations or the FDIC would have taken it over and paid off depositors as necessary." Bernanke, supra n. 9, at 252; Blinder, supra n. 8, at 122.

145. Crisis Report, supra n. 7, at 326; Paulson, supra n. 24, at 125, 136.
146. Crisis Report, supra n. 7, at 331–337; Paulson, supra n. 24, at 137, 161, 172–175, 180–183, 195–211; Bernanke, supra n. 9, at 253–255.
147. Paulson, supra n. 24, at 191–213, 216; Geithner, supra n. 9, at 185–187.
148. Crisis Report, supra n. 7, at 327–330.
149. Crisis Report, supra n. 7, at 330, 333; Paulson, supra n. 24, at 188, 224. See generally id. at 224–232.
150. Paulson, supra n. 24, at 181, 187; Geithner, supra n. 9, at 187 ("It's going to be a calamity").
151. Paulson, supra n. 24, at 181; Geithner, supra n. 9, at 179.
152. Bernanke, Geithner & Paulson, supra n. 17, at 65; Geithner, supra n. 9, at 178–181, 212–213, 343.
153. Geithner, supra n. 9, at 207; Paulson, supra n. 24, at 199, 209. In 2018, Lehman would settle security holder claims for $2.4 billion. Lehman to Pay $2.4 Billion to End Crisis-Era Mortgage Claims, 50 Sec. Reg. & L. Rep. (BNA) 376 (2018).
154. Bernanke quoted in Wallison, supra n. 19, at 331; Bernanke, supra n. 9, at 205.
155. Crisis Report, supra n. 7, at 339, 356; Blinder, supra n. 8, at 127.
156. Crisis Report, supra n. 7, at 353–354. See generally id. at 353–356.
157. Paulson quoted in Sorkin, supra n. 22, at 417. In his memoir, Paulson recalled a conversation with his wife: "What if the entire system collapses? Everybody is looking to me, and I don't have the answer. I'm really scared." Paulson, supra n. 24, at 215. See generally Bernanke, Geithner & Paulson, supra n. 17, at 2–15.
158. Bank of America Buys Merrill Lynch, Experts See More Concentrated Segment, 40 Sec. Reg. & L. Rep. (BNA) 1480 (2008).
159. Paulson, supra n. 24, at 217.
160. Blinder, supra n. 8, at 150–153.
161. Paulson, supra n. 24, at 219; Geithner, supra n. 9, at 188, agreed the Bank of America acquisition of Merrill was "in the nick of time."
162. Paulson, supra n. 24, at 258.
163. Bernanke, supra n. 9, at 179.
164. Crisis Report, supra n. 7, at 142, 145.
165. Crisis Report, supra n. 7, at 146.
166. McLean & Nocera, supra n. 37, at 269–284.
167. Crisis Report, supra n. 7, at 360.
168. Crisis Report, supra n. 7, at 360–362; Sorkin, supra n. 22, at 410; Lowenstein, supra n. 35, at 211, 219.
169. Crisis Report, supra n. 7, at 362.
170. Geithner, supra n. 9, at 198.
171. Geithner, supra n. 9, at 204–205; Sorkin, supra n. 22, at 459–460, 473–474, 480–481; Lowenstein, supra n. 35, at 232–234.

172. Crisis Report, supra n. 7, at 362–363; Bernanke, supra n. 9, at 310–311. Both Bernanke and Geithner made the point that because of commercial banking subsidiaries, both Morgan Stanley and Goldman already could borrow through the PDCF (Prime Dealer Credit Facility) and TSLF (Term Securities Lending Facility) federal loan programs. The key point was the one made by Mack in the text, as Geithner stated Bank Holding Company status "would create the impression that they were under the umbrella of Fed protection." Geithner, supra n. 9, at 205.
173. Sorkin, supra n. 22, at 412, 483.
174. 40 Sec. Reg. & L. Rep. (BNA) 1476 (2008). See also Fed Again Invokes Emergency Powers with $37.8 Billion in New Loans to AIG, 40 Sec. Reg. & L. Rep. (BNA) 1643.
175. Troubled Asset Relief Program: Status of Government Assistance Provided to AIG (GAO-09-975), Sept. 2009 at 47. Why 79.9 percent in equity? Economist Alan Blinder suggested that below 80 percent AIG would not require consolidation of AIG's financials into the federal government's balance sheet as would be required under generally accepted accounting principles. Blinder, supra n. 8, at 136.
176. Bush, supra n. 126, at 458; Blinder, supra n. 8, at 130–140; Barney Frank quoted in Blinder at 140.
177. Regarding AIG, see generally Crisis Report, supra n. 7, at 139–132, 201, 243–244, 265–274, 344–350; GAO, Financial Crisis: Review of Federal Reserve Assistance to American International Group (*GAO AIG Report*), at x–xiii, 270–288, 364–367, 421–425; Paulson, supra n. 24, at 191–198, 217–241; Geithner, supra n. 9, at 184–198; Blinder, supra n. 8, at 131–136; Ron Shelp, Fallen Giant: The Amazing Story of Hank Greenberg and the History of AIG (John Wiley & Sons 2006); Bandler, AIG: Risky Business, Fortune, Oct. 20, 2008, at 112; Sorkin, supra n. 22, at 152–165, 207–208, 225–227, 292–293, 330–339, 353–365, 382–403.
178. Crisis Report, supra n. 7, at 139–140, 200–202; Bernanke, Geithner & Paulson, supra n. 17, at 71–75; Blinder, supra n. 8, at 100–133; Lowenstein, supra n. 35, at 121; McLean & Nocera, supra n. 37, at 69–81, 188–191.
179. Crisis Report, supra n. 7, at 350–351; Bernanke, supra n. 9, at 271–274; Blinder, supra n. 9, at 131–132; Geithner, supra n. 9, at 184.
180. Crisis Report, supra n. 7, at 243, 346; McLean & Nocera, supra n. 37, at 190–191, 324–326.
181. McLean & Nocera, supra n. 37, at 191–199.
182. Sorkin, supra n. 22, at 155; Shelp, supra n. 177, at 2–3, 162–172; Bandler, supra n. 177, at 118; McLean & Nocera, supra n. 37, at 324–326.

183. Crisis Report, supra n. 7, at 242–244, 265–274; GAO AIG Report, supra n. 177, at 17–18; McLean & Nocera, supra n. 37, at 324–326.
184. Sorkin, supra n. 22, at 162–165.
185. Lowenstein, supra n. 35, at 158.
186. Kevin Coffey quoted in Crisis Report, supra n. 7, at 346. See Crisis Report generally at 344–350.
187. Crisis Report, supra n. 7, at 347–349; Geithner, supra n. 9, at 191; Sorkin, supra n. 22, at 397.
188. Paulson, supra n. 24, at 217–218, 223–224, 228–241; Bernanke, supra n. 9, at x–xi, 270, 283–284; Geithner, supra n. 9, at 188–198; Crisis Report, supra n. 7, at 347–350; GAO AIG Report, supra n. 177, at 25–45; Lowenstein, supra n. 35, at 206–217; Sorkin, supra n. 22, at 330, 382–385, 391–397, 401–403.
189. Bernanke, supra n. 9, at 286–287, 422–423.
190. Inv. Co. Act Rel. 30,551 (2013) (nn. 79–89); Crisis Report, supra n. 7, at 356–360; Paulson, supra n. 24, at 234; Bernanke, supra n. 9, at 300; Geithner, supra n. 9, at 195; Bernanke, Geithner & Paulson, supra n. 17, at 76–77.
191. Paulson, supra n. 24, at 252–264; Bernanke, supra n. 9, at 300–302; Bair, supra n. 43, at 108–109; Blinder, supra n. 8, at 142–149.
192. 7 Louis Loss, Joel Seligman & Troy Paredes, Securities Regulation 176–181 (5th ed. 2017); Paulson, supra n. 24, at 238, 246–247, 263–264, 342, 345; Geithner, supra n. 9, at 203; Bernanke, supra n. 9, at 299; Sorkin, supra n. 22, at 421–423, 434–435; Lowenstein, supra n. 35, at 220. There were unintended consequences. Sheila Bair believed that the SEC short selling bar "had stanched the short sales in the stocks of behemoths such as Citigroup and Goldman Sachs, but it had also redirected short-selling activity to the smaller, publicly traded banks such as WaMu." Bair, supra n. 43, at 86.
193. Bernanke, supra n. 9, at 299. See also Geithner, supra n. 9, at 218 ("The stability of the entire banking system was at risk"); Paulson, supra n. 24, at 244.
194. Paulson, supra n. 24, at 256; Bernanke, Geithner & Paulson, supra n. 17, at 78–92.
195. Crisis Report, supra n. 7, at 305–307, 365–366; Bair, supra n. 43, at 75–78, 84–94; Lowenstein, supra n. 35, at 239–241.
196. Blinder, supra n. 8, at 178, 181; Crisis Report, supra n. 7, at 371; United States Treasury, "Break the Glass" Bank Recapitalization Plan (Discussion draft Apr. 25, 2008).
197. Bernanke, supra n. 9, at 302–303.
198. Geithner, supra n. 9, at 225.
199. Treasury's Bailout Proposal, CNN Special Rep. 1 (Sept. 20, 2008) (complete test of three page bill); Paulson, supra n. 24, at 254–261, 265–267, 287–290; Bernanke, supra n. 9, at 302–317; Sorkin, supra

n. 22, at 488; Blinder, supra n. 8, at 185–187; Geithner, supra n. 9, at 224; Bush, supra n. 126, at 439–440.

200. Paulson, supra n. 24, at 294–300; Bernanke, supra n. 9, at 320–322; Blinder, supra n. 8, at 203–205. President Bush had opposed holding the meeting in the first place and recalled so had Paulson. Bush, supra n. 126, at 461–462.

201. Crisis Rep. supra n. 7, at 365–366; Bair, supra n. 43, at 75–78, 84–94.

202. Geithner, supra n. 9, at 213–214.

203. Bernanke, supra n. 9, at 322–324. Blinder agreed. See Blinder, supra n. 8, at 155–157.

204. Crisis Report, supra n. 7, at 304–305, 366–371; Paulson, supra n. 24, at 301–302, 314–318, 326–328; Bernanke, supra n. 9, at 298, 327–332; Geithner, supra n. 9, at 217–220, 222–223; Bair, supra n. 43, at 95–105; Sorkin, supra n. 22, at 448–450, 467; Blinder, supra n. 8, at 157–161; Lowenstein, supra n. 35, at 245–249.

205. Emergency Economic Stabilization Act of 2008, 122 Stat. 3765, 110th Cong., 2d Session (2008), esp. §§ 104, 109, 110, 111, 115, 116, 119, 121, 125, 135, 302; Crisis Report, supra n. 7, at 372; Paulson, supra n. 24, at 320–322, 328; Bernanke, supra n. 9, at 318–320, 332–375; Lowenstein, supra n. 35, at 247; Geithner, supra n. 9, at 220–222.

206. Bernanke, supra n. 9, at 336; Crisis Report, supra n. 7, at 373; Geithner, supra n. 9, at 227–228.

207. McDonald & Robinson, supra n. 60, at 334–335.

208. Lowenstein, supra n. 35, at 258.

209. McDonald & Robinson, supra n. 60, at 335–336; Tooze, supra n. 40, at 188–191.

210. Paulson, supra n. 24, at 333, 336; Bernanke, supra n. 9, at 326–327; Blinder, supra n. 8, at 168–171, 196–197, 411–412.

211. Bernanke, supra n. 9, at 347–348, 358–359; Crisis Report, supra n. 7, at 373; Paulson, supra n. 24, at 336; Lowenstein, supra n. 35, at 259; Geithner, supra n. 9, at 228–229.

212. Bernanke, supra n. 9, at 349–352; Paulson, supra n. 24, at 348–351.

213. Bernanke, supra n. 9, at 337–339; Geithner, supra n. 9, at 224–227; Bush, supra n. 126, at 464.

214. Crisis Report, supra n. 7, at 373–375; Paulson, supra n. 24, at 358–366; Bernanke, supra n. 9, at 353–357; Geithner, supra n. 9, at 236–239; Bair, supra n. 43, at 1–7, 115–116; Lowenstein, supra n. 35, at 270–272; Blinder, supra n. 8, at 200–203; Sorkin, supra n. 22, at 521–528.

215. Crisis Report, supra n. 7, at 374–375; Bernanke, supra n. 9, at 340–343; Paulson, supra n. 24, at 357–370; Geithner, supra n. 9, at 230–239; Bair, supra n. 43, at 111–119. FDIC Chair Bair initially was not happy with this program. Initially she called a broader

proposal made by Paulson, Geithner, and Bernanke for the FDIC to guarantee all liabilities of the banking system "an ambush." "It was amazing how eager and willing other agencies were willing to expose us [the FDIC] to risk."

216. GAO, Review of Federal Reserve System Financial Assistance to American International Group, Inc., (GAO-11-616 Sept. 2011); GAO, Troubled Asset Relief Program: Government's Exposure to AIG Lessens as Equity Investments Are Sold (GAO-12-574 May 2012); Special Inspector General for TARP, AIG Remains in TARP as TARP's Largest Investment (July 25, 2012); Crisis Report, supra n. 7, at 376–379; Paulson, supra n. 24, at 342, 376, 387, 392–395; Geithner, supra n. 9, at 227–228, 245–247, 303–306; Bernanke, supra n. 9, at 364–367; Reuters, U.S. Could Make $15.1 Billion on AIG Bailout: GAO (May 8, 2012).
217. Bernanke, supra n. 9, at 368–371; Crisis Report, supra n. 7, at 65, 137–139, 195–200, 379–382; Geithner, supra n. 9, at 222, 252; Paulson, supra n. 24, at 403–404, 407, 409–417; Bair, supra n. 43, at 73–74, 96, 98, 105, 121–128; Lowenstein, supra n. 35, at 66–67, 251–252; Blinder, supra n. 8, at 163; Treasury, Federal Reserve & FDIC Joint Press Release on Citigroup (Nov. 23, 2008).
218. Bush, supra n. 126, at 468; Crisis Report, supra n. 7, at 375; Paulson, supra n. 24, at 361–362, 387, 391-392, 424–425, 427–428; Blinder, supra n. 8, at 212–213; Bernanke, supra n. 9, at 376–377.
219. Paulson, supra n. 24, at 405, 421.
220. Crisis Report, supra n. 7, at 382–386; Paulson, supra n. 24, at 335, 425, 432; Bernanke, supra n. 9, at 373–376; Bair, supra n. 43, at 203–204.
221. 10 Louis Loss, Joel Seligman & Troy Paredes, Securities Regulation 662–700 (4th ed. 2013); Geithner, supra n. 9, at 393; Diana Henriques, The Wizard of Lies: Bernie Madoff and the Death of Trust (2011); SEC Off. of Inspector General, Investigation of Failure of the SEC to Uncover Bernard Madoff's Ponzi Scheme Public Version (OIG No. 509 Aug. 31, 2009); SEC Off. of Compliance, Inspections and Examinations: Examination of Bernard L. Madoff Investment Securities (Rep. No. 468, Sept. 29, 2009); Off. of Inspector General, Semiannual Report to Congress (April 2009–Sept. 30, 2009); FINRA Special Review Committee (including the author), Report on FINRA's Examination Program in Light of the Stanford and Madoff Schemes (Sept. 2009); Complaint, *SEC v. Madoff*, 08 CIV 10,791 (S.D.N.Y. 2008) (alleging $50 billion Ponzi scheme); Complaint, *United States v. Madoff*, 08 Mag. 2735 (S.D.N.Y. 2008) (related criminal matter); Lichtblau, Federal Causes of Stock Fraud Drop Sharply, *N.Y. Times*, Dec. 25, 2008 at A1; SEC Press Rel. 2008-297, Statement Regarding Madoff Investigation (Dec. 16, 2008); Labaton, SEC

Image Suffers in a String of Setbacks, *N.Y. Times*, Dec. 15, 2008 at B6; Norman Poser, Why the SEC Failed: Regulators against Regulation, 3 Brook. J. Corp., Fin. & Comm. L. 289 (2009).

222. Citigroup to Buy Back Billions of ARS in Deals with SEC, State Regulators, 40 Sec. Reg. & L. Rep. (BNA) 1249 (2008); Wachovia Becomes Fifth Bank to Settle with States in ARS Probe, Cuomo Reports, 40 Sec. Reg. & L. Rep. (BNA) 1309 (two units of Wachovia agreed to repay investors more than $8.5 billion and to pay a $50 million penalty); Citigroup, UBS Agree to Pay Record $30 Billion in ARS Settlement, 40 Sec. Reg. & L. Rep. (BNA) 2049; Wachovia, Citi to Return $4.7B to Investors in Calif. ARS Settlement, 41 Sec. Reg. & L. Rep. (BNA) 625; Citigroup, Wachovia to Pay $880 Million to Settle Mich. ARS Dispute, 41 Sec. Reg. & L. Rep. (BNA) 728; SEC, Cuomo Announce Final Settlements in 2008 Auction Rate Securities Disputes, 41 Sec. Reg. & L. Rep. (BNA) 1070 (2009) (total buybacks of $56 billion of illiquid auction rate securities at par from retail investors and $522.5 million in penalties).

223. Geithner, supra n. 9, at 255–256, 276–277; Blinder, supra n. 8, at 166–167; Crisis Report, supra n. 7, at 390–400.

224. Lowenstein, supra n. 35, at 281; Paulson, supra n. 24, at 431; Geithner, supra n. 9, at 273, 294, 336, 360.

225. Geithner, supra n. 9, at 263, 278–279, 281–286; Bernanke, supra n. 9, at 387–389; A. Schlesinger, The Coming of the New Deal 337–341 (1958); Blinder, supra n. 8, at 217–220, 223–234; Tooze, supra n. 40, at 296: "What was remarkable in 2009 was how little the Obama administration asked in return for the protection it offered."

226. Steven Rattner, Overhaul: An Insider's Account of the Obama Administration's Emergency Rescue of the Auto Industry (2010); Crisis Report, supra n. 7, at 375; Geithner, supra n. 9, at 336–339, 356; Bernanke, Geithner & Paulson, supra n. 17, at 105–108; Lowenstein, supra n. 35, at 274, 279; Shao, Steven Rattner: The 2009 Auto Bailout Was Necessary, Stanford Grad. Sch. of Bus. Insights (Mar. 1, 2011); Kiley, As Obama Takes Victory Lap Over Auto Industry Rescue, Here Are the Lessons of the Bailout, Forbes (Jan 20, 2016); U.S. Dep't of Treasury, TARP Program Reports: Auto Industry (Mar. 20, 2018).

227. Crisis Report, supra n. 7, at 396; Bernanke, supra n. 9, at 359, 393; Geithner, supra n. 9, at 280.

228. Geithner, supra n. 9, at 306–307, 314–315; Bair, supra n. 43, at 165–170, 205–208; Dash, U.S. Agrees to Raise Its Stake in Citigroup, *N.Y. Times* (Feb. 27, 2009); GAO, Review of Federal Reserve System Assistance to American International Group, Inc. (GAO-11-616 Sept. 2011); GAO, Government's Exposure to AIG Lessens as Equity

Investments Are Sold (GAO-12-574 May 2012); Associated Press, Citigroup Stock Falls Below $1 a Share (Mar. 5, 2009).

229. Bernanke, supra n. 9, at 421–424; Geithner, supra n. 9, at 303–305, 315–318, 327–331.

230. Crisis Report, supra n. 7, at 396; Geithner, supra n. 9, at 357-358; Bair, supra n. 43, at 178-180; CNN, CIT Files for 5th Largest U.S. Bankruptcy (Nov. 1, 2009); McGraw, CIT Leaves Bankruptcy, with Questions, *N.Y. Times* (Dec. 10, 2009).

231. Geithner, supra n. 9, at 266–275, 286–294, 311–314, 323, 334, 345–347, 352–355, 523–524; Bernanke, supra n. 9, at 392–397; Blinder, supra n. 8, at 256–260; Bair, supra n. 43, at 156–164; Secretary Geithner Introduces Financial Stability Plan, Remarks, Feb. 10, 2009, Dep't of Treasury TG-18; Joint Statement by Secretary of Treasury Timothy F. Geithner, Chairman of the Board of Governors of Federal Reserve System Ben S. Bernanke, Chairman of FDIC Sheila Bair, Feb. 10, 2009, Dep't of Treasury (*Joint Statement*) TG-21; Federal Reserve Sys., The Supervisory Capital Assessment Program (Apr. 24, 2009); Joint Statement by Federal Reserve, Treasury, FDIC, and OCC on Treasury Capital Assistance and Supervisory Capital Assessment Program (May 6, 2009); Statement Regarding Supervisory Capital Assessment Program by Ben S. Bernanke (May 7, 2009); Andrews, Ailing Banks Need $75 Billion, U.S. Says, *N.Y. Times* (May 7, 2009); CNN Special Report, Ellis, Stress Test: Banks Need $75 Billion (May 8, 2009); Paul Krugman, Does He Pass the Test: N.Y. Rev. of Books (July 10, 2014), Lizza, The Obama Memos, New Yorker (Jan. 30, 2012); Lizza, Inside the Crisis, New Yorker (Oct. 12, 2009).

232. Geithner, supra n. 9, at 334–335; Elliot, The Public-Private Investment Program: An Assessment, Brookings Initiative on Bus. & Pub. Policy (Mar. 23, 2009); Akin Gump, U.S. Treasury Announces New Public-Private Investment Program (Mar. 26, 2009); Bair, supra n. 43, at 161–164; Joint Statement, supra n. 228, at 3; Once Weak, U.S. Banks Ride High, *N.Y. Times*, June 23, 2018, at B1.

233. Tooze, supra n. 40, at 53, 105, 156, 159; Bernanke, supra n. 9, at 418–421; Bernanke, The Economic Outlook and Monetary Policy, Fed. Reserve Bank of Kansas City Econ. Symposium (Aug. 27, 2010, Jackson Hole, Wyo.); Geithner, supra n. 9, at 277–278; Paulson, supra n. 24, at 417–418; Quantitative Easing: How Well Does This Tool Work?, St. Louis Fed. Reserve Bank (2d Quarter 2017).

234. Bernanke, supra n. 9, at 418–421; Bernanke, The Economic Outlook and Monetary Policy, Fed. Reserve Bank of Kansas City Econ. Symposium (Aug. 27, 2010, Jackson Hole, Wyo.); Geithner, supra n. 9, at 277–278; Paulson, supra n. 24, at 417–418; Williamson, Quantitative Easing, How Well Does This Tool Work?, St. Louis Fed. Reserve Bank (3d Quarter 2017); Tooze, supra n. 40, at 99–100,

324–325, 408, 515; Greece's Bailout is Ending: The Pain is Far From Over, *N.Y. Times*, Aug. 20, 2018, at B1; Matt Phillips, Risky Lending Is Back, And It's Bypassing Banks, *N.Y. Times*, June 12, 2019.

235. Crisis Report, supra n. 7, at 375–376, 400; Dep't of Treasury, TARP Monthly Report to Congress 5 (Apr. 2018); National Employment Monthly Update 2008-2018; United States Federal Deficit by Year; Bernanke, supra n. 9, at 476–482, 524; Geithner, supra n. 9, at 364, 441–450, 472–477, 496, 500–501; Blinder, supra n. 8, at 234–235, 409–428.
236. Shiller, supra n. 61, at viii.
237. Crisis Report, supra n. 7, at xviii–xxvii, 417, 435, 443–447. One dissenter on the National Commission further expounded his views in his book, Wallison, Hidden in Plain Sight, supra n. 19.
237. In Wall Street and the Financial Crisis: Anatomy of a Financial Collapse (Apr. 13, 2011), the Senate Permanent Subcomm. on Investigations conducted studies for four root causes of the financial crisis. The majority Staff Report, with which some have taken issue, focused in part on what it termed "high risk lending," "regulatory failures," "inflated credit ratings," and "investment bank abuses." Id. at 2–11.
238. Bush, supra n. 126, at 448–449.
239. Bush, supra n. 126, at 440, 442–443, 445, 453, 458–460, 463, 470.
240. Bush, supra n. 126, at 439, 449–450; Geithner, supra n. 9, at 154; Bernanke, supra n. 9, at 128–129; Sorkin, supra n. 22, at 47–49, 187–188, 373–375; Lowenstein, supra n. 35, at 83–84; McLean & Nocera, supra n. 37, at 245–247.
241. Ben Bernanke, Essays on the Great Depression (Princeton Univ. Press 2000); Greenspan, supra n. 109, at 51–53, 228–233, 256–257, 370–376, 430; Bob Woodward, The Maestro (Simon & Schuster 2001); Robert Shiller, Irrational Exuberance (Broadway Books 2000); Bernanke, supra n. 9, at 70, 81–84, 108, 526–530, 571–573; Geithner, supra n. 9, at 46–67, 119, 141–143; Blinder, supra n. 8, at 57, 165–166, 382; Lowenstein, supra n. 35, at 286, 295.
242. Geithner, supra n. 9, at 75–76, 90–94, 131; Bair, supra n. 43, at 99–100, 110–111, 113, 283, 304–305; Bernanke, supra n. 9, at 78, 380–381; Sorkin, supra n. 22, at 62–66.
243. GAO, Financial Regulation: Complex and Fragmented Structure Could Be Streamlined to Improve Effectiveness (GAO-16-175 R016); Greenspan, supra n. 109, at 488–492; Geithner, supra n. 9, at 96–98; Bernanke, supra n. 9, at 94, 402–403; Crisis Report, supra n. 7, at xxi, 111–113, 204–206, 308; Bair, supra n. 43, at 45, 96; McLean & Nocera, supra n. 37, at 243–249; Paulson, supra n. 24, at 66–68; Blinder, supra n. 8, at 58–59; Wallison, supra n. 19, at 84–85, 250–263.

2

Before the New Deal

The Birth of the United States Economic System

The United States was born in financial crisis. Hamilton bemoaned in Federalist Paper No. 15:

> We may indeed, with propriety, be said to have reached almost the last stage of national humiliation. There is scarcely any thing that can wound the pride, or degrade the character, of an independent people, which we do not experience.... Do we owe debts to foreigners, and to our own citizens, contracted in a time of imminent peril, for the preservation of our political existence? These remain without any proper or satisfactory provision for their discharge.... Are we in a condition to resent, or to repel the aggression? We have neither troops, nor treasury, nor Government.
>
> ... Is commerce of importance to national wealth? Ours is at the lowest point of declension....
>
> Is private credit the friend and patron of industry? That most useful kind which relates to borrowing and lending, is reduced within the narrowest limits, and this still more from an opinion of insecurity than from a scarcity of money.

Government under the Articles of Confederation was a shambles. Hamilton continued: The Continental Congress had "an indefinite discretion to make requisitions for men and money, but they have no authority to raise either, by regulations extending to the individual citizens of America. The consequence of this is, that, though in theory, their resolutions concerning those objectives are laws, . . . yet, in practice, they are mere recommendations, which the States observe or disregard at their option." In 1781, the Continental Congress had resolved that the states provide $8 million in 1782 — by 1783, the states had provided only $420,000.

The Continental Congress had not implemented a plan to repay the Revolutionary War debt. Business historian Thomas McCraw wrote: "The United States started out on a shoestring and almost immediately went bankrupt." The debt of the Continental Congress was over $200 million. No one knew the exact amount of the debt because there was no national currency, but instead a plethora of locally issued bills and certificates. The Revolutionary War had cost about $160 million in 1780 dollars, more than the total budget of the national government would be during the 20 year period 1790–1810. The Colonies had printed Bills of Credit in excess of $200 million. Lack of confidence in the financial system, in turn, had led to rampant inflation that devalued the ability of these bills and certificates to pay off debt.

Direct taxation was impracticable. Federalist Paper No. 12 explained:

> Tax laws have in vain been multiplied; new methods to enforce the collection have in vain been tried; the public expectation has been uniformly disappointed, and the treasuries of the States have remained empty. The popular system of administration, inherent in the nature of popular government, coinciding with the real scarcity of money, incident to a languid and mutilated state of trade, has hitherto defeated every experiment for extensive collections, and has at length taught the different legislatures the folly of attempting them.

"A nation," Hamilton asserted, "cannot long exist without revenue. Destitute of this essential support, it must resign its independence, and sink into the degraded condition of a province."

The United States relied on duties on imports. Other ameliorative steps taken by the Continental Congress too often had been ineffectual. The Articles of Confederation authorized the Continental Congress to coin money, issue Bills of Credit and borrow money. Paper money issued by the Continental Congress in 1780 was worth two cents on the dollar, giving rise to the phrase "not worth a Continental."

What was to constitute money represented an issue of fundamental political significance. Specie, meaning gold and silver, was a legal tender. When paper money was issued by the Continental Congress or the states without being backed by specie, it rapidly depreciated during this period. Farmers often were required to take paper money in return for Revolutionary War supplies and frequently were victimized by its devaluation. Shay's Rebellion in 1786 has been characterized as a response to the dearth of specie from which they could pay taxes.

In a nation that Benjamin Franklin estimated after the Revolution had 100 farmers for each artisan or merchant, the agrarian interest often was dominant. Jefferson's idyllic view, "those who labor in the earth are the chosen people of God," was widespread. In colonial Virginia, in Jefferson's view, paper money was unnecessary. A planter could consign shipments of tobacco to correspondents in England and obtain "all his supplies from his merchant," Jefferson wrote in 1813, "and liquidate them at the end of the year by the sale of his produce to him without the intervention of a single dollar of cash."

The Revolutionary War transformed the dominant sentiment. To Hamilton writing in his 1790 Report on Public Credit: "[T]he debt of the United States . . . was the price of liberty." Without paper money during the Revolutionary War, "there was no practicable alternative to issuing them," Bank historian Bray Hammond wrote, "except giving up the struggle."

In 1785, the Continental Congress adopted the dollar as the Confederation's official monetary unit, but it was not the exclusive currency. Shops in New York City, historian Ron Chernow wrote, "quoted prices in pounds, shillings and pence. . . . To make matters worse, exchange rates differed from state to state." In all, when Hamilton began as Secretary of the Treasury in 1784, there were at least 50 different currencies from different countries, the states, and private companies in circulation.

In 1781, the Continental Congress incorporated the Bank of North America, which it called a "National Bank." Banking historian Bray Hammond more aptly recognized, "it was scarcely ever . . . the National Bank it was designed to be." The Bank received a second identical charter from Pennsylvania in 1782. The Bank issued bank notes that were the equivalent to paper currency that could be taken to the Bank and exchanged for gold or silver. In 1785, the agrarian majority of the Pennsylvania legislature repealed the State charter for the Bank of North America, causing its cash accounts to decline from $59 to $37 million. A Legislative Report explained: "[T]he accumulation of enormous wealth in the hands of a society who claim perpetual duration will necessarily provide a degree of influence and power which cannot be entrusted in the hands of any set of men whatsoever without endangering the public safety." The Bank continued to operate under the authority of the Continental Congress. After the Bank of North America obtained a charter from Delaware in 1786, Pennsylvania rechartered the Bank and dissuaded the Bank from moving to Delaware. The Bank of North America, however, was more limited under its new charter. No longer was the charter perpetual, now only for 14 years. The capital of the Bank was limited to $2 million, not $10 million as before. To Hamilton, these restrictions and other aspects of its governance disqualified the Bank of North America from becoming the United States' first National Bank. In fact, the Bank of North America only had capital in 1786 with a par value of $870,000. The Bank perennially was short of capital.

The Bank of North America survived because of the vital support its founder Robert Morris provided. Morris served as Superintendent of Finance of the Continental Congress beginning in 1781. He accepted the position of Superintendent on condition he could continue his private investments. The Bank of North America was a hybrid with the government owning five-eighths of its stock and private investors providing $400,000 for shares. The Bank was pivotal in financing the Revolutionary War. The Bank of North America issued Bills of Credit. Given the limited amount of specie available to the Bank to back the Bills of Credit, the Bank's Bills of Credit sold at a discount. During the Revolutionary War, Morris would buy back notes to boost them to par value. In 1781, on the eve of the Revolutionary Army's decisive battle at Yorktown, Morris personally signed 6000 Bills of Currency to enable Washington to provide supplies and fund the march from New York and Pennsylvania to Yorktown. Morris' use of his personal fortune to support the fledging government helped stabilize the finances of the colonies and Continental Congress when they were on the verge of collapse.

The finances of the Continental Congress remained extraordinarily weak. When the colonies' army was disbanding after independence was won, the Continental Congress did not have enough specie to buy paper certificates with which to promise to pay the wages of the victorious army. The Continental Congress, incapable of an effective system of taxation, could not pay interest on the national debt. Throughout the war, the Bank of North America helped, but only marginally. For Washington, there was not enough money or credit to pay his soldiers or buy needed supplies. Independence was won in the Revolutionary War. Financial stability was not.

Banks were politically controversial. Hamilton petitioned the New York State legislature to grant a charter to the Bank of New York and drafted Articles of Association. Hamilton's petition was denied for seven years because of the fervent opposition of Governor George Clinton, who feared the Bank would favor merchants and ignore farmers. The Bank of New York began operations in 1784 as a private bank. Hostility to banks was widespread. For Jefferson, in historian Chernow's view, "banks were devices to fleece the poor, oppress farmers, and insure a taste for luxury that would subvert republican simplicity." John Adams, Jefferson's political rival, held equally critical beliefs. "Every bank in America is an enormous tax upon the people for the profit of individuals." Adams dismissed bankers "as swindlers and thieves" and feared that banks would release "the gangrene of avarice" into the American atmosphere.[1]

The United States Constitution, adopted in 1787, would respond to several of the Federalist critiques of the Articles of Confederation. Congress had the power: "To lay and collect taxes, duties, imposts and excises, to pay the debts and provide for the common defense and general welfare of the United States;" "to borrow money on the credit of the United States;" "to regulate commerce with foreign nations, and among the several States, and with the Indian Tribes;" "to coin money, regulate the value thereof, and of foreign coin;" "to raise and support armies, but no appropriation of money to that use shall be for a longer term than two years;" "to provide and maintain a navy;" and "to make all laws which shall be necessary and proper for carrying into Execution the foregoing Powers."

The States were prohibited from coining money, emitting Bills of Credit, making anything but gold and silver coin a tender in payment of debts or enact "Law impairing the Obligation of contracts", laying any imposts or duties on exports, "except what may be absolutely necessary for executing its inspection laws." "No State shall, without the consent of Congress, lay any Duty of Tunnage, keep troops, or ships of war in time of peace . . . or engage in war unless actively invaded, or in such imminent danger as will not admit of delay;" "full faith and credit shall be given each State to the public Acts, Records and Judicial Proceedings of every other State." The Duty of Tunnage was an additional tariff on merchandise carried on foreign ships.

The extent of the transformation from a Confederacy of States to a Nation was underlined by the Supremacy Clause: "The Constitution and the Laws of the United States . . . shall be the Supreme Law of the Land; and the Judges in every State shall be bound thereby."[2]

No individual would figure more prominently in the creation of the United States as a viable financial entity than Alexander Hamilton. Along with Morris, who was widely viewed as the most able financier in the pre-Constitutional period, Hamilton had been a proponent of a National Bank as early as 1779. On April 30, 1781, Hamilton wrote Morris, whom he had supported to be the Superintendent of Finance of the Continental Congress, a lengthy letter that set out "some ideas relative to the object of your departments." The letter was a *tour de force.* In detail, Hamilton calculated colonial aggregate revenues between $6 and $7 million and aggregate expenses of $11 million and a "difference between our revenues and expenses . . . from four to four and a half million."

Hamilton discounted the likelihood that foreign or domestic loans could cover this amount. His primary solution then and later as Secretary of Treasury was: "[T]he institution of a National Bank." Hamilton was a true believer:

> The tendency of a national bank is to increase public and private credit. The former gives power to the State for the protection of its rights and interests, and the latter facilitates and extends the operations of commerce among individuals. Industry is increased, commodities are multiplied, agriculture and manufactures flourish, and herein consist the true wealth and prosperity of a State.

Hamilton laid out a 20 article plan for a National Bank. He proposed a bank with stock of 3 million pounds, raised by subscription. The bank would be a corporation with the United States, any State or foreigner eligible to become subscribers "and participate [in] its profits for any sums not exceeding in the whole half the stock." "The United States collectively and particularly [would] become responsible for all transactions of the bank conjointly with the private proprietors." The bank would have the power to lend money to the public or to individuals, borrow up to one half of its stock, and the power to loan up to half its stock and receive deposits. More specifically, "The bank [was intended] to loan Congress $1,200,000 lawful at eight percent for the payment of which with its interest a certain inalienable fund of $110,400 per annum to be established for twenty years." Hamilton then consistently relied on currency other than continental dollars. The inalienable fund was a national debt that Hamilton envisioned extinguishing with a sinking fund. "This loan will enable Congress to get through the expenses of the War."

Later in the letter, Hamilton effused:

> A national debt if it is not excessive will be to us a national blessing: it will be powerful cement of our union. It will also create a necessity for keeping up taxation to a degree which without being oppressive, will be a spur to industry; remote as we are from Europe and shall be from danger, it were otherwise to be feared our popular maxims would incline us to too great parsimony and indulgence.

The plan for a national bank was a plan also for a new national currency and assumption of State debt. Hamilton recommended:

> The Bank [was] to become responsible for the redemption of all the paper now emitted; the old, at forty for one in thirty years, the new at par, with gold and silver, according to the terms promised by Congress in their resolution of March, '80. One-third of the first to be redeemed at the end of every ten years; and the whole of the last to be redeemed at the expiration of the six years specified by Congress, with the interest of five per cent. The United States, in compensation for this responsibility, to establish certain funds for an annuity, payable to the Bank equal to the discharge of the whole amount of the paper currency in thirty years, with an interest of two per cent per annum.

The bank was to have a 30-year term during which: "No other bank public or private to be permitting during that period." The explanatory Note explained: "Other banks might excite a competition prejudicial to the interests of the National Bank and multiply and diversify paper credit too much." "Three banks to be erected in Massachusetts, Pennsylvania and Virginia to facilitate the circulation and payment of bank notes." "The affairs of the bank to be managed by twelve general directors, men of reputation and fortune, eight of them to be chosen by the private proprietors and four by Congress. The Minister of Finance to have the privilege of inspecting all their proceedings."

Hamilton's 1781 plan for the national bank was the embryo of the plan to create a viable national economy that Hamilton would implement beginning in 1789 as Secretary of Treasury.

Hamilton's inspiration for the national bank, in 1781 and as Secretary of Treasury, was European banks. He, like Morris, was most deeply impressed by the Bank of England.[3]

The Bank of England

Established in 1694 to help finance the war effort against France, the initial purpose of the Bank of England was to lend money to the government during wartime. War long was the begetter of centralized bank power. Walter Bagehot, long the leading analyst of the Bank of England, in *Lombard Street: A Description of the Money Market in 1873*, described the Bank's origins and initial powers:

> The Government of Charles II ... had brought the credit of the English State to the lowest possible point. It has perpetrated one of those monstrous frauds, which are likewise gross blunders. The goldsmiths, who then carried on upon a trifling scale what we should now call banking, used to deposit their reserve of treasure in the "Exchequer," with the sanction and under the care of the Government.... Charles II ... shut up the "Exchequer," would pay no one, and so the "goldsmiths" were ruined.
>
> The credit of the Stuart Government never recovered from this monstrous robbery, and the Government created by the Revolution of 1688 could hardly expect to be more trusted with money than its predecessor.... In 1694, the credit of William III's Government was so low in London that it was impossible for it to borrow any large sum; and the evil was the greater, because in consequence of the French war the financial straits of the Government were extreme. At last a scheme was hit upon which would relieve their necessities. "The plan," says Macaulay, "was that twelve hundred thousand pounds should be raised at what was then considered as the moderate rate of 8 per cent." In order to induce the subscribers to advance the money

> promptly on terms so unfavourable to the public, the subscribers were to be incorporated by the name of the Governor and Company of the Bank of England. They were so incorporated, and the 1,200,000 [pounds] was obtained.

In return for the substantial benefit of the loan to the government, the Bank of England was given three important privileges:

First, the Bank had the exclusive possession of the government balances with the implicit promise that it would lend money to the government.

Second, until much later, the Bank had a monopoly of limited liability in England, meaning in the event of its failure, only the Bank's assets were subject to suit in bankruptcy proceedings, not that of its investors.

Third, the Bank had the privilege of being the sole joint stock company permitted to issue bank notes in England.

Later, in 1844, the Bank Charter Act granted the Bank of England what in essence was a monopoly in issuing bank notes that were the legal tender. The Bank was not created to manage the British currency, but as the decades passed, its bank notes became the country's dominant form of paper money. Smaller banks trusted the Bank of England, sometimes called "The Old Lady of Threadneedle Street." The Bank was managed by 26 directors, including a full time Governor and Deputy Governor. The directors "were substantial city merchants and members of the leading city companies." The Bank's charter long was limited to 20 year terms and it did not establish branches outside of London.

By Bagehot's time: "All London banks keep their principal reserve on deposit of the Banking Department of the Bank of England." Indeed by then, the Bank of England had become the center reserve depository for all of England, Ireland, and Scotland and for most of European reserves as well. "In consequence, all our credit system depends on the Bank of England for its security."

In his 1790 Report on a national bank, Hamilton recognized as strengths of the Bank of England, the size of the capital of the Bank, by 1790, between 11 and 12 million Pounds, the use of the capital to fund a public debt, and "[t]he confining of the right of the Bank to contract debts [limited] to the amount of its capital."

The Bank had developed some techniques similar to those of a modern central bank. The Bank of England could raise the interest rates it paid to attract more legal tender. "[I]t is proven by experience that money [then] does come in. . . ."

During the debate over the Bank's charter renewal in 1781, the Bank was criticized for excessive charges for managing the government's finances. Lord Marsh, the Prime Minister, defended the Bank as: "from long habit and the usage of many years . . . a part of the Constitution; all the money business of the Exchequer being done at the Bank, and as experience had proved, with much greater advantage to the public than when it had formerly been done at Exchequer." In 1797, Sir Francis Baring, founder of the Bank that bore his name, called the Bank of England, the country's *dernier resort.*

To Bagehot, the Bank of England's role as lender of last resort during a financial panic was critical:

> . . . [T]he Bank of England . . . must in time of panic do what all other similar banks must do; that in time of panic it must advance freely and vigorously to the public out of the reserve.
>
> And with the Bank of England, as well as other Banks in the same case, these advances, if they are to be made at all, should be made so as if possible to obtain the object for which they are made. The end is to stay the panic; and the advances should, if possible, stay the panic. And for this purpose there are two rules: First, That these loans should only be made at a very high rate of interest. This will operate as a heavy fine on unreasonable timidity, and will prevent the greatest number of applications by persons who do not require it. . . .
>
> Secondly, That at this rate these advances should be made on all good banking securities, and as largely as the public ask for them. The reason is plain. The object is to stay alarm, and nothing therefore should be done to cause alarm. But the way to cause alarm is to refuse someone who has good security to offer. The news of this will spread in an instant through all the money market at a moment of terror; no one can say exactly who carries it, but in half an hour it will be carried on all sides, and will intensify the terror everywhere. No advances indeed need be made by which the Bank will ultimately lose.[4]

These two rules would influence Bernanke, Geithner, and Paulson in 2007–2009.

Before being sworn in to be the first President of the United States, George Washington approached Robert Morris to be the Secretary of Treasury. "The Treasury, Morris, will of course be your berth. After your invaluable services as Financier of the Revolution, no one can pretend to contest the office of Secretary of Treasury with you." Morris declined, but recommended "a far cleverer fellow than I am for your Minister of Finance . . . Colonel Hamilton." Washington was startled: "I always knew Colonel Hamilton to be a man of superior talents, but never supposed that he had any knowledge of finance." Morris replied: "He knows everything, sir. To a mind like his, nothing comes amiss."

Hyperbole is common in political discourse and personnel recommendations. In this instance, Hamilton in the initial two years of Washington's first Presidential term would establish, as Chernow declaimed, the "machinery of a modern nation-State — including a budget system, a funded debt, a tax system, a central bank, a customs service and a coast guard." Daniel Webster would go even further in his praise: "The fabled myth of Minerva from the brow of Jove was hardly more sudden or more perfect than the financial system of the United States as it burst forth from the conception of Alexander Hamilton."[5]

This financial success was accompanied by an almost Platonic view of a wealthy guardian class. Presidential historian Arthur Schlesinger summarized Hamilton's deeply skeptical view of the American democracy:

> . . ."All Communities," [Hamilton] told the men gathered in Philadelphia to ponder a constitution for the 13 States," divide themselves into the few and the many. The first are rich and well-born, the other the mass of the people. . . . The people are turbulent and changing; they seldom judge or determine right." The formula for government was simple. "Give, therefore, to the first class a distinct, permanent share in the government. They will check the unsteadiness of the second, and, as they cannot receive any advantage by a change, they therefore will ever maintain good government."

Hamilton personified the "energy in the executive" that he had written about in Federalist No. 70, where he called it "a leading character in the definition of good government." Hamilton was nominated and confirmed on September 11, 1789. Hamilton would serve until 1795. When he began, he was 34 years old. The next day, he arranged a $50,000 loan for the federal government from the Bank of New York and sought a $50,000 loan from the Bank of North America. On his second day, he effectively took over administration of the Customs Service. Within a short period, he had 39 employees. After two years, counting the employees in Hamilton's office, the Comptroller, the Auditor, the Registrar, the Treasurer, and those in the Revenue Cutter Service, later the United States Coast Guard, the payroll of the Treasury Department exceeded 500 employees. Hamilton ultimately would have 570 employees, the great majority of the United States government. In 1791, the War Department had 12 employees; the State Department, eight.

Hamilton propounded his vision of a thriving United States and his operational plans in three reports to Congress: The *Report on Public Credit* (January 14, 1790), the *Report on a National Bank* (December 13, 1790), and the *Report on the Subject of Manufacturers* (December 5, 1791).

On September 21, Hamilton's tenth day in office, a Resolution of the House of Representatives requested that the Secretary prepare a plan for the support of the public credit, a matter the Resolution explained, "of high importance to the prosperity of the United States."

The Assumption of Public Debt

Within four months, Hamilton delivered his *Report on Public Credit.* By then, the national debt of the United States was $54 million, including $11.7 million in foreign debt. Hamilton characterized the debt of the states as "not equally well ascertained." He presumed the total debt of the states could be estimated to be $25 million, making a total national and state debt of approximately $79 million.

The election of George Washington in January 1789 set off a speculative frenzy in the market for public debt. "From January to November [1789], they rose thirty-three and a third per cent; and from that period to this time, they have risen fifty per cent more."

The impact on holders of debt securities was painfully divisive. Many Revolutionary War veterans had sold securities that they had received for wartime service to speculators for as few as 15 cents on the dollar. If the national government assumed public debt, who would benefit, the soldiers or the speculators?

Equally divisive was the position of the States. "Four states," Jon Meacham explained, "(Virginia, North Carolina, Georgia and Maryland) had already been fiscally responsible and paid off much of their Revolutionary debts. Others (chiefly Massachusetts, South Carolina, and Connecticut) had not, and were therefore quite happy to send their bills to Hamilton in New York. The more fiscally responsible states believed that they would inevitably end up paying federal taxes to bail out their lagging neighbors."

The essence of Hamilton's plan in the *Report on Public Credit* was to assume the debt of the national government and have the national government assume the debt of the states, honoring the debt contracts in good faith, meaning that speculators, not war veterans, foreign debt holders, and states that had not fully paid their debt would be paid nearly in full.

Hamilton argued that the good faith repayment of public debt was required by the United States Constitution, whose Article VI, Section 1 provided: "All Debts contracted . . . before the Adoption of this Constitution, shall be as valid against the United States under this Constitution, as under the Confederation." Hamilton stressed: "Every breach of the public engagements, whether from choice or necessity is, in different degrees, hurtful to the public credit."

Public credit was essential to a nation for "which there will be a necessity for borrowing. . . . For, when the credit of a country is in any degree questionable, it never fails to give an extravagant premium, in one shape or another, upon all the loans it has occasion to make. Nor does the evil end here; the same disadvantage must be sustained on whatever is to be bought on terms of future payment."

Public debt would serve as a form of money. "Transfers of stock or public debt are [the] equivalent to payments in specie."

Hamilton particularly highlighted the effect which the funding of the public debt would have upon landed property: "The present depreciated state of that species of property is a serious calamity. The value of cultivated lands, in most of the states, has fallen, since the Revolution, from twenty-five to fifty per cent. In those farther south, the decrease is still more considerable."

Hamilton stoutly rejected the argument for discrimination among debt holders: "It is inconsistent with justice, because, in the first place, it is a breach of contract — a violation of the right of a fair purchaser."

He adumbrated this point:

> Every buyer therefore stands exactly in the place of the seller, has the same right with him to the identical sum expressed in the security; and, having acquired that right by fair purchase and in conformity to the original *agreement* and *intention* of the

> government, his claim cannot be disputed without manifest injustice.
>
> That he is to be considered as a fair purchaser, results from this: Whatever necessity the seller may have been under, was occasioned by the government, in not making a proper provision for its debts. The buyer had no agency in it, and therefore ought not to suffer. He is not even chargeable with having taken an undue advantage. He paid what the commodity was worth in the market, and took the risks of reimbursement upon himself. He, of course, gave a fair equivalent, and ought to reap the benefit of his hazard, a hazard which was far from inconsiderable, and which, perhaps, turned on little less than a revolution in government.

Hamilton agreed that "the case of those who parted with their securities from necessity is a hard one," but their claim should be against the government, not the buyers in due course.

Discrimination would be "destructive of the *quality* of public debt . . . which is essential to its capability for answering the purposes of money — that is, the *security* of *transfer*." When there is a breach of faith, "it renders property in the funds less valuable, consequently [inducing] lenders to demand a higher premium for what they lend [that is, higher interest]."

For similar reasons, Hamilton rejected discrimination among the states for their public debt:

> If all the public creditors receive their dues from one source, distributed with an equal hand, their interest will be the same. And having the same interests, they will unite in the support of the fiscal arrangements of the government: As these, two, can be made with more convenience where there is no competition: These circumstances combined will insure to the revenue laws a more ready and more satisfactory execution.

Hamilton did make one fundamental exception to his recommendation to pay all debt in full. The immediate repayment of all debt, using 6 percent interest on Confederate and state debt, was "impracticable." "Effective measures were taken to establish public credit, that the government rate of interest in the United States will, in a very short time, fall at least as low as five percent; and that in a period not exceeding twenty years, it will sink still lower, probably to four."

Accordingly, Hamilton recommended to Congress a loan for the full amount of national and state debt. The holders of debt either could receive two-thirds of their existing debt at 6 percent interest and receive the other third in lands in the Western territory at the rate of 20 cents per acre, or to have the whole sum funded at an interest rate of 4 percent with a variety of optional "sweeteners" such as a receipt of $15.80 per $100 of debt payable in lands. "The fund to be established ought, for the present, to be confined to the existing [not future] debt of the United States."

Hamilton also proposed a separate loan of $10 million, payable one half in debt and one half in specie, the subscriber to the new debt would receive an interest of 5 percent.

"Foreign debt," in the opinion of Hamilton, "ought to be paid by new loans abroad." This was a critical point. Unlike all other funds available to the United States, foreign loans were worth their face value.

Hamilton estimated that the payout of interest on the $54 million national debt of $2,239,163 plus $600,000 for "current services," meaning that the amount of interest on the United States portion of the debt and cost of government, was anticipated initially to be $2,839,163.

State debt would be assumed in exchange for securities of the United States.

Hamilton believed that the costs of the assumption of national and state debt could be "obtained from the present duties on imports and tonnage, with [proposed] additions which, without any possible disadvantage, either to trade or agriculture, may be made on wines, spirits (including those distilled within the United States), teas and coffee."

Here the policy of Hamilton was unabashedly mercantile rather than free trade. Hamilton read and quoted Adam Smith and *The Wealth of Nations,* but followed instead the high tariff policies then dominant in Europe. He recommended "a sound policy to carry duties upon articles of this kind as high as will be consistent with the practicability of a safe collection."

Hamilton justified funding the national debt largely through higher duties as a luxury tax, adding: "The consumption of ardent spirits, particularly, no doubt very much on account of their cheapness, is carried to an extreme which is truly to be regretted, as well in regard to the health and morals . . . of the community."

Regardless of whether Hamilton's view on the sin tax or higher duties on ardent spirits was fair or wise, Hamilton had little choice but to rely on customs revenue. Duties then accounted for 90 percent of government revenue.

To ensure safe collection of duties, Hamilton proposed a Customs Service.

The *Report on Public Credit* then laid out several pages of specific duties upon wines, distilled spirits, teas, and coffee that he proposed be charged after May 1790, starting with: "Upon every gallon of Madera wine, the quality of London particular, thirty-five cents."

Hamilton estimated in a schedule to the *Report on Public Credit* "the net product of the duties proposed in this report of about [$1,703,400]."

Hamilton proposed borrowing up to $12 million first to pay the current year interest and installments of foreign debt. Second, to pay "any deficiency which may happen in the product of the funds provided for paying the interest of the domestic debt." Third, to finance the change in the foreign debt to a reduced 5 percent interest. The new loan after paying 1790 installments would cost $3,888,888. Fourth, to purchase the public debt "at the price it shall bear in the market while it continues below its true value." This would strengthen public creditors "as it would tend to raise the value of stock," and frustrate speculation, including foreign speculators. "By the Government's entering into competition with them, it will not only reap a part of the profit itself, but will contract the extent, and lessen the extra profit of foreign purchasers."

In creating this new debt, Hamilton disavowed his earlier view that the national debt could be a national blessing. In the *Report on Public Credit,* he now urged that "the proper funding of the present debt will render it a national blessing." "[T]he creation of debt should always be accompanied with the means of extinguishment. This [Hamilton regarded] as the true secret for rendering public credit immortal."

Hamilton, working with the Postmaster General, proposed that revenues to the Post Office, a sum not exceeding $1,000,000 per year, be used in a fund to pay off the national debt. Chernow estimated that the fund could retire about 5 percent of the debt each year until it was paid off.

Hamilton foreshadowed the need for a national bank with a single sentence: "The Secretary contemplates the application of this money through the medium of a national bank, for which, with the permission of the House, he will submit a plan in the course of this session."

He concluded the *Report on Public Credit* by recommending that Congress with "no further delay" adopt concurrent Resolutions:

> That the United States do assume, and will, at the first session in the year 1791, provide, on the same terms with the present debt of the United States, for all such parts of the debts of the respective States, or any of them, as shall, prior to the first day of January, in the said year, 1791, be subscribed toward a loan to the United States, upon the principles of either of the plans which shall have been adopted by them, for obtaining a reloan of their present debt.
>
> Provided, that the provision to be made, as aforesaid, shall be suspended, with respect to the debt of any State which may have exchanged the securities of the United States for others issued by itself, until the whole of the said securities shall either be re-exchanged or surrendered to the United States....
>
> That the amount of the debt of each State, so assumed and provided for, be charged to such State in account with the United States, upon the same principles upon which it shall be lent to the United States.
>
> That subscriptions be opened for receiving loans of the said debts, at the same times and places, and under the like regulations, as shall have been prescribed in relation to the debt of the United States.[6]

The market reaction to the *Report on Public Credit* was "electrifying.... Securities began to change hands with a speed never before seen in America."

But the political consequences of the *Report* were deeply divisive. Debate began on February 8, 1790. The Funding Act Assuming National and State Debt would only be enacted on August 4, 1790. James Madison, Hamilton's principal co-author of the Federalist Papers and close ally in the ratification of the Constitution, aggressively opposed Hamilton's plan for assumption. Hamilton felt betrayed. Madison earlier had, according to Hamilton, supported funding the debt, not discriminating between original and present holders, and the expediency of assuming the state debt.

On four separate occasions between February and July 1790, Madison thwarted Hamilton's attempts to enact debt assumption, defeating the proposal altogether in the House on April 12, 1790.

Madison viewed Hamilton's arguments in favor of assumption of state debts as "unsupported." He rejected the argument that State debt should be viewed as the debt of the United States and noted that at the Constitutional Convention on August 18–19, 1787, the Convention had considered but not proceeded with a plan to assume state debt. He was pointed in his denunciation of the unequal effects Hamilton's plan would have on the states. Virginia could pay off its debt for $3 million. Hamilton's plan would raise the cost to Virginia to $5 million.

In contrast, Connecticut would save two-thirds the cost of its state debt; New York, 36 percent.

Madison was outraged that the recent rise in public debt securities prices would redound to speculators rather than to the original holders of the securities. An amendment offered by Madison to require the original holders to be fully repaid, despite their sale of the debt securities, was voted down by the House on February 22 by a vote of 36 to 13. Madison's proposal was unpopular in part because as Massachusetts Representative Fisher Anzo insisted: "If government has this right, what right of property is safe?"

Madison categorically rejected the assertion that assumption of state debts would strengthen the national government. "There is no man more anxious for the success of the government than I am, and no one who will join more heartily in curing its defects; but I wish these defects to be remedied by additional constitutional powers, if they should be found necessary. This is the only proper, effectual, and permanent remedy."

The strict construction of the Constitution's national powers was critical to Madison.

Moreover, Madison was of the opinion that the "public debt is a public evil, an assumption of the State debts [by the national government] will enormously increase, and, perhaps perpetuate it. . . . [T]he United States and the several States could discharge a debt of eighty million with greater ease and in less time than the United States alone could do it."

Madison went so far as to urge in response to a representative from Massachusetts who implied that the rejection of assumption would lead to a break up of the United States itself, that this would be of less harm than adoption of assumption: "It is my opinion, sir, that if the refusal to assume the State debts would produce dangerous consequences to the union from the discontents that it is apprehended will grow out of the measure, much more have we to fear from an assumption, particularly if hazarded by a small majority."

The possibility of break up was further than allies of Madison were prepared to go. Critically, Jefferson held the view: "[I]f everyone retains inflexibility his present opinion, there will be no bill passed at all for funding the public debts will . . . without funding, this is an end of the government." Jefferson, along with legislators from Pennsylvania and Virginia, engineered a compromise that ended the impasse over assumption of national and state debt. Madison was persuaded by Jefferson and Hamilton at a celebrated dinner at Jefferson's lodgings on June 20, 1790, to support assumption, or at least not decisively oppose it, in return for what today is known as Washington, D.C. becoming the national capitol after temporarily being located in Philadelphia, rather than permanently being located in New York as Hamilton earlier sought.[7]

On July 16, 1790, Congress passed An Act for Establishing the Temporary and Permanent Start of the Government, which provided that Congress would move from New York to Philadelphia in December 1790 and then to its permanent capitol on the Potomac River in 1800 in "a district of territory, not exceeding ten miles square, to be located as hereafter directed on the river Potomac, at some place between the mouths of the Eastern branch and Connogochegue, be, and the same is hereby accepted for the permanent seat of the Government of the United States," meaning a location near Washington's plantation in Mount Vernon.

A few weeks later, on August 4, 1790, Congress enacted An Act for Making Provision for the Payment of the Debt of the United States. The Assumption Act generally was consistent with Hamilton's *Report on Public Credit.* The domestic and foreign debt was to be paid in full to each creditor who voluntarily accepted the new loan terms. "[N]othing in this act contained shall be construed in any wise to alter, abridge or impair the right of those creditors of the United States, who shall not subscribe to the said loan, or the contracts upon which their respective claims are founded; but the said contracts and rights shall remain in full force and virtue."

Loans were authorized for the full amount of the domestic national and state debt.

For two-thirds of the domestic national debt, the United States would pay subscribers to the new loan 6 percent subject to redemption of up to 8 percent of principal and interest redemption in any year. The remaining one-third would only be paid 6 percent interest beginning in 1808, also subject to 8 percent redemption in any year.

Congress authorized payments of up to $21.5 million for state debt. Since not all of the state allocations were used, the total actually assumed by the national government ultimately equaled $18.3 million.

The interest for repayment on state debt was different than that on national debt. Certificates were issued for 4/9 of the debt at 6 percent beginning at the time of issuance, for 2/9 for payments would be at 6 percent beginning in 1808, and for the remaining one-third, interest would begin at issuance at 3 percent.

For domestic debt solely for the payment of past due interest, "commonly called indents of interest," a new loan would pay 3 percent interest.

The President was authorized to borrow up to $12 million to pay off in full foreign debt.

The first $600,000 of duties on goods, wares and merchandise imported into the United States and on the tonnage of ships or vessels would be allocated to the support of the United States government, including the cost of defense. Additional duty payments would pay interest and arrears of interest on foreign debt until payment of the foreign debt was fully satisfied.

The proceeds from the sales of lands in the Western territories "now belonging, or that may hereafter belong to the United States" were appropriated to create a sinking fund to pay off the principal on the debt until the debt was fully satisfied.

Assumption of the national, state, and foreign debt for the period preceding the beginning of the United States would prove to be irreversible. While Hamilton and the Assumption Act provided mechanisms to extinguish the new debt to repay the old, the Assumption Act also created the first national debt for the United States, a taxing power through the duty system, a means to make the states to a limited degree dependent upon the national government. For proponents of limited national government and the primacy of the states, there was subsequent bitterness over the Residence Act-Assumption Act compromise. Jefferson, for one, bemoaned, "we can pay off [the new] debt in fifteen years; but we can never get rid of the financial system."[8]

Hamilton further implemented his *Report on Public Credit* with a December 1790 proposal for an excise tax on distilled spirits, a "sin" tax largely on whiskey. With Madison's support, the Excise or Duties on Distilled Spirits Act was enacted in March 1791 by a vote of 35 to 21. Madison supported a tax on distilled spirits "as direct taxes would be still more generally obnoxious." He shared with Hamilton the view that "the tax might have collateral social benefits such as increasing sobriety and thereby [preventing] disease and untimely death." The new tax was wildly unpopular, beginning later in 1791 in Western Pennsylvania and elsewhere when federal agents began to seek to collect duties on whiskey and other distilled spirits. Discontent reached an apogee in 1794 with the Whiskey Rebellion, which led to President Washington federalizing a military force of 12,950 men, a huge army in its day. Resistance to the tax in western Pennsylvania dissipated when the troops arrived.[9]

Opposition to the excise tax on distilled spirits further hardened the division between agrarian interests in the country and the South and the urban and mercantile interests associated with Hamilton, which were generally in the North.

The First National Bank

Hamilton's *Report on a National Bank*, published December 13, 1790, would prove more divisive and lead in principal part, as John Marshall wrote in 1807, to the formation of rival political parties. Marshall wrote: Hamilton's economic plans, especially for a national bank, "made a deep impression on many members of the legislature; and contributed, not inconsiderably, to the complete organization of these distinct and visible parties." As with Assumption and the Whiskey Tax, Economic Professor John Wood wrote: "Opposition to a national bank came from two overlapping groups: rural elements, especially in the South, who disliked banks in general because they were associated with trade and manufacturers and threatened a way of life, and constitutionalists, also primarily Southern, who saw national banks as part of the central government's assault on states' rights and personal liberties."[10]

The case for a National Bank was crisply stated by Hamilton in the *Report on a National Bank*:

> First. The augmentation of the active or productive capital of a country. Gold and silver, when they are employed merely as the instruments of exchange and alienation, have been not improperly denominated dead stock; but when deposited in

> banks, to become the basis of a paper circulation, which takes their character and place, as the signs or representatives of value, they then acquire life, or, in other words, an active and productive quality.... It is a well established fact, that banks in good credit can circulate a far greater sum than the actual quantum of their capital in gold and silver. The extent of the possible excess seems indeterminate; though it has been conjecturally stated at the proportions of two and three to one....
>
> Secondly. Greater facility to the government in obtaining pecuniary aids, especially in sudden emergencies. This is another and an undisputed advantage of public banks: one, which as already remarked, has been realized in signal instances, among ourselves. The reason is obvious: The capitals of a great number of individuals are, by this operation, collected to a point, and placed under one direction....
>
> Thirdly. The facilitating of the payment of taxes. This advantage is produced in two ways. Those who are in a situation to have access to the bank can have the assistance of loans to answer with punctuality the public calls upon them.

Hamilton was aware of several arguments being articulated against a national bank. These most significantly included that a national bank would impede lending by other institutions, which meant state banks. Here Hamilton stressed: "The capital of every public bank will of course be restricted within a certain defined limit."

Hamilton recognized the temptations to over trade and to make loans to "unsuccessful adventures and fraudulent traders." Hamilton trusted the self-corrective properties of the bank and its board: "The bank itself is in so much jeopardy of being a sufferer by it, that it has the strongest of all inducements to be on its guard.":

> If banks, in spite of every precaution, are sometimes betrayed into giving a false credit to the persons described; they more frequently enable honest and industrious men, of small or perhaps of no capital to undertake and prosecute business, with advantage to themselves and to the community; and assist merchants of both capital and credit, who meet with fortuitous and unforeseen shocks, which might without such helps prove fatal to them and to others; to make head against their misfortunes, and finally to retrieve their affairs: Circumstances, which form no inconsiderable encomium on the utility of banks.

Finally, Hamilton responded to the concerns that banks promoting paper currency would "banish" gold and silver, then the most trusted basis of money:

> It may be said, that as bank paper affords a substitute for specie, it serves to counteract that rigorous necessity for the metals, as a medium of circulation, which in the case of a wrong balance, might restrain in some degree their exportation; and it may be added, that from the same cause, in the same case, it would retard those [ ]economical and parsimonious reforms, in the manner of living, which the scarcity of money is calculated to produce, and which might be necessary to rectify such wrong balance.

To Hamilton, paper money based on a ratio to their gold and silver would:

> enable the government to pay its foreign debts, and to answer any exigencies, which the external concerns of the community may have produced. They enable the merchant to support his credit, (on which the prosperity of trade depends) when special circumstances prevent remittances in other modes. They enable him also to prosecute enterprises, which ultimately tend to an augmentation of the species of wealth in question. It is evident, that gold and silver may often be employed in procuring commodities abroad; which, in a circuitous commerce, replace the original fund, with considerable addition.

A key consideration in creating a national bank was the Constitution's prohibition on the emitting of paper money by individual States: "Among other material differences between a paper currency, issued by the mere authority of government, and one issued by a bank, payable in coin, is this: That, in the first case, there is no standard to which an appeal can be made, as to the quantity which will only satisfy, or which will surcharge the circulation; in the last, that standard results from the demand."

While Hamilton's arguments were cogent, he underestimated the intensity of opposition on these points then and in the future.

He also articulated other views in the *Report on the National Bank* that were politically unwise.

He rejected having "a plurality of branches," instead seeking a single national bank in Philadelphia. This view itself would be rejected by the Directors of the National Bank who in the 20 year life of the Bank would establish eight branches, a set of decisions believed to be politically expedient.

Hamilton objected to loans to proprietors of land. "Land is alone an unfit fund for a bank circulation. If the notes issued upon it were not to be payable in coin, on demand, or at a short date; this would amount to nothing more than a repetition of the paper emissions, which are now exploded by the general voice. If the notes are to be payable in coin, the land must first be converted into it by sale, or mortgage."

Land as collateral for loans later would prove to be a common and effective basis of debt, when the landholder overcollateralizes the debt by providing more in fair market value of the land than the debt. In Hamilton's day, this unnecessary swipe at land as the basis of debt reflected a preference, like the single national bank he commended in Philadelphia, for Northern merchants, rather than Southern landholders. Historian Gordon Wood would write that Hamilton's resistance to the needs of farmers and small businessmen was an "insensitivity" that over time galvanized support for competitive state banks that "give them the credit they wanted."

Hamilton also objected to the profits of the Bank redounding to the immediate benefit of the state. His priority was to establish the credit of the United States:

> To attached full confidence to an institution of this nature, it appears to be an essential ingredient in its structure, that it shall be under a *private* not a *public* direction, under the guidance of *individual interest,* not of *public policy;* which would be supposed to be, and in certain emergencies, under a feeble or two sanguine administration would, really, be, liable to being too much influenced by *public necessity*.... It would indeed be little less, than a miracle, should the credit of the bank be at the disposal of the government, if in a long series of time, there was not experienced a calamitous abuse of it. It is true, that it would be the real interest of the government not to abuse it; its genuine policy to husband and cherish it with the most guarded circumspection as an inestimable treasure. But what government ever uniformly consulted its true interest, in opposition to the temptations of momentary exigencies? What nation was ever blessed with a constant succession of upright and wise Administrators?

> The keen, steady, and, as it were, magnetic sense, of their own interest, as proprietors, in the directors of a bank, pointing invariably to its true pole, the prosperity of the institution, is the only security, that can always be relied upon, for a careful and prudent administration.

Hamilton's trust in the "keen, steady and . . . magnetic sense of . . . the directors of [the] bank" was unblinking. Later, the bank would be assaulted for corruption, encouraging speculation and fraud, and Northern bias. Both politics and the fallibility of those associated with the bank would undermine its support.

But that was later. In 1790, Hamilton, generally backed by the First Congress of the United States, was in control.

In his plan for the Constitution of a national bank, Hamilton proposed 24 points, most significantly:

> I. The capital stock of the bank shall not exceed ten millions of dollars, divided into twenty-five thousand shares, each share being four hundred dollars. . . .
>
> II. The amount of each share shall be payable, one fourth in gold and silver coin, and three fourths in that part of the public debt, which according to the loan proposed by the Act making provision for the debt of the United States, shall bear an accruing interest at the time of payment of six per centum per annum. . . .
>
> VI. The totality of the debts of the company, whether by bond, bill, note, or other contract, (credits for deposits excepted) shall never exceed the amount of its capital stock. . . .
>
> VII. The company may sell or demise its lands and tenements, or may sell the whole, or any part of the public debt, whereof its stock shall consist; but shall *trade* in nothing, except bills of exchange, gold and silver bullion, or in the sale of goods pledged for money lent: nor shall take more than at the rate of six per centum, per annum, upon its loans or discounts.
>
> VIII. No loan shall be made by the bank, for the use or on account of the Government of the United States, or of either of them to an amount exceeding fifty thousand dollars, or of any foreign prince or State; unless previously authorized by a law of the United States. . . .
>
> X. The affairs of the bank shall be under management of twenty-five directors, one of whom shall be the resident. . . .
>
> XII. Not more than three-fourths of the directors in office, exclusive of the President, shall be eligible for the next

> succeeding year. But the director who shall be President at the time of an election may always be re-elected.
>
> XIII. None by a stockholder being a citizen of the United States, shall be eligible as a director. . . .
>
> XVII. Not less than seven directors shall constitute a board for the transaction of business. . . .
>
> XX. The bills and notes of the bank originally made payable, or which shall have become payable on demand, in gold and silver coin, shall be receivable in all payments to the United States.
>
> XXI. The Officer at the head of the Treasury Department of the United States, shall be furnished from time to time, as often as he may require, not exceeding once a week, with statements of the amount of the capital stock of the bank and of the debts due to the same; of the monies deposited therein; of the notes in circulation, and of the cash in hand; and shall have the right to inspect such general account in the books of the bank as shall relate to the said statements; provided, that this shall not be construed to imply a right of inspecting this account of any private individual or individuals with the bank.
>
> XXII. No similar institution shall be established by any future act of the United States, during the continuance of the one hereby proposed to be established. . . .
>
> XXIV. And lastly, The President of the United States shall be authorised to cause a subscription to be made to the Stock of the said company, on behalf of the United States, to an amount not exceeding two millions of dollars, to be paid out of the monies which shall be borrowed by virtue of either of the acts, the one entitled "An act making provision for the debt of the United States," and the other entitled "An Act making provision for the reduction of the public debt"; borrowing of the bank an equal sum, to be applied to the purposes for which the said monies shall have been procured reimbursable in ten years by equal annual installments; or at any time sooner, or in any greater proportion, that the Government may think fit.

In his comments on the plan, Hamilton particularly emphasized two points. First:

> The combination of a portion of the public debt in the formation of the capital, is the principal thing, of which an explanation is required. . . .
>
> This part of the fund will be always ready to come in aid of the specie. It will more and more command a ready sale; and can therefore expeditiously be turned into coin if an exigency of

> the bank should at any time require it. This quality of prompt convertibility into coin, renders it an equivalent for that necessary agent of bank circulation; and distinguishes it from a fund in land of which the sale would generally be far less compendious and at great disadvantage. . . .
>
> The debt composing part of the capital, besides its collateral effect in enabling the bank to extend its operations, and consequently to enlarge its profits, will produce a direct annual revenue of six per centum from the Government, which will enter into the half yearly dividends received by the stockholders.

Second, the right of the bank to contract debts was limited to its capital, "an important precaution, which is not to be found in the Constitution of the Bank of North America" [then the largest state bank].[11]

The Bank Bill as introduced and later enacted largely followed Hamilton's *Report*. The National Bank was to have capital of $10 million "divided into twenty-five thousand shares, each share being four hundred dollars." Shares for the bank were to be paid one-fourth in gold and silver and three-fourths as part of the public debt. The bank would pay interest of 6 percent annually.

The Bank would be formed as a corporation with a 20-year duration until March 4, 1811.

Critically, the Bank Bill and subsequent Act limited:

> . . . The total amount of the debts, which the said corporation shall at any time owe, whether by bond, bill, note, or other contract, shall not exceed the sum of ten millions of dollars, over and above the monies then actually deposited in the bank for safe keeping, unless the contracting of any greater debt shall have been previously authorized by a law of the United States.

But "the bills or notes of the said corporation, originally made payable, or which shall have become payable on demand, in gold and silver coin, shall be receivable in all payments to the United States." "[N]o other bank shall be established by any future law of the United States, during the continuance of the corporation hereby created; for which the faith of the United States is hereby pledged."

The Secretary of Treasury would receive as proposed, statements of account no less frequently than once a week.

Within five weeks, the Senate enacted the Bank Bill.

As with the Assumption Bill, Madison led the opposition to the bank in the House. On February 1, 1791, Madison offered a detailed critique based both on economic and Constitutional objections.

His economic objections were terse:

> The principal disadvantages consisted in, first, banishing the precious metals, by substituting another medium to perform their office: This effect was inevitable. It was admitted by the most enlightened patrons of banks, particularly by Smith on the Wealth of Nations. The common answer to the objection was, that the money banished was only an exchange for something equally valuable that would be imported in return. He admitted the weight of this observation in general, but doubted whether, in the present habits of this country, the returns would not be in articles of no permanent use to it.
>
> Second. Exposing the public and individuals to all the evils of a run on the bank, which would be particularly calamitous in so great a country as this, might happen from various causes, as false rumors, bad management of the institution, an unfavorable balance of trade from short crops, &c.
>
> It was proper to be considered also, that the most important of the advantages would be better obtained by several banks properly distributed, than by a single one. The aids to commerce could only be afforded at or very near the seat of the bank. The same was true of aids to merchants in the payment of customs.

His more forceful objections were based on the Constitution, on which Madison, as a principal participant in its drafting at the Constitutional Convention, author of the Bill of Rights and co-author of the Federalist Papers, could speak with considerable authority.

First, he rejected the argument that a bank could be incorporated. "[A] power to grant charters of incorporation had been proposed in the general convention and rejected." The power to create a bank or a banking corporation was not expressly granted to the national government in the Constitution.

The powers granted to the national government were limited. "It is not a general grant, out of which particular powers are excepted; it is a grant of particular powers only, leaving the general mass in other hands." Madison stressed: "An interpretation that destroys the very characteristic of the Government cannot be just."

Could a power to incorporate a bank be implied?

The only clauses, Madison argued, under which an implicit power to incorporate a bank could be implied, or as he put it "pretended" were:

> 1. The power to lay and collect taxes to pay the debts, and provide for the common defence and general welfare: Or,
>
> 2. The power to borrow money on the credit of the United States: Or,
>
> 3. The power to pass all laws necessary and proper to carry into execution those powers.
>
> The bill did not come within the first power. It laid no tax to pay the debts, or provide for the general welfare. It laid no tax whatever. It was altogether foreign to the subject.
>
> No argument could be drawn from the terms "common defence, and general welfare." The power as to these general purposes, was limited to acts laying taxes for them; and the general purposes themselves were limited and explained by the particular enumeration subjoined. To understand these terms in any sense, that would justify the power in question, would give to Congress an unlimited power; would render nugatory the enumeration of particular powers; would supercede all the powers reserved to the state governments. . . .
>
> It had been said that "general welfare" meant cases in which a general power might be exercised by Congress, without interfering with the powers of the states; and that the establishment of a national bank was of this sort. There were, he said, several answers to this novel doctrine.
>
> 1. The proposed bank would interfere so as indirectly to defeat a state bank at the same place. 2. It would directly interfere with the rights of the states, *to prohibit* as well as to establish banks, and the circulation of bank notes. . . . 3. Interference with the power of the states was no constitutional criterion of the power of Congress. . . .
>
> The case of the bank established by the former Congress, had been cited as a precedent. This was known, he said, to have been the child of necessity. It never could be justified by the regular powers of the articles of confederation. Congress betrayed a consciousness of this in recommending to the states to incorporate the bank also . . .
>
> The second clause to be examined is that, which empowers Congress to borrow money.
>
> Is this a bill to borrow money? It does not borrow a shilling. Is there any fair construction by which the bill can be deemed an exercise of the power to borrow money? The obvious meaning

> of the power to borrow money, is that of accepting it from, and stipulating payment to those who are *able* and *willing* to lend. . . .
>
> The *third* clause is that which gives the power to pass all laws necessary and proper to execute the specified powers.
>
> Whatever meaning this clause may have, none can be admitted, that would give an unlimited discretion to Congress.
>
> Its meaning must, according to the natural and obvious force of the terms and the context, be limited to means *necessary* to the *end*, and *incident* to the *nature* of the specified powers.
>
> The clause is in fact merely declaratory of what would have resulted by unavoidable implication, as the appropriate, and as it were, technical means of executing those powers. In this sense it had been explained by the friends of the constitution, and ratified by the state conventions.
>
> The essential characteristic of the government, as composed of limited and enumerated powers, would be destroyed: If instead of direct and incidental means, any means could be used, which in the language of the preamble to the bill, "might be conceived to be conducive to the successful conducting of the finances; or might be *conceived* to *tend* to give *facility* to the obtaining of loans." . . .
>
> But the proposed bank could not even be called necessary to the government; at most it could be but convenient. Its uses to the government could be supplied by keeping the taxes a little in advance — by loans from individuals — by the other banks, over which the government would have equal command; nay greater, as it may grant or refuse to these the privilege, made a free and irrevocable gift to the proposed bank, of using their notes in the federal revenue.

On February 8, 1791, the House of Representatives enacted the Bank Bill by a vote of 39 to 20. "Most of the ayes — 33 out of 39 — were from New England, New York, New Jersey, and Pennsylvania; most of the nays — 15 out of 20 — were from Virginia, the Carolinas, and Georgia."[12]

Given the hotly pressed views of Madison, President Washington sought the opinion of his Attorney General Edmund Randolph on the constitutionality of the Bank Act. His analysis, though plodding, was thorough and deserves more respect than history has accorded it.

Randolph wrote two papers on the Act's constitutionality, on both summarizing at length powers "which bear any analogy to that of incorporation" and the arguments in favor and in opposition to the Act's constitutionality. Randolph did not believe that the "power to lay and collect taxes," "borrow money" or "regulate commerce," as well as "the general qualities of the Federal Government" provided a Constitutional basis for a national bank:

> [W]e come to the last enquiry . . . , whether it be sanctified by the power to make all laws which shall be necessary and proper for carrying into execution the powers vested by the Constitution. To be necessary is to be incidental, or in other words may be denominated the natural means of executing a power.
>
> The phrase, *and proper*, if it has any meaning, does not enlarge the powers of Congress, but rather restricts them. For no power is to be assumed under the general clause, but such as is not only necessary but proper, or perhaps expedient also. But as the friends to the bill ought not to claim any advantage from this clause, so ought not the enemies to it, to quote the clause as having a restrictive effect: both ought to consider it as among the surplusage which as often proceeds from inattention as caution.
>
> . . .
>
> In every aspect therefore under which the attorney general can view the act, so far as it incorporates the bank, he is bound to declare his opinion to be against its constitutionality.

Washington then sought the opinion of Secretary of State Thomas Jefferson. Jefferson emphasized state powers and the strict construction of the Constitution:

> I consider the foundation of the Constitution as laid on this ground: That "all powers not delegated to the United States, by the Constitution, nor prohibited by it to the States, are reserved to the States or to the people." . . . To take a single step beyond the boundaries thus specially drawn around the powers of Congress, is to take possession of a boundless field of power, no longer susceptible of any definition.
>
> The incorporation of a bank, and the powers assumed by this bill, have not, in my opinion, been delegated to the United States, by the Constitution.
>
> 1. They are not among the powers specially enumerated: for these are: 1. A power to lay taxes for the purpose of paying the debts of the United States; but no debt is paid by this bill, nor any tax laid. . . .
>
> 2. *To borrow money*. But this bill neither borrows money nor ensures the borrowing it. The proprietors of the bank will be just as few as any other money holders, to lend or not to lend their money to the public. . . .

II. Nor are they within either of the general phrases, which are the two following:

1. To lay taxes to provide for the general welfare of the United States, that is to say, "to lay taxes for *the purpose of* providing for the general welfare." For the laying of taxes is the *power*, and the general welfare the *purpose* for which the power is to be exercised. They are not to lay taxes *ad libitum, for any purpose they please*; but only *to pay the debts or provide for the welfare of the Union.* In like manner, they are not *to do anything they please* to provide for the general welfare, but only to *lay taxes* for that purpose. To consider the latter phrase, not as describing the purpose of the first, but as giving a distinct and independent power to do any act they please, which might be for the good of the Union, would render all the preceding and subsequent enumeration of power completely useless.

It would reduce the whole instrument to a single phrase, that of instituting a Congress with power to do whatever would be for the good of the United States; and, as they would be the sole judges of the good or evil, it would be also a power to do whatever evil they please....

2. The second general phrase is, "to make all laws *necessary* and proper for carrying into execution the enumerated powers." But they can all be carried into execution without a bank. A bank therefore is not *necessary*, and consequently not authorized by this phrase.

[It] has been urged that a bank will give great facility or convenience in the collection of taxes. Suppose this were true: yet the Constitution allows only the means which are "*necessary*", not those which are merely "convenient" for effecting the enumerated powers. If such a latitude of construction be allowed to this phrase as to give any non-enumerated power, it will go to everyone, for there is not one which ingenuity may not torture into a *convenience* in some instance *or other*, to *some one* of so long a list of enumerated powers. It would swallow up all the delegated powers, and reduce the whole to one power, as before observed. Therefore it was that the Constitution restrained them to the *necessary* means, that is to say, to those means without which the grant of power would be nugatory....

Besides, the existing banks will, without a doubt, enter into arrangements for lending their agency, and the more favorable, as there will be a competition among them for it; whereas the bill delivers us up bound to the national bank, who are free to refuse all arrangement, but on their own terms, and the public not free, on such refusal, to employ any other bank. That of

> Philadelphia I believe, now does this business, by their post-notes, which, by an arrangement with the treasury, are paid by any State collector to whom they are presented. This expedient alone suffices to prevent the existence of that *necessity* which may justify the assumption of a non-enumerated power as a means for carrying into effect an enumerated one. The thing may be done, and has been done, and well done, without this assumption, therefore it does not stand on that degree of *necessity* which can honestly justify it.
>
> It may be said that a bank whose bills would have a currency all over the states, would be more convenient than one whose currency is limited to a single state. So it would be still more convenient that there should be a bank, whose bills should have a currency all over the world. But it does not follow from this superior conveniency, that there exists anywhere a power to establish such a bank; or that the world may not go on very well without it.

Washington requested that Madison draft a veto message and asked Hamilton to opine on the constitutionality of the Bank Act. Hamilton's opinion would persuade Washington to sign the Act and in 1819, would provide a basis for United States Supreme Court Justice Marshall's celebrated opinion in *McCulloch v. Maryland*, upholding the constitutionality of the Second Bank of the United States.

If Jefferson anchored his opinion on the limited power of the national government and states' rights, Hamilton diametrically premised his argument on the sovereignty of the national government:

> . . . [E]very power vested in a government is in its nature sovereign, and includes, by force of the term, a right to employ all the means requisite and fairly applicable to the attainment of the ends of such power, and which are not precluded by restrictions and exceptions specified in the Constitution, or not immoral, or not contrary to the essential ends of political society. . . .
>
> If it would be necessary to bring proof to a proposition so clear, as that which affirms that the powers of the federal government, as to its objects, were sovereign, there is a clause of its Constitution which would be decisive. It is that which declares that the Constitution, and the laws of the United States made in pursuance of it, and all treaties made, or which shall be made, under their authority, shall be the [supreme] law of the land.

> The power which can create the supreme law of the land in any case, is doubtless sovereign as to such case....

Hamilton rejected the analysis of Jefferson and Rudolph:

> The first of these arguments is, that the foundation of the constitution is laid on this ground: "That all powers not delegated to the United States by the Constitution, nor prohibited to it by the states, are reserved for the states, or to the people." Whence it is meant to be inferred, that Congress can in no case exercise any power not included in those enumerated in the Constitution. And it is affirmed, that the power of erecting a corporation is not included in any of the enumerated powers....
>
> It is not denied that there are implied [as] well as express powers, and that the former are as effectually delegated as the latter....
>
> ... Then it follows, that as a power of erecting a corporation may as well be implied as any other thing, it may as well be employed as an instrument or mean of carrying into execution any of the specified powers, as any other instrument or mean whatever. The only question must be in this, as in every other case, whether the mean to be employed or in this instance, the corporation to be erected, has a natural relation to any of the acknowledged objected or lawful ends of the government....
>
> To this mode of reasoning respecting the right of employing all the means requisite to the execution of the specified powers of the government, it is objected, that none but necessary and proper means are to be employed; and the Secretary of State maintains, that no means are to be considered as necessary but those without which the grant of the power would be nugatory....
>
> It is certain that neither the grammatical nor popular sense of the term requires that construction. According to both, necessary often means no more than needful, requisite, incidental, useful, or conducive to. It is a common mode of expression to say, that it is necessary for a government or a person to do this or that thing, when nothing more is intended or understood, than that the interests of the government or person require, or will be promoted by, the doing of this or that thing. The imagination can be at no loss for exemplifications of the use of the word in this sense. And it is the true one in which it is to be understood as used in the Constitution. The whole turn of the clause containing it indicates, that it was the intent of the Convention, by that clause, to give a liberal latitude to the exercise

of the specified powers. The expressions have peculiar comprehensiveness. They are, "to make all laws necessary and proper for carrying into execution the foregoing powers, and all other powers vested by the Constitution in the government of the United States, or in any department or officer thereof."

To understand the word as the Secretary of State does, would be to depart from its obvious and popular sense, and to give it a restrictive operation, an idea never before entertained. It would be to give it the same force as if the word absolutely or indispensably had been prefixed to it. . . .

This restrictive interpretation of the word *necessary* is also contrary to this sound maxim of construction, namely, that the powers contained in a constitution of government, especially those which concern the general administration of the affairs of a country, its finances, trade, defense, etc., ought to be construed liberally in advancement of the public good. . . .

It leaves, therefore, a criterion of what is constitutional, and of what is not so. This criterion is the end, to which the measure relates as a mean. If the end be clearly comprehended within any of the specified powers, and if the measure have an obvious relation to that end, and is not forbidden by any particular provision of the Constitution, it may safely be deemed to come within the compass of the national authority. There is also this further criterion, which may materially assist the decision: Does the proposed measure abridge a pre-existing right of any state or of any individual? If it does not, there is a strong presumption in favor of its constitutionality, and slighter relations to any declared object of the Constitution may be permitted to turn the scale. . . .

It shall now be endeavored to be shown that there is a power to erect one of the kind proposed by the bill. This will be done by tracing a natural and obvious relation between the institution of a bank and the objects of several of the enumerated powers of the government; and by showing that, politically speaking, it is necessary to the effectual execution of one or more of those powers. . . .

A bank relates to the collection of taxes in two ways — indirectly, by increasing the quantity of circulating medium and quickening circulation, which facilitates the means of paying directly, by creating a convenient Species of medium in which they are to be paid. . . .

A bank has a direct relation to the power of borrowing money, because it is an usual, and in sudden emergencies an essential, instrument in the obtaining of loans to government.

> A nation is threatened with a war, large sums are wanted on a sudden to make the requisite preparations. Taxes are laid for the purpose, but it requires tine to obtain the benefit of them. Anticipation is indispensable. If there be a bank the supply can at once be had. If there be none, loans from individuals must be sought. The progress of these is often too slow for the exigency ill some situations they are not practicable at all. Frequently when they are, it is of great consequence to be able to anticipate the product of them by advance from a bank....
>
> The institution of a bank has also a natural relation to the regulation of trade between the states, in so far as it is conducive to the creation of a convenient medium of exchange between them, and to the keeping up a full circulation, by preventing the frequent displacement of the metals in reciprocal remittances. Money is the very hinge on which commerce turns. And this does not merely mean gold and silver; many other things have served the purpose, with different degrees of utility. Paper has been extensively employed.

Chief Justice Marshall later in 1819 in the United States Supreme Court decision in *McCulloch v. Maryland* pungently amplified Hamilton's key points: "[W]e must never forget that it is a constitution we are expounding":

> ... Congress is not empowered by it to make all laws, which may have relation to the powers conferred on the government, but such only as may be "*necessary and proper* for carrying them into execution....
>
> ... Does it always import an absolute physical necessity, so strong, that one thing, to which another may be termed necessary, cannot exist without that other? ... To employ the means necessary to an end, is generally understood as employing any means calculated to produce the end, and not as being confined to those single means, without which the end would be entirely unattainable....
>
> It must have been the intention of those who gave these powers, to insure, as far as human prudence could insure, their beneficial execution.... This provision is made in a constitution intended to endure for ages to come, and, consequently, to be adapted to the various *crises* of human affairs....
>
> We admit, as all must admit, that the powers of the Government are limited, and that its limits are not to be transcended. But we think the sound construction of the constitution must

> allow to the national legislature that discretion, with respect to the means by which the powers it confers are to be carried into execution, which will enable that body to perform the high duties assigned to it, in the manner most beneficial to the people. Let the end legitimate, let it be within the scope of the constitution, and all means which are appropriate, which are plainly adopted to that end, which are not prohibited, but consist with the letter and spirit of the constitution, are constitutional.

On February 25, 1791, Washington signed the Bank Bill. In his remarks at the opening of the Second Congress, Washington would praise the "rapid subscriptions to the Bank of the United States" as a sign of the nation's progress.[13]

Hamilton completed the development of the initial United States monetary system with his January 28, 1791, *Report on the Establishment of a Mint.* In this Report, Hamilton proposed to replace the cacophony of Spanish reals, British pounds, and other foreign and domestic coins with the dollar, which earlier had been adopted by the Continental Congress. The United States dollar would be backed by gold and silver at a fixed ratio of 15 units of silver for one unit of gold, which then was international practice. Hamilton recommended $10 gold coins, silver dollars, silver pence equal to one-tenth of a dollar, copper pence equal to one-hundredth of a dollar, and other copper coins equal to one-half what we now know as the penny. To produce the coins, there would need to be a Mint.

Only the federal government was empowered by the Constitution to produce coins. The states were forbidden to do so.

Hamilton's *Mint Report* had the support of Jefferson. On April 2, 1792, Congress enacted a law establishing a Mint and regulating coins of the United States. The Mint was to be established "for the time being" at "the seat of government of the United States," meaning Philadelphia. Ten dollar gold coins were denominated Gold Eagles, with $5 Half Eagles and $2.50 Quarter Eagles. Ten cent coins were denominated dimes, one cent coins, cents. Hamilton's recommendation of silver-gold ratio of 15-1 was adopted.[14]

Hamilton's third fundamental Report, his December 1791 *Report on Manufacturers,* was an anthem to the United States industrial revolution. It is hard to overstate how primitive United States manufacturing was in 1791. Hamilton listed 17 types of then existing manufacturing, which demonstrated the "[practicability] of success in manufacturing establishments in the United States." These included "tanned and tawed leather dressed skins," "bricks and coarse tiles," "ardent spirits," "writing and printing paper," "hats of fur," "refined sugars," "oils of animals", carriages of all kinds," "snuff, chewing and smoking tobacco," "start and hair powder," "lampblack and other painted colors." The United States, Hamilton wrote, was "addicted to agriculture." He began his *Report on Manufacturing* by rebutting the belief "that agriculture is, not only, the most productive, but the only productive species of industry."

Hamilton envisioned a mixed economy with "the establishment of manufacturers . . . calculated not only to increase the general stock of useful and productive labor, but even to improve the state of agriculture" by increasing the domestic market for "the surplus produce of the soil." Such a mixed economy with a stronger manufacturing base would allow the United States to "exchange with Europe on equal terms" rather than be "the victim of a system" under which the lack of domestic manufacturing fled to "difficulty [obtaining] from abroad manufactured supplies." Hamilton emphasized:

> . . . The extreme embarrassments of the United States during the late War, from an incapacity of supplying themselves, are still matter of keen recollection: A future war might be expected again to exemplify the mischiefs and dangers of a situation, to which that incapacity is still in too great a degree applicable, unless changed by timely and vigorous exertion. To effect this change as fast as shall be prudent, merits all the attention and all the Zeal of our Public Councils; 'tis the next great work to be accomplished.

Business historian Thomas McCraw emphasized the extent that weakness in manufacturing made the United States dependent on Europe, especially Great Britain:

> Even after the war ended in 1782, America's external economy was still tied to the British Empire almost as tightly as it had been before the Revolution. And while the country's imports rose by more than 69 percent during the twenty years from 1770 to 1790, its exports grew by only 2.7 percent, one twenty-sixth as much. This was a path to disaster. For the period 1787–1792, more than 90 percent of all imported manufactures came from Britain.

Hamilton's *Report* proposed two primary means to promote manufacturing—protective duties and bounties.

Protective duties or tariffs "enable the national manufacturers to undersell all their foreign competitors." Hamilton recommended increasing tariffs on several specific commodities such as "steel, raw", whose 1789 tariff would be increased from 75 cents per cubic ton to 100 cents. Hamilton's list included iron, nails, and spikes, manufactured steel and firearms and weapons (in which he recommended tripling the tariff from 5 percent to 15 percent). The selection of items focused on finished goods that could be manufactured in the United States. Hamilton simultaneously recommended lowering or eliminating duties on specific raw materials, such as sulfur (for gunpowder), wood, copper, and cotton. Congress in May 1792 adopted virtually all of Hamilton's recommendations on tariffs.

Hamilton's more ambitious recommendations concerned bounties or subsidies for specific domestic manufacturing to stimulate the growth of manufacturing, which Hamilton characterized as "one of the most efficacious means of encouraging manufacturers, and it is in some views, the best." In Hamilton's *Report*, surplus income from tariffs could provide "a fund paying the bounties which shall have been decreed."

Hamilton targeted bounties to a selective list: Coal, raw wood, sail cloth, cotton, and glass. In Hamilton's analysis, this was necessary given the behavior of competitive foreign nations:

> But the greatest obstacle of all to the successful prosecution of a new branch of industry in a country, in which it was before unknown, consists, as far as the instances apply, in the bounties premiums and other aids which are granted, in a variety of cases, by the nations, in which the establishments to be imitated are previously introduced. It is well known (and particular examples in the course of this report will be cited) that certain nations grant bounties on the exportation of particular commodities, to enable their own workmen to undersell and supplant all competitors, in the countries to which those commodities are sent. Hence the undertakers of a new manufacture have to contend not only with the natural disadvantages of a new undertaking, but with the gratuities and remunerations which other governments bestow. To be enabled to contend with success, it is evident, that the interference and aid of their own government are indispensable.

As Hamilton anticipated in the *Report on Manufacturers*, he ran into a buzzsaw of criticism based on the by then familiar regional opposition of the agrarian South. Madison and Jefferson argued that bounties were not authorized for the national government in the Constitution and only could be provided by state governments. The resistance to bounties was sufficiently effective in 1792 that Congress tabled the full *Report on Manufacturers*, which included Hamilton's bounty recommendations and separate recommendations for inland navigation. In time, each of Hamilton's more far reaching initiatives would be adopted, such as the 3000 mile intracoastal waterway stretching from Boston to Florida that was recommended in 1802 by President Jefferson's Secretary of Treasury Albert Gallatin or the many federal subsidy programs that had been developed in the 20th century such as the National Institutes of Health or National Science Foundation.

Hamilton's promotion of manufacturing occurred simultaneously with the growth of an entrepreneurial economy. Before the United States was formed, only eight for-profit corporations were chartered in the United States. During the 1790s, 311 for-profit corporations were formed, creating banks, insurance companies, canals, bridges and turnpikes, among other purposes. By 1816, Jefferson had been converted from someone who argued "let our workshops remain in Europe" to believing "we must now place the manufacturers by the side of the agriculturist." "A people," Henry Adams would write, "which had in 1787 been indifferent or hostile to roads, banks, funded debt, and nationality, had become in 1858 habituated to ideas and machinery of the sort on a great scale."

To facilitate this transformation, Hamilton underlined his earlier proposal for funded debt and the national bank.[15]

It was with respect to development of a national bank and banking system that the Hamiltonian model stuttered. Throughout much of the 19th and early 20th centuries, the states' rights and strict Constitutional arguments proposed by Jefferson and Madison generally prevailed.

The Bank of the United States (soon to be known as the First Bank of the United States) opened for business in Philadelphia on December 12, 1791, with $10 million in initial capitalization, larger than that of any other corporation in the country. The $8 million the Bank raised from previous investors made this the largest initial public offering in our country's history. When the National Bank opened, there were only four state banks in the country, with a fifth opened in December 1791.

The $2 million invested by the United States in the Bank meant that the United States would receive 20 percent of the Bank's profits. The Bank also accepted deposits from private individuals and businesses and made loans to private citizens and firms.

The Bank was the most prominent actor in United States finance, serving as sole fiscal agent for the United States government economic historians recounted as fiscal agent: The Bank:

> effected payments of interest on the public debt, at home and abroad; it received subscriptions to new issues of government securities; it effected payment of the salaries of government officials, including Thomas Jefferson himself and the numerous Congressmen who believed it to be unconstitutional; "it facilitated the incessant and complicated foreign exchange operations of the Treasury"; it moderated the outflow of specie; and it supplied bullion and foreign coins to the Mint. It helped collect customs bonds, which was a very important part of its business; ... The Bank's notes provided a uniform part of the circulating medium, receivable for all payments due the government. The Bank was the principal depository of government funds, which it transmitted without charge at the Treasury's request, and, in accordance with the act incorporating it, submitted weekly reports of its condition to the Secretary of the Treasury.

The Bank was not the equivalent to a modern central bank such as the Federal Reserve Board. The Bank of the United States did not officially set monetary policy or regulate banks and bank holding companies. A 2009 Federal Reserve history recognized:

> Nonetheless, its prominence as one of the largest corporations in America and its branches' broad geographic position in the emerging American economy allowed it to conduct a rudimentary monetary policy. The bank's notes, backed by substantial gold reserves, gave the country what passed for a more stable national currency. By managing its lending policies and the flow of funds through its accounts, the bank could — and did — alter the supply of money and credit in the economy and hence the level of interest rates charged to borrowers....
>
> In addition, banknotes issued by the First Bank were widely accepted throughout the country. And unlike notes issued by

> state banks, First Bank notes were the only ones accepted for payment of federal taxes.

The Bank supported the United States government "whenever called upon." By the close of 1795, the Bank had lent the United States government $6.2 million, close to two-thirds of its $10 million capital.

The Bank, however, was the subject of intense controversy from the first public subscription for its stock. The Bank's public offering was in multiple steps. Bank stock cost $400 per share, one-fourth in specie (gold or silver), three-fourths in United States debt securities. Initially investors bought *scrips,* a $25 per share down payment towards the full $400 balance due over a two-year period. The *scrips* soon were selling at twice the $25 price with investors borrowing money in order to obtain the Bank's stock.

Historian Ron Chernow described the frenzy of the Bank's first stock offering on July 4, 1791:

> . . . On that memorable day in Philadelphia, the subscription to the stock of Hamilton's central bank was thrown open to an expectant public, and the public promptly went berserk. Speculation was rife that the stock would pay rich dividends of 12 percent or more, and people had been flocking to the capital for a week in anticipation of this first offering. So lusty was the pent-up demand that mobs, dazzled by visions of riches, stormed the building, overwhelming the clerks. The heavily oversubscribed issue sole out within an hour, leaving many disgruntled investors empty-handed. . . .
>
> . . . Even Hamilton never dreamed that the response would be so giddy that it would take less than an hour to complete the offering. . . .
>
> . . . So frenzied was the trading in scrip that many investors doubled their money within days, and the resulting madness was dubbed "scrippomania."

The trading price of scrip was subject to wild gyrations. By early August, scrip with an initial sale price of $25 per share was trading for more than $300 per share. On August 17, when banks stopped offering loans for investors to buy scrip, the United States experienced its first equivalent to a stock market crash, with prices for scrip and for government securities in some cases falling by more than $100. The bursting of the scrip bubble also led to the first government directed stabilization of a private market when Hamilton instructed the cashier of the Bank of New York, a private bank Hamilton earlier had helped form, to purchase $150,000 in government debt securities. Hamilton met with fellow members of the Treasury's Sinking Fund Commission — Thomas Jefferson, Edmund Randolph, John Adams and John Jay — who authorized direct Treasury purchase of Government securities in the marketplace. This set in motion another speculative frenzy with scrip and Government securities reaching even higher prices during the winter of 1791–1792.

For Jefferson, Madison, and others critical of the National Bank, the speculative frenzy alone was evidence that the speculators buying scrip and government securities prices were a "corrupt squadron," who had transformed the Nation's nascent financial markets into a "gaming table." Jefferson wrote: "The spirit of gaming, once it has seized a subject, is incurable. The tailor who has made thousands in one day, tho[ugh] he has lost them the next, can never again be content with the slow and moderate earnings of his needle." Worse yet, was the belief that money invested in scrip could have been used for productive purposes. Jefferson also wrote: "Ships are lying at the wharves, . . . buildings are stopped, capitals are withdrawn from commerce, manufacturers, arts, and agriculture to be employed in gambling, and the tide of public prosperity almost unparalleled in any country is arrested in its course and suppressed by the rage of getting rich in one day."

The concerns of the Bank critics were not purely theoretical, but had some basis in fact. Hamilton had limited the initial subscriptions to the bank stock to Philadelphia, Boston, and New York where existing banks could facilitate sales through private loans. This pattern of sales was consistent with the fervent Madison-Jefferson complaint that the Bank would be used to enrich the North at the expense of the South.

The most fervent Jeffersonian critique was trading in bank stock would lead to insider trading and other forms of corruption by Hamilton's cronies and members of the government. This indeed happened. William Duer was Hamilton's Assistant Secretary of the Treasury until forced to resign in April 1790 after politician William Maclay charged him with providing advance information to friends such as Hamilton's mentor Robert Morris during the Assumption legislation debate. Duer then entered into a partnership with Alexander Macomb, a wealthy land speculator with the intent of "making speculation on the debt of the United States, and in the stock of the bank . . . and at the . . . Bank of New York." Duer planned to form a new bank, the Million Bank and merge the Bank of the United States and the Bank of New York. Duer, it was believed, also sought to corner the market in government securities and bank stock. Hamilton's association with Duer was well known. Hamilton had chosen Duer to be a Governor of the Society for Establishing Useful Manufacturers where Macomb also served as Director. But Hamilton testified with some heat against the proposed merger of Million Bank, the Bank of New York, and the Bank of the United States: "I sincerely hope that the Bank of New York will listen to no coalition with this newly engendered merger." Hamilton characterized the frenzied trading as a "dangerous tumour" in New York's economy.

Duer had borrowed heavily, on occasion at interest rates as high as 6 percent per month. On March 9, 1792, Duer stopped payment to the Treasury and some creditors. On March 12th, the Comptroller of the Treasury wrote to New York's District Attorney requesting that he recover money Duer owed or file suit against him. Duer was jailed two weeks later and subsequently died in prison.

Hamilton used the Treasury's Sinking Fund to stabilize prices in Treasury debt, but the damage to the reputation of the Bank and to Hamilton was done, soon compounded by the failure of Alexander Macomb to pay for stock worth $500,000 and the bankruptcy of 25 New York financiers on March 10, 1792, the day after Duer stopped payment. For Jefferson, Duer was the "King of the Alley," "the fate of the nation seemed to hang on the desperate throws and plunges of gambling scoundrels." Jefferson wrote in cataclysmic terms about "the criminality of this paper system": "[A]t length our paper bubble is burst, the failure of Duer in New York soon brought on others, and there [will be] still more, like nine-pins knocking one another down, till at that place the bankruptcy is become general, every man concerned in paper being broke, and most of the tradesmen and farmers, who lend it to them at an interest of from .3 to 6. per cent a month, have lost the whole."

Jefferson, who harbored the belief that Hamilton sought to orchestrate a monarchial plot met with Washington in October 1792. Hamilton had been vulnerable to this type of charge since he made extended remarks at the Constitutional Convention in June 1787 characterizing the British government as "the best in the world."

Washington rebuffed Jefferson's accusation — presumably he would have been the first King — and defended Hamilton as having revitalized the United States economy when its affairs were desperate and national credit was lost.

Repeated allegations that Hamilton had participated in insider trading in Treasury and Bank securities or misused funds in the Treasury persisted. On December 15, 1792, the Speaker of the House of Representatives Frederick Muhlenberg, accompanied by House Representatives James Monroe and Abraham Veneble, met with Hamilton at his office and presented evidence of "a very improper connection between Hamilton and a Mr. Reynolds." Before presenting a letter to President Washington, they gave Hamilton the opportunity to explain why he had paid over $1000 to James Reynolds, who earlier had been charged with "an infamous crime," by the Department of Treasury, and subsequently had fled the country. Hamilton produced substantial correspondence with James and Maria Reynolds to demonstrate that payments made to James Reynolds were not to facilitate improper pecuniary speculation — the charge Hamilton most feared — but "an amorous connection with his wife for a considerable period with his privity and connivance."

When James Callender later published *The History of 1796* including allegations that Hamilton had engaged in improper financial transactions with James Reynolds, Hamilton published in July 1797 a lengthy pamphlet "fully refuting" "the charge of speculation."[16]

America's first sex scandal badly tarnished Hamilton's reputation and his defense did little to assuage critics of the Bank.

But the mortal risk to the Bank of the United States was not corruption, but that it competed with a growing number of state banks. This risk evolved over 20 years.

The first six years of the Bank's duration were served under United States Presidents and Secretaries of Treasury who were supporters of the Bank — Washington, Secretaries of the Treasury Hamilton and Oliver Wolcott, a close ally of Hamilton. Wolcott continued as Secretary of Treasury under the second President John Adams, who abhorred banks, but was neutral towards the Bank of the United States during a Presidency focused on other issues.

President Jefferson was congenitally hostile to banks, characterizing the Bank of the United States as possessing "the most deadly hostility . . . against the principles and form of our Constitution," once telling Madison that the United States chartering of the Bank of the United States was "an act of treason" against the states and that anyone who tried to "act under authority of a foreign legislature [meaning the Congress of the United States]" ought to be "adjudged guilty of high treason and suffer death accordingly, by the judgment of the state courts" — a view so extreme Madison dismissed Jefferson's opinion as one of his "impressions of the moment." Jefferson was not recorded again as characterizing support for the banks as "high treason," but during and after his Presidency, he continued to excoriate the Bank: "[N]o government [is] safe which is under the vassalage of any self-constructed authorities," "a blot in all our constitutions, which, if not covered, will end in their destruction." It was notable that the most important land transaction in United States history, President Jefferson's Louisiana Purchase in 1803 for $15 million, was handled not by the Bank of the United States, but by the British Barings Bank.

Despite Jefferson's personal antipathy towards the Bank of the United States, his Administration did not act hostilely. Albert Gallatin, Secretary of the Treasury during Jefferson's eight years as President beginning in 1801 and under President Madison until 1814, a 13-year career as Treasury Secretary that was the longest in United States history, was the critical financial leader in their Presidencies. Just as Hamilton was indispensable to Washington, in finance, without Gallatin Henry Adams wrote, "Jefferson would have been helpless." Gallatin, historian Claude G. Bowers wrote, "was the only member of the [Jeffersonian] opposition capable of coping with Hamilton in the field of finance." During his brief term as United States Senator before being forced to resign for failure to satisfy the nine-year citizenship requirement and as a leader in the House, the Swiss born Gallatin was honest, often more interested in what worked than ideology, and fair. In 1801, Jefferson requested that Gallatin investigate Hamilton's blunders and frauds at the Treasury Department. Gallatin did so and later reported to Jefferson: "I have found the most perfect system ever formed. Any change that should be made in it would injury it. Hamilton made no blunders, committed no frauds. He did nothing wrong." In 1809, Gallatin would prepare his own *Report on Manufacturing*, echoing Hamilton's enthusiasm for encouraging and promoting domestic industry. In 1808, Gallatin proposed $20 million in infrastructure improvements to roads and canals, projects that ultimately were achieved beginning with the Cumberland Road running from Maryland and later reaching Illinois.

The bond between Jefferson and Gallatin was a close one. Jefferson deferred to Gallatin on financial matters and always asked Gallatin to prepare the financial portion of his annual message. Gallatin supported Jefferson's goals for "frugal government," paying off the $112 million national debt—which Jefferson informed Gallatin was the highest priority of his Presidency—and eliminating internal taxation including the hated Whiskey Tax, as well as large reductions on spending on the military and the Louisiana Purchase. When Jefferson proposed an embargo against Great Britain in 1807, Gallatin disagreed with Jefferson's course: "In every point of view, privations, sufferings, revenue, effect on the enemy, politics, home, etc., I prefer war to a permanent embargo." Jefferson persisted: "What is *good* in this case cannot be effected. . . . [W]e have therefore, only to find out what will be *least bad*." Gallatin deferred to Jefferson and Jefferson got his embargo. The embargo led to a drastic curtailment of foreign trade. Imports had been $138 million and exports $108 million declined by 1814 to $13 million in imports and $7 million in exports.

Gallatin's support for the National Bank was decisive in tempering Jefferson's abject hostility during the Bank's initial 20-year charter. Gallatin had helped prepare the charter of the Bank of Pennsylvania as a Pennsylvania legislator and in 1796 had argued that banks were essential in a country far from capital markets and with little gold and silver of its own. Gallatin wrote in 1809 in a *Report to Congress* urging the rechartering of the Bank of the United States: "The affairs of the Bank, considered as a moneyed institution, have been wisely and skillfully managed." Jefferson begrudgingly was convinced in 1803 to support a branch of the Bank in New Orleans. Jefferson wrote: "[I]t mortifies me to be strengthening principles which I deem radically vicious [but Gallatin was probably correct] that we can never completely get rid of [Hamilton's] financial system."

To mollify Jefferson and other critics of the Bank, Gallatin's 1809 *Report on the Bank of the United States*, published the day before Jefferson left office, proposed giving both the national and state governments power to appoint directors, expressly requiring the National Bank to lend up to three-fifths of its capital to the national government—taking away the implicit power of the Bank to withhold funds. Gallatin further proposed caps on interest rates charged to the United States and on monthly payments.

Gallatin in 1803 persuaded Jefferson to support the National Bank branch in New Orleans and in his 1809 Report favoring rechartering, stressed the positive advantages of the Bank: It was:

> 1st. A safe place of deposit for the public moneys.
> 2d. The instantaneous transmission of such moneys from any one part of the continent to another, the Bank giving us immediately credit at New York, if we want it, for any sum we may have at Savannah or any other of their offices, and *vice versa.*
> 3d. The great facility which an increased circulation and discounts give to the collection of the revenue.

Gallatin proposed increasing the Bank's capital to $30 million and allowing the states to invest up to $15 million of the expanded capital, with the added sweetener that the Bank would pay interest on government deposits in excess of $3 million. Under Gallatin's proposal, the government could borrow up to $18 million.

The Failure to Recharter the First National Bank

In the 1808 petition for rechartering the National Bank, the Bank's directors highlighted that the United States government as a stockholder had regularly received dividends through the difference between its loan from the Bank at 6 percent and the Bank's dividends on stock which averaged about 8 percent. When the United States sold its stock, it would receive a further profit of over $650,000.

By the time of his Presidency, James Madison no longer opposed the National Bank, but remained silent during the campaign for its rechartering. Gary Wills believed: "By 1811, Madison had changed his mind on the bank though he did not want to make an open break with Jefferson on the issue. He privately assured people that his arguments against the bank, though sound at the time, had been rendered inapplicable by long usage."

Congress did not act on the National Bank's 1808 petition or Gallatin's 1809 report. The National Bank submitted a second petition on December 10, 1810. Gallatin again expressed support on January 30, 1811 after the House had voted not to consider the bill for rechartering on January 24, 1811. A bill to review the charter of the Bank of the United States was introduced on February 5, 1811 in the Senate and defeated on February 20th by a vote of 18 to 17 with George Clinton, Madison's Vice President, casting the deciding vote as President of the Senate. The Bank of the United States closed its doors on March 3, 1811 as a National Bank.

The major Congressional opposition combined two types of opponents. First, Jeffersonian agrarians who continued to challenge the Bank's constitutionality and were critical of the large holdings of Bank stocks owned by foreigners, opening the Bank up to criticism that it was a British bank created by Federalists who no longer held the White House or majorities in Congress.

The major new source of opposition came from the state banks. The number of state banks had grown from four in 1791 when the initial National Bank charter had been issued to 88 in 1811. The National Bank was a creditor of state banks and acted as a check on state bank circulation of paper currency. Historian Gordon Wood aptly recognized:

> [T]he more important enemies of the [Bank of the United States] were the state banks. By regularly redeeming the outstanding notes of the state banks, the [Bank of the United States] had checked their ability to issue notes too far in excess of what they could cover with specie, that is, their reserves; and this had become a deep source of anger. In addition, the state banks resented the monopolistic position the [Bank of the United States] had in holding the national government's deposits and condemned it for being Federalist and British-dominated.

The failure to renew the charter of the Bank of the United States set in motion a stampede of new state banks, from 88 to 246 by 1816. The limits to circulation of paper money in the 1791 Bank of the United States charter or the Constitution's Article I § 10 prohibition on state emission of bills of credit were ignored. "The American economy," as Gordon Wood wrote, "floated on paper." Easy, long-term credit was provided to farmers and small businesses. The benefits of the National Bank were soon sorely missed. Gallatin wrote in 1831: "The dissolution of the Bank of the United States deprived the country of foreign capital of over $7,000,000." More consequentially, the state banks were incapable of helping the United States fund the War of 1812. state bank notes often could not be passed from one part of the country to another, but were limited to local use. The national debt grew from a low of $45 million during Jefferson's Presidency to $127 million in 1815.[17]

Before the closure of the Bank of the United States, Gallatin had arranged for state banks to assume the business of the National Bank. "[T]hey were a poor substitute at best." The Treasury no longer could turn to a bank for quick loans. A total of $61 million in debt was authorized by Congress between 1812 and 1814. Only $45 million could be sold with most of the debt sold at 12 to 20 percent discounts. The United States would borrow $80 million between 1812 and 1816, but receive specie value of only $34 million. As in the Revolutionary War, soldiers were paid in depreciated money which sometimes they would not accept.

The War of 1812 severely aggravated the weaknesses of the state banking system. When Great Britain raided Washington in 1814 and burned the Capitol, White House (then called the President's Mansion) and Treasury and threatened Baltimore, a financial panic ensued. State banks lacked the specie to pay bank customers and in 1814 led to suspension of Species payments in most of the country. The value of bank notes deteriorated with notes trading for 75 to 80 cents in Washington and Baltimore and at discounts elsewhere. The state banks, unlike the Bank of the United States, could issue debt greater than their capital. By 1816, the state banks had issued $170 million of paper currency on $87 million of capital. Economic historian Bray Hammond generalized: "The champions of the Bank of the United States had been justified by the miserable experience consequent on the dissolution of 1811. With the restraints of the old Bank out of the way, private banks had rushed into business, extended too much credit, and suspended *en masse* when trouble came."

"The machinery of government," wrote Second Bank historian Ralph Catterall, "threatened to come to a disastrous stop." Without a national bank, state banks would neither pay specie nor accept each other's notes at par (meaning initial price). The country had no common medium of exchange. The United States government received state revenues in depreciated state bank paper currency. State bank notes in one area of the country would only be traded at a heavy discount in other areas of the country. "The result was that the [federal] government found itself with an enormous mass of depreciated paper currency only in the immediate vicinity of its issue."

Catterall continued:

> In November, 1814, [Treasury] Secretary Dallas was compelled to announce to the holders of government securities in Massachusetts that the treasury could no longer pay the interest on the national debt held in that section, having neither specie nor New England bank notes with which to pay. At the same moment the administration failed to redeem treasury notes at Boston, Philadelphia, and New York; it actually paid some of its soldiers in bank notes which were not receivable in discharge of taxes; it could not obtain funds "to defray the current ordinary expenses of the different departments." The State Department was unable to discharge its stationery bill; "the [T]reasury was obliged to borrow pitiful sums, which it would disgrace a merchant in tolerable credit to ask for;" the War Department could not pay a bill for $3,500; "the paymaster was unable to meet demands for paltry amounts — not even for $30;" the deficit for the coming year would probably reach $40,000,000. Meanwhile, the government "was subsisting upon the drainings of unchartered banks in the District," and on the proceeds of temporary loans procured from various state banks, as a matter of grace on their part.

The War of 1812 led to hyper-inflation. Domestic commodity prices spiked by 20 to 30 percent, cotton doubled in price, imported commodities rose by about 2 percent.

At the state level, some states, most notably Kentucky, passed "relief" legislation designed to delay or stop collection of debts. This was held by the Kentucky Court of Appeals to be unconstitutional on the ground that such legislation impaired the United States Constitution prohibition of state impairment of obligations of contracts. In New York, future President Martin Van Buren would champion legislation as early as 1817 to repeal legislation calling for imprisonment for debt, except in cases of fraud. In 1830, five-sixths of the individuals in New England and middle states jails were debtors, most owing less than $20.

The Second Bank of the United States

President Madison called on Congress to establish a new national bank, which he now endorsed in terms of "expediency and almost necessity." Madison called it "essential . . . that the benefits of a uniform national currency should be restored to the community. The absence of the precious metals will, it is believed, be a temporary evil; but until they can again be rendered the general medium of exchange, it devolves on the wisdom of Congress to provide a substitute."

Congress enacted an initial version of a Second Bank of the United States that Madison vetoed in January 1815 because it provided too little guaranteed support for the National Government, did not necessarily "provide a circulating medium," without which taxes could not be collected, "nor . . . furnish loans, in anticipation of public revenue."

After the War of 1812 was ended by the Treaty of Ghent, Madison and Secretary of Treasury Dallas again proposed a national bank, with Madison emphasizing: "The benefits of a uniform national currency should be restored to the community."

Senator John Calhoun, Chair of the Finance Committee, amplified Madison's critique in remarks on February 26, 1816 on the Senate floor. The state of the currency, he explained, "was a stain on the public and private credit and injurious to the morals of the community." Calhoun urged the state of the currency also was opposed to the principles of the United States Constitution:

> The power was given to Congress by that instrument, in express terms, to regulate the currency of the United States. In point of fact, he said, that power, though given to Congress, is not in their hands. The power is exercised by banking institutions, no longer responsible for the correctness with which they manage it. Gold and silver have disappeared entirely. There is no money but paper money; and that money is beyond the control of Congress. No one, he said, who referred to the Constitution, could doubt that the money of the United States was intended to be placed entirely under the control of Congress. . . . There then existed, he said, a depreciated paper currency, which could only be regulated and made uniform by giving a power for that purpose to the General Government. The states could not do it.

Within five years, state paper currency, Calhoun stated, had increased from $80 or $90 million to $200 million. State banks had issued more paper than they could redeem.

In April 1816, Congress enacted and Madison signed An Act to Incorporate the Bank of the United States. In role reversal the minority Federalists and the Northeast opposed the Second National Bank; Jefferson's party, the Republicans, and the South supported the new Act.[18] Unlike with the First Bank, there was scarcely any discussion about the constitutionality of the Second Bank during Congressional debate.

The Act incorporating the Second Bank in many respects were similar to that of the First Bank. Both banks were not only the largest corporations in the country, they were the only corporations capable of operating nationwide. Both banks had their head offices in Philadelphia and were the principal depository of the United States Treasury. The Second Bank, like other banks of the time, issued its own paper currency. But unlike state banks, the Second Bank's Notes were legal tender that always could be exchanged for gold or silver.

The $10 million in capital in the First Bank had now grown to $35 million in the Second Bank. But the proportion of United States ownership remained 20 percent, meaning the $2 million investment in the First Bank was now $7 million.

As with the First Bank, 80 percent of the subscription was to be held by individuals, companies, corporations or states, with one-fourth payable in gold or silver (now denominated "gold or silver coin of the United States, or in gold of Spain or the denomination of Spain"), three-fourths in funded debt of the United States. Notably when the First Bank was authorized to commence operations when $400,000 in specie was received, the Second Bank was required to receive $8.4 million in specie and public debt.

The length of the charter of both banks was 20 years.

Both banks' minimum amounts of property to be held was capped, $15 million including capital stock in the First Bank, $55 million in the Second Bank. Both banks' ownership of real estate was identically limited.

Bank indebtedness "whether by bond, bill, note or other contract" was limited to $10 million above deposits in the First Bank, to $35 million above deposits in each case unless otherwise authorized by law.

In both banks, the scope of business was limited to banking and dealing in trade or sale of goods was precluded.

Neither bank could purchase public debt. Both banks could sell their government stock for coin or bullion subject to limitations.

In both banks, the rate of interest could not exceed 6 percent.

In both banks, loans to the United States government, states, or foreign states were limited, unless authorized by law.

Both banks were managed by a 25-person board, all directors to be resident citizens of the United States. Both banks had provisions requiring rotation of directors. In the Second Bank, as in the First, no more than three-fourths of the directors could be elected for the following year and no director, except the director who was President of the Bank, could serve more than three years out of four. In both banks, no less than seven directors constituted a board to transact business.

Both banks were required to report to the Treasury weekly statements of account.

In both Acts incorporating the First and Second Banks, no other bank was to be established by the United States during the continuance of the bank.

The Second Bank was nonetheless strikingly different in its organization, context and performance than the First Bank. Over time, it fared less well.

Hamilton's Report that led to a national bank and the formation of the First Bank had emphasized central control of the First Bank. Hamilton had sought to preclude bank branches. His initial subscriptions to the bank stock in three Northern cities had fed the Jeffersonian narrative that the bank was a Northern conspiracy against the South organized to follow hated British models of governance and finance.

The Second Bank, in contrast, provided that subscriptions for the $28 million of stock would be held in 19 geographically dispersed locations:

> Portland, in the District of Maine; at Portsmouth, in the State of New Hampshire; at Boston, in the State of Massachusetts; at Providence, in the State of Rhode Island; at Middletown, in the State of Connecticut; at Burlington, in the State of Vermont; at New York, in the State of New York; at New Brunswick, in the State of New Jersey; at Philadelphia, in the State of Pennsylvania; at Wilmington, in the State of Delaware; at Baltimore, in the State of Maryland; at Richmond, in the State of Virginia; at Lexington, in the State of Kentucky; at Cincinnati, in the State of Ohio; at Raleigh, in the State of North Carolina; at Nashville, in the State of Tennessee; at Charleston, in the State of South Carolina; at Augusta, in the State of Georgia; at New Orleans, in the State of Louisiana; and at Washington, in the District of Columbia.

The subscription process was democratized, the par value of stock was reduced from $400 per share in the First Bank to $100 per share in the Second, shares in the Second Bank could be purchased for an initial per share installment of $5 in specie and $25 either in specie or government securities.

Bank branches were skeletally described in the Act creating the First Bank. The bank directors could establish offices for the purposes of discount and deposit where they thought fit. A discount was the equivalent to an interest payment deducted from the sum lent in advance. In contrast, the Act required the Second Bank's directors to establish "a competent office of discount and deposit in the District of Columbia whenever any law of the United States shall require such an establishment" and an Office of Discount and Deposit in any state in which 2000 shares have been subscribed or held. The Second Bank directors also could establish such bank branches "wheresoever they shall think fit." Or the bank directors could employ any other bank or banks — meaning state banks — with the approval of the Secretary of the Treasury to perform branch office functions. As with the Second Bank's directors, the new Act specified the number of directors in the branches ("not more than thirteen nor less than seven") would be approved for one year terms. The branch bank directors would choose their own president. Each director would be both a United States citizen and a resident of the state, territory, or district in which any branch was established. No more than three-fourths of the directors could be reappointed for the next year. No director, other than the president, could serve for more than three years out of four.

The Second Bank branch bank provision would vastly add to the complexity of managing the Second Bank. By October 1817, 19 branches had been established in: Portsmouth, N.H.; Boston, Mass.; Providence, R.I.; Middletown, Conn.; New York, N.Y.; Baltimore, Md.; Washington, D.C.; Richmond, Va.; Norfolk, Va.; Charleston, S.C.; Savannah, Ga.; New Orleans, La.; Cincinnati, Ohio; Chillicothe, Ohio; Lexington, Ky.; Louisville, Ky.; Pittsburgh, Pa.; Fayetteville, N.C.; and Augusta, Ga. Later, eight other branch banks would be established in Mobile, Ala.; Nashville, Tenn.; Portland, Me.; St. Louis, Mo.; Buffalo, N.Y.; Burlington, Vt.; Utica, N.Y.; and Natchez, Miss.

This meant that every state on the Atlantic seaboard had a branch except New Jersey and Delaware, and in the interior every district, except Indiana and Illinois, similarly had a branch.

From the start, this was decidedly a mixed blessing. Losses in the bank branches in proportion to their capital would be ten times greater than that of the Second National Bank.

The National Bank used the branches to transfer capital among the branches, where the capital would be subject to local management. Sometimes, contrary to Bagehot's admonitions, capital was shifted to those sections of the country where there was weakness. The branch banks, especially during the first two years of the Second Bank, controlled the powers to lend with the national bank unable or unwilling to exert close control.

Governance in the Second Bank was different than in the First. Five directors were appointed by the President with the advice and consent of the Senate. No more than three of these directors could be residents in any one state. There was no preamble in the Second Bank's enabling Act like that in the First National Bank. But the objective of the bank had demonstratably changed. The First Bank of the United States sought a bank to achieve Hamiltonian objectives: "To be conducive to the successful conducting of the national finances; tend to give facility to the obtaining of loans for the use of the government in sudden emergencies; and to be productive of considerable advantage to trade and industry in general."

The overarching objective of the Second Bank was the restoration of an effective currency system through gold or silver or specie payments. The Second Bank Incorporation Act specified: "[T]he [Second Bank] shall not at any time suspend or refuse payment in gold and silver, of any of its notes, bills or obligations; nor of any moneys received upon deposit in said bank, or in any of its offices of discount and deposit."

The Second Bank was obligated to transfer public funds without charging commissions or fees. Deposits of public funds could be made in branches unless the Secretary of Treasury otherwise ordered. The Second Bank was obligated to redeem in specie or pay a 12 percent interest until the demand was satisfied. The Second Bank also was required to pay the United States government $1.5 million for its monopoly as a national bank and in holding United States government resources.[19]

The context in which the Second Bank operated had dramatically changed. There were now hundreds of state banks. The Act incorporating the Second Bank did not eliminate local bank notes.

During its initial years, the Second Bank was badly managed. The Bank was chartered on April 10, 1816, and less than three weeks later on April 30, 1816, Congress ordered specie payments to go into effect on February 20, 1817. The initial president of the Second Bank, William Jones, was appointed in 1816 and proved unequal to the job. Jones, earlier Secretary of the Navy, had succeeded Gallatin as Secretary of the Treasury, where he served until 1814 with what one historian characterized as his "helpless inefficiency." By the time of his appointment as president of the Second Bank in 1816, Jones, a Pennsylvania politician and merchant, had been bankrupt. He was a political appointee. Madison named all five of his directors from his Republican Party.

The Second Bank's most immediate task was to resume specie payments and transfer United States deposits in state banks to the Second Bank. Both tasks were handled clumsily. Secretary of Treasury Alexander Dallas wrote to state banks on July 22, 1816 requesting that they resume payment of specie on all notes with a denomination of less than $5 beginning in October 1816. The state banks refused to do so until July 1, 1817, which was months after Congress's February 20, 1817, deadline. William Crawford, Dallas's successor as Secretary of Treasury, sent a new Circular to the state banks on December 20, 1816, which also "was declined without hesitation." On February 1, 1817, at the invitation of the Second Bank, representatives of key state banks in Philadelphia, New York, Baltimore, and Richmond agreed to a compromise by which state banks would transfer their debt to the Second Bank, but the actual transfer of funds over $8.8 million would not be made until July 1, 1817, when the state banks also would pay interest. Other balances against the State Banks would not be called until the Second Bank had made loans to individuals in the banks — $2 million in New York and Philadelphia, $1.5 million in Baltimore, and $500,000 in Virginia. If the discounts were not taken by individuals, they could be taken by the relevant state banks. While the agreement did succeed in providing a currency in which to pay taxes, the agreement reduced the burden on the state banks and required the Second Bank to defer collecting balances in the ordinary course of business until it had loans of $6 million to individuals or to state banks. Awkward though this compromise was, it did cause state banks to resume specie payments.

The Second Bank February 1, 1817 compromise was, in the words of David Dewey's *History of the Second Bank*:

> a one-sided agreement, with the advantages largely in favor of the local banks. The bank assumed at once the responsibility of paying on a specie basis all drafts which might be drawn by the Government on its deposits, and yet the bank could not draw specie from the local banks by the presentation of their notes for redemption until July 1. Moreover, it forced the [Second] bank to make large loans on the supposition that the local banks would reduce their discounts in order to be enabled to pay over the public funds. By making these loans the [Second] bank endangered its own specie reserve, since the local banks could, in accumulating the bills of the bank, drain it of its specie.

Effective resumption of a currency system required a reduction of state bank loans and state note circulation. Jones' policies to encourage rapid expansion of Second Bank branches, lending freely, and allowing its own branches, especially in the South and West to extend discounts, was inconsistent with the needed contraction of state bank loans and note circulation.

The *raison d'etre* of the Second Bank was to restore an effective currency system by ending what Dewey termed "the evils of the depreciated local currency." The Second Bank's policies here also were counterproductive. The Bank agreed to redeem the notes of all branches at any other branch. The branches had inadequate specie holdings; discounts were made "without limits." The branches in the South and West were encouraged to make large loans. Frequently notes from the Western branches were presented to Northern offices which were ill prepared to redeem them. Early in 1818, the Boston branch refused to receive Southern branch bills. When Northern branches did redeem the Southern and Western notes, they did so in the notes of local banks that became heavily indebted to the branch office.

Indiscriminate redemption did aid in the resumption of specie payments and helped create an acceptable currency throughout the United States. But the policy of indiscriminate redemption could not be justified in financial terms. On August 26, 1818, the Second Bank adopted a new policy prohibiting its branches from taking the notes of other branches except in payments due to the United States.

The initial $28 million subscription was not as rapidly subscribed as had been the subscriptions to the First Bank. With specie requirements at an 8 percent premium, the Second Bank facilitated many sales instead accepting promissory notes, frustrating the intent of Congress to bolster the Bank with gold and silver. Rather than receive $7 million in gold and silver coin, the Bank initially only received $2 million and ended up with $12 million in promissory notes and $14 million (of the $21 million due) in government securities.

Despite these measures after 24 hours, subscriptions were $3 million short to the initial public subscription. Under the Act creating the Second Bank, no shareholder was allowed to own more than 3000 shares nor more than 30 votes. Philadelphia banker Stephen Girard easily circumvented both limitations by employing a phalanx of nominees to purchase shares. Girard bought all $3 million of the initially unsubscribed stock and then resold some of his holdings to associates including John Jacob Astor.

During Jones' term as president, his weakness as an administrator served the bank badly. "Blind ignorance was probably," historian Ralph Catterall opined, "the chief factor in putting the bank in peril." Jones did not fix the capital for the burgeoning number of bank branches or compel the branches to settle accounts periodically. In April 1817, specie in the Second Bank was $1,811,839, half of what it should have been. Nonetheless, a semiannual dividend of 4 percent was declared in January 1818.

A post-War of 1812 economic boom encouraged the Second Bank and United States Treasury to accept and use state bank notes to receive its revenue. This, in turn, encouraged the rapid growth in state banks from 246 in 1816 to 392 in 1818. The laxity of the Second Bank and United States Treasury was particularly egregious. Historian Murray Rothbard explained:

> Bank expansion was spurred by the decision of the Bank of the United States and the Treasury to treat the notes of nominally resuming banks as actually equivalent to specie. The Bank thereby accumulated balances and notes against the private banks without presenting them for redemption. Many of these notes were original Treasury balances which had been deposited with the Bank.

The Jones presidency would be scandalized by bank branch stock loans. Banks in Philadelphia, Cincinnati, and Western and Southern offices discounted the sale of stock loans — a form of mismanagement facilitated by the lack of fixed capital in the branch banks and lack of supervision of their trading. Mismanagement was compounded by fraud. The Baltimore branch allowed a small number of insiders to subscribe to 40,141 shares of Second Bank stock using 15,628 persons as proxies. Insiders in Baltimore were allowed by branch bank officers to borrow from the Bank up to 100 percent of their purchases. The stock was bought at marked discounts meaning the stock for which no money was paid by the insider was likely to achieve an initial profit. Total discounts on the bank stock by three key insiders equaled over $1.5 million which was later characterized as the amount by which the Baltimore bank branch was looted.

In aggregate, the total losses to the Second Bank from mismanagement, speculation and fraud was many millions. In 1818–1819, a House Committee concluded that the Second Bank had violated its charter in purchasing $2 million of public debt, in not requiring all stockholders to pay the second and third installments of their stock in coin and funded debt, in paying dividends to stockholders who had not completed their installments and allowing some stockholders to cast more votes than the charter allowed. A resolution to repeal the charter of the Bank, nonetheless, was defeated by a vote of 121 to 30.

A searing judgment of Jones' presidency was made by economic historian Bray Hammond:

> The Bank yielded. It yielded first to its own greedy stockholders, by helping them get their stock the easiest way possible. It yielded to borrowers in general, living up to the open-handed philosophy which its president . . . expressed . . . ; though by doing so it enlarged its liabilities and exposed its specie to withdrawal. It yielded to the state banks, which sought to frustrate its pressure upon them for the current redemption of their notes. Unreasonable and preposterous though the private banks' position was, the federal Bank itself, in this period, was scarcely better.[20]

Langdon Cheves, the second president of the Bank, was more competent than Jones. Cheves, a former Speaker of the House of Representatives, served from 1819 until 1823. Cheves came to understand that the problem of the Second Bank involved more than "a great want of financial talent":

> I had not the faintest idea that its power had been so completely prostrated or that it had been thus unfortunately managed or grossly defrauded. I never imagined that when it had at so much

> expense and loss imported so many millions of specie, they had been entirely exhausted and were not yet paid for: nor that the Bank was on the point of stopping payment.

Cheves aggressively reformed management of the bank. Salaries were reduced, current expenses cut. By January 1819, 14 new directors were elected to the Second Bank's board. Former President Jones, among others, resigned from the bank in January 1819. Cheves "remorselessly" weeded out incompetent officers and sought prosecution of those who had looted or defrauded bank branches. Litigation and often branch bank board changes occurred in Baltimore, Louisville, Richmond, Fayetteville, and Cincinnati.

Cheves took control with alacrity. The greatest areas of weakness for the Second Bank involved the Southern and Western branches. Within his first 70 days, he ordered branches in the South and West "not to issue their notes" and the Second Bank to cease "to purchase and collect exchange on the South and West." Cheves insisted that balances due from state banks were to be collected. As an emergency measure, the Second Bank borrowed $2 million in Europe. Earlier fears of curtailment or suspension dissipated.

To restore the capital of the Second Bank, Cheves determined that no dividends would be paid until the original capital was intact. These were short term objectives.

Cheves sought three long term objectives: The reduction of active funds; a proper and controlled distribution of capital to the branches; and supervision to ensure that the branches retained capital to which they had been assigned.

To reduce active funds, Cheves insisted that the insolvency debts of Baltimore and elsewhere of 37,954 shares be charged off in full, reducing the Second Bank's capital by $3,795,400. He coordinated investment as far as practicable in the funded debt of the United States. This reversed the Jones policy of selling United States government securities. Cheves increased the Second Bank's investment in United States stock with $6 million in government loans in 1820 and 1821. He further reduced active capital by charging off $10 million in suspended debt, leaving in 1822 only $8 million in active capital, strictly limiting the Bank's ability to make loans.

Cheves' second objective focused on how Second Bank capital would be managed. He transferred funds in the Western and Southern branches to Northern ones, "putting an end to most of the business of Southern and Western offices and . . . compelling them to remit in specie or bills of exchange in Europe or the North, the [Second] Bank by October 1819," correcting to a considerable extent the injurious distribution of the capital by former mismanagement.

To keep the capital stationary in the branches, Cheves created a system in which the Eastern branches were not using specie to redeem Western and Southern branch notes. Cheves initially sought to cease the receipt of branch paper in the Eastern branches in payment of government dues. Secretary of Treasury Crawford declined to support this draconian approach since it would transform the Western and Southern paper into local currencies, capable of circulating at par only within an immediate neighborhood of the relevant branch. Cheves instead using regulatory powers instructed the Western branches not to issue notes larger than five dollars. Cheves required all offices to draw bills of exchange upon other offices only when the branch had established a fund upon which to draw.

Simultaneously, Cheves moved to hold state banks to a strict accountability by insisting upon an immediate reduction of state bank debt and a regular settlement of balances in the future at fixed intervals.

Collectively, these efforts stabilized the Second Bank's finances. By January 1, 1821, the Bank's initial capital was restored in part because of $3.55 million in profits after 1819. By 1821, permanent capital was fixed in the cases of the Southern and Western branches, with the exception of Baltimore. By limiting Second Bank capital to $8 million, "no extensive business was done, and under [Cheves'] management little could be done, for his policy was one of continuous restriction. Since the Western and Southern offices could rarely issue notes, they could not make material discounts, and the measures thus adopted checked Western business almost entirely." Indeed the West and South were almost entirely deprived of the Second Bank's notes because of a September 1819 policy which forbade their issue if the cost of exchange was adverse.[21]

Cheves' presidency occurred during the Panic of 1819, the nation's first depression. Commodity prices fell almost by half because of an unrelated financial crisis in England. Flour prices plummeted to their lowest level since the Revolution. The public would largely blame the Second Bank because of its demands for specie and constriction of currency. The Second Bank also was the object of hostility because of its foreclosure on many real estate properties following the panic. Historian Murray Rothbard explained:

> The Panic of 1819 intensified hostility against the Bank of the United States, and enmity toward the bank grew throughout the country. Aside from long-standing hostility on general political or constitutional grounds, opponents of the bank consisted of the uncompromising wings of two diametrically opposed camps: the inflationists who wanted inconvertible government paper, and the hard money forces who criticized the bank for acting as a national force for monetary expansion.

By 1821, the impact of the Panic of 1819 largely would be over, but the hostility to the Second Bank would endure.

Politically by limiting the Bank's ability to issue notes and bills of credit that could be transferred for specie, Cheves' work in the memorable phrase of bank critic William Gouge: "The Bank was saved, and the people were ruined." The damage to the people and the economy was exaggerated by Gouge, but his remark captured the intensity of branch and state bank opposition to Cheves' rescue of the Second Bank. Cheves' policy of limiting note circulation led to charges that he was creating an unnecessary scarcity of money, denying all regions equality of exchange, leaving currency at the mercy of local state banks, nearly all of whose bills were at a discount except at the place where they were issued.

State bank and regional opposition to first the expansion then the contractionist policies of the Second Bank was heated. Former Presidents Jefferson and Adams and future President John Quincy Adams denounced paper money, with both Adamses excoriating paper money beyond the value of specie, in the words of the elder Adams, as "theft" and bound to depreciate. In several then Western states — Tennessee, Kentucky, Illinois, and Missouri — the response to the tight money policies of the National Bank had been the expansion of new state banks. "In each of these states," historian Murray Rothbard reported, "all the banks had suspended specie payment during the depression. After controversy, they had been allowed to continue in operation, but their notes depreciated rapidly. The legislatures then turned, despite heavy opposition, to establishing the new state-owned banks." Most of the state banks in Ohio failed by 1819:

> The depth of sentiment throughout the West against banks in general and the Bank of the United States in particular, for their excessive expansionist and contractionist activities, was revealed by incidents in rural Ohio. In the fall of 1819, General William Henry Harrison, later President of the United States, was a successful candidate for the Ohio State Senate. A citizens' meeting before the elections criticized him for being a director of a local branch of the Bank of the United States. Harrison, in a lengthy reply, insisted he was a sworn enemy of all banks and especially the Bank of the United States. He declared that he was unalterably opposed to the establishment and continuance of the United States Bank.

These views were not limited to Harrison. In July 1819, the Bank of Nashville campaigned against the Bank of the United States for seeking to "destroy every state bank."

Underlying the state opposition to the Second Bank was a fundamental question of Federalism: Who governed the financial system: The federal government or the states? Most conspicuously, this debate played out in Maryland, Tennessee, Georgia, North Carolina, Kentucky, and Ohio, which had adopted state taxes that applied to the Second Bank. The logic of the state taxes was simple: State banks had to pay state taxes, the Second Bank when it conducted business within a state, did not. National government was accused of "invading the states." As one commentator paraphrased: If the Second Bank could "create a monied institution in the very bosom of the states, paramount to their laws, then indeed is state sovereignty a mere name."

In *McCulloch v. Maryland,* as earlier discussed, Chief Justice John Marshall definitively resolved in 1819 that it was constitutional for the United States Congress to incorporate the Second Bank under the *necessary and proper* clause of the Constitution. Marshall brushed aside the argument that the incorporation of the Bank "invaded state sovereignty" by opining:

> The nation, on those subjects on which it can act, must necessarily bind its component parts. But this question is not left to mere reason: the people have, in express terms, decided it, by saying,

> "this constitution, and the laws of the United States, which shall be made in pursuance thereof," "shall be the supreme law of the land," and by requiring that the members of the state legislatures, and the officers of the executive and judicial departments of the states, shall take the oath of fidelity to it.

McCulloch was most immediately consequential for Marshall's resolution of the second issue: Could a state enact a tax on any bank not chartered by the State?

Writing for a unanimous Court, Marshall decisively rejected the power of states to tax the national government as "the power to destroy":

> If the states may tax one instrument, employed by the government in the execution of its powers, they may tax any and every other instrument. They may tax the mail; they may tax the mint; they may tax patent rights; they may tax the papers of the custom-house; they may tax judicial process; they may tax all the means employed by the government, to an excess which would defeat all the ends of government. This was not intended by the American people. They did not design to make their government dependent on the states.

Marshall's conclusions in *McCulloch* were affirmed in 1824 in *Osborn v. Bank of the United States,* a decision involving an attempt by Ohio to tax the Second Bank, whose law Marshall wrote was "certainly much more objectionable than that of Maryland." Ohio's position was that it did not seek to tax the Bank, but its trade or operations. Chief Justice Marshall firmly rejected this distinction:

> The distinction between destroying what is denominated the corporate franchise, and destroying its vivifying principle, is precisely as incapable of being maintained, as a distinction between the right to sentence a human being to death, and a right to sentence him to a total privation of sustenance during life. . . .
>
> This distinction, then, has no real existence. To tax its faculties, its trade, and occupation, is to tax the bank itself. To destroy or preserve the one, is to destroy or preserve the other.[22]

In the short term, the Second Bank won the battle, but for most of the next 95 years, the claims of the states to regulate national finance would prevail.

Nicholas Biddle

In 1823, Cheves was succeeded by the most talented of the Second Bank's presidents, Nicholas Biddle, who served until the closure of the Bank in 1836. Biddle was 37 years old when he assumed the presidency. He had served as a Senator in the Pennsylvania legislature and as a government director since 1819. Biddle had been an editor of the Lewis and Clark expedition journals. He was admitted to Princeton at the age of 10 and graduated at 13. A lawyer, he also edited a commercial digest and as one historian put it: "Having a taste for economic subjects, and being thoroughly read in Smith, Ricardo and the French economists, he threw himself with enthusiasm into the study of banking and monetary questions."

Biddle's presidency had two distinct periods. The first seven years, 1823 to roughly 1830, was a period in which his skill as an early central banker achieved striking results. During most of these years, the services of the Bank were valued by the administrators of Presidents Monroe and John Quincy Adams. The last six years were dominated by Jackson's War on the Bank. Throughout both periods, the Second Bank was the largest corporation in the United States, indeed, one of the largest in the world.

Much would be made of the defects of Biddle's character during the Jacksonian assault, but no serious criticism could be made of his extraordinary ability or indefatigable work habits. He was, as Ralph Catterall wrote, "a man of intense energy, autocratic in temper, and possessing supreme confidence in his own judgment."

From the start, Biddle pursued markedly different policies than Cheves.

First, in stark contrast to Cheves who sought to decrease the Second Bank's circulation of funds and starve the South and West of currency, Biddle systematically worked to enlarge currency circulation. Biddle, in 1832, testified to Congress that "the great object . . . to which the bank has for many years directed its anxious attention, has been to identify itself thoroughly with the real business of the country." Biddle reversed Cheves focus on branches in the Northern and Middle states and primarily sought to employ the Second Bank funds "in those sections of the Union where there is less banking capital [meaning the Southern and Western states] and where production of the great staples of the country seen to require [the] most assistance in bringing them into the commercial market."

Biddle employed several techniques to achieve greater circulation of currency. To create state bank notes that could be safely received in all branches of the Second Bank, Biddle focused on ending the depreciation of state bank notes by having Second Bank branches engage in constant settlement of state bank notes and the issue of the branch bank's own notes. When this was done, the Second Bank branches could receive each other branch's notes with less risk.

At the same time, the Second Bank expanded the purchase of bills of exchange in the South and West. Bills of exchange historically had allowed a merchant to ship goods to a distant city and receive payment for the goods before they were sold and money in the sale returned to the merchant. "The proceeds from the bills," wrote Second Bank historian Ralph Catterall, "provided a fund for the redemption of the note issues of the Southern and Western offices, and thus made possible extensive loans in those sections without threatening the danger of transferring capital thither from the other offices." Monthly Note circulation when Biddle began his presidency was $4,432,000; by June 1826, it had increased to $9,616,000.

Second, Biddle sought to strengthen the currency of the United States by diminishing the issues of state banks. Biddle saw a basic purpose of the Second Bank was to furnish "a sound currency to the Union, and that could only be done by forcing the state banks to redeem their [notes] in specie on demand." To provide the West and South with funds without the risk of requiring his branches to settle accounts in specie, Biddle popularized branch drafts or bills of exchange. The bank drafts looked like bank notes in design, color, and texture and like notes were in five, ten, and after 1831 twenty dollar denominations. The drafts were accepted by the Treasury to pay taxes and generally operating as a form of currency. Unlike notes, which could be settled by specie, branch drafts could only be issued on a deposit of money in a bank. In actual use, the Second Bank made no distinction between branch notes and branch drafts. Biddle explained: "The branch draughts being, in practice, substitution for branch notes, are considered in all respects the same." But critically, branch drafts added to the circulation of currency in the South and West without removing specie from these regions. Between 1823 and 1836, investment in bills of exchange at the Second Bank increased from $1.9 to $19.3 million.

Third, Biddle ran the Second Bank on conservative and profit-making principles. In an early official letter, Biddle wrote: "We have had enough, and more than enough of banking in the interior. We have been crippled and almost destroyed by it. It is time to concentrate our business — to bank where there is some use and some profit in it, . . . to make at present the large commercial cities the principal scene of our operations."

The capital of the Second Bank was employed where it would be most useful and safe, largely in cities along the Atlantic coast. Historian Ralph Catterall explained:

> New York was made the center of extensive operations, being instructed to secure all the good paper it possibly could, while the funds of the bank were so managed as to protect it against inimical action by state banks and brokers. To make this possible, the office was to cease the issue of state-bank notes, using its own exclusively; to reduce the balances of the city banks due to it, and compel them to settle all their debts in specie at least once a week.

The Second Bank itself controlled the specie held at individual branches, which were prohibited from selling it.

Biddle reduced Second Bank risk by requiring loans to be for short periods and only on good commercial paper. The New York Branch was directed to loan on paper only for 60 and 90 days with exceptions up to 120 days, if "beyond all exception and for a good customer." In 1825, Biddle rejected the request of a branch president to lend for longer periods in an effort to achieve larger profits. "Let us not," Biddle wrote, "by the hope of doing better or getting more business risk the prosperity and safety of the institution." Loans and real estate or stock were forbidden because of their "tendency to lock up the funds of the institution."

To ensure conservative management, Biddle kept the branches under a close supervision. Cheves had sought to restrict runaway branch operations by restricting their business. This prevented loss, but the Bank of the United States was virtually nonexistent in the West and Southwest. Biddle viewed Cheves's approach as intolerable and instead designed strict measures of control for the branches as a basis of allowing them to subsequently expand their business. Biddle enlarged the functions of the branch cashiers, making them the confidential officers of the Second Bank's board.

Biddle sought to accumulate surplus. In 1823 there was not a dollar of accumulated profits. By the end of his 13-year term, the surplus had grown to $6 million. He sold forfeited stock in 1825 to achieve a profit of $481,000. He charged a 1½ percent premium for purchasing bills of exchange, which would be criticized as usurious since this premium for a 90-day bill equaled 12 percent per annum. Dividends to shareholders were stabilized at 6 percent in 1826 to 1828 and subsequently at 7 percent.

Biddle's management of the Bank was a success in financial terms. During Biddle's terms, the United States began an industrial revolution with phenomenal growth in transportation projects such as the Erie Canal completed in 1825 and the Baltimore and Ohio Railroad begun in 1828. By 1825, steamboats "were found everywhere from the Hudson to the Mississippi — the result," Catterall wrote, "was a tremendous reduction in the cost of transportation, an enormous increase in the volume of production, and a marked diminution of the price of the commodities transported. The American industry most profoundly affected was the cultivation of cotton, a commodity in great request after 1824. . . . Times were good and everyone wanted to borrow."

Jon Meacham in his biography of Jackson rhapsodized:

> In Jackson's era, America was moving from a way of life based on farms to one fundamentally linked to a larger industrialized economy. Railroads, canals, and roads were tying the country together. Factories were growing, manufacturing burgeoning. When Jackson became President, the railroad was hardly more than a dream; by the end of the 1830s, there were 3,200 miles of track. The cotton textile workforce more than tripled from 1820 to 1840, and the number of iron wage earners increased fivefold. . . . Regular transatlantic steamship travel began in 1838.

"Paper money," biographer Arthur Schlesinger wrote, "underwrote and stimulated the contagion of enterprise." Between 1828 and 1833, the ratio of paper money to specie grew from 3 to 1 to 8.5 to 1.

The Second Bank was highly profitable, earning more than $3 million in net profits by 1824 while conducting 20 percent of the nation's banking business. Between 1820 and 1832, total Bank assets including notes, bills of exchange, loans, and cash grew from $73.6 million to $131.9 million. Much of the Bank's growth occurred in the Southwest and West. In 1832, it was calculated that the discount and exchange dealings of bank branches in the Southwest and West had grown to $36.4 million of a total of $70.4 million, 52 percent. Biddle had largely secured control of the banking business on inland exchange, offering better interest rates than competitive state banks. This was explicable. The Second Bank had advantages over its competition, including branches throughout the United States, notably in New Orleans, Nashville, Louisville, and Lexington, and capital large enough for the Bank to deal in exchange more extensively than state banks. In 1831–1832, the Second Bank had to contract because of overexpansion of Western loans, but troublesome as these difficulties were, the bank itself continued on sound financial footing.[23]

Andrew Jackson and the War on the Bank

The most consequential actor in United States financial regulation through 1913 was not Hamilton, Gallatin or Biddle, but Andrew Jackson, whose 1832 veto of the bill to extend the charter of the Second Bank of the United States decisively changed the course of financial regulation for the next eight decades.

Jackson was a larger than life figure, a military leader and hero of the War of 1812 where in New Orleans in 1815 Jackson won a legendary victory, a victory as Meacham put it "reminiscent of Shakespeare's Henry V at Agincourt." The British lost nearly 300 men with 1200 wounded and hundreds more taken prisoner or missing. Only 13 Americans died. Jackson was more than a war hero — a lawyer who served in the United States House of Representatives and United States Senate and from 1798 to 1804 on the Tennessee Supreme Court. Unlike the more genteel first six presidents, Jackson also was a Westerner, a self-made man, owner of the Hermitage plantation near Nashville, Tennessee, "landed, proud, individualistic, slave-owning and more bound," wrote economic historian Bray Hammond, "by the cruder conventions than the political ones. Cock-fighting, betting, horse racing, and the punctilio of the duel seem to have satisfied [his] cultural needs." To the more refined Albert Gallatin, Jackson was a pugnacious animal. "Jackson," as biographer Arthur Schlesinger wrote, "did indeed bear the reputation of being intemperate, arbitrary and ambitious for power." He also could be urbane, reserved, and formal rather than the border savage his political opponents made him out to be.

By nature, used to getting to the heart of the matter rather than scholarly, Jackson above all else in the decisive battles of his presidency could be uncompromising. He played to win. He was known as Old Hickory by his soldiers because of his toughness.

Jackson had led United States state militias in the Creek War, decisively won by Jackson at the Battle of Horseshoe Bend in 1814 in revenge for the Creek massacre of American settlers in 1813 at Fort Mims.

Jackson's memory of the massacre of American settlers would influence his presidency. Jackson's victory required the Creeks to surrender 23 million acres of land to the United States in Alabama and Georgia. From 1816 until 1818, Jackson led United States troops in Florida against the Seminole Indians. After Jackson captured Pensacola, Spain sold Florida to the United States in 1819.[24]

In 1824, Jackson ran for president in a four way race against Secretary of State John Quincy Adams, Speaker of the House Henry Clay, and Secretary of the Treasury William Crawford. Jackson won a plurality of the popular vote but did not secure an Electoral College majority. The House of Representatives chose John Quincy Adams to be the nation's sixth president. Jackson never forgave Henry Clay, whom Jackson characterized as "certainly the basest, meanest scoundrel that even disgraced the image of his God." The feelings were mutual. Clay opposed Jackson on principle — he was an heir to Hamilton's view of the national government. Clay also distrusted Jackson's temperament, which Clay feared might turn the United States into a dictatorship.

In 1828, Jackson ran again and decisively defeated President Adams winning 56 percent of the popular vote and the Electoral College by 178 to 83. The Second Bank was not an issue in the 1828 election. Among others, Nicholas Biddle voted for Jackson.

Jackson rose to power as a champion of American democracy. What was then termed universal suffrage would be adopted by nearly all of the states by 1828. This meant that all white males were eligible to vote. Property ownership and tax payment requirements were eliminated. National turnout increased from 27 percent in the 1824 election to 57 percent in 1828.

Jackson in 1828 was buoyed by a social movement as well as founding what became the Democratic Party. Bray Hammond wrote: "[T]he Jacksonian revolution signified that a nation of democrats was tired of being governed, however well, by gentlemen from Virginia and Massachusetts."

De Touqueville in his celebrated 1835 *Democracy in America* began:

> Amongst the novel objects that attracted my attention during my stay in the United States, nothing struck me more forcibly than the general equality of conditions. I readily discovered the prodigious influence which this primary fact exercises on the whose course of society, by giving a certain direction to public opinion, and a certain tenor to the laws; by imparting new maxims to the governing powers, and peculiar habits to the governed. I speedily perceived that the influence of this fact extends far beyond the political character and the laws of the country, and that it has no less empire over civil society than over the government; it creates opinions, engenders sentiments, suggests ordinary practices of life, and modifies whatever it does not produce. The more I advanced in the study of American society, the more I perceived that the equality of conditions is the fundamental fact from which all others seem to be derived, and the central point at which all my observations constantly terminated.

Daniel Walker Howe, author of *What Hath God Wrought: The Transformation of America, 1815–1848*, in contrast characterized:

> Andrew Jackson's greatest legacy to posterity was the Democratic Party. His popular appeal had created it; the decisions he reached in the White House became its politics. . . . Until the Civil War transformed America, the Democratic Party continued along the trajectory Jackson had set, endorsing popular sovereignty, opposing a national economy and national economic planning, promoting continental expansion, and protecting slavery.

Jackson framed his core beliefs tersely in his second inaugural address on March 4, 1833: "In the domestic policy of this government there are two objects which especially deserve the attention of the people and their representatives, and which have been and will continue to be the subjects of my increasing solicitude. They are the preservation of the rights of the several states and the integrity of the Union."

By his second term, Jackson held, Arthur Schlesinger believed, a "deepening belief that the economic problem, the balance of class power, overshadowed all other questions of the day."

For his second term, Jackson chose Martin Van Buren to be Vice President. Van Buren had been elected New York governor in

1828 and in a short term supported ending monopoly privileges for state banks and creating a Safety Fund plan to fortify state bank paper currency by requiring each bank to contribute to a fund that could be drawn upon to redeem the notes of any bank that became insolvent. Jackson earlier had virulently opposed a Tennessee relief statute in 1819, acting then like a representative of the landholding aristocracy. Van Buren had been an early proponent of abolishing imprisonment for debt and in 1832, the same year Jackson chose Van Buren to be his Vice President, Jackson successfully supported a federal law to abolish such imprisonments on the logic that "it should be the care of the republic not to exert a grinding power over misfortune and poverty."

For Jackson, payment in full of the national debt in 1835 was a proud achievement. This was pursued relentlessly through his Presidency. "I will not borrow a cent," Jackson insisted, "except in cases of absolute necessity." This meant that Jackson in some instances favored internal improvements such as roads, bridges and canals being funded solely by the states. In May 1830, Jackson vetoed a bill that authorized the federal government to subscribe to the stock of a Kentucky company for a turnpike from Maysville to Lexington, Kentucky. In his autobiography, Van Buren would characterize Jackson's refusal of federal aid for internal improvements as one of the administration's leading lines of policy. Van Buren believed that government aid to private companies should end. By 1830, this was a significant change in federal policy and frustrated for a time a link in a national road that connected the Natchez Trace to the South and the Ohio with the Tennessee river systems. This was justified on states' rights principles. Jackson also was pleased to veto the Maysville Road that passed through Henry Clay's hometown.

Jackson memorably would adumbrate his view of limited federal government in his 1837 Farewell Address:

> It is well known that there have always been those amongst us who wish to enlarge the powers of the General Government, and experience would seem to indicate that there is a tendency on the part of this Government to overstep the boundaries marked out for it by the Constitution. Its legitimate authority is abundantly sufficient for all the purposes for which it was created, and, its powers being expressly enumerated, there can be no justification for claiming anything beyond them. Every attempt to exercise power beyond these limits should be

> promptly and firmly opposed, for one evil example will lead to other measures still more mischievous; and if the principle of constructive powers or supposed advantages or temporary circumstances shall ever be permitted to justify the assumption of a power not given by the Constitution, the General Government will before long absorb all the powers of legislation, and you will have in effect but one consolidated Government.

Jackson was no angel. He popularized the spoils system and viewed "[o]ffice . . . as a species of property." During Jackson's time, New York Senator William Marcy would declaim: "To the victors belong the spoils." Jackson was repulsed by the possibility that Second Bank branches in Lexington, Charleston, and Portsmouth had sought his defeat in the 1828 election and may not have been assuaged by Biddle's sanctimonious response to the Postmaster General in 1829 that bank branch directors should be selected from both parties. Biddle decried political appointments and argued that a system of political balance would result "almost inevitably" in the selection of "incompetent or inferior persons."

The historical judgment of the Jackson presidency was most critical of the enthusiasm with which Jackson pursued Indian removal. Starting with his First Annual Message to Congress in December 1829, Jackson sought voluntary emigration of Indians inhabiting parts of Georgia and Alabama to "a home in a distant land." The policy was unequivocally racist. In his Second Annual Message in December 1830, Jackson reported:

> that the benevolent policy of the Government, steadily pursued for nearly 30 years, in relation to the removal of the Indians beyond the white settlements is approaching to a happy consummation. Two important tribes [the Choctaw and Chickasaw] have accepted the provision made for their removal at the last session of Congress, and it is believed that their example will induce the remaining tribes also to seek the same obvious advantages.

In Jon Meacham's view:

> Jackson believed in removal with all his heart, and by refusing to entertain any other scenario, he was as ferocious in inflicting harm on *a* people as he often was in defending the right of those he thought of as *the* people. To Jackson the interests of whites were paramount in the removal question. To those who argued

> for Indian rights, he justified his course by arguing that removal would guarantee the survival of the tribes, which would otherwise be wiped out, and by asserting that coexistence was impossible.

Jackson, contrary to the claim of Horace Greeley, probably did not state "John Marshall has made his decision, now let him enforce it" in response to the Supreme Court decision in *Worcester v. Georgia*, which held that a Georgia law to prosecute an individual living in the Cherokee Nation was "repugnant to the Constitution, laws and treaties of the United States." But Jackson was responsible for the Trail of Tears under which in 1838 16,543 Cherokees were forcibly removed from Georgia to Oklahoma and an estimated 2000 to 8000 died along the way. In all, between 1831 and 1842, close to 60,000 Choctaw, Creek, Chickasaw and Cherokee were removed from the United States, mostly to territories west of the Mississippi River.

Jackson similarly would be ferocious in opposing South Carolina and his first Vice President John C. Calhoun, who sought the state power to nullify federal laws with which they disagreed. The crisis in the 1830s was triggered by South Carolina's opposition to federal tariffs. Jackson was a strong friend of States' rights, but adamant in his opposition to any act that threatened to undermine the nation. In April 1830, Jackson had memorably declared: "Our Union — it must be preserved" as nullification fever escalated. Vice President Calhoun supported a nullification doctrine that would enable a state to void a federal law within its borders and announced in May 1832 that he would not be a candidate for Vice President later that year and returned to his native South Carolina to champion nullification. In November 1832, South Carolina's legislature adopted the Ordinance of Nullification, declaring that the United States 1828 and 1832 tariffs would be unenforceable in South Carolina after February 1, 1833. Jackson led Congress in enacting the Force Act in March 1833 under which the president was authorized "to employ such part of the land or naval forces, or militia of the United States, as may be deemed necessary for the purpose of preventing the removal of such vessel or cargo [used to collect duties on imports], and protecting the officers of the customs in retaining the custody thereof." A compromise tariff of 1833 defused the 1830s crisis. Jackson had been prepared to use military force if a peaceful resolution proved impossible.[25]

Jackson's campaign against the Second Bank of the United States began less definitively. He did not mention the Bank in his March 4, 1829, Inaugural Address, although he did address several other leading policy topics including the management of the public revenue, standing armies, the Navy, the national militia and relations with Indian tribes.

In November 1829, Second Bank President Biddle visited Jackson in Washington and presented a plan to pay off the national debt which Jackson supported. "But," the President informed Biddle:

> I think it right to be perfectly frank with you — I do not think the power of Congress extends to charter a bank out of the ten mile square. I do not dislike your bank any more than all banks. But ever since I read the history of the South Sea Bubble I have been afraid of banks. I have read the opinion of John Marshall, who I believe was a great and pure mind — and could not agree with him.

Biddle expressed his gratitude for Jackson's frank explanation and for his willingness to mention the Bank's role in paying off the national debt in the President's Annual Message to Congress.

In December 1829, Jackson delivered his First Annual Message to Congress, which emphasized foreign relations, tariffs, extinguishment of the national debt, made possible in part by the aid of "the judicious arrangements of officers in the Bank of the United States," sharing of the subsequent surplus with the states according to their ratio of representation, states rights, discharge of imprisoned debtors, and Indian removal. Only in two paragraphs near the end of his message did Jackson address the Second Bank where he stated *in toto*:

> The charter of the Bank of the United States expires in 1836, and its stock holders will most probably apply for a renewal of their privileges. In order to avoid the evils resulting from precipitancy in a measure involving such important principles and such deep pecuniary interests, I feel that I cannot, in justice to the parties interested, too soon present it to the deliberate consideration of the legislature and the people. Both the constitutionality and the expediency of the law creating this bank are well questioned by a large portion of our fellow citizens, and it must be admitted by all that it has failed in the great end of establishing an uniform and sound currency.

> Under these circumstances, if such an institution is deemed essential to the fiscal operations of the Government, I submit to the wisdom of the Legislature whether a national one, founded upon the credit of the Government and its revenues, might not be devised which would avoid all constitutional difficulties and at the same time secure all the advantages to the Government and country that were expected to result from the present bank.

The references to the constitutionality of the Bank, the failure to establish a uniform sound currency, and the potential of a different kind of national bank prompted both Houses of Congress to refer Jackson's assertions to committees. Both the Senate and House committees upheld the Bank. The Senate Committee concluded in part:

> On the whole the committee are of opinion that the present state of the currency is safe for the community and eminently useful to the Government; that for some years past it has been improving by the infusion into the circulating medium of a larger portion of coin and the substitution of the paper of more solvent banks in lieu of those of inferior credit; and that if left to the progress of existing laws and institutions, the partial inconveniences which still remain of the paper currency of the last war will be wholly and insensibly remedied. Under these circumstances they deem it prudent to abstain from all legislation, to abide by the practical good which the country enjoys, and to put nothing to hazard by doubtful experiments.

The House Committee directly addressed each of Jackson's concerns, amplifying the Senate's support of bank operations, asserting that the bank "actually furnished a circulating medium more uniform than specie" and derided Jackson's proposed bank "founded upon the credit of the government and revenues" as likely inefficient, "a patronage," "dangerous in its character," and "a centralizing agency of enormous potency."

With respect to constitutionality, the House Committee described the unanimous United States Supreme Court opinion in *McCulloch v. Maryland*, the acquiescence of Jefferson, the reversal by Madison of his original opinion, and the approval of the Bank's constitutionality by both parties.

Jackson was annoyed by the House Committee's criticism of his embryonic Bank plan and privately wrote in June 1830 that the Second Bank was "the present hydra of corruption, so dangerous to our liberties by its corrupting influences everywhere and not the least in the Congress of the Union."

Jackson next communicated publicly about the Bank in his Second Annual Message to Congress in December 1830. Here he wrote with greater precision about his plan for a new national bank:

> The importance of the principles involved in the inquiry whether it will be proper to recharter the Bank of the United States requires that I should again call the attention of Congress to the subject. Nothing has occurred to lessen in any degree the dangers which many of our citizens apprehend from that institution as at present organized. In the spirit of improvement and compromise which distinguishes our country and its institutions it becomes us to inquire whether it be not possible to secure the advantages afforded by the present bank through the agency of a Bank of the United States so modified in its principles and structures as to obviate constitutional and other objections.
>
> It is thought practicable to organize such a bank with the necessary officers as a branch of the Treasury Department, based on the public and individual deposits, without power to make loans or purchase property, which shall remit the funds of the government, and the expense of which may be paid, if thought advisable, by allowing its officers to sell bills of exchange to private individuals at a moderate premium. Not being a corporate body, having no stock holders, debtors, or property, and but few officers, it would not be obnoxious to the constitutional objections which are urged against the present bank; and having no means to operate on the hopes, fears, or interests of large masses of the community, it would be shorn of the influence which makes that bank formidable. The states would be strengthened by having in their hands the means of furnishing the local paper currency through their own banks, while the Bank of the United States, though issuing no paper, would check the issues of the state banks by taking their notes in deposit and for exchange only so long as they continue to be redeemed with specie. In times of public emergency the capacities of such an institution might be enlarged by legislative provisions.
>
> These suggestions are made not so much as a recommendation as with a view of calling the attention of Congress to the possible modifications of a system which cannot continue to exist in its present form without occasional collisions with the local authorities and perpetual apprehensions and discontent on the part of the states and the people.

Jackson's references to "dangers which many of our citizens apprehend from that institution [the Second Bank] as at present organized" and his skepticism as to whether the bank could be "modified in its principles and structures as to obviate constitutional and other objections," sounded ominous. But in context less alarming than they might appear. Jackson in fact made no recommendation to Congress but rather called "the attention of Congress to the possible modifications of a system which can not continue in its present form without occasional collisions with local authorities and perpetual apprehension and discontent on the part of the states and the people."

Biddle knew he had ample majorities in both Houses of Congress to enact a new charter but not enough to override a presidential veto. Jackson's critical remarks in his Second Annual Message were near the end of a lengthy Annual Message with an even longer list of topics to address than the First Message. In Jackson's Third Annual Message delivered in December 1831, his one muted paragraph about the Bank was the next to last in the text and simply stated:

> Entertaining the opinions heretofore expressed in relation to the Bank of the United States as at present organized, I felt it my duty in my former messages frankly to disclose them, in order that the attention of the legislature and the people should be seasonably directed to that important subject, and that it might be considered and finally disposed of in a manner best calculated to promote the ends of the Constitution and subserve the public interests. Having thus conscientiously discharged a constitutional duty, I deem it proper on this occasion, without a more particular reference to the views of the subject then expressed to leave it for the present to the investigation of an enlightened people and their representatives.[26]

It was after Jackson's timorous Third Annual Message to Congress that Biddle and supporters of the Bank badly misplayed their hand. In January 1832, Biddle supported the Bank's petition for rechartering four years before the Bank's Charter would expire and 10 months before the November 1832 Presidential election. The nominee of what was then the Republican Party would be Henry Clay, whom Jackson loathed. Clay was an unabashed supporter of rechartering.

By 1832, opposition to the Bank within Jackson's Administration and in the states had intensified.

Within Jackson's closest circle of advisers, editor Amos Kendall; Roger Taney, Attorney General, who in June 1832 wrote Jackson an influential letter denying the constitutionality of the Second Bank; Congressmen Churchill Cambrelang; Senator Thomas Hart Benton and Vice President Van Buren, all supported ending the Bank. Jackson ardently championed this view. In 1832, Jackson complained to Van Buren: "The Bank, Mr. Van Buren, is trying to kill me, but I will kill it."

In some states, opposition to banks had long been building. A New York legislative committee in 1818, for example, stated:

> Of all aristocracies, . . . none more completely enslave a people than that of money; and in the opinion of your committee, no system was ever better devised so perfectly to enslave a community, as that of the present mode of conducting banking establishments. Like the Syren of the fable, they entice to destroy. They hold the purse strings of society; and by monopolizing the whole of the circulating medium of a country, they form a precarious standard, by which all property in the country, houses, lands, debts and credits, personal and real estate of all descriptions, are valued; thus rendering the whole community dependent on them; proscribing every man who dares to expose their unlawful practices: if he happens to be out of their reach, so as to require no favors from them, his friends are made the victims. So no one dares complain.

The power of the state banks had grown. By 1830, there were 330 state banks, each capable of circulating notes. In 1830, collectively, the state banks had issued roughly three times as much paper currency ($61.3 million) as they had specie ($22.1 million). In some states, such as Kentucky, there was opposition to the Second Bank's efforts to restrain state bank note circulation. Some states and state banks were covetous of United States deposits in the Second Bank. New York State banks long resented the location of the Second Bank in Philadelphia, which stunted New York City's opportunity to be the nation's financial capital.

Jabez Hammond, a contemporary and admirer of Martin Van Buren and Andrew Jackson, later wrote that the state bank attack on the Bank of the United States had the support of state banks in different states and especially New York banks subject to the expense and regulation of the Safety Fund:

> More than two-thirds of the revenue of the United States, amounting to many millions annually, was paid into the United States Branch Bank and when there was under the absolute control of the mother Bank at Philadelphia. The state banks

> believed that if the United States Bank should be annihilated, these immense deposits would be made in their own vaults, and hence all the benefits arising from deposits and also the whole profits of the very great circulation of the United States to the state banks—without compelling them to increase their own capital to the amount of a single dollar.

There was bitter resentment of the power of the Second Bank. Arthur Schlesinger, in *The Age of Jackson*, wrote of the Bank's power:

> ...It enjoyed a virtual monopoly of the currency and practically complete control over credit and the price level. Biddle's own testimony disclosed its extent:—
>
> > Q.3. Has the bank at any time ever oppressed any of the state banks?
> >
> > A. Never. There are very few banks which might not have been destroyed by an exertion of the powers of the bank. None have ever been injured.
>
> To radical Democrats like Taney, Biddle's tone implied that he thought himself entitled to credit for his forbearance. "It is this power concentrated in the hands of a few individuals," Taney declared, "—exercised in secret and unseen although constantly felt—irresponsible and above the control of the people or the government for the 20 years of its charter, that is sufficient to awaken any man in the country if the danger is brought distinctly to his view.

In the period of Jackson's veto, the Bank was frequently charged with winning support from members of Congress and other politicians by providing them loans, sometimes with insufficient collateral, and extending other favors not granted to other individuals. It was asserted that the Bank "subsidized the press" by granting printers and publishers loan accommodations on easy terms. Catterall, who made the most exhaustive investigation of these charges, having reviewed not only public documents but also Biddle's private papers found no evidence of Biddle or the Bank spending a dollar corruptly.

The most detailed assault on the Second Bank would be made by journalist William Gouge, widely viewed as the Jacksonian antibank authority. In 1833, Gouge published *A Short History of Paper Money and Banking in the United States.* "Probably no work in economics," Schlesinger found, "had ever circulated so widely in the United States." The book was printed in three editions by 1837, including a cheap stereotyped edition that sold for 25 cents, serialized in numerous papers, and inspired the popular ditty:

> Of modern books, the best I know—
> The author all the world is thanking—
> One written more for use than show,
> Is quaintly titled "Gouge on Banking."
>
> But still improvements might be made,
> Whilst books on books the world is scourging,
> Let *Biddle* try to help the trade,
> And write one titled Banks on *Gouging*.

Paper money, in Gouge's view, was "the foundation of the American Banking System." Gouge saw paper money, which allowed banks to lend multiples of their capital in gold or silver, as responsible for the frequent patterns of economic expansion and contraction that typified the United States:

> Nothing is gained by this forced extension of the credit system. It does, indeed, increase the gambling trade of speculation; and that kind of trade in which sheriffs, constables, and assignees, are the active agents. It also increases, in particular years, the trade of consumption; but then it draws from the productive capital of the country, and diminishes the trade of consumption in the following years....
>
> As in the case of all public evils, the system bears with the most hardship on the poor. The rate of wages is ... the last thing that is affected by an expansion; and one necessary consequence of a contraction is, to deprive some men of employment. If a rich man cannot sell his merchandise today, he can sell it tomorrow; and if he cannot sell it for full price, he can sell it for half price. But labor is the poor man's only commodity. If he cannot sell it today, it is lost to him forever.

Gouge was emphatic in a broad critique of banks as corporations:

> Against corporations of every kind, the objection may be brought, that whatever power is given to them, is so much taken from either the government or the people.
>
> As the object of charters is to give to members of companies powers which they would not possess in their individual capacity, the very existence of monied corporations is incompatible with equality of rights....

> [Banks as corporations] are protected, in most of the states, by direct inhibitions on individuals engaging in the same business.
>
> They are exempted from liabilities to which individuals are subjected. If a poor man cannot pay his debts, his bed is, in some of the states, taken from under him. If that will not satisfy his creditors, his body is imprisoned. The shareholders in a bank are entitled to all the gain they can make by banking operations; but if the undertaking chances to be unsuccessful, the loss falls on those who have trusted them. They are responsible only for the amount of stock they may have subscribed. . . .
>
> They coin money out of paper. What has always been considered one of the most important prerogatives of government, has been surrendered to the banks.

Bankruptcies were more frequent when there was paper money and banks. Paper money depreciated where specie did not. The existence of banks contributed to wealth disparity — "rendering the condition of some members of society almost helpless."

Our American banks, Gouge concluded, "have found that for which the ancient alchemists sought in vain; they have found that which turns everything into gold — in their own pockets."

In Gouge's view, banks were not necessary and should gradually be phased out in favor of a system of private credit.

There also was an intense personal hostility in Jackson's opposition to Second Bank rechartering. Historian Daniel Walker Howe explained: "Years before, Jackson had speculated extensively in land and promissory notes. When some of the complicated deals soured, he narrowly escaped financial ruin. From these youthful experiences the old man derived his distrust of banks and promissory notes and his horror of debt." Jackson was convinced by 1832 "that the bank concentrated too much power in private hands. The ensuing 'Bank War' in origin a struggle over sovereignty, turned out to inflame hostility of party and class." But Jackson personalized his opposition to the Bank with what one historian characterized as "paroxysms of rage." In response to a request for a Baltimore delegation to relief from the war on the bank, Jackson insisted: "The government will not bow to the monster." Jackson would "put his foot upon the head of the monster and yet crush him to the dust."

Jackson's personalization focused on Biddle. Jackson opposed his spirit of independence, his efforts to be above politics, which meant not accountable to the government or the people. In an extreme view, Roger Taney advised Jackson that renewing the Second Bank charter was tantamount to giving:

> Nicholas Biddle, the President of the Bank, his executors, administrators, and assigns . . . all the powers, privileges, and immunities now intended to be conferred on the individuals who happen to be the stockholders in the existing bank. . . . What is called renewing this charter is in fact and in law nothing more nor less than granting a new charter to certain favored and designated persons instead of leaving the privileges it confers equally open to the competition of all and giving to every citizens an equal opportunity of sharing in the advantages which the government is about to sell.

In a weak attempt to compromise with Jackson, the Bill to Extend the Second Bank Charter was limited to 15 additional years, after renewal in 1836; the Bank or its branches could not circulate, pay out or issue bank drafts or other paper currency in amounts less than $50, except at the place where issued; real estate holdings were limited to that for the conduct of its business; no more than two branch offices could be established or continued in any State; the Bank would pay an annual annuity to the United States of $200,000; Congress was authorized to prohibit the Bank from issuing bank notes or bills less than $20; and the Bank annually was required to report to the Secretary of Treasury a list of all foreign shareholders, "and an application of the Treasurer of any state, shall make out and transmit to such Treasurer a list of stockholders resident in, or citizens of such state, with the amount of stock owned by each." Otherwise, the Second Bank's 1816 Act of Incorporation remained in force.

On June 11, the Senate passed the rechartering Bill by a vote of 28 to 20, on July 3, the House by a vote of 107 to 85.[27]

Jackson's veto of the rechartering of the Second Bank on July 10, 1832 is "the most important Presidential veto in American history." It also is a deeply frustrating document, as Bray Hammond wrote: "legalistic, demagogue and full of sham. Its economic reasoning was said by Professor Catterall over fifty years ago, to be beneath contempt. Its level is now no higher."

Arthur Schlesinger, generally a champion of Jackson's politics, recognized the inadequacy of the veto as economic policy:

> Jackson's real opposition, of course, and that of Benton, Taney and Kendall, arose from their hard-money views. Yet, a great

> part of their backing came from cheap-money men. Thus powerful hard-money arguments — the economic argument that the paper system caused periodic depressions, and the social argument that it built up an aristocracy — were unavailable because they were as fatal to the debtor and state banking positions as to the Bank itself.
>
> The veto message was brilliantly successful in meeting this dilemma. It diverted attention from the basic contradiction by its passages of resounding and demagogic language; it played down the strictly economic analysis; and it particularly sought to lull Western fears by dwelling on the hardships worked by the long arm of the Bank in the Mississippi Valley.

Jackson's veto message had five main themes.

First, Jackson continued to assert that a Bank of the United States was not authorized by the Constitution. Jackson was well aware that the Supreme Court in *McCulloch v. Maryland* had ruled otherwise, but turned his losing Constitutional law argument into a powerful political one: "The powers and privileges possessed by the existing bank... are subversive of the rights of the states and dangerous to the liberties of the people.... Nor is our government to be maintained or our Union preserved by invasions of the rights and powers of the several states in thus attempting to make our General Government strong, we make it weaker."

In his Second Inaugural Address, delivered March 4, 1833, Jackson would make this point more crisply: "In proportion, therefore, as the General Government encroaches upon the rights of the states, in the same proportion does it impair its own power and detract from its ability to fulfill the purposes of its creation."

Second, the Second Bank not only would be granted monopoly privileges, but the value of these privileges would be increased:

> [T]he Bank of the United States... enjoys an exclusive privilege of banking under the authority of the General Government, a monopoly of its favor and support, and, as a necessary consequence, almost a monopoly of the foreign and domestic exchange. The powers, privileges, and favors bestowed upon it in the original charter, by increasing the value of the stock far above its par value, operated as a gratuity of many millions to the stockholders.

Jackson estimated that rechartering of the Bank, minus the $200,000 annual annuity to the United States government, would increase the value of the stock by 20, 30 or 50 percent, a profit as much as $14 million.

Jackson hammered this point:

> Every monopoly and all exclusive privileges are granted at the expense of the public, which ought to receive a fair equivalent. The many millions which this act proposes to bestow on the stockholders of the existing bank must come directly or indirectly out of the earnings of the American people.... If we must have such a corporation, why should not the government sell out the whole stock and thus secure to the people the full market value of the privileges granted? Why should not Congress create and sell twenty-eight millions of stock, incorporating the purchasers with all the powers and privileges secured in this act and putting the premium upon the sales into the Treasury?

Third, with unmitigated xenophobia, Jackson denounced the fact that the rechartering allowed the Bank to continue to have foreign stockholders. At the time of the veto, $8,405,000 of the $28 million of private stock in the Bank was held by foreigners. Jackson zeroed in on the provision requiring the cashier of the Second Bank annually to transmit a list of stock holders in a state to the Treasury of each state who so requested. This meant that not only could foreigners own stock in the Second Bank, but they also potentially could receive a tax exemption by not being subject to state taxation which was limited to citizens or residents of a state:

> As it is only the stock *held* in the states and not that *employed* within them which would be subject to taxation, and as the names of foreign stockholders are not to be reported to the treasurers of the states, it is obvious that the stock held by them will be exempt from this burden. Their annual profits will therefore be 1 per cent more than the citizen stockholders, and as the annual dividends of the bank may be safely estimated at 7 per cent, the stock will be worth 10 or 15 per cent more to foreigners than to citizens of the United States.

Jackson emphasized:

> Thus will this provision ... make the American people debtors to aliens in nearly the whole amount due to this bank, and send across the Atlantic from two to five millions of specie every year to pay the bank dividends....

> If we must have a bank with private stockholders, every consideration of sound policy and every impulse of American feeling admonishes that it should be *purely American.* [Italics in original.]

Fourth, the election of directors and selection of the Bank's leaders was not subject to the control of the democratically elected president and executive branch, but concentrated power in the hands of a few citizens irresponsible to the people. Only five of the Bank's 25 directors were chosen by the government. Rather than taking comfort, given his xenophobia, that foreigners could not vote for the other 20 directors, Jackson saw this as increasing the likelihood that power would fall into the hands of a few leading shareholders:

> There is danger that a president and directors would then be able to elect themselves from year to year, and without responsibility or control, manage the whole concern of the bank during the existence of its charter:
>
> Is there no danger to our liberty and independence in a bank that in its nature has so little to bind it to our country? The president of the bank has told us that most of the state banks exist by its forbearance. Should its influence become concentrated, as it may under the operation of such an act as this, in the hands of a self-elected directory whose interests are identified with those of the foreign stockholders, will there not be cause to tremble for the parity of our elections in peace and for the independence of our country in war?

Fifth, Jackson characterized the modifications in the rechartering bill as "not consistent with the right of the states or the liberties of the people:"

> The qualifications of the right of the bank to hold real estate, the limitation of its power to establish branches, and the power reserved in Congress to forbid the circulation of small notes are restrictions comparatively of little value or importance. All the objectionable principles of the existing corporation, and most of its odious features, are retained without alleviation.

Jackson believed: "[t]hat a bank of the United States, competent to all the duties which may be required by the government, might be so organized as not to infringe on our own delegated powers or the reserved rights of the states[,] I do not entertain a doubt. Had the executive been called upon to furnish the project of such an institution, the duty would have been cheerfully performed."

After criticizing the haste and inadequacy of a Congressional investigation of the Bank, Jackson closed with a much quoted peroration:

> It is to be regretted that the rich and powerful too often bend the acts of government to their selfish purposes. Distinctions in society will always exist under every just government. Equality of talents, of education, or of wealth can not be produced by human institutions. In the full enjoyment of the gifts of Heaven and the fruits of superior industry, economy, and virtue, every man is equally entitled to protection by law; but when the laws undertake to add to these natural and just advantages artificial distinctions, to grant titles, gratuities, and exclusive privileges, to make the rich richer and the potent more powerful, the humble members of society—the farmers, mechanics, and laborers—who have neither the time nor the means of securing like favors to themselves, have a right to complain of the injustice of their government. There are no necessary evils in government. Its evils exist only in its abuses. If it would confine itself to equal protection, and, as Heaven does its rains, showers its favor alike on the high and the low, the rich and the poor, it would be an unqualified blessing. In the act before me there seems to be a wide and unnecessary departure from these just principles.

The die was cast. In transforming what could have been a debate on the wisest course to extend the charter of the Second Bank into a Manichaean struggle between good and evil, the veto message was, as one historian wrote, "prodigiously popular." Let Biddle complain that the veto message "has all the fury of a chained panther biting the bars of his cage. It is really a manifesto of anarchy, such as Marat or Robespierre might have issued to the Mob of Faubourg St. Antione." Or David Webster could beseech the Senate: The veto "manifestly seeks to influence the poor against the rich. It wantonly attacks whole classes of the people, for the purpose of turning against them the prejudices and resentments of other classes."

For Jackson and his many proponents, this was, as Hammond wrote, "their finest accomplishment. [The veto] redistributed vested rights. It established *laissez faire.* It freed banks from federal credit regulation.... It furthered the interests of New York City, Boston and Baltimore at the expense of Philadelphia."

And most of all, in political terms, the veto worked. A Senate vote to override, requiring a two-thirds majority, failed 22 to 19. The veto had lifted "Jackson to the summit of popularity." He was reelected in 1832, with a crushing 219 electoral votes against Clay's 49.[28]

Jackson's *War on the Bank* and the bitterness of Biddle's response accelerated after the 1832 election.

One month after the election in his Annual Message, Jackson recommended sale of the United States government stock in the Second Bank and Congressional inquiry as to whether government deposits should be removed from the Bank in view of the Bank's mismanagement and possible insolvency. By then, Jackson, in Woodrow Wilson's view, considered his 1832 reelection "a deliberate verdict against the Bank — a command to destroy it." The House of Representatives rejected both the proposal to sell the government's stock and the inquiry as to the safety of leaving Government deposits in the Bank.

Jackson remained determined to remove the deposits. Key members of his Cabinet, including Louis McLane, Secretary of the Treasury until June 1, 1833 when he became Secretary of State, and his successor William Duane, as well as Vice President Van Buren opposed removal. Jackson worked with Amos Kendall to attempt to overcome their reluctance. Kendall met with state bank officials in Baltimore, Philadelphia, New York, and Boston in July 1833 to ascertain their willingness to accept government deposits then in the Second Bank. Most banks in Baltimore, Philadelphia, and New York were eager to accept government deposits.

Jackson was gratified by Kendall's report that "the state banks were not only not afraid," but would provide the government "the same services on substantially the same terms as the Bank of the United States."

On September 18, 1833, Jackson read a paper prepared by Attorney General Taney in which Jackson stated his intention to remove government deposits. The paper was published in the *Washington Globe* newspaper on September 20. Taney in a December 1833 Report to Congress would state that the Bank had increased its loans and discounts from $42 million in 1831 to $70 million during the first half of 1832 while renewal was pending. These actions had "justly forfeited the confidence of the government," demonstrating that the Bank "was using its money for the purpose of obtaining a hold upon the people of this country in order to operate upon fears and to induce them by the apprehension of ruin, to vote against the candidate which [the Bank] desired to defeat." Taney's September paper for Jackson stressed that the election in 1832 in effect had been a referendum on Bank termination and therefore "with due attention to the interests of the people, [Bank termination] could be no longer postponed." Moreover, Taney believed that public funds had become unsafe in the custody of the Bank which had hindered payments to specified stockholders, frustrated access to Bank records by Jackson appointed government directors, waged a public relations campaign using Bank funds and sometimes conducted business with fewer than the required quorum of seven directors.

Under the Bank's 1816 incorporation statute, only the Secretary of Treasury could remove government funds. Secretary of Treasury Duane shortly after Jackson's presentation to the Cabinet refused to do so, writing to Jackson: "I refuse to carry your directions into effect... not because I desire to favor the Bank of the United States to which I have been, am, and always shall be opposed" but because Duane recognized that the House of Representatives had "pronounced the public money in the Bank of the United States safe." Duane believed that "a change to local and irresponsible banks would shake public confidence and promote doubt and mischief in the operations of society." Jackson fired Duane on September 23 and replaced him with Roger Taney as Interim Secretary of Treasury. The controversial Taney later would not be confirmed as Secretary of Treasury, but in 1835 would become Chief Justice of the United States.

On September 26, Treasury Secretary Taney began a process of removal of funds from the Bank. Instead of removing the funds in one step, the Treasury discontinued making deposits in the Bank and paid down funds with the Bank by paying its bills with drafts on the Bank. This reduced government deposits in the Bank to zero by the end of 1833. Taney put federal tax receipts in state banks sometimes chosen on the basis of political friendship and soon derided as "pet banks." Daniel Walker Howe described the furious response:

> Jackson had defied the wishes of Congress and most of his cabinet; he had violated the spirit, perhaps the letter, of the law. McLane and Cass, the secretaries of state and war, both

> tendered their resignations, which the President persuaded them to withdraw by publicly declaring that removal of the deposits was his personal decision, for which they shared no responsibility. Vice President Van Buren stayed out of town, distancing himself both literally and figuratively from the removal policy, which he feared would divide the Democratic party and jeopardize his hopes to succeed Jackson. The political and business communities were shocked. No parallel episode would occur again until 1973, when President Nixon fired two attorneys general in order to find one who would obey his order to dismiss the special prosecutor Archibald Cox.

Jackson was scorned as King Andrew the First, the Republican Party soon renamed itself the Whig Party, the British Party named for opposition to monarchial usurpation.

On March 28, 1834, the Senate, led by Henry Clay, voted 26 to 20 to censure Jackson, the only censure in United States history of a President. The Resolution read in full: "Resolved that the President in the late Executive Proceedings in relation to the public revenue, has assumed upon himself authority and power not conferred by the Constitution and laws but in derogation of both." In another first, the Senate refused to receive Jackson's protest of the Censure Resolution. To Senator Webster, Jackson's protest was the equivalent of Louis IX's "I am the State."

Clay persuaded the Senate in June 1834 to adopt Resolutions declaring that Taney's reasons for removing funds in the Second Bank were insufficient and directing the funds to be restored after July 1, 1834. The House did not adopt these Resolutions. Jackson's Censure was expunged in January 1837, a vote that caused Clay to lament: "The Senate is no longer a place for any decent man."

Biddle again badly miscalculated the depths of public anger. Between August 1833 and June 1834, the Second Bank curtailed its operations in a campaign to pressure Congress and Jackson to restore deposits and renew the Second Bank charter. In October 1833, the Bank began calling loans and restricting credit. Biddle stated: "The ties of party allegiance can only be broken by the actual conviction of existing distress in the community. Nothing but the evidence of suffering will produce any effect in Congress. . . . Our only safety is in pursuing such a steady course of firm restriction—and I have no doubt that such a course will ultimately lead to restoration of the currency and the recharter of the Bank."

Between August 1833 and April 1834, the contraction of the Second Bank's currency amounted to $18.3 million of a total of $62 million. The Second Bank declined to take the notes of state banks outside of the city in which the state bank was established. State bank debts were to be paid in specie or on drafts of Atlantic cities and state bank debts were not permitted to accumulate.

"[T]he country suffered bitterly," Catterall wrote. Money became scarce. Wages declined. Notes of state banks were depreciated from 1.5 to 12 percent. Money could only be borrowed at 12 to 18 percent during periods of the contraction. Biddle cavalierly maintained the view that no misguided leniency or relief should be exercised. "On general principles," he wrote in January 1834, "I believe that if the Bank were to suffer itself to be misled into the measure of making money plenty, it will only give to its enemies the triumph of having robbed it with impunity, and only confirm what those enemies have said that their act of violence would be attended with no inconvenience to the public."

In March 1834, Biddle wrote: "The Executive by removing the public revenues had relieved the Bank from all responsibility for the currency." Biddle's approach, Gallatin wrote in 1841, meant that the Second Bank "ceased to be a regulator of the currency as early as the years 1832–1833, when its discounts and other investments were increased from fifty-five to sixty-five millions. That is to say, at the rate of 85 percent beyond its capital, compared to lower rates at the sound banks of our great commercial cities."

Speaker of the House James K. Polk pointedly contributed to the debate in the House of Representatives: "The Bank of the United States has set itself up as a great irresponsible rival power of the government. . . . The present is, in substance and in fact, the question of recharter or no recharter. The question is, in fact, whether we shall have the republic without the bank, or the bank without the republic."

Historian Arthur Schlesinger concluded: "Somewhere along the way, Biddle had lost his grip on reality. Ambition, vanity and love of power had crossed the line to megalomania." This is an overstatement, but Biddle had overestimated the patience of the business world. In March 1834, Gallatin organized a committee of New York City's most prominent financiers to demand that Biddle relax the contraction. As a correspondent to Biddle explained in February 1834, if the pressure went so far as to ruin merchants, it would alienate that class, and convince people that the Bank was at fault. The *St. Louis Republican* on February 10th published an editorial explaining: "We have been and still are fast friends of this institution [the Bank]. But when we see it adopting a course fraught with distress and ruin to our community, we shall not hesitate to condemn it."

The Jacksonian System of Banking

On April 4, 1834, House Democrats, Jackson's party, achieved a majority of the House in favor of Resolutions upholding removal (118 to 103) and opposing rechartering (by a larger vote of 134 to 82). The "Bank War" was effectively over.

Beginning with Resolutions in June 1834, the Second Bank ended the contraction. The Second Bank wound up its affairs as a national bank in 1836, but in 1835 note circulation reached a higher level than any other year in the Bank's history. Debt increased through July 1835.

In Daniel Walker Howe's historical verdict:

> The great Bank War turned out to be a conflict both sides lost. The government ended up without the services of a central bank, with an uncontrolled and fluctuating paper currency, and powerless to mitigate the swings of the business cycle. The Bank of the United States ended up with a far inferior Pennsylvania charter and on a road that led to bankruptcy.[29]

Daniel Walker Howe's verdict was apt in its judgment of the Jackson-Biddle melodrama. Jackson's war on the Bank fundamentally altered financial regulation for the next 70 years. Until the Civil War, the states provided the sole framework for banking and banking regulation.

The initial consequence of the bank veto was a state bank mania. Approximately 200 state banks were created between 1834 and 1837. In 1837, there were 627 state banks. By 1848, some 40 state banks had over 200 branch banks, typically in distant states. Between 1830 and 1838, state bank loans and discounts rose from $200,451,214 to $525,115,702.

Accelerating the rapid growth in state banks was "free banking." Since the first corporations had been formed in the United States, the legislature established a bank or other corporation by the terms of a special charter, often secured as a result of political wrangling.

The war on the bank soon broadened into a general attack on corporate privileges.

The essence of this Jacksonian assault was not against the corporate form per se, but against the monopoly privileges that so often accompanied the special charter. Rather than abolish the corporation, most Jacksonians sought to make its advantages freely available. The constitutions of several states were amended to enjoin their legislatures from creating corporations by special Act "when the object of the incorporation is attainable by general laws." Under the new general incorporation Acts, the privileges of the special Acts were unavailable. The corporate form became automatically available to anyone who satisfied minimum capital and registration requirements.

Free banking intended to end the political favoritism or corruption believed to be associated with special charters and encouraged a more competitive, *laissez faire* system of state banks. Both in the 18 states that adopted free banking laws by 1860 and the 15 states that did not, there were limited forms of state regulation. Free banks could open when they had a minimum capital without a vote of the state legislature. The stockholders were protected by limited liability provisions that meant they could lose all of their investment, but unlike partnership investors, were not further personally liable for a bank's debts if the bank failed.

The states generally required free banks to post bonds as collateral for all notes issued or to hold reserves and required free banks to pay gold or silver on demand for notes. A few state banks were "wildcat" banks that issued notes without adequate reserves. State banks in major cities such as New York settled balances with each other initially typically on a weekly basis.

New York's 1838 free banking laws, Hammond explained:

> [were] taken to enthusiastically. The number of free-banking associations set up in the first three years nearly doubled the number of banks in the state. A hundred and thirty-four were chartered in about twenty months — and this in a period when times were hard. Over fifty applicants for free-bank charters were ready in the first six months, and how sanguine they were about the future is indicated by requests in all but four cases for charters to run at least 100 years; fourteen sought a corporate life of 400 years or more, and of these, two specified 1,000 years and one 4,050 years. But of the eighty or so first organized, more than twenty failed to survive even three years.

The brave new world of state banking regulation was associated with perils. The nation's economic boom in 1835–1836 occurred concomitantly with state bank increases in paper money by 32 percent between January 1, 1835 and December 1, 1836 from $82 million to $108 million. Land speculation was rife, as speculators and pioneers in the West borrowed money from local banks and used this to purchase millions of acres. More plentiful, less reliable paper currency fed inflation. The transfer of the Second Bank's deposits to state banks fueled land speculation. Historian Wyman Boardman wrote: "Jackson and the Democrats favored a policy that made land available easily and cheaply. This contradicted the hard money policy because it called for cheaper money and expansion of credit so that those with little or no savings could take up enough acreage for a self-sufficient farm. In addition, the more liberal the policy, the more it encouraged speculators to buy up large tracts and hold them until they rose in value."

Congressional and Jacksonian policies further exacerbated inflation. The Act to Regulate the Deposits of Public Money, enacted on June 23, 1836, required the Treasury to return federal surplus funds to the states after the national debt was paid off in 1835.

The Jackson Administration cut the other way in July 1836 by issuing a Specie Circular requiring gold and silver to be used to pay for public lands. This prevented the payment for public lands by notes of questionable banks, including some organized by land speculators. Since there was little specie in the West, the demand for specie from Eastern banks threatened the solvency of some of them. The specie reserves of New York City banks decreased from $7.2 million on September 1, 1836 to $1.5 million by May 1, 1837.

The Specie Circular would be among the most self-destructive actions of the Jacksonian period. The Circular was an overreaction that required state banks to redeem their notes in specie on demand and prohibited state banks from issuing notes of less than $5, later raised in steps to $20, crippled the state bank system.

Hammond caustically concluded:

> At the President's direction, 11 July 1836, less than three weeks after approval of the distribution [of the federal government surplus], Secretary Levi Woodbury issued the "specie circular," which directed land agents to accept only gold and silver in payment for public lands. This document was notable for being the only administrative act of President

> Jackson that was consistent with the hard-money doctrine absorbed from his agrarian background and always professed by him. It was a step toward blessing America, the most progressive and dynamic of economies, with an exclusively metallic circulation such as Europe had had in the Middle Ages; but its immediate purpose was to prevent "frauds, speculations, and monopolies in the purchase of the public lands and the aid which is said to be given to effect these objects by excessive bank credits." This purpose was laudable. But the measure itself was unconscionably clumsy and taken too late to do anything but harm. It was intended to protect poor settlers and to curb the land speculators, whom, however, it largely spared because they were better able to get control of specie than the poor settlers were; and, by permitting less public land to come on the market, it gave the speculators who had land in their possession already a further advantage.

New York banks suspended specie payments on May 10, 1837, refusing any longer to redeem bank notes in specie. Within a few days, all banks in the country were engaged in a general suspension. After the May 1837 general suspension of specie, many states which earlier had adopted legislation requiring state banks to redeem their notes in specie relaxed these repayment requirements.

Jackson vetoed legislation that would have rescinded the Specie Circular the day before leaving office in March 31, 1837. The Specie Circular would be rescinded in 1840. By then, considerable damage had been done. Many banks resumed specie payments in 1839 but a few months later, suspended payments again until 1842. Many state banks failed, including Nicholas Biddle's United States Bank of Pennsylvania, successor to the Second Bank of the United States and still at the time of its failure, the largest bank in the United States, which failed in 1841.

Jackson also supported the revaluation of gold from the 15 to 1 ratio of silver to gold that Hamilton had supported four decades earlier to 16 to 1. Congress enacted the Coinage Act in June 1834. This effectively set the price of silver below international market prices and stimulated the coinage of gold. In October 1833, there had been only $30 million in specie in the country, of which $28 million was in banks. By December 1836, specie had grown to $73 million, of which $45 million was in banks.

By 1863, when the Civil War National Bank Acts created national bank notes, there was no paper currency issued by the federal government that traded at par. State banks by then had issued 1500 different bank notes that traded in the economy at varying discounts from par. Historically James Haxley calculated there had been as many as 72,000 different bank notes issued between 1782 and 1862. Gary Gorton, a Yale Management Professor, explained:

> This is hard to imagine today — a ten-dollar bill issued by a particular bank in New Haven, Connecticut, for example, might have been worth only $9.90 in gold in New York City, $9.40 in Baltimore, and so on. The discounts from par were not certain; they changed and could not be known for sure by users of the banknotes (everyone in the economy). The discounts were determined in the market for banknotes, where brokers traded notes.[30]

A combination of the deterioration of exports of United States products between 1835 and 1837, most notably cotton, caused by crop failures and the failure of some leading United States cotton dealers, the Specie Circular, inflation spurred by distribution of federal surplus to state banks and the hyperactive Western public land sales created the Panic of 1837. Some 158 New York firms went bankrupt in March and April 1837. In the South, economic activity "lay prostrate under an avalanche of debt with no hope of recovery as long as the planters were unable to dispose of their crops profitably." Schlesinger summarized:

> Crop failures in 1835 toppled the first domino. Farmers could not pay merchants and speculators, who in turn could not pay banks; and the decline of agriculture exports, making the international balance of trade unusually heavy against the United States, caused an unexpected demand abroad for payment in specie. Meanwhile, the Specie Circular called the bluff of banks issuing their notes on the public land.

Inflation soared between 1835 and 1837: Flour, which had sold at $5.62 a barrel in March, 1835 rose to $7.75 in March, 1836, and $12 in March, 1837. Pork climbed from $10 in March, 1835, to $16.25 a year later and to $81.25 in March, 1837. The wholesale price of coal mounted from $6 a ton in January, 1835, to $10.50 in January, 1837, and rents increased proportionately.

Total federal government receipts, largely from customs duties, fell from $50.8 million in 1836, when the federal government had a $19.9 million surplus to $25 million in 1837 when the federal government had a $12.2 million deficit. In the fall of 1837, the Treasury ended the Jacksonian policy of returning surplus net revenues to the states.

Protests were held in New York City including a February 1837 assembly of 4000 to 5000 persons who gathered under the motto, "As the currency expands, the loaf contracts," before a mob of 1000 stormed the Eli Hart & Co. store, trampling flour and wheat on the floor. "The Flour Riots" reminded some of the bread riots of the French Resolution. In May, the *New Era* reported of New York: "At no period of its history has there been as great a degree of general distress as there is at this day." That month, Boston businessmen met in Boston's Faneuil Hall and protested against a law requiring the payment of specie at post offices, "peaceably" if possible, "forcibly if necessary." Representative Lawrence insisted: "There is no people on the face of God's Earth that is so abused, cheated, plundered and trampled by their ruler as are the people of the United States." The Whig party's press articulated similar denunciations throughout the country. A few days after Philadelphia state banks suspended specie payments in 1837, 20,000 people met in Independence Square. "I have never seen the working class more deeply agitated and roused," Henry Gilpin wrote to President Van Buren.

Van Buren's response to the panic was hamstrung. Henry Clay unrelentingly criticized Jackson and his successor Van Buren for contributing to the Panic through the veto of the Second Bank's rechartering and withdrawal of deposits, the Gold Coinage Act and the Specie Circular. Jackson, the most charismatic leader among the Democrats, in contrast, urged Van Buren to remain firm in his opposition to a "corrupt paper currency system." On July 9, 1837, Jackson wrote Van Buren:

> Now is the time to separate the government from all banks, receive and disburse the revenue in nothing but gold and silver coin, and the circulation of our coin through all public disbursements will regulate the currency forever hereafter, keep the government free from all embarrassment, whilst it leaves the commercial community to trade upon its own capital, and the banks to accommodate it with such exchange and credit as best suits their own interests, both being money making concerns, devoid of patriotism, looking alone to their own interests, regardless of all others.

Van Buren, popularly known as the Little Magician for his political dexterity, generally sided with Jackson and, as Daniel Walker

Howe wrote, "offered his suffering country nothing by way of relief." His response was so inept by the end of his one term in 1841, he had acquired the sobriquet, Martin Van Ruin.

On May 15, 1837, Van Buren called for a special session of Congress, which Van Buren would characterize as "imperative" as a result of "[t]he general and almost simultaneous suspension of specie payments by the banks in May." On September 4, 1837, Van Buren delivered a message that Woodrow Wilson characterized as proposing "nothing . . . for the relief of business." Van Buren proposed no new National Bank:

> We have no emergencies that make banks necessary to aid the wants of the Treasury; we have no load of national debt to provide for, and we have on actual deposit a large surplus. No public interest, therefore, now requires the renewal of a connection that circumstances have dissolved. The complete organization of our government, the abundance of our resources, the general harmony which prevails between the different states and with foreign powers, all enable us now to select the system most consistent with the Constitution and most conducive to the public welfare.

He opposed receipt by the Treasury of state bank notes not redeemed in specie: "It would destroy without the excuse of war or public distress that equality of imposts and identity of commercial regulation which lie at the foundation of our Confederacy, and would offer to each state a direct temptation to increase its foreign trade by depreciating the currency received for duties in its ports."

Van Buren viewed the Constitutional prohibition on the states making anything but gold or silver a legal tender as decisive in his support of the specie circulation: "There can be no doubt that those who framed and adopted the Constitution, having in immediate view the depreciated paper of the Confederacy — of which $500 in paper were at times only equal to $1 in coin — intended to prevent the recurrence of similar evils, so far at least as related to the transactions of the new government."

Van Buren instead proposed a separation of the federal government from the banking system. The federal government role should be limited to individuals and corporations:

> They are, to regulate by law the safe-keeping, transfer, and disbursement of the public moneys; to designate the funds to be received and paid by the government; to enable the Treasury

> to meet promptly every demand upon it; to prescribe the terms of indulgence and the mode of settlement to be adopted, as well in collecting from individuals the revenue that has accrued as in withdrawing it from former depositories; and to devise and adopt such further measures, within the constitutional competency of Congress, as will be best calculated to revive the enterprise and to promote the prosperity of the country.
>
> For the deposit, transfer, and disbursement of the revenue national and State Banks have always, with temporary and limited exceptions, been heretofore employed; but although advocates of each system are still to be found, it is apparent that the events of the last few months have greatly augmented the desire, long existing among the people of the United States, to separate the fiscal operations of the government from those of individuals or corporations.

Van Buren anticipated his proposed Treasury system could be achieved without additional expense. "[U]nder our present form of government, the intervention of the executive officers in the custody and disbursement of the public money seems to be unavoidable."[31]

In July 1840, after failing to adopt Van Buren's Independent Treasury legislation in October 1837 and June 1838, Congress enacted the Independent Treasury Act, providing that the Treasury should have vaults and places of sole deposit for revenue in Washington and elsewhere and critically, that payments should be made to the United States only in gold or silver. Conservative Democrats resisted Van Buren's lack of support for the state banks and breathtaking quiescence. In his September 4, 1837 Special Message, Van Buren had insisted: "All communities are apt to look to government for too much. If, therefore, I refrain from suggesting to Congress any specific plan for regulating the exchanges of the country, relieving mercantile embarrassments, or interfering with the ordinary operations of foreign or domestic commerce, it is from a conviction that such measures are not within the constitutional province of the General Government."

The Independent Treasury Act did not effectively address the Panic of 1837. The election of 1840 represented what Schlesinger termed The Whig Counterreformation. William Henry Harrison, military victor of the 1811 defeat of Shawnee Indians in Tippecanoe, Indiana, campaigned as a war hero who shared down to earth values. A Democratic Party leaning newspaper attempted to ridicule Harrison as a dull rustic. "Bring him a barrel of hard [meaning alcoholic] cider and settle a pension of two thousand a year on him, and take my word for it, he will sit the remainder of his days in his log cabin." Harrison was inspired to campaign as the log cabin and hard cider candidate under the inimitable slogan, "Tippecanoe and Tyler Too."

Harrison and John Tyler won the 1840 election over Van Buren decisively with 53 percent of the popular vote and an Electoral College margin of 234 to 60.

His Presidency was the shortest in American history. Until Ronald Reagan won the 1980 election, the 67-year-old Harrison was the oldest President in United States history. He delivered the longest Inaugural speech in United States history, one hour and forty-five minutes, on March 4, 1841, on a cold Washington D.C. day. One month later, on April 4, 1841, Harrison died of pneumonia.

In his Inaugural Address, Harrison criticized an exclusive metallic currency and disparaging state government efforts to respond to "the embarrassed state of business and the currency." On March 17, 1841, "the condition of the revenues and finances of the country" prompted Harrison to call an extra session of Congress on May 31, 1841. Henry Clay submitted legislation to repeal the Independent Treasury Act which Congress passed and President Tyler signed. But Tyler was unwilling to sign either Clay's initial version of the new Bank of United States Charter or a compromise version with a headquartered office in Washington, D.C. and branch offices in only states where the state did not refuse permission.

This was a decisive moment in the history of United States financial regulation. No successful effort would be made to create a central bank until the establishment of the Federal Reserve System in 1913. While other significant actions would be taken, the Hamiltonian vision of a Bank of the United States to guide and stimulate our economy was ended for the next seven decades.[32]

The United States economy paid a steep price for the termination of the federal central bank. "In destroying the Bank," Arthur Schlesinger would write in his generally celebratory *The Age of Jackson*, "Jackson had removed a valuable brake on credit expansion; and in sponsoring the system of deposit in state banks, he had accelerated the tendencies toward inflation." Bray Hammond, more clinically, would write:

> But at the middle of the 19th century banks had still to stand on their own. There was no longer a Federal Bank restraining the expansion of their liabilities, and the insurance of those liabilities after an imperfect attempt had been abandoned. To the United States government, banks had become untouchable, and though they were under conservative restraint in some states, they were mostly at large in a jungle of *laissez faire.* Too many let themselves be tempted into taking risks that were incongruous with the nature of the economy in its current stage. When business was good too many thought it was bound to be still better, and when they judged it might be poor it proved to be worse.... So in the extraordinarily dynamic period of business enterprise extending from the election of Andrew Jackson in 1828 to the election of Abraham Lincoln in 1860, blunders in banking were profuse. So was dishonesty, though neither blundering nor dishonesty predominated.

The cost of federal passivity was substantial. Bank panics occurred in 1853, 1857, 1873, 1884, 1890, 1893, 1895, 1899, and 1907; recessions between 1845 and 1847, 1851, and 1854–1855; a "Great Depression" followed the Panic of 1893, believed to have been "one of the worst financial crises that has occurred in the business history of the United States." The financial and business community repeatedly suffered. In 1857, specie payments were suspended by virtually every bank in New York, stock prices fell approximately 50 percent, more than 5000 businesses failed nationwide. Law Professor Jerry Markham wrote: "Between 1864 and 1879, the number of national banks increased from some 500 to 2,000.... From the Civil War to the end of the century, 352 of these banks failed. The depositors in those failed banks were not protected by government account insurance." Between 1873 and the beginning of recovery in 1878, more than 47,000 businesses and 400 banks failed. On September 20, 1873, the New York Stock Exchange suspended operations because its settlement systems were not operating. Bank runs intermittently occurred with depositors making a "run" to the bank and demanding full return of their deposits. When banks could not satisfy depositor demands, the banks would either suspend operations or fail. Approximately 11,000 banks failed in the aftermath of the Panic of 1884. The "Great Depression" of 1893 lasted until 1897. Six hundred banks and 15,000 businesses failed during that period. Four million people were unemployed.

It is not a fair historical judgment to opine that an effective Federal central bank could have presented this entire cavalcade of economic dysfunction. More aptly, it is appropriate to conclude that an effective regulatory system could have responded more rapidly than a largely *laissez faire* approach and better mitigated damage to the economy.

Nor is it fair to suggest that the federal government did nothing from 1841 to 1913. The federal government took many steps but none during this period were sufficient to tame the intense volatility of the United States economy.[33]

In 1844, the Democratic Party swept back into office. President Polk campaigned in part on a plan to revive Van Buren's Independent Treasury Act, which had operated between 1840 and 1841. In August 1846, Polk signed a new Independent Treasury Act, officially titled An Act To Provide for the Better Organization of the Treasury, and for the Collection, Safe-keeping, Transfer, and Disbursement of the Public Revenue. As with the 1840 Independent Treasury Act, the purpose of the 1846 Act was to separate Treasury receipt and distribution of public funds from private banking and to reduce speculation and inflation by requiring receipts of "all duties, taxes, sales of public lands, debts and sums of money accruing or becoming due to the United States . . . to be paid in gold and silver coin only, or in Treasury notes issued under the authority of the United States" and to similarly limit to specie and Treasury notes all disbursements by the United States.

Banking historian Bray Hammond explained:

> The Treasury notes mentioned here were interest-bearing obligations of the government receivable in payments to the government, but not being a legal tender they could not be forced upon the government's creditors. They were not, in the customary sense, a part of the money in circulation. The use of Treasury drafts between depositories was authorized and so even was their restricted sale for private transactions, but the Secretary of the Treasury was told "to guard as far as many be against those drafts being used or thrown into circulation as a paper currency or medium of exchange.

Through the Civil War, the Independent Treasury worked reasonably well for the federal government. In the aftermath of the Panic of 1857, President James Buchanan said in his December 7, 1857 State of the Union address: "Thanks to the independent treasury, the government has not suspended [specie] payments, as it was compelled to do by the failure of the banks in 1837. It will continue to discharge its liabilities to the people in gold and silver. Its disbursements in coin pass into circulation and materially assist in restoring a sound currency."

Buchanan's remarks, however, were premised upon his fervent beliefs:

> It is apparent that our existing misfortunes have proceeded solely from our extravagant and vicious systems of paper currency and bank credits, exciting the people to wild speculations and gambling in stocks. These revulsions must continue to recur at successive intervals so long as the amount of the paper currency and bank loans and discounts of the country shall be left to the discretion of 1,400 irresponsible banking institutions, which from the very law of their nature will consult the interest of their stockholders rather than the public welfare.

Occluded in Buchanan's statements was the overriding reality that while the federal government did not suspend specie payments in 1857, state banks generally already had done so.

Even before the Civil War, state banks in major cities such as New York had taken steps to mitigate risk. In 1853, 62 banks in New York City created the New York Clearing House Association to provide daily settlement of net balances among New York banks by exchanging checks and drafts between member banks. "Great as the benefits of the New York Clearing House were and much as it accomplished in correcting 'relaxation' and 'improper expansion' as [former Secretary of Treasury] Gallatin had thought it might, and in exercising 'a restrictive power over the general currency of trade' throughout the country . . . , it did not prevent or obviously mitigate, four years later, the Panic of 1857."

In August 1857, the New York Office of the Ohio Life Insurance and Trust Company, which effectively was a bank, failed. Several New York banking firms who were creditors of the Ohio Life Insurance and Trust Company failed. "Toward the end of September," Hammond explained, "the banks in Pennsylvania and Baltimore suspended, then in Pennsylvania, Maryland and Virginia generally. Then in New England." On October 13, heavy runs on all New York banks began. The next day, all banks except the Chemical stopped specie payments. The Chemical followed suit on October 15. The suspension soon prevailed throughout the entire country.

Specie payments were resumed in New York and New England in December 1857 and by the summer of 1858 throughout the country. In March 1858, the New York Clearing House required all members to hold "coin equal to not less than twenty percent of our net deposits of every kind." Again, this was a salutary step that proved unable to resist the stresses that soon buffeted the national economy, as was the New York Clearing House decision in 1860, just after Lincoln's election, for its members to pool their specie reserves.

By the end of the century, clearinghouses were in most major cities and added other services including loans to member banks and sometimes to governments. The National Monetary Commission later would praise "the great value of clearing-house loans" is that the net settlements reduce the need for actual cash. In 1878, the Department of the Treasury's New York Subtreasury became a member of the New York Clearing House.[34]

The Civil War

The Civil War would be the greatest financial crisis in the United States since the Revolutionary War. Almost instantly, the economy and national government were overwhelmed. By 1861, Northern banks and merchants had advanced $100 million to the South. With seven Southern states seceding within four months of Lincoln's election, a panic seized first New York City and the other banks and soon the West that interregional finance threatened to grind to a halt. Bankruptcies soon commenced with close to 6000 businesses failing as hostilities commenced. Loan rates in the New York securities market rose to 24 percent.

The existing state banking system was chaotic. The *Chicago Tribune* during the Civil War would calculate there were 1,395 banks in the United States that had issued 8370 different bills of various denominations. Some banks, stated Jay Cook, soon to be a legendary federal bond promoter, issued notes equal to 25 times their capital "with no other security than the good faith of their institution."

Lincoln and his Secretary of Treasury, Salmon Chase, led a national government initially unable to address a crisis of this magnitude. When Chase began as Secretary of Treasury, the total resources of the Treasury were less than $2 million, which had already been appropriated ten times over.

In June 1861, Chase calculated the needs of the national government for the fiscal year ending June 30, 1862, to be $318,519,581. This projected expenditures of $874,000 per day. Later in the War, expenditures would reach nearly $4 million per day. By October 1865, the debt of the United States would be $2.8 billion.[35]

The imperatives of Civil War finance were defined by military expenditures. On April 15, 1861, at the commencement of the Civil War, President Lincoln issued a proclamation calling upon the military of the several states of the Union to provide 75,000 troops to suppress the rebellion in South Carolina, Georgia, Alabama, Florida, Mississippi, Louisiana, and Texas.

On July 4, 1861, in a special session of Congress, Lincoln elaborated:

> At the beginning of the present Presidential term, four months ago, the functions of the federal government were found to be generally suspended within the several states of South Carolina, Georgia, Alabama, Mississippi, Louisiana, and Florida excepting only those of the Post-Office Department.
>
> Within these states all the forts, arsenals, dockyards, customhouses, and the like, including the movable and stationary property in and about them, had been seized and were held in open hostility to this government, excepting only Forts Pickens, Taylor, and Jefferson, on and near the Florida coast, and Fort Sumter, in Charleston Harbor, South Carolina.

In what turned out to be a vain hope to make "this contest a short and decisive one," Lincoln called upon Congress to "place at the control of the government . . . at least 400,000 men and $400 million."

From his first public remarks as a 23-year-old Whig candidate for the Assembly in 1832, Lincoln had supported a National bank and, at critical moments in his presidency, a national currency. But in the exigencies of Civil War, Lincoln largely deferred finance to Secretary of Treasury, Chase. As Lincoln put it to an economist with a proposal for issuing greenbacks: "You must go to Chase. He is running that end of the machine."

Chase sought on July 4, $320 million to fund the next year's war effort, of which $240 million would be in loans and $80 million from duties and imports, sales of public lands, direct taxes on lands and buildings, and excise taxes on luxuries and consumer goods.

On July 17, 1861, Congress enacted Chase's program, authorizing the Secretary of Treasury to borrow up to $250 million during the next year in the form of bonds or Treasury notes. Of this amount, the Secretary could borrow up to $100 million in a loan in Europe or in the United States. A separate $50 million, later increased to $60 million, was to be raised by issuing Treasury notes payable in coin on demand.

Chase sought to borrow $150 million of the $250 million loans from banks in New York, Philadelphia, and Boston. He successfully negotiated $50 million bond issuances on August 19, 1861, October 1, 1861, and November 16, 1861.

Compared to the more modest borrowings of the Treasury in the pre-Civil War period, these were staggering sums. On August 5, 1861, Congress suspended provisions of the 1846 Independent Treasury Act:

> to allow the Secretary of the Treasury to deposit any of the moneys obtained on any of the loans now authorized by law, to the credit of the Treasurer of the United States, in such solvent specie-paying banks as he may select; and the said moneys, so deposited, may be withdrawn from such deposit for deposit with the regular authorized depositories, or for the payment of public dues, or paid in redemption of the notes authorized to be issued under this act, or the act to which this is supplementary, payable on demand, as may seem expedient to, or be directed by, the Secretary of the Treasury.

Until December 1861, leading banks, while willing to buy and resell bonds to the public, balked at the requirement of forwarding gold to the Treasury. Even with gold in greater abundance in leading United States banks after the California gold rush, the total gold holdings in New York, Philadelphia, and Boston banks in August 1861 amounted to only $63 million. The banks interpreted the suspension of the specie collection requirements in the August 5th Act as authorizing the Treasury to receive loans in the form of credits on the bank's books and allow the Treasury to pay its creditors by check. This would protect the gold reserves of the banks.

For some months, Chase insisted upon payments to the Treasury and disbursements to the government's creditors to be solely in specie, meaning gold. Chase did not view the August 5th Act as changing the requirement that the United States government be paid and disburse specie and "until Congress shall decide otherwise, I must execute the law as it exists and receive and pay only coin and government notes." Bray Hammond recognized: "This was like killing the goose that laid the golden eggs. By refusing bank credit and demanding cash, the Secretary was forcing the banks to abandon banking." Chase's compromise was to permit payments to the Treasury to be made over time.

Further complicating the machinery of the nation's finances in 1861 was Chase's determination to have Treasury demand notes accepted for payment of Government expenditures while retaining gold reserves in the Treasury to support the notes. This meant the Treasury was competing with the banks for gold. This also increased the pressure on the banks. Hammond explained:

> The effort to pay his bills in demand notes and retain his gold increased the demand for gold and the objection to [Chase's] notes. The banks were triply the victims of the procedure,... being required to maintain reserves of gold in proportion to their liabilities, to pay their depositors in gold, and to deliver in gold what they lent the Secretary of the Treasury.

By December, aggregate bank gold reserves were half what they had been in August despite the belief the bank gold reserves could be replenished by sales of the new government bonds for gold to the public. Between December 7 and 28, New York Bank gold reserves shrank almost one-third. In late December, New York's bankers voted to suspend specie payments, soon joined generally by banks in the North.

Matters became even worse in November when the U.S.S. San Jacinto stopped the R.M.S. Trent and forcibly removed Confederate Commissioners to Britain and France, James Mason and John Slidell, as well as their secretaries. This caused prices on already anxious stock markets to fall sharply out of fear of British retribution:

> In this state of confused dismay, money went into private hoards or fled abroad. The heavy exports of farm products, despite the blockade of cotton, did not fall off, but the gold receipts paying for them did; brokers left their funds abroad instead of fetching them home. And California gold was diverted to London after the *Trent* seizure, lest complications arise from its being captured by the British on its usual course from San Francisco to New York. In other words, money was considered safer with the prospective enemy than it was at home or homeward bound.

By late 1861, it was apparent that the Jacksonian specie based monetary system was unsustainable. On December 9, 1861, Chase proposed a new path in his First Report as Secretary of Treasury to Congress. By then, Congress had authorized a Union Army of 500,000 men. This would increase to 961,600 by 1865. In December 1861, Chase anticipated: "To meet these increased demands, arising almost wholly from the increase of the Army and Navy and the increase of pay and rations beyond the original estimates, large additional appropriations have been and will be necessary." Chase estimated that for 1862 and 1863 fiscal years, loans of $655 million would be necessary. The public debt which had been $90.9 million in July 1861 was anticipated to grow to $897.4 million by July 1863. Other means of addressing debt such as taxation or retirement of federal expenditures only marginally could address these metastasizing figures.

Chase in December 1861 proposed a fundamentally new approach to debt. He sharply criticized existing bank note circulation governed by 34 States and 1600 state banks: "Under such a system, or rather lack of system, great fluctuations, and heavy losses in discounts and exchanges, are inevitable; and not unfrequently, through failures of the issuing institutions, considerable portions of the circulation become suddenly worthless in the hands of the people."

Chase recommended the creation of national notes secured by the pledge of United States bonds.

An initial step toward national notes had been taken in July when Congress authorized the Secretary of the Treasury to issue $50 million in notes payable in coin. Chase was reluctant to transform the earlier issued Treasury notes into a national currency "without adequate provision for redemption" given "the risk of a depreciated, depreciating and finally worthless paper money." A critical weakness of the partial step towards a national currency taken in June 1861 was the requirement of a gold reserve when the Treasury lacked the gold reserves to support a national currency.

Instead, Chase proposed national notes with "the security of . . . redemption by the pledge of United States stocks, and an adequate provision of specie." United States bonds would not prove to be as secure as gold reserves, but they could be provided as necessary to fund the War. In the state of national emergency, that was the decisive point.[36]

During the first six months of 1862, Senator John Sherman estimated $350 million had to be obtained by the Treasury and disbursed. Already, Sherman explained, $100 million was due and payable to "soldiers, to contractors, to the men who have furnished provisions and clothing for your army, to your officers, your judges, and your civil magistrates." No more money could be raised under the July 1861 authorization. The debt markets were wobbly — bonds were trading at 88 below the par of 100, and Treasury notes were worth half their face value in parts of the country.

With no real choice, Congress in February 1862 approved the first paper currency in United States history. The Secretary of Treasury was authorized to issue "on the credit of the United States" $150 million in Treasury notes in July 1861. The new notes, soon popularly known as greenbacks after the design selected by the Department of Treasury, were authorized to be legal tender in payments of all public and private debts within the United States, except duties on imports and interest upon bonds and notes which would continue to be paid in coin. Greenbacks were intended to be like paper money, payable on demand with a value intended to be equal to the denominations specified on the currency such as $5, $10, and so on.

On one face of the greenbacks, text was to express "that they are secured by United States bonds, deposited with the Treasury of the United States" and the notes also were to "express upon their face the promise that the [banking] associations receiving the same to pay on demand." In other words, the new national currency was to be issued by state banks but subject to national quality standards. This was essential at a time when state banks generally issued notes, the equivalent to paper currency today, and as much as 80 percent of all bank notes in 1862, according to the *New York Times*, were estimated to be counterfeit.

With successive Congressional actions on July 11, 1862, January 17, 1863, and March 3, 1863, a total of $450 million in greenbacks would be issued during the Civil War. Greenbacks were prone to depreciation. By January 1863, it took $164 in greenbacks to get $100 in gold. On December 18, 1865, eight months after Appomattox, Congress resolved as early as possible to resume "specie payments as the business interests of the country will permit."[37]

The February 1862 Legal Tender Act and the issuance of greenbacks were consequential first steps towards building a new federal system of finance. In 1871, by which time Salmon Chase was Chief Justice of the Supreme Court, the Court upheld the constitutionality of the 1862 Act in the *Legal Tender Cases,* employing the logic of the necessary and proper clause discussion in *McCulloch v. Maryland.* The Supreme Court emphasized the necessity of the new paper currency:

> ... [A] civil war was then raging which seriously threatened the overthrow of the government and the destruction of the Constitution itself. It demanded the equipment and support of large armies and navies, and the employment of money to an extent beyond the capacity of all ordinary sources of supply. Meanwhile the public treasury was nearly empty, and the credit of the government, if not stretched to its utmost tension, had become nearly exhausted.... The necessity was immediate and pressing. The army was unpaid. There was then due to the soldiers in the field nearly a score of millions of dollars. The requisitions from the War and Navy Departments for supplies exceeded fifty millions, and the current expenditure was over one million per day. The entire amount of coin in the country, including that in private hands, as well as that in banking institutions, was insufficient to supply the need of the government three months, had it all been poured into the treasury. Foreign credit we had none.... It was at such a time and in such an emergency that the legal tender acts were passed.

Notably the *Legal Tender Cases* held that the new paper currency was legal tender both for contracts before and after the February 25, 1862, enactment date of the legislation. In holding that the new legal tender could be applied to obligations before the enactment date, the Court overruled its 1870 decision in *Hepburn v. Griswold* which had held, in a decision written by Chase, that while there was no question of "the general constitutionality... of the legislation", "an act making promises to pay... a legal tender in payment of debts previously contracted... is prohibited by the Constitution."

The prohibition in *Hepburn* lasted 15 months. The *Legal Tender Cases* easily swatted aside its holding of unconstitutionality with the observation that *Hepburn* "was decided by a divided court, and by a court having a less number of judges than the law in existence provided this court shall have." The constitutionality of legal tender in payment of private debts in time of peace was subsequently established in 1884 in *Julliard v. Greenman* and in 1935 in *Norman v. Baltimore & Ohio Railway.*[38]

When Chase delivered his Second Report as Secretary of the Treasury in December 1862, the state of United States finances had become more perilous. The estimate of the public debt on July 1, 1863, "in view of the unexpected increase of expenditures" was anticipated to be $1,122,297,403.24. If the War continued with undiminished disbursements until July 1, 1864, the projection was forecast to grow to $1,744,685,586.80. The 1864 estimate was double his estimate for 1863, one year earlier.

Chase took pride that the new national currency had "worked well": "Not a single requisition from any department upon the Treasury remained unanswered."

But competition from the continued existence of state bank notes had increased state currency then in circulation from $130 million to $167 million in the year ended November 1, 1862, on top of $210 million in United States notes. The aggregate of state and United States currency had contributed to inflation in many products: "Wheat, quoted at $1.38 to $1.45 per bushel on the 1st of November, 1861, was quoted at $1.45 to $1.50 on the 1st of November, 1862. . . . Corn sold on the 1st of November 1861 at 62 to 65 cents per bushel, and on the 1st of November, 1862, at 71 to 73 cents." Similar increases in prices of hay, beef, and other staples of domestic produce also were exhibited between those two dates.

Chase then proposed the second fundamental step in his program to transform the national currency:

> Under these circumstances, the path of wisdom and duty seems very clear. It leads to the support of a United States note circulation, and to the [state] bank note circulation. A comparatively small reduction of the latter will allow ample room for the whole increase of the former, authorized by existing laws; and as the reduction proceeds the increase may be extended, never, however, passing the point which admits the negotiation of loans at reasonable rates.

To facilitate the substitution by the current state banks of national currency for state bank notes, Chase proposed what he termed a "moderate" tax on the circulation of State currency.

Chase recommended that the United States government furnish the national currency, but the greenbacks should be issued by what were then state bank associations, which voluntarily would be converted into United States banks:

> The central idea of the proposed measure is the establishment of one sound, uniform circulation, of equal value throughout the country, upon the foundation of national credit combined with private capital. . . .
>
> It is proposed that these associations be entirely voluntary. Any persons, desirous of employing real capital in sufficient amounts, can, if the plan be adopted, unite together under proper articles, and, having contributed the requisite capital, can invest such part of it, not less than a fixed minimum, in United States bonds, and, having deposited these bonds with the proper officer of the United States, can receive United States notes in such denominations as may be desired, and employ them as money in discounts and exchanges.

The United States banks would be "restricted mainly to investing United States notes in bonds." The immediate advantage of what Chase viewed initially as a war time emergency measure "will be found in the market created for bonds, and the support thereby given to national credit." The long term general advantage of the new system of currency "will only be fully apparent when the national circulation given to them shall become the established and sole note circulation of the country."

With Hamiltonian fervor, Chase argued: "Had the system been possible, and had it actually existed two years ago, can it be doubted that the national interests and sentiments enlisted by it for the Union would have so strengthened the motives for adhesion derived from other sources that the wild treason of succession would have been impossible?"

Chase stressed:

> The Secretary recommends, therefore, no mere paper money scheme, but, on the contrary, a series of measures looking to a safe and gradual return to gold and silver as the only permanent basis, standard, and measure of values recognized by the Constitution — between which and an irredeemable paper currency, as he believes, the choice is now to be made.

On January 17, 1863, President Lincoln added his powerful voice in support of Chase's new system of financial regulation:

> It seems very plain that continued issues of United States notes without any check to the issues of suspended banks and without adequate provision for the raising of money by loans and for funding the issues so as to keep them within due limits must soon produce disastrous consequences; and this matter appears to me so important that I feel bound to avail myself of this occasion to ask the special attention of Congress to it.
>
> That Congress has power to regulate the currency of the country can hardly admit of doubt, and that a judicious measure to prevent the deterioration of this currency, as a seasonable taxation of bank circulation or otherwise, is needed seems equally clear. Independently of this general consideration, it would be unjust to the people at large to exempt banks enjoying the special privilege of circulation from their just proportion of the public burdens.
>
> In order to raise money by way of loans most easily and cheaply, it is clearly necessary to give every possible support to the public credit. To that end a uniform currency, in which taxes, subscriptions to loans, and all other ordinary public dues, as well as all private dues, may be paid, is almost, if not quite, indispensable.... The securing of this circulation by the pledge of United States bonds... would still further facilitate loans by increasing the present and causing a future demand for such bonds.

The National Currency Act of 1863

On February 25, 1863, after close votes in the House and Senate, Congress enacted the National Currency Act, the first of three laws necessary to effectively achieve Chase's new system of financial regulation.

The core provisions of the National Currency Act established the Office of the Comptroller of the Currency, a separate bureau within the Treasury "under the general direction of the Secretary of the Treasury" "charged with the execution of this and all other laws... respecting the issue and regulation of a natural currency secured by United States Banks." The Office of the Comptroller was the first enduring banking regulator in the United States.

Several sections of the National Currency Act addressed banking associations that would be regulated by the Comptroller, soon called national banks. The National Currency Act envisioned a system of free banking under which any persons, "not less in number than five," could form a banking association as long as they had capital stock of at least $50,000 if the bank was in a city with a population of less than 10,000 people or $100,000 if the city had a population over 10,000 people. Each association could increase this amount.

The Comptroller was required to approve the commencement of the bank's business operations when 30 percent of the capital stock was paid in and there was compliance with other applicable provisions of the Act.

> Each bank could seek authorization for a life of up to 20 years, and shall have the power to carry on the business of banking by obtaining and issuing circulating notes in accordance with the provisions of this act; by discounting bills, notes, and other evidences of debt; by receiving deposits; by buying and selling gold and silver bullion, foreign coins, and bills of exchange; by loaning money on real and personal security, in the manner specified in their articles of association, for the purposes authorized by this act, and by exercising such incidental powers as shall be necessary to carry on such business[.]

The banks were intended to be a means to strengthen the United States Treasury during war-time emergencies. Even before commencement of banking business, each association was required to transfer to the Treasury United States bonds equal to one-third of the capital stock paid in. The Comptroller would then provide the association "notes of different denominations in blank, registered and countersigned . . . equal to the amount up to ninety percent of the current market value of the United States banks so transferred and delivered."

The entire amount of notes issued under the 1863 Act was not to exceed $300 million. Similar to the 1862 Legal Tender Act, the association notes were intended to "be received at par in all parts of the United States in payment of taxes, excises, public lands, and all other dues to the United States, except for duties on imports and also for all salaries or other debts and dues owing by the United States to individuals, corporations and associations with the United States, except interest on public debt."

Each bank was required to have on hand in lawful United States money in "at least twenty-five percent of the aggregate amount of its outstanding notes of circulation and its deposits."

No bank was allowed to be indebted in an amount greater than its paid capital stock and the total of four specified accounts:

> First. On account of its notes of circulation.
>
> Second. On account of moneys deposited with, or collected by, such association.
>
> Third. On account of bills of exchange or drafts drawn against money actually on deposit to the credit of such association, or due thereto.
>
> Fourth. On account of liabilities to its stockholders, for money paid in on capital stock, and dividends thereon, and reserved profits.

Clearing house certificates representing specie or lawful money deposited by a bank were deemed in the possession of the bank. For banking associations in Boston, Providence, New York, Philadelphia, Baltimore, Cincinnati, Chicago, St. Louis, or New Orleans, clearing house certificates were viewed to be part of the bank in other cities to the extent of three-fifths of the required 25 percent reserve.

The total liabilities of any person, company, or firm to a bank association "shall at no time exceed one-third, exclusive of liabilities as accepted, one fifth; and exclusive of liabilities and . . . bills of exchange, one tenth part of the capital stock of such association actually paid in."

The Act specifically provided that any state bank established either by a special charter or free banking law, upon a two-thirds vote of its capital stock could convert to a national bank and transfer to the United States Treasury United States bonds "in the manner provided by this act."

The greatest weakness of the 1863 and subsequent Civil War National Banking Acts was the relationship between national law and state banks. Chase had hoped that patriotism, among other reasons, would prompt state banks to convert to national banks. It did not. Initially nearly 700 banks were chartered under the 1863 Act, most of which were new banks. "It became evident," Hammond wrote, "that the state banks, if they could not be enticed, must be driven."

1864 National Banking Act

Hugh McCulloch, the first Comptroller of the Currency, previously President of the Bank of the State of Indiana, led efforts to revise the

National Currency Act of 1863 through the enactment of the National Banking Act of 1864, which succeeded the 1863 Act. The 1863 Act was repealed by the 1864 National Banking Act with the 1864 Act expressly providing that the repeal of the 1863 Act did "not affect any appointment made, acts done, proceedings had, or the organizing acts of any association organized or in the process of organization under the [1863] Act."

In its structure, the 1864 National Banking Act was the same as the 1863 National Currency Act. Both Acts established the Office of the Comptroller of the Currency and charged the Comptroller and her or his staff with responsibility for the design and production of notes used as currency; receipt and deposit of required bonds from national banks; ensuring compliance by the banks with paid-in capital, reserve, loan and liability limits; dividend restrictions; reporting; examination of bank financial records; distribution of notes to each bank; destruction of worn-out or mutilated notes; the national depository system; collection of fees; supervision of commencement and liquidation of operations, default procedures, including appointment of special agents to ascertain whether banks have paid money for its notes, and identification of cases of bank officer embezzlement, mutilation of bank bills, drafts, notes or other evidence of indebtedness and counterfeit; and the Comptroller's annual report to Congress.

This was a broad national regulatory role but limited compared to a modern central bank, which has consequential roles in setting interest rates and money supply, reducing unemployment and financial stability.

The 1864 Act, as with the 1863 Act, also established banking associations under a free banking system, meaning any five or more persons could form a national bank when they satisfied specified capital and regulatory requirements.

The bank capital requirements in the 1864 Act were modified — rather than \$50,000 or \$100,000 per bank depending on whether it was located in a city with fewer or more than 10,000 people, the 1864 Act had three levels of capital requirement — \$50,000 for banks organized in any place with fewer than 6,000 inhabitants; \$100,000 for banks in cities between 6,000 and 50,000; and \$200,000 for banks in larger cities.

Banks in 1864 were only authorized to commence operations when at least 50 percent, not 30 percent, of the required capital stock was paid in.

The new association's banking powers were similar in the 1864 Act, but more tightly phrased. Every association organized under the National Banking Act could "carry on the business of banking by discounting and negotiating promissory notes, drafts, bills of exchange, and other evidences of indebtedness; by receiving deposits, by buying and selling exchange coin, and bullion, by loaning money on personal security; by obtaining, issuing and circulating notes according to the provisions of this act." Banks also were authorized to purchase, hold and convert real estate for specified purposes, including mortgages and loans made by the associations.

Before commencing operations, each bank was required to transfer and deliver to the Treasurer of the United States bonds both equal to but not less than one-third of paid-in capital not less than $30,000 and in return, as in the 1863 Act, for notes of different denominations.

As with the 1863 Act, the entire amount of notes that could be issued under the 1864 Act was not to exceed $300 million. Somewhat different than the 1862 Legal Tender Act, the notes were to be in $1, $2, $3, $5, $10, $20, $50, $100, $500, and $1,000 denominations, "[p]rovided that not more than one-sixth part of the notes furnished shall be of a less denomination than five dollars, and that after specie payment shall be resumed no association shall be furnished with notes of less denomination than five dollars."

In the 1864 Act, the notes were expressly authorized "to issue and circulate as money" and similar to the 1863 Act for all payments to the United States, "except for duties on imports" and all payments by the United States "except interest on the public debt, and in redemption of the national currency."

Both Acts had ratios between capital and total liabilities of any association, person, company or firm for money borrowed. In the 1863 Act, a tripartite formula limited the total liabilities to 3 to 1, exclusive of liabilities as acceptor, 5 to 1 and exclusive of bills of exchange, 10 to 1.

The 1864 Act was simpler with a 10 to 1 ratio between total liabilities of covered persons and entities to the paid-in capital stock of the bank, with the provision "[t]hat the discount of bona fide bills of exchange drawn against existing values, and the discount of commercial or business paper actually owned by [the covered person or entity] shall not be considered as money borrowed."

The reserve requirements in the 1864 Act were substantially modified. The 1864 Act had a three-level system of reserve and depository requirements. At the lowest level were what popularly came to be known as country banks with a 15 percent reserve requirement and the expectation that 60 percent of balances due for redemption of its notes would be held by banks or clearing associations in St. Louis, Louisville, Chicago, Detroit, Milwaukee, New Orleans, Albany, Leavenworth, San Francisco, Washington, Charleston, or Richmond. Banks in the cities designated in the Act for redemption of country bank notes had a 25 percent reserve requirement. Each of these banks in turn had to select "subject to the approval of the Comptroller of the Currency" a bank in New York "at which it will redeem its lawful money reserve at par." Each of these designated banks "may keep one half of its lawful money reserve in cash deposits in New York."

There were three noteworthy new provisions in the 1864 Act.

To pay for the costs of the Office of the Comptroller including printing costs, each association was required each half year to pay duties "one half of one per centum . . . in circulation," one quarter of one upon the average amount of its deposits and one quarter of the average amount invested in United States bonds.

Each national bank designated by the Secretary of Treasury could be designated a depository of public money "except receipts from customs" and a financial agent of the government.

As under the 1863 Act, any state bank on a two-thirds vote of its capital stock could convert to a national bank "subject to the same duties, responsibilities and rules . . . for other associations under the [Act]." State banks that subsequently chose to subject themselves to the 1864 Act were subject to added capital requirements:

> [S]hareholders of any banking association now existing under state laws, having not less than five millions of dollars of capital actually paid in, and a surplus of twenty per centum on hand, both to be determined by the comptroller of the currency, shall be liable only to the amount invested in their shares; and such surplus of twenty per centum shall be kept undiminished, and be in addition to the surplus provided for in this act[.]

To the extent the heightened capital and regulatory oversight of converting state banks might discourage the conversion of state banks, a national tax ultimately set at 10 percent on "notes of any person, state bank or state banking associations used for circulation and paid out by them after the 1st day of August 1866," created a far more powerful incentive to convert. The constitutionality of the 10 percent tax was approved by the Supreme Court, in a decision written by the ubiquitous Salmon Chase. When Chief Justice Marshall in *McCulloch v. Maryland* had insisted "the power to tax is the power to destroy," Chief Justice Chase, who as Secretary of Treasury *had* designed this tax to destroy State Banks and create a system of national banks and national currency. In 1869, Chase wrote:

> It is insisted, however, that the tax in the case before us is excessive, and so excessive as to indicate a purpose on the part of Congress to destroy the franchise of the bank, and is, therefore, beyond the constitutional power of Congress.
>
> The first answer to this is that the judicial cannot prescribe to the legislative departments of the Government limitations upon the exercise of its acknowledged powers. The power to tax may be exercised oppressively upon persons, but the responsibility of the legislature is not to the courts, but to the people by whom its members are elected. So if a particular tax bears heavily upon a corporation, or a class of corporations, it cannot, for that reason only, be pronounced contrary to the Constitution.

State banks were deprived of the authority to issue national currency under the 1864 Act or to act as depositories under the Act.

The objective of the Chase National Banking Acts and punitive taxation initially largely was achieved. The number of state banks sharply declined from 1059 in 1864 to 297 in 1868. Senator Sherman, the leader of efforts to enact national banking and related tax legislation, stated in February 1865: "The national banks were intended to supersede the State banks. Both can not exist together; yet while the national system is extending, the issues of State banks have not materially decreased. . . . If the State banks had power enough in Congress to prolong their existence beyond the present year, we had better suspend the organization of national banks." Less eloquently, the *Chicago Tribune* beseeched Congress: "Tax the banks out of existence."[39]

Weaknesses in the National Bank Act of 1864 led to the rebound of state banks and the development of the dual banking system that operates to this day.

The largest point was the creation of the dual banking system with national banks subject to national control and state banks subject to state control and with banks given the choice as to which jurisdiction to which they will be subject. This choice, as Professor Redford recognized in 1966, "distinguishes banking regulation from all other fields of regulation in this country."

State banks circumvented the 10 percent tax on currency by emphasizing services that allowed their customers to pay bills with checks and deposit balances, avoiding issuing bank notes altogether. By 1874, state bank total deposits exceeded total note issuances of national banks. State deposit banking was profitable and demonstrated the nonessentiality of note issuance. State minimum capital and regulatory requirements for state banks were less demanding than the National Banking Act's minimum $50,000 capital requirement and examination by the Comptroller of the Currency. Surveys of state bank minimum capital requirements in 1895 and 1909 found with very few exceptions state capital requirements were lower than those for national banks, in some instances as low as $5,000 or $10,000 required capital, more often $25,000 or $50,000. Reserve requirements for state banks long were undemanding. Eugene White, author of *The Regulation and Reform of the American Banking System, 1900–1929*, reports that in 1887, only three states had reserve requirements. In 1895, 31 states and territories had no reserve requirements. The National Banking Act, wrote White, "had severely encumbered national bank operations by restricting their capacity to lend on security or real estate." The 1864 Act permitted National Banks to issue mortgages "for debts previously contracted" but otherwise not to make loans on real estate. White added: "[E]nforcement of federal laws was stricter than that of state laws where supervision was noticeably lax." In 1885, only ten states authorized regular examination of banks.[40]

Currency Wars

In the period after the enactment of the Civil War National Banking Acts, Congress, the President, and the public focused on what constituted money, not the structure of federal banking regulation.

Until 1873, there were two competing bases of United States currency. The Revolutionary War with its much derided "Continental" dollars and the Civil War with its greenbacks were periods of paper money, when the currency was backed by the credit of the national government. These periods proved to be inflationary with the currency depreciating markedly relative to "hard" currency or specie, meaning gold or silver. Authors of *A Monetary History*, Milton

Friedman and Anna Schwartz, calculated that in June 1867, of a total of $979 million in total currency, the vast majority, $788 million, was in national bank notes ($292 million), United States notes meaning greenbacks ($372 million) or other United States currency ($124 million).

The more frequently used alternative basis of currency was bimetal, meaning currency backed by silver and gold. Initially, the enactment of Hamilton's 1792 Law Establishing a Mint in Regulating Coins, the United States had been based on a bimetal model, with the United States dollar backed by gold and silver at a fixed ratio of 15 units of silver to one unit of gold, which then was international practice.

Until 1834, only silver in fact was used as the legal basis for United States money. Friedman explained:

> The reason was simple: There was and is a market for silver and gold outside the U.S. Mint: for jewelry, industrial use, coinage by other countries, and so forth. In 1792, the ratio of the market price of gold to the price of silver was almost exactly 15 to 1, the ratio Hamilton recommended. But shortly thereafter, the world price ratio went above 15 to 1 and stayed there.... As a result, anyone who had gold and wanted to convert it to money would do better by exchanging the gold for silver at the market ratio and taking the silver to the mint than by taking the gold directly to the mint.

In 1834, the 1792 Coinage Act was amended to change the silver to gold ratio to 16 to 1. The world market silver to gold ratio then was 15.625 to 1. Whether the purpose of the changed ratio was "to do something for gold" with four Southern states having recently discovered gold or at the height of the Jackson war on the Bank to weaken the Second Bank's notes by making gold an effective substitute for the notes, "the adoption of the 16 to 1 ratio," Friedman wrote:

> spelled the end of the reign of silver. From then to the Civil War, little silver was coined.... From 1834 on, gold coins circulated and gold was the effective standard. Despite the increased demand for gold for monetary use, the gold-silver price ratio fell after the Californian and Australian gold discoveries of the 1840s and 1850s so that its status as "cheap money" seemed secure.

After 1834, the silver dollar was no longer in circulation and soon became an unknown coin to most Americans. Between 1834 and 1873, no silver Dollars were used to pay duties of customs houses.

During the Civil War, the major monetary use of gold was for foreign transactions. Because Europe, most significantly England since 1815, was on a gold standard, gold was essential to financing United States trade. New York banks engaged in foreign transactions had two kinds of deposit accounts, those payable in greenbacks and those payable in gold. Gold deposits were expressed in dollars, but this meant the physical amount of gold that corresponded to the pre-Civil War dollar. At times during the Civil War, the physical amount of gold was equal to more than two dollars in greenbacks, reaching a peak of over $2.50 in greenbacks in 1864.

In 1873, Congress enacted a new Coinage Act, elaborately styled An Act Revising and Amending the Laws Relative to the Mint, Assaying Office and Coinage of the United States. The 1873 Act when debated and enacted was noncontroversial and passed by overwhelming majorities — 110 to 13 in the House, 36 to 10 in the Senate. The Coinage Act discontinued the standard silver dollars, although silver trade dollar coins could "be a legal tender at their nominal value for any amount not exceeding five dollars in any one payment." Trade dollars were only available for commerce with countries on a silver standard, then meaning China. By the 1870s, China and India were the only major countries on a silver standard.

The price of silver determined the significance of the demonetization of silver. After 1836, the price of silver generally had been above the 16 to 1 ratio to gold. This meant that the Coinage Act of 1873 had little practical consequence on the utility of silver and initially inspired little contemporary comment. Beginning in 1872, however, the price of silver began to sharply fall as a result of new highly productive mines led by the Comstock Mine in Nevada and because other European countries followed the lead of the United States and abandoned silver as a basis of money in favor of gold. By 1879, the marketplace silver to gold ratio was 18.4 to 1, by 1896; when Bryan first was nominated for president, it was 30 to 1.

The Panic of 1873, with over 5000 bankruptcies that year alone, including leading investment bank Jay Cooke & Company, the closure of the New York Stock Exchange in September 1873, and unemployment estimated to be 25 percent of New York's workers by the Society for Improving the Conditions of the Poor in the Winter of 1873–1874, was deeply unnerving.

The conversion to a gold standard after 1873 also was coincident with systemic deflation at a rate of 1.7 percent per year in the

United States between 1875 and 1896. In rural and agricultural areas of the country, the wholesale prices of agriculture and other basic commodities fell at a greater rate, in one estimate 3 percent per year. Financial journalist and author Roger Lowenstein believed: "[F]rom 1867 to 1897, prices skidded relentlessly lower, and over the whole of that period, they tumbled well more than 50 percent."

The majority of our population was then involved in farming and were, as Friedman put it, "generally net monetary debtors," who were harmed by a fall in prices. Those in debt benefitted from inflation and soon politicians were declaiming that the 1873 demonetization of silver was a result of a cabal of Wall Street bankers and English and other European nations and banks who earlier were on the gold standard.[41]

Senator William M. Stewart in 1889 would decry the demonetization of silver as "the Crime of the Nineteenth Century." Senator John Reagan more fervently in 1890 would insist: "I am persuaded history will write it [the Act of 1873] down as the greatest legislative crime and the most stupendous conspiracy against the welfare of the people of the United States and of Europe or any other age has witnessed." William Jennings Bryan's 1896 Democratic Party Convention "Cross of Gold" address had its origins in the demonetization of silver in 1873; even Frank Baum's *Wizard of Oz*, some argue, was supposedly inspired by the late 19th century currency battles, with kindhearted Dorothy from Kansas representing the virtuous and beleaguered nature of agrarian America: the Land of Oz, with its emphasis on gold and the very name Oz inspired by the ounces in which gold was customarily measured epitomized the gaudiness and excess of Wall Street; and Dorothy protected in the novel, but not the Technicolor movie, by silver slippers. The yellow brick road (symbol of gold) led to Emerald City (Washington D.C.) where no answers are found. Fortunately, Dorothy by then had allied with the Scarecrow (symbol of the farmer), the Tin Woodsman (labor), and the Cowardly Lion, who in the literary analysis is William Jennings Bryan, the roaring lion of 1896 when he championed free silver, who by the 1900 publication date, seemed less inclined to refight that battle for free silver.

The Free Silver and Bimetal Movements intensified in the decades after 1873. Even before 1873, the end of greenbacks and resumption of a specie-based currency was associated with deflation. Indeed, after the hyperinflation of the Civil War, that was one of the very points of specie resumption. Secretary of Treasury McCulloch in December 1865 forcefully made the case for withdrawing greenbacks as rapidly as the Secretary of Treasury can "dispose of securities":

> The present legal-tender acts were war measures, and while the repeal of those provisions which made the United States notes lawful money is not now recommended, the Secretary is of the opinion that they ought not to remain in force one day longer than shall be necessary to enable the people to prepare for a return to the constitutional currency. It is not supposed that it was the intention of Congress, by these acts, to introduce a standard of value, in times of peace, lower than the coin standard, much less to perpetuate the discredit which must attach to a great nation which dishonors its own obligations by unnecessarily keeping in circulation an irredeemable paper currency.

On December 18, 1865, the House by a vote of 144 to 6 adopted a resolution expressing a concurring view on the need to resume a specie-based currency as soon as possible.

On April 12, 1866, Congress enacted legislation to reduce greenback circulation ($414,892,156 on May 1, 1866) by not more than $10 million within six months and after that, no more than $4 million in any one month. "The sharp decline in business prices and the business contraction after the Civil War," wrote Friedman and Schwartz, "produced after some lag, a marked change in sentiment." In February 1868, Congress suspended the retirement of greenbacks, prompting a debate on whether the $44 million in greenbacks already retired should be reissued.

Ulysses Grant, the highly popular Republican President elected in 1868, stressed the need to return to a specie-based currency "paid in gold" in his March 4, 1869, Inaugural Address: "A great debt has been contracted in securing to us and our posterity the Union. The payment of this, principal and interest, as well as the return to a specie basis as soon as it can be accomplished without material detriment to the debtor class or to the country at large, must be provided for. To protect the national honor, every dollar of government indebtedness should be paid in gold, unless otherwise expressly stipulated in the contract."

In December 1869, Grant amplified these themes:

> Among the evils growing out of the rebellion, and not yet referred to, is that of an irredeemable currency. It is an evil which I hope will receive your most earnest attention. It is a duty, and one of the highest duties, of government to secure to the citizen a medium of exchange of fixed, unvarying value. This implies a return to a specie basis, and no substitute for it can be devised. . . . Immediate resumption, if practicable, would not be desirable. It would compel the debtor class to pay, beyond their contracts, the premium on gold at the date of their purchase and would bring bankruptcy and ruin to thousands. Fluctuation, however, in the paper value of the measure of all values (gold) is detrimental to the interests of trade. It makes the man of business an involuntary gambler, for in all sales where future payment is to be made both parties speculate as to what will be the value of the currency to be paid and received. I earnestly recommend to you, then, such legislation as will insure a gradual return to specie payments and put an immediate stop to fluctuations in the value of currency.

The Republican Party, then with a strong majority in Congress similarly supported, as the 1872 party platform wrote "a speedy resumption of specie payment."

The Panic of 1873 rapidly reordered national politics. In April 1874, Congress passed an inflation bill to increase paper circulation by $100 million. On April 22, 1874, Grant vetoed the bill, reiterating the above quoted text from his December 1869 message to Congress and pointedly adding: "I shall adhere to the views then expressed."

The Republican Party suffered an unprecedented defeat in the Congressional elections of 1874, losing 93 seats in the House of a total of 293. This meant the Republicans went from a 70 percent majority party to a minority party with 36 percent of the House. Historian Richard White described the electoral wipeout: "Republicans had not simply failed to meet the economic crisis, they had raised hopes only to have Grant dash them. Democrats could, and did, attack the Republicans as tools of rich Northern bankers and merchants."

In the lame duck session of the outgoing Congress in January 1875, the badly defeated Republican Party enacted the Specie Payment Resumption Act of 1875, requiring the Secretary of Treasury on January 1, 1879 to redeem United States legal tender notes "in sums of not less than fifty dollars."

The Resumption Act authorized the Secretary of Treasury to use surplus revenues and the proceeds of bond sales to build Treasury gold reserves.

The 1875 Resumption Act both strengthened the Greenback Party and the Free Silver Movement, each representing an inflationary currency alternative to gold.

The Greenback Party, formed in 1874 as the Independent Greenback Party, was one of several third parties that participated in national elections in the late 19th century, most prominently including the Populist Party. In 1876, the Greenback Party Platform called for repeal of the Specie Resumption Act of 1875 and renewed use of greenbacks to restore currency through an expanded money supply: "We demand the immediate and unconditional repeal of the Specie Resumption Act of January 14, 1875, and the rescue of our industries from ruin and disaster resulting from its enforcement." The Greenback Party in 1876 drew much support from farmers and in the late 1870s was able to help elect 21 members to Congress, securing about 10 percent of the vote in the 1878 election. The Party did even better in 1880, electing 26 members of Congress.

In 1877, the House of Representatives passed a bill to repeal the 1875 Resumption Act. The House Bill was defeated in the Senate by a single vote.

Rutherford B. Hayes, winner of the contested, some argue stolen, 1876 Presidential election, sought to pursue a specie-based currency, but was pressed to compromise. Hayes supported "honest money," which meant a return to the gold standard. In his March 5, 1877, inaugural address, Hayes repeated:

> [T]he statement made in my letter of acceptance, that in my judgment the feeling of uncertainty inseparable from an irredeemable paper currency, with its fluctuation of values, is one of the greatest obstacles to a return to prosperous times. The only safe paper currency is one which rests upon a coin basis and is at all times and promptly convertible into coin.

Secretary of Treasury John Sherman's views were more nuanced. The United States Monetary Commission organized under a Joint Resolution of Congress adopted in August 1876 had recommended a bimetallic standard including the coinage of what Sherman termed "the old silver dollar" which Sherman acknowledged "would greatly add to the convenience of the people." "A gold coin of the denomination of one dollar is too small for convenient circulation, while such a coin in silver would be convenient for a multitude of daily transactions." But Sherman vehemently objected to the free coinage of silver or to making silver legal tender:

> Of the metals, silver is of most general use for coinage. It is a part of every system of coinage even in countries where gold is the sole legal standard. It best measures the common wants of life, but, from its weight and bulk, is not a convenient medium in the larger exchanges of commerce. Its production is reasonably steady in amount. The relative market value of silver and gold is far more stable than that of any other two commodities — still, it does vary. It is not in the power of human law to prevent the variation. This inherent difficulty has compelled all nations to adopt one or the other as the sole standard of value, or to authorize an alternative standard of either, or to coin both metals at an arbitrary standard, and to maintain one at par with the other by limiting its amount and legal-tender quality, and receiving or redeeming it at par with the other.

Congress, in 1878, dominated by a soft money majority, enacted the Bland-Allison Act which directed United States mints to coin silver dollars which would become "a legal tender, at their nominal value, for all debts, public and private, except where otherwise expressly stipulated in the contract." The Act was a compromise. The Secretary of the Treasury was authorized to purchase between $2 and $4 million of silver bullion per month. The President was directed to invite Latin American and European nations to a conference "to adopt a common ratio between gold and silver for the purpose of establishing, internationally, the use of bi-metallic money."

President Hayes vetoed the Bland-Allison Bill:

> The bill provides for the coinage of silver dollars of the weight of 412½ grains each, of standard silver, to be a legal tender at their nominal value for all debts and dues, public and private, except where otherwise expressly stipulated in the contract. It is well known that the market value of that number of grains of standard silver during the post year has been from 90 to 92 cents as compared with the standard gold dollar. Thus the silver dollar authorized by this bill is worth 8 to 10 per cent less than it purports to be worth, and is made a legal tender for debts contracted when the law did not recognize such coins as lawful money.

> The right to pay duties in silver or in certificates for silver deposits will, when they are issued in sufficient amount to circulate, put an end to the receipt of revenue in gold, and thus compel the payment of silver for both the principal and interest of the public debt. . . .
>
> It is my firm conviction that if the country is to be benefited by a silver coinage it can be done only by the issue of silver dollars of full value, which will defraud no man. A currency worth less than it purports to be worth will in the end defraud not only creditors, but all who are engaged in legitimate business, and none more surely than those who are dependent on their daily labor for their daily bread.[42]

Congress overrode Hayes' veto and in 1878 the United States resumed bimetallism. In December 1878, the premium on gold disappeared for the first time since 1861. The Hayes Administration begrudgingly complied with the Bland-Allison Act by purchasing the minimum of $2 million of silver bullion each month. Secretary of the Treasury Sherman emphasized gold. By the end of 1878, the Treasury had purchased over $100 million in gold, enough to resume specie payments.

There was widespread revulsion at the McKinley Tariff of 1890, which increased duties from 38 to 50 percent to protect United States manufacturers, and dramatically raised costs to United States consumers and harshly impacted American farmers. A pivotal consequence of the tariff was the Congressional election of 1890, which historian Richard White has characterized as "the greatest midterm reversal in American history." The Democrats gained 86 seats to become the majority party with 238 Representatives in Congress compared to just 86 for the Republicans, who in 1888 had been the majority party with 179 representatives.

Declining market prices for silver earlier had led some Western mines to shut down. Enduring deflation, as White wrote, hurt farmers twice: "It made money scarce and it also made the money they eventually paid to creditors more valuable than the money they had received." With new states that had silver mining joining the Union between 1886 and 1889 and an ongoing recession, exports fell and with this decline concomitantly duties paid in gold also fell.

In July 1890, before the stunning 1890 election, Congress enacted the Sherman Silver Purchase Act of 1890, named after then Senator John Sherman, Chair of the Senate Finance Committee. The Act secured enactment of the 1890 McKinley Tariff Act. Support for the Silver Purchase Act came from the West, especially Western miners, and from farmers perennially eager to reduce debt through inflationary silver backed currency.

The Silver Purchase Act directed the Secretary of the Treasury to purchase 4.5 million ounces of silver bullion each month at the market price and to pay for the silver with Treasury notes. The Treasury notes were redeemable either in gold or silver at the discretion of the Secretary of Treasury and were legal tender in payment of all public and private debts, "except where otherwise expressly stipulated in the contract." Critically, the Act provided that it was "the established policy of the United States to maintain the two metals on a parity with each other upon the present [16 to 1] legal ratio or such ratio as may be provided by law."

Until July 1891, the Secretary of Treasury was required to coin two million ounces of silver bullion per month into standard silver dollars and after that, as many silver dollars as were necessary to provide for the redemption of the Treasury notes created by the Silver Purchase Act.

Much of the Bland-Allison Act that required the monthly purchase of $2 to $4 million of silver bullion was repealed.

From enactment, the Silver Purchase Act was a catastrophe. Between 1891 and 1893, bullion purchases and coinage of silver dollars equaled $68 million. The price of silver rose by December 1890 to $1.21 from 93 cents. But by the iron consequences of Gresham's Law, bad money drove out the good. In 1893, $60 million in gold would be exported from the United States. By August 1894, United States gold reserves would decline to $52 million. World gold prices fell sharply. Europe feared a flight from the United States gold standard, aggravated by the enactment by the Senate in 1890 of a Free Silver Coinage Bill without any limit and Treasury purchases and coinage. The Senate Bill did not become law, but Europe's anxiety continued.

A recession climaxed by the Panic of 1893 ensued. Whether coincident or causal, the 1890 Silver Purchase Act was blamed for a rise in unemployment from an estimated 4 percent in 1890 to 18.4 percent in 1894; the February 1893 collapse of the Pennsylvania & Reading Railroad; in all, 119 railroads would go into receivership in 1893; the failure of 360 national and state banks in 1893 with subsequent restrictions by banks of cash payments.

To halt the flight of gold and stabilize the economy, President Grover Cleveland called for repeal of the Sherman Silver Purchase Act on August 8, 1893:

> Our unfortunate financial plight is not the result of untoward events nor of conditions related to our natural resources, nor is it traceable to any of the afflictions which frequently check national growth and prosperity. With plenteous crops, with abundant promise of remunerative production and manufacture, with unusual invitation to safe investment, and with satisfactory assurance to business enterprise, suddenly financial distrust and fear have sprung up on every side....
>
> I believe these things are principally chargeable to Congressional legislation touching the purchase and coinage of silver by the General Government.

In October 1893, Congress repealed the Sherman Silver Purchase Act.

Repeal did little to restore confidence in the economy. The period 1893 to 1896, Friedman and Schwartz characterized as years of "dragging deflation, interrupted only by a brief cyclical revival from June 1894 to December 1895. This is one of the few revivals in the cyclical history of the United States in which aggregate output probably did not reach the level of the preceding cyclical peak, and in which per capita output almost surely did not."

In historical biographer Ron Chernow's view, expressed in *The House of Morgan*:

> Among the indebted farmers of the South and West, the gold standard generated fanatic hatred. The United States was still an agrarian debtor nation, and poor, rural debtors far outnumbered big city bondholders. These farmers had many legitimate grievances, for they contended with the curse of steadily falling prices in the late nineteenth century. Deflation meant they had to repay debt in dearer money — a recipe for ruin. There was no central bank to expand credit during hard times. At the same time, because of tariffs and industrial trusts, the prices of finished goods didn't fall as fast as the price of food.... So farmers welcomed inflation — specifically, higher prices for their own produce — as the only way to remain equal in the contest against bankers and industrialists.
>
> This discontent made bankers the favorite bogeyman in rural political demonology. So venomous was the mood that several

western states outlawed bankers, and Texas banned them altogether until 1904.

Gold could be attacked because it was deflationary, because it removed control of our financial system from New York to London, capital of the world's greatest creditor nation, Great Britain, and because it concentrated United States money and credit in the Northeast, leaving the West and South often desperately short of funds.

So intense was the distrust of Wall Street bankers and enthusiasm for free silver coinage that President Cleveland initially was rebuffed in 1894 and early 1895 in his efforts to replenish the gold reserve. Chernow explained: "Populist fury made resorting to private banks like Morgan unthinkable." By February 1895, Cleveland had no choice. With only $9 million in gold coin remaining in government vaults on Wall Street, Cleveland and Treasury Secretary John Carlisle met with Morgan, who informed the President that a $10 million draft was about to be presented, which meant the United States would be in default.

Believing Morgan, Cleveland asked: "What suggestions have you to make, Mr. Morgan?" Morgan proposed that the House of Morgan and the London-based House of Rothschild could obtain 3.5 million ounces of gold, at least half from Europe, in exchange for approximately $65 million worth of 30-year gold-backed bonds. Morgan also promised that the gold obtained by the government would not leave again. When the bonds were issued on February 20, 1895, they sold out in 22 minutes in New York and two hours in London. The financial markets steadied.

The bond's promoters earned profits of $6 to $7 million, prompting further populist outcry and anti-Semitism because of the Rothschild participation. Mary Lease called Cleveland a tool "of Jewish bankers and British gold." Congressman William Jennings Bryan directed the House Clerk to read Shylock's bond from the *Merchant of Venice.* A separate, more telling point was made by the *New York World*: The Cleveland Administration had "gratuitously given to a syndicate in a secret conference" what amounted to a $5 million bonus with little risk on their part "and it will be paid out of the public Treasury." The newspaper, as American historian Richard White pointed out, underestimated the bonus.

Political opposition intensified before and after Cleveland's successful lobbying for the repeal of the Silver Purchase Act in 1893 and his 1895 approval of the Morgan gold reserve rescue plan.

In March 1894, Jacob Coxey led 400 members of the Army of the Commonwealth of Christ from Massillon, Ohio to Washington, D.C. to demand that the government provide jobs to the unemployed and issue $500 million in legal tender notes to do so. Coxey's Army also sought the power for states, cities, and towns to issue paper money. Coxey's Army was dispersed by the police, but support for an alternative to gold continued to grow. The American Bimetallic League organized a Silver Convention in August 1893. In 1895, Republicans favoring silver coinage formed the National Bimetallic Union which merged with the American Bimetallic League in 1896 to form the American Bimetallic Union, popularly known as the National Silver Party.[43]

The decision by President Cleveland to send federal troops to repress the Pullman Strike in 1894 further infuriated labor.

At the ballot box, Cleveland's Democratic Party suffered historic losses in the United States House of Representatives in 1894, losing 127 seats to become again the minority party with the Republicans now holding a 253 to 93 majority. In the Senate, the Democratic Party majority in 1894 declined from 44–37 in 1892 to a razor-thin 40–39 in 1894. Among others, Congressman William Jennings Bryan was defeated in 1894 in his run for the Senate in Nebraska. Both parties were bitterly divided over silver coinage and bimetallism.

The battle lines for the 1896 Presidential election hardened in June 1896 when the Republicans selected William McKinley to be their nominee. McKinley was a strong supporter of "sound money" and with his strong support, the Republicans adopted a platform rejecting the free coinage of silver:

> The Republican party is unreservedly for sound money. It caused the enactment of a law providing for the redemption [resumption] of specie payments in 1879. Since then every dollar has been as good as gold. We are unalterably opposed to every measure calculated to debase our currency or impair the credit of our country. We are therefore opposed to the free coinage of silver, except by international agreement with the leading commercial nations of the earth, which agreement we pledge ourselves to promote, and until such agreement can be obtained the existing gold standard must be maintained.

A number of "Silver Republicans" subsequently walked out of the convention led by Colorado Senator Henry Tella.

In 1896, Cleveland did not seek re-election, leaving the choice of the Democratic Party nominee open at the 1896 convention.

On July 7, 1896, the Democratic Party proposed a platform that unequivocally demanded "the free and unlimited coinage of both silver and gold at the present legal ratio of 16 to 1 without waiting for the aid or consent of any other nation:"

> Recognizing that the money question is paramount to all others at this time, we invite attention to the fact that the federal Constitution named silver and gold together as the money metals of the United States, and that the first coinage law passed by Congress under the Constitution made the silver dollar the monetary unit and admitted gold to free coinage at a ratio based upon the silver-dollar unit.
>
> We declare that the act of 1873 demonetizing silver without the knowledge or approval of the American people has resulted in the appreciation of gold and a corresponding fall in the prices of commodities produced by the people; a heavy increase in the burdens of taxation and of all debts, public and private; the enrichment of the money-lending class at home and abroad; the prostration of industry and impoverishment of the people.
>
> We are unalterably opposed to monometallism which has locked fast the prosperity of an industrial people in the paralysis of hard times. Gold monometallism is a British policy, and its adoption has brought other nations into financial servitude to London....
>
> ...We demand that the standard silver dollar shall be a full legal tender, equally with gold, for all debts, public and private, and we favor such legislations as will prevent for the future the demonetization of any kind of legal-tender money by private contract.

The majority of delegates to the Democratic Convention were pro-silver, but there were several potential nominees including former Congressman Richard Bland, sponsor of the 1878 Bland-Allison Act, Iowa Governor Horace Boies, Vice President Adlai Stevenson, Senator Joseph Blackburn, Senator Teller, and Bryan.

In the folklore, Bryan's Cross of Gold speech on July 8, 1896, with its stirring peroration led to a one hour demonstration in which "bedlam broke loose, delirium reigned supreme," and Bryan's nomination on July 10th.

Matters were not that simple. Bryan was nominated on the fifth ballot after trailing Bland in the first three ballots.

Bryan's charisma was infectious, his voice "deep and powerfully musical," "clear as a cathedral bell." Historian Richard White wrote of the most effective convention speech ever delivered, that Bryan's "demeanor matched his speech, it radiated strength, youth, and vigor."

But the substance of Bryan's address deeply mattered to the delegates and the nation. His address was an unadulterated effort to revive the fervor and the policies of the Jackson Presidency:

> They say that we are opposing national bank currency; it is true. If you will read what Thomas Benton said, you will find he said that, in searching history, he could find but one parallel to Andrew Jackson; that was Cicero, who destroyed the conspiracy of Cataline and saved Rome. Benton said that Cicero only did for Rome what Jackson did for us when he destroyed the bank conspiracy and saved America. We say in our platform we believe that the right to coin and issue money is a function of government. We believe it. We believe that it is a part of sovereignty, and can no more with safety be delegated to private individuals than we could afford to delegate to private individuals the power to make penal statutes or levy taxes.

Bryan reached out to Labor and the Populists:

> Upon which side will the Democratic party fight; upon the side of "the idle holders of idle capital" or upon the side of "the struggling masses"? That is the question which the party must answer first, and then it must be answered by each individual hereafter. The sympathies of the Democratic party, as shown by the platform, are on the side of the struggling masses who have ever been the foundation of the Democratic party. There are two ideas of Government. There are those who believe that if you will only legislate to make the well-to-do prosperous, their prosperity will leak through on those below. The Democratic idea, however, has been that if you legislate to make the masses prosperous, their prosperity will find its way up through every class which rests upon them. . . .
>
> . . . [W]e care not upon what lines the battle is fought. If they say bimetallism is good, but that we cannot have it until other nations help us, we reply, that instead of having a gold standard because England has, we will restore bimetallism, and then let England have bimetallism because the United States has it. If they dare to come out in the open field and defend the gold standard as a gold thing, we will fight them to the uttermost.

> Having behind us the producing masses of this nation and the world, supported by the commercial interests, the laboring interests and the toilers everywhere, we will answer their demand for a gold standard by saying to them: You shall not press down upon the brow of labor this crown of thorns, you shall not crucify mankind upon a cross of gold.

As with McKinley, Bryan's nomination divided the Democrats; "Gold" Democrats bolted from the party and nominated John Palmer to run as the candidate of the splinter National Democratic Party. Bryan's campaign on his theme of free silver gained the support of some Populists and Silver Republicans.

The 1896 election has been characterized as the first modern presidential election. Mark Hanna, McKinley's campaign manager, raised a prodigious $4 million to support the McKinley campaign, and as Theodore Roosevelt scoffed, "Hanna advertised McKinley as if he were a patent medicine." Hanna used 1400 speakers on behalf of McKinley, produced 275 separate campaign pamphlets, and emphasized that McKinley was the "Advance Agent for Prosperity." McKinley's campaign emphasized sound money, the tariff as a solution to unemployment, and the argument that Bryan was waging a campaign of class warfare.

The indefatigable Bryan delivered as many as 600 speeches to as many as five million listeners, made four extended railroad trips covering 18,000 miles in three month—in contrast to McKinley's front porch campaign—and did what he could to counter the Republican Party financial and organization advantages. Bryan could not counter the enduring pain of the Panic of 1893 or belief manifest in the 1894 congressional elections that the Democrats had failed to produce the stable economy that Cleveland had promised.

McKinley decisively won the popular vote with 7,111,607 votes (51 percent) to Bryan's 6,509,152 (46.7 percent) and the Electoral College with 271 votes to 176. The regionalization of the election was evident in the results. McKinley won the Northeast and Midwest, Bryan the South and West, with the exception of California and Oregon, then relatively small in population.

The 1896 election represented the high water mark of the campaign for free silver coinage and bimetallism. To have adopted Bryan's 16 to 1 silver to gold ratio in 1896 would have been lunacy. The price ratio was 30.8 to 1 in 1896, meaning that silver could have purchased from the Treasury for gold and resold on the market for nearly twice the official exchange ratio, producing as Friedman wrote, "major disturbances in both price levels and international trade."

The political enthusiasm for bimetallism also dissipated after the 1896 election as the United States gold reserves dramatically increased as a result of discoveries in South Africa, Alaska, and Colorado, nearly quadrupling from $502 million in government and private holdings in June 1896 to $1891 million in 1914 as a result of "cheap gold." The 1897 failure of European crops also created a strong market for American farmers, converted a grade deficit into a surplus and brought European gold into the United States. Unemployment declined to 5 percent by 1900, when McKinley was reelected over Bryan.

In 1900, Congress adopted the Gold Standard Act, effectively declaring gold to be the monetary standard of the United States and directing the Treasury to redeem United States and Treasury notes with gold coin, maintaining a $150 million reserve in gold coin and bullion "for such redemption purposes only." With brief exceptions, the United States would remain on the gold standard until 1971 when President Nixon ended the convertibility of dollars into gold.

Currency, whether in the form of greenbacks, free silver coinage, or bimetallism, faded as a political issue after 1900.[44]

The Transformation of the United States Economy

By 1900, the United States was a nation transformed. Thirteen former colonies with a total population of 3.9 million in 1790 had grown to 45 States spanning the continent, with 76 million people in 1900. The land area of the United States had more than tripled between 1790 and 1900, from 867,980 to 2,974,154 square miles. The United States in 1900 was knitted together by 258,784 miles of railroad track and 933,000 miles of telegraph wire.

During the decades after the Civil War, the character of the United States economy was radically transformed. On May 10, 1869, the first transcontinental rail line was completed at Promontory Point, Utah. This linkage symbolized the great age of railway construction. In the next decade, a staggering 20 percent of United States capital formation was devoted to extending rail line systems.

Trunk lines burgeoned in the Middle Atlantic states and the North Central states and then across the Great Plains and finally into the South.

By greatly broadening the markets of an agrarian economy, the railroads quickened the growth of such established commercial centers as New York, which by 1900 had a population of 3,437,202 people, Philadelphia, and St. Louis and helped populate such new centers as Chicago, Minneapolis, Kansas City, Dallas, and Atlanta. Between 1790 and 1900, the proportion of urban population grew from 5 to 40 percent. This great urban expansion increased the demand for consumer goods such as clothing, food, and whiskey. At the same time, railroad construction created the first large market for producers' goods such as steel.

The genesis of a national transportation network and an expanding urban market made possible a new type of business corporation. For the first time, a single manufacturer could dominate not just a local market, not just a regional one, but an entire national market.

The Eastern railroad corporations were the first to secure important national monopolies. Exploiting their strategic position by discriminatory freight rates and refusals to deal, eight railroad corporations were able to wrest ownership of 95 percent of the anthracite coal industry by 1893.

Beginning in 1871, John D. Rockefeller set out to consolidate the oil refining industry under a more effective legal form. Rockefeller already had become a leading refiner in Cleveland by combining several local refineries and then persuading two of three competitive railroad lines to secretly rebate 37½ percent of the freight tariff on crude oil shipments from the Pennsylvania oil region and on refined oil shipments from his Cleveland refinery to the Eastern states.

In 1874, Rockefeller traded Standard Oil stock to purchase leading refineries in Philadelphia and Pittsburgh. Shortly later, he bought a major refinery in New York City. Within five years, Rockefeller controlled 95 percent of all refined oil shipments in the United States.

But Rockefeller did so through a corporate form that altered the course of American history. Effectively blocked by the law of every state from organizing any one corporation large enough to possess the assets of 95 percent of the nation's oil refineries, Rockefeller's legendary counsel, S.C.T. Dodd, devised the corporate trust. Under a trust, several legally separate corporations deposited a controlling interest of their stock with a common board of trustees in return for a contractual right to dividends.

The dimensions of the Standard Oil Trust's success were not lost on the business community. In 1884, a Cotton Oil Trust was organized in the State of Arkansas. In 1887, three great trusts, the "Whiskey Trust," the "Sugar Trust," and the "Lead Trust" were created. By 1890, 24 trusts with a total capitalization of $376,000,000 had been formed.

The trust form of business organization proved enormously controversial. By 1890, the United States, through the Sherman Antitrust Act, and 27 states and territories had enacted laws to prevent or limit trusts and monopolies. These laws largely would prove to be ineffectual in retarding the growth of nationwide enterprise. New Jersey in 1888 soon followed by Delaware and other states enacted laws to allow corporations to achieve unrestricted size through holding companies that held the stock of other corporations and mergers. In the 1890s, business historian Jerry Markham described a "merger mania":

> The American Smelting and Refining Company, the American Woolen Company, the American Car and Foundry Company, the American Hide and Leather Company, and the International Paper Company were all industry amalgamations. The iron and steel industries began merging and consolidating into the Federal Steel Company, the Illinois Steel Company, the Minnesota Iron Company, and the Lorain Steel Company. Other companies that were formed as a part of the consolidation of the steel business were the American Steel Hoop Company, the National Steel Company, the National Tube Company, and the American Bridge Company. Between 1898 and 1902, 198 trusts or giant new corporations were created in coal, sugar, and other industries.

Between 1894 and 1904, more than 1800 corporations were consolidated into 93 firms.

In 1904, John Moody published *The Truth about the Trusts,* in which Moody described 440 large industrial, franchise and transportation trusts of an important and active character, with a total floating capital of $20,379,162,511. These 440 trusts were led by seven Greater Industrial Trusts: The Copper Trust, the Smelters Trust, the Sugar Trust, the Tobacco Trust, the Shipping Trust, the Oil Trust and the Steel Trust. Moody was not a critic of the Trusts but acknowledged that he used the term *Trust* to describe "any act, agreement or combination believed to possess the intention, power or tendency to monopolize business, interfere with trade, fix prices, etc." In their then current form, holding companies in the seven Greater Industrial Trusts were formed in six instances between 1899 and 1902; in the seventh, in 1891. Moody characterized three trusts as dominated by Standard Oil or Rockefeller (Oil, Copper, and Smelters), and a fourth as affiliated with Standard Oil (Tobacco), and two as dominated by J.P. Morgan (Shipping and Steel).

Underlying the post-Civil War national economy was a system of finance with 13,053 banks in 1900, of which 3731 were national and 8696 were state chartered. These data, while capturing one reality of the nation's dual banking system, obscured much else.

By 1900, at the apex of the nation's system of finance were a small number of giant banking companies led by National City Bank of New York, then the nation's largest bank, and J.P. Morgan & Company. After the panic of 1907, these and other giant banking institutions would be investigated as part of a Money Trust. In 1900, leading banks performed functions that both involved commercial banking and investment banking.

Most banks at the turn of the 19th century were state banks, usually local, without branches, and prohibited from issuing national bank notes. The national currency was accessible to only a minority of the nation's banks.

Both national and state banks were subject to new forms of competition. With national banks after the 1864 National Banking Act prohibited from lending on real estate, savings banks, thrift institutions, or building and loan companies were formed to facilitate real estate lending. Over 500 thrift institutions including savings and loans had been formed by 1888, with assets of approximately $450 million. Markham wrote: "These institutions were located principally in New York and Massachusetts. In 1899, there were 130 savings banks in New York alone. They were the largest financial institutions in the State. By 1900, deposits in savings banks exceeded $1 billion."

More consequential during the Panic of 1907 were trust companies, which were established under State incorporation laws that did not limit activities of corporations. Initially trust companies, as their name suggested, focused on administering estates and wills.

But by the beginning of the 20th century, they had begun to compete with commercial banks by holding customer deposits. Trust company activities by 1907 included a number of business activities not permitted by national banks and often state banks, such as managing estates and trusts, safe deposits, securities underwriting, acting as transfer agents for stock issues, and issuing fidelity and title insurance. Trust companies also could make uncollateralized loans or loans against securities and held lower cash reserves than national banks, often 5 percent compared to the national bank requirement of 25 percent. They had other competitive advantages over the national banks, including the ability to pay higher interest rates and invest in riskier assets including real estate. Their greater flexibility proved highly profitable by the turn of the 20th century. By 1900, trust companies held approximately 26 percent of banking assets in New York. The number of trust companies increased from seven in 1865 to over 250 in 1890. Critically, the trusts were not subject to national banking regulation or members of the New York Clearing Association. In the view of co-authors Milton Friedman and Anna Schwartz, and of historian Ron Chernow, the recklessness of what Friedman called the "mushrooming trust companies in New York City" played "a notable part in the Panic of 1907."[45]

Between the Panic of 1893 and the Panic of 1907, securities markets experienced a period of intense volatility. The Dow Jones Industrial Average with an initial close of 62.76 on February 16, 1885, would plunge to its historical low of 28.48 on August 8, 1896, then nearly quadruple to 100.25 on January 12, 1906. During the next 22 months, the Dow Jones Industrial Average collapsed 48.5 percent, closing at 53 on November 15, 1907.

The Panic of 1907

Some 2000 business firms would fail in the wake of the 1907 Panic, including 100 state and 30 national banks. Beginning in October 1907, banks first in New York City, then Nationally, suspended convertibility of bank deposits into currency, instead issuing loan certificates and other emergency currency. Harvard's Professor Andrew estimated that $500 million of cash substitutes were circulated nationwide. Two-thirds of cities with populations over 25,000 suspended cash withdrawals "to a greater or lesser degree." Annual net national product figures would fall over 11 percent from 1907 to 1908.

Business historian Jerry Markham elaborated on the depths of the Panic of 1907:

> Long lines formed outside of banks overnight as depositors sought to obtain funds. Many failures followed, including the National Bank of America. A run by depositors began on the Trust Company of America on October 23, 1907 and lasted for two weeks. During that period $34 million was paid out to depositors. Another run began on the Lincoln Trust Company. Both of these trust companies had engaged in reckless practices. "Their methods of attracting business, absurdly high interest on deposits and the collection of out-of-town checks without charges were generally regarded as unsafe and even piratical." The situation worsened when the country banks started demanding their funds from the New York banks. This caused a scarcity of money, and the rate on call loans rose to 125 percent. This placed further pressure on the securities market as brokers began demanding margin that customers could meet only by selling their securities.

Volatility increased in 1907. Business historian Vincent Carosso described "[a] severe stock market break occurred ... in March 1907, forcing some of the highest grade stocks to tumble as much as twenty-nine points in less than a month. That shock was followed by two other serious setbacks in July and October." Two billion dollars was lost in the March 1907 Panic. Union Pacific lost $25 million in a single day. "In the fall of 1907," Roger Lowenstein in his history of the creation of the Federal Reserve wrote, "America suffered the worst breakdown in the history of the National Banking System. Overnight, banks were stripped of reserves and the country was plunged into a severe depression."

The existing means to ameliorate financial panic were inadequate.

In March 1907, leading industrialists and financiers Henry Clay Frick, Edward Harriman, William Rockefeller, and Jacob Schiff tried to assemble a $25 million fund to calm the market. J.P. Morgan declined to participate, concerned that this would appear to be stock price manipulation and the plan was abandoned.

In August 1907, the Department of Treasury deposited $28 million in banks across the United States, steps more than countervailed by President Theodore Roosevelt's speech that month decrying "malefactors of great wealth."

The New York Clearing House was somewhat more effective. Copper speculators, led by Frederick Heinze, president and majority stockholder of the Mercantile National Bank, had attempted to corner, that is manipulate, the copper market. In October, short sales — sales made by traders who profited from stock price declines — had pummeled the prices of United Copper, which fell $35 in two hours and Amalgamated Copper. Heinze's stock brokerage firm failed and depositors made a run on Heinze's Mercantile Bank. The New York Clearing House was able to provide assistance to save the Mercantile Bank.

The New York Clearing House was unable to prevent the more consequential failure in October 1907 of the Knickerbocker Trust, which unlike commercial banks was not a member of the Clearing House Association and did not maintain sufficient reserves. On October 22, 1907, Knickerbocker with total deposits of $60 million, suspended operations after paying out $8 million to depositors.

Wall Street and the Department of Treasury turned to J.P. Morgan, then legendary for his protection in 1895 of United States gold reserves, which were near a bankruptcy level for the United States. Morgan's leadership in 1907 in rescuing key trust companies, bailing out New York City and the New York Stock Exchange, would become, as Columbia History Professor Adam Tooze wrote in 2018, "the stuff of Wall Street legend."

But the more important point was that Morgan's heroics, as extraordinary as they were, were transitory in impact, and set in motion a multifaceted movement for reform that in 1913 led to the creation of the Federal Reserve. "The 1907 panic," Morgan biographer Ron Chernow would write, "was Pierpoint's last hurrah.... Its victory was pyrrhic ... as America decided that never again would one man wield such power."

As the Knickerbocker Trust deteriorated, on October 20, 1907, Morgan assembled a consortium of banks, including James Stillman of National City Bank and George Baker of First National Bank of New York, who along with Morgan, served as presiding officers of the rescue consortium. Morgan, in his son-in-law's words "allocate[d] to each one the sum of money which he felt was appropriate and necessary to make up the total amount needed to carry the weaker institutions through the panic." Morgan's efforts were viewed as so pivotal that Treasury Secretary George Cortelyou placed $25 million in government funds at Morgan's disposal. This type of transference of money by the United States government reflected Roosevelt and Cortelyou's confidence in Morgan as the "banker of bankers," and the limits of United States government powers to deal with the Panic. Later in the crisis, President Roosevelt would direct the deposit of another $50 million into commercial banks. The United States government was not alone. John D. Rockefeller also would provide $25 million to support the Morgan consortium, and $10 million to National City Bank.

After an audit of Knickerbocker's financial books, the Morgan consortium wrote off Knickerbocker as hopeless, leading to its October 22nd failure. When Morgan a few weeks later refused to meet with Knickerbocker President Charles Barney, Barney committed suicide. The failure of Knickerbocker set off a chain reaction of other potential failures.

On October 23, Morgan, Stillman, and Baker each provided $3 million to stabilize the heathier Trust Company of America, then New York City's second largest trust. As Morgan put it, "[t]his is the place to stop the trouble, then."

On October 24, with New York Stock Exchange President Ransom Thomas informing Morgan that 60 brokerage firms were nearing bankruptcy and that Thomas would have to close the Exchange that day unless $25 million was raised immediately, Morgan led a collocation of banks in securing a $23.5 million pledge. On October 25, the group provided another $13 million. "If twenty millions had been needed that day," Morgan partner George Perkins later testified, "the stock exchange and a hundred or more firms would have gone up, it was just that close."

On October 28, with New York City finances near default, Morgan, Baker, and Stillman raised $30 million through municipal revenue bonds to provide funds to New York to meet payroll and immediate obligations.

Borrowing costs were out of control with call money rates reaching 150 percent. Despite the heroics of the Morgan consortium, eight banks and trust companies failed that week.

By late October with the Panic, as Roger Lowenstein wrote, reaching "epic proportions," the New York Clearing House authorized member banks to settle accounts with loan certificates, in effect, promises to pay cash when cash became available. Loan certificates, in a period of financial panic and money hoarding, were used through the nation by banks and by some ordinary depositors. The certificates provided a measure of relief, but usually only in the city of issue. Drafts on Philadelphia, Boston, and other banks during this period were returned from New York banks during this period.

The issuance of clearinghouse loan certificates would prove, as Rutgers Professor of Economics Eugene White recognized:

> poor substitutes for a full-fledged central bank as they could not freely expand the monetary base. Even in their surrogate role, their ability to cope with a crisis depended on the mutual trust and cooperation that was fostered by their daily exchanges. The exclusive character of the clearinghouses promoted cooperation in the face of crises, yet the proliferation of national and state banks and trust companies to meet the growing demand for banking services threatened their ability to cope with the extraordinary needs for increased liquidity in bad times.

Morgan was responsible for one more complex financial legerdemain. Moore and Schley, a securities brokerage firm, by November 2, 1907 was $25 million in debt. The firm held majority ownership of Tennessee Coal and Iron Company and had used this stock as collateral for its loans. If Moore and Schley had to liquidate its stock ownership in Tennessee Coal, that might further collapse stock market prices. Morgan assembled Trust Company executives in the ornate East Room of his mansion and arranged for United States Steel, a favorite J.P. Morgan creation, to privately buy Moore and Schley's Tennessee Coal and Schley's holdings for $45 million on condition that the assembled trust company executives contribute to a $25 million pool to support the weaker trusts. The next day, President Roosevelt agreed not to bring an antitrust action against U.S. Steel for its purchase of the Tennessee Coal and Iron stock majority.

The Morgan U.S. Steel transaction later would be bitterly criticized. John Moody would estimate that the Tennessee Coal stock purchased for $45 million had a potential value of approximately $1 billion. As with Morgan's 1895 restoration of gold reserves to the United States Treasury, his 1907 leadership of the consortium that ended the Panic was at a price.

The Response to the 1907 Panic

The United States economy was in disarray after the Bank Panic of October 1907. Stock prices fell approximately 40 percent. Financial journalist and author Lowenstein captured the abrupt shift in national sentiment:

> Quickly on the heels of the Panic, the economic contraction deepened. As bank reserves dwindled, banks were forced to curtail loans.... Iron and steel production was severely reduced. Many factories shuttered or went part-time due to the lack of currency for wages. The severity of the depression astonished businesspeople, not least because it had struck during a period of prosperity. The country's railroads had been profitable, its farmers rich.

Senator Nelson Aldrich later would declaim: "The country escaped by the narrowest possible margin from a total collapse of all credit and a wholesale destruction of all values."[46]

Over the next six years, a virtually nonstop series of investigations and legislation occurred in response to the 1907 Panic.

New York Governor Charles Evans Hughes, having made his reputation as Chief Counsel of New York State's 1905 Armstrong Committee investigation of the life insurance industry, in June 1907 created a Committee to Investigate Speculation in Securities and Commodities.

Before the Hughes Committee on Speculation could issue its Report, Congress in May 1908 enacted the Aldrich-Vreeland Act to amend the national banking laws. In the hyper-partisan atmosphere of the day, the Act was adopted with no Democrat supporting the Act in the House and by a vote of 47 to 20 vote in the Senate with the Republicans voting 43 to 4 in favor and the Democrats voting 16 to 4 against the Act.

The Aldrich-Vreeland Act was heavily compromised.

Republican Senator Aldrich, after consultation with J.P. Morgan and other New York financiers, introduced S. 3023, which authorized creation of the National Currency Association and empowered the Secretary of Treasury to authorize emergency currency based on local government and railroad bonds. This was of benefit to New York banks and banks in other leading financial centers which held railroad bonds and state and municipal bonds, but was widely opposed by banks elsewhere whose assets were based to a greater degree on commercial transactions. It soon became apparent the House would not adopt the original Aldrich Bill. The Senate, after amendments, did so.

Congressman Vreeland led a House Committee created to fashion a compromise in substitution for a more radical proposal introduced by Congressman Fowler, Chair of the House Banking Committee. Fowler's Bill sought the creation of not more than 20 bank redemption districts, empowered to require all United States banks with unsecured notes to the limit of bank capital, "provided the bank had arranged for the redemption of its notes in gold at a redemption center, and had deposited with the Treasury in gold, or lawful money, 5 per cent, of its notes, and 5 per cent, of its deposits, as guaranty funds."

The Fowler Bill went considerably further and contained provisions to guarantee deposits, empower national banks to engage in a trust business, abolish the Independent Treasury System and eventually retire greenbacks.

The Fowler Bill also proved incapable of adoption.

Vreeland, ultimately in H.R. 21871, introduced legislation that was adopted by the House by a large majority. Similar to the Aldrich Bill, the Vreeland Bill provided for issuance of additional notes by National Clearing House Associations based in a notable difference from the Aldrich Bill on "any securities, including commercial paper, held by a national banking association." The new notes were limited to 75 percent of the cash value of the securities or commercial paper and had a lien on all the assets of the banks in the Clearing House Association.

The Senate declined to adopt the Vreeland Bill. Both the Aldrich and Vreeland Bills were referred to a conference that reported the heavily compromised legislation in the last days of the first session of the 60th Congress in May 1908. The Act awkwardly threaded its way between the Senate's initial insistence on limiting the Department of Treasury's emergency power to issue additional currency to local government and railroad bonds and the House's intent to provide for new currency based on commercial assets.

The Aldrich-Vreeland Act as enacted provided that no fewer than 10 national banks, each with unimpaired capital and a surplus of not less than 20 percent and a surplus of at least $5 million voluntarily could form a National Currency Association. No more than one National Currency Association could be formed in any one city.

The members of a National Currency Association could be taken from a single state, part of a state, or contiguous parts of one or more states.

The National Currency Associations under the direction and control of the Secretary of Treasury were empowered under specified conditions "to render available . . . additional circulation of any securities . . . held by a national banking association." This emergency power would be used only once in the short life of the Act at the start of World War I in 1914.

There were limits on the power to create additional securities. Each bank receiving such additional securities had to deposit with the Currency Association United States bonds equal to not less than 40 percent of its capital and to have unimpaired capital and surplus of not less than 20 percent.

After the deposit, the Currency Association could seek additional notes up to 75 percent of the cash value of the securities or commercial paper that was deposited. State, city, town, county or other municipal bonds that were deposited with the Association could receive notes up to 90 percent of the market value of the deposited municipal bonds after additional approval by the Secretary of Treasury.

Under the Act, the total amount of additional notes that could be issued at any time could not exceed $500 million.

When national banks circulated bonds other than United States bonds, they were subject in the first month to a 5 percent tax on the average amount of notes in circulation and an additional tax of 1 percent for each subsequent month until a total tax of 10 percent was reached.

National banks also were required to maintain a redemption fund of 5 percent of its additional circulation other than that based on United States bonds.

United States notes would state that they were secured by "United States bonds or other securities."

There were two critical weaknesses of the Act. First, the ability of a national bank association to receive additional circulating notes based on commercial paper provided a question begging form of collateral. In the Act, *commercial paper* was defined "to include only notes representing actual commercial transactions," with fewer than four months to run and commercial paper for a national bank could not exceed 30 percent of unimpaired capital and surplus.

This was a bitter pill for Senator Aldrich, who opposed any issue of notes based on bank commercial assets and initially insisted on a bond secured currency or nothing. Only when acceptance of some form of bank assets, other than notes, became essential to the bill, did Aldrich yield.

The larger limitation of the Act was its incapacity to fully address the Bank Panic of 1907 and the accompanying economic recession. Besides the powers in the Act to provide additional currency, there was little to address financial crises. The Act had a six-year term and was scheduled to expire on June 30, 1914, which was later extended to June 30, 1915.

What the Aldrich-Vreeland Act did provide, however, was the creation of a National Monetary Commission to address "what changes are necessary or desirable in the monetary system of the United States or in the laws relating to banking and currency." This was a Blue Ribbon commission comprised of nine members of the Senate and nine members of the House. The National Monetary Commission would be the most consequential part of the otherwise little used Aldrich-Vreeland Act. Nelson Aldrich would chair the Commission. Edward Vreeland would be Vice Chair. After several studies, its Final Report would be submitted to Congress in 1912 and provide a proposal that was one basis for the 1913 Federal Reserve Act.[47]

The National Monetary Commission was dominated by a Republican Party, then criticized for favoring high tariffs and alignment with J.P. Morgan and Wall Street. With Nelson Aldrich chairing the Commission, the party selected a highly competent legislator, once labeled "the ablest man in the U.S. Senate," but one who would be excoriated after his leadership in August 1909 enacting the Taft-supported Payne-Aldrich Tariff, as one journalist wrote, "distrusted, disliked, even hated and vilified as few other men in public are hated and vilified." The Payne-Aldrich Tariff raised tariffs on iron ore and coal. "Effectively," Roger Lowenstein concluded, "Payne-Aldrich marked the beginning of a civil war within the Republican Party." Aldrich and Taft were characterized as leading the conservative wing of the Party. Progressives, later most significantly Theodore Roosevelt and Robert La Follette, would be alienated.

Aldrich would meet in 1910 at the Jekyll Island Club in Brunswick, Georgia, "the richest, most exclusive, most inaccessible club in the world," with a small coterie of bankers and academics selected by

Morgan senior partner, Henry Davison. The advisors included Paul Warburg, a partner in the Kuhn Loeb Investment Bank and a fervent advocate of a central bank who in 1907 had published *A Plan for a Modified Central Bank,* and subsequently, *A Plan for a United Reserve Bank*; Frank Vanderlip, President of the National City Bank of New York, who also supported a central reserve; and Professor Piatt Andrew, then an Assistant Professor at Harvard. The secrecy of the Jekyll Island meeting and the Morgan influence later would add to conspiracy theories of the origins of the Federal Reserve, most elaborately presented in 1994 by G. Edward Griffin, sometime writer for the John Birch Society, in *The Creature from Jekyll Island,* which argued that the bankers on the Island sought to establish a cartel with the aim of dominating competition in banking and confiscating the people's wealth. This was sheer fantasy, but the tilt of the Jekyll Island Plan, presented to the National Monetary Commission, was towards centralization of banking albeit without using the term "central bank."

> The Commission made a thorough study of the defects of the United States banking system, and the disasters that were the consequence of the Panic of 1907, which was summarized in its 1912 Report:
>
> 1. We have no provision for the concentration of the cash reserves of the banks and for their mobilization and use whatever needed in times of trouble. Experience has shown that the scattered cash reserves of our banks are inadequate for purposes of assistance or defense at such times. . . .
>
> 4. Of our various forms of currency the bank-note issue is the only one which we might expect to respond to the changing needs of business by automatic expansion and contraction, but this issue is deprived of all such qualities by the fact that its volume is largely dependent upon the amount and price of United States bonds.
>
> 5. We lack means to insure such effective cooperation on the part of banks as is necessary to protect their own and the public interests in times of stress or crisis. . . .
>
> 6. We have no effective agency covering the entire country which affords necessary facilities for making domestic exchanges between different localities and sections, or which can prevent disastrous disruption of all such exchanges in times of serious trouble.
>
> 7. We have no instrumentality that can deal effectively with the broad questions which, from an international standpoint,

> affect the credit and status of the United States as one of the great financial powers of the world....
>
> 8. The lack of commercial paper of an established standard, issued for agricultural, industrial, and commercial purposes, available for investments by banks, leads to an unhealthy congestion of loanable funds in great centers and hinders the development of the productive forces of the country....
>
> 12. Our system lacks an agency whose influence can be made effective in securing greater uniformity, steadiness, and reasonableness of rates of discount in all parts of the country....
>
> 14. We have no power to enforce the adoption of uniform standards with regard to capital, reserves, examinations, and the character and publicity of reports of all banks in the different sections of the country.
>
> 15. We have no American banking institutions in foreign countries. The organization of such banks is necessary for the development of our foreign trade.
>
> 16. The provision that national banks shall not make loans upon real estate restricts their power to serve farmers and other borrowers in rural communities.

Based upon this critique, the National Monetary Commission proposed in January 1912 a bill, popularly known as the Aldrich Bill, providing a comprehensive reorganization of credit and a thorough reconsideration of our banking system and its methods.

Bowing to political reality, the National Monetary Commission did not propose a central bank, but instead a National Reserve Association in which all national and state banks were eligible to be members.

The Association was to have an authorized capital of 20 percent of the paid-in and unimpaired capital of all eligible banks. The head office of the Association would be in Washington. When $200 million of capital was subscribed, $100 million paid in cash, the Association would commence business and select 15 cities to be branches of the National Reserve Association. The branches would be distributed throughout the country, with one branch in New England, two branches in the Eastern states meaning New York, New Jersey, Pennsylvania, and Delaware, four branches in the Southern states, four branches in the Midwestern states, and four branches in the Western states.

Each branch would be in an Association district. All subscribing banks within a district would form local associations of not fewer than 10 banks with an aggregate capital of not less than $5 million. "It is proposed," the National Monetary Commission Report explained, "to group into local associations all subscribing banks located in contiguous territory."

The National Monetary Commission Report emphasized the democratic dimension of the local Associations, "analogous in their organization to our political divisions, into counties, states and the United States."

The National Reserve Association would be led by a Board of 39 directors. Fifteen would be from the Boards of the 15 branches, meaning bankers. Fifteen would be elected by the Boards of Director of each branch to "represent the agricultural, commercial, individual and other interests of the district" and not be officers of banks, trust companies, insurance companies, or other financial institutions. Nine additional directors would be elected by voting representatives of the branch boards. No more than one director of this class could be chosen from any one district. In addition, there would be seven *ex officio* members of the National Reserve Association Board: The Governor and two Deputy Governors of the National Reserve Association, the Secretary of Agriculture, the Secretary of Treasury, the Secretary of Commerce and Labor, and the Comptroller of the Currency.

The Governor of the Association also would serve as Chair of the Association Board. The Governor would be selected by the President of the United States from a list of no fewer than three nominees submitted by the Association and serve for a term of 10 years, subject to removal for cause by a two-thirds vote of the Association Board.

The Directors of the Association annually would elect from the Board a nine member Executive Committee with "all the authority which is vested in the board of directors, except the power of nomination, appointment and removal of the governor and deputy governor."

The National Reserve Association would be the principal fiscal agent of the United States into which the United States would "deposit its general funds with said association and its branches."

Critically, there would be no further issue of notes by any national banks beyond the amount then outstanding. When a national bank retired any part of its existing issue, there was no right to reissue the circulating notes.

The National Reserve Association itself would issue its own notes on behalf of the United States, "it being the policy of the United States to retire as rapidly as possible, consistent with the public interest, bank-secured circulation and to substitute therefor notes of the National Reserve Association."

The notes of the National Reserve Association in circulation at any time in excess of $900 million and not covered by an equal amount of lawful money, gold bullion, or foreign gold coin would result in the Association paying a special tax of 1.5 percent on notes up to $1.2 billion and 5 percent on notes greater than $1.2 billion. The $900 million limit was then $200 million above the normal level of bank notes outstanding.

The notes of the National Reserve Association were intended to be received in payment of all taxes, excises, and other dues of the United States and to be used for all salaries, debts, or demands owing by the United States, "excess obligations of the government which are by their terms specifically payable in gold, and for all debts due from or by one bank or trust company to another."

The National Monetary Commission viewed the then current system of bank note issues based upon government banks as "defective and that a change in the manner and character of the issues must take place at an early date." At the time of the Report, there were outstanding less than $200 million of United States bonds not owned by the banks and held for circulation. The Report explained:

> We propose that while the national banks shall have the right to retain their existing circulation all new issues shall be made by the National Reserve Association. We propose that the authority now exercised by seven or eight thousand national banks shall be vested in this cooperative association of all the banks. We propose to relieve the United States from the obligation to redeem the outstanding national-bank notes based on the bonds which are taken over by the reserve association. The association is required to redeem in gold or its equivalent, at any of its branches, upon presentation, such notes and all notes of its own issue.

The National Monetary Commission Report underlined its purpose to "remove all danger of a currency famine in any section of the country" by adopting "every provision that the experience of the world has shown to be necessary for the security and convertibility of a paper currency:"

> We have provided that the reserve association, through its branches, shall at once, upon application and without charge for transportation, forward the circulating notes of the association to any subscribing bank against its credit balance. We assume that there will be but few banks in the United States — certainly none in central communities — that will be more than 24 hours away from a positive source of supply of notes for use for crop moving or other purposes.

Only the United States and banks owning stock in the National Reserve Association would be depositors in the Association. The National Reserve Association would not pay dividends on deposits.

The National Reserve Association through its branches could discount notes and bills of exchange arising out of commercial transactions, "that is, notes and bills of exchange issued or drawn for agricultural, industrial or commercial purposes, and not including notes or bills issued or drawn for the purpose of carrying stocks, bonds or other investment securities." The National Reserve Association also through a branch, after approval of the Secretary of Treasury, could discount the direct obligations of a depositing bank provided that there was a pledge and deposit of satisfactory securities and the amount loaned did not exceed three-fourths of the actual value of the securities pledged. The National Reserve Association would fix or adjust rates of discount uniformly throughout the United States.

This power to discount against such products as cotton, wheat, or products in transit would give a new and wider market to domestic bills of exchange drawn on foreign countries, the National Monetary Commission predicted, and help pay for our purchases abroad.

National banks were authorized to accept drafts or bills of exchange arising out of specified commercial transactions, limited to not more than one-half of the capital and surplus of the bank.

The National Reserve Association also "whenever its own condition and the general financial condition warrant" could "purchase from a subscribing bank acceptances of banks or acceptors of unquestioned financial responsibility arising out of [specified] commercial transactions."

The National Association could invest in United States bonds or in obligations with less than one year to run of the United States, any state, or of foreign government.

The power of the National Reserve Association to deal with foreign countries were striking. The Association could purchase checks or bills of exchange arising out of specified commercial transactions payable in foreign countries. The Association could open and maintain banking accounts in foreign countries and "establish agencies in foreign countries for the purpose of purchasing, selling, and collecting foreign bills of exchange." The Association also would be authorized to buy or sell checks or foreign bills of exchange arising out of commercial transactions with fewer than 90 days to run. Banking corporations could be formed to carry on the business of banking in foreign countries and to aid in commerce with foreign countries and act as fiscal agents of the United States. There was a minimum capital requirement of not less than $2 million to form such a corporation.

The National Monetary Commission characterized the then current matters of financial foreign trade as "disgraceful to a progressive nation:"

> We export of domestic products about two thousand million dollars annually, and our annual imports amount approximately to fifteen hundred million dollars. Very much the larger portion of this international trade is financed by and pays tribute to foreign bankers. Take one illustration: Last year we exported about six hundred and fifty million dollars in value of cotton; it was largely financed by 60 or 90 day bills drawn on Liverpool, London, Paris, or Berlin. This business was practically all done by foreign banks or bankers. The banks in the South and perhaps in New York were enabled to collect a small commission on a part of the business en route, but the lion's share of the profits accruing from the transactions, millions of dollars in amount, were paid to European merchants and bankers, and this large sum was in the last analysis paid by the cotton planter.

National Banks could loan up to 30 percent of time deposits upon improved and unencumbered real estate, the loans not to exceed 50 percent of the actual value of the real estate.

Any bank doing business in the United States and being the owner of stock in the National Reserve Association could invest in the stock of any other bank organized under the Act, but no bank could hold more than 10 percent of the capital stock of another subscribing bank.

Subscribing banks could count their deposit balance in the National Reserve Association and notes of the Association as part of its required reserve. The National Monetary Commission Report stressed the significance of this provision:

> Perhaps the most important defect in our monetary system is to be found in its unscientific treatment of the reserves of individual banks. . . . We propose that all or any portion of the cash reserves of the banks, including those which are now required by law to be held in their vaults, may be deposited with the reserve association, and when so deposited shall be counted as a part of their legal reserve. This will transform money which is now deprived of potency and defensive power into a condition of vitality and effectiveness. It is proposed that the reserves thus concentrated may be used by the reserve association, through its branches, for the assistance and support of any bank or section when needed.

All demand liabilities, including deposits and circulating notes of the National Reserve Association, "shall be covered to the extent of fifty per centum by a reserve of gold (including foreign gold coin and gold bullion) or other money of the United States which the national banks are now authorized to hold as part of their legal reserve."

Earnings of the Association would be divided among its shareholders who were entitled to receive an annual dividend of 4 percent on paid-in capital, a $2 million contingency fund, and "one-half of additional net earnings shall be paid into the surplus fund of the National Reserve Association until said fund shall amount to twenty per centum of the paid-in capital [when] one-fourth shall be paid to the United States as a franchise tax, and one-fourth shall be paid to the shareholders until the shareholders' dividend shall amount to five per centum on paid-in capital." The United States would receive one-half of additional earnings after that as a franchise tax until the National Reserve Association surplus fund equaled 20 percent of paid-in capital at which time all excess earnings would be paid to the United States as a franchise tax.

Any member of a local Association could apply for a guaranty of commercial paper that it sought to rediscount at the branch of the National Reserve Association in its district.

A local Association with a vote of three-fourths of the local Association Members and the approval of the National Reserve Association also could serve as a clearinghouse.

The National Monetary Commission's legislative proposal was heavily influenced by Eastern banker preferences, with the National Reserve Association Board dominated by bankers and businesspeople chosen by bankers, sharp focus on facilitating foreign trade and rejection of alternative proposals for a banking system based on separate state or district organizations, each with independent functions. "The fatal objection, in the opinion of the Commission, to any plan of this kind is found in the lack of affiliation or means to insure cooperation between these different local organizations."

The ghost of Jackson haunted the Commission. The unprecedented system of 15 districts involved in governance and financial decisions was highlighted:

> [T]he National Reserve Association differs radically from the First and Second Banks of the United States and from European central banks. Its sources of authority are democratic and not autocratic. Instead of overshadowing banks, it is their representative; its controlling forces, acting in the public interests, impose policies upon and grant powers to its managers.

The National Monetary Commission recognized the necessity of "inserting provisions that would prevent beyond question the possibility of control by any corporation or combination of corporations, banks or otherwise, by any individual or combination of individuals for selfish or sinister purposes. No provision of the bill . . . is of more vital importance than this." To guard against Wall Street control, the New York district with 29 percent of the banking resources of the country would have 8 percent of the representation on the National Reserve Association Board. Each of the 15 districts would be equally represented in electing Board members of the Association.

After the Democrats won control of the House in 1910, the tenor of the debate over banking and currency legislation fundamentally changed. Congressman Charles August Lindbergh, father of the famous aviator, in July 1911 published a *New York Times* opinion piece decrying the Money Trust, which the *Wall Street Journal* aptly characterized as a code name for J.P. Morgan. Lindbergh supported a plan which "if adopted would make the people the master of the world, instead of the present master — The Money Trust."

In February 1912, the House of Representatives adopted a Resolution, H.R. 429, "to obtain full and complete information on the banking and currency condition of the United States for the purpose of determining what legislation is needed."

Arsénee Pujo, Democrat from Louisiana, who served on the National Monetary Commission, was authorized to form a Subcommittee of the House Committee on Banking and Currency. Samuel Untermyer, a successful corporate and merger lawyer who had become a fierce critic of Wall Street, was selected to be staff counsel. Untermyer would so sharply question J.P. Morgan that Morgan would feel humiliated and angered by the interrogation. When he died just a few weeks after the hearing, some of his family would believe his death was the consequence of Untermyer's relentless questioning. While this diagnosis is debatable, the well-publicized and sensational nature of the Pujo Committee hearings, furthered the rapidly growing movement for reform legislation to address banking and currency. J.P. Morgan's testimony that there was no growing concentration of stocks or credit in recent years was inconsistent with that of other witnesses. Morgan's insistence that commercial credit primarily was based not on money or property, but on character, would be ridiculed. Frank Vanderlip, President of National City Bank of New York, would characterize Morgan's performance as "blundering."

In April 1912, the House adopted H.R. 505, submitted by Pujo, which echoed the critique of opponents of a Money Trust: "[I]t has been charged, and there is reason to believe, that the management of the finances of many of the great industrial and railroad companies of the country . . . is rapidly concentrating in the hands of a few groups of financiers in the City of New York . . . and other cities. . . ."

After extensive Public Hearings in 1912, the Pujo Committee published its *Report on its Investigation of Control of Money and Credit* early in 1913. While the Report also addressed clearinghouse associations and the New York Stock Exchange, "[t]he bulk of the oral and documentary evidence . . . was directed toward ascertaining whether, in common parlance, there is a 'money trust'."

The majority of the Committee found no evidence of a definitive agreement between designated persons to concentrate into themselves control of money and credit. But the Pujo Committee did find:

> an established and well-defined identity and community of interest between a few leaders of finance, created and held together through stock ownership, interlocking directorates, partnership and joint account transactions, and other forms of domination over banks, trust companies, railroads, and public-service and

> industrial corporations, which has resulted in great and rapidly growing concentration of the control of money and credit in the hands of these few men.

The Report described five processes of concentration:

> First, through consolidations of competitive or potentially competitive banks and trust companies, which consolidations in turn have recently been brought under sympathetic management.
>
> Second, through the same powerful interests becoming large stockholders in potentially competitive banks and trust companies.
>
> . . .
>
> Third, through the confederation of potentially competitive banks and trust companies by means of a system of interlocking directorates.
>
> Fourth, through the influence which the more powerful banking houses, banks, and trust companies have secured in the management of insurance companies, railroads, producing and trading corporations, and public utility corporations, by means of stockholdings, voting trusts, fiscal agency contracts, or representation upon their boards of directors, or through supplying the money requirements of railway, industrial, and public utilities corporations and thereby being enabled to participate in the determination of their financial and business policies.
>
> Fifth, through partnership or joint account arrangements between a few of the leading banking houses, banks, and trust companies in the purchase of security issues of the great interstate corporations, accompanied by understandings of recent growth . . . which have had the effect of effectually destroying competition between such banking houses, banks, and trust companies in the struggle for business or in the purchase and sale of large issues of such securities.

The Pujo Committee's reported that JP Morgan & Co., First National Bank of New York, National City Bank of New York, Lee, Higginson & Co. of Boston and New York, Kidder Peabody & Co. of Boston and New York, and Kuhn Loeb & Co. through these processes were the principal agents of concentration:

> The parties to this combination or understanding or community of interest, by whatever name it may be called, may be conveniently classified, for the purpose of differentiation, into four separate groups.

First. The first, which for convenience of statement we will call the inner group, consists of JP Morgan & Co., the recognized leaders, and George F. Baker and James Stillman in their individual capacities and in their joint administration and control of the First National Bank, the National City Bank, the National Bank of Commerce, the Chase National Bank, the Guaranty Trust Co., and the Bankers Trust Co., with total known resources, in these corporations alone, in excess of $1,300,000,000, and of a number of smaller but important financial institutions. This takes no account of the personal fortunes of these gentlemen.

Second. Closely allied with this inner or primary group, and indeed related to them practically as partners in many of their larger financial enterprises, are the powerful international banking houses of Lee, Higginson & Co. and Kidder, Peabody & Co., with three affiliated banks in Boston — the National Shawmut Bank, the First National Bank, and the Old Colony Trust Co. — having at least more than half of the total resources of all the Boston banks; also with interests and representation in other important New England financial institutions.

Third. In New York City, the international banking house of Messrs. Kuhn, Loeb & Co., with its large foreign clientele and connections, whilst only qualifiedly allied with the inner group, and only in isolated transactions, yet through its close relations with the National City Bank and the National Bank of Commerce and other financial institutions with which it has recently allied itself has many interests in common, conducting large joint-account transactions with them, especially in recent years, and having what virtually amounts to an understanding not to compete, which is defended as a principle of "banking ethics." Together they have with a few exceptions preempted the banking business of the important railways of the country.

Fourth. In Chicago this inner group associated with and makes issues of securities in joint account or through underwriting participations primarily with the First National Bank and the Illinois Trust & Savings Bank, and has more or less friendly business relations with the Continental & Commercial National Bank, which participates at times in the underwriting of security issues by the inner group. These are the three largest financial institutions in Chicago, with combined resources (including the two affiliated and controlled state institutions of the two national banks) of $561,000,000.

The Pujo Committee Hearings focused on JP Morgan & Co.

JP Morgan & Co. was a private bank, meaning that it was not subject to the National Bank Act reporting and examination processes, but records available to the Pujo Committee found that Morgan had acted as a commercial bank, accepting deposits and paying interest, half for 78 interstate corporations, which had deposited $82 of the $162 million total deposits in the firms. JP Morgan significantly had been involved in securities sales to the public. "During the years 1902 and 1912 inclusive, the firm directly procured the public marketing of securities issues of corporations amounting in round numbers to $1,950,000, including only issues of interstate corporations."

J.P. Morgan had systematically developed affiliations with a number of financial firms, including Bankers Trust, whose entire Board of Directors, J.P. Morgan had selected, and Guaranty Trust Co., which Morgan controlled through a voting trust. These were the first and second largest trust companies in the nation, as well as several relatively smaller banks. In aggregate, "Morgan & Co. and their nominees thus control or have a powerful voice in banks and trust companies in the City of New York with resources of $723,000,000. Its own resources are unknown, but adding only its deposits, $162,000,000, the answer becomes $885,000,000, adding the resources of Equitable Life, it becomes $1,389,000,000."

JP Morgan & Co. also owned a majority of the stock in Equitable Life Assurance Co., a "great company" as the Pujo Report phrased it, with resources of $500 million and had directorships and other membership of several railroads, led by the New York Central & Hudson River Railroad, for which Morgan & Co. had raised $550,000,000 in 67 stock issues since 1897; the New York, New Haven & Hartford Railroad, for which Morgan & Co. had raised $188 million in 17 stock issues since 1904; Northern Pacific, Southern Railway, Reading Co., and Erie Railroad, each of which Morgan & Co. reorganized.

Morgan & Company's largest organization had been United States Steel, with an underwriting of $1,014,446,000 of stock and $304,000,000 of bonds. In the Pujo Report's description: The underwriting was "directed and absolutely dominated by Morgan & Co. Mr. Morgan . . . named the entire first board of directors. No director has been chosen since without his approval." Morgan & Co. also organized International Harvester and helped organize General Electric.

The Pujo Report also found Morgan directors on Western Union, the First National Bank of New York, and National City Bank of New York.

In aggregate, JP Morgan & Co., the First National Bank, National City Bank, and Bankers and Guaranty Trust held:

> One hundred and eighteen directorships in 34 banks and trust companies having total resources of $2,679,000,000 and total deposits of $1,983,000,000.
>
> Thirty directorships in 10 insurance companies having total assets of $2,293,000,000.
>
> One hundred and five directorships in 32 transportation systems having a total capitalization of $11,784,000,000 and a total mileage (excluding express companies and steamship lines) of 150,200.
>
> Sixty-three directorships in 24 producing and trading corporations having a total capitalization of $3,339,000,000.
>
> Twenty-five directorships in 12 public utility corporations having a total capitalization of $2,150,000,000.
>
> In all, 341 directorships in 112 corporations having aggregate resources or capitalization of $22,245,000,000.

In 1913, $22 billion was more than three times the assessed value of all the property in New England, nearly three times the assessed value of all real estate in New York City, twice the assessed value of all property in the 13 Southern states, and more than the assessed value of all property in the 22 states west of the Mississippi River.

No one did more to popularize the findings of the Pujo Committee than Louis Brandeis. In 1913, Brandeis was a nationally known lawyer for progressive causes who published articles in *Harper's Weekly* entitled *Breaking the Money Trust.* Later, the articles would be published as the book, *Other People's Money and How the Bankers Use It.* Brandeis highlighted "the vicious circle of control — the endless chain — through which our financial oligarchy now operates":

> J.P. Morgan (or a partner), a director of the New York, New Haven & Hartford Railroad, causes that company to sell to J.P. Morgan & Co. an issue of bonds. J.P. Morgan & Co. borrow the money with which to pay for the bonds from the Guaranty Trust Company, of which Mr. Morgan (or a partner) is a director. J.P. Morgan & Co. sell the bonds to the Penn Mutual Life Insurance Company, of which Mr. Morgan (or a partner) is a director. The New Haven spends the proceeds of the bonds in purchasing

> steel rails from the United States Steel Corporation, of which Mr. Morgan (or a partner) is a director. The United States Steel Corporation spends the proceeds of the rails in purchasing electrical supplies from the General Electric Company, of which Mr. Morgan (or a partner) is a director. The General Electric sells supplies to the Western Union Telegraph Company, a subsidiary of the American Telephone and Telegraph Company; and in both Mr. Morgan (or a partner) is a director. The Telegraph Company has an exclusive wire contract with the Reading, of which Mr. Morgan (or a partner) is a director. The Reading buys its passenger cars from the Pullman Company, of which Mr. Morgan (or a partner) is a director. The Pullman Company buys (for local use) locomotives from the Baldwin Locomotive Company, of which Mr. Morgan (or a partner) is a director. The Reading, the General Electric, the Steel Corporation and the New Haven, like the Pullman buy locomotives from the Baldwin Company. The Steel Corporation, the Telephone Company, the New Haven, the Reading, the Pullman and the Baldwin Companies, like the Western Union, buy electrical supplies from the General Electric. The Baldwin, the Pullman, the Reading, the Telephone, the Telegraph and the General Electric companies, like the New Haven, buy steel products from the Steel Corporation. Each and every one of the companies last named markets its securities through J.P. Morgan & Co.; each deposits its funds with J.P. Morgan & Co.; and with these funds of each, the firm enters upon further operations.

The Pujo Committee Report proposed its own legislation. The four most consequential recommendations specified:

> *A. Consolidations of banks.* — Two or more banks should not be permitted to consolidate unless such consolidation shall have been approved by the Comptroller of the Currency as in the public interest. He should have plenary power to forbit it where it threatens to result in undue concentration of control.
>
> *B. Interlocking bank directorates.* — No person should be permitted to be a director in more than one national bank serving the same community or locality, nor should any person who is a director of any State bank or trust company, or is a partner or associate of any private banker or banking firm, be eligible as a director of any national bank serving the same community or locality, except that a director in a national bank may have one partner who is a director in a trust company.

C. Interlocking stockholdings amongst banks. — No part of the stock of any national bank should be permitted to be owned or held directly or indirectly by any other bank or by any trust company or holding company; and no national bank should be permitted to own or hold any part of the stock of any other bank or trust company.

D. Voting trusts in banks. — The transfer of any part of the stock of national banks to trustees solely or primarily in order that they may vote the same at annual elections and other stockholders' meetings — "voting trusts," as they are generally known — should be expressly prohibited.[48]

The Federal Reserve System

The 1910 and 1912 national election results dramatically increased the momentum for reform. In 1908, Republican William Howard Taft, Theodore Roosevelt's handpicked successor, had decisively been elected with 321 electoral votes to Democrat William Jennings Bryan's 162. Republicans held a 59 to 31 majority in the Senate, and a 219 to 172 member majority in the House.

In 1910, the burgeoning split between the more conservative Taft and the more progressive Republicans contributed to Democrats winning control of the House by a 230 to 163 Majority and narrowing the Republican Majority in the Senate to 50 to 40.

The Democratic Party majority in the House grew to a 2 to 1 majority in 1912, 291 to 134, and simultaneously Democrats gained a narrow 47 to 45 majority in the Senate. While much of the focus in 1912 was Democrat Woodrow Wilson's victory with a 41.8 percent of popular vote over Progressive or Bull Moose nominee Theodore Roosevelt, who gathered 27.4 of the vote, and William Howard Taft, who painfully lost with 23.2 percent, the most consequential element of the Democratic 1912 party sweep was that the Democratic Party now controlled the White House, the Senate, and the House and had the ability to enact legislation strikingly different than the approach favored by Taft.

The Democratic Party 1912 platform was emphatic in denouncing "[t]he high Republican tariff [as] the principal cause of unequal distribution of wealth" and the achievement of the "two most important reforms demanded in the last national platform, namely the amendment of the Federal Constitution authorizing an income tax, and the amendment providing for the popular election of senators." But the Platform was skeletal on banking legislation: "We oppose the so-called Aldrich Bill or the establishment of a central bank; and we believe our country will be largely freed from the panics and consequent unemployment and business depression by such a systematic revision of our banking laws as will render temporary relief in localities where such relief is needed, with protection from control of dominion by what is known as the Money Trust.... We condemn the present methods of depositing government funds in a few favored banks, largely situated in and controlled by Wall Street, in return for political favors, and we pledge our party to provide by law for the deposit by competitive bidding in the banking institutions of the country, national and State, without discrimination as to locality, upon approved securities and subject to call by the Government."

The platform, largely written under the direction of William Jennings Bryan, channeled Jacksonian enthusiasm for states' rights: "[W]e denounce as usurpation the efforts of our opponents to deprive the States of any of the rights reserved to them, and to enlarge and magnify by indirection the power of the Federal government." For the many Democrats at the Convention aligned with Bryan, the essence of the party approach could be crystalized in three overarching negative imperatives: No Central Bank, no system controlled by J.P. Morgan or Wall Street, and no legislation written by Aldrich.

Wilson, though the standard bearer of the party, was instinctively different in his politics. He shared in more temperate terms Bryan's rejection of banker control. On January 8, 1912, at the Jackson Day Dinner, Wilson praised William Jennings Bryan, who like Andrew Jackson, for basing his career "not... upon calculation, but has based it upon principle." As with both Jackson and Bryan, Wilson asserted that "the government of this country was privately controlled and that the business of this country was privately controlled." "What do we stand for here tonight and what shall we stand for as long as we live? We stand for setting the government of this country free and the business of this country free." Wilson emphasized striking at the trusts as necessary to "[rescue] the businesses of this country." Implicitly, Wilson criticized Morgan and his ilk: "[T]he real danger is the combination of the combinations, the real danger is that the same group of men control chairs of banks, systems of railways, whole manufacturing enterprises, great mining projects, great enterprises for developing of the natural water power of this country and that threaded together in the personnel of a series of boards of directors is a community of interest more formidable than any conceivable combination in the United States." "[W]hat we have got to do is to disentangle this colossal community of interest." In 1911, Governor of New Jersey, Wilson similarly had claimed:

> The great monopoly in this country is the money monopoly. So long as that exists, our old variety and freedom and individual energy of development are out of the question. A great industrial nation is controlled by its system of credit. Our system of credit is concentrated. The growth of the nation, therefore, and all our activities are in the hands of a few men.

Wilson read Brandeis's *Harper's Weekly* articles and was influenced by them. Brandeis, among other acerbic points, wrote:

> The dominant element in our financial oligarchy is the investment banker. Associated banks, trust companies and life insurance companies are his tools. Controlled railroads, public service and industrial corporations are his subjects. Though properly but middlemen, these bankers bestride as masters America's business world so that practically no large enterprise can be undertaken without their participation....
>
> The goose that lays golden eggs has been considered a most valuable possession. But even more profitable is the privilege of taking golden eggs laid by somebody else's goose. The investment bankers and their associates now enjoy that privilege. They control the people through other people's money.

Brandeis concluded: "We must break the Money Trust or the Money Trust will break us."

Wilson's approach to banking regulation was critically different from that of Bryan and the 1912 Democratic Party Platform.

Before his March 4, 1913 inauguration, Wilson had been convinced: "The banking system of this country does not need to be indicted. It is convicted."

Wilson was not hesitant to invoke federal power to address national problems. In the first years of his administration, Congress would enact the Clayton Act to strengthen federal antitrust laws, created the Federal Trade Commission to outlaw unfair methods of competition, signed a new Revenue Act that significantly reduced tariffs in the Aldrich Tariff Act of 1909 as well as an income tax, which, among other things, reduced the nation's reliance on tariff duties to support its operations.

Wilson, like Brandeis, generally favored competition rather than direct regulation. Given Wilson's strong views on Wall Street and the Money Trust, "the most pernicious of all trusts," Wilson viewed destruction of the Money Trust as essential to restoring competition. As Wilson stated in 1913, early in his presidency: "You must put the credit of this country at the disposal of everybody upon equal terms."

In June 1913, Wilson addressed a joint session of Congress on the banking system. His tone remained emphatic. "The tyrannies of business, big and little, lie within the field of credit."

Wilson emphasized: "The principles upon which we should act are also clear:"

> We must have a currency, not rigid as now, but readily, elastically responsive to sound credit, the expanding and contracting credits of everyday transactions, the normal ebb and flow of personal and corporate dealings. Our banking laws must mobilize reserves; must not permit the concentration anywhere in a few hands of the monetary resources of the country or their use for speculative purposes in such volume as to hinder or impede or stand in the way of other more legitimate, more fruitful uses. And the control of the system of banking and of issue which our new laws are to set up must be public, not private, must be vested in the government itself, so that the banks may be the instruments, not the masters, of business and of individual enterprises and initiative.

Wilson was insistent that the initial proposal of the House Banking Committee Panel, Carter Glass, for a series of 15 to 20 privately controlled reserve banks organized along regional lines, was inadequate. There had, Wilson informed Glass, to be a "capstone," "that is, a central board in Washington supervising the Reserve Banks." Wilson rejected banker control of the proposed national banking system and instead sought a Federal Reserve Board made up entirely of presidential appointees.

On the pivotal issue of control of what became the Federal Reserve Board, Wilson sided with William Jennings Bryan and Louis Brandeis. As Brandeis had urged Wilson on June 11, 1913: Nothing would do so much to establish confidence in the business community "as the assurance that the government will control the currency issue and the conviction that whatever money is available, will be available for business generally, and not be subject to the control of the favored few."

Wilson rejected the arguments of the American Bankers Association representatives Festus Wade and Sal Wexler later in June who criticized Wilson's all political Federal Reserve Board: "Will one of you gentlemen," Wilson countered, "tell me in which civilized country of the earth there are important government boards of control on which private interests are represented?"

The initial Federal Reserve Bill, H.R. 7837, was introduced on June 26, 1913, by Representative Carter Glass in the House and Senator Robert Owen, Chair of the Banking and Currency Committee in the Senate. The language of both the House and Senate bills was identical and popularly called either the Glass-Owen or Owen-Glass Bill.

On September 18, 1913, H.R. 7837 was passed by the House by a vote of 287 to 85. Before passage in the House, there had been considerable opposition to the bill on the part of the banking community which principally opposed political, rather than banker, control of the Federal Reserve Board, the number of Reserve Banks rather than a single central bank, the requirement that banks subscribe to stock in their local Reserve Banks and the ending of the power for banks to deposit reserves in private banks.

Frank Vanderlip, President of National City Bank of New York, the nation's largest bank, melodramatically asserted that if the ultimate Act contained this degree of federal control, the nation's 7500 national banks might consider rechartering as state banks, taking $11 billion in assets out of the National banking system. In August, the Currency Commission of the American Bankers Association meeting in Chicago unanimously adopted proposals for far-reaching amendments to H.R. 7837, including either a central bank or far fewer Reserve Banks than the 12 proposed in the initial version of H.R. 7837, that three Reserve Board directors be chosen by bankers and that membership in the Reserve System be voluntary. Roger Lowenstein further elaborated the depths of bank opposition to H.R. 7837:

> When the ABA held its annual convention in Boston, on October 8, some two thousand delegates ratified the criticisms drafted in Chicago and denounced Glass-Owen as "socialistic." A week later, Senator Nelson Aldrich emerged from the obscurity of his retirement and savaged the bill as a triumph of "Bryanism."

A different type of opposition to the initial version of the Glass-Owen Bill developed in the House. Agrarian interests led by Robert Henry, Chair of the House Rules Committee, wanted the Federal Reserve to include farm and a labor representative and that agricultural assets should also be the basis of Federal Reserve Notes. On July 23, 1913, agrarian representatives on the House Banking Committee pushed through a ban on bank interlocking directors. Carter Glass unsuccessfully opposed the ban as likely to extinguish any bank support of the bill. The House agrarian revolt was quelled on August 22, 1913, when Glass read a letter from William Jennings Bryan who long had advocated a ban on interlocking directorship, but now urged the House to enact H.R. 7837 without a ban. "[C]are must be taken not to overload a good measure with amendments, however good these amendments may be in themselves." Bryan authorized Glass to say that he entirely supported the President, who regarded H.R. 7837 as the Administration's bill: "I am with him on all the details." Wilson promised to address bank interlocks in a subsequent antitrust law. The Clayton Act of 1914 subsequently prohibited bank directors from service on more than one bank. The Glass-Owen Act shortly later was overwhelmingly approved in the House.

The Legislative Report accompanying H.R. 7837 was critical both of the National Monetary Commission and the Aldrich Bill:

> Without going further into the detailed analysis of the Aldrich bill, it may be stated that the committee objects to the plan fundamentally on the following points:
>
> 1. Its entire lack of adequate governmental or public control of the banking mechanism it sets up.
>
> 2. Its tendency to throw voting control into the hands of the larger banks of the system.
>
> 3. The lack of adequate provision for protecting the interests of small banks and the tendency to make the proposed institution subserve the purposes of large interests only.
>
> 4. The intricate system by which the reserve institution it created was prevented from doing any business that might compete with that of existing banks.

Nonetheless, H.R. 7837 often echoed aspects of both the Commission and the Aldrich Bill. In specific respects, the initial version of H.R. 7837 was more inclined to echo bank sentiments than Wilson earlier appeared to be. The bill should be recognized as the product of a complex political process and proceeded through unique approaches given the earlier history of United States banking.

H.R. 7837 did not propose a single central bank nor like the Aldrich Bill — a confederation of currency associations — but instead a hybrid structure with a relatively weaker supervisory Federal Reserve Board and at least 12 regional Federal Reserve banks, which initially had greater powers than they were to have after later amendments to the Federal Reserve Act. As the Legislative Report explained:

> 1. The idea of centralization or cooperation, or combined use of banking resources, is the basic idea at the root of central banking argument.
>
> 2. It is not necessary in order to obtain the benefits of the application of this idea that there should be one single central bank whose activities should be coterminous with the limits of a nation's territory.
>
> 3. Equally good results can be obtained by the federating of existing banks and banking institutions in groups sufficiently large to afford the strength or cooperating power which is the chief advantage of the centralization.
>
> 4. In the United States, with its immense area, numerous natural divisions, still more numerous competing divisions, and abundant outlets to foreign countries, there is no argument either of banking theory or of expediency which dictates the creation of a single central banking institution, no matter how skillfully managed, how carefully controlled, or how patriotically conducted.

In the initial version of H.R. 7837, Wilson's capstone was achieved in a Federal Reserve Board, comprised of seven members: The Secretary of Treasury, the Secretary of Agriculture and the Comptroller of the Currency, and four members appointed by the President of the United States with the advice and consent of the Senate. The Secretary of Treasury was to be Chair of the new Board.

The four Presidential appointees were meant to be bipartisan — no more than two could be from the same political party — but in a notable difference from Wilson's insistence that there was to be no banker on the new Board, "at least one of [the Presidential appointees] shall be a person experienced in banking." The Legislative Report added: "This, of course, does not mean that other members of the board would be inexperienced in or ignorant of banking."

The Federal Reserve Board powers compared to later were limited. The Board principally was empowered to conduct examinations of Federal Reserve banks. This was substantially "the same limit of authority which is today exercised by the Comptroller of the Currency with respect to national banks." The proposed Act included sections that strengthened the existing banking examination requirements.

In times of emergency, the Board could permit or require Federal Reserve banks to rediscount the discounted prime paper of other Federal Reserve banks. The Board also could suspend reserve requirements in the proposed Act and supervise and regulate the issue and retirement of Federal Reserve notes. The Board could levy assessments upon Federal Reserve banks to pay for its estimated expenses.

H.R. 7837 proposed creation of not less than 12 Federal Reserve banks within separate districts throughout the country. No Federal Reserve bank could begin operating with less than $5 million in paid-up and unimpaired capital. The proposed Act revised the existing reserve system for national banks. The Legislative Report explained:

> The present reserve system recognizes three classes of banks: (*a*) Country banks, (*b*) reserve city banks, (*c*) central reserve city banks. Country banks are required to hold 6 per cent of their deposit liabilities in lawful money and may hold 9 per cent in balances with other banks. Reserve city banks are required to hold 12½ per cent of their deposits in lawful money and may hold 12½ per cent in balances with other banks in central reserve cities. Central reserve city banks are required to hold 25 per cent of their deposits (including those of other banks with them) in lawful money in their own vaults.

The objective of the proposed bill was to reduce reserves in private banks with bank reserves held in part in the Federal Reserve bank in their districts.

Under the proposed Act, a country bank was required to hold a reserve equal to 12 percent of aggregate amount of deposits, not including savings deposits.

A reserve bank or a central reserve city bank would hold a reserve equal to 20 percent of the aggregate amount of its deposits, less savings deposits and after that, 18 percent. Three years after enactment, the 18 percent reserve would consist of either of reserve money in the bank's own vault or of credit balance with the Federal Reserve bank in its district.

The Legislative Report recognized that this approach to reserves meant:

> that the Government shall retain a sufficient power over the reserve banks to enable it to exercise a directing authority when necessary to do so, but that it shall in no way attempt to carry on through its own mechanism the routine operations of banking which require detailed knowledge of local and individual credit and which determine the actual use of the funds of the community in any given instance. In other words, the reserve-bank plan retains to the Government power over the exercise of the broader banking functions, while it leaves to individuals and privately owned institutions the actual direction of routine.

Every Federal Reserve bank would be required at all times to have in its own vaults 33⅓ percent of its outstanding demand liabilities in gold or lawful money.

Each Federal Reserve bank would operate under the oversight and control of a Board of Directors whose power would be the same as those conferred upon the directors of a national bank under then existing law. The Federal Reserve bank boards would be comprised of bankers from member banks in the district.

After payment of all necessary expenses and taxes, the member banks in a Federal Reserve bank district were entitled to receive a 5 percent annual dividend based on paid-in capital stock with greater earnings initially going into a surplus fund. When the surplus fund of a Federal Reserve bank amounted to 20 percent of its paid-in capital, 60 percent of additional earnings would go to the United States, 40 percent to the member banks.

Every Federal Reserve bank and the capital stock held by member banks would be exempt from federal, state and local taxes, "except in respect to taxes upon real estate."

Each of the 7473 National Banks then in existence was given the choice to either become a Federal Reserve bank or become a state bank under state law. The Legislative Report to H.R. 7837 rejected the argument that the current national banks would be "compelled" to become Federal Reserve banks. The Report urged that the reduction of bonds National Banks then were required to have and deposit with the Treasury would make becoming a Federal Reserve bank attractive:

> By the terms of the National Banking Act banks must, in order to become national banks, purchase and deposit with the Treasurer of the United States government bonds as security for circulation. This requirement is nominally 25 per cent of capitalization for banks up to $150,000 capital and $50,000 for all above that level.
>
> . . . [T]his volume of bonds is now something like $750,000,000, or very nearly three-quarters of the capital stock of the banks. The proposed bill arranges for releasing the banks from this required investment and substitutes in lieu of it a required investment equal to 10 per cent of their capital (paid up), or not to exceed $105,000,000. This is one-seventh of the amount now invested in bonds.

Similarly, any state bank or transfer could become a Federal Reserve bank if it had a paid-up unimpaired capital sufficient to become a national bank in the place where it is situated and conforms to the other regulations of the Federal Reserve Board.

Each Federal Reserve bank could receive deposits of current funds in lawful money, national bank notes, Federal Reserve notes, or checks and drafts upon solvent banks.

The Federal Reserve banks could discount notes and bills of exchange arising out of commercial transactions including notes and bills of exchange drawn for agricultural, industrial, or commercial purposes with a maturity of fewer than 90 days. Notes and bills could not be discounted to carry or trade in stocks, bonds or other investment securities.

Federal Reserve banks could also discount eligible notes and bills of exchange with a maturity of more than 90 days but fewer than 120 days when the bank's own cash reserves exceeded 33⅓ percent of its total outstanding demand liabilities exclusive of its outstanding Federal Reserve notes. No more than 50 percent of the eligible notes and bills of exchange so discounted could have a maturity of more than 90 days.

The Legislative Report stressed:

> The purpose of the new act is to develop a commercial paper market, and if successful in this endeavor the legislation will

> entirely transform the conditions under which paper is bought and sold, loans contracted between banks, and funds transferred from one part of the country to another.

Federal Reserve banks in addition could discount acceptances of banks used in export or import of goods and mature in no more than 6 months as long as the amount discounted did not exceed 50 percent of the capital stock of the bank. Acceptances previously were forbidden to national banks. Acceptances were futures contracts, allowing banks to agree to pay bills of exchange at a future date. The Legislative Report explained: "The acceptance form of loan is, however, very common in Europe, and has been found exceedingly serviceable. It is the opinion of expert bankers that it could be applied in the United States to excellent advantage."

The aggregate of these notes and bills for any one person, company, firm, or corporation rediscounted at any one bank shall not exceed 10 percent of the unimpaired capital and surplus of the bank.

Federal Reserve banks that were national banks and not located in a reserve city or central reserve city could make loans secured by improved and unencumbered farmland for more than 12 months as long as the amount of these loans was less than 50 percent of the actual value of property offered as security.

Each Federal Reserve bank was empowered to deal in gold coin and bullion, to invest in United States, state and local bonds, to purchase or sell from member banks bills of exchange arising out of commercial transactions payable in foreign countries, to establish, subject to review, and determination of the Federal Reserve bank "a rate of discount charged by such banks for each class of paper" and with the consent of the Federal Reserve Board to open and maintain banking accounts and agencies in foreign countries "for the purpose of purchasing, selling and collecting foreign bills of exchange."

The proposed Act directed the transfer of all moneys now held in the general fund of the Treasury to Federal Reserve banks. The Secretary of Treasury subject to the approval of the Federal Reserve Board was directed to apportion government funds in Federal Reserve banks "equitably between different regions."

H.R. 7837 proposed a new system of Federal Reserve notes in place of the then current national bank notes:

> In its essence the plan now recommended by the committee for a new note issue contains the following points:
>
> 1. Ultimate withdrawal of the circulation privilege from the government bonds of all classes.
> 2. Issue of notes by the government through Federal reserve banks upon business paper held by such banks.
> 3. Redemption of such notes and regulation of their amount outstanding at any moment through Federal reserve banks.

The Federal Reserve notes would be obligations of the United States to be paid out solely through Federal Reserve banks, protected by commercial paper and with redemption insured through the holding of a reserve of gold equal to 33$^1/_3$ percent of the notes outstanding at any time. The Federal Reserve notes would be receivable for all taxes, customs and other public dues: "They shall be redeemed in gold or lawful money on demand at the Treasury Department of the United States, in the City of Washington, District of Columbia, or at any Federal reserve bank."

The Legislative Report both emphasized the safety of the new notes given that they were obligations of the United States and the contributions the notes would make to currency elasticity:

> Elasticity must be considered from two standpoints — that of expansion and that of contraction. As to expansion, the regulatory mechanism is the Federal reserve board, which is given the power to veto applications for notes. . . . The contraction feature is more difficult. In attempting to guard against the danger that the notes might remain in circulation after the need for them had passed, the bill makes the following provisions: (1) The notes can not be used in bank reserves; (2) the notes are not to be legal tender; (3) the notes can not be paid out by any Federal reserve bank (when not at first issued by it) under penalty of a tax of 10 per cent on their face value; (4) every Federal reserve bank is directed, upon receiving the note of another reserve bank, to (*a*) either send it direct to the bank that issued it, (*b*) to send it to the Treasury, charging it off against deposits, or (*c*) to present it to the Treasury for redemption in lawful money.

The proposed Act provided for the refunding of existing United States bonds now held by national banks that backed national bank notes. The 2 percent United States bonds could be exchanged for 3 percent notes payable after 20 years, with the national banks permitted to convert annually 5 percent of their 2 percent bonds into the new 3 percent bonds.

After lengthy Hearings, which resulted in a majority of the Senate Banking Committee initially favoring a single central bank with eight branches or a Federal Reserve Board with four Federal Reserve banks as proposed by Senator Gilbert Hitchcock, both Senate Owen's version of H.R. 7837 and the Hitchcock Bill were referred to the full Senate. The Hitchcock Bill was rejected by a close vote of 43–41. The full Senate then proceeded to adopt Senator Owen's version of H.R. 7837.

In Owen's Bill, there were to be no fewer than 8, nor more than 12 Federal Reserve banks. Individual, partnerships or corporations could subscribe for up to $10,000 stock in any Federal Reserve bank. Federal Reserve banks could commence business with a subscribed capital of $3 million or more, rather than the House requirement of $5 million in paid-up and unimpaired capital. In the Owen version of the bill, Class B Federal Reserve bank directors would "be actively engaged in their districts respectively in commerce, in agriculture, and in some other pursuit."

The Owen Bill increased the dividend to the Federal Reserve bank stockholders to 6 percent, and decreased payments to the United States by the split of earnings of the Federal Reserve banks to 50, not 60, percent.

As with the House bill, there would be a seven person Federal Reserve Board, but its membership would be different. In addition to the Secretary of Treasury, six members would be appointed by the President with the advice and counsel of the Senate. Two would be persons experienced in banking or finance.

Where the House version of the Federal Reserve Bill empowered the Federal Reserve Board to supervise and regulate the issue and retirement of Federal Reserve Notes, the Senate version directed the Federal Reserve Board to operate "under the charge of the Comptroller of the Currency the issue and retirement of Federal Reserve notes."

The Owen Bill empowered the Federal Reserve Board to authorize member banks to use as reserves not only Federal Reserve notes, but also bank notes based on United States bonds.

The Federal Reserve could authorize Federal Reserve banks to discount the direct obligations of member banks, secured by the pledge and deposit of satisfactory securities with a limit on the amount so loaned of three-fourths of the actual value of the pledged securities.

The Owen Bill eliminated the language in the provision requiring moneys held in the general fund of the Treasury that were deposited in Federal Reserve banks *be equitably allocated.*

In contrast to the House version requiring a special reserve account of 33⅓ percent of the reserve notes paid out, the Owen version provided:

> Every Federal reserve bank shall maintain reserves in gold or lawful money of not less than thirty-five per centum against its deposits and its Federal reserve notes in actual circulation, but the amount of gold in the Federal reserve bank together with the amount deposited by it with the Treasury, shall be at least equal to thirty-three and one-third per centum of the Federal reserve notes issued to said bank and in actual circulation and not offset by gold or lawful money deposited with the Federal reserve agent.

In lieu of the House provision for retirement of the 2 percent United States bonds, the Owen Bill had a provision granting discretion to the Treasury and Federal Reserve Board to purchase bonds after a member bank had filed an application to sell its bonds.

The Owen Bill replaced the House bill tripartite reserve requirements with requirements that banks not in a reserve or central reserve city hold and maintain reserves equal to 12 percent of the aggregate amount of its demand liabilities and 5 percent of its total deposits. After 24 months, certain of the required reserves could be held in banks in reserve or central reserve cities "as now defined by law."

Banks in reserve cities were required to hold 15 percent of the amount of its demand liabilities and 5 percent of time deposits.

Banks in central reserve cities were required to hold as reserve 18 percent of the aggregate amount of its demand liabilities and 5 percent of time deposits.

The Owen Bill struck the provision in the House Bill requiring each Federal Reserve bank to have in its own vaults in gold or lawful money, 33⅓ percent of its outstanding demand liabilities.

After a House-Senate Conference Committee resolved differences between the House and Senate versions of H.R. 7837, the Federal Reserve Act was enacted in the House by a vote of 298 to 60 and in the Senate by a vote of 43 to 25. On December 23, 1913, Woodrow Wilson signed the Federal Reserve Act into law. Wilson's Secretary of Agriculture David Houston exclaimed in his diary:

> The impossible has happened. Today, Tuesday, December 23d, the currency measure became a law. The President approved it a few minutes after six o'clock in the afternoon. It was passed by a Congress dominated by the Democrats, two-thirds of whom had been unsound on currency questions and a majority of whom can scarcely be said to have understood what the measure meant and would accomplish. The majority of the Republicans had also had an unenviable record on the currency. Bryan and several other members of the Cabinet had supported free silver, as had Vice President Marshall, The Speaker, Champ Clark, and many Democratic Senators. The measure itself was the result of the labours of many men, extending over a long period, but its passage at this time in its present form was due to Woodrow Wilson, ably supported by [Secretary of Treasury] McAdoo, Glass, and a few others.

To Wilson biographer Arthur Link, the creation of the Federal Reserve System "was the crowning achievement of the first Wilson Administration," "the greatest single piece of constructive legislation of the Wilson era."

The Act, in its structure and key provisions, could be traced to the House adopted initial version of H.R. 7837 that was adopted in September 1913. Some of these provisions were amended to incorporate the language of the Senate adopted version of the Owen Bill, adopted by the Senate five days earlier on December 18, 1913. The language of the Conference Draft that became the Federal Reserve Act further refined and tightened the final text.

The Federal Reserve Act was an amalgam of Wilson's insistence on a publicly controlled supervisory capstone: the bankers preferences, for elasticity of currency, foreign trade, and a large place, if not control, of the governance the 12 Federal Reserve banks; the farmer's interest in support for agriculture; and Senator Aldrich and the National Monetary Commission's detailed provisions dealing with the reorganization of credit, new notes to act as currency and discounting systems for notes and bills of exchange. The enduring ideology of Andrew Jackson was influential. There was no private central bank. Paper currency was limited by Federal Reserve and member bank reserves. Each of the proponents of the Act won something. No proponent won everything.

The Federal Reserve Act of 1913 began with a brisk articulation of objectives in a preamble:

> To provide for the establishment of Federal reserve banks, to furnish an elastic currency, to afford means of rediscounting commercial paper, to establish a more effective supervision of banking in the United States, and for other purposes.

The most important achievement of the Federal Reserve Act was the creation of a new structure for banking regulation. Not since 1836, with the expiration of the charter of the Second Bank of the United States, had there been a national bank, in this case with some of the powers of a modern central bank.

The Act's structure of banking regulation was unique. The Federal Reserve Board, located in Washington, shared power with not less than 8 nor more than 12 Federal Reserve banks, as well as with the Department of Treasury and the Comptroller of Currency. Uncertainty as to the relationship of the Federal Reserve Board to the Secretary of Treasury, and the Federal Reserve Bank of New York would undercut the effectiveness of the Federal Reserve Board during the 20 year period preceding the New Deal. New Deal legislation in 1933 and 1935 would clarify these critical power relationships and strengthened the Fed's ability to help prevent another catastrophe such as the 1929–1933 Stock Market Crash strengthened, but these steps alone did not complete creation of the modern Fed, but instead were critical milestones.

The structure of the Federal Reserve Act was unique in a second sense, combining national regulatory requirements and a largely presidentially appointed Federal Reserve Board with the largely private and banker dominated Federal Reserve banks.

Jacksonian fear of an all-powerful central bank led Congress and Wilson to limit the initial powers of the Federal Reserve Board and to cabin its authority through the private interests represented on the Federal Reserve banks and the powers retained by member banks in the Federal Reserve districts. Even Wilson, who had insisted on a Federal Reserve Board as a "capstone" to the new regulatory system, said of the Federal Reserve banks: "We have purposely scattered the regional reserve banks and shall be intensely disappointed if they do not exercise a very large measure of independence." This was political rhetoric, in all probability only somewhat believed by Wilson. But in the political climate of the day, this was rhetoric he needed to recite.

After more than a century, the Federal Reserve System has proved more politically sustainable than the earlier banks of the United States. But its initial complex structure combined without what Ben Bernanke would term "strong clear oversight or clear lines of authority" would make the Federal Reserve Board and the Federal Reserve banks, particularly the Federal Reserve Bank of New York, disastrously ineffectual in being a lender of last resort in 1929–1933, or effectively responding to the United States' greatest financial crisis, the Great Depression.

In the Federal Reserve Act, the Federal Reserve Board consisted of seven members, including the Secretary of Treasury and Comptroller of Currency as members *ex officio.* The other five Federal Reserve Board members were Presidential appointees with the advice and consent of the Senate. No more than one Board member could be from any one Federal Reserve district. The President "shall have due regard to a fair representation of the different commercial, industrial and geographic divisions of the country." At least two of the five Presidential appointees were to be persons experienced in banking or finance. From these five Board members, the President was to designate one as Governor, who would be the active executive officer, and one as Vice Governor. All of the Board members appointed by the President were expected to work full time for the Fed. Once the Federal Reserve Board had all five members in place, each Board member would serve a ten-year term unless removed for cause by the president. To dampen partisanship, the terms of one of the five Board members would expire each two years.

The Federal Reserve Board was empowered "[t]o exercise general supervision over... Federal Reserve Banks" and had the power "to levy semiannually upon the Federal reserve banks, in proportion to their capital stock and surplus, an assessment sufficient to pay its estimated expenses and the salaries of its members and employees." At later times, this power of self-funding would distinguish the Fed from many of the independent regulatory agencies, such as the Securities and Exchange Commission, and would strengthen the independence of the Fed.

In 1913, however, the specific Federal Reserve Board powers of most consequence were the powers:

> (a) To examine at its discretion the accounts, books and affairs of each Federal reserve bank and of each member bank and to require such statements and reports as it may deem necessary.
>
> . . .
>
> (b) To permit, or, on the affirmative vote of at least five members of the Reserve Board to require Federal reserve banks to rediscount the discounted paper of other Federal reserve banks at rates of interest to be fixed by the Federal Reserve Board.
>
> (c) To suspend for a period not exceeding thirty days, and from time to time to renew such suspension for periods not exceeding fifteen days, any reserve requirement specified in this Act. . . .
>
> (d) To supervise and regulate through the bureau under the charge of the Comptroller of the Currency the issue and retirement of Federal reserve notes, and to prescribe rules and regulations under which such notes may be delivered by the Comptroller to the Federal reserve agents applying therefor.
>
> (e) To add to the number of cities classified as reserve and central reserve cities under existing law in which national banking associations are subject to the reserve requirements set forth in section twenty of this Act; or to reclassify existing reserve and central reserve cities or to terminate their designation as such.

The Federal Reserve Board was to receive the advice of a Federal Advisory Council, whose members were selected by the Federal Reserve Board.

A Reserve Bank Organization Committee comprised of the Secretary of Treasury, the Secretary of Agriculture, and the Comptroller of the Currency was created to designate the 8 to 12 cities in the Act known as Federal Reserve cities, and to divide the United States into districts, each containing one of the Federal Reserve cities. The Organization Committee chose 12 cities which remain the same today: Boston, New York, Philadelphia, Cleveland, Richmond, Atlanta, Chicago, St. Louis, Minneapolis, Kansas City, Dallas, and San Francisco.

Every national bank, every other eligible bank, and every trust company in the District of Columbia could signify within 60 days of the Federal Reserve Act's passage whether it sought to be a member bank of the Federal Reserve. Member banks were required to subscribe to the capital stock of the district Federal Reserve bank 6 percent of the paid-up capital and surplus of the bank. Any national bank that failed to become a Federal Reserve member bank within one year would lose all of its rights, privileges, and franchises under the National Banking Act.

If member bank subscriptions to the Federal Reserve bank in their district proved inadequate, a public sale of Federal Reserve bank stock would occur. No individual, partnership, or corporation, other than a member bank, was permitted to subscribe to more than $25,000 of stock in a Federal Reserve bank. This public stock would not be entitled to voting power. If total subscriptions by banks and the public to a Federal Reserve bank were insufficient, the Department of Treasury would subscribe for the balance.

Federal Reserve banks were required to have subscribed capital of at least $4 million to commence business. The Federal Reserve banks, but not the member banks, could establish branch banks within their Federal Reserve district and in any district in which a Federal Reserve bank operations were suspended. By 2019, there were 24 branches supporting the 12 Federal Reserve banks.

While the Act was phrased in terms of a mandate for national banks to become member banks of the Federal Reserve, membership was in fact optional. National banks could become state banks if they so choose. To encourage the national banks to become Federal Reserve member banks, required reserve percentages were reduced, member bank contributions to their district Reserve Banks were reduced, and dividends to member bank stockholders were increased.

State banks also were given the option to become stockholders of the Federal Reserve bank in their district if they complied with the same reserve and capital requirements as the national banks converting to Federal Reserve member banks. State banks had to agree to submit to the same examination and other regulatory requirements applicable to national banks. This state bank affiliate status in the Federal Reserve System initially would be little used. By June 1917, only 53 state banks had entered the Federal Reserve System.

While the Federal Reserve bank and member bank system was new, it was notable that the Federal Reserve Act did not change the status of reserve cities and central reserve cities. The initial Federal Reserve Act attempted, when possible, to build on the existing framework of National Banking Act.

The Federal Reserve banks initially had a 20-year term, which in 1927 was extended in perpetuity or "until dissolved by Act of Congress or until forfeiture of franchise for violation of law."

The Boards of Directors of Federal Reserve banks had the Classes A, B and C earlier proposed in both the House and Senate version of H.R. 7837. Each Federal Reserve bank director would serve for three years:

> Class A shall consist of three members, who shall be chosen by and be representative of the stock-holding banks.
>
> Class B shall consist of three members, who at the time of their election shall be actively engaged in their district in commerce, agriculture or some other industrial pursuit.
>
> Class C shall consist of three members who shall be designated by the Federal Reserve Board.

One of the Class C Directors also would be designated as Chair of the Reserve Bank Board and serve as Federal Reserve agent required to make regular reports to the Federal Reserve Board.

No Class B Director could be an officer, director, or employee of any bank.

No Class C Director could be an officer, director, employee, or stockholder of any bank. Nonetheless, both the Class C Directors selected to be Chair and a second appointed as Deputy Chair, were required to be persons of "tested banking experience."

Federal Reserve bank directors would serve three-year terms, with one member of each class up for election or re-election each year.

The capital stock of each Federal Reserve bank was set at a manageable $100 per share. Member bank shares could not be transferred or hypothecated (that is pledged to support a loan).

The Federal Reserve Act raised the annual dividend to member banks to 6 percent "[a]fter all necessary expenses of a Federal Reserve bank have been paid or provided for." After the member bank dividend was paid, the net earnings of the Federal Reserve bank were paid to the United States as a franchise tax, "except that one-half of such net earnings shall be paid into a surplus fund until it shall amount to forty per centum of the paid-in capital of such bank."

Federal Reserve banks, including their capital stock and surplus, were exempt from all federal, state, and local taxes, except taxes upon real estate.

Federal Reserve banks were given broad banking powers:

> (1) To receive from any member bank in the United States deposits of current funds in lawful currency, National Bank Notes, Federal Reserve Notes or checks from "solvent" member banks.
>
> (2) Upon indorsement of any of its member banks, any Federal Reserve Banks could discount Notes, drafts and Bills of Exchange arising out of commercial transactions, defined to mean Notes, drafts and Bills of Exchange "issued or drawn for agricultural, industrial or commercial purposes." In contrast, "Notes, drafts and bills of exchange covering investments or issued or drawn for the purpose of carrying or trading in stocks, bonds, or other investment securities, except bonds and Notes of the Government of the United States" were excluded. Covered Notes, drafts and bills admitted to discount were required to have a maturity of not more than 90 days, with the proviso that agricultural Notes, drafts and bills based on livestock could have a maturity up to 6 months.
>
> (3) Acceptances based on the import or export of goods with a maturity up to 3 months, when indorsed by at least one member bank were permitted if limited to no more than one-half the paid capital stock and surplus of the bank.
>
> (4) No one person, company or corporation in any one bank could be responsible for rediscounting equal to more than 10 percent of the unimpaired capital and surplus unless the discount of bills was drawn against actually existing values.
>
> (5) Any member bank could accept drafts or Bills of Exchange for import or export of goods with not more than 6 months to run with the aggregate limit for such bills of no more than one-half of the bank's capital and surplus.

Federal Reserve banks also were given powers to purchase and sell in the open market, at home and abroad, either from or to domestic or foreign banks, firms, corporations, or individual bankers' acceptances and bills of exchange with or without the indorsement of a member bank.

Federal Reserve banks were empowered to deal in gold coin or bullion at home or abroad or make loans based on gold; exchange Federal Reserve notes for gold, gold coin, or gold certificates.

The Federal Reserve banks could buy or sell, at home or abroad, bonds and notes of the United States and bills, notes, revenue bonds and warrants with a maturity from date of purchase of not more than six months issued in anticipation of collection of taxes or other assured revenues by any state, county, district, political subdivision or municipality in the continental United States.

Federal Reserve banks in the open market could purchase from member banks and sell bills of exchange arising out of commercial transactions.

Each Federal Reserve bank, "subject to review and determination of the Federal Reserve Board" could determine the discount rates charged by the bank for each class of paper, "which shall be fixed with a view of accommodating commerce and business."

Each Federal Reserve bank could establish accounts with other Federal Reserve banks for exchange purposes and with the consent of the Federal Reserve Board, could open and maintain accounts in foreign countries, and:

> establish agencies in such countries wheresoever it may deem best for the purpose of purchasing, selling, and collecting bills of exchange, and to buy and sell with or without its indorsement, through such correspondents or agencies, bills of exchange arising out of actual commercial transactions which have not more than ninety days to run and which bear the signature of two or more responsible parties.

The Federal Reserve Act contained a simpler provision on deposit of the general fund of the Treasury. All moneys upon direction of the Secretary of Treasury would be deposited in Federal Reserve Banks which would act as fiscal agents of the United States "and the revenues of the government... may be deposited in such banks, and disbursements... made by checks drawn against such deposits." There were no geographical limits placed upon the Secretary of Treasury. Five percent of the United States general fund was required to be held for the redemption of outstanding national bank notes.

The Federal Reserve Board was authorized to issue its own Federal Reserve notes, which were obligations of the United States, intended to replace the privately issued national bank notes, which then were a basic currency in the United States. The Federal Reserve Notes were "receivable by all national and member banks and Federal reserve banks and for all taxes, customs, and other public dues. They shall be redeemed in gold on demand at the Treasury Department of the United States, in the city of Washington, District of Columbia, or in gold or lawful money at any Federal reserve bank."

The new Federal Reserve notes were to be issued to each Federal Reserve bank, which could apply "for such amount of the Federal reserve notes . . . as it may require" as long as the Federal Reserve bank provided collateral equal to the sum of the Federal Reserve Notes received.

Each Federal Reserve bank was required to maintain gold or lawful money of not less than 35 percent against its deposits and of not less than 40 percent against its Federal Reserve notes in circulation.

Given the anxiety of Carter Glass and others about inflation in paper currency, the Federal Reserve Act initially did not authorize notes in denominations of $1 or $2, considered at the time more inflationary, but solely in denominations of $5, $10, $20, $50, and $100.

The Federal Reserve Act established a means to retire national bank notes after two years, during a period of 20 years. This was to be achieved by the Federal Reserve Board authorizing Federal Reserve banks to acquire the United States bonds that secured circulation to the national bank note to be retired. Each Federal Reserve bank could purchase no more than $25 million of the United States bonds each year. As this was done, the Federal Reserve banks could take out of circulation national bank notes equal to the par value of the United States bonds and receive Federal Reserve Notes equal to the par value of the United States bonds so deposited.

The Act also provided a refunding mechanism for United States 2 percent gold bonds, which could be exchanged by Federal Reserve banks once approved by the Federal Reserve Board for a combination of Treasury one year gold notes (up to 50 percent of the 2 percent bonds tendered) and 30 year 3 percent United States gold bonds for the balance of the 2 percent bonds tendered.

The Federal Reserve Act required reserves after a 30-month period to be held in the vaults of the member bank or in the Federal Reserve bank at the option of the member bank except for reserves required either to be in the vaults of the member bank or in the Federal Reserve bank.

Reserve requirements were lowered.

Country banks, those not in a reserve or central reserve city, were required to hold 12 percent of the aggregate of its demand deposits and 5 percent of time deposits.

A bank in a reserve city was required to hold 15 percent of the aggregate amount of demand deposits and 5 percent of time deposits.

A bank in a central reserve city was required to hold 18 percent of the aggregate amount of demand deposits and 5 percent of time deposits.

Any national bank not situated in a central reserve city could make loans secured by improved and unencumbered farm land situated within its Federal Reserve district for up to five years for an amount not exceeding 50 percent of the actual value provided as collateral. Banks making these loans could do so to an aggregate amount equal to 25 percent of its capital and surplus or to one-third of its time deposits.

A national bank also possessing capital and surplus of $1 million or more, with approval of the Federal Reserve Board, could establish foreign business "for the furtherance of the foreign commerce of the United States."

Banking in the United States involved three types of banks: National banks that were members of the Federal Reserve whose 7530 banks in aggregate in 1929 held $21.586 billion in total deposits; state member banks whose 1177 banks held $14.279 billion in total deposits; and state nonmember banks whose 15,797 banks held $13.170 billion in total deposits. Unlike other banking systems, each bank could choose its status. In contrast to Canada, national banks in the United States in 1915 had virtually no bank branches, a total of 26, with state bank branches growing to 2207 branches by 1925, creating an additional incentive for state banks to remain state banks.

Banking regulation remained dispersed with a supervising Federal Reserve Board, 12 Federal Reserve banks, remnants of the National Banking Acts and state banking regulations with variable regulating and examination standards.

Banking regulation had begun a gravitation from a largely state-based system with the enactment of the Federal Reserve Act of 1913, but this gravitation remained begrudging and limited by the banking ideology of Jackson, who would continue to be a force in banking regulation for 100 years after his 1832 veto of the charter of the Second Bank of the United States.[49]

* * * * * * *

Securities Regulation

Securities regulation, in contrast, proceeded at the state level, through private organizations, and to a limited extent through the federal government before the New Deal, but more slowly, less decisively, and in some instances with the distinction between commercial and investment banking quite blurred.

Throughout United States history, no business corporation could begin operations until it filed a certificate of incorporation obliging it to operate subject to a state's corporation laws. Often, the early state corporate statutes had been restrictive, limiting, among other things, the amount of capital a business firm could raise. Under the United States Constitution, a business firm was permitted to incorporate in any state, regardless of where the firm actually did business. By the turn of the 20th century, "chartermongering" states led by New Jersey, Delaware, and Nevada, had stimulated a "race for the bottom," removing the restrictive features of their corporate statutes in order to induce out-of-state firms to incorporate within their increasingly hospitable borders. In return, the chartermongering States received from each firm an annual franchise tax. In Delaware, where chartermongering was elevated to a high art, corporate franchise taxes and related fees averaged 31 percent of the state's total revenues from 1913 to 1934.

Throughout the 19th century, corporate securities sales had been supervised by state corporate laws. Each shareholder was required to contribute not less than a stated amount — called a par value — for shares. Stock not paid for by the minimum contribution could not legally be issued. Although the par value originally was intended to protect creditors by ensuring that a firm would not run up bills before raising sufficient capital to pay them, it protected shareholders as well by guaranteeing that "every stockholder in a corporation is entitled to insist that every other stockholder shall contribute his ratable part of the company's capital."

The requirement that a firm could sell its shares at no less than par value was inconvenient if the value of a firm's assets declined and the firm needed to raise additional capital. Firms took to employing a loophole implicit in the corporate statutes by selling "low par" stock with a stated capital as low as a penny and most of the price paid for a share denominated as "surplus." The practice received legislative blessing in 1912, when New York became the first state to authorize "no par" stock. The practical consequence of both low par and no par shares was that a board of directors was no longer bound by the requirement of selling all shares at a stated par value price, and had discretion to raise or lower the sales price of corporate shares.

The concept that each shareholder must contribute his "ratable part of the company's capital" also was challenged by the facility with which directors could issue stock in exchange for property or services, rather than for cash. Crucial amendments to state corporate statutes gave color of law to the issuance of "watered" stock (or stock valued at more than the property exchanged for it). By the 1920s, state corporate statutes often provided: "The judgment of directors as to the value of property purchased shall be conclusive."

Occasionally stock watering was effectively challenged by a shareholders' fraud suit. But by the 1920s, the ability of the judiciary to protect noncontrolling shareholders from management self-favoritism had been outrun by a series of statutory innovations that allowed corporate insiders to achieve profits from securities distributions without risking a fraud suit. Many of these enactments came into being as the result of 1927 and 1929 amendments to the Delaware General Corporation Law.

Corporations could issue stock options or stock purchase warrants, either of which permitted a corporation to distribute rights to buy corporate stock at a designated price regardless of how high above the option price the stock's market price rose. Stock option warrants first received legislative sanction in March 1929, when the Delaware General Assembly amended § 14 of its General Corporation Law. Alternatively, under § 13 of the revised Delaware General Corporation Law a corporation could issue blank stock, whose "voting powers, designations, preferences, and relative, participating, optional or other rights" could be fixed by a board of directors after original subscribers had purchased their shares. Adolf Berle scathingly concluded in 1930 that the effect of these and kindred corporate law devices could accord corporate management "the power of confiscation": "By using them, or a combination of them, appropriately, the profits of the enterprise and also in a considerable measure the underlying assets may be shifted from one group of stockholders to another."

A few states early in United States history more directly had attempted to regulate sales of securities. Massachusetts in 1852 had required railroad companies to file a certificate "stating that all of the stock named in its charter has been subscribed for by responsible parties, and that twenty per cent of the par value of each and every share of the stock thereof has been actually paid into the treasury of the company."

In 1879, the California Constitution of 1879 voided all contracts for the sale of stock on margin, that is, stock purchased by borrowed money.

A Georgia statute of 1904 required companies selling "investment securities of any kind on the partial payment, installment or any other plan of payment, and providing for the redemption and retiring of the same, or any part thereof," to deposit in a trust company at least $25,000, to establish a redemption fund of at least 75 percent of the amount collected in premiums, and to file annual financial statements with the Comptroller General.

A Missouri statute in 1907 outlawed the keeping of places for dealing in stocks, bonds, and commodities for future delivery "without at the time of sale the seller shall cause to be made a complete record of the things sold, the purchaser and the time of delivery in a book for that purpose," and deliver a written memorandum (or confirmation) with a stamp affixed.

Connecticut in 1903 adopted a brief statute that made it unlawful for any mining or oil corporation to offer its shares, directly or through an agent or broker, until it had filed in the office of the Secretary of State a certificate showing its financial condition, the location and plans of its properties, the amount of work done and cash expended for improvements, and the condition of its plant and machinery. The legislature generously provided that the Act should not "in any way affect any corporation all of whose mines are situated within this state." It was not until 1911 that this Act was replaced by a new statute that conditioned the sale of oil or mining shares upon prior administrative permission.

Nevada enacted a statute in 1909 that was primarily intended to achieve full disclosure in the sale of mining stock. This Act was watered down in 1911 and repealed in 1915, and Nevada had no securities law of any kind until 1963.

In 1910, the Rhode Island corporation law was amended to include a provision regulating the issuance of "stock, shares, or installment shares, in any investment company or in any real estate, mining, or co-operative corporation, society, association, or organization, other than building and loan associations, or notes or bonds or other securities thereof."

Kansas became the first state to enact a comprehensive and enduring form of state securities regulation. The origin of the law could be traced to Midwestern farm prosperity. Between 1900 and 1910, business historian Vincent Carosso wrote:

> [T]he total estimated value of farm land and buildings in the United States more than doubled, while the index of wholesale prices for all farm products rose approximately 50 percent. Many farmers paid off their debts and accumulated cash savings. Prosperity attracted to Kansas numerous promoters, [and] swindlers . . . determined to separate the affluent farmer form his savings by enticing him to invest in fraudulent, financially unsound, or highly speculative enterprises. Suffering heavy losses, the victims of these frauds and misrepresentations agitated for protection, then joined with other dissatisfied Midwesterners to elect reform administrations that promised them relief from such abuses. . . .

In 1911, Kansas enacted the best known state securities law before 1933, popularly known as a "Blue Sky" law, since it was intended to check stock swindlers so barefaced they "would sell building lots in the blue sky." It is one of the more improbable ironies of corporate law that the man who initially popularized securities regulation in the United States was not a sophisticated reform attorney like Louis Brandeis, but, rather, a retired grocer and populist politician named J. N. Dolley.

Appointed Bank Commissioner in 1910, Dolley organized a Special Department to investigate securities offered for sale in Kansas. His action was in response to a wave of recent land, mining, and insurance company stock frauds. Dolley asserted that firms selling securities should be subject to "the very strictest of supervision. Why should the bank be regulated and supervised any more so than the stock selling company?" he wrote. "History and statistics show that losses through banks are but a drop in the bucket compared with the money which is loss through investment in worthless stocks and bonds." So prodded, the Kansas legislature in 1911 enacted a sweeping securities licensing statute. By its terms, no "investment company" could sell securities in Kansas until it filed a description of its operations with the Bank Commissioner and received a permit. The Bank Commissioner was given broad discretion not to grant a permit if he found any aspect of a company's business to be "unfair, unjust, inequitable, or oppressive to any class of contributors, or if he decides from his examination of its affairs that said investment company is not solvent and does not intend to do a fair and honest business, and in his judgment does not promise a fair return on the stocks, bonds or other securities by it offered for sale."

Dolley broadly advertised the law's "wonderful results," estimating, in one often quoted statement, that the Act in its first year of operation had saved the citizens of Kansas "at least six million dollars" and that fewer than 100 of the 1400 to 1500 companies investigated by his Banking Department had been granted a permit.

Each of these claims was a fantastic exaggeration. A 1913 Report by Thomas Mulvey, Canada's Undersecretary of State, found, on the basis of an examination of Dolley's own records, no substantive basis for Dolley's estimate that Kansas citizens had been saved at least $6 million, and that, through May 1913, only 62 firms had been refused a permit.

At the time, Mulvey's sobering appraisal was ignored. Within two years after the Kansas Blue Sky Act had been adopted, 23 states enacted securities regulation statutes, all but six of which were either identical with the Kansas law or modeled on it. After the Kansas type of Blue Sky law was held to be Constitutional in the *Blue Sky Cases* by the United States Supreme Court in 1917, the movement swept the country. By 1933, every state except Nevada had adopted a securities law.

Rarely have statutes enacted with such fanfare and general support subsequently been so universally deprecated. In the brutal glare that followed the 1929–1933 Stock Market Crash, it was evident that the Blue Sky laws never really had a chance to succeed. As early as 1915, the Investment Bankers Association had reported to its members that they could "ignore" all Blue Sky laws by making offerings across state lines through the mails. Unscrupulous securities promoters soon adopted the technique. A 1933 Department of Commerce study found, "[t]he most effective and widely used method of evading the provision of State Blue Sky laws consists in operating across state lines." Robert Healy, Chief Counsel to the Federal Trade Commission, testified before Congress that same year that over 90 percent of the securities sold in Pennsylvania were sold through the mails.

Nor were purely intrastate securities sales much better policed. Effective lobbying, principally by the Investment Bankers

Association, had riddled most state Blue Sky laws with exemptions. Typically, an Act might exempt the securities of all corporations listed on a stock exchange and all securities issued by a public utility subject to the regulation of a federal or state agency. The more porous statutes also exempted the securities of all firms incorporated intrastate, bank corporations, insurance companies, investment companies, cooperative associations, building and loan associations, business trusts, as well as issued "guaranteed by friendly foreign governments," mortgage bonds and notes secured by property within the state, short term commercial paper, "isolated" securities transactions, one year debentures, and a myriad of other types of securities or transactions.

Only eight states appropriated sufficient funds to support securities commissions that could work full time investigating suspected frauds and prosecuting violators. In 40 states, administration of the Blue Sky Act was "a football of politics" as the Chair of the Conference on Prevention of Fraudulent Transactions in Securities put it in 1931. Enforcement responsibilities were assigned to unspecialized attorneys working for state officials as disparate as the Railroad Commission or the State Auditor. When political administrations changed, responsibility for Blue Sky enforcement frequently was reassigned.

Even in New York, which was widely regarded as having the most effective Blue Sky agency, enforcement was inadequate. In 1932, the Attorney General's Bureau of Securities employed more than 100 people, secured injunctions against 1522 persons and firms, and instituted 146 criminal prosecutions. At approximately the same time, officials of the New York Stock Exchange estimated that of the $1 billion or so of fraudulent securities annually sold in the United States, about half were sold in New York State.[50]

With state law largely a nullity during the period before the New Deal, regulation of securities firms to a greater degree remained in private organizations.

The New York Stock Exchange (*NYSE*) had grown exponentially since stock traders on May 17, 1792, had signed an agreement under a proverbial buttonwood tree on Wall Street, essentially to do what today would be viewed as an antitrust violation. The traders pledged not to buy or sell securities in any public stock from any person "at a rate less than one-quarter per cent commission on the special value, and that each will give preference to each other in our negotiations." At the time, there were five public securities traded in the New York market.

The telegraph transformed securities trading. By the time of the Civil War, stock exchanges had been established in Baltimore, Philadelphia, and Boston. Some 10 exchanges were formed between 1861 and 1869 including the Chicago Stock Exchange and San Francisco Stock and Exchange Board. In New York, the NYSE faced competition from the Consolidated Stock Exchange, causing the NYSE, according to the Pujo Report, to "wage bitter warfare" prohibiting a member of the Consolidated Exchange to sell securities on the NYSE.

In June 1909, the Hughes Committee *Report on Speculation in Securities and Commodities* was published. It was an odd, bloodless document, with few specific examples to bring its analysis to life and relatively little data. The Committee sought to address "[t]he problem, whenever speculation is strongly rooted, is to eliminate that which is wasteful and morally destructive, while retaining and allowing free play to that which is beneficial." The Committee acknowledged: "The difficulty in the solution of the problem lies in the practical impossibility of distinguishing what is virtually gambling from legitimate speculation."

The Hughes Committee *Report on Speculation* was most notable for what it did not recommend. There was no proposal for federal legislation to address stock markets or stock issuances. The Report did not recommend abolishing margin trading, that is, purchasing securities on borrowed money, although it did recommend increasing the amount of collateral required from customers to 20 percent. After the federal securities laws were enacted in the New Deal, margins have been raised to 50 percent or more. The Hughes Committee did not recommend prohibiting or limiting short selling. The Report did encourage the NYSE to take steps to prevent the worst form of stock price manipulation "by exercising its influence and authority over the [Exchange's] members to prevent them." Even here the Hughes recommendations were remarkably measured. The Report expressly opposed state authority to examine the books of exchange members "analogous to that required of banks," because of the confidentiality of the relationship between brokers and customers. Nor did the Committee support a proposal to require verification of facts contained in applications for listing securities on the Exchange.

In its most far-reaching recommendations, the Hughes Committee did recommend:

> the Exchange should, however, adopt methods to compel the filing of frequent statements of the financial condition of the companies whose securities are listed, including balance sheets, income and expense accounts, etc., and should notify the public that these are open to examination under proper rules and regulations. The Exchange should also require that there be filed with future applications for listing a statement of what the capital stock of the company has been issued for, showing how much has been issued for cash, how much for property, with a description of the property, etc., and also showing what commission, if any, has been paid to the promoters or vendors. Furthermore, means should be adopted for holding those making the statements responsible for the truth thereof. The unlisted department, except for temporary issues, should be abolished.

The Hughes Committee recommendations largely were ignored. Unlisted trading — that is, trading on the NYSE of securities not listed there — would be abolished by the NYSE in 1910.

In 1909, the Hughes Committee had characterized the NYSE as "today probably the most important financial institution in the world."

The Pujo Report endorsed this characterization, terming the NYSE:

> [T]he New York Stock Exchange is the primary market for securities in the United States and as such is a vital part of the financial system. . . . In the past decade the average annual sales of shares on that exchange have been 195,500,000, at prices involving an annual average turnover of nearly $15,500,000,000; and of bonds $800,000,000. . . .
>
> Quotations on its floor determine the current value of all securities there traded in, which means the securities of all the greater corporations of the country. . . .
>
> The business conducted upon this exchange is not only nation wide, but international in its scope. Its members maintain private wires to all the principal cities of the United States and the transactions conducted by its members are for the account of customers from all parts of the country and from foreign countries.
>
> . . .

> It is a voluntary, unincorporated association, with a written constitution. Its chief functionaries are a President, a secretary, a governing committee, a law committee, a committee on admissions, a committee on arrangements, a committee on stock list, and a finance committee. This governing committee is its principal organ of administration. Its membership is now limited to 1100, which under the constitution, can only be increased by the governing committee. There has been no increase in this limitation since 1879, although the volume of sales has grown from 75,000,000 shares and $418,000,000 of bonds in that year to 129,824,169 shares and $684,942,420 of bonds in 1912; and the number of listed securities, as roughly estimated by a high official of the exchange, is fifty times greater now than at that time.
>
> As no complete record is kept, the amount loaned on the floor of the exchange in a day can not be definitely stated. One of the leading brokers estimated the amount at not more than $50,000,000, and often much less. . . . The chief lenders are the National City Bank, the Hanover National Bank, J.P. Morgan & Co., and Kuhn, Loeb & Co. . . . Such loans are mainly payable on demand and are made upon collateral that is listed on the exchange. . . . This loan stand constitutes the only open market for the lending of money in the United States. Most of the loans made to stock exchange members are, however, negotiated directly between the banks and the brokers at the offices of the banks and not at the loan stand of the exchange.

The New York Stock Exchange Committee and Stock List provided some oversight to listed securities.

Before a security could be offered for sale on the NYSE, the corporate issuer had to file an application describing in detail the firm's capital structure, history, liabilities, properties, financial statements over the past five years, and officers. The firm had to forward, along with the application, copies of its charter, by-laws, leases, franchises, relevant director and shareholder resolutions, an opinion of an independent legal counsel as to the legality of the corporate organization and the immediate securities issuance, and a copy of a report of a qualified engineer describing the actual physical condition of properties at a recent date. Not only were the stock exchange listing requirements far more precise than any found in the Blue Sky laws, they more closely resembled the standards subsequently adopted in Schedule A of the 1933 Securities Act than those found in the English Companies Act, which proponents of the

Federal Securities Act usually identified as their model. Even the most unrelenting critics of corporate finance lauded the NYSE's listing requirements. Harvard's Professor William Z. Ripley, for example, declaimed unequivocally in his influential 1927 work, *Main Street and Wall Street,* "Beyond peradventure of doubt the New York Stock Exchange is today the leading influence in the promotion of adequate corporate disclosure." Similarly, Adolf Berle believed that "the most forward-looking steps in finance taken during the 1925–1929 boom were not taken by government, but by that most maligned institution, the New York Stock Exchange."

Nonetheless, the NYSE's listing requirements proved little more effective than the Blue Sky laws. Being purely voluntary standards, they could be avoided by any corporation that chose to register as an *unlisted* security on the New York Curb Exchange [which in 1953 was renamed the American Stock Exchange] or any of the other 17 securities exchanges which permitted securities to be traded on an *unlisted* basis. An *unlisted* security was one about which the corporate issuer had supplied no information whatever, but which had been admitted to trading on an exchange on the application of a member of that exchange.

Nor did the NYSE scrupulously enforce its listing requirements. As a number of new stock applications approved increased to 300 in 1926, 571 in 1928, and 759 in the first nine months of 1929, responsibility for enforcing the requirements remained with the eight Exchange members who composed the Listing Committee and a small investigative staff. Testifying in 1934, Frank Altschul, Chair of the Exchange's Committee on Stock List, conceded that the NYSE ceased making any independent investigation of an application for the listing of additional stock by a firm whose stock was previously listed unless there appeared patently suspicious matters in the listing application. In at least one instance, the Stock List Committee did not respond when an application *did* include patently suspicious matter. When Ivar Kreuger's Kreuger and Toll Company in 1929 applied to list a 30-year debenture, reserving the right to substitute new pledged securities for those listed as collateral on the application, Altschul and the Stock List Committee were aware that no American firm had ever been accorded so sweeping a substitution privilege. The Stock List Committee did not make an independent investigation of Kreuger and Toll, nor did it consult an attorney as to the legality of the substitution provision. When Ivar Kreuger subsequently replaced the French debentures serving as collateral with less valuable Yugoslavian ones, Altschul could only testify that the New York Stock Exchange had been "deceived."

The Pujo Report in 1913 offered three other examples where a pool of stock traders manipulated listed share prices by "wash sales," that is, simultaneously placing buy and sell orders to create a false appearance of activity that would artificially increase the price of the security on the exchange. The Pujo Report included testimony of two New York Stock Exchanges demonstrating knowledge of this type of transaction. The Pujo Report summarized:

> The practices thus approved by the authorities of the exchange not only deceive the great body of the public as to the true state of the market and whet their appetite for speculation, but debase and make impossible of fulfillment the high office of the exchange as a register of the current values of securities, and draw from the channels of legitimate trade and commerce millions of the country's capital.

The Pujo Report excoriated the "scandalous practices of officers and directors in speculating upon inside and advance information as to the action of their corporations."

The Pujo Committee concluded "[t]he facilities of the New York Stock Exchange are employed largely for transactions producing moral and economic corruption; and it is fair to assume that in lesser and varying degrees that this is true or may come to be true of other institutions throughout the country similarly organized and conducted."

The Pujo Committee recommended that the United States Congress regulate stock exchanges using its powers "unconditionally to prohibit the mails, the interstate telegraph and telephone, the national banks and all other instrumentalities under its control, from being used in executing, negotiating, promoting, increasing or otherwise aiding transactions or such exchanges."

The Committee principally recommended that the objectionable features of operations and stock exchanges would be eliminated if the exchanges were incorporated in the states or territories in which they are located rather than allowed to operate a voluntary organization "with the privileges and freedom of action of a private club."

Margin requirements were proposed to be raised to 20 percent.

Manipulation through wash sales would be prohibited.

In the period before the New Deal, none of the stock exchange recommendations of the Pujo Report were adopted.[51]

Parallel to the NYSE's oversight of listed securities were rudimentary improvements in corporate reporting. In 1923, over 30 percent of the firms listed on the NYSE were not subject to an agreement to provide shareholders with either annual or quarterly financial statements, and only 242 of the 957 listed firms provided both annual and quarterly financial reports. A decade later all 1157 firms listed on the Exchange provided at least annual financial reports, and over 60 percent provided quarterly reports as well. By 1933, at least 85 percent of the firms listed on the NYSE were periodically audited by independent certified public accountants.

The rapidity with which periodic audited financial statements became commonplace masked the continuing unreliability of financial reporting. Through 1933, no government or private agency effectively defined *generally accepted accounting principles.* Instead, individual corporate managements retained broad discretion to choose among alternative accounting principles. On occasion this discretion was employed to create an exaggerated impression of a firm's worth. Federal Trade Commission attorneys testified before Congress in 1933 that public utilities investigated by the FTC had "written up" assets by more than $1 billion by substituting an estimated appraisal or reproduction value for the preferred method of recording the assets' original cost on the firm's balance sheet. At the very least, commonly employed accounting practices did not provide investors with a reliable tool with which to compare the worth and performance of different firms. Through 1933, there were several commonly employed methods of recording inventory value or depreciating the value of perishable assets. Any period's earnings could be swollen by a firm's selling a corporate asset, since the distinction between operating income and other income was not regularly made. In some states, dividends could be paid out of invested capital when a firm was not earning profits. A 1929 survey of 580 leading firms actively traded on the NYSE found that only 323 reported gross income.[52]

Only once had the federal government before the New Deal regulated on a comprehensive basis corporate securities sales. In April 1918, Congress authorized the Wartime Capital Issues Committee "to investigate, pass upon, and determine" whether each securities sale of more than $100,000 was "compatible with the national interest." This was not securities legislation intended to protect investors. This was a wartime measure designed to ration capital to support the government's policy of "war business first." All proposed securities issues that did not have "an immediate military or economic necessity" either were disapproved or subjected to conditions that would prevent their competition with the government's fund-raising activities.

The Committee's authority was voluntary, not compulsory. Its purpose was to direct the flow of capital toward "essential uses" by disapproving securities issuances that interference with the government's wartime use of credit, labor, and materials. Although the Committee functioned for only six months, it reviewed 2289 applications involving new securities with a par value of $2,564,021,000, of which $499,218,000 of securities were disapproved.

In two Reports, the Capital Issues Committee emphasized its limitations. "In the absence of specific power either to compel submission to its jurisdiction or to enforce its findings," the Committee reported, it was "unable to deal effectively with many enterprises whose promoters or managers remained deaf to every appeal to their patriotism. This situation permitted the continuance of a considerable traffic in worthless or fraudulent securities," which the Committee "conservatively" estimated to equal $500 million annually and predicted would rise as investors exchanged Liberty Bonds issued to finance the war for more speculative securities. Accordingly, the Capital Issues Committee was "unanimously of the opinion that Federal supervision of security issues, here undertaken for the first time, should be continued by some public agency, preferably by one of the Government departments, in such a form as to check the traffic in doubtful securities, while imposing no undue restrictions upon the financing of legitimate industry." Indeed, the government was so concerned with the amount of fraudulent stock selling during the war that the Secretary of the Treasury, the Chairman of the Federal Reserve Board, and the Capital Issues Committee asked the Federal Trade Commission to take jurisdiction in the emergency. The FTC briefly did so, on the theory that the bad securities were in unfair "competition with the good."

President Wilson in August 1919 recommended the adoption of a Federal Securities Act "to prevent the fraudulent methods of promotion by which our people are annually fleeced of many millions of hard-earned money." Numerous securities bills were introduced in Congress between 1919 and 1927, the most important of which was first offered by Congressman Edward Dennison in December 1920. The Dennison Bill would have plugged the largest loophole in the enforcement of state Blue Sky laws by making it illegal for any person to use the mails or any of the facilities of interstate commerce to sell securities in any state until there had been compliance with the formalities of that State's Blue Sky law. Although there was doubt as to whether a federal statute whose sole purpose was to aid in the enforcement of state laws was constitutional, Dennison won the grudging support of the Investment Bankers Association by agreeing to exempt a wide range of securities transactions. After being favorably reported out by the House Commerce Committee, the bill was passed nearly unanimously by the House of Representatives. In the Senate, the Dennison Bill was referred to the Judiciary Committee, which never reported out the measure to the full Senate.[53]

The greatest demand for investment banking services in the 19th and early 20th century came from the railroad industry. Between 1873 and 1878, new railroad construction exceeded 5000 miles per year. During the 15-year period, 1878–1893, total railroad mileage nearly tripled. The combined total outstanding issues of railroad bonds and stock more than doubled from $4.8 to $9.9 billion. By 1913, when the Pujo Report was published, railroad capitalization would have doubled again to $19.8 billion.

For much of the period before the Pujo Report, railroad issues "dominated" securities trading. Charles Dow, later creator of the Dow Jones Industrial Average, in 1884 created the Dow Jones Transportation Average, 9 of whose 11 component companies were railroads.

Robber Barons such as Cornelius Vanderbilt, Daniel Drew, and Jay Gould would fight bare knuckle struggles for control of several railroads including the Harlem, the New York Central, and Erie beginning in the 1850s and 1860s. In the 1860s, Union Pacific construction by Crédit Mobilier, according to business historian Jerry Markham, "would be forever associated with financial fraud and intrigue."

Efforts led by populist and agrarian politicians to end railroad price discrimination in 1887 would result in the creation of the Interstate Commerce Commission (*ICC*).

Using 1903 data, John Moody would describe six groups of financiers who controlled 81 percent of steam railroad mileage through holding companies: The Morgan, Vanderbilt, Pennsylvania, Gould-Rockefeller, Harrison-Kuhn-Loeb, and Moore groups. Of Moody's $20,379,162,511 attributed to 440 large industrial, franchise and transportation trusts, these six groups then controlled $9,017,016,907 or 44 percent of all the trusts' capitalization. Largely through mergers, the six groups had increased their mileage between 1897 and 1903 by 102,753 miles, from 61,833 to 164,586 miles.

The ICC was the first United States independent regulatory agency and continued until abolition in 1995. Brandeis' *Other People's Money* would be less restrained than Moody and excoriated "a curse of bigness," criticizing Big Railroad Systems and the Money Trust for securities issuances and mergers involving Union Pacific, which acquired Southern Pacific in 1901. The Great Northern Railroad acquired the Chicago, Burlington & Quincy railroad. The New Haven Railroad acquired 121 companies. In 1913, the Pujo Report recommended that interstate railroad security issues should be placed under the supervision of the ICC.

In 1920, Congress did so and passed the Transportation Act. Its purposes were described by Supreme Court decisions as "the establishment of a new federal railway policy to insure adequate transportation service by means of securing a fair return on capital devoted to the service, restoration of impaired railroad credit, and regulation of rates, security issues, consolidations and mergers in the interest of the public." The new Act adopted a long-standing recommendation of the ICC, going back to 1907, by adding § 20a to the former Interstate Commerce Act. This was the first federal securities legislation. The new provision made it unlawful for any common carrier by railroad to issue its own securities or to assume obligations (as lessor, lessee, guarantor, or otherwise) with respect to the securities of any other person or corporation, without the authorization of the ICC based on an investigation of the purposes and uses of the proposed issue or assumption.

The investor protection aspects of this requirement were indirect. It was neither a Blue Sky law, in the sense that the ICC's primary interest was in giving investors a *fair shake* for their money, nor a disclosure statute. The provision took its coloration from the former Interstate Commerce Act and its purpose of preventing a recurrence of the notorious financial scandals with their destruction of confidence in railroad investment. The statutory standards were phrased in terms of the contribution that the particular plan of financing would make to a healthy railroad system for the nation. Initially, the ICC had to find that the particular issue or assumption of obligations by the application "(a) is for some lawful object within its corporate purposes, and compatible with the public interest, which is necessary or appropriate for or consistent with the proper performance by the carrier of service to the public as a common carrier, and which will not impair its ability to perform that service, and (b) is reasonably necessary and appropriate for such purpose."[54]

However salutary ICC regulation of railroad finance may have been, until the New Deal, this left a majority of the United States economy without federal oversight.

Between 1898 and 1902, 2600 firms merged with a total capitalization of $6 billion, including American Telephone and Telegraph, United States Steel, and International Harvester. In the next few years, Ford Motor Corporation, American Tobacco, and General Motors would be formed.

Growth spurred the financial needs of General Electric, United Cigar Manufacturing, Sears Roebuck, and B.F. Goodrich and led to a dramatic increase in investment banking. By 1914, securities trading involved 250 institutions, led by private banks including J.P. Morgan and Kuhn Loeb, joined by new securities firms such as Goldman Sachs, Lehman Brothers, Kidder Peabody, and Lee Higginson.

As early as 1876, the United States Supreme Court had interpreted the phrase in the National Banking Act authorizing a national bank to exercise "all . . . incidental powers as shall be necessary to carry on the business of banking" as not permitting a national bank generally to engage in the securities business. The Court held in *First National Bank of Charlotte v. Exchange National Bank of Baltimore* that: "Dealing in stocks is not expressly prohibited; but such prohibition is implied from the failure to grant the power." In that case, a national bank was permitted to accept stock in compromise of a debt when it was "honestly believed" that a loss would otherwise accrue from the transaction. In 1879, the Supreme Court in *National Bank v. Case* held that a bank could accept stock as collateral. But in that decision and in 1892 in *California Bank v. Kennedy*, the Court affirmed that a national bank could not acquire the stock of another corporation.

In 1902, the Comptroller of the Currency ruled that a national bank could not act as an investment bank and underwrite securities.

Commercial banks responded by forming unregulated securities affiliates including the First National Bank of Chicago, which established the First Trust and Savings Bank in 1903, First National Bank which formed the First Securities Corporation in 1908, and National City Bank which in 1911 formed the National City Company, which would underwrite 20 percent of all bond offerings in the United States during the 1920s. "Doubt about the legality of security affiliates failed to stop their use," explained business historian Vincent Carosso:

> In 1911, when the National City Bank organized its affiliate, the National City Co. to transact "business which though often very profitable may not be within the express corporate authority of a National Bank," both Solicitor General Frederick W. Lehman and Attorney General George W. Wickersham informed President Taft that security affiliates were illegal and dangerous. "Examples are recent and significant," Lehman wrote Wickersham, "of the peril to a bank, incident to the dual and diverse interests of its officers and directors." But since Treasury Secretary Franklin MacVeagh and Secretary of State Philander C. Knox thought otherwise, Taft chose not to challenge the National Banks.

Had the federal government done so, it is uncertain it would have made a difference. State chartered commercial banks and private banks under the law then would have been unaffected by such a ruling.[55]

* * * * * * *

Insurance Regulation

The third pillar of finance in the period before the New Deal was the insurance industry. The industry was demonstrably smaller at the time of the Pujo Investigation and at the time of the 1929–1933 Stock Market Crash than commercial banking. In 1913, the nation's 27,285 national and state banks possessed $26.1 billion in assets. By 1929, total bank assets had approximately tripled to $72.3 billion. In contrast, in 1913, the nation's 302 life insurance companies possessed assets of $935 million. The life insurance industry would expand to 438 companies by 1929, but with assets of $4.3 billion, the life insurance held 6 percent of commercial bank assets.

The development of the United States insurance industry had proceeded slowly. Initially in the colonial and first decades of the United States, the industry was dominated by marine and fire insurance. Between 1721 and 1796, there were 21 offices in Philadelphia for underwriting marine insurance. Benjamin Franklin organized a fire insurance enterprise in 1730. The Philadelphia-based Contributorship for Insuring Houses from Loss by Fire was chartered in 1748. Aetna Fire Insurance Company of New York held a shareholder's meeting in 1835. The Mutual Insurance Company was formed earlier and, as with Aetna, initially was a fire insurer. Only later would Aetna and Mutual become life insurers.

After the 1840s, life insurance played a pivotal role in the industry's growth. Twenty-three life insurance companies would be founded between 1812 and 1842. In 1843, Mutual Life Insurance Company of New York, a firm owned by its policyholders, rather than shareholders, was formed in New York City. In 1860, there would be $205 million of life insurance in force. The growth of an urban population and a less self-sufficient nonagrarian population dramatically expanded life insurance sales. By 1900, $7.6 billion in life insurance was in force.

Economist Douglass North described the post-Civil War growth in life insurance:

> With an increase of over five hundred per cent in insurance in force between 1865 and 1905, the total income of all reporting life insurance companies had grown from $25 million to $642 million annually and the excess of total income over total expenditures had grown from $14 million to $230 million annually. During the two decades preceding the Armstrong Investigation [1885–1905], the assets of life insurance companies increased by more than $2 billion. Five companies were responsible for two-thirds of this growth. The Metropolitan and the Prudential, pioneering in the new industrial insurance, were soon to overtake the leaders in the field. However, in 1905 it was the big three, the Mutual, the Equitable, and the New York Life, that dominated the life insurance world.

Total assets of these five insurers increased from $228 million in 1885 to $1.46 billion in 1905, an increase of 640 percent.

There were close links between the big three life insurance firms and investment banks. In 1905, 74 percent of New York Life assets, 57 percent of the Equitable assets, and 54 percent of the Mutual assets were in securities. North wrote: "Life insurance companies suited perfectly the need of the investment banker. They possessed large amounts of liquid funds, not subject to call for long periods of time. Moreover, they were expanding at such a rate that there was a continuous flow of such funds for Morgan in steel or Harriman and Schiff in railroad consolidation."

Much of the growth of Equitable, New York Life, and Mutual would be through the sale of tontine insurance, which was estimated to be responsible in 1905 for 80.3 percent of Equitable insurance in force, 87.9 percent of New York Life's insurance in force, and 82.6 percent of Mutual's life insurance in force as well as 64 percent of all insurance in force in the industry.

Tontine insurance was first sold by Equitable in 1868. The subsequent "phenomenal expansion" of life insurance sales in the United States in the period before the Armstrong Investigation, discussed below, was driven by the popularity of the tontine insurance, inspired by the aggressive marketing techniques of Equitable and other insurance firms.

Tontine insurance had two distinct purposes. First, the insurance policy provided the same type of insurance as standard life insurance or "level premium insurance." But tontine also invested additional premium dollars in an investment fund: "This fund grew both from the continuing receipt of payments and from the earnings received on investments. After a stipulated period had elapsed (usually twenty years), the entire amount accumulated in the tontine fund was divided among the surviving policyholders."

The cost of tontine insurance exceeded the cost of standard insurance, but for most purchasers of the tontine policies, this seemed justified by the accumulated savings of tontine insurance for the survivors.

Effusively, a 2013 Report prepared for the National Association of Insurance Commissioners and the Center for Insurance Policy and Research would claim:

> Tontines revolutionized the industry. Their popularity with the emerging middle-class, which was seeking investment options, helped to propel demand. Through tontine deposits, insurers began to amass large amounts of money not backed by reserves, which they used to purchase controlling shares in banks and other corporations. Insurers' close ties to banks also allowed them to participate in investment syndicates to buy bonds at cheaper prices.

The disparate requirements of state insurance regulation became a matter of contention for the insurance industry. In the early 19th century, some states relied on reporting on the financial status of insurance corporations. Other states imposed substantive requirements. Massachusetts, beginning in 1817, for example, prohibited fire insurers from engaging in other types of insurance and limited their insurable risks to one-tenth of their capital. New York in 1851 required a $100,000 deposit for corporations seeking to underwrite insurance in New York State. Insurance boards were formed beginning with New Hampshire in 1851. In 1859, New York established the New York Insurance Department led by a Superintendent of Insurance.

After the National Banking Act of 1864 was enacted, some insurance companies sought to persuade Congress to enact a National Insurance Act to simplify regulation. The National Board of Fire Underwriters in 1868 urged the adoption of a National Insurance Law.

The insurance corporations' efforts to persuade Congress to adopt a National Insurance Law were unsuccessful in part because of the United States Supreme Court in 1869 in *Paul v. Virginia* in which the Court held issuing fire insurance across state lines could not be considered a transaction subject to the Interstate Commerce Clause of the Constitution: "Issuing a policy of insurance is not a transaction of commerce. The policies are simple contracts of indemnity against loss by fire, entered into between the corporations and the assured, for a consideration paid by the latter."

This meant that Congress had no constitutional authority to regulate interstate insurance companies.

Subsequent Supreme Court decisions affirmed the power of the states to comprehensively regulate insurance carriers, including premium rates, forbid price discrimination, publicize basic schedules and conditions that affect rates, require reserves, limit dividends, protect investment, and generally limit risks.

In 1905, a bitter control fight at the Equitable Life Assurance Company, then second in size among life insurers, boiled over to a public scandal that prompted disclosure of broad mismanagement in New York insurance companies generally. The Armstrong Committee named after its chair, New York State Senator William Armstrong, would vault Committee Counsel Charles Evans Hughes, to National prominence.

Morton Keller, author of *The Life Insurance Enterprise, 1805–1910,* would generalize:

> The legislative investigation is the morality play of American Society. Like any well-wrought drama, the successful investigation produces a great catharsis — of the presumed social ill, of an aroused public indignation. The Armstrong life insurance investigation of 1905 was one of the most spectacular of its genre. Never before had a legislative committee subjected a group of major corporations to such thorough and searching scrutiny. Never before had so vigorous and disinterested an investigator as Charles Evans Hughes worked with such freedom and to such effect. Never before, and scarcely since, has an inquiry produced such substantial corrective legislation.

Fifty-seven sessions of Public Hearings were held between September and December 1905, focusing on the 15 leading New York State insurers selling standard or level premium insurance. The 440-page Armstrong Committee 1908 Report harshly criticized several insurance companies, including Mutual Life Insurance Company, for lobbying payments which included "to control legislation in this and other states which could affect their investors" and political contributions largely made to the Republican Party ($15,000 in 1896, $35,000 in 1900, $40,000 in 1904) denominated "legal expense." The Report stated: "The accounts and vouchers both of 'Legal Expense' and of the 'Supply Department' are not in satisfactory condition. It may be questioned whether in many cases the persons signing the vouchers have actually received the moneys receipted for."

The Armstrong Commission explained:

> The business of the *Mutual* has enormously expanded within recent years. In twenty years its outstanding insurance has increased from $368,952,337 to $1,547,611,660, and its annual premium income from $14,768,902 to $62,932,097, and during the same period its surplus has risen from $6,943,764 to $74,357,818 (including surplus to be apportioned in 1905). But this notable expansion has not been of advantage to its policy holders. It has served as an excuse for the increase of expenses and for lavish payments to officers and agents. . . .
>
> . . . In 1885, when the premium income was $14,768,902 and the total income $20,214,954, the dividends to policy holders

> were \$3,183,023 and the total payments to policy holders \$14,403,050, the expenses being only \$3,134,452. In 1904, when the premium income was \$62,932,097 and the total income \$81,002,984, the dividend to policy holders were \$2,674,207, the total payments to policy holders were \$34,484,275, and the expenses \$16,898,456.

The Armstrong Committee similarly examined New York Life Insurance Company: "The scheme of supervision through committees of the Board of Trustees has left in practice a wide field for the arbitrary exercise of executive power. The executive officers have been permitted to disburse enormous sums of money without proper accounting."

As with the Mutual, New York Life contributed lavishly to the Republican Party (\$48,702.50 in 1904, an inference that a similar amount was contributed in 1896 and 1900).

New York Life Vice President and Finance Committee Chair George Perkins, previously a member of JP Morgan, had directed New York Life to invest \$3 million in 1901 in the Morgan organized United States Steel Syndicate and \$1.8 million in U.S. Steel Bonds in 1902, as well as \$4 million in International Mercantile Marine, of which Morgan was Syndicate Manager.

The Armstrong Committee leveled its most damning criticism at the Equitable. Since its organization in 1859, the Equitable had grown by 1904 to an industry leader with 564,594 policies representing \$1,495,542,942 of insurance.

Henry Hyde long ran the Equitable as an autocracy. While the Equitable was a corporation with stockholders given voting rights, these were nullified in the Equitable by Hyde's ownership of a majority of the stock which he held until his death in 1899.

In 1895, Hyde placed his shares in a trust, providing for himself beneficial ownership, that is voting rights, while he lived. In the event of his death, his son James Hazen Hyde became beneficiary of the Trust until he attained the age of 30 when he would own the majority stock interest directly.

James Hyde was 23 years old when his father died. When he reached 25, James Alexander, Louis Fitzgerald, and James became Trustees.

In 1905, Alexander, the President of the Equitable, led a revolt. Alexander, with 25 Equitable officers and agents, petitioned the

Board to replace the Trust's control with a system of policyholder voting:

> The petitioners stated that from "their practical experience in the conduct of the society's business" they "have become convinced that its continued welfare and progress and the due administration of the trust funds in its charge render a change necessary, and that it is incompatible with present public opinion, as well as with the interests of the society and its beneficiaries, that the policy holders as the real parties in interest should continue to be without any voice in the administration of these funds, but that the entire power of selecting directors should be vested in and exercised solely by the holder for the time being of a majority of the society's nominal capital stock."

In March 1905, the Board substantially agreed and recommended that Equitable's charter be amended to provide that 28 of its 52 directors be elected by the policyholders. The charter amendment required the approval of the New York Superintendent of Insurance. A stockholder suit was brought which at the time of the preparation of the Armstrong Report enjoined Equitable's directors from amending its charter as proposed. An appeal to New York State's highest court then was pending.

Simultaneous with the initial proposal to mutualize the Equitable and give policyholders the right to elect directors, Equitable's Board appointed a committee led by H.C. Frick to investigate Equitable's management. The Frick Committee's conclusions were brutal:

> The committee found that owing to the practice of nominal transfers to qualify directors the title of a great majority of the Board was open to doubt; that the relations of the Board to the exercise of the society's powers had been practically nominal, these powers having been delegated to officers and committees which had been guilty of serious irregularities; that the society's methods of doing business were unsystematic, and that there was a "general looseness in the administration of its affairs requiring prompt and thorough rectification." There were "excessive salaries, excessive commissions, excessive expenses, superfluous offices," and "a general lacking in the organization of that strong moral fibre so essential for the accomplishment of satisfactory results."

Supposedly to restore confidence in the Equitable, the controlling interest in the Trust was sold to Thomas F. Ryan for $2.5 million in cash. This transaction was question-begging. Two offers, Frick at $5 million and George Young of the United States Mortgage & Trust at $7 million exceeded Ryan's $2.5 million successful bid. E.H. Harriman, formerly active on the Equitable board and a member of the Frick Committee, resigned the day the Frick Committee Report was produced and strongly objected to the sale to Ryan.

Sharper questions were raised about the failure of the Trustees to put in operation the plan of mutualization. Ryan later testified that he would do all in his power to aid the policyholders in acquiring the right to elect a majority of the board if the ongoing litigation established that the New York legislature was competent to confer it.

Against this backdrop, the New York Superintendent of Insurance began an investigation of Equitable in May 1905 and issued Reports in June and October, 1905 calling "attention to grave abuses of management and additional irregularities of the former administration."

In July 1905, the New York Joint Committee of the Senate and Assembly adopted a concurrent Resolution directing the Armstrong Committee "to investigate and examine into the business and affairs of life insurance companies doing business in the State of New York."

The Armstrong Committee found that the directors of Equitable had not performed the functions with which they were charged, but "[f]or the most part they have been figure-heads invited by those in control of the stock to listen to such annual reports as might be submitted by the officers."

Senior executive "salaries were unwarrantably increased." Henry Hyde received $75,000 from 1886 to 1894, and subsequently until his death in 1899, $100,000 per year. James Alexander began as president at $75,000 in 1903. James Hyde, who graduated from college in 1898, also received $100,000 per year in 1903. "[T]he salary of this young man, only twenty-six and comparatively inexperienced, was plainly a recognition of his stock control."

"Disbursements for so-called legal expenses have been unwarrantably large and would seem to be no doubt that many improper expenditures have been charged to this account. Irregular practices have been facilitated and the absence of proper vouchers detailing with suitable particularity in the legal services reserves.... In some cases vouchers have referred to fictitious legal proceedings. There has been no check upon the discretion of the executive officers." Those disbursements included large amounts expended in connection with legislative matters. In 1904, the Equitable contributed $50,000 to the Republican National Committee and an annual $10,000 contribution to the Republican State Committee.

Equitable maintained irregular accounts at the Mercantile Trust Company, 65 percent of whose stock the Equitable owned, and Equitable Trust Company, in which Equitable held 45 percent of the stock. In both Trusts, moneys from syndicate participations were deposited. In 1905, $1,874,996.60 was debited in the Trusts. No record was kept on Equitable's books of these loans.

Financial statements filed with the Insurance Department included false statements, in 1904, Equitable reported $412,438,380.84 in assets, a surplus of $80,394,861.31, but a deduction of only $1,514,639.90 for agents' balances, which the Insurance Department did not characterize as assets. To evade this Insurance Department policy, Equitable for many years made assignments to trust companies of large portions of its advances to agents and received cash credits from the trust companies which were counted as assets. In 1904, the assignments to the Equitable Trust Company and the Commercial Trust Company of Philadelphia aggregated $5,813,184.87, roughly four times the reported agent balances. When Equitable's accounts were reappraised in 1905, including adjustments for agents' balances, and revaluation of real estate holdings and collateral loans in excess of those actually made, its surplus was found to be $67,142,865.42, meaning the surplus was overstated by about 20 percent.

In 1904, a transfer of $10,250,000 was made to Kuhn Loeb, which returned this and earlier sums to the Equitable. Equitable listed the $10,250,000 as a loan to Kuhn Loeb for which no collateral and no note was given.

Irregular accounts in the Trusts also were used to further the self-interest of the Equitable control group. In 1902, when stock was increased in the Equitable Trust from $500,000 to $1,000,000, the Equitable declined to take the majority of shares offered (1670 or 2335 offered shares), all of the shares not purchased by Equitable were purchased by James Hyde, Hyde relatives, or other members of the Equitable executive committee.

Similar transactions occurred at the Lawyers' Title Company and the Lawyers' Mortgage Company. In March 1901, Equitable purchased

2000 shares of Lawyers' Title Company. Eleven hundred of these shares were distributed at cost to James Hyde, his mother, and several associates. In May 1901, a similar transaction occurred at Lawyers' Mortgage Company for 1500 shares, of which 850 went to James Hyde and associates. "The shares of both these companies greatly increased in value within a short period to the benefit of the officers of the society who had received those allotments."

James Hyde and other Equitable officers claimed $950,000 of the $1.5 million allotment that J.P. Morgan made to the Equitable for the Chicago, Burlington & Quincy, which was "expressed to be, and was in fact, a profitable venture."[56]

The Armstrong Committee was sharply critical of the earlier supervision of Equitable by the Insurance Department of New York:

> The *Equitable Life Assurance Society* was examined in 1902. Like the others it was conducted through the New York office and purported to be a complete examination. But its perfunctory character is sufficiently shown by the fact that the report of the examiner fails to give the slightest intimation of the existence of any of the abuses which, recently disclosed, have outraged public sentiment. There is no hint of extravagant expenditures, of irregular accounts, or of the manipulation of corporate investments for the profit of the officers. The palpable evasion of the law governing the annual statement in the making of the pretended "end of the year" loans, although known to the examiner, was left unchallenged.

The Armstrong Committee ridiculed the purported justification for Ryan buying $50,200 of the Equitable stock with dividends limited to 7 percent per year or $3514 for $2.5 million "despite an unequivocal statement of [Ryan's] absence of selfish intention."

The Committee championed policyholder voting and recommended a comprehensive plan for policyholder governance, specifically proposing a new law that should provide:

> (1) For accessible lists of policy holders.
> (2) For the nomination of candidates representing the administration.
> (3) For independent nominations whenever desired.
> (4) For the circulation by the company of ballots containing names of all candidates.
> (5) For the cancellation of existing proxies.

> (6) For voting either in person, by mail or by proxy, but for the limitation of the life of proxies to two months preceding a given election....

The Committee quoted at length the Appellate Court decision in *Lord v. Equitable Life Assurance*, urging the constitutionality of policyholder voting as well as the unfairness of solely entrenching life insurance company stockholders:

> ... [A]s a practical proposition, although the policy holders technically occupy the relation of creditors to the corporation they are the capitalists; they are the ones who furnish the money upon which the business is conducted.... The original stock subscription of $100,000, under the provisions of the law as it stood at the time of the organization of the defendant company, was invested in securities and deposited with the Comptroller, and this capital has never been employed in the business, except as it has stood as a guarantee fund for the payment of policies. All the rest of the capital, with a surplus of $80,000,000, has been contributed by the policy holders in a company which pledged itself in its charter to conduct its business on the mutual plan and to distribute at intervals an equitable proportion of the surplus after providing for all the liabilities of the company.

The Armstrong Committee recommended that policyholders should be given the opportunity to vote to convert life insurance stock corporations into purely mutual companies.

The Committee proposed several limits upon life insurance investments. The Committee castigated "flagrant abuses in connection with investments in real estate": "Under the guise of procuring suitable accommodations for the transaction of business excessive amounts have been expended in the acquisition of land and buildings not necessary in any proper sense for the uses of the corporation, which yield a poor return upon the amount expended."

The Armstrong Committee unequivocally recommended: "Investment in stocks should be prohibited." Life insurance companies "were not incorporated to make money by speculation, by barter, by purchase for resale or by the development of industry. They were chartered to furnish life insurance, and the true measure of their power and their duty in the handling of their funds is to invest them with due conservatism, to the end that they may be able to discharge their obligations."

Existing New York law had "tempted life insurance companies to engage indirectly in enterprises foreign to the purpose of their organization. Through the control of subsidiary corporations, by means of stock ownership, some have practically transacted the business of banks and trust companies." Life insurance companies had participated in the securities industry through syndicates that underwrote or marketed corporate securities.

The Armstrong Committee specifically recommended:

> (1) That no investment in the stock of any corporation shall be permitted, except in public stocks of municipal corporations.
>
> (2) That investments in bonds secured to the extent of more than one-third the value of the entire security therefor by the hypothecation of corporate stocks shall be prohibited.
>
> (3) That no loans shall be made upon stocks and bonds which are not the subject of purchase under the above provisions.
>
> (4) That every company now owning stocks or bonds of the prohibited classes shall be required to dispose of the same within five years from December 31, 1906, and each year prior thereto shall make a reduction of the amount of such investments to an extent approved by the Superintendent of Insurance.
>
> (5) The statute should also forbid all syndicate participations, transactions for purchase and sale on joint account, and the making of any agreement providing that the company shall withhold from sale, for any time, or subject to the discretion of others, any securities which it may own or acquire.
>
> (6) It should also be provided that no officer or director should be pecuniarily interested either as principal, co-principal, agent or beneficiary in any purchase, sale or loan made by the corporation, except in case of a loan upon his policy.

The Armstrong Committee anticipated Brandeis's assault upon the curse of bigness with proposals to limit new business:

> The business of the *Mutual*, the *Equitable* and the *New York Life* has grown beyond reasonable limits. Notwithstanding the fact that they have long since passed the point where further enlargement can benefit their policy holders, they have resorted to every effort to obtain new business, regardless of the expense which is reflected in diminishing dividends. Fearful of losing prestige, the chief concern of each has been to keep up with the others. Extravagant commissions have been paid and these

> have been supplemented by liberal bonuses and prizes. Clubs have been formed, conventions held, and money lavishly expended for the entertainment of agents to excite them to their utmost endeavor.

While the prohibition of issuance of new policies whenever the assets of a life insurance company reached a prescribed volume was "impracticable," the Armstrong Committee proposed limiting the amount of new business that each life insurance company could undertake each year as a means "to maintain a requisite vitality and a suitable agency organization, while precluding a further and unnecessary increase of business."

The "Big Three" then in life insurance, Equitable, New York Life, and Mutual, were proposed to be limited to $150,000,000 per year. Smaller companies would be limited based on a sliding percentage of total insurance in force at the end of each calendar year:

> Total insurance less than $50,000,000, no limit.
>
> Total insurance between $50,000,000 and $100,000,000, 30 percent, thereof.
>
> Total insurance between $100,000,000 and $300,000,000, 25 percent, thereof.
>
> Total insurance between $300,000,000 and $600,000,000, 20 percent, thereof.
>
> Total insurance between $600,000,000 and $1,000,000,000, 15 percent, thereof.
>
> If the total insurance in force shall be in excess of $1,000,000,000, the new business shall not exceed $150,000,000 annually.

Contributions by insurance corporations for political purposes "should be strictly forbidden."

The Armstrong Committee was especially critical of lobbying expenses:

> Nothing disclosed by the investigation deserves more serious attention than the systematic efforts of the large insurance companies to control a large part of the legislation of the state. They have been organized into an offensive and defensive alliance to procure or to prevent the passage of laws affecting not only insurance, but a great variety of important interests to which, through subsidiary companies or through the connections of their officers, they have become related.... Enormous sums

> have been expended in a surreptitious manner. Irregular accounts have been kept to conceal the payments for which proper vouchers have not been required. This court of conduct has created a widespread conviction that large portions of this money have been dishonestly used.

The Armstrong Committee recommended restricting, but not eliminating, lobbying expenses:

> The laws against bribery and corruption, offences which are difficult of proof, are sufficiently stringent, but an effort should be made to strike at the root of the evil by requiring under proper penalties full publicity with regard to moneys expended in connection with matters before the Legislature. Corporations should be required to keep accounts and vouchers in which all such payments should be fully detailed and receipted for, and an adequate statement regarding them should form a part of such reports as may be required.
>
> In the case of insurance corporations the remedy lies first, generally, in the requirement of a proper authorization of all expenditures and vouchers, stating in detail the purposes for which moneys paid for legal expenses or in connection with legislative matters have been expended. And, further, the company should be compelled to set forth in its annual statement to the Superintendent of Insurance all sums so disbursed, giving the names of the payees, the amounts paid and the specific purpose of the payment.

The Committee recommended that all insurance company counsel or agents register with the Secretary of State in a docket of legislative appearances that would be publicly available.

Fees contingent upon legislative action would be prohibited.

The Armstrong Committee devoted 16 pages to regulation of life insurance company expenditures. The Committee believed "that the most wasteful expense lies in the amount paid for new business." By limiting the new business of the Big Three life insurers, the Commission believed that agent expenses would "very largely . . . diminish." The Committee did not propose setting commission rates by law, but did recommend prohibiting loans and advances to agents.

Aggregate expenses for New York life insurance companies were proposed to be limited to the "total loadings" of insurance premiums: "[T]he expense of new business should not exceed the loading on first year's premiums plus the present value of the mortality savings on a conservative basis for five years after admission. These two items arise directly from the new business. Were there no new business, neither the loading on new premiums nor these mortality gains would be realized." Under this method, the Armstrong Committed predicted new business "in effect pays for itself and the general gains of the company are available for distribution as dividends."

The Commission pointedly sought to limit life insurance surplus and reserves: "It is manifest that all gains or surplus in excess of such contingent fund should, in equity, be returned to the holders of participating policies at such appropriate times as may be practicable for their ascertainment."

The Committee recommended the prohibition of tontine insurance policies. Nearly all life insurance companies operated under charters providing for the ascertainment of surpluses and periodic distributions. Tontine insurance created an exception to withhold distribution of gains under deferred dividend plans.

The Armstrong Committee sharply criticized "the wasteful methods of the companies" selling tontine insurance, "which have been made possible by the vast accumulations permitted by this form of insurance:"

> It is the opinion of the Committee that dividends should be distributed annually, being applied either in reduction of premiums or to the purchase of additional insurance, or paid in cash, at the option of the insured. No attempt should be made to disturb rights under existing contracts, but the issue of so-called deferred dividend policies in the future should be forbidden.

The Committee recommended that the results of life insurance management should be compelled by publication of annual accounting. Each year, a statement was proposed to be filed with the New York Superintendent of Insurance disclosing 17 categories of information, including all property owned by the company, commissions paid to any person, legal expenses, compensation to any director or officer greater than $5000 per year, a complete statement of profits and losses upon the business transacted during the year, and a statement of any and all reserve or surplus funds held by the company.

Contingency reserves of life insurance companies would be limited to 2 percent for the largest insurers with net value of $500,000,000 or more, with levels from 2½ percent to 20 percent scaled for firms with net value of $500,000,000 down to firms with net value of not more than $100,000.

Policyholders, without first seeking approval from the State Attorney General, "should have free access to the courts to have their rates determined."

The Armstrong Committee notably proposed limiting the forms of life insurance policies to four basic types:

(1) Ordinary life, providing for a continuous payment of premiums until death, when the policy matures;

(2) Limited payment life, providing that premiums shall be fully paid in a certain number of years, *e.g.*, in ten, fifteen or twenty, and that the policy shall mature at death;

(3) Endowment, providing for the payment of the policy at a fixed time or in the event of earlier death; and

(4) Term policies, or those providing for insurance against death during a specified period.

New types of life insurance could be sold in New York only after approval by the Superintendent of Insurance.

Within three months, the New York Legislature enacted many of the recommendations of the Armstrong Committee.

Policyholder voting both in life insurance corporations and mutual companies was established. Life insurance companies were authorized by a majority vote of their directors to confer upon policyholders the right to vote "for all or any less number of directors in such manner . . . as may be authorized by a vote of the stockholders representing at least a majority of the capital stock." Life insurance corporations similarly could reorganize and be reincorporated as mutual companies.

Mutual insurance companies were required to provide for director elections using the governance standards specified by the Armstrong Committee, including accessible lists of policyholders, management and independent nominations of directors when 100 or more qualified policyholders made independent nominations for directors, circulation by mail of the nominees for directors, the right of policyholders to revoke earlier proxy votes, and the right to vote by proxy or in person.

Life insurance companies were restricted in their right to acquire real estate to a specified list of transactions including mortgages "in good faith by way of securing for loans previously contracted or for moneys due." The Superintendent of Insurance was required to approve the acquisition or disposal of specified real estate transactions.

Stock investments were prohibited, other than stock in a municipal corporation after June 1, 1906. Life insurance corporations similarly were prohibited from subscribing to or participating in the underwriting of the purchase or sale of securities or property.

New business was limited with adoption of a schedule of restrictions as prescribed by the Armstrong Committee. For life insurers with $1 billion or more insurance in force, no more than $150 million of new insurance was permitted each year.

In a separate Act, the New York Legislature prohibited all corporations or joint stock companies doing business in the state from making direct or indirect contributions to any political party or candidate for office.

A different separate act required all lobbyists, defined as persons retained or employed for compensation acting on behalf of any person, firm, corporation, or association when engaged in promoting or opposing the passage of any bill, resolution, or executive approval of a bill or resolution, to file with the Secretary of State her or his name and a brief description of the legislation to which such service was to be rendered. The Secretary of State then was required to publish for public inspection a Docket of Legislative Appearances.

Life insurance expenditures were regulated. No New York life insurance corporation could expend $100 or more without a voucher signed by or on behalf of the person, firm or corporation receiving the money, "correctly describing the consideration for the payment" and if the payment was for services, "an itemized statement of disbursements made."

Commissions and advances to life insurance agents were limited in accordance with the Armstrong Committee. Loans and advances to agents or any other person soliciting applications for insurance were prohibited "except advances against compensation for the first year of insurance." The Armstrong Committee formula for limiting the expense of new business to the "total loadings" and insurance premiums was adopted as the limit on advances to agents.

Life insurance company salaries, compensation, or emoluments in excess of $5000 per year were required to be approved by the Board of Directors. Pensions to the family of any officer, director or trustee were prohibited. Life insurance directors and officers also were prohibited from receiving "any money or valuable thing for negotiating, procuring, recommending or aiding in, any purchase by or sale to such corporation, or any loan from such corporation" with an exception for loans upon life insurance policies.

Tontine insurance was ended for all policies after January 1, 1907, by the requirement that every life insurance company annually distribute surplus. Surplus was to be calculated each December 31st.

Each life insurer was allowed to maintain a contingency reserve in addition to the net value of its policies. As in the Armstrong Committee report, the highest permissible level of contingency reserve was 20 percent for firms with net values of $100,000. The permissible percentages of contingency reserve then decreased as the size of an insurer's net value increased.

Consistent with the Armstrong Committee's recommendations, each life insurer was required to file an annual report with the Superintendent of Insurance. The Act specified 16 required statements, most of which were identical to the Armstrong Committee recommendations.

The New York Legislature most conspicuously went further than the Armstrong Committee Report with respect to specifications of permissible types of life insurance. As with the Armstrong Committee Report, there were four standard forms of policies: (1) an ordinary life policy; (2) a limited payment life policy; (3) an endowment policy; and (4) a term policy. Unlike the Committee Report, the Legislature then specified required language for each type of policy. As with the Armstrong Committee Report, the Superintendent of Insurance could authorize other kinds of policies after a public hearing with notice given to every life insurer.

The Armstrong Investigation and New York 1906 Insurance Legislation had a profound impact in increasing confidence in the insurance industry in the period before the New Deal. Life insurance sales declined between 1905 and 1907 from $2.283 billion to $1.782 billion, before experiencing a period of ten-fold growth by 1929, with annual sales reaching $17.755 billion. This growth in part was the consequence of new insurance products introduced after the Armstrong Committee Report, including group insurance and annuities. Limits on life insurers owning stock and underwriting securities would lead the Equitable and other insurance companies to sell trust companies and reduce aggregate life insurance assets in stock from 6 percent to 1 percent between 1906 and 1922. Those limits would provide an enormous advantage to the life insurance industry when the stock market crashed in 1929–1933. Only 20 out of 350 insurers or 5.7 percent went into receivership during the Great Depression.

New York insurance regulation would become a model for the insurance industry. The Massachusetts Insurance Commissioner aptly explained: "In a certain sense, [New York's] supervision will become a national supervision, as its companies do business in all states." Within a short period, new insurance departments were recommended or created in Colorado, Indiana, Washington, Georgia, and South Carolina. History professor Morton Keller generalized:

> Considerable legislation expanded the powers, duties, salaries, and staffs of the state insurance officers. Deposit and report requirements and agent or company responsibility for legal service and process grew apace, as did laws forbidding the removal of litigation to federal courts....
>
> Most spectacularly, legislatures turned their attention to corporate political activity, company control, and marketing matters. Everywhere, campaign contributions were forbidden and lobbying was regulated. Considerable legislation dwelt on the problems of corporate democracy in such matters as the selection of directors and proxy voting....
>
> Agents and policies came under new and more stringent control. There was an increase in the number of laws subjecting agents to licensing, certifying, and residence requirements; making the solicitor the agent not of the insured but of the company; and forbidding rebating and rate discrimination. Before 1905, occasional legislation specifically allowed corporations to be licensed as insurance agents or brokers; after that date, laws just as specifically forbad companies from so doing.

After the enactment of the 1906 Armstrong Report inspired New York insurance legislation, there was no serious federal effort to regulate life insurance.[57]

ENDNOTES:

1. Alexander Hamilton, James Madison & John Jay, The Federalist No. 15 at 79, No. 12 at 66–67, 69–70, No. 30 at 159–160 (Barnes & Noble Classics 2006); Bray Hammond, Banks and Politics in America: From the Revolution to the Civil War 3–39, 48–71 (Princeton Univ. Press 1957); Treasury Department, Second Report on the Further Provision Necessary for Establishing Public Credit (Report on a National Bank) (13 Dec. 1790); Ron Chernow, Hamilton 157, 199–201, 220–221, 346–347 (Penguin Press 2004); 1 Jerry Markham, A Financial History of the United States 68–72, 75, 83–88 (Routledge 2015); Jerry Markham, Banking Regulation: Its History and Future, 4 N.C. Banking Inst. 221 (2000); William Gouge, A Short History of Paper Money and Banking in the United States 25–27, 32 (Banking) (T.W. Ustick 1833, reprinted from the Collection of the University of Michigan Library); Ben Bernanke, The Courage to Act (W.W. Norton & Co. 2015); Fritz Redlich, The Molding of American Banking: Men and Ideas (1781-1910) (Martino Publishing 2012).
2. Constitution of the United States, Art. I, §§ 8(1)–(3), (5), (12), (13), (18); § 10(1)–(3); Art. IV § 1; Art. VI § 2. See generally Thomas McCraw, The Founders and Finance: How Hamilton, Gallatin and Other Immigrants Forged a New Economy 1, Ch. 5–8 (Belknap Press of Harvard Univ. Press 2012).
3. Letter to Robert Morris from Alexander Hamilton (Apr. 30, 1781); Chernow, supra n. 1, at 155–157, 170–171. Hamilton in 1779 had written an earlier version of his letter to General John Sullivan proposing a National Bank with a capital of $200 million, "a fantastic sum," Hammond wrote, "save that it represented the current depreciated Continental paper money." Hammond, supra n. 1, at 41. In this letter, he cited the Bank of England and the French Council of Commerce as models for a central bank. Chernow, supra n. 1, at 137–138. In 1780, Hamilton wrote to James Duane, a representative to the Continental Congress, urging the Confederation "should have complete sovereignty in all that relates to war, peace, trade, finance . . . [it should have] the right of coining money; establishing banks on such terms and with such privileges as they think proper." Hammond, supra n. 1, at 46. See generally Richard Sylla & David Cowen, Alexander Hamilton on Finance, Credit, and Debt (Columbia Univ. Press 2018); McCraw, supra n. 2, at 45–73.
4. Walter Bagehot, Lombard Street: A Description of the Money Market 3–31, 41–44, 85–86 (Createspace, North Charleston, SC, USA 1873); Liaguat Ahmed, Lords of Finance 76–80 (Penguin Press 2009); Michael Barr, Howell Jackson & Margaret Tahyar, Financial

Regulation: Law and Policy 868–870 (Foundation Press 2016); John Wood, Central Banking in a Democracy 11–16 (Routledge 2015).

5. Chernow, supra n. 1, at 4, 286–287, 302.
6. Treasury Department, First Report on Public Credit (Jan. 9, 1790); McCraw, supra n. 2, at 56–109; Chernow, supra n. 1, at 288–306, 339; Markham, Financial History, supra n. 1, at 75–80; Jon Meachem, Thomas Jefferson: The Art of Power 242–245 (Random House 2012); Arthur Schlesinger, The Age of Jackson 10 (Little Brown 1945).
7. Chernow, supra n. 1, at 303–306; Madison remarks in House of Representatives, Apr. 22, 1790; McCraw, supra n. 2, at 139–142; Meachem, supra n. 6, at 243–244; Chernow, supra n. 1, at 304–306, 319–323, 326–331; Markham, Financial History, supra n. 1, at 77–80; Lynne Cheney, James Madison: A Life Reconsidered 209–211 (Penguin Books 2015).
8. An Act Making Provision for [Payment of the] Debt of the United States, 1st Cong., 2 Sess. (Aug. 4, 1790); Paul Trescott, Federal-State Financial Relations 1790–1860, 15 Journal of Econ. Hist. 227 (1955); Markham, Financial History, supra n. 1, at 77–80; Chernow, supra n. 1, at 327–330.
9. An Act Repealing after the Last Day of January Next, the Duties Laid Upon Distilled Spirits Imported from Abroad, and Laying Others in their Stead, and Also upon Spirits Distilled Within the United States, H.R. 110, 1st Cong., 3d Sess. (March 3, 1791); Thomas Slaughter, the Whiskey Rebellion: Frontier Epilogue to the American Revolution (Oxford Univ. Press 1986); Chernow, supra n. 1, at 341–343; Markham, Financial History, supra n. 1, at 80–81; Meacham, supra n. 6, at 288–289.
10. Marshall quoted in Wood, supra n. 4, at 31; Hammond, supra n. 1, at 118–122; Chernow, supra n. 1, at 344, 349–355.
11. Report on a National Bank (Dec. 13, 1790); Hammond, supra n. 1, at 124–143; Chernow, supra n. 1, at 347–349.
12. An Act to Incorporate the Subscribers to the Bank of the United States, 1st Cong., 3d Sess. (Feb. 25, 1791); Chernow, supra n. 1, at 349–355; Madison Remarks on House of Representatives on the Bank Bill (Feb. 2, 1791); Federalist Paper No. 44; Hammond, supra n. 1, at 114–143; McCraw, supra n. 2, at 110–121; Gordon Wood, Empire of Liberty: A History of the Early Republic, 1789–1815 99 (Oxford Univ. Press 2009); Markham, Financial History, supra n. 1, at 88–89.
    In Federalist Paper No. 44, Madison had viewed the necessary and proper clause more latitudinously:

    > Had the convention attempted a positive enumeration of the powers necessary and proper for carrying their other

powers into effect; the attempt would have involved a complete digest of laws on every subject to which the constitution relates; accommodated too not only to the existing state of things, but to all the possible changes which futurity may produce: for in every new application of a general power, the *particular powers,* which are the means of attaining the *object* of the general power, must always necessarily vary with that object; and be often properly varied whilst the object remains the same....

Had the constitution been silent on this head, there can be no doubt that all the particular powers requisite as means of executing the general powers, would have resulted to the government, by unavoidable implication. No axiom is more clearly established in law, or in reason, than that wherever the end is required, the means are authorized; wherever a general power to do a thing is given, every particular power necessary for doing it, is included.

13. Walter Dellinger & J. Jefferson Powell, The Constitutionality of the Bank Bill: The Attorney General's First Constitutional Law Opinions, 44 Duke L.J. 110 (1994) (including Randolph's two opinions on the Bank Bill (Feb. 12, 1791); Thomas Jefferson Opinion on the Constitutionality of the National Bank (Feb. 15, 1791); Alexander Hamilton Opinion on the Constitutionality of a National Bank (Feb. 23, 1791); McCulloch v. Maryland, 17 U.S. (4 Wheat) 316 (1819)); Chernow, supra n. 1, at 351–355; Markham, Financial History, supra n. 1, at 88–89; Meacham, supra n. 6, at 249–250; Cheney, supra n. 7, at 225–227; Schlesinger, supra n. 6, at 29. In 1824, Jefferson went further: "The federal [government] is, in truth, our foreign government, which department alone is taken from the sovereignty of the separate states."
14. Report on the Establishment of a Mint (Jan. 28, 1791); An Act Establishing a Mint, and Regulating the Coins of the United States, 2d Cong., 1st Sess. (Apr. 2, 1791); Chernow, supra n. 1, at 355–357; Hammond, supra n. 1, at 92.
15. Alexander Hamilton's Final Version of the Report on the Subject of Manufactures (Dec. 15, 1791); Journal of United States House of Representatives (Jan. 15, 1790); Federalist Paper No. 60; Douglas Irwin, The Aftermath of Hamilton's "Report on Manufacturers" (NBER Working Paper 9943 2013); Hammond, supra n. 1, at 8–9; Joel Seligman, Corporations: Cases and Materials 3–10 (Little Brown 1995); Chernow, supra n. 1, at 344–345.
16. First Fed. Bank of Philadelphia, The First Bank of the United States: A Chapter in the History of Central Banking 5–8 (2009); Alexander

Hamilton, Observations on Certain Documents Contained in No. V & VI of the History of the United States for the Year 1796, in which the Charge of Speculation against Alexander Hamilton, Late Secretary of the Treasury is Fully Refuted, Written by Himself (July 1797); McCraw, supra n. 2, at 80–81, 145, 156–163; Wood, supra n. 4, at 33–36; Hammond, supra n. 1, at 125–134; Chernow, supra n. 1, at 293–294, 357-361, 379–384, 408–418; Markham, Financial History, supra n. 1, at 90, 108–114. Near adjournment of the Second Congress, a resolution drafted by Jefferson was introduced to censure Hamilton for misuse of funds. The resolution received little support. Cheney, supra n. 7, at 238.

17. Hammond, supra n. 1, at 205–226; First Fed. Bank of Philadelphia, supra n. 16, at 10 n. 26; Jefferson Letter to John Taylor (May 28, 1816); John Steele Gordon, We Banked on Them, 46 American Heritage No. 4 (July-Aug. 1995); James Wettereau, New Light on the First Bank of the United States, 61 Penn. Mag. of History & Biography 263 (1937); John Holdsworth & David Dewey, The First and Second Banks of the United States, National Monetary Commission, 61st Cong., 2d Sess. (GPO 1910); Gordon Wood, supra n. 12, at 98–99, 143–145, 293–298; Cowen, The First Bank of the United States and the Securities Market Crash of 1792, 60 J. Econ. Jist. 1041 (2000); Lehman Inst., The Founding Economist: Alexander Hamilton and Albert Gallatin, quoting Henry Adams, Claude G. Bowers, Thomas McCraw, James Hamilton; Joseph Ellis, American Sphinx: The Character of Thomas Jefferson 151–157, 185–186, 230–235 (Vintage Books 1998); Gary Wills, James Madison 76 (Times Books 2002); Meacham, supra n. 6, at 354, 366–369, 383–392, 417, 425–432; McCraw, supra n. 2, at 274–283, 290–297; Wood, supra n. 4, at 37; Cheney, supra n. 7, at 302–303; Murray Rothbard, The Panic of 1819 2–8 (Columbia Univ. Press 1962 reprinted by Ludwig von Mies Inst. 2007).

18. Hammond, supra n. 1, at 231–255; Wood, supra n. 4, at 37–39; Daniel Howe, What Hath God Wrought 81 (Oxford Univ. Press 2007); Ralph Catterall, The Second Bank of the United States (Univ. of Chicago Press 1902, reprinted by Forgotten Books 2012); Rothbard, supra n. 17, at 1–9.

19. An Act to Incorporate the Subscribers to the Bank of the United States, 14th Cong., 1st Sess. Ch. 44 (1816); Holdsworth & Dewey, supra n. 17, at 148–178; Catterall, supra n. 17, at 1–30; Howe, supra n. 18, at 374; Schlesinger, supra n. 6, at 31, 134–135.

20. Holdsworth & Dewey, supra n. 17, at 156–163, 175–181, 188–191, 220–224; Hammond, supra n. 1, at 244–257; Markham, Financial History, supra n. 1, at 134–138, 367; Catterall, supra n. 18, at 31–61; Rothbard, supra n. 17, at 10–18; Gouge, supra n. 1, at 101–110.

21. Hammond, supra n. 1, at 262–263; Catterall, supra n. 18, at 70–91; Holdsworth & Dewey, supra n. 17, at 224–227.
22. McCulloch v. Maryland, 17 U.S. (4 Wheat) 316 (1819); Osborn v. Bank of the United States, 23 U.S. (19 Wheat) 738, 862 (1824); Hammond, supra n. 1, at 263–268, 279–285; Holdsworth & Dewey, supra n. 17, at 227; Gouge, supra n. 1, at 110 (Banking in the United States); Catterall, supra n. 18, at 17–27, 88–91; Howe, supra n. 18, at 144–146. Besides the six states that adopted taxes that applied to the Second Bank, 14 states passed legislation that sought to prevent the Second Bank from collecting states' debts. Barr, Jackson & Tahyar, supra n. 4, at 34–35. See also Markham, Financial History, supra n. 1, at 137–138.
23. Caterall, supra n. 18, at 93–163, 274–275; Hammond, supra n. 1, at 286–325; Holdsworth & Dewey, supra n. 17, at 227–237, App. F.; Wood, supra n. 4, at 39–41; Jon Meacham, American Lion: Andrew Jackson in the White House 46 (Random House 2009); Gouge, supra n. 1, at 18–19 (History of Paper Money); Schlesinger, supra n. 6, at 9, 172; Markham, Financial History, supra n. 1, at 141–142.
24. Schlesinger, supra n. 6, at 36–42; Meacham, supra n. 6, at 32–36; Hammond, supra n. 1, at 346–349.
25. Mecham, supra n. 6, at 43–44, 48–49, 54–58, 77, 116, 135–139, 184–186, 201–205, 216–217, 226–239, 298, 307, 317–318; Howe, supra n. 18, at 357–359, 375, 488–490; Schlesinger, supra n. 6, at 19, 36–37, 46–49, 58–59, 135–136; Hammond, supra n. 1, at 327–328, 331–332, 347–348, 351–352, 386–387; Catterall, supra n. 18, at 171–172, 186–187, 251; Bray Hammond, Sovereignty and an Empty Purse 13 (Princeton Univ. Press 1970); de Touqueville, Democracy in America (Bantam Classic 2000, originally published 1835); Jackson Second Inaugural Address (March 4, 1833); Jackson First Ann. Message (Dec. 8, 1829; Jackson Second Ann. Message (Dec. 6, 1830); Worcester v. Georgia, 31 U.S. 515 (1832); Force Bill of 1833 (Mar. 2, 1833).
26. Jackson First Inaugural Address (Mar. 4, 1829); Jackson First Ann. Message (Dec. 8, 1829); Jackson Second Ann. Message (Dec. 6, 1830); Jackson Third Ann. Message (Dec. 6, 1831); Hammond, supra n. 1, at 372–378, 382; Schlesinger, supra n. 6, at 80–85; Catterall, supra n. 18, at 198–199, 203–204; Holdsworth & Dewey, supra n. 17, at 248–249.
27. Bill to Continue the Second Bank Charter, Senate Journal, 22d Cong., 1st Sess. 451–453 (July 11, 1832); Gouge, supra n. 1, at 5–8, 30–31, 40–45, 94–96, 100–101, 114–123, 132–133, 223–224; Hammond, supra n. 1, at 335, 351–352, 356–359, 385–397, 443–444; Mecham, supra n. 6, at 201; Schlesinger, supra n. 6, at 75–79, 85–87; Holdsworth & Dewey, supra n. 17, at 250–252, 255–257, 264–265; Catterall, supra n. 18, at 190–192.

28. Jackson Veto Message (July 10, 1832); Jackson Second Inaugural Address (Mar. 4, 1833); Howe, supra n. 18, at 379–385, 394–395, 410; Hammond, supra n. 1, at 361–362, 405, 410; Catterall, supra n. 18, at 239–242; Schlesinger, supra n. 6, at 90–94.
29. Second Bank Act of Incorporation, 14th Cong., 1st Sess. Ch. 44 (1816); Resolution of Censure (Mar. 28, 1834); Hammond, supra n. 1, at 411–439; Mecham, supra n. 24, at 265–270, 278–279, 286–288, 335–337; Schlesinger, supra n. 6, at 101, 103–129; Catterall, supra n. 18, at 292–296, 302, 314–315; Howe, supra n. 18, at 383, 388–390, 394–395; Lehman Inst., Andrew Jackson, Banks and the Panic of 1837 16–22 (2005).
30. Hammond, supra n. 1, at 474–487, 572, 603; Markham, Financial History, supra n. 1, at 148–151, 168–179; McCraw, supra n. 2, at 5; Seligman, supra n. 15, at 5–6; J. Willard Hurst, The Legitimacy of the Business Corporation 30 (Lawbook Exchange Ltd. 1979); E. Merrick Dodd, American Business Corporations until 1860: With Special Reference to Massachusetts 183, 287–288 (Harvard Univ. Press 1954); Liggett v. Lee, 288 U.S. 517, 549–550 n. 4 (N.Y. 1933) (Brandeis dissent); Seligman, supra n. 15, at 5–6; Gary Gorton, Misunderstanding Financial Crises 11–17 (Oxford Univ. Press 2012); Schlesinger, supra n. 6, at 129–131, 218; Lehman Inst., supra n. 29, at 21–24; Howe, supra n. 18, at 505.
31. Martin Van Buren, Special Session Message (Sept. 4, 1837); Hammond, supra n. 1, at 451–497; Lehman Inst., supra n. 29, at 25–31; Markham, Financial History, supra n. 1, at 149; Howe, supra n. 18, at 505; Schlesinger, supra n. 6, at 217–239; John Platt, United States Independent Treasury Systems 11 (Dep't of Treasury 1968).
32. William Henry Harrison, Inaugural Address (Mar. 4, 1841); William Henry Harrison, Proclamation Convening an Extra Session of Congress (Mar. 17, 1841); John Tyler, June 1, 1841: Special Session Message to Congress Regarding General Affairs of the Country (June 1, 1841); John Tyler, Veto Message (Aug. 16, 1841); Lehman Inst. supra n. 29, at 28–29; Hammond, supra n. 1, at 496–497; Markham, Financial History, supra n. 1, at 150–152; Schlesinger, supra n. 6, at 267–305, 391–401; William Freehling, William Harrison, Campaign and Elections, Miller Center.
33. Schlesinger, supra n. 6, at 218; Hammond, supra n. 1, at 675–676, 698, 707–717; Markham, Financial History, supra n. 1, at 167, 201–203, 293–296, 301–303, 331–333; Vincent Carosso, Investment Banking in America: A History 29 (Harvard Univ. Press 1970); Gary Gorton, Slapped by the Invisible Hand: The Panic of 2007 30–33 (Oxford Univ. Press 2010).
34. Independent Treasury Act of 1846 §§ 18–20, ch. 90, 9 Stat. 59, 29th Cong., 1st Sess. (1846); James Buchanan, First Ann. Message to

Congress in the State of the Union (Dec. 8, 1857); Platt, supra n. 31, generally; William Gouge, Report on Public Depositories, Dec. No. 30, Senate Exec. Documents, 33d Cong., 2d Sess. (May 26, 1854); Hammond, supra n. 1, at 705–717, 721–722; Hammond, supra n. 25, at 20; Markham, Financial History, supra n. 1, at 368–370.

35. Hammond, supra n. 1, at 718–722; Hammond, supra n. 25, at 18–28, 325; Markham, Financial History, supra n. 1, at 207–208, 213, 220; Roger Lowenstein, America's Bank: The Epic Struggle to Create the Federal Reserve 12 (Penguin Press 2015); Report of the Secretary of the Treasury, 37th Cong., 2d Sess. 7 (Dec. 9, 1861).
36. Lincoln Proclamation (Apr. 15, 1861); Lincoln Special Session Message (July 4, 1861); Hammond, supra n. 25, at 37, 98, 112–125, 239–243; Hammond, supra n. 1, at 720–724; Evan Sparks, Lincoln and the Banks, ABA Banking J., Feb. 11, 2018; In His Own Words: Abraham Lincoln and Banking, Office of Comptroller of the Currency; An Act to Authorize a National Loan and for Other Purposes, ch. 5, 37th Cong., 1st Sess. (July 17, 1861); Report of the Secretary of Treasury, supra n. 35; Report of the Secretary of the Treasury, 37th Cong., 3d Sess. (Dec. 4, 1862); Markham, Financial History, supra n. 1, at 207–210; An Act to Authorize a National Loan, and for Other Purposes, ch. 46, 27th Cong., 1st Sess. (Aug. 5, 1861); Claudia Goldman & Frank Lewis, The Economic Costs of the American Civil War: Estimates and Implications, 35 J. Econ. Hist. 299 (1975).
37. An Act to Authorize the Issue of United States Notes, and for the Redemption or Funding Thereof, and for Funding the Floating Debt of the United States, ch. 33, 27th Cong., 2d Sess. (Feb. 25, 1862); Hammond, supra n. 25, at 211, 218, 252, 355; Shelby Foot, 2 The Civil War: A Narrative 109 (Random House 1963).
38. Legal Tender Cases, 79 U.S. 457 (1871); Hepburn v. Griswold, 75 U.S. 603 (1870); Julliard v. Greenman, 110 U.S. 421 (1884); Norman v. Baltimore & Ohio R. Co. 294 U.S. 240 (1935); Milton Friedman & Anna Schwartz, A Monetary History of the United States, 1857–1960, 24–25 (Princeton Univ. Press 1963).
39. Report of the Secretary of Treasury, supra n. 36 (Dec. 4, 1862); Lincoln Message to Congress on Printing Money (Jan. 17, 1863); Hammond, supra n. 25, at 328, 332; An Act to Provide a National Currency, Secured by a Pledge of United States Stocks, and to Provide for the Circulation and Resumption Thereof, ch. 58, 37th Cong., 3d Sess. (Feb. 25, 1863); National Bank Act, ch. 106, 13 Stat. 99 (1864); Veazie v. Fenno, 75 U.S. 533 (1869), quoting § 9 of Act of Congress (July 13, 1866); Hammond, supra n. 1, at 727–734; Markham, Financial History, supra n. 1, at 217–220, 365; Office of the Comptroller of the Currency, A Short History; Redford, Dual Banking: A Case Study in Federalism, 31 Law & Contemp. Prob. 749 (1986).

40. Eugene White, The Regulation and Reform of the American Banking System: 1900–1929, 10–62 (Princeton Univ. Press 1983); Office of the Comptroller, A Short History, supra n. 39, at 12; Barr, Jackson & Tahyar, supra n. 4, at 39–40; Markham, Financial History, supra n. 1, at 219–220, 365, 368–371; Redford, supra n. 39, at 749–765; Davis v. Elmira Sav. Bank, 161 U.S. 275, 283 (1896); An Act to Provide Internal Revenue to Support the Government, to Pay Interest on the Public Debt, and for Other Purposes, ch. 78, 13 Stat. 484 (Mar. 3, 1865).
41. Friedman & Schwartz, supra n. 38, at 16–17, 26, 58–59, 85, 114; Milton Friedman, The Crime of 1873, 98 J. Pol. Econ. 1159, 1160–1172 (1990); An Act Revising and Amending the Laws Related to the Mints, Assaying Office and Coinage of the United States, ch. 131, 43d Cong. 3d Sess. (Feb. 12, 1873); Lowenstein, supra n. 35, at 18.
42. An Act to Provide for the Resumption of Specie Payments, ch. 15, §§ 14–15, 43d Cong., 2d Sess. (1875); Grover Cleveland, Message on the Repeal of the Sherman Silver Purchase Act (Aug. 8, 1893); Richard White, The Republic for Which It Stands: The United States during Reconstruction and the Gilded Age, 1865–1896 at 246, 263–274, 369–371 (Oxford. Hist. of the United States 2007); Hugh Rockoff, The "Wizard of Oz" as a Monetary Allegory, 98 J. Pol. Econ. 739 (1990); Report of the Secretary of the Treasury (Dec. 12, 1865); Friedman & Schwartz, supra n. 38, at 44–50; Markham, Financial History, supra n. 1, at 339–349; Ulysses S. Grant, Inaugural Address (Mar. 4, 1869); Ulysses Grant, First Ann. Message (Dec. 6, 1869); Republican Party Platform of 1868 (May 20, 1868); Republic Party Platform of 1872 (June 5, 1872); Ulysses S. Grant, Veto Message (Apr. 22, 1874); Independent Greenback Platform (May 17, 1876); Rutherford B. Hayes, Inaugural Address (Mar. 5, 1877); Ann. Report of Secretary of the Treasury for the Year 1877; Report and Accompanying Documents of the United States Monetary Commission Organized under the Joint Resolution of Aug. 15, 1876; S. Rep. No. 703, 44th Cong. 2d Sess. (1877); Rutherford B. Hayes, Veto of Bland-Allison Act (Feb. 8, 1878).
43. An Act Directing the Purchase of Silver Bullion and the Issue of Treasury Notes Thereupon and for Other Purposes, ch. 708, 51st Cong., 1st Sess. (July 14, 1890); White, supra n. 42, at 618–635, 649–654, 771–773, 832–836; Friedman & Schwartz, supra n. 38, at 104–133; Wood, supra n. 4, at 52–53; Markham, Financial History, supra n. 1, at 345–348; Rockoff, supra n. 42, at 742–743; Grover Cleveland Message on the Repeal of the Sherman Silver Purchase Act (Aug. 8, 1893); Ron Chernow, The House of Morgan: An American Banking Dynasty and The Rise of Modern Finance 71–78 (Atlantic Monthly Press 1990; Karen Hoffman, "Going Public" in the

Nineteenth Century: Grover Cleveland's Repeal of the Sherman Silver Purchase Act, 5 Rhetoric & Public Affairs 57 (2002).

44. Republican Party Platform (June 18, 1896); Democratic Party Platform (July 7, 1896); William Jennings Bryan, Cross of Gold Speech (July 8, 1896); White, supra n. 42, at 841–849; Friedman & Schwartz, supra n. 38, at 8, 90–119, 135–140; Rockoff, supra n. 42, at 743–745; Karl Rove, The Triumph of William McKinley: Why the Election of 1896 Still Matters (Simon & Schuster 2015); H. Wayne Morgan, The View from the Front Porch: William McKinley and the Campaign of 1896 (12th Hayes Lecture on the Presidency, Feb. 12, 2001); Friedman & Schwartz, supra n. 38, at 1177; An Act to Define and Fix the Standard of Value, to Maintain the Parity of All Forms of Money Issued or Coined by the United States, to Refund the Public Debt, and for Other Purposes, ch. 41, 56th Cong., 1st Sess. (Mar. 14, 1900).

45. 1 Historical Statistics of the United States: Colonial Times to 1970 Series A1-5, 55–72, 210–263 (U.S. Dept. of Commerce 1975); 2 Historical Statistics of the United States: Colonial Times to 1970 Series Q284-312, R46-55, W96-106, X580-587, X610-619 (U.S. Dept. of Commerce 1975); Joel Seligman, A Brief History of Delaware's General Corporation Law of 1899, Del. J. Corp. L. 249 (1976); John Moody, The Truth about the Trusts: A Description and Analysis of the American Trust Movement (Moody Pub. 1904); Alfred Chandler, The Beginning of "Big Business" in American Industry, 33 Bus. Hist. Rev. 1 (1959); Ida Tanbell, 1–2 The History of the Standard Oil Company 33, 38–52 (1925); Standard Oil Co. v. United States, 221 U.S. 1 (1911); Markham, Financial History, supra n. 1, at 356–359, 365–367, 371–372, 375–377; Barr, Jackson & Tahyar, supra n. 4 at 42–43; Lowenstein, supra n. 35 at 61–63; Friedman & Schwartz, supra n. 38, at 149; Chernow, supra n. 43 at 122.

46. Wikipedia, Closing Milestones of the Dow Jones Industrial Average; Friedman & Schwartz, supra n. 38, at 156–157; Lowenstein, supra n. 35, at 59, 63–70; Markham, Financial History, supra n. 1, at 29–34; Carosso, supra n. 33, at 128–131; Address of President Roosevelt on the Occasion of the Laying of the Corner Stone of the Pilgrim Memorial Monument, Provincetown, Massachusetts (Aug. 1907); Chernow, supra n. 43, at 121–128; White, supra n. 40, at 76–83; Adam Tooze, Crashed: How a Decade of Financial Crises Changed the World 170 (Viking 2018); A. Piatt Andrew, Substitutes for Cash in the Panic of 1907, 22 Quarterly J. Econ. 497 (1908); Edwin Perkins, The Divorce of Commercial and Investment Banking: A History, 88 Banking L.J. 483, 487–488 (1971); Robert Bruner & Sean Carr, The Panic of 1907 (John Wiley & Sons 2017).

47. Report of Governor Hughes' Committee on Speculation in Securities and Commodities (State of New York June 7, 1909); 7 Louis Loss, Joel Seligman & Troy Paredes ch. 8.B.4.b (Wolters Kluwer 5th ed. 2017); 7 id. ch. 8.B.4.b (2017); An Act to Amend the National Banking Laws, ch. 229, 60th Cong., 1st Sess. (May 30, 1908); Laughlin, The Aldrich-Vreeland Act, J. Pol. Econ. 489 (1908); Roosevelt, Eighth Ann. Message (Dec. 8, 1908); Markham, Financial History, supra n. 1, at 35–38; Chernow, supra n. 43, at 110; Lowenstein, supra n. 35, at 78–79; Friedman & Schwartz, supra n. 38, at 169–172; White, supra n. 40, at 65.
48. 1 Paul Warburg, Federal Reserve System: Its Origin and Growth chs. 1–4 (MacMillan Co. 1930); Lowenstein, supra n. 35, at 92–197; Chernow, supra n. 43, at 149–156; Markham, Financial History, supra n. 1, at 47–50; Peter Conti-Brown, The Power and Independence of the Federal Reserve 20 (Princeton Univ. Press 2016); Report of the National Monetary Commission (1912); Report of the Committee Appointed Pursuant to House Resolutions 429 and 504 to Investigate the Concentration of Control of Money and Credit, H. Rep. No. 1593, 62d Cong., 2d Sess. (1913) (*Pujo Report*); White, supra n. 40, at 90–95; Charles Lindbergh, The Money Trust, New York Times, July 24, 1911; Charles Lindbergh, Banking and Currency and the Money Trust (National Capital Press, 1913); Louis Brandeis, Other People's Money and How the Bankers Use It (National Home Lib. Found. 1933).
49. 1912 Democratic Party Platform (June 25, 1912); Wilson Jackson Day Dinner Speech (Jan. 8, 1912); Brandeis, supra n. 48, at 1–19, 23, 25, 36–37, 137; Arthur Link, Woodrow Wilson and the Progressive Era 1910–1917 at 43–53 (Harper & Row 1954); Melvin Urofsky, Louis D. Brandeis: A Life chs. 12–13, 16, esp. at 381–384 (Pantheon Books 2009); Lowenstein supra n. 35, at 141–142, 181–183, 217–263; Federal Reserve Act, Pub. L. No. 63–43, 38 Stat. 251, ch. 6, 63d Cong., 2d Sess. (Dec. 23, 1913); Wilson Inaugural Address (Mar. 4, 1913); Wilson, Address to a Joint Session of Congress on the Banking System (June 23, 1913); White, supra n. 40, at 96–97, 130–165; Wood, supra n. 4, at 63–68; Markham, Financial History, supra n. 1, at 45–46; Sarah Binder & Mark Spindel, The Myth of Independence: How Congress Governs the Federal Reserve 8–10, 52–81 (Princeton Univ. Press 2017); Carosso, supra n. 33, at 137–155; Friedman & Schwartz, supra n. 38, at 189–192; Bernanke, supra n. 1, at 46–47; H.R. 7837, 63d Cong., 1st Sess. (Aug. 1913); H. Rep. No. 69, 63d Cong., 1st Sess. (Sept. 9, 1913); S. Rep. No. 133, 63 Cong., 1st Sess. (Nov. 22, 1913); S. Doc. No. 264, 63d Cong. 2d Sess. (Dec. 9, 1913); Warburg, supra n. 48, at 129; Act of Feb. 25, 1927, 44 Stat. 1234.

50. Joel Seligman, The Transformation of Wall Street: A History of the Securities and Exchange Commission and Modern Corporate Finance 42–46 (3d ed. Aspen Pub. 2003); Loss, Seligman & Paredes, supra n. 47; Carosso, supra n. 33, at 156–173, 189–192; Liggett v. Lee, 288 U.S. 517 (1933); Adolf Berle & Gardiner Means, The Modern Corporation and Private Property 119–128 (Harcourt, Brace & World 1968); Berle, Corporations and the Public Investor 20 Am. Econ. Rev. 62 (1930); William Ripley, Main Street and Wall Street 46–54 (Little Brown 1927); James Bonbright, The Dangers of Stock without Par Value, 24 Colum. L. Rev. 449 (1924); Berle, Investors and the Revised Delaware Corporation Act, 29 Colum. L. Rev. 570 (1929); Mass. Acts & Resolves 1852, ch. 303; California Const. Act IV § 26 (1879); Ga. L. 1904 No. 592 at 74; Missouri L. 1907, S.B. 109 at 392; Conn. Pub. Acts 1903, ch. 196; Conn. Pub. Act 1911, ch. 232; Nev. Stat. 1909, ch. 56; Nev. Stat. 1911, ch. 202; Nev. Stat. 1915, ch. 49; R.I. Acts & Resolves 1910, ch. 557 § 39; Kansas Laws 1911 ch. 133; Louis Loss & Edward Cowett 7-17 Blue Sky Law (Little Brown 1958); J.N. Dolley, The Kansas Blue Sky Law, 75 Cent. L.J. 221 (1912); Mulvey, Company Capitalization Control lxvii–lxviii (1913); Mulvey, Blue Sky Law, 36 Can. L. Times 37 (1916); Hall v. Geiger-Jones Co., 242 U.S. 539 (1917); Caldwell v. Sioux Falls Stock Yards Co., 242 U.S. 559 (1917); Merrick v. N.W. Halsey & Co., 242 U.S. 568 (1917); Michael Parrish, Securities Regulation and the New Deal 21–30 (1970); Dep't of Commerce, A Study of the Economic and Legal Aspects of the Proposed Federal Securities Act, and Federal Securities Act Hearings, House Commerce Comm., 73d Cong., 1st Sess. (1933); Forrest Ashly, The Economic Effects of Blue Sky Laws (Univ. of Pa. 1926); Paul Mahoney, The Origins of the Blue Sky Laws: A Test for Competing Hypotheses, 46 J. L. & Econ. 229 (2003). For a critique of the Blue Sky Laws, see Jonathan Macey & Geoffrey Miller, Origins of the Blue Sky Laws, 70 Tex. L. Rev. 347 (1991).
51. Seligman, supra n. 50, at 46–49; Pujo Report, supra n. 48, at 33–54, 114–128; Markham, Financial History, supra n. 1, at 114–125, 241–248, 288–290; 2 Jerry Markham, A Financial History of the United States: From J.P. Morgan to the Institutional Investor (1900–1970) 3–10, 50–54 (Routledge 2015); J. Edward Meeker, The Work of the Stock Exchange 549–567 (Ronald Press 1930); Ripley, supra n. 50, at 210–214; Rudolph Weissman, The New Wall Street 111 (Harper & Bros. 1939); Stock Exchange Practices Report, Senate Rep. No. 1455, 73d Cong., 2d Sess. 68–73 (1934); 19–20 George V ch. 23.
52. Seligman, supra n. 50, at 48–49; Twentieth Century Fund, The Security Markets 579–609 (Twentieth Century Fund 1935); David

Hawkins, The Development of Modern Financial Reporting Practices among American Manufacturing Corporations, 37 Bus. Hist. Rev. 135 (1963); Frank Smith, Accounting Requirements of Stock Exchange 1933, 17 Acct. Rev. 145 (1937); Ripley, supra n. 50, at 156–208; Testimony of Robert Healey, FTC Chief Counsel, Federal Securities Act Hearings, House Commerce Comm., 73d Cong., 1st Sess. 231–232 (1933); Berle & Means, supra n. 50, at 135–138.

53. Seligman, supra n. 50, at 49–50; War Finance Corporation Act, Pub. L. 121, 65th Cong. §§ 201–206 (1918); Loss, Seligman & Paredes, supra n. 47; Report of Capital Issues Comm., H.R. Doc. No. 1485, 65th Cong., 3d Sess. 1–5 (1918); FTC Ann. Rep. for Fiscal Year Ended June 30, 1919, H.R. Doc. No. 751, 66th Cong., 2d Sess. 47–48 (1920); Woodbury Willoughby, The Capital Issues Committee and War Finance Corporation (Johns Hopkins Univ. Studies in Hist. & Pol. Sci. Series 52, No. 2, ch. 1 (1934); Markham, Financial History, supra n. 51, at 80–85.

54. Loss, Seligman & Paredes, supra n. 47; Pujo Report, supra n. 48, at 164–165; Carosso, supra n. 33, at 29, 33–47; Brandeis, supra n. 48, at 110–123; Schwabacher v. United States, 334 U.S. 182, 191–192, 195 n. 15 (1948); Turner, Federal Regulation of Carrier Securities, 25 Law & Contemp. Prob. 106 (1960); 41 Stat. 494 (1920), later 49 U.S.C. § 11301; 1 I.L. Sharfman, The Interstate Commerce Commission 190 (1931); 4 Interstate Commerce Act, Ann. 2615, S. Doc. No. 166, 70th Cong., 1st Sess. (1930); 2 Historical Statistics of the United States, supra n. 45, at 735; Interstate Commerce Act of 1887, Pub. L. 49-104, 24 Stat. 379 (1887); Markham, Financial History, supra n. 1, at 251–264, 290–293; Moody, supra n. 45, at 429–450.

55. Markham, Financial History, supra n. 51, at 12–13, 23–27, 57–58, 63–65, 115–118; Brandeis, supra n. 48, at 16–18, 93–102; Carosso, supra n. 33, at 82–98; First Nat'l Bank v. National Exch. Bank, 92 U.S. 122 (1816); National Bank v. Case, 99 U.S. 628 (1879); California Bank v. Kennedy, 167 U.S. 362 (1897); Note, National Banks and The Brokerage Business: The Comptroller's New Reading of The Glass-Steagall Act, 69 Va. L. Rev. 1303 (1983).

56. Report of the Joint Comm. of the Senate & Assembly, New York State, Appointed to Investigate the Affairs of Life Insurance Companies, Assembly Doc. No. 41 (1906); 2 Historical Statistics of the United States, supra n. 45, at 1019, 1056, 1065; Morton Keller, The Life Insurance Enterprise, 1885–1910 at 245 (Harv. Univ. Press 1963); Markham, Financial History, supra n. 1, at 181–194, 279–282; Barr, Jackson & Tahyar, supra n. 4, at 339–344; Paul v. Virginia, 75 U.S. 168 (1869); German Alliance Ins. Corp. v. Lewis, 233 U.S. 389 (1914); Douglass North, Life Insurance and Investment Banking at the Time of the Armstrong Investigation of 1905–1906,

14 J. Econ. Hist. 209 (1954); Roger Ransom & Richard Sutch, Tontine Insurance and the Armstrong Investigation: A Case of Stifled Innovation, 1868–1905, 47 J. Econ. Hist. 379 (1987); Carosso, supra n. 33, at 113–127.

57. Joint Comm. of Senate & Assembly, State of New York, Appointed to Investigate the Affairs of Life Insurance Companies, supra n. 56; An Act to Amend Insurance Law Generally, Ch. 326 (N.Y. Senate & Assembly, Apr. 27, 1906); Ch. 239 (N.Y. State Senate & Assembly, Apr. 16, 1906); Ch. 321 (N.Y. State Senate & Assembly Apr. 26, 1906); National Association of Insurance Commissioners & Center for Insurance Policy and Research, State of the Life Insurance Industry: Implications of Industry Trends 3–10 (Aug. 2013); Keller, supra n. 56, at 257–258; Markham, Financial History, supra n. 51, at 18–20; Historical Statistics, supra n. 45, at 1056–1057.

3

The New Deal Revolution

The post-World War I period began with the Roaring Twenties and ended with the three greatest economic crises in United States history: The 1929–1933 Stock Market Crash, the Banking Crisis, and the Great Depression.

In response, the Roosevelt New Deal significantly strengthened banking regulation, revolutionized securities regulation, dramatically improved federal housing programs, and overthrew the concept of limited national power to regulate the economy that had been the hallmark of the Jacksonian dominance of federal policy during the prior 140 years as part of an effort to restore and transform the American economy.

The calamity of World War I had left the United States with the strongest economy in the world. Germany and France had seen 3.4 million of their citizens die in the carnage of the Great War; their economies contracted by 30 percent. Britain had lost 900,000 citizens and its economy contracted by 5 percent.

The prognosis for Europe was dire. The 1919 Versailles Peace Treaty had left Germany with crippling debt—an initial $5 billion by May 1, 1921 with a Reparations Commission authorized to determine Germany's ultimate liability and how reparations were to be collected. In 1920, the Commission initially estimated reparations at $33 billion, triggering what Liaquat Ahamed, author of *Lords of Finance*, characterized as "the single greatest destruction of monetary value in human history." The German mark which traded at

4.2 to the dollar in 1914, "[b]y August 1923, a dollar was worth 620,000 marks and by early November, 630 billion."

Less devastated, but still bereft, was Britain, which owed the United States $5 billion and in turn was owed $11 billion by 17 countries, $3 billion from France and $2.5 billion from Russia, which after the war was uncollectible from the new Bolshevik government. France separately owed the United States $4 billion.

John Maynard Keynes, in his influential *The Economic Consequences of the Peace,* was brutal in his criticisms of the Carthaginian Peace imposed on Germany, which was subject to impossibly large reparation terms, loss of one-eighth of its territory including Alsace and Lorraine, its coal mines in the Saar Basin, and merchant marine. Keynes ranged beyond economic facts to conclude:

> The policy of reducing Germany to servitude for a generation, of degrading the lives of millions of human beings, and of depriving a whole nation of happiness should be abhorrent and detestable — abhorrent and detestable, even if it were possible, even if it enriched ourselves, even if it did not sow the decay of the whole civilized life of Europe.

Less well remembered was Keynes' pessimism about the other nations of Europe:

> The Treaty includes no provisions for the economic rehabilitation of Europe — nothing to make the defeated Central Empire into good neighbors, nothing to stabilize the new states of Europe, nothing to reclaim Russia; nor does it promote in any way a compact of economic solidarity amongst the Allies themselves; no arrangement was reached at Paris for restoring the disordered finances of France and Italy, or to adjust the systems of the Old World and the New.

The United States policy post-World War I was strikingly different than its Marshall Plan to rebuild Europe after World War II. In March 1922, Congress created the World War Foreign Debt Commission chaired by Secretary of the Treasury Andrew Mellon and including Secretary of Commerce Herbert Hoover to negotiate the terms on which American war loans were to be repaid. Congress was demanding. The Commission was directed not to accept less than 90 cents on the dollar lent. The French publication *L'éclair* expressed the outrage felt by many in Europe: "Has America which but yesterday we acclaimed for her generosity and her idealism fallen to the role of Shylock?"

In economic terms, the United States was the victor of the Great War. Before World War I in 1915, the gross national product (*GNP*) of the United States was $40 billion, roughly equal to Britain, France, and Germany combined. By 1920, the United States GNP was $91.5 billion, 50 percent greater than these three leading European nations combined.[1]

John Kenneth Galbraith, a critic of the excesses of 1920s finance, was one of many economic historians who recognized the achievements of subsequent Coolidge prosperity:

> ... [T]he twenties in America were a very good time. Production and employment were high and rising. Wages were not going up much, but prices were stable. Although many people were still very poor, more people were comfortably well-off, well-to-do, or rich than ever before. Finally, American capitalism was undoubtedly in a lively phase. Between 1925 and 1929, the number of manufacturing establishments increased from 183,900 to 206,700; the value of their output rose from $60.8 billion to $68 billion. The Federal Reserve index of industrial production which had averaged only 67 in 1921 (1923-25 = 100) had risen to 110 by July 1928, and it reached 126 in June 1929. In 1926, 4,301,000 automobiles were produced. Three years later, in 1929, production had increased by over a million to 5,358,000, a figure which compares very decently with the 5,700,000 new car registrations of the opulent year of 1953 [the year Galbraith wrote]. Business earnings were rising rapidly, and it was a good time to be in business.

Political rhetoric articulated the United States self-confidence. In his last Message to Congress on December 4, 1928, President Coolidge reassuringly began:

> No Congress of the United States ever assembled, on surveying the state of the Union, has met with a more pleasing prospect than that which appears at the present time. In the domestic field there is tranquility and contentment, harmonious relations between management and wage earner, freedom from industrial strife, and the highest record of years of prosperity. . . . The great wealth created by our enterprise and industry, and saved by our economy, has had the widest distribution among our own people, and has gone out in a steady stream to

> serve the charity and the business of the world. The requirements of existence have passed beyond the standard of necessity into the region of luxury. Enlarging production is consumed by an increasing demand at home and an expanding commerce abroad. The country can regard the present with satisfaction and anticipate the future with optimism.

Nor were politicians alone in their optimism. The rosy glow was also communicated by financier Bernard Baruch who in June 1929 declaimed: "[T]he economic condition of the world seems on the verge of a great forward movement." Yale economist Irving Fisher in the autumn of 1929 boldly asserted: "Stock prices have reached what looks like a permanently high plateau."

The 1929–1933 Stock Market Crash

The stock market roared in the 1920s decade. The Dow Jones, which closed 1920 at 72, reached 200 by the early summer of 1928. This was an impressive rise, but not markedly out of line with corporate profits that rose over 80 percent during the 1920s decade. It was only during the final year of the Coolidge Presidency that the market began to exhibit a manic quality. In an 18-month period commencing in March, the Dow Jones Industrial Average nearly doubled again, reaching a high of 381 on September 3, 1929.

"Everybody ought to be rich," General Motors Director and Democratic National Committee Chair John J. Raskob explained in 1929:

> The common stocks of this country have in the past ten years increased enormously in value because the business of the country has increased. Ten thousand dollars invested ten years ago in the common stock of General Motors would now be worth more than a million and a half dollars. And General Motors is only one of many first-class industrial corporations.

The "Everybody Ought to be Rich" enthusiasm touched many during a decade derided in retrospect for speculative excess. A great Florida land boom buoyed selected land lot prices in Miami, from $800 in the early days of a real estate development to $150,000 in 1924, only to crash ignominiously in the late 1920s. Frederick Lewis Allen, the journalist historian of the period wrote in *Only Yesterday*:

> By the middle of 1930, after the general business depression had set in, no less than twenty-six Florida cities had gone into default of principal or interest on their bonds, the heaviest defaults being those of West Palm Beach, Miami, Sanford, and Lake Worth; and even Miami, which had a minor issue of bonds maturing in August 1930, confessed its inability to redeem them and asked the bondholders for an extension.

The bubble in common stocks was more widespread. New issues of stock increased from $275 million to $6.757 billion between 1921 and 1929. Borrowed money or brokers' margin loans to customers increased from $1.08 billion on March 31, 1920, to $8.52 billion on October 4, 1929, with customers generally providing 20 to 50 percent of the value of the stock price. This meant if you placed 20 percent down, your profits could be 500 percent higher than had you paid full price. Leverage, however, worked both ways. If stock prices fell, your losses also would be 500 percent greater.

Confidence in investment bankers such as the JP Morgan firm or National City Bank's Charles Mitchell was endemic to the investing public. When the Federal Reserve Board attempted to discourage member banks from making loans to facilitate securities speculation on February 2, 1929, Mitchell, a newly elected Director of the Federal Reserve Bank of New York in March 1929, in effect, overruled Washington's Federal Reserve by telling the press on behalf of the nation's largest commercial bank: "We feel that we have an obligation which is paramount to any Federal Reserve warning, or anything else, to avert any dangerous crisis in the money market." The next day, National City put up to $25 million into the margin loan market beginning at an interest rate of 16 percent on the first $5 million and $5 million for each additional interest rate increase of 1 percent.

Brokerage bulletins and letters reassured investors that leading stocks such as Radio Corporation of America or General Motors would be "taken in hand" by pools of stock market traders supposedly protecting against precipitous stock price declines and galvanizing further stratospheric price rises.

While the relatively small number of individual investors actually bought stock, later estimates would be approximately 1.5 million out of a national population of 120 million, "[t]he striking thing about the stock market speculation of 1929 was not the massiveness of the participation," Galbraith wrote in *The Great Crash.* "Rather, it was the way . . . the market . . . dominated the culture." Frederick Lewis Allen almost poetically described:

> As one walked up the aisle of the 5:27 local, or found one's seat in the trolley car, two out of three newspapers that one saw were open to the page of stock market quotations. Branch offices of the big Wall Street houses blossomed in every city and in numerous suburban villages. In 1919 there had been five hundred such offices; by October, 1928, there were 1,192; and throughout most of 1929 they appeared in increasing numbers. The broker found himself regarded with a new wonder and esteem. Ordinary people, less intimate with the mysteries of Wall Street than he was supposed to be, hung upon his every word. Let him but drop a hint of a possible split-up in General Industries Associates and his neighbor was off hot-foot the next morning to place a buying order.[2]

In September 1929, the great bull market began to come undone. It was a crash unique in financial history. When the mania in overseas investments and joint stock companies crashed in London in 1720, it burst with a suddenness that forever afterward caused it to be known as the South Sea Bubble. The same had been true of the 1719 Mississippi Bubble in France, and the collapse of the Florida land boom in 1926. But matters were different in the stock markets in 1929. "When the crash finally came," financial historian John Brooks wrote almost lyrically, "it came with a kind of surrealistic slowness — so gradually that, on the one hand, it was possible to live through a good part of it without realizing that it was happening, and, on the other hand, it was possible to believe one had experienced and survived it when in fact it had no more than just begun."

The decline accelerated in October. Substantial losses occurred on Friday, October 18, Saturday, October 19, and Monday, October 21. The market advanced Tuesday, but on Wednesday, October 23, *The New York Times* Average lost a breathtaking 18 points. In less than a week, the average surrendered 30 of its 291 points.

On October 24, a bankers' pool organized by JP Morgan and Company's Thomas Lamont purchased $20 to $30 million worth of securities to stabilize the market. But within a few days share prices again collapsed. Losses on Monday, October 28, far exceeded those previously recorded. The *Times* Average fell 29 points, individual securities like General Electric lost as many as 50 points. This time bankers' support did not materialize. On Tuesday, the 29th, the *Times* Average fell another 24 points. In the eight weeks after Labor Day, the average collapsed 111 points (36 percent), nearly as much as it had gained in the preceding 18 months. In all, the two month loss on the New York Stock Exchange totaled $18 billion. And the price collapse had, in fact, just begun.[3]

From the White House Herbert Hoover anxiously regarded the 1929 Crash. As early as 1925, Hoover had been concerned about "the growing tide of speculation." On a few occasions while he was Secretary of Commerce, Hoover had complained to President Coolidge about the Federal Reserve Board's "easy money policies."

But at the time, Hoover did not care to press such views too firmly. Calvin Coolidge had achieved his substantial popularity not by criticizing the booming economy, but by identifying himself with it. Hoover campaigned for president in 1928 as the candidate who would sustain "Coolidge prosperity." Praising Coolidge for "introducing a new basis in government relation with business," Hoover maintained that for prosperity to last, "a continuation of the policies of the Republican Party is fundamentally necessary." Once elected, Hoover symbolized his association with Coolidge's economic views by reappointing, as the Secretary of the Treasury, Andrew Mellon, the Coolidge Administration's most visible link to the business community.

Hoover's economic views were never as doctrinaire as those of Coolidge or Mellon. Denounce "bureaucraticizing of business" he might, but Hoover also insisted that the American economy "is no system of *laissez faire*." To prevent credit inflation from jeopardizing industrial employment and farm prices, Hoover, in theory, endorsed limited federal intervention.

It was only in practice that he hesitated. Twice in February 1929, the Federal Reserve Board cautioned member banks against borrowing money "for the purpose of making speculative loans," statements that President-elect Hoover supported. Hoover was appalled when President Coolidge, just a few days before leaving office, had helped undermine the Board's tentative efforts at "moral suasion" by assuring the country that stocks were "cheap at current prices."

Throughout the summer of 1929, share prices soared by nearly 25 percent, brokers' loans increased at a rate of $400 million per month. Hoover did not intervene.

A similar ambivalence characterized Hoover's response to the October stock market crash. By then, Hoover feared an "inevitable collapse which will bring the greatest calamities upon our farmers, our workers, and legitimate business." But Hoover's initial response was to join Charles E. Mitchell, Thomas Lamont, John D. Rockefeller, and other business leaders in reassuring the country. On October 25 Hoover informed the press, "The fundamental business of the country, that is, production and distribution, is on a sound a prosperous basis." In his memoirs Hoover would attribute his reluctance to propose direct action concerning the securities markets to a deep split among his advisers. Secretary of the Treasury Mellon and others advocated the traditional *laissez-faire* formula: let the slump liquidate itself. Even a panic was not, in Mellon's view, altogether a bad thing. "It will," Hoover recalled the Secretary explain, "purge the rottenness out of the system. High costs of living and high living will come down. People will work harder, live a more moral life. Values will be adjusted and enterprising people will pick up the wreck from less competent people." What gave Mellon's argument particular force was Hoover's awareness that it reflected the beliefs of many Republicans. Hardhearted as Hoover may have found the Treasury Secretary's advice, he was well aware of the political risk of attacking the financiers who were the bulwark of his party.

There were additional reasons for Hoover to urge volunteerism. For most of the next three years, he remained convinced that there was "doubtful constitutional authority . . . [for] federal regulation of the sale of securities," and that, in any event, "the primary responsibility for initiation of official action lay on Governor Franklin Roosevelt of New York."[4]

The Democratic minority in Congress did not share Hoover's reluctance either to criticize the financial community or to propose regulation of the securities markets. Having seen the Republicans prevail in 1928 by claiming responsibility for "general prosperity," Democratic Party spokesmen claimed that the incumbent administration was equally responsible for the market collapse. On November 1, 1929, Senator Joseph T. Robinson, the Democrat's minority leader, issued a statement to the press:

> If the foundation of the belief of ruined investors was faith in the strong position of American industry, it is also true that the prophets and high priests of American prosperity, represented

> by no less personalities than a former President of the United States, the Secretary of the Treasury, and the former Secretary of Commerce, now President, contributed, by unduly and repeated optimistic statements, to the creation of enthusiastic, if not frenzied adventures in stocks.

Within ten weeks of the October stock market crash, six Members of Congress introduced bills to regulate corporate financial statements, margin loans, or short sales of securities.[5]

The Democratic Party's criticisms were soon muted. In December 1929, and the first four months of 1930, the stock market experienced a sustained advance, recovering by April 1930 about one half of what had been lost in October and November of 1929.[6]

Hoover claimed that the "systematic, voluntary measures of cooperation with business" he instituted "have re-established confidence." At first, Hoover's tone was tentative. In his December 1929 State of the Union address, he suggested that it might, nonetheless, be desirable for Congress to "consider the revision of some portions of the banking law." But as "the Little Bull Market" galloped on, Hoover became more emphatic. In mid-February, he indicated to the press that the preliminary shock of the collapse had abated. By March he was predicting that the worst effects of the crash on unemployment would be over within 60 days. Addressing the United States Chamber of Commerce on May 1, Hoover engaged in what he termed "some moderate optimism," stating, "We are not through the difficulties of our situation [but] I am convinced we have passed the worst and with continued effort we shall rapidly recover." On May 28, Hoover was reported to have said that he believed business conditions would be normal by fall.

These were Hoover's most often quoted statements on the stock market crash and the economic depression. Not only did they give rise to the erroneous belief that Hoover said, "Prosperity is just around the corner," they tightened the public's association between Hoover's policies and responsibility for the economy's health.[7]

This time the reaction of the Democrats in Congress was a serious threat to Hoover. Congressional elections were only four months away. The flurry of bills introduced were not just the hastily drawn creations of relatively obscure junior members.[8]

Leading the critics was the Senator whose voice mattered most on financial issues, Virginia's Carter Glass. A lifelong conservative, Glass generally opposed "centralized" federal power. But the Senator's conservatism permitted one consistent exception. By the time of the Crash, Senator Glass had built his career around application of federal controls against the New York City "money crowd."

In June 1930, Glass attacked Republican financial policies. The assault was important not just because of the Senator's reputation. Glass was the first national politician effectively to move beyond the vague charge that Hoover's excessive optimism had contributed to the Crash to an enumeration of some of the causes of the debacle. Glass introduced a banking bill "to prevent the undue diversion of funds into speculative operations."[9]

However, the Senator's more publicized challenge concerned foreign bonds. Under President Harding, the State Department had adopted a procedure requiring American banks to clear loans to foreign countries with the Department. The bankers soon found it to their advantage to do so. After receiving State Department clearance, the banks could advertise the Department's approval when selling foreign bonds in the United States. On June 16, Glass secured Senate endorsement of a resolution requesting "the Secretary of the Senate . . . to inform the Senate upon what authorization of law . . . does the State Department base its right either to approve or disapprove investment securities offered for sale in the money markets of the United States." Glass had known about the procedure for close to three years. But now, with newspapers regularly reporting foreign bonds near default, he firmly reiterated his protest "against another dangerous centralization of power in the Federal Government, and particularly against usurpation of a power with which the Executive Government is not legally clothed, and which, exercised without responsibility . . . may easily be frightfully prostituted in various ways."

Secretary of State Henry L. Stimson attempted to mollify Glass by characterizing the procedure as an "informal scrutiny" permissible because of the "voluntary cooperation of American investment bankers" and the President's Constitutional authority respecting foreign affairs. Glass immediately labeled Stimson's contention that the State Department did not approve loans "an affront to the intelligence" of the Senate, and secured passage of a second resolution advising the Department to "desist from the dangerous practice of involving the United States government in any responsibility of whatever nature, either by approval or disapproval, for foreign investment loans floated in this country."[10]

As the 1930 Congressional elections neared, Hoover felt a growing sense of exasperation. The market continued to fall; his earlier optimistic predictions about business conditions were being quoted by Democratic Congressional candidates with withering irony. Soon after the market declined in October 1930, the White House confirmed that President Hoover had entertained New York Stock Exchange President Richard Whitney at a "secret" dinner on October 12. According to the White House, the two had been consulting on methods to curb "bear raids" for some time.

Hoover's belated effort "to do something" about the securities market had no appreciable effect on the 1930 election. For the first time since 1919, the Democrats won control of the House and came within one vote of controlling the Senate. By the time the 72nd Congress officially convened 13 months later, in December 1931, Hoover's "voluntary" approach to the securities markets was no longer credible.

But the President continued to side with the faction within his Administration that advocated Mellon's *laissez-faire* approach. Bitterly, Hoover would recall in his memoirs his statement to Whitney "that I preferred to let American institutions and the states govern themselves, and that the Exchange had full power under its charter to control its own members and to prevent it from being used for manipulation against the public interest. Mr. Whitney made profuse promises, but did nothing." In fact, the NYSE did call for daily reports on short sales in May 1931, after a number of newspaper accounts "reported" that bear raiders were selling short to depress the market. For a few days after the Bank of England suspended gold payments, in September 1931, the NYSE banned short sales altogether. But the ban was soon lifted. And on October 16, 1931, in a nationally broadcast address from Hartford, Connecticut, Whitney insisted that short selling was "essential to an open market for securities."

Whitney's Hartford address fed a vengeful mood in Congress. In the first three days of the 72nd Congress alone, ten separate bills to regulate securities markets were introduced. Most of these bills were intended to regulate short selling. Senator Arthur Capper introduced two bills, one of which would have imposed a 25 percent tax on all short sale profits, the second of which declared that "short sales . . . exert a vicious influence and produce abnormal and disturbing declines of prices that are not responsive to actual supply and demand." Not to be out done, Senator Smith W. Brookhart proposed a bill to imprison each investor who sold stock short.[11]

More significant to Hoover than the number of bills introduced was the growing impatience of the Republicans in Congress. Two months before the session convened, Senator James E. Watson, the Republican floor leader, publicly warned the President that a resolution to investigate the stock markets was all but certain to be adopted in the Senate. Hoover made no public response. When Congress convened, the Progressive Republicans — acknowledged by Hoover to hold the balance of power in the Senate — led the clamor for securities law reform. Early in the Session, Hiram Johnson sought approval for a Finance Committee investigation of foreign bonds. The aging Progressive was a long-time foe of both Herbert Hoover and international bankers, but his determination personally to supervise an examination of "the terms and conditions" of all foreign debt securities sold in the United States was a striking illustration of the new political climate. Within a day the Senate approved Johnson's enabling resolution. Hearings began on December 18.

For 15 hearing days, Johnson led the Finance Committee's investigation. Told was a story he would later characterize as "at once grotesque and tragic." Between 1923 and 1930 American investors had purchased close to $6.3 billion of foreign bonds. This equaled approximately 10 percent of new securities sales in the United States during those years. Then, in rapid order, the collapse of the world economy had led to substantial depreciation in over 90 percent of all foreign bonds sold in the United States. By December 1931, the aggregate market price for 14 Latin American nations' bonds was 26 percent of their face value. Peruvian bonds were selling at less than 7 percent of their par value.

Johnson's Hearings focused on the role of the American investment banks that distributed these securities. By the late 1920s, investment banks issuing foreign bonds were earning commissions as high as 14 percent. These commission rates, unusually high for bonds, prompted an intense competition among the investment banks. Reversing the historic rule that the borrowing nation contact the underwriting house, by the late 1920s as many as 20 investment banks were sending representatives to a South American capital to solicit the opportunity to make a loan. On occasion, the bankers' methods were less than scrupulous. The J. & W. Seligman firm, not related to the author, paid the son of the President of Peru $415,000 for his aid in securing for it the right to sell Peruvian bonds.

What particularly outraged Senator Johnson, as it had earlier galled Carter Glass, was the role of the United States government in foreign bond sales. In spite of Senator Glass's resolution, the State Department continued to clear foreign bonds. Pressed hard by Senators Johnson and Edward P. Costigan, Assistant Secretary of State Francis White conceded that the Department's practice in many cases led the public to assume that "the security is ample and the investment is a good one," even though the Department would not object to a loan if it knew the loan "was absolutely rotten."[12]

Early in February 1932, Andrew Mellon resigned as Secretary of the Treasury and left for London to become Ambassador to the Court of St. James. This was a clear signal that Hoover's ambivalence toward federal regulatory programs as distinguished from the subsidy programs, such as the Reconstruction Finance Corporation, was being resolved in favor of intervention. Mellon had a much derided formula to describe his *laissez-faire* approach: "Liquidate labor, liquidate stocks, liquidate the farmers, liquidate real estate."[13]

In January 1932, Hoover met with directors of the New York Stock Exchange (*NYSE* or *Exchange*). This time no "pleasant dinner" was reported. Hoover demanded that the Exchange take immediate action against pool operators and bear raiders. He offered Whitney "curative amendments" that had been formulated by "responsible members of the Exchange." With evident disgust the former President later would recall, "the directors repeatedly promised they would adopt these amendments, but made only minor changes." On February 16, Hoover again met with Whitney. The President was uncharacteristically blunt. Unless the New York Stock Exchange effected substantial reforms, Hoover would ask Congress to investigate the Exchange "with a view to federal control legislation."[14]

The following day the Stock Exchange adopted a new rule requiring brokers to secure written permission from clients before lending their shares to short sellers. Although a few brokers predicted that the new rule might reduce short sales by as much as 50 percent, most commentators in Congress and the financial press disagreed.

Business Week labeled the rule a "grandiose gesture" by the Exchange to satisfy the President and thwart Congressional action. The rule's endurance, suggested the magazine, "will depend upon the political need for a burnt offering." *Wall Street Journal* columnist Thomas Woodlock questioned whether it would have much effect even if it did last. Richard Whitney, testifying at House Judiciary Committee hearings on short selling, on February 24, all but implied that the rule was meaningless: "I do not believe in the last analysis that it will prevent stocks being available for loaning purposes."[15]

Hoover's patience wore out. At a press conference on February 19, Hoover sharply warned "the managers of the Exchange that they should take adequate measures to protect investors from artificial depression of the price of securities for speculative profit. Individuals who use facilities of the Exchange for such purposes are not contributing to recovery of the United States." When "the managers of the Exchange" did not respond, Hoover summoned Frederick Walcott and Peter Norbeck, Republican members of the Senate Banking Committee, to a highly publicized meeting at the White House. Walcott, a former investment banker, had served as Hoover's assistant in the U.S. Food Administration during World War I and was one of Hoover's closest personal friends, besides being an ally in Congress. During the meeting, Hoover repeated rumors he had received concerning "vicious pools . . . in which corporation and even bank directors were manipulating their own stocks." He asked Walcott to take charge of an investigation of stock exchange practices.

Although Hoover insisted in his memoirs that he meant the investigation to be undertaken "with a view to legislation," this is doubtful. The beleaguered President still believed federal control of the stock exchange might be unconstitutional. In several public statements, Senator Walcott emphasized that the purpose of the hearing should be to call "some of the outstanding bear raiders" to testify and then the Hearings should then adjourn. It may be reasonably inferred that Hoover wanted to pressure Whitney to adopt effective stock exchange reforms and to demonstrate to voters early in an election year that leading Democrats like National Party Chair John J. Raskob and Bernard Baruch had contributed to the recent share price decline.[16]

The Banking Crisis

Concomitant with the Stock Market Crash of 1929–1933 was a Banking Crisis first evident in 1930, a year in which 1300 banks failed including the Bank of the United States, a private bank quite different than the embryonic Central Banks of the 19th century. The Bank of the United States had 400,000 depositors and $286 million in deposits. Milton Friedman and Anna Jacobson Schwartz in *A Monetary History of the United States, 1857–1960* characterized the December 1930 failure of the Bank of the United States as "of special significance":

> The Bank of the United States was the largest commercial bank, as measured by volume of deposits, ever to have failed up to that time in U.S. history. Moreover, though an ordinary commercial bank, its name had led many at home and abroad to regard it somehow as an official bank, hence its failure constituted more of a blow to confidence than would have been administered by the fall of a bank with a less distinctive name. In addition, it was a member of the Federal Reserve System. The withdrawal of support by the Clearing House banks from the concerted measures sponsored by the Federal Reserve Bank of New York to save the bank — measures of a kind the banking community had often taken in similar circumstances in the past — was a serious blow to the System's prestige.

The initial phase of the Banking Crisis did not last long. Bank failures declined sharply in early 1931, but as with the Stock Market Crash and its Little Bull Market, this provided little sustained relief. In all, 2000 banks would fail by the end of 1931. "By 1932," business historian Jerry Markham found, "one in four banks in the United States had failed."

What Friedman and Schwartz labeled "the second banking crisis of 1931" had "far more severe effects on the stock of money than the first":

> In the six months from February to August 1931, commercial bank deposits fell by $2.7 billion or nearly 7 per cent, more than in the whole eighteen-month period from the cyclical peak in August 1929 to February 1931. In the seven months from February to September 1931, commercial bank deposits fell by 9 per cent, one percentage point more than the maximum decline in deposits during the whole of the 1920–21 contraction.

A burgeoning global economic crisis amplified the domestic Banking Crisis. On May 8, 1931, Austria's largest bank, the Creditanstalt, with 50 percent of Austria's bank deposits, suffered a loss of $20 million in its 1930 accounts, depleting most of its equity. In 1933, Creditanstalt would be liquidated with aggregate losses by then of $150 million. The failure of Creditanstalt precipitated a run on gold reserves in Germany, which lost half its gold reserves in the first three weeks of June 1931. During the Summer of 1931, with Germany unable to fully repay scheduled reparations, its banking system collapsed. By early 1932, German production was running at 60 percent of 1928 levels. One-third of the workforce was unemployed. Political discontent escalated leading to the January 1933 appointment of Adolf Hitler as Chancellor.

On September 21, 1931, Britain abandoned the gold standard after a run on its standing currency precipitated by France and the Netherlands. Twenty-five other nations abandoned the gold standard within a year. To attempt to withstand the need to do so, several nations, led by France, Belgium, Switzerland, Sweden, and the Netherlands, initially converted their Dollar assets into gold. Between September 16 and October 28, United States gold reserves declined by $725 million, adding an external pressure on United States bank gold reserves.

In August and September, 1931, United States banks with deposits of $414 million, approximately 1 percent of the total of commercial bank deposits, closed their doors. The outflow of gold in September accelerated pressure on bank reserves. "Currency," Friedman and Schwartz explained, "was being withdrawn internally by depositors justifiably fearful for the safety of banks and gold was being withdrawn externally by foreigners fearful for the maintenance of the gold standard."

To stem the external drain on gold, the Federal Reserve System increased its rediscount rate from 2½ to 3½ percent, the sharpest rise within so brief a period in the history of the Federal Reserve System. This abrupt policy change had rapid consequences. In October 1931, 522 commercial banks with $471 million of deposits closed. During the next three months, another 875 banks did so. "All told in the six months from August 1931 to January 1932," Friedman and Schwartz wrote, "1860 banks with deposits of $1449 million suspended operations, and the deposits of those banks that managed to keep afloat fell by a much larger sum," that Friedman and

Schwartz estimated *in toto* to be five times the deposits in suspended banks or "no less than 17 percent of the initial levels of deposits in operating banks."

As the Banking Crisis continued, the Fed only reluctantly in April 1932 made a large scale $1 billion open market purchase to increase its reserves. The effect of this purchase again was temporary. Over 4000 banks failed in 1933, bringing the total to 9000 banks that failed between 1930 and 1933, with total losses of about $2.5 billion. Between 1929 and 1933, the rate of operating banks that failed more than doubled from 5.6 to 12.9 percent. Between December 31, 1929 and the end of February 1933, 5500 banks, more than one bank in every five, suspended operations, with deposit liabilities of approximately $5.5 billion. In the years 1930 to 1932, the reported volume of total loans and investments by Federal Reserve Member Banks declined by nearly $8.5 billion. The total stock of money fell by $18 billion between 1929 and 1933, over 42 percent. Bank failures were important not only because of the losses imposed on bank stockholders, depositors, and creditors, but also because they contributed to a substantial decline in money being circulated.[17]

President Hoover supported limited steps to address the Banking Crisis. In October 1931, Hoover had persuaded a reluctant banking community to create the National Credit Corporation, a private association to extend loans to individual banks against collateral not ordinarily acceptable. By December 1931, the Corporation had lent less than $10 million. At the end of January 1932, the National Credit Corporation had lent a total of $155 million to 575 banks. The Corporation soon died. Hoover wrote: "It had not exerted anything like its full possible strength. Its members — and the business world — threw up their hands and asked for government action."

Hoover then focused his support on the Reconstruction Finance Corporation (*RFC*), created by Congress on January 22, 1932, with an initial authorization to have capital stock of $500 million subscribed by the United States from funds in the Department of Treasury. The RFC was modeled on the earlier War Finance Corporation and authorized to extend loans to all financial institutions in the United States, including state chartered banks that were not members of the Federal Reserve System as long as the RFC deemed the loans amply secured. Management of the RFC was vested in a Board of Directors consisting of the Secretary of the Treasury, the Governor of the Federal Reserve Board, and the Farm Loan Commissioner and four other persons appointed by the President with the advice and consent of the Senate. The RFC could have up to three times its subscribed capital or $1.5 billion by issuing debt securities. In the period of February 2, 1932, to March 4, 1933, the RFC lent $951,440,497 to banks and trust companies.

In February 1932, Congress enacted An Act to Improve the Facilities of the Federal Reserve System, initially called the Glass-Steagall Act before the name was appropriated by the more far-reaching Banking Act of 1933, which authorized the 12 Federal Reserve banks upon receiving consent of no less than five members of the Federal Reserve Board to broaden eligible collateral for groups of at least five member banks and banks with at least $5 million in assets borrowing from the Federal Reserve Board. The release of funds on these terms was small.

A separate Emergency Relief and Construction Act of July 21, 1932, permitted the Federal Reserve banks to discount to individuals, partnerships, and corporations that had no source of funds eligible for discount by member banks. Discounts under this little used provision reached a maximum of $1.4 million in March 1933. The 1932 Emergency Relief and Construction Act commendably had as its primary purpose the provision of $300 million to relieve destitution.[18]

Collectively, these efforts by Hoover and Congress in 1931 and 1932 were too little, too late. By the time of Roosevelt's Inauguration on March 4, 1933, the economy had collapsed. The Great Depression had begun. Unemployment had been approximately 3 percent of the labor force during the summer of 1929. By 1933, nearly 13 million people were out of work, approximately 25 percent of the labor force.

The gross national product which had been $103.1 billion in 1929 was cut nearly in half to $55.6 billion in 1933, a decline of 46 percent. Total national wealth similarly had declined 25 percent, from $439.4 billion in 1929 to $330.5 billion in 1933. New private and public construction fell more precipitously, from $10.8 billion in 1929 to $2.9 billion, a shrinkage of 79 percent. National income shrank by 52 percent between 1929 and 1932, from $87.4 billion to $41.7 billion. New corporate offerings shrank from almost $6.8 billion in 1929 to less than $400 million in 1933.[19]

In 1932 Democratic Party platform focused on what it termed "the disastrous policies" pursued by Republican Administrations since 1920:

> In this time of unprecedent economic and social distress the Democratic Party declares its conviction that the chief causes of this condition were the disastrous policies pursued by our government since the World War, of economic isolation, fostering the merger of competitive businesses into monopolies and encouraging the indefensible expansion and contraction of credit for private profit at the expense of the public.

In the realm of financial regulation, the platform stated:

> We advocate protection of the investing public by requiring to be filed with the government and carried in advertisements of all offerings of foreign and domestic stocks and bonds true information as to bonuses, commissions, principal invested, and interests of the sellers.
>
> Regulation to the full extent of federal power, of:
>
> (a) Holding companies which sell securities in interstate commerce;
> (b) Rates of utilities companies operating across state lines;
> (c) Exchanges in securities and commodities.
>
> We advocate . . . a more rigid supervision of national banks for the protection of depositors and the prevention of the use of their moneys in speculation to the detriment of local credits.
>
> The severance of affiliated security companies from, and the divorce of the investment banking business from, commercial banks, and further restriction of federal reserve banks in permitting the use of federal reserve facilities for speculative purposes.

Franklin Roosevelt, the Democratic Party nominee for President, endorsed the Party platform "100 percent." He framed his campaign primarily in economic terms: "[I]t is inevitable that the main issue of this campaign should resolve about the clear fact of our economic condition, a depression so deep that it is without precedent in modern history."

Roosevelt's acceptance speech would best be remembered for his peroration: "I pledge you, I pledge myself to a new deal for the American people," but Roosevelt emphasized:

> . . . I list an important place for that prize statement of principle in the platform here adopted calling for the letting in of the light of day on issues of securities, foreign and domestic, which are offered for sale to the investing public.
>
> My friends, you and I as common-sense citizens know that it would help to protect the savings of the country from the dishonesty of crooks and from the lack of honor of some men in high financial places. Publicity is the enemy of crookedness.

Seven weeks later on August 20, 1932, in a key campaign address in Columbus, Ohio, Roosevelt charged Hoover with responsibility for "encouraging a vast speculative boom." "Much of our troubles," claimed Roosevelt, "came from what [Hoover] described as a 'new basis in government relation with business' . . . The administration lined up with the stock market." When the market broke, Hoover's Administration "attempted to minimize the crash . . . it erroneously charged the cause to other Nations . . . it delayed relief; it forgot reform." For his part, Roosevelt pledged himself to a comprehensive program of securities law reform. "First . . . to inspire truth telling, I propose that every effort be made to prevent the issue of manufactured and unnecessary securities of all kinds which are brought out merely for the purpose of enriching those who handled their sale to the public." Second, he proposed federal regulation of securities exchanges and holding companies that sell securities in interstate commerce. Third, he urged the complete divorce of investment and commercial banking. And finally, Roosevelt recommended prevention of Federal Reserve funds from being used for speculative enterprises. Periodically throughout the campaign, Roosevelt returned to the issue of securities law reform, scorning "the reckless promoter, the Ishmael or Insull whose hand is against every man's." A centerpiece of his address on public utilities was the call for "full publicity" in securities sales. Repeatedly, Roosevelt admonished, "Let in the light!"

The 1932 Elections were a landslide for Roosevelt and the Democrats. Roosevelt won the popular vote by a 56.9 to 39.7 percent and the electoral college by 472 to 59 votes, sweeping all but six states from Hoover.

In 1928, the Republicans had mastery of the Senate by a 53 to 39 majority. The Democrats had narrowed the Republic majority to 50 to 45 in 1930 before sweeping to a 59 to 36 dominance in the Senate in 1932.

In 1928, the Republicans had held a 270–164 seat majority in the House of Representatives. In 1930, the Democrats had almost secured control of the House with 216 of the 218 seats necessary. In 1932, the Democrats added 97 seats to achieve a 313 to 117 seat Majority.

Roosevelt had a mandate for decisive action. He began his Inaugural Address echoing Biblical themes to respond to a state of near paralytic terror that gripped the nation:

> . . . [L]et me assert my firm belief that the only thing we have to fear is fear itself—nameless, unreasoning, unjustified terror which paralyzes needed efforts to convert retreat into advance. . . .
>
> . . . Values have shrunken to fantastic levels; taxes have risen; our ability to pay has fallen; government of all kinds is faced by serious curtailment of income; the means of exchange are frozen in the currents of trade; the withered leaves of industrial enterprise lie on every side; farmers find no markets for their produce; the savings of many years in thousands of families are gone.
>
> More important, a host of unemployed citizens face the grim problem of existence, and an equally great number toil with little return. Only a foolish optimist can deny the dark realities of the moment.
>
> Yet our distress comes from no failure of substance. We are stricken by no plague of locusts. Compared with the perils which our forefathers conquered because they believed and were not afraid, we have still much to be thankful for. Nature still offers her bounty and human efforts have multiplied it. Plenty is at our doorstep, but a generous use of it languishes in the very sight of the supply. Primarily this is because the rulers of the exchange of mankind's goods have failed, through their own stubbornness and their own incompetence, have admitted their failure, and abdicated. Practices of the unscrupulous money changers stand indicted in the court of public opinion, rejected by the hearts and minds of men.
>
> True, they have tried, but their efforts have been cast in the pattern of an outworn tradition. . . . They know only the rules of a generation of self-seekers. They have no vision, and when there is no vision the people perish.
>
> The money changers have fled from their high seats in the temple of our civilization. We may now restore that temple to the ancient truths. The measure of the restoration lies in

> the extent to which we apply social values more noble than mere monetary profit.

His major policy point was stated plainly: "This Nation asks for action, and action now." He tersely hinted at the legislative program that would become the hallmark of the First 100 Days:

> Our greatest primary task is to put people to work. This is no unsolvable problem if we face it wisely and courageously. It can be accomplished in part by direct recruiting by the Government itself, treating the task as we would treat the emergency of a war, but at the same time, through this employment, accomplishing greatly needed projects to stimulate and reorganize the use of our natural resources.
>
> . . . We must act and act quickly.
>
> . . . [I]n our progress toward a resumption of work we required two safeguards against a return of the evils of the old order; there must be a strict supervision of all banking and credits and investments; there must be an end to speculation with other people's money; and there must be provision for an adequate but sound currency.

At a time when many were questioning whether the United States Constitution and American capitalism could survive, Roosevelt reaffirmed his commitment to the United States Constitution, "the most superbly enduring political mechanism the modern world had produced," stating, however, that if it was necessary, he would ask Congress for a "temporary departure from the normal balance of public procedure," by which he meant "broad executive power to wage a war against the emergency, as great as that would be given to [the President] if we were in fact invaded by a foreign foe."

Roosevelt fervently rejected calls for revolution or actions comparable to those occurring in Stalin's Soviet Union, Mussolini's Italy, or starting in Hitler's Germany: "We do not distrust the future of essential democracy. The people of the United States have not failed. In their need they have registered a mandate that they want direct, vigorous action. They have asked for discipline and direction under leadership. They have made me the present instrument of their wishes. In the spirit of the gift, I take it."[20]

Thirty-six hours after taking the oath of office, Roosevelt issued Proclamation 2039, declaring a bank holiday from March 6 to March 9. All banking transactions were suspended for all Federal

Reserve banks, national banks, trust companies, savings and loan companies, credit unions and other business enterprises operating in any form of the banking business. At the same time, Roosevelt called a Special Session of Congress to meet on March 9 to enact emergency legislation to reopen the banks.

Roosevelt had little choice. In November 1932, Nevada had declared a 12-day bank holiday, meaning banks were closed, after the suspension of a bank chain that held 65 percent of the state's deposits. Bank holidays occurred in Iowa in January and Louisiana in early February. When the Reconstruction Finance Corporation declined to lend money to Guardian Trust Company of Detroit, owned by Edsel Ford, a statewide run on the banking system began. On February 14, 1933, the Governor of Michigan, by Proclamation, closed all of the state's 550 banks for eight days. Indiana closed its banks on February 23rd; Maryland, on the 25th; Arkansas, on the 27th; Ohio, on the 28th. A third of all United States currency was withdrawn from banks in February and early March.

By March 1, 1933, an international currency panic had reduced the New York Federal Reserve Bank's gold reserve below the 40 percent statutory requirement. On Friday, March 3rd, $350 million was withdrawn from the Federal Reserve Bank of New York. That day, the New York Federal Reserve Bank adopted a Resolution urging that the Federal Reserve Board request President Hoover proclaim a nationwide bank holiday.

At 2:30 a.m. on March 4th, New York Governor Lehman declared a three-day banking holiday. At 3:30 a.m., Illinois followed New York's lead and declared its own bank holiday. By the time of Roosevelt's inauguration on March 4th, the bank systems in 28 states were completely closed and in the remaining 20 states, partially closed.

On March 9, Roosevelt presented to Congress Public Law No. 1, the Emergency Banking Act. Roosevelt's Message to Congress could not "too strongly urge upon Congress the clear necessity for immediate action. A continuation of the strangulation of banking facilities is unthinkable."

In the mood of panic, Congress responded with virtually unprecedented celerity. Only one copy of the proposed legislation was available in the House of Representatives after it convened at noon on March 9, 1933. House Banking and Currency Committee Chair Henry Steagall read the text aloud. The House adopted the emergency bill unanimously on a voice vote shortly after 4:00 p.m. The

Senate shortly later proceeded to debate the House bill. Just before 7:30 p.m., the Senate passed the Emergency Banking Bill by a vote of 73 to 7. One hour later, it was in the White House. The entire process took fewer than eight hours.

The Emergency Banking Act had three primary objectives.

First, initially on an emergency basis, the Act transformed the United States currency system, requiring any and all individuals, partnerships, associations, and corporations to deliver their gold coin, gold bullion, or gold certificates to the Treasury and accept an equivalent amount in coin or currency issued under the laws of the United States. A separate provision of the Act substituted for the nation's gold backed currency, new circulating notes equal to the face value of the direct obligations of the United States. When the new notes were issued against the security of the notes, drafts, bills of exchange, and bankers' acceptances, the Treasury would provide up to 90 percent of their estimated value. "Such notes shall be . . . receivable . . . in all parts of the United States for the same purposes as are national bank notes, and shall be redeemable in lawful money of the United States on presentation at the United States Treasury or at the bank of issue."

Roosevelt on March 9 characterized the additional currency as being "adequately secured . . . to meet all demands for currency and at the same time to achieve this end without increasing the unsecured indebtedness of the government of the United States."

On March 10, Roosevelt issued an Executive Order prohibiting the export of gold except in accordance with regulations issued by the Secretary of Treasury.

By Joint Resolution on June 5, the Senate and House affirmed Roosevelt's Executive Order and provided:

> [E]very provision contained in or made with respect to any obligation which purports to give the oblige a right to require payment in gold or a particular kind of coin or currency, or in an amount in money of the United States measured thereby, is declared to be against public policy; and no such provision shall be contained in or made with respect to any obligations hereafter incurred. Every obligation, heretofore or hereafter incurred, whether or not any such provision is contained therein or made with respect thereto, shall be discharged upon payment, dollar for dollar, in any coin or currency which at the time of payment is legal tender for public and private debts.

The Joint Resolution added: "All coin and currencies of the United States (including Federal Reserve notes and circulating notes of Federal Reserve banks and national banking associations) heretofore or hereafter coined or issued, shall be legal tender for all debts, public and private, public charges, taxes, duties, and dues."

The June 5 legislation abrogated the gold clauses found in many contracts requiring payment in gold, an abrogation affirmed by a 5-4 majority of the United States Supreme Court in 1935 in *Norman v. Baltimore & Ohio Railroad*. The majority decision characterized gold clauses in private contracts as "an attempted frustration" of the Constitutional powers of Congress over the monetary system of the country.

The purpose of the requirement that gold be returned to the Treasury was to end hoarding and restore currency to banks for circulation. During the ensuing months, this purpose coincided with a broader Congressional and New Deal initiatives to devalue the dollar to support commodity prices.

On May 12, 1933, Congress enacted the Agriculture Adjustment Act. Title III of the Act, popularly known as the Thomas Amendment, after its sponsor Oklahoma Senator Elmer Thomas, gave the President discretion to purchase up to $3 billion in Treasury and other obligations of the United States government, to issue up to $3 billion in United States notes, under the authority of the 1862 Act that had originally created greenbacks solely for the purpose of meeting maturing federal obligations, to repay United States loans, bonds and other interest-bearing obligations of the United States, and most consequentially to fix the weight, meaning the dollar value, of gold as a standard unit of value for all forms of money issued or coined by the United States with the President expressly empowered to reduce the value of gold by no more than 50 percent. At that time, the legal price of gold was $20.67 per ounce.

After a controversial period of variable prices for gold, including three months during which Roosevelt, in effect, managed the world's gold price, Roosevelt supported the Gold Reserve Act of 1934, enacted on January 30, which prohibited private ownership of gold and bullion by individuals or business entities, "[e]xcept to the extent permitted in regulations issued by the Secretary of the Treasury, with the approval of the President, no currency of the United States shall be redeemed in gold," transferred all gold then held by the Federal Reserve to the Treasury, and empowered the President to devalue gold by up to 40 percent.

On January 31, 1934, Roosevelt issued Proclamation No. 2072 effectively fixing the value of dollars as convertible to gold at $35 per ounce, the full 40 percent permitted by the Act, where it remained until 1971 when President Nixon definitively closed the gold window.

After February 1, 1934, the United States returned to a gold standard, but in a limited way. The Treasury subsequently bought all gold offered to it at $35 per ounce, but only sold gold for the purpose of foreign payment. Effectively, United States reliance on gold-backed currency ended in 1933. As Professor and author John Wood put it: "The gold standard . . . was irrelevant to policy after 1933. A constraint that has been relaxed, and is expected to be relaxed when it threatens to bind, is not a constraint. The legal gold requirements on Federal Reserve deposits and notes were terminated in the 1960s."

The second paramount objective of the Emergency Banking Act was "to reopen all sound banks." In his March 9th Message to Congress, Roosevelt stressed:

> In order that . . . the opening of banks for the resumption of business may be accomplished, I ask of the Congress the immediate enactment of legislation giving to the Executive branch of the Government control over banks for the protection of depositors; authority forthwith to open such banks as have already been ascertained to be in sound condition and other such banks as rapidly as possible; and authority to reorganize and reopen such banks as may be found to require reorganization to put them on a sound basis.

The Emergency Banking Act achieved bank reopening through several means. Congress approved and affirmed "all actions, regulations, rules, licenses, orders and proclamations heretofore or hereafter taken, promulgated, made or issued by the President of the United States or the Secretary of the Treasury since March 4."

The Act empowered the President during this "period of national emergency" to investigate, regulate or prohibit "any transactions in foreign exchange, transfers of credit between or payments by banking institutions as defined by the President and export, hoarding, melting or earmarking of gold by any person within the United States."

The Emergency Bank Act further provided:

> In order to provide for the safer and more effective operation of the National Banking System and the Federal Reserve System, to preserve for the people the full benefits of the currency provided for by the Congress through the National Banking System and the Federal Reserve System, and to relieve interstate commerce of the burdens and obstructions resulting from the receipt on an unsound or unsafe basis of deposits subject to withdrawal by check, during such emergency period as the President of the United States by proclamation may prescribe, no member bank of the Federal Reserve System shall transact any banking business except to such extent and subject to such regulations, limitations and restrictions as may be prescribed by the Secretary of the Treasury, with the approval of the President.

Collectively, these powers gave the President near total control over the national banking system. Roosevelt and his Secretary of Treasury, William Woodin, rapidly employed these powers.

After enactment of the Emergency Banking Act, Roosevelt issued a proclamation indefinitely extending the bank holiday.

On March 10th, by Executive Order, Roosevelt empowered the Secretary of the Treasury with the power to license Federal Reserve banks found to be in satisfactory conduct to conduct usual banking business.

On March 11th, Roosevelt announced:

> [A] definite program has been arranged consisting of successive steps by which banks throughout the country will be opened progressively on Monday, Tuesday, and Wednesday mornings.
>
> The Secretary of the Treasury will issue licenses to banks which are members of the Federal Reserve System, whether national bank or State, located in each of the twelve Federal Reserve Bank cities, to open Monday morning [March 13].
>
> So also the State authorities having supervision over State banks which are not members of the Federal Reserve System will be asked to permit any such State institutions located in any one of the twelve Federal Reserve Bank cities to open for business on Monday morning if in their judgment they deem it wise to do so.
>
> Under this progressive plan, banks located in any city having an active, recognized clearing house association, of which there are 250 cities, will receive licenses for reopening on Tuesday

> morning, and banks located elsewhere will receive their licenses permitting reopening for Wednesday.

Roosevelt explained later with respect to banks in smaller places: "On Wednesday and succeeding days, banks in smaller places all through the country will resume business, subject of course, to the Government's physical ability to complete its survey."

Roosevelt's powers to close or license banks were amplified by powers in the Emergency Act to fund banking operations of the Federal Reserve and national banks.

National banks were authorized to issue preferred stock "in such amounts and with such par value as shall be approved by the Comptroller" with the then potentially high interest rate "not exceeding six per centum" per year. Critically, the Act provided:

> If in the opinion of the Secretary of the Treasury any national banking association or any State bank or trust company is in need of funds for capital purposes either in connection with the organization or reorganization of such association, State bank or trust company or otherwise, he may, with the approval of the President, request the Reconstruction Finance Corporation to subscribe for preferred stock in such association, State bank or trust company, or to make loans secured by such stock as collateral, and the Reconstruction Finance Corporation may comply with such request.

Any Federal Reserve bank could "in exceptional and exigent circumstances and when any member bank has no further eligible and acceptable assets" was empowered to "make advances to such member bank on its time or demand notes secured to the satisfaction of such Federal Reserve Bank." The Act permitted the 12 Federal Reserve banks to provide loans for up to 90 days "to any individual, partnership, or corporation" or promissory notes "secured by direct obligations of the United States."

The Secretary of the Treasury issued a Statement on March 11 explaining:

> By amendments to the Federal reserve act it is made possible for Federal reserve banks to make loans direct to corporations, firms and individuals on their notes secured by direct obligations of the United States Government. There are approximately $11,000,000,000 of such securities outstanding with the public other than with banking institutions. In order to enable

> the reopened banks to secure currency sufficient to meet demands, Federal reserve banks are authorized to lend to any member bank, regardless of its size, on sound assets. To provide adequate Federal reserve bank currency to satisfy the possible demands under this program, Federal reserve banks are authorized to issue Federal reserve bank notes, not only against Government securities, but also against any member bank note secured by sound assets.

Unlike other Federal Reserve notes, no reserve was required to be held against these notes.

In a separate telegram dated March 11, 1933, to New York Federal Reserve Governor George Harrison, Roosevelt promised to protect the Federal Reserve banks against losses:

> It is inevitable that some losses may be made by the Federal Reserve banks in loans to their member banks. The country appreciates, however, that the 12 regional Federal Reserve banks are operating entirely under Federal Law and the recent Emergency Bank Act greatly enlarges their powers to adapt their facilities to a national emergency. Therefore, there is definitely an obligation on the federal government to reimburse the 12 regional Federal Reserve Banks for losses which they may make on loans made under these emergency powers. I do not hesitate to assure you that I shall ask the Congress to indemnify any of the 12 Federal Reserve banks for such losses.

On May 24th, the Emergency Banking Act was amended to authorize any state bank or trust company that was not a member of the Federal Reserve System to apply for loans from the Federal Reserve bank in the district in which it is located if the application was accompanied by the written approval of its state banking commission.

The third primary objective of the Act was achieved by empowering the Comptroller of the Currency to provide conservators to take possession of banks and to take such actions as may be necessary to conserve their assets. Conservators were directed to examine the affairs of covered banks and then report to the Comptroller on the bank's financial condition. The conservator then either could permit the bank to resume banking "subject to such terms, conditions, restrictions and limitations as he may proscribe" or reorganize any national banking association. The Federal Reserve Board 1933 Annual Report explained: "The principal duty of a conservator, like that of a receiver, is to conserve the assets of the bank for the benefit of depositors, but in performance of this duty he is not under the same obligation as a receiver to liquidate the assets."

On March 12, 1933, President Roosevelt delivered his first Fireside Chat, addressing the bank situation. The Chat, one of the most influential of Roosevelt's public addresses, succeeded in reassuring the public about what "has been done in the last few days, why it was done, and what the next steps are going to be." As with his Inaugural Address, Roosevelt stressed: "[T]here is an element in the readjustment of our financial system more important than currency, more important than gold, and that is the confidence of the people. Confidence and courage are the essentials of success in carrying out our plan.... Let us unite in banishing fear."

Roosevelt began by explaining in simple terms why the banking situation had deteriorated into crisis by March 3:

> First of all let me state the simple fact that when you deposit money in a bank the bank does not put the money into a safe deposit vault. It invests your money in many different forms of credit-bonds, commercial paper, mortgages and many other kinds of loans. In other words, the bank puts your money to work to keep the wheels of industry and of agriculture turning around. A comparatively small part of the money you put into the bank is kept in currency—an amount which in normal times is wholly sufficient to cover the cash needs of the average citizen. In other words the total amount of all the currency in the country is only a small fraction of the total deposits in all of the banks. What, then, happened during the last few days of February and the first few days of March? Because of undermined confidence on the part of the public, there was a general rush by a large portion of our population to turn bank deposits into currency or gold. A rush so great that the soundest banks could not get enough currency to meet the demand....
>
> By the afternoon of March 3 scarcely a bank in the country was open to do business.

Roosevelt emphasized that the bank holiday and subsequent Emergency Banking Act and related rules, orders, and proclamations provided the best path forward:

> This bank holiday while resulting in many cases in great inconvenience is affording us the opportunity to supply the currency necessary to meet the situation. No sound bank is a dollar

> worse off than it was when it closed its doors last Monday. Neither is any bank which may turn out not to be in a position for immediate opening. The new law allows the twelve Federal Reserve banks to issue additional currency on good assets and thus the banks that reopen will be able to meet every legitimate call. The new currency is being sent out by the Bureau of Engraving and Printing in large volume to every part of the country. It is sound currency because it is backed by actual, good assets. . . .
>
> . . . I know that many people are worrying about state banks not members of the Federal Reserve System. These banks can and will receive assistance from member banks and from the Reconstruction Finance Corporation. These state banks are following the same course as the national banks except that they get their licenses to resume business from the state authorities, and these authorities have been asked by the Secretary of the Treasury to permit their good banks to open up on the same schedule as the national banks. . . .
>
> . . . It needs no prophet to tell you that when the people find that they can get their money — that they can get it when they want it for all legitimate purposes — the phantom of fear will soon be laid. People will again be glad to have their money where it will be safely taken care of and where they can use it conveniently at any time. I can assure you that it is safer to keep your money in a reopened bank than under the mattress.

The Emergency Banking Act of 1933 and Roosevelt's March 12 Fireside Chat succeeded in dissipating the fear and helped restore confidence in commercial banks. By mid-April 1933, deposits at Federal Reserve banks increased by approximately $1 billion, and by June, the increase was greater than $2 billion. Between March 4 and March 15, $370 million in gold coin and gold certificates was returned to the Federal Reserve banks and the Treasury. Another $260 million was returned in the second half of March, $175 million in May and June, 1933, and about $60 million more in the last six months of 1933. The Federal Reserve Board concluded: "The return flow of money was principally from hoards rather than active circulation."

On March 15, 1933, the first day of stock trading after an extended closure of securities and commodities exchanges, the New York Stock Exchange recorded a gain of 15.34 percent, the largest one day percentage gain in its history to that date.

At the same time, a substantial number of banks were reorganized or closed. On January 1, 1933, there had been 17,800 commercial banks in operation. By the end of 1933, fewer than 12,000 commercial banks were licensed to do business and open. Of the 5000 unlicensed banks, 3000 reopened later, 2000 were either liquidated or consolidated with other banks.

The Reconstruction Finance Corporation (*RFC*) was pivotal in the restoration of the banking system. The RFC invested over $1 billion in bank capital, some one third of the total capital of all United States banks in 1933, and purchased preferred stock, notes and other debt securities in 6139 commercial banks, roughly one-half of the operating banks at the end of 1933. The RFC also made loans to depositors and closed banks of over $90 million on the security of the best assets of these banks. In aggregate, 5811 open banks and 2773 closed banks received RFC loans totaling more than $2 billion.[21]

Raymond Moley would later claim of the start of the Roosevelt Administration: "Capitalism was saved in eight days." In the sense of demonstrating a preference for reform rather than Nationalization, capitalism could be viewed as saved by Roosevelt's First 100 Day legislative achievements, beginning with the Emergency Banking Act.

But in terms of structural reform, the Emergency Banking Act accomplished little.

The United States system of commercial banking had generated an extraordinary number of weak local banks by 1920s. Nearly 30,000 banks operated in the United States in 1922. The vast majority, some 20,000, were state banks, 8210 in 1922 were national banks. In the 1920s, approximately 5000 country banks failed with $1.5 billion in deposits. In seven states, more than 40 percent of all the banks in 1920 failed. The suspension rate of state institutions, 4228 (or 86 percent of all state and national bank failures) in the 1920s far exceeded the failure of 697 national banks. The failure of any one bank could have a domino effect, freezing assets in other banks until bank customers received their deposits.

The inefficiency and dysfunction of the commercial banking structure was appreciated both by the state and national banks. One method of mitigation was merger. Approximately 350 bank mergers occurred each year between 1921 and 1925, reaching a high point of over 500 mergers in 1929.

The need for consolidation to reduce risk pitted the smaller state banks against the Federal Reserve member banks, most of which were national banks. In June 1923, the Federal Reserve Board calculated that of the 19,354 nonmember (that is, state) banks, less than one half, some 9633, possessed sufficient capital to be eligible under the Federal Reserve Act's capital requirements.

State banks in states with appropriate legislation had a key advantage over national banks. They could grow through branching. The 1913 Federal Reserve Act had left intact earlier restrictions in national bank branching, which dated back to an interpretation of the 1864 Banking Act by Freeman Clark, the second Comptroller of the Currency, and were slightly broadened by subsequent legislation. These restrictions largely limited national banks to branches in state banks with branches that had rechartered in the federal system.

State branching developed slowly. In 1898, New York authorized New York City banks to branch in a five county area. In 1909, only ten states permitted branching, including California which allowed state-wide bank branching in 1909. Over time, bank branching took on greater significance. In 1966, California had 98 state banks with 666 branches; New York similarly had 133 state banks with 1069 branches.

This meant a state bank could establish multiple branches throughout the state, a flexibility that national banks long did not possess. During the decades preceding the New Deal, the number of state banks matched and then far exceeded national banks. In 1895, there were 3715 national banks and 3774 state banks, a rough parity. State banks with increasing frequency in the 1920s amended their bank charter laws to permit branching. By 1925, 720 banks were operating 2525 branches, accounting for 10.5 percent of all bank offices and a notable 35.2 percent of commercial bank loans and investments. A vast majority of branches, 2207 or 87 percent, were affiliated with state banks. By 1930, there were 7197 national banks and 13,352 state banks, meaning state banks constituted 65.4 percent of total national and state branches.

In 1924, the United States Supreme Court held in *First National Bank in St. Louis v. State of Missouri* that a state law could frustrate the formation of national bank branches by the enactment of a state antibranching statute. Justice Sutherland wrote:

> National banks are brought into existence under federal legislation, are instrumentalities of the federal government and are necessarily subject to the paramount authority of the United States. Nevertheless, national banks are subject to the laws of a state in respect of their affairs, unless such laws interfere with the purpose of their creation, tend to impair or destroy their efficiency as federal agencies, or conflict with the paramount law of the United States.... The question is whether the Missouri statute falls within the rule or within the exception.
>
> Does it conflict with the laws of the United States? In our opinion, it does not. The extent of the powers of national banks is to be measured by the terms of the federal statutes relating to such associations, and they can rightfully exercise only such as are expressly granted or such incidental powers as are necessary to carry on the business for which they are established.

The decision in *First National Bank* increased concerns within the Federal Reserve that national banks would relinquish their national charters to take advantage of state statutory advantages, including branching. By the end of the 1920s, 22 states had adopted anti-branching legislation.

With the states generally opposing national bank branching and the Federal Reserve concerned that the absence of this power threatened the national banking system, Congress in 1927 enacted the McFadden Act.

The McFadden Act attempted to strengthen the relative position of the Federal Reserve system by reducing the capital requirement to form a national bank with the approval of the Secretary of Treasury to $50,000 in any place where the population did not exceed 6000 and $25,000 in any place where the population did not exceed 3000. In the outlying districts of cities with a population that exceeded 50,000 where the capital requirement was $200,000 and state law permitted a state bank to be organized with capital of $100,000 or less, the Comptroller could approve formation of a national bank with $100,000 capital.

The McFadden Act also augmented national bank branching powers to permit national banks to establish and operate new branches within the city, town, or village in which the bank was situated if state law permitted state banks to operate branches in these locations. While this increased national bank branch powers, it was done begrudgingly. The one location limit was restrictive. Moreover, a subsequent provision of the McFadden Act denied national banks the power to establish any branch in a city, town, or village with less than 25,000 population. No more than one branch could be established in locations where the population was less than 50,000, no more than two branches could be established where the population did not exceed 100,000.[22]

The structural weaknesses of the Federal Reserve Board also weakened United States banking in the years before the New Deal. The 1913 Federal Reserve Act left uncertain who was in charge of open market operations to sell Treasury securities and bring cash to the coffers of the United States Government and the rediscount rate, which is the interest rate at which commercial banks borrow from Federal Reserve banks and which effectively sets interest rates for other forms of borrowing.

The Federal Reserve was not operational when World War I commenced. During World War I, Secretary of Treasury William McAdoo dominated national financial policy, authorizing banks to issue emergency currency in 1914 and persuading the New York Stock Exchange to close for several months. Throughout the War, McAdoo pressured the Federal Reserve to maintain low interest rates.

The authority of the central Federal Reserve Board remained contested during the 15 years after World War I. The Federal Reserve Act had created a weak Federal Reserve Board with 12 regional Federal Reserve banks, each of which to some degree acted as a Federal Reserve within their region. During a period when the central Federal Reserve Board, in John Kenneth Galbraith's phrase "was a body of startling incompetence" or as Milton Friedman agreed "monetary policy [was] . . . inept," the Federal Reserve was divided by a power struggle between the central Fed and the regional Federal Reserve banks. The 12 Federal Reserve banks were dominated by the New York Federal Reserve Bank. Until 1928, when he prematurely died, Benjamin Strong, the Governor of the New York Fed, was the dominant personality in the entire Federal Reserve, a man whom finance author Liaquat Ahamed labeled as a Lord of Finance because of his role coordinating international central bank policy with Montague Norman, Governor of the Bank of England, Hjalmar Schacht of the German Reichebank, and Émile Moreau of the Banque de France.

Throughout post-World War I years, Secretary of Treasury Andrew Melon "[i]n international finance . . . left all currency matters to Benjamin Strong." As Galbraith put it, Strong was "the first American since Nicholas Biddle to make an important reputation as a central banker. Strong's views were regarded throughout the system with only little less awe than the gold standard." Biographer Lester Chandler characterized Strong as "one of the world's most influential leaders in the fields of money and finance, . . . his was the greatest influence on American monetary and banking policies; he had no close competitors."

Strong served as chair of the Governors Conference comprised of the 12 Federal Reserve bank governors and after 1922, as chair of the five member Governors Committee on Open Market Operations, where he was universally recognized to be the most influential member.

Until New Deal revisions of the Federal Reserve Act, the 1913 Act only empowered the central Federal Reserve Board to approve discount rate requests from the regional Federal Reserve banks. Strong, an advocate of low rates to help Europe recover from World War I, and George Harrison, his successor as Governor of the New York Fed, were dilatory in seeking to raise rates as security speculation heated up in the late 1920s, and the central Board was even more reluctant to raise rates when in February 1929, after the central Federal Reserve Board had issued a statement on February 2, 1929, explaining that member banks were not "within its reasonable claims for rediscount facilities of its Federal Reserve bank when it borrows . . . for making speculative loans," the New York Fed raised its rediscount rate from 5 to 6 percent. In this, and 10 subsequent occasions through May 23, 1929, the Federal Reserve Board declined to approve the interest rate increase, preferring to proceed through direct action or jawboning of individual banks.

Matters deteriorated further in June 1929 when the New York Fed presented a program for the midyear period allowing the New York Fed, in Milton Friedman and Anna Schwartz's summary:

> (1) to discount freely for member banks, whether or not they had outstanding collateral loans; (2) to provide monetary ease by purchasing government securities or acceptances, if legitimate demands could not be met adequately by rediscounting; (3) to raise the discount rate, if there was evidence of speculation in securities, real estate, commodities, or inventories; and (4) to reduce rates again promptly as conditions permitted.

On June 12, the central Federal Reserve Board rejected the New York Fed program, informing the bank: "Since February the policy of the Federal Reserve System has expressed itself primarily through what is called 'direct action' and this position was taken deliberately by the Federal Reserve Board. To this position it holds fast. It is satisfied with the reasonableness of its policy and with its necessity."

Only on August 9 did the central Board approve the increase to 6 percent rediscount rate for the New York Federal Reserve Board. In retrospect, it is evident that direct pressure alone was a policy failure.

The quiescence of the Federal Reserve System became even more dysfunctional in the 1929 to 1933 period. Contrary to economist Bagehot's admonition that a central bank should be a lender of last resort for an economy during a financial panic, "[advancing] freely and vigorously to the public out of the reserve." This was the period during which, as Friedman and Schwartz explained, a Great Contraction occurred, during which the stock of money declined by over one-third between August 1929 and March 1933 and the monetary system collapsed. Friedman and Schwartz ascribed "the passive, hesitant policy [of the Federal Reserve Board] from 1929 to 1933 in measurable part and the premature death of Strong." Economics Professor John Wood would generalize in 2015: "It is widely agreed that the Fed failed in the Great Depression, although whether because of sins of omission or commission, for causing the money stock to fall by one-third between 1929 and 1933, or for failing to contest a fall due to other causes, is not settled." Columbia History Professor Adam Tooze later would add: "The deflationary misery of the 1930s was the defining event in the Fed's history. This was the history that Bernanke [as Chair decades later] had pledged not to repeat." Bernanke also emphasized the pervasiveness of debtor insolvency in the 1929–1933 period: "[T]he ratio of debt service to national income went from 9 percent in 1929 to 19.8 percent in 1932–33. The resulting high rates of default caused problems for both borrowers and lenders."

Compounding the quiescence of the Federal Reserve System was the aggressive financial engineering of investment and commercial banks. Commercial banks were able to form investment bank affiliates in states where this was permitted. As early as 1908, First Security Company had been established with a $10 million capital investment by First National Bank, which was aligned with JP

Morgan. In 1911, National City Bank created the National City Company, which subsequently transformed itself into a more specialized investment business until 1918, which it absorbed N.W. Halsey & Company, a private investment bank, and combined its operations with National City Bank's bond department. This allowed Charles E. Mitchell, President of National City Bank, to use National City Company to become "the largest agency in the world for the distribution of securities." Several other investment banking affiliates were created by commercial banks and trust companies during the post-World War I period, including the Guaranty Trust organized by the New York Guaranty Trust Company in 1920, and the First National Corporation, an affiliate of the First National Bank of Boston, created in 1918.

In 1927, the McFadden Act alternatively allowed commercial banks to purchase investment securities without recourse up to 25 percent of their capital.

Business historian Vincent Carosso generalized in his *History of Investment Banking*:

> The functions of affiliates became so varied that, together with their sponsors, they could offer so-called "department store" banking facilities. The more active ones developed large sales organizations and actively solicited business, seeking the securities business as an end in itself. The variety of types of affiliates developed has been summarized as follows:
>
> (1) Wholesalers of security issues, purchasing entire offerings or participating in purchase and banking groups which acquire whole issues of securities from governmental bodies or corporations.
>
> (2) Retailers of securities, maintaining corps of salesmen and often branches in other states than that in which the bank operates for the distribution of stocks and bonds to institutions and private investors.
>
> (3) Holding and finance companies, carrying blocks of securities for control or otherwise, which the bank could not or would not list among its own investments.
>
> (4) Investment trusts, buying and selling securities acquired purely for investment or speculative purposes.
>
> (5) An asset realization company, to take over from the parent bank loans and investments which prove doubtful or nonliquid.

(6) A medium for supporting the market for the bank's own stock.
(7) A real estate holding company.

In 1922, there were 10 affiliates underwriting and distributing securities, 62 national banks had bond departments, 8 state banks and trust companies had securities affiliates, 197 had bond departments. By 1929, nearly every large urban commercial bank had one or more securities affiliates. Carosso found: "Through their bond departments or affiliates, commercial banks originated 22 percent of new issues in 1927; in 1930, it was 44.6 percent."

Affiliations of securities affiliates were dominated by the larger commercial banks and trust companies. A 1934 *Harvard Business Review* article summarized the eight largest private investment banks and largest affiliates of commercial banks:

Investment Banks	***Affiliates of Commercial Banks***
JP Morgan & Co.	Guaranty Co.
Bonbright & Co., Inc.	Continental Illinois
Harris, Forbes & Co.	National City Co.
Kuhn, Loeb & Co.	Chase Securities
Dillon, Read & Co.	Bankers Trust
Blair & Co.	First National — Old Colony
Halsey, Stuart & Co.	Equitable Trust
Lee, Higginson & Co.	Union Trust

Collectively, these firms were responsible for 2500 security issues with an aggregate value of $28 billion between 1921 and 1932, roughly one half of the total value of all securities issues during that period.

A separate financial innovation popularized during the 1920s was the investment trust. Trusts held a portfolio of securities in other securities, usually stocks and bonds. Investment banks or commercial bank security affiliates became heavily involved in organizing investment trusts. Investment banks actively promoted trusts in part to create a demand for securities they underwrote. The trusts and their sponsors did not publish much financial information. The propensity of investment banks and their affiliates to unload inferior securities on the trusts became more evident after the 1929–1933 crash as did weaknesses in trust organizations and the level of fees charged for management contracts, fees based on percentage of capital or earnings, and commissions on securities purchases or sales of the trust.

A third fundamental development in finance of the 1920s was the domination of state public utilities by public utility holding companies led by Electric Bond & Share formed in 1905, the Morgan-backed United Corporation organized in 1929, and Samuel Insull's utility empire, which by 1932 were responsible for 45 percent of electric energy generated in the United States. Sixteen holding companies had ownership interests in properties producing 92 percent of electrical output of the nation's private utilities.[23]

With the 1933 Banking Act, the Roosevelt Administration began an assault on the structure of finance that would be a key pillar of the New Deal transformation.

The dominant figure in the Senate during this transformation before the New Deal was Senator Carter Glass, who had chaired hearings beginning 1931 of a Subcommittee of the Senate Banking and Currency Committee, which conducted a broad investigation of commercial and investment banking and proposed S. 4412. S. 4412 was passed by the Senate in 1932 and was reintroduced as S. 1681 during the 1933 Bank Holiday Crisis. The Glass Bill was premised on the assumption "that the United States will never have a complete and strong [banking] system until such time as it shall succeed in fully harmonizing and adjusting state and federal laws on banking questions." The Glass Bill and an accompanying Report specifically criticized inflation of bank credit "(1) in carrying and inflating the prices of securities, especially common stocks, (2) the overdevelopment of real estate and real estate enterprises, and (3) in the upbuilding of a large capital equipment paid for with short-term accommodation but not funded at the time into longer-term loans." The Senate Report correlated bank insolvencies after 1924 until 1929 as a result of "a gradual disintegration of banking under present conditions."

The Glass Bill sought:

> (1) To separate as far as possible national and member banks from affiliates of all kinds.
>
> (2) To limit the amount of advances or loans which can be obtained by affiliates from the parent institutions with which they are connected.

> (3) To install a satisfactory examination of affiliates, working simultaneously with the present system of examination applicable to the parent banks.

The bill also intended "to provide some check upon the abnormal growth of all security loans of banks," and more opportunities for national banks to establish branches "not merely in the towns and cities in which they are located but also outside of such limits at any point within the borders of the state in which they exist." The Glass Bill further proposed to increase the independence of the central Federal Reserve Bank and to establish an Open Market Committee to effectuate greater central Fed powers with respect to speculative transactions.

The 1931 Senate Subcommittee Hearings on the Glass Bill exhibited a sharp divide on the issue of separating commercial and investment banking. Eugene Meyer, then Governor of the Federal Reserve, presented the Committee with a memorandum supporting the entire Glass Bill, but in testimony characterized the unanimous Board support of separation after three years not as a firm recommendation but as a suggestion. Meyer testified that the wisdom of separation was "in the realm of the unknown to a certain extent, because of the absence of full information." Leading bankers, some members of the New York Fed and the Comptroller of the Currency testified against separation, especially when the economy was in such a perilous condition. George Harrison, Governor of the New York Fed, disagreed with even the tepid suggestion of the central Fed, expressed concern that the "confusion and embarrassment [of separation might] be worse than the evil itself." Owen Young, Chairman of General Electric and a member of the New York Fed, in turn disagreed with Harrison and favored separation as did George Davidson, President of Central Hanover Bank & Trust Company and Harvard Professor William Z. Ripley, author of *Main Street and Wall Street.* Albert Wiggin, President of the Chase National Bank, and the ubiquitous Charles E. Mitchell led a long list of bankers opposed to separation.

The House of Representative Committee on Banking and Currency chaired by Henry Steagall introduced H.R. 5661, a separate bill in 1932, to provide for deposit insurance for bank customers and the creation of the Federal Bank Deposit Insurance Corporation. A House Committee Report explained:

> The bill provides for a Federal Bank Deposit Insurance Corporation which shall insure all deposits of all member banks, and also of all state banks complying with the conditions proscribed to the extent of 100 percent of the first $10,000 of any deposit and 75 percent of the next $50,000 thereof, and 50 percent of the amount of any deposits in excess of $50,000. Provision is made that when a bank is closed the amounts of the deposits insured as herein stated shall be immediately available to the depositors through the medium of a temporary national bank, which shall be created to assume and discharge the insured deposit liabilities of the closed bank. . . .
>
> The bill requires that the deposits in all banks which are members of the Federal Reserve System shall be insured under the limitations before stated and provides that any state bank, or trust company not a member of the Federal Reserve System, with the approval of the state authority and after examination by and approval of the Federal Deposit Insurance Corporation, shall be entitled to the privileges of insurance provided for member banks upon agreeing to comply with the law and upon subscribing for the same amount of stock as would be required if such bank or trust company became a member bank. . . .
>
> It is believed that the bill thus makes absolutely safe and adequate provision for the protection of depositors in the thousands of nonmember banks, without facing any undue risk or burden upon the member banks.

As with the Glass Bill, Steagall's Bill was adopted by the House in 1932 and again in 1933. President Roosevelt did not initially support deposit insurance, expressing doubt about the wisdom of making "the United States Government liable for the mistakes and errors of individual banks." But John Garner, his Vice President, Jesse Jones, Chair of the Reconstruction Finance Corporation, and influential Senator Arthur Vandenberg fervently did support deposit insurance as did the public generally. Roosevelt ultimately supported deposit insurance as well.

The Glass-Steagall Act

The momentum of Roosevelt's first 100 days and the Senate's Stock Exchange Practice Hearings helped build decisive momentum for new banking legislation. The Glass-Steagall Act was enacted on June 16, 1933, combining the Senate's Glass Bill and the House's Steagall Bill.

Several sections of the Act achieved Senator Glass's aspiration to separate national bank commercial bank functions from investment banking. The Act provided: "After one year from the date of the enactment of this Act, no member bank shall be affiliated in any manner . . . with any corporation, association, business trust, or other similar organization engaged principally in the issue, flotation, underwriting, public sale, or distribution at wholesale or retail or through syndicate participation of stocks, bonds, debentures, notes, or other securities."

The term *affiliate* was defined for this section to include any corporation, business trust, association, or other similar organization of which a member bank or a member bank owning or controlling another bank "directly or indirectly, owns or controls either a majority of the shares" or "a majority of its directors, trustees or other persons exercising similar functions are directors of any one member bank."

This section was amplified by a separate provision that barred any person, firm, corporation, association, business trust, or other similar organization engaged in issuing, underwriting, selling, or distributing securities simultaneously "to engage at the same time to any extent whatever in the business of receiving deposits. . . ."

The Act expressly did permit member banks to purchase and sell investment securities "solely upon the order, and for the account of customers, and in no case for its own activity." A proviso permitted a bank to purchase investment securities, here meaning debt securities but not stock, for its own account subject to a 15 percent limit of its capital stock and a 25 percent limit of its unimpaired surplus.

The Act separately addressed private bankers as JP Morgan and prohibited them and financial institutions generally from receiving deposits unless the institution was subject to examination or regulation under state or federal law and submitted to periodic examination by the Comptroller of the Currency or by the Federal Reserve bank of the relevant district and made and published detailed periodic reports of its resources and liabilities.

The Glass-Steagall Act limited member banks from:

> (1) [making] any loan or any extension of credit to, or purchase securities under repurchase agreements from, any of its affiliates, or (2) invest any of its funds in the capital stock, bonds,

> debentures, or other such obligations of any such affiliate, or (3) accept the capital stock, bonds, debentures, or other such obligations of any such affiliate as collateral security for advances made to any person, partnership, association, or corporation, if, in the case of any such affiliate, the aggregate amount of such loans, extensions of credit, repurchase agreements, investments, and advances against such collateral security will exceed 10 per centum of the capital stock and surplus of such member bank, or if, in the case of all such affiliates, the aggregate amount of such loans, extensions of credit, repurchase agreements, investments, and advances against such collateral security will exceed 20 per centum of the capital stock and surplus of such member bank.

Additionally, the Act provided that "no national bank, without the approval of the Comptroller of the Currency, and no State member bank, without the approval of the Federal Reserve Board, shall (1) invest in bank premises, or in the stock, bonds, debentures, or other such obligations of any corporation holding the premises of such bank, or (2) make loans to or upon the security of the stock of any such corporation, if the aggregate of all such investments and loans will exceed the amount of the capital stock of such bank."

The Glass-Steagall Act separation of commercial and investment banking had a powerful and rapid impact on the banking industry. Banking historian Vincent Carosso explained:

> A major reorganization of the investment banking industry immediately resulted from the Banking Act. Affiliations were eliminated; the bond departments of commercial banks were cut in size and their activities greatly reduced; and private bankers were forced to choose between deposit and investment banking. Two-thirds of these partnerships, according to one estimate, decided to stay in the securities business. . . . The Morgan firm and its Philadelphia office, Drexel & Co., as well as Brown Brothers Harriman & Co., were notable exceptions. These three old investment houses abandoned the securities business and opted for deposit banking.

Subsequently, three Morgan partners and two Drexel partners resigned from the JP Morgan commercial bank and organized Morgan Stanley, an investment bank. Several other offshoots of commercial banks were created in 1934 and 1935:

> The officers and directors of Brown Harriman & Co., Inc., organized in June 1934, came from the National City Co., and Brown Brothers Harriman & Co. Officials of Harris, Hall & Co., founded in October 1934, came from the defunct affiliate of Chicago's Harris Trust & Savings Bank. In June 1935, Charles E. Mitchell, the one-time head of the National City Co., was named board chairman of Blyth & Co., the successor to Blyth, Witter & Co., originally a San Francisco banking house founded in 1914.

Representative Steagall achieved his priority with the creation of deposit insurance and the Federal Deposit Insurance Corporation (*FDIC*). This was the world's first effective deposit insurance system and in the post-World War II period would be internationally emulated.

Milton Friedman and Anna Schwartz were effusive in their praise of this aspect of the 1933 Banking Act:

> Federal insurance of bank deposits was the most important structural change in the banking system to result from the 1933 panic, and, indeed in our view, the structural change most conducive to monetary stability since state bank note issues were taxed out of existence immediately after the Civil War.

By the time deposit insurance became available for Federal Reserve member banks on July 1, 1934, 14,000 of the nation's 15,438 commercial banks, accounting for 97 percent of all commercial bank deposits, would be insured by the Deposit Insurance Fund.

Deposit insurance would be credited with the virtual elimination of bank runs and bank failures until the 2007–2009 debacle. Commercial bank failures would drop from 4000 in 1933 to 31 by 1935 and in the post-World War II period, long would remain in the single digits.

As enacted by the Glass-Steagall Act, the FDIC was established to purchase, hold and liquidate national banks closed by the Comptroller of the Currency or their directors or state member banks closed by appropriate state authorities on their directors. The FDIC had a three-person Board of Directors, appointed by the President, subject to Senate confirmation, including the Comptroller. Initially, the FDIC was funded by $150 million from the Treasury and by capital stock required to be purchased by Federal Reserve banks and member and nonmember banks who sought protection by deposit insurance. The FDIC was authorized to issue and have outstanding up to three times its capital in the form of notes, debentures, bonds, or other obligations.

The FDIC created the Temporary Deposit Insurance Fund in 1934. Every member bank licensed before January 1, 1934, automatically became a member of the Fund. Each Federal Reserve national bank subsequently licensed and each state bank, trust company, or mutual savings bank that became a Federal Reserve bank and each state bank that was not a member of the Federal Reserve System with appropriate state or FDIC Certification of Solvency also could become members of the Fund.

Initially the Fund was directed to pay up to $2500 for net approved claims of depositors in covered banks.

Member and nonmember banks protected by deposit insurance were Class A stockholders in the FDIC and could receive dividends up to 6 percent per year.

State banks, trust companies, and mutual savings banks could become Class A stockholders. The initial Class A stockholders were required to provide the FDIC an amount equal to one half of one percent of their total deposits at the date of admission and one half of one percent of total deposits a month from the period of the last Class A dividend. Later, Class A stockholders were required to provide 5 percent of capital and surplus.

The Federal Reserve banks were Class B stockholders and were required to subscribe to an amount equal to one half of its surplus as of January 1, 1933, but did not receive any dividends.

If a Class A stockholder became insolvent or ceased to be a member bank, all of its cash paid subscriptions to capital stock would first be applied to pay its debts.

The Act provided:

> [W]henever any national bank which is a class A stockholder of the Corporation shall have been closed by action of its board of directors or by the Comptroller of the Currency, as the case may be, on account of inability to meet the demands of its depositors, the Comptroller of the Currency shall appoint the Corporation receiver for such bank. As soon as possible thereafter the Corporation shall organize a new national bank to assume the insured deposit liabilities of such closed bank, to receive new deposits and otherwise to perform temporarily the functions provided for it in this paragraph. For the purposes of this

> subsection, the term *insured deposit liability* shall mean with respect to the owner of any claim arising out of a deposit liability of such closed bank the following percentages of the net amount due to such owner by such closed bank on account of deposit liabilities: 100 per centum of such net amount not exceeding $10,000; and 75 per centum of the amount, if any, by which such net amount exceeds $10,000 but does not exceed $50,000; and 50 per centum of the amount, if any, by which such net amount exceeds $50,000.

The FDIC was authorized to have all the rights, powers, and privileges of receivers of insolvent national banks. When permitted by state law, the FDIC also could serve as receiver of a state member bank. When state law did not permit the appointment of the FDIC as receiver, the FDIC would organize a new national bank to assure the insured deposit liabilities of the closed state banks and receive new deposits.

Under the Glass-Steagall Act, the powers of the central Federal Reserve Board were enhanced, most significantly by the amendment to the Federal Reserve Act to create the Federal Open Market Committee. "No Federal Reserve Bank shall engage in open market operations — except in accordance with regulations adopted by the Federal Reserve Board." The Open Market Committee included one member of each Federal Reserve bank, but no member of the central Federal Reserve Board.

As amended, the Federal Reserve Act, upon affirmative vote of six members of the Federal Reserve Board, could fix "the percentage of individual bank capital and surplus which may be represented by loans secured by stock or bond collateral made by member banks within such district, but no such loan shall be made by any such bank to any person in an amount in excess of 10 per centum of the unimpaired capital and surplus of such bank."

Federal Reserve banks could make advances to member banks for up to 90 days at rates set by the Federal Reserve banks, "subject to the review and determination of the Federal Reserve Board."

The Federal Reserve Act was revised to empower the Federal Reserve Board to prescribe:

> [R]egulations . . . defining within the limitations of this Act the conditions under which discounts, advancements, and the accommodations may be extended to member banks. . . .

> Whenever, in the judgment of the Federal Reserve Board, any member bank is making such undue use of bank credit, the Board may, in its discretion, after reasonable notice and an opportunity for a hearing, suspend such bank from the use of the credit facilities of the Federal Reserve System and may terminate such suspension or may renew it from time to time.

The Federal Reserve Board also was authorized to:

> exercise special supervision over all relationships and transactions of any kind entered into by any Federal reserve bank with any foreign bank or banker, or with any group of foreign banks or bankers, and all such relationships and transactions shall be subject to such regulations, conditions, and limitations as the Board may prescribe.

The term of Federal Reserve Board members was extended to 12 years, but membership on the Board was unchanged.

Consistent with the advocacy of Senator Glass, the limits on national bank branches were broadened:

> A national banking association may, with the approval of the Comptroller of the Currency, establish and operate new branches: (1) Within the limits of the city, town or village in which said association is situated, if such establishment and operation are at the time expressly authorized to State banks by the law of the State in question; and (2) at any point within the State in which said association is situated, if such establishment and operation are at the time authorized to State banks by the statute law of the State in question by language specifically granting such authority affirmatively and not merely by implication or recognition, and subject to the restrictions as to location imposed by the law of the State on State banks. No such association shall establish a branch outside of the city, town, or village in which it is situated unless it has a paid-in and unimpaired capital stock of not less than $500,000: *Provided,* That in States with a population of less than one million, and which have no cities located therein with a population exceeding one hundred thousand, the capital shall be not less than $250,000: *Provided,* That in States with a population of less than one-half million, and which have no cities located therein with a population exceeding fifty thousand, the capital shall not be less than $100,000.

National bank branching still remained restricted. No interstate branching was authorized by the 1933 Act.

The Glass-Steagall Act limited member bank officers or directors from simultaneously serving as officers, directors or managers of any business primarily engaged in purchasing or selling or negotiating securities. No member bank could perform the function of a correspondent bank of any such individual, partnership, corporation, or association.

The 1914 Clayton Act was amended to prohibit directors, officers, or employees of banks, bank associations, or trust companies organized under United States law from serving at the same time as a director, officer, or employee of any corporation or partnership (other than a mutual savings bank "which shall make loans secured by stock or bond collateral to any individual, association, partnership or corporation other than its own subsidiaries."

No member bank executive officer could borrow or otherwise become indebted to any member bank of which he or she was an executive officer and no member bank could make a loan or extend credit in any other manner to any of its executive officers.

Capital requirements for national banks were amended. After the Glass-Steagall Act took effect:

> [N]o national banking association shall be organized with a less capital than $100,000, except that such associations with a capital of not less than $50,000 may be organized in any place the population of which does not exceed six thousand inhabitants. No such association shall be organized in a city the population of which exceeds fifty thousand persons with a capital of less than $200,000, except that in the outlying districts of such a city where the State laws permit the organization of State banks with a capital of $100,000 or less, national banking associations now organized or hereafter organized may, with the approval of the Comptroller of the Currency, have a capital of not less than $100,000.

Morris Plan banks, designed to enable employees to take out small, short-term loans, were made subject to the Federal Reserve Act. Mutual savings banks similarly could be subject to the Act without capital stock when they had surplus and undivided profits not less than the capital required for the organization of a national bank "in the same manner and subject to the same provisions of law as state banks and trust companies."[24]

Two years later, the Banking Act of 1933 itself was substantially amended by the Banking Act of 1935. The 1934 Congressional Elections had been a validation of the New Deal. The Democratic Party majority in the House of Representatives increased from 313 to 117 to 322 to 103, with the Democrats gaining 9 seats and the Republicans losing 14. The Progressives won 7 seats. In the Senate, the results were even more decisive. The Democratic Party Majority swelled from 60 to 35 to a veto proof 69 to 25. The midterm gains for the Democrats strengthened Roosevelt's ability to seek a substantial realignment of federal-state relations.

With the recommendation of Treasury Secretary Henry Morgenthau, Roosevelt in 1934 nominated Marriner Eccles to be Governor and then Chair of the Federal Reserve Board. Eccles was a highly successful Utah banker and industrialist who had served with Morgenthau in the Treasury Department. Eccles would serve as Chair of the Federal Reserve Board until 1948.

Eccles unequivocally sought to centralize Federal Reserve power in Washington. He regarded the regional Federal Reserve banks, especially the New York Federal Reserve Bank, as subservient to private interests. Eccles also favored national bank branching, which Roosevelt quickly rejected. After a two-hour meeting with Eccles, who had intimated that being a Governor on the Federal Reserve would not be worth it unless the power of the regional Federal Reserve banks was broken, Roosevelt generally endorsed Eccles's approach.

Eccles aggressively challenged a core tenet of the Federal Reserve's first 20 years: The insistence that the Federal Reserve was not a central bank. Roosevelt authorized Eccles to draft a new Banking Act that significantly strengthened the central Federal Reserve Board.

Roosevelt and Eccles both were aware that this view would be vehemently resisted by Senator Glass, widely viewed as "the father of the Fed." In July 1935, before the August enactment of the new Banking Act, Glass heartily disapproved of Eccles's draft, as earlier adopted by the House because Eccles proposed:

> that the Federal Reserve banks be stripped of every particle of local self-government and that we should establish here in Washington practically a central bank, to be operated by people who are not bankers, and have no technical knowledge of the banking business. That suggestion was so repugnant to the

> original purpose of the Federal Reserve Banking System that those who propounded the suggestion soon found it convenient to abandon their indefensible attitude. If anything was deliberately and decisively determined in 1913, . . . it was that this country did not want a central bank.

The 1935 Banking Act

As enacted, the 1935 Banking Act had three titles.

Title I addressed Federal Deposit Insurance and was relatively noncontroversial. The insured deposit was raised from $2500 to $5000 per deposit or deposits in an insured bank, an amount that the House Report determined would provide full insurance for 98 percent of the depositors in insured banks. Over subsequent years, the insured amount would be periodically raised to $250,000 per depositor in 2008. The Temporary Federal Deposit Insurance Fund as well as a separate Fund for Mutual were consolidated into a permanent Insurance Fund. The burden upon insured banks was reduced to an assessment rate of 1/12 of 1 per centum per year. By 1935, the FDIC had received capital funds of approximately $240 million from the sale of its stock to the United States and to Federal Reserve banks.

The House had considered, but rejected, the earlier requirement that:

> every bank must become or apply to become a member bank of the Federal Reserve System by July 1, 1937, in order to continue as an insured bank after that date. More than 7500 insured banks are not now members of the Federal Reserve System. The committee . . . has come to the conclusion that membership in the Federal Reserve System, however desirable it may be from the viewpoint of bringing about a unified banking system, should not be rendered practically compulsory by requiring insured banks to either join the system or terminate their insurance. The committee has therefore eliminated this requirement of existing law.

In the final Act, only state nonmember banks with average deposits of $1 million or more after July 1, 1942, were required to join the Federal Reserve System in order to continue their insured status. Some 6500 state nonmember banks with deposits of less than

$1 million could continue to receive deposit insurance without joining the Federal Reserve System.

The 1935 Act extended the benefits of deposit insurance to banks in Puerto Rico and the Virgin Islands.

The Conference Committee resolved a difference in approaches in the House and Senate versions with respect to financing the FDIC:

> The House bill authorized the Secretary of the Treasury to purchase the guaranteed obligations of the Corporation. The Senate amendment authorized the Secretary to purchase any of the obligations of the Corporation and provided that if the Reconstruction Finance Corporation failed for any reason to purchase such obligations as required by . . . the Reconstruction Finance Corporation Act, the Secretary should purchase such obligations in an amount equal to the amount the Reconstruction Finance Corporation so failed to purchase. The conference agreement retains the provisions of the Senate amendment and adds a provision requiring the Secretary of the Treasury to purchase an additional $250,000,000 of the obligations of the Corporation.

Title III of the 1935 Banking Act provided technical amendments to the banking laws, most of which were adopted in identical form in the House and Senate bills. The Clayton Act, as amended by the 1933 Banking Act, had been a broad prohibition on bank, banking associations, or trust company directors, officers, or employees serving as directors, officers, or employees of virtually any corporation that received loans secured by virtually any individual, association, partnership, or corporation. The 1935 Act substituted new language in the Clayton Act exempting seven relationships from the prohibition on interlocking directors, officers, or employees.

The heart of the 1935 Banking Act was Title II, which revamped the powers of the central Federal Reserve and regional Federal Reserve banks and made the central Federal Reserve bank more independent of the Executive Branch.

Symbolically, the Federal Reserve Board was renamed the Board of Governors of the Federal Reserve System. Board members now had 14-year terms and were led by a Chair and Vice Chair, not a Governor and Vice Governor. The Chair and Vice Chair were selected by the President for four-year terms. The Chair was the Executive Officer of the Board. The Federal Board now had seven, not eight, members. After February 1, 1936, neither the Secretary of Treasury or the Comptroller of the Currency were members of the Board. In selecting Board members, the President could not select more than one member from any one Federal Reserve district and now was subject to a hortatory requirement to have "due regard to the fair representation of the financial, agricultural, industrial and commercial interests, and geographic division of the country," rather than the earlier language that this was a requirement.

The Open Market Committee, previously solely composed of representatives of the 12 Federal Reserve banks, now included the seven members of the Federal Reserve Board and five representatives of the Federal Reserve banks:

> Such representatives of the Federal Reserve banks shall be elected annually as follows: One by the boards of directors of the Federal Reserve Banks of Boston and New York, one by the boards of directors of the Federal Reserve Banks of Philadelphia and Cleveland, one by the boards of directors of the Federal Reserve Banks of Chicago and Saint Louis, one by the boards of directors of the Federal Reserve Banks of Richmond, Atlanta, and Dallas, and one by the boards of directors of the Federal Reserve Banks of Minneapolis, Kansas City, and San Francisco.

In 1942, Congress amended this provision to make the New York Fed's President a permanent member of the Open Market Committee.

The previous provision requiring Federal Reserve banks to engage in Open Market Operations "in accordance with the directions and regulations adopted by the [Open Market] Committee" was retained. A provision in the 1933 Act permitting a Federal Reserve bank to decline to participate in approved Open Market Operations upon filing a notice of its decision within 30 days was eliminated.

United States notes, bonds, or other obligations or obligations guaranteed by the United States could "be bought and sold without regard to maturities but only in open market." There was no longer a requirement that federal notes be secured at all times by a specific pledge of collateral.

The Federal Reserve Board now on a majority vote of four members could change the regulations as to reserves to be maintained against demand or time deposits by member banks.

These enhancements of the Federal Reserve Board's powers with respect to the Open Market Committee had been a critical source of controversy between the House and the Senate. The Eccles inspired House bill had sought to displace the earlier Open Market Committee with an Advisory Committee composed of five Federal Reserve bank representatives. The Advisory Committee was intended to be purely consultative. "It had no vote in determining open-market policies, but the Board was required to consult this Committee before making any changes on its own initiative in open-market policies in rates of interest and discounts to be charged by Federal Reserve banks, or in the reserve balances to be maintained by member banks." The Senate Committee had proposed the language adopted as a compromise between the earlier decentralized process and Eccles's preference for a more powerful Federal Reserve Board.

The Federal Reserve Board was empowered to appoint regional Federal Reserve bank presidents for five-year terms with the power to dismiss regional bank presidents "at pleasure," meaning with or without cause.

The Board could waive requirements for insured banks to become members of the Federal Reserve System.

Advances to member banks made by regional Federal Reserve banks could be made for no more than four months "under rules and regulations prescribed by the Board of Governors of the Federal Reserve System."

These were the major structural changes in banks and the Federal Reserve during the New Deal and provided the basis for the more active Federal Reserve Board of the post-World War II period.[25]

Securities Regulation

The most far reaching aspect of the New Deal transformation of financial regulation involved securities regulation. Between 1933 and 1940, Congress enacted six federal securities laws. This revolution began with the Senate Banking and Currency Committee's 1932–1934 Stock Exchange Practices Hearings, popularly called the Pecora Hearings in recognition of the decisive role played by the Committee's Counsel, Ferdinand Pecora.

Ultimately the Senate Banking Committee's Hearings would transform American capitalism. They would be directly responsible for the Securities and Banking Acts of 1933, the Securities Exchange Act of 1934, and the creation of the Securities and Exchange Commission. But the hearings began like a Keystone Kops comedy.

Peter Norbeck was the dominant figure in the stock exchange inquiry for the first nine months. The South Dakotan characterized himself as a "Theodore Roosevelt Republican." John T. Flynn, both a political radical and a leading financial journalist of the day, more colorfully styled the Senator "one of those Prairie Republicans — half Democrat, half other ingredients — but less than one-half of one percent Republican." Party labels were not particularly relevant. The former well driller was an unabashed sectionalist and champion of farm relief legislation. Norbeck's most visible achievement as Senator would be helping to secure funds for the carving of the monument on Mount Rushmore.

By his own admission, Peter Norbeck was not qualified to be Chair of the Banking Committee. He knew little about finance. He had been named to the Committee in 1921 in an attempt to give it greater geographic balance. At least once he tried to resign. However, in 1926, when unexpected election results made him the ranking Republican member, Norbeck feared he would suffer too great a loss of prestige if he did not accept the Chairmanship of the influential committee. Besides, he observed, "as an authority on banking and currency he was the ablest well-driller in Congress."

Whatever Norbeck's technical limitations as Chair, he brought to the Senate Banking Committee as clear an anti-Wall Street bias as a prairie Progressive could muster. Flynn would go so far as to write, "It was Norbeck, big, honest, calm, filled with common sense, who made this an investigation of Wall Street, who kept doggedly at the probe . . . and who, more than any other man, gave to the investigation its tone, its character, and direction."[26]

Such an encomium could come only in retrospect. It was nearly impossible to find anything in the Senator's performance to praise at the start of the hearings.

The Stock Exchange Hearings officially began on Monday, April 11, 1932.[27] For the first two days they were a near total disaster. A smooth, haughty Richard Whitney was the lead off witness. The self-confident New York Stock Exchange President dazzled the 500 or so reporters and spectators jammed into the modestly proportioned Committee room. He denied knowledge of a bear raid scheduled for the previous Saturday. Indeed, Whitney testified, "constant investigations have shown . . . bear raids [do] not exist." Nor did short selling have much effect on market prices, accounting as it did for less than 5 percent of all stock exchange transactions. If they wanted culprits to blame for the exaggerated price movements of the great bull market and succeeding crash, Whitney suggested they look at "the high-powered political agents of prosperity," who misled the country into a "state of mind that . . . thought poverty was about to be abolished in our country forever."[28]

Norbeck labored to revitalize the hearings. At the conclusion of the second hearing day, he began easing out Temporary Counsel Claude Branch in favor of Branch's assistant, William Gray, a Philadelphia trial attorney with a reputation as a forceful cross-examiner. When the hearings resumed on April 18, the determined Gray attempted to show that short selling artificially depressed the market. But Gray had no investigative base to draw on. When he argued that Whitney's view of short selling was "opposed . . . by a great many intelligent, clear thinking people, who know as much as can be known . . . about market conditions," the Stock Exchange President stated flatly, "Mr. Gray, I have never denied that intelligent people might not have a different opinion than I, but in this I would say they are wrong."

Usually Whitney did not concede even that much. Throughout protracted testimony on April 18 and again on the 21st, he denied that stock exchange members spread false rumors to depress the market, denied that large operators traded under fictitious names, and at one point all but denied that he knew what a pool operation was. Gray's questioning proved so ineffective that Whitney could barely conceal his amusement. When the Counsel asked Whitney on the fourth Hearing day, "Would you like to get home tonight?" Whitney replied, "I do not particularly care, Mr. Gray. I will say that I am very happy here in Washington."[29]

Whitney's testimony discouraged several Senators on the Banking Committee. Having initially expected hard evidence of "a giant bear raid," they saw instead the sophisticated Whitney easily deflect accusations based on rumor, gossip, or unsubstantiated suspicion.

The Stock Exchange Practices Hearings effectively began on April 26. After two days of entertaining but uncorroborated testimony from such notorious Wall Street traders as Ben "Sell'em" Smith and Matthew Brush (who explained with Runyonesque logic that "nobody is in Wall Street for their health"), Norbeck promised "sensational disclosures" at the following day's Session. Rumors swirled that Fiorello La Guardia would be a "surprise witness" and that the Congressman recently had received documents so inflammatory that he had them placed under guard at police headquarters.

The next morning, La Guardia arrived accompanied by a squad of uniformed policemen and two plainclothes policemen carrying a heavy brown trunk. From the trunk, La Guardia produced cancelled checks and news clippings showing that, over a ten-year period, publicist A. Newton Plummer had received $286,279 for planting favorable news stories to boost the prices of 61 separate stocks. Among other beneficiaries of Plummer's payments were reporters for *The New York Times,* the *Wall Street Journal,* the *New York Herald Tribune,* the *New York Evening Post,* and the *New York Evening Mail.* In return, these reporters had published as fact articles written by Plummer, such as ones stating that Superior Oil's production has increased "approximately 200 percent since the first of the year" and Indian Motorcycle "orders [were] 65 percent ahead of business a year ago." "Shocking as these facts may seem," La Guardia told the Senators, "I believe that the same sordid story could be told about nearly every stock in which there has been a pool and in which there have been efforts to shoot up the price."[30]

The Senate Banking Committee resumed the hearings in mid-May. Among other revelations, Gray showed a pool organized by the firm of M.J. Meehan and Company had generated profits equal to nearly $5 million by trading Radio Corporation of America stock during one week in March 1929. Profit participants included Mrs. David Sarnoff, the wife of RCA's Chief Executive Officer, John J. Raskob, and Mrs. M.J. Meehan. Gray demonstrated that film magnate Harry Warner saved $9.25 million by selling Warner Brothers stock before the elimination of dividend payments, then repurchasing the securities after the price dropped. David Lion, a publicist, it was disclosed, had earned at least $2 million from 30 pool operations. And Fox Film's William Fox caused his corporation to take ownership of 210,300 shares of company stock after the October 1929 Crash reduced their value by $3.3 million, but personally claimed the loss on his New York State income tax return.[31]

These revelations were widely reported by the nation's press, but Gray's scattershot approach led to serious evidentiary gaps. For example, Gray was unable to corroborate his suspicions that the

RCA pool had been aided by planted news stories and "wash sales," that is, sales and purchases by the same person or group to artificially create the appearance of activity in a stock, or to prove the effect of David Lion's publicity on share prices or even that the publicity was fraudulent.

By mid-June, Senatorial attention was waning. Norbeck barely was able to persuade a majority of the Banking Committee members to seek $50,000 in additional funds to continue the Stock Exchange inquiry until March 3, 1933, when the 72nd Congress would adjourn.

Norbeck then made his final contribution to securities law reform. After consultation with Senator Fletcher, the senior Democrat on the Banking Committee, who would succeed Norbeck as Committee Chair, Norbeck hired Ferdinand Pecora to be the Committee's Counsel. Born in Nicosia, Sicily, in 1882, Pecora had immigrated to New York City at the age of four. The future "hellhound of Wall Street" briefly applied himself to the pursuit of the Episcopal ministry, before a factory injury incapacitated his shoemaker father, requiring him to leave college and help support his family. His career in law began when, at the age of 15, Pecora became a junior clerk in a one man law office diagonally across the street from JP Morgan and Company. Five years later Pecora started part-time study at New York Law School. After graduating in 1906, Pecora served as a managing clerk in several firms before passing the bar in 1911.

He entered public life via local politics. In 1912, Pecora joined Theodore Roosevelt's National Progressive Party. An astute district leader, Pecora became Vice President of the Bull Moose Party in New York State. Impressed with Woodrow Wilson's policies, Pecora switched his allegiance to the Democrats in 1916. The following year, the Mayor of New York City rewarded Pecora's campaign efforts with a position in the office of New York City's District Attorney.

There, Pecora thrived. District Attorney Joab J. Banton, who named Pecora his Chief Assistant in 1922, credited Pecora with successful prosecution of over 150 fraudulent securities salesmen, and with the conviction of corrupt politicians in the City's Health Department and the Office of Comptroller of the State of New York. In a 1933 telegram to Senator Norbeck, Banton praised Pecora as "the best qualified lawyer" in the country to lead the Banking

Committee's investigation. Bainbridge Colby, Secretary of State under Wilson, after declining the Counsel position himself, recommended Pecora to Senator Fletcher as "the most brilliant cross-examiner in New York."

Pecora was undeniably among the most theatrical. A compact, swarthy man with curling black and gray hair, he punctuated his courtroom appearances with the vigorous jabbing of a stubby finger. During the Stock Exchange Hearings, Pecora's manner alternately could be genial, courtly, mocking, or belligerent. It was always relentless. So relentless, in fact, that a startled J.P. Morgan, Jr., later would protest that Pecora pursued him as if he were "a horse thief." He was given to intellectual excesses as well. A wholesale subscriber to the Brandeis bigness-is-badness thesis, he often treated Wall Street witnesses as if they had something to hide.[32]

Hearings resumed on February 15, with the long-delayed examination of the Insull public utility empire. Before its collapse, the Insull group of utility companies had been the third largest utility group in the country, producing approximately 10 percent of the nation's total electrical power. The local level of the system comprised over 100 gas, electricity, and transportation firms scattered throughout 30 states. These operating companies were largely administered through five holding companies, in each of which the Insull family owned a minority controlling interest. When financier Cyrus Eaton in 1927 began purchasing large blocks of Insull holding company securities, Insull reacted defensively by forming two super-holding companies "to perpetuate," a press release explained, "the existing management of the Insull group of securities."

The collapse of the stock markets in September 1931 toppled the heavily indebted Insull system. Newspapers claimed that the fall of the $3 billion empire was "the biggest business failure in the history of the world." Insull's personal fortune of over $150 million vanished. An early advocate of "customer ownership," Insull took down with him 600,000 shareholders and 500,000 bondholders. On learning, in October 1932, that he was about to be indicted in federal court on charges of mail fraud, Insull fled to Greece.

Pecora's three-day inquiry focused on the securities sales that accompanied the formation of the final two super-holding companies, Insull Utility Investment and the Corporation Security Company. Documentary evidence demonstrated that, besides thwarting

Eaton, Insull, in the words of his most sympathetic biographer, "was not entirely immune to the intoxification" of wealth. The Insull Utility Investment Corporation had been organized with 3,000,000 shares of common stock in December 1928. Of these, 750,000 shares were sold to the Insull family at $7.54 per share. By a January 17, 1929, agreement, the Insull family had the option to purchase 200,000 more shares at $15 per share; Samuel Insull personally agreed to buy an additional 250,000 shares at the price of $12 per share. That same day, trading commenced in the common stock on the Chicago Stock Exchange with an opening price of $30 per share. The reorganization gave the Insull family an immediate $24.4 million paper profit merely for trading their shares in the next lower rung of holding companies for Insull Utility common stock. The second day, Insull Utility stock reached $40 a share. On August 2, 1929, it reached a peak price of $149 or a paper profit for Insull of $166 million.

By comparing Insull Corporation annual reports with Insull Corporation federal tax returns, Pecora was able to suggest that at least part of this remarkable accretion could not be attributed to the great bull market. The Insull Utility Investment Company 1930 Annual Report to Shareholders, for example, indicated a $10.3 million profit. The same year's tax return reported a $6.5 million loss. Allied efforts "to protect the market" in Insull securities were undertaken by the Halsey Stuart investment bank, then the nation's largest dealer in corporate bonds. The Halsey Stuart firm organized two trading syndicates to maintain designated market prices during the initial issuance of securities in Insull's superholding companies without disclosing its own investment in Insull securities (which at one point would have yielded a profit of more than $36 million). By fragmenting operations in over 100 separate corporations, Insull, in addition, induced virtually every major bank in Illinois, including one managed by Charles Dawes, a former Vice President of the United States, to exceed the state's 15 percent limit on the amount of loan money that a bank could advance to any single borrower.[33]

Four days after Pecora completed taking testimony from Halsey Stuart, he began an examination of the National City Bank that would make his a household name. The National City Bank only recently had been surpassed as the largest bank in the country by the Chase National. Charles E. Mitchell was the Bank's President and Chairman of the Board. To a far greater degree than J.P. Morgan, Jr., whose reputation was derived from his father, Mitchell was the representative banker of his generation. In the preceding two decades, he had helped transform commercial banking.

Before Mitchell, commercial banks generally limited themselves to the familiar functions of receiving deposits and making loans to home buyers or business firms. Commercial banks rarely invested their funds in stocks or corporate bonds, or originated or underwrote profitable, investment banking practices were left to "private" investment houses, such as JP Morgan and Company or Kuhn, Loeb. Such restraint not only reflected the historic conservatism of commercial bankers, it was required by state and national laws, which prohibited banks from engaging in "nonbanking" (meaning non-commercial banking) functions.[34]

In 1911, the National City Bank became one of the first commercial banks to circumvent these restrictions. The Bank's senior executives incorporated the National City *Company*, a securities investment firm, which, under the General Incorporation Law of New York State, was permitted to engage in almost any business but commercial banking. Technically, the new securities affiliate was an entirely separate institution. But as Frederick Lewis Allen drolly observed, to consider an affiliated firm like the National City Company independent was "a masterpiece of legal humor." All of the National City Company's $10 million in start-up capital was advanced by the National City Bank, which declared a special 40 percent dividend and persuaded the bank's shareholders to invest "their money" in the new firm. The shareholders also agreed that they would not exercise voting rights in the new company, but by a trust agreement permanently vested voting control in three senior officers of the National City Bank. Shareholders could not even sell their nonvoting shares in the National City Company without simultaneously selling their shares in the bank. The nonvoting shares in the company were printed on the reverse side of the stock certificates of the bank, "physically as well as legally indivisible," Ferdinand Pecora would write. The bank and the company were "like one body with two heads."

Sharply questioned by President William Taft's Department of Justice, the National City Company remained a relatively small operation until 1916, when Charles E. Mitchell accepted its Presidency. In 13 years, Mitchell boosted a four person office into the largest investment house in the country, complete with 1900 employees, 69 branch offices, a private wire stretching 11,300 miles, its own engineers, accountants, bookkeepers, policemen, and annual securities sales averaging over $1.5 billion per year. To accomplish this, Mitchell simply ignored time honored banking practices. "Instead of waiting for investors to come," an admiring business executive wrote, "he took young men and women, gave them a course of training on the sale of securities, and sent them out to *find* the investors. Such methods, pursued with such vigor and on such a scale were revolutionary." To lure investors, the National City Company advertised extensively in National magazines, had its salesmen selling bonds door to door like Fuller brushes or Hoover vacuum cleaners or clerking in brightly lit downtown securities offices. "To keep the salesmen on their toes," Mitchell's headquarters sent out a daily stream of demands, pep talks, and inducements known as "flashes." The most welcome flashes offered cash prizes to the salesmen who earned the most points selling a list of hard-to-move securities. When sales lagged, Mitchell displayed a harsher side. "I should hate to think," he once telegraphed, "there is any man in our sales crowd who would confess to his inability to sell at least some of any issue of either bonds or preferred stock that we think good enough to offer. In fact, this would be an impossible situation and in the interest of all concerned, one which we would not permit to continue."

So esteemed was Mitchell's leadership that in 1921 the National City Company President was also made President of the considerably larger National City Bank; in 1929, he became the Bank's Chairman as well. He was, by then, one of the nation's most influential bankers. Even as scornful a critic as Edmund Wilson would concede, "He was the banker of bankers, the salesman of salesmen, the genius of the New Economic Era." A more coveted judgment was that of the advertising pioneer Bruce Barton. Nearly every social historian of the 1920s has paused to ridicule Barton's 1924 best seller, *The Man Nobody Knows,* in which Barton acclaimed Jesus of Nazareth as "the founder of modern business." "He picked up twelve men from the bottom ranks of business and forged them into an organization that conquered the world." What is intriguing about Barton's tract is that many of the virtues he attributed to Christ — personal magnetism, blazing conviction, power to pick men, patience, humility, and faith in good advertising — he had attributed to Mitchell the previous year in a magazine article, *Is There Anything Here That Other Men Couldn't Do?*[35]

On February 21, the seemingly indomitable Mitchell strode into the Banking Committee's Hearing room flanked by a retinue of senior associates. Ten days later, Pecora would spy Mitchell walking to Union Station alone, carrying his own grip, a discomfited and beaten man.

The banker's fall occurred with astonishing quickness. Pecora commenced his examination by focusing on Mitchell's remuneration. The President and each of several Vice Presidents of the National City Company received an annual base salary of $25,000. But the investment company's executives also shared in a management fund. After 80 percent of the company's net profits were set aside as retained earnings, senior executives were given 20 percent of annual profits. Twice a year the executives themselves voted on how to distribute the management fund — with Mitchell regularly receiving about one third of the pay-out both from the investment affiliate and from a similar fund administered by the National City Bank. In 1927, Charles E. Mitchell's portion of the investment company's fund was $529,230 and his share from the bank was $527,000, or a total of $1,056,230. In 1928, his pay-out from the two funds came to $1,316,634.14; in 1929, approximately $1,108,000. When the October 1929 Crash eliminated the possibility of profit-sharing during the latter half of that year, National City established a "morale loan fund" for officers who might have been overextended in the securities markets. Without interest or collateral, $2 million was loaned to about 100 National City Bank and National City Company officers. Only 5 percent had been repaid by the end of February 1933. Additionally, Mitchell and National City senior executives periodically also were allowed to purchase new securities issues at bargain prices. For example, when Boeing Airplane's common stock was first sold on the New York Curb Exchange at $57 in November 1928, National City executives held 45,000 shares, which they had earlier purchased privately for $30 per share. At the time when a concerted effort was being made to reduce the salary of $1600 a year paid to many federal employees, Mitchell's remuneration seemed astronomical.

The least expected revelation was saved for the late afternoon of the first day's testimony. After persistent questioning by Pecora and Senator Brookhart, Mitchell conceded that in 1929 he had sold

18,300 shares of National City stock to a relative, later revealed to be his wife, to establish a loss of $2,872,305.50 "for tax purposes." Since Mitchell later repurchased all 18,200 shares at the initial sale price even though the market price was considerably lower, it was widely assumed that the banker had violated federal income tax laws. Within three days, George Medalie, the United States Attorney for New York City, publicly launched an investigation of the transaction. Mitchell resigned from all National City positions on February 26. In late March, Mitchell was indicted for willfully evading the payment of $573,312.81 in income taxes in 1929.

The investigation of the Bank continued. It was Pecora's thesis that National City's extravagant incentive salary arrangements had encouraged bank officers to engage in unsound security selling and unsound banking practices. The Counsel now turned to what Mitchell had labeled the "production" side of National City Company operations, that is, "the manufacture of long-term credits." Fourteen months before, Senator Johnson had won headlines for revealing that the J. & W. Seligman investment house had bribed the son of a Peruvian President to secure the right to sell the country's bonds in the United States. The Seligman house had turned to the National City Company for help in marketing the bonds. By cross-examining several National City officers, Pecora adduced the background of the company's participation in the sale of $90 million worth of Peruvian bonds, which at one point in 1933 would sell for less than 5 percent of their offering price.

In March 1927, the National City Company joined the Seligman investment house and others to sponsor a $15 million Peruvian bond issue. When the bond issue was quickly absorbed by the public, National City telegraphed its Latin American representatives for updated reports. The replies were uniformly unfavorable. In July 1927, the overseas manager of the National City Bank wrote Mitchell: "As I see it, there are two factors that will long retard the economic importance of Peru. First, its population of 5,500,000 is largely Indian, two-thirds of whom reside east of the Andes, and a majority consume almost no manufactured products. Second, its principal sources of wealth, the mines and oil wells, are nearly all foreign-owned, and excepting for wages and taxes, no part of the value of their production remains in the country." The Manager pointedly added, "The country's political situation is equally uncertain." Six months later, National City received another report that "the balance of internal payments is unfavorable to Peru"; in March 1928, "the whole taxation system is a hodge-podge." The Manager of the Lima branch of the bank concluded a September 1928 cablegram: "We have assumed (a) no further national loan can be safely issued and (b) integrity Republic's finances threatened until floating debt problem solved." The National City Company nonetheless cosponsored a December 1927 $50 million Peruvian bond issue, and a $25 million Bond distribution in October 1928.

In none of the prospectuses that accompanied the three bond issues did the Bank describe Peru's bad debt record or the other adverse economic information on file. Instead, National City printed a disclaimer at the bottom of the first page: "The above statements are based on information received partly by cable from official and other sources. While not guaranteed, we believe them to be reliable, but they are in no event to be construed as representations by us." By the time of the Senate Banking Committee Hearings in February 1933, investors had lost nearly $75 million on Peruvian bonds; Pecora showed that the bankers' initial commissions had been worth $4.5 million.[36]

In 1927, with the great bull market beginning its final manic phase, National City abandoned a long-held policy and commenced selling common stock to the public for the first time, including common stock in the National City Bank. Under the National Banking law, it was illegal for a National Bank to purchase its own stock. To minimize the possibility of speculation in bank securities, the law forbade banks even from lending money when their own stock was used as collateral. The National City Bank's investment affiliate persistently evaded these strictures. In 1928, the Company began the sale of Bank stock worth $650 million. To establish what Flash No. 3873 called "working control of this market," the Bank's stock was removed from the New York Stock Exchange and traded on the more volatile over-the-counter market. There, by making purchases for its own account as frequently as every three or four minutes in quantities as large as 30,000 to 40,000 shares a day, the Company helped push up the Bank's stock price from $785 in January 1928 to the equivalent of $2925 ($585 per share after a five-for-one split) in 1929. At the same time as the Company manipulated the Bank's stock price, Company salesmen were offered special bonuses for hawking the stock. National City Company securities customers were encouraged to sell other securities and switch to the Bank's stock. In February 1929, prospective purchasers were offered the opportunity to purchase Bank stock for $5.00 below the rapidly rising market price. After the October 1929 Crash, the Bank's stock price fell from its peak of nearly $3000 to just over $100.[37]

The National City Hearings were conducted against the backdrop of the Bank Holiday Crisis. With depositors nearing panic, as state after state ordered banks to close their doors, Mitchell in particular, and New York City bankers in general, became the objects of a near hysterical public rage. Surveying press response at the conclusion of the National City hearings, the *Literary Digest* recorded an unforgiving mood: "Apologies, even resignations, do not satisfy listening editors." The mood in Congress rivaled that of the editors. Senator Burton Wheeler argued, "The best way to restore confidence in our banks, is to take these crooked presidents out of the banks and treat them the same as they treated Al Capone when Capone avoided payment of his tax."[38]

By mid-March, Roosevelt had established himself as political patron of the Pecora hearings. Roosevelt persuaded Duncan Fletcher to remain on the Banking Committee as Chair, rather than use his seniority rights to claim the Chairmanship of the Commerce Committee. The 75-year-old Floridian was so soft spoken, his voice was barely audible during the Banking Committee hearings. Often during the Hearings, he appeared to doze in his chair. But Fletcher, a party loyalist, had actively campaigned for Franklin Roosevelt. A proverbially hard worker, Fletcher had, since 1908, favored regulation of the "gambling sharks and rascals in Wall Street." Soon after his Inaugural, Roosevelt privately began meeting with Pecora as well. At Roosevelt's suggestion, Pecora and Fletcher agreed to make JP Morgan and Company the next target of the investigation.[39]

The public investigation of the House of Morgan began on May 23. Days before, telegraph lines were installed in the Senate Office Building so that reporters could wire intermittent reports. Because the noise of spectators inside and outside the Senate Banking Committee room repeatedly disrupted the hearings, the investigation was moved to the cavernous Senate Caucus Room. Klieg lights were installed in the Caucus Room's chandeliers to aid photographers. For 12 hearing days, newspapers gave the testimony front page coverage, many printing it verbatim. "So completely," reported *The New Republic*, "has the Senate probe into the great House of Morgan blanketed all other issues on the Washington stage that it is impossible at this time to arouse interest in any other topic." News sources generally tinted their coverage in purple. *Time* magazine characterized the House of Morgan as "the greatest and most legendary private business of modern times." *Business Week* termed "Morgan & Co. . . . unique in the magnitude of its operations and in the world prestige it enjoys." The *Richmond Times-Dispatch*, like many daily newspapers, seemed unable to contain its awe: "J. Pierpont Morgan, the twentieth-century embodiment of Croesus, Lorenzo the Magnificent, Rothschild; the lordly Mr. Morgan, financier and patron of arts; the unreachable Mr. Morgan, with his impregnable castle at Broad and Wall Streets and his private army of armed guards; the austere Mr. Morgan, to whose presence only the mighty are admitted, in a committee-room and upon his bare brow the gaze of the 'peepul.' Truly an extraordinary event!"[40]

Although J.P. Morgan, Jr., dominated the attention of news reporters, the real target of Pecora's probe was the firm built by his father. JP Morgan and Company was the nation's leading private bank. Compared to commercial banks like the Chase or National City, Morgan and Company was a minuscule operation. As late as 1933, "the house on the corner" included only 20 partners. Drexel and Company, an allied company in Philadelphia, added but four partners to that number. Yet the firm's reputation for financial acumen persisted for two decades after the elder Morgan's death. These 24 partners held 126 directorships and trusteeships in 89 firms with well over $20 billion in total resources. Most significantly, between January 1919 and May 1933, Morgan and Company had helped offer $6 billion in new securities.

This enormous sum was sold without the high pressure sales efforts that characterized more aggressive firms, such as Mitchell's National City Company. Morgan and Company did not employ salesmen. To maintain its status as a private bank totally exempt from state or federal regulation, it did not advertise even to the extent of placing a sign on the outer door of its Wall Street office. The firm's success, Morgan argued in an uncompromising opening statement written for him by John W. Davis, was the result of "the respect and esteem of the community." The private banker was "a national asset and not a national danger," because he was subject to a code of professional ethics so exacting that "we have never been satisfied with simply keeping within the law." Echoing his father's celebrated argument to the 1912 Pujo Committee that commercial credit was based on "character," not on "money or property," the younger Morgan insisted: "As to the theory that [a private banker] may become too powerful, it must be remembered that any power which he has comes, not from the possession of large means, but from the confidence of the people in his character and credit, and that that power, having no force to back it, would disappear at once if people thought that the character had changed or the credit had diminished."

It was Morgan and Company's reputation as a "national asset" that Pecora challenged in the Stock Exchange Practices Hearings. Five years later, Pecora would write, "In truth, the investigation of the Morgan firm elicited no such glaring abuses" as he uncovered in his investigation of "other great banking institutions and personalities." But the fact that the name J.P. Morgan was, as *The New York Times* put it, "a magic one in American finance" caused the Morgan revelations to be the most influential of the Stock Exchange Practices Hearings.

As with Mitchell, Pecora began the Morgan Hearings with a probe of income taxes. The revelation that the partners in the House of Morgan paid only $48,000 in income taxes in 1930 and none at all in 1931 and 1932 was treated by the press as the most sensational disclosure of the Morgan hearings. Even newspapers sympathetic to Morgan, like *The New York Times*, printed front-page headlines proclaiming, MORGAN PAID NO INCOME TAX FOR THE YEARS 1931 AND 1932 or TAX "EVASION" BY MORGAN IN LEGAL STOCK DEALINGS IS NOT HUNTED BY PECORA. But there was a crucial difference between the income tax disclosures about Morgan and the disclosures about Mitchell. J.P. Morgan, Jr., had violated no laws. Between 1917 and 1929, Morgan partners had paid over $57 million in income taxes, largely on their stock market profits. When the market plummeted, the Morgan partners reported no taxable income in 1931 and 1932, since their stock market losses exceeded all other taxable income. In fact, the net worth of Morgan and Company and Drexel and Company fell 55 percent between 1929 and 1931, declining from $119 million to $53 million.[41]

Nearly as widely publicized as the Morgan tax returns was the disclosure, the next day, of Morgan and Company's "preferred lists." During securities distributions for at least five firms, Morgan and Company had offered stock to firm members and influential individuals at cost or nearly at cost shortly before the security was expected to be traded on a public securities market at a substantially higher figure. This allowed the investors on the preferred list almost immediately to dispose of the security with a sure profit. In June 1927, for example, JP Morgan and Company acquired 400,000 shares of Johns-Manville common stock for $47.50, 344,000 shares of which later were resold to a private list at cost, and 56,000 sold at $57.50. The week after the offerings were made to the individuals on the preferred lists, market quotations for Johns-Manville fluctuated between $78 and $84. On January 28, 1929, JP Morgan and Company purchased 1.25 million shares of common stock from Alleghany Corporation. During the next weeks, the Morgan firm privately sold 575,000 of these shares to a preferred list at the purchase price of $20 per share. At the same time, the stock was being traded on the New York Stock Exchange on a "when issued" basis at prices ranging from $33 to $37 per share. Later in 1929, 723,000 shares of Standard Brands were sold to a favored list at the original cost of $32 per share. Within five days, Standard Brands shares were publicly traded at $44.

Those on the lists who were not members of JP Morgan and Company were people who seemed to have the ability to benefit the firm. There were a striking number of prominent political figures, led by former President Calvin Coolidge, Wilson's Secretary of War, Newton D. Baker, and Senator William McAdoo, Wilson's Secretary of the Treasury, who to his embarrassment was serving on the Senate Banking Committee investigating Morgan and Company. Also listed were Franklin Roosevelt's Secretary of the Treasury, William Woodin, who had received his shares when he was President of the American Car and Foundry Company, former Republican National Committee Chairman Charles D. Hilles, and Democratic National Chairman John J. Raskob. Other influential public figures listed included Silas Strawn, former President of both the U.S. Chamber of Commerce and the American Bar Association, John C. Martin, General Manager of the *New York Evening Post*, Democratic Party adviser Bernard Baruch, and attorney Owen Roberts, who since had been elevated to the United States Supreme Court. E.H.H. Simmons and Richard Whitney, while President and Vice President of the New York Stock Exchange, had been favored. So had fellow bankers Charles E. Mitchell, Albert Wiggin, and George Baker, and the officers of dozens of the nation's largest firms, beginning with the chief executive officers of the very largest: Alfred P. Sloan of General Motors, Walter Teagle of Standard Oil, Myron C. Taylor of U.S. Steel, Owen D. Young of General Electric, and Walter Gifford of American Telephone and Telegraph.

Morgan and Company partner George Whitney vehemently denied that any *quid pro quo* was expected of anyone on a preferred list, prompting an astonished Senator James Couzens to exclaim, "I never heard of anybody quite so altruistic in my life before." One letter offering shares did state, "There are no strings tied to this stock, so you can sell it whenever you wish." But it was difficult to accept such disclaimers at face value. At least one recipient of preferred shares, John J. Raskob, accompanied his return check with a note to George Whitney, stating, "I appreciate deeply the many courtesies shown me by you and your partners, and I sincerely hope the future holds opportunities for me to reciprocate." Albert Wiggin, Chairman of the Chase National Bank, would testify that when he received the opportunity to buy 10,000 shares of Alleghany Corporation at $20 while the shares were publicly traded at $35, "I assumed it was a favor and I was very glad to take it." At the very least, Morgan and Company's private security sales seem to have been employed to create a hospitable political and business climate for its banking operations. Even if the preferred lists accomplished no more than that, their existence fortified the belief that most investors entered the marketplace at a disadvantage.[42]

It was a sobering reflection of the limited ability of a Congressional inquiry to educate the public about a technical subject that the most serious case built against the House of Morgan received considerably less press attention than the preferred lists. The crux of Pecora's presentation was that late in the 1920s, Morgan and Company, too, had surrendered its traditional austere standards and helped organize three giant holding companies whose primary function was to increase promoters' profits. Most significant was the evidence Pecora developed over the course of several hearing days concerning the United Corporation. Before January 1929, Morgan and Company owned substantial blocks of stock in the United Gas Improvement Company, the Public Service Corporation of New Jersey, and the Mohawk Hudson Power Corporation, three gas and electricity firms whose operations were centered in New York and New Jersey. Each was a holding company; the United Gas Company, for example, owned stock in 60 separate local operating companies. Such local or regional part holding and part operating utility firms often had been defended as contributing to the most efficient generation of power in a local market.

Early in 1929, however, JP Morgan and Company joined with Bonbright and Company to create the United Corporation, which ultimately held shares in public utility holding and operating companies in localities as widely dispersed as Connecticut, Illinois, Mississippi, Georgia, and France. Even Morgan and Company's George Whitney was able to identify but one "useful public purpose . . . served by the incorporation of the United Corporation": the opportunity for investors to diversify their holdings in public utility firms.

Pecora belittled that purpose. Persistent questions contrasted the opportunities accorded the Morgan and Bonbright firms and favored individuals on Morgan's United Corporation preferred list with the opportunities offered the public investor. United Corporation's initial capital structure had been formed in January 1929, when Morgan and Company traded its utility corporation shares and a small quantity of cash for 600,000 preferred shares, 800,000 common shares, and 714,200 perpetual option warrants issued by United. United also sold 400,000 shares of common stock and 1,000,000 option warrants to the Morgan and Bonbright firms in return for $10 million in cash investment from each. Theoretically, the aggregate market value of United's preferred and common stock should have equaled approximately the value of the shares United held in other firms plus United's other assets. But the 2,714,200 perpetual option warrants gave the Morgan and Bonbright firms the chance to buy up to that many common shares at the option price of $27.50 at any time in the future. In effect, the options placed a ceiling on how much of the common stock's price appreciation the two investment firms had to share with other United Corporation shareholders. Any time the common stock price exceeded $27.50, the investment banks could exercise their warrants, obtaining an instant profit equal to the difference between the market price and option price for the stock, and reducing the proportion of earnings and assets available for each common share.

Pecora documented that the combination of the frenzied 1929 stock market and public confidence in the "magic" Morgan name had swiftly elevated the United common stock from an initial market price just over $25 to a price of $72 at one point in 1929. By selling some of its United preferred stock, common stock, and option warrants, Morgan and Company was able to realize over $19 million in profits by 1933, including profits of $8.5 million on the sale of 200,000 option warrants between June and September 1929.[43]

Public reaction to the Morgan Hearings was almost as condemnatory as that to the Charles E. Mitchell and National City Company revelations. Although the failure of the Morgan partners to pay income taxes and their use of the preferred lists won the greatest attention from journalists, the most serious editorial judgment was that the House of Morgan had forfeited its right to remain unregulated. "Why It Hurts" *The New York Times* titled an editorial as sorrowful as if it were describing the fall of the House of Thebes: "Here was a firm of bankers, perhaps the most famous and powerful in the whole world, which was certainly under no necessity of practicing the small arts of petty traders. Yet it failed under a test of its pride and prestige. By a mistake which had with the years swollen into a grievous fault, it sacrificed something intangible, imponderable, that had to do with the very highest repute." Walter Lippmann termed "the system of favoritism to insiders... a system which can be explained but not defended." He called on Washington to "reduce the sheer power of so much privately directed money." Though guilty of "no crude crime against the law," the House of Morgan, according to the *New York World-Telegram*, was guilty of "the far deeper, more dangerous offense of what Lord Bryce well calls 'The submarine warfare which wealth can wage.' The country, the tone of its business, finance, and government, the whole capitalistic structure will be better, safer, and more stable when this long-standing notion of wealth's high prerogatives and immunities has gone finally into the discard." "No banking is private," *Business Week* insisted flatly. William Allen White summed up the Hearings in his *Emporia Gazette*: "If the turmoil in the courts and in the Congressional committee stops, changes, or modifies the great thimble-rigging game of Wall Street, the depression of the last four years will have been worth all its cost."[44]

The public response to the Morgan Hearings was directly responsible for the passage of the Glass-Steagall Act in 1933, which required private banks to limit themselves either to receiving deposits or to providing investment services. Roosevelt initially had offered the bill only lukewarm support. Treasury Secretary Woodin favored delaying its adoption. But on the third day of the Morgan

Hearings, the Senate unexpectedly enacted the bill by a voice vote. The House soon followed suit.[45]

The Hearings also galvanized support for a new $100,000 appropriation for Pecora's investigation.[46] But the most enthusiastic appreciation of Pecora's work came from the Executive Branch. On May 27, President Roosevelt signed into law the Securities Act of 1933, the most important outcome to that date of the Stock Exchange Hearings. With a sideward glance toward Capitol Hill, Roosevelt stated:

> The new law will also safeguard against the abuses of high-pressure salesmanship in security flotations. It will require full disclosure of all the private interests on the part of those who seek to sell securities to the public. The Act is thus intended to correct some of the evils which have been so glaringly revealed in the private exploitation of the public's money.[47]

The Securities Act of 1933

The Securities Act of 1933 was a conservative response to the 1929–1932 Stock Market Crash. As with the Pecora investigation, a primary enduring mission of the Securities and Exchange Commission (*SEC*) created the following year, has been to compel disclosure of data by firms involved in the securities markets, indirectly inducing these firms to avoid illegal or embarrassing activities. The Commission's "disclosure philosophy" became so well established, it was generally regarded as an inevitable method of regulating corporate finance.

Each of Roosevelt's principal 1932 Presidential campaign advisers favored the creation of a very different type of federal agency to direct the flow of new investment in private industry. Raymond Moley, chief of the Presidential campaign "brains trust," was an admirer of the regulatory approach urged by Charles Van Hise, University of Wisconsin President, in his celebrated 1912 book, *Concentration and Control.* Agreeing with Van Hise that the growth of large corporations was inevitable, Moley disparaged any attempt to "atomize" big business because it would threaten "America's greatest contribution to a higher standard of living for the body of its citizenry — the development of mass production." Instead, Moley recommended a turning away "from the nostalgic philosophy of the trust busters" toward the development of federal "controls to stimulate and stabilize economic activity." At the same time, Moley was convinced that Roosevelt's financial policies would have to shore up business confidence in order to stimulate private investment. In retrospect, Moley would term the 1933 Securities Act "a grave mistake" that had "only a negative effect upon recover," since it lacked the support of the investment banking community it regulated.[48]

Economist Rexford Tugwell, Moley's colleague at Columbia University and a fellow brains truster, agreed with Moley that "we were . . . a long way on the road to a system of monopolies . . . we should allow it to evolve and should manage it publicly, rather than go back to a more primitive state where no social management existed." In Tugwell's view, the Great Depression had been caused, in part, by the misallocation of capital. Overexpansion of plant facilities had raised prices, but there was no corresponding increase in consumer purchasing power. Where industries had as much as twice the plant, machinery, materials, and men needed for current production, Tugwell regarded the need for a "system of planning" as all but self-evident. After Roosevelt's nomination, Tugwell presented him with a "proposal for an Economic Council" to provide "integrated industrial planning." A chief function of the Council would be to "encourage or discourage the flow of capital into various industries."[49]

Adolf Berle, a Columbia University Law School Professor and the brains truster with the greatest technical familiarity with corporate finance, urged Roosevelt in May 1932 to establish a federal board that would "exact full information about securities sold" and would also "exercise a real control over undue expansion of groups of credit instruments, where issue of these reached a point threatening the safety of the financial structure."[50]

Roosevelt disagreed. He approached the problem of securities regulation with the instincts of a progressive politician in the Wilson and Brandeis tradition, rather than of a economist concerned with the larger questions of capital allocation and economic recovery. Rarely did Roosevelt speak about the stock market without invoking the title of Louis Brandeis's much quoted book, *Other People's Money.* Like Brandeis, Roosevelt viewed the need to reform securities sales practices primarily as stemming from the self-interest of investment bankers, particularly the House of Morgan. Like Brandeis, Roosevelt believed the moral delicts of the bankers would be curbed when fully exposed to public scrutiny. Frequently Roosevelt's speeches paraphrased the first sentence of Chapter 5 of the Brandeis book: "Publicity is justly commended as a remedy for social and industrial diseases. Sunlight is said to be the best of disinfectants; electric light the most efficient policeman."

The process of transforming Roosevelt's securities policy into a bill began within hours of Roosevelt's election. On November 9, 1932, Roosevelt received a telegram from Huston Thompson requesting a conference to discuss an "outline to cover platform pledge regarding sale of securities and holding companies." Thompson, a Western populist transformed into a Wilsonian Democrat, had been much affected by Brandeis's arguments for local government and small scale industry when he had served in the Wilson Administration as an Assistant Attorney General and a Commissioner of the Federal Trade Commission (*FTC*). From 1920 to 1921 and again from 1923 to 1924 he had been the FTC's Chair. While at the FTC, Thompson had publicly supported the efforts of the Capital Issues Committee to prevent, as he wrote, a "speculative orgy in 'wild cat' investments." When the Capital Issues Committee disbanded, Thompson directed an FTC securities fraud program, although he came to believe it had doubtful legal authority.

"As I see it," Thompson had written in a magazine article much influenced by *Other People's Money*, "the solution must be effected through a system of publicity which shall protect the public by informing the investors as to the securities to be sold by giving the prospective purchaser a full opportunity to be enlightened and then leaving to him the responsibility of purchase." Thompson personally had written the 1932 Democratic Party platform plank calling for control of the sale of securities and had urged Roosevelt to deliver campaign speeches both on securities sales and holding companies. In 1933, at the age of 58, Thompson was a courtly, distinguished looking man of considerable presence, not unaware that Louis Howe, Roosevelt's political mentor, and Progressive Senator George Norris were encouraging the President-elect to nominate Thompson as his Attorney General. Roosevelt met with Thompson, whose abilities as a courtroom attorney Roosevelt admired, and Thompson soon forwarded a memorandum outlining his approach to securities, holding companies, and amendments to the antitrust laws.[51]

Roosevelt also authorized Moley to elicit from Samuel Untermyer suggestions regarding regulation of the stock exchanges and securities issues. At 74, Untermyer was the grand old man of the corporate reform movement. His crusading service as counsel to the 1912 Pujo investigation of the "Money Trust" had won him Moley's regard as a "colorful, voluble John the Baptist preparing the way for the solemnities of Wilson, Brandeis, and Glass."

Moley was soon disappointed. In mid-January 1913, Untermyer forwarded a bill "to prevent the use of the mails or of the telegraph and telephone in furtherance of fraudulent and harmful transactions on stock exchanges." As convinced in 1933 as he had been in 1914 that the only method to guarantee the constitutionality of the bill was to grant enforcement powers to the Post Office, Untermyer formulated his bill to give the Postmaster General sweeping powers to issue regulations and prohibitions concerning transactions on the stock exchanges, new securities issuances, periodic corporate financial statements, and the membership of the stock exchanges. Moley's first impression was horror. "The Post Office Department was essentially a service organization," he later wrote. "The idea of sticking an immense regulatory machine into it horrified my sense of the administrative and legal proprieties."[52]

Roosevelt shared Moley's doubt that empowering the Post Office to supervise such matters as a uniform system of accounting would be wise. According to one subsequent news account, Roosevelt also was annoyed with Untermyer for leaking a self-serving story to a New York City newspaper just before a scheduled meeting with Roosevelt. But the factor that finally persuaded Roosevelt to shelve the Untermyer Bill was the unique opportunity rapidly to enact legislation created by the favorable public and Congressional response to his handling of the Banking Crisis just after his inauguration on March 4. Roosevelt's entire legislative program was accelerated. After making the previously unplanned decision to keep Congress in session, Roosevelt indicated to Moley on March 18 that among his legislative priorities for the first session of the 73rd Congress would be "regulation of corporations," by which he meant a securities bill.[53] From about that date onward, Roosevelt was determined to draft and quickly submit to Congress a securities bill that could be voted on while he still enjoyed the extraordinary political support generated by the Banking Crisis. Without initially informing Moley, Roosevelt began discussing alternative securities proposals with other drafting teams.

Shortly after taking office on March 4, Roosevelt had directed his Attorney General, Homer Cummings, and his Secretary of Commerce, Daniel Roper, to work with Huston Thompson in preparing another draft of the securities bill. Apparently, Thompson was well aware of Roosevelt's self-imposed deadline. After studying Blue Sky laws and earlier federal proposals, he and his team hurriedly assembled a draft of a bill that combined features of several of these precedents, as well as provisions modeled on the English Companies Act. Thompson then consulted with Justice Brandeis and officials of the Federal Reserve Board and Interstate Commerce Commission before presenting his draft to Roosevelt, Moley, and Roper on March 19. Roosevelt almost immediately indicated to Thompson that the draft was acceptable.[54]

Roosevelt submitted Thompson's bill to both Houses of Congress the following day. In an accompanying Message, which borrowed heavily from Brandeis's *Other People's Money*, the Final Report of the Capital Issues Committee and the 1932 Democratic Party platform, Roosevelt emphasized:

> The Federal Government cannot and should not take any action which might be construed as approving or guaranteeing that newly issued securities are sound in the sense that their value will be maintained or that the properties which they represent will earn profit.
>
> There is, however, an obligation upon us to insist that every issue of new securities to be sold in interstate commerce shall be accompanied by full publicity and information, and that no essentially important element attending the issue shall be concealed from the buying public.
>
> This proposal adds to the ancient rule of caveat emptor the further doctrine: "Let the seller also beware." It puts the burden of telling the whole truth on the seller. It should give impetus to honest dealing in securities and thereby bring back public confidence.[55]

As originally submitted to Congress, Thompson's draft empowered the FTC to investigate and prosecute fraudulent securities sales. With respect to corporate security issuances made by firms with $100,000 or more of a capital stock, except for securities sold by common carriers or public utilities already supervised by the federal government and other limited exemptions, no sale or offer to sell a security would be lawful until a registration statement was filed with the FTC. Thompson's draft stipulated that securities sales could commence immediately, without the Commission's prior approval. However, the Commission was vested with powers to revoke the registration of any security whose issuer "has been or is about to engage in fraudulent transactions . . . is not conducting its business in accordance with law . . . is in any other way dishonest," or whose business is "in unsound condition or insolvent." It also could revoke a security's registration when "the enterprise or business of the issuer . . . is not based upon sound principles, and . . . the revocation is in the interest of the public welfare."

In addition, the FTC was given unlimited power to investigate the sale of all securities, including those otherwise exempt from the Act, if it suspected that any firm or promoter was willfully attempting to defraud a purchaser, and to forward any evidence uncovered to the Justice Department for criminal prosecution.[56]

In the House of Representatives, Thompson's bill was claimed by Commerce Committee Chairman Sam Rayburn. This was fortunate for Roosevelt. Rayburn was just beginning his most effective years in Congress. In the next three years he would be the member of the House of Representatives most responsible for the enactment of the SEC's first three basic enabling laws. Although by inclination Rayburn was a conservative cut-the-federal-budget-and-don't-interfere-with-the-private-economy Southern Democrat, once branded by the AFL "the workingman's enemy," his intense loyalty to Roosevelt and his populist suspicion of Wall Street soon led Rayburn to consider himself "a helluva New Dealer." Besides being one of the ablest legislative tacticians ever to serve in Congress, Rayburn had some technical familiarity with securities law as a result of an eight year campaign, ultimately successful in 1920, to subject railroad stocks and bonds to the regulation of the Interstate Commerce Commission.[57]

Like Roosevelt, Rayburn was convinced of the strategic advantage of moving for rapid enactment of a securities bill. Hearings began on March 31, with only two days of testimony scheduled. Initially, Rayburn invited no opposition witnesses to appear. Thompson led off the hearings by urging that the combination of an estimated $25 billion worth of "undesirable or worthless" securities sold between 1919 and 1932 and the failure of Blue Sky laws to be enforced across state lines made adoption of a federal securities bill imperative. Almost immediately, however, Thompson's bill was subjected to a buzz saw of criticism, first from members of Congress on the Commerce Committee, then from the opposition witnesses Rayburn reluctantly allowed to testify. Most harshly criticized were the provisions permitting the FTC to revoke any security it found "not based upon sound principles" and the section subjecting directors to strict liability to any securities purchaser for an indefinite period of time for any material misstatement of fact in the registration statement. Also criticized were the provisions about fraud in the resale of securities after the securities were first issued, the section empowering the FTC to enforce Blue Sky laws, and the failure to exempt short term bank loans, commonly called commercial paper.

By April 4, the day before the House Hearings concluded, Rayburn was convinced that the Thompson Bill was too stringent and would have to be thoroughly revised or replaced. That day, Rayburn called on Raymond Moley and through him swiftly won President Roosevelt's agreement to alter drastically Thompson's bill.[58]

Roosevelt acquiesced to Rayburn's view that the bill was too far reaching, because the substantive feature of the legislation he felt most strongly about was the basic disclosure principle, and Rayburn persuaded him that so stringent a bill might prove unnecessarily divisive.

On April 4, when Rayburn communicated his unhappiness with Thompson's draft to Moley, Moley contacted Harvard Law Professor Felix Frankfurter. Within hours, Frankfurter wired back: "Three of us will arrive at the Carlton Friday morning." From the time of that telegram onward, Frankfurter was the man Roosevelt and Moley relied on to supervise the drafting and enactment of a securities bill. Long after the legislation was on the statute books, the Harvard Law Professor would retain Roosevelt's near total confidence in matters concerning securities law reform. Frankfurter would help select the draftsmen of the SEC's three basic statutes, the FTC officials who enforced the Securities Act during its first year, most of the original SEC Commissioners, and many of the Commission's top staff appointees. It would be Frankfurter's ideas, more than the simpler slogans of Louis Brandeis, that would dominate the Commission during the New Deal.

Felix Frankfurter, as Raymond Moley later would explain to Huston Thompson, "was . . . in the eyes of the administration the leading lawyer of this country." Such encomiums are nearly always subject, but there was considerable evidence that Roosevelt so regarded Frankfurter. During Roosevelt's two terms as Governor of New York, Frankfurter periodically visited Albany or Hyde Park and was a frequent correspondent. An admiring Roosevelt observed to a close associate, "Felix has more ideas per minute than any man of my acquittance. He has a brilliant mind, but it clicks so fast it makes my head fairly spin. I find him tremendously interesting and stimulating." Frankfurter was Roosevelt's initial choice to be Solicitor General, a position that Roosevelt urged Frankfurter to accept explicitly because "I can't put you on the Supreme Court from the Harvard Law School." Frankfurter stunned Roosevelt by declining, but Frankfurter believed, and arguably demonstrated, "that I can do much more to be of use to you by staying in Cambridge than by becoming Solicitor General." Roosevelt chided Frankfurter for being "an independent pig," but never wavered in his determination to nominate Frankfurter to the highest Court, a nomination ultimately telephoned to Cambridge early in 1939.[59]

Frankfurter's primary academic interest was administrative law. In Frankfurter's unromantic reckoning, the advent of modern industry made inevitable the growth of government bureaus and a diminution of the role of the courts as the basic arbiter of private rights. Prefacing one of the first administrative law casebooks in 1932, Frankfurter characterized this transformation as "the distinctive development of our era":

> Governmental regulation of banking, insurance, public utilities, industry, finance, immigration, the professions, health and morals, in short, the inevitable response of government to the needs of modern society, is building up a body of enactments not written by legislatures and of adjudications not made by courts, and only to a limited degree subject to their revisions. These powers are lodged in vast congeries of agencies. We are in the midst of a process still largely unconscious and unscientific, of adjusting the play of these powers to the traditional system of Anglo-American law and courts.[60]

In retrospect, it is obvious that the emergence of "vast congeries of agencies" was the most fundamental transformation to have occurred in 20th century American governance. Indeed, it long was commonplace to assume that most routine Executive Branch decisions in a modern democracy will be made by its Fourth Branch, the administrative agencies. Precisely because Franklin Roosevelt ushered into existence an "alphabet" of regulatory agencies, political scientists usually identify him as the pivotal figure in the development of the modern federal government.

But in 1933, Felix Frankfurter was one of a comparatively few scholars who were thinking seriously about how the administrative agencies themselves should be administered. Frankfurter's approach to the agencies was premised on his skepticism that Congress by legislative enactment could effectively administer the structure or behavior of a modern economy. On the other hand, Frankfurter was even more skeptical of the wisdom of nearly unlimited delegations of power to administrative agencies along the lines proposed by Tugwell. An authority on Constitutional Law, Frankfurter had strong grounds for believing that too broad a grant would be unconstitutional, a belief confirmed in 1935 when the National Recovery Administration Act was so ruled. But his thought was based upon an even more fundamental consideration. Rule by experts simply could not survive without popular support:

> The expert [Frankfurter insisted] should be on tap, but not on top.
>
> . . . In a democracy, politics is a process of popular education — the task of adjusting the conflicting interests of diverse groups in the community, and bending the hostility and suspicion and ignorance engendered by group interests toward a comprehension of mutual understanding. For these ends, *expertise* is indispensable. But politicians must enlist popular support for the technical means by which alone social policies can be realized.

The problem of administrative law was to persuade Congress to adopt laws that both particularized substantive legal goals so specifically that these ends could survive hostile or indifferent interpretation by the courts or political appointees and were sufficiently flexible in means that a creative agency could adjust to changed or newly discovered circumstances. The success of Frankfurter's approach to administrative governance was dependent on the creation of a new class of expert administrators. By 1930, this instinct has grown into a theory memorialized in Frankfurter's book *The Public and Its Government*:

> The staples of contemporary politics — the organization of industry, the course of public utilities, the well-being of agriculture, the mastery of crime and disease — are deeply enmeshed

> in intricate and technical facts, and must be extricated from presupposition and partisanship. Such matters require systematic effort to contract the area of conflict and passion and widen the area of accredited knowledge as the basis of action.

"There are some things we can no longer afford," Frankfurter would write in 1934. "Above all we can no longer afford to do without a highly trained, disinterested governmental personnel. What this Administration has had to do is to create something like the English Civil Service overnight." "The greatest immediate need," Frankfurter would write Walter Lippmann while lobbying for the 1933 Securities Act, is "qualified men for key jobs."[61]

By April 7, when he arrived in Washington to meet with Roosevelt and Moley, Frankfurter had selected three younger associates, James M. Landis, Benjamin V. Cohen, and Thomas G. Corcoran, to help draft the Securities Act. In time, each of the three would achieve political prominence in his own right, but in the spring of 1933, Landis, Cohen, and Corcoran still were considered Frankfurter's aides, sympathetically referred to as "Felix's boys," derided as "Frankfurter's little hot dogs."

Of the three, the most prominent in the history of the SEC was Landis. Landis was Frankfurter's protégé. The son of a Presbyterian missionary, Landis was born and lived until the age of 13 in Japan. After working his way through Cicero, Horace, and solid geometry under the tutelage of a knuckle cracking pedant, Landis "ran out of schooling" and was shipped to the United States for further education. Here, his intellectual prowess was readily apparent: He graduated first in his high school class, was "first group" in every subject at Princeton but German, and received such high marks at the Harvard Law School that Dean Roscoe Pound would have to remind journalists that Landis "wasn't the brightest student at Harvard since Mr. Justice Brandeis, as has been said," Landis had merely led all students in the Class of 1924.

A decisive moment in Landis's career occurred in his second year at Harvard Law School, when he met Frankfurter. Frankfurter championed him, making it possible for Landis to spend a fourth year as a special fellow in Cambridge, where the two began collaborating on articles, then sending him to Washington to serve as a clerk to Justice Brandeis. In 1926, at the age of 27, Landis began teaching at Harvard Law School as an assistant Professor. His advance thereafter, even Dean Pound would concede, was "meteoric, almost unheard of." Two years later, Landis coauthored with Frankfurter *The Business of the Supreme Court* and became the youngest full Professor in the Law School's history and the school's first Professor of Legislation.

In time, Landis would be responsible for a memorable articulation of Frankfurter's view of government-by-administrative-agency. In 1938, responding to criticism that the independent administrative agencies had become "a headless fourth branch of the government, a haphazard deposit of irresponsible agencies and uncoordinated powers," Landis would defend the administrative process as "the most significant development in legal history in the last century," essential because of "the inadequacy of a simple tripartite form of government to deal with modern problems." As Landis put it: "With the rise of regulation, the need for expertness became dominant; for the art of regulating an industry requires knowledge of the details of its operations, ability to shift requirements as the condition of the industry may dictate." Disparaging legislation that attempted to prescribe in too great detail "the conditions of administrative action" and administrators who took "the legislative approach" of reading "a governing statute with the hope of finding limitations upon authority," Landis argued that the appropriate relationship of the democratic legislature to the expert agency was to define the agency's area of expertise and recite the appropriate problems for it to solve, leaving it broad discretion as to means. Exceeding even Frankfurter's faith in administrative experts, Landis would recommend in his seminal work, *The Administrative Process*, greater insulation of the agency from court review and an increase in the sanctions agencies could enforce. He would urge that the "singleness" of an agency's function would lead to "a professionalism of spirit" that would justify its greater independence.[62]

Cohen, at the age of 39, was the eldest of the three men Frankfurter brought to Washington. Although he later would secure William Douglas's judgment as "the best and most intelligent man in the New Deal," Cohen's shyness camouflaged his exceptional legal talents. Impressed with Cohen's intelligence, Frankfurter considered him "perhaps the most brilliant graduate of the Chicago Law School, one of the most brilliant doctors we [meaning the Harvard Law School] ever had."[63]

The more personal Corcoran also had been a Frankfurter favorite while at Harvard Law School. Not only had he coauthored articles with Frankfurter, but he had assimilated Frankfurter's view of the decisive significance of agency staffing. Five years later, at his apogee in the Roosevelt Administration, he would state that his highest ambition was to be Civil Service Commissioner. Already by the spring of 1933 he was operating out of an attorney's office in the Reconstruction Finance Corporation as "a sort of Washington general manager for Frankfurter," wrote Raymond Moley, "demoniacally attempting to staff the entire federal government," in the view of journalists Joseph Alsop and Robert Kintner. Frankfurter had sought out the 33-year-old Corcoran primarily to help lobby for the securities bill that Landis and Cohen would draft.[64]

Rayburn quickly gave the nod for Landis and Cohen to set to work. Both agreed with Frankfurter that the English Companies Act should constitute the basis of their draft. Working feverishly, Landis and Cohen were able to assemble a new bill within two days. The core of the Securities Act of 1933, Landis would recall 25 years later, was "to be found in that hurried draft of ours":

> Our draft remained true to the conception voiced by the President in his message of March 29, 1933, to the Congress, namely, that its requirements should be limited to full and fair disclosure of the nature of the security being offered and that there should be no authority to pass upon the investment quality of the security. . . . We also provided for the passage of a period of time before a registration statement could become effective, giving the Commission power during that period to issue a stop-order because of misrepresentation or inadequacy of disclosure. . . . This device of a waiting period, then completely novel, in our opinion would accomplish several things. It would slow up the procedure of selling securities and the consequent pressures that the underwriters could exert upon their selling group or other dealers to take sight unseen an allotment of the issue. It would give an opportunity for the financial world to acquaint itself with the basic data underlying a security issue and through that acquaintance to circulate among the buying public as well as independent dealers some intimation of its quality.[65]

By April 21, Landis and Cohen had completed a revised draft. Significantly, the FTC was to be given the power to define accounting concepts used in preparation of registration statements. Pivotal matters, such as the Act's distinction between regulated "public offerings," versus unregulated "private offerings" and a definition of fraud, had reached polished form. Rayburn was impressed, and later that day wrote Frankfurter of his belief that "we are going . . . to get out a good, workable bill."

Earlier, Rayburn named a Commerce Committee Subcommittee to supervise preparation of the new securities bill. Rayburn insisted that railroad securities — subject to regulation under the Congressman's 1920 amendment to the Interstate Commerce Act — be added to the list of exempted securities. Municipal securities also were exempted, Landis explained in a letter 30 years later, because "the mayors of our various cities rose up en masse when we tried to bring the issuance of municipal securities under the 1933 Act." But Rayburn dissuaded the subcommittee from adopting other significant changes. No public subcommittee hearings were held. Only after Moley repeatedly insisted did Rayburn agree that the subcommittee would hold a private meeting to consider the objections of leading corporate lawyers John Foster Dulles, Arthur H. Dean, and Alexander I. Henderson. Dulles, leading the group, insinuated that Rayburn was sponsoring legislation that would undermine the financial system. Rayburn, incensed, retorted that all that was being demanded was that capitalism live up to its pretensions. The more low keyed Dean and Henderson also failed in attempts to persuade the Subcommittee to soften the civil liability provision and eliminate the 30-day waiting period.

Although local commercial banks had some success in broadening the exemptions under the Securities Act, the Wall Street investment banking community and the New York State Stock Exchange were almost entirely ineffective in their lobbying efforts. To reverse a popular saying of the day, the period of the First Hundred Days of the Roosevelt Administration was that rare time when money talked and nobody listened. Rayburn, after 12 years in the Washington of Harding, Coolidge, and Hoover, was fully aware of the period's uniqueness. Like Roosevelt, he was animated by a conviction that the moment could not last, that he had to move swiftly or it might be too late.

After further technical refinements, Rayburn formally introduced the Landis-Cohen draft on May 3. The full Commerce Committee modestly added to the list of exemptions securities issued by state banks, then reported out the bill to the House on May 4. The following day Rayburn moved that the entire House enact the measure.

The House debate was an anticlimax. There was almost no discussion of the provisions of the bill itself. Many Members of Congress were inclined to accept Congressman Arthur H. Greenwood's conclusion: "I have never read a bill that appeared to be more carefully drawn.... This bill should not be mutilated or garbled by amendments that have not been thought out." Shortly before 5:00 p.m., the House of Representatives unanimously adopted the Landis-Cohen Bill on a voice vote. Even Rayburn seemed a little startled by how easily it had been pushed through, gleefully saying to Cohen, who had sat with him during the final debate, that he "did not know whether the bill passed so readily because it was so damned good or so damned incomprehensible."[66]

Cohen's pleasure could only have been short lived. In the Senate, the Landis-Cohen Bill was in serious trouble. Duncan Fletcher, Chairman of the Senate Banking Committee, did not share Rayburn's anxieties about Thompson's securities bill. During the course of eight hearing days, early in April, Thompson had shown considerable flexibility, agreeing to remove the controversial revocation Section, eliminate the provision empowering the federal government to enforce state Blue Sky laws, limiting the bill to prospective applications, exempting commercial paper, and expanding the items to be disclosed — changes cumulatively so fundamental that Fletcher later would inform his Senate colleagues that "there are not a great many differences" between the revised Thompson draft and the House backed Landis-Cohen Bill. In fact, the differences that did remain were significant. Thompson's bill was considerably sketchier in detail, imposed strict liability on persons signing a registration statement "false or deceptive in any material respect," did not include a waiting period between the time a firm registered a security with the FTC and was allowed to sell the security to the public, and was ambiguous in its characterization of many items that needed to be disclosed. Obviously moved by Pecora's revelations before the Banking Committee, Fletcher seemed all but unwilling to consider Wall Street objections to Thompson's bill, at one point snapping at the bill's most articulate opponent, Arthur Dean, "We do not want to spend our time hearing criticism of the bill, with people picking it to pieces here and there and getting nowhere."[67]

As Thompson's bill progressed toward Senate Banking Committee approval in late April, Frankfurter made an unsuccessful attempt to have it withdrawn. Using Banking Committee member Senator James Byrnes as an intermediary, Frankfurter attempted to convince Fletcher of the Thompson Bill's deficiencies. Byrnes failed, and the Banking Committee official reported out the bill on April 27.

Thereafter, Frankfurter assumed a much more active role in lobbying on behalf of his disciples' bill. On April 28, he wired Moley an analysis of the Thompson draft, beginning, "Detailed consideration of Senate securities bill proves that in essential aspects it is partly innocuous and partly unconstitutional." With Roosevelt's approval, Moley showed Frankfurter's telegram to Senate majority Leader Joseph T. Robinson and impressed on Robinson Roosevelt's preference for Frankfurter's bill. Nonetheless, with little debate, the Senate enacted the revised Thompson ill on May 8, three days after the House had adopted the Landis-Cohen Bill.

The decisive Conference Committee began on May 15. Fletcher led the five man Senate contingent, which included Carter Glass and Hiram Johnson. Rayburn led the five members from the House. Landis and Cohen attended as technical experts for the House, and Ollie Butler and Walter Miller, coauthors of Thompson's bill, as advisers to the Senate. Fletcher graciously accepted the inevitable, and suggested that the younger Rayburn act as Conference Committee Chairman. As a practical matter, this ensured that the Landis-Cohen draft would be the basis of the Committee's negotiation.

Because meetings of Conference Committees are the penultimate step in the enactment process, when legislators are particularly eager to reach a mutually satisfactory compromise, they often result in the weakening of regulatory measures. Precisely this occurred in the securities bill conference. Members of both Houses' negotiating teams agreed to compromise and make the bill less stringent in order to ensure rapid passage. For the Senate conferees, this primarily meant surrendering their more severe civil liability. For the House, it meant agreeing to shorten the waiting period from 30 to 20 days and surrendering the provision, originally proposed in the Thompson Bill, empowering the federal government to enforce the Blue Sky laws when securities were sold across state lines.[68]

As enacted, the 1933 Securities Act granted regulatory power to the Federal Trade Commission. The heart of the Act was the detailed list of data in Schedule A that an issuer of securities had to disclose in the registration statement filed with the FTC and in prospectuses available to investors before it offered securities to the public. Schedule A attempted to do more than give an investor detailed financial records of the issuer; it called for disclosure of information about the firm's business, need for capital, officers, and the costs of the securities issuance. In discouraging fraud or unfairness, the Act was most likely to be effective. A subsequent *Columbia Law Review* study, for example, demonstrated that virtually every undisclosed aspect of the option warrants issued by JP Morgan in connection with the United Corporation would have been revealed by Schedule A. If the FTC found the registration statement "on its face incomplete or inaccurate in any material respect," it could seek a stop order barring public sale of the securities. A corporation's board of directors, principal executive, financial or accounting officers, outside accountants, engineers or appraisers who certified a part of the registration statement, and the firm's underwriters (investment bankers) could be held liable for any untrue statement or omission of a material fact in the registration statement after it became effective unless they could prove they had acted with due diligence.

The Act, however, did not invest the FTC with power to pass on the quality of securities issued, and did not attempt to direct capital to those industries where it was most needed. It did not give the Commission authority to enforce state Blue Sky laws even for issues that were exempt from the filing provisions of the federal Securities Act. It totally exempted all securities already issued, all securities issued intrastate, all securities issued by the United States, any state, or political subdivision of a state, all securities issued or guaranteed by national or state banks, building and loan associations, or similar institutions, securities issued by railroads, insurance annuity contracts, securities to be repaid in less than nine months, and, if the FTC saw fit, securities issuances of less than $100,000.

No one better understood the modest nature of the statute than Felix Frankfurter. "The New Federal Securities Act," he explained in an August 1933 *Fortune* magazine article, "is a belated and conservative attempt to curb the recurrence of old abuses which, through failure of adequate legislation, had attained disastrous proportions." It was "a modest first installment of legislative controls to assure commerce and industry a continuous flow of their necessary capital . . . strong insofar as publicity is potent; it is weak insofar as publicity is not enough." Yet Frankfurter discerned more in his creation than a federal Blue Sky law. The Act's greater import was the opportunity it offered for a modern administrative agency to evolve. Far more significant than the detailed Schedule A was the little discussed residual authority granted to the FTC to evolve uniform accounting standards; it was this power, more than any other part of the Act, that Frankfurter calculated would "have far-reaching beneficial effects on American corporate practices."[69]

Virtually from the date of its legislation, the Securities Act was controversial. Initially it was assailed by disappointed reformers. As early as April 26, *The New Republic*'s T.R.B. informed his readers, "The bankers rewrote the bill." This was arrant nonsense, but no more sweeping in its condemnation than Moley's privately held opinion that the Act "had been hurried through with inadequate debate," or Berle's published condescension that the Act "leaves unsolved the major questions." Sharing this view was William O. Douglas, then a young Yale Law Professor, who, like Berle, was one of the nation's leading authorities on corporate finance. Doubtful that most investors had "the time, money, or intelligence to assimilate the mass of information in the registration statement," he characterized the Securities Act as "wholly secondary in any thorough-going and comprehensive program for social control in this field":

> There is no machinery provided for obtaining subsequent reliable information either in the form of annual reports or otherwise.... There is nothing in the Act which controls the power of the self-perpetuating management group which has risen to a position of dominance in our industrial organization. There is nothing in the Act which purports to deal with the protection of the rights of minorities. There is nothing which concerns the problem of capital structure, its soundness or unsoundness. There is nothing that deals with the problem of mobilizing the flow of capital to various productive channels. And, finally, there is nothing which deals with the fundamental problem of the incremental power and profit inherent in our present forms of organization.

Later, Douglas would express himself quite differently, but in 1933 he spoke for many corporate law reformers when he criticized the Securities Act as "a nineteenth-century piece of legislation" since it did not "perfect a plan for control of our present forms of organization."[70]

The hostility of the business community to the Securities Act, especially its civil liability provision, was every bit as intense as that of the frustrated reformers. But in May 1933, Wall Street and business in general were on the defensive, daily embarrassed by the Pecora investigation's revelations. Only later would the New York Stock Exchange, investment banks, and corporate spokesmen effectively respond; and when they did, their collective discontent would become a maelstrom of criticism, eventually requiring even the compromise Securities Act Roosevelt endorsed to be further pruned. At issue, basically, was the political question of who should regulate the economy, or, as Berle wrote, whether high finance would be master or servant. The securities legislation of 1933 was a modest Act, but it constituted the first effective regulation of corporate finance. It was as much in bitterness at being regulated at all, as because of the details of the Securities Act, that Wall Street soon rebelled.

The Securities Exchange Act of 1934

The battle for the Securities Exchange Act of 1934, the most important enduring federal securities law, would be far more controverted.

"A perfect institution," Richard Whitney called the New York Stock Exchange. In November 1937, SEC Chairman William O. Douglas would offer a less sanguine opinion, implying that it was a "private club" with "elements of a casino." However characterized, there was no real dispute that the New York Stock Exchange was the primary object of the Securities Exchange Act of 1934 and in that year the Exchange was forced to compromise some of its independence as a result of one of the most bruising lobbying struggles ever waged in Washington.[71]

On Wall Street, it was known simply as "the Exchange." By 1932, there were at least 33 other organized securities exchanges in the country; in addition, thousands of unlisted stock and bond issues were traded in unorganized over-the-counter markets. But the New York Stock Exchange alone accounted for as much as three-fourths of all listed securities transactions, and in the period between 1928 and 1933 over 90 percent of securities brokerage commissions were received by its members. With a few exceptions, the securities of the nation's largest publicly owned firms were listed there.

Technically, the New York Stock Exchange was an unincorporated association whose 1375 members had paid as much as $625,000 for the privileges of membership. But the Exchange was effectively governed by a loose alliance of floor members called specialists and floor traders. In a quite literal sense, the NYSE revolved around its 300 or so specialists. Their function was to make a market in a particular stock by serving as brokers through whom other brokers could buy and sell securities and as dealers who themselves would buy or sell stock for their own accounts when other investors would not. Often floor brokers were able to execute orders to buy or sell securities at the market price by trading with other floor brokers in the crowd. When, however, floor brokers were not requested to execute orders at the market price but, instead, were presented with orders to buy or sell when a security price ascended or descended to a given price, these future orders would be entered into the specialist's book and executed when the market reached the designated price. This central role made the specialist highly controversial. Throughout the Pecora Hearings, allegations were made that specialists used their pivotal position to orchestrate pool operations or exploited their knowledge of the specialist books in trading for their own accounts.

Closely allied with the specialists in Exchange politics were the floor traders, approximately 170 members who traded solely for their own accounts, rather than serving as brokers executing orders for others. Since floor traders were vulnerable to the charge that they performed no socially useful function, they drew even heavier criticism from the New Deal reformers than did the specialists. Thomas Corcoran, for example, testified:

> They take no chances. They take no position against the market. They simply follow the market the way sea birds follow a ship, following the trend and picking up what they can on the way. They sense the market and follow the pools, whether the market is long or short. . . . They serve no purpose, in the long run, to make the market any better for the investor on the outside, but rather because they are quick and on the inside, they help to accentuate the swings of pools. They are naturally pool operators.

By contrast, the majority of Exchange members who were floor brokers, or members of the broker-dealer firms that had direct contact with the public, exerted comparatively less influence on Exchange politics in 1933. The floor brokers' function was largely ministerial — to execute purchase and sell orders wired to them by customers' men located in the broker-dealer firm offices throughout the country. Since the Exchange's broker-dealer firm members were not physically present on the Exchange floor, they usually deferred to the leadership of the specialists and floor traders.[72]

Throughout the 1933–1934 battle over the Securities Exchange Bill, the New York Stock Exchange's membership was almost entirely unified in opposition to the New Deal's stock exchange proposals. President Richard Whitney reflected the uncompromising opposition to federal regulation characteristic both of the Exchange's floor members and of private investment banks, such as JP Morgan and Company, for whom his brother worked and for whom Whitney's own firm, Richard Whitney and Company, served as a bond broker.

In lectures, radio broadcasts, and Congressional testimony Whitney's message was consistent: "The Exchange by maintaining . . . a free and open market for securities, rendered a great service to the nation." The New York Stock Exchange should not be made "a goat" for the Depression. Like the financiers he represented, Whitney's distrust of Washington was instinctive; his was a near certain conviction that government regulation could only be crude, vengeful, and ultimately destructive.[73]

With the conclusion of the JP Morgan Hearings in June 1933, the momentum for stock exchange legislation perceptibly slowed. Then, in late June, a jury found Charles Mitchell "not guilty" of income tax evasion — a setback to the New Deal so totally unexpected that Attorney General Homer Cummings felt compelled to acknowledge publicly: "Nevertheless, I still believe in the jury system."[74] After the Pecora Hearings recessed in July for the summer, Wall Street's long dampened opposition to the 1933 Securities Act began to be expressed vehemently.

In August, leading corporate attorney Arthur Dean published a slashing attack in *Fortune*, anticipating that the law would be "drastically amended at the next session" because of its complexity and severe civil liability sections, which were such "as to render financing exceedingly difficult, if not actually impossible, in the case of corporations with extensive interests." Dean predicted dire results from the Securities Act: It alone might "seriously retard economic recovery... result in unemployment because corporations may be forced to make drastic economies and to suspend the payment of dividends in order to obtain necessary working capital," make it difficult for "new and speculative corporations [to obtain] long-term capital," increase the cost of selling securities to all corporations, and discourage underwriters from helping issue securities, forcing "American corporations to go abroad for capital." "With the purposes of the Act," Dean concluded, "the writer is in full sympathy, but it seems hardly necessary to burn down the house to exterminate vermin." Dean's call to amend the 1933 Securities Act was roundly echoed. Frank Gordon, President of the Investment Bankers Association, soon won unanimous support from the Association for a resolution seeking "redefinition" of the Act "so as to make it possible for responsible enterprises to meet their requirements for new capital and to cooperate with the recovery program."[75]

Publicly, Roosevelt adamantly opposed any significant amendments to the Act. At an October 18 Press Conference, he scornfully insisted:

> There is a very definite drive being made by certain elements to have the Securities Act modified or repealed. They would much rather have it repealed. They would much rather have the old, free use that they had before — being able to sell watered stocks to you and me. Well, they are not going to have that right anymore.... There will be mighty few changes, if any, in the Securities Act this winter.

Roosevelt was able to ignore the Wall Street campaign against the Securities Act because of the stunning revelations of the Pecora Hearings in the autumn of 1933, including evidence that Albert Wiggin, President of the Chase National Bank, then the Nation's largest bank, had formed six private corporations that had earned over $10 million between 1928 and 1932, by, among other transactions, receiving a cut from the Chase Securities Corporation's investment and pool operations and by short selling stock in the Chase National Bank itself during the 1929 Stock Market Crash.[76]

A far more influential lobby to amend the Securities Act developed within the Roosevelt Administration. Before the year was out, Lewis Douglas, Roosevelt's Director of the Budget, Secretary of the

Treasury William Woodin, National Recovery Administration Chair Hugh Johnson, top officials of the Commerce Department, and Secretary of Agriculture Henry A. Wallace would urge Roosevelt to amend the Act. The intra-Administration opposition began with the conservative Budget Director Douglas, whom Thomas Corcoran considered "instinctively hostile" to the securities law. Before a September 8 Cabinet meeting, Douglas circulated a memorandum prepared by Paul Mazur, an economist for Lehman Brothers, that criticized the Act as standing in the way of "needed long-term financing." Agriculture Secretary Wallace wrote to Roosevelt that he agreed with Mazur "about the necessity for amending the securities bill." Although he would endorse the Act in its full rigor if the economy were functioning as well as it had in 1924 or 1929, Wallace wrote, "I am really fearful of its influence at the present time." By November, Secretary of the Treasury Woodin and NRA Administrator Hugh Johnson also were urging modification.[77]

Senator Fletcher, Congressman Rayburn, Felix Frankfurter, and James Landis sharply defended the securities law. The advocacy of Frankfurter and Landis was particularly influential. As early as July 6, Frankfurter warned Roosevelt of "the fray that is ahead." He wrote, "There are still too many in 'the Street' who think that . . . the 'green goods business' . . . will flourish as of old. It is hard for some folk to realize that new social and economic standards ever come into play." When leading financiers and corporate attorneys assailed the Act in August and September, Frankfurter wrote to Roosevelt again: "There is no question but that leading bankers and the big law firms are trying to create a bankers' strike," employing the act as an "opportunity publicly to oppose the New Deal."[78]

About a week after the Securities Act was signed, Landis received an emergency call in Cambridge, requesting him to return as a consultant to the Federal Trade Commission to help set up a special division to enforce the Act. Then in October, when a vacancy unexpectedly developed on the FTC, Roosevelt named the Harvard Law School Professor an FTC Commissioner. In late October, Landis made a spirited defense of the Securities Act in an address to the New York State Society of Certified Public Accountants. Castigating "the attack of selfish and short-sighted interests," Landis asserted that "if half of the energy that has been expended in fulminating against the Act and propagandizing for amendments were enlisted in the effort to advise the Commission in the wise exercise of its powers, the government and issuers, bankers, lawyers, and accountants would be far nearer a solution of their problems."[79]

Characteristically, Roosevelt attempted to conciliate the warring Administration factions by initiating two studies of the effect of the Act on capital formation. Neither effort succeeded, but out of the failure grew a renewed impetus for a stock exchange bill. The first Study was initiated late in October, after Henry Bruere, a friend of Roosevelt and President of the Bronx Bank, who was acting as an adviser on credit issues, wrote the President: "There seems to be an honest belief that the liability and certain other provisions of the Securities Act in its present form has actually prevented or limited and will prevent and limit the natural flow of capital into industry." Roosevelt urged Bruere "to get working on the problem of possible revision" by meeting with a Committee including Landis and his fellow FTC Commissioner George Mathews, but Roosevelt insisted that "this should be done quietly," since he "wished to take his position after further consideration of matured recommendations from the Committee."[80]

At approximately the same time Roosevelt asked Commerce Secretary Daniel Roper to revitalize his interagency Stock Exchange Study Group. Roosevelt's charge to Roper was considerably broader and more formal than his request of Bruere. The Secretary of Commerce was expected to investigate claims that the 1933 Securities Act obstructed new securities sales, and was also to return with recommendations for a securities exchange bill. Roper requested Assistance Commerce Secretary Dickinson to study Samuel Untermyer's much discredited stock exchange bill.

No revision was completed before Congress adjourned, and during the summer Dickinson seemed content to let the project drop. Then in early October, after Roosevelt again asked Roper to study the securities laws, Roper once more turned to Dickinson. Dickinson, a former corporate attorney unsympathetic to securities law reform, invited James Landis and Adolf Berle to join a committee Dickinson stacked against reform by adding his former Sullivan and Cromwell partner Arthur Dean and a conservative Washington attorney, Henry Richardson.

Dickinson, Dean, and Richardson strongly favored amending the Act. In time, Roper would forward to Roosevelt recommendations of the majority of the Dickinson Committee that liability under the Act be limited to the amounts caused by an untrue statement or omission, that most underwriters be exempt from liability, and that courts have the power to assess both costs and a $500 penalty on the losing party in securities law litigation to discourage bad-faith litigation.

By November, it was also clear that the majority of the Dickinson Committee favored as well a limited stock exchange bill. Early that month, Landis had presented to the Committee what he considered the "irreducible minima" of a stock exchange bill: A requirement of periodic publicly filed corporate reports; public reports of stock transactions of directors, principal officers, and the corporation itself when it was dealing in its own stock; "police regulation" of specialists, brokerage houses, customers' men, pool operations, short selling, and fraudulent "washed" sales or matched orders; regulation of over-the-counter transactions; and "any other proposals necessary to give effectiveness to any of the above." Rather than requesting Landis to prepare a draft statute, Dickinson had turned to Henry Richardson, who, on November 16, 1933, had circulated the outline of a much different bill. "The general idea of the draft here presented," Richardson explained, "is that the bill is to be drawn on the theory that insofar as possible each exchange will discipline its own members and conduct its own affairs." The heart of Richardson's proposal was the recommendation that each securities exchange's rules be approved by a seven member Securities Exchange Commission, which would include two representatives of the general investing public, two members of stock or commodities exchanges, one representative from industry, one representative from agriculture, and a Chairman who would be a member of the Federal Reserve Bank of New York.[81]

Shortly after Landis received Bruere's recommendation to amend the 1933 Securities Act and Richardson's proposal for an industry dominated stock exchange bill, he requested a meeting with President Roosevelt. This may have been the decisive meeting in the history of the 1934 Securities Exchange Act. Landis was seeking Roosevelt's encouragement to develop proposals for a stock exchange bill outside the president's official committee. Roosevelt, by this time, was aware that conciliatory efforts within his Administration would fail and that he would soon have to side with one of the contending factions.

On the same day as the Dickinson Committee met with Richard Whitney to hear his view on stock market reform, Landis forwarded to Roosevelt a blistering memorandum defending the Securities Act. Taking issue with the argument that the dearth of new private security issues could be attributed to the Act, Landis argued that "an examination of situations where the Act is alleged to have caused the non-flotation of an issue brings forcibly to the forefront the recognition that so many factors are responsible for this non-flotation that isolation of the fear of the Act is impossible." However, even when the FTC had "intimated its willingness to relax registration requirements on refunding issues wherever that can be done," no firm had registered with the Commission. Instead, corporate attorneys had lobbied for "changes" that, though "seemingly innocuous, may open wide opportunities for evasion." For example, Landis asserted that the frequent suggestion that recovery under the Act be limited to situations where an investor directly "relied" on a falsehood might fully subvert the Act, since the Act did not, and Landis believed constitutionally could not, compel securities dealers to deliver to each investor a copy of the firm's registration statement or prospectus. Similarly, limitation of damages to those directly "caused" by a false statement or omission might make it nearly impossible for investors to prove damages. Without the stringent civil liability sections, Landis asserted, the FTC would not have been able to compel firms attempting to sell securities to the public to acknowledge "such facts as the pendency of damaging litigation" or the existence of "outstanding liabilities, misleading accounting practices . . . and the like."

In Landis' view, the tactics of the opponents of the Act "created a situation where the only safe course seems to be that of remaining adamant on the Securities Act. Not only would there be the danger of appearing not to be able to withstand the pressure of financial interests," but if Roosevelt agreed to amend the Act in the face of a bankers' strike, "the 'strike' may very well be continued until further modifications again take place."[82]

Roosevelt, aware of Fletcher's and Rayburn's strong support of the Act, sided with Landis. Early in December Roosevelt twice denied that he would support any changes in the Securities Act that could weaken the law. Privately, Landis directed an FTC associate, I.N.P. Stokes, to continue previously initiated efforts to draft a securities exchange bill that would place the securities exchanges under FTC control. Roosevelt informed Raymond Moley "of his intention to get securities exchange legislation through the coming [congressional] session." Moley was asked to contact Benjamin Cohen and Thomas Corcoran and ask that they also begin drafting a stock exchange measure. Another young attorney, Telford Taylor, then joined Stokes in drawing up drafts of a stock exchange bill; these were reviewed by both Landis and Cohen. By mid-January, Stokes and Taylor were collaborating on a revised draft bill, which, on January 23, was circulated for comment to Senator Fletcher and his Banking Committee counsel, Ferdinand Pecora.[83]

Significantly complicating the reformers' efforts was the Dickinson Committee. By January 23, its Report, *Stock Exchange Regulation,* had been forwarded to the White House. Roosevelt, attempting to play down the importance of the Report, transmitted it to Senator Fletcher with a public letter stating, "I shall leave with you and your associates the matter of the construction of the legislation," but this was a caveat virtually no one appreciated when the Report was publicly released on January 27. News accounts universally assumed that the Report was meant to embody Roosevelt's recommendations for stock exchange reform, an impression buttressed by the fact that both Landis and Berle had signed the Report, indicating "general accord" with its contents.

The Dickinson Report recommended that a new federal Stock Exchange authority or new Division of the FTC be empowered to license securities exchanges, but that the federal agency should be "constituted as to place responsibility to the fullest extent possible on the private bodies now handling the work of the stock exchanges." The Report then listed several powers it recommended that the Stock Exchange Authority *not* exercise. Among other things, the Committee said that it was "not... desirable to require the licensing of individual brokers [since] there is a distinct danger that such a system would break down the controls exercised by the stock exchanges"; it was not feasible to regulate "unorganized" or over-the-counter securities markets, because this would entail "building up a federal policing agency on such a scale as to be impracticable"; it was not appropriate to give the new stock exchange authority power to limit margin loans beyond the opportunity "to consult" with the district Federal Reserve banks, "which should be empowered to prescribe margin requirements"; and short sales should not be "curbed," since they acted "as a stabilizing influence on the downside of the market." The problems associated with stock market pools, specialists, and the non-segregation of brokerage from underwriting and dealing firms were recognized as serious concerns. But Dickinson's Report insisted that additional studies should be conducted before any prohibitory rules were established. Only with respect to a few matters, like fraudulent "matched orders" and the need for periodic corporate reporting, did Dickinson's Committee unequivocally recommend immediate regulation.[84]

Senator Fletcher, his colleague on the Banking Committee, Senator Couzens, and Pecora were appalled by the Dickinson Report. Pecora soon let it be known that he personally favored a bill that severely restricted short selling, pools, and margin trading. By February 1, the latest Stokes-Taylor draft had been delivered to Benjamin Cohen for a final rewrite. Pecora instructed Cohen to toughen the draft by establishing fixed margin requirements, segregating brokers from dealers, and flatly outlawing all pools, wash sales, matched orders, and short sales. Landis was uncomfortable with so rigid an approach. He had been sympathetic to the Dickinson Report's recommendation of further study of several stock exchange controversies. But Cohen, in part influenced by the view that a reform bill should initially seek far broader reforms than Congress was likely to enact so that the bill's proponents would have room to compromise, incorporated most of Pecora's stringent prohibitions.[85]

On February 9, two weeks after the Dickinson Report had been submitted, Roosevelt sent a Message to Congress formally recommending the enactment of legislation to regulate the securities exchanges. In deference to the divisions within his Administration, Roosevelt did not publicly endorse Cohen's final revision. But his frequent subsequent public and private comments that he would not be satisfied with a bill unless it had "teeth in it" left little doubt about his personal preference.[86]

Simultaneously with Roosevelt's message, Senator Fletcher and Congressman Rayburn introduced Cohen's stock exchange proposal, called the Fletcher-Rayburn Bill. The breadth and severity of the Fletcher-Rayburn Bill startled both official Washington and Wall Street. *The New York Times,* for example, reflected the view of many with its headline "DRASTIC STOCK MARKET BILL."[87]

The proposed law primarily was addressed to the regulation of securities exchanges. Each securities exchange was required to register with the FTC, which was given the power to approve or disapprove exchange rules and regulations. The Bill itself, however, proscribed nine specific types of market manipulation, including the carrying out of wash sales or matched orders or otherwise creating a "false and misleading appearance of active trading" in a security, or disseminating false or misleading information to influence investors to buy or sell a particular security.

Section 6 of the bill forbad brokers to lend investors margin credit equal to more than 80 percent of the lowest price of a security during the preceding three years or 40 percent of current prices. The Federal Trade Commission could mandate more severe loan limits if "appropriate in the public interest or for the protection of investors." These provisions were consonant with the conviction of Roosevelt and the draftsmen that "the two real causes of trouble in the stock market are speculation with borrowed money, that is, on margin, and lack of adequate publicity." The vesting of the FTC with discretion to impose even more severe loan limits reflected the New Dealers' doubts that the Federal Reserve Board possessed sufficient political independence from the New York financial community to adequately regulate margin limits.

Section 10 of the bill proposed to revolutionize stock exchange membership. Floor traders were to be abolished. Explained Corcoran, "The only interest the public has in a stock exchange is that it should be a place where the outside public can buy and sell its stocks. There is no public interest to be served by giving an inside seat to a small group of men who are trading for their own account." Similarly, specialists were to be barred from trading for their own accounts or disclosing the contents of their future order books to anyone, unless the data were available to all members of the exchange. Indeed, Section 10 invited the Exchanges to go further and replace the specialists altogether with exchange officers or employees who could perform "the functions of specialists" but would have no rights to trade for their own accounts. Finally, to prevent brokers from touting new securities issued by their own firms when consulted for disinterested investment advice, Section 10 would have prohibited brokerage houses from acting as dealers or underwriters.

To the floor traders and specialists who dominated New York Stock Exchange governance, Section 10 was tantamount to a declaration of war. If enacted, it would have ended all private transactions on the Exchange floor, permanently transforming the Exchange into a clerical agency for the execution of off floor orders. But the Section had equally radical implications for the stock brokerage firms that were the floor members' rivals in Exchange politics. Brokerage firms permanently would have lost the opportunity to share in the new securities issuance business. Rarely was a statutory proposal so well calculated to unite its opposition. The furor engendered by Section 10 briefly jeopardized the possibility of enacting any stock exchange proposal.

There was much more to the omnibus bill. The FTC also was to be given a general authority to regulate the interstate transactions of the over-the-counter markets. Since most over-the-counter transactions were intrastate, this provision was unlikely to be of much consequence, but Landis and Cohen were doubtful that purely intrastate securities sales could be regulated constitutionally.

Three related provisions of the bill empowered the FTC to require corporations selling securities traded on an exchange to file a registration statement with the exchange similar to that required by the 1933 Act for new securities, update the statement with annual and periodic reports, and conduct corporate elections that employed mailed proxies subject to FTC regulations. The electoral rules were recommended, Corcoran explained, because "proxies, as solicitations are made now, are a joke. The persons who control the machinery for sending out the proxies, with practically no interest in the corporation, can simply keep other people from organizing [and] get enough proxies to run the company." It soon became known that the Roosevelt Administration also was considering the possibility of developing a comprehensive Federal Corporation Bill to fully replace the ineffective corporate governance provisions of state law. The Senate Banking Committee, the Twentieth Century Fund, the Dickinson Report, and the New York Stock Exchange would each separately recommend a Federal Corporation Act — although it was widely assumed that the NYSE's enthusiasm for corporate law reform was a tactic to deflect the momentum for a securities exchange law.

Finally, the "anti-Wiggin" provisions of the Fletcher-Rayburn Bill required corporate directors, officers, or owners of 5 percent or more of a class of stock to file public reports of their trading in their own firm's stock and precluded their realizing "insiders' profits" by buying or selling securities and earning a profit within any six-month period.[88]

Pecora, by then a master at scheduling hearings for maximum political advantage, attempted to galvanize support for the Fletcher-Rayburn Bill by holding hearings highly embarrassing to the NYSE just after the bill's introduction. From February 14 to the 22nd, the Senate Banking Committee heard evidence that the NYSE had been unable or unwilling to effectively investigate pool operations in alcohol stocks after Congress had voted to repeal Prohibition. Between July 18 and July 21, 1933, the price of American Commercial Alcohol abruptly fell from a high of 89⁷/₈ to a low of 29¹/₈. Pecora immediately had taken a train to New York City and personally requested Richard Whitney to initiate a NYSE investigation. Whitney reluctantly agreed, but then three months later reported to Pecora that "there were no material deliberate improprieties" in stock transactions in American Commercial Alcohol or five other alcohol firms investigated: "The repeal situation appears to have created a public interest in these stocks great enough to account for their activity." Incredulous, Pecora had assigned his own investigators to study American Commercial Alcohol's price fluctuations. They soon uncovered evidence that between May 3 and July 24, 1933, American Commercial's Chair of the Board, Russell Brown, its specialist on the NYSE, Charles Wright, and such notorious market operators and Thomas Braff and Ben "Sell'em" Smith had organized a pool operation that had helped push American Commercial's stock price up from a quotation near $20 to almost $90 by participating in as much as 75 percent of the stock's trades during that period. As the market rose, Brown had arranged to issue approximately 45,000 new shares of American Commercial stock to himself and other pool members. After the pool had sold off these and other shares, the pool ceased trading in American Commercial stock and its share price collapsed. During the February 1934 Hearings, Pecora emphasized that the NYSE neither at the time nor after the stock's suspicious market quotations had been called to its attention had been able to identify even the existence of a pool. How, Pecora suggested, could it be trusted to police its own member?[89]

This time Pecora's political theater failed him. He had come to view Richard Whitney and other officials of the NYSE as obstructionists. Roosevelt, too, believed that "the fundamental trouble with this whole Stock Exchange crowd is their complete lack of elementary education. I do not mean lack of college diplomas, etc., but just inability to understand the country or the public or their obligation to their fellow men." For months, relations between Richard Whitney and the New Deal had deteriorated. The past October, Whitney had been incensed when Pecora hired John Flynn, an acerbic critic of the Exchange, and asked Flynn to deliver personally to Whitney a draft of a questionnaire Pecora wanted the NYSE to distribute to its members. On seeing Flynn, Whitney had abruptly left his office, returning several minutes later to deliver a furious lecture on why the NYSE did not require government regulation, during the course of which Whitney delivered the memorable observation that "the Exchange is a perfect institution." Some days later, Whitney formally refused to distribute the questionnaire. This required the much irritated Pecora to subpoena 11 stock exchange firms before successfully distributing his questionnaire to the balance of the Exchange's members. Whitney had his own causes for irritation. Late in October, the Exchange had tightened its auditing standards. By February, Whitney was ready to announce three new Exchange Rules barring members from participating in pools and prohibiting specialists from accepting stock options from anyone or disclosing information in their future order books. These rules were considerably more stringent than those recommended in the Dickinson Report. Yet in the days before his Stock Exchange message, Roosevelt had refused to speak to Whitney about the new Exchange rules or to discuss the Administration's impending legislation.[90]

Whitney struck back. In February and March, he directed a highly effective business lobby. In spite of initial popular and press opinion in favor of stock exchange legislation, Whitney was able to force Pecora and Landis to withdraw their bill.

The campaign began four days after the Fletcher-Rayburn Bill was introduced, when Whitney met with representatives of 30 brokerage firms. The following day Whitney wrote each member of the Exchange that the bill would "have very disastrous consequences to the stock market." A similar letter was forwarded to the Presidents of all corporations listed on the New York Stock Exchange, emphasizing the "serious" effects the bill would have on their firm and its directors, officers, and principal shareholders. Soon Whitney had organized the 46,000 New York City brokerage house employees to protest the bill.

The stock exchange lobby swiftly made itself felt in Washington. Congressmen reported receiving vast numbers of letters, telephone calls, and telegrams, variously warning that the bill "provides for the wholesale 'goose-step' regimentation of industry and commerce under the control of the Federal Trade Commission," "aids foreign competitors of American corporations to the detriment of American stockholders by making available confidential information not presently obtainable," "attempts an impossible degree of regulation of the credit agencies and business enterprises of the country, even to the point of requiring small and large companies to sign away constitutional rights as a condition to the continuance of their securities upon the public markets." "The issue involved," summed up the Standard Commercial Tobacco Company, "is whether political bureaucracy shall be permitted to stifle the initiative and creative genius of American enterprise." Even Roosevelt's successor as Governor of New York, Herbert Lehman, was persuaded to write the President that the State was counting on $40 million in stock transfer taxes in 1934–1935, and Lehman hoped that the interests of the Exchange "will be given careful and sympathetic consideration."[91]

Nowhere was the effectiveness of Whitney's lobbying campaign more evident than in the parallel House and Senate Hearings on the initial Fletcher-Rayburn Bill, held between February 14 and March 16. From the moment Landis and Corcoran completed their detailed explanation of the Bill to Rayburn's House Commerce Committee, both sets of Hearings were dominated by Whitney.

The Stock Exchange President broadly outlined his position in similar opening statements to both Committees. The FTC's powers under the bill, Whitney argued, were so great that the Commission might not regulate but might "actually . . . supervise and manage all stock exchanges [and] establish indirectly a form of nationalization of business and industry which has hitherto been alien to the American theory of Federal Government." Even if the FTC exercised its powers with restraint, the bill would "destroy the free and open market for securities."

This was especially likely, Whitney urged, because of the rigidity of the proposed margin requirements and the arbitrariness of the rule barring specialists from trading in securities for their own accounts, which might lead to erratic oscillations in share prices heretofore prevented by specialists' purchasing and selling shares to ensure orderly price quotations.

Whitney was succeeded at the witness table by Thomas Gay, outside counsel to the NYSE, who opined that the Fletcher-Rayburn Bill was "not Constitutional," then momentarily stunned the House Commerce Committee by producing an opinion letter James Landis had written for the New York Stock Exchange in 1932 while a Law Professor at Harvard; in it, he stated that a bill to regulate short selling introduced by Congressman La Guardia was not constitutionally acceptable. Landis refuted Gay's argument, noting that his letter concerning the La Guardia Bill had included the reservation "I am as yet unconvinced that a bill could not be drafted to regulate security transactions on stock exchanges which would be Constitutional." Landis insisted that the Fletcher-Rayburn proposal was that bill.

Then Whitney presented his most convincing argument: opposition to the bill was national; it was not limited to Wall Street bankers. The NYSE was hardly a popular institution in 1934. Indeed, next to JP Morgan, it was the most obvious symbol of New York City's by then highly resented financial community. But the same hostility was not felt toward the smaller regional stock exchanges, whose continued existence few employment conscious Congressman could afford to dismiss entirely. On five successive House Hearing days, well-rehearsed representatives of 24 separate local exchanges echoed Whitney's testimony. The tone of the local representatives' testimony was set by Eugene Thompson, President of the Association of Stock Exchanges, who, either paraphrasing or misstating a frequently expressed criticism of the Fletcher-Rayburn Bill, told the House Commerce Committee that it was hardly necessary "to cure a case of hiccups by severing the head of the patient." Less morbid, but presumably more persuasive, was the prediction of the Cincinnati Stock Exchange's W.D. Gradison that the bill might "eliminate from existence" most regional exchanges. Several of the regional exchange representatives specifically criticized the draftsmen for so focusing on the model of the New York Stock Exchange that they failed to appreciate that a small exchange could not afford a segregation of brokers and dealers. Virtually every local exchange "heartily" endorsed Whitney's proposal of a Stock Exchange Coordinating Authority.[92]

Before either the House or Senate hearing on the initial Fletcher-Rayburn Bill were completed, James Landis conceded in a letter to Felix Frankfurter that "the Stock Exchange Bill is taking a terrific beating." By then, Congressional support was beginning to slip away. The flight from the bill was not slowed by statements of Corcoran and Pecora in late February indicating a willingness to modify the bill, or by Rayburn's subsequent remark that the measure merely had been "introduced as a basis for consideration," and the House Commerce Committee soon would rewrite it. On March 5, Senate Majority Leader Joseph Robinson took the Senate floor to announce "As to whether the Stock Exchange Regulation Bill may be ready for disposition during this session of Congress, no assurance at this time can be given." With these words, the initial Fletcher-Rayburn Bill was effectively dead.

The conspicuousness of the bill's defeat elevated the lobbying battle for a stock exchange Act into a crucial test of Roosevelt's leadership. If no stock exchange bill could be adopted during the 73rd Congress, Roosevelt would have suffered his first major legislative defeat.

With the prestige of his Administration directly challenged, Roosevelt assumed personal direction of the effort to rewrite the bill. On March 7, the White House sharply responded to Senator Robinson, by announcing that President Roosevelt expected Congress to pass at the present session legislation for federal regulation of stock exchanges. After a conference with Roosevelt the following day, Robinson concurred, with the face saving proviso that "the bill would be simplified as much as practicable."[93]

The revised Fletcher-Rayburn Bill was introduced into the House on March 19. Roosevelt's personal intervention had resulted in unified Administration support for the bill. Tom K. Smith, a St. Louis banker then serving as Assistant to Secretary of the Treasury, Henry Morgenthau, Jr., informed the House Committee that now, since most of the Treasury Department's "suggestions and changes . . . have been incorporated into the bill," the Department "approved" the bill. Federal Reserve Board governor Eugene Black unequivocally informed both Committees that "the Board is . . . prepared to approve the bill as revised." Robert E. Healy, the FTC Chief Counsel, emphatically testified in favor of the bill's grant of authority to the Commission to prescribe corporate accounting standards. Jesse Jones, Reconstruction Finance Corporation Chairman, held a press conference at which he predicted that banks would soon lose their fear of both the 1933 Securities Act and the proposed stock exchange bill.

The bill's most effective advocate was Roosevelt himself. Four days after the revised bill was introduced, he informed reporters that he favored a stock exchange bill "with teeth in it." Roosevelt demonstrably considered this an apt metaphor. On March 26, just before departing for a vacation, he publicly released letters to Rayburn and Fletcher repeating his certitude "that the country as a whole will not be satisfied with legislation unless such legislation has teeth in it." Noting that "a more definite and more highly organized drive is being made against effective [stock exchange] legislation . . . than against any similar recommendation made by me during the past year," Roosevelt made his first specific declaration of support for the revised Fletcher-Rayburn Bill. "I do not see," he wrote, "how any of us could afford to have [the bill] weakened in any shape, manner, or form."[94]

The stock exchanges remained adamantly opposed. As long as the Fletcher-Rayburn Bill threatened to eliminate floor traders and the specialist system, it represented a personal threat to a substantial portion of the members of every stock exchange. Whitney signaled the intensity of the bill's opposition on March 22, when he began testimony to the House Commerce Committee by stating: "Our basic objections to the old bill apply with equal force to the new one." Twenty-five regional exchanges concurred with Whitney that they could support the Fletcher-Rayburn Bill only if it was sweepingly altered to create a new federal Stock Exchange Commission in place of the FTC to enforce the Act, grant the Federal Reserve Board unfettered discretion in setting margins, leave largely unchanged the existing system of specialists and floor traders, and not regulate corporate proxy elections.

The perceived "punitive" nature of the bill continued to unify widely disparate elements of the business community in opposition. The commission brokers were especially antagonistic. Acting through Raoul Desvernine, a New York City attorney, they had attempted to negotiate with Landis and Cohen a compromise revision bill containing provisions similar to those Richard Whitney had proposed. Desvernine had offered the support of the moderate leaders of the brokerage houses if the New Dealers would agree to substitute a three person National Securities Exchange Commission, including "at least one commissioner . . . thoroughly experienced in stock exchange practices" for FTC enforcement, give the Federal Reserve Board a flexible power over margin limits, only modestly alter exchange membership, and eliminate sections in the bill dealing with corporate reports, corporate insider trading, and over-the-counter markets, since these were not "pertinent to exchange regulation." Each of Desvernine's proposals was rejected. Paul Shields, a leading commission broker and exchange moderate, angrily wrote Rayburn that the revised bill intended "to punish all people dealing in securities." His sentiment was widely shared. By early April, the Chambers of Commerce or Boards of Trade of 43 cities had organized to arouse public opinion against the bill. Twenty-eight prominent industrialists, claiming to speak for the nation's 486,000 corporations, soon also wrote to protest "provisions . . . unnecessarily severe."[95]

By the time the revised Fletcher-Rayburn Bill was reported out, the respective House and Senate Committees had revised it to incorporate several of the amendments publicly recommended by Richard Whitney. The most fundamental changes occurred in the Senate Banking Committee. By a vote of 10-8, the Committee adopted a proposal by Carter Glass to replace the Federal Trade Commission and Federal Reserve Board as enforcement agencies with a new three person Securities Exchange Commission. Glass insisted that the amendment was offered to ensure that the Federal Reserve Board would not be "allied or aligned in any way with stock exchange transactions." That Glass had long been concerned with maintaining the Board "as far from stock exchange transactions as possible" was well known, but this explanation of why he championed Whitney and Desvernine's proposal for a new commission was ingenuous. A more probable explanation was that he, like the exchange leaders, feared the FTC. With the 1933 appointments of Landis and George Mathews as Commissioners, and the continued service of Robert Healy as Chief Counsel, the FTC, as Landis candidly put it, was controlled by "our group." Glass, deeply distrustful of Pecora and the New Deal reformers, initially recommended that the new Securities Exchange Commission include members experienced with exchange practices, a proposal intended to ensure that Landis could not control the new Commission.

Ultimately, as a consequence of NYSE lobbying to weaken the Securities Exchange Act and Senator Glass's antipathy to the New Deal, the SEC would be born. Later Landis would acknowledge that he had been wrong to oppose the creation of a separate commission, since an agency, Landis came to believe, with a narrow jurisdiction, like the SEC, had advantages in providing administrative expertise that an agency with a broader jurisdiction, like the FTC, lacked. But at the time, the SEC had not been sought by the New Deal. Its birth, in a sense, was an accident.

The Senate Banking Committee also adopted a second Glass amendment replacing fixed margin limits with a substitute provision empowering the Federal Reserve Board to specify margin requirements for loans from member banks to brokers. The proposed Securities Exchange Commission was to specify margin requirements for loans from brokers to investors. In the House, less significant changes were made. The FTC was retained as the enforcement agency, and the Federal Reserve Board's discretion to regulate margins was still subject to a fixed formula, although the Board could set loan limits as high as 55 percent of the current price of a security, or 100 percent of its lowest market price during the preceding 36 months.

With these amendments, the stock exchange bill was assured of passage. Rayburn angrily defended the revised bill during the ensuing floor debate. Decrying "the most vicious and persistent lobby that any of us have ever known in Washington," he charged that some of the letters received in opposition to the bill were coerced, other forgeries. Without further amendment, the House adopted the Stock Exchange Bill on May 4, by a vote of 281-84 with 66 abstentions.[96]

Fletcher soon demonstrated a comparable control over the Senate. After successfully appending to the revised Bill James Landis's amendments to the 1933 Securities Act, and a Pecora proposal to require disclosure documents from bankruptcy, reorganization, and other protective committees, Fletcher frustrated attempts to add over 20 other amendments to the bill. By a vote of 62–13, the Senate approved the Fletcher-Rayburn Act on May 12. "Not in years," reported *The New York Times*, "has a bill of such a controversial nature been passed by so overwhelming a majority."[97]

Roosevelt and Fletcher, buoyed by the huge Senate majority, made a final attempt to restore the FTC as the administrative agency and to set fixed margin limits. Ignoring long standing custom, Fletcher chose not to name senior Banking Committee members Glass and Robert Wagner to the Conference Committee, since both favored the new Securities Exchange Commission, and selected instead Senators Alben Barkley and James Byrnes, whom Fletcher described as "sympathetic to the legislation." Nearly simultaneously, Roosevelt informed a press conference that he "personally" preferred the House margin rules and FTC enforcement.

The move to reinstate the FTC badly misfired. After learning that he had not been named to the Conference Committee, Carter Glass fumed to the press, "It was a direct affront and a gratuitous indignity, and deliberately intended to be," and resigned from the Senate Banking Committee. Senator Barkley, a personal friend of Glass's, promptly also resigned from the Conference Committee. Majority Leader Robinson refused to accept either resignation, but agreed with Barkley that he could vote as a "free agent" on the Conference Committee, not bound by the usual unit rule. He pledged to support Glass's new commission. Roosevelt, embarrassed by accusations that he had attempted to influence the Conference Committee and had not originally objected to Glass's proposal for a new Commission, awkwardly retreated, informing the press that it was "not a frightfully important thing, one way or the other" which agency enforced the Stock Exchange Bill. In the Conference Committee, the slightly more dignified Securities *and* Exchange Commission was brought into existence by compromise, the House Conferees giving up the struggle for FTC enforcement, their Senate counterparts surrendering most of the Glass margin limit amendment.[98]

By late May, the long legislative battle was over. As reported out by the Conference Committee and swiftly enacted, the Securities Exchange Act of 1934 was a marvel of irresolution. On most controversial substantive issues, Congress had been stalemated. Rather than providing the new Commission with a clear mandate, the legislators often had granted the agency authority to study the controversy or issue its own rules. In effect, Congress had broadly defined the Commission's areas of expertise and invited it to forge its own mandate. The political processes that produced the jerry built statute were allowed to continue.

The heart of the Act was the Glass inspired Section 4, which created the Securities and Exchange Commission (*SEC*). Related Sections empowered the Commission to enforce the new law and to assume jurisdiction over the 1933 Securities Act. The new agency was to be composed of five Commissioners appointed by the President, with the advice and consent of the Senate. No more than three Commissioners could be members of the same political party.

Each would serve a five year term. This was a significant legislative victory for the Roosevelt Administration, which succeeded, as Will Rogers phrased it, in putting "a cop on Wall Street" without agreeing that any member of the Commission would be a stock exchange member, as Whitney, John Dickinson, and Carter Glass had urged.

The Administration also succeeded in retaining important portions of Benjamin Cohen's original draft. The Act required the registration of stock exchanges, vesting the SEC with authority to approve stock exchange rules. Firms issuing securities traded on an exchange were directed to file registration documents with that exchange. These firms also had to file annual and quarterly reports with the SEC. The Commission additionally was empowered to issue rules regarding corporate proxy elections and the over-the-counter markets. But with the exception of the noncontroversial anti-market-manipulation rules and the anti-Wiggin short-term profit sections, virtually all of the provisions retained from Cohen's original draft conferred on the SEC vague powers to use its discretion in issuing rules where appropriate "in the public interest or for the protection of investors."

Several other substantive provisions drafted by Cohen at Pecora's behest had been weakened. Where the bill originally had set fixed margin loan limits, the Act reversed this formula by providing that the initial extension of margin to investors could be no greater than the higher of 55 percent of the current market price of a security or 100 percent of the lowest price during the preceding 36 months, and adding that the Federal Reserve Board was empowered to raise or lower these limits whenever it deemed appropriate. The NYSE achieved an almost total victory regarding exchange membership. Floor traders were allowed to continue, subject to SEC rules. The specialist system was nearly unchanged. Broker-dealer segregation was not achieved. Congress deferred resolution of each of these issues until the SEC completed studies of exchange membership and broker-dealer segregation, in 1935 and 1936 respectively. The Commission was directed to make a similar study of unlisted securities by 1936. The Senate Banking Committee Counsel failed in his ambition to outlaw or severely limit short selling.

Nonetheless, Pecora, like most in the New Deal, regarded the Securities Exchange Act of 1934 as a "happy compromise." With the creation of the SEC, the proponents of securities law reform had secured an ongoing agency to enforce the new statute and to continue studying the need for further reforms. With such considerations in mind, Pecora emphasized to Roosevelt the day the President signed the Act, "It will be a good or bad law depending upon the men who administer it."[99]

The SEC

With the passage of the 1934 Securities Exchange Act, it was widely assumed that James Landis would be the first Chair of the Securities and Exchange Commission. As early as May 27, *The New York Times* had headlined a front page article "J.M. LANDIS SLATED FOR STOCK MARKET CHIEF"; *Newsweek* reported that Washington "confidently expected" the appointment; *Time* echoed the prediction, adding that Landis would "dominate" the Commission's proceedings; *Business Week* took to referring to the SEC as "Landis' New Commission." Endorsing the prevailing opinion, *Fortune* published a feature article, "The Legend of Landis."[100]

Roosevelt's desire to conciliate the growing business opposition to his Administration precluded Landis's appointment. As the Securities Exchange Act battle neared its conclusion, Roosevelt and Moley agreed there would "be a rather complete examination and realignment of policy before September 1st [1934]." Corcoran reported to Frankfurter, "The plan of battle is to avoid any further attempt at reforms that might bring down more criticism during the present Congress, arrange a 'truce of God,' reorganize the machinery down here to help along a business recovery this summer, and in every other way postpone all other considerations to the necessarily primary objective of winning the congressional elections." New Deal historians Arthur Schlesinger, Jr. and James MacGregor Burns would write that Roosevelt sought to reclaim his role "of National Father, of bipartisan leader, of President of all the people"; "to present himself as above the party battle."[101]

The "truce of God" with the business community lasted nearly a year, and was particularly apparent in the months preceding the 1934 election. Addressing a bankers' convention on October 24, Roosevelt, for example, stated, "The time is ripe for an alliance of all forces intent upon the business of recovery," generously conceding to his earlier scapegoats, "The Government is bending every effort through the Treasury, the Federal Reserve system, the Reconstruction Finance Corporation, the Securities and Exchange

Commission, and the Federal Housing Administration to facilitate and encourage the revival of private investment . . . all of these new agencies are seeking consultation and cooperation with you bankers."[102]

The architect of Roosevelt's conciliatory strategy was Raymond Moley, who, though no longer a full time government employee, remained one of Roosevelt's most influential policy advisers. Long an apostle of the need to revive business confidence, Moley had publicly reassured the New Deal's conservative opponents in May 1934: "With the passage of the Stock Exchange Bill, the New Deal is practically complete." When, shortly after, Roosevelt turned to Moley to suggest a list of people suitable for appointment to the Commission, the President implicitly took another step to fashion his truce of God with business. Arguing that James Landis was "better as a member than as chairman because he is essentially a representative of strict control and operates best when defending that position against opposition from contrary view," Moley joined such Democratic Party conservatives as Bernard Baruch in successfully recommending Joseph P. Kennedy for Chair of the SEC "because of executive ability, knowledge of habits and customs of business to be regulated, and ability to moderate different points of view on Commission."[103]

From the point of view of many New Deal reformers, the choice of Kennedy to be the SEC's first Chair was absolutely, totally incredible. Throughout his varied business career, Kennedy had been a pool operator and a bear raider, periodically collaborating with Charles Wright and other market manipulators whom the SEC soon would indict. Never accepted by J.P. Morgan and the financial establishment, Kennedy had amassed his fortune largely by running the stock department for the Hayden, Stone investment firm, reorganizing film companies, then exploiting his friendship with Franklin D. Roosevelt to secure the appointment as U.S. importer for British distillers Haig and Haig, John Dewar, and Gordon's once Prohibition was lifted. In his day, it would be attributed to the "Irish" in Kennedy that he would inform *The New York Times* columnist Arthur Krock that he had been a "famous ballplayer" at Harvard who turned down a professional contract and achieved all of his success in administrative work, "not in market operations" — each of which statements was just as false as Joseph P. Kennedy's 1936 declaration that "I have no political ambitions for myself or for my children."

Most of this was known by Roosevelt in 1934, who took seriously Louis Howe's adamant opposition to Kennedy's appointment. But Roosevelt also was able to recognize much else. However questionable some of Kennedy's business career had been, Roosevelt believed Kennedy when he claimed that his greatest ambition was to be "a credit to his family." Crude though Kennedy sometimes might be in his speech and morals, his loyalty to Roosevelt in the 1930–1932 campaign for the Presidency had been unflagging. Forsaking his fellow Roman Catholic Al Smith, Kennedy had raised money for Roosevelt and served as his conduit to the politically powerful publisher William Randolph Hurst for close to two years. At the Nominating Convention, the influential Arthur Krock credited Kennedy with helping persuade Hearst to release the decisive California delegates to Roosevelt. By the early New Deal period, Kennedy was Roosevelt's best known advocate among businessmen. As conservative opposition to the New Deal's "regimentation" of business grew, Kennedy stood almost alone in the business community when he wrote:

> An organized functioning society requires a planned economy. The more complex the society the greater the demand for planning. Otherwise there results a haphazard and inefficient method of social control, and in the absence of planning the law of the jungle prevails.

In time, Kennedy would write articles supporting the National Recovery Administration, the Social Security Act, the federal securities laws, the need for a federal corporation law, the need to reform investment trusts, and the need to eliminate private investment banking. It was this ideological affinity that led to Kennedy's appointment as SEC Chair. Roosevelt needed an appointee who would conciliate and reassure the financial community, but he also wanted an SEC Chair he could trust. Joseph P. Kennedy, an improbable amalgam of political liberal and business opportunist, market operator and loyal party servant, of earthy directness and Harvard education, shrewd intelligence and amorality, seemed to Roosevelt the best available man to symbolize his politics of business conciliation.[104]

As word of the impending Kennedy Chairmanship began to circulate, liberal and radical criticism of the choice mounted. To Roy

Howard of the Scripps-Howard newspapers, naming a stock manipulator to be SEC Chair was a breach of faith. In a personal meeting with Roosevelt, and then in a *Washington News* editorial, Howard insisted that the President "cannot with impunity administer such a slap in the face to his most loyal and effective supporters as that reported to be contemplated in the appointment of Joseph P. Kennedy." Roosevelt stuck by his choice, announcing that Kennedy, Landis, Pecora, FTC Commissioner George Mathews, and FTC Chief Counsel Robert Healy were his nominees. As stipulated by the 1934 Securities Exchange Act, the initial Commission appointments were for staggered terms of five, four, three, two, and one years. Roosevelt publicly signified his preference for a Kennedy Chairmanship by naming Kennedy to the five year term. Since the statute also provided that the SEC Commissioners themselves chose their Chair, Roosevelt had no power directly to install Kennedy as Chair. But privately, Roosevelt summoned Landis, Mathews, and Healy to his office and urged them to "take a good look at Kennedy." Landis was disappointed, but led the three FTC officials in agreeing to do so. After a long meeting with Kennedy on the morning of July 2, Landis also persuaded Pecora to accept the one-year appointment on the Commission and to support the Kennedy Chairmanship.[105]

With the Kennedy Chairmanship officially confirmed, liberal fury reached firestorm proportions. "Had Franklin D. Roosevelt's dearest enemy accused him of making so grotesque an appointment as Joseph P. Kennedy to the Chairmanship of his Stock Exchange Commission," *The New Republic* editorialized, "the charge might have been laid to malice. Yet the President has exceeded the expectations of his most ardent ill wishers." "The appointment is appalling," scolded an incredulous John T. Flynn. "I say it isn't true. It is impossible. It could not happen." Even naming Kennedy to the Commission, explained Jerome Frank, General Counsel of the Agricultural Adjustment Administration and himself a future SEC Chairman, was "like setting a wolf to guard a flock of sheep."

Among the indignant, Thomas Corcoran was one of the first to grasp the larger significance of Roosevelt's SEC appointments. "Oh well," he noted to Moley, "we've got four out of five anyhow."[106]

Corcoran's calculation was telling. Kennedy began his time as Chair on the defensive, distrusted by his colleagues and contemptuously regarded by an important faction of the nation's press. That in the next 431 days as SEC Chair he was able to convert such critics as Pecora, Fletcher, John T. Flynn, and Roy Howard into begrudging admirers was a testament to his shrewdness and personal diplomacy. Kennedy's own version of the truce of God began even before he was sworn in. In separate *ententes cordiales,* he made his peace with Landis and with Pecora.

The alliance of greatest consequence was with Landis. Kennedy reassured Landis that the FTC Securities Division would be fully welcomed at the SEC on September 1, 1934, when the new Commission assumed responsibility for the 1933 Securities Act. Praising Landis as "one of the outstanding authorities in the country on the interpretation and application of statutes," Kennedy delegated to Landis primary responsibility for supervising all of the studies, reports, and regulations of the Commission. Landis also wrote most of the SEC's first opinions. In the areas that mattered most to Landis, he would have had little more authority had he been Chair.[107]

Somewhat more surprising was the speed with which Kennedy achieved an effective working relationship with Pecora. In the July 2 showdown between the two, Kennedy agreed to give Pecora primary responsibility for supervising the Stock Market Trading Division, the SEC Division that would investigate market manipulations and regulate stock exchange floor members. Kennedy soon also impressed Pecora with his zeal in seeking out stock market fraud. So much so that Pecora wrote in his valedictory article about the Commission, "The chairman, Joseph P. Kennedy, is a business man with a wide experience in the practical affairs of Wall Street. I did not see any Wall Street brokers or experts come down to Washington who knew any more about the mechanisms of the Exchange and the methods of the Street than he does."[108]

The appearance of harmonious working relationships with the other SEC Commissioners and a close personal relationship with Roosevelt enabled Kennedy rapidly and effectively to organize the Commission. This was Kennedy's most significant achievement as Chair. He was appointed shortly after Roosevelt's Budget Bureau had communicated to Congress a $300,000 estimate for the Commission's first fiscal year budget. Disagreeing, Landis had written Roosevelt of the need "to start off this new Commission with an appropriation in the neighborhood of $1,500,000." Seizing the initiative, Kennedy demanded that the Budget Bureau recommend an appropriation of greater than $4 million for the Commission's second year. The Bureau gagged at this staggering increase, but eventually approved a $2.3 million budget, which represented a considerable Kennedy victory. When the House Appropriations Committee reduced the recommended appropriation to $1.7 million, a week of Kennedy's lobbying resulted in Congress restoring virtually all of the Budget Bureau's recommended $2.3 million appropriation.[109]

A sufficient budget is the minimum requirement of an effective governmental agency. What distinguished the SEC was its ability to attract talented staff attorneys. In early understandings with Landis and Pecora, Kennedy had bargained away three of the five top staff positions of the Commission. Landis's two top assistants in the FTC Securities Division, Baldwin Bane and Donald Montgomery, were named, respectively, SEC Executive Assistant and Chief of the Examination Division (soon renamed the Registration Division), which enforced the 1933 Securities Act. David Saperstein, Pecora's Chief Associate Counsel on the Senate Banking Committee, assumed the leadership of the Stock Market Trading Division. Kennedy insisted on naming his own General Counsel and chose Judge John J. Burns. Burns, a full Professor at Harvard Law School by the age of 29, had been the youngest man ever appointed a Massachusetts Superior Court judge when he was so named at 30.[110]

Kennedy also deferred to Landis in the fifth top staff appointment. The 1934 Securities Exchange Act authorized the SEC to make a detailed Study of bankruptcy, reorganization, and protective committees, a project intended to be a continuation of Pecora's Senate Banking Committee investigation. Landis urged Kennedy to appoint Yale Law School Professor William O. Douglas. With the possible exception of Aldolf Berle, Douglas was the nation's leading law Professor of Corporate Finance. Between 1931 and 1934, he had written or coauthored five casebooks and nine law review articles on bankruptcy and corporate and securities law, an extraordinary achievement. Especially important to Landis was a February 1934 *Harvard Law Review* article of Douglas's entitled *Protective Committees in Railroad Reorganizations,* which had run intellectual circles around a less sophisticated article written earlier by Pecora staffer Max Lowenthal, who was the only other serious candidate for the appointment.[111]

Each of the Commission's top staff appointments was made by July 17, 1934, approximately two weeks after the Commissioners themselves had been sworn in. During Kennedy's 14-month tenure, the staff expanded to 692 employees. Regional offices were established in New York City, Boston, Atlanta, Chicago, Fort Worth, Denver, San Francisco, and Seattle.[112]

Kennedy's primary substantive goal as SEC Chair was to revive the foundering securities markets. By late July, he had convinced his fellow Commissioners that the SEC could aid Roosevelt's business recovery policies only if it won stock exchange and corporate acceptance. The policy of the SEC, Kennedy insisted, should be "balanced." Prosecution of security fraud should go hand in hand with encouragement of honest enterprise.[113]

On July 25, Kennedy heralded the Commission's "balanced" approach in his maiden address as SEC Chair, a speech nationally broadcast by radio. Kennedy reassured Wall Street:

> We of the SEC do not regard ourselves as coroners sitting on the corpse of financial enterprise. . . .
>
> We are not working on the theory that all the men and all the women connected with finance, either as workers or investors, are to be regarded as guilty of some undefined crime. . . .
>
> We regard ourselves, as the President has said, as partners in a cooperative enterprise. We do not start off with the belief that every enterprise is crooked and that those behind it are crooks.
>
> We want to see the wheels turn over and gather speed. We want to see the security business, by far the greatest in volume and most important in its effects of any in the country, go forward on a broad scale.[114]

The Commission quickly put Kennedy's cooperative approach into action. Before each of the SEC's initial regulations was issued, conferences were held with representatives of the affected industry. In retrospect, Kennedy would explain that, the Commission "realized that the most effective enforcement of the Act would follow from the cooperation of people in the business."[115]

In public addresses, New York Stock Exchange President Whitney built on the obvious implication of the SEC's "balanced" policy to urge investors to "realize . . . the necessity of dealing with financial houses of reputation" like those associated with the Exchange and "shun the wandering security salesman."[116]

Whitney's attempted use of the Commission to sanitize the NYSE seemed all the more plausible in light of the SEC's highly publicized campaign against stock manipulations and what Kennedy termed "fraudulent get rich schemes." During the SEC's first year, 10 minor securities exchanges closed, including the New York Mining Exchange, known as "the penny stock exchange," and the Boston Curb Exchange, which Kennedy described as "a famous old playground for skip shop promoters." An eleventh exchange, the New York Produce, discontinued its Securities Division. A twelfth, the Baltimore Stock Exchange, was denied all unlisted trading privileges when evidence showed that firms not granted unlisted trading privileges were being traded on an unlisted basis. Twenty-three hundred individual cases of possible securities fraud were investigated. Yet, for all of the Commission's much publicized enforcement efforts, and Kennedy's recurrent threats to prosecute "sham securities" and "financial racketeers," not one major member of the New York Stock Exchange was civilly or criminally prosecuted the first year. This was not a policy decision, and several exchange members soon would be. But the coincidence of the Commission's enforcement activities being directed primarily against minor exchanges and local traders enabled Kennedy to seek a détente with the leaders of the most influential exchange while maintaining a reputation for rigorous enforcement of the securities laws.[117]

The first dividend from the SEC's policy of détente came in September. By promulgating initial regulations for the registration of securities exchanges that did little more than require the description of the exchanges' rules and procedures, the Commission avoided an early Constitutional challenge to the 1934 Securities Exchange Act. Twenty-four exchanges, led by the New York Stock Exchange, duly applied for registration and on September 27 were certified as National Securities Exchanges. Sensitivity to industry concerns also guided the Commission in its promulgation of requirements for listing business corporations on securities exchanges and the Commission's early unlisted trading regulations. Before issuing the permanent listing requirements, for example, the Commission met repeatedly with the New York Stock Exchange's accounting and corporate officials. The requirements ultimately issued preserved for corporations and their accountants "a wide latitude in the manner of presenting the required data." A Commission Press Release "call[ed] attention to that portion of the Securities Exchange Act which permits [the SEC] to honor the requests of corporations to keep certain information confidential." By the end of the first year, 2776 securities had been approved for unlisted trading, and 3345 securities were permanently registered, with another 1048 applications for registration still being processed.[118]

Securing a working relationship with the leading investment banks was far more difficult for the Commission. The passage of the 1934 Securities Exchange Act did not end the capital strike. As late as November 1934, JP Morgan partner Russell Leffingwell was still trying to prove to President Roosevelt that the "Securities Act and the Banking Act have pretty much closed [the capital markets]." Roosevelt refused to consider repeal or amendment of the Securities Act, and the bankers' strike continued. New securities effectively registered under the 1933 Securities Act dwindled from $113 million in July 1934, the month when the Commission began operations, to a minuscule $11 million in January 1935.[119]

Initially, Kennedy pursued a low keyed approach in attempting to revive the securities market, emphasizing that the total expense of issuance of new securities under the 1933 Act was averaging only 0.38 of 1 percent of the gross proceeds of the securities issuance. That argument had no discernible impact, and on December 5, the Commission instructed John J. Burns, the General Counsel, to study the revision of the basic A-1 Registration Form and make "recommendations to the Commission . . . as soon as possible." Sensitive to the criticism that only new, speculative firms were issuing securities under the 1933 Act, the Commission focused its revision efforts on the development of a new Form A-2, to be available only to seasoned firms that had already issued securities.[120]

"This is our answer," Kennedy stated in announcing the new Form A-2 on January 13, "to our pledge to make less onerous, less expensive, and more practical the registration of securities. We have tried this out with the most vociferous opponents of the Securities Act and with accountants. . . . They feel that there is nothing in it which is unreasonable and will advise their clients to go ahead." Although the new form required all of the information specified in Schedule A of the Securities Act, it permitted summary responses and eliminated several questions concerning the history of the issuing firm.[121]

The "capital logjam" ended on March 7, 1935, when Swift and Company registered a $43 million bond issue after the Commission directed new rules be drafted to assure the firm's Directors that they would not be subject to an SEC enforcement action for earlier private offering negotiations. Kennedy employed the Swift and

Company registration both as a carrot and a stick. To potential corporate issuers, he stressed that the firm's 59-page Registration Statement was considerably simpler to assemble than the "about 20,000 pages" filed under the requirements of the earlier registration form by Republic Steel Corporation.[122]

Two days after Swift's filing, Pacific Gas and Electric registered a $45 million issue; on April 1, Southern California Edison filed for $73 million. The "trickling little stream of private corporation finance" soon reached "flood tide," as Kennedy put it. In April 1935, $142 million of securities were effectively registered; in July, $530 million. The aggregate 1935 total of $2.7 billion of securities effectively registered was better than four times greater than the 1934 total of $641 million.[123]

The success of Kennedy's campaign to register new securities won him considerable praise. *Time* magazine reported that the SEC "has won the distinction of being the most ably administered New Deal agency in Washington."[124]

The only major institution that the Commission did challenge during Kennedy's term was the New York Stock Exchange. And against the Exchange, the challenge was modest, and achieved, at best, indecisive results. Section 19(c) of the Securities Exchange Act of 1934 directed the SEC to "make a study and investigation of the rules of national securities exchanges with respect to the classification of members, the methods of election of officers and committees to insure a fair representation of the membership, and the suspension, expulsion, and disciplining of the members of such exchanges." The Commission's Report was published in late January 1935. Although the statutory section referred to the "rules of national securities exchanges," the SEC Report specifically treated only the New York Stock Exchange. Generally moderate in tone, the Report was an undisguised attempt to lessen floor member domination of Exchange governance by removing the obstacles to the Commission brokers' exercising their numerical strength.

This in itself was the more conservative of the alternative strategies considered by the Commission. Under the New York Stock Exchanges' Constitution, only Exchange members who had purchased a seat could be members of the Governing Committee. No outside interest was directly represented in the government of the Exchange. But because "a successful administration of the [Securities Exchange] Act will be hampered if the governing boards are not inclined to give the Commission effective cooperation," the SEC chose not to demand that outsiders be allowed to serve on the Exchange's Governing Committee. For the same reasons, the SEC was not yet prepared to recommend that there be a nonmember President of the Exchange or a paid President.

But the Report did make clear recommendations concerning the members of the Exchange's Governing Committee. As of 1934, the brokerage firms that dealt directly with the public owned 52 percent of the 1375 seats on the New York Stock Exchange. But only 14 Governors, about one-third of the Governing Committee, were representatives of the commission houses. The commission brokers' influence was also reduced by the requirement that only floor members of the Exchange could serve on the Governing Committee. Explained the Report: "An anomalous condition thus exists. The less influential partners of large firms, who execute orders on the Exchange as the floor member partners, are eligible for participation in the administration of exchanges, while the more consequential and significant partners, charged with the vital duties of managing these firms as office partners, may not participate in the government of the Exchanges." A twofold "correction" was urged. First, commission brokers should hold a larger proportion of the Governing Committee's seats. Second, office partners of registered firms should be eligible for membership on the Governing Committee.

Closely related to the problem of fair representation on the Governing Committee was the method of electing members. A five-member Committee of the New York Stock Exchange annually nominated the following year's members. Members of the Exchange theoretically could name an independent nominee if a petition was signed by 40 members, but this was considered "open revolt" and infrequently done. This nomination system, insisted the SEC's Report in its sharpest words, was "subject to just criticism. The results of its operation have been the self-perpetuation of the 'in' group.... In its place should be substituted... nomination to the Governing Board by some method of petition and... a vote on the candidates so nominated by ballot of the membership."

Other recommendations were made to increase from one-fourth to one-third the proportion of the Governing Committee annually elected, nominate the Exchange President by petition, end restriction of membership of Standing Committees to members of the

Governing Committee, and reform complaint proceedings. But consistent with Kennedy's "cooperative" approach, none of the SEC's 11 proposals was to be imposed. The Report concluded: "The Commission does not now suggest that legislation be enacted to bring about these recommendations. Its recommendations can be put into effect by the voluntary action of the Exchanges themselves without resort to legislation. It hopes that, in the main, these recommendations will be found acceptable and put into effect by the Exchanges themselves."[125]

Over the next few weeks, the Exchange agreed to increase the number of members on the Governing Committee from 40 to 48 by adding 8 brokerage house office partners, and voluntarily adopted several of the SEC's other recommendations.[126]

Emboldened, the Commission house leaders decided to challenge Whitney directly in the 1935 Exchange elections. Pierce, at a February 25 meeting with the Nominating Committee, proposed that the Exchange hire a paid President and a press agent to replace its unpaid member President. A fair measure of the difference between the New Deal and even the most reform minded Exchange members was Pierce's suggestion for President — "a man of the type of the late Calvin Coolidge." Acknowledging that it had heard a "considerable divergence of opinion," the Nominating Committee soon took the unusual step of proposing three nominees for Exchange President: Whitney, a critic of Whitney, John Hanes, and a compromise nominee, Charles Gay, a brokerage house senior partner, personally friendly to Whitney. Hanes promptly withdrew. Gay, however, like Pierce, believed that the Exchange needed better "public relations" if its slack share volume was to revive. Although cordial to Whitney and his emissaries, Gay insisted that he would stay in the race. Two days before the April 8 meeting at which Exchange officer nominees were officially announced, Whitney withdrew from the campaign for the Presidency and accepted a nomination to a seat on the Governing Committee.[127]

Whitney's withdrawal had little practical effect on Exchange governance. Gay, a self-made man educated in Brooklyn's public schools, outwardly could not have appeared less like the patrician Whitney. Yet a decade's experience on the Exchange's Governing Committee had inculcated Gay with views similar to Whitney's. As Gay's statement accepting nomination emphasized, in lines Whitney himself could have delivered, "There is a widespread misunderstanding of the Exchange; what it really is . . . It is not a private club. It is a national institution filing [*sic*] a national need of first importance." The May election results were a further vindication of the Old Guard. The former Exchange President received more votes than any other candidate, including Gay, who ran unopposed. Except for the symbolic loss of the top office, the Old Guard's domination of Exchange politics was undiminished.[128]

There was, in April 1935, an indication of how little the Exchange's policies were affected by the elections. The 1934 Securities Exchange Act empowered the SEC to regulate exchange floor members. In the fall of 1934, Kennedy had persuaded the Commission to defer consideration of segregation of brokers and dealers and reform the role of specialists until 1936, when a statutorily directed Study was required to be delivered to Congress. Trading rules, however, were negotiated with the exchanges. But given the Commission's strong desire not to jeopardize its "cooperative" relationship with the NYSE, and the continuing domination of the Exchange by the specialists and floor traders of the Old Guard, the 16 trading rules promulgated succeeded only in outlawing the best known devices for manipulating share prices through pool operations. Whitney's firm stance prevented the issuance of a rule that measurably limited short selling. A last minute telegram from Whitney prompted the SEC to rewrite the Tenth Rule, "Trading by Specialists," to avoid the possibility of interference in specialists' market making functions. After Whitney's faction triumphed in the May 8 elections, the Commission agreed that the NYSE could adopt its rules after making additional minor modifications. Somewhat defensively, the Commission in its *First Annual Report* characterized the trading rules as "experimental" and noted that they might "be changed if further study indicates a necessity therefor."[129]

Kennedy's period as Chair ended less happily than it began. As a market operator, political operative, and Hollywood mogul, Kennedy had exhibited an extraordinary sense of timing. By May 1935, he sensed that it was time to resign. His reputation by then was secure. It then must have seemed doubtful that any SEC Chair soon could surpass Kennedy's achievements in his organization of the Commission or in breaking the capital logjam. He anticipated that the work of the Commission would be increasingly technical. "Consequently," Kennedy would write, it would be "necessary that lawyers should predominate in the Commission." A nonlawyer, easily wearied by detail work, Kennedy on May 27 literally was walking to the White House to resign when he learned from a *Washington Star* newsboy that the Supreme Court had declared the National Industrial Recovery Act unconstitutional. Because of personal loyalty to Roosevelt, Kennedy returned to his office and tore up his resignation letter.

The Supreme Court's unanimous *Schecter* decision did more than end the NRA, the most heralded of Roosevelt's early recovery programs; it placed in question the constitutionality of a host of New Deal statutes, including the Securities Act of 1933 and the Securities Exchange Act of 1934. Although the New York Stock Exchange's Governing Committee announced that it did "not contemplate any action looking toward a test of the Securities Exchange Act," the SEC soon conceded that its plan to register the over-the-counter brokers and dealers by July 1 had been thwarted as a result of *Schecter.* By late June, J. Edward Jones, a securities promoter, had mounted a constitutional challenge to the 1933 Securities Act. Until April 1936, when the Supreme Court upheld the constitutionality of the 1933 Act in the *Jones* case, no one at the Commission could be entirely confident that the agency would survive.[130]

Kennedy was routinely re-elected Chair on July 1, 1935. But changes in the tenor of Roosevelt's policy direction continued to make him uncomfortable. Roosevelt's truce of God with business had ended. The combination of the Supreme Court's Constitutional challenge to the New Deal and the business community's unremitting hostility signified to Felix Frankfurter and others close to Roosevelt that "the Administration plainly has reached a new stage." On June 10, 1935, Frankfurter reflected the President's own mood when he wrote to Jerome Frank, "From now on it must be to a large extent trench warfare."[131]

Roosevelt, personally, had been in part responsible for exacerbating the hostility between the New Deal and business. Soon after the Democrats' unexpected gains in the 1934 Congressional elections, he had directed Administration drafting teams to prepare anti-public utility holding company legislation. Even as moderated before enactment by Congress, the Public Utility Holding Company Act of 1935 was the most radical securities reform measure of the Roosevelt Administration. To deal with the sprawl and inefficiency of public utility empires, such as that of Samuel Insull, Section 11, the controversial "death sentence" provision of the Act, empowered the SEC to limit each holding company "to a single integrated public utility system" by compelling divestiture of most geographically dispersed subsidiaries.

Kennedy was opposed to the breadth of the proposed death sentence provision. Soon after the enactment of the Public Utility Holding Company Act of 1935, Kennedy resigned. Under his leadership, the SEC had played a conciliatory role, achieving prominence for its stimulation of private investment. With the enactment of the Holding Company Act, the agency's emphasis would shift to business reform; its character inevitably would become more confrontational.

Kennedy's resignation officially was accepted on September 20. His last act as Chair was to participate in the unanimous election of James Landis as his successor.[132]

A year and three months before, *Times* had characterized James Landis as a "true economic radical"; Henry Stimson had labeled him "the most dangerous man in the country." Yet after Landis had served for 15 months as an SEC Commissioner, Wall Street had come to view him with something close to approbation. By then his support of Kennedy's policy of business government cooperation was well known. It was assumed that Landis as Chair would be cautious, undogmatic, a mediator between the conflicting claims of such parties as investors and securities issuers, the New York Stock Exchange and the smaller, regional exchanges, exchange floor members, and commission house members.[133]

Still, there was something to be said for *Time's* initial perception of Landis. As a theorist, James Landis was no radical. But he was an articulate advocate of an expanded role for the federal regulatory agencies. Doubtful that unregulated firms in industries like banking, insurance, utilities, shipping, or communications could function adequately to meet public needs, or even function efficiently in the narrower economic sense, Landis viewed the primary purpose of an administrative agency to be "the guidance and supervision of the industry as a whole," rather than to play the simpler role of policeman.

So that the administrative agencies effectively could perform this supervisory role, Landis urged the agencies' right to a near exclusive jurisdiction over technical regulatory problems and the agencies' right to combine in a single regulatory body the functions historically embodied by the Constitution's three conceptually separate branches of government.[134]

The combination of Landis's theoretical beliefs about government by administrative agency and his personal self-doubts precluded his being either punitive or evangelical as Chair. Landis sought instead to reform the securities industry on the basis of "findings arrived at as scientifically as seemed possible."[135]

Landis's insistence on the professional excellence of the SEC gave the Commission staff its *esprit de corps*, its enduring standards of high quality, its attractiveness to talented attorneys. But Landis's effectiveness was limited by a tactical conservatism that increasingly was to isolate him from the forefront of the Roosevelt Administration's reform efforts — efforts that Landis earlier had helped lead. In particular, Landis was reluctant to confront industry leaders the SEC was required to regulate, and he had difficulty articulating the substantive goals needed to galvanize political support. It was with such considerations in mind that William O. Douglas, the SEC's third Chair, disparagingly assessed his predecessor: "James M. Landis . . . was born to be dean of a law school."[136] By dint of his intellect, preparation, and commitment, Landis also had been born to be SEC Chair. But he lacked the toughness and political flair that were to make Douglas, his successor, a more accomplished SEC Chair.

Public Utility Holding Company Act of 1935

The greatest showdown between Washington and Wall Street did not concern the Securities Act of 1933 or the Securities Exchange Act of 1934, but rather the Public Utility Holding Company Act of 1935. The restructuring of the public utility industry long was the SEC's single most far reaching accomplishment. It was also by far the most difficult to attain.[137]

The structure of few industries was so influenced by investment banking practices as that of the public utility industry before the 1929 Stock Market Crash. By 1932, three super-holding companies, JP Morgan's United Corporation, Insull's utility empire, and the Electric Bond and Share Company, were responsible for 45 percent of the electric energy generated in the United States. Sixteen holding companies had ownership interests in properties producing about 92 percent of the electrical output of the nation's privately owned companies. Four holding company groups controlled more than 56 percent of the total mileage of the country's natural gas transportation system. Natural and manufactured gas production was concentrated in a similar handful of dominant firms. Persuasive arguments were made that utility firms larger than local operating plans were necessary to finance efficiently local construction and least expensively maintain central engineering, construction, and managerial staffs. But the far flung geographic dispersion of the utility holding companies and their immense size far exceeded economies of scale. And the Stock Market Crash and ensuring Depression rebutted the utilities' claims of efficiency. Although, between 1929 and 1936, utility operating companies' revenues dropped only about 15 percent from their highest historical levels, 53 utility holding companies with $1.7 billion worth of securities outstanding went into receivership or bankruptcy. Twenty-three other utility holding companies with about $535 million of outstanding securities defaulted on interest payments and voluntarily offered readjustment plans. During the same seven-year period, 53 operating companies with $600 million of outstanding securities either were forced into bankruptcy or receivership or voluntarily sought a readjustment plan.[138]

The concentration of the utility industry precipitated what was the most extensive study of an American industry ever conducted. Between 1928 and 1935 the FTC published 84 volumes of hearings and documentary evidence on utility corporations. Beginning with the populist assumptions that "no large holding company structure has grown to its present size without the aid of investment bankers" and that "managements apparently often give greater attention to the counsel of bankers than to the interests of widely scattered stockholders," the FTC's concluding Report depicted in detail how individuals like Insull and banks like JP Morgan and Company were able to control holding company empires with minority common stock ownership through such means as stock "pyramiding," nonvoting stock, voting trusts, classified boards of directors, interlocking directorates, and contractual relationships. Most often minority control was achieved by the purchase of voting control only in a top holding company, most of whose capital was raised by the selling of bonds or nonvoting preferred stock. To control the entire holding company system, the top holding company then would buy a majority voting interest in a series of subholding companies, each of which also largely would be capitalized through the sale of bonds or nonvoting stock. The subholding companies, in turn, would own voting control in the utility operating companies. Through such pyramiding of control, five public utility holding company systems were controlled in 1931 by the holders of common stock worth less than 1 percent of the entire system's assets. In the most extreme case, Standard Gas and Electric Company, with a total investment of $1.2 billion, was controlled by $23,100 of common stock. A principal consequence of financing public utility systems with large proportions of debt securities was a significant increase in the risk of business failure, since the fixed interest charges on debt securities had to be paid, regardless of the earnings of the utility. By contrast, dividends to stockholders usually were paid at the discretion of a board of directors and may not be paid at all when a firm lacks an available "surplus." Excessive debt to equity ratios were the primary cause of the utility holding company bankruptcies during the 1929–1936 period.

The FTC *Utility Corporations Report* also emphasized the unsound accounting techniques employed by those who controlled the top holding companies. It was found that the combined capital assets of the 151 firms studied were written up by $1.4 billion (16 percent of claimed aggregate capital assets of $8.6 billion) to inflate earnings and justify dividends. Top holding companies further swelled their profits by providing engineering, construction, accounting, and managerial services to operating firms, exacting in some instances profits ranging from 50 percent to over 300 percent of the actual cost of such services. The appearance of even greater profits was created by such unsound accounting methods as failing to recognize adequately depreciation expenses for physical assets, recognizing income from the undistributed earnings of subsidiaries, and recognizing income from the sale of properties to controlled subsidiaries at figures higher than market value. The FTC's exhaustive Report concluded with recommendations that Congress seek to abolish all top holding companies and many subholding companies through tax measures or statutory prohibitions.[139]

Roosevelt, himself an uncompromising advocate of holding company abolition, created the National Power Policy Committee in the Summer of 1934 to formulate his Administration's legislative proposals. Secretary of the Interior Harold Ickes was named Chairman. Benjamin Cohen soon was hired as General Counsel; Robert Healy, among others, served on the Committee. In March 1935, shortly before the conclusions of the FTC *Utility Corporations Report* were published, the Power Policy Committee recommended to Congress the practical abolition of most holding companies. It asked for legislation directing a Federal Administrative Commission to see to "the elimination of unnecessary corporate complexities and of properties which do not fit into an economically and geographically integrated whole." The Committee recommended that a federal administrative agency supervise the issuance of securities by utility companies, the acquisition of new securities and properties, prevent utility holding companies from owning nonutility ventures, prevent electric utility and interstate gas transmission or production firms from being commonly owned, and police holding company service, sales, and construction arrangements to ensure that controlled operating companies received "the performance of their work at cost."[140]

The Public Utility Holding Company Act of 1935,[141] as enacted, achieved most of the policy aims of the National Power Policy Committee. Drafted chiefly by Benjamin Cohen, the Act followed the by then familiar general structure of the 1933 and 1934 Securities Acts. After a section declaring that public utility holding companies were engaged in interstate commerce and had committed a long catalogue of abuses, the Act went on to forbid the utilities from engaging in interstate commerce unless they registered with the Securities and Exchange Commission. There was only one significant exemption for intrastate holding company systems.

The most far reaching provision of the Act was Section 11, the controversial death sentence provision. The final compromise version of the section required the SEC as soon as practicable after January 1, 1938, to limit the operations of each holding company system to a single integrated system "and to such other businesses as are reasonably incidental or economically necessary or appropriate to the operations of such integrated public utility system," provided, however, that a holding company system could continue to control one or more additional public utility systems if it could show that the additional systems were in the same state or an adjoining state and that joint control would result in substantial economies. At the same time, the corporate simplification subsection of § 11 vested the SEC with the power to restructure any holding company whose structure was unduly or unnecessarily complicated.

The Act additionally empowered the SEC to regulate the sale of all utility securities issuances, in the manner of a Blue Sky Law Commission, requiring truth in prospectuses and barring altogether new securities issuances when the SEC considered the securities not reasonably adapted to the financial structure of the firm, or when it considered the underwriting costs too great or found any other terms of the issues "detrimental to the public interest." Similar grants of power authorized the SEC to regulate the purchase by a utility system of any securities, utility assets, or interest in any other business. The Commission was directed to bar altogether loans by one utility firm in a holding system to a second utility in the same system and to prohibit utility company dividends unless the Commission was satisfied that they could be made without jeopardizing a utility firm's "financial integrity." Section 13 authorized the SEC to supervise all utility services, sales, and construction contracts performed by subsidiaries of holding companies or independent mutual service companies to ensure that they were performed "economically" and "at cost" for the benefit of operating companies. All remaining holding companies and each new mutual service company was required to report periodically to the SEC, employing a uniform system of accounts if the Commission deemed it in the public interest to develop uniform accounting methods.

In the broadest sense, the Holding Company Act gave the SEC power to refashion the structure and business practices of an entire industry. Except in wartime, the federal government never before had assumed such total control over any industry, not even in banking, railroad transportation, or communications, over which federal regulatory powers long had existed. As with the two federal antitrust laws, the emphasis of the Holding Company Act was a significant one shot intervention into a dysfunctional industry, rather than the continuing regulation of an industry's structure. By directing the SEC to simplify the public utility systems "as soon as practicable after January 1, 1938," Roosevelt acted on the belief that changing an industry significantly had to be done swiftly after the passage of an enabling Act, while its political supporters remained in power.

There never was any real likelihood that the utility industry would cooperate with the SEC in the enforcement of the Holding Company Act. Throughout the bitter legislative battle leading to the enactment of the Act, the Edison Electric Institute, the public utilities' principal lobbying organization, steadfastly had maintained that "the true purpose of the Bill is to socialize the business of providing homes of the nation with electric light and power."[142]

On September 12, 1935, just 17 days after the passage of the Holding Company Act, the Edison Electric Institute announced that it had retained, in addition to John W. Davis, former Secretary of War Newton Baker and former Solicitor General James Beck to test the constitutionality of the Act "as soon as possible."[143] The test came with unexpected suddenness. Although no utility was required to register with the SEC until December 1, 1935, on September 16 the Trustees of the American States Public Service Company, a minor utility system then being reorganized under the provisions of the Bankruptcy Act, and one Fred Lautenbach, a dentist who owned $2500 of the firm's bonds, petitioned Federal District Court Judge William Coleman for a declaration that the Public Utility Holding Company Act was unconstitutional.

Landis's time as Chair began a few days later in an atmosphere of crisis. None of the conciliatory tactics that had worked so effectively for Kennedy in enforcing the Securities Laws aided Landis in enforcing the Holding Company Act. After summoning the leading utility executives to Washington in an attempt to develop a cooperative approach to the Act, Landis was informed on September 25 that the utility firms intended to fight the Act "to the last legal ditch."[144]

The destiny of the Public Utility Holding Company Act was decided by the federal courts. And in the courts, the SEC at first found itself outmaneuvered. By September 27, when SEC General Counsel Burns, flanked by Cohen and Corcoran, arrived in Judge Coleman's Baltimore Federal District Court to appear in the *American States Public Service Company* proceeding, it was already obvious that the Judge intended to declare the Act unconstitutional.

On November 7, the inevitable Coleman decision was handed down. Condemning the Act as "grossly in excess of any lawful Congressional power [and] the extreme of dictatorial control," the Judge declared the Public Utility Holding Company Act "void in its entirety." "So devoid," Coleman opined, "are its provisions of any attempt properly to distinguish between intrastate and interstate commerce that, were dissection attempted, scarcely a clause would survive, save perhaps the preamble."[145]

The next day public utility stocks rose between one and three points. From the date of the passage of the Holding Company Act,

John Foster Dulles, Managing Partner of the leading Wall Street firm of Sullivan and Cromwell, had urged the major utility firms not to register with the Commission, but to "resist the law with all your might." The Coleman decision precipitated a stampede among the utility firms to follow Dulles's advice. Fifty-eight separate lawsuits were brought on behalf of over 100 companies in 13 different federal district courts to enjoin the enforcement of the Act. Three hundred and seventy-five firms sought a Declaration of Exemption. As the Act's December 1, 1935, deadline for temporary registration expired, a mere 57 utilities, mostly minor firms, had formally registered with the SEC. Nearly all of these firms availed themselves of the Commission's offer to file while reserving their constitutional rights, including the right simultaneously to bring an action to have the Act declared unconstitutional.[146]

With unexpected suddenness, on November 26 the Commission began its own test case to establish the constitutionality of the Holding Company Act, catching its chosen defendant as surprised as the Commission itself had been by the commencement of the *American States Public Service Company* proceeding.

The chosen target was the Electric Bond and Share Company, the nation's second largest utility system, responsible in 1932 for production of 14 percent of national electrical generation and, significantly for the Constitution's Interstate Commerce Clause, an undeniably interstate system, operating in 31 separate states stretching from Florida to Washington. By beginning the suit, the SEC was able to limit the case to a test of the constitutionality of two less controversial provisions, §§ 4 and 5, which prohibited a utility from engaging in interstate commerce until it had filed a Registration Statement with the SEC.

In this posture, there was little likelihood that Electric Bond and Share could prevail even before "the horse and buggy" Supreme Court of the day. Electric Bond and Share was a super-holding company with controlling interests in five multistate holding companies, which, in turn, controlled 187 domestic subsidiaries that provided electricity and gas to a population of nearly 14 million people in the United States and served approximately 13 million additional people abroad. Electric Bond and Share also held 100 percent interests in 8 service and construction company subsidiaries. Through these service companies, the firm systematically had milked its operating company subsidiaries. During the seven years 1922–1938,

64 percent of Electric Bond and Share's income had been derived not from the yield on securities it held in its subholding companies, but from fees for providing construction, engineering, management, and underwriting services to its controlled operating firms. As best as the FTC could calculate, the profit on such service relationships averaged over 100 percent. Further to inflate Electric Bond and Share's apparent worth, the assets of operating subsidiaries frequently were written up with the firms were initially organized, merged, or reorganized. The same assets regularly were under depreciated. In 1929, the capital surplus account of Electric Bond and Share appeared to be overstated by as much as $383 million.[147]

In January 1937, Judge Mack's decision affirming the constitutionality of §§ 4 and 5 of the Act was published.[148] In the immediate aftermath of Mack's ruling, two major utility systems, the North American Company and the American Water Works and Electric Company, withdrew suits against the SEC and announced that they would register. In mid-March, a third major system, American Light and Traction Company, registered. But when, in June 1937, the United States Supreme Court refused to expedite review of the *Electric Bond and Share* case and instead directed that Mack's decision first be considered by the Second Circuit Court of Appeals, the resolve of the remaining unregistered utility systems stiffened. Even the Fourth Circuit Court of Appeals' earlier partial reversal of Coleman's ruling in the *American States Public Service* proceeding encouraged few firms to register. When Landis resigned his Chairmanship in September 1937, only 90 or so utility firms, holding about one-third of the assets of all companies subject to the Holding Company Act, had registered. It would not be until 1938, when the United States Supreme Court affirmed Judge Mack's decision in *Electric Bond and Share*, that enforcement of the Public Utility Holding Company Act effectively began.[149]

Within a week of the Supreme Court's *Electric Bond and Share* decision, every major utility system had registered.[150] This set the stage for a second showdown between the utility industry and the SEC over enforcement of the Holding Company Act.

On August 3, Douglas requested that 66 major public utility systems submit plans no later than December 1, 1938, describing what steps they intended to take to comply with the Public Utility Holding Company Act. Douglas's letter and a related Press Release offered to accept "tentative suggestions, plans, and programs," conceded that full geographic integration and corporate simplification would "take years," but emphasized, "to get on with our task we must insist on progress."[151]

Douglas's effort to secure voluntary compliance with § 11 almost totally failed. Although nearly every utility system submitted a "plan" for geographic integration, only a few of the utilities' integration proposals were to prove adequate.[152]

The SEC dramatically shifted its strategy. The Commission, supported by Roosevelt, proceeded "to institute proceedings practically simultaneously against all the major [holding company] systems" beginning in early 1940, rather than to continue attempting to negotiate compliance with the Act or proceed through test cases, proved to be the key to the effective enforcement of § 11 of the Public Utility Holding Company Act.[153]

By 1940 the SEC had less reason to fear the judiciary. Five of the nine Supreme Court Justices — Hugh Black, Stanley Reed, Felix Frankfurter, William Douglas, and Frank Murphy — were Roosevelt appointees, and they reasonably could be assumed to favor the Act's enforcement. Throughout the duration of Roosevelt's Administration, the process of replacing pre-New Deal Justices with Roosevelt appointees continued. By the time of Roosevelt's death, in 1945, only two of the nine Justices then sitting had not been appointed by him. Parallel changes occurred in the lower federal courts. This contributed to the success of the SEC's aggressive litigation strategy after 1940. In the 280 judicial proceedings completed under the Public Utility Holding Company Act by June 30, 1952, only two were terminated adversely, a record so one-sided that Second Circuit Judge Learned Hand once introduced an SEC attorney with the caustic observation, "Now we will hear from that sacred cow, the Securities and Exchange Commission." Although the SEC's Public Utilities Division included extraordinarily talented attorneys, the Commission's Holding Company Act litigation record would have been inconceivable before a less sympathetic judiciary.[154]

Lack of a Supreme Court quorum during World War II delayed a definitive construction of the Holding Company Act's integration and simplification section until 1946, deferring full realization of the results of the SEC's restructuring of the utility industry until the Truman Administration.[155] Much of the work necessary for the industry's restructuring, however, was accomplished before the definitive Supreme Court decisions.

In February and March 1940, the SEC initiated integration proceedings against 9 of the 13 largest registered holding company systems. By June 1943, the SEC had instituted 127 § 11 proceedings, involving almost all of the 55 utility systems registered with the Commission in 1940. Given the number of holding company systems registered under the Act and the time required for contesting antitrust litigation, it never was considered desirable by the SEC to impose divestiture plans on each utility. The SEC's § 11(e) strategy quietly commenced in 1939, when Chairman Douglas persuaded Congress to postpone the recognition of capital gains or losses under the Internal Revenue Code when the securities or property of registered holding companies were exchanged "in obedience to an order of the Securities and Exchange Commission." In 1942, Congress exempted public utilities that complied with § 11(b) of the Holding Company Act from the Tax Code's stamp tax on issuances and exchanges of securities.[156]

The key to the SEC's § 11(e) strategy was doctrinal. Largely between 1941 and 1943, the Commission construed §§ 11(b)(1) and 11(b)(2) in an uncompromising manner, making plain to any utility that required the SEC to enforce those provisions that it would be subjected to as comprehensive a divestiture order as was permissible under a reasonable interpretation of the Act. Three lines of cases were of paramount significance in interpreting the geographic integration of § 11(b)(1). First, the SEC held in its 1941 *Columbia Gas and Electric* and *United Gas Improvement* opinions that a "single integrated public utility system" could not retain both electric and gas properties. Second, in its *United Gas Improvement* and 1942 *North American Company* opinions, the SEC construed the language permitting an integrated public utility system to retain "such other businesses as are reasonably incidental, or economically necessary or appropriate" as allowing retention of other businesses only when they resulted in "economies in the operation of an integrated utility system." "Other businesses" without a functional relationship to an integrated electric or gas system could not be retained. Third, Commission opinions in the *United Gas Improvement, Engineers Public Service,* and *North American Company* cases stringently limited the opportunities for a holding company to retain an additional public utility system beyond the single physically interconnected utility system permitted by definitional § 2(a)(29).

Simultaneously, the Commission interpreted the proscription against "unduly or unnecessarily complicated corporate structures" in § 11(b)(2) as requiring the elimination of holding or subholding companies "which serve no useful purpose." Under the SEC's interpretation, heavily leveraged holding company systems such as *Electric Bond and Share* could be dismantled if it was shown that specific constituent firms had no productive function or had been used primarily to increase the leverage of the controlling shareholders in the top holding company.[157]

The cumulative effect of these interpretations gave the SEC the bargaining power to persuade many holding company systems to offer a sufficiently far reaching voluntary divestiture plan to satisfy the Commission. This was often done in one of two ways. By agreeing to divest additional integrated utility systems, several major holding companies, including the Middle West Corporation, the Columbia Gas and Electric Corporation, American Gas and Electric Company, and the Commonwealth and Southern Corporation, were allowed to retain geographically larger principal integrated systems than they otherwise might have. In other instances, divested operating companies were allowed to retain both gas and electric properties, although the Commission usually forbade a registered holding company to do so.[158]

The tendency of an SEC-approved plan to increase both preferred and common share values was widely recognized in the aftermath of the Commission's March 1943 approval of United Gas Improvement's plan. UGI was a subholding company of the United Corporation, which itself controlled 80 subsidiaries. To facilitate the retirement of UGI's preferred stock, the SEC approved a plan under which UGI's preferred shareholders exchanged their shares for cash and common stock with a dividend preference in the Philadelphia Electric Company, UGI's largest subsidiary. In dollar terms, UGI common stock rose from $4.00 per share before UGI filed its plan to nearly $10 just before UGI completed its recapitalization. By mid-1943, financial analysts like Standard and Poor's, Moody's Stock Survey, and Barron's predicted that comparable financial benefits would be enjoyed by security holders of other holding companies after they filed plans under the Public Utility Holding Company Act.[159]

After Supreme Court decisions in 1945 and 1946 held that §§ 11(b)(1) and 11(b)(2) were constitutional and approved SEC interpretations of these subsections, the pace of voluntary compliance accelerated. Between 1945 and 1948, holding companies divested themselves of assets worth approximately $7 billion. By the end of the Truman Administration, the SEC's mission under § 11 was over 90 percent completed. At one time or another, holding companies registered with the SEC had controlled 1983 subsidiaries. By June 30, 1952, 1603 had been divested. On July 1, 1940, 15 separate holding companies supplied electric or gas service in 10 or more states. By June 30, 1951, no utility holding company operated in 10 or more states; only 7 operated in 5 to 9 states. In 1959, when § 11 enforcement was almost complete, only three registered holding companies would operate in more than four States.[160]

In 1938, at the time of the Supreme Court's decision in the *Electric Bond and Share* case, three holding company systems — Electric Bond and Share, the United Corporation, and the nonbankrupt holding companies once controlled by Samuel Insull — directly or indirectly controlled 50 percent of the $15 billion of assets owned by registered holding companies. The cumulative effect of the SEC's proceedings against Electric Bond and Share, the United Corporation, and the Insull interests was to transform three superholding companies that directly or indirectly had controlled about half of the nation's electrical generation into approximately 45 regional, state, or local utility companies.[161]

Taking into account the compromises the SEC made to enforce § 11, the Commission's geographic integration and corporate simplification of the utility industry remains the most comprehensive structural relief ever achieved by an agency of the federal government. The SEC's enforcement of the Holding Company Act also was an illustration of the advantages of the administrative process. Crucial to the SEC's effort was a large and sophisticated staff in its Public Utilities Division able to study not just a single case, but an industry. Equally crucial was the ability of the Commission to coordinate doctrine, timing of litigation, and negotiations with holding companies in such a manner as to persuade an entire industry ultimately to comply voluntarily with the geographic integration provisions of the Act. It is highly unlikely that the initial prosecution of several separate holding company actions before separate federal district court judges would have led to an equally effective dissolution program, for the Act's effective enforcement required, above all else, continuity of effort. Beginning with the FTC's comprehensive study of the utility industry and continuing through the legislative battle to enact Benjamin Cohen's draft of the Holding Company Bill, the 1935–1938 litigation battle to establish the constitutionality of the Act and then stretching for another 14 years during which the SEC substantially completed its § 11 program, the effort to restructure the holding company industry was pursued by highly competent people with generally similar political ends. Such a continuity of objective and competence is the hallmark of an effective administrative agency.[162]

Stock Market Regulation

The other major priority for the New Deal's SEC was stock market regulation. In interpreting and expanding the mandate of the 1934 Securities Exchange Act, Landis made his most enduring contributions to the Commission.

The New York Stock Exchange had been the logical first concern of stock market regulation. It was the largest and most influential securities exchange. But merely to regulate listed securities on the organized stock markets would not have effectively reduced securities fraud so much as rechanneled it to the unlisted departments of the smaller exchanges and to the over-the-counter markets.

By definition, unlisted securities were securities admitted to trading privileges on an exchange at the initiative of an exchange member instead of the issuing corporation. Since unlisted securities typically had not provided investors with financial reports comparable with those of listed securities on the New York Stock Exchange, the initial 1934 Securities and Exchange bill had called for the abolition of all unlisted trading. Unified opposition by 24 regional exchanges had resulted in a compromise provision of the Act. The SEC was directed to study unlisted trading and report to Congress by January 3, 1936. But unless Congress adopted new legislation, all unlisted trading was to end on June 1, 1936, the death sentence date for unlisted securities.

By January 1936, Landis had come to regard the problem of unlisted trading as more complex than a matter of unequal investor information. Discarding a draft of the Unlisted Trading Report prepared by A. Wilfred May under the supervision of Kemper Simpson, the Commission's Economic Adviser, Landis had directed an assistant, attorney Milton Katz, to prepare a new report, focusing on the structure of the securities markets.[163]

The Katz draft, published as the SEC's *Report on Trading in Unlisted Securities Upon Exchanges,* and related Commission statements depicted the organized stock market system on the verge of becoming noncompetitive. In the period from July 1, 1935, to June 30, 1936, 85 percent of the market value of securities transactions on all organized exchanges occurred on the NYSE, which traded only listed securities. Eleven percent of the market value of securities transactions on an organized exchange took place on the New York Curb Exchange, 80 percent of whose trading was in unlisted securities. About half the securities traded on the other 22 exchanges were unlisted. If unlisted trading were to be abolished, Landis testified, the New York Curb Exchange "would suffer seriously [and] many small exchanges would be forced to close." Ultimately, the previously unlisted shares would be largely redistributed to the NYSE, which would then account for an even higher proportion of transactions on the organized stock exchanges, or to the over-the-counter markets, some of which Landis had recently described as persisting in "practices which could not have been indulged in even on the least reputable of our stock exchanges." Such a stock market system would also be more difficult to police. As the SEC's Report emphasized:

> Exchanges constitute an organized mechanism of control which can be utilized to good advantage. Manipulative or deceptive practices in the comparatively unorganized over-the-counter markets are more difficult to detect and prevent. In consequence, if our purpose is the effective regulation of trading practices, it would be profitless to drive securities from the exchanges into the over-the-counter markets.

Both to increase interexchange competition and to ensure more effective regulation, the Commission's January 1936 Report recommended retention of unlisted trading.[164]

The 1934 Securities Exchange Act granted the SEC *carte blanche* authority to regulate the over-the-counter markets as long as its rules and regulations gave investors protection "comparable" with that provided by the Act "in the case of national securities exchanges.

Through 1936, the amount of over-the-counter trading dwarfed securities transactions on the organized exchanges. Although the Commission found "authentic data were lacking," it was estimated that two to four times the amount of trading on the exchanges was transacted over the counter. Where 6260 issues were traded on all exchanges registered with the SEC, 90,000 issues were quoted for over-the-counter trading in the National Quotation Bureau's semi-annual stock and bond summaries. The SEC termed the over-the-counter markets "one of the enigmas of our financial system," not so much because of the size of the over-the-counter markets as because of their variety. The 1934 Securities Exchange Act described over-the-counter trading with the phrase "otherwise than on a national securities exchange." Within this capacious definition coexisted several distinct types of securities trading. At one extreme the over-the-counter markets were "preeminent in those securities having the least amount of risk." Virtually all United States Treasury bonds and notes, federal farm loan bonds, home owners loan bonds, and state and municipal bonds were traded over the counter. Similarly, in 1958 it would be estimated that about 80 percent of all transactions in corporate bonds were traded over the counter. At the other extreme were over-the-counter markets trading local issues or new issues where trading volume was too sparse to justify the issues being listed on an exchange. His experience in enforcing the 1933 Securities Act for the Federal Trade Commission had convinced Landis that the most speculative oil and gas, gold mine, and liquor securities usually were traded by local, sometimes fly-by-night, over-the-counter dealers. Finally, the over-the-counter markets provided some competition with the exchanges by trading bonds, preferred stock, and other fixed income securities. "Even with respect to some common stocks admitted to exchange trading," reported a 1936 SEC Study, "the volume of trading over the counter frequently exceeds that on the exchange."

But over-the-counter trading did not occur on a discrete number of exchange floors. Each of the nation's 5000 to 6000 over-the-counter brokers and dealers could become a market maker in a designated security merely by signifying to other over-the-counter traders an intent to deal in particular securities. No seat on an exchange need be purchased. No exchange disciplinary rules need be obeyed. The principal over-the-counter firms were unified only by "a nationwide web of telephone and telegraph wires."

The very informality of the over-the-counter markets invited sharp dealing, particularly in small, local common stock trading. Even the most wide open of the pre-Crash securities exchanges functioned as an "auction market," requiring specialists to match the highest bid and lowest offer in each transaction. When trading was sufficiently active in a security, the funneling of most transactions to a specialist resulted in price quotations being relatively stable, rarely including erratic price jumps. By contrast, over-the-counter dealers were not bound to deal with any particular market maker. Purchase transactions typically occurred when the over-the-counter dealer bought a security from a market maker at one price and resold it to a customer at a higher price. The customer was not informed of the price at which the over-the-counter dealer had purchased the security, and the SEC later learned of a great many instances in which over-the-counter firms pocketed profits as high as 25 percent or more per transaction. In one notorious instance, the Commission found that an over-the-counter dealer had taken a profit of 380 percent by purchasing a security at $5.00 and reselling it to a customer at $24.[165]

Landis focused the Commission's efforts on regulating the over-the-counter brokers and dealers whose activities often clearly were in interstate commerce. In a November 1935 speech, Landis proposed a two-pronged approach to regulation of the over-the-counter dealers. Landis called first for the Commission to seek the registration of all brokers and dealers active in the over-the-counter markets, "together," Landis explained, "with the imposition of a few regulations mainly confirming their fiduciary duties." The registration program, in fact, had already begun, and by December 31, 1935, would result in the registration of 5083 over-the-counter brokers and dealers. But Landis emphasized that such "large scale" registration could accomplish little more than "winnowing out . . . the black sheep" by denying registration to brokers or dealers who had criminal records or were guilty of violating the securities laws. Landis stressed "the second method of control," an SEC attempt "to help in the organization of a self-disciplinary agency of dealers. Just as the Disciplinary Committees of the Exchanges have been invaluable to us in our efforts to supervise the activities on the Exchanges," Landis explained, "similar machinery would seem to be of value for the over-the-counter markets." Protracted negotiations first conducted by Landis would result in 1938 in Congressional approval of a self-disciplinary agency for over-the-counter dealers.[166]

The SEC's February 1936 legislative proposals were directed primarily toward rationalizing the relationships among listed securities, unlisted securities, and the over-the-counter markets. The Commission proposed amending the Securities Exchange Act to permit continued trading of unlisted securities if trading had occurred before March 1, 1934, if the security was listed on a second exchange, or if the SEC found that the issuer voluntarily provided information to investors "substantially equivalent" to that required by the 1933 and 1934 Acts. The new section strengthened the New York Curb and the regional exchanges. Not only was each of the smaller exchanges allowed to continue trading in unlisted securities that had been traded before the 1934 Act, but each was allowed to trade the most active listed securities on other exchanges if it could convince the SEC that there would be "sufficient public trading activity" on its floor to provide an orderly market.

A proposed amendment to the 1934 Act codified the SEC's earlier system of registering over-the-counter brokers and dealers. It also required each over-the-counter security with a share value of $2 million or more, registered under the 1933 Securities Act, to provide periodic financial statements, as if it were listed on an exchange. With little modification, the 1936 amendments to the 1934 Act were passed unanimously by both Houses of Congress and signed into law by President Roosevelt on May 26.[167]

The very qualities that led Landis's success in extending the 1934 Act to unlisted trading and the over-the-counter markets — his aversion to dogmatic positions, his insistence on thorough study, his preference for moderate, incremental action — soon led him to issue the most controversial Study of his Chairmanship, the SEC's June 1936 *Report on the Feasibility and Advisability of the Complete Segregation of the Functions of Dealer and Broker.*

The bitterest defeat for Ben Cohen and Pecora, as well as for Flynn, in the lobbying for the 1934 Securities Exchange Bill had been the deletion of the original uncompromising section on segregation and the enactment of a section that directed the SEC to study the feasibility and advisability of the complete segregation of the functions of dealer and broker and to report the results of the Study to Congress. The Segregation Study represented the second, and presumably last, chance for Flynn and a fair number of like-minded stock exchange reformers to remake the New York Stock Exchange in the image of a public utility.

Kemper Simpson, the Commission's Chief Economic Adviser, and Willis Ballinger, Chief of Special Studies, were assigned to prepare the Report on Segregation. Although the Simpson-Ballinger draft of the Segregation Report did not call for complete segregation, it did recommend an almost total elimination of members floor trading for their own accounts, the barring of brokerage houses from also underwriting new securities, and the strengthening of the smaller regional exchanges at the expense of the less well organized over-the-counter markets. Landis, appalled by the Report's cursory consideration of the practical consequences of segregation in the organized exchanges, persuaded the Commission to reject the Simpson-Ballinger draft and assign David Saperstein, Director of the Trading and Exchange Division, and Thomas Gammack, his Executive Assistant, to work with Landis in rewriting the Report. The withdrawal of the Report embittered all concerned. A copy of the Simpson-Ballinger draft found its way to the *Herald Tribune*. In late 1936, the full Commission eliminated the positions of Economic Adviser and Chief of Special Studies, effectively dismissing Simpson and Ballinger. A bitter Simpson departed, publicly railing against a "Commission dominated by those interested primarily in technical detail and legal phraseology."

The final Segregation Report released in June 1936 was not so much technical in detail as cautious in its conclusions. In language that even Flynn and Simpson could approve, the Report began with an extensive criticism of stock exchange floor traders and specialists. Approximately 24 percent of trading on the New York Stock Exchange between June 24, 1935, and December 14, 1935, the Report found, had been trading by members for their own accounts. When trading on the stock exchange floor, a member enjoyed extraordinary advantages over nonmember investors, primarily because his physical presence on the floor gave him the advantage of having crucial information. The Report stated:

> He sees instantly the outbreak of activity in a stock, the nature of the trading, and the direction of prices. He is in a position to discount or revise his market appraisals almost instantaneously.

> Upon the basis of information which he derives while on the floor he can increase, decrease, or cancel his orders more rapidly than a nonmember to whom the same information is only made available at a later time.

The SEC Report recommended that no legislation be enacted requiring the complete segregation of the functions of dealer and broker. The Commission would use its existing rulemaking authority to effect "partial segregation" primarily through the functional segregation of all members on an exchange floor with the exception of specialists. "Under such a requirement floor traders could not act as brokers, and commission brokers could not . . . initiate orders for their own account." This was a significant "evolutionary step," which would have reduced the number of NYSE floor brokers dealing for their own accounts. But its significance was considerably reduced by the fact that the recommended "functional segregation" did not extend to dealing that took place off the floor. Thus, a commission broker barred from trading for his own account on the exchange floor could do so in the over-the-counter market. Nor did the Report specify any new limitations on specialist trading beyond indicating that the SEC would study "appropriate restrictions governing the conditions under which the specialist may trade with his book." Finally, and by far most significantly, the Segregation Report shied away from the most important implication of its empirical findings. Given the Report's findings concerning the abuses of member trading and its insistence that liquidity should not be regarded as a "fetish," the Report well might have renewed the call for the abolition of floor traders, the stock exchange members who traded only for their own accounts.[168]

To the stock exchanges, the Segregation Report, even with its limited recommendations, was, as both Landis and *The Literary Digest* independently judged it, "a bombshell." When Landis made plain to a NYSE Committee on November 18, 1936, that the SEC intended to see its plan for functional segregation of exchange members put into effect regardless of the wishes of the exchange, the value of a seat on the exchange began a precipitous drop, declining $38,000, to a value of $89,000 by December 1, 1936. W.W. Spald, President of the Associated Stock Exchanges, lambasted the SEC for subjecting the organized stock market to a greater degree of regulation than the over-the-counter markets. "Stock exchanges," claimed Spald, "have entered the dying industries classification by reason of the discriminatory operation of the Securities and Exchange laws." For the exchanges, partial segregation of brokers and dealers was almost as intense a pocketbook issue as the proposed abolition of floor traders had been in 1934.[169]

Even before securities prices sharply slumped in the fall of 1937, NYSE President Charles Gay publicly blamed SEC and other federal regulatory bodies for creating "abnormal market conditions" that threatened to destroy a "broad, liquid market." At his final Press Conference, Landis scornfully dismissed Gay's remark that excessive regulation had lessened the liquidity of the market and sharply questioned the objectivity of stock exchange officials like Gay, whose living depended on creating the greatest possible share volume. Against the strong opposition of the exchange, however, Landis was unable to negotiate a partial segregation rule during his Chairmanship. And when the market began a severe slump in mid-August 1937, the SEC, in spite of his earlier insistence, did not impose such a rule.[170]

The defeat of partial segregation was a rare setback in the SEC's efforts during the Landis Chairmanship to reduce fraud on the securities exchanges. Although Landis personally disliked the policeman's role, the SEC he led was imaginative and effective in its enforcement activities. By the end of his Chairmanship, the SEC had evolved a strategy of informal enforcement procedures and occasional highly publicized exemplary prosecutions that allowed the Commission to maximize the impact of its enforcement resources.

The effectiveness of the Commission's enforcement activity, combined with the primitiveness of its initial Hearing procedures, engendered intense animosity. The anti-SEC hostility became evident in the aftermath of the Supreme Court decision in *Jones v. SEC.* J. Edward Jones, then the nation's largest dealer in oil royalty securities, in May 1935 had filed a Registration Statement that the SEC considered so misleading that it telegraphed Jones one day before the statement was to become effective and demanded that he show cause why a Stop Order should not be issued. Instead, Jones moved to withdraw the Registration Statement. When the SEC refused to permit him to do so, citing a Commission rule that withdrawal could occur only with SEC consent, Jones began a federal court challenge to the constitutionality of the 1933 Securities Act and the SEC's rule preventing withdrawal of his Registration

Statement. In March 1936, his case reached the Supreme Court. Justice Sutherland's subsequent decision ignored questions of the Act's constitutionality, allowing Court of Appeals holdings affirming the Act's constitutionality to stand as controlling law. But a 6-3 Court majority ruled that, the Act being silent on the appropriate procedure, the SEC should have followed controlling Equity Court rules and permitted withdrawal. This was a defeat for the SEC, but on a technical point, remediable in the future by waiting until the Registration Statement became effective before instituting a Stop Order proceeding.

Although Sutherland's decision implicitly acknowledged that the SEC's actions were at most "petty encroachments" or "minor invasions of personal rights," he closed his decision by comparing the Commission's procedures with the "unlawful inquisitorial investigations" and "intolerable abuses of the Star Chamber." Landis attributed Sutherland's tirade to the anti-New Deal sentiments of the Court's majority, taking some pleasure in telegraphing Roosevelt the bristling rejoinder to Sutherland in Justice Cardozo's dissent. "A Commission which is without coercive powers, which cannot arrest or amerce or imprison though a crime has been uncovered or even punish for contempt, but can only inquire and report, the propriety of every question in the course of the inquiry being subject to the supervision of the ordinary courts of justice, is likened with denunciatory fervor to the Star Chamber of the Stuarts. Historians may find hyperbole in the sanguinary simile."[171]

Precisely because their discretion overlapped the traditional responsibilities of each of the three branches of government, Roosevelt's agencies even in what Landis called their "lusty youth" were jealously regarded. Sutherland's tirade against the SEC was as much a defense of judicial supremacy as a polemic against the New Deal. The fevered excesses of the Liberty League and Alf Landon's 1936 "Down with the Alphabet [Agencies]" Presidential campaign would draw their justification from the traditional tripartite scheme of the Constitution that Landis's theoretical writings and the SEC in practice disputed as inevitable. Even Roosevelt's own Committee on Administrative Management early in 1937 would inveigh against the independent regulatory commissions that threatened in time to become "a headless fourth branch of government, not contemplated by the Constitution, and not responsible administratively either to the President, to Congress, or to the Courts." Lacking the legitimacy accorded by the Constitution through periodic election or judicial appointment, agencies like the SEC were inherently vulnerable.

Beginning in 1934, the American Bar Association began a 12-year campaign to reduce the judicial powers of the administrative agencies. A 1938 American Bar Association Committee's legislative proposals were the inspiration for the Walter-Logan Administrative Law Bill, introduced in 1939. The Walter-Logan Bill proposed to increase dramatically judicial review of administrative agency actions. Significantly, the proposal would have permitted judicial review of virtually all decisions of a procedural or administrative nature, such as a Commission decision to file an injunction or a Trial Examiner's ruling on the admissibility of evidence. "If this is a correct interpretation of the bill," one official SEC Comment insisted, "administrative proceedings may thereby be interminably hampered and delayed in a manner not permitted with respect to judicial proceedings in the lower [federal] courts." James Landis, by then Dean of Harvard Law School, asserted, in a slashing attack on the Walter-Logan Bill, that it would "cut off here a foot and there a head, leaving broken and bleeding the process of administrative law." But despite the combined opposition of the Roosevelt Administration, Sam Rayburn, and such Wall Street stalwarts as John Foster Dulles and the Administrative Law Committee of the Association of the Bar of the City of New York, the Walter-Logan Bill was passed by both Houses of Congress late in 1940.

Roosevelt vetoed the Bill. In a December 17, 1940 Message, he urged that it was advisable to await the Report of a Committee on Administrative Procedure, earlier appointed by the Attorney General, before adopting new legislation. The 1941 Report of the Committee — known as the Acheson Committee, after its Chairman Dean Acheson — effectively ended the movement to enact procedural legislation to hamstring such controversial agencies as the SEC and the NLRB. The 474 page final Report began with an elaborate case against interference with the administrative agencies. Pointedly noting that 34 of the existing 51 administrative agencies had been created before the New Deal, the Acheson Report argued that the agencies were a pragmatic necessity to handle routine governmental matters, enforce preventive rather than punitive legislation (such as the SEC's securities registration statute), and carry out a vast range of discretionary rulemaking functions. The less restrictive legislative recommendations of the Acheson Committee became the basis of the Administrative Procedure Act enacted in 1946. Since the SEC by then had voluntarily adopted sophisticated hearing rules and independent trial examiners, the Act itself resulted in little change in the Commission's procedures.[172]

On January 11, 1937, it was publicly announced that Landis would become Harvard Law School's next Dean. During eight subsequent months as a lame duck, Commissioner Douglas campaigned to succeed Landis as Chair. With the completion of the first five parts of his massive Protective Committee Study by May 1937, and introduction of three proposed bills incorporating the Study's legislative recommendations, Douglas believed that he had earned the Chairmanship. He was miffed that Landis refused to support him.

As the rivalry between Landis and Douglas heated up, Douglas began making speeches far more critical of Wall Street than Landis as SEC Chair was prepared to make, winning praise from the same John T. Flynn, *New Republic,* and *Nation* that regularly assailed Landis. Increasingly, Douglas dissented from SEC opinions. He cultivated relationships with Joseph P. Kennedy and Thomas Corcoran, who, in 1937, were particularly influential in advising Roosevelt on financial issues. It was characteristic of Douglas that when Roosevelt stunned his own Administration in February 1937, by proposing the "packing" of the Supreme Court, Douglas quickly joined Corcoran and Cohen in helping Roosevelt mobilize his Administration to lobby for the proposal. Landis, by contrast, had to be persuaded to deliver a speech endorsing the plan. Douglas later attributed his selection as the SEC's third Chair to Joseph Kennedy's supportive "intervention."

When Landis officially tendered his resignation as Chair on September 11, 1937, he wrote Roosevelt a gracious letter, concluding, "Our Commission and our work sprang from your mind, your utterances, your ideals." An equally appropriate encomium could have been stated of Landis for his role in helping to draft the 1933 and 1934 Securities Acts and the regulations, opinions, and reports issued during the SEC's first three years. Yet both sympathetic and critical commentators concurred with the assessment in a *New York Times* editorial that, as an administrator, he had been "diligent, unsensational and, on the whole, conservative." Douglas lost no time in emphasizing at his first press conference that his Chairmanship would "be a period of action"; on issues such as segregation and regulation of the over-the-counter markets, Douglas considered the Commission's steps to that date to have been a "prologue." His own SEC would "move more swiftly."[173]

The Douglas Chairmanship

William Orville Douglas's career as a Supreme Court Justice was so long and so controversial that it all but obliterated memory of the achievements during the Roosevelt Administration that led to his elevation to the Court. This is unfortunate. As distinguished as Douglas's contributions as a Justice were, they would never have occurred but for his 19 months as Chair of the Securities and Exchange Commission. Between March 1938, when the Richard Whitney embezzlement scandal broke (discussed in further detail, below), and April 1939, when he was elevated to the Supreme Court, Douglas led the SEC on a crusade that attempted to complete the Commission's logical mandate by consolidating SEC enforcement of the over-the-counter markets, commencing enforcement of the geographic integration and corporate simplification provisions of the Public Utility Holding Company Act, and replacing state standards of corporate finance, accounting, and corporate governance with SEC-enforced federal rules. No other SEC Chair ever addressed so many fundamental problems simultaneously. Not all of Douglas's initiatives succeeded. But his Chairmanship was the most accomplished in the SEC's history.

Douglas had a more adversarial conception of the role of the SEC than had Landis. In his first press conference as Chair, Douglas would emphasize that the SEC should be "what I might call 'the investor's advocate.' We have got brokers' advocates; we have got Exchange advocates; we have got investment banker advocates; and we are the investor's advocate." Douglas's hostility to "the goddam bankers" was scathing and passionate. His first public bid to succeed Landis as SEC Chair was made in a luncheon address to New York City's Bond Club on March 24, 1937. The audience, primarily New York City investment bankers, was reported to have been "shocked" by Douglas's unrelenting attack on the noncompetitive conditions prevailing in the investment banking business. Douglas pointedly insisted that competitive bidding for corporate securities sales was necessary to stop "bankers . . . dispensing to themselves the patronage of a monopoly," that investment banking had severely disrupted "economic balance and stability" through "overissuance and oversalesmanship" of securities, and that "the key to the solution of current industrial problems is to be found in large measure in a process of democratization of industry" by making corporate managements more responsive to labor, the investor, and the consumer.

Yet no matter how passionate were Douglas's public statements, he always exhibited a shrewd operational sense. Alone among New Deal reformers he had opposed the "*in terrorem*" liability provisions of the 1933 Securities Act as being self-defeating.

His *bel idéal* was industry self-regulation under the close supervision of a government agency. The concept seemed at odds with his Brandeis-like enthusiasm for economic and governmental deconcentration. But it was typical of Douglas to prefer a pragmatic solution, one that would be effective and enduring, to a philosophically pure solution. To Douglas, industry self-regulation under government supervision was profoundly different from the "cooperative" approach espoused by Kennedy and Landis. Industry, in Douglas's view, had to retain the initial responsibility for preventing fraud or government bound by due process standards and could avoid "the bureaucratic blight" of a too intrusive government police force. But an agency like the SEC had to move aggressively when industry self-discipline failed to maintain high ethical standards.[174]

The 19 months of Douglas's Chairmanship coincided with the political epigee of the Roosevelt Administration. It began eight months after Roosevelt unveiled his Court-packing plan, the worst miscalculation of his Administration and a political fiasco from which the New Deal never fully recovered. Just before Douglas's SEC Chairmanship commenced, the economy began the most serious recession since 1929–1933. Between May 1937 and June 1938, the Federal Reserve Board's index of total industrial production fell 33 percent. During the same period, durable goods' production declined over 50 percent; profits, 78 percent; payrolls, 35 percent. The rate of unemployment doubled. Almost six million people lost their jobs. "Roosevelt's recession" shattered the President's claim that the 1933–1937 recovery occurred "because we . . . planned it that way." The 1938 Congressional Elections were another New Deal debacle. The number of Republicans in the

House of Representatives swelled from 88 to 170 and increased in the Senate by eight.[175]

Douglas's Chairmanship of the SEC was to prove one of the few bright spots in the New Deal's waning years. Like the rest of the Roosevelt Administration, Douglas began his Chairmanship on the defensive. The 1937–1938 recession was accompanied by a stock market crash almost as severe as that of 1929. Stock prices plummeted 38 percent between August 14 and October 18, 1937, as compared with a price collapse of 45 percent between September 7 and November 13, 1929. Leading financial spokesmen sought to blame the stock market collapse on the SEC. Within the Commission, it was then widely believed that if a Republican were elected President in 1940, a serious attempt would be made to repeal the securities laws, or cripple their effectiveness with inhibitory amendments or unsympathetic Commission appointments. Abe Fortas, Douglas's closest aide, would urge that Douglas's greatest achievement as Chair was in changing business' attitude toward the SEC. "Douglas was primarily responsible for completing the acceptance of public responsibility by financial institutions, for persuading a reluctant Wall Street that it was an appropriate subject for legal mandates."[176] Douglas's "revolution" or "domestication of Wall Street," as Fortas alternatively termed it, was by no means foreordained.

Roosevelt's initial response to the rising criticism of the SEC was an attempt to appease the business community. On October 25, 1937, he received Commerce Secretary Roper's Business Advisory Council. The following day, after Douglas met with Roosevelt, Douglas informed reporters that matters were in a state of flux, an oblique way of conceding that Roosevelt had prevailed on Douglas to accept a Federal Reserve Board recommendation, which Douglas had vehemently opposed, lowering margin rates from 55 to 40 percent. Six weeks later, simultaneous with the nomination of Douglas's long-time friend Jerome Frank, Roosevelt nominated John W. Hanes to be an SEC Commissioner. Hanes was the first member of the New York Stock Exchange selected for the position. Although he was a reformer among exchange members, his appointment was recognized as a conciliatory gesture; as Douglas put it in his autobiography, Hanes was chosen because of great pressure on Roosevelt "to 'protect' the interests of Wall Street."

Once on the Commission, Hanes spearheaded an in-house campaign to repeal those sections of the 1933 Securities Act that required a 20-day waiting period, barred solicitation of orders before registration was effective, and required dealers to deliver a prospectus to investors before each new security's initial sale.[177]

That Douglas under these circumstances was able to initiate a program of stock exchange reform primarily was a consequence of the deepening division among the NYSE's members. That Douglas's reform program succeeded as completely as it did was the result of the Richard Whitney embezzlement scandal.

The events leading to stock exchange reform began in August 1937, when Charles Gay published the New York Stock Exchange Annual Report accusing the SEC and other federal regulatory bodies of endangering the securities market. Gay's Report ended the appearance of SEC–NYSE "harmony" that had prevailed since the creation of the Commission by abruptly spurning James Landis's effort to negotiate a rule at least partially segregating exchange floor members.

The looming confrontation caused Paul Shields, E.A. Pierce, John Hanes, and other leading Commission brokers who had maneuvered Gay's election in 1935 to break with Gay. By August 1937, the securities brokerage business was badly sagging. Bond trading in 1937 was to reach its lowest level, with two exceptions, since 1918. In August 1937, new securities issuances were running at a rate 50 percent of a year before. In the vernacular, "grass was growing on Wall Street" and "the market was dead." Brokers were asking: "How can we keep from starving to death?" The Shields-Pierce faction insisted that only the appearance of cooperation between the SEC and Wall Street could rebuild investor confidence. Shields had been furious when Gay rationalized his uncompromising rejection of Landis's partial segregation initiative as unavoidable, since the floor traders and specialists associated with Richard Whitney's Old Guard commanded a majority of the Exchange's Governing Committee. Having labored to deprive Whitney of the Exchange presidency in 1935, the Shields-Pierce faction made no attempt to hide its bitterness that Whitney continued to dominate the Exchange through a factotum.[178]

At his first press conference, Douglas emphasized his intent to confront the NYSE by repeatedly asserting that the SEC would "proceed immediately on a course of swift and direct action where the facts justify it," coupling to this implied threat a none-too-subtle signal: "I should think that the best elements in finance... would find here the fullest cooperation." On October 16, Shields and Pierce journeyed to Washington to respond to Douglas's implicit invitation with an explicit invitation of their own: Would the SEC back them in a fight to reorganize the Exchange? Douglas, flanked by fellow Commissioners Robert Healy and George Mathews, promised full support. Joseph Kennedy, on whom Douglas then heavily relied for advice and communications with the White House, also agreed and soon informed Shields of Roosevelt's support. To symbolize Roosevelt's commitment, Douglas, Kennedy, and Shields made a well-publicized trip to Hyde Park and met with the President the following week.

At Shield's initiative, the SEC began negotiations with the NYSE in an effort to restore a cooperative relationship. Three matters dominated the next month's discussions. First, Douglas's insistence that the management of the NYSE had to be removed from the Old Guard's control and placed in the hands of a paid president with his own professional staff. Second, Douglas's threat that unless the NYSE agreed to reorganization, the Commission would impose new trading rules. And third, the SEC's insistence that the NYSE draft a letter to the Commission formally requesting reorganization discussions and including a paragraph acknowledging that the Commission had not been responsible for the 1937 market break. To the Commission, retraction of Gay's accusation was critical. With the market in a near collapse, Douglas feared that Congress would investigate Gay's charges to see whether they could be corroborated. This could lead to the repeal of some of the Commission's powers. Throughout the discussions, Douglas emphasized his belief that the NYSE had failed to make and enforce effective antimanipulation rules. To substantiate this belief, early in October Douglas had instructed the SEC's New York Regional Office to examine the records of over 100 exchange members to determine the extent to which floor member trading had accelerated the market's steep decline between September 7 and 25, 1937, through short sales or concerted activity. Whether Douglas directly discussed the Regional Office's Study in his negotiations or not, the extent of the SEC investigation alone implied that unless the NYSE retracted the criticism made by Gay, the SEC was prepared to publish a Report blaming the market's abrupt decline on floor member trading.[179]

On November 22, 1937, the negotiations collapsed. Although as many as 20 draft letters for the NYSE to forward publicly to the Commission were prepared by SEC and Exchange lawyers, the Exchange's Old Guard, which dominated the Law and Governing Committees, refused to commit themselves to a paid president or to language exonerating the SEC from responsibility for the 1937 market crash.

The following day, Douglas, with the unanimous approval of the Commission, issued a press release strongly implying the nature of new trading rules that the SEC would issue unless the NYSE committed itself to reorganization.

The first paragraph succinctly made public Douglas's private threat. The Commission had reached a point where it had to decide whether to continue "the past policy of leaving to the Exchanges much of the regulation of their own business" or to seek "an immediate and more persuasive administration directly by the Commission of all phases of Exchange business coming within the purview of the Securities Exchange Act of 1934":

> Operating as private-membership associations, exchanges have always administered their affairs in much the same manner as private clubs. For a business so vested in the public interest, this traditional method has become archaic. The task of conducting the affairs of large exchanges, especially the New York Stock Exchange, has become too engrossing for those who must also run their own businesses. And it may also be that there would be greater public confidence in exchanges (and the prices made thereon) which recognized that their management should not be in the hands of professional traders but in fact, as well as nominally, in charge of those who have a clearer public responsibility.

In Douglas's view, the conflicts of interest of the professional floor traders created problems more "fundamental" than archaic governance. Describing at length the results of the Regional Office's Study of Exchange member trading in September and October 1937, Douglas implied "that members of the Exchange trading for their own account — particularly the specialists — either create the daily price fluctuations or else contribute materially to their severity" specifically by accentuating a "declining market by short selling for speculative profit." The Regional Office's Study of trading in selected leading securities on the New York Stock Exchange then was summarized to document "that short selling represented as much as 31 percent of the total trading in one of these market leaders and constituted almost a quarter of the trading in . . . five leading stocks." Strongly suggesting a willingness to limit or abolish most members' floor trading for their own accounts and severely to restrict short selling, Douglas argued:

> These figured as a group or a challenge to the validity of the common assertion that the existence of the specialist and the floor trader is justified on the basis of their stabilizing influence on the market, and their resultant benefits to the members of the public who enter the market. In a market in which there is such an enormous public interest — in which not only 300,000 small traders but 10,000,000 investors have a stake, it is essential that no element of the casino be allowed to intrude and that all such elements be obliterated.[180]

Douglas's November 23 Press Release soon achieved its desired effect of shocking the NYSE into reorganization. This was not the consequence of Douglas's tough words alone. Tough words can always be answered in kind. Rather, President Gay and much of the Old Guard realized how much more financially expensive SEC-imposed trading rules and a public feud with the Commission would have than reorganization. No one after the issuance of the release could seriously believe that Douglas, like his predecessor Landis, was bluffing when he threatened to impose new rules. This reality rendered all but irrelevant the Old Guard's confidence that the 1940 Presidential Election would eliminate "the SEC problem." For over three years they might first have to live with Douglas. And Douglas had made obvious that the rules the SEC might impose could abolish or substantially reduce much of the exchange's floor members' business.

Six days after Douglas's Press Release was issued, Gay capitulated, not so much to the SEC as to the Shields-Pierce reform faction of exchange members. Responding "in the friendliest spirit, and in the firm belief that cooperation between the Exchange and the Commission is essential," Gay promised to begin reorganization by appointing "a special committee to study this whole matter and to report as promptly as possible."[181]

On December 10, 1937, Gay appointed a nine-man committee "to consider all aspects of a further development of the organization and administration of the Exchange, including, among others, the advisability of making the Presidency a salaried office, of transferring greater administrative responsibility to executives, and of making the function of standing committees supervisory rather than administrative." The Committee's membership was most notable for its failure to include a single exchange member associated with Whitney's Old Guard. Instead, the Exchange's future organization was placed in the hands of three corporate executives: Carle Conway, Chairman of the Board of Continental Can, known to favor Exchange reorganization; Kenneth Hogate, President of the *Wall Street Journal*; and Thomas McInnerney, President of National Dairy; three current Exchange members, one of whom, 30-year-old William McChesney Martin, Jr., had made no secret of his reform sentiments; and three outside members, Adolf Berle, who had been a charter member in Roosevelt's brains trust and was an enthusiastic supporter of Douglas, Trowbridge Callaway, an investment banker who was then President of the Better Business Bureau of New York, and John Prentiss, a partner in Hornblower and Weeks, who had once been President of the Investment Bankers Association. Four days later, Conway was named Chair of the Committee and immediately traveled to Washington to solicit Douglas's advice and to promise a report by the end of January.[182] Ganson Purcell, Director of the SEC's Trading and Exchange Division, soon delivered to the Conway Committee an outline of the Commission's recommendations, most of which subsequently were adopted. The SEC recommended proportional representation on the Board of Governors of the various classes of members "(such as specialists, commission brokers, etc.), each such class to be entitled to representation on the Committee in the ratio which it bears to the entire body of members." This was meant to increase considerably the power of the underrepresented commission brokers. To provide the exchange "with a degree of executive efficiency of as nearly a disinterested nature as possible," the Purcell outline provided "for a full time salaried President with a background of executive and business experience, who should not be, or have been, a member of the Exchange . . . or in any way engaged in the securities or banking business."[183]

The very composition of the Conway Committee ensured that its report would recommend a substantial reorganization of NYSE governance. But precisely because Gay had excluded Old Guard representatives from the Conway Committee, the reception a reform report would be accorded by the Exchange's Old Guard dominated Governing Committee was less predictable. Cognizant of the Exchange floor members' general hostility to reorganization, on January 24, 1938, the SEC forcefully indicated what type of trading rules it was likely to adopt if the Conway Committee Report was rejected. Invoking its own rulemaking authority, the Commission significantly limited short sales in a declining market by requiring each short sale to be made at a price above the last transaction in the security. This precluded floor members from accentuating general market declines by the systematic short sale of leading securities. The Short Sale Rule was the first that the SEC imposed, rather than persuading the Exchange to issue as its own trading rule. It also was the first trading rule promulgated without any prior consultation with the NYSE, a distinct departure from the "cooperative" policy of predecessor Chairs Kennedy and Landis.[184]

Three days later, the Conway Commission issued its report recommending a nearly complete adoption of the reorganization proposals urged by the SEC. Ultimate governing power was to be removed from the existing Old Guard dominated 50 member Board of Governors and vested in a reconstituted 32 member Board. The new Board's electoral rules were meant to ensure that it would be controlled by the Commission house brokers. Besides the Exchange President and the Board of Governors' Chairman, three of the new Board Members would be public representatives and 12 would be nonmember partners of firms doing a brokerage business for the public. The Old Guard faction of floor traders and specialists would be eligible to seek election only to the minority of 15 slots on the Board reserved for NYSE members. But they could not secure even all of these slots, for the Conway Report insisted that "these governors should be selected with due regard to the various interests represented in membership." The most important function of the reconstituted Board of Governors was to select a full time paid President, who would serve as the Exchange's Chief Executive Officer and "be the point of contact with governmental agencies and the general public." The President was to have his own staff and general responsibility for public relations.[185]

By choosing to reconstitute Exchange self-governance, not to supplant it, Douglas made a decisive compromise. In return for a more cooperative Exchange management, the SEC, as a practical matter, restricted its ability to impose rules. As the Conway Report explained, "a close working relationship" between the SEC and the Exchange was conditioned on the understanding that "standards of conduct must be largely self-executed, rather than imposed." Subsequently, this would prove a highly expensive compromise. The SEC's deference to Exchange rulemaking in the two decades after World War II would result in the Commission long ignoring the costs to investors of the Exchange's fixed brokerage commission rate structure. But in early 1938, with the Conway Committee Plan for Exchange governance in effect, the SEC had the security of knowing that regardless of how the 1940 elections turned out, the Exchange's Governors would profess to be sympathetic to the Commission's existence. Had the SEC instead sought more direct control of the Exchange, it would have united all factions of the Exchange in a general opposition that could have proved decisive after the 1940 elections. As it was, by choosing to support the leading Commission brokers in their effort to take over the governance of the Exchange, the Commission received an immediate political dividend. The Conway Report concluded by publicly repudiating the accusations in Gay's 1937 Annual Report: "Neither the Stock Exchange nor the SEC," explained the Report, "can be held responsible for major fluctuations in the price of securities. These depend on fundamental business and economic conditions."[186]

The Exchange's Board of Governors adopted the Conway Committee's Report on January 31, 1938, a mere four days after its publication. By late February, a three-man committee, named by Charles Gay and comprising Conway Committee Secretary William McChesney Martin, Jr., former Exchange President E.H.H. Simmons, and commission broker Charles Harding, had drafted proposed Constitutional amendments based on the Report.[187]

The Whitney Scandal

It was then that the Whitney scandal broke. During the afternoon of March 7, 1938, Exchange President Gay telephoned Douglas that he would arrive in Washington that evening. With him would be Howland Davis, Chairman of the Exchange's Disciplinary Committee. They had a matter of importance to discuss with Douglas that could not be explained over the telephone. At approximately eight o'clock that evening Douglas met Gay and Davis at the Carleton Hotel. Douglas was informed that shortly before Gay and Davis had left New York City, the Exchange's Board of Governors had held a Special Meeting and voted charges of misconduct against Richard Whitney. Although they were not yet sure of the full extent of Whitney's illegal activities, they had heard evidence that Whitney had embezzled or unlawfully pledged securities belonging to the New York Stock Exchange Gratuity Fund (which paid $20,000 to the heirs of each Exchange member on his death) and at least two customers. A public hearing before the Exchange's Board of Governors was scheduled for March 17.

At 10:05 the next morning, Robert L. Fisher, the Secretary of the Exchange, unexpectedly rang the gong that suspends trading. As puzzled Exchange members crowded around the rostrum, Charles Gay read a letter from Richard Whitney and Company that stated, in its entirety, "We regret to advise you of our inability to meet our engagements." Gay tersely announced that the Whitney firm had been suspended for insolvency, but he could not bring himself to state publicly that Whitney had been involved in criminal misconduct. Immediately after Gay hurried from the rostrum, an Exchange press release was distributed. It began, "In the course of an examination of the affairs of Richard Whitney & Company, the Committee on Business Conduct discovered on March 1, 1938, evidence of conduct apparently contrary to just and equitable principles of trade and on Monday, March 7, 1938, at 1:30 p.m., presented to a Special Meeting of the Governing Committee charges and specifications." That sentence meant that Whitney was not only bankrupt, but allegedly dishonest. Two journalists reported, "There was a dead silence, then a wild babble of voices." Market prices jolted sharply lower; then trading in the afternoon all but ceased.

The immediate effect of the Whitney scandal was momentous. It was as if the floor had dropped out from under Wall Street. Chester Lane, SEC Assistant General Counsel, was in San Francisco to give a speech the day the scandal broke:

> You could see the change overnight in the attitude of the San Francisco financial community [he recalled]. They saw the handwriting on the wall. This was not a fraud in securities practice; it was not financial immorality of the kind which the SEC was set up to eliminate; it was nothing but out-and-out stealing by the most respected and prominent of all the figures of the financial world in the country.... You could see a deepening sense of gloom over just those few days in the faces of the people

> I was meeting. They knew Douglas was preparing to buck, and they knew now that he was going to be successful.[188]

After the scandal broke, events began to move with dizzying rapidity. On March 9, 1938, Richard Whitney issued a statement assuming personal responsibility for all "actions [that] have been wrong." The next day New York County District Attorney Thomas E. Dewey personally arrested Richard Whitney and indicted him for grand larceny and misappropriating $105,000 of securities from a trust fund established by his later father-in-law. Within 24 hours, New York State's Attorney General secured a second grand larceny indictment, charging Whitney with the theft of $153,200 of securities from the New York Yacht Club, of which Whitney was Treasurer. By March 17, Whitney had pleaded guilty to both indictments and had been expelled from the New York Stock Exchange by unanimous vote.[189]

In his memoirs, Douglas would describe Roosevelt as close to tears when informed that his fellow Groton graduate had pleaded guilty to larceny. "Not Dick Whitney!" Douglas recalled he exclaimed. "Dick Whitney — Dick Whitney," Roosevelt repeated. "I can't believe it."[190]

Douglas's own reaction was totally without sentiment. The scandal offered him and the SEC a once-in-a-lifetime opportunity. As long as Douglas could protract and publicize the revelations of the Whitney scandal, he would neutralize the ability of the financial community to oppose SEC efforts further to reform the NYSE or seek additional enabling legislation. Douglas immediately seized this opportunity. Within minutes of being informed by Charles Gay on March 7 of Whitney's defalcations, Douglas had directed Commissioner John W. Hanes and General Counsel Allen Throop to initiate an investigation of Whitney. A formal investigative order was voted by the full Commission the next morning, 45 minutes before Gay made the first public disclosure of the scandal.

Although Richard Whitney, the New York Stock Exchange, and Thomas Dewey were eager to end the scandal as quickly as possible on the basis of Whitney's repeated assertion that "none of my partners, none of my business associates or connections, in fact no one but myself has or had any responsibility," Douglas was determined to show that Whitney's conduct was not just that of a single self-destructive individual; it also implicated other financiers, in particular J.P. Morgan, Jr., in whose firm Richard Whitney's brother, George, was a partner.

On April 6, 1938, the SEC unanimously ordered a public hearing "to examine the circumstances surrounding the failure of the firm of Richard Whitney and Company," stating that the primary purpose of the hearing would be to enable the Commission to recommend additional rules, regulations, or legislation. To preserve the ability of the Justice Department subsequently to bring criminal indictments, the Commission took the unusual step for a legislative hearing of permitting counsel for each witness to conduct cross-examination and present exculpatory evidence.[191]

For 14 hearing days between April 8, 1938, and June 28, 1938, SEC attorneys publicly examined 52 witnesses, focusing on the knowledge or complicity of other Exchange members in Whitney's misconduct. It was shown that over a 12-year period, Whitney had borrowed, without collateral, $6,172,800 from 16 Exchange members, mostly to cover financial losses he experienced in disastrous investments in firms distilling applejack, marketing peat humus, and mining colloids. At least 18 other individuals had refused to make loans. To one non-Old Guard Exchange member, this pattern of loans was evidence that Whitney was "broke and borrowing money all over the street." But almost no other Exchange member considered the loans a cause for official concern. Not until January 1938, did a single creditor demand repayment from Whitney. What made such forbearance suspect was the Gratuity Fund incident, which Dewey and the State Attorney General failed adequately to investigate. Since 1935, Whitney had served as one of five elected trustees who managed the $2.5 million fund to provide death benefits to Exchange members. Whitney also served as the fund's broker. Beginning in February 1937, Whitney had retained some $900,000 of the fund's bonds entrusted to his care and misappropriated $221,508 in cash. On November 22, 1937, the failure of Whitney to return the fund's assets was brought to the attention of the other trustees by the fund's accountant. Promptly after the meeting, one of the trustees, Whitney's friend and predecessor as Exchange President, E.H.H. Simmons, requested that Whitney return the fund's cash and bonds. Since Whitney had pledged most of the misappropriated securities, he could not immediately comply. Desperate, on November 23 Whitney had called on his brother George to secure an emergency loan of $1,082,000. Whitney informed his brother that he had misappropriated the trust fund's assets. To save his brother, George Whitney had sought help from Thomas Lamont, the Morgan firm's Managing Partner, informing him of Richard Whitney's defalcations from the trust fund. George Whitney and Thomas Lamont delivered the $1,082,000 to Richard Whitney on November 24, enabling him to return the wrongfully pledged securities to the Gratuity Fund. Neither reported his knowledge of Richard Whitney's embezzlement to any responsible figure.[192]

The Commission aggressively urged the Exchange to discipline George Whitney, Thomas Lamont, and E.H.H. Simmons. The day the Report on Whitney was published, Douglas forwarded a copy to the Board of Governors, directing its attention "specifically to the possibility of violation by persons who appeared and testified (of the section in the Exchange's Constitution granting the Board power) to suspend any member adjudged guilty of any act determined . . . to be 'detrimental to the interest or welfare of the Exchange.'" By then, Douglas's close friend, University of Chicago President Robert Hutchins, had been selected as one of the three public representatives on the Board. At the December 14, 1938, meeting of the Governors, Hutchins requested that the Exchange conduct a public hearing to determine whether George Whitney, Lamont, or Simmons had violated the Exchange's Constitution.

Not one member of the Board agreed with Hutchins. By a vote of 27-1, the Board decided not to proceed, in part because of a statement from JP Morgan and Company asserting that in late November 1937 Exchange officials were aware of Richard Whitney's embezzlement. The Morgan statement, quite simply, was false and contradicted earlier testimony given by George Whitney and Thomas Lamont. Hutchins promptly resigned.[193]

Douglas's reaction to what he termed the Whitney whitewash was Vesuvian. On December 18, he prepared a draft of a statement to be released by the Commission, including the accusation:

> When persons of outstanding wealth are involved, the Exchange cannot be trusted to do its own house cleaning. Unhappily we are forced to conclude that discipline by the Exchange authorities of its own members will be exerted only if the offending person is of relatively little importance, that there is, so far as the Exchange is concerned, one law for the very powerful or wealthy and another for those of little wealth and influence.

Since the publication of such a statement would have discredited the NYSE reform government that Douglas had helped elect eight months before, the SEC instead issued a brief reassurance that "the action on the Whitney case has not caused a change in the cooperative program which we launched."

Douglas's fury did not subside. His last major action as Chair was to persuade Roosevelt to name Robert Hutchins as his successor. This would have been a symbolic act almost as humiliating to the Exchange's reform government as the unpublished December 18 draft statement. Hutchins declined. To many, including some senior officers of the SEC, Douglas's relentless pursuit of the Old Guard was unnecessarily vindictive.

Yet it was exactly Douglas's reputation for uncompromising toughness that made possible the 1938 reform of the New York Stock Exchange. Kennedy's "cooperative approach" had moved the NYSE but little. Landis's patient negotiation has resulted in stalemate. It was Douglas's exploitation of the political differences among the NYSE members and the Whitney scandal that got things done. Douglas himself would justify his approach in purely operational terms. "Political and economic power only rarely diverge," he once explained to Milton Katz, a Landis Executive Assistant, "and when they do, you must move rapidly."[194]

The second phase of Douglas's efforts to reform the NYSE began within hours of Richard Whitney's expulsion on March 17, 1938. That afternoon the constitutional revisions inspired by the Conway Committee were adopted by a vote of 1013-22.[195]

On April 11, 1938, the Exchange's Nominating Committee named a genuine reform slate for election to the reconstituted Board of Governors. Old Guard representatives were almost totally excluded. Of the 32 Chairmen and Vice Chairmen of the 17 Exchange standing committees in existence before the Whitney scandal, only three were nominated for re-election to the Board of Governors. Even former Exchange Presidents Simmons and Gay were denied customary "elder spokesmen" nominations. Within a month, all 28 of the reform slate's nominees had won unopposed election to the Board of Governors. Paul Shields, the leader of the reform slate, soon claimed a slot on the three-person committee to name a new full time Exchange President as well as the Chairmanship of the new Committee on Public Relations. As many as 200 candidates were considered by Shields's Presidential Selection

Committee before it determined to retain its interim figure of self-rectitude, temporary President William McChesney Martin, Jr., as President.[196]

Martin unquestionably was a publicist's dream. Profoundly religious, he did not smoke, drink, or gamble, and was wont to refer to the Exchange as a "savings bank for securities." At 31, he was a symbolic antidote to the Whitney scandal. A plethora of magazine feature articles soon explained to readers that Martin had been a tennis champion at Yale, lived a spartan existence in New York City's Yale Club, often eating at automats, had been shocked by the machinations of floor traders when he first joined the Exchange, voted for Roosevelt in 1932, and never missed a Broadway play, although, true to form, he always sat in the balcony to save money and would repair to Sardi's afterward to drink a hot chocolate. A *Time* cover story accordingly dubbed him Mr. Chocolate. *Collier's* hailed "the Lamb of Wall Street."

William McChesney Martin also was a serious student of economics, and for this reason won Douglas's support. He was the son of a president of the St. Louis Federal Reserve Bank. After graduating from Yale, he had briefly worked for his father as a Federal Reserve bank examiner before joining A.G. Edward & Sons, a commission brokerage house, as head statistician. In May 1931, he had moved to New York City to work as A.G. Edward's floor broker while taking graduate courses in economics at Columbia and the New School of Social Research. In 1935, he was a successful reform candidate for the Exchange Board of Governors.

Like Douglas, Martin viewed the NYSE "as a vital and indispensable part of the national economy," with no other legitimate purpose. "The days of the Exchange as a private business are past," he would explain in July 1938. The Exchange is a "public service institution [that] will be operated as a public business. To avoid SEC imposition of rules, the Exchange had to "demonstrate by action . . . [that] it would be unnecessary for government to interfere."[197]

With a reform Board of Governors elected, Douglas used the occasion of a May 20, 1938, dinner honoring the Conway Committee to outline the balance of the SEC's program for Exchange reform. To Douglas, the course of immediate action was clear. The Exchange would have to assume the primary burden of policing manipulative trading, withdraw the trading advantages of insiders, and prevent broker misuse of customer funds. If the Exchange would eliminate these last sources of irritation, Douglas promised that the SEC would not only be the investors' advocate, but also "your advocate."[198]

In private round table conferences with Martin, the ubiquitous Paul Shields, and other Exchange representatives, beginning on May 18, 1938, Douglas bargained hardest for two principal concerns. To protect customers from the kind of losses resulting from broker misconduct or insolvency illustrated by the Whitney scandal, Douglas proposed the establishment of a brokers' trust company to handle "those aspects of the brokerage business having to do with receipts and deliveries of securities, receipts and payments of cash, the obtaining of credit for security purchases, [and] clearing of securities." Both in his May 20 speech honoring the Conway Committee and in the private negotiations, Douglas emphasized that a brokers' trust institution was his first priority. In late August, he deferred publication of Part II of the Report on Whitney for what turned out to be a two-month period to give Martin and Shields time to use their "best efforts" to persuade the Exchange "to bring about the adoption, first, of a central depository for customers' funds and securities and, secondly, of a trust institution which would assume, subject to customers' order, full control of customers' funds and securities." The Central Depository had "great appeal" to Douglas because "it would simplify the [SEC's] task of making inspections of the margin accounts of our far flung brokerage community and also the handling of the other details which are the necessary incidents of enforcement or self regulation," as well as reduce or eliminate the risks associated with brokers "holding and commingling of the funds and securities of their customers."

With considerably less vehemence Douglas also proposed complete segregation of all floor members of the Exchange. Douglas urged both that floor members be limited to performing the function either of broker or dealer and that specialists be permitted to perform only dealers' functions. Since this proposal went well beyond Landis's earlier efforts to secure partial segregation of floor members, and also exceeded the recommendations of the Douglas Commission's Trading and Exchange Division, it apparently was meant to be a bargaining chip with which to induce the Exchange's floor members to support the brokers' trust institution. As such, it proved only modestly effective. After five months of negotiation, the SEC and the Exchange agreed to an elaborate compromise. In return for the Commission's not then imposing any segregation rule, the Exchange's Board of Governors on October 26, 1938, adopted a 13-point reform program. The key features of the program committed the Exchange to more frequent and detailed audits of member firms; prohibited brokers doing business with the public from maintaining margin accounts; established a 15 to 1 ratio between a broker's indebtedness and his working capital; required members to report all uncollateralized loans to other members; reported that the Exchange had hired Haskins & Sells, an accounting firm, to study the feasibility of a Central Depository; and encouraged each member firm to form a corporate affiliate to handle dealer and underwriter activities, as a compromise means of insulating brokerage customers from the risks inherent in underwriter and dealer operations.[199]

Nearly simultaneously, the SEC published "In the Matter of Richard Whitney." While praising the Exchange for "a constructive approach," the SEC publicly repeated its "opinion that full realization of effective regulation of the industry in the public interest is to be found in the establishment of trust institutions to assume the banking and custodial functions of the brokerage business." Although the SEC Annual Reports of the next two years were highly critical, the Exchange and leading Commission house brokers, including Pierce and Shields, continued to oppose the brokers' trust institution because of its initial cost and tendency to disrupt the broker-customer relationship. In August 1939, an Exchange Committee recommended an alternative program to protect brokerage customers: It required that customers' accounts be fully segregated and that the Exchange's examining force be increased and conduct audits on a surprise basis.

When Douglas had first contemplated reform of the Exchange in September 1937, his paramount concern had been reducing insider manipulation. He had indicated his approach to the problem with the colorful phrase "You need a snoop to catch a jiggle." Within 13 months, the Douglas SEC put into effect reforms different from those Douglas had originally contemplated. Instead of floor segregation or a brokers' trust institution, he had forced the Exchange floor members to accept an in-house "snoop" in the form of a broker-dominated Board of Governors, a full-time President, and an increased Exchange disciplinary force. Over time, the significance of these reforms dissipated. Within a few years after Douglas left the SEC, Exchange floor members again dominated Exchange governance. Repeatedly during the next three decades the SEC would attempt to abolish floor traders; in the late 1960s the need for a Central Stock Depository again would be evident.

Yet Douglas's "revolution in financial morality" should not be underestimated. Until Douglas and the Whitney scandal, the politics of the Exchange had been dominated by its concern to preserve the trading privileges of floor members. After Douglas, the Exchange exhibited a greater commitment to the philosophy of the major brokerage houses, which emphasized the need to assure customers that they could invest safely on the NYSE. In part, the enormous post-World War II expansion in securities trading occurred because Douglas-type reforms did reduce the likelihood of manipulation on the New York Stock Exchange.[200]

The Maloney Act

The Whitney scandal eased passage of the 1938 Maloney Act amendments to the Securities Exchange Act, which led to the creation of the private National Association of Securities Dealers, succeeded in 2007 by the Financial Industry Regulatory Authority, to police over-the-counter brokers and dealers. In this project, as in several others, Douglas built on studies initiated during Landis's time as Chair. As early as November 1935, Landis publicly had promoted "the organization of a self-disciplinary agency of dealers." Douglas's contributions to the Maloney Act were tactical. Adopting Landis's approach to enforcement of OTC regulations, Douglas lobbied the bill through the Roosevelt Administration and Congress within a few months after its introduction by rapidly recognizing what compromises were necessary to its passage and by exploiting the legislative opportunity created by the Whitney scandal.

In December 1937, Douglas invited leaders of the investment banking community to discuss means of better coordinating enforcement activities. At the meeting several bankers agreed with an SEC proposal to amend the Securities Exchange Act to give voluntary associations an official status similar to that of the organized exchanges "in order to enable the associations to undertake effective programs of enforcement." Douglas emphasized to a congressional committee that if effective self-regulation of the securities exchanges was to succeed, the SEC could not compromise its enforcement role, but should play a residual role: "Government would keep the shotgun, so to speak, behind the door, loaded, well oiled, cleaned, ready for use but with the hope it would never have to be used." Amplifying this theme in a January 7, 1938, address to the Hartford Bond Club, Douglas urged allowing voluntarily organized over-the-counter associations "ample contractual powers over members to take a hand in enforcing the law." Self-regulation would have "unquestioned advantages" over direct SEC enforcement: "By and large, government can operate satisfactorily only by proscription. That leaves untouched large areas of conduct and activity; some of it susceptible of government regulation but in fact too minute for satisfactory control; some of it lying beyond the periphery of the law in the realm of ethics and morality. Into these large areas self-government, and self-government alone, can effectively reach."[201]

Virtually simultaneously, Connecticut Senator Francis Maloney introduced SEC drafted legislation to implement Douglas's approach to over-the-counter regulation. The Maloney Bill permitted the formation of National Associations of Brokers and Dealers if it appeared to the Commission that each association permitted all over-the-counter brokers and dealers (or all within specific geographic areas) the right to membership, assured democratic voting procedures, and enforced disciplinary rules to prevent fraud, promote just and equitable principles of trade, and "to perfect the mechanism of a free and open market" by forbidding price discrimination "between customers, or issuers, or brokers or dealers" and barring rules designed to permit the fixing of minimum profits or commission rates. The SEC's "shotgun in the closet" was emphasized. The Commission was given the power to review all disciplinary decisions, abrogate any association rule or request, then itself alter or supplement most rules. In late January 1938, Douglas secured Roosevelt's support with the argument that the Maloney Bill would "afford . . . investors in the over-the-counter markets protection comparable to that afforded under the Exchange Act in the case of exchanges [at] a small fraction of the sum which would be necessary, should the alternative system of direct Commission action be adopted."[202]

Negotiations with the securities industry were more difficult. Soon after Douglas's December 1937 meeting with the industry's leading investment bankers, both the Investment Bankers Association and the Investment Bankers Conference approved the Maloney Bill "in principle." In part, industry support was the consequence of a subsection that provided that if the Maloney Act conflicted with "any provision of any law of the United States," the Maloney Act "shall prevail." This subsection was intended to shield the governance of the over-the-counter markets from the reach of the antitrust laws, a protection that only an act of Congress could provide a "self-regulatory" group.[203]

The SEC fared less well against a more potent political opponent. During the Roosevelt Administration, no business lobby proved nearly as effective against the SEC as the nation's municipal securities issuers and municipal securities dealers. Strengthened by the appearance of defending local government, not big business, with political allies in both parties and almost every state, the municipal securities lobby was able to wrest exemption from the 1933 Securities Act and the 1934 Securities Exchange Act.

When the municipal securities lobby began its campaign for exemption from the Maloney Bill, Senator Maloney made a nationwide radio address to argue that the general pattern of exemptions for municipal securities dealers could be justified on no principled basis:

> What claim have municipal dealers to a holier-than-thou attitude? If they engage in fraudulent practices, should they escape regulation? If their acts are deceptive or manipulative, should not investors be protected against them also? Should not they be held to the same conservative standards of financial responsibility as other dealers? . . . The answers are obvious. If they are exempted from this type of regulation, it would be the grossest form of discrimination against other dealers, fully as reputable, fully as honest, fully as competent as they.

As was always the case during the New Deal, such logic proved unpersuasive. On March 1, 1938, the Senate Banking Committee voted 7-3 to exempt dealers in municipal securities from the Maloney Bill. This placed Douglas in a quandary. Commissioner Healy undoubtedly reflected the full Commission's belief when he publicly stated that the exemption for municipal securities dealers "smack[ed] of unfair competition." But Douglas as SEC Chair had to balance ethical considerations with operational ones. By the spring of 1938 he had fully assimilated the advice Felix Frankfurter wrote in January 1934 to the considerably more idealistic Professor William Douglas: "The French proverb 'Let not the better be the enemy of the good' has marked application in the history of legislation."

Douglas refused to allow the unfairness of the municipal securities dealer exemption to jeopardize passage of the Maloney Bill. Soon after the Whitney scandal broke in early March, Douglas committed the SEC to seeking the bill's earliest possible enactment. No attempt was made to reverse the municipal securities dealer exemption on the Senate floor, and it passed the Senate on the unanimous consent calendar on March 31, 1938. When the House Commerce Subcommittee considering the Maloney Bill communicated to Douglas its preference for the Senate-passed municipal securities dealer exemption on April 29, 1938, "in order that the chances of the Bill's passing the House would not be prejudiced," the SEC drafted the necessary amendment. With only a few minor concessions to the Investment Bankers Association necessary for steering the Maloney Bill through the House Rule Committee, the SEC draft was enacted and signed in June 1938.

Fourteen months later, the SEC approved the registration of the National Association of Securities Dealers (*NASD*) as the over-the-counter regulatory organization. Within two decades, NASD's membership exceeded 80 percent of the over-the-counter brokers registered with the SEC, in large measure because of an important economic advantage of NASD membership. Broker-dealers who were members of NASD were charged a "wholesale" price when they purchased or sold securities from other NASD members; non-NASD members had to pay the same price as the public.[204]

Self-regulation of the over-the-counter industry did not come without cost. By creating NASD to serve as the over-the-counter dealers' disciplinarian, the SEC granted quasi-official status to a trade association that would often oppose — frequently successfully — further SEC legislative initiatives. A greater weakness in SEC "self-regulation" of the over-the-counter market was the risk that during periods when the Commission was led by less activist Chairs than Douglas or hamstrung by budget stringency, the SEC would cease to prod NASD to discipline its members vigilantly. As Douglas recognized, without an SEC "shotgun in the closet," there was lessened incentive for an industry self-regulatory organization to perform the unpleasant task of disciplinarian. During the Truman and Eisenhower Administrations, the SEC did not effectively oversee NASD self-regulation. The lack of disciplinary vigor both of the SEC and of

NASD was responsible in part for the discernible increase in securities fraud during the 1950s.

The Protective Committee Study

Until he assumed the position of Chair in September 1937, Douglas's principal work at the SEC was supervising the Commission's Protective Committee Study, a study notable, like the Pecora investigation, for its protracted Public Hearings. Eventually the Study produced an eight part, 4000 page report, which, in the manner of Brandeis's *Other People's Money* and the Senate Banking Committee's 1934 "Stock Exchange Practices Report," was an adversarial brief, largely devoted to making the case for displacement of insider control of corporate bankruptcies, reorganizations, and debt security sales. The report urged stringent reform of foreign and municipal debt adjustments, and of real estate bond sales. The cumbersome length of the report and its adversarial excesses — ridiculed by Robert T. Swaine, a leading corporate bankruptcy attorney, as giving the Study the "colorful verbiage of a dime novel of the nineties" and the "dramatic excitement" of "a modern Hollywood gangster thriller" — reduced the legislative impact that the Protective Committee Study otherwise might have enjoyed. The Study did lead to the enactment of two minor corporate reform measures, Chapter X of the Chandler Bankruptcy Revision Act and the Trust Indenture Act. But when introduced in May 1937, both were meant to complement a more far-reaching measure proposed by Congressman Clarence Lea called the Committee Bill.[205]

As drafted by Douglas and his Protective Committee Study staff, the Lea Committee Bill would have subjected all municipal and foreign debt arrangements, corporation reorganizations, and voluntary corporate readjustments to similar patterns of regulation. In each type of reorganization, there would have been required disclosure of material background information, including the fees to be paid Protective Committee members. Incumbent corporate management, underwriters, and other interested persons would have been barred from serving on the Reorganization Committees. On request of a court, the SEC would have been empowered to file a report concerning the fairness of a reorganization plan. Where a reorganization involved more than $5 million, the SEC would have had the power to intervene in a court proceeding and, under some circumstances, to arbitrate differences between protective committees and security holders. The Committee Bill well realized the law professor's favored virtues of constitutionality, unambiguous language, internal consistency, remedial provisions rationally related to the "necessity for regulation" described in the bill's findings of fact, and efficiency, in the sense that the proposal addressed technically similar problems under a generic regulatory framework. The Committee Bill, however, was politically artless. Having made no serious effort, even within the Roosevelt Administration or Congress, to build a coalition to support the bill, the drafters hopelessly overreached themselves. Provisions like that forbidding incumbent management to direct a reorganization when it was voluntary and effected through means such as a merger that could instantly infuse a hard pressed firm with adequate capital were opposed as inflexible and counterproductive, even by such usually reform minded commentators such as Harvard Law School Professor E. Merrick Dodd. By seeking to regulate in one bill such diverse debtors as foreign governments, municipalities, and business corporations, the Committee Bill achieved the improbable result of uniting in opposition liberal Congressman Adolph Sabath, the Foreign Bond Associates, Incorporated, and myriad spokesmen for municipal corporations with such predictable opponents as the Investment Bankers Association.[206]

By contrast, the SEC's 1937–1938 campaign for enactment of Chapter X of the Chandler Bankruptcy Revision Bill was an illustration of Douglas's political maturity. As early as 1926, there had been considerable bipartisan support for amendment of the Bankruptcy Act of 1898. In 1929, Federal District Court Judge Thomas Thatcher of the Southern District of New York appointed Colonel William J. Donovan to conduct a comprehensive investigation into the administration of bankruptcy proceedings. Donovan's Report roundly criticized both the courts and bankruptcy trustees for a system that "has been ineffective, burdensome, and generally inefficient." Subsequent studies by the Department of Commerce, Judge Thatcher when he became President Hoover's Solicitor General, the House Judiciary Committee, and Yale University's Institute of Human Relations reached similar conclusions. By 1932, a private bar dominated National Bankruptcy Conference was established to develop a revised Bankruptcy Bill. But the Conference's efforts soon were overtaken by events. Hastily drafted emergency Bankruptcy

Acts were passed in 1933 and 1934. Bills drafted by the National Bankruptcy Conference were the subject of extensive House Judiciary Committee Hearings in 1935 and 1936.

William Douglas became the dominant figure in the bankruptcy reform efforts. In no corporate related field were Douglas's intellectual abilities more widely recognized than bankruptcy. Between 1928 and 1934, he had been a Special Adviser to Colonel Donovan, had collaborated with the Department of Commerce in its Bankruptcy Studies, had directed Bankruptcy Studies for Yale's Institute of Human Relations, and had written on the subject the leading law school casebook, articles for the *Encyclopedia Britannica* and the *Encyclopedia of the Social Sciences*, as well as several law review articles. Congressman Walter Chandler agreed to hold up an effort to pass a new Bankruptcy Act until Douglas's Protective Committee Study completed its relevant reports and to allow Douglas to participate in drafting the revision bill.

Douglas's Protective Committee Study group wrote virtually all of the bill. On May 10, 1937, the Protective Committee Study published Part I of its Report, a 900 page document entitled *Strategy and Technique of Protective and Reorganization Committees*. The Protective Committee Study made 14 specific legislative recommendations, two of which were of fundamental importance. First, the Study recommended that in every corporate bankruptcy a qualified and disinterested trustee should be appointed to "supplant the system of leaving [the corporate bankrupt's insiders] in possession or of appointing 'friendly' trustees." Independent counsel also should be required. The independent trustee should be responsible not only for preparing a reorganization plan, but for investigating:

> the condition of the company and of the events antedating the failure, with the threefold objective (1) of ascertaining the facts necessary for formulation of a plan; (2) of evaluating the worth of the existing management and the desirability of its retention by the reorganized company; and (3) of disclosing and diligently pursuing corporate assets in the form of claims against directors, officers, their affiliated interests and others who may have misused corporate control for their personal benefit.

Second, the SEC was to be available to the federal court "as an aid in the administration of the [bankruptcy reorganization] and in the analysis of the fairness, equity, and soundness of plans."

At Chandler's direction, Douglas compromised differences with the National Bankruptcy Conference. In return for Douglas's agreement to support repeal of a provision in an emergency Bankruptcy Act allowing creditors with claims as small as $1000 to institute a federal court bankruptcy proceeding and other technical concessions, the Conference agreed to support virtually all of the Protective Committee Study draft of what came to be known as Chapter X of the Chandler Bankruptcy Revision Act.

As enacted, Chapter X of the Chandler Act required a court to appoint an independent trustee to investigate the background of each bankruptcy involving $250,000 or more of indebtedness. The trustee could not be a director, officer, employee, or underwriter of the bankrupt firm, but the trustee was required to report any evidence that corporate insiders had been involved in fraud, misconduct, mismanagement, or other irregularities. Where the bankruptcy involved more than $3 million of indebtedness, the federal district court judge conducting the bankruptcy proceeding was required to submit to the SEC for examination and advisory review any reorganization plan the judge deemed worthy of consideration. On request or approval of the bankruptcy judge, the SEC was allowed to intervene and participate in other phases of the bankruptcy proceeding. SEC insistence secured passage of a novel provision giving labor unions or employees' associations the right to be heard on the economic soundness of the reorganization plan where it affected the interests of employees. A comparable "democratization" gave corporate insiders, any creditor, and any stockholder the right to be heard in a bankruptcy proceeding. Other SEC inspired provisions barred the issuance of nonvoting stock by the reorganized firm and required full disclosure of all fees and expenses incurred in a bankruptcy reorganization.[207]

The second legislative consequence of the Protective Committee Study was the Trust Indenture Act of 1939. In June 1936, the Protective Committee Study published the most influential of its eight reports, entitled *Trustees Under Indentures.* This Report benefited from several fortuities. Even in the most generous view, an analysis of corporate debt securities was tangential to the Protective Committee Study's mandate. Mindful of this, the main body of *Trustees Under Indentures* was a mere 112 pages in length — a pamphlet by Protective Committee Study standards — and limited to discussion of a "few exemplary major points," editorial decisions that had the result of making the Report the easiest to read Protective Committee Study document. Unlike the rest of the Protective Committee Study's work, which ranged in somewhat desultory fashion over several different legislative topics, such as municipal debt adjustment, foreign bonds, and real estate bond protective committees, *Trustees Under Indentures* was focused on a single legislative problem: long-term corporate debt. This meant not only that the Report could be easily translated into a legislative proposal, but also that the legislative proposal would be opposed only by a single group of industry lobbyists. Finally, and most fortuitously, much of the Report was inspired by Edward Levi, then a Yale Law School graduate student, later President of the University of Chicago and Attorney General of the United States, whom Douglas allowed to review the Protective Committee Study's debt security research for a school paper he was preparing. The paper was never published, but Douglas, with Levi's permission, incorporated many of Levi's arguments into the Trust Indenture Report.[208]

The thesis and tone of *Trustees Under Indentures* was similar to that of the Bankruptcy Report: Disorganized and scattered investigators often were treated unfairly by self-interested inside management and allied bankers. As the Trust Indenture Report explained, when corporate bonds and other long-term debt securities were sold, the investors' basic protector was a trustee, usually a commercial bank, which was required by a formal indenture agreement to enforce remedial provisions if the corporate issuer defaulted on its obligations to investors. But *Trustees Under Indentures* found that "typically the trustees do not exercise the elaborate powers which are the bondholders' only protection." Instead, the "so-called trustee" typically acts as "merely a clerical agency." This trustee passivity jeopardized the investors' position throughout the life of a debt security. Usually the trustee did not participate in drafting the indenture, allowing the corporate issuer and its underwriter to decide what safety features would protect investors. Not surprisingly, these protective features often proved illusory. For example, when corporate debt securities were sold, it was common for the issuer to advertise negative pledge clauses by which it promised not to incur other debts during the life of the loan. Because an investors' representative did not participate in the drafting of negative pledge clauses, these clauses often contained ingenious loopholes. Trustee inaction could be equally dangerous to investors after the initial indenture agreement was written, as investors in Kreuger and Toll discovered shortly after the 1929 Stock Market Crash, when they learned that their trustee had permitted Ivar Kreuger to substitute as collateral for $25 million worth of sound European bonds, Yugoslavian and other poorly rated bonds with an identical face value but an actual value of $9.75 million.

The Report was most critical of passive trustees when a corporation defaulted on its indenture obligations. In 63 percent of the indentures studied, trustees were not required to complain of a default, even if they had actual knowledge of it, unless formally requested by holders of a specified percentage of the outstanding debt securities. As "a general practice," trustees often exercised their discretion and ignored known defaults. Since the trustee often as a practical matter had the exclusive power to bring a lawsuit to enforce investigators' rights, this usually meant investors had no effective legal protection unless holders of specified percentages of outstanding debt securities (usually 50 percent or more) compelled the trustee to institute a lawsuit.

Dismal as the performance of passive trustees was, the Protective Committee Study argued, it was inevitable. The trustee of a corporate debt security usually was selected by the corporate issuer or the underwriter or both. Invariably the trustee was inadequately remunerated for the assumption of more than minimal duties. In a typical example, the Chase National Bank received $1100 a year for acting as trustee for $10 million of the debentures of the National Electric Power Company. Yet even this minimal fee was characterized as "grotesquely exorbitant for the negligible services performed" by Judge Samuel I Rosenman in the *Hazzard v. Chase National Bank* case, because exculpatory clauses with which most debt indentures "fairly bristle" exonerated a trustee from all misconduct except that caused "by its own gross negligence or bad faith," a level of misconduct almost never proven in a court of law.

Enactment of the Trust Indenture Act of 1939 was facilitated by policy differences between the principal bank lobby organizations, which Douglas skillfully exploited. Douglas worked closely with an American Bankers Association Committee. Soon after *Trustees Under Indentures* was published, R.G. Page, Chairman of an ad hoc committee of the American Bankers Association, the commercial bankers' lobbying organization, wrote his fellow commercial bankers that the Report was "most drastic" and "astonishingly unfair to corporate trustees as a class," but since "any fair minded person must admit that there have been abuses," he had accepted an SEC invitation to confer. Between October 1936 and March 1938, Douglas and the American Bankers Association negotiated the provisions of what ultimately became the Trust Indenture Act.

Passage of the bill became inevitable in early May 1939, when the Senate voted 40–19 in favor of a final SEC-American Bankers Association draft. The Trust Indenture Act of 1939 itself, to invoke a favorite phrase of James Landis, was closely articulated. Most corporate debt securities were required to comply with the Trust Indenture Act, as well as with the disclosure provisions of the Securities Act of 1933. The Trust Indenture Act, when applicable, required each corporate debt security to be protected by at least one trustee with a net worth of $150,000, free of nine specified conflicting associations with other debt issues, the corporate issuer, the underwriter, or voting stockholders. Although a commercial bank also could be a creditor of the corporation, a detailed section of the Act, laboriously negotiated by the SEC and the American Bankers Association, prohibited the bank trustee from improving its creditor position at the expense of debt security holders within four months of a default unless a genuine "reserve" or "distress" loan was made. To facilitate debt security holders' enforcement of their rights, the Act required lists of debt security holders to be readily available, required periodic reports both from the trustee and the issuer (including certificates of fair value when collateral was substituted), barred exculpatory provision after known defaults, and allowed debt security holders direct rights of action whenever principal and interest payments were past due.[209]

Accounting and Corporate Governance Standards

Douglas also sought to address accounting standard setting and corporate governance. In these areas, his efforts were less successful.

While an SEC Commissioner, William Douglas had disagreed with the Kennedy-Landis policy of leaving the promulgation of accounting principles almost entirely to the accounting profession. In 1936 and 1937, Douglas and fellow Commissioner Robert Healy pressed the Commission to "take the lead in formulating accounting principles as it was empowered to do under the 1933 Act." Douglas was the first SEC Chair to challenge the laxness of the Commission's accounting policies, raising questions for SEC internal study and modestly reforming the Commission's accounting policies. But his efforts were not sufficiently far reaching to be fully effective. By default, Douglas would contribute to the SEC's historic reluctance to assume direct responsibility for accounting principles, a reticence that long endured as a weak link in the Commission's corporate disclosure program.

Kennedy and Landis had viewed accounting reform as subordinate in importance to capital flotation. Following the Commission's November 1934 *Northern States Power* decision, the SEC permitted, in the words of a 1937 Staff Study, "financial statements reflecting improper accounting practices to remain unchanged provided such statements were footnoted to set forth the proper procedure which should have been followed together with a statement of the manner in which the accounts would have been altered had they been set up properly."

Douglas recalled in his autobiography that in late December 1937, Healy, an enthusiast of the common law's method of incremental case-by-case development, spoke also for Douglas when he described "the next step in accounting":

> The staff as the result of instructions has for some time been studying the proposal to issue some rules dealing with accounting principles. We are not thinking of a mass of rules or innovations in accounting. We are trying to express a few standards as to principles which we believe are accepted by a majority of good accountants, especially of those who do not assume the role of special pleaders for their more lucrative clients.

This approach proved inadequate. The ideal of comparable corporate financial statements, as distinguished from the common law's ideal of individualized justice, can be effectively pursued only within a comprehensive accounting framework. Chief Accountant Blough, however, had convinced a majority of the Commission that his Office lacked sufficient time and staff to do "the extensive research necessary to formulate the correct accounting principles" even in individual accounting controversies. Nor was the limited Healy-Douglas policy ever fully effected. A majority of the SEC Commissioners (Mathews, Frank, Hanes) opposed Commission formulation of accounting principles.

A compromise was engineered among the five SEC Commissioners in late March by which the Chief Accountant was authorized periodically to issue Accounting Releases expressing his interpretation of accounting standards on major accounting questions "for the purpose of *contributing* to the development of uniform standards" (italics added). One month later, the Commission, with Mathews dissenting, modestly tightened the looseness of the Kennedy-Landis footnote policy with the adoption of Accounting Series Release No. 4, which stated in its entirety:

> In cases where financial statements filed with this Commission pursuant to its rules and regulations under the Securities Act of 1933 or the Securities Exchange Act of 1934 are prepared in accordance with accounting principles for which there is not substantial authoritative support, such financial statements will be presumed to be misleading or inaccurate despite disclosures contained in the certificate of the accountant or in footnotes to the statements provided the matters involved are material. In cases where there is a difference of opinion between the Commission and the registrant as to the proper principles of accounting to be followed, disclosure will be accepted in lieu of correction of the financial statements themselves only if the points involved are such that there is substantial authoritative support for the practices followed by the registrant and the position of the Commission has not previously been expressed in rules, regulations, or other official releases of the Commission, including the published opinion of its chief accountant.

The advance in accounting rigor portended by this Release proved to be slight. Two SEC staff attorneys pointedly noted in 1939 that the Commission had left unresolved virtually all accounting controversies by failing to define *substantial authoritative support.* Accordingly, standards for such basic accounting concepts as cost of sales, depreciation, inventories, and surplus continued to "seem very inadequate."[210]

The chief unfinished business in the Roosevelt Administration's program of federal securities law was the enactment of a statute regulating corporate governance. There was irony in this omission. Many of the unethical or illegal actions reported by the Pecora Committee, the SEC's Protective Committee Study, and SEC enforcement programs involved the misconduct of senior corporate managers and directors, not investment bankers. Section 14 of the

1934 Securities Exchange Act, which gave the SEC power to regulate corporate proxy elections, had been widely recognized as a minor first step, to be succeeded by a more comprehensive federal corporate governance statute. President Roosevelt favored such an Act. So did many in his cabinet, as well as a majority of the people questioned in public opinion polls, the AFL, several members of Congress, the SEC, and even the New York Stock Exchange. Nevertheless, until the very end of the New Deal, a federal corporate governance statute was not a Roosevelt Administration priority. And when the Roosevelt Administration did commit itself to the enactment of such a law, it all but defeated its own efforts by linking enactment of provisions regulating corporate governance to an omnibus corporate licensing bill intended also to revitalize the antitrust laws and broaden employees' rights.

Professor William Douglas was a leader in the movement to secure enactment of a federal corporate governance statute. Indeed, as early as 1934, he was the most prominent academic proponent of a Federal Incorporation Act. In an expansive 1934 letter to Frankfurter, Douglas explained:

> Federal incorporation does not mean to me merely drafting a statute and determining what the rule of *ultra vires,* stock dividends, directors' liability, etc. to adopt. Those are next to clerical in significance. The real problem is to determine what social and economic values are at stake; What is wanted; What should be destroyed? What types of holding companies do you want? What room shall be left for the little fellow, the Henry Fords of the future or the corner grocery store of the new decade?

Douglas never proposed a legislative formula to answer these questions. But in June 1934, he published what has endured as his best known law review article, *Directors Who Do Not Direct.* The primary concern in regulating large corporations, Douglas insisted, was "[to avoid] or [make] impossible the vicious practice of having the board controlled or dominated by the managers." While disparaging as well "inside" directors who were corporate executives subservient to senior management and "outside" or nonemployee directors chosen solely for their prestige, Douglas saw a solution in taking away control and dominance of the board from executive management and vesting it instead in an independent board with sufficient power and responsibility to "supervise those who [manage the enterprise] and [formulate] the general commercial and financial policies under which the business is to be conducted." Douglas meant such directors to be "experts . . . sufficiently detached from the business to be able to see it in relation to its competitors, trade trends, etc.," not merely public representatives to serve as "corrective influences." They should have a position of dominance and power on the board rather than the subordinate position to which some reformers would relegate them. As a "partial agenda" of means to create such a supervisory board, Douglas urged preventing management domination over corporate elections by withdrawing their control of the proxy machinery (by which shareholders could not personally attend meetings were required to sign over their votes to incumbent management's representatives), barring nonvoting stock, and magnifying the opportunities for scattered minorities to express themselves through cumulative voting.[211]

While he was SEC Chair, Douglas delivered a related address urging paid directors, whose primary business would be to serve on the boards of a few corporations so that each director could "acquire a thorough knowledge of the corporation."

> With no conflicting interests whatsoever, the paid director could give his full attention to his company's affairs. He could visit the factories and the warehouses. He could know if the plant was being carried at too high a value; he could look not merely at statements of inventory but at the inventory itself. He would be able to penetrate the mysteries of the balance sheet and see the realities that lie behind it. He would not be merely a director at board meetings; he would be a director between board meetings as well. He could give the directing job more time in a week than many a director give it in a year.[212]

As SEC Chair, however, Douglas initially did not seek a federal corporate governance statute. With so many initiatives already begun, Douglas was reluctant to begin an additional campaign for a corporate governance statute.

In August 1935, shortly after the Supreme Court's *Schecter* decision held unconstitutional the National Industrial Recovery Act, Wyoming's populist Senator Joseph O'Mahoney had proposed in its stead a federal incorporation act, meant simultaneously to achieve the disparate goals of more effective antitrust enforcement, advancement of employees' right, and protection of shareholders by requiring every firm engaged in interstate commerce to secure a license from the FTC. Each license, in addition to requiring equal treatment for female employees, barring child labor, and guaranteeing employees the right to bargain collectively, would have barred dishonest or fraudulent trade practices. A second title would have guaranteed stockholders equal voting rights, disallowed bonuses or commissions to corporate officers unless voted by stockholders, required the distribution to stockholders of corporate surplus above a specified percentage of capital stock, and authorized the Civil Service Commission to accredit corporate representatives to serve as proxy holders. A final title would have excluded the interstate shipment of goods produced in whole or in part by child labor. The concept of a federal licensing act, though not O'Mahoney's admixture of provisions, appealed to Roosevelt.[213]

In January 1937, Idaho's William Borah, a Senator more respected by the Roosevelt Administration than O'Mahoney, introduced a second corporate licensing bill. Having as its basic purpose the prevention of monopolies, the bill authorized the FTC to refuse to license or to revoke the license of any interstate firm violating the antitrust laws.

The Borah approach, basically a death sentence for antitrust law violators, was consonant with Roosevelt's own view. With Roosevelt's tacit support, Assistant Attorney General Robert Jackson and Interior Secretary Harold Ickes delivered a series of virulent antimonopoly addresses in December 1937 and January 1938. At approximately the same time, O'Mahoney and Borah decided to combine the substantive features of their respective bills into a new jointly sponsored Corporate Licensing Bill. However, as the 1937–1938 recession deepened, the policy differences among Roosevelt's principal economic advisers sharpened. The administration's leading conservatives, including Treasury Secretary Morgenthau, Commerce Secretary Roper, the Reconstruction Finance Corporation's (*RFC*) Jesse Jones, and Joseph Kennedy, urged the President to conciliate business by, among other actions, declaring a moratorium on reform initiatives.[214]

Roosevelt resolved this conflict within his administration with his ill-fated Temporary National Economic Committee (*TNEC*) proposal. In April 1938, Roosevelt asked Congress to appropriate $500,000 so that the FTC, the SEC, and the Department of Justice could make a comprehensive study of the concentration of economic power in American industry. By linking the passage of any new federal corporation statute to Borah's death sentence for antitrust law violators, and implicitly to O'Mahoney's labor reform legislation — and deferring passage of each until a major interdepartmental economic study was completed — Roosevelt doomed the chance of any federal corporate governance law being enacted during the New Deal. Roosevelt requested funding for an Executive Branch Study, whose direction would have been controlled by men such as Robert Jackson, Thurman Arnold, and Douglas. In their hands, the appropriation likely would have been used to conduct public hearings dramatizing the need for new legislation in much the same fashion as Pecora earlier had used the Stock Exchange Practices Hearings to build support for the securities laws. Instead, Congress authorized $500,000 for the unwieldy TNEC, composed of six members of Congress and representatives from six federal agencies.[215]

Practical control of the TNEC rested with Senator O'Mahoney, who remained wedded to the omnibus concept of national charters for national business. Through the conclusion of the TNEC investigation, in March 1941, O'Mahoney remained an advocate of a single generic law embracing antitrust, shareholder, labor, and ultimately consumer reforms as the basic legislative aim of TNEC. However, much sense O'Mahoney's all embracing corporate licensing proposal might have made as a liberal political party's platform, it divided the TNEC. Eventually even the final SEC representatives, Sumner Pike, voted against it, in part because O'Mahoney, in order to secure a TNEC majority in favor of the corporate licensing concept, made his description of the proposal increasingly vague.[216]

The Investment Company and Investment Advisers Acts

Early in 1939, Douglas was confirmed as a Supreme Court Justice. With Douglas's departure, the SEC passed its historic zenith. Never again would the Commission receive such strong support from the White House, Congress, and the public. As the memory of the 1929 Stock Market Crash, Pecora's investigation, and the Whitney scandal faded, the Commission's ability to initiate new reforms would dissipate. Increasingly, it would be known for its technical proficiency, not for its legislative reform role. Washington also would change. During the New Deal, the SEC had loomed large because it was the lead agency in addressing one of the half dozen or so major problems that the Roosevelt Administration was committed to solve. But the federal government would expand enormously in the post-World War II period, reducing the Commission to one of the smallest of the alphabet of agencies.

During the balance of the pre-World War II period under the Commission's fourth Chair, Jerome Frank, the SEC was able to secure enactment of its final two New Deal enabling acts, the Investment Company Act of 1940 and the Investment Advisers Act.

The SEC's greatest legislative defeat during the Roosevelt Administration involved the compromises necessary to win enactment of the Investment Company Act of 1940. The SEC officially would observe that the law represented "the minimum workable regulation of investment companies," in part justified because it provided the Commission with a basis from which to seek "major amendments . . . if and when amendment seems advisable." Unofficially, the Act represented the most the SEC could achieve in the anti-New Deal 76th Congress, a half-a-loaf compromise made with the investment company industry because of uncertainty that any law could be enacted after the November 1940 Presidential elections or the start of American participation in World War II.[217]

Before the 1929 Stock Market Crash, the history of American investment companies had been comparatively brief. Although one Massachusetts investment trust may have been formed as early as 1823, investment companies played a relatively minor role in the United States economy until 1926. It was only in the frenzied years just before the Stock Market Crash that investment companies became, in John Kenneth Galbraith's words, "the most notable piece of speculative architecture of the late twenties, and the one by which, more than any other device, the public demand for common stocks was satisfied." Where approximately 160 investment trusts with combined assets of less than $1 billion were actively in business in 1926, close to 600 new investment companies were formed in the next three years, increasing total assets to over $8 billion just before the 1929 market break.

Three considerations were emphasized in the high pressure sales campaigns that stimulated the investment companies' accelerated growth. First, American promoters stressed the successful record of the earlier formed English and Scottish investment trusts. Second, small investors were informed that only through an investment company could they economically diversify their shareholdings and reduce their risk. Finally, tremendous emphasis was placed on the quality of the investment company's management. As one saying went, the investment companies formed by Dillon, Read investment bank provided "an opportunity to let the public in on [Clarence] Dillon's investment brains."

Given the nature of the pre-Stock Market Crash sales promotion, it was hardly surprising that 97 percent of the industry's assets in 1929 were held by investment companies that provided little or no restriction on the type or frequency of investments a company could make, almost all of the largest investment companies were organized and managed by leading investment banks, and a majority of common shareholders held investments of $500 or less.

Because the virtually unregulated investment companies provided obvious opportunities for their managers to exploit ill informed small investors, the firms were suspiciously regarded even before the 1929 Stock Market Crash. A prescient March 1929 *Atlantic Monthly* article by investment company manager Paul Cabot complained of the "dishonesty; inattention and inability; and greed" in the investment trust movement, warning that without the remedies of publicity and education, a period of "disaster and disgrace" would be "inevitable." Similar considerations, less melodramatically expressed, dissuaded the NYSE from permitting even the tentative listing of investment trust securities until June 1929.[218]

After the 1929 Stock Market Crash, the reputation of the investment companies declined even more precipitously than it had grown in the previous three years. With aggregate investment company assets shrinking to $2.8 billion and at least 22 companies declaring bankruptcy, the investment companies were criticized by the *New York Journal of Commerce,* the *American Bankers Association Journal,* and *Barron's* between October 1929 and February 1930. *The New Republic*'s John T. Flynn effectively commenced his career as the generation's best known critic of Wall Street with an April 1930 article *Investment Trusts Gone Wrong.* Soon Flynn was joined by the *Harvard Law Review,* which in November 1930 published a discussion of the need for statutory regulation of investment trusts.[219]

Legislation was to be almost a decade in coming. Although the Pecora Hearings would investigate several investment companies and the final report denounce the "veritable epidemic of investment trusts [that] afflicted the nation," the abuses of the investment companies were overshadowed by the far more publicized misdeeds of JP Morgan and Company, Charles E. Mitchell, pool market operators, and purveyors of then near worthless foreign bonds. The SEC was responsible for sustaining concern. In July 1935, Paul Gourrich, the Commission's Technical Adviser, prepared at Commissioner James Landis's request a memorandum summarizing "prima facie evidence of the need of a thorough investigation of the investment companies." The memorandum stated: "So many misdeeds and malpractices are revealed in this study, so shocking are some of the findings, that the following summary is virtually a bill of indictment." At approximately the same time, Commissioner Robert Healy, who had directed the FTC's seven-year investigation of Public Utility Holding Companies, communicated his belief that investment companies subsequently might be employed by those seeking to evade the Public Utility Holding Company Bill, then nearing enactment. At the recommendation of the SEC, a section was added to the Holding Company Act. It directed the Commission to deliver a study of investment companies to Congress no later than January 4, 1937.[220]

The SEC's six year *Study of Investment Trusts and Investment Companies* closed a decade of government investigation of financial scandals with a 5100 page report. By delaying publication of most of the Report until 1939 and 1940, the SEC was able to describe two generations of investment company misconduct and to show that the unsupervised reorganization of the industry after the Crash had created problems almost as serious as the promoters' abuses that stimulated the investment companies' 1927–1929 growth.

The basic sin of the investment bankers who formed investment companies before the 1929 Crash had been self-interest. Excessive fees were commonplace in the period, with promoters often profiting from the distribution of securities in the investment companies themselves and from the purchase and sale of a portfolio of securities, as well as from management contracts, stock options, and the unloading of slow moving securities.

Illustrative were Dillon, Read's two giant investment companies, the United States and Foreign Securities Corporation and the United States and International Securities Corporation. When it was begun in 1924, the United States and Foreign Securities Corporation was considered by Hugh Bullock, an investment company executive, to be "by far the most eminent of the trusts of the early 1920s." The public was sold 250,000 shares of first preferred stock at $100 a share for $25 million; Dillon, Read purchased 50,000 shares of second preferred stock for $5 million. Anyone purchasing the preferred stock received as a bonus a common stock share with each share of preferred. Dillon, Read also awarded itself 250,000 common shares for its considerably smaller preferred stock investment and sold itself an additional 500,000 shares of common stock for $100,000. Thus, at the formation of the firm, Dillon, Read not only received a $1 million underwriting fee, but also locked up 75 percent of the possible profits of the company on an investment one-fifth as large as that made by public investors. In a rising market, Dillon, Read's common stock was worth over $17 million by September 1928. Dillon, Read also would profit from the United States and Foreign Securities Corporation by acting as its broker in purchasing and selling securities for its investment portfolio, directing the investment company in at least 16 instances to purchase blocks of new securities originated by Dillon, Read, and causing the firm to buy large blocks of railroad securities from Dillon, Read in a slumping market.

In October 1928, Dillon, Read amplified its opportunities to profit from captive brokerage and underwriting sales by using $10 million of the surplus profits of the United States and Foreign Securities Corporation to purchase all of the second preferred stock and two million shares of common stock in a new subsidiary investment firm, the United States and International Securities Corporation. With public investors advancing $50 million for first preferred stock and a minority of the common shares, Dillon, Read, by that date, had succeeded in creating a controlled pool of $80 million on its own initial investment of $5.1 million. As long as the market rose, the public investors did receive a 6 percent annual return on their preferred stock investment. But after the Crash, the excessively leveraged United States and International Securities Corporation went bankrupt, and the original United States and Foreign Securities Corporation sustained losses amounting at one time to $26 million. Such results were common for the more highly leveraged investment companies. "By the end of 1937," the SEC would report, "the average dollar which had been invested in July 1929 in the index of leverage investment company common stocks was worth 5 cents, while the nonleverage dollar was worth 48 cents."

Following the Stock Market Crash, approximately half of the investment companies organized between 1927 and 1936 went out of business.[221]

Even before the introduction of the SEC-drafted bill, its provisions for regulating investment companies were compromised in order to increase the possibility of the bill's enactment by the anti-New Deal 76th Congress. After conferences of SEC staff with investment company industry leaders, beginning in late January 1940, SEC proposals to divorce completely investment companies from the investment banking firms, impose a death sentence on previously issued debt securities and preferred stock, and redistribute securities voting rights were dropped. As introduced, the SEC's Bill was judged "moderate and well considered" by *The New York Times.* Unlike the Public Utility Holding Company Act, it directed no reorganization of an industry. Instead, a variety of techniques employed in earlier securities laws were to be used to ensure that investors would receive fair value in future investment company transactions. Following the examples of the 1933 Securities Act and the Maloney Act amendments to the 1934 Securities Exchange Act, for instance, investment companies and their directors, managers, and advisers were to be registered with the SEC. Conflicts of interest were to be minimized by the flat prohibition of such practices as investment company underwriters' selling the investment company other securities. The companies would be internally policed through a requirement that a majority of each investment company's Board of Directors be composed of outside, unaffiliated people. Excessive promotion of investment companies was to be discouraged by barring persons from service as officers of an investment company if they had promoted a second investment company within the preceding five years. To prevent investment companies from serving as disguised holding companies, maximum size limits were to be imposed. Shareholders were to have the opportunity to approve any fundamental change in an investment company's policy and its manager's remuneration contract. In the future, with very few exceptions, all new issues of investment company securities were to be common stock with equal voting and dividend rights. The most far reaching provisions to the bill focused on investment banking arrangements. Stock options and warrants for investment company underwriters were to be proscribed. Investment banker exploitation also was to be prevented by prohibiting underwriters from buying investment company securities except at the same price they were sold to the public and by empowering the SEC to stop "unconscionable or grossly excessive sales loads." Fairness in the reorganization or dissolution of investment firms was to be realized by a comparable Commission power to block such transactions if found "not fair and equitable to all persons . . . affected."

Although even the SEC's most conservative Commissioner, George Mathews, considered the Commission's bill barely adequate, it was clear, after 18 hearing days before a Senate Banking Subcommittee in April 1940, that the initial SEC bill would not be adopted by the 76th Congress. Many conservatives in Congress shared with Senator Robert Taft a dislike of giving the SEC or any regulatory agency "infinite . . . discretionary power . . . to tell a man how he shall conduct his business."

Other Congressional opponents of the bill were impressed by the arguments of the Lehman Corporation's Arthur H. Bunker, who during the hearings was the investment company industry's leading spokesman. Addressing himself primarily to the dozen most far reaching provisions of the bill, Bunker argued that the SEC draft when "further than is necessary to safeguard the interests of investors," with the result that "it is quite possible [the] legislation [may] hamstring and shackle the operations of investment companies to such an extent that their usefulness may cease to exist." Paradoxically, however, Bunker and most other investment company industry leaders were as eager as the SEC to secure passage of an investment company bill before the 76th Congress adjourned. Only by enactment of a law, Bunker believed, could "the cloud" under which the industry long had operated be removed and investment companies regain the ability to market new securities. With Bunker's pledge that the investment company industry was "not only willing, but anxious to cooperate" with the SEC, backed by a joint statement of investment company leaders accepting nearly all of the less consequential provisions of the SEC draft, David Schenker, the SEC Investment Company Study Director, and investment company attorneys Alfred Jaretzki and Warren Motley began in early April to negotiate a compromise bill.[222]

The Investment Company Act was the product of five weeks of subsequent SEC-industry negotiations. The final bill, though not purely a disclosure measure, contained several major SEC concessions. Principally, the SEC agreed to the following: It would not require registration of investment company officers; it would require that only a 40 percent minority of each investment firm's directors be disinterested outsiders; it would eliminate investment company maximum size limits; eliminate limitations on the number of investment companies a person could sponsor; withdraw the flat prohibition against issuance of new debt securities or preferred stock in favor of a limitation on the amount each firm could issue; and would all but totally eliminate the Commission's fairness jurisdiction by limiting its power to enjoin reorganizations to instances where investment company security holders requested SEC intervention and a federal district court found a reorganization plan "grossly unfair." Since most of these concessions had been publicly requested by Arthur Bunker, and the investment companies' own concessions were comparatively less significant, one law review commentator condemned the compromise "for removing the most important features of the original bill." The Investment Company Bill was the only New Deal securities law unequivocally endorsed by the Investment Bankers Association. The SEC supported the watered-down bill, employing the Election year logic that if it failed to secure the Investment Company Act in the 76th Congress, it ran the risk of getting no investment legislation in the foreseeable future.

Two months after the compromise bill publicly was endorsed by the SEC and the investment company industry, it was unanimously passed by both Houses of Congress. Senator Wagner noted with approval that the bill "has the distinction of having the virtually unanimous support of the persons for whose regulation it provides, as well as of the regulatory agency by which it is to be administered."[223]

Besides providing less effective regulation of the investment company industry, the legislative defeat had a second and broader significance. Throughout the New Deal period, the Commission's draftsmen had evolved a more sophisticated concept of the SEC's appropriate enduring role. The Securities Act of 1933, the Commission's initial enabling Act, popularly had been termed an antifraud measure because it explicitly required the SEC to ensure accurate dissemination of material facts to investors, rather than approve or disapprove securities issued. It soon had been recognized that the principal usefulness of the Act was not in preventing fraud, but in discouraging such activities as investment banker or corporate executive overreaching, which were not, as a matter of law, fraudulent, but often were deterred when held up to public scrutiny. Subsequent SEC statutes had more directly addressed the question of insider unfairness. Notably, the 1935 Holding Company Act empowered the Commission to impose fairness standards in reorganizing the capital structures of holding companies; the 1938 Chandler Act directed the SEC to advise federal courts concerning the fairness of bankruptcy reorganizations. Underlying the drafting of these Acts was the New Deal SEC's recognition that disclosure alone often did not effectively protect investors.

When the 76th Congress refused to grant the SEC power to enforce fairness requirements for investment companies, it sealed the impression that the SEC's primary role was to monitor a corporate disclosure system. As the character of the investment company industry before 1940 well illustrated, this was a second best solution, permitting the Commission to be an effective "investor's advocate" when it could prove fraudulent misrepresentations or omissions, but often making it a toothless watchdog when investors were exploited because they had less ability to appraise the worth of a securities transaction than did corporate insiders. Thirty-four years later, former Chairman William Cary would urge that a Federal Corporate Uniformity Act be enacted to provide minimum federal fiduciary standards and "prescribe fairness as a prerequisite to any transaction." Echoing the SEC's arguments for the original Investment Company Bill, Cary would write:

> Disclosure alone is not enough. It is absurd that a corporate transaction, clearly unfair though perhaps not fraudulent, should be subject to attack in the federal courts only upon the ground that it has not been disclosed to the shareholders rather than because of its inherent inequity. . . . Even if it said that the securities laws focus exclusively upon protection of the securities market, confidence in the market generally and in any particular stock may depend as much upon the probity of management as upon the mechanism of the market. If we accept the soundness of the securities laws, then there should be a federal interest in providing a standard of conduct for management and the corporation on which much of the economy depends.[224]

Accompanying enactment of the Investment Company Act was enactment of the final New Deal securities enabling law, the Investment Advisers Act.

As with investment trusts, investment advisers only emerged as an independent profession after World War I. The Commission found only 20 investment advisers in business before 1919. But by the time of the 1940 Acts, the Commission was able to document enough evidence of abuse by fringe operators to persuade the Senate Banking and Currency Committee to state:

> Not only must the public be protected from the frauds and misrepresentations of unscrupulous tipsters and touts, but the bona fide investment counsel must be safeguarded against the stigma of the activities of these individuals. Virtually no limitations or restrictions exist with respect to the honesty and integrity of individuals who may solicit funds to be controlled, managed, and supervised. Persons who may have been convicted or enjoined by courts because of perpetration of securities fraud are able to assume the role of investment advisers. Individuals assuming to act as investment advisers at present can enter profit-sharing contracts which are nothing more than *heads I win, tails you lose* arrangements. Contracts with investment advisers which are of a personal nature may be assigned and the control of funds of investors may be transferred to others without the knowledge or consent of the client.[225]

As enacted, the Advisers Act was bare bones, requiring registration of persons engaged for compensation in the business of providing advice or issuing analysis or reports regarding securities. The Act also outlawed investment adviser fraudulent or deceptive practices and prevented assignment of advisory contracts without the client's consent. There were several exclusions from the Act, including banks, lawyers, accountants, publishers, and broker-dealers, under specified conditions.

The Roosevelt Administration did not achieve all it sought in federal securities regulation. But what it did achieve fundamentally transformed finance. Six federal securities acts were adopted. The SEC was created. The framework for further expansion of federal securities regulation after World War II was in place. And when the Supreme Court ruled in 1938 in *United States v. Carolene Products* that regulatory legislation in ordinary commerce was to be presumed constitutional, the risk that the federal securities laws would be declared unconstitutional essentially ceased.[226]

Housing Regulation

Throughout his Presidency, Franklin Roosevelt emphasized a third pillar of financial regulation, mortgage relief and a national housing policy. On January 20, 1937, in his Second Inaugural Address, Roosevelt memorably declaimed: "I see one-third of a nation ill-housed, ill-clad, ill-nourished." Business historian David Mason described the housing crisis when Roosevelt took office four years earlier:

> By the time Franklin D. Roosevelt took the oath of office on March 4, 1933, the problems facing homeowners were reaching epidemic proportions. According to federal statistics, roughly 45 percent of the more than 10.6 million homes in the country had either first, second, or third mortgages. The government estimated that 43 percent of all first mortgages were in default with an average arrearage of fifteen months. Furthermore, more than half of all homes with second and third mortgages were in default and in arrears an average of eighteen months. Officials concluded that nearly 25 percent of all homeowners with mortgages were in danger of losing their property. In fact, lenders were initiating an average of 24,000 foreclosures per month by 1933, a rate that was nearly five times more than that of just six years earlier.

Roosevelt viewed the challenge of housing as more than a problem of finance, but a challenge to the health and well-being of the nation. On January 6, 1937, in his State of the Union message, Roosevelt had urged Congress:

> There are far reaching problems still with us for which democracy must find solutions if it is to consider itself successful. For example, many millions of Americans still live in habitations which not only fail to provide the physical benefits of modern civilization but breed disease and impair the health of future generations. The menace exists not only in the slum areas of the very large cities, but in many smaller cities as well. It exists on tens of thousands of farms, in varying degrees, in every part of the country.

Throughout his presidency, Roosevelt prioritized housing finance, beginning with the Emergency Home Owners Loan Act of

1933 and continuing with the National Housing Acts of 1934 and 1937.

Roosevelt dramatically expanded earlier initiatives of Hoover. In 1931, Hoover had initiated White House Conferences on Home Building and Home Ownership to review the National housing crisis and make recommendations, among other topics, for a mortgage reserve bank.

In 1932, with Hoover's strong support, Congress had enacted the Federal Home Loan Bank Act, which created the Federal Home Loan Bank Board, whose five members were appointed by the President with the advice and consent of the Senate. The 1932 Act authorized the Federal Home Loan Bank Board to divide the country into eight to twelve districts, each with a Federal Home Loan Bank. Any building or loan institution other than a national bank or trust company, including savings and loan associations, cooperative banks, homestead associations, insurance companies, or savings banks was eligible to become a member of a Federal Home Loan Bank or a nonmember borrower if the borrowing institution made long-term home mortgage loans. The United States was authorized to purchase up to $125 million of stock under the Act with additional stock subscriptions anticipated from members. When the Federal Home Loan Bank system became operational in October 1932, $122 million had been provided by the federal government, $12 million from savings and loan institutions. Within a few months, $98.8 million had been lent. By March 1933, lending volume exceeded $5 million per day.

The mission of the Federal Home Loan Bank System was to facilitate collateralized mortgage loans up to $20,000 with the Federal Loan Bank Board channeling money to member and nonmember borrowers. Despite the power to make direct loans to homeowners, the Federal Home Loan Bank Board largely limited itself to the wholesale function of lending money to the district Federal Home Loan Banks, which, in turn, funded homeowners. Through March 1933, only three of 41,000 homeowner requests for direct loans had been approved.

The Roosevelt Administration sharply criticized the Federal Home Loan Bank Board for adopting policies "not designed to give help in cases of emergency distress."

In June 1933, during Roosevelt's first one hundred days, Congress adopted the Home Owners Loan Act: "To provide emergency relief with respect to home mortgage indebtedness, to refinance home mortgages, to extend relief to thee owners of homes occupied by them and who are unable to amortize their debt elsewhere, to amend the Federal Home Loan Bank Act, to increase the market for obligations of the United States and for other purposes."

The purpose of the Act unabashedly was to provide immediate debt relief to homeowners in danger of losing their homes by refinancing loans, extending the time for repayment of principal and interest, and reducing interest rates.

The Home Owners Loan Act directed the Federal Home Loan Bank Board to create the Home Owners Loan Corporation, funding the Corporation with up to $200 million from the RFC and up to $2 billion in bonds. These amounts would be increased to $400 million in direct RFC support by 1935 and $4.7 billion in bonds in 1937. The Home Owners Loan Corporation was authorized to refinance home mortgages up to 80 percent of the value of real estate with a cap of $14,000; extend principal and interest payments and make loans in cash up to 50 percent of the collateralized real estate.

The Home Owners Loan Act also authorized the Federal Home Loan Bank Board to reincorporate Federal Savings and Loan Associations "giving primary consideration to the best practices of local thrift, mutual thrift, and home-financing institutions in the United States." The Federal S&L Associations were empowered to lend funds up to $20,000 only on the security of mortgages upon homes or combinations of homes and businesses within 50 miles of the Association's home office. Each S&L Association automatically became a member of the district Federal Home Loan Bank and was eligible for a key sweetener. The Secretary of Treasury could subscribe for preferred stock in an S&L Association up to $100,000.

Buttressing the Home Owners Loan Corporation were the 1934 and 1937 National Housing Acts.

The 1934 National Housing Act focused on reviving housing construction and housing mortgages. The Act created a Federal Housing Administration (*FHA*) to administer three programs. First, banks, thrift companies, personal finance companies, mortgage companies, building and loan associations, and other financial institutions that lent money to finance real estate alterations, repairs, and improvements could have up to 20 percent of their loans insured up to $2000 per loan. Revitalizing housing construction was a New Deal priority. Total new housing construction that had exceeded $12 billion in 1926 and 1927 had slumped to less than $3 billion by 1933. Home improvement loans were even lower—just 12.5 percent of pre-Stock Market Crash levels. Two million housing industry workers in construction were without jobs in 1933. The Roosevelt Administration committed up to $200 million in RFC funds to insuring financial institutions making housing loans.

Second, the Act empowered the FHA to create a system of national mortgage insurance to provide individual mortgage holders borrowing up to 80 percent of the approved value of housing obligations up to $16,000. The mortgage insurance provided debentures, that is, debt securities, to the financial institutions for "all claims arising out of the mortgage transaction," meaning that the S&L or other lending institution risk largely could be eliminated. Typically, FHA mortgage insurance covered 96.5 percent of the appraised value of the home or business. The Federal Housing Administration also was authorized to insure public or private low cost housing projects. In aggregate, the FHA could provide up to $1 billion insurance for home mortgages and low cost housing projects.

After three years, 18 percent of all mortgages had FHA insurance. In 1938, Congress made the insurance more attractive, allowing mortgage holders to receive insurance up to 90 percent of property value, increasing the term of a mortgage to 25 years, decreasing monthly payments, and cutting the insurance premium in half. By the end of World War II, 34 percent of all mortgages had FHA insurance.

Third, the 1934 National Housing Act authorized the FHA to establish National Mortgage Associations to purchase and sell housing mortgages. S&L lobbying had defeated a greater power proposed by the Roosevelt Administration to allow the National Mortgage Association to make direct mortgage loans, which the S&L's feared would be a mortal threat. As it was, explained historian Mason, there were fears that the new National Mortgage Association would have "access to low-cost government funds that would drive down all mortgage rates and hurt thrift profitability." Only one Association operated through 1937. In 1938, Congress ended the National Mortgage Association program and created the Federal National Mortgage Association to strengthen the secondary market for home loans made by private institutions that were insured by the FHA.

In 1937, the United States Housing Act or Wagner-Steagall Act was adopted primarily to provide financial assistance to the states for the purpose of eliminating unsafe and unsanitary housing, the eradication of slums, and sanitary housing for low income families. Initially, the Act was administered by the United States Housing Authority in the Department of Interior with borrowing capacity up to $300 million. The Housing Authority was empowered to make loans, annual contributions, or capital grants to state public housing authorities "to assist the development, acquisition or administration of low-rent housing or slum-clearance projects by such agencies." Between 1937 and 1941, the Housing Authority lent $800 million as part of construction of 587 low rent housing developments, creating 170,000 new units. Tenants generally were expected to pay one-half the rent with federal, state, or local programs contributing to the balance.

Over time there were several reorganizations of the plethora of New Deal housing agencies including the 1942 Executive Order 9070, which established a National Housing Agency to consolidate the Federal Home Loan Bank Board, the Federal Housing Administration and the United States Housing Authority.[227]

Throughout his entire presidency, housing remained a Roosevelt priority. In his 1944 State of the Union address, Roosevelt envisioned an Economic Bill of Rights, including the "right of every family to a decent home." While the Roosevelt Administration did not achieve that, his contributions to housing were substantial.

The Home Owners Loan Corporation (*HOLC*) received support from the Roosevelt administration and Congress, in the words of economist Alan Blinder, that was "colossal . . . equal to about 5 percent of GDP." S&L historian Mason adumbrated this point:

> At its peak in 1934, the HOLC operated 458 local, state, and regional offices, employing nearly 21,000 people. When lending operations ended in 1938, it had processed more than 1.88 million applications worth nearly $6.2 billion. The agency approved more than one million of these requests totaling $3.1 billion, and thrifts eventually acquired $770 million in HOLC bonds, an amount that represented 13 percent of total thrift industry assets. While the majority of these loans were repaid in full, the

> HOLC did foreclose on almost 20 percent of its borrowers. Remarkably, when it wound up its business in 1946, HOLC operations did not cost taxpayers any money, and it even returned a profit to the United States Treasury.

Private residential construction between 1933 and 1940 increased six fold.[228] Through 2019, the Federal Housing Administration had insured over 34 million home mortgages and 47,205 multifamily projects.

The New Deal Revolution in Finance

There were other New Deal financial regulatory initiatives. In 1934, Congress enacted the Federal Credit Union Act. In 1936, the Grain Futures Act of 1922 was replaced by the Commodity Exchange Act, which created the Commodity Exchange Commission, whose mission then was limited to agricultural products.[229]

The core of the New Deal transformation in finance remained banking, securities, and housing. Underlying this transformation was a fundamental shift in the Supreme Court's interpretation of the Constitution. In 1905, the Court had decided in *Lochner v. New York* that a state could not adopt a 60 hour maximum work week because of the doctrine soon known as substantive due process. "There is no reasonable ground for interfering with the liberty of persons or right of free contract by determining the hours of labor" in this case for the occupation of baker. The Court viewed this interpretation of the Constitution to supersede the power of a legislature to enact labor laws. As the Court memorably wrote: Are we "at the mercy of legislative majorities?"

Between 1934 and 1936, the Supreme Court struck down 12 New Deal economic programs including the National Industrial Recovery Act and the initial Agricultural Adjustment Act. The New Deal appeared stymied by what Roosevelt characterized as a "horse and buggy" Supreme Court. From April 1937, on, however, the Supreme Court upheld every New Deal law presented to it including some that were similar to those earlier struck down.

The judicial reversal of its strict interpretation of congressional and state powers to regulate the economy was epitomized by decisions such as *United States v. Carolene Products*, which in 1938 declared that the will of the legislature in any instance with "some rational basis" was presumed constitutional, or *Wickard v. Filburn*, which in

1942 held that under the Interstate Commerce Clause of the Constitution Congress had the power even to regulate farm products consumed on the premises because of their potential impact on market prices and market conditions that were interstate.

The "Switch in Time Saved the Nine" Supreme Court Justices from Roosevelt's heavy handed Court packing plan. Instead Roosevelt achieved a more sympathetic judiciary through a president's conventional powers to appoint justices.

The enduring consequence of the post-1938 interpretation of federal and state legislative powers was not only to fortify the New Deal economic programs untouched by the 1934–1936 Supreme Court decisions declaring 12 programs unconstitutional, but to make possible broad further extensions of national and state regulatory laws in the post-World War II period, including the Social Security Act, enacted in 1935, and the Fair Labor Standards Act of 1938, which created federal minimum wage and maximum work hour standards.[230]

The financial regulatory model that was created by the New Deal was aligned with the atomized economy that emerged after the New Deal. At the national level, the leading banks were overseen by the Federal Reserve System, the Comptroller of the Currency, and the Federal Deposit Insurance Corporation; securities, investment banks, broker-dealers, investment advisers, and investment companies were regulated by the Securities and Exchange Commission; housing finance was subject to the Federal Home Loan Bank Board, the Federal Housing Administration as buttressed by capital infusions from the Reconstruction Finance Corporation and the United States Housing Authority by Savings & Loan Institutions, which in turn were subject to the Federal Savings and Loan Corporation.

Despite this degree of alignment, the fragmentation of New Deal financial regulatory model over time would prove to be the model's greatest weakness.

By 1945, there were 5015 Federal Reserve national banks, with $81.5 billion in assets, 1822 Federal Reserve state member banks with assets of $44.9 billion, and 7289 state nonmember banks with assets of $19.8 billion. By 1945, there were also 6149 savings and loan associations with total assets of $8.7 billion; 8615 credit unions, 3757 at the federal level, 4858 at the state level, with total assets federal and state credit unions of $435 million.[231]

This meant that in 1945 there were at the national level five regulatory agencies addressing banks or depository agencies: The Federal Reserve, the Comptroller, the FDIC, the Federal Savings and Loan Insurance Corporation, and the Bureau of Federal Credit Unions. But this only was at the national level. Concurrent systems of regulation existed for banks, savings and loans, and credit unions at the state level.

Securities regulation also was concurrent at the national level with the SEC and in each of the states with Blue Sky Commissions.

Housing finance also was subject to both federal and state regulatory law.

Insurance remained subject solely to state law.

If companies and regulators stayed in their lanes, for decades the system worked well. The challenge would build over decades as financial firms achieved ways to escape regulatory silos and a new financial order emerged.

ENDNOTES:

1. John Maynard Keynes, The Economic Consequences of the Peace (1919); Liaquat Ahamed, The Lords of Finance: The Bankers Who Broke the World 100, 108–110, 114–124, 130–132, 139–140 (Penguin Press 2009); 1 Historical Statistics of the United States Colonial Times to 1970 224 (Bureau of the Census 1975); Vincent Carosso, Investment Banking in America: A History 248–249 (Cambridge: Harvard University Press 1970); Ron Chernow, The House of Morgan 227 (Atlantic Monthly Press 1990).
2. Ahamed, supra n. 1, at 270–279, 308–312, 341–348; Joel Seligman, The Transformation of Wall Street: A History of the Securities and Exchange Commission and Modern Corporate Finance 2 (Wolters Kluwer 3d ed. 2003); Frederick Lewis Allen, Only Yesterday: An Informal History of the 1920s 180–181, 194–197, 226–265 (Harper & Row 1931); John Kenneth Galbraith, The Great Crash 1929 1–7, 15, 33–38, 52, 70–79 (Houghton Mifflin 1954); Calvin Coolidge State of the Union Address (Dec. 4, 1928); John J. Raskob, Everybody Ought to Be Rich, Ladies Home J. (Aug. 1929); Carosso, supra n. 1, at 243; Gene Smilley & Richard Keehn, Margin Purchases, Brokers' Loans and the Bull Market of the Twenties, 17 Bus. & Econ. Hist. 129 (1988).
3. See generally Seligman, supra n. 2, at Ch. 1; Galbraith, supra n. 2, at 83–92, 98–103, 109–121, 126, 135–141; Ahamed, supra n. 1, at 352–360; Carosso, supra n. 1, at 300–318; Allen, supra n. 2, at

266–281; Robert Sobel, The Great Bull Market (W. W. Norton 1968); John Brooks, Once in Golconda (Harper & Row 1969).

4. Herbert Hoover, Memoirs: The Great Depression 5–20, 30–31, 126 (MacMillan 1952); Herbert Hoover, The Cabinet and the Presidency 203–204 (MacMillan 1952); Arthur Schlesinger, The Crisis of the Old Order 88 (Houghton Mifflin 1957); Galbraith, supra n. 2, at 33–38; William Starr Myers & Walter Newton, The Hoover Administration 14 (Scribner's 1936); Ray Lyman Wilbur & Arthur Mastick Hyde, The Hoover Policies (Scribner's 1937).
5. *Congressional Record,* 71st Cong., 1st Sess., Nov. 1, 1929, at 5063; Myers & Newton, supra n. 4, at 21; The six bills were, in chronological order, H.R. 5060, 71st Cong., 1st Sess. (Nov. 11, 1929); H.R. 5412, 71st Cong., 1st Sess. (Nov. 21, 1929); H.R. 5658, 71st Cong., 2d Sess. (Dec. 2, 1929); H.R. 6122, 71st Cong., 2d Sess. (Dec. 3, 1929); H.R. 6985, 71st Cong., 2d Sess. (Dec. 9, 1929); and S. 2846, 71st Cong., 2d Sess. (Jan. 6, 1930).
6. Compare the 147 point drop in *New York Times* Average of 50 stocks between September 3, 1929, and November 13, 1929, with the 81 point gain between November 13 and April 10, 1930.
7. William Starr Myers, ed., The State Papers and Other Public Writings of Herbert Hoover, vol. 1 (Garden City, N.Y.: Doubleday, Doran, 1934), at 154; Hoover, Memoirs: The Great Depression, supra n. 4, at 57–58; Allen, supra n. 2, at 283–284.
8. *New York Times,* June 17, 1930, at 1; June 23, 1930 at 4; H.R. 12,171, 71st Cong., 2d Sess. (May 5, 1930), discussed in the *Congressional Record,* May 6, 1930, at 8456–8457, and June 19, 1930, at 11,228–11,229.
9. S. 4273, 71st Cong., 2d Sess. (1930).
10. *Congressional Record,* 71st Cong., 2d Sess., June 16, 1930, at 10,874–10,879; Carosso, supra n. 1, at 248–249; *Congressional Record,* 71st Cong., 2d Sess., June 25, 1930 at 11,647; *Congressional Record,* 71st Cong., 3d Sess., Feb. 26, 1931, at 6103.
11. Hoover, Memoirs: The Great Depression, supra n. 4, at 17; *New York Times,* Oct. 15, 1930, at 1, May 27, 1931, at 39, June 6, 1931, at 26, July 1, 1931, at 44, Sept. 24, 1931, at 1; Myers & Newton, supra n. 4, at 51–52; Whitney's Hartford speech was reprinted in Stock Exchange Practices Hearings, 72d Cong. at 187–193. Each of the following bills was presented on December 8, 9, or 10, of the 1st Sess. of the 72d Cong.: H.R. 4, H.R. 5, H.R. 348, H.R. 4604, H.R. 4638, H.R. 4639, H.R. 4642, S. 127, S. 1309, and S. 1311.
12. *New York Times* Oct. 1, 1931, at 15. A brief biography of Senator Johnson appears in the *Dictionary of American Biography,* Supplement Three (New York: Scribner's 1973), at 383–398; Sale of Foreign Bonds or Securities in the United States, Hearings before the

Committee on Finance, U.S. Senate, 72d Cong., 1st Sess. (1931–1932), at 1–2, 324–327, 395, 615–616, 621–622, 727, 743, 748, 852, 1273–1274, 1356, 1620–1621, 1903, 1911, 6060; *Congressional Record,* 72d Cong., 1st Sess. Dec. 9, 1931, at 213, Dec. 10, 1931, at 271, Mar. 15, 1932, at 1279–1280, 1772–1773, 6052, 6054–6057; Stock Exchange Practices Report, at 89; 1 Historical Statistics of the United States, supra n. 1, at 1106; Henry Doyle, Investors' Losses in South America, Current History, Feb. 1932 at 720–721.

13. Mellon quoted in Hoover, Memoirs: The Great Depression, supra n. 4, at 30; 1 Historical Statistics, supra n. 1, at 135, 235; 2 id. at 666, 1006; Brooks, supra n. 2, at 137; Allen, supra n. 2, at 416–418; Frederick Lewis Allen, Since Yesterday: The 1930s in America 59 (Harper & Row 1939).
14. Hoover, Memoirs: The Great Depression, supra n. 4, at 126; David Saul Levin, Regulating the Securities Industry: The Evolution of a Government Policy 116–117 (Colum. Univ. Ph.D. 1969); Allen, supra n. 2, at 59.
15. *New York Times,* Feb. 19, 1932, at 1–2; Short Selling of Securities, Hearings before the House Judiciary Committee, 72d Cong., 1st Sess. (1932), at 121; *Business Week,* Mar. 2, 1932, at 7; *Wall Street Journal,* Feb. 26, 1932, at 1.
16. Wilbur & Hyde, supra n. 4, at 344–346; *New York Times,* Feb. 27, 1932, at 2, Feb. 29, 1932, at 2, Mar. 2, 1932, at 1, Mar. 4, 1932, at 2, Mar. 5, 1932, at 1, 5, Apr. 28, 1949, at 31; Hoover, Memoirs, The Great Depression, supra n. 4, at 127; *Wash. Post,* Mar. 4, 1932, at 4; *Barron's,* Mar. 7, 1932, at 16; Brooks, supra n. 3, at 137–140; John Flynn, Wall Street Medicine, Colliers, Nov. 11, 1933 at 12–13.
17. 2 Jerry Markham, A Financial History of the United States 161–165 (Routledge 2015); Milton Friedman & Anna Jacobson Schwartz, A Monetary History of the United States 1857–1960 279–287, 308 (Princeton Univ. Press 1963); Ben Bernanke, Essays on the Great Depression 8–9, 15–16 (Princeton Univ. Press 2000); Ahamed, supra n. 1, at 155–164, 170–172, 393–434. Friedman and Schwartz also published an abridged version of their Monetary History entitled The Great Contraction (Princeton Univ. Press 2008), with Anna Jacobson Schwartz's Preface quoted at ix.
18. Friedman & Schwartz, supra n. 17, at 320–321, 381; James Olson, The End of Voluntarism: Herbert Hoover and the National Credit Corporation, 41 Annals of Iowa 1104 (1972); An Act to Provide Emergency Financing Facilities for Financial Institutions, to Aid in Financing Agriculture, Commerce and Industry, and for Other Purposes, Pub. L. No. 2, 72d Cong., 1st Sess. (Jan. 22, 1932); Markham, supra n. 17, at 161–163; B.W. Patch, The RFC under Hoover and Roosevelt, 2 Editorial Research Reports (1935), reprinted by

CQ Press; Alejandro Komai & Gary Richardson, A Brief History of Regulations Regarding Financial Markets in the United States 1789 to 2009, NBER Working Paper 17,443 (2011); An Act to Amend the Facilities of the Federal Reserve System, Pub. L. No. 44, Ch. 58, 72d Cong., 1st Sess. (Feb. 27, 1932); An Act to Relieve Destitution, to Broaden the Lending Powers of the Reconstruction Finance Corporation, and to Create Employment by Providing for and Expediting Public-Wage Programs, Pub. L. No. 302, Ch. 520, 72d Cong., 1st Sess. (July 21, 1932); Bernanke, supra n. 17, at 44.

19. 1 Historical Statistics, supra n. 1, at 224, 255; 2 Historical Statistics, supra n. 1, at 618; Ahamed, supra n. 1, at 361; Galbraith, supra n. 2, at 168; Allen, supra n. 2, at 45; Schlesinger, supra n. 4, at 248; Carosso, supra n. 1, at 352–353.

20. Democratic Party Platform (June 27, 1932); Franklin Roosevelt, Address Accepting the Presidential Nomination at the Democratic National Convention in Chicago (July 2, 1932); Governor Franklin D. Roosevelt's Speech at Columbus, Ohio (Aug. 20, 1932); First Inaugural Address of Roosevelt (Mar. 4, 1933); Arthur Schlesinger, The Coming of the New Deal Foreword, 1–8 (Houghton Mifflin 2003).

21. An Act to Provide Relief in the Existing National Emergency in Banking, and for Other Purposes, Ch. 1, 73d Cong., 1st Sess. (Mar. 9, 1933); Pub. L. No. 4, H.R. 3757, An Act to Provide for Direct Loans by Federal Reserve Banks to State Banks and Trust Companies, 73d Cong., 1st Sess. (Mar. 24, 1933); An Act to Amend the Emergency Banking Act, Pub. L. No. 4, 73d Cong., 1st Sess. (Mar. 24, 1933); Agriculture Adjustment Act, Pub. L. No. 10, 48 Stat. 31, 73d Cong., 1st Sess. (May 12, 1933); Gold Reserve Act of 1934, Pub. L. No. 87, 48 Stat. 337, 73d Cong., 2d Sess. (Jan. 30, 1934); Executive Order 6102 (Apr. 4, 1933); Executive Order Relating to the Hoarding, Export and Earmarking of Gold Coin, Bullion or Currency and to Transactions in Foreign Exchange (Aug. 28, 1933); Proclamation 2039 — Declaring Bank Holiday (Mar. 6, 1933); Presidential Proclamation No. 2072 (Jan. 31, 1934); Gold Repeal Joint Resolution, 48 Stat. 12 (June 5, 1933); Franklin D. Roosevelt, Message to Congress (Mar. 9, 1933); Statement by President Roosevelt (Mar. 11, 1933); Franklin D. Roosevelt, On the Banking Crisis, Fireside Chat 1 (Mar. 12, 1933); Statements by Secretary of Treasury Woodin (Mar. 10, 11, 13, & 31, 1933); Norman v. Baltimore & Ohio Railroad, 294 U.S. 240 (1935); Ahamed, supra n. 1, at 442, 446; Allan Meltzer, A History of the Federal Reserve: Volume 1: 1913–1951 at 442–462, 573 (Univ. of Chicago Press 2003); Sarah Binder & Mark Spindel, The Myth of Independence: How Congress Governs the Federal Reserve 98–106, 110–113 (Princeton Univ. Press 2007);

Dan Bryan, The 1933 Banking Crisis: From Detroit's Collapse to Roosevelt's Bank Holiday, American Hist. USA; Friedman & Schwartz, supra n. 17, at 442–448, 462–483; Stephen Green, Emergency Banking Act of 1933, Federal Reserve Hist. (Nov. 22, 2013); Robert Jabaily, Bank Holiday of 1933, Federal Reserve Hist. (Nov. 22, 2013); Markham, supra n. 17, at 165–166; Schlesinger, supra n. 20, at 4–8; John Wood, Central Banking, A Democracy 90–94 (Routledge 2015); Ann. Rep. of Federal Reserve Bd. for the Year 1933; Silber, Why did FDR's Bank Holiday Succeed?, Econ. Policy Rev. (June 16, 2009);

22. McFadden Act, Pub. L. No. 639, ch. 191, 44 Stat. 1228 (1927); The National Bank Bill, H.R. Rep. No. 83, 69th Cong., 1st Sess. (1926); The National Bank Bill, S. Rep. No. 473, 69th Cong., 1st Sess. (1926); Amendments to Banking Laws, H.R. Rep. No. 1481, 69th Cong., 1st Sess. (1926); Amendments to Banking Laws, H.R. Rep. No. 1796, 69th Cong., 2d Sess. (1927); First National Bank in St. Louis v. State of Missouri, 263 U.S. 640 (1924); Carosso, supra n. 1, at 242; Galbraith, supra n. 2, at 179; Markham, supra n. 17, at 111–115; Eugene White, The Regulation and Reform of the American Banking System, 1900–1929 at 138–141, 156–165 (Princeton Univ. Press 1938).
23. Seligman, supra n. 2, at 127; Friedman & Schwartz, supra n. 17, at 189–419; Ahamed, supra n. 1, at 1–2, 173–176, 291–298, 315, 365–366; Roger Lowenstein, America's Bank: The Epic Struggle to Create the Federal Reserve 260–263 (Penguin Press 2015); Galbraith, supra n. 2, at 27–33, 41–51; Peter Conti-Brown, The Power and Independence of the Federal Reserve 23–24 (Princeton Univ. Press 2016); Binder & Spindel, supra n. 21, at 87–92; Wood, supra n. 21, at 70–87; Adam Tooze, Crashed: How a Decade of Financial Crisis Changed the World 366 (Viking 2018); Bernanke, supra n. 17, at 46–47; Carosso, supra n. 1, at 271–299; Terris Moore, Security Affiliates Versus Private Investment Banks — A Study in Security Originations, 12 Harv. Bus. Rev. 478 (1934).
24. Banking Act of 1933, Pub. L. No. 66, 73d Cong., 1st Sess. (1933); S. Rep. No. 584, 72d Cong., 1st Sess. (1932); S. Rep. No. 77, 73d Cong., 1st Sess. (1933); H.R. Rep. No. 150, 73d Cong., 1st Sess. (1933); H.R. Rep. No. 254, 73d Cong., 1st Sess. (1933); 20th Ann. Rep. of Federal Reserve Bd. 40–50 (1934); Meltzer, supra n. 21, at 429–434; Carosso, supra n. 1, at 368–375; Friedman & Schwartz, supra n. 17, at 434–438; Binder & Spindel, supra n. 21, at 106–110; Diamond & Dyburg, Bank Runs, Deposit Insurance and Liquidity, 91 J. Pol. Econ. 401 (1989); Kunt & Detragiache, Does Deposit Insurance Increase Banking System Stability: An Empirical Investigation, 49 J. Monetary Econ. 1373 (2002); Perkins, The Divorce of

Commercial and Investment Banking: A History, 88 Banking L.J. 483, 505–524 (1971); Schlesinger, supra n. 4, at 20–21, 442–443.

25. Banking Act of 1935, Pub. L. No. 305, 74th Cong., 1st Sess. (1935); H.R. Rep. No. 742, 74th Cong., 1st Sess. (1935); S. Rep. No. 1007, 74th Cong., 1st Sess. (1935); H.R. Rep. No. 1822, 74th Cong., 1st Sess. (1935); *Cong. Rec.*, 74th Cong., 1st Sess. (July 2, 1935) quoted in Wood, supra n. 21, at 95; Melzer, supra n. 21, at 463–488, 559; Binder & Spindel, supra n. 21, at 113–121; Friedman & Schwartz, supra n. 17, at 445–449, 511–543; Peter Conti-Brown, The Power and Independence of the Federal Reserve 28–32 (Princeton Univ. Press 2016); Markham, supra n. 17, at 171.
26. The section on securities regulation in this chapter is an abridgment and update of Seligman, supra n. 2, Chapters 2–8. With respect to Peter Norbeck, see Gilbert Fite, Peter Norbeck: Prairie Statesman (Columbia: University of Missouri Press, 1948); John T. Flynn, The Marines Land in Wall Street, *Harper's Monthly* magazine, July 1934, at 148–149; and Flynn, Wall Street Medicine, *Collier's*, Nov. 11, 1933, at 12–13.
27. Fite, supra n. 26, at 173–174; *New York Times*, Apr. 5, 1932, at 18.
28. Stock Exchange Practices Hearings before Senate Banking Comm., 72d Cong. (1932), at 1–106, esp. at 16, 18, 32, 43–44; *New York Times*, Apr. 14, 1932, at 33.
29. Stock Exchange Practices Hearings, supra n. 28, at 111, 134, 145, 171–179, 219, 225, 253, 277–279.
30. Stock Exchange Practices Hearings, supra n. 28, at 307, 444–464; *New York Times*, Apr. 21, 1932 at 1, Apr. 26, 1932 at 1–2, Apr. 27, 1932 at 1.
31. Stock Exchange Practices Hearing, supra n. 28, at 466–476, 493–494, 518, 627–653, 677–689, 985–987.
32. Michael Perrino, The Hellhound of Wall Street: How Ferdinand Pecora's Investigation of the Great Crash Forever Changed American Finance (2010); *New York Times*, Nov. 18, 1932, at 27, Jan. 25, 1933, at 23, May 21, 1933, VIII at 2; David S. Levin, Regulating the Securities Industry: The Evolution of a Government Policy 196–198 (Colum. Univ. Ph.D. Dissertation 1969); *Newsweek*, June 10, 1933, at 16; William Leuchtenburg, Franklin D. Roosevelt and the New Deal 59 (Harper & Row 1963); Ralph DeBedts, The New Deal's SEC 41 (Colum. Univ. Press 1964).
33. Stock Exchange Practices Hearings, supra n. 28, at 1401–1532, 1615–1626, 1660–1666; Stock Exchange Practices Report, S. Rep. No. 1455, 73d Cong., 2d Sess. 360–362 (1934); Ferdinand Pecora, Wall Street Under Oath 224–233 (Simon & Schuster 1939); Forrest McDonald, Insull 273–315 (Univ. of Chicago Press 1962).
34. Carosso, supra n. 1, at 84–85, 97–98, 271–281.

35. Pecora, supra n. 33, at 71–92; Frederick Lewis Allen, The Lords of Creation 311–315 (Harper & Bros. 1935); Stock Exchange Practices Hearings, supra n. 28, at 1774–1775, 2028–2030; Bruce Barton, Is There Anything Here that Other Men Couldn't Do?, *American Magazine*, Feb. 23, 1923 at 16, 128–135; Bruce Barton, The Man Nobody Knows (Bobbs-Merrill 1924); Edmund Wilson, Sunshine Charley, *New Republic*, June 28, 1933, at 59, 177–178; Charles Mitchell, *Sound Inflation, Magazine of Wall Street*, June 9, 1917, at 295–296.
36. Pecora, supra n. 33, at 100–102, 127–129; Stock Exchange Practices Report, supra n. 33, at 107–109, 126–135; Stock Exchange Practices Hearings, supra n. 28, at 1779, 1811–1814, 2058–2069.
37. Stock Exchange Practices Report, supra n. 33, at 168–171; Stock Exchange Practices Hearings, supra n. 28, at 2000–2001, 2022; Pecora, supra n. 33, at 110–111.
38. Literary Digest, Mar. 11, 1933, at 11–12; Leuchtenburg, supra n. 32, at 22.
39. Wayne Flynt, Duncan Fletcher, Dixie's Reluctant Progressive 50, 169–170 (Florida St. Univ. Press 1971); DeBedts, supra n. 32, at 41–42; *New York Times*, May 6, 1933, at 98; Ernst Lindley, The Roosevelt Revolution 138–143 (Viking Press 1933).
40. Stock Exchange Practices Hearings, supra n. 28, at 3–4, 18, 76, 189; *New York Times*, May 24, 1933, at 1; *Literary Digest*, June 10, 1933, at 3; *New Republic*, June 7, 1933, at 98; *Newsweek*, June 3, 1933, at 1; *Time*, June 5, 1933, at 51–56; Lindley, supra n. 39, at 138–143; Pecora, supra n. 33, at 4–5; Levin, supra n. 32, at 231; Chernow, supra n. 1, at 356–391.
41. Pecora, supra n. 33, at 5; Stock Exchange Practices Hearing, supra n. 28, at 3–6, 22, 44–53, 72–80, 879; Stock Exchange Practices Report, supra n. 33, at 329–331; *New York Times*, May 24, 1933 at 1, June 2, 1933 at 1; William Harbaugh, Lawyer's Lawyer: The Life of John W. Davis 327–320 (Oxford Univ. Press 1973); Brooks, supra n. 3, at 191.
42. Stock Exchange Practices Hearings, supra n. 28, at 138–221, 370–373, 824–877; Stock Exchange Practices Report, supra n. 33, at 101–105; Pecora, supra n. 33, at 27–35; *New York Times*, May 25, 1933, at 14–15.
43. Stock Exchange Practices Hearings, supra n. 28, at 307–497; John Flynn, Security Speculation 155–157 (Harcourt, Brace 1934); Pecora, supra n. 33, at 21–25; Note, High Finance in the Twenties: The United Corporation, 37 Colum. L. Rev. 785 (1937).
44. *New York Times*, May 27, 1933, at 12; *New York Herald Tribune*, May 26, 1933, at 21; *Literary Digest*, June 10, 1933, at 4–5; *Business Week*, June 7, 1933, at 32.
45. *New York Times*, May 26, 1933, at 1; *New Republic*, June 7, 1933, at 98.

46. S. Resolution No. 93, *Cong. Rec.*, 73d Cong., 1st Sess. 5233 (June 8, 1933).
47. 2 The Public Papers and Addresses of Franklin D. Roosevelt at 213–214.
48. Raymond Moley, After Seven Years 23–24, 370–371 (Harper & Row 1939); Raymond Moley, The First New Deal 225, 306, 314 (Harcourt Brace & World 1966).
49. R.G. Tugwell, The Brains Trust 277–278, 525–528 (Viking Press 1968); R.G. Tugwell, The Industrial Discipline and the Government Arts 203–207 (Colum. Univ. Press 1933).
50. Adolf Berle, Navigating the Rapids 45–59 (Harcourt Brace Javanovich 1973).
51. Telegram to Hon. Franklin D. Roosevelt, Roosevelt Papers, PPF 1333; Michael Parrish, Securities Regulation and the New Deal 45–46 (Yale Univ. Press 1970); Carosso, supra n. 1, at 354–355; Homer Cherrington, The Investor and the Securities Act 43 (American Council on Pub. Affairs 1942); Huston Thompson, Regulation of the Sales of Securities in Interstate Commerce, 9 ABA J. 157 (1923); Letters to Roosevelt from Thompson, June 11, 1932, July 7, 1932, Nov. 25, 1933, Houston Thompson Papers, Container No. 3, Library of Congress & Roosevelt Papers PPF 1333; Letter to Thompson from Norris, Apr. 8, 1933, Container No. 3; Huston Thompson Diary, Apr. 21, 1933, Container No. 1.
52. Moley, After Seven Years, supra n. 48, at 176–177; Moley, The First New Deal, supra n. 48, at 308–309; Frank Friedel, Franklin D. Roosevelt: Launching the New Deal 77, 341–343 (Little Brown 1973); The Legend of Landis, *Fortune,* Aug. 1934, at 118.
53. Moley, After Seven Years, supra n. 48, at 165–166, 177; Moley, The First New Deal, supra n. 48, at 232, 310; Friedel, supra n. 52, at 342; The Legend of Landis, supra n. 52, at 118; Parrish, supra n. 51, at 44–47.
54. Hunter Thompson Diary, March 13, March 19, and March 20, 1933, Hunter Thompson Papers, Container No. 1, Library of Congress; Parrish, supra n. 51, at 44–51.
55. *Cong. Rec.*, 73d Cong., 1st Sess. 937, 954 (Mar. 29, 1933), reprinted in Federal Securities Act Hearings, House Commerce Comm. 1st Sess. 1 (1933).
56. The Text of Thompson's Bill, H.R. 4314, is in Federal Securities Act Hearings, supra n. 55, at 1–9, with accompanying analysis at 107–111. See also James Landis, The Legislative History of the Securities Act of 1933, 28 Geo. Wash. L. Rev. 29, 30–33 (1959); Parrish, supra n. 51, at 47–51.
57. Dwight Darrough, Mr. Sam (Random House 1962); Alfred Steinberg, Sam Rayburn: A Biography (Hawthorne Books 1975);

Raymond Moley, 27 Masters of Politics 242–249 (Funk & Wagnalls 1949).

58. Federal Securities Act Hearings, supra n. 55, at 9–91, 116–248; *New York Times*, Apr. 6, 1933, at 3; Moley, After Seven Years, supra n. 48, at 178–179; Friedel, supra n. 52, at 346–347; Parrish, supra n. 51, at 56–57.
59. Moley, The First New Deal, supra n. 48, at 312; Moley, After Seven Years, supra n. 48, at 179; Frankfurter Diary, May 8, 1933, Frankfurter Papers, Container No. 1, Library of Congress; Liva Baker, Felix Frankfurter 155 (Coward McCann 1969); Huston Thompson, Diary, May 5, 1933, Huston Thompson Papers, Container No. 1, Library of Congress; Joseph Lash, From the Diaries of Felix Frankfurter 44–47 (W.W. Norton 1975).
60. Felix Frankfurter & J. Forrester Davison, Cases and Materials on Administrative Law VII (CCH 1932).
61. Felix Frankfurter, The Public and Its Government 144, 152, 161 (Yale Univ. Press 1930); Parrish, supra n. 51, at 61; Letter to Lippmann quoted in Lash, supra n. 59, at 53; Frankfurter Letter to Lippmann, Apr. 17, 1933, Frankfurter Papers, Container No. 78, Library of Congress.
62. The Reminiscences of James Landis 1–146 (Colum. Univ. Oral History 1964); The Legend of Landis, supra n. 52, at 44–47, 118–120; Donald Ritchie, James M. Landis (Harvard Univ. Press 1980); James Landis, The Administrative Process (Yale Univ. Press 1938); James Landis, Crucial Issues in Administrative Law, 53 Harv. L. Rev. 1077 (1940); James Landis, Significance of Administrative Commissions in the Growth of the Law, 12 Indiana L.J. 474 (1937).
63. Landis, supra n. 56, at 34; William O Douglas, Go East, Young Man 369 (Dell 1974); Parrish, supra n. 51, at 59; Frankfurter Diary, May 8, 1933, Frankfurter Papers, Container No. 1, Library of Congress.
64. Joseph Aisop & Robert Kintner, Men Around the President 54–61 (Doubleday Doran 1939); Parish, supra n. 51, at 59–60; Letters to Frankfurter from Cohen, Jan. 1, 1934, and from Corcoran, Dec. 11, 1933, Frankfurter Papers, Container No. 116, Library of Congress.
65. Landis, supra n. 56, at 34–35; Landis, Reminiscences, supra n. 62, at 159–161.
66. Landis, supra n. 56, at 37–41; Parrish, supra n. 51, at 64–68; Letter to Manuel Cohen from Landis, Cohen SEC Papers, Vol. 41, Item 7; Landis Reminiscences, supra n. 62, at 164–167; Moley, The First New Deal, supra n. 48, at 312–313; Moley, After Seven Years, supra n. 48, at 181; *Cong. Rec.*, 73d Cong., 1st Sess. 2838 (May 3, 1933), 2907 (May 4, 1933), 2911–2954 (May 5, 1933); *New York Times*, May 6, 1933, at 1; Letter to Landis from Cohen, May 5, 1933, Landis Papers, Container No. 4, Library of Congress.

67. Thompson Testimony, Securities Act Hearings, Senate Banking Comm., 73d Cong., 1st Sess. 98, 103–105, 116 (1933), see also 145; Levin, supra n. 32, at 279–281; *Cong. Rec.* 2978 (May 8, 1933), 3801 (May 20, 1933); see generally for comparison of House and Senate Bills, Landis, Legislative Genesis of the 1933 Act.
68. Frankfurter Letters to Moley, Apr. 27, 1933, May 16, 1933, Frankfurter Papers, Reel 7, Harvard Law School; Telegram, Frankfurter Papers, Reel 7, Harvard Law School; Moley, The First New Deal, supra n. 48, at 313; *Cong. Rec.* 2978–3000 (May 8, 1033); Landis, supra n. 56, at 43–49; Landis Reminiscences, supra n. 62, at 169–172; Parrish, supra n. 51, at 70; Levin, supra n. 32, at 288–292; *Cong. Rec.* 3900–3903 (May 22, 1933).
69. Note, High Finance in the Twenties (III), 37 Colum. L. Rev. 1161 (1939); Felix Frankfurter, The New Federal Securities Act, Fortune 53–55, 106–111 (Aug. 1933).
70. New Republic, Apr. 26, 1933, at 309; Moley, The First New Deal, supra n. 48, at 314; Adolf Berle, High Finance: Master or Servant?, 23 Yale Rev. 42 (1933); William O Douglas, Protecting the Investor, 23 Yale Rev. 528 (1933); William O. Douglas & George Bates, The Federal Securities Act of 1933, 43 Yale L.J. 171 (1933).
71. Whitney quoted in Joseph Alsop & Robert Klutner, The Battle of the Market Place, *Saturday Evening Post,* June 15, 1938, at 9; SEC Press Release Nov. 23, 1937, reprinted in William O. Douglas, Democracy and Finance 65, 70 (Yale Univ. Press 1940).
72. Stock Exchange Practices Report, supra n. 33, at 5–6, 25, 47–50; Testimony of Richard Whitney, National Securities Exchange Hearings, House Commerce Comm., 73d Cong., 2d Sess. 216–217 (1934), see also 124; Twentieth Century Fund, Stock Market Control 18–19 (Appleton-Century 1934); Flynn, supra n. 43, at 24–26, 28, 62–69, 229–243; J. Edward Meeker, The Work of the Stock Exchange 63, 443–444 (Ronald Press rev. ed. 1930); Raymond Vernon, The Regulation of Stock Exchange Members 58–96 (Colum. Univ. Press 1941); Robert Sobet, NYSE 18–20 (Weybright & Talley 1975).
73. Matthew Josephson, Groton, Harvard, Wall Street, *New Yorker,* Apr. 2, 1932, at 19–22; *Literary Digest,* Apr. 23, 1932, at 42–43; Brooks, supra n. 3, at 124–128, 130–132, 142–143.
74. *Literary Digest,* July 1, 1933, at 6.
75. Arthur Dean, The Federal Securities Act: I, Fortune, Aug. 1933, at 104, 106; *New York Times,* Oct. 18, 1933, at 29.
76. See Parrish, supra n. 51, at 131–187.
77. Letter to Roosevelt from Wallace, Sept. 2, 1933, Roosevelt Papers, OF 396; Levin, supra n. 32, at 326, 329; Landis Reminiscences, supra n. 62, at 177.

78. Letters to Roosevelt from Frankfurter, July 6, 1933, Roosevelt Papers, PPF 140, Oct. 1, 1933, Felix Frankfurter PSF.
79. Landis Address to New York State Accountants reprinted in *Commercial & Fin. Chron.*, Nov. 4, 1933, at 3243.
80. *New York Times,* Oct. 11, 1933 at 33, Dec. 8, 1933 at 1; Jesse Jones, Fifty Billion Dollars 31 (MacMillan 1951); Letter to the President from Bruere, Oct. 27, 1933; Landis, Legislative History of the 1934 Securities Exchange Act, Vol. 8; Henry Bruere Memorandum, Roosevelt Papers, OF 213.
81. *New York Times,* Oct. 7, 1933, at 30; Letter to Roosevelt from Roper, Feb. 2, 1934, Roosevelt Papers, OF 242; Report to Secretary of Commerce of Committee on Stock Exchange Regulation, Roosevelt Papers, OF 242; Memorandum included in Landis, supra n. 80.
82. Letters to Roosevelt from Landis, Nov. 24, 1933, Roosevelt Papers, OF 100, Dec. 4, 1933, Landis Papers, Box 9, File 5; Landis Reminiscences, supra n. 62, at 197–198; Landis, supra n. 56, at 40 n. 18; Levin, supra n. 32, at 338–339; *New York Times,* Dec. 5, 1933, at 35.
83. *New York Times,* Dec. 3, 1933 at 1, Dec. 7, 1933 at 2, Dec. 14, 1933 at 35; *Wall St. J.*, Dec. 13, 1933, at 1; Landis, Legislative History of the 1934 Securities Exchange Act, Vol. 2; Levin, supra n. 32, at 347–348; Moley, After Seven Years, supra n. 48, at 284; Moley, The First New Deal, supra n. 48, at 517.
84. The Dickinson Report was reprinted in *Commercial & Fin. Chron.*, Feb. 10, 1934, at 925–930.
85. *New York Times,* Dec. 3, 1933, at 1; Donald Ritchie, The Legislative Impact of the Pecora Investigation, 5 Capital Studies 97 (1977); Landis, Legislative History of the 1934 Securities Exchange Act, Vol. 2.
86. *Cong. Rec.*, 73d Cong., 2d Sess. at 2264 (Feb. 9, 1934), 2356 (Feb. 10, 1934); *New York Times,* Feb. 10, 1934, at 1; *Nation,* Feb. 28, 1934, at 250; *Newsweek,* Feb. 17. 1934, at 26; Roosevelt Letter to Rayburn, Mar. 26, 1934, reprinted in H.R. Rep. No. 1383, 73d Cong. 2d Sess. 2 (1934).
87. *Cong. Rec.*, 73d Cong., 2d Sess. 2264–2272 (Feb. 9, 1934), 2378 (Feb. 10, 1934); *New York Times,* Feb. 10, 1934, at 1.
88. A copy of the Bill appears at 1–15, see also 134, 163, 480, 782 National Securities Exchange Hearings, House Commerce Comm. 73d Cong., 2d Sess. (1934); Stock Exchange Practices Hearings, Senate Banking Comm., 73 Cong., 2d Sess. 6356–6340 (1934); see also Parrish, supra n. 51, at 119; Pecora, supra n. 33, at 269; Roosevelt Press Conferences, Vol. 3, Feb. 28, 1934, at 210–211; Stock Exchange Practices Report, supra n. 33, at 391; Twentieth Century Fund, supra n. 72, at 170–173; *Commerce & Fin. Chron.*, Feb. 10, 1934, at 926.

89. *Cong. Rec.*, 73d Cong., 2d Sess. 8169–8174 (May 7, 1934); Stock Exchange Practices Report, supra n. 33, at 55–69, see also 189–203.
90. Ferdinand Pecora, Wall Street under the Flag, Mar. 30, 1935, at 12–13; Berle, supra n. 50, at 103–104; *New York Times,* Oct. 17, 1933, at 31, Oct. 19, 1933, at 12, Oct. 26, 1933, at 29, Oct. 31, 1933, at 29; Feb. 14, 1934, at 29, 31; Joseph Alsop & Robert Kintner, The Battle of the Market Place, *Saturday Evening Post,* June 11, 1938, at 9; Whitney Letter to Roosevelt, Feb. 8, 1934, Roosevelt Papers, PPF 1275.
91. Whitney's lobbying efforts are described in *New York Times,* Feb. 15, 1934, at 27, Feb. 17, 1934, at 21, and Mar. 12, 1934, at 1; Senate Stock Exchange Practices Hearing, supra n. 88, at 7281–7286; *Commercial & Fin. Chron.*, Mar. 31, 1934, at 2170, Apr. 14, 1934 at 2501; *Cong. Rec.*, 73d Cong., 2d Sess., Apr. 30, 1934, at 7689–7697, May 2, 1934, at 7925, 7934–7935, May 4, 1934, at 8097, May 7, 1934, at 8196–8197; *Newsweek,* May 19, 1934, at 27; Statement of the Board of Directors, U.S. Chamber of Commerce, Mar. 3, 1934, and Statement of the Standard Tobacco Company, both in Carter Glass Papers, Box No. 329; "SEC," *Fortune,* June 1940, at 123; Letter to Roosevelt from Herbert Lehman, Mar. 24, 1934, quoted in Ralph De Bedts, The New Deal's SEC 67 (Colum. Univ. Press 1964).
92. House National Stock Exchange Hearings, supra n. 88, at 187, 209–215, 237–246, 252, 272, 278–279, 298, 809–890; Senate Stock Exchange Hearings, supra n. 88, at 6584.
93. Letter to Frankfurter from Landis, Mar. 6, 1934, Frankfurter Papers, Container No. 117, Library of Congress; *New York Times,* Feb. 28, 1934, at 1, 2, Mar. 6, 1934, at 1, Mar. 8, 1934, at 1; House National Stock Exchange Hearings, supra n. 88, at 395.
94. House National Securities Exchange Hearings, supra n. 88, at 701–704, 809, 845; Senate Stock Exchange Practices Hearings, supra n. 88, at 7577–7578; Press Conferences of President Franklin D. Roosevelt, Vol. 3, Mar. 23, 1934, at 256; *New York Times,* Mar. 14, 1934 at 27, Apr. 3, 1934, at 1.
95. House National Securities Exchange Hearings, supra n. 88, at 723; Letter to Roosevelt from Whitney, Apr. 12, 1934, Roosevelt Papers, OF 34; Devesnine revised Bill and Memorandum, Landis Papers, Container No. 150, Library of Congress; Letter to Rayburn from Paul Shields, Mar. 22, 1934, Roosevelt Papers, OF 34; *New York Times,* Apr. 3, 1934, at 4, May 7, 1934, at 1.
96. *New York Times,* Apr. 10, 1934, at 1, Apr. 12, 1934, at 19, Apr. 15, 1934, II at 11; Senate Stock Exchange Hearings, supra n. 88, at 7555; *Wall St. J.*, Apr. 10, 1934, at 1; Parrish, supra n. 51, at 133–138; Levin, supra n. 32, at 388–394; *Cong. Rec.*, 73d Cong., 2d Sess., May 7, 1934, at 8286.

97. *Cong. Rec.*, 73d Cong., 2d Sess., Apr. 30, 1934, at 7693–7699, May 4, 1934, at 8116, May 12, 1934, at 8667–8669, 8710–8713; *New York Times*, May 13, 1934, at 1.
98. *New York Times*, May 16, 1934, at 1, 24, May 20, 1934, IV, at 1, May 26, 1934, at 25; *Commercial & Fin. Chron.*, May 19, 1934, at 3360–3361; Newsweek, May 26, 1934, at 24; Roosevelt Press Conferences, Vol. 3, May 16, 1934, at 348–350; Landis Memorandum, Reasons for Making the Federal Trade Commission the Administrative Agency for Securities Exchange Legislation, Carter Glass Papers, Box No. 316.
99. House Report No. 1383, 73d Cong., 2d Sess. (1934); *Cong. Rec.*, 73d Cong., 2d Sess., June 1, 1934, at 10,185, 10,269; Donald Ritchie, James M. Landis 59 (Harvard Univ. Press 1980); *New York Times*, June 7, 1934, at 7.
100. *New York Times*, May 27, 1934, at 1; *Newsweek*, June 9, 1934, at 28; *Time*, June 11, 1934, at 62; *Business Week*, June 9, 1934, at 9–10; *Fortune*, Aug. 1934, at 44–47, 118–120.
101. Thomas Corcoran Letter to Felix Frankfurter, May 10, 1934, Frankfurter Papers, Container No. 16, Library of Congress; James MacGregor Burns, Roosevelt: The Lion and the Fox 183–208 (Harcourt Brace & World 1956); Schlesinger, supra n. 20, at 503.
102. The Public Papers and Addresses of Franklin D. Roosevelt, Vol. 3 438–439 (Random House 1938).
103. Raymond Moley, And Now Give Us Good Men, *Today*, May 19, 1934, at 12; Moley, The First New Deal, supra n. 48, at 517–520; Moley, After Seven Years, supra n. 48, at 286–290.
104. Richard Whalen, The Founding Father: The Story of Joseph P. Kennedy 3–161 (New American Library 1964); David Koskoff, Joseph P. Kennedy: A Life and Times 42–69 (Prentice-Hall 1974); Moley, The First New Deal, supra n. 48, at 379–382; Joseph P. Kennedy, I'm for Roosevelt 7–8, 14–15, 106–107 (Reynal & Hitchcock 1936); Mr. Kennedy, the Chairman, *Fortune*, Sept. 1937, at 56–59, 138–144; Joseph P. Kennedy, Big Business: What Now?, *Saturday Evening Post*, Jan. 16, 1937, at 10–11, 78–82.
105. Whalen, supra n. 104, at 139–140; Moley, After Seven Years, supra n. 48, at 287–288; Moley, The First New Deal, supra n. 48, at 519; Koskoff, supra n. 104, at 57; Landis Reminiscences, supra n. 62, at 191–193.
106. *New Republic*, July 11, 1934, at 220, 236, July 18, 1934 at 265; Koskoff, supra n. 104, at 59; Moley, After Seven Years, supra n. 48, at 289.
107. Kennedy, I'm for Roosevelt, supra n. 104, at 97; *SEC Minutes*, Oct. 24, 1934, Oct. 26, 1934, Oct. 30, 1934, Dec. 10, 1934, Jan. 1, 1935.
108. Pecora, supra n. 90, at 60; *New York Times*, Dec. 21, 1934, at 43, Jan. 15, 1935, at 27, Jan. 17, 1935, at 32; *Commercial & Fin. Chron.*, Sept. 22, 1934, at 1787–1788, July 21, 1934, at 362.

109. *Cong. Rec.*, 73d Cong., 2d Sess., June 13, 1934, at 11, 238; Landis, Letter to Roosevelt, June 14, 1934, Roosevelt Papers, OF 1060; *New York Times*, Jan. 10, 1934, at 2, Jan. 11, 1935, at 36, Jan. 12, 1935, at 2, Jan. 13, 1935, II at 15, Jan. 18, 1935 at 3; *Commercial & Fin. Chron.*, Jan. 12, 1935, at 235.
110. *Commercial & Fin. Chron.*, July 27, 1934, at 362; *SEC Minutes*, July 16 & 17, 1934; Whalen, supra n. 104, at 150; *New York Times*, July 17, 1934, at 29; Burns Telegram to Frankfurter, May 10, 1935, Frankfurter Papers, Reel 10, Harvard Law School.
111. Landis, Reminiscences, supra n. 62, at 232–233; Douglas, supra n. 63, at 258–259; Letter to Landis from Douglas, July 12, 1934, Douglas Papers, Container No. 6, Library of Congress; *SEC Minutes*, Nov. 7, 1934, July 1, 1935, July 20, 1935.
112. *SEC First Ann. Rep.* 6–7, 38.
113. Kennedy, I'm for Roosevelt, supra n. 104, at 98–100; Joseph P. Kennedy, Regulation of Security Exchanges, Vital Speeches of the Day, Dec. 17, 1934, at 187–191.
114. *New York Times*, July 26, 1934, at 13.
115. *SEC First Ann. Rep.* at 20–21; *Commercial & Fin. Chron.*, July 28, 1934, at 522; *New York Times*, July 19, 1934, at 27, July 21, 1934, at 17, July 27, 1934, at 23, Aug. 8, 1934, at 29, Aug. 10, 1934, at 28, Aug. 17, 1934, at 23, Sept. 11, 1934, at 29, Sept. 12, 1934, at 40, Sept. 13, 1934, at 13, Sept. 14, 1934, at 34; *SEC Minutes*, Nov. 27, 1934, Nov. 28, 1934; Kennedy, I'm for Roosevelt, supra n. 104, at 99–100.
116. *Commercial & Fin. Chron.*, July 28, 1934, at 522, Feb. 2, 1935, at 719; *Literary Digest*, Nov. 24, 1934, at 40; *New York Times*, Feb. 8, 1935, at 7.
117. *New York Times*, July 4, 1934, at 25, Jan. 20, 1935, IX, at 2; *SEC Minutes*, Oct. 1, 1934, (Kansas City Board of Trade), Oct. 5, 1934 (New York Mining Exchange), Oct. 16, 1934 (Los Angeles Curb Exchange), Nov. 22, 1934 (California Stock Exchange), June 21, 1935 (Merger of two Seattle Exchanges), July 29, 1934 (Pacific Stock Exchange), and Aug. 5, 1935 (Louisville Stock Exchange); *New York Times*, July 1, 1935, at 31 (Boston Curb Exchange, Hartford Stock Exchange, and Philippine Stock Exchange). See also 1934 Sec. Ex. Act Rels. No. 62 (1934), 78 (1934), and 183 (1935); Joseph P. Kennedy, "Shielding the Sheep," *Saturday Evening Post*, Jan. 18, 1936, at 64,068. The New York Produce Exchange's discontinuance of securities operations is described in 1934 Sec. Ex. Act Rel. 76 (1035). The termination of unlisted trading on the Baltimore Stock Exchange is described in *SEC Minutes*, July 17, 1935; *SEC First Annual Report*, at 31; Joseph Alsop & Robert Kintner, The Battle of the Market Place, *Saturday Evening Post*, June 11, 1938, at 76.
118. *SEC Minutes*, Aug. 11, 1934, Aug. 28, 1934, Sept. 27, 1934, Nov. 28, 1934, Dec. 5, 1934, Dec. 11, 1934, Dec. 12, 1934, Dec. 17, 1934,

Dec. 18, 1934; Sec. Ex. Act Rels. 5 (1934), 18 (1934), 66 (1934); *New York Times*, Aug. 14, 1934, at 1, 30, Sept. 15, 1934, at 21; *SEC First Ann. Rep.* at 17, 24.

119. Compare Sec. Act Rel. 224 (1934), with 299 (1935).
120. Joseph P. Kennedy, Regulating the Securities Exchanges, Vital Speeches of the Day, Dec. 17, 1934, at 189; *SEC Minutes*, Dec. 5, 1934, Dec. 12, 1934, Jan. 5, 1935, Jan. 10, 1935, Jan. 11, 1935, Jan. 12, 1935; *New York Times*, Dec. 9, 1934, IV, at 1.
121. *New York Times*, Jan. 14, 1935, at 1; *Commercial & Fin. Chron.*, Jan. 19, 1935, at 382; Sec. Act Rel. 276 (1935).
122. *New York Times*, Mar. 9, 1935, at 1; Sec. Act Rel. 322 (1935); *SEC Minutes*, Feb. 28, 1935; Paul Gourrich, Investment Banking Methods Prior to and Since the Securities Act of 1933, 4 Law & Contemp. Prob. 69 (1937).
123. Sec. Act Rels. 317 (1935), 328 (1935), 381 (1935), 389 (1935), 458 (1935), 470 (1935); R.W. Goldschmidt, Registration under the Securities Act of 1933, 4 Law & Contemp. Prob. 28 (1937).
124. *Time*, July 22, 1935; see also *New Republic*, Oct. 9, 1935, at 244.
125. Report on the Government of Securities Exchanges, H.R. Doc. No. 85, 74th Cong., 1st Sess. (1935).
126. *New York Times*, Mar. 19, 1935, at 31, Mar. 21, 1935, at 33; Sec. Ex. Act Rel. 131 (1935).
127. *New York Times*, Feb. 26, 1935, at 27, Mar. 5, 1935, at 33, Mar. 8, 1935, at 31, Mar. 23, 1935, at 23, Apr. 6, 1935, at 1, Apr. 9, 1935, at 31; DeBedts, supra n. 32, at 146–147.
128. *New York Times*, Apr. 14, 1935, at 8, May 14, 1935, at 29, May 15, 1935, at 31; DeBedts, supra n. 32, at 148; *Business Week*, May 18, 1935, at 2021.
129. The Rules are reprinted in an Appendix to the *SEC First Ann. Rep.*; see also *SEC Minutes*, Oct. 2, 1934, Jan. 3, 1935, Apr. 12, 1935, Apr. 15, 1935, Apr. 16, 1935, May 22, 1935.
130. Kennedy, I'm for Roosevelt, supra n. 104, at 97; Whalen, supra n. 104, at 174–175; Public Papers and Addresses of Franklin D. Roosevelt, Vol. 4, at 220; *New York Times*, June 2, 1935, III, at 1, June 13, 1935, at 39; *SEC First Ann. Rep.* at 32; Jones v. SEC, 298 U.S. 1 (1936).
131. Frankfurter letter to Jerome Frank, June 10, 1935, Frankfurter Papers, Container No. 55, Library of Congress.
132. *New York Times*, July 10, 1935, at 7; Memorandum for Missy LeHand (for Roosevelt) from Kennedy, July 15, 1935, Douglas SEC Commissioner Files; *Wall St. J.*, Aug. 24, 1935, at 1; *New York Times*, Aug. 24, 1935, at 3; Douglas, supra n. 63, at 267; Kennedy letter to Roosevelt, Sept. 6, 1935, Roosevelt Papers, PPF 207.

133. *Time,* June 11, 1934, at 62; Corcoran letter to Frankfurter, May 11, 1934, Frankfurter Papers, Container No. 116, Library of Congress; *New York Times,* Sept. 24, 1935, at 37.
134. Landis, The Administrative Process, supra n. 62, at 2, 10, 12, 14–16.
135. Landis letter to Arthur Hays Sulzberger, July 3, 1936, SEC Commissioner Files, Container No. 1.
136. Douglas, supra n. 63, at 265–266.
137. Utility Corporation Summary Report of the FTC to the Senate, 70th Cong., 1st Sess. Doc. No. 92, Pt. 72-A, at 38–39, 46–49, 118–126 & Pt. 73-A at 32–33, 57; *SEC 26th Ann. Rep.* at xvii–xviii.
138. FTC Utility Corporation Report, supra n. 137, Pt. 72-A at 75, 136–154; Twentieth Century Fund. Electric Power and Government Policy 35–36 (Twentieth Century Fund 1948).
139. FTC Utility Corporation Report, supra n. 137, Pt. 72-A at 298–303, 496–515, 845, Pt. 73-A at 64.
140. Report of National Power Policy Committee, 74th Cong., 1st Sess. (1935), H. Doc. No. 137, at 8–12; Parrish, supra n. 51, at 153–159.
141. 1 Louis Loss, Joel Seligman & Troy Parades, Securities Regulation 382–398 (6th ed. 2019); Ellis Hawley, The New Deal and the Problem of Monopoly 325–337 (Princeton Univ. Press 1966); Parrish, supra n. 51, at 145–178; Schlesinger, supra n. 4, at 302–324; DeBedts, supra n. 32, at 112–143; Philip Fungiello, Toward a National Power Policy 3–121 (Univ. of Pittsburgh Press 1973).
142. Edison Elec. Inst., Federal Domination of Local Business, Landis Files, Box 11, File 10, Harvard Law School.
143. *New York Times,* Sept. 13, 1935, at 9.
144. *New York Times,* Sept. 25, 1935, at 35, Sept. 26, 1935, at 33.
145. American States Pub. Serv. Co., 12 F. Supp. 667 (D. Md. 1935).
146. *New York Times,* Nov. 9, 1935, at 4, Dec. 2, 1935, at 1; Parrish, supra n. 51, at 219–220; Douglas, supra n. 63, at 277–278; *SEC Minutes,* Oct. 7, 1935; SEC Second Ann. Rep. at 37, 52; SEC Third Ann. Rep. at 49.
147. FTC Utility Corporation Report, supra n. 137, at 56, 84–92, 169–170, 215, 258–265, 322–323, 335–336, 363–365, 394–395, 405–407, 427, 462–466, 476, 486–487, 510–519, 599–621, 844; H. Rep. No. 827, 73d Cong., 2d Sess. Pt. 3, 437–468 (1934).
148. SEC v. Elec. Bond & Share, 18 F. Supp. 131 (S.D.N.Y. 1937).
149. Electric Bond & Share Co., 303 U.S. 419 (1938).
150. *New York Times,* Apr. 5, 1938, at 43.
151. *SEC Fifth Ann. Rep.* at 70, *New York Times,* Aug. 5, 1938, at 21.
152. *New York Times,* Dec. 2, 1938, at 35; *Business Week,* Dec. 10, 1938, at 20; Parrish, supra n. 51, at 236.
153. Pub. Utility Holding Co. Act. Rel. 1946 (1940); Letter to Seligman from Robert O'Brien, Sept. 10, 1980.

154. *SEC 18th Ann. Rep.* at 136; Milton Freeman, A Private Practitioner's View of the Development of the Securities and Exchange Commission, 28 Geo. Wash. L. Rev. 23 (1959).
155. *SEC Tenth Ann. Rep.* at 115, n. 56; Robert Ritchie, Integration of Public Utility Holding Companies 21–23 (U. Mich. Law School 1954).
156. Internal Rev. Code, Feb. 10, 1939, Supp. R. §§ 371–372 and 1942 Amendments, 56 Stat. Ch. 619 at 960.
157. Columbia Gas & Elec. Corp., 8 SEC 460 (1941); United Gas Improvement Co., 9 SEC 218 (1942); Engineers Pub. Serv. Co., 7 SEC 774 (1941); North Am. Co., 11 SEC 206 (1942); Ritchie, supra n. 155, at 25–33, 230–292.
158. Ritchie, supra n. 155, at 220–229; Ernst Adams, Ten Years of the Public Utility Act of 1935, *Pub. Util. Fortnightly*, Nov. 8, 1945, at 619; Middle Co. Corp., 15 SEC 309 (1944); Columbia Gas & Elec. Corp., 17 SEC 494 (1944); American Gas & Elec. Corp., Holding Co. Act Rel. 6333 (1945); Commonwealth & S. Corp., Holding Act Rel. 7615 (1947); Milton Cohen Interview, Aug. 4, 1980.
159. *SEC Tenth Ann. Rep.* at 97.
160. North Am Co. v. SEC, 327 U.S. 686 (1946); American Power & Light v. SEC, 329 U.S. 90 (1946); *SEC 13th Ann. Rep.* at 225; *14th Ann. Rep.* at 57; *25th Ann. Rep.* at xxv–xxvii; *SEC 18th Ann. Rep.* at 83–86.
161. *SEC Fourth Ann. Rep.* at 7–8; *15th Ann. Rep.* at 115–116; United Corp., 13 SEC 854 (1943); United Corp., Holding Co. Act. Rel. 13,088 (1956); Ritchie, supra n. 155, at 99–103.
162. Pub. L. No. 109–58, 119 Stat. 594. In 2005, the Public Utility Holding Company Act, long having since spent its force, would be repealed.
163. SEC, Report on Trading in Unlisted Securities Upon Exchanges 1–3 (1936); Milton Katz Interview, Oct. 6, 1979; *New York Times*, Oct. 5, 1937, at 35.
164. SEC, Report on Trading in Unlisted Securities Upon Exchanges, at 4–6, 8, 12–13, 15–16; SEC *Second Annual Report*, at 116; *Business Week*, May 16, 1936, at 37–38; *New York Times*, May 20, 1936, at 33; Landis Testimony, Trading in Unlisted Securities Upon Exchanges Hearings, Senate Banking Committee, 74th Cong., 2d Sess. (1936), at 1–15, 19–46; Landis, Address Before the National Association of State Security Commissioners, Nov. 12, 1934, at 5, on file with the SEC; *New York Times*, Jan. 1, 1936, at 41. See also Parrish, supra n. 51, at 213–214; Landis letters to Manuel Cohen, Cohen SEC Papers, Vol. 32, item 25, and Vol. 33, item 6.
165. SEC, Report on the Feasibility and Advisability of the Complete Segregation of the Functions of Dealer and Broker 65–77 (1936); SEC *Second Annual Report*, at 21; Rudolph Weissman, The New Wall Street 175 (Harper & Brothers 1939); William Taft Lesh, Federal Regulation of Over-the-Counter Brokers and Dealers in Securities, 59 Harv.

L. Rev. at 1237–1243 (1946); *Time*, July 22, 1935, at 42–43; *New York Times*, Mar. 1, 1936, IV, at 7.

166. James Landis, Address before New England Council, Boston, Mass., Nov. 22, 1935, on file with SEC; Sec. Ex. Act Rel. 451 (1935).

167. *SEC Minutes*, Dec. 14, 1936, Jan. 16, 1937, May 10, 1937, June 29, 1937; *New York Times*, May 21, 1936, at 39, Oct. 5, 1937, at 35 and 42; Parrish, supra n. 51, at 210; Ritchie, supra n. 62, at 73–74. The Simpson-Ballinger Report, entitled Studies on the Feasibility and Advisability of the Complete Segregation of the Functions of Dealer and Broker, is on file at the SEC.

168. SEC, Report on the Feasibility and Advisability of the Complete Segregation of the Functions of Dealer and Broker, at 16–17, 101–102, 108–113.

169. *SEC Minutes*, Nov. 19, 1936; *New York Times*, Nov. 19, 1936, at 39; Nov. 20, 1936, at 35, Jan. 4, 1937, at 37, Apr. 7, 1937, at 40.

170. Jones v. SEC, 298 U.S. 1 (1936).

171. Landis, The Administrative Process, supra n. 62, at 136–140; Robert Kintner, The SEC Dictatorship, American Mercury, June 1936, at 180–187; *New York Times*, Apr. 8, 1936, at 22; Roland Richmond, The Securities Exchange Act of 1934: An Experiment in Administrative Law, 47 Yale L.J. 622, 635–646 (1938);The Public Papers and Addresses of Franklin D. Roosevelt, Vol. 5, at 679; Kenneth Culp Davis, Handbook on Administrative Law 6–9 (West. Pub. 1951); George Warren, ed., The Federal Administrative Procedure Act and the Administrative Agencies 10–13 (New York University School of Law 1947); Jerome Frank, If Men Were Angels, at 18–32, 51–52, 141–146, 163, 179, 184–185 (Harper & Brothers 1942); *SED 12th Annual Report*, at 128–129; James Landis, Crucial Issues in Administrative Law, 53 Harv. L. Rev. 1102 (1940); Note, The Federal Administrative Procedure Act, 56 Yale L.J. 670–674, 703, n. 203 (1947); Administrative Procedure in Government Agencies (The Acheson Committee Final Report), Senate Doc. No. 8, 77th Cong., 1st Sess. (1941), especially at 7024; S. 915 and H.R. 6324 (The Walter-Logan Bill), 76th Cong., 1st Sess. (1939); Comments of the SEC on Enrolled Bill H.R. 6324, and letter to Henry Ashhurst from Jerome Frank, May 6, 1940, Frank SEC Commissioner Files, Container No. 26; Memo on the Administrative Law Bill, July 22, 1939, Either SEC Commissioner Files, Container No. 33; Letter to James Landis from Sam Rayburn, May 14, 1940, Landis Papers, Container No. 27, Library of Congress.

172. Kenneth Culp Davis, Handbook of Administrative Law 6–9 (West Publishing 1951); George Warren, ed., The Federal Administrative Procedure Act and the Administrative Agencies 10–13 (New York Univ. School of Law 1947); Jerome Frank, If Men Were Angels 18,

32, 51–52, 141–146, 163 (Harper & Brothers 1942); SEC Twelfth Ann. Rep. at 128–129; James Landis, Crucial Issues in Administrative Law, 53 Harv. L. Rev. 1102 (1940); Note, The Federal Administrative Procedure Act, 56 Yale L.J. 607–674, 703, n. 203; Administrative Procedure in Government Agencies, Senate Doc. No. 8, 77th Cong., 1st Sess. (1941); S. 915, H.R. 6324, 76th Cong., 1st Sess. (1939); Comments of the SEC on Enrolled Bill H.R. 6324, Letter to Henry Ashhurst from Jerome Frank, May 6, 1940, Frank SEC Commissioner Files, Container No. 26; Memo on the Administrative Law Bill, July 22, 1939, Eicher SEC Commissioner Files, Container No. 33; Letter to James Landis from Sam Rayburn, May 14, 1940, Landis Papers, Container No. 27, Library of Congress.

173. Landis letter to Roosevelt, Jan. 13, 1937, Landis Papers, Container No. 13, Library of Congress; Ritchie, supra n. 155, at 75; *New York Times*, Jan. 12, 1937, at 25, May 22, 1937, at 21, May 25, 1937, at 41, Sept. 16, 1937, at 24, Sept. 23, 1937, at 45; *New York Herald Tribune*, Jan. 12, 1937, at 16; *New Republic*, Jan. 27, 1937, at 384; Douglas, supra n. 63, at 258–281; William O. Douglas, Democracy and Finance (Yale Univ. Press 1940); *New Republic*, Jan. 20, 1937, at 357; *Nation*, Jan. 23, 1937, at 86–87; Holding Co. Act Rels. 486 (1936), 521 (1937); Landis Reminiscences, supra n. 62, at 302–303; Milton Katz Interview, Oct. 6, 1979; Douglas Papers, Container No. 21, Library of Congress; Landis Letter to Roosevelt, Sept. 11, 1937, Roosevelt Papers, OF 1060 and PPF 4858.

174. Douglas, supra n. 63, Douglas, supra n. 173, Foreword 28 Geo. Wash. L. Rev. at 1–5 (1959); DeBedts, supra n. 32, at 152–159; Parrish, supra n. 51, at 179–186; Chester Lane, Oral History, Memoir (Columbia Univ. Oral History Research Office 1957), at 330–331, 343–344, 413; Douglas Papers, especially biographical materials in Containers Nos. 6, 10, 13, 16, 24, Library of Congress; John T. Flynn, Washing Wall Street's Face, *Collier's*, Jan. 29, 1938, at 12–13; Max Lerner, Wall Street's New Mentor, *Nation*, Oct. 23, 1937, at 429–432; Transcript of Douglas's Press Conference Sept. 22, 1937, Douglas Papers, Container No. 21, Library of Congress; Memorandum to the President from Douglas, Feb. 24, 1938, Roosevelt Papers, OF 1060; Frankfurter-Douglas correspondence dated Dec. 8, 1933, Jan. 16, 1934, Feb. 19, 1934, Douglas Papers, Container No. 6, Library of Congress; Letter to Willis Ballinger from Douglas, Douglas Papers, Container No. 10, Library of Congress; Interview with Abe Fortas, Dec. 28, 1979, Washington, D.C.

175. James MacGregor Burns, Roosevelt: The Lion and the Fox 291–380 (Harcourt, Brace & World 1956); William E. Leuchtenburg, Franklin D. Roosevelt and the New Deal 231–274 (Harper & Row 1963); Ellis Hawley, The New Deal and the Problem of Monopoly

380–419 (Princeton University Press 1966). The economic background is described in Kenneth Roose, The Economics of Recession and Revival 20–55 (Yale University Press 1954); Charles Kindleberger, The World in Depression 271–277 (Berkeley: University of California Press 1973).

176. Interview with Abe Fortas, Dec. 28, 1979.
177. *SEC Minutes*, Oct. 18, 1937; *New York Times*, Oct. 15, 1937, at 12, Dec. 11, 1937, at 25; *Time*, Dec. 20, 1937, at 53; *Business Week*, Dec. 18, 1937, at 18; Douglas, supra n. 63, at 267; Parrish, supra n. 51, at 199; Memorandum to Frank from Hanes, Apr. 15, 1938, Frank Papers, Box 28, File No. 290, Yale; *New Republic*, Dec. 15, 1937, at 169.
178. Alsop & Kintner, supra n. 90, June 25, 1938, at 10; Wall Street Itself, *Fortune*, June 1937 at 160; *Business Week*, June 18, 1938, at 22; Rudolph Weissman, The New Wall Street 283 (Harper & Brothers 1939); Lane, Oral History Memoir at 330–331; Fred Rodell, Douglas Over the Stock Exchange, *Fortune*, Feb. 1938, at 120–122; Memorandum to Douglas from Milton Katz, Oct. 11, 1937, Douglas SEC Commissioner Files; Douglas Press Conference, Sept. 22, 1937, Douglas Papers, Container No. 21, Library of Congress.
179. Alsop & Kintner, supra n. 90, June 25, 1938, at 78–80; DeBedts, supra n. 32, at 160–163; Memorandum to Douglas from SEC New York Regional Office, Oct. 15, 1937, Douglas SEC Commissioner Files.
180. Douglas Nov. 23 Press Rel. reprinted in Douglas, Democracy and Finance, supra n. 173, at 63–73.
181. *New York Times*, Nov. 30, 1937, at 12.
182. Sobel, NYSE 37–38 (Weybright & Talley 1975); *New York Times*, Dec. 11, 1937, at 25, Dec. 15, 1937, at 39; *Time*, Aug. 15, 1938, at 44, 46.
183. Ganson Purcell Memorandum, Problems of Organization and Administration of the New York Stock Exchange, Undated, Douglas SEC Commissioner Files.
184. Sec. Ex. Act Rels. 1548 (1938) (adoption); 2039 (1939) (modification of rule).
185. *New York Times*, Jan. 28, 1938, at 1.
186. *New York Times*, Feb. 2, 1938, at 27.
187. *New York Times*, Feb. 1, 1938, at 25, Feb. 24, 1938, at 29; Alsop & Kintner, supra n. 90, at 81–82; Sobel, supra n. 182, at 42–45.
188. SEC, Richard Whitney Vol. I at 1, 51; Douglas, supra n. 63, at 289; Alsop & Kintner, supra n. 90, at 82; *New York Times*, Mar. 9, 1938, at 1; Lane, supra n. 178, at 330–331; Douglas & John W. Hanes Memoranda, Mar. 7, 9 (1938), Douglas SEC Commissioner Files; *SEC Minutes*, Mar. 8, 1938.

189. *New York Times*, Mar. 10, 1938, at 1, Mar. 11, 1938, at 1, 4, Mar. 12, 1938, at 1, 18, Mar. 15, 1938, at 1, 12, Mar. 17, 1938, at 22, Mar. 18, 1938, at 29; SEC, Richard Whitney, supra n. 188, at 1–3, 53–55.
190. Douglas, supra n. 63, at 289–290.
191. Ibid; Telegram to Thomas E. Dewey from Douglas, Mar. 22, 1938, Douglas SEC Commissioner Files; I.F. Stone, Questions on the Whitney Case, *Nation*, Jan. 14, 1938, at 55–58; *SEC Minutes*, Apr. 1–6, 1938; Sec. Ex. Act Rel. 1640 (1938); SEC, Richard Whitney, supra n. 188, at 2–3.
192. Richard Whitney, supra n. 188.
193. Letter to William McChesney Martin from Douglas, Jan. 26, 1939, Douglas Papers, Container No. 30, Library of Congress; Letter to Douglas from Hutchins, Jan. 26, 1939, Douglas Papers, Container No. 30, Library of Congress; Letter to John Hanes from Jerome Frank, Frank Papers, Box 28, File No. 290, Yale.
194. Douglas Memorandum, Possible Alternative Courses by SEC Re: the Whitney Case in the Light of Recent White-Wash, Dec. 18, 1938, Douglas SEC Commissioner Files; *SEC Minutes*, Dec. 22, 1938; Letter to William McChesney Martin from Douglas, Dec. 27, 1938, Douglas SEC Commissioner Files; Interview with Milton Katz, Oct. 6, 1979; Memorandum to Douglas from Paul Gourrich, Oct. 31, 1938, Douglas SEC Commissioner Files.
195. *New York Times*, Mar. 18, 1938, at 29.
196. *New York Times*, Apr. 12, 1938, at 33; Sobel, supra n. 182, at 55; *Fortune*, Aug. 1938, at 48.
197. *Fortune*, Aug. 1938, at 47–48, 85–86; *Time*, Aug. 15, 1938, at 40–47; John Flynn, Lamb of Wall Street, *Collier's*, July 30, 1938, at 11, 41–42; *Business Week*, July 9, 1938, at 13–14; *New York Times*, May 14, 1938, at 2, July 1, 1938, at 25, July 2, 1938, at 17.
198. Douglas Address reprinted in Douglas, supra n. 173, at 79–91.
199. *SEC Minutes*, May 17 & 19, 1938; Memorandum of Conference Between Representatives of the Commission and Representatives of the New York Stock Exchange at the Hotel Powhatan, May 18, 1938, Douglas SEC Commissioner Files; *SEC Minutes*, Mar. 18, 1938, July 19, 1938, July 28, 1938, Aug. 6, 1938, Oct. 20, 1938, Nov. 22, 1938; *New York Times*, July 23, 1938, at 17, July 24, 1938, at 3, Dec. 23, 1938, at 27; Memorandum to the Commission from Ganson Purcell Re: Broker-Dealer Segregation Experiment Proposed by New York Stock Exchange Committee on Floor Procedure, July 27, 1938, Douglas SEC Commissioner Files; Memorandum of NYSC Conference, Aug. 25, 1938, Douglas SEC Commissioner Files; SEC, Richard Whitney, Pt. II, supra n. 188.
200. SEC Fifth Annual Rep. at 44, Sixth Ann. Rep. at 82–87, Tenth Ann. Rep. at 38–39; Alsop & Kintner, supra n. 90, at 10.

201. *New York Times,* Dec. 21, 1937, at 35; *SEC Minutes,* Oct. 11, 1937; Douglas, supra n. 63, at 82; Douglas Hartford Speech quoted in Weissman, supra n. 165, at 186–188; *New York Times,* Jan. 8, 1938, at 21.
202. Regulation of Over-the-Counter Markets Hearings before Senate Banking Comm., 75th Cong., 3d Sess. 1–6 (1938); Memorandum for Douglas from Roosevelt, Feb. 1, 1938, OF 1060.
203. *New York Times,* Jan. 23, 1938, III, at 1; § 15A of the Act as adopted.
204. *New York Times,* Feb. 26, 1938, at 19, Mar. 2, 1938, at 29, Mar. 11, 1938, at 27; § 15A(m) of the Maloney Act; Letter to Douglas from Frankfurter, Jan. 16, 1934, Douglas Papers, Container No. 6, Library of Congress; Memorandum to Roosevelt from Douglas, Mar. 16, 1938, Douglas SEC Commissioner Files; *SEC Minutes,* Apr. 22, 1935, Apr. 29, 1938.
205. Robert T. Swaine, "Democratization" of Corporate Reorganizations, 38 Col. L. Rev. 257–262 (1938); E. Merrick Dodd, The Securities and Exchange Commission's Reform Program for Bankruptcy Reorganizations, 38 Col. L. Rev. 225, 245–255 (1938); a copy of the Lea Committee Bill and related hearings appear in To Amend the Securities Act of 1933, Hearings, House Commerce Committee, 75th Cong., 1st Sess. (1937).
206. To Amend the Securities Act Hearings, supra n. 205, at 307–320.
207. The Chandler Bankruptcy Revision Act appears in 52 Stat. 840. Its legislative history is discussed in H. Rep. No. 1409, 75th Cong., 1st Sess. (1937); S. Rep. Nos. 1916 and 2073, 75th Cong., 3d Sess. (1938); Revision of the Bankruptcy Act Hearings, House Judiciary Com., 76th Cong., 1st Sess. 1–8, 162–197 (1939); Revision of the National Bankruptcy Act Hearings, Senate Judiciary Subcommittee, 75th Cong., 2d Sess. 1–16 (1937–1938); Edward Altman, Corporate Bankruptcy in America 5–19 (D.C. Heath, 1971); Dodd, supra n. 205, at 223–245; SEC Fifth Annual Report at 7–9, 14–15; SEC Protective Committee Study Report at 868–869, 897–902.
208. Letter to Arthur Corbin from Douglas, Mar. 12, 1938, Douglas Papers, Container No. 23.
209. Regulation of Sale of Securities Hearings, Senate Banking Committee, 75th Cong., 1st Sess. 15–42, 87–88, 185–195 (1937); Trust Indentures Hearings, House Commerce Committee, 75th Cong., 3d Sess. 16–43, 72–75 (1938); Trust Indentures Hearings, House Commerce Committee, 76th Cong., 1st Sess. 35–56 (1939); Trust Indenture Act Hearings, Senate Banking Committee, 76th Cong., 1st Sess. 17–71, 99–123 (1939); Letter from R.G. Page to President of the Member Addressed, American Bankers Association, Aug. 26, 1936, Douglas SEC Commissioner Files; Letter to Senator Robert F. Wagner from Franklin D. Roosevelt, May 24, 1937, Douglas Papers, Container No. 20, Library of Congress; *SEC Minutes,* Mar. 7, 8, 1938;

Memorandum to Mr. Burke and Mr. McKellar from Chairman Douglas, Dec. 28, 1938, Douglas SEC Commissioner Files; and *New York Times,* May 3, 1939, at 35. The Trust Indenture Act is at 53 Stat. 1149–1178.

210. Douglas, supra n. 63, at 274–276; George Mathews, Accounting in the Regulation of Security Sales, 13 Acct. Rev. 226 (1938); *SEC Minutes,* Feb. 12, 1938, Mar. 25, 1938, Apr. 13, 1938; Maurice Kaplan & Daniel Reaugh, Accounting Reports to Stockholders and the SEC, 48 Yale L.J. 965, 978 (1939); Carman Blough, The Relationship of the Securities and Exchange Commission to the Accountant, 63 J. Acct. 23 (1937).

211. *New York Times,* May 25, 1938, at 6, Mar. 1, 1939, at 14; Testimony of William Greer, Federal Licensing of Corporations Hearings, Senate Judiciary Subcommittee, 75th Cong., 1st Sess. 87–89 (1937); Letter to Frankfurter from Douglas, Feb. 19, 1934, Douglas Papers, Container No. 6, Library of Congress.

212. William O Douglas, Directors Who Do Not Direct, 47 Harv. L. Rev. 1315 (1934); Douglas, supra n. 63, at 46–55.

213. Cong. Rec., 74th Cong., 1st Sess. 12,452, 12,551–12,556 (1938); Federal Licensing of Corporations, Senate Judiciary Subcommittee, 75th Cong., 1st Sess. (1937).

214. Cong. Rec., 75th Cong., 1st Sess. 178–179 (Jan. 12, 1937), 494–498 (Nov. 30, 1937); Harold Ickes, The Secret Diary: Vol. 2, 263, 283–287 (Simon & Schuster 1954); *New York Times,* Dec. 31, 1937, at 1, Jan. 2, 1938, at 1; Hawley, supra n. 175, at 388–419; Burns, supra n. 175, at 319–328; Leuchtenburg, supra n. 175, at 246–259; Joseph Alsop & Robert Kintner, We Shall Make America Over, *Saturday Evening Post,* Nov. 19, 1938, at 14–15, 85–92.

215. The Public Papers and Addresses of Franklin D. Roosevelt 305–320 (1938); Pub. Res. No. 113, 75th Cong., 3d Sess. (1938); Hawley, supra n. 175, at 411–419.

216. TNEC Final Report, at 24–29, 681–684; Dwight McDonald, The Monopoly Committee: A Study in Frustration, 8 American Scholar 295 (1939).

217. SEC Protective Committee Study, supra n. 207, Pt. 7, at 412–413; *SEC Minutes,* Dec. 30, 1938, Feb. 1, 1939; Memorandum to Jerome Frank from Thomas Lynch, Mar. 24, 1939, Douglas SEC Commissioner Files.

218. Tamar Frankel, The Regulation of Money Managers, Vol. 1 at 21–28 (Little Brown 1978); SEC Seventh Ann. Rep. at 29–35; Hugh Bullock, The Story off Investment Companies 14 (Columbia Univ. Press, 1959); Galbraith, supra n. 2, at 51; Stock Exchange Practices, Report of the Senate Banking Committee, Rep. No. 1455, 73d Cong., 2d

Sess. 333–359 (1934); SEC, Investment Trusts and Investment Companies, I, 1–2 and 36, II 363, 386–387, III 40, 43.

219. Investment Trusts and Investment Company Hearings, Senate Banking Subcomm., 76th Cong., 3d Sess. 34 (1940); SEC Investment Trusts, supra n. 218, I at 4, III at 44–47; John Flynn, Investment Trusts Gone Wrong (New Republic 1931).

220. Investment Trust Study, Aug. 7, 1935, Landis Papers, Container No. 6, Files 10–11, Harvard Law School; Interview with Harry Heller, May 20, 1980; SEC, Investment Trusts, supra n. 218, II at 27–38, III at 48.

221. SEC, Investment Trusts, supra n. 218, III at 34, 276, 879, 943, 1598–1603, 1665–1667; Stock Exchange Practices Report, supra n. 218, at 334–359; Pecora, supra n. 33, at 206–214; Flynn, supra n. 219, at 56–58; Jerome Frank, If Men Were Angels 149 (Harper & Bros. 1942); Henry Heller Interview, May 20, 1980; House Investment Trust and Investment Companies Hearings, House Commerce Subcommittee, 76th Cong., 3d Sess. 62–63, 71–75, 95–100 (1940).

222. Senate Hearings, supra n. 219, at 1–32, 132, 326, 345, 399, 401, 1049, 1052–1059, 1105–1109; Janetski, The Investment Company Act of 1940, 26 Wash. U. L. Q. 308 (1941); *New York Times*, Mar. 12, 1940, at 33, Mar. 16, 1940, at 14.

223. Pub. L. No. 768, 54 Stat. ch. 686, 76th Cong., 3d Sess. (1940); Senate Hearings, supra n. 219, at 1109–1177; House Investment Trust Hearings, supra n. 221, at 75; S. Rep. No. 1775, 76th Cong. 3d Sess. 2 (1940); Jaretski, supra n. 222, at 310–347; J. Woodrow Thomas, The Investment Company Act of 1940, 9 Geo. Wash. L. Rev. 918 (1941); SEC Tenth Ann. Rep. at 158.

224. William Cary, Federalism and Corporate Law, 83 Yale L.J. 700–703 (1974).

225. SEC, Investment Counsel, Investment Management, Investment Supervision, and Investment Advisory Services 3 (1939); SEC Tenth Ann. Rep. at 180; S. Res. No. 1775, 76th Cong., 3d Sess. 21–22 (1940); Lowe v. SEC, 472 U.S. 181, 190–202, 219–224.

226. United States v. Carolene Products, 304 U.S. 144 n. 4 (1938).

227. Roosevelt Second Inaugural Address (Jan. 20, 1937); David Mason, From Building and Loans to Bail-Out: A History of the American Savings and Loan Industry, 1831–1995, at 93–97, 78–117 (Cambridge Univ. Press, 2004); Roosevelt State of the Union Address (Jan. 6, 1937); Roosevelt State of the Union Address (Jan. 11, 1944); Federal Home Loan Bank Act, Pub. L. No. 72–304, 47 Stat. 725 (1932); Home Owners Loan Act, Pub. L. No. 73–43, 48 Stat. 128 (1933); National Housing Act of 1934, Pub. L. No. 93–479, 48 Stat. 1246; An Act to Provide Additional Home Mortgage Relief, Pub. L. No. 76, 49 Stat. 293 (1935); Alan Blinder, After the Music Stopped 324–325 (Penguin Books, 2014); Markham, supra n. 17, at 172.

228. Wagner-Steagall Housing Act, Pub. L. No. 75–412, 50 Stat. 888 (1937); FDR Library & Museum, 75th Anniversary of the Wagner-Steagall Act of 1937; Living New Deal, United States Housing Act of 1937; Mason, supra n. 227, at 123; Historical Statistics of the United States: Colonial Times to 1970, Pt. 2, at 618.
229. Federal Credit Union Act, Pub. L. No. 467, 49 Stat. 1216, 73d Cong., 2d Sess. (1934); Amendment to Grain Futures Act of 1922, Pub. L. No. 675, 49 Stat. 1491, 74th Cong., 2d Sess. (1936); Jerry Markham, The History of Commodity Futures Trading and its Regulation (Praeger 1987).
230. Lochner v. New York, 198 U.S. 45 (1905); United States v. Carolene Products, 304 U.S. 144, n. 4 (1938); Wickard v. Filburn, 317 U.S. 111 (1942). On the Switch in Time That Saved the Nine and the underlying judicial decisions, see generally Ronald Rotunda, Modern Constitutional Law: Cases and Notes ch. 4 (West Academic 11th ed. 2015); Arthur Schlesinger, The Politics of Upheaval (Houghton Mifflin, 1960); Social Security Act of 1935, Pub. L. No. 74–271, 49 Stat. 620 (1935); Fair Labor Standards Act of 1938, Pub. L. No. 75–218, Ch. 672, 52 Stat. 1060 (1938).
231. Historical Statistics, supra n. 228, at 1023, 1047.

4

The Deterioration of the New Deal Model

In the post-World War II period through 2007–2009, the United States system of financial regulation was widely heralded for overseeing unprecedented economic expansion without bank holidays or a recurrence of the 1929–1933 Stock Market Crisis, Banking Crisis, or Great Depression.

The United States ended World War II with the dominant economy in the world. In 1938, the United States economy, with a gross national product (*GNP*) of $84.7 billion, already was the largest in the world with 33 percent of world GNP of $255.8 billion. By the end of World War II in 1945, United States GNP had dramatically increased to $211.9 billion, an inflation adjusted increase of 84 percent. During the same period, most of the leading war powers declined in GDP: France by 46 percent; Germany by 12 percent; the Soviet Union by 4 percent; Japan by 15 percent. This meant that United States GDP which had equaled 40 percent of the principal combatants (the United Kingdom, France, Italy, the Soviet Union, Germany, Austria, and Japan) in 1938 equaled 53 percent of these nations' GDP in 1945.

The United States relative percentage of world GDP declined in the period through 2006 to 27 percent as production throughout the rest of the world returned to competitive levels. But what was most striking about the post-World War II period was the staggering increase in United States GDP to $13.85 billion in 2006, an increase of over 60 fold in the post-World War II period.

Within the United States, each of the principal financial sectors experienced concomitant growth between 1945–2006. Total bank assets grew from $162.2 billion in 1945 to $11.9 trillion in 2006; the market value of all stocks traded on all exchanges in 1945 was $16.3 billion, in 2006, $19.3 trillion; life insurance in force increased from $115.5 billion in 1945 to $10.1 trillion in 2006.[1]

The post-World War II period of financial regulation was a period of substantial consolidation and expansion of the powers of principal financial regulatory agencies, most notably the Federal Reserve, the SEC, the CFTC, state insurance commissions, and the federal housing agencies. But it also was a period of insufficient coordination of these and other financial regulators, acceptance of a multiplicity of new regulators, and unregulated lines of business and products, bureaucratization of regulation which too often delayed or ignored fundamental change in the underlying dynamics of those that were regulated and intermittent political pressure to deregulate the New Deal model. Gradually throughout this period, there emerged a new financial order, not atomized as the New Deal model assumed, but financial supermarkets in multiple businesses and nations, able to circumvent regulatory controls. The New Deal model deteriorated because it was incapable of keeping up with these much faster growing principal economic actors.

The Aftermath of World War II

In the post-World War II period, the Federal Reserve Board (the *Fed*) achieved its prominent role in national monetary policy, but this achievement was not inevitable and through 1951, the Fed functioned as a junior partner to the Department of Treasury, constrained by the President and the Treasury.

Between 1933 and 1941, the Fed rarely changed its open market portfolio and discount rate. Monetary policy was controlled by the Treasury and President Roosevelt through changes in the United States gold stock and the devaluation of the dollar against gold. In 1934, the revaluation of gold had led to the establishment of the Exchange Stabilization Fund that, along with Treasury Trust Funds such as Postal Savings and Railroad Retirement, gave the Treasury the power to engage in open market operations, which was the statutory role of the Fed. Treasury Secretary Morgenthau used the threat of Treasury open market operations to insist that any Fed decision on open market transactions would be approved by the Treasury. Economics Professor Allan Meltzer concluded: "Despite the legislative changes that had increased *de jure* Federal Reserve independence, the Federal Reserve was less independent of the administration from 1934 to 1941 than in any other peacetime period." The Fed largely functioned as a fiscal agent making purchases for the Treasury, generally to exchange earlier issued long-term debt for new short-term debt.

With the Treasury purchasing gold consistent with Roosevelt's policies after 1933, the size of United States gold holdings rose rapidly, at times exceeding the total Fed open market portfolio. By 1940, the Treasury owned almost 80 percent of the world's monetary gold. In December 1936, Roosevelt approved a Treasury proposal to sterilize gold, meaning the Treasury would issue gold certificates or debt rather than the Federal Reserve banks increasing bank reserves. If gold later was withdrawn, the Treasury could buy back the gold certificates. Responsibility for this program was solely in the hands of the Treasury. Gold sterilization continued until the 1937–1938 recession began.

During the period 1933–1937, the Fed's policy changed. In the 1929–1933 period, the Fed had relied unsuccessfully on open market purchases and rediscounting to use interest rates as its primary means of stimulating the economy or dampening speculation.

Congress and the Roosevelt Administration provided the Fed with two new tools that were emphasized throughout the New Deal: margin control, that is control over how much could be lent to securities purchasers, and the ability to lower the reserve requirements of member banks. Both powers were solely vested in the Fed.

Section 7 of the Securities Exchange Act of 1934 empowered the Federal Reserve to specify the amount of credit that Exchange members or broker-dealers could extend to or maintain for any customer. The emphasis of the Roosevelt Administration and Congress then was on "preventing the excessive use of credit . . . which can be directed by speculation into the stock market and out of other more desirable uses of commerce and industry." For two decades, the Fed used these powers aggressively beginning in 1934 with loans between 55 and 75 percent of the securities market value, effectively decreasing the amount of customer loans that could be made. In

1937, maintenance margin loans were reduced to 40 percent and initial margin to 50 percent during that year's recession, when post-war inflation was considered the greater risk; maintenance and initial margin loan requirements were increased to 75 percent in July 1945, then 100 percent in January 1946, "to curb inflationary developments brought about by speculative activity in the stock markets," as Fed Chair Eccles explained.[2]

The Federal Reserve Board's second new exclusive power was authorized by the 1935 Banking Act, which granted the Fed the power to raise or lower member bank reserve requirements between those set by Congress in the 1933 Banking Act and twice that level. As reserves grew in the period before 1936, the Fed substantially increased reserve requirements in three steps in 1936 and 1937, while maintaining in a January 1937 press release: "Member banks will have excess reserve requirements of approximately $500 million to finance further recovery and to maintain easy conditions." A decrease in reserve requirements gave member banks the power to make more loans or as the euphemism went, allowed the Fed to print money.

The 1937–1938 recession was blamed on the Fed by Secretary of Treasury Morgenthau and others who believed that Fed policies, such as those increasing reserve requirements, had led to a rise in interest rates. Allan Meltzer in his multivolume *History of the Federal Reserve* opines that the increase in reserve requirements and the failure to offset this by such monetary factors as open market purchases contributed to the causes of the 1937–1938 recession. There also "were two large contractive changes in fiscal policy in 1937. One was the reduction of soldiers' bonus payments and passage of the undistributed profits tax; the other was the beginning of Social Security tax payments. Passed in 1935, Social Security taxes became effective in fiscal 1936 (calendar 1937)."

After a sharp stock market fall in March 1938, Roosevelt committed to $2 billion in additional construction and welfare expenditures and the Federal Reserve reduced reserve requirement ratios, effectively releasing $750 million. Central Reserve and Reserve City bank reserve requirements were set at 22.75 and 17.5 percent. In 1942, prodded by the Treasury, the Fed again reduced reserve ratios in three steps for Central Reserve banks, from 26 to 20 percent, releasing $1.2 billion or 6 percent of the monetary base at the time. After the War, in 1948–1951, the Fed made several changes in reserve ratios, raising ratios, for example, for Central Reserve banks from 20 to 24 percent in 11 separate adjustments.

In May 1940, Roosevelt began placing the United States on a war footing seeking to gear production of war planes from approximately 6000 planes the prior year to 12,000 that year with a plan to "turn out at least 50,000 planes a year." Roosevelt sought an appropriation of $896 million for four primary purposes:

> First, to procure the essential equipment of all kinds for a larger and thoroughly rounded-out Army;
>
> Second, to replace or modernize all old Army and Navy equipment with the latest type of equipment;
>
> Third, to increase production facilities for everything needed for the Army and Navy for national defense. We require the ability to turn out quickly infinitely greater supplies;
>
> Fourth, to speed up to a 24-hour basis all existing Army and Navy contracts and all new contracts to be awarded.

After Italy on June 10, 1940, joined Germany in its war effort in France, betraying Roosevelt's effort to secure Italian neutrality, Roosevelt decried "the hand that held the dagger has stuck it into the back of its neighbor." Roosevelt pledged to extend aid to England, then undergoing bombing by the German Air Force, and to "harness and speed up the use of those resources in order that we ourselves in the Americas may have equipment and training equal to the task of any emergency and every defense."

In September 1940, Japan joined Germany and Italy "in the threat that if the United States of America interfered with or blocked the expansion program of these three nations — a program aimed at world control — they would unite in ultimate action against the United States."

Roosevelt called for the United States to "be the great arsenal of democracy":

> We are planning our own defense with the utmost urgency, and in its vast scale we must integrate the war needs of Britain and the other free nations which are resisting aggression. . . .
>
> And on the economic side of our great defense program, we are, as you know, bending every effort to maintain stability of prices and with that the stability of the cost of living.

On May 27, 1941, two months after Congress enacted the Lend-Lease Act with an appropriation of $7 billion to provide for material aid "for the government of any country whose defenses the President deems vital to the defense of the United States," Roosevelt issued "a proclamation that any unlimited national emergency exists and requires the strengthening of our defense to the extreme limit of our national power and authority."

On December 7, 1941, "a day," Roosevelt declared, "which will live in infamy," the United States was suddenly and deliberately attacked by naval and air forces of the Empire of Japan in Pearl Harbor, with other Japanese attacks against Malaya, Hong Kong, Guam, the Philippine Islands, and Midway Island.

On December 8, 1941, Roosevelt requested and Congress declared a State of War "existed between the United States and the Japanese Empire."

On December 11, 1941, Germany "pursuing its course of world conquest, declared war against the United States." Roosevelt sought and received from Congress War Declarations against Germany and Italy.

World War II would be the most expensive war in United States history, with estimated costs to the United States of $334 billion or $4.7 trillion in 2019 dollars. Defense spending during World War II equaled 37.5 percent of GDP. During World War II, the United States was responsible for the production of "two-thirds of all Allied military equipment used in World War II. That included 86,000 tanks, 2.5 million trucks and a half million jeeps, 286,000 warplanes, 8800 naval vessels, 5600 merchant ships, 434 million tons of steel, 2.6 million machine guns, and 41 *billion* rounds of ammunition—not to mention the greatest superbomber of the war, the B-29, and the atomic bomb," reported historian Arthur Herman.

Secretary of Treasury Morgenthau and President Roosevelt had three major objectives for War finance: (1) to finance 50 percent of the War by taxation; (2) to finance most of the rest through bond sales; and (3) to maintain low interest rates.

These objectives were largely achieved. Some 45 percent of War expenditures were funded by taxes. Individual tax rates soared to 91 percent for individuals with income over $200,000. Corporate tax rates were raised to 40 percent, with additional profits or "excess profits," and a 5 percent victory tax. In 1942, it was estimated that taxes took two out of every three dollars earned by corporations. Total taxation rose from less than $7 billion in 1941 (7 percent of GNP) to $45 billion in 1945 (21 percent).

World War II government bond sales totaled over $150 billion. These were in all seven War Bond sales and a Victory Loan Drive.

Morgenthau succeeded in financing more than $200 billion in World War II at an average cost of 1.94 percent compared to World War I average interest costs of 4.22 percent.[3]

To achieve these results, the United States established a comprehensive system of control.

In September 1939, Roosevelt created the Office for Emergency Management to avoid profiteering and unwarranted price rises.

In January 1941, the President established an Office of Production Management to coordinate the powers and priorities of several federal agencies. The Office of Production Management included a Division of Civilian Supply to formulate plans and programs for the equitable allocation among civilians of materials, power, fuel, and other commodities.

In April 1941, within the Office for Emergency Management, Roosevelt established an Office of Price Administration and Civilian Supply, later the Office of Price Administration.

In May 1941, Roosevelt directed the Office of Emergency Management to ensure effective coordination of the priority powers and supply allocation activities of the federal government during the unlimited national emergency.

In August 1941, the Office of Emergency Management, by Executive Order, established the Supply Priorities and Allocations Board to:

> Serve as the coordinating center for the execution of the powers and activities of the several departments and agencies relating to priorities; in this connection, review, clear, and approve for execution all requests or proposals originating from other Federal agencies, private industry, or other sources for Priority action with respect to the procurement, production, transmission, or transportation of materials, articles, power, fuel, and other commodities; issue or provide for the issuance of all priority orders, warrants, certificates, or ratings with respect to the supply, production, transmission, or transportation of materials, articles, power, fuel, and other commodities.

In January 1942, the War Production Board was created to exercise general direction over war procurement and production. The War Production Board's primary function was to convert a civilian economy to war production by allocating scarce materials such as steel, aluminum, and rubber, controlling wages and prices and organizing scrap metal drives. As Arthur Herman colorfully explained: "Factories that made silk ribbons now produced parachutes, automobile factories built tanks, typewriter companies converted to machine guns, undergarment manufacturers sewed mosquito netting, and a roller coaster manufacturer converted to the production of bomber repair platforms." Between 1942 and 1945, the Board would supervise production of $183 billion of weapons and supplies, roughly 40 percent of the world's output using 12 regional offices and 120 field offices.

In January 1942, Congress enacted the Emergency Price Control Act to stabilize prices and prevent speculation, unwarranted and abnormal increases in prices and rents, and to eliminate and prevent profiteering, hoarding, manipulation, speculation, and other disruptive practices resulting from abnormal market conditions or scarcities caused by or contributing to the national emergency. The Act authorized the Office of Price Administration to establish maximum commodity prices utilizing voluntary agreements in conjunction with producers, manufacturers, retailers, wholesalers, and other groups having to do with commodities.

In October 1942, Congress amended the Emergency Price Control Act, authorizing Roosevelt to issue a general order stabilizing prices, wages, and salaries affecting the cost of living. "Such stabilization as far as practicable [shall] be on the basis of the levels which existed on September 15, 1942." The Office of Price Administration was authorized to regulate prices on 60 percent of all civilian food items and 90 percent of the goods sold in 600,000 United States retail stores until the Act was repealed in 1946.

Voluntary selective commodities price controls under the January 1942 Act price controls were justified by inflation. In the six months before selective controls began in April 1942, inflation increased by 10.3 percent. During the period of controls from April 1942 to June 1946, inflation was reduced to 3.5 percent. The program had substantial bureaucratic costs and by 1945 and 1946, there were 28,826 and 32,209 price control cases brought to curb black market activity, nearly as many as civil cases brought under the other federal statutes when combined. Price controls did achieve their purpose of keeping inflation and war time costs lower than they otherwise would have been.

During World War II, wage and price controls were coordinated with rationing. Across the country, 8000 ration boards were created by the Office of Price Administration to administer a system of ration books, coupons, and stamps. More than 91 percent of the United States population registered to receive War Ration Books that covered food and nonfood items as varied as sugar, coffee, typewriters, gasoline, bicycles, silk, nylon, fuel oil, meat, cheese, butter, processed foods, dried fruits, canned milk, whiskey, and cigarettes that could be used at all relevant retail stores. New car production was banned in 1942.[4]

During World War II, the Fed assumed a limited role supporting the Roosevelt Administration by working with the Treasury to keep interest rates low, albeit with occasional friction. The Fed viewed its primary duty as supporting financing the military. The dominant economic policy mechanisms of World War II were tax policy, price and wage controls, production conversion to military purposes, and rationing. The Fed's role was ancillary.

In September 1941, the Federal Reserve Board adopted consumer credit regulation through Regulation W, which required a 20 percent down payment on installment sales on several durable goods, ultimately including shoes, hats and haberdashery, with loans initially limited to 18 months.

In 1942, the Treasury agreed to peg interest rates on short- and long-term government securities at predetermined and low levels. The Fed announced on April 30, 1942, its commitment to purchase all 90-day Treasury Bills offered at a rate no higher than 0.375 per annum. One year, Treasuries were held to a rate of 0.875 percent. Long-term Treasury securities with terms of 25 years or more were limited to a 2.5 percent maximum rate. "With rates fixed," Meltzer found after these decisions, the "FOMC [Federal Open Market Committee] had little to do. . . . By the end of the war, short-term government securities had become the Federal Reserve's principal asset." Throughout the War, the regional banks also agreed to a uniform discount rate of 1 percent.

In 1942, Congress amended the Federal Reserve Act to authorize the Fed to underwrite Treasury debt during the War. Regional banks were allowed to purchase government securities directly from the Treasury. By lifting the earlier ban on regional bank purchase of government debt, the Fed helped finance the War even when the market would not do so.

The consequence of pegged interest rates and Fed authority to directly purchase government securities meant, as Sarah Binder and Mark Spindel wrote: "[T]he Fed ended up buying—first in the market and then directly from the Fed after 1942—most of the short term war debt. In other words, the Fed monetized the country's debt; it printed money (that is, created bank reserves) to buy up Treasuries."

The most notable new development in international finance during World War II was the 1944 Bretton Woods Agreement, on which the Fed offered little substantive comment. As Meltzer tartly put it: "The Fed never formally considered the Bretton Woods Agreement and was not asked to do so." The Bretton Woods Agreement created the International Monetary Fund and International Bank for Reconstruction and Development, later part of the World Bank. The purpose of the Agreement was to reconstruct the international monetary system, fixing the dollar to gold ratio at $35 an ounce. Negotiation of the Bretton Woods Agreement was led by the Treasury, culminating in 730 delegates from 44 Allied Nations gathering in Bretton Woods, New Hampshire July 1-22, 1944, signing the Agreement on the final day. The United States, then with two-thirds of the world's gold, succeeded in its insistence that a fixed rate exchange system tie gold to the United States dollar. The Allies were united in a desire to avoid a repetition of the disastrous financial terms of the World War I Treaty of Versailles, whose draconian terms had destroyed European stability. The participants in the Agreement pegged their currencies to the fixed exchange rate with a 1 percent band to stabilize parity by purchasing or selling foreign currency. The Treasury used its Exchange Stabilization Fund and tax revenues to pay its initial $2.75 billion subscription to the International Monetary Fund. The United States policy of subsidizing international monetary policy was taken further in the 1948 Marshall Plan in which the United States provided 16 Western European countries $17 billion in grants.[5]

When World War II ended, unemployment was less than 2 percent, inflation was controlled by wage and price controls. The end of war time production and controls widely was feared to be calamitous. In October 1945, Secretary of Commerce Henry Wallace, for example, estimated that the drop in the GNP over the next months would be $40 billion, the drop in wages $20 billion, and unemployment would reach 7 or 8 million in the spring of 1946. The twin objectives of continuing to control inflation and preventing large scale unemployment would dominate the Truman Presidency post-war plans.

Post-World War II demobilization and the initial decline in industrial production occurred rapidly after the War ended in Europe on May 8, 1945, and Japan on September 2, 1945. Government purchases of goods and services declined from $83 billion in 1945 to $30 billion in 1946. Military spending in aggregate shrank from $97.3 billion in the fiscal year ending June 30, 1945, or 38 percent of GNP to $28.2 billion the following year. Deficit spending of $54 billion in 1945, was succeeded by a $700 million surplus in 1947, and $8 billion in 1948.

Immediately after the Japanese surrender in September 1945, the Office of Price Administration moved to eliminate rationing on gasoline, fuel oil, processed foods, and stoves. By the end of 1945, rationing was ended on all foods except sugar. The War Production Board by September 1945 had removed 229 of its remaining controls. Most World War II price controls were ended by June 1946. Effective November 1, 1947, Regulation W, with its control of consumer credit, largely ceased. Individual income tax rates declined from a highest rate of 90 percent for incomes of $1 million or more during World War II to 77 percent in 1948–1949.

Within months, with controls ending and consumer spending rising, inflation accelerated. Economist Hugh Rockoff calculated that inflation in the six months following the end of the war, wage and price increased in June 1946 increased by 28 percent. During the same six months, wholesale prices rose by 45 percent. Whole prices increased by an annualized rate of 16.4 percent between January 1946 and August 1948, before a recession in 1949 caused prices to stabilize or fall until the Korean War began in June 1950. Congress, in July 1945, enacted a new price control law that included exceptions on a short-term basis for meat and on a longer term basis for other items. In October and November 1946, facing a tough midterm election, Truman terminated price controls, except on rents, wages, and salaries.

The Truman Presidency

In September 1945, President Truman delivered a Special Message to Congress recommending a 21 points program for reconversion. Truman built on Roosevelt's proposed Economic Bill of Rights to call for a national policy of full employment:

> A national reassertion of the right to work for every American citizen able and willing to work — a declaration of the ultimate duty of government to use its own resources if all other methods should fail to prevent prolonged unemployment — these will help to avert fear and establish full employment.

Congress enacted the Employment Act of 1946 that forewent Truman's proposal that the government take responsibility to provide full employment in favor of the commitment "to promote maximum employment, production and purchasing power." This would be the basis of the dual mandate to both fight inflation and limit unemployment applicable to the Fed.

The Employment Act created the Council of Economic Advisers, whose three members were intended to be independent both of the Treasury and the Fed and to be "as a result of his training, experience and attainments exceptionally qualified to analyze and interpret economic developments." The Chair of the Council of Economic Advisers in the post-World War II period, along with the Treasury Secretary, and Fed Chair, would become a key figure in coordinating fiscal and monetary policy.

In 1946, Republicans, with a preference for a less activist federal government, gained control of the House and Senate with a broad electoral sweep, converting a 1944 Democratic majority in the House of 242-191 to a 1946 Republican House majority of 246 to 188 by adding 55 seats. In the Senate, the Republican sweep was just as decisive. The 1944 Democratic majority of 56-39 was succeeded by a Republican majority of 50 to 46, with the Republicans adding 11 Senators. Truman's popularity had suffered in part because of unprecedented labor stoppages. In the year after World War II, 5 million employees would be involved in strikes and 120 million days of labor would be lost. Aggregate wages and salaries declined between 1945 and 1946 from $117.5 to $112 billion.

The 1946 Republican majorities were short lived. In 1948, along with Truman's unexpected election, the Democrats added 75 House seats to take a 263-171 majority and 9 Senators to reclaim a 54–42 majority.

After the 1946 elections, Congress frustrated Truman's proposals to address inflation, including proposals in the autumn of 1947, calling for the restoration of price, wage, and credit controls.

In August 1948, Truman again asked for price and credit controls, rationing, and an excess profits tax, in effect, a return to wartime controls. Congress only enacted a return to credit controls through Regulation W, "which," Truman complained, "is but a tiny fraction of what we need." Earlier in March 1948, Congress had enacted a one-year extension of rent controls. In 1949, rent controls were extended until 1950.

Consistent with Truman's proposals to curb inflation was his preference and that of the Department of Treasury to maintain pegged interest rates in the post-World War II period. This set in motion a sharp conflict with the Fed, especially Fed Chair Marriner Eccles, until 1948 when Truman replaced him as Chair. A decisive tool to combat inflation is the power to raise interest rates.

Between 1946 and 1951, the Treasury opposed ending pegged rates. Only in July 1947, was the Fed initially able to secure Treasury concord to raise the 0.375 percent Treasury bill interest rate. Treasury certificates with up to one year maturity long were capped at 1.125 percent interest. In December 1947, Treasury agreed with a Fed proposal to raise long-term Treasury debt yields but only up to the 2.5 percent ceiling. Further interest rate increases were put on hold by the 1948–1949 recession.

Under the Fed's new Chair, Thomas McCabe, the Fed continued to meet Treasury opposition. In March 1949, Treasury Secretary John Snyder rejected a Fed proposal to increase short-term interest rates by 0.125 percent. In 1950, Snyder declined to permit the Fed to raise the certificate rate above 1.125 percent.

This meant that the Fed's monetary role largely was limited to changes in member bank reserve requirements. Between 1948 and 1951, the Fed made 19 changes in member bank reserve requirements. Reserve requirement changes, however, were made in a narrow band. The effective average of reserve requirements for member banks moved between 14.22 percent in 1950 and 15.86 in 1949.

The authority to raise or lower reserve requirements without authority to increase or decrease interest rate levels alone was not sufficient to reestablish the Fed's statutory role in monetary policy.

The Korean War brought matters to a head. Over $150 billion would be appropriated to fund the Korean War. The Defense Production Act of 1950 authorized the Fed to control consumer credit and real estate construction credit and regulate prices and wages, with Government data showing that prices for a basket of 218 products had increased by 25 percent in the first three months of the

War. The Fed reinstituted Regulation W for consumer durables and Regulation X for real estate credit. Truman, by Executive Order in September 1950, created the Economic Stabilization Agency, which in January 1951, created the Office of Price Stabilization, and the Wage Stabilization Board to reinstitute price and wage controls. Wages and salaries were frozen in 1951. Prices also were frozen in January 1951 in a move that proved unpopular and unwieldy.

Marriner Eccles, Vice Chair of the Fed on January 25, 1951, testified to the Congressional Joint Committee on Economic Report that "the main issue of today [is] inflation." Eccles urged that the existing system of capped interest rates and Fed purchases of Treasury securities threatened the United States economy:

> As long as the Federal Reserve is required to buy Government securities at the will of the market for the purpose of defending a fixed pattern of interest rates established by the Treasury, it must stand ready to create new bank reserves in unlimited amount. This policy makes the entire banking system, through the action of the Federal Reserve System, an engine of inflation.

In September and October 1950, the Fed was required to purchase $8 billion of a $13 billion refunding issue to avoid its failure.

In five Fed Open Market Committee Meetings between August and December 1950, the Fed urged the Treasury to issue a 2.5 percent long-term nonbank debt instrument and pressed for higher rates in Treasury refundings.

In September 1950, the Open Market Committee voted to raise the one-year Treasury rates to 1.75 percent. The Treasury did not accede until November 1950 when the Treasury refunded a $7.9 billion issue of bonds and certificates at 1.75 percent.

Antagonism between the Fed and Treasury was widely reported in the national press. On January 18, 1951, Treasury Secretary Snyder spoke in New York and unilaterally stated after a meeting with President Truman and Fed Chair Thomas McCabe: "The Treasury has concluded, after a joint conference with President Truman and Chairman McCabe . . . that the funding and new money issues will be financed within the pattern of that [2.5 percent] rate," flatly contradicting McCabe's statement to the President: "We have some doubt as to whether a long-term bond can maintain itself at the 2.5 percent level."

A journalist in the *Washington Post* soon memorably opined:

> In the opinion of this writer, last Thursday constituted the first occasion in history on which the head of the Exchequer of a great nation had either the effrontery or the ineptitude, or both, to deliver a public address in which he has so far usurped the function of the central bank as to tell the country what kind of monetary policy it was going to be subjected to. For the moment at least, the fact that the policy enunciated by Mr. Snyder was, as usual, thoroughly unsound and inflationary, was overshadowed by the historic dimensions of this impertinence.

President Truman, frustrated by the friction between the Fed and the Treasury, sternly lectured the members of the Fed Open Market Committee on January 31, 1951, in the Oval Office, later releasing a press release that the Fed would "fully support the Treasury defense financing program." According to a separate Treasury statement, this meant that interest rate levels would be maintained during the Korean War. New York Fed President Allan Sproul concluded that the Treasury had lied: "[P]ublication concerning yesterday's meeting with the President... doesn't align with the facts." Eccles released his personal notes from the meeting that directly challenged Truman's misstatement. Newspapers, including the *New York Times* and *Washington Post* printed articles declaring that President Truman and Treasury Secretary Snyder had lied. The *Times* added: "The President has ordered the Federal Reserve Board to take its orders in the future from the Secretary of the Treasury. We can recall no instance where the independent central banking system in a democracy has been subjected to similar public degradation."

After the Fed Open Market Committee met on February 6-8, 1951, and wrote to Truman about its belief that the continued cap on interest rates would weaken confidence in the integrity of the United States dollar and government securities "by a flood of newly created dollars [that] will overwhelm whatever price, wage and similar controls, including selective credit controls, that might be contrived.... The inevitable result [of supporting bond prices] is more and more money and cheaper and cheaper dollars. This means less and less confidence." The letter sharply responded to the President and Treasury's recent statements: "Mr. President, you did not ask us in our recent meeting to commit ourselves to continue on this dangerous road. Such a course would seriously weaken the financial stability of the United States and encourage a further flight from money into goods."

Bankers, economists, and Secretary of Defense James Forrestal also expressed concerns that consumer prices had risen by 14 percent, adding to the pressure to unshackle the Fed from the Treasury.

The Fed had received further crucial support from a Subcommittee of the Joint Committee on the Economic Report, chaired by Senator Paul Douglas [D-IL], which in June 1950, issued a unanimous report urging Congress to issue general instructions to the Federal Reserve and the Treasury stating that:

> [I]t was the will of Congress that the primary power and responsibility for regulating the supply, availability, and cost of credit in general shall be vested in the duly constituted authorities of the Federal Reserve System, and that Treasury action relative to money, credit, and transactions in the Federal debt shall be made consistent with the policies of the Federal Reserve.

The full Joint Committee did not adopt the Subcommittee's Report, but Douglas succeeded in securing three Republican Senators to join three Democratic Senators in Douglas's March 5, 1951, introduction of legislation requiring the Treasury to manage debt according to policies set by the Fed. Douglas's threatened legislation was credible in a Congress with Democrats holding fragile majorities in the Senate (49-47, down from 54 to 42 in 1948) and the House (235 to 199, down from 263 to 171 in 1948) and an unpopular president.

On March 4, the day before Douglas's legislative threat was introduced in Congress, the Treasury and Fed issued a bland announcement which came to be known as the 1951 Accord: "The Treasury and the Federal Reserve System have reached full accord with respect to debt management and monetary policies to be pursued in furthering their common purpose to assume the successful financing of the Government's requirements and, at the same time, to minimize monetization of the public debt."

Beneath this opaque announcement, President Truman and Treasury Secretary Snyder had agreed that the Fed would approve no change in the discount rate during the rest of the 1951 calendar year "without prior consultation with the Treasury," but after that could conduct monetary policy without the approval of the Treasury.

In its 1951 Annual Report, the Federal Reserve Board amplified the significance of the 1951 Accord:

> The Treasury and Federal Reserve felt that everything possible should be done to terminate the unwholesome situation that had developed and to coordinate the debt management responsibility of the Treasury with the Federal Reserve responsibility for restraining credit expansion. It was the immediate object of the Treasury to restore conditions in the market that would be favorable to refinancing the large volume of maturing obligations, as well as financing several billions of new money required during the remainder of the year. It was the immediate object of the Federal Reserve to endeavor to curb the unprecedented inflationary loan expansion that had continued uninterruptedly since Korea by minimizing the monetization of the public debt and by making it necessary for member banks to borrow from the Federal Reserve in order to obtain additional reserves.

Several specific steps soon were taken to reduce the pressure of long-term Treasury bonds overhanging the market. The Fed and the Treasury "agreed that a substantial portion of these bonds could be taken off the market by a Treasury offer to exchange for them a nonmarketable $2^3/_4$ percent, 29-year bond, redeemable at the holder's option before maturity only by conversion into a 5-year marketable Treasury note." This would minimize the need to monetize the public debt through liquidation of Treasury 1967–1972 bonds. The Fed withdrew from the market for bank eligible Treasury obligations after the Accord, but did continue to purchase Fed $2^1/_2$ percent restricted Bonds to facilitate the exchange offer. The conversion would prove successful and \$13.5 billion in $2^1/_2$ percent Treasuries would be exchanged for $2^3/_4$ percent nonmarketable Treasuries. The Fed purchased \$5.6 billion of the exchange offer or 41 percent. Fixed support for long term Treasury bonds "was abandoned following the close of the books on the conversion offering on April 6, 1951."

Short-term interest rates on Treasury securities no longer would be pegged. As the 1951 Federal Reserve Board Annual Report explained:

> [T]he pending task of refunding the large volume of short-term securities maturing or callable in the near future presented difficult problems both for the Treasury and for the Federal Reserve. It was agreed that the Committee, in order to minimize

monetization of the debt, would immediately reduce or discontinue purchases of short-term securities and permit the short-term market to adjust to a position at which banks would depend upon borrowing at the Federal Reserve to make needed adjustments in their reserves.

In William McChesney Martin's view:

> In monetary history the accord was a landmark. In withdrawing from supporting fixed prices in the Government bond market, the Federal Reserve System regained its influence over the volume of money. It ceased to be the residual buyer who, by purchases of Government securities, however reluctantly made, furnished bank reserves indiscriminately and thus abetted inflationary overexpansion of the money supply.

By relying on the principle of a free market to determine interest rates, Martin also believed that the pressure on the Fed was reduced "to inject periodically into credit markets large amounts of reserve funds which are difficult to withdraw before they have resulted in undesirable credit developments." This reduced the pressure on the Fed to be the handmaiden of the Treasury's debt management. The Treasury would no longer rely on the Fed to ensure low interest costs but instead would pay competitive rates.

In the view of Allan Meltzer, a leading historian of the Federal Reserve System:

> The March 1951 Accord with the Treasury changed the Federal Reserve's formal status from subservient to co-equal partner with the Treasury. The Treasury remained responsible for debt management; the Federal Reserve gradually regained authority to change market interest rates, reserves, and money. The two institutions shared responsibility for the success of the Treasury's offerings. The Treasury had to price its issues to attract buyers; the Federal Reserve accepted that it had to assist the Treasury by supplying additional reserves, if offerings failed to attract buyers in sufficient number to sell the issues at the offering price.

This is a fair generalization. But it understates several points. The 1951 Accord only became the talismanic charter of the modern Fed because Martin as Chair between 1951 and 1970 successfully defended the Fed's independence from repeated challenges during the Eisenhower, Kennedy, and Johnson presidencies. The 1951 Accord did not control efforts by Congress or by the President to influence interest rate levels and Fed policies more generally. These efforts did not relent after 1951, but the Accord, with exceptions, gave the Fed greater confidence in responding to them. While the Accord gave the Fed control over interest rates relative to the Treasury, it did not control how market forces responding to such factors as government deficits, tax policy, or balance of payment imbalances could influence Fed interest rate levels. In the perpetual tug of war between the Fed with its emphasis on independence and political administrations with their conflicting preference for political success, which meant lower interest rates or a larger money supply, the results were never foreordained. And vital as the Accord was, it never prevented a presidency ultimately from controlling the Fed through the appointment process.

A few days after the public disclosure of the 1951 Accord, Fed Chair Thomas McCabe resigned and Truman named William McChesney Martin as Chair. Martin would serve as Fed Chair for 19 years until 1970 during the presidencies of Truman, Eisenhower, Kennedy, Johnson and Nixon.[6]

Martin's Chairmanship

Martin was unlike the Kennedy and Johnson administrations, which were unabashedly Keynesian. Keynesian policy emphasized the need for fiscal stimulants such as tax cuts, spending increases, or lower interest rates to ameliorate recessions and achieve low levels of employment. Martin also was not an advocate of Milton Friedman's monetary approach, which focused on the behavior of money and its impact on economic activity, price levels, and income. Martin, in Meltzer's characterization "had little interest in economic theories or analysis of how the changes that the FOMC initiated reached beyond the money market to prices, unemployment, or exchange rates."

All this was true and as Meltzer further explained, Martin "did not have a single measure or set of measures by which it judged what happened or specified what should happen." This, also, was true, but more explicable during the Martin Chairmanship when statistical analysis was more primitive than it subsequently became.

More significantly, Meltzer's critique understates the extent to which Martin was guided by core beliefs. Martin disliked controls such as interest rate pegs or price or wage controls, and frequently spoke in favor of free markets and competition as superior means to oversee an economy. He viewed low inflation as a key to sustainable economic growth. He was wary of pro-growth or Keynesian economists such as Paul Samuelson, Walter Heller or John Kenneth Galbraith who viewed Martin's degree of emphasis on avoiding inflation as retarding economic growth and preventing higher levels of employment. Martin sought to avoid boom-bust periods of economic growth, and recession. Martin's objective was sustainable economic growth, not the highest rate of growth.

The Eisenhower Presidency

The Fed during the Eisenhower administration largely freed itself from the pressure to support long-term Treasury debt by adopting a "Bills Only" or after 1960, a "Bills Preferable" policy, which meant it limited its open market purchases to short-term Treasury bills except when there was a risk that a long-term Treasury issue would fail, such as occurred in December 1955 or during the unsettled market after the dispatch of Marines to Lebanon in July 1958. This policy would be criticized for contributing to higher long-term interest rates, but it was justified by the Fed as addressing the broadest government securities market and interfering least with the operation of the debt markets. It is notable that until 2008, the Fed made few purchases or loans on long term debt.

On March 4, 1953, the Federal Open Market Committee (*FOMC*) resolved, in Meltzer's summary:

> that: (1) operations for the System account would be confined to the short end of the market; (2) purchases and sales would be made only to meet the objectives of monetary and credit policy (not to support any pattern of yields and prices); and (3) during periods of Treasury financing, the System would not purchase maturing issues, when-issued securities, or issues with comparable maturity.

The bills only policy strengthened the Fed's independence from the Treasury. Martin viewed the Fed in political terms. He viewed the Fed as independent within the government, not independent of the government: "Congress appropriates the money; they levy the taxes; they determine whether or not there should be deficit financing. The Treasury then is charged with the responsibility of raising whatever funds the Government needs to meet its requirements. . . . I do not believe it is consistent to have an agent so independent that it can undertake, if it chooses, to defeat the financing of a large deficit, which is a policy of the Congress."

This meant while the Fed was independent and could determine interest rates and member bank reserve requirements to increase available credit, the Fed could not refuse to finance a deficit that Congress approved.

Independent with government also recognized the realpolitik of a regulatory agency's independence. Congress could change the statutes that created or empowered a regulatory agency and derogate an agency or its leaders through hearings. The president could change an agency's policy over time through appointments, and in many instances, but not that of the Fed, could control its budget.

George Schultz, later President Nixon's Treasury Secretary, would generalize:

> The Federal Reserve is an "independent" agency, and therefore monetary policy should be expected to be free of some of the institutional and political constraints that plague fiscal policy. Independence is, however, a relative matter. The Federal Reserve is part of the government. The chairman meets with the President and with fiscal policy officials, seeking to gain acceptance for policies the Fed favors. It is questionable whether the Federal Reserve can remain entirely independent of administration views about domestic monetary policy; and, of course, the Fed takes direction from the President, through the Treasury Department, on international monetary affairs.

Martin centralized Federal Reserve authority in Washington through the Chair and the FOMC. This move most specifically strengthened the central Fed relative to Federal Reserve Bank of New York, which under its highly respected leader Allan Sproul, posted a significant challenge to Martin's authority, only fully ended in 1956 when Sproul retired. Sproul, in the manner of Ben Strong, had the ability and the inclination to make the New York Federal Reserve Bank the functional center of Fed operations.

The FOMC approved Federal Reserve bank requests for discount rate changes. At FOMC meetings, Martin augmented his influence by listening or writing first to FOMC members and only then stating a consensus view. Martin, according to Meltzer, "was never defeated once the new procedure was in place." In 1955, Martin persuaded the FOMC to end its Executive Committee which biographer Robert Bremner characterized as "the last vestige of unrestricted influence of the New York Federal Reserve Bank President over the Fed's open-market policy making process."

Martin was a consensus builder. He often would wait several FOMC meetings until a majority agreed with him or a consensus formed. The FOMC beginning in 1952 relied on member bank borrowing to adjust reserve positions, rather than imposing borrowing limits as before. Martin, in Bremner's view, held the view that the best solution to government regulation of financial markets depended on men of goodwill working together. He rejected a proposal for additional legislation from Senator Douglas: "We will sit around a table and hammer it out. Solutions require some experimentation, some probing, some accommodation of views. Constructive public policy in the financial field is something that can come only from long, tortuous, persistent, humble study."

For his first 15 years as Chair, Martin's consistent policy emphasis was on fighting inflation. As he stated at the FOMC meeting in December 1957, the Federal Reserve "System was the only instrument of Government that was fighting inflation." Open market purchases and sales by the time of Martin's Chairmanship "had become the dominant means of changing bank reserves and the monetary base." The discount rate, set by the Central Fed, was the interest rate at which the regional Federal Reserve banks lent to commercial banks.

The Fed emphasized control over interest rates to constrain inflation when economic activity heated up increasing the discount rate from 1.5 to 3.5 percent in seven separate steps between 1954 and 1957, or to stimulate the economy by reducing interest rates or reserve requirements, as it did it during the 1953–1954 and 1957–1958 recessions.

Alternatively, the Fed used cuts in member bank reserve requirements to generate greater money supply in 1953 concomitant with an initially unpopular Treasury issue as a measure of active ease designed to "avoid deflationary tendencies."

Martin well understood that Fed actions alone could not prevent inflation if government deficits created pressures to increase interest rates or money supply or both. But Martin believed that the Fed could "lean against the wind," or as he memorably put it: The job of the Fed was to "take away the punch bowl just when the party gets going." Martin sought to use preemptive rate increases early during an economic recovery to ameliorate inflation. In the period before President Johnson's deficit spending of the Great Society and Vietnam War caused Martin to shift his emphasis to the priority of seeking a tax increase to cut a burgeoning federal deficit, Martin's Fed was highly alert to signs of inflation, holding, for example, a Special Open Market Committee meeting on January 11, 1955, to discuss "the possibility that inflationary seeds may be germinating" or in August 1955, expressing concerns that "all the danger signals [for inflation] . . . are now flashing red." In 1958, Martin defended 1958 Fed rate increases, urging if inflation were allowed to persist, it would create "maladjustments of such severity to lead to a protracted period of liquidation and structural realignment in the country." Consistently, the Fed would increase interest rates to minimize or forestall inflation and subsequent recession.

When an increase in interest rates appeared to be politically infeasible in 1958 at a time when inflation posed a problem "bigger . . . than anything he had faced in his own lifetime," Martin urged the Open Market Committee to achieve the same type of constraint by moving the System's free reserves toward zero. Free reserves were held by Federal Reserve banks in excess of those required to be maintained by the Fed's reserve requirements minus member bank borrowing and could be the basis of additional bank loans, the proverbial creation of money.

Martin and several members of the Fed similarly believed that to prevent long-term inflation, the Fed should keep money growth close to the average growth of real output. The Fed during this period sought to maintain stable prices believing that low inflation contributed to economic growth.

The Fed's power to use interest rates or money growth to maintain price stability was limited by Martin's commitment to coordinate the Treasury's debt management. Independence within government meant the Fed helped the Treasury sell its securities. In a 1956 speech, Martin explained:

> The Federal Reserve's task of managing the money supply must be conducted with recognition of the Treasury's requirements, for two reasons: One, the Federal Reserve has a duty to

> prevent financial panics, and a panic surely would follow if the Government, which represents the people as a whole, could not pay its bills; second, it would be the height of absurdity if the Federal Reserve were to say in effect that it didn't think Congress was acting properly in authorizing expenditures, and therefore it wouldn't help enable the Treasury to finance them.

"Independence," Meltzer generalized, "was not absolute. The Federal Reserve was a creature of Congress. Congress had created (or permitted) the deficit the Treasury had to finance. The Federal Reserve shared that responsibility, and it had to balance it against its responsibility for preventing inflation." The Federal Reserve's job was to prevent the bond market from failing to accept a Treasury issue. This meant the Fed supplied enough reserves to keep interest rates from rising or rising too much when the Treasury sold its offering. This was what Martin and the Fed meant by an "even keel" or "neutral" policy. The Fed defined independence to mean it was not bound by the Treasury's limits on interest rates.

Coordination with Treasury under Martin involved weekly meetings with the Secretary of Treasury. At times, these meetings would be joined by the Council of Economic Advisers Chair and after 1960, by the White House Budget Director, giving rise to the phrase *Quadriad* to describe what the *New York Times* called the "first semi-formal machinery ever devised for bringing the Federal Reserve into contact with the Chief of State." Martin after 1956 met with Eisenhower approximately three times a year and Kennedy an average of six time a year. These meetings helped avoid the open warfare of the Truman period and gave Martin an opportunity to weigh in on administration fiscal plans such as in May 1958 when Martin argued to Eisenhower's Treasury Secretary Robert Anderson that a contemplated "tax cut will only add to the difficulties of dealing with the wage-cost spiral." Later in the Johnson presidency, Martin frequently addressed the need for a tax increase as budget deficits spiraled ever higher.

During the Eisenhower administration, the Fed's relations with Treasury generally improved. The Treasury usually accepted Martin's or FOMC's suggestions about the pricing and maturity of Treasury debt issues.[7]

In economic terms, the first 15 years of Martin's Chairmanship of the Federal Reserve were remarkably successful. Inflation was kept under control. Wholesale prices for all commodities grew from a level of 81.8 in 1950 to 96.6 in 1965, an annual average of less than 1 percent. Consumer price levels for all items grew only slightly more, from 72.1 in 1950 to 94.5 in 1965, an annual average of about 1.5 percent. The GNP during these same years more dramatically increased from 248.8 in 1950 to 684.9 in 1965, an aggregate increase of 275 percent. Personal income during this period increased by an aggregate of 237 percent. Unemployment during these years ranged from a low of 2.9 percent in 1953 to a high of 6.8 percent during the 1957–1958 recession, numbers that were not equal in most years to the economist's assumption of full employment at 4 percent or lower unemployment rates, but not numbers that were substantially out of bounds as they later would become. Average annual earnings of employees grew from $2292 in 1950 to $5710 in 1965, or 249 percent during that period. Total new construction between 1950 and 1965 soared, increasing 220 percent; the value of residential structures in constant 1958 dollars similarly increased by 207 percent; total financial assets of households, personal trusts, and nonprofit organizations increased by 332 percent in part because the market value of stocks and bonds registered on national securities exchanges increased by 409 percent during these 15 years.

The 1959 *Staff Report on Employment, Growth, and Price Levels of the Joint Economic Committee of the United States* Congress would explain: "No economy can match the record of growth of the American economy over the past 120 years. It has been estimated that real gross national product grew 4.3 percent per year from 1839 to 1879; 3.7 percent per year from 1879 to 1919; and 3 percent per year from 1919 to 1959." But the Staff Report, as with the Keynesian economists of the day and John Kennedy viewed the 2.7 percent growth rates between 1954 and 1959 as inadequate because of the Fed's emphasis on an anti-inflation policy. The Staff Report urged had the federal government instead emphasized policies that facilitated growth and maintaining aggregate demand, the economy could grow at 3.9 to 4.5 percent.[8]

Pressures on the Fed during Martin's full Chairmanship were manifold.

After the enactment of the Employment Act in 1946 and Senator Douglas's leadership in 1951 helping to free the Federal Reserve Board from subservience to the Treasury in setting interest rates, Congress assumed a greater role overseeing the Fed's commitment to maintaining maximum employment and often worked to maintain or lower interest rate levels. Senator Douglas, previously an Economics Professor at the University of Chicago, wrote in 1953 to retired Chair Marriner Eccles criticizing the Federal Reserve for allowing money growth to slow. In 1955, Douglas criticized the Fed for buying Treasuries when issued securities in a $12 billion refunding offer that was failing. Douglas viewed these purchases as inconsistent with the independence he had helped secure in 1951 for the Fed. In effect, Douglas urged if the Treasury mispriced an issue, Treasury should assume responsibility for the failure and not depend on the Fed to rescue them. In 1956, at the Senate Banking Committee Hearing on Martin's reappointment as Governor and Chair of the Federal Reserve System, Douglas criticized four decisions in 1955 to raise discount rates instead of increasing reserve requirements. Douglas was dissatisfied with Martin's explanation that "our policies are not directed to rewarding or punishing banks" and abstained on the vote to reconfirm Martin as he had earlier abstained on the vote to initially confirm Martin. Congressional criticism of the Fed's persistence in allowing interest rates to rise in the 1958–1960 period led to several members of Congress calling the Fed doctrinaire and inflexible.

Representative Wright Patman, later 1960 Chair of the House Committee on Banking and Currency, brought a populist's zeal for keeping interest rates low, telegraphing Martin on May 31, 1957, urging the Fed to boost prices on Treasury bonds from a 12 percent discount below par of sales price to reach par. This, in effect, was a demand that the Fed return to the pegged interest rate policy of 1942–1951, or as Patman wrote: "The time has come for the Open Market Committee to make a decision. Will the Federal Reserve be restored to its intended function of providing the economy with the money and credit necessary to carry on commerce and trade, and of aiding the Treasury in its borrowings . . . or shall the System insist on standing aloof."

Patman introduced nonbinding resolutions beginning in the mid-1950s calling for an audit of the Federal Reserve Board, abolition of the FOMC with transfer of its functions to the full Board and expansion of the Board to 12 members, each with a six-year term. In 1960, Patman proposed returning $15 billion of the Fed's $25 billion debt in exchange for non-interest bearing Treasury securities, a proposal the Fed beat back by reminding members of Congress that since

1947, the Fed had paid 90 percent of its excess earnings to the Treasury. Patman's criticism did cause the Fed to require its reserve banks to discontinue the practice of holding contingent reserves and pay to the Treasury in 1959 accumulated reserves of $261 million. None of Patman's legislative proposals were adopted.[9]

In 1959, the *Staff Report on Employment, Growth and Price Levels of the Joint Economic Committee,* chaired by Senator Douglass with Wright Patman as Vice Chair, while affirming Douglas's long-held belief that "changes in the rate structure . . . should lie with the Federal Reserve," was critical of the increased reliance on monetary policy. Especially since 1953, that is, Martin's Chairmanship:

> The Federal Reserve System has relied almost entirely upon so-called general credit controls, including changes in discount rates, changes in member bank reserve requirements, and open market operations. Reserve requirements have been gradually lowered in several stages in the recessions of 1953–54 and 1957–58, and have not been raised since 1951. Since early 1953, the Federal Reserve has confined its open market operations almost entirely to short-term securities — the so-called bills-only policy. The System has shown a decided antipathy for selective credit controls.
>
> General credit controls have been rather slow to exert their effects on aggregate demand, even in dealing with inflation, the job for which they are alleged to be most suited.

Senator Douglas, in particular, favored an end to the bills only policy and no further reduction in reserve requirements. In 1960, 21 Senators led by Douglas urged the Federal Reserve to adopt four reforms, as summarized by Meltzer, to: "(1) tighten regulation of government security dealers including margin requirements for their customers, (2) end bills-only, (3) permit the money supply to increase on average at the rate of output growth, and (4) use open market operations (not reserve requirement changes) to provide secular growth of money."

Martin, replying for the Fed, did not endorse the first, second, or fourth proposal, but agreed with the third: "As I have testified to the Congress on various occasions, it is the Board's position that we should provide for such increases in the money supply as can be absorbed by a growing economy without generating inflationary pressures."

Powerful committee chairs such as Paul Douglas or Wright Patman could influence the Fed's policy and priorities by scheduling hearings, conducting investigations, or questioning specific decisions. A more significant measure of the impact of Congress on the Federal Reserve System was the legislation that was enacted into law. Legislation did not reflect the sometimes idiosyncratic views of committee chairs or individual members, but majorities in both houses of Congress.

During the first 15 years of Martin's Chairmanship, the legislation adopted by Congress generally supported the Fed.

In 1956, Congress enacted the Bank Holding Company Act. In its initial form, the Act granted the Federal Reserve Board regulatory authority over all bank holding companies owning or controlling two or more banks. Control generally referred to ownership of power to vote 25 percent or more of the voting shares of each of the subsidiary banks or control in any manner of the election of a majority of the directors of each of the subsidiary banks.

Each bank holding company had to register and periodically report to the Fed and was subject to "such regulations and orders as may be necessary to enable [the Fed] to administer and carry on the purpose of this Act and prevent evasions thereof."

The Fed was empowered to approve each transaction that resulted in a company becoming a bank holding company, each holding company acquisition of more than 5 percent of the shares of any bank, and any merger of one bank holding company with another bank holding company. In exercising these powers, the Fed was required to notify and hear the views of the Comptroller of the Currency and each relevant State banking authority.

No bank holding company was permitted to acquire any voting shares or substantially all of the assets of any bank located outside the state in which the bank holding company maintained its principal office and place of business or where it conducted its principal operations unless the out-of-state acquisition was authorized by the law of the State in which the acquired bank was located.

The Act initially also prohibited a bank holding company from acquiring direct or indirect ownership or control of any voting shares of any company that was not a bank.

There were limited exceptions to the prohibition on bank holding companies owning nonbanks such as that for a company that was involved in a safe deposit business or shares held in a fiduciary capacity or for purchases of less than 5 percent of the outstanding voting shares of a company.

The Bank Holding Company Act prohibited:

> [A]fter two years from the date of enactment of this Act or from the date as of which it becomes a bank holding company, whichever is later, retain direct or indirect ownership or control of any voting shares of any company which is not a bank or a bank holding company or engage in any business other than that of banking or of managing or controlling banks or of furnishing services to or performing services for any bank of which it owns or controls 25 per centum or more of the voting shares.

A reciprocal provision prohibited a bank to invest any of its funds in the capital stock, bonds, debentures, or other obligations of a bank holding company of which it is a subsidiary or to accept any such capital stock, bonds, debentures, or other obligations, purchase such securities or other assets or other obligations through a repurchase agreement or make any loan, or discount of credit to a bank holding company of which it is a subsidiary.

Since 1938, when President Roosevelt urged "legislation that will effectively control the operation of bank holding companies," nearly annual efforts had been made in Congress to authorize the Fed to regulate bank holding companies.

When enacted in 1956, the Bank Holding Company Act expanded the Fed's regulatory authority and was a significant step towards a more logical scheme to regulate banks. In 1970, the logic of the Bank Holding Company Act regulation was furthered by an amendment authorizing the Fed to regulate one bank holding companies. During the period 1956 to 1970, the number of one bank holding companies grew from 117 with commercial deposits of $11 billion to 890 one bank holding companies with commercial deposits of $181 billion, roughly 43 percent of all insured commercial banks in the United States. Between 1956 and 1970, one bank holding companies were not subject to the requirement of the Bank Holding Company Act and could engage in activities that were not incidental to banking such as selling commercial paper. The 1970 Amendment to the 1956 Act was intended to close this loophole.

Over time, the logic of the Bank Holding Company Act was turned on its head. The Senate Report accompanying the Bank

Holding Company Bill in 1955 had emphasized: "In general, the philosophy of this bill is that bank holding companies ought to confine their activities to the management and control of banks and that such activities should be conducted in a manner consistent with the public interest. Your committee believes that bank holding companies ought not to manage or control nonbanking assets having no close relationship to banking."

Federal Reserve Chair Martin had noted two principle problems the Fed sought to address:

> (1) The unrestricted ability of a bank holding company group to add to the number of its banking units, making possible the concentration of commercial bank facilities in a particular area under a single control and management; and
>
> (2) The combination under single control of both banking and nonbanking enterprises, permitting departure from the principle that banking institutions should not engage in business wholly unrelated to banking. Such a combination involves the lending of depositors' money, whereas other types of business enterprise, not connected with banking, do not involve this element of trusteeship.

In subsequent decades, the holding company would be the principal vehicle by which financial supermarkets would circumvent the atomized structure of financial regulation. These efforts would succeed because of a combination of regulatory decisions by the Fed and other regulators, judicial opinions, and Congress. Congress would be a key actor in this transformation of finance. In 1999, Congress would enact the Gramm-Leach-Bliley Act, which would repeal the Glass-Steagall Act, that is, separation of the commercial and investment banking businesses, and authorize bank holding companies to own other financial institutions. After the Gramm-Leach-Bliley Act, bank holding companies could elect to become financial holding companies and engage in the full scope of securities underwriting as well as insurance underwriting and sales.

By the second quarter of 2018, bank holding companies in the United States held $19 trillion in assets and included eight domestic global systemically important banks (JP Morgan Chase, Citigroup, Morgan Stanley, Bank of America, Goldman Sachs, Wells Fargo, Bank of New York Mellon, and State Street). Most of the largest United States broker-dealers then were affiliated either with a United States bank holding company or a foreign banking organization. At year end 2017, 4470 bank holding companies controlled 4423 commercial banks with 97 percent of all insured commercial bank assets in the United States. As of year end 2017, 492 domestic bank holding companies operated as financial holding companies.[10]

The most consequential check on Fed independence was the president and the Department of Treasury.

Truman had appointed William McChesney Martin to be Chair of the Fed just a few days after the 1951 Accord in an effort to rein in the Fed. Martin had served as head of the Export-Import Bank between 1946 and 1949 and as Assistant Secretary of the Department of Treasury between 1949 and 1951 during the time of greatest friction between the Fed and the Treasury. He was viewed by the Truman Administration, particularly Treasury Secretary John Snyder, as an ally. Martin served as the Treasury's negotiator of the 1951 Accord. While Truman had been troubled by Martin's unwillingness to make a promise to keep interest rates low, Truman was persuaded by Snyder's loyalty to his Assistant Secretary.

Martin's commitment to Fed independence would be viewed as apostasy by the Truman's administration. In a 1952 chance encounter reported by Martin to an associate, Truman had responded to Martin's salutation "Good Afternoon Mr. President" with one word: "Traitor." Truman's Chief Economist would state that Martin "double crossed" the President by doggedly pursuing Fed independence. This mattered little during the last two years of Truman's beleaguered second term.[11]

The 1952 elections were a decisive rejection of Truman. Dwight Eisenhower won a landslide, capturing 55.2 percent of the popular vote and a 442-89 victory in the electoral college. He carried every state outside of the South. The Senate changed little, from a 49–47 Democratic Party majority in 1950 to a 48–48 tie in 1952, but with the new Vice President, Richard Nixon, as tie-breaker, the Republicans controlled the Senate. Republican control of the House was more definitive. With 22 seats going to the Republicans, the Democratic 235 to 199 majority in 1950 was converted to a 221–213 Republican majority.

President Eisenhower's views on the economy were more consonant with those of Martin than any other President during Martin's Chairmanship. No domestic political goal was more cherished by Dwight Eisenhower than the reduction of the federal budget.

Eisenhower had inherited projected deficits of nearly $7 billion in 1953 and $9.9 billion in 1954, after Korean War military spending increased the defense budget from $14 billion in fiscal year 1950 to $42 billion in 1952. In his 1952 Campaign, Eisenhower set as "a goal of the new administration to cut federal spending, to eliminate the budget deficit, and to reduce taxes." This was a goal Eisenhower unrelentingly pursued. "When my administration took over the reins of government in 1953," Eisenhower recalled, "there was no one among my immediate associates not dedicated, in principle, to the proposition that both federal expenditures and the public debt must be reduced." On February 2, 1953, Eisenhower stressed "the elimination of the annual deficit" as his first order of business. In 1958, Eisenhower derived satisfaction from his belief that "over the past five years it seems to be that I have put in two-thirds of my time fighting increased expenditures in government." Sherman Adams, long Eisenhower's closest associate, memorialized the administration with a similar observation: "Eisenhower was more deeply concerned with economics than most people realized. He once told the Cabinet that if he was able to do nothing as President except balance the budget he would feel that his time in the White House had been well spent." During the Eisenhower Administration, Budget and Treasury officials attended regular National Security Council meetings, because as Adam explained: "The pressure of the government's fiscal watchdogs at the meetings reflected the President's belief, often voiced, that the nation could be destroyed by spending itself to death as well as by force of arms." Secretary of the Treasury Humphrey spoke for the President when he repeatedly emphasized Eisenhower's belief that government deficits and borrowing were the major causes of inflation.

Eisenhower made his most uncompromising efforts to balance the 1954 and 1955 budgets. The 1954 budget for the period from July 1, 1953, to June 30, 1954, had been drafted by the Truman administration and called for $78.6 billion in expenditures, $71 billion of which were for national security program, or such "uncontrollable" major items as interest on the national debt. In spite of this lack of "elbow room," Eisenhower's Budget Bureau scaled down the 1954 budget to $72 billion in the early months of 1953. Efforts to reduce the 1955 budget began almost immediately. In November 1953, Eisenhower approved a memorandum prepared by his Budget Director, Joseph Dodge, meant, in Eisenhower's words, "to serve as a weapon in his economizing efforts with federal agencies." The memorandum's three principal points read:

> (1) . . . Both appropriations and the level of expenditures for fiscal year 1955 must be reduced substantially below those for the 1954 fiscal year.
>
> (2) To achieve this objective every possible reduction will have to be made and every item included in the Budget must meet the test of necessity rather than of desirability. This policy of reduction must be applied with relative uniformity, though equitably, to all agencies.
>
> (3) Pressures to protect favored expenditures or programs must give way, except in the most unusual cases, to the greater pressure to reduce overall Government expenditures.

In what may be a unique event in United States history, Treasury Secretary Humphrey in 1958 criticized the Eisenhower administration's proposed 10 percent increase in spending in 1958 during a recession, urging Congress to reduce spending to avoid "a depression that will curl your hair." Eisenhower supported his Secretary of Treasury.

President Eisenhower also supported the Fed's independence, but sometimes reluctantly. In 1956, after the Fed raised discount rates during an election year, prompting Eisenhower's intense anger, Secretary of Treasury George Humphrey told Martin that he should resign instead of opposing the President. Martin replied that he would resign if his leadership were violently opposed by the Administration. Eisenhower, after talking to Martin and receiving a promise to ease credit if the economy slowed, concluded that dismissing Martin would be unwise. At a subsequent press conference, Eisenhower memorably explained: "The only comment I can logically make is this: the Federal Reserve Board is set up as a separate agency of Government. It is not under the authority of the president, and I really personally believe it would be a mistake to make it definitely and directly responsible to the political head of the state."

This did not prevent the Eisenhower or subsequent administrations from seeking to cajole or pressure the Fed. The Department of Treasury jawboned the Fed to ease its tight money policies in 1957, threatening to shift its balances from reserve banks to commercial banks to increase bank reserves, prompting Carl Allen, President of the Chicago Federal Reserve Bank, to characterize the Treasury as wanting a bailout from the Fed. In August 1957, the 1957–1958 recession reached its peak. Throughout the entire recession, industrial production would fall 13.5 percent, GNP, 3.3 percent. Unemployment would climb to 7.5 percent. Treasury Secretary Anderson and R.J. Saulnier, Chair of the Council of Economic Advisers, repeatedly urged Martin to ease interest rates. Martin long declined, more concerned about short-term inflation than a future recession.

In this emphasis, Martin's approach generally was consonant with Eisenhower. In early 1955, Arthur Burns, then head of the Council of Economic Advisers, Treasury Secretary Humphrey, and Eisenhower agreed that inflation was reemerging as the economy's major problem and the economy's growth rate could not be sustained. Martin and Eisenhower's economic advisers agreed on the need to prevent the type of "excesses" as Burns put it, that led to the 1956–1957 inflationary boom.

In several FOMC meetings in 1957, signs of an economic slowdown were evident. During the April-June 1957 period, the GNP declined 0.1 percent. Martin was more concerned about the 3 to 4 percent annual increase in consumer prices and persuaded the Committee not to change policy. In August 1957, a divided Fed increased the discount rate, a rare instance when Martin forewent his commitment to consensus and instead prioritized his determination to control inflation. As Martin explained in supporting a rate increase from the Chicago Reserve Bank on July 30, he was willing "to assume the risk of being charged with precipitating a downturn, rather than take any action except one [that I] believe correct." Two weeks later, the Fed by an unusually close 4-3 vote approved a 0.5 percent discount rate increase.

Only in January 1958 did the Fed take several steps to deal with the 1957–1958 recession, including two rate reductions and a $1 billion reduction in required member bank reserves, increasing the money supply.

Eisenhower's 1958 budget resulted in a $3.3 billion deficit as he used increased aid to agriculture, extended unemployment compensation, and accelerated defense spending to respond to the recession.

In March 1960, the Fed did increase free reserves, the basis of additional member bank loans. Only in August 1960, did the Fed support the Cleveland Fed's reduction of its discount rate to 3 percent, prompting New York, Richmond, and Kansas City that day to similarly reduce their rates with the other Federal Reserve banks soon following.

After a two-year expansion, the economy experienced a mild 10 month recession in 1960–1961. The Fed declined requests from Vice President Nixon and Arthur Burns to ease its interest rate levels to avoid a recession. After the 1960 election, Nixon told Martin that he blamed the Fed for his defeat.[12]

The Kennedy Presidency

The 1960 presidential election was nail bitingly close with Senator John F. Kennedy defeating Vice President Richard Nixon by 112,827 votes (49.72 to 49.55 percent), but more decisively in the electoral college, 303–219. Critically, Kennedy defeated Nixon by 9000 votes in Illinois and 46,000 votes in Texas. Had both states gone for Nixon, Nixon would have been elected. Kennedy was buoyed by his self-confidence and vigor in four televised debates, each of which was viewed by over 60 million people and the consequences of the 1957–1958 and 1960–1961 recessions in tamping down support for Nixon. The Democrats retained substantial majorities in the Senate, 64–36, and in the House, 262–175.

Close as the presidential election was, Kennedy campaigned for office and began his presidency with a broad agenda for a new generation. His campaign slogan was "The New Frontier," the title of his acceptance speech on July 15, 1960, at the Democratic National Convention. Kennedy self-consciously sought to build on the legacies of Franklin D. Roosevelt and Harry Truman:

> Today our concern must be with that future. For the world is changing. The old era is ending. The old ways will not do. . . .
>
> . . . The New Deal and the Fair Deal were bold measures for their generations, but now this is a new generation. . . .
>
> It is time, in short — It is time, in short, for a new generation of leadership. . . .
>
> The New Frontier is here whether we seek it or not.
>
> Beyond that frontier are uncharted areas of science and space, unsolved problems of peace and war, unconquered problems of ignorance and prejudice, unanswered questions of poverty and surplus. It would be easier to shrink from that new frontier, to look to the safe mediocrity of the past, to be lulled by good intentions and high rhetoric — and those who prefer that course should not vote for me or the Democratic Party. . . .

The platform emphasized an aggressive pro-growth critique of the Eisenhower-Nixon administration and the Fed:

> We Democrats believe that our economy can and must grow at an average rate of 5% annually, almost twice as fast as our average annual rate since 1953. We pledge ourselves to policies that will achieve this goal without inflation....
>
> As the first step in speeding economic growth, a Democratic president will put an end to the present high-interest, tight-money policy.
>
> This policy has failed in its stated purpose — to keep prices down. It has given us two recessions within five years, bankrupted many of our farmers, produced a record number of business failures, and added billions of dollars in unnecessary higher interest charges to government budgets and the cost of living.
>
> A new Democratic administration will reject this philosophy of economic slowdown. We are committed to maximum employment, at decent wages and with fair profits, in a far more productive, expanding economy....
>
> We vigorously reject the notion that America, with a half-trillion-dollar gross national product, and nearly half of the world's industrial resources, cannot afford to meet our needs at home and in our world relationships.
>
> We believe, moreover, that except in periods of recession or national emergency, these needs can be met with a balanced budget, with no increase in present tax rates, and with some surplus for the gradual reduction of our national debt.

In emphasizing maximum employment at decent wages, the platform invoked Roosevelt's Economic Bill of Rights with its aspiration of full employment and contrasted this objective with the Eisenhower-Nixon administration: "For nearly 30 months the rate of unemployment has been between 5 and 7.5% of the labor force. A pool of three to four million citizens, able and willing to work but unable to find jobs, has been written off by the Republican administration as a 'normal' readjustment of the economic system. The policies of a Democratic administration to restore economic growth will reduce current unemployment to a minimum."

Kennedy's Inaugural Address with its much quoted phrase: "Ask not what your country can do for you... ask what you can do for your country," similarly included a harsh critique of Eisenhower and Fed economic policy:

> The present state of our economy is disturbing. We take office in the wake of seven months of recession, three and one-half years of slack, seven years of diminished economic growth, and nine years of falling farm income.
>
> Business bankruptcies have reached their highest level since the Great Depression. Since 1951 farm income has been squeezed down by 25 percent. Save for a brief period in 1958, insured unemployment is at the highest peak in our history. Of some five and one-half million Americans who are without jobs, more than one million have been searching for work for more than four months. And during each month some 150,000 workers are exhausting their already meager jobless benefit rights....
>
> Our recovery from the 1958 recession, moreover, was anemic and incomplete. Our gross national product never regained its full potential. Unemployment never returned to normal levels. Maximum use of our national industrial capacity was never restored.
>
> In short, the American economy is in trouble. The most resourceful industrialized country on earth ranks among the last in the rate of economic growth. Since last spring our economic growth rate has actually receded. Business investment is in a decline. Profits have fallen below predicted levels. Construction is off. A million unsold automobiles are in inventory. Fewer people are working — and the average work week has shrunk well below 40 hours. Yet prices have continued to rise — so that now too many Americans have less to spend for items that cost more to buy.

Kennedy biographer Robert Dallek characterized the economy as Kennedy's biggest domestic worry during the first 100 days of the presidency: "The 1960 recession that had helped elect him continued into 1961. In his State of the Union message on January 30, he made economic expansion his primary domestic goal."

Kennedy's appointments to the Council of Economic Advisers and White House were consistent with a Keynesian "New Economics" intended to make a sharp break from what was regarded as the too cautious policies of the Eisenhower period.

On January 27, 1961, one week after the inauguration, Kennedy named to his Council of Economic Advisers two prominent

Keynesians: Walter Heller, previously Professor of Economics and Chair of the University of Minnesota Business School's Department of Economics to be Chair and Yale Economics Professor James Tobin. Both were harshly critical of the Fed.

Heller came to Washington determined to end the independence of the Fed, although he later came to believe "after working with the Fed under both Presidents [Eisenhower and Johnson] . . . that it isn't too bad an arrangement provided there is good will, competent people and reasonably systematic consultation." James Tobin, who along with Council consultants, Kenneth Arrow, Robert Solow, and Paul Samuelson, would be one of four of Heller's team who later would win the Nobel Prize in Economics, published a magazine article in January 1961 shortly before he was appointed, warning that the Fed may "resist and frustrate any effort by the Kennedy Administration to gear the federal budget and other instruments of economic policy to higher levels of employment and production." In a 1996 interview, Tobin would opine: "I think some aspects of the Federal Reserve are inconsistent with democratic political theory. . . . I don't think that there should be votes on the Federal Open Market Committee for people who are not appointed as public servants by the President and who are not subject to confirmation by the Senate. . . . I also think the four-year term of the Chairman of the Fed and the four-year term of the President should be better synchronized." Tobin also recommended that the Secretary of the Treasury and the Chair of the Council of Economic Advisers be members of the Fed, each of which proposals would have reduced the independence of the Fed.

Samuelson was the most renown economist of his time, winner of the first Nobel Prize in Economics, author of what long was the most widely acclaimed textbook in economics. Beginning in 1958, Samuelson, along with Tobin, Seymour Harris, and John Kenneth Galbraith, advised Kennedy in economics. After the election, Samuelson:

> warned that storm clouds were gathering on the nation's economic horizon. Unemployment was high and rising, approaching 7 percent as Inauguration Day grew near. Economic output was consequently subpar, leaving the nation with considerable economic slack. According to some estimates, the nation was using only 80 percent of its economic capacity.

Samuelson warned Kennedy that the nation might be headed into a recession. The diagnosis was unwelcome, as was the prescription. Samuelson, like most of the nation's leading economists, had embraced a version of post-war Keynesianism that emphasized the stabilizing role of fiscal policy. Faced with a looming slowdown, Samuelson and his colleagues suggested a program of expansionary spending.

Samuelson declined the opportunity to be Chair of the Council of Economic Advisers but did chair a Special Study Committee on Economic Policy, which in January 1961, issued *Prospects and Policies for the 1961 American Economy*, recommending that policymakers should rapidly increase and accelerate spending programs, boost unemployment benefits, foster residential housing construction, and pursue other expansionary programs that were "desirable for their own sake," including urban renewal and natural resource development.

Samuelson delineated temporary but expansionary tax cuts as a second line of defense. This was contrary to the orthodoxy of the Eisenhower-Martin period when increasing deficits by reducing taxes was counterintuitive.

Given these beliefs, it was hardly surprising that Samuelson also favored replacing Martin.

The Keynesian policy preferences of Kennedy's Council of Economic Advisers was most memorably articulated in the 1962 Economic Report of the President. The Report emphasized coordination of monetary and fiscal policies with a paramount emphasis on four goals: "(1) The achievement of full employment and sustained prosperity without inflation, (2) the acceleration of economic growth, (3) the extension of equaling of opportunity, and (4) the restoration of balance of payments."

The first goal was decisively different than the Eisenhower-Fed emphasis on balanced budgets and low interest rates as the path to prosperity. The Kennedy Council of Economic Advisers was more willing to employ such Keynesian means as tax cuts and government spending to address maximizing employment and increasing economic productivity. The Council was willing to accept some deficits and inflation if this buoyed employment and productivity. The Council had no qualms about reducing the Fed's independence.

The Kennedy Keynesians believed that coordination of fiscal and monetary policies could smooth out economic volatility, achieving high growth, maximum employment, and low inflation even with deficit spending during periods of actual or threatened recession. There was a profound trust in policymakers to choose and adjust the right levels of inflation and employment. There was confidence that: "Prosperity shrinks budget deficits" through higher tax revenues. In its accompanying 1962 Economic Report, the Council of Economic Advisers emphasized several automatic defenses against recession and inflation:

> Given the tax rates, tax revenues move up and down with economic activity, since most taxes are levied on private incomes or sales. Indeed, tax revenues change proportionally more than GNP. Furthermore, certain Federal expenditures, such as unemployment compensation payments, are automatically affected by the state of the economy. Economic fluctuations, therefore, result in substantial changes in Federal expenditures and revenues, even when basic expenditure programs and tax rates remain unchanged. With the present system of tax rates and unemployment compensation payments, a one-dollar reduction in GNP means a reduction in Federal tax receipts and an increase in transfer payments totaling about 30 cents. Therefore, private incomes after Federal taxes fall by only 70 cents for each reduction of one dollar in GNP. For this reason, any initial decline in spending and output is transmitted with diminished force to other sectors of the economy.
>
> These automatic or built-in stabilizers moderate the severity of cyclical swings in the economy. If the forces causing a downturn in economic activity are weak and transient, the automatic stabilizers cushion the severity of the decline and give the basic recuperative powers in the private economy a better opportunity to produce a prompt and full recovery.

In 1962, Kennedy subscribed to this approach. In his 1962 Economic Report, Kennedy wrote:

> Our postwar economic growth — though a step ahead of our record for the last half century — has been slowing down. We have not in recent years maintained the 4 to 4½ percent growth rate which characterized the early postwar period. We should not settle for less than the achievement of a long-term growth rate matching the early postwar record. Increasing our growth rate to 4-1/2 percent a year lies within the range of our capabilities during the 1960's. It will lay the groundwork for meeting both our domestic needs and our world responsibilities.

On February 2, 1961, Kennedy proposed a detailed Program to Restore Momentum to the American Economy. To stimulate the economy, Kennedy in this and related addresses directed federal agencies to pursue 17 separate actions, including accelerating procurement and construction planned for 1961 using existing funds, accelerating 1961 tax refunds, raising price supports on corn, cotton, butterfat and milk, and other price-supported commodities, expansion of free food distribution for needy families, decreasing Federal Housing Administration and Small Business Administration interest rates and two new export-import programs to make available credit guarantees, insurance, and financing for semifinished and consumer durable goods.

Kennedy laid out a detailed legislative agenda including extending temporary unemployment compensation, new unemployment compensation coverage to include over 3 million more workers, aid to dependent children, liberalizing Social Security to increase Social Security benefits, and create an earlier retirement age for workers, increasing the minimum wage to $1.25 and expanding coverage to 3.6 million additional workers. Kennedy proposed housing legislation including a 4 year commitment of $2.5 billion for urban renewal, expansion of federal aid to highways, increased aid for waste treatment facilities and air pollution, an increase in aid to education, and medical care for the aged.

Kennedy also recommended two modest tax proposals, specifically to enact an investment tax credit for the modernization of private plant and equipment and withholding taxes on interest and dividends.[13]

No president has a totally free hand in economic policy in our two party, separation of powers, system of governance. From the start, Kennedy appreciated that his substantial majorities in the House and Senate on economic issues were illusory. Democrats in the House, led by House Ways and Means Chair Wilbur Mills, were more conservative than Kennedy's Keynesian advisers. Seymour Harris calculated that 102 of the 262 House Democrats were from the Deep South, "with at least one-half hostile to the president on domestic issues." The Senate, where Kennedy had served for eight years, included some who regarded Kennedy as a lightweight.

To countervail the Keynesian Council of Economic Advisers, Kennedy appointed Douglas Dillon to be Secretary of Treasury. Dillon, former Chair of the investment firm of Dillon, Read, had served as Eisenhower's Ambassador to France beginning in 1953 and subsequently as Eisenhower's Under Secretary of State for Economic Affairs and Under Secretary of State. Dillon was well respected in Republican and financial circles. He was rumored to have been Nixon's choice for Secretary of Treasury. Dillon believed that the Eisenhower Administration had limited economic growth and not sufficiently reduced wartime taxes. While not a Keynesian, his views were not opposed to those of Kennedy. Arthur Schlesinger highlighted Kennedy's preference for competing policy voices:

> "I need you both," he told Heller, "for a proper balance in economic matters." Diverging policy interests created in any case a balance, or at least a tug of war, between the Council, charged by statute with working "to promote maximum employment, production and purchasing power," and the Treasury, primarily involved in taxation, the management of the debt, and the protection of the dollar.

Kennedy's relationship with Martin began as a rocky one. Kennedy's approach to spending, deficits, and inflation was at odds with that of Martin. Several Kennedy advisers had urged replacement of Martin and dissipation of the independence of the Fed. Seymour Harris, a consultant to the Council of Economic Advisers, most shrilly criticized the "absurdity" of the Eisenhower Administration "rigidly insisting on an independent Federal Reserve Board":

> [T]he Eisenhower administration voluntarily tied its own hands. The President failed to use all weapons that might contribute toward the attainment of his economic objectives. He failed to recognize the fact that monetary policy cannot be divorced from political considerations and that an independent policy of the Federal Reserve not only blunts other weapons but in the long run is likely to weaken monetary policy....
>
> ...The aura of independence has been carried so far that when the Congress proposes that the Federal Reserve should reconsider its "bills only" policy, the Federal Reserve authorities announce that they are not willing to go along. Is it expedient to allow an agency which can influence prices, output, employment and generally the allocation of resources, to operate without adequate public accountability?

This type of comment prompted Martin in an unusual outburst in December 1960, to complain within earshot of a newspaper reporter: "The President has a chip on his shoulder about the Federal Reserve System." A spokesman for Kennedy responded: "The President-elect has remarked that 'Mr. Martin's got a chip on his shoulder and I'm going to knock it off.'" The ensuing press brouhaha was so intense that Kennedy publicly disclaimed that he had requested Martin's resignation. As Martin biographer Robert Bremner put it: "Kennedy and Martin managed to get off to the worst start imaginable."

During his first meeting with Kennedy on February 1, 1961, Martin expressed regret for his "chip on the shoulder" remark and affirmed that the Fed was in the process of reappraising its monetary policies. Martin believed that he could find opportunities to cooperate with Dillon and others in Kennedy's administration.

Kennedy believed and wrote in his 1962 Economic Report "that a new President [should] be able to nominate a Chairman of his choice for a term of four years coterminous with his own." Martin not only championed the Fed's independence, but could be obstinate in defending it. He was, as John Wood wrote in a reevaluation of Martin, "the most determined fighter in the history of the Fed." Wood recounted:

> Evidence of his backbone was shown during a meeting of the "quadriad" (President Kennedy, Treasury Secretary Douglas Dillon, Chairman of the Council of Economic Advisers Walter Heller, and Martin), when the "exasperated" President asked Martin "why he would not agree with his other advisers" and "Martin responded that he was the only person in the room that did not work for the President."

Kennedy chose not to replace Martin. As with Douglas Dillon, Martin was viewed as a symbol of orthodoxy in monetary management. Before Kennedy's inauguration, Kennedy asked Walter Heller to meet with Martin and assess "whether he would be cooperative or obstructionist." Heller recalled "being enormously taken with him. [Martin] pledged, 'I'm not going to give up on the independence of the Fed.' [Heller responded], 'Well I'm sure that is not what the President is going to ask you to do.' . . . Martin added 'There's plenty of room here for cooperation.'"

Martin frequently sought to work constructively with the new administration. This involved several accommodations by the Fed. In 1961, the Fed increased member bank reserves by about $1 billion.

In his February 2, 1961, Economic Message to Congress, Kennedy articulated what came to be known as "Operation Twist," which required the Fed to support lower long-term and higher short-term interest rates. Martin on February 7, 1961, told the FOMC that the change would "enable the system to escape from the change of doctrinaire commitment to *laissez faire*, free enterprise position."

Over the next two years, the Fed purchased nearly $4 billion of longer term securities with one- to five-year maturities with the intent to lower long term interest rates, that is, twist the yield curve. While Martin and several members of the FOMC were skeptical that the purchase of longer term Treasury debt could materially lower interest rates, Martin continued to cooperate.

This brought a formal end to the policy of bills only. By 1961, the policy was in disfavor with the Kennedy administration because it limited available monetary options and with economists generally. In 1959, the Joint Economic Committee Staff Report recommended abandoning the bills only policy "to increase the effectiveness of monetary policy." The privately funded Commission on Money and Credit had been formed in 1957, by the Chair of the Committee for Economic Development, to make the first extensive investigation of the United States monetary system since the Adrien Commission of 1908–1911. In June 1961, the Monetary Commission also recommended the modification or abandonment of bills only. With the 1961 purchases of one- to five-year Treasuries, the Fed ended bills only.[14]

During his presidential campaign and throughout his presidency, Kennedy committed to maintaining gold at $35 per ounce and supporting the Bretton Woods Agreement. On February 6, 1961, Kennedy sent a message to Congress committing to reduce the deficit in the balance of payments. Kennedy was determined to safeguard the dollar. As he emphasized on February 6, 1961:

> This loss of gold is naturally important to us, but it also concerns the whole free world. For we are the principal banker of the free world and any potential weakness in our dollar spells trouble, not only for us but also for our friends and allies who rely on the dollar to finance a substantial portion of their trade.

By 1961, the global dominance of the world economy that the United States possessed after World War II had dissipated. In 1949, the United States held 70 percent of the world's monetary gold stock. That year, United States gold resources were $24.56 billion. Claims against the reserves equaled $18.38 billion.

By 1960, United States gold reserves declined by 10 percent to less than $17.8 billion, the lowest level in 20 years. Claims against gold reserves by then equaled $35.14 billion. By the end of 1962, United States gold holdings declined by $5.32 billion on a trajectory to fall to $11.07 billion by 1970.

Simultaneously, the United States balance of payments had deteriorated. In 1958–1960, the deficit in international payments averaged $3.7 billion annually, improving only somewhat in 1961 to approximately $2.5 billion. In large part, this was because of an average of $3 billion of United States military operations during the previous six years. Between 1951 and 1957, the balance of payments had averaged about $1 billion and was concomitant with popular programs such as the Marshall Plan that helped rebuild Western European economies. "Deficits in the U.S. balance of payments," the Council of Economic Advisers explained in 1962, "are financed either by drawing down our gold reserves or by increasing foreign claims against them in the form of liquid dollar liabilities to foreigners, official and private."

Countervailing the enduring vulnerabilities of the deterioration of United States gold reserves and an increasing balance of payment deficits were compensatory United States assets. In 1961, the United States could draw upon $4.1 billion in its quota at the International Monetary Fund. United States government and private short-term assets were substantial. Western European countries owed the United States long-term government debt of $2.9 billion. Private short-term assets were $2.9 billion. Total long-term private investments in foreign countries totaled over $44 billion, far exceeding foreign investment in the United States of $28 billion.

On February 6, Kennedy sent Congress a Special Message on Gold and the Balance of Payments in which he sought to "gain control of our balance of payments so that we can achieve over-all equilibrium of our international payments." Kennedy placed "maximum emphasis on expanding our exports." He proposed several initiatives including amending the Federal Reserve Act to permit the Fed to establish separate maximum rates of interest paid by member banks on time and savings deposits held in this country by foreign governments or monetary authorities to enable American banks "to make a maximum competitive effort to attract and hold dollar balances which might otherwise be converted into gold."

With Kennedy's support, the United States, Canada, and 18 European nations agreed to form an Organization for Economic Cooperation and Development to mutually coordinate economic policy. On March 16, 1961, the Senate ratified the Treaty.

In October 1961, Congress also approved Kennedy's Trade Expansion Act, broadening Kennedy's power to cut tariffs, and separate legislation to authorize the Fed to set higher interest rates on foreign deposits in American banks.

During the 1961–1963 Kennedy administration, Martin and a sometimes reluctant Fed largely supported a series of administration initiatives, often acting in tandem with the Treasury.

The consequences of this collaboration were significant. The Fed's ability to increase or decrease interest rates in response to the domestic economy was constrained. In 1961, during Operation Twist, the Fed did not decrease short-term interest rates even when unemployment rose to 7 percent.

In January 1962, the Fed for the first time assisted the Treasury in purchasing foreign currencies. This represented a policy reversal by the Fed which long had interpreted the Federal Reserve Act as precluding Fed foreign currency purchases. Martin's Fed did not ask Congress for new legislation when the Treasury decided not to seek new legislation. Martin treated this as an urgent matter at the September 12, 1961, FOMC and reminded the Committee that the Fed "was often accused of being obstructive." Martin viewed the Exchange Market Stabilization Plan as highly advantageous: It would "defend the dollar . . . reduce the drain on gold and . . . promote confidence in the dollar."

The Fed authorized currency stabilization agreements between central banks. Martin was keenly aware of the significance of the Fed's Currency Exchange Program. In February 1962, he stated at a FOMC: "Ten years from now, foreign exchange operations will likely be as much a part of the system as are open market operations." The Treasury began the Fed's participation in currency exchange with an initial limit of $500 million in what it could sell to the Fed in foreign currency. Within a decade, the limit was $20 billion. Fed participation allowed the Treasury to expand the program. The Fed and Treasury collaborated in their operations. The Fed-Treasury collaboration continued until 1998, when it was formally ended after 15 years of disuse.

In June 1962, the Fed also initiated currency swap arrangements to support the dollar, exchanging $60 million of Belgian francs and Dutch guldens to purchase dollar holdings of the two banks. By August, total swap agreements equaled $700 million and would increase to $11.7 billion in currency swap lines by August 1971.

In December 1961, the United States joined a gold pool in the London Gold Market, providing $135 million or one half of $270 million to keep the price of gold below $35.20, the delivery price of gold purchased in New York and sold in London. Participating central banks agreed to purchase gold solely from other central banks or the United States Treasury, not from the market. During its life until 1968, the pool, Meltzer wrote: "[P]revented central banks from competing for gold, lowered the price paid to producers, and kept the gold price close to $35. It may have reduced demand on U.S. gold stock by encouraging countries to hold additional dollars." A net total of $2.5 billion in gold was sold by member countries and the London Market, of which the United States share was $1.6 billion.

None of the monetary measures adopted by the United States Treasury or the Fed prevented the further deterioration of the United States gold reserves, balance of payments, or the ultimate breakup of the Bretton Woods Agreement, but collectively they delayed the day of reckoning until 1971.

Kennedy sometimes was frustrated. Clumsily in 1962, he threatened to pull United States troops out of Europe if France converted its excess dollars into gold to pressure the Kennedy administration into changing its European policies. French President De Gaulle regarded this as an idle threat. Had United States troops been withdrawn, Europe would be lost and the United States weakened.

The Kennedy administration rejected a 1959 plan proposed by Robert Triffin in Testimony to the Joint Economic Committee, reprinted in his book *Gold and the Dollar Crisis.* Triffin believed that the Bretton Woods system contained what Paul Volcker would characterize as a "potentially fatal flaw in its dependence on the dollar":

> [Triffin] argued that as the volume of trade expanded over time, any fixed exchange rate system would need an increase in usable reserves, in other words, an increase in acceptable international money to finance increased trade and investment. Future gold production at the established price could not be enough to meet the need, so the source of

> the international liquidity necessary to lubricate growth within the Bretton Woods system would have to be dollars. The only avenue for putting those dollars in the hands of the rest of the world was the American balance of payments deficit.

Triffin proposed to transform the International Monetary Fund into a type of international central bank:

> Let the United States, the United Kingdom, and other major countries bar the use of their national currency as monetary reserves by other countries. Give all countries, instead, the choice of keeping in the form of international, gold-convertible, deposits at the International Monetary Fund, any portion of their reserves which they do not wish to hold in the form of gold. Attach to these reserve deposits at the Fund exchange rate guarantees that would make them a far safer medium for reserve investment than any national currency holdings, always exposed to devaluation, inconvertibility, blocking, or even default by the debtor country.

Otherwise, Triffin believed that countries concerned about the ability of the United States to redeem dollars in gold would demand gold and the system would collapse.

Undersecretary of State George Ball developed a more limited proposal that if NATO countries agreed to hold excess dollars for two years, rather than convert to gold, the United States would work to eliminate its balance of payments deficit and negotiate a new agreement to replace Bretton Woods, as well as agree to sell $1 billion of gold to participating countries during the two-year period. James Tobin, on behalf of the Council of Economic Advisers, proposed a plan in support of Ball's proposal. To succeed Bretton Woods, under the Tobin plan the special role of the dollar would be eliminated and each participating nation, including the United States, would agree to hold a fixed proportion of their reserves in dollars. This would be a different way to internationalize world currency. During the two-year transition period, the United States would increase its swap lines to $2.5 billion to purchase dollars and increase forward exchange operations to reduce the quantity of dollars private holders offered central banks.

The Treasury and the Fed both opposed the Ball-Tobin proposal as unnecessary because of several steps already underway, including exchange market operations, swaps, and the gold pool. In addition,

Martin was concerned that beginning this type of negotiation would reduce confidence in the United States ability to maintain dollar convertibility into gold and precipitate a run.

With divided advisers, Kennedy sought a halfway house, supporting Ball's plan if European nations made this their proposal to the United States. The European nations would not and the initiative failed.

The Federal Reserve took other steps to address the balance of payments deficit. In July 1963, the Federal Reserve increased discount rates to 3.5 percent and the Regulation Q ceiling rate on commercial bank time deposits to 4 percent. Many Board members were skeptical that small increases in the discount rate would make much difference and expressed anxiety about slowing the economy. They favored the Kennedy Administration reducing foreign commitments.

On July 18, 1963, Kennedy delivered his second Special Message on Balance of Payments. He sent a mixed message. There had been some progress. "Our gold outflow has been halved.... The deficit in our balance of payments has been reduced—from $3.9 billion in 1960 to $2.4 billion in 1961 and $2.2 billion in 1962." He emphasized an "urgent need for further efforts" while "[making] it equally clear that this nation will maintain the dollar as good as gold, freely interchangeable with gold at $35 an ounce, the foundation-stone of the free world's trade and payment system." Kennedy also reiterated his administration's "vigorous efforts to restrain overseas expenditures, without reducing military effectiveness." Despite the Berlin building of 1961, net overseas outlays for defense had been decreased from $2.7 billion in 1960, to $1.9 billion in 1962.

Kennedy praised the role of the Fed in Operation Twist in helping reduce the United States payment deficit: "From February 1961 through July 12, 1963, the rate on newly issued 3-month Treasury bills rose 76 basis points, while the rise in long-term Treasury bond yields was held to only 22 basis points and the yields on high-grade corporate bonds and mortgages actually declined."

To address an increase in long-term capital outflows, "up from $850 million in 1960 to $1.2 billion in 1962 and so far this year is running an annual rate of well over $1.5 billion," Kennedy made a new proposal for an Interest Equalization Tax that would increase the cost of United States persons investing in foreign securities by 15 percent of the actual value of stock and by 2.75 percent to

15 percent of the actual value of debt depending on the debt's years to maturity. The tax did not apply to debt with fewer than three years to maturity. The Interest Equalization Tax Act was estimated by Kennedy to increase the interest cost to foreigners of obtaining capital in the United States by 1 percent. Kennedy characterized the tax as preferable to "[a] substantial increase in our whole long-term interest rate structure which would throw our economy into reverse, increase unemployment and substantially reduce our import requirements" or direct capital controls, which Kennedy viewed as "contrary to our basic precept of free markets."

The Interest Equalization Tax, enacted in 1964 and lasting until 1974, was heartily disliked by investors who criticized the tax as "[bringing] American investment activity in foreign markets to a virtual standstill." After a strong initial effect, the Interest Equalization Tax led to considerable circumvention by shifting lending and deposits abroad. Advocates of the tax considered it one of many programs that decreased the balance of payments deficit from an average of $2.5 billion between 1961 and 1964, to $1.1 billion in 1965 and 1966.[15]

Martin and the Fed were outmaneuvered by James Saxon, Kennedy's Comptroller of the Currency, who in 1962 took steps to dissipate the Glass-Steagall Act separation of investment and commercial banking. Saxon explained in the Comptroller's 1963 Annual Report entitled *Years of Reform: A Prelude to Progress*:

> Early in 1962, we undertook a broad-scale inquiry into the functioning of the National Banking System under the laws, policies, practices, and procedures which then had been in effect for many years. . . .
>
> One central theme has guided our efforts to reform the structure of banking regulation and procedures. In our review of past policies and practices, we have put them to the fundamental test of whether they were needed in order to maintain the solvency and liquidity of the banking system. Wherever a restrictive control did not meet this test, we have endeavored to broaden the discretionary powers of the national banks, insofar as this appeared desirable and was permissible under existing law. Wherever existing law appeared unduly restrictive in terms of this basic philosophy, we have advocated legislative changes to the Congress.

Saxon saw himself as in the vanguard of a deregulatory movement. In 1966, he explained:

> Burdened by vague fears inherited from the past, hampered by narrowly conceived regulatory policies, and constantly distracted by parental admonitions from the public authorities — banking initiative had for many years been stilted or discouraged. A new spirit now abounds. Banking has responded forcefully and imaginatively to its new challenges and its new opportunities. It is confident in its outlook, aggressive in its conduct, and optimistic of its future.

Saxon did not hesitate to challenge the Fed. In 1966, for example, he wrote to the Senate Committee for Banking and Currency of his opposition to the Fed's regulation of bank acquisition of stock in another bank: "While there is reason for retaining jurisdiction in the Federal Reserve Board over otherwise unregulated nonbank holding companies, such reasons do not apply to parent companies which are themselves regulated banks." Saxon criticized the Fed for blocking Chase Manhattan Bank's acquisition of 80 percent of the voting stock of Liberty National Bank.

In September 1962, Congress enacted legislation transferring authority over national bank trust departments from the Federal Reserve System to the Office of the Comptroller of the Currency. The Comptroller, among other expansionary steps, authorized national banks and state chartered banks that were members of the Federal Reserve System to underwrite municipal revenue bonds. Martin separately opposed enabling legislation to permit national banks to underwrite municipal bonds on the ground that this created a conflict of interest for the banks that both held deposits, provided trust services and advised municipal governments. "[T]hose who advise should not be also selling things that were on their shelves."[16]

Kennedy and Martin achieved a sufficiently effective working relationship that Kennedy reappointed Martin in 1963 as Fed Chair. As Kennedy explained to Martin when the two met on January 26, 1963: "I know you don't always agree with what we're doing and that my people don't always like what you're doing. But in our dealings, I've found you to be independent-minded and willing to speak up for your position. There are too few of such people and they are what a president needs above all."

Martin had the strong support of the business community, Treasury Secretary Dillon, and after some initial opposition, Walter Heller of the Council of Economic Advisers. Dillon stressed:

"Martin's support of our fiscal policy will be of vital importance in holding foreign opinion in line during the coming months and avoiding any loss of confidence in the dollar." Dillon also recognized the role that Martin could play in pursuing Kennedy's most significant unenacted fiscal goal, the 1963 tax cut. "He can," Dillon said of Martin, "be a tower of strength, in support of our tax program."

Kennedy regarded his 1963 comprehensive tax reduction and revision program as "the single most important step that can be taken to achieve balance [of payments] abroad as well as growth here at home. Along with his Civil Rights Bill, the Kennedy Tax Cut Bill would be one of the two most important laws that Kennedy failed to achieve during his presidency.

On December 14, 1962, Kennedy had stated at the Economic Club of New York:

> The final and best means of strengthening demand among consumers and business is to reduce the burden on private income and the deterrents to private initiative which are imposed by our present tax system; and this administration pledged itself last summer to an across-the-board, top-to-bottom cut in personal and corporate income taxes to be enacted and become effective in 1963. I am not talking about a "quickie" or a temporary tax cut, which would be more appropriate if a recession were imminent. Nor am I talking about giving the economy a mere shot in the arm, to ease some temporary complaint. I am talking about the accumulated evidence of the last 5 years that our present tax system, developed as it was, in good part, during World War II to restrain growth, exerts too heavy a drag on growth in peace time; that it siphons out of the private economy too large a share of personal and business purchasing power; that it reduces the financial incentives for personal effort, investment, and risk-taking.

In his January 14, 1963, State of the Union address, Kennedy further explained:

> America has enjoyed 22 months of uninterrupted economic recovery. But recovery is not enough. If we are to prevail in the long run, we must expand the long-run strength of our economy. We must move along the path to a higher rate of growth and full employment. . . .

> To achieve these greater gains, one step, above all, is essential — the enactment this year of a substantial reduction and revision in federal income taxes.
>
> For it is increasingly clear — to those in government, business, and labor who are responsible for our economy's success — that our obsolete tax system exerts too heavy a drag on private purchasing power, profits, and employment. Designed to check inflation in earlier years, it now checks growth instead. It discourages extra effort and risk. It distorts the use of resources. It invites recurrent recessions, depresses our federal revenues, and causes chronic budget deficits.

Kennedy proposed a permanent lowering of tax rates by $13.5 billion. Individual income taxes, which then ranged from 20 to 91 percent, would be reduced "to a more sensible range of 14 to 65 percent." Corporate tax rates would be reduced from 52 to 47 percent.

Kennedy viewed the tax cut as likely to increase national income "which in time will result in still higher federal revenues."

Martin's support for the tax cut was qualified. He was skeptical that the tax cut would expand consumer demand and tax revenues or reduce unemployment. While Martin agreed that the economy had grown during the first two years of the Kennedy administration, he was troubled by swelling federal deficits — $6.3 billion in 1962, $7.8 billion in 1963, and if Kennedy's Tax Plan was adopted as proposed in his State of the Union address, $11.7 billion.

In 1958, fear of inflation had prompted Martin to oppose an Eisenhower administration tax cut. In 1963, inflationary pressures were weak and growing weaker. Martin pragmatically supported the tax cut. On July 15, 1963, at a meeting of the Quadriad, Kennedy asked Martin: "Is it Federal Reserve policy to prevent a rise in long term rates?" Martin responded favorably: "I cannot be certain that the effect of the [anticipated increase in the discount rate from 3 to 3.5 percent] will be confined to short term rates, but we will make a major effort to achieve this goal." Kennedy supported the Fed's short term rate increase, but pointedly said to Martin: "The rate increase makes the passage of the Tax Program even more urgent. It would be especially useful if Bill could offer his public support for it." Martin had succeeded in developing a closer relationship with the Kennedy administration through several cooperative efforts, but he well understood as he explained to the

FOMC in March 1963: "The [Federal Reserve] System is considered off the team when it does not do everything that is wanted by the administration."

Wilbur Miller, Chair of the House Ways and Means Committee, was at best a sometime ally of the Kennedy administration. But Mills shared Kennedy's view that tax rates were too high in August 1962, and persuaded Kennedy to seek a permanent, not temporary, set of tax rate reductions. On September 25, 1963, the House passed the Kennedy tax cuts by a vote of 271 to 155.

Kennedy failed to secure the support of Harry Byrd, the Chair of the Senate Finance Committee, who, as early as December 14, 1960, had warned Kennedy against proposing a substantial tax cut given the deficit. The *New York Times* included an *Associated Press* story in which Byrd told Kennedy that a tax cut "would be the worst thing we could do."

The Johnson Presidency

The enactment of the Kennedy tax cut only occurred in February 1964, after Lyndon Johnson championed the bill. Within days after Kennedy's assassination on November 22, 1963, Johnson committed to making Kennedy's Tax Cut Bill "the first priority . . . nothing should stand in its way."

On November 27, 1963, Johnson spoke to Congress five days after Kennedy's assassination:

> . . . [N]o memorial oration or eulogy could more eloquently honor President Kennedy's memory than the earliest possible passage of the civil rights bill for which he fought so long . . .
>
> And second, no act of ours could more fittingly continue the work of President Kennedy than the early passage of the tax bill for which he fought all this long year. This is a bill designed to increase our national income and federal revenues, and to provide insurance against recession. That bill, if passed without delay, means more security for those now working, more jobs for those now without them, and more incentive for our economy.

Johnson understood that the only way to secure enactment of the Kennedy Tax Bill was to persuade Senator Byrd [D-VA] to engineer its release from the Senate Finance Committee. Johnson believed that Byrd's control of the Finance Committee was absolute.

"[N]othing could be done that he opposed." And the only way to persuade Byrd to support the bill was to reduce the budget from $102 billion to below $100 billion. Byrd, as Treasury Secretary Dillon recalled, "would have no truck with Keynesian theories." Byrd tied enactment of a tax cut to the budget. Johnson understood that the stakes were higher than that. Without enactment of the Kennedy tax cut, Kennedy's civil rights legislation also was imperiled. Robert Caro, in *The Years of Lyndon Johnson: The Passage of Power*, describes in detail Johnson's success in persuading Heller and the Council of Economic Advisers to make substantial budget cuts to secure the 1964 Tax Cut Bill and then persuade Byrd to support the tax cut.

Johnson explained in his memoir, *The Vantage Point*:

> I worked as hard on that budget as I have ever worked on anything.... The budget determines how many unemployed men and women are going to be trained; how many hungry schoolchildren are going to be fed; how many poor people are going to be housed... how our entire population is going to be protected against a possible enemy attack. Day after day I went over that budget.... I studied every line, nearly every page, until I was dreaming about the budget at night.

Johnson stressed to Byrd: "You can tell your grandchildren you were the senator who finally got a President to cut his budget."

On January 8, 1964, Johnson delivered his first State of the Union address in which, along with articulating support for many of the programs that became pillars of his Great Society, Johnson sought Kennedy's Tax Bill, "the most far-reaching cut of our time." Johnson had secured Byrd's support by limiting total expenditures to $97.9 billion, $500 million below the prior year's $98.4 billion and cutting the deficit in half from $10 billion to $4.9 billion. Johnson stressed:

> Above all, we must release $11 billion of tax reduction into the private spending stream to create new jobs and new markets in every area of this land....
>
> ... [E]very individual American taxpayer and every corporate taxpayer will benefit from the earliest possible passage of the pending tax bill from both the new investment it will bring and the new jobs that it will create.

> That tax bill has been thoroughly discussed for a year. Now we need action. The new budget clearly allows it. Our taxpayers surely deserve it. Our economy strongly demands it. And every month of delay dilutes its benefits in 1964 for consumption, for investment, and for employment.

On January 28, 1964, the Senate Finance Committee reported out Kennedy's tax cut legislation, the Revenue Act of 1964. It was enacted by the Senate on February 7 and signed into law by Johnson on February 26, 1964. While the Senate made several amendments in the lengthy Act, the essence of Kennedy's tax cut proposal remained intact. The highest individual tax rates were reduced from 91 to 70 percent, corporate tax rates were reduced from 52 to 48 percent. The Act also created a minimum standard deduction of $300 for individual taxpayers. The Senate deleted a provision for lower capital gains taxes.

As Kennedy had predicted, the 1964 Tax Cut had a substantial stimulative impact. Kennedy already had achieved his 5 percent growing rate, low inflation, and declining unemployment. Total federal tax receipts which were $112.6 billion in 1964, increased to $130.9 billion in 1966, and $153.7 billion in 1967.

By September 30, 1963, the expansion was in its 33rd month with a growth rate of 6 percent for the first nine months of 1963. In the 1960s, the United States would enjoy almost nine years of growth. Industrial production increased an average of 6.4 percent, GNP, 4.3 percent. Inflation remained under control through 1965, below 1.5 percent until midyear. Unemployment fell from 5.7 percent in 1963, to 3.8 percent in 1966. Walter Heller in 1977 testimony to the Joint Economic Committee would credit the tax cut as "the major factor that led our running a $3 billion (budget) surplus by the middle of 1965 before escalation in Vietnam struck us." Meltzer would characterize the two and one half years ending in 1965 as "probably the best under the Federal Reserve Act and for many years to come."[17]

Stylistically, there were vast differences between Johnson and Martin. Johnson viewed bankers with suspicion and saw higher interest rates and denials of access to credit as harmful to labor, small business, and a growing economy. He envisioned a Great Society, replete with a "War on Poverty," civil rights, and education and health care programs. He was a man who got things done, the Master of the Senate, as Caro described his years as Senate majority leader. He had little interest in economic analysis or theory. He wanted results and focused with laser-like intensity on the politics of achieving what he sought. To Johnson, Walter Heller and the Council of Economic Advisers were fellow travelers. As Johnson explained to Heller on the second day of his Presidency: "I'm no budget slasher. . . . I am a Roosevelt New Dealer." Johnson championed the Kennedy tax cut as critical to stimulating the economy, ensuring his 1964 election, and creating resources and momentum for the Great Society.

Martin, in contrast, at the beginning of Johnson's Presidency, seemed an anachronism. At the first Quadriad meeting with Johnson, Treasury Secretary Dillon, and Hiller on January 10, 1964, Martin had intended to distribute a memorandum, Monetary Policy and Cost-Push Inflation, in which Martin wrote: "The immediate goal of monetary policy should be to provide the resources needed to support a rate of growth in bank credit and money which will foster stable economic growth. . . . It must take into account price developments and the possibility of inflation, *or the widespread expectation of inflation,* which would do great damage to health growth." (Emphasis in original.) Johnson, in contrast, warned the Fed in his 1964 Economic Report: "It would be self-defeating to cancel the stimulus of tax reduction by tightening money."

When Johnson and Martin publicly disagreed in December 1965, about Fed discount rate increases, the *Washington Post* cartoonist Herb Block caricatured Martin scowling in an 1890s suit replete with a bowler hat and stiff collar facing one way on a bicycle built for two, with Johnson in shorts and a t-shirt facing the other. The bicycle was labeled "U.S. Economic Policy." Martin biographer Robert Bremner believed: "Their differing personal philosophies and goals put Martin and Johnson in conflict throughout most of Johnson's five years in the presidency. It is unlikely that Johnson ever had to work continually with anyone with [whom] he disagreed more frequently, and the same can be said for Bill Martin."

Johnson and Martin formed an awkward relationship, coordinating policies that would prove ineffectual in curbing the late 1960 inflation or the 1969–1970 recession.

As with Kennedy, Johnson understood that his strongest leverage over the Fed was through the appointments process. The Keynesian policies of the Kennedy Council of Economic Advisers continued under Walter Heller and Gardner Ackley, who was appointed Chair in 1964. Ackley was a Professor at the University of Michigan and Department of Economics and had been President of the American Economic Association. He was well-regarded by Paul Samuelson as "one of the leading micro-economists of the time." Ackley was outspoken in his hostility to the Fed. In a 1973 oral history, Ackley acknowledged "I don't believe that the Federal Reserve System ought to have any real independence. It is part of the government and should be responsible to the administration."

The appointment as Fed Governors in 1965 of Sherman Maisel, a Keynesian University of California Economic Professor, and in 1967 of Andrew Brimmer, meant that four of the seven Fed Governors in 1967 had been selected by Kennedy or Johnson. Both Maisel and Brimmer supported expansionary Fed policies as did two earlier appointments, George Mitchell and James Robertson. After 1967, Martin often was uncertain whether he could secure a majority of the Board.

In November 1964, the Fed approved increases in the discount rate from 3.5 to 4 percent for all Federal Reserve banks, and maximum bank interest rates to 4 percent for time deposits with less than 90 days to maturity and 4.5 percent for long-term deposits. The increase was in response to a November 24, 1964 by the United Kingdom to raise the U.K. discount rate from 5 to 7 percent to support the pound. At that time, this increase was considered so significant that a Swiss banker, quoted in *Time* magazine, predicted: "A seven percent increase will drag money from the moon." The Fed explained that the rate increases were taken "to maximize the international strength of the dollar" and were "aimed at counteracting possible capital outflows that might be prompted by any widening spread between interest rates in this country and the higher rates abroad and also at ensuring the flow of savings through commercial banks remains ample for the financing of domestic investment."

The Fed moved with the strong support of the Treasury, which on November 25, 1964, also helped orchestrate $3 billion of emergency assistance from the Fed, the Bank of England, and the United States Export-Import Bank to help stabilize the British exchange rate.

Johnson erupted when Treasury Secretary Dillon informed him about the Fed's imminent increases on November 22. The president demanded to know how the Fed and Treasury "would guarantee that the higher rates will not hurt the economy." Dillon and Martin advised Johnson that this type of guarantee was not possible. Martin, to help calm the president, held an unprecedented press conference at the time of the rate increase and stressed that the increase was precautionary and should not impact the availability of credit. Johnson reluctantly agreed to the Fed rate increases but was described in newspaper accounts as "unhappy and upset." Gardner Ackley earlier had sent a memorandum to Johnson criticizing the rate increase as "unwelcome." "[T]he high discount rate will cost us production and jobs in 1965. . . . Some academic studies suggest that losses for 1965 could run as high as $1 billion in GNP and 100,000 jobs."

After Johnson's landslide election in 1964, Douglas Dillon announced in March 1965, his retirement as Treasury Secretary. Dillon had been an ally with Martin moderating the economic policies of the Kennedy and Johnson administrations. By then, Martin's relationship with Council of Economic Advisers Chair Gardner Ackley was less comfortable than the relationship Martin had with Walter Heller. Martin was invited to fewer Quadriad meetings and conversations with the Johnson administration to work on complementary monetary and fiscal policies occurred less frequently.

Shortly after Dillon announced his resignation, Martin on March 10, 1965, offered to resign as Fed Chair. Johnson brusquely declined the offer: "I can't lose more than Doug at the moment." Martin did not then press the issue, but on at least three other occasions offered to resign. Johnson rejected each offer and in March 1967, Johnson reappointed Martin for a fifth four-year term as Chair of the Fed. In 1967, Martin had overwhelming business community support. John Macy, head of the Civil Service Commission, advised Johnson: Martin's "world prestige is unequaled. More on the hill are pro-Martin than against him." A Council of Economic Advisers member reported that 95 percent of the Business Council supported Martin's reappointment. Gardner Ackley, who frequently disagreed with Martin on monetary policy, informed Johnson that at least four and probably five Fed Governors supported Martin's reappointment. George Mitchell, who on the Fed often disagreed with Martin, explained his support: "Martin is increasingly becoming a follower of new (meaning Keynesian) economics. Bill is very much inclined to go along with the majority of the Board. . . . Now that the new economics is firmly in the saddle . . . , Bill can be counted on to cooperate."

In a remarkable private conversation on May 14, 1967, Martin again offered to resign. In his diary, Martin wrote that he said to Johnson: "You and I have had some sharp disagreements. I do not want to complicate the problems you are facing." Johnson acknowledged: "Bill, you and I have had our differences." But then Johnson said: "I am convinced that you're the best man available for the job. The country has confidence in you. I desperately need you to continue. I am going to have a very difficult time in the next two years, and I am pleading with you to continue. The Vietnam War is going to get hotter. . . . If it were not for Vietnam, I would be willing to let you retire." Johnson then surprised Martin: "Now I am going to tell you something that I want you to keep in complete confidence. I have decided not to run in 1968. . . . I am asking you to stay with me, if your conscience permits, until the inauguration of a new President in 1969."

Martin agreed after securing Johnson's assurance that he would not appoint a successor to Fed Governor Charles Shepardson, a Martin ally, who was not acceptable to Martin. Johnson reassured Martin that "he would not appoint anyone until [Martin] gave his approval." Martin also secured Johnson's assurance that Johnson would not try to run the Fed "by indirection," a promise Martin presumably realized was unlikely fully to be kept.[18]

By the end of 1965, unemployment was down to 4 percent, inflation measured by the Consumer Price Index remained low in 1965, beginning and ending that year at 2.1 and 2 percent. The GNP increased 6.6 percent in 1964.

Johnson in his 1965 economic report sought to address "the unfinished task of prosperous America . . . to build a Great Society" by achieving full employment without inflation, restoring external equilibrium in balance of payments, and defend the $35 exchange rate, widening the benefits of prosperity through such means as the war on poverty and a 7 percent increase in Social Security, and improving the quality of American life and strengthening national defense. Johnson sought a modest reduction in excise taxes, repeal of the 25 percent gold reserve requirement against reserve bank deposit liabilities, and most importantly, "a budget that will continue expansionary force rather than restrictive pressure on our economy."

Beginning in mid-1965, Johnson and Defense Secretary McNamara and Budget Director Charles Schultze took steps to hide the increase in Vietnam War military spending to reduce the publicly reported level of federal government deficit.

In October 1965, Schultze wrote a memorandum to the president stating "I have instructed my staff not to divulge the budgetary outlook with the Fed." Johnson sought to delay any further tax increase until January 1966, when his administration announced its 1967 budget estimates. In November 1965, the Johnson administration estimated total spending in 1967 at $105 billion, a wildly understated number. In his January 12, 1966 State of the Union address, the 1967 budget was estimated to be $112.9 billion, based on the assumption that the Vietnam War ended midyear, December 1966, and defense spending was calculated to be $58.3 billion. The actual 1967 budget expenditures would be $137 billion with defense spending equal to $71 billion.

Increases in budget deficits were made inevitable by plans Johnson implemented to nearly double the 190,000 troops in Vietnam. Johnson reported in his January 12, 1967 State of the Union that the troop level would reach 455,000 in 1967. General Westmoreland had sought 600,000 troops by year end 1967. McNamara falsely informed Ackley that the budget cost in Vietnam in 1967 would be $10 billion, while privately informing Johnson he expected the cost to be $15 to $17 billion.

By July 1965, Martin had been informed by Senator Richard Russell [D-GA] that the budget deficit would be much larger than Johnson had described to the Treasury, the Council of Economic Advisers, or Martin at the Quadriad. In July 1965, Johnson had rejected the recommendation of the Joint Chiefs of Staff to use traditional budgetary procedures to prosecute the war in Vietnam. This meant higher taxes. Johnson rejected their advice, the advice of his Council of Economic Advisers, and Fed Chair Martin. As Johnson explained in an account written by David Halberstam:

> I don't know much about economics, . . . but I do know the Congress. And I can get the Great Society through right now — this is a golden time. We've got a good Congress and I'm the right President and I can do it. But if I talk about the cost of the war, the Great Society won't go through and the tax bill won't go through. Old Wilbur Mills will sit down there and he'll thank me kindly and send me back my Great Society, and then he'll tell me that they'll be glad to spend whatever we need for the war.

Senator Stennis [D-MS] and Representative Mendel Rivers [D-SC] similarly had informed Gardner Ackley that the 1966 fiscal year deficit was likely to be $10 billion, not the $3 to $5 billion he estimated after discussions with Defense Secretary McNamara.

Johnson wanted "Guns and Butter," the Great Society, and increased Vietnam War expenditures without reducing spending, raising taxes, or having the Fed raise interest rates. At the October 1965 Quadriad meeting, Ackley and Treasury Secretary Fowler urged Martin to delay any interest rate increase until the evidence was clearer. Martin delayed a rate increase until December 3, 1965, as yields on five-year Treasury rates increased .4 of a percent to 4.52 percent between August 1 and December 1. The debt market was signaling that government interest rates needed to rise to continue to make Federal debt marketable. A November 4, 1965, Treasury issue of 18-month 4.25 notes had not been well received. Simultaneously, the balance of payments deficit in 1964 grew from $3.85 billion in 1960, to $8.06 billion.

At a divided FOMC on November 23, 1965, Martin, after expressing his view that it was "unfortunate that the [Federal Reserve] System had divided and continued to be divided" stated that "he wanted the record to reflect his opinion that it was not possible to run away continually from making a decision." "[H]e thought the financial problem was acute when conditions reached a point where . . . it was necessary to support a Treasury financing in order to make it successful. . . . Except for [Federal Reserve] support, the latest offering of the Treasury would not have been successful. . . . This created a real problem. The Treasury expected to announce another financing on the 16th of December. Therefore, if the [Fed] was going to make any move now, it must do so before that time."

Martin favored discount rate increases and coordinating Regulation Q ceiling rate increases because "he believed the country was in a period of creeping inflation already. And he believed the balance of payments situation would be benefited by more restraint in the over-all economy. In short, he thought the economy was going too fast at the moment."

On December 3, 1965, a divided Fed voted 4-3 to raise the discount rate from 4 to 4.5 percent and to increase the Regulation Q ceiling rate on bank time deposits and certificates of deposit having a maturity of more than 30 days to 5.5 percent. In a subsequent

December 1965 speech, Martin explained why the Fed's 4–3 majority believed that inflation was now a threat: "[O]ver little more than twelve months, a crucial index of industrial wholesale prices has risen about 1¾ percent, after four years of virtual stability."

The three dissenters included George Mitchell, who warned that the Fed "appeared to be on a collision course with the administration." The dissenters felt "that it was at least premature in the absence of more compelling evidence of inflationary dangers."

Martin cast the decisive vote. Martin well understood the risk to the Fed's independence if it rejected the president's intent to avoid an interest rate increase: "There is a question," he explained, "whether the Federal Reserve is to be run by the administration in office." The Fed announcement of the rate increase emphasized that the intent was to slow excessive demands for credit and maintain price stability.

The Fed statement issued on December 6, 1965, announced:

> In sum, the actions taken should have the three-pronged impact of:
>
> 1. Backing up the Government's efforts to prevent inflationary excesses from damaging an economy now carrying the added burden of military operations in Vietnam;
> 2. Bolstering the Government's programs to overcome the persistent deficit in the United States balance of payments; and
> 3. Demonstrating a new United States determination to maintain the international strength of the dollar.

Johnson summoned Martin to his ranch in Johnson City, Texas on December 5, euphemistically for "a trip to the woodshed." Johnson was enraged. He accused Martin of placing himself above the president. "You went ahead and did something that I disapproved of... and can affect my entire term here.... You've got me in a position where you can run a rapier into me and you've done it.... You took advantage of me and I just want you to know that's a despicable thing to do."

Martin did not back down: "Mr. President, we were not precipitous about this. I warned you about this. We discussed this [increase] and you asked me to give you another chance and we couldn't wait any longer." Martin concluded: "I do have a very strong conviction that the Federal Reserve Act placed the responsibility for interest rates with the Federal Reserve Board. This is one of the few occasions where the Federal Reserve Board decision had to be final."

Martin succeeded in that instance in defending the Fed's independence and maintaining a rate increase that the 4-3 Fed majority believed necessary. But Martin and the Fed paid a price. By the end of November 1965, Martin and Council of Economic Advisers Chair Gardner Ackley were no longer talking to each other. In January 1966, Martin complained to top Johnson aide Joe Califano that he felt "closed out of the decision-making process" because of his show of independence. In February 1966, Johnson rejected Martin's recommended candidate for the seventh Federal Reserve governorship and named Andrew Brimmer, who was expected to have an expansionary view of the economy.

Martin and Johnson in late February came to an uneasy peace. In late January, Martin informed Treasury Secretary Fowler that if Johnson wanted him to resign, "all that is needed . . . is a quiet nudge and I'll resign." The day after his initial unsuccessful conversation with Johnson about what became the Brimmer seat on the Fed, Martin told Johnson, "But as I think over our talk . . . I become more discouraged with the programs as I see them." In late February, after a second conversation about the Brimmer nomination, a calmed down Johnson came to terms with the Fed Chair. Johnson told Martin: "I have great respect for you and business and bankers have a high regard for you. You have educated three Presidents before me . . . and I want you to continue to be frank with me."[19]

The December 1965 rate increase failed to stem inflation. After the Johnson City confrontation with Johnson, Martin, presiding over a divided Federal Reserve Board, was unable to then use discounts or bank reserve requirements to address inflation or ultimately to prevent the 1969–1970 recession. Inflation would increase 3.8 percent in the first six months of 1966, compared to 1.9 percent in 1965. The Consumer Price Index would reach 7 percent in the April-June months of 1968. In July-August 1967, wage settlements averaged a 6 percent increase, generating further cost-push pressures for further price increases. In 1969, the inflation rate would hit an annual 18-year high of 5.75 percent.

Historians have harshly criticized Martin's timidity after December 1965. Meltzer articulated this view when he wrote of the December 1965 rate increase: "Martin had shown courage and determination by refusing to back down under intense pressure from the president. Then he retreated." To stimulate the economy, the Fed increased the growth rate of the monetary base from an average of 4.3 percent during 1960–1963 and 7 percent by mid-1971. Between 1960 and August 1971, the federal debt increased from $287.7 billion to $413.8 billion with Fed Reserve holdings growing by $39.5 billion, from $27.4 to $66.9 billion. The Fed purchases were a major source of the increase in the monetary base made inevitable by the federal government's deficit spending.

One reason for some of the delay in Fed steps to address inflation was the 1966–1967 credit crunch. The Fed had followed up its December 1965 rate increases with several further steps to tighten credit. In February 1966, limiting the System's holdings of government securities to $1.5 billion, prompted bank borrowings to increase an average by nearly $600 million. In July and August 1966, the Fed raised reserve requirements in two steps on time deposits (other than savings accounts) from 4 to 6 percent. This increased total required reserves by $900 million. In September, the Fed in its summary required "member banks to moderate their rate of expansion of loans, particularly business loans; indicated that bank use of Reserve Bank discount facilities would be expected to be in a manner consistent with this objective; and noted the continuing availability of discount facilities to cushion deposit shrinkages."

By the summer of 1966, credit was being squeezed in the financial community by the Fed's tight money policies. Treasury Secretary Fowler recalled leading investment bankers in August 1966 "expressing great fear that a financial panic is likely if something weren't done to relieve the Fed's tightening." Martin indicated to Fowler that he could relieve the pressure but "needed to see some sign of fiscal restraint first."

The Fed's 1966 Annual Report was more discrete: "As a continued high volume of credit demands and increased monetary restraint resulted in rising market rates of interest, commercial banks found themselves less able to accommodate business and other credit demands by competing for the liquid funds of corporations."

In November 1966, the FOMC shifted gears and sought to stimulate "a moderate reserved expansion of bank credit and easier conditions in financial markets." In December 1966, the Fed discontinued "the special discount arrangements of the September 1 letter." During the first five months of 1967, money supply increased an average rate of 10 percent and bank credit of 12 percent. This caused the interest rate on three-month Treasury bills to fall from 5.5 percent in October 1966, to 3.5 percent in June 1967. Most significantly, in June 1967, the Fed cut the discount rate from 6 to 5.5 percent, the first cut since 1960. The several Fed steps to stimulate the economy rapidly worked. After July 1967, industrial production began to increase. GNP growth was 7 percent in the period April-June 1968. There was little slack in the economy. Unemployment was 3.5 percent that quarter. The Consumer Price Index would rise from zero in early 1967 to an annual rate of 7 percent in June 1968. By mid-September 1967, three-month Treasury bill interest rates rose from 3.71 to 4.32 percent in four months, five-year Treasury bonds from 4.58 to 5.38 percent.

In 1968, Martin delayed seeking a rate increase when GNP growth had reached 7 percent and the Consumer Price Index measure of inflation was at 7 percent in June 1968 to avoid the possibility of creating a new 1966 credit squeeze by tightening credit too soon. The subsequent 1968 Fed rate increases alone were too little, too late.

Martin had been outspoken in stressing the need between 1966 and 1968 for a tax increase as the most important means to reduce deficit spending and inflation. In December 1965, Martin had informed the Quadriad that lower interest rates were dependent on a tax increase. He repeated this argument frequently. Fowler recalled in his oral history that Martin told the president late in 1966: "I feel now, as in every meeting [with you] since January [1966] that you should go forward with a tax increase on the assumption that expenditures in Vietnam are going to rise." This was a widely held view. Paul Samuelson publicly backed a tax increase in February 1966. Five of the Treasury Department's six economists and its consultant board favored an increase at the end of February. The *Washington Post* reported in April 1961, 70 percent of a poll of 30 economists favored an increase. Gardner Ackley, Johnson's Chair of the Council of Economic Advisers, told the president that he could not have the Vietnam War and the Great Society without a tax increase. In December 1965, the Council of Economic Advisers and Ackley sent memoranda to Johnson seeking a tax increase based on the growing needs for the Vietnam War and additional domestic requirements. Ackley believed there was a sense of urgency. He believed that the economic situation could get out of control.

Johnson initially was unpersuaded. He resisted seeking a tax increase because of his concerns that it would be tied to cuts in Great Society programs.

Martin persisted, taking the extraordinary step in May 1967, of being anonymously interviewed by *Washington Post* reporter Hobart Rowen on "escalation of U.S. troop commitments in Vietnam [that] might require a substantial 1968 tax increase." In a June 5, 1967, Quadriad Meeting, Martin informed Johnson: "There should be no shilly-shallying around about [a tax increase], it is essential to make clear that the size of the deficit makes this action necessary." In a June 26, 1967, speech, Martin stated: "I would support income tax increases amounting to 10 percent to bring federal income and expenditures closer to balance."

During the second half of 1967, Martin, in biographer Bremner's words, "adopted a remarkably risky tactic to force consideration of a tax increase. He concluded that the FOMC [Federal Open Market Committee] should not tighten credit because it would encourage Congress to avoid action on the tax increase by letting the Fed do the job of slowing the economy." On March 18, 1968, Martin addressed the Economic Club of Detroit, with a sense of heightened urgency:

> What we're confronted with today is a budgetary problem that's been getting progressively worse. I have said this repeatedly, and I'm sure some of you will have tired of hearing me say it: what we are moving toward gradually is not deficit finance for a temporary period, but perpetual deficit. This is a very sad progression toward undermining the currency....
>
> The heart of our budgetary problem — and I have no hesitation in saying this — is that this country today is over extended and overcommitted.

Against a backdrop of rising interest rates in the credit markets, with 20-year Treasury Bonds rising to a peak of 5.8 percent in mid-November, the Fed did raise the discount rate from 4 percent to 4.5 percent on November 19, 1967, and March 14, from 4.5 to 5 percent. On April 19, 1968, the Fed increased the discount rate to 5.5 percent and the Regulation Q ceiling rate on certificates of deposit from 60 to 89 days from 5.5 to 6 percent, and to 6.25 percent for 180 days or more.

Ultimately, the federal budget deficit overwhelmed Johnson's unwillingness to seek a tax increase. By December 12, 1966, the total federal budget was skyrocketing from an original estimate of $112 billion for the 1968 fiscal year to a forecast $140 billion. The 1967 deficit was $9.8 billion. The 1968 deficit was projected to be $19 billion, the largest deficit in absolute and percentage term since World War II. On January 9, 1967, Johnson telephoned Martin and informed him: "I've decided to bite the bullet on taxes. . . . I have decided to follow your advice."

In his January 10, 1967, State of the Union address, Johnson proposed a surcharge of 6 percent on both corporate and individual income taxes "to last for 2 years or so long as the unusual expenditures associated with our efforts in Vietnam continue." At the time of his January 1967 State of the Union address, Johnson estimated the 1967 deficit to be $9.7 billion and with the surcharge, $8.1. billion in 1968.

Johnson closed the July 21, 1967, Quadriad meeting by committing "to the 10 percent surtax increase recommended by Chairman Martin."

On August 3, 1967, Johnson sent a special message to Congress on the state of the budget and the economy. By then, expenditures had grown $8.5 billion from $135 to $143.5 billion, revenues, even if a 6 percent tax surcharge was enacted, were estimated to be $7 billion lower than in January, meaning "the deficit could exceed $28 billion. Johnson recommended:

— A temporary surcharge of 10% should be placed on corporate income tax liabilities, effective July 1, 1967.

— A temporary surcharge of 10% should be placed on individual income tax liabilities, effective October 1, 1967.

In a separate August 3, 1967, press conference, Johnson anticipated that "as much as $4 billion" could be achieved through budget cuts. Combined with $7.4 billion that could be generated by the 10 percent tax surcharges, this would reduce the deficit by $11.4 billion, but still leave a hefty $17 billion deficit.

Wilbur Mills, Chair of the House Ways and Means Committee, was unimpressed by the size of the budget cuts, stating in 1967: "It seems to me that the position we are in shows an increasing awareness on the part of the administration of the need for expenditure cuts. I think we are making progress, but I feel that we still have some distance to go."[20]

Simultaneous with the burgeoning budget deficit was a continuing deterioration of the United States balance of payments and gold reserves. Johnson responded to the November 1967, British devaluation of the pound by "[reaffirming] unequivocally the commitment of the United States to buy and sell gold at the existing price of $35 per ounce," but by then the United States commitment to a $35 gold price was in its terminal phase.

The International Monetary System, as the Federal Reserve wrote, "was subject to greater strains during 1967 than at any time since the 1930s." These strains became acute on November 18, 1967, when Great Britain responded to its balance of payments deficit by devaluing the pound by 14.3 percent from $2.80 to $2.40. In the prior month, the Bank of England had raised its discount rate from 5.5 to 6.5 percent. The day after the devaluation, the Bank of England raised its discount rate to 8 percent.

The United States took several steps to stabilize the British pound and its own balance of payments deficit. On November 30, 1968, the Federal Reserve increased to $1.5 billion its reciprocal currency arrangement with the Bank of England and increased by $1.75 billion its swap lines with eight central banks and the Bank of International Settlements.

On December 5, 1967, $475 million of gold was withdrawn from the United States Treasury.

On January 1, 1968, President Johnson issued Executive Order 11,387, authorizing the Fed to impose regulations on the foreign transactions of banks and other financial institutions. On that same day, the Fed issued revised guidelines to reduce nonexpert credits to developed countries in Western Europe and to produce at least a $500 million net capital inflow to United States banks and other financial institutions. United States banks were requested in 1968, not to make new loans with greater than one year maturities to developed countries in Western Europe, except for bona fide export credits or for legally binding commitments. Nonbank financial institutions were requested to reduce their holdings of liquid funds abroad during 1968 to zero or the absolute minimum necessary to cover working balances and to make no new loans to developed countries of Western Europe except to finance bona fide export credits or to meet legally binding commitments.

The run on gold continued in London on March 7, 1968, with $180 million of gold changing hands. In March 1968, United States gold stock declined $1.2 billion. United States and ally gold reserves were declining to dangerous levels through their unlimited support of the London gold pool. By 1968, United States monetary gold stock had declined to $10.9 billion from $17.8 billion in 1967. At the 1968 level, potential claims on United States gold had increased from twice the gold supply in 1965, to three times the supply.

The most consequential response was taken in mid-March 1968 when the United States, working with the leaders of seven central banks and the International Monetary Fund (*IMF*), created a new two-tiered system to replace the Bretton Woods United States gold on demand at a $35 price. The United States for three more years was able to maintain the $35 gold exchange rate for official settlements. Martin and Treasury Secretary Fowler "forcefully rejected" the White House and Council of Economic Advisers recommendation to expand existing Fed swap credits by $2 billion.

Instead, on March 14, 1968, a decision was made to suspend operations in the London gold pool that had been one means by which the United States supported the international $35 gold exchange rate.

On March 18, 1968, Johnson signed legislation eliminating the 25 percent gold reserve requirement behind Federal Reserve notes, ending the last gold reserve requirement of the 1913 Federal Reserve Act. By then, the Treasury had only $3.5 million of free gold left.

Nearly simultaneously, after four years of discussion and negotiation, the United States, leading central banks, and the *IMF* issued a draft of a new supplementary form of international reserve assets, Special Drawing Rights (*SDRs*), allowing any IMF country to participate in the new paper reserve system and receive SDRs, not gold. The IMF became a type of universal banker, not holding national currencies, but guiding the international flow of funds to finance balance of payments.

On June 19, 1968, Congress enacted the Special Drawing Rights Act, authorizing the president to accept amendments to the IMF for the purpose of establishing Special Drawing Rights. The IMF formally created SDRs in 1969, distributing SDRs to IMF participants in proportion to their IMF quotas. Participating IMF countries could use SDRs whenever it had a balance of payment or reserve need to do so without resulting in any exchange of gold. SDRs were neither a currency nor a claim on the IMF, but a claim on the freely usable currencies of IMF participants. The value of SDRs was based on a basket of international reserve currencies issued by IMF members with the largest exports of goods and services over the previous five-year period.

Robert Triffin in 1959 testimony to the Joint Economic Committee and his book *Gold and the Dollar Crisis*, described what came to be known as Triffin's Dilemma, as summarized by a subsequent Treasury Report to Congress:

> In the 1960s, the supply of reserve assets — mainly gold and U.S. dollars — was constrained by the Bretton Woods system of fixed exchange rates. Demand for international liquidity had to be met through U.S. balance of payments deficits, which risked undermining confidence in the value of the dollar in relation to the value of gold. However, elimination of U.S. deficits risked causing a shortage of reserves, a slowdown in global economic activity, and deflation. Hence, the dilemma facing economic policy makers was a choice between an international liquidity shortage and a loss of confidence in the dollar.

Martin, in a September 14, 1970, speech in Basel, would praise the SDR system, likening the creation of international reserve assets to the creation of a national central bank to address the uncontrolled creation of credit by the national banking system.

For an interim period, the SDR system did help relieve the run on gold. But it was never widely used because of the requirement that foreign reserve assets had to be exchanged into a currency to use SDRs. A country must be a willing party to buy SDRs. Paul Volcker later would write: "Great hopes were placed on the imaginative new instrument, which promptly was labeled 'paper gold' but was neither paper nor gold: as one wit at the IMF said, the SDR was 'not minted, not printed.' Rather, the SDR could be found only in the blips on an IMF computer, and many restrictions were placed on activating the computer."

SDRs did not address the more serious problem, the overvalued dollar. The simultaneous end of gold sales to nongovernmental or central banks achieved through ending support of the gold post, in contrast, was highly significant. This was a consequential step towards the end of the $35 gold fixed exchange system in 1971.

On March 31, 1968, Johnson announced at the end of a speech in the aftermath of the January 1968, Tet Offensive in Vietnam and a renewed call to move toward peace, that he would not seek or accept the nomination of the Democratic party for another term as president. In making this surprise announcement, Johnson stressed: "With America's sons in the fields far away, with America's future under challenge right here at home, with our hopes and the world's hopes for peace in the balance every day, I do not believe that I should devote an hour or a day of my time to any personal partisan causes or to any duties other than the awesome duties of this office — the presidency of your country."

In his remarks, Johnson also stated that he would "approve appropriate reductions in his January 1968, budget when and if Congress so decides this should be done."

Johnson's announcement, the gold reserve crisis, the overheating United States economy with nominal economic growth increasing 10 percent in the first quarter of 1968, and the Consumer Price Index up 4.1 percent that quarter galvanized the Senate on April 2, 1968, to adopt legislation by a vote of 57–31 that included Johnson's 10 percent tax increase and $6 billion in expenditure cuts demanded by Wilbur Mills. The House followed suit and on June 20, 1968, after a conference committee chaired by Wilbur Mills, Congress enacted the Revenue and Expenditure Control Act of 1968, which included the 10 percent tax surcharge on individual and corporate income taxes and a reduction of $6 billion in expenditures in Fiscal Year 1969. The final vote in the House was 268 to 150 and in the Senate, 64 to 16. The full impact and the 10 percent tax surcharges lasted fewer than two years. Congress reduced the surcharges to 5 percent effective January 1, 1970, and eliminated them entirely in July 1970.

The Revenue and Expenditure Control Act of 1968 on top of the new Special Drawing Rights contributed to a reversal of the $3.4 billion balance of payments deficit in 1967, and a $1.6 billion surplus in 1968.

The United States economy continued to overheat. Real GNP accelerated to 6 percent during the first six months of 1968 compared to under 4 percent in the last six months of 1967. With unemployment declining to 3.3 percent in 1968, unit labor costs rose significantly by approximately 4 percent. Average hourly wages in private nonfarm industries increased to 7.3 in 1968, more than the 5 percent in 1967. Wholesale prices of initial commodities averaged 2.5 percent higher in 1968, compared to 1.5 percent in 1967. Consumer prices rose 4.7 percent in 1968.

The federal deficit remained staggeringly high, increasing $21 billion in 1968, $6 billion in 1969, $17 billion in 1970, and $27 billion in 1971. Prime bank loan rates would increase to 6.75 percent in December 1968, 7.5 percent in March 1969, as high as 8.5 percent in June 1969.

The denouncement of Martin's Chairmanship was a sad one. In February 1969, he apologized to the Joint Economic Committee for past errors:

> It appears that the Federal Reserve was overly optimistic in anticipating immediate benefits from fiscal restraint... but now we mean business in stopping inflation.... A credibility gap exists in the business and financial community as to whether the Federal Reserve will push restraint hard enough to check inflation. The Board means to do so and is unanimous on that point.

"It is more important to settle the problems of inflation than to settle the War in Vietnam," Martin informed international bankers in Copenhagen on June 20, 1969. "There will be a good deal of pain and suffering before the U.S. eliminates inflation.... I might favor even sterner restraints such as voluntary credit controls, forced savings, and a high tax increase, if these should be needed to bring the severe United States inflation under control."

Nixon, still smarting from the Fed's tight money policies in 1960, which he believed cost him election as president in 1960, informed Martin at their first meeting in December 1968, that he intended to replace Martin as Chair with Arthur Burns, whom Paul McCracken, Nixon's initial Chair of the Council of Economic Advisers, described as "a long-time friend of the President." Martin disappointed Nixon by telling him that he would serve out his term as Chair until January 31, 1970.

In Martin's final FOMC on January 25, 1970, the meeting notes would report: "Growth in real gross national product came to a halt in the fourth quarter of 1969 [October-December], according to preliminary Commerce Department estimates, but prices and costs were continuing to rise.... Average wholesale prices rose considerably further from mid-November to mid-December for both commodities and farm and food products." Federal Fund Rates were as high as 9.75 percent for dollar auctions in the short-term money market. Effective January 5, 1970, the ceiling rate on federally underwritten home mortgages rose from 7.5 to 8.5 percent.

By the time Martin retired, he had come to believe: "I've failed." As Federal Open Market Secretary Bob Holland wrote: "[Martin] felt that the inflation that had crept into the American economy was too much. It had happened on his watch and he saw it as a failure." At a lavish farewell party at the White House, Martin said: "I wish I could turn the bank over to Arthur Burns as I would have liked. . . . But we are in very deep trouble. We are in the wildest inflation since the Civil War."

Martin's self-assessment was an unduly critical one, reflecting his disappointment in the last period of his Chairmanship, rather than a fair historical assessment.

Martin created the contours of the modern Federal Reserve System and effectively made the Fed a central bank. He deserves particular credit for implementing the 1951 Accord in ways that both achieved Fed qualified independence to determine interest rates and money supply and securing "a seat at the table" for the Fed Chair on national fiscal policy such as the debate on acceptable-levels of federal budget deficit and the need to resist or support tax cuts or tax increases. Martin modernized the internal structure of the Fed, and significantly expanded the Fed's international role. Paul Samuelson, a frequent Martin critic, saluted Martin on his retirement: "Martin enters the Valhalla of American central bankers." *Time* magazine similarly lauded Martin as "the pivotal economic figure of two tumultuous decades."

Others such as 23 professors who appeared before congressional hearings on the Federal Reserve System after Fifty Years supported Wright Potman's attack on the extent of the Fed's independence. Federal historian Allan Meltzer, *pro contra,* criticized Martin for accommodations made to achieve coordination with administration fiscal policy. Meltzer wrote: "A puzzle of the 1960s is that Martin, who successfully resisted inflation in the 1950s, permitted and abetted the increase. A principal reason is that he accepted coordination with the administration's fiscal policy even to the point of increasing money growth and lowering interest rates after Congress passed the 1968 tax surcharge." The .25 percent interest rate cut, it should be noted, was soon reversed. Martin later regretted even this modest interest rate cut. The notes from his final Quadriad Meeting on January 23, 1970, quoted Martin: "The System had pulled a boner after the tax increase last year by pursuing for a time an easier monetary policy. This decision heavily reflected projections of their staff that the tax increase might produce an overkill effect, causing substantial slack in the economy. In retrospect this evaluation of prospects was in error."

There are larger points worth stressing. Under Martin, changes in the discount rate and money supply again were fortified as the principal weapons of the Fed's monetary policy. His consensus and evidence-based approach to discount rate and reserve changes had generally subsequently been followed while Fed doctrine evolved and economic analysis substantially improved. Martin or any Chair's ability to act was limited by the membership of the Fed. Political context inevitably weighs on Fed decision making. It was easier for Martin to "successfully [resist] inflation in the 1950s," when President Eisenhower's balanced or near balanced budgets reduced inflationary pressures. It was not feasible for Martin or any Fed Chair fully to control the escalating deficits of the Johnson presidency.

A different critique of the Fed during and after Martin's chairmanship is appropriate. The Fed during his chairmanship had less interest in issues outside of monetary policy. Between 1951 and 1970, the number and assets of Federal Reserve national and state member banks roughly stayed the same:

	National Banks		State Member Banks		Nonmember Banks	
Year	**Number**	**Assets (in billions)**	**Number**	**Assets (in billions)**	**Number**	**Assets (in billions)**
1951	4946	$94.3	1910	$47.2	7251	$23.9
1970	4620	$314.3	1147	$117.2	7683	$98.4

These data means that in 1951, the 4620 Federal Reserve national banks possessed 57 percent of banking assets. In 1970, the 4638 national banks possessed a similar 59 percent of these banks' assets.

Beneath these placid data, the world was changing. Ceiling interest rates on customer accounts for national banks under Regulation Q and after 1966 savings and loans but with a 0.75 percent higher ceiling than banks. This created an institutional context in which different bank and savings and loan interest rate ceilings could impact bank versus savings and loan (*S & L*) competition. Regulation Q did not apply to foreign euro dollar accounts. Nonbanking institutions such as mutual funds were not subject to Regulation Q. As inflation raised interest rates Regulation Q posed an increasing challenge to the structure of financial institutions. Interest rate regulation would be a key factor blamed for the massive losses by savings and loans in later decades. At no time during Martin's period did the Fed effectively champion allowing free markets, to determine interest rates. Relying on market forces, in contrast, was Martin's strong preference with the discount rate.[21]

The Nixon Presidency

The Presidency of Richard Nixon (1969–1974) primarily focused on foreign policy, most significantly the prosecution of the war in Vietnam until the withdrawal of United States troops in 1973 and the 1972 rapprochement with China. Nixon would be the first president to resign after the Watergate Scandal.

Throughout his presidency, Republican Richard Nixon faced a Democratic party controlled Congress. In 1968, Nixon had been elected president with a thin 43.4 percent of the popular vote compared to 42.7 percent for Vice President Hubert Humphrey, and 13.5 percent for Segregationist third party candidate George Wallace. His victory in the electoral college in 1968 was 301 to 191 for Humphrey and 46 for Wallace.

In 1972, Nixon was reelected in a landslide with 60.7 percent of the popular vote and the 520 electoral college votes of 49 states to 37.5 percent of the popular vote and one state and the District of Columbia for Senator George McGovern.

The variable size of Nixon's 1968 and 1972 presidential elections had little impact on Democratic party control of Congress. In 1968, the Democrats held a 58-42 Majority in the Senate; in 1970, a 53–45 majority; and in 1972, a 56–42 majority. Similarly, in the House of Representatives, the Democrats had a 243–192 seat majority in 1968; in 1970, a 255–180 majority; and in 1972, a 242–192 majority.

Nixon appointed Arthur Burns to be Chair of the Federal Reserve System early in 1970 after Burns served in the White House as Counsellor to the president during the final year of Martin's term. Burns became Chair on February 1, 1970, and after reappointment, served as Chair until March 31, 1978.

Burns was a Columbia University Professor who had served as Eisenhower's Chair of the Council of Economic Advisers between 1953 and 1956 and wrote major economic works on business circles, propounding an atheoretical analysis of economic history to find patterns of cyclical coherence. Burns viewed himself neither as a Monetarist nor a Keynesian.

As Fed Chair, Burns believed wage and price controls were the preferred means to combat inflation rather than Martin's emphasis on interest rate and bank reserve adjustments, or Milton Friedman's focus on money supply. Burns believed that labor unions, high wage settlements, and government social programs made inflation difficult to control using monetary policy. He knew that increasing unemployment to combat inflation was unacceptable to Nixon. Burns was skeptical of Friedman's preference for adjusting money growth as the key mechanism to combat inflation. Friedman had urged that any reduction in unemployment achieved by increasing inflation would be temporary.

On June 22, 1971, Burns wrote a nine-page letter to Nixon summarizing his view:

> There was a time when the onset of a business recession was typically followed in a few months by a decline in the price level and in wage rates, or at least by a moderation of the rise. That is no longer the case. The business cycle is still alive, indeed too much so; but its inner response mechanism, which has never stood still, is now very different from what it was even ten or twenty years ago....
>
> ... Why are the old rules not working: Why is inflation continuing at a virtually undiminished rate in the face of substantial unemployment of men, machinery, plant and equipment?
>
> The answer is to be found in the changed character of our labor and product markets....
>
> > ... The past decade has witnessed a vast growth of trade unionism in the public sector — mainly among state and local employees but also federal employees. We have had innumerable illegal strikes of public employees, among them the postal strike. These strikes have been preponderantly successful, in the sense that the employees got pretty much what they asked for. In this environment, both the trade union leaders and the rank and file have come to believe that the

> government lacks either the power or the will to resist their demands. They have therefore become progressively bolder in pushing wage and other demands.
>
> ... During the past decade, we have also had a vast expansion of welfare programs. When subsidies are provided by government to strikers — and this is what we have been doing more and more — workers on strike can hold out longer. Business managers are fully aware of this, and they are therefore less inclined to take a strike than was the case ten or twenty years ago....
>
> What I recommend, as a way out of the present economic malaise, is a strong wage and price policy.

On January 30, 1970, Burns wrote in a private letter: "I wish the world was as simple as the Friedmanites and Keynesians wish to make it, but it never has been and, I dare say, never will be." On April 7, 1970, Burns would state that inflation came "mainly from wage increases that reduced supplies and raised prices.... It was a mistake for the Federal Reserve to attempt to deal with cost-push inflation through monetary policy."

Burns brought to the Fed an arrogance that made him unpopular with some fellow senior economic leaders in the Nixon administration, some fellow Fed governors, and some senior staff. By October 1970, after Burns was formally appointed to be Fed Chair, Burns asked Martin, who remained Chair, to inform the FOMC that "he would not feel bound by any decisions made before his term." He had little patience with those that disagreed with his analysis. He was a dominant Chair who left little doubt that he sought to be in control. Burns criticized Nixon as being moved "mainly, if not entirely, by a political motive" playing "a dangerous game" in which Nixon set his advisers in conflict with each other, "quite Rooseveltian." Burns characterized National Security Adviser Henry Kissinger as "a brilliant political analyst but admittedly ignorant of economics," Secretary of Treasury John Connally as "a thoroughly confused politician, and future Treasury Secretary George Shultz as "a no less confused amateur economist."

Burns would be sharply criticized for subordinating the Fed's statutory mission to control inflation to Nixon's preference for rapid economic growth to improve Nixon's probability of reelection in 1972. Nixon believed that rising unemployment had cost him the presidency in 1960. At Herbert Stein's first meeting with

President Nixon, Nixon had put it simply: "[W]e must not raise unemployment."

Nixon was heavy handed in his approach to Burns and the Fed's independence. He stated: "I respect [Burns'] independence. However, I hope that independently he will conclude that my views are the ones he should follow." In 1970 and 1971, Nixon repeatedly questioned Burns about his commitment to the Nixon administration policies, in 1970 urging Treasury Secretary Connally to find "an opponent of Arthur Burns to fill the next vacancy."

On November 24, 1971, according to a tape recording, Burns reassured the President:

> *Burns*: There is a campaign on to write me letters to urge more expansion. I will make good on my promises.
>
> *Nixon*: I have no doubt about it. I just want to be sure I'm not misreading you.
>
> *Burns*: Burns does not forget.
>
> *Nixon*: I'll keep them off your back.

In January 1972, Nixon sent Burns an "eyes only" letter commending Burns' efforts to increase money growth and promising to appoint a new Fed Governor "who will follow your leadership." But Nixon continued if the money supply did not "move adequately to fuel the expanding economy in 1972 . . . What could happen out of all of this is that a major attack on the independence of the Fed will eventually develop. I do not want this to happen — particularly I do not want it to happen when the Chairman of the Fed is a man in whom I have such enormous confidence and for whose economic advice I have such great respect."

On February 3, 1972, Burns wrote to the president: "I am confident that monetary policy will promote rather than impede economic expansion this year." On September 7, 1972, Burns informed the president that monetary growth using the Fed's M-1 monetary aggregate, then the basic measure of money supply measuring currency in circulation plus commercial bank deposits, had averaged 8 percent in 1972 and Burns "promised" that it would remain expansive until November. As Meltzer generalized: "The presidential tape recordings and letters and the Ehrlichman notes leave little doubt that President Nixon urged Burns to accelerate money [growth] to aid his election and that Burns agreed."

On November 4, 1972, just before the 1972 election, Nixon wrote to Burns:

> I do want you to know that there is nothing I feel stronger on than this money supply problem and that the crescendo of complaints that I have been receiving, not only from the New York financial community but from other places ... expressing the same concern convinces me that you owe it to yourself, as well as to our goal of getting the economy to move smartly up in the months ahead, to re-evaluate your decision with regard to holding the money supply down and to take some action to move it up.

In February 1971, former Democratic Texas Governor John Connally was appointed Treasury Secretary. Nixon biographer Stephen Ambrose explained:

> Connally was a politician with no experience in banking or economics. When a reporter asked him his qualifications to be Secretary of the Treasury, he quipped, "I can add." What he could add was not so much money as votes, which was one reason Nixon liked him so much — he put first things first.

Connally was a more vibrant and forceful personality than Nixon's first Treasury Secretary David Kennedy and had a politician's preference for what worked rather than economic theory. As a Democrat, Connally brought to the Nixon administration a bipartisan appeal and served as the administration's primary economic spokesman.

Nixon's economic policies would prove to be incoherent and ineffectual. Between his January 20, 1969, Inauguration and August 15, 1971, Nixon promoted three fundamentally inconsistent economic policies. Nixon's economic policies would amplify the unemployment and inflation of the last years of the Johnson presidency. Between his 1969 inauguration and 1974 resignation, unemployment would rise from 3.5 to 5.6 percent, inflation from 4.7 to 8.7 percent, giving rise to a scornful characterization of his policies as that of stagflation, combining high unemployment and high inflation.

Some of these adverse consequences were caused by external events. In 1973–1974, an energy crisis triggered by Arab nation anger at United States support for Israel in the Six Day War had resulted in long gas lines and a 45 percent increase in fuel prices.

The price of oil jumped from $2.80 to $9.60 a barrel between September 1973 and March 1974.

But much of the economic calamity of the Nixon period was self-inflicted. Generally supportive economists such as Milton Friedman would excoriate Nixon's economic policies, asserting that "in the long run, the president's economic decisions will prove to have been more harmful to the nation than the misdeeds he had been responsible for in Watergate."

Nixon's first economic policy was articulated on February 17, 1969, when the Council of Economic Advisers appeared before the Joint Economic Committee and testified the Nixon administration, like its predecessors, was committed to the national objectives found in the Employment Act of 1946 of "maximum employment, production and purchasing power," knowing the term *purchasing power* here was a reference to "the problem of inflation." McCracken, Chair of the Council of Economic Advisers, later wrote:

> In this initial statement the council said the Nixon administration confronted a choice among three strategies. It could lock the brakes and stop the inflation dead in its tracks, an option which almost certainly would produce a substantial rise in unemployment. It could continue the policies of recent years, endeavoring to avoid any rise in unemployment, but this would mean a further acceleration of inflation. Third, it could pursue a policy "gradually and persistently" reducing the rate of inflation. Since the first alternative would have courted the risk of substantial economic and social disarray and the second could have meant a yet further acceleration of inflation, the gradualism approach became the strategy.

Nixon, like Eisenhower, initially emphasized his commitment to a balanced budget. On January 22, 1970, in his first State of the Union address, Nixon stated with pride:

> We had a balanced budget in 1969.
>
> This administration cut more than $7 billion out of spending plans in order to produce a surplus in 1970, and in spite of the fact that Congress reduced revenues by $3 billion, I shall recommend a balanced budget for 1971.

As the 1970 election season began, Burns and Nixon became disillusioned with gradualism.

On May 26, 1970, in a FOMC meeting, Burns warned of a financial crisis, then said: "It was necessary temporarily to put aside the objective of moderate growth in the monetary aggregates [that is, the money supply] and undertake the classical functions of a central bank when a crisis existed or was near at hand."

Nixon repeatedly asked McCracken "to explain why we had not solved the inflation problem." But his focus was elsewhere, Nixon said that "he never heard of losing an election because of inflation, but lots were lost because [of] unemployment or recession. Point is, he's determined not to let the War or inflation get carried to the point that it will lose us House or Senate seats in November." Nixon's priority was reelection. Fed Governor Sherman Maisel would record in his diary Burns' "clear feeling... that the president has gone all out to be re-elected in 1972. As a result he has subordinated inflation control to this idea."

Federal Reserve historian Allan Meltzer agreed: "More than any other president, President Nixon tried to use monetary policy to create conditions favorable to his reelection. In Arthur Burns, he had a chairman who shared his views and was willing to accommodate his president."

More brutally, William Greider in *Secrets of the Temple*, a work critical of the Federal Reserve System, would write:

> The Burns era, furthermore, produced the most damaging accusation of political collusion in the Federal Reserve's history — the economic pump priming that helped Richard Nixon win a landslide re-election victory in 1972. The President's federal budget was highly stimulative, and despite objections from senior governors, the Fed contributed its part to the campaign boom — rapid money growth that reached 11 percent three months before the election.

Economist Robert Hetzel was more sympathetic to Burns describing near universal support for expansionary monetary policy among economists and in Congress.

Burns did not follow a linear path of simply seeking more stimulus, but the consequences of his leadership of the Fed during the first years of the Nixon Presidency on balance were expansionary. There would be instances of disapproval of rate decreases and some rate increases, but on balance, the expansionary pattern of the Fed's policies during Nixon's first term was clear.

In July 1970, Burns sought and received support on a 7-3 vote of the FOMC not to prevent money growth above 5 percent. On August 17, 1970, the Fed reduced bank reserve requirements for commercial paper at banks with time deposits totaling $5 million or more from 6 to 5 percent. This was expected to release $350 million from required reserves. The increase or decrease of bank reserve requirements was a key means by which the Fed could expand or contract money supply. During 1971 as a whole, total bank reserves increased by 7.3 percent.

In May 1972, the Fed proposed for comment comprehensive reserve reductions for national banks, which became effective on November 9, 1972, decreasing, for example, reserve city banks, which had been 17 percent on the first $5 million of deposits and 17.5 percent after that to a ratio of 8 percent below $2 million, 10 percent for $2 to $10 million, 12 percent for $10 to $100 million, 13 percent for $100 to $400 million, and 17.5 percent for more than $400 million. The change in reserve requirements applied the same reserve requirements to member banks of like size regardless of the bank's location.

Each FOMC meeting from August to November included a directive to "promote some easing of conditions in credit markets." On November 17, Burns was one of four members of the Open Market Committee who favored lowering the federal funds rate to achieve 7 to 8 percent growth in the M1 measures of money supply. Between mid-June and late November, the federal funds rate was reduced from 7.8 percent to 5.2 percent. By year end, it would be 4.8 percent. By the end of December 1970, the Fed had decreased the discount rate to 4.5 percent for all Reserve banks.

After the Democratic party House majority was expanded in the 1970 elections and with unemployment rising to 5.9 percent during the last three months of 1970, Nixon abruptly shifted his policy as he explained in his second State of the Union address on January 22, 1971. With a new-found Keynesian enthusiasm, Nixon proposed "an expansionary budget this year — one that will stimulate the economy and thereby open up new job opportunities for millions of Americans. . . . By spending as if we were at full employment, we will help to bring about full employment."

Nixon proposed six goals: welfare reform, full prosperity in peacetime, restoring and enhancing our natural environment, improving the nation's health care, strengthening and renewing state and local governments with a $18 billion revenue sharing investment, and reform of the federal government itself, among other things, shrinking the 12 Cabinet departments to eight, "[organized] around the great purposes of government." During Nixon's presidency, Congress would enact a revenue sharing program and create the Environmental Protection Agency and the Occupational Safety and Health Agency.

But the most immediate consequence of Nixon's expansionary budgeting beginning in 1970 was a swelling of the Federal deficit to $23 billion in 1971.

Nixon announced: "[W]e are all Keynesians now." In June 1971, Burns was informed the federal government would have to run a large deficit because growth had been insufficient. Money growth had been more than 10 percent in the first six months of 1971.

Economic conditions did not improve during the next seven months. By mid-1971, inflation was up to 6 percent. On April 6, 1971, the FOMC was informed that $4.5 billion in dollars had been acquired by foreign central banks in the prior four weeks. On May 11, the Open Market Committee was informed that $4 billion had moved abroad in the prior two days.

The United States capital outflow neared crisis proportions in 1971. After running a $12 billion deficit in 1970, the capital deficit would total $30 billion in 1971. Dollar reserves in other countries increased by approximately $40 billion in 1970 and 1971, with Japan and Germany each accumulating $11 billion and Great Britain $10 billion.

As McCracken would write:

> ... [T]he U.S. external payments position was weakening. By the late 1960s our merchandise trade account was showing only a hairline surplus, and our net balance on current account was negative. In the formal sense the dollar standard for the international monetary structure remained, but major foreign official holders understood that they should not show up at the U.S. gold window to exchange their dollars for gold. A *de facto* gold exchange standard no longer existed, but the pretense did. This make-believe could not last, and in early August 1971 the British requested a conversion of $3 billion into gold.

The British gold request was pivotal. Had it been honored, United States gold reserves would have fallen below $10 billion. In May 1971, Germany had left the Bretton Woods system, prompting the dollar to drop 7.5 percent against the Deutsch mark. In August, as the dollar declined against other European currencies, Switzerland also left the Bretton Woods system.

On August 15, 1970, Congress enacted the Economic Stabilization Act, which authorized the president to issue orders and regulations to set price, rent, wage, and salary controls until February 28, 1971.

Nixon long resisted wage and price guidelines or controls. Speechwriter William Safire stated that at a March 26, 1971, Cabinet meeting, Nixon explained that he believed "the idea of a wage-price review board is wrong." Council of Economic Advisers Chair McCracken recalled that Nixon did not believe wage and price guidelines would work. In June 1971, at a Quadriad meeting, McCracken reluctantly changed his view and now supported wage and price controls. Burns long had held this view and stressed again that "it is doubtful we have made any progress moderating the pace of inflation." Burns proposed a six month wage and price freeze and a wage-price review board. Nixon in June 1971 again rejected wage and price controls: "I am not going to — and this is against all the recommendations that I take very much to heart — I am not going to go on the wage-price board, and I'm not going to go on the wage-price freeze."

But there was increasing public support for guidelines or controls that from the business community's point of view could reduce labor costs and from labor's point of view could control prices. On March 13, 1971, 49 percent of Americans, according to a Gallup Poll, favored a wage and price freeze as long as the Vietnam War lasted. Only 38 percent opposed a wage and price freeze. McCracken recalled: "It was very clear that the President's popularity rating was low, in part because there was this almost tidal wave of demand for wage and price control."

Between August 2 and 12, 1971, Nixon met with Treasury Secretary Connally, Peter Peterson, Nixon's Assistant for International Economic Policy, and George Schultz, then Labor Secretary, to fashion a radically different new plan. In his 1978 memoirs, Nixon wrote:

> There were signs of improvement ahead, but patience had worn thin, and we ran out of time. Demands for action poured down on the White House from all sides. Media criticism of our policies became intense.... Most of the critics and many of

> the economists hammered away on one theme: the need to have some program of mandatory government control of prices and wages.

On August 13, 1971, Nixon and a broader group of 15 advisers including Arthur Burns, Paul McCracken, and Paul Volker joining Connally from Treasury and met at Camp David to act upon a plan developed by Connally and delivered to Nixon on August 6. Connally informed Nixon when he presented his recommendations: "I am not sure this program will work. But I *am* sure that anything less will not work." McCracken later would recall of the weekend at Camp David: "In terms of melodrama, it was the high point of economic policy in the Nixon years. It is tempting to suggest that in terms of substantive economic policy decision, it was probably the low point." Burns was similarly critical: "The weekend confirmed my growing feeling that the President needs to act in a way that satisfies his hunger for drama and novelty, that he lacks true self-assurance and that therefore required some dramatic act to convince himself that he is a strong leader."

There was rapid agreement to virtually all of the elements of Nixon's new economic policy at Camp David with the exception of the proposal to fully end the convertibility of gold for dollars held by foreign official holders. Paul McCracken recalls:

> The most controversial element of the president's proposed program turned out to be closing the gold window by refusing to sell gold to foreign official holders in exchange for their dollars. And the opposition came from Burns, a man who did not hold his views casually. He argued forcefully that the other elements of the program would so strengthen confidence in the dollar and the U.S. economy that risks associated with unilaterally terminating the Bretton Woods international monetary system need not be incurred.

Burns' handwritten notes of the meeting record: "I expressed fear that a closing of gold window would lead to chaotic financial markets, and that it might be followed by trade wars, currency wars, and political friction—such as occurred during the thirties."

Nixon recalled in his 1978 memoirs: Burns warned "that I would take the blame if the dollar was devalued. *Pravda* would write that this was a sign of the collapse of capitalism."

Nixon paused for several hours on August 13 to consider concerns raised about closing the gold window before deciding later that evening to proceed with all elements of the proposed new economic policy.

On August 15, 1971, Nixon shocked the world in a nationally televised address with a third abrupt policy change, his new economic policy. Nixon pledged to "attack" three targets: "Unemployment, inflation and international speculation."

Nixon proposed several new economic stimulants. "I shall ask Congress, when it reconvenes after its summer recess, to consider as its first priority the enactment of the Job Development Act of 1971." He proposed "the strongest short-term incentives in our history to invest in new machinery and equipment that will create new jobs for Americans: a 10 percent Job Development Credit for 1 year, effective as of today, with a 5 percent credit after August 15, 1972." Nixon proposed a repeal of the 7 percent excise tax on automobiles, effect that day and to accelerate personal income tax exemptions scheduled for January 1, 1973, to January 1, 1972.

Nixon directed the Treasury Secretary to recommend new tax proposals to stimulate research and development in new industries as well as new techniques to help provide 20 million new jobs for young people entering the job market during the next decade.

As 1972 began, with unemployment still in Nixon's reckoning too high at 6 percent, Nixon proposed a budget with a deficit of $25.2 billion. The Fed later would be accused of working to reelect Nixon by expanding the money supply by approximately 9 percent in 1972.

Second, with inflation in May and June of 1971 running at 6 to 7 percent, Nixon proposed "decisive action — action that will break the vicious circle of spiraling prices and costs." Nixon froze all United States prices and wages for a 90-day period and appointed a Cost of Living Council to propose mechanisms to continue price and wage stability after the 90-day freeze.

In economics, Nixon's imposition of wage and price controls was as unexpected and sharp a policy change as his 1972 trip to China would be. Nixon soft pedaled the magnitude of wage and price controls on August 15, 1971:

> Let me emphasize two characteristics of this action: First, it is temporary. To put the strong, vigorous American economy into a permanent straitjacket would lock in unfairness; it would stifle

> the expansion of our free enterprise system. And second, while the wage-price freeze will be backed by government sanctions, if necessary, it will not be accompanied by the establishment of a huge price control bureaucracy. I am relying on the voluntary cooperation of all Americans — each one of you: workers, employers, consumers — to make this freeze work.

Milton Friedman long had prophesized that wage and price controls would end "in utter failure and the emergence into the open of the suppressed inflation."

Friedman's prophecy would prove all too accurate. In 1972, the United States experienced its worst inflation since the end of World War II. Wholesale prices increased by 18 percent, consumer prices by nearly 9 percent. As 1974 began, overall inflation was proceeding at an annual rate of 8 to 9 and rose 12 to 14 percent in the first three months of 1974, led by a rise in petroleum and other energy products of about 20 percent during the whole of 1974. The phasing out of price controls by August 1974 triggered a massive inflation of wholesale prices of producers finished goods. These prices had averaged a 5 percent increase in the last six months of 1973, but increased 13 percent in the first three months of 1974, 27 percent in the next three months, and 32 percent in the third trimester of 1974. Wages increased by 9 percent in 1974. These would be the largest increase in consumer goods since 1947.

Fed actions to increase bank reserves by a total of $750 million in November 1974, and reduce the rate of interest in the money supply did little to slow skyrocketing interest rates. The federal funds rate peaked at 13.5 percent shortly after midyear 1974. Prices on the New York Stock Exchange declined by 25 percent between a high point in January 1973 and a low in December 1973.

The United States entered into a recession. After a 6 percent increase in GNP in 1973, the real GNP declined by more than 2 percent in 1974. Unemployment reached a 34-year high of 8.2 percent in early 1975.

In the short run, however, the wage and price freeze controls in the new economic policy would be an economic and political success. Inflation would decline from 5.8 percent in 1970, to 3.3 percent in 1972. Unemployment would fall from 6 percent on January 1, 1972, to 5 percent by year end of 1972 with 2.4 million new jobs created. Real GNP would increase 6 percent between July and September 1972, then 8 percent in the first three months of 1972.

The day after Nixon's remarks, the Dow Jones Industrial Average would rise 32.9 points, its largest one day increase in dollar value.

Nixon was decisively reelected in 1972. In the long run, the Nixon economic policy would be a disaster in terms of combating inflation, which would double in 1973 to 6.2 percent and soar to 11.1 percent in 1974, the year Nixon resigned. In 1972, the United States balance of payments rose to $6.8 billion, approximately $4 billion higher than in 1978. McCracken gave considerable credit for Nixon's 1972 reelection to wage and price controls: "Whether Nixon would have won in November 1972 without the controls program is a question that can never be given a definitive answer, but it is difficult to avoid the conclusion that the initial popularity of the program to control wages and prices significantly contributed to the lopsided character of his decisive 1972 victory." Nixon seemed to agree calling the wage and price controls "a political necessity" in his 1978 memoir:

> What did America reap from its brief fling with economic controls? The August 15, 1971, decision to impose them was politically necessary and immensely popular in the short run. But in the long run I believe that it was wrong. The piper must always be paid, and there was an unquestionably high price for tampering with the orthodox economic mechanisms.

Wage and price controls would proceed through four phases.

On October 7, 1971, with the freeze remaining very popular, Nixon announced initiation of Phase II, with the creation of a seven member Price Commission to limit prices to no more than 2.5 percent each year and a 15 member Pay Board, with five members each from labor, management, and the public, to reduce increases in annual wage increases on average of 5.5 percent. Privately Nixon, according to Herb Stein, explained that if he did not maintain wage and price controls, "the Democrats would win the presidency and then would impose permanent controls." Burns was informed by one White House aide: "The White House has formulated a plan to blame the Fed if Phase II turns out to be a failure."

In December 1971, Congress amended the Economic Stabilization Act of 1970 to authorize the president until April 30, 1973, to control prices, rents, wages, salaries, and interest rates with specified exceptions at levels not less than those prevailing on May 25, 1970. This Act provided the statutory basis for the Nixon wage and price controls.

In January 1973, Phase III was adopted after Nixon's decisive 1972 reelection, when inflation had fallen to 3.4 percent. Phase III replaced the Phase II controls and relied more on voluntary compliance. The Pay Board and the Price Commission ended and their role was assumed by the Cost of Living Council. In announcing Phase III, Nixon established a goal of reducing price inflation to no more than 2.5 percent by the end of 1973. This goal proved to be a chimera. Wholesale prices of farm products and foods rose at a seasonally adjusted rate of almost 50 percent from December 1972 to June 1973. At the end of March in order to restrain rapidly rising meat prices, ceilings on red meat were imposed. "This," as the Federal Reserve Annual Report for 1973 explained, "slowed the increase of meats, but food prices as a whole continued to rise very fast." Simultaneously shortages in livestock, poultry, eggs, and milk, which had begun in 1972, were aggravated by the on again, off again price controls and price freezes.

On June 13, 1973, Phase III was ended and a general price freeze was instituted for 60 days. In 1972, George Shultz had succeeded John Connally as Secretary of the Treasury and in 1971 Herb Stein had become Chair of the Council of Economic Advisers, replacing McCracken. Shultz had served as Dean of the University of Chicago Business School where Milton Friedman had, as Paul Volcker wrote, "a pervasive influence on the intellectual life of the school. In many areas — including monetarism and its informational corollary of floating exchange rates — Shultz was among those captivated."

Shultz objected to the new freeze and was deeply upset by the Watergate scandal and resigned as Treasury Secretary in 1974. The price freeze proved ineffectual. In mid-July, to avoid shortages, the price freeze on food other than beef was relaxed. Livestock and meat prices rose dramatically after the mid-July relaxation. World shortages in wheat, corn, and soybeans added to the inflationary pressure. Between mid-July and mid-August, the cost of farm products increased at the most rapid rate since World War I. While wholesale prices of farm products declined between mid-August and December, they remained 36 percent higher in December 1973, than they had been a year earlier. This time, Hetzel reported: "[T]he controls produced shortages. Farmers drowned baby chicks rather than sending them to market at a loss. As the *Congressional Quarterly*... wrote, "You may have chicken prices at 59 cents a pound during the freeze but you may not have any chickens." Meat disappeared from the shelves of supermarkets."

Public opinion turned sharply against Nixon's economic policies. On May 15, 1973, Lou Harris reported that the public had a 25 percent positive, 70 percent negative result in a survey on his handling of the economy. On controlling the cost of living, the results were worse: 12 percent positive, 79 percent negative.

Nixon era price and wage controls lumbered to a conclusion in Phase IV, which lasted from August 12, 1973, after the 60-day freeze until April 30, 1974, with a progressive lifting of price controls on such items as cement and nonferrous metals when congressional authority under the Economic Stabilization Act ended. In early 1974, the Nixon Administration announced that it would end all price controls except for health care and petroleum.

Nixon's third major initiative on August 15, 1971, involved far reaching steps to protect "the American dollar as a pillar of monetary stability around the world" by beginning a process that would take the United States off the fixed gold-dollar exchange. Nixon directed Treasury Secretary Connally "to suspend temporarily the convertibility of the American dollar except in amounts and conditions to be determined to be in the interest of monetary stability and in the best interests of the United States." He sought to work "[i]n full cooperation with the International Monetary Fund and those who trade with us [to] press for the necessary reforms to set up a new International Monetary System."

To further protect the dollar and United States balance of trade, Nixon imposed an additional 10 percent temporary tax on goods imported into the United States.

As with wage and price controls, devaluation of the dollar and the end of the fixed gold exchange rate would proceed in phases. European nations reacted vehemently to the 10 percent surcharge. Several complained that they could not negotiate new exchange rates until the United States removed the surcharge. Paul Volcker representing the Treasury had further shocked the Europeans when he informed them the United States sought to transform the United States $4 billion deficit into a $9 billion surplus, a massive $13 billion change in one year. In the initial period between August 15 and December 17–18, the currencies of other industrial nations were allowed to float above Bretton Woods parity levels. European controlled banks discontinued operations in foreign exchange markets.

For a period of months, as leading European nations and Japan pressed for devaluation of the United States dollar in exchange for an increase in a fixed price of gold, Nixon opposed any change in the gold price. He changed his mind after stock prices fell sharply in October and November 1971, and Pete Person presented data estimating that an increase in the dollar gold exchange rate that devalued the dollar would increase net exports and employment.

In December 1971, at the Group of Ten Ministers at the Smithsonian Institution in Washington, the United States agreed to an 8.57 percent devaluation of the dollar, increasing the price of gold from $35 to $38. Leading trading partners other than Canada agreed to new fixed exchange rates. The Agreement was estimated to increase United States exports by $8 billion. Nixon vastly exaggerated the significance of the Smithsonian Agreement, calling it "the most significant monetary agreement in the history of the world."

The Smithsonian Agreement proved unworkable. The dollar devaluation had not gone far enough and the lack of convertibility of dollars into gold caused a sharp increase of foreign exchange reserves from $146 billion in 1972, to $337.3 in 1980.

On February 12, 1973, the United States agreed to a further 10 percent devaluation of the dollar, setting the official gold price at $42.22, which within 11 days would be approximately one half the market value of gold. On February 23, 1973, the market price reached $89. The fixed dollar exchange system continued to deteriorate. By mid-1973, the dollar had depreciated an average of 15 percent from its February 1973 level.

In March 1973, the six members of the European community agreed to fix their currencies against each other and jointly floated their currencies against the United States dollar. This effectively ended the Bretton Woods and fixed exchange system in favor of floating rates. The new floating rate system was recognized in the Jamaica Accords at the January 1976 IMF meeting in Kingston, Jamaica. George Shultz observed of the 1976 Jamaica Accord that it achieved three major changes: (1) the legitimation of floating, (2) the recognition that domestic economic stability is a prerequisite to exchange rate stability, and (3) a reduction in the role of gold in the International Monetary System.

Hetzel wrote in retrospect:

> If the Bretton Woods system encouraged the instability that its founders had hoped to avoid, how did it survive until March

> 1973? . . . [T]he United States ran the system in a way that did not force deflation on other member countries. After 1949, it maintained an overvalued dollar. The United States could afford to allow persistent gold outflows because it had accumulated most of the free world's monetary gold stocks by the end of World War II.

After a sharp appreciation against other currencies in the last three months of 1973 and into January 1974, the dollar declined between January and May an average of 10 percent. By the first months of 1974, the price of gold reached $180 per ounce.

On December 31, 1974, the United States private ban on gold ended. After that date, United States citizens could own or trade gold as they could any other commodity. The Treasury auctioned part of its gold reserve in 1975, 1978, and 1979.

In August 1975, the IMF agreed to abolish an official price of gold and eliminated requirements to use gold in transactions with the IMF.

These steps ended the fixed gold exchange system. Gold prices would now be determined by market forces. The special place of gold in the monetary system was over.

In 1996, Princeton Economics Professor Paul Krugman, later a Nobel laureate in economics, would summarize what he believed the end of a fixed gold-dollar exchange system meant:

> The current world monetary system assigns no special role to gold; indeed, the Federal Reserve is not obliged to tie the dollar to anything. It can print as much or as little money as it deems appropriate. There are powerful advantages to such an unconstrained system. Above all, the Fed is free to respond to actual or threatened recessions by pumping in money.

In 1992, Volcker would bemoan the end of Bretton Woods:

> In sum, the fact that the world has had a mostly unmanaged system of floating exchange rates over the past twenty years while it also experienced slower growth, greater inflation, and stronger pressures for protectionism does not strike me as entirely accidental. No doubt other factors have also played an important role, notably the oil crises of the 1970s and worldwide tendencies toward lower savings and less fiscal discipline. But on the evidence, it is hard to believe that we have found anything like an optimal set of international monetary arrangements.

In 2011, Fed Chair Paul Volcker was more succinct, regretting the end of Bretton Woods: "Nobody's in charge. . . . The Europeans couldn't live with the uncertainty and made their own currency [the euro] and now that is in trouble."

For many, August 15, 1971, would be A Day Which Lived in Infamy. A *Forbes* article would quote Fed Chair Arthur Burns that August week as exclaiming: "What a tragedy for mankind," by which he meant ending the fixed exchange system. The end of the fixed exchange system also ended the overvalued dollar but strengthened the ability of the Fed to respond to emergencies.[22]

Banking During the Nixon Administration

During the Nixon presidency, the nature of bank competition fundamentally changed. There were two primary reasons for this.

The Fed during the Nixon Presidency step by step reduced the restrictions on permissible bank activities under the 1970 Amendment to the Bank Holding Company Act using its authority to define which activities were so closely related to banking or controlling banks. On May 20, 1971, the Fed amended Regulation Y and permitted bank holding companies to acquire or retain an interest in a company solely engaged in one of seven activities:

> 1. Making or acquiring, for its own account or for the account of others, loans and other extensions of credit (including issuing letters of credit and accepting drafts), such as would be made, for example, by a mortgage, finance, credit-card, or factoring company.
>
> 2. Operating as an industrial bank, Morris Plan bank, or industrial loan company in the manner authorized by state law so long as the institution would not both accept demand deposits and make commercial loans.
>
> 3. Servicing loans and other extensions of credit for any person.
>
> 4. Performing or carrying on any one or more of the functions or activities that may be performed or carried on by a trust company . . . in the manner authorized by State law so long as the institution would not both accept demand deposits and make commercial loans.
>
> 5. Acting as investment or financial adviser. . . .

> 6. Leasing personal property and equipment, or acting as agent, broker, or adviser in leasing of such property. . . .
>
> 7. Making equity and debt investments in corporations or projects designed primarily to promote community welfare, such as the economic rehabilitation and development of low-income areas.

In June 1971, the Board added an eighth activity:

> (1) providing bookkeeping or data processing services for the internal operations of the holding company and its subsidiaries and (2) storing and processing other banking, financial, or related economic data, such as performing payroll, accounts receivable or payable, or billing services.

In August 1971, the Fed approved insurance agency activities:

> Acting as insurance agent or broker in offices at which the holding company or its subsidiaries are otherwise engaged in business (or in an office adjacent thereto) with respect to the following types of insurance:
>
> (i) any insurance for the holding company and its subsidiaries;
>
> (ii) any insurance that (A) is directly related to an extension of credit by a bank or a bank-related firm of the kind described in this regulation; or (B) is directly related to the provision of other financial services by a bank or such a bank-related firm, or (C) is otherwise sold as a matter of convenience to the purchaser, so long as the premium income from sales within this subclause (C) does not constitute a significant portion of the aggregate insurance premium income of the holding company from insurance sold pursuant to this clause (ii);
>
> (iii) any insurance sold in a community that (A) has a population not exceeding 5000, or (B) the holding company demonstrates has inadequate insurance agency facilities.

In January 1972, the Fed authorized bank holding companies to act as investment advisers to mutual funds and other investment companies. The Board concluded "that a bank holding company might exercise all functions customarily permitted an investment adviser except to the extent limited by the Banking Act of 1933." The Board interpreted the Glass-Steagall provisions of the 1933

Banking Act "as prohibiting a bank holding company from sponsoring, organizing or controlling a mutual fund."

In December 1972, the Fed further amended Regulation Y to authorize bank holding companies to sell credit life and credit health insurance when it extended credit to a borrower.

In December 1973, a bank holding company was authorized to sell thrift notes to supply capital to a wholly-owned nonbanking subsidiary.

In February 1974, the Fed amended Regulation Y to authorize bank holding companies to provide general management consulting services to nonaffiliated banks.

In March 1974, the Fed broadened its June 15, 1971 Regulation Y amendments that permitted the leasing of personal property and equipment to also include the leasing of real property, acting as an agent, broker or adviser under specified conditions.

Cumulatively, Regulation Y amendments and interpretations furthered the erosion of the separation of commercial banking from the securities and insurance industries.[23]

Interest rate ceilings and variable regulation of banks, S & L and securities firms created a separate competitive pressure. As the differential between the market rate of interest and federal deposit interest rates ceilings widened, there was an increased incentive for bank customers and business to seek higher yields elsewhere.

By the time of Nixon's presidency, the Fed placed a ceiling on savings and time deposits through Regulation Q. The Fed had sought to protect bank solvency by keeping a lid on Regulation Q rates while market rates had risen dramatically. Since 1965, the Federal Home Loan Bank Board similarly had tried to prevent increases in savings and loan interest first with its authority to deny credit for S & Ls to pay dividends, then after 1966 legislation with required interest ceilings on customer accounts to be developed in coordination with the Fed and the Federal Deposit Insurance Corporation.

Between 1945 and 1965, commercial banks, S & Ls and mutual savings banks had paid average annual rates on savings accounts that were consistently higher than commercial banks. Then in 1965 and 1970, the interest rate differential narrowed:

AVERAGE ANNUAL RATES OF INTEREST PAID ON SAVINGS ACCOUNTS BY COMMERCIAL BANKS, SAVINGS AND LOAN ASSOCIATIONS, AND MUTUAL SAVINGS BANKS, 1945–70
(in percent)

Year	Commercial Banks	Savings and Loan Associations	Mutual Savings Banks
1945	0.87	2.46	1.70
1950	0.94	2.52	1.90
1955	1.38	2.94	2.64
1960	2.56	3.86	3.47
1965	3.69	4.25	4.11
1966	4.04	4.48	4.45
1967	4.24	4.68	4.74
1968	4.48	4.71	4.76
1969	4.87	4.81	4.89
1970	4.95	5.14	5.01

A process of disintermediation occurred in 1945–1965 between Fed regulated commercial banks on the one hand and savings and loans and state regulated mutual savings banks on the other. During these years, total assets of commercial banks had increased from $158 billion to $375 billion; total assets at S & Ls had increased from $9 billion to $130 billion; total assets of mutual savings banks from less than $17 billion to over $58 billion. This meant that the proportion of all assets held by commercial banks fell from 86 percent to less than 67 percent, the percent of S & L assets rose from 5 to 23 percent, and mutual savings bank assets rose slightly from 9 to 10 percent.

For extended periods between 1966 and 1971, bank and S & L deposit rate interest minimums were below market rates. The growth rate of S & Ls then was less than that of banks and serious questions were raised about the ability of thrift institutions to survive. In 1971, the President's Commission on Financial Structure and Regulation would bluntly state:

> The power of the rate ceilings to isolate deposit markets from the rest of the short-term money market has eroded with continued reliance on this regulation. In time, they will probably have little effectiveness. Thus the major deterrent to losses of income and liquidity and the possible failures of thrift institutions during past periods of rising interest rates will not provide the same protection in the future.

As interest rate ceilings in the 1960s squeezed the ability of banks to finance United States corporations, firms increasingly turned to large negotiable Certificates of Deposit (*CDs*) often borrowed from European sources and short-term corporate debt, typically commercial paper rather than relying on noninterest paying bank checking accounts or low interest paying bank deposits. By 1966, investors held $15 billion of CDs, second only to $64 billion in Treasury bills held by investors. Commercial paper grew from $8.4 billion year end 1964 to $39.7 billion in May 1970.

Commercial paper, unlike FDIC guaranteed accounts, carried risk. In 1970, the Penn Central Railroad, then the largest railroad and sixth largest industrial corporation in the United States, went bankrupt, after defaulting on over $80 million of its outstanding $200 million of commercial paper, prompting a $3 billion shrinkage in the commercial paper market. This not only created a crisis in the commercial paper market but also a perplexing challenge for Fed regulated banks. The Fed estimated that it would require between $7 to $10 billion of additional reserves to fully replace commercial paper with bank loans.

Banks responded by using a number of new techniques to attract funds including CDs, savings certificates, and special notice accounts. In December 1975, the Fed amended Regulation Q to permit Individual Retirement Accounts (*IRAs*) at member banks.

In 1970, the Consumer Savings Bank in Worcester, Massachusetts sought to create NOW accounts, or Negotiable Orders of Withdrawal, which were not subject to Regulation Q but were essentially a checking account that paid competitive rates of interest. After an initial denial of the right to offer NOW accounts, a Massachusetts court ruled in favor of the savings bank and beginning in June 1972, Massachusetts savings banks could offer these accounts.

In 1973, Rhode Island also authorized NOW accounts. By February 1976, NOW accounts would be permissible at all depository institutions except credit unions in each New England state.

The Fed sought to stymie NOW accounts in member banks in December 1973. The Fed limited member commercial banks to 5 percent interest and limited the number of transactions that could be processed against a NOW account to no more than 150 per year after Congress in August 1973, had authorized NOW accounts by depository institutions in Massachusetts and Rhode Island. In October 1974, the Fed removed the 150 transaction limit on member bank NOW accounts. By March 1, 1976, the Fed permitted member banks in Connecticut, Maine, Rhode Island, and Vermont to offer NOW accounts.

On June 16, 1970, Nixon created the President's Commission on Financial Structure and Regulation to "review and study the structure, operation, and regulation of the private financial institutions in the United States, for the purpose of formulating recommendations that would improve the functioning of the private financial system." The Commission, popularly known as the Hunt Commission after its Chair, Reed Hunt, retired Chair of Crown Zellerbach, would include 15 business leaders, notably Alan Greenspan, two economists, one state senator, and Lane Kirkland, the Secretary-Treasurer of the AFL-CIO.

In its December 1971 report, the Hunt Commission broadly addressed problems relating to commercial banks, mutual savings banks, savings and loan associations, credit unions, private pension plans, and life insurance companies. The Commission focused on the consequences of inflation during the late 1960s and the "severe effects" of high interest rates.

The Hunt Commission Report was most notable for its recommendation to abolish ceiling interest rates on time and savings accounts as well as CDs over $100,000 and move toward full abolition of interest rate ceilings for banks after a ten-year transition. The Commission Report also recommended broadening the loan and investment powers of S & Ls and mutual savings banks to make them more competitive with commercial banks. Both commercial banks and S & Ls would be given broader powers to make real estate loans and equity investments in community rehabilitation and development corporations up to 5 percent of capital, surplus and undivided profits, and "leeway provisions" to invest no more than

3 percent of total assets or 30 percent of total capital, whichever was less in other equity investments.

Commercial banks also would be authorized to manage and sell mutual funds and commingle funds subject to SEC regulation. The mutual fund and commingling of funds recommendations were meant to open avenues for commercial banks to compete more effectively for trust and investment funds from persons of moderate and low incomes:

> Bank trust departments now manage nearly $300 billion of assets. The commercial banking industry has developed a high level of skill in financial management and investing funds for the account of customers. At the present time, however, because of restrictions on commingling of funds, only customers with large estates or substantial funds are usually accepted as customers. Thus the inability of banks to service the needs of persons with only moderate amounts to invest discriminates against most of the public.

The Hunt Commission Report recommendations were not acted upon. But high market interest rates led to intensified competition for the banking industry. Most significantly, money market funds would be invented in 1971 and popularized during the 1970s by securities brokerage firms and mutual funds. Money market funds were the equivalent to bank deposit and checking services, with check writing privileges, direct electronic deposits and debit cards. Money market funds were not subject to Regulation Q and paid higher interest rates, typically by investing in Treasury Bills and commercial paper. In 1975, money market funds would hold $3 billion in assets. By 1979, over one million Merrill Lynch customers would invest over $70 billion in Merrill Money Market Funds. The total customer investments in money market funds would grow exponentially. On September 9, 2018, money market funds would be worth $3.523 trillion and had long been the most popular investment in the United States.

The share of total private financial assets held by insured depository institutions dropped from around 60 percent in 1970 to less than 35 percent in 2000, calculated Professor Jerry Markham in a law review article on *Banking and Regulation: Its History and Future.*

Throughout the Nixon Administration, as competition with banks increased because of interest rate ceilings, the Fed was largely reactive.

On January 21, 1970, for the first time in several years, the Fed raised maximum rates payable on member bank savings deposits from 4 to

4.5 percent and raised the maximum rate payable on time deposits, depending on the time to maturity, to 5.5 to 7.5 percent. The Fed explained when it adopted the January 1970, maximum rate ceilings:

> More broadly, these actions were designed to bring rates payable by banks and other savings institutions more into line with rates prevailing on competing market securities, in expectation that this would help to generate the deposit funds needed to finance a moderate pick-up in credit flows through financial institutions and encourage longer-term savings within the framework of continued over-all credit restraint.

On June 23, 1970, the Fed suspended maximum rate ceilings on large denomination CDs with maturities of 30 to 89 days.

In 1973, with increased risk of disintermediation because of a boom in the housing market, the Fed took several additional steps. On July 5, 1973, the Fed in coordination with the FDIC and the Federal Home Loan Bank Board, increased ceiling rates on several types of time and savings deposit accounts generally by 0.5 percent and suspended interest rate ceilings on time deposits of $1000 or more with a maturity of four years or more.

After Congress enacted legislation requiring the Fed, FDIC, and Federal Home Loan Bank Board to impose an interest rate limitation on consumer type time deposits with a maturity of four years or more, the three federal depository regulatory institutions set a 7.25 percent ceiling on these accounts with a denomination of at least $1000 to less than $100,000.

In April 1974, when savings and loans had to borrow heavily to cover disintermediation of deposits, the Fed estimated the borrowing at $50 million a day, meaning that the Federal Home Loan Bank Board would exhaust its liquid assets by May and then borrow against a $4 billion line of credit with the Treasury. The Federal Home Loan Bank Board asked the Fed to offer emergency standby assistance, which the Fed agreed to do as a lender of last resort, as it had in principal agreed in September 1973, to an emergency plan for S & Ls and other nonmember depository institutions.[24]

The Ford Presidency

Gerald Ford's brief presidency, which began August 9, 1974, after the Watergate scandal led to President Nixon's resignation and ended January 20, 1977, with the inauguration of his successor Jimmy Carter, was marked by a worsening of the economic crisis begun under Nixon.

Ford would be a weakened president because of the combination of his full and unconditional pardon of Richard Nixon on September 8, 1974, the fall of Vietnam in April 1975, his apparent heartlessness when New York City neared bankruptcy, prompting the long remembered *New York Daily News* headline: "Ford to City: Drop Dead," and his administration's inability to reverse the Nixon Presidency stagflation.

On August 13, the *New York Times* aptly characterized Ford as beginning his presidency with "the worst inflation in the country's peacetime history, the highest interest rates in a century... utterly demoralized securities markets, a stagnant economy with large-scale unemployment in prospect and a worsening international trade and payments position."

Voter dissatisfaction led to further dominance by the Democrats in Congress after the 1974 elections. In the Senate, the Democratic majority would grow from a 56–42 to 60–38, in the House from 242–192 to an overwhelming 291–144 seat advantage.

Throughout the balance of 1974, and several months into 1975, the early months of Ford's presidency, the economy grew measurably worse.

The inflation adjusted GSP fell 7.5 percent in the last three months of 1974, and 9.2 percent in the first three months of 1975. In May 1975, industrial production would be 12.5 percent below September 1975. Unemployment, which was 5.6 percent in August 1974, when Ford took office, reached 8.9 percent in May 1975, a 35-year high, declining only to 7.8 percent in 1976. Between December 1973 and December 1974, inflation measured by the Consumer Price Index would increase 12.2 percent before declining to 7 percent in 1975, and 4.6 percent in 1976. The Dow Jones Industrial Average during that period would fall 28 percent from 828 to 596.5. The Federal deficit would swell to $53 billion in 1975, and $66 billion in 1976.

Ford's economic policy team was led by Treasury Secretary Bill Simon, appointed by Nixon in May 1974, who testified to Congress: "[F]ree competitive markets are the most effective way to increase output" and who opposed most stimulus programs but favored tax reduction. Simon saw inflation and federal expenditures as a major threat to free enterprise. He observed in December 1974: "History is littered with the wreckage of societies that failed to come to grips with inflation." Simon worked with the President's Office of Management and Budget to encourage Ford to veto a substantial number of spending bills enacted by Congress.

Alan Greenspan was appointed Chair of the Council of Economic Advisers in 1974, and urged that inflation grew when the Fed increased the money supply to avoid stresses in credit markets. The Council's 1976 Economic Report explained:

> Rapid and sustained inflation requires a continual inflationary increase of the supply of money. The main reason why expansionary fiscal operations are among the factors generating sustained inflation is that when fiscal deficits are large the money authorities, in an attempt to offset the interest rate and credit availability effects of large increases in government debt, tend rapidly to increase their security holdings and hence to inject new money.

Fed Chair Burns was the longest serving Ford Senior Economic Adviser. Compared to his service under Nixon, who tried "to interfere with the Federal Reserve both in ways that were fair . . . and unfair [,] Mr. Ford . . . was truly angelic." During the Ford administration, there would be no attacks on Fed independence. In an August 12, 1974, memorandum, sent three days after Ford became President, Burns stressed: "[T]he nation is in the grip of a dangerous inflation." Burns recommended a $5 billion spending reduction (outlays in 1975 were $132 billion), a pledge of a balanced budget in 1976, avoidance of price and wage controls, reconstitution of the Cost of Living Council, tough antitrust enforcement, and an enlarged public service program to reduce unemployment.

Both Burns and Greenspan rejected the Keynesian trade-off between inflation and unemployment. Greenspan believed: "Unemployment was never seen as a necessary condition for bringing down the rate of inflation. . . . [S]ince the unemployment rate and inflation rate both went up together, we always argued that it was possible to bring them both down together."

Ford's senior economic team initially rejected economic stimuli to end the recession, confident that a long-range focus on dampening inflation would be preferable.

On August 12, 1974, three days after becoming president, Ford addressed a Joint Session of Congress and emphasized: "My first priority is to work with you to bring inflation under control. Inflation is domestic enemy number one."

On September 28, 1974, Ford issued Executive Order 11,808 establishing the President's Economic Policy Board, chaired by the Secretary of Treasury with eight secretaries of departments, as well as the Director of the Office of Management and Budget, and Chair of the Council of Economic Advisers. The Chair of the Fed was invited to attend meetings of the Economic Policy Board:

> The Economic Policy Board shall provide advice to the president concerning all aspects of national and international economic policy, will oversee the formulation, coordination, and implementation of all economic policy of the United States, and will serve as the focal point for economic policy decision-making. The Chairman of the Board shall act as the principal spokesman for the Executive Branch on matters of economic policy.

The Economic Policy Board also had an Executive Committee also chaired by the Secretary of Treasury and consisted of the Assistant to the President for Economic Affairs, the Director of the Office of Management and Budget, the Chair of the Council of Economic Advisers, and the Executive Director of the Council on International Economic Policy. The Fed Chair also was invited to attend meetings of the Executive Committee.

Ford later would describe the Economic Policy Board "as the most important institutional innovation of my administration." During its first year, the Executive Committee of the Economic Policy Board met almost daily.

Ford's most definitive initial policy was his nationally televised address October 8, 1974, which popularly came to be known as the WIN Speech. After holding a two-day bipartisan Inflation Conference on September 27–28 and listening or reviewing hundreds of proposals, Ford in his October 8th speech echoed Roosevelt's March 4, 1933, Inaugural address and promised "direct, vigorous action." Ford laid out a 10-point program to "put our own economic house in order." The first nine initiatives provided a comprehensive roadmap for joint action. Ford sought to address food production, energy production, reliance on foreign sources, which had risen from 19 percent of American energy consumption in 1960 to 38 percent in 1974, international interdependency, restrictive business practices that he sought to confront by a "return to the vigorous enforcement of antitrust laws," and reducing inflation caused by federal government actions. Ford asked Congress to establish a National Commission on Regulatory Reform "to undertake a long-overdue total reexamination of the independent regulatory agencies." He addressed the need for more capital, here stating: "I have personally been assured by the Chairman of the Independent Federal Reserve System that the supply of money and capital will expand sufficiently to meet the needs of our economy and that in no event will a credit crunch occur" Ford proposed a 10 percent investment tax credit to create more jobs and liberalization of the capital gains.

He proposed expanding unemployment benefits and creating a new Community Improvement Corps to provide work for the unemployed "through short-term useful projects to improve, beautify and enhance the environment of our cities, our towns and our countryside." Ford earlier had signed the Housing and Community Development Act of 1974 and urged more stimulus for housing.

Ford addressed thrift institutions:

> Savings and loan and similar institutions are hard hit by inflation and high interest rates. They no longer attract, unfortunately, adequate deposits. The executive branch, in my judgment, must join with the Congress in giving critically needed attention to the structure and the operation of our thrift institutions which now find themselves for the third time in 8 years in another period of serious mortgage credit scarcity.

To fund his new programs, Ford sought a one year 5 percent tax surcharge on corporations and upper level individual incomes while simultaneously he indicated that he would seek sufficient spending deferrals and rescissions to limit the 1975 budget to $300 billion. "It is my judgment that fiscal discipline is a necessary weapon in any fight against inflation."

Ford concluded by asking his fellow Americans to become volunteer inflation fighters and make "a list of 10 ways to fight inflation and save energy, to exchange your list with your neighbors, and to send me a copy." Ford urged: "Unless every able American pitches in, Congress and I cannot do the job." He encouraged housewives "to cut the food you waste by 5 percent." Ford proposed a nationwide volunteer mobilization to *Whip Inflation Now* and displayed his own WIN button on his lapel during his remarks.

Reaction to the October 8 speech was almost uniformly negative. The WIN volunteer mobilization was widely ridiculed as a publicity stunt and soon abandoned. The public reaction to the 5 percent surcharge was overwhelmingly disdainful. The *New York Times* dismissed the 10 point plan, stating they "in no sense add up to a program for an emergency." Ford did not effectively address growing unemployment and the recession. An October 1974, Harris Survey found that 65 percent of the American people believed that we already were in a recession.

The 1974 election results in which the Democrats gained 49 seats in the House of Representative in Ford's recollection were "shocking." By December, a Harris Poll found that "86 percent of Americans surveyed had no confidence in the ability of the President to manage the economy." The Democratic Conference on Party Organization and Policy on December 6, 1974, characterizing the 1974 elections as "[providing] a mandate for change and proposed attacking recession and unemployment with greater public works than Ford had proposed and a comprehensive package for tax reductions."

In his January 15, 1975, State of the Union address, Ford reoriented his priorities to focus on recession. He proposed a $16 billion one-year tax reduction, with $12 billion going to individuals in the form of tax rebates based on their 1974 income taxes and $4 billion to business in the form of a liberalized investment tax credit. He proposed that future individual taxes be reduced by $16.5 billion by raising the low income allowance and reducing individual tax rates. He also proposed reducing the corporate tax rate from 48 to 42 percent.

Congress largely adopted Ford's tax proposals on May 29, 1975, with the enactment of the Tax Reduction Act of 1975. The Act provided $22.8 billion of tax cuts, $12 billion of which was in the form of tax rebates and $10 billion of which was for increases in the 1975 low income allowance, an increase in the income limit for child care expenses, a 5 percent tax credit for new home purchases, as well as an increase in the business investment tax credit.

As with President Ford, the Fed tilted its policy both seeking "to ensure that conditions in money and credit markets would continue to a good recovery in economic activity" and to what it continued to describe as "the urgent need to make further progress in dampening inflation."

The 1975 Tax Reduction Act pumped incomes by approximately $12 billion between the last three months of 1974 and June 1975. Interest rates dropped with the Fed approving four discount rate reductions in 1975, which lowered the rate from 7.75 percent in January 1975, to 5.5 percent in early 1976. The basic M1 measure of money supply would decline to 4.4 percent in 1974 but expand in the last three months of 1975, until the end of 1976, at 5.7 percent. This was still lower than the Nixon era monetary stimulus but trended in an expansionary direction. Money growth in part had been stimulated by several 1975 Fed reductions in the commercial bank 1 percent reserve requirement for demand deposits and reductions from 8 to 4 percent for euro-dollar borrowings and loans made by member bank foreign branches to United States citizens, reduction from 3 to 1 percent on member bank time deposits with an original maturity of four years or more and 3 to 2.5 percent for member bank time deposits with a maturity of 180 days to four years.

Ford had become an expansionist. The 1975 Tax Reduction Act contributed to massive federal deficits of $53 billion in 1975, and $73.7 billion in 1976. In October 1975, he proposed a $28 billion tax cut to extend the 1975 tax reductions.

The Carter Presidency

Ford was defeated running for president by former Georgia Governor Jimmy Carter in 1976, after surviving an intense challenge for the Republican nomination by the more conservative Ronald Reagan. The improvement of economic conditions in 1976, with inflation whipped and unemployment somewhat decreased and GDP growing 5 percent between late 1975 and 1976, helped Ford narrow as much as a 33 percent gap to a 2 percent loss, 50.1 to 48 percent to Carter. Carter's electoral college majority was more decisive. The Democratic majorities in the House and Senate were virtually unchanged. The Democrats in the Senate remained 61 to 38 in 1976 after having been 61 to 37 in 1974; Democrats in the House 292 to 143 in 1976, after having been 291 to 144 in 1974.

Congress was less patient with the Fed in 1973 and 1974. As the Nation was headed into a recession, the Fed had reduced the money supply. The Fed employed three measures of money. M1 was the most widely followed and measured currency held in the Treasury, Federal Reserve banks, and the vaults of all commercial banks plus most demand deposits. Between 1972 and the first three months of 1975, M1 would dramatically fall from 8.4 percent to 0.6 percent. Interest rates in 1974 would skyrocket.

On April 24, 1974, the Fed raised the discount rate from 7.5 to 8, reducing the rate only slightly to 7.75 percent in December 1974. During 1974, short-term corporate borrowing would be exorbitant. The interest rate for commercial paper would be 12 percent in July 1974 and the prime rate by which business could borrow from banks also would be 12 percent.

The Fed's deflationary policies did whip inflation. The Consumer Price Index, which was 12.2 percent between December 1973 and December 1974 would fall to 7 percent in 1975, and 4.6 percent in 1976.

The costs of whipping inflation would be staggering. Unemployment, which was 5.6 percent when Ford assumed office in August 1974, averaged 8.2 percent in 1975, peaking at 8.9 percent in May 1975, and declining only moderately to 7.8 percent in 1976. The inflation adjusted GDP would fall 7.5 percent in the last three months of 1974, and 9.2 percent in the first three months of 1975. In May 1975, industrial production would be 12.5 percent below September 1975. The Dow Jones Industrial Average between January 1973 and December 6, 1974, would decline 45 percent. With the international economy in 1975, according to the Fed, "[suffering] the deepest worldwide recession since the 1930's," the United States Merchandise Trade deficit would grow from $5.4 billion in 1974, to $9 billion in 1975, and $9.2 billion in 1976.

On March 24, 1975, Congress adopted House Concurrent Resolution 133, which Burns had opposed. The Resolution stated in part:

> Whereas the United States economy is now suffering from excessively high unemployment and a decline in production and the gross national product, together with inflation; and
>
> Whereas the economy's performance in part is affected by changes in the rate of growth of the monetary and credit aggregates: Now, therefore, be it
>
> *Resolved by the House of Representatives (the Senate concurring),*
>
> That it is the sense of Congress that the Board of Governor of the Federal Reserve System and the Federal Open Market Committee —
>
> (1) pursue policies in the first half of 1975 so as to encourage lower long term interest rates and expansion in the monetary

> and credit aggregates appropriate to facilitating prompt economic recovery; and
>
> (2) maintain long run growth of the monetary and credit aggregates commensurate with the economy's long run potential to increase production, so as to promote effectively the goals of maximum employment, stable prices, and moderate long term interest rates.

The Resolution required the Fed to publicly state 12 month targets for money growth and increased congressional oversight by requiring the Fed every six months to report to Congress in open hearings.

The Resolution was unusual in that Congress as a whole, not just individual committee chairs or members criticized the Fed's performance. The Resolution stressed the goals of maximum employment and facilitating prompt economic recovery.[25]

The 1976 Democratic Party platform characterized replacing Republican mismanagement as the Nation's leading problem with a return to the politics of Roosevelt, Truman, Kennedy, and Johnson as the solution:

> During the past 25 years, the American economy has suffered five major recessions, all under Republican administrations. During the past eight years, we have had two costly recessions with continuing unprecedented peacetime inflation. "Stagflation" has become a new word in our language just as it has become a product of Republican economic policy. Never before have we had soaring inflation in the midst of a major recession....
>
> In contrast to the record of Republican mismanagement, the most recent eight years of Democratic leadership, under John F. Kennedy and Lyndon B. Johnson, produced economic growth that was virtually uninterrupted. The unemployment rate dropped from 6.7 percent in 1961 to 3.6 per cent in 1968, and most segments of the population benefited. Inflation increased at an average annual rate of only 2 per cent, and the purchasing power of the average family steadily increased. In 1960, about 40 million people were living in poverty. Over the next eight years, 14-1/2 million people moved out of poverty because of training opportunities, increased jobs and higher incomes....
>
> We have met the goals of full employment with stables prices in the past and can do it again.

Carter was a man of many parts. A 2006 biography by Burton Kaufman and Scott Kaufman captured some of his complexity, explaining:

> Jimmy Carter is a southerner, an engineer, an agribusinessman, and a politician. He is not a nuclear physicist, a populist, or even a dirt farmer, as he and his followers have sometimes claimed. He is a Southern Baptist and an evangelical but not a fundamentalist. He is deeply religious but not theological. He can be — and most of the time is — courteous, compassionate, and gracious, but he can also be — and frequently has been — sarcastic, short-tempered, calculating, and opportunistic. He is a person of deep moral conviction and principle; at the same time, during his career, he has often been devious and politically pragmatic. He is highly intelligent, introspective, and thoughtful, but he is not ideological, philosophical, or conceptual.

A 1946 graduate of Annapolis, Carter served for seven years in the Navy, most of which was spent in the fledging nuclear navy working on Admiral Hyman Richover's legendary team. Kaufman and Kaufman believed:

> The qualities that Rickhover displayed as a naval officer and that Carter so admired were the same qualities that helped define Carter's approach to his presidency. Rickover was a loner who never cared much for the social life of the navy or of the Washington, D.C., establishment. He had seemingly inexhaustible energy. He approached problem solving through a mastery of detail. He was not prone to compromise. He demanded excellence. He micromanaged. He believed that self-fulfillment meant something more than material gain and that he served some singular purpose other than his own ambitions.

W. Carl Biven, who wrote *Jimmy Carter's Economy*, qualified these views:

> Much has been made of his engineering mentality. A description of Jimmy Carter would be incomplete if one did not go on to say that the engineer is a part of the Carter personality, but not all. After he graduated from Annapolis, he applied for a Rhodes scholarship to study political science and history. He was a finalist but didn't receive the scholarship. He balanced his formal training in the physical sciences with extensive

> reading in history, literature, philosophy, and theology— that part of knowledge which is not emphasized at Annapolis.... He developed an intense interest in classical music. His love of classical music carried over into the White House, where pieces he selected were played each day in his office. "He was to an astonishing extent a self made man," Bert Carp, deputy to Stuart Eizenstat, has said. "I might conceivably order the great books but I wouldn't read them all. He's ordered them and read them and taught himself Spanish off a record."

When his father died in 1953, Carter took over his father's peanut farm in Plains, Georgia. The business prospered and within a few years, Carter was one of Plains' most respected business and civil cadre. After serving in the Georgia Senate between 1963 and 1967, Carter was elected governor in 1970 as a staunchly anti-segregation moderate.

Carter's religious faith was deeply woven into his life. Carter admired Reinhold Neibuhr's theology, including the work *Courage and the Courage to Change,* in which Niebuhr wrote: "The sad duty of politics is to establish justice in a sinful world." In accepting the Democratic Party nomination on July 15, 1976, Carter spoke in moral terms about a nation "shaken by a tragic war abroad and by scandals and broken promises at home." He ran for president as an outsider against "a political economic elite."

Carter would win the Democratic Party nomination and defeat Ford in the general election by running as the anti-Watergate, anti-Washington candidate. He emphasized restoring trust in government by reforming the bureaucracy, reducing secrecy in decision making and passing strong ethics laws. Carter's commitment to fiscal discipline and aspirations for a balanced budget would be dominating considerations in his approach to economic issues.

As president, Carter contrasted himself with the "free-spending policy" that some Democratic leader sought. He would have serious disagreements with Congress beginning in late February 1977, when he sought to eliminate 19 water projects in 17 states that Carter considered "worthless" or "pork-barrel." He would take pride that he reduced a 1976 federal deficit of $66 billion or 4 percent of GNP to a 1971 proposed deficit of 0.5 percent with his "new goal to reduce the deficit to zero." His determination to balance the budget was pervasive. When Council of Economic Advisers Chair Charles Schultze sent him a memorandum on inflation in March 1977,

Carter responded: "There is nothing in your inflation memo involving government spending restraints — future impact of initiating new programs — balancing the budget, etc. Why?"

As a centrist in the Democratic Party, Carter sought to unite as Stuart Eizenstat wrote, "as best he could his diverse and often incompatible coalition of Southern conservatives and Northern liberals and blue-collar industrial-state workers and their unions." His religious faith and anti-segregation views would help him win every state in the South except Virginia by uniting African-American voters with religious white voters. His fiscal conservatism would include a determination to cut the defense budget, which appealed to Northern liberals.

Carter would oppose mandatory wage and price controls in favor of voluntary cooperation and jawboning in part because organized labor then was the backbone of the Democratic Party and opposed wage controls or tight wage guidelines. In the 1976 election, 62 percent of unionized labor supported Carter. "In that era," Stuart Eizenstat, Carter's Chief Domestic Policy Adviser, would write, "it was difficult if not impossible for a Democrat to win the presidency without the big labor unions. Mobilizing thousands of field workers to organize on the ground, especially to turn out voters on Election Day."

Carter and his economic team rejected the trade-off between inflation and unemployment, but initially sought job creation as a top economic goal, not curbing inflation. As with Harry Truman, Carter set full employment as a national goal. During the 1976 campaign, Carter would quantify this goal as "bringing unemployment down to 3 percent among adults, 4 to 4½ percent for the whole labor force." In an interview with the editors of *Fortune* magazine during the campaign, Carter explained: "I would proceed aggressively, with the first emphasis on jobs. My economic advisers and I agree that until you get the unemployment rate down below 5 percent, there's no real danger of escalating inflationary pressures." He arrived at the White House determined to stimulate the economy.

As with Roosevelt, Truman, Kennedy, and Johnson, Carter sought to rein in the Fed's independence, but decorously as the 1976 Democratic Party platform put it, by making the Federal Reserve "a full partner in national economic decisions . . . responsive to the economic goals of Congress and the President."

Carter's presidency would be weakened by his distant attitude toward Congress and sometimes obsessive micromanaging. Carter buried himself in an endless flow of reading material. The amount of time he spent on the minutiae of Governance left him with less time to meet with members of Congress, interest group leaders, or the public.

Carter's inaugural address on January 20, 1977, was short on policy specifics, but began his presidency in spiritual terms:

> Here before me is the Bible used in the inauguration of our first president, in 1789, and I have just taken the oath of office on the Bible my mother gave me a few years ago, opened to a timeless admonition from the ancient prophet Micah:
>
> "He hath showed thee, O man, what is good: and what doth the Lord require of thee, but to do justly, and to love mercy, and to walk humbly with thy God." . . .
>
> . . . And I join in the hope that when my time as your President has ended, people might say this about our Nation:
>
> - that we had remembered the words of Micah and renewed our search for humility, mercy, and justice;
> - that we had torn down the barriers that separated those of different race and region and religion, and where there had been mistrust, built unity, with a respect for diversity;
> - that we had found productive work for those able to perform it;
> - that we had strengthened the American family, which is the basis of our society;
> - that we had ensured respect for the law, and equal treatment under the law, for the weak and the powerful, for the rich and the pool;
> - and that we had enabled our people to be proud of their own government once again.

Carter's economic team before his inauguration emphasized the need for a stimulus package. Arthur Burns was odd man out. Carter's economic advisers were concerned that the Federal Reserve would offset the stimulus package with monetary restraints. Burns was, as a critical memorandum prepared in December 1977 by Treasury Secretary Michael Blumenthal and Charles Schultze explained: "more concerned with inflation than unemployment," willing to "thwart administration goals to reduce unemployment." Burns they believed "has stirred up opposition to many of your policies." Schultze separately criticized Burns' lack of cooperation. Burns "is an intellectually stubborn man." Blumenthal and Schultze added: Burns "is fundamentally unsympathetic towards giving joint priority to reducing unemployment and inflation, he will not hesitate to frustrate the unemployment goal if he thinks there is the slightest risk for the inflation goal." Carter was predisposed to replace Burns: "He's the one who, when Nixon was facing reelection, was the most eager or willing to use the Fed policy to help Nixon with a stimulus for the economy, an action which I don't think was good for the economy."

The Carter administration initially opposed any increase in interest rates. During 1977, Burns' final year as Fed Chair, inflation measured by consumer prices rose to 6.75 percent, wholesale prices similarly rose to 6.5 percent. The Fed approved two discount rate increases in 1977—from 5.25 to 5.75 percent effective August 30, 1977, and from 5.75 to 6 percent effective October 26, 1977. Given Burns' reputation as the Nation's "Number One Inflation Fighter," those were modest increases, some believed motivated by Burns' desire to be reappointed.

In December 1977, Carter nominated G. William Miller to be Burns' successor ad Fed Chair. Miller began in March 1978. He was Chief Executive Officer of Textron, a major aerospace and defense firm. Miller earlier had served as a lawyer in a leading New York City firm, Cravath, Swaine & Moore, was a Democrat and long-time advocate of equal employment opportunities for minorities. Between 1963 and 1965, Miller had been Chair of the Industry Advisory Group to the Presidential Adviser on Equal Employment Opportunity. In 1968, Miller had Chaired a National Business Group campaign for Democratic Party nominee Hubert Humphrey.

Miller had served as a Director of the Boston Federal Reserve Bank for eight years and unlike Burns in his public remarks, Miller emphasized that he believed that coordinated fiscal policy and the Fed could help reduce unemployment without triggering inflation. Carter's economic advisers recommended Miller because: "Miller shares your basic goals and views. He would be an independent Chairman, but he would be cooperative and easy to work with."

On March 8, 1978, at Miller's confirmation hearing, Miller declined to choose whether reducing unemployment or fighting inflation should be the Fed's priority. "[W]e can tackle both to achieve what we really need—full employment with price stability."

Unlike Burns, Miller would maintain a constructive relationship with Carter during his chairmanship.

Michael Blumenthal earlier had been named Treasury Secretary and would serve with Miller, Stuart Eizenstat, the Chief Domestic Adviser, and Charles Schultze, Council of Economic Advisers on Carter's Economic Policy Group. Blumenthal, whose family escaped from Nazi Germany in 1939, arriving near penniless in San Francisco after the War, would earn a Ph.D. in economics from Princeton in 1956, and teach there between 1954 and 1957. Subsequently, Blumenthal served under Presidents Kennedy and Johnson in the State Department as Assistant Secretary of State for Economic Affairs and during Kennedy's Presidency as Chair of the United States Delegation to the Geneva Tariff Negotiations. In 1967, Blumenthal left government to join Bendix, a major aerospace manufacturer. He was appointed Chair and Chief Executive Officer in 1977. Blumenthal was an accomplished business leader who was a Democrat.

But Blumenthal would not prove to be successful as Treasury Secretary either in reducing inflation or unemployment. Blumenthal soon would be at odds with Carter, Vice President Mondale, and Eizenstat in believing that inflation was a greater threat to the country than unemployment. His views on tax reform would not be considered sufficiently protective of lower and middle class taxpayers. Carter viewed Blumenthal as ineffective as Chair of the Economic Policy Group and in August 1979, Carter replaced Blumenthal as Treasury Secretary with G. William Miller, who served as Fed Chair for only 17 months. As Treasury Secretary, Miller would be more conciliatory than Blumenthal.

Charles Schultze, Chair of the Council of Economic Advisers, was the third pivotal Carter economic adviser. When his appointment was announced, Carter had called Schultze his Chief Economic Adviser, which caused tensions with Blumenthal. Schultz and Blumenthal ultimately fashioned an awkward sharing of leadership on economic policy. Schultze would serve as Chair of the Council of Economic Advisers throughout Carter's four-year presidency. He had earned a Ph.D. in economics from the University of Maryland and was an Assistant Professor of Economics at Indiana University between 1959 and 1962. Unlike Gardiner Ackley, his predecessor in Johnson's Administration, Schultze sought policy coordination with the Fed, by which he meant "really talking together frankly," not subordination. Carter felt "compatible" with Schultze: "Charlie would sit down with me in the Oval Office and just say in his inimitable way, 'you know me Mr. President. These are the practical things that I believe we can extract from the various sources of advice and information and these are the options that you have.' "

At the outset of his work for Carter, Schultze acknowledged that the deficits inherited by Ford "limited room for maneuver in terms of new programs," but he did not believe that Carter or his senior advisers fully appreciated "the risks when you're dealing with inflation. That is, if you're a little bit too conservative in your economic policy and you make a mistake, it's easy to cure. So next year you have a little bit bigger tax cut. But if you make a mistake on the inflationary side, the inflation becomes very hard to pull down. We didn't appreciate that. Sure, we were aware of it, but we weren't aware enough."[26]

Until Carter's appointment of Paul Volcker as Fed Chair on August 6, 1979, the fiscal and monetary policies of his administration would be an abysmal failure. In 1978, the Federal Reserve's Annual Report acknowledged: "Inflation emerged clearly as the nation's most urgent economic concern in 1978." Inflation was aggravated by the 1978 Organization of Petroleum Exporting Countries (*OPEC*) oil price spike and the ensuing United States energy crisis. In 1979, consumer inflation averaged 13 percent, briefly rising in February and March 1980 to a virtually unimaginable 18 percent. The GNP declined sharply from a 5.75 percent increase in 1977 to 1 percent increase in 1979. Unemployment which had declined to 5.7 from 5.9 percent in 1979, rose to a peak 7.8 percent in 1980. In retrospect, Stuart Eizenstat, Carter's Director of Domestic Policy, would write: "Our bigger mistake on economic policy was . . . misjudging the strength of inflationary forces in early 1977, and having an economic policy which overstimulated the economy."

The deteriorating economy would parallel the deterioration in Carter's public support. In March 1977, a Harris poll found that 75 percent of the American people favorably viewed his ability to "inspire confidence." By October, only 46 percent in an NBC survey approved of Carter's performance as president. In April 1978, with 63 percent of the American people viewing inflation as their greatest concern, only 32 percent in a *New York Times*-CBS poll approved of Carter's record on the economy. In August 1978, an ABC-Harris poll reported 69 percent of the American people disapproved of Carter's performance. By the summer of 1979, a Yankelovich poll found that only 23 percent of respondents believed that things were going well in the economy, 64 percent believed that the country was "in deep and serious trouble."

The failure to tame stagflation and the deterioration of public support was the result of the poorly fashioned and ineptly implemented 1977 and 1978 stimulus and anti-inflation programs. As Stuart Eizenstat in retrospect would write: "We . . . lacked a consistent, coherent policy and had no clear framework within which individual decisions could be made and explained to the public."

Before his inauguration, Carter and his economic team developed a stimulus package. Charles Schultze recalled it was 90 percent complete before Carter's January 20, 1977, inauguration. Carter reluctantly supported a stimulus package at a December 1, 1976, meeting at the Pond House in Plains. Stuart Eizenstat recalled:

> Carter himself believed that the nation's economic imbalances would be righted by balancing the federal budget — a belief that was shared by many in America and which he stood by to the end. He proposed to achieve balance by the end of his first term through a "quick and effective stimulus" that would not tie his hands during the rest of his term.

On January 7, 1977, in a follow up meeting with congressional leaders in Plains, Carter rejected recommendations for more spending and fewer tax cuts. Eizenstat paraphrased Carter's remarks: "This was not going to be the Great Society redux. He explained that he was proposing a tax cut for low and medium-income taxpayers, but he expected it to be paid for, first by tax reform that he would [propose later] in 1977, and then by higher tax revenues that would be a growth dividend for the stimulus itself." Compared to the Kennedy stimulus package, which equaled 1.7 percent of GNP or that of Ford at 1.5 percent, Carter's proposal was less than 1 percent.

On January 31, 1977, Carter sent Congress a message outlining his proposals for stimulating the economy. There were five main components: (1) A $50 rebate for each taxpayer, each family who filed for the earned income credit, and every beneficiary of Social Security or railroad retirement. This was a one-time benefit intended to provide $11.4 billion in 1977. Carter favored a one-time rebate to save future revenues for balancing the budget, which he sought to achieve by the end of his first term. (2) Tax credits for businesses equal to 4 percent of Social Security payroll taxes paid by the business or alternatively each business could choose a 2 percent credit for new investment in machinery or equipment. (3) An additional $4 billion for emergency public works beyond the $2 billion authorized by Congress in 1976. (4) An increase in public jobs under the Comprehensive Employment and Training Act (*CETA*) from 310,000 already authorized to 725,000 by 1978, and an increase in CETA youth training programs by 176,000 slots and an increase of 92,000 jobs in Vietnam-era veteran CETA retraining and employment programs. And (5) a near doubling of the $1.25 billion countercyclical revenue sharing for states and localities when unemployment exceeded 6 percent.

Carter anticipated the total net costs in 1977 and 1978 of his stimulus program net of savings on unemployment insurance and welfare to be just over $20 billion.

On March 8, 1977, the House of Representatives approved Carter's stimulus package. There was little enthusiasm for the $50 rebate, but early in the Carter presidency, a House majority went along.

There was less enthusiasm in the Senate. Charles Schultze described a call from Senator Humphrey: "The [rebate] idea won't do us any good; it's terrible; it's like a bribe; you're just dropping fifty-dollar bills all over the place." Senator Long belittled the rebate as "throwing $50 bills off the top of the Washington Monument."

The United States Conference of Mayors and AFL-CIO echoed the liberal Congressional leaders in criticizing the stimulus as not going far enough and as "a retreat from the goals we understood President-elect Carter to have set during last year's election campaign." By March, some in unionized labor were in rebellion against Carter because of dislike of his stimulus campaign and Carter's unwillingness to support their proposed increase in the minimum wage from $2.30 to $3.00 an hour.

With food prices rising and the risk of inflation increasing in the early months, Carter unexpectedly withdrew the $50 rebate proposal on April 14, 1977, despite advice from several senior economic and political advisers that he would pay a price for abandoning the rebate, as Eizenstat wrote, "in a way that showed his inexperience in dealing with Congress." Senator Ed Muskie, former Democratic presidential candidate, now Chair of the Senate Budget Committee, was outraged when he learned from a press leak that the hard work his Committee had done to support Carter's original stimulus package partly was for naught. Carter later would recall: "I almost lost a friend in that episode with Ed Muskie." The abrupt policy switch on the stimulus package on top of his political ineptitude in rolling out the water projects cuts two months earlier undercut Carter's credibility. Without the $50 rebate, the $20 billion net stimulus package was reduced to $14.3 billion. The revised Carter stimulus package also dropped the investment tax credits for business in favor of tax credits for businesses that hired additional employees, as championed by Al Ullman, Chair of the House Ways and Means Committee.

On May 13, 1977, Carter signed the Economic Recovery Act, which provided $20.1 billion in public works programs to increase employment and a one-year extension of the Comprehensive Employment and Training Act. Separate legislation established new job projects for disadvantaged youth. On May 23, 1977, the Tax Reduction and Simplification Act raised the standard deduction to $2200 for single taxpayers and $3200 for taxpayers filing jointly and created a new jobs credit for employers of up to $100,000, equal to 50 percent of the first $4200 of wages paid to each additional employee in 1977 and 1978 and provided $2.25 billion in countercyclical revenue sharing with states and localities.

By then, the economic priority of the Carter administration had shifted from a stimulus program to an anti-inflation program. In his memoirs, Carter would acknowledge: "The overall inconsistency in my policy during this rapid transition from stimulating the economy to an overall battle against inflation was to plague me for a long time. . . . [F]or more than three and a half years, my major economic battle would be against inflation, and I would stay on the side of fiscal prudence, restricted budgets, and lower deficits."

The flaw in Carter's anti-inflation policy was that he long handcuffed the means to succeed. Under Carter, there would be no mandatory wage and price controls. Until the 1979 appointment of Volcker as Fed Chair, his administration would resist massive interest rate rises to end what by then had become runaway inflation. Carter regarded fighting inflation through high unemployment as "morally unacceptable." "Inflation must not be attacked by causing additional human misery." Eizenstat eulogized the Carter policy failure:

> Carter realized before most of his advisers, myself included, that inflation was the greatest danger to the nation and its growth. He employed everything from two anti-inflation czars, tight budgets, increasingly tough wage and price guidelines, a labor-management advisory board, and deregulation. These measures were like using a toy gun against a raging elephant.

On April 15, 1977, Carter delivered his first anti-inflation message. The message contained 11 specific actions to be taken by the federal government, including a two-year extension of the statutory authority of the Council on Wage and Price Stability, and deregulating specific industries such as trucking and airlines to allow competition to lower prices. But the core of the document was Carter's call for the voluntary cooperation of management and labor "and not be based on coercive or self-defeating controls." He announced that he had appointed George Meany, President of the AFL-CIO and Reginald Jones, Chair of General Electric, to "help coordinate new cooperation between labor, management and the government."

Reliance on voluntary cooperation did not work. Charles Schultze concluded after he left office: "We had an anti-inflation program, so-called in April 1977, which had all kinds of bits and pieces in it, none of which meant anything." Eizenstat, also in retrospect, characterized the labor-management group led by Meany and Jones as "a toothless tiger, because the AFL-CIO refused to talk about specific numbers or to agree to restrain their wage demands to catch up with inflation."

In 1977, Carter named economist Barry Bosworth Director of the President's Council on Wage and Price Stability, in part to monitor wage and price inflation. In 1977, the Consumer Price Index rose 6.8 percent. In 1978, the Consumer Price Index shot up 9.3 percent. Food inflation was rising 16.4 percent in 1977. In May 1978, the Council on Wage and Price Stability reported that: "Labor costs, which had been increasing at an annual rate of 6.0 percent, rose 8.2 percent over the past four quarters, "the year since the first Carter anti-inflation program was announced.

In his first State of the Union message on January 19, 1978, Carter proudly stated: "Last year was a good one for the United

States. . . . Four million jobs were created, . . . an all time record and the number of unemployed dropped by more than one million."

But Carter explained: "[W]e must lower the rate of inflation and keep it down." He renewed the attack on inflation. He then asked "government, business, labor, and other groups to join in a voluntary program to moderate wage and price increases in each sector of the economy during 1978 below the average increase of the last 2 years." Carter repeated: "I do not believe in wage and price controls. A sincere commitment to voluntary constraints provides a way — perhaps the only way — to fight inflation without government interference."

Cutting the other way were Carter's stimulus proposals — a $17 billion income tax cut to go to individuals and $2 billion cuts in excise taxes.

In March 1978, Blumenthal and Schultze advised Carter: "The price outlook is deteriorating."

In April 1978, in an Address to the American Society of Newspaper Editors, Carter announced the appointment of Robert Strauss, former Chair of the Democratic National Committee, then serving as Carter's Special Trade Representative, to be his Counsellor on Inflation. Carter also announced a freeze on pay increases for all 2300 political appointees in the federal government. All other federal white collar salaries, which in 1977 had risen by more than 7 percent, would be limited in 1978 to pay hikes of 5.5 percent as an "example for labor and industry to moderate price and wage increases."

Again, the unions balked. Secretary of Labor Ray Marshall and Strauss reported to Carter at a meeting with George Meany and other labor leaders: "The unions . . . are unwilling to practice wage deceleration prior to any indication of a slowdown in price inflation." At a May meeting with Carter, Sol Chaikin, President of the International Ladies Garment Workers, echoed Meany's point: His union "will cooperate only when the Consumer Price Index is dropping."

On October 24, 1978, in a nationally televised address, Carter characterized inflation as "our most serious domestic problem. . . . Inflation can threaten all the economic gains we've made, and it can stand in the way of what we want to achieve in the future."

Carter acknowledged that earlier efforts to control inflation had "not been successful." He again rejected wage and price controls and a deliberate recession.

He pledged to concentrate his "efforts within the government," which he termed one of the "causes of inflation. . . . We are going to hold down government spending, reduce the budget deficit, and eliminate government waste."

Carter opposed "any further reduction in federal income taxes until we have convincing prospects that inflation will be controlled." The federal deficit had been reduced from $66 billion in 1976, to $40 billion for the 1979 budget. He pledged to reduce the deficit in the following year to $30 billion or less. He ordered a 20,000 person reduction in the federal government's permanent employees. He enthusiastically recognized the benefits of the recent deregulation of the airline industry: "Free market forces drove prices down, record numbers of passenger travelers, and profits went up. . . . Of all the weapons against inflation, competition is the most effective."

Carter announced more specific wage and price standards, asking all but the lowest paid workers to limit total wage increases to a maximum of 7 percent per year and setting a basis target for economy-wide price increases at 5.75 percent. "To reach this goal, I'm tonight setting a standard for each firm in this nation to hold its price increases at least one-half of one percentage point below what they averaged during 1976 and 1977."

Carter recognized: "The difficulty with a voluntary program is that workers fear if they cooperate with the standards while others do not, then they will suffer if inflation continues." To assuage this concern, "I will ask Congress next January to enact a program that workers who observe the standards would be eligible for a tax rebate if the inflation rate is more than 7 percent."

Carter stated with respect to the $80 billion worth of purchases the government makes from private industry each year: "We will require firms that supply goods and services to the government to certify their compliance with the wage and price standards. We will make every effort, within legal limits, to deny government contracts to companies that fail to meet our wage and price standards."[27]

Council of Economic Advisers Chair Charles Schultze would characterize "the guts of [Carter's] speech was the guidelines" and the commitment that next year's deficit would be no more than $30 billion. Neither commitment worked.

Carter followed up what came to be known as the Phase II Guidelines by appointing Alfred Kahn to be his new Anti-Inflation Czar. Robert Strauss by then had resigned, explaining: "I can't go further with only a smile and sunshine. I need more government help." Kahn, a Cornell Professor of Economics, author of the influential 1970 work, *The Economics of Regulation: Principles and Institutions*, had served as Chair of the New York Public Service Commission and had revised the state's utility rates to reflect true costs. He had achieved a signal success in the Carter administration as Chair of the Civil Aeronautics Board in leading airline deregulation, but Kahn did not want the job, openly paraphrasing, *The Treasure of Sierra Madre* in derision of the "stinking guidelines." In order to persuade the reluctant Kahn to accept the assignment as Anti-Inflation Czar, Carter also appointed Kahn to be Chair of the Council of Wage and Price Stability. In these two roles, Kahn was, as Eizenstat wrote: "A capable person . . . great in one job . . . miscast in another."

Public, congressional and stock market reaction to the Phase II Wage and Price Guidelines was highly negative. The public and Congress scorned the Guidelines as too weak, the same approach that had not earlier worked. As Meltzer wrote: "The public had learned a main lesson about guidelines — they don't control inflation." The Dow Jones Industrial Average declined by nearly 10 percent after Carter's speech.

Robert Higgs, after a review of selected business and labor compliance with the Phase II Guidelines, concluded: "Patently, the guidelines did not slow the rate of inflation: During 1979, the decline in the purchasing power of money actually accelerated. That the program failed to achieve its ostensible objective therefore is beyond argument."

The ongoing deterioration of the dollar against international currencies accelerated. In December 1977, New York Federal Reserve President Paul Volcker had urged Carter to make a presidential statement because "there is a risk of a snowballing impact on the dollar." This, in fact, occurred in 1978. The United States merchandise trade deficit widened from $35 billion in 1977 to an annual rate of more than $45 billion in the first three months of 1978, giving impetus to the decline of the dollar. The trade-weighted value of the dollar against 10 leading currencies declined from 107 in June 1976 to 86 in September and October 1978, some 19.6 percent. "By late October," the Federal Reserve reported, "the decline of the dollar had become precipitous, and it imperiled the international financial system."

On November 1, 1978, President Carter announced that the Secretary of Treasury Blumenthal and Fed Chair Miller would jointly implement a $30 billion rescue plan, including an increase in the gold auction to 1.5 million ounces beginning in December, a $7.6 billion increase in Federal Reserve swap lines with Germany, Switzerland, and Japan, and sale of $2 billion of special drawing rights to these three countries, a drawdown of $3 billion of foreign currencies from the International Monetary Fund, and a sale by the Treasury of up to $10 billion of foreign currency.

The initial stock and money market reactions to the November 1 rescue plan were quite favorable. The stock market rose 35 points in a single day, the dollar appreciated 7 to 10 percent against other leading currencies.

On November 1, the Fed increased the discount rate by a full percentage point to 9.5 percent, the largest increase in 45 years "developed as a part of a broad government program to strengthen the dollar in foreign exchange markets and thereby counter continuing domestic inflationary pressures."

Since taking office as Fed Chair in March 1978, Miller generally had been more accommodating of administration fiscal policy than Burns had been. Rather than take a sharp anti-inflation approach, the Fed in the period before Volcker's appointment as Fed Chair generally increased discount rates and federal fund rates to follow the money market and inflation. In 1978, the Fed would increase the discount rate seven times from 6 percent to 9.5 percent. In the first six months of 1979, the federal funds rate increased from 10.1 to 10.5 percent while consumer price inflation rose from 10.6 to a high of 14.7 percent in May 1978.

In 1979, when oil prices spiked prompting greater concerns about a deepening recession, the Fed became reluctant to increase the discount rate and further weaken the economy. A minority of Federal Reserve Governors, including Volcker, dissented from the Fed majority's reluctance to more aggressively use interest rate interest to combat inflation. On April 17, 1979, Governor Henry Wallich pointedly remarked: "[W]e have had several months now of status quo and in that several months, we've had at least a 3 percentage point increase in the inflation rate." At the May 22, 1979 Open Market Committee, Volcker objected to what he believed to be the Fed majority anxiety about recession: "If we're going to balance these risks of inflation and recession, we have to run not too scared that the recession is going to be worse than we expected."[28]

Congress was less accommodating. On October 27, 1978, Congress enacted the Full Employment and Balanced Growth Act, popularly known as the Humphrey-Hawkins Act, after its Congressional sponsors, liberal stalwarts Hubert Humphrey who died in January 1978, and Representative Augustus Hawkins. The bill had first been introduced in 1974 and tempered in 1975 into Concurrent Resolution No. 133 with its goals of "maximum employment, stable prices and moderate long term interest rates." When originally reported out of the House Education and Labor Committee in 1976, the bill provided for joint planning by Congress and the administration to achieve a 3 percent unemployment rate within four years and federally funded jobs programs to make the federal government the employer of last resort.

In 1977, Congress had enacted the Federal Reserve Act amendments which had codified the 1946 Employment Act implicit goals into a dual mandate of "maximum employment" and "stable [meaning noninflationary] prices," adding a third goal of "moderate long-term interest rates."

The 1978 Humphrey-Hawkins Act dual mandate built on the earlier 1977 Federal Reserve Act amendments and the 1946 Employment Act. Humphrey-Hawkins went further than the 1946 and 1977 legislation and specified explicit numerical goals for the President's Economic Report reducing the rate of unemployment to no more than 3 percent among individuals 20 and over and 4 percent for individuals over 16 within five calendar years and reducing the inflation rate to no more than 3 percent within five years. The president was directed, as he or she deemed appropriate, to recommend countercyclical employment policies to reduce unemployment.

The Fed also was required no later than February 20 and July 20 of each year to provide a Report to Congress, among other things, setting forth monetary and credit aggregated for the calendar year during which the Report is transmitted.

Two weeks later, Congress took another large step towards emphasizing maximum employment, rather than fighting inflation, as its leading economic priority. On November 6, 1978, Congress enacted a new $18.7 billion set of tax cuts in the Revenue Act of 1978, which reduced individual income taxes by increasing the standard deduction from $3200 to $3400, increasing the size of the lower income tax bands, reduced the corporate tax rate from 48 to 46 percent, and increased the capital gains exclusion from 50 to 60 percent.

Carter's support of the stimulus package — by then in flat contradiction to his anti-inflation campaign — had softened in May when he reduced the size of his initial stimulus package from a net of over $20 billion to $14.3 billion. With the size of the projected deficit growing and Congress unwilling to tie the tax cut to reform of the tax code, Carter on October 14, 1978, had informed Treasury Secretary Blumenthal, Council of Economic Advisers Chair Schultze, and Domestic Policy Adviser Eizenstat: "I am hoping I can veto the tax bill, and use this as an example for my anti-inflation program. Tax reform is so screwed up. I am feeling better knowing I can veto the bill." In the 1977 campaign, Carter had called the tax code "a disgrace to the human race." Shortly before the November 7, 1978, midterm elections, Carter signed the Revenue Act after Members of Congress expressed concerns a veto would harm the Democratic Party's reelection fortunes.

The 1978 elections results were mixed. The Democratic majority in the Senate declined slightly from 61–38 to 58–41 after the general election and a special election. Their House majority declined from an overwhelming 292–143 to a still formidable 277–158. The Republicans picked up six governorships.

Underlying the 1978 election results was an incipient tax revolt that had begun in 1976 and 1977 with enactments in New Jersey and Colorado to limit government spending. California voters in 1978, had supported Proposition 13, which rolled back property taxes to their 1975 levels and imposed a 2 percent limit on yearly increases in property taxes. This reduced California property tax revenues by close to 60 percent. Representative Jack Kemp and Senator William Roth introduced a bill calling for a 10 percent cut in federal taxes for three years. Ronald Reagan, running for president in 1980, would endorse the Kemp-Roth Bill.[29]

Things went from bad to worse. With Carter in May 1978 promising NATO allies that he would increase Defense spending by 3 percent and the 1978 Revenue Act cutting tax revenues by nearly $19 billion, Carter's promise to hold the 1980 budget deficit to $30 billion was shredded. The budget message Carter delivered to Congress on January 23, 1979, projected a $60 billion deficit, an increase, in Eizenstat's recollection that "shocked" the financial community.

More confusing yet, on January 24, 1979, Carter now considered "the most important priority this year was to reduce the burdens on taxpayers" and proposed $35 billion in "progressive tax reduction . . . to help assure continued economic recovery and reduction in unemployment."

After the economy, Carter considered energy his most important domestic policy. Solving the energy crisis was "the moral equivalent of war." During the four years of his presidency, Congress would enact three energy laws, in 1978 create the Department of Energy, set the nation on a path to decontrol of natural gas prices, and secure a large Windfall Profit Tax on Energy.

Dwarfing these achievements would be an energy crisis that would by December 1978, doom his Phase II Wage and Price Guidelines to ineffectuality. During the first four months of 1979, energy prices rose at an annual rate of 32 percent.

Oil producing nations within the Organization of Petroleum Exporting Countries (*OPEC*) had quadrupled oil prices during the 1973–1974 oil shock. The cost of oil imports had risen from $4.7 billion in 1972 to $45 billion in 1977, leading to a five-fold increase at the gas pumps.

After Carter's 1976 election, the nation faced natural gas shortage in the winter of 1976–1977, causing many schools and factories to close and the layoff of several hundred thousand employees. Carter directed James Schlesinger, soon the first Secretary of Energy, to develop a plan to address the energy crisis. Schlesinger recommended a complex set of proposals to, among other things, tax domestic oil production and gasoline consumption, create tax credits for energy conservation, and tax automobiles with low fuel efficiency. A watered down version of these proposals was adopted after intensive horse trading in November 1978, as the National Energy Act, which deregulated natural gas.

Carter's efforts to deregulate domestic oil production would not be successful. Domestic oil prices then were set by complex price controls established by the 1975 Energy Policy and Conservation Act.

In December 1978, OPEC raised prices by 15 percent, crippling any chance that voluntary wage price guidelines would work.

On January 16, 1979, the Shah of Iran was overthrown by Ayatollah Khomeini, spiritual head of Iran's 31 million Shiite Muslims, setting in motion a second oil shock. Iranian oil production declined from 6 million barrels a day in 1978, to 1.5 million in 1980, reducing the world oil production of 60 million barrels by over 7 percent. OPEC raised oil prices by another 17 percent. Within days of the Shah's overthrow, spot market prices for oil nearly doubled from $22 a barrel to $42 a barrel, over ten times the $4 price a decade earlier.

Over 50 percent of United States gas stations closed in the summer of 1979. On July 4, 1979, 90 percent of New York City area gas stations were closed because of gas shortages. Stuart Eizenstat reported "something close to a national hysteria in energy shortages:"

> While we were considering decontrolling gasoline and diesel fuel, the Teamsters Union and the long-haul drivers they represented were up in arms against it. Frustrated truckers were literally shooting gas station attendants who had run out of fuel. These burly drivers shut down the Pennsylvania Turnpike, leading to riots injuring more than one hundred people, and more than 150 arrests. They then converged on the White House with their heavy vehicles in a massive demonstration demanding a meeting with the president, or at least someone on the White House staff.

On April 5, 1979, Carter announced that he would decontrol oil prices on June 1 and "continue at a fairly uniform rate over the next 28 months. The immediate effect of this action will be to increase production of oil and gas in our own country."

Carter further announced a windfall profits tax on oil companies to capture part of the huge profits that these companies would reap: "[a]s government controls end, prices will go up on oil which has already been discovered." It was estimated that raising the price of oil to world levels would increase oil company profits by $13 billion. The windfall profits tax would pay about half the amount to the government.

Carter understood the short-term adverse political consequences of decontrol: "Phased decontrol will gradually increase the price of petroleum products. In the short run, it will add a small amount to our rate of inflation, but that is the cost we must pay to reduce our dependence on the foreign oil cartel."

The overheated rhetoric of Carter's address criticizing the oil companies as profiteers, the stark contradiction between a two-year campaign to fight inflation and rising oil prices backfired. Liberal

Democrats in Congress led by Senator Ted Kennedy began a legislative effort to end a presidential power to end oil and gas controls. A May 1970 Gallup poll found Kennedy leading Carter among Democrats for the 1980 presidential nomination 54 to 31 percent. By June 1979, only 33 percent of the American people viewed Carter favorably, according to a *New York Times-CBS* Survey, 45 percent rated Carter unfavorably. Pat Caddell, Carter's pollster, termed these results "staggering:" "Almost no candidate whose personal rating has been negative has survived reelection." By July 1979, the Consumer Price Index, which had increased at an annualized rate of 12.5 percent in April and May, rose to an annual rate of 13.9 percent. Carter biographers Burton Kaufman and Scott Kaufmann recount an increasingly rebellious Democratic congressional party majority: "In early April Congress killed Carter's wage insurance plan by slashing $2.5 billion slated for the program from the budget. The next month it defeated Carter's standby gasoline rationing plan. At the end of May Democrats sent a message to Carter by voting in caucus, 139 to 69, to reinstate controls on oil."

The combination of the looming oil price increases, the doubling of the budget deficit, the confusion about the priority of fighting inflation, Charles Schultze recalled: "really sort of hit the papers. It reinforced the view of the administration as essentially disorganized.... [T]here was a sense that we were going downhill; and are not getting our message across."

On July 4, 1979, Carter cancelled without public explanation another address on energy. He wrote in his diary that day: "I had already made four speeches to the nation on energy and they had been increasingly ignored."

Carter's pessimism was reinforced by an April 23, 1979, memorandum from Patrick Caddell warning of a "nation deep in crisis... a crisis in confidence marked by a dwindling faith in the future [and] growing real despair of elites and ordinary citizens alike as they struggle to articulate in concepts the malaise which they themselves feel." Among others, Caddell had taken to heart University of Rochester Professor Christopher Leach's recently published book, *The Culture of Narcissism* which depicted the United States as a self-indulgent society. Carter termed Caddell's memorandum "one of the most brilliant analyses of sociological and political interrelationships I have ever seen."

Carter met for 11 days at Camp David with government, business, labor, academic, and religious leaders seeking a new way to galvanize public support for his flagging political agenda.

A *New York Times-CBS* poll the week after the cancellation of Carter's speech found his approval rating at 26 percent, lower than Nixon during Watergate.

Carter rejected the view of Vice President Mondale and others that the Caddell Memo was "the craziest goddamn thing that I have ever read. There is not a psychiatric problem with America, but real problems with coping economically."

On July 15, 1979, Carter delivered what popularly came to be known as "The Malaise Speech," a national address entitled "Energy and National Goals—A Crisis of Confidence."

Carter's address was informed by Caddell and softened by the critique of Mondale and others:

> I want to speak to you first tonight about a subject even more serious than energy or inflation. I want to talk to you right now about a fundamental threat to American democracy. . . .
>
> It is a crisis of confidence.
>
> It is a crisis that strikes at the very heart and soul and spirit of our national will. We can see this crisis in the growing doubt about the meaning of our own lives and in the loss of a unity of purpose for our nation. . . .
>
> The symptoms of this crisis of the American spirit are all around us. For the first time in the history of our country a majority of our people believe that the next five years will be worse than the past five years. Two-thirds of our people do not even vote. . . .
>
> What you see too often in Washington and elsewhere around the country is a system of government that seems incapable of action. You see a Congress twisted and pulled in every direction by hundreds of well-financed and powerful special interests.

Carter made several specific proposals:

> In little more than two decades we've gone from a position of energy independence to one in which almost half the oil we use comes from foreign countries, at prices that are going through the roof. Our excessive dependence on OPEC has already taken a tremendous toll on our economy and our people. This is the direct cause of the long lines which have made millions of you spend aggravating hours waiting for gasoline. It's a cause of the

increased inflation and unemployment that we now face. This intolerable dependence on foreign oil threatens our economic independence and the very security of our nation. . . .

Point one: I am tonight setting a clear goal for the energy policy of the United States. Beginning this moment, this nation will never use more foreign oil than we did in 1977 — never.

Point two: To ensure that we meet these targets, I will use my presidential authority to set import quotas. I'm announcing tonight that for 1979 and 1980, I will forbid the entry into this country of one drop of foreign oil more than these goals allow.

. . .

Point three: To give us energy security, I am asking for the . . . commitment of funds . . . to develop America's own alternative sources of fuel — from coal, from oil shale, from plant products for gasohol, from unconventional gas, from the sun.

I propose the creation of an energy security corporation to lead this effort to replace two and a half million barrels of imported oil per day by 1990. The corporation will issue up to five billion dollars in energy bonds, and I especially want them to be in small denominations so average Americans can invest directly in America's energy security. . . .

These efforts will cost money, a lot of money, and that is why Congress must enact the windfall profits tax without delay.

. . .

Point four: I'm asking Congress to mandate, to require as a matter of law, that our nation's utility companies cut their massive use of oil by fifty percent within the next decade and switch to other fuels, especially coal, our most abundant energy source.

Point five: To make absolutely certain that nothing stands in the way of achieving these goals, I will urge Congress to create an energy mobilization board which, like the War Production Board in World War II, will have the responsibility and authority to cut through the red tape, the delays, and the endless roadblocks to completing key energy projects. . . .

Point six: I'm proposing a bold conservation program to involve every state, county, and city and every average American in our energy battle. This effort will permit you to build conservation into your homes and your lives at a cost you can afford.

I ask Congress to give me authority for mandatory conservation and for standby gasoline rationing. To further conserve energy, I'm proposing tonight an extra ten billion dollars over the next decade to strengthen our public transportation systems.

Carter's speech led to the enactment of a $27 billion Windfall Profits Tax, and creation of the Synthetic Fuel Corporation, with a production goal equivalent to at least 2 million barrels per day of crude oil by 1992, and the 1980 Energy Security Act. Although Congress rescinded Carter's surcharge on imported oil and rejected the Energy Mobilization Board, the Malaise Speech as it came to be known after Caddell's Memo was leaked to journalist Elizabeth Drew, did lead to important energy policy achievements.

Public perception of Carter as an effective leader was undercut on July 17, 1979, when Carter asked for resignations of his entire Cabinet and within two days accepted the resignations of Treasury Secretary Michael Blumenthal, Energy Secretary Schlesinger, Health, Education and Welfare Secretary Joseph Califano, Attorney General Griffin Bell, and Secretary of Transportation Brock Adams. The forced resignations, eventuated in Eizenstat's words to "a near mutiny by his valued Vice President."

There was one positive personnel change. To succeed Fed Chair G. William Miller who became Secretary of Treasury, Carter in Eizenstat's words "made perhaps the most significant and lasting economic decision of his presidency by appointing Paul Volcker as Chairman of the Federal Reserve." Miller was viewed as too lax on monetary policy. *Fortune Magazine*, for example, had entitled an article: "Bill Miller is a Faint-Hearted Inflation Fighter." Schultze and Blumenthal had privately met with Miller urging him to increase interest rates. Later they leaked to the press their view that the Fed needed to tighten its monetary policy. Carter had rebuked their effort then, but by the summer of 1979, Carter too realized there had to be a change at the Fed.[30]

Fed Chair Paul Volcker and the Battle to Tame Hyperinflation

Volcker was a *summa cum laude* graduate of Princeton, who had earned a Master's degree from Harvard's Graduate School of Public Administration. He began his career in 1952 at the New York Federal Reserve Bank as a junior economist and government securities trader. Volcker left the Fed to work five years as a financial economist at Chase Manhattan Bank, resuming his government career in 1962 at the Department of Treasury. In 1963, Volcker became the Deputy Secretary for Monetary Affairs, before returning in 1965 to Chase Manhattan as Vice President and Director of Planning.

From 1969 to 1974, Volcker was Treasury Under Secretary of International Affairs, where he played a pivotal role in the suspension of gold convertibility in August 1971. In 1975, Volcker became President of the New York Federal Reserve Bank, then and now viewed as the second most important position in the Fed and served as Vice Chair on the Federal Open Market Committee.

Volcker, after 30 years of service in government and a leading bank, was better prepared for the position as Fed Chair than any person in the Fed's history. But he also was well known for his independence. Volcker had dissented several times during Miller's period as Chair, pressing Miller and the Fed to raise interest rates. The fear of recession long had kept Miller and the Fed majority from tightening monetary policy to the extent necessary to definitively end inflation.

At the February 1979, FOMC, Volcker would not rule on the possibility of a recession in the second half of the year, but emphasized: "But in terms of the recession outlook itself, I think the number one problem continues to be the concerns about the price level. The greatest risk to the economy . . . is people having the feeling that prices are getting out of hand."

At the April FOMC Meeting, Volcker went further:

> [Inflation] clearly remains our problem. In any longer-range or indeed shorter-range perspective, the inflationary momentum has been increasing. . . . We talk about gradually decelerating the rate of inflation over a series of years. In fact, it has been accelerating over a series of years and hasn't yet shown any signs of reversing.

Volcker made no secret of his views when he was interviewed by Carter. Volcker stressed that he was "mainly concerned that the President not be under any misunderstanding about my own concern about the importance of an independent central banker and the need for the tighter money — tighter than Bill Miller had wanted."

Volcker by the time of his chairmanship had some views similar to those of the monetarists. Volcker accepted the Milton Friedman view on the decisive importance of controlling money growth by controlling inflation. Volcker would testify at his confirmation hearing: "If the growth of money is excessive over a period of time, we're going to have inflation."

Friedman and his acolytes stressed that the role of the Fed was to prevent sustained price level changes. Fed monetary actions to change money supply or lower interest rates had increased both inflation and subsequent recessions. Monetarists insisted on the importance of policy perseverance.

Volcker was not a monetary purist. In a 1976 article in the *Federal Reserve Bank of New York Monthly Review,* Volcker elaborated on his pragmatism:

> It is hardly a satisfactory answer to say that central banks in principle can always resist inflationary pressures by simply refusing to provide enough money to finance them. Set against persistent expansionary pressures, aggressive wage demands, monopolistic or regulatory patterns that resist downward price adjustments, and other factors affecting cost levels, such an approach would threaten chronic conflict with goals of growth and employment that must rank among the most important national objectives. In a democracy, the risk would not be just to the political life of a particular government, but to our way of government itself.

Volcker stressed the need to change inflationary expectations. On October 17, 1979, testifying to the Joint Economic Committee, Volcker elaborated on the "serious inflation environment we are now facing":

> An entire generation of young adults has grown up since the mid-1960s knowing only inflation, indeed an inflation that has seemed to accelerate inexorably. In the circumstances, it is hardly surprising that many citizens have begun to wonder whether it is realistic to anticipate a return to general price stability, and have begun to change their behavior accordingly. Inflation feeds in part on itself. So part of the job of returning to a more stable and more productive economy must be to break the grip of inflationary expectations.

Volcker well understood that with inflation and unemployment at unacceptable levels, the time was ripe for a strong anti-inflation program, "that's as convincing as we can make it." Volcker emphasized: "The worst thing we could do is to indicate some backing off—when we have an announced anti-inflation program."

Inflation would rise from an average of 2.6 percent between 1964 and 1968, 5 percent in 1969–1973, 8 percent in 1974–1978 to

14.6 percent from May 1979 to April 1980. The 14.6 percent rate was the highest percentage rate in United States history.

In February 1980, a four-month recession began with GNP declining 2.5 percent and unemployment rising to 7.8 percent. With inflation also worsening, the Dow Jones Industrial Average would fall from 904 on February 13, 1980, to 785 in the third week of March. In March, housing starts were down 42 percent from a year before. Car sales were off 24 percent from the previous year. By March, the federal funds rate was up to 17 percent. With the discount rate at the 12 percent level set in October 1979, borrowing rose from $1.2 billion on average in January to $2.8 billion in March. The Fed only then increased the discount rate to 13 percent. At its March 18 meeting, the FOMC set a range for federal funds between 13 and 20 percent.

Volcker would be widely lauded for leading efforts to reduce inflation to 3.7 percent by 1983. But there were enormous social costs in ending inflation. Unemployment would nearly double from 5.8 percent during the first nine months of 1979 to 10.8 percent late in 1982. The United States would experience its worst recession since 1929–1933.

Carter understood the social costs of squeezing inflation out of the economy. By the summer of 1979, he had diminished confidence in the anti-inflation remedies his economic advisers had recommended during the previous two and one-half years. Carter knew what he was facing — higher interest rates in the run-up to the 1980 election. Carter recalled: "Facing reelection I was about to make a political decision of momentous importance, and my advisers were very concerned." He chose Volcker because he sought "the strongest effort to control inflation, which was dangerously high and about to go higher." In Eizenstat's recollection, Carter:

> told Schultze and others of us among his inner circle that he had tried everything else to fight inflation and nothing worked — presidential messages, deregulating transportation, tight budgets, jawboning, two inflation czars, and increasingly tough voluntary wage and price guidelines. He would rather lose the election than leave the country a legacy of high inflation without having taken every possible step, however politically poisonous.

The conventional way for the Fed to signal a tightening of monetary policy was to raise its discount rate. On August 16th, at Volcker's first board meeting as Chair of the Fed, the Fed raised the discount rate from 10 to 10.5 percent "as a timely indication of the system's concern about the persisting strength of inflationary forces in the economy."

On September 18th, on a 4–3 vote, the Fed Board again raised the discount rate from 10.5 to 11 percent.

The market reaction to the two increases was negative. John Berry in the *Washington Post* reported:

> Many money market analysts have been expecting the FOMC to seek to tighten credit in an effort to slow down sharp increases in the money supply.... However, the split vote, with its clear signal that from the Fed's own point of view interest rates are at or close to their peak for this business cycle, might forestall any more increases in market interest rates.

Robert Bennett in the *New York Times* similarly opined: "[T]he vote left uncertain whether Paul A. Volcker, who became Federal Reserve Chairman early in August, could continue to command a majority for his high-rate policies. The split was seen as indicating a fundamental division within the board over whether inflation remained a more pressing problem than recession."

Commodities prices soared. Gold rose $24 an ounce in one day to a high of $375.75 in London, and then jumped another $6.25 in later trading in New York. At an October 4 Fed meeting: "[O]ne Board Member referred to the outburst of speculation activity in the gold market which appeared to be spilling over into other commodity markets as well and to the very sensitive condition in domestic financial and dollar exchange markets." The 1979 Federal Reserve Annual Report explained: "In foreign exchange market the weighted average value of the dollar against major foreign currencies had declined substantially since the Committee's meeting in mid-September." This was on top of a 12 percent decline of the dollar against major foreign currencies between late 1976 and January 1979.

Public opinion increasingly expressed concern about inflation. In 1970, when inflation was 6 percent, a Gallup poll found only 14 percent named "the high cost of living" as one of the nation's most important problems. By 1980–1981, inflation would be characterized as one of the country's most important problems by 70 percent of Gallup respondents.

In 2001, Volcker would recall the market and press reaction to the September 18 discount rate increase: "That's the last increase . . . we'll see. . . . [T]he market reacted badly. Then I realized we had this credibility problem worse than I thought."

The three Federal Reserve governors who voted against the rate increase, Nancy Teeters, Emmett Rice, and Charles Partee, soon came to share Volcker's view that there needed to be a dramatic change in monetary policy.

Governor Partee who voted against the September 18th discount rate increase shortly later addressed market analysts in New York and received extremely hostile questions: "I was chastised for not voting for the discount increase. Didn't I realize the metal markets were going wild? Didn't I realize the Mexican peso was now favored over the dollar?" Fed Vice Chair Frederick Schultz, who voted for the increase, came to believe: "Every day you got this sense that the world was coming apart at the seams. You saw it in every market. There was a genuine flight from the currency — people investing in tangibles, art, jewelry, stamps, gold. Everything that was tangible was increasing in value."

By the time of the FOMC October 6, 1979 meeting, the Federal Reserve governors were ready to switch from policies perceived as incrementalist to a decisive approach.

On September 29, 1979, Volcker traveled to Belgrade for the annual International Monetary Fund Meeting. Then German Chancellor Helmut Schmidt reinforced Volker's belief that the time had come to act. Treasury Secretary Miller and Chair of the Council on Economic Advisers were briefed on the direction Volcker intended to pursue and were not enthusiastic. Schultze echoed the concerns of Mondale and earlier those of Carter. He feared that Volcker's tighter monetary policy would increase unemployment and lead to a recession. Schultze also was worried that the Fed would not retreat in a recession, which likely would occur in the 1980 election year.

Carter stood by Volcker, taking no action in opposition to the impending policy change. Volcker later wrote: "My reading of the situation was that while the president would strongly prefer that we not move in the way we proposed, with all its uncertainties, he was not going to insist on that judgment in an unfamiliar field over the opinion of his newly appointed Federal Reserve chairman."

When the president of the AFL-CIO in late October 1979 urged Carter to "[get] rid of Mr. Volcker," Carter responded:

> Well, first of all, it's not possible to get rid of Mr. Volcker under the American law. And, secondly, the Federal Reserve has very wisely been isolated from political influence exerted by the White House or the Congress. It's an independent agency, and I think it should be independent. Interest rates are almost directly related to the rate of inflation, and I think it would be expecting too much for the interest rate charges to be lower than the rate of inflation. The best way to get interest rates down is to lower inflation.[31]

On October 6, 1979, Volcker called an emergency Saturday meeting of the Federal Reserve Board. At that meeting, Volcker later wrote: "We meant to slay the inflationary dragon." In the last few months, money supply had begun to increase rapidly in excess of federal targets. The Fed had become less confident that its use of the federal funds rate was effective to restrain money growth. The Fed announced a major policy change:

> [M]ost members strongly supported a shift in the conduct of open market operations to an approach planning emphasis on supplying the volume of bank reserves estimated to be consistent with the desired rates of growth in monetary aggregates, while permitting much greater fluctuations in the federal funds rate than heretofore.

The Fed would no longer solely rely on an indirect method to determine money supply, but now intended to cut off money supply growth at its source, bank reserves. At a rare press conference after the special October 6, 1979, Fed Board meeting, Volcker amplified this point:

> The Federal Reserve for some years has ordered a good deal of its emphasis in actual day-to-day operations to maintaining a high degree of stability in the federal funds rate which we most directly influence. That rate, of course, has been influenced in one direction, but generally by small increments in order to effect the growth in the money supply. Now what is implied here is a somewhat differen[t] approach where the primary emphasis is put on the supply of reserves which ultimately controls the money supply. . . . But by emphasizing the supply of reserves and constraining the growth of the money supply through the reserve mechanism, we think we can get firmer controls over the growth in the money supply in a shorter period of time — greater assurance of that result.

Volcker warned that the daily federal funds rate was likely "to fluctuate over a wider range than has been the practice in recent years." This meant that the federal funds rate at which was likely to go up and the Fed would accept higher short-term interest rates to achieve a definitive reduction of the money supply and ultimately an end to inflation. As Volcker explained: "[A]s the Federal Reserve will take less interest . . . in the daily fluctuation of the very important short-term rate."

The Fed on October 6 announced three complementary actions to curb inflation.

First, a change in the methodology used to conduct monetary policy that now placed "primary emphasis on restraining expansion of . . . monetary aggregates [that is, money supply] over the year from the [last three months] of 1978 to the [last three months] of 1979 within the Committee's range for that period." The Fed had sought to limit the growth of its various methods of calculating money supply within specific ranges. For these 12 months, the most watched money aggregate, M1, had a growth range of 1.5 to 4.5 percent. M1, in fact, had grown at 9.5 percent during the July-September 1979 period and its growth rate had accelerated in 1979. The Fed announced that it would restrain bank reserves to reduce the M1 growth rate to 4.5 percent during the last three months of 1979.

Volcker explained the need for the change in operating procedures in his memoir in 1992:

> Every six months our objectives were laid out in terms of desired growth in certain measures of the money supply, as a law passed a few years earlier required us to do. But the actual operational target, day by day, week by week, from one federal Open Market Committee meeting to another, was the short-term rate of interest. Specifically, it was the federal funds rate, in effect the "wholesale" market price for overnight loans among banks and their largest customers.
>
> In that focus on interest rates lay a psychological trap, and the implications became worse as the inflationary momentum grew. With the best staff in the world and all the computing power we could give them, there could never be any certainty about just the right level of the federal funds rate to keep the money supply on the right path and to regulate economic activity.

A further advantage of restraining bank reserves rather than asking the Fed periodically to approve new money supply growth ranges was that it meant that the pivotal control device could be activated or adjusted by senior Fed staff without repeatedly putting the Fed Board of Governors on the spot. Governor Henry Wallich recognized this after the new procedure was adopted: "At the policy level, the reserve-based procedure has the advantage of minimizing the need for Federal Reserve decisions concerning the funds rate. Interest rates become a byproduct, as it were, of the money-supply process." In an interview with W. Carl Biven, Schultze later acknowledged: "Either consciously or unconsciously, Volcker was dead right on the politics of it. In order to do what had to be done and stop and reverse inflation, the Fed had to jack interest rates up to unprecedented heights." A decade after October 6, 1979, Schultze explained: "For Carter to stop the inflation, unemployment would have had to go from 6 percent to 10 percent. No democratically elected president can or would do it (neither Carter nor Reagan). You have to have an independent central bank."

Volcker agreed. Interest rates soon rose higher than he or his fellow Fed governors anticipated. "I would not have had support for deliberately raising short-term rates that much."

To emphatically signal the market about the significance of the new orientation, the Fed increased by 8 percent the marginal reserve requirements on specific major liabilities of member banks when they exceeded base amounts with $100 million of these assets. This would increase the cost of bank borrowing as the Fed anticipated slowing the growth rate of these deposits. The 8 percent reserve requirement applied to forms of money that the Fed had had difficulty affecting through federal funds rates such as euro-dollar borrowing, which occurred abroad, repurchase agreements against federal government securities, and borrowings from nonmember institutions. Previously, reserve requirements for euro-dollar borrowings were zero and repurchase agreements against government securities were exempt from reserve requirements.

Third, the Fed on October 6 increased the discount rate by 1 percent to 12 percent.

The White House on October 6 issued a supportive presidential statement: "The administration believes that the actions decided upon today by the Federal Reserve Board will help reduce inflationary expectations, contribute to a stronger U.S. dollar abroad, and curb unhealthy speculations in commodity markets."

In contrast, the initial market reaction to what would come to be viewed as an epochal policy change would be skeptical. On the Monday and Tuesday after the October 6, 1979, announcement, the Dow Jones Average fell approximately 4.5 percent. Interest rates on 10-year federal bonds rose from 10.43 percent on October 5, 1979, to a peak of 13.2 percent in February 1980. Bank prime rates at which they lent to their best customers reached 15.25 percent in February 1980, subsequently rising to 19 percent later in 1980.

Nor was money growth restrained, in aggregate, using all Fed measures of money, reaching a 14 percent annual rate in October 1979.

There was some good news. With interest rates 2.5 to 3 percent higher in December than one year earlier, credit flow slowed, dropping approximately 18 percent below the average of the first nine months of 1979. The value of the dollar experienced a sharp and rapid recovery.

But the financial markets doubted that the Fed would persist in the new policy. Volcker recounted at the November FOMC meeting that the first question the public asked was: "Are you going to stick with it?" Alan Greenspan, Chair of the Council of Economic Advisers to Nixon and Ford, expressed his skepticism to *The Wall Street Journal* on October 9, 1979, that the Fed would have the fortitude to stick to its policy if unemployment began to climb significantly. Senator William Proxmire, Chair of the Senate Committee on Banking, Housing and Urban Affairs, approved of the "aggressive" policy under Volcker but was concerned whether "the Federal Reserve will continue to pursue a tight monetary policy in a presidential election year." At the January 1980, FOMC meeting, even Volcker conceded: "I don't think we've made as much expectational progress . . . as conceivably might have been hoped."

The public reaction to the new policy, as the United States economy descended into a severe recession, was furious. Bill Medley of the Federal Reserve Bank of New York in a brief history described: "Farmers protested at the Federal Reserve's headquarters, and car dealers, who were especially affected by high interest rates, sent coffins containing car keys of unsold vehicles. Many people also wrote letters to Volcker telling him how they had saved for many years to purchase a home but were now unable to because of high rates."

On October 19, 1979, Senate Majority Leader Robert Byrd declared: "Attempting to control inflation or protect the dollar by throwing legions of people out of work and shutting down shifts in our factories and mines is a hopeless policy."

In 1981, during the initial year of Reagan's presidency, Treasury Secretary Donald Regan pointedly criticized the Fed's new policy: "What I'm suggesting is that if (money supply growth) stays here, you're going to have a severe recession." Regan then suggested how the money supply needed to be adjusted going forward. The same year, Congressman George Hansen accused Volcker of "destroying the small businessman. We are destroying middle class America. We are destroying the American dream." In 1982, House Majority Leader James Wright called for Volcker's resignation.[32]

The new monetary policy succeeded because of presidential support from Carter and then from Reagan and Fed perseverance. But the path to success was a wild roller coaster ride.

By January 1980, contrary to expectations, the economy was not slowing down. In fewer than three months, the Fed increased the federal funds rate from 11 to 20 percent. Short-term rates also rose. Far from causing the overheated economy to cool, in January 1980, the Consumer Price Index rose 16.8 percent. Gold, which had sold at $400 an ounce in the early fall of 1979, more than doubled to $875 per ounce. Silver quadrupled.

Facing a difficult challenge for the 1980 Democratic presidential nomination from Senator Ted Kennedy, Carter announced a New Economic Plan on March 14, 1980, which included a balanced budget for the next year, achieved by cutting $13 billion, freezing federal civilian employment, and reducing ongoing spending programs through the federal government. Carter vowed to "veto any legislation that exceeds the spending limits which I consider to be inconsistent with a balanced budget."

Carter also committed to a credit restraint program:

> The traditional tools used by the Federal Reserve to control money and credit expansion are a basic part of the fight against inflation. But in present circumstances, these tools need to be reinforced so that effective constraint can be achieved in ways that spread the burden reasonably and fairly.
>
> I'm therefore using my power under the Credit Control Act of 1969 to authorize the Federal Reserve to impose new restraints on the growth of credit on a limited and on a carefully targeted basis.

Carter's credit restraint program in part was reactive. Unlike Ted Kennedy, his challenger for the Democratic Party presidential nomination, he continued to champion voluntary wage and price standards. On January 28, 1980, Kennedy in contrast had endorsed mandatory wage and price controls.

A mid-January 1980 *New York Times/CBS* poll found that 65 percent of adult Americans were willing to have the government enforce limits on wage and price increases to slow inflation. January inflation data was available in mid-February and was dismal. The Producer Price Index rose at an annual rate of 19 percent, the Consumer Price Index, 18 percent.

By February 1980, Carter was revising his 1981 budget, which the Office of Management and Budget earlier had estimated was 50 percent higher than Carter's $30 billion deficit promised in August 1979. Volcker participated in budget meetings and Carter followed Volcker's advice to cut the deficit. Carter also wanted direct controls on consumer credit. Volcker opposed the controls: "While the economy had been expanding right through the end of the year despite the extremely high interest rates and the earlier forecasts of recession, credit-financed consumption was at best sluggish, and the idea of getting involved in the administrative morass of direct controls on millions of consumer credit transactions had no appeal to us for economic or practical reasons."

But Volcker ultimately acceded to the consumer credit controls:

> I repeatedly conveyed our concerns to the president and his staff. In the end, however, I found it impossible to resist the implied argument that, at a time when the president had publicly supported our risky and unprecedented monetary policy, and when he was responding to our urging that he take tough steps to tighten the budget, we in the Federal Reserve ought to respect his political judgment that consumer credit controls were needed to convey the right sense of urgency.

Volcker persuaded the Fed Board to support the controls by making the controls as mild as the Fed possibly could make them.

After Carter spoke on March 14, Volcker introduced the Fed's Credit Restraint Program. As part of what the Fed called "a general government program to help curb inflationary pressures," the Fed unanimously adopted a six part program:

First, the Board established "a Special Credit Restraint Program that encouraged all creditors to comply voluntarily with the Board's overall objectives of reducing credit availability and dampening inflationary pressures."

Second, the 8 percent marginal reserve requirement on bank managed liabilities established in October 1979, was raised to 10 percent. This requirement had had only limited effectiveness since October 1979, because slowing in bank credit in the first three months of 1979 had reduced the total of managed liabilities subject to the managed reserve requirement above base levels. The reserve requirement also had not applied to foreign affiliates of banks subject to the reserve requirements or to deposits with greater than one year maturities. This and other loopholes convinced the chief financial officer of a major New York bank: "If someone really doesn't want to carry the extra reserves, he doesn't have to."

Third, nonmember banks were now subject to the same 10 percent noninterest bearing marginal reserve requirement established for member banks in October 1979.

Fourth, creditors who provided at least $2 million in consumer credit were required to maintain noninterest bearing deposits with the Fed equal to 15 percent of the growth in assets after March 14, 1980. This requirement covered credit cards, notably MasterCard and Visa, bank overdraft and revolving credit, unsecured personal loans, retail merchant credit and credit secured by financial assets other than savings deposits. Mortgage and car loans were not subject to this requirement. Approximately 85 percent of all covered consumer credit, provided by 10,108 firms, of which 6000 were banks, were covered. This requirement was intended to raise the cost of credit extensions and discourage credit growth. This requirement had the broadest impact of the Fed's six part program, covering $184 billion of the $381 billion in outstanding consumer credit at the end of 1979.

Fifth, money market funds and similar creditors were required to maintain noninterest bearing deposits equal to 15 percent of the growth in assets after March 14, 1980. The 15 percent reserve requirement was expected to reduce the return on new money market funds by 2 percent and to slow the outflow of funds from thrift institutions and smaller banks.

Finally, the Fed established a voluntary Credit Restraint Program "that urged intermediaries, other creditors and borrowers to take into account the Federal Reserve's anti-inflationary efforts when making credit decisions. Lenders were asked to continue to meet the essential credit needs of their established customers, but to avoid lending for speculative or nonproductive purposes and to limit overall growth in credit to a range of 6 to 9 percent."

The 6 to 9 percent range was considerably lower with the Fed's announced target range for money growth of 17.75 in January and February 1980.

The March 14, 1980, Credit Restraint Program unexpectedly hit like a bombshell. Total bank loan growth for March 1980 fell to an annual adjusted rate of 2.5 percent compared to rates of 15 to 20 percent a year earlier. A *New York Times* poll taken in April found that 50 percent of respondents were using credit cards less than they did in 1979, only 5 percent were using them more. Carter reported: "[M]any card holders began to believe that it was almost unpatriotic to buy items on credit."

Volcker recalled later:

> [A]ll of a sudden after the president's announcements, consumers stopped spending. No one had ever seen anything like it. The consumer credit controls we had decided upon were not intended to bite hard. Mechanically, they did not. Credit was exempted for autos and things related to housing, which are the principal uses for consumer credit; the effect therefore should have been limited to credit card purchases and general-purpose installment loans. Even then, our special new reserve requirements would only apply to increases in loans and was designed only to raise the cost of credit moderately. But the president was interpreted as saying that the country was in a national emergency and that consumer spending should be restrained. So a lot of consumers stopped spending. They certainly stopped using credit cards, some cutting their cards into little pieces and sending them to the White House. "Mr. President," the letters said, "we will cooperate."

In March, the money supply was flat. In April, the money supply declined by 17 percent. Interest rates began a precipitous decline. The 3-month Treasury bill fell from 16.5 percent at the end of March to 13.8 percent on April 18, reaching a low of 6.37 percent in July. By May, interest rates were plummeting an average of 2 percent per week. The prime rate, which had been 19.5 percent on April 18, 1980, was 11 percent in July.

The GNP dropped 9.1 percent between April and June 1980, unemployment rose from 6.3 percent in March to 7.8 percent in

July. An additional 1.6 million people were out of work. More 1980 data showed that consumer installment credit fell 13 percent in May. Consumer credit extensions were 25 percent lower than the September 1979 peak.

The Fed backpedaled. On May 22, 1980, the Fed amended its Credit Restraint Program to reduce by one-half its limits on credit growth. The marginal reserve requirement was cut in half from 10 to 5 percent, as were the 15 percent deposit requirements for covered consumer credit and money market mutual funds.

The Fed also took a position contrary to credit restraint in the 1980 Silver Crisis. On March 26, 1980, the Fed was informed by Bache Halsey, a securities brokerage firm, that it had lent $200 million to billionaires Herbert and Nelson Hunt to buy silver. The Hunt Brothers had tried to corner the silver market and through their purchases had helped drive the price from $10.61 per ounce in August 1979 to over $50 an ounce on January 18, 1980. The silver bubble collapsed and the Hunt Brothers, as well as the banks and brokerage firms who had lent the Hunts over $800 million, faced default and in some cases, such as Bache Halsey, bankruptcy. First National Bank, the ninth largest commercial bank in the United States, had lent the Hunts $175 million and was vulnerable.

On March 27, 1980, silver fell to a low of $10.80 an ounce.

The Hunts also had bought futures contracts in London from the mineral firm, Engelhard. With the precipitous price decline, the Engelhard firm demanded the Hunts deliver an additional $665 million in cash on Monday, March 31.

Over the weekend, Volcker approved the terms negotiated by 13 banks for a $1.1 billion loan to extinguish the Hunts' debts, including those to Engelhard, with remaining obligations over ten years. As a 1980 Securities and Exchange Commission *Report on the Silver Crisis* found: "[F]or six days in March 1980, it appeared to government officials, Wall Street and the public at large that a default by a single family in the fermenting silver market might disrupt the U.S. financial system."

This was inconsistent with the March 14 credit controls, but Volcker and the Fed were determined to avoid precipitating a bank panic that might have occurred had the silver market collapsed on March 31, 1980, and bank customers pulled deposits out of banks such as First Chicago that had lent money to the Hunts.

On July 1, 1980, the Fed rescinded its Credit Restraint Program altogether.

By the end of 1980, Congress would repeal the legislation authorizing credit controls, effective June 30, 1982.

The economy responded rapidly. The money supply measured by M1, which had been flat in May, grew by 11 percent in June, 22.8 percent in August. Interest rates similarly began a rapid climb, with the federal fund, which averaged 10.6 percent on July 2, 1980, rising to 14 percent by Election Day in November.

The Fed increased the discount rate from 10 to 11 percent on September 25, prompting an election campaign critique by Carter: "The Fed is independent of the President. It's just like the judicial system. I don't have influence on it, but that doesn't mean I have to sit mute. My own judgment is that the strictly monetary approach to the Fed's decision on the discount rate and other banking policies is ill-advised."

Volcker privately would characterize 1980 as "[a] false start.... At very considerable cost, at very considerable turbulence, we more or less held inflation at bay, preventing it from getting worse." He would describe 1980 as "a mostly wasted year [for] restoring credibility in the attack on inflation."[33]

On November 4, 1980, former California Governor Ronald Reagan defeated Jimmy Carter and was elected president, winning a lop-sided 50.7 percent of the popular vote and 489 electoral college votes to Carter's 41 percent of the popular vote and 49 electoral college votes. Independent Candidate John Anderson received 6.6 percent of the popular vote. Reagan's victory was attributed by Carter and historians generally to a public perception that Carter's handling of the Iranian hostage crisis reflected ineptitude, or as Carter stated: "The sense of impotence... that was generated from those hostages not being released." The hostage crisis included a botched rescue attempt in April 1980, the resignation of Secretary of State Cyrus Vance, and nightly news coverage of the hostage crisis. Carter also attributed his defeat to the bitter Democratic primary battle with Senator Ted Kennedy and his inability to effectively address the economy. Reagan memorably asked in the one Presidential debate with Carter on October 28, 1980: "Are you better off than you were four years ago?" Carter implicitly acknowledged the sting of Reagan's question when he acknowledged in a Town Hall meeting in October 1980: "If I had to do it over again, I'd put more emphasis on inflation."

Reagan's victory had long coat tails. The Senate, where Democrats had a 58–41 majority in 1978, flipped to a Republican majority of 53 to 46, a net gain of 12 seats with the loss of nine incumbents, including George McGovern, 1972 Democratic party nominee for president. The Democrats lost 34 seats in the House but held onto a diminished majority of 243–192.

After the Election, the Fed raised the discount rate to 12 percent on November 14, 1980, with a 2 percent surcharge for frequent borrowing of large institutional banks with at least $500 million in deposits, then to 13 percent by December 4, increasing the surcharge to 3 percent.

None of these changes had a rapid impact. By Christmas week of 1980, the bank prime rate would hit a record of 21.5 percent. The federal funds rate peaked at 19.8 percent in December.

In 1981 and 1982, Volcker and the Fed would consistently restrain money supply despite a recession which lasted from July 1981 to November 1982. As Volcker wrote later: "By the time Ronald Reagan took office in January 1981, monetary policy was again fully engaged in restraint." Volcker would express his gratitude to Reagan and his administration for "generally supporting our efforts to restrain money growth in 1981, even at the expense of seriously high interest rates."

In 1981, Fed monetary policy was highly restrictive. Growth in the money supply as measured by the M1 metric declined from 7.5 to 7.3 percent in 1979 and 1980 to 2.3 percent. Between January and March 1981, the federal funds rate briefly fell to 14.7 percent before resuming a rise to 19.1 percent in June 1981. With a recession gathering force, the Fed took an anti-Keynesian position and increased the discount rate to 14 percent in May 1981 with a surcharge of 4 percent before decreasing the rate to 12 percent in December 1981. Meltzer explained: "By increasing interest rates in the middle of a recession, the FOMC increased its credibility. This was clearly a change in practice. Never before had the public seen an increase in interest rates with unemployment rates at 7.5 percent."

By December 1981, unemployment would reach 8.8 percent. The Consumer Price Index declined 9.5 points in 1981. On February 25, 1981, the Fed summarized its monetary policy in uncompromising terms:

> The basic premise of the System's policy is the broadly accepted notion that inflation can persist over appreciable

> spans of time only if it is accommodated by monetary expansion. The strategy to which the System has committed itself is to hold monetary growth to rates that fall short of such accommodation and thus encourage adjustments consistent with a return to price stability over time.

Economic growth declined in 1982 with the GNP dropping 1.1 percent. Unemployment rose to 10.8 percent in December 1982, but inflation as measured by the Consumer Price Index declined to 4.5 percent in 1982. The federal funds rate declined to 8.95 percent in December 1982. Short-term and long-term interest rates declined 3 to 5 percentage points in 1982. The Fed in an environment of declining interest rates approved seven half percent reductions in the discount rate, which was lowered from 12 percent in July 1982, to 8.5 percent by year's end.

"Conditions in the national economy," the Federal Reserve would begin its 70th Annual Report, "took a decided turn for the better in 1983." GNP rose 6 percent in 1982 and again in 1984. Unemployment was reduced by 2.5 percent, falling to 8.2 percent by year end, declining to 5.3 percent at the close of 1988. Stock prices increased by 20 percent. "The years of high inflation," Meltzer would report, "were over" by the end of 1982. Price measures rose 4 percent on average in 1983 and 1984, 3.5 to 3.75 percent in 1985, 2.5 percent in 1986, 4 percent in 1987, and 4 to 4.5 percent in 1988.

In 1983, the Fed deemphasized its focus on controlling money supply. In Reports to Congress in February and July 1983, the Fed "indicated that monetary policy during that year would be conducted with the aim of fostering a recovery in economic activity and encouraging further progress toward price stability."

In 1988, the Fed would state: "[As] in other recent years, the Federal Reserve maintained a flexible approach to monetary targeting by responding to emerging conditions in the economy and in financial markets as well as to growth of the monetary aggregates themselves.[34]

The Reagan Presidency

Ronald Reagan had been a popular movie star beginning in the 1930s and television host of General Electric Theatre from 1953 to

1962. In his autobiography, Reagan would attribute his enthusiasm for tax cuts to his career as a film actor:

> At the peak of my career at Warner Bros., I was in the ninety-four percent tax bracket; that meant that after a certain point, I received only six cents of each dollar I earned and the government got the rest. The IRS took such a big chuck of my earnings that after a while I began asking myself whether it was worth it to keep on taking work. Something was wrong with a system like that: When you have to give up such a large percentage of your income in taxes, incentive to work goes down. . . .
>
> The same principle that affected my thinking applied to people in all tax brackets: The more government takes in taxes, the less incentive people have to work. What coal miner or assembly-line worker jumps at the offer of overtime when he knows Uncle Sam is going to take sixty percent or more of his extra pay. . . .
>
> If, on the other hand, you reduce tax rates and allow people to spend or save more of what they earn, they'll be more industrious; they'll have more incentive to work hard, and money they earn will add fuel to the great economic machine that energizes our national progress. The result: more prosperity for all — and more revenue for government. . . .

Reagan served as president of the Screen Actors Guild eight times. Reagan gravitated to conservatism during the 1950s. He made a recording for the American Medical Association opposing Medicare after legislation was introduced in 1961. If Medicare was not prevented, Reagan warned: "[W]e will awake to find that we have socialism." He opposed the Peace Corps and food stamps.

He became a leading conservative spokesman during the unsuccessful 1964 presidential campaign of Barry Goldwater. On October 27, 1964, Reagan broadcast a speech similar to those he had frequently made in the past, entitled, *A Time for Choosing*:

> [T]he full power of centralized government was the very thing the Founding Fathers sought to minimize. They knew you don't control things; you can't control the economy without controlling *people*. So we have come to a time for choosing. Either we accept the responsibility for our own destiny, or we abandon the American Revolution and confess that an intellectual belief in a far-distant capitol can plan our lives for us better than we can plan them ourselves.

Individual freedom could only be achieved in Reagan's view through tax reform and rolling back government regulation:

> We need tax reform that will at least make a start toward restoring for our children the American dream that wealth is denied to no one, that each individual has the right to fly as high as his strength and ability will take him.... But we cannot have such reform while our tax policy is engineered by people who view the tax as a means of achieving changes in our social structure....
>
> No nation has survived the tax burden that reached one-third of its national income. Today in our country the tax collector's share is thirty-seven cents of every dollar earned. Freedom has never been so fragile, so close to slipping from our grasp.

Reagan's self-confident, charismatic delivery elevated him in 1966 to the first of two terms as governor of California. He almost wrestled the 1976 Republican nomination for president from Gerald Ford, receiving 1070 delegates to Ford's 1187 at the Convention. Jim Baker, at that time working for Ford, said of Reagan's challenge: "He damn near took us down. It was really close."

In 1980, Reagan ran on a Republican platform that stressed the dangers of inflation and the ineptitude of President Carter:

> We consider inflation and its impact on jobs to be the greatest domestic threat facing our nation today. Mr. Carter must go! For what he has done to the dollar; for what he has done to the life savings of millions of Americans; for what he has done to retirees seeking a secure old age; for what he has done to young families aspiring to a home, an education for their children, and a rising living standard. Mr. Carter must not have another four years in office.
>
> In his three and one-half years in office, Mr. Carter has presented and supported policies which carried inflation from 4.8 percent in 1976 to a peak of 18 percent during 1980....
>
> He has through both inaction and deliberate policy permitted or forced tax increases of more than 70 percent, more than $250 billion, directly increasing the cost of living and the costs of hiring and producing. This has crippled living standards, productivity, and our ability to compete in the world. It has led to reduced output, scarcity, and higher prices.

Accepting the Republican Party nomination on July 17, 1980, Reagan emphasized "I believe it is clear our federal government is overgrown and overweight. . . . [M]y first act as Chief Executive will be to impose an immediate and thorough freeze on Federal hiring," and then conduct a detailed review of every department and bureau that lives by federal appropriation with the aspiration "of initiating action to get substantial relief for our paying citizens:"

> I've long advocated a 30 percent reduction in income tax rates over a period of three years. This phased-in tax reduction would begin with a 10 percent "down payment" tax cut in 1981, which the Republicans in Congress and I have already proposed.

Reagan's inaugural address, January 20, 1981, would best be remembered for the line: "In this present crisis, government is not the solution to our problem, government is the problem". He elaborated:

> It is my intention to curb the size and influence of the Federal establishment and to demand recognition of the distinction between the powers granted to the Federal Government and those reserved to the States or to the people. All of us need to be reminded that the Federal Government did not create the States; the States created the Federal Government.
>
> Now, so there will be no misunderstanding, it's not my intention to do away with government. It is rather to make it work—work with us, not over us; to stand by our side, not ride on our back. Government can and must provide opportunity, not smother it; foster productivity, not stifle it.

Reagan, by the time of his presidency, ritualistically incanted: "We fully recognize the independence of the Federal Reserve System and will do nothing to interfere with or undermine that independence." As with his predecessors dating back to Eisenhower, while acknowledging the Fed's autonomy, Reagan also sought coordination with the Fed over interest rates and money supply. In 1981 and 1982, tight Fed monetary policies caused Reagan on one occasion to tell a Republican audience: "The Fed is independent, but they're hurting us in what we're trying to do as much as they're hurting everyone else." Reagan nonetheless did not unduly pressure the Fed. In 1982, Volcker would write: "President Reagan must have received lots of advice to take on the Fed himself, but he never did despite plenty of invitations at press conferences. . . . I had the sense that, unlike some of his predecessors, he had a strong visceral aversion to inflation and an instinct that, whatever some of his advisers might have thought, it wasn't a good idea to tamper with the independence of the Federal Reserve."

Reagan's three closest advisers were two Californians, Ed Meese, Counsel to the President for Policy with Cabinet rank, and Deputy Chief of Staff Mike Deaver, as well as Chief of Staff Jim Baker.

Meese had worked with Reagan since Reagan began as governor in 1966, at times as Legal Adviser, Executive Secretary, and Chief of Staff. Reagan felt philosophically more comfortable with Meese, according to Biographer H. W. Brandt, than anyone else. "He totally understood Ronald Reagan ideologically, because they're so much alike ideologically." Meese coordinated and supervised in tandem with Baker the Office of Management and Budget and the Council of Economic Advisers. Meese participated as a principal in all policy group meetings and separately had responsibilities in foreign policy including the National Security Council.

Deaver also had served with Reagan during Reagan's time as governor. He was personally closer to both Ronald and Nancy Reagan than anyone else in the White House. Deaver knew how to approach Reagan and was never afraid to tell him bad news or that he thought Reagan was wrong. David Stockman, who initially led the Office of Management and Budget during Reagan's presidency, would grow to loathe Deaver and his crowd as someone who "never read anything. They lived off the tube. They understood nothing about the serious ideas underlying the Reagan Revolution." Reagan had the closeness of friends with Meese and Deaver, but neither had Washington experience.

Jim Baker was the third member of Reagan's inner Troika and initially was distrusted because of his service to President Ford and Presidential Candidate George H.W. Bush during the period when Bush had scorned Reagan for Voodoo Economics. Baker claimed not to have been bothered by the opinions of him felt by some of Reagan's senior staff: "President Reagan understood what many of his followers did not: that it's more important for the chief of staff to be competent and loyal than to be a so-called true believer. I had more faith in his ideas than I was given credit for, and that faith grew stronger over the years." Baker added: "He also understood that one of the most important tasks of a White House chief of staff is to look at policy questions through a political prism. After watching me at work in 1976 and 1980, he apparently believed I could do this." Baker negotiated a pact with Meese, under which Baker alone controlled hiring and firing of the White House staff, coordination and control of all paper flow to the president, and presidential scheduling. Meese was suspicious, but Baker insisted to Meese: "You've got the policy: I'll just make the trains run on time." Uneasily, the Troika served Reagan.

Reagan's economic team was led by Treasury Secretary Don Regan from 1981 to 1985, when he switched jobs at the beginning of President Reagan's second term with White House Chief of Staff James Baker. Regan in 1981 was Chair of the Nation's best known stock brokerage firm, Merrill Lynch. In 1972, Regan had endorsed Nixon's wage and price controls and had contributed to several liberal Democrats. But he would regularly align himself with Reagan's economic views and would be one of Reagan's most effective economic spokesmen. Regan believed that he knew as much about money as Volcker and did not hesitate to criticize Volcker when he felt Volcker's policies had been too restrictive. "Paul, you're a nanny!" Baker was less abrasive and more pragmatic than Regan.

Both Meese and Baker opposed the reappointment of Volcker in 1983, because each viewed Volcker as difficult to work with and too independent. Volcker's refusal to reduce discount rates two weeks before the 1982 Elections in Baker's view had led to a sharp stock market decline and dimmed Republican Party prospects. Regan was adamant about not reappointing Volcker: "There's no way we're going to put that guy back in there. He won't take orders." President Reagan surprised many in his administration by reappointing Volcker on June 18, 1983. Reagan credited the Fed for reducing the prime interest rate by six points during his first year and "thanks in part to a tight money policy (which I supported) and the part of the Federal Reserve Board, inflation was below ten percent for the first time in three years." By 1983, the financial markets viewed Volcker as the nation's top inflation fighter and generally supported him. Office of Management and Budget Director David Stockman and the Council of Economic Advisers Chair Martin Feldstein supported Volcker as did key Republican Senators including Howard Baker, the Majority Leader, and Bob Dole, the Senate Finance Committee Chair.

Within the Reagan White House during the critical early years, Reagan's key economic adviser was not Harvard economist Martin Feldstein, the Chair of the Council of Economic Advisers in 1982 and 1983, but David Stockman, the *wunderkind* Director of the Office of Management and Budget (*OMB*). At 34, Stockman had served two terms in Congress, where he had become the Republican Party's most prominent authority on the federal budget. It was said that he read the entire federal budget as a congressional staff member and had read ten years of back issues of the *Congressional Quarterly*, driven by an almost monomaniacal desire to dismantle the federal welfare state. His initial 1981 budget called for abolishing 144 programs. Stockman was considered by Congressman Phil Gramm to "be the smartest member of Congress." He was championed to lead OMB by influential Congressman Jack Kemp. By 1981, Stockman was widely believed by fellow supply side conservatives to be deeply committed, dedicated, as Stockman wrote, "to the cause of shrinking Big Government," despite his flirtation with Marxism and membership in the Radical Students for a Democratic Society while an undergraduate at Michigan State University. To avoid the draft, he attended Harvard Divinity School, where he became the live in babysitter for Daniel Patrick Moynihan, then a Harvard professor working for Nixon. Moynihan would help Stockman find work for Republican Congressman John Anderson in 1970, as Executive Director of the House Republican Conference. By then, Stockman had completed the journey, as Moynihan quipped, "from preaching the infallibility of Ho Chi Minh [to] proclaiming the immutability of the Laffer Curve." The Laffer Curve was a popular supply side theory developed by economist Arthur Laffer, urging in its most extreme articulations that tax cuts would pay for themselves because the Treasury would receive more revenue even with lower tax rates from an expanded economy.

Reagan had been impressed by Stockman when Stockman had served as a stand-in for his former boss, Congressman John Anderson in a September 1980, debate rehearsal for a debate that later was cancelled, and as a stand-in for Jimmy Carter in debate rehearsals in October 1980. As with Meese, Stockman held Cabinet rank.

The policy differences among Reagan's economic advisers were consequential.

In a broad sense, all of the Reagan economic team viewed Keynesian economics as a failure as revealed by the last several years in which efforts to manage the economy had resulted in rising high inflation and high unemployment. Three broad strands of economic theory were supported by various Reagan economic advisers.

Monetarists favored nondiscretionary rules to limit or reduce money supply as the key to minimizing perturbations in output. Supply siders emphasized the incentive effects of reducing marginal tax rates. Traditional free market conservatives sought to reduce the role of government in the economy.

To Volcker, more meaningful than economic theory was the extent to which advisers were doctrinaire or pragmatic. Some of the more doctrinaire monetarists early in the Reagan administration "wanted to write very specifically about our monetary policy, for example, one favored formulation was that money growth should be 'predictably and assuredly' reduced by 1 percent a year for several years." Treasury Secretary Regan pressed Volcker and the Fed to maintain a steady, gradual decline in money. Volcker talked the administration out of "that kind of language. . . . I knew that such precision would be impossible to achieve in the real world, and achievable or not, it would look like the administration was trying to order the Fed."

Ronald Reagan was not well versed in economics or a theoretician. He was, as Jim Baker put it, "much more interested in the big picture than in the details, a big-idea man who left the fine points to others." He was, biographer Richard Reeves wrote: "[A] President of big things. Baker, Meese, and Deaver handled smaller things." But Reagan unabashedly sought to roll back the New Deal regulatory state, a Reagan revolution that combined what Reagan termed "four commonsense fundamentals: continued reduction of the growth in Federal spending; preserving the individual and business tax reductions that will stimulate saving and investment; removing unnecessary Federal regulations to spark productivity; and maintaining a healthy dollar and a stable monetary policy, the latter a responsibility of the Federal Reserve System." Each of these four cornerstones was considered part of an integrated plan for recovery and the policy implications of these initiatives, not the theoretical debate, would dominate the Reagan economic policy.

In his autobiography, Reagan would call his most immediate priority on his first day in Office was "dealing with double-digit inflation, high unemployment, and a prime interest rate of 21.5 percent, the highest since the Civil War."[35]

The hallmark of Reagan's economic policy was the 1981 and 1986 tax laws and a revised approach to the federal budget that initially proposed reducing nondefense spending by 15 percent less in 1984 than 1980 while substantially increasing defense spending.

On February 5, 1981, Reagan made the case for the new budget and 1981 tax legislation in an address, entitled *The State of the Nation's Economy*:

> The Federal budget is out of control, and we face runaway deficits of almost $80 billion for this budget year that ends September 30th. That deficit is larger than the entire Federal budget in 1957, and so is the almost $80 billion we will pay in interest this year on the national debt.
>
> Twenty years ago, in 1960, our Federal Government payroll was less than $13 billion. Today it is $75 billion. During these 20 years our population has only increased by 23.3 percent. The Federal budget has gone up 528 percent. . . .
>
> . . . By 1960, our National debt stood at $284 billion. . . . Today the debt is $934 billion.

Reagan reiterated that he would "ask for a 10-percent reduction across the board in personal income tax rates for each of the next three years."

This proposal was essentially the same as the Roth-Kemp Bill. Reagan's proposed income tax cut would reduce federal revenues by $44 billion in fiscal year 1982, and by $118 billion in 1984.

Reagan's revision of Carter's budget for the next fiscal year, 1982, represented what the Congressional Budget Office (*CBO*) termed "a dramatic change in government policies." The new budget proposed to increase the share of defense in the budget from 23.4 in 1980 to 33.2 percent in 1984. Increased defense spending the CBO then calculated would average 9 percent per year in real terms between 1980 and 1986. Nondefense spending cuts were proposed to increase from $48 billion to $138 billion in 1984 compared to Carter's January 1981 budget. The federal spending cuts were concentrated in grants, to State and local Governments and in cuts to Social Security benefits for the elderly, Medicare, railroad retirement, unemployment insurance, and veterans' benefits.

Underlying the president's March 1981 budget revisions was a rosy scenario forecast, as a *Washington Post* headline declared on February 7, 1981, with real GNP at 4.2 to 5 percent between 1982 and 1986 compared to Carter's optimistic January 1981 Budget forecast at 3.5 to 3.7 percent and the CBO forecast of 2.5 to 3.8 percent. The consequence of this and other administration's budget assumptions was a $1 billion surplus in 1984 compared to the CBO anticipated $49 billion deficit.

Stockman and those preparing the budget were boxed in. As John Anderson had taunted Reagan during the 1980 campaign: How was it possible to raise defense spending, cut income taxes, and balance the budget at the same time? Reagan had promised each would be achieved. Reagan promised to increase military spending by 7 percent a year, adjusted for inflation, over five years. Reagan also was adamant that the main benefit programs of Social Security and Medicare would not be touched. In February 1981, the over-optimism of Stockman and others in the Reagan administration that "inflation [would] melt away like the morning mist." as the financial markets early in 1981, generated a bull market of historic proportions, led the Reagan administration to revise Carter's budget forecast replacing double digit inflation with a swift decline in prices and interest rates.

In time, the phrase rosy scenario would be as much criticized as Lyndon Johnson's credibility gap, Nixon's pressure on the Fed in 1982, to increase the money supply, or Jimmy Carter's Malaise Speech.

On March 30, 1981, John Hinckley unsuccessfully attempted to assassinate Reagan, generating enormous public sympathy for the president. A mid-April NBC News/Associated Press poll found that 77 percent of respondents had a favorable opinion of Reagan compared to 58 percent on Inaugural Day. Among Democrats, Reagan's approval rating was an astonishing 64 percent. Biographer Richard Reeves recounts: "When Regan called, most members of Congress reacted as if they were hearing the voice of God himself."

Reagan responded to an April 10, 1981, rejection of his initial budget plan by the Senate Budget Committee with an April 28, 1981, address before a joint session of Congress:

> It's been half a year since the election that charged all of us in this Government with the task of restoring our economy. Where have we come in this 6 months? Inflation, as measured by the Consumer Price Index, has continued at a double-digit rate. Mortgage interest rates have averaged almost 15 percent for these 6 months, preventing families across America from buying homes. There are still almost 8 million unemployed. The average worker's hourly earnings after adjusting for inflation are lower today than they were 6 months ago, and there have been over 6000 business failures.
>
> Six months is long enough. The American people now want us to act and not in half-measures. They demand and they've earned a full and comprehensive effort to clean up our

> economic mess.... [T]he budgetary actions taken by Congress over the next few days will determine how we respond to the message of last November 4th. That message was very simple. Our government is too big, and it spends too much.

For speeches like this, Reagan would earn the sobriquet The Great Communicator. One week later, 63 Democrats in the House would join all 190 Republicans to pass the Gramm-Latta Budget Resolution favored by Reagan. The Senate followed. Tip O'Neill recognized: "We can't argue with a man as popular as [Reagan] is."

Between the first Gramm-Latta Resolution, which directed Congressional Committees on the limits of relevant expenditures and the second Gramm-Latta Resolution, Reagan and his team made a critical mistake seeking to cut federal expenditures by another $50 billion by, among other cuts, raising the Social Security retirement age. The *New York Times* explained in a front page story on May 13: "The Reagan Administration today announced details of a proposal for the first significant reduction in Social Security benefits since the retirement system was adopted 46 years ago." Jim Baker later would acknowledge: "We shot ourselves in the foot." On May 19, 1981, the Senate killed Social Security reform unanimously 96-0 by adopting a Resolution: "The Congress shall not precipitously and unfairly punish early retirees."

In June 1981, as early actual financial data became available, Larry Kudlow and Council of Economic Advisers member Jerry Jorden presented a gloomier forecast in a meeting with Jim Baker, Don Regan, and Ed Meese. Kudlow and Jordan echoed Volcker's concern that even with inflation subsiding, the economy was heading towards recession. The supply siders anticipated miracle of "rational expectations" by which business and consumers generated substantial new investments had not occurred. In William Greider's account, Kudlow declared: "The forecast is garbage. We're going to take a recession and huge deficits." With lower tax revenues, Stockman, in Baker's account, estimated minimum deficits of $60 billion in each of the next four years. "There's no such thing as a painless cure for inflation," Kudlow said. "Jordan and I argued that the costs were coming first and the long-term benefits would come later. It would be better to acknowledge it instead of being embarrassed later."

Treasury Department Assistant Secretary for Economic Policy Paul Craig Roberts strenuously opposed changing the administration forecast: "Lowering the growth projections would widen the deficit at an inopportune time—just at the point of congressional decision on the president's tax bill. Treasury did not think Congress would pass the tax bill if it seemed that the administration expected the deficit to grow rather than the economy."

Reagan repeatedly indicated that he would not give up on a balanced budget. "Deficit spending is how we got into this mess." Nor would he cut the proposed 7 percent annual increase in the Defense Budget: "There must be no perception by anyone in the world that we're backing down an inch on the defense budget. When I was asked during the campaign about what I would do if it came down to a choice between defense and deficits, I always said national security had to come first, and the people applauded every time."

Jim Baker believed that Kudlow's analysis was correct but sided with the Treasury. "The President wants a tax cut, and I can't publish [a revised] forecast now." Budget Director David Stockman would regard the decision not to revise the forecast as a fateful turning point that led to the massive deficits of the 1980s. Volcker separately would conclude:

> The more starry-eyed Reaganauts argued that reducing taxes would provide a kind of magic elixir for the economy that would make the deficits go away, or at least not matter. This was an extreme version of what I had argued as a young official in the Treasury in 1963. But some of their arguments made me wonder why we bothered to collect taxes at all. The more realistic advisers (everything is relative) apparently thought the risk of a ballooning deficit was a reasonable price to pay for passing their radical program; any damage could be repaired later, helped by a novel theory that the way to keep spending down was not by insisting taxes be adequate to pay for it but by scaring the Congress and the American people with deficits.

Reagan would recall in his autobiography that: "Opinion polls showed ninety-five percent of the American people were behind the proposed spending cuts and almost as many supported the thirty-percent, three year tax cut." The Democrats in the House led by Speaker Tip O'Neil, in contrast, felt Reagan's intent to dismantle New Deal and Great Society programs would "destroy everything [Tip O'Neil] had worked his entire life for."

To secure the votes necessary to enact the Reagan budget, Stockman and the administration papered over future deficits with what came to be known as The Magic Asterisk, denoting future unidentified budget cuts that would have to be enacted. There also were several compromises with individual members of Congress to achieve the final vote.

On July 27, 1981, Reagan took again to the airwaves to reassure Social Security recipients that they would "continue to receive your checks in the full amount due you" and make his final appeal for the 1981 tax reduction legislation and budget.

On August 13, 1981, Reagan signed into law the Economic Recovery Act, the largest tax cut in 35 years, more than twice as large as any post-1967 Tax Bill. The Senate overwhelmingly supported the Tax Bill 89 to 11. The House was closer, 238-195, a victory for Reagan made possible by 40 Democratic House Member votes.

The Economic Recovery Act reduced the top tax bracket from 70 to 50 percent and the bottom bracket from 14 to 11 percent. Congress had been unwilling to enact three years of 10 percent increases, but largely gave Reagan and the proponents of the Kemp-Roth Bill what they sought: A 5 percent cut on October 1, 1981, followed by 10 percent cuts on July 1, 1982, and July 1, 1983.

In 1986, the Tax Reform Act significantly further dropped the top bracket to 28 percent, with concomitant capital gains taxes increasing from the highest brackets from 20 to 28 percent. The top tax brackets remained for three years at 28 percent before being increased to 39.5 percent. Reagan would characterize the 1986 bracket reductions as "the tax reform bill we wanted":

> Knowing they could now keep seventy percent of what they earned instead of paying seventy percent of it to the government, the most affluent Americans invested in new projects and new ideas; but contrary to what some of the tax-and-spend liberals have said, tax reform didn't create a windfall for the rich at the expense of the poor; instead, it was the other way around.
>
> Under the new laws, more than eighty percent of Americans paid the lowest tax rate, fifteen percent, or no tax at all; the households of four million lower-income working Americans were excused from paying federal income taxes altogether. Meanwhile, the proportion of personal income taxes paid by the top-earning one percent of Americans increased by more than a third between 1981 and 1987—from 17.9 percent to almost

twenty-five percent. During the same period, the tax burden on the poorest half of American taxpayers fell by almost twenty percent—from 7.4 percent of the total to 6.1 percent.

The 1981 Act indexed tax brackets beginning in 1985 to obviate the impact of inflation. The Department of Treasury's Office of Tax Analysis explained:

> Without indexation, inflation can push taxpayers into higher tax brackets without any increase in real income. This phenomenon is called "bracket creep," and it increases federal revenue as a percentage of GDP without any legislative action. In fact, when inflation is relatively high and bracket creep is particularly intense, as it was through much of the 1970s, policymakers have to cut taxes repeatedly to maintain the desired level of taxes. Of the 9 major tax bills enacted between 1968 and 1981, 6 reduced federal revenue.

The 1981 Act accelerated depreciation, which allowed businesses to claim larger expenses and pay lower corporate taxes. Depreciation allows a business to set aside throughout the useful life of a building or equipment or other covered assets enough each year to cover the replacement cost. A building's useful life actually might be 25, 50, or more years. The 1981 Act replaced earlier useful life categories with four shorter categories: 3, 5, 10 or 15 years.

The 1981 Act also created a 10 percent exclusion up to $3000 for two earner married couples; increased the exemption for estate tax from $175,625 to $600,000 in 1987; reduced the windfall profits tax; replaced the $200 interest exclusion with a 15 percent net interest exclusion beginning in 1985, with a $900 lap; and allowed all working taxpayers to establish individual retirement accounts.

For the 1982 to 1986 period, the Treasury's Office of Tax Analysis estimated the average reduction in federal tax revenues from the Economic Recovery Act to be $110.4 billion each year or 2.89 percent of prior tax revenues.

On November 10, 1981, the *Atlantic* published a cover story by *Washington Post* Assistant Managing Editor William Greider entitled *The Education of David Stockman.* Stockman had met with Greider on a weekly basis for months and provided Greider an unguarded commentary on the development and enactment of the 1981 budget and tax reduction. That Stockman agreed to do so and permit publication while he was still working for Reagan showed remarkably poor judgment. His candor would almost end his White House career. With respect to the OMB's forecasts, Stockman explained:

> None of us really understands what's going on with all these numbers. You've got so many different budgets out and so many different baselines and such complexity now in the interactive parts of the budget between policy action and the economic environment and all the internal mysteries of the budget, and there are a lot of them. People are getting from A to B and it's not clear how they are getting there. It's now clear how we got there.

Stockman criticized the Kemp-Roth Tax Bill with its supply side premise that a reduction in the higher tax brackets would stimulate the economy. Stockman recognized the theory of rational expectations was not working. "But I mean," Stockman acknowledged, "Kemp-Roth was always a Trojan horse to bring down the top rate.... It's kind of hard to sell 'trickle down,' so the supply side formula was the only way to set a tax policy that was really 'trickle down.' Supply-side is 'trickle-down' theory:"

> Supply-side was the wrong atmospherics — not wrong theory or wrong economics, but wrong atmospherics.... The supply-siders have gone too far. They created this nonpolitical view of the economy, where you are going to have big changes and abrupt turns, and their happy vision of this world of growth and no inflation with no pain.

There was fury in the White House about the Stockman interview. Nancy Reagan, Ed Meese, and Mike Deaver wanted Stockman immediately fired. Jim Baker saved his job because the administration needed his skill with the federal budget but took Stockman to the woodshed in an epithet filled preparation for a meeting with Reagan. "You're going to have lunch with the President. The menu is humble pie." Reagan recorded in his diary that Stockman "tendered his resignation. I got him to tell the whole thing about his supposed friend who betrayed him; then refused to accept his resignation."

Stockman's bitter 1986 memoir, *The Triumph of Politics: When the Reagan Revolution Failed,* emphasizes a quite different narrative. Reagan, in Stockman's view, was "too kind, gentle and sentimental" to lead a real revolution in American economic policy:

> The true Reagan Revolution never had a chance. It defied all of the overwhelming forces, interests, and impulses of American democracy. Our Madisonian government of checks and balances, three branches, two legislative houses, and infinitely splintered power is conservative, now radical. It hugs powerfully

> to the history behind it. It shuffles into the future one step at a time. It cannot leap into revolutions without falling flat on its face. . . .
>
> The fact was, due to the efforts of myself and my supply-side compatriots, Ronald Reagan had been made to stumble into the wrong camp on the eve of his final, successful quest for the presidency. He was a consensus politician, not an ideologue. He had no business trying to make a revolution because it wasn't in his bones. . . .
>
> To make a revolution required defining fairness in terms of exacting, abstract principles — not human hard-luck stories. It meant complete elimination of subsidies to farmers and businesses. It required an immediate end to welfare for the able bodied poor. It meant no right to draw more from the Social Security fund than retirees had actually contributed, which was a lot less than most were currently getting.
>
> These principles everywhere clashed with the political reality. Over the decades, the politicians had lured tens of millions of citizens into milking . . . cows, food stamps, Social Security, the Veterans Hospitals, and much more. They were getting more than they deserved, needed, or were owed. For the Reagan Revolution to add up, they had to be cut off. The blueprint was thus riddled with the hardship and unfairness of unexpected change. Only an iron chancellor would have tried to make it stick. Ronald Reagan wasn't that by a long shot.

In 1981 and 1982, the recession continued and deficits worsened. Reagan acknowledged in his first State of the Union address on January 26, 1982, that deficits during his presidency would start "at less than a hundred billion dollars." Congress in 1982 enacted the Tax Equity and Fiscal Responsibility Act of 1982, which to that date was the largest tax increase in recent history. Baker recalls Reagan agreeing to the 1982 tax increase after hearing dire deficit forecasts in the spring of 1982 from his Troika of key advisers, Ed Meese, Jim Baker, and Mike Deaver: "All right, I'm gonna do it, but it's wrong. . . . [Reagan] later said he regretted capitulating."

Taxes in total were increased for the four years after enactment by an annual average of $37.5 billion or 0.98 percent, 34 percent of the 1981 tax cut. The tax increases largely were achieved by repealing the 1981 Act's increases in accelerated depreciation deductions, requiring taxpayers to reduce the basis by 50 percent for investment tax credits and instituting 10 percent withholding on dividends and interest paid to individuals. The withholding on dividends and interest was repealed in 1983.

During the balance of the Regan Administration, there would be six new tax laws, most significantly the Tax Reform Act of 1986. The cumulative impact of these six tax laws would be small, approximately .73 percent, or 25 percent of the 1981 Tax Cut. The net consequence of the 1981 Economic Recovery Act and subsequent Reagan era tax legislation would be a net decrease in the tax revenue of approximately 1.18 percent tax revenues compared to the last Carter budget. Between 1980 and 1989, total federal income tax receipts increased at an average rate of 8.2 percent from $308.7 to $549 billion.

Reagan was less successful through his presidency at budget cutting, which Reagan would call "one of my biggest disappointments as President." In 1981, Congress enacted $39 billion of budget cuts. During his first term, 1981–1985, inflation-adjusted nondefense expenditures fell by 9.7 percent, including cuts to Medicaid, food stamps, federal education programs, federal housing programs, and a 22 percent cut to the Environmental Protection Agency. In his first year, he ended price controls on domestic oil which led to lower oil prices. But the nondefense expenditure cuts were overwhelmed by a $140 billion increase in defense expenditures and the $124.6 billion cost to the United States government of the savings and loan crisis.

Reagan's aspiration for a constitutional amendment to balance the budget was never enacted, although the Senate did vote to support the amendment by a vote of 69 to 31 on August 4, 1982. Subsequently, the Gramm-Rudman-Hollings Act of 1985 created automatic statutory spending reductions. In 1986, the United States Supreme Court declared Gramm-Rudman-Hollings unconstitutional in *Bowsher v. Synar*, which held that the power of Congress to remove the Comptroller General, an Executive Branch officer, violated the separation of powers in the Constitution. A revised version of Gramm-Rudman-Hollings was enacted in 1987 and again revised in 1990 in the Budget Enforcement Act, but none of these Acts effectively controlled budget deficits.

Reagan would take pride in the 1980s economic expansion that began in November 1982. Inflation adjusted GDP averaged 3.5 percent during his eight years in office, with a high of 7.3 percent in 1984. Unemployment declined to 5.3 percent in 1988, approximately one-half its 1982 peak of 10.8 percent. Sixteen million new jobs were created. Inflation declined substantially from 13.6 percent in 1980, to 4.1 percent in 1988.

Reagan's tax cuts and domestic policy popularized the phrase trickle down. The share of the top 5 percent of United States households increased from 16.5 to 18.3 percent, the highest fifth declined to 44.1 to 46.3 percent. Reagan was the only post-war president not to raise the minimum wage. The number of children 18 years old and younger living below the poverty level grew from 18.3 to 19.5 percent between 1980 and 1988.

Reagan's popularity limited House losses in 1982 to 26 seats, a number that Kevin Phillips would write: "Never before has the party out of power scored such piddling gains in the face of massive and increasing unemployment." In the Senate, the Republicans held their 54 seat majority.

By June 1984, with inflation down to 3.2 percent and economic growth at 7.4 percent, as a Reagan television spot put it "It's morning again in America." Reagan briefly stumbled in the first presidential debate with Walter Mondale on October 7, 1984, saying during the debate: "I'm all confused now," prompting the *Wall Street Journal*, among others, to ask in a front page headline: "Is Oldest U.S. President Now Showing His Age?" Reagan memorably disarmed this concern in the second presidential debate on October 21, 1984, with a stronger performance and the much quoted assertion about former Vice President Mondale: "I am not going to exploit, for political purposes, my opponent's youth and inexperience."

On November 6, 1984, Reagan was reelected in one of the greatest landslides in United States history, winning 49 states and 58.8 percent of the popular vote. The Republicans held their Majority in the Senate, 53–47 and gained 16 seats in the House, leaving the Democrats with a still large 253–182 majority.

But as Garry Wills would write with some overstatement: "[T]he more the White House succeeded politically, the more it failed economically. . . . Tax reductions did not make for a broader base of productivity to be based."

The national debt would triple during Reagan's two terms from $997 billion to $2.85 trillion. More than any other post-war president to that date, Reagan inculcated the belief that even during peacetime without a financial emergency, it was permissible to finance the federal government through debt. The budget deficit would be $207.8 billion in 1983, or approximately 6 percent of

GDP, in 1985, $212.3 billion, in 1986, the deficit would be $221.2 billion or 5.7 percent of GDP. Debt as a percentage of GNP would increase from 25.2 percent in 1981 to 39.8 percent in 1988.

To pay for the massive budget deficits, the United States relied increasingly on foreign purchase of our debt. In 1985, the peak year of the Reagan presidency, debt financed from abroad would equal $103 billion. By April 2019, foreign holdings of the United States debt would equal $6.2 trillion or 28 percent of the total United States debt of $21.8 trillion.[36]

The Accelerating Transformation of Banking

The combination of volatile, often high, interest rates, interest rate ceilings, antiquated federal financial regulatory requirements and a belated embrace of new technology such as electronic funds transfer and automated teller machines led to a 1980s decade that began to fundamentally change the structure of the banking industry.

Savings and loan institutions were affected by interest rate volatility and Regulation Q interest rate ceilings. Billions of dollars in deposits and potential deposits gravitated to money market accounts that grew from $9.5 billion in 1978, to $236 billion by the end of 1982. Since S & Ls largely held fixed rate mortgages, the income generated by these mortgages often was insufficient to attract new deposits. Aggregate S & L profits precipitously fell from $3.6 billion in 1979, to $781 million in 1980.

Simultaneously, Paul Volcker on behalf of the Fed articulated concern that federal member banks were leaving the Federal Reserve System because they were required to keep reserves in non-interest paying accounts with the 12 Federal Reserve banks. In February 1980, Volcker testified that 69 banks with $7 billion in deposits had left the Federal Reserve System with another 320 banks "considered certain or probable to withdraw" and 350 more "actively considering withdrawals." Deposits covered by the Fed system then 70 percent were on track to decline to 64 percent and potentially as low as 57 percent.

The concern was taken seriously by Congress. In 1979, national member banks had declined by 116 and in 1980 would decline by another 23 banks.

A total of 107 S & Ls failed in 1981 and 1982. The number of insolvent S & Ls with risk of failure increased from 43 of the 3993

S & Ls insured by the Federal Savings and Loan Insurance Corporation to 415 in 1982, with $220 billion in assets. These S & Ls held 32 percent of industry assets.

In contrast, national banks and state member banks in the Federal Reserve System increased by 305 between 1981 and 1983, from 5474 to 5807.

Separately, in 1979, the United States Circuit Court in the District of Columbia in *American Bankers Ass'n v. Board of Governors of the Federal Reserve System* held that fund transfer systems authorized by the Fed, Federal Home Loan Bank Board, and the National Credit Union Administration to permit electronic transfer of funds from savings to checking accounts or implicitly to permit automated teller machines were in violation of the underlying enabling statutes.

On March 31, 1980, Congress enacted the Depository Institutions Deregulation and Monetary Control Act to address each of these disparate legislative needs and to address the perceived unfairness of bank customers being trapped in a depository system where interest payments on bank accounts were substantially less than inflation and borrowing costs.

Title I of the Act, the Monetary Control Act of 1980, fortified the Fed's oversight powers. The Fed was granted the power to require all depository institutions to maintain reserves. The term depository institution was broadly defined and authorized the Fed to exercise power over member banks, FDIC-insured banks, mutual savings banks, credit unions, S & Ls, and insured institutions under the National Housing Act.

The Fed lowered reserve requirements for all depository institutions to 3 percent for total transaction accounts of $25 million or less and 12 percent for deposit accounts and NOW accounts in excess of $25 million. For time deposits, the Fed had discretionary power to require reserves of 3 percent or in such other instances up to 9 percent "solely for the purpose of implementing monetary policy." The reduction in required reserves from 16.25 percent to 12 percent was a major inducement to secure member bank support. In one estimate, when the new reserve requirements were fully phased-in, member banks would be freed from nearly $14.5 billion in reserve requirements, which, for example, at a 5 percent return on these funds if deposited in private banks would generate for the industry annual income of $725 million per year.

There also were sweeteners for depository institutions who accepted Fed oversight. All depository institutions with either transaction accounts or time deposits whose reserves were held by the Fed "shall be entitled to the same discount and borrowing privileges as member banks."

Title II of the Act broadened the lending powers of federal S & Ls, which were permitted to loan up to 20 percent of their assets in a combination of commercial real estate, secured or unsecured loans for personal, family, or household purposes, commercial paper and corporate debt. Federal S & Ls also could issue credit cards and were given trust powers to the same extent as competitive state banks, trust companies or other corporation and permitted to act under the laws of the state in which the S & L was located.

State usury laws no longer could be applied to limit the interest and related charges on any loan, mortgage, credit sale, or advance that was secured by a first lien on residential real estate by any depository institution except in any specific state which in the three years, April 1, 1980 to April 1, 1983, adopted a law opting out of the end of usury limits on loans, mortgages, credit sales or advances within the state.

FDIC deposit insurance was increased from $40,000 to $100,000 per account.

In the future, the Fed could charge fees to cover the actual direct and indirect costs of services it provided to depository institutions for:

1) Currency and Coin Services;
2) Check Clearing and Collection Services;
3) Wire Transfer Services;
4) Automated Clearinghouse Services;
5) Settlement Services;
6) Securities Safekeeping Services;
7) The Federal Reserve Float; and
8) Any New Services which the Federal Reserve System offered, including but not limited to payment services to effectuate the electronic transfer of funds.

Required charges for fees were essential for the Fed when the total of its required reserves was reduced from $27 to $16 billion. Charges for its services were anticipated to initially generate $200 million a year rising to nearly $600 million a year by 1985.

Title III of the Depository Institutions Deregulation and Monetary Control Act decisively addressed the impact of interest rate ceilings on bank customers, "particularly those with modest savings" and depository institution's ability to compete for funds, implicitly with money market funds that were impeding "the ability of depository institutions to compete for funds."

Senator Proxmire, chair of the Senate Banking Committee, and the Banking Committee itself highlighted the impact high borrowing costs and low bank deposit interest rates had on bank depositors. "It is ridiculous for the savings rate to be a maximum of 5-1/4 at a bank for a small saver or 5½ percent at a savings and loan, when the inflation rate . . . is about 13 percent," Proxmire argued on the floor of the Senate, October 31, 1979. A Senate Committee Report earlier in October 1979 insisted: "Regulation Q now sanctions blatant discrimination against the small saver to justify its continued existence. It is grossly unfair. . . . Small savers should not be forced by a system of government rate controls to subsidize borrowers."

The Deregulation Act eliminated limitations on the maximum rates of interest that could be paid by depository institutions through an "orderly phase-out" over six years to be administered by a Deregulation Committee consisting of the Treasury Secretary, the Chairs of the Fed, the FDIC, the Federal Home Loan Bank Board, and National Credit Union Administration as voting members and the Comptroller of the Currency as a nonvoting member. The charge to the Deregulation Committee was to "work toward providing all depositors with a market rate of return on their savings with due regard for the safety and soundness of depository institutions."

The 1980 Act authorized all depository institutions to pay interest and issue NOW accounts nationwide to lure funds back from money market funds. The Act also authorized banks to use Automatic Transfer Services (*ATS*) to permit automatic transfers of funds from savings accounts to other bank accounts. By the end of 1980, the Fed reported "actual growth of ATS and NOW accounts substantially exceeded" the amount the FOMC had anticipated in their monetary aggregates.

The initial consequences of the 1980 Monetary Control Act were overwhelmed by the continued spike in interest rates. By 1981, new mortgages were less than half what they had been three years earlier. Housing starts, vital to S & L mortgage loans, fell from 1.8 billion in September 1979 to .85 million in January 1982. In 1981, the industry lost $4.6 billion and $4.3 billion in 1982.

S & Ls in 1982 were required to give up the interest rate ceiling differential that favored them by January 1, 1984, and compete on a level playing field with banks in mortgages, commercial real estate, and personal, family, or household loans, as well as trust business. "It's a matter of survival of the fittest," Henry Reuss, chair of the House Banking Committee, explained.

The response to the gathering S & L crisis by Congress, the Fed, the Reagan Administration, and the Supreme Court was strikingly inconsistent.

In March 1982, Congress enacted a Joint Resolution stating that the Full Faith and Credit of the United States would stand behind the Federal Savings and Loan Insurance Corporation (*FSLIC*) and the FDIC if either ran out of funds to insure covered S & L and bank deposits.

In October 1982, Congress enacted the Garn-St. Germain Depository Institutions Act. The Act combined two opposing concepts.

On the one hand, the Act authorized the FDIC with respect to insured banks, the Federal Home Loan Bank Board with respect to S & Ls, and the National Credit Union Administration with respect to insured credit unions to exercise new far reaching power to prevent the closing of these institutions. The regulatory agencies could make loans or deposits, purchase their assets or securities or assume liabilities of these depository institutions, or facilitate a merger, consolidation or sale of assets of an endangered institution with another insured institution.

The FDIC and Federal Home Loan Bank Board were authorized to convert state-chartered savings banks into federal savings banks and federal mutual S & Ls into stock S & Ls or savings banks.

The FDIC acting as receiver could arrange the sale of assets of a closed insured bank with total assets of $500 million or more including a sale to an out-of-state bank or bank holding company with a depository institution located in the state where the closed bank was chartered. The FDIC was granted a similar power to sell assets or arrange a merger of a mutual bank with total assets of $500 million or more to an out-of-state bank or bank holding company. The federal bank or S & L regulators also could increase or maintain the capital of these federal banks and S & Ls by making purchases of net worth certificates or authorize these institutions to issue net worth certificates. A qualified institution was a troubled bank or S & L with net worth equal to less than 3 percent of its assets and losses during the previous two quarters. The FDIC also could provide assistance to qualified uninsured state institutions if the state indemnified the FDIC for any losses it might incur.

At the same time, S & Ls were granted new powers to make residential or commercial real estate loans up to 40 percent of their assets, secured or unsecured commercial loans up to 10 percent of their assets, investments in tangible personal property "including without limitation, vehicles, manufactured homes, machinery, equipment or furniture, for rental or sale" up to 10 percent of S & L assets, and investments in small business investment companies up to 1 percent of S & L assets. S & Ls were authorized to establish branches, including out-of-state branches, when the branch was authorized before the enactment of the Depository Institutions Amendments Act of 1982 and the laws of the state in which the branch was located permitted establishment of the branch by a state S & L.

The Garn-St. Germain Act authorized banks, S & Ls and credit unions and nonfederally chartered housing creditors to issue adjustable rate mortgages. For S & Ls, that in total had lost $8.7 billion in 1981 and 1982, this was particularly consequential. In 1980, the total assets of the S & L industry was $604 billion, of which $480 billion was in mortgage loans, most of which provided fixed rate interest lower than the 11 percent average cost for S & Ls to borrow money.

All depository institutions were authorized to create money market deposit accounts "directly equivalent to and competitive with money market mutual funds registered with the Securities and Exchange Commission."

National and state member banks also were granted new powers to discount real estate loans as commercial paper, engage in transactions with affiliates up to 20 percent of the capital stock and surplus of the member bank, exempted from reserve requirements any combination of reservable liabilities up to $2 million.

The Bank Holding Company Act was amended to preclude most life insurance activities of bank holding companies.[37]

When Reagan signed the Garn-St. Germain Act of 1982, he would characterize the Act as "the most important legislation for financial institutions in the last 50 years." Reagan's words would prove to be prophetic, but for reasons quite different than he believed.

Between 1982 and 1985, the S & L industry went on a buying binge in nontraditional S & L assets. Total S & L assets during those years expanded by 56 percent compared to 24 percent for commercial banks. S & Ls who invested most heavily in nontraditional assets grew most rapidly. In 1984, S & Ls with an annual growth rate of less than 15 percent held 68 percent of their assets in residential loans. S & Ls with growth rates over 50 percent held 53 percent of their assets in mortgages.

The Bipartisan National Commission on Financial Institution Reform, Recovery and Enforcement, established by Congress in 1990, to examine the causes of the problems in the savings and loan industry before 1989, reported in July 1993:

> During the 1930s, Congress transformed S & Ls into agents of national housing policy. Federal deposit insurance was provided as a subsidy allowing S & Ls to raise large amounts of funds at less than market interest rates so that they could finance long-term, fixed-rate, home mortgage loans. For the next 30 years they admirably performed the role that Congress had assigned them of providing the financing for realization of the American dream of home ownership. Government regulation sheltered S & Ls from competition, allowing the industry to be profitable- and failures to be rare. As long as interest rates did not rise substantially, S & Ls faced little risk. . . .
>
> During the early 1980s, the S & L industry was swept up in a movement to deregulate American business. But "deregulating" S & Ls was not like that of, say, airlines or trucking in which power was given to market forces in the interest of economic efficiency. . . . The industry obtained substantial new investment powers, and it was subjected to less supervision; but government-backed deposit insurance was retained and even increased.

The Federal Home Loan Bank Board decreased the capital S & Ls were required to maintain from 5 percent to 4 percent of net worth in November 1980, then lowered required capital to 3 percent, at a time when the Federal Deposit Insurance Corporation retained 5 percent minimum capital requirements, which it proposed to raise to 6 percent.

Even the 3 percent net worth requirement overstated the effective S & L requirement. Most business firms, including banks, were subject to Generally Accepted Accounting Principles (*GAAP*) then established by the Financial Accounting Standards Board. The Federal Home Loan Bank Board had developed a more latitudinous Regulatory Accounting Principles (*RAP*). Under GAAP, in 1983 there were 293 insolvent S & Ls. Under RAP, only 48 S & Ls were insolvent.

The Federal Home Loan Bank Board also eliminated restrictions on the minimum number of S & L stockholders. Previously there were required to be at least 400 stockholders, of whom at least 125 had to be from the local community served by the S & L and no individual could own more than 10 percent of the stock. A new regulation allowed the stock of an S & L to be held by a single owner. The National Commission on Financial Institution Reform, Recovery and Enforcement harshly criticized this change: "This allowed developers, others with conflicts of interest, and out-and-out crooks to take over S & Ls. Takeovers were made even easier by allowing acquirers to put up land and other real estate, often at inflated appraised values, rather than cash. Small institutions could be acquired at low cost and quickly expanded into large ones through growth of insured deposits."

Until 1982, the Federal Home Loan Bank Board encouraged goodwill mergers under which Richard Pratt, Federal Home Loan Bank Board chair, testified in 1992: "[T]wo institutions with massive negative earnings could merge and the combined entity could show positive income without the operation of either institution changing." This was done with the authorization of the Federal Home Loan Bank Board by treating the higher than market price the acquiring firm paid to acquire the second firm was treated as goodwill and considered an asset. The National Commission excoriated this type of account as "pervert[ing] the concept of goodwill, producing a sham. . . . There was no arm's length transaction as required by [the Financial Accounting Standards Board]. This goodwill was a sham method of increasing net worth of the acquirer while making it look as though the problems of the insolvent S & L had been solved."

The National Commission underlined: "Perversely the more insolvent the acquired institution, the greater its value to the acquirer as a vehicle for inflating income and draining off cash. These activities were made easier because the acquirer typically received regulatory forbearance as a reward for taking over an insolvent S & L." Between 1980 and 1982, there were 752 S & L acquisitions before the Financial Accounting Standards Board tightened its standard of goodwill.

In May 1983, S & Ls were allowed by the Federal Home Loan Bank Board to invest up to 10 percent of their assets in high yield, high risk junk bonds popularized by Michael Milken and the securities firm of Drexel Burnham Lambert to finance high risk corporations. In 1983, S & Ls then limited to mortgage loans within their home state were authorized to engage in nationwide lending.

Nor was the Federal Home Loan Bank Board alone during the early 1980s in encouraging latitudinous regulation.

In 1982, the Comptroller of the Currency interpreted the Glass-Stegall Act to authorize a national bank to establish a discount brokerage service for both bank and nonbanking customers. This decision was quickly embraced by national banks. In December 1983, the American Bankers Association estimated that there were approximately 1000 banks engaged in discount brokerage.

Fed Chair Paul Volcker during this period frequently opposed shadow banks or nonbank banks as he called them in 1984 Testimony on Banking Legislation, but favored expansion of bank holding company powers to permit holding companies to sponsor and distribute mutual funds, underwrite and distribute municipal security revenue bonds and mortgage backed securities, engage in insurance brokerage, and own S & Ls. In 1982, the Fed approved the application of J.P. Morgan and Bankers Trust to establish futures merchant affiliates. In 1983, the Fed amended its list of permissible bank holding company activities to add: "(1) issuing money orders, (2) arranging equity financing, (3) underwriting government securities and money market instruments, (4) acting as a futures commission merchant, and (5) providing foreign exchange services."

In 1986, the Fed further increased authorized bank holding company insurance activities by adding to permitted activities:

> (1) selling credit-related life, accident, and health insurance and insurance for involuntary unemployment; (2) selling, through finance-company subsidiaries, property insurance on

> collateral of $10,000 or less (or $25,000 for manufactured homes); (3) continuing and expanding certain agency activities authorized before specified grandfather dates; (4) acting as a managing general agent for group insurance for the holding company; (5) acting as a general insurance agent if the holding company has $50 million in assets or less; and (6) acting as a general insurance agent in towns with inadequate insurance agency facilities or fewer than 5,000 residents.

The new S & L and banking powers were subject to judicial challenge, but the courts often interpreted the Glass-Steagall and Bank Holding Company Acts expansively. The Supreme Court in 1984 unanimously affirmed the Federal Reserve Board Order authorizing Bank of America's acquisition of leading discount securities broker Charles Schwab, writing in part:

> In this case, the Board held that the securities brokerage services offered by Schwab were "closely related" to banking within the meaning of § 4(c)(8) [of the Bank Holding Company Act]. . . . The Board found that banks currently offer, as an accommodation to their customers, brokerage services that are virtually identical to the services offered by Schwab. . . .
>
> . . . The general nature of the statutory language . . . suggests that Congress vested the Board with considerable discretion to consider and weigh a variety of factors in determining whether an activity is "closely related" to banking. In this case, the Board concluded that Schwab's brokerage services were "closely related" to banking because it found that the services were "operationally and functionally very similar to the types of brokerage services that are generally provided by banks and that banking organizations are particularly well equipped to provide such services." . . . The Board acted well within its discretion in ruling on such factors. . . .
>
> The legislative history demonstrates that Congress enacted § 20 to prohibit the affiliation of commercial banks with entities that were engaged principally in "activities such as underwriting."

In 1985, the Supreme Court held that national banks could serve as agents in the sale of variable insurance annuities interpreting this as an incidental power to the business of banking under the Glass-Steagall Act.

In 1987, the Supreme Court affirmed a Comptroller of Currency order permitting two national banks to operate discount brokerage services outside their home states not hindered by the branch office limitations of the McFadden Act.

In 1986, the Federal Reserve Board approved the application of National Westminster Bank, PLC, and its subsidiary, NatWest Holdings, Inc., to provide investment advice and securities brokerage to institutional customers through a newly formed subsidiary. This authorization was affirmed in 1987 by the District of Columbia Circuit Court.

In 1988, the Second Circuit Court of Appeals upheld new powers approved by the Fed to allow bank holding companies to underwrite and deal in specified municipal revenue bonds, mortgage related securities and commercial paper.

Law Professor Donald Langevoort would write in 1987 that the Glass-Steagall Act by then was "obsolete" except with respect to securities underwriting by banks.

The deregulation at the federal level was exceeded in several states, most significantly California, Texas, and Florida. The loosening of federal S & L regulation had set off, what the National Commission on Financial Institution Reform, Recovery and Enforcement, called "a competition in laxity in state regulation:"

> With federal charters so attractive, state-chartered S & Ls converted to federal charters in droves. In 1981, there were $81 billion of assets in state-chartered institutions. By 1983 only $34 billion remained — a 58 percent decline. The California Department of S & Ls depended on assessments on state-chartered institutions for its funding. In 1981, it had a 150-member regulatory staff; by 1983 the staff dropped to 30 professionals and 55 persons in total. In an effort to entice institutions back to state charters, Governor Jerry Brown signed into law in 1982 provisions giving state-chartered S & Ls unlimited authority to invest in service corporations subject only to approval of the S & L Commissioner. In effect, this allowed California S & Ls to engage in virtually any activity they chose. In 1983, the state suspended restrictions on the types of loans that could be made on non-residential real estate.

The National Commission was even more critical of Texas:

> The most dismal supervisory performance was in Texas, where some of the most egregious practices and greatest losses occurred. Texas S & Ls had authority to do virtually anything, and many did. Responding to boom conditions in the state and to the incentives to milk their cash cows, many institutions grew by over 100 percent per year, and 40 tripled in size from 1982–86. . . . Forty of the fastest growing institutions had over 30 percent of assets in these activities. All these S & Ls later failed. State supervision was virtually nonexistent.[38]

With the economy rebounding in 1983 and 1984, the Reagan Administration's major policy initiative, *Blueprint for Reform: The Report of the Task Group on Regulation of Financial Services*, was chaired by Vice President George Bush with Treasury Secretary Don Regan as Vice Chair, and future SEC Chair Richard Breeden, then Deputy Counsel to Bush, as Staff Director.

The Bush Report was quiescent and largely accepted the status quo of the financial industry. By December 31, 1983, the nation's $5.079 trillion system of finance included:

Commercial Banks	$1.753 Trillion	34.5%
S & Ls	$.825 Trillion	16.2%
Mutual Savings Banks	$.194 Trillion	3.8%
Credit Unions	$.1 Trillion	2%
Life Insurance Companies	$.638 Trillion	12.6%
Other Insurance Companies	$.29 Trillion	4.5%
Money Market Funds	$.1.6 Trillion	3.2%
Mutual Funds	$.13 Trillion	2.6%
Securities Broker-Dealers	$.05 Trillion	1%
Private Pension Plans	$.41 Trillion	8.1%
Government Retirement Plans	$.32 Trillion	6.3%
Finance Companies	$.27 Trillion	5.1%
Real Estate Investment Trusts	$.04 Trillion	1%

Approximately 70 percent of all banks and 50 percent of thrifts combining S & Ls and mutual savings banks were regulated by the states. By 1983, bank holding companies had grown to nearly 5400 from the initial 53 in 1956 and held more than 80 percent of United States bank assets. Approximately 93 percent of the nation's commercial banks were regulated by the Comptroller or FDIC with 7 percent of state member banks regulated by the Fed.

The Bush Report recognized three ongoing dynamics of the federal regulatory structure:

> First, most federal restrictions on pricing by depository institutions will end. Indeed, federal price controls on interest rates for time deposits have already been virtually eliminated....
>
> Second, the distinctions between different types of depository institutions, and between depository and other financial services institutions, will continue to fade. The Garn-St. Germain Act greatly expanded the bank-like powers of thrift institutions, while retaining the legal distinction of these institutions as a separate industry....
>
> Third, depository institutions will continue to expand their geographic scope of operations through increased electronic services, expansion of subsidiary activities, acquisitions of failed institutions, changes in state laws and possibly federal regulatory changes.

By July 1984, 12 states had enacted national or regional interstate banking laws. Interstate banking also was being dramatically expanded through technology. By 1983, the number of automated teller machines had increased exponentially to 50,000, and would nearly double again by 1990.

The Bush Report focused on the four types of depository institutions (commercial banks, S & Ls, mutual savings banks, and credit unions) that comprised 56.5 percent of the American system of finance. As of December 31, 1983, banks, S & Ls, and mutual savings banks were categorized:

Type	Number	% of Banks	Assets (in billions)	% of Total Bank Assets
National Banks (OCC)	4772	33%	$1400	60%
State Member Banks (FRB)	1059	7%	$426	18%
State Non-Member Banks (FDIC)	8632	60%	$516	22%
Total Banks	**14,463**	**100%**	**$2342**	**100%**
Federal S & Ls	1553		$498	
State S & Ls	1487		$255	
Mutual Savings Banks	436		$234	

The Bush Task Force ignored the ongoing crisis in the S & L industry and proposed a modest set of reforms.

Most prominent were its ideas to create functional bank regulation by eliminating the FDIC's role in examining, supervising, and regulating state nonmember banks and creating a new Federal Banking Agency (*FBA*) within the Treasury Department, incorporating and upgrading the Office of the Comptroller of the Currency. Three federal bank agencies would be reduced to two. The new FBA would regulate all national banks, and the Fed would regulate all state members of the Fed. All antitrust responsibilities would be centralized in the Department of Justice and all securities regulation would be centralized in the SEC rather than divided among the Office of the Comptroller, FDIC, Fed, and Federal Home Loan Bank Board as well as Department of Justice and SEC. The Fed would continue to supervise the holding companies of the largest domestic banks, as well as specified international holding companies.

The Fed would transfer its authority to designate permissible activities of bank holding companies to the FBA, which meant to the Treasury. But the Fed "should maintain a sufficient level of supervisory and regulatory authority to back up its responsibilities as the Central Bank."

The role of the FDIC in providing deposit insurance would be retained, but the FDIC and Federal Savings and Loan Insurance Corporation would be required to establish common minimum capital requirements.

The separate federal regulatory system for S & Ls and mutual savings banks would be retained with a new portfolio asset test measuring the percentage of an institution's assets in housing and housing related financial instruments as the basis of qualification for federal S & L and mutual savings bank regulation.

Consistent with the theory of empowering states, federal supervision of state banks and S & Ls, as well as their holding companies would be transferred to state regulatory agencies that were certified to have sufficiently strong and reliable regulatory programs. The Bush Report included an encomium to the dual banking system:

> Through the years, the existence of this "dual" federal and state system has provided a safety valve against outdated or inflexible regulatory controls being imposed by either federal or state authorities. Acting as laboratories for change, the states have frequently developed new forms of financial services, which then spread nationally through federal action. For example, the states originated both checking accounts and branch banking. In recent years states began the chartering of credit unions and invented the NOW account as a device to permit the payment of interest to consumers on funds essentially equivalent to checking accounts.

Deregulation was emphasized with a series of specific recommendations to eliminate requirements for prior approval of bank holding companies, branch locations, capital requirements for each branch as well as other forms of deregulation that were further afield from banking regulation, such as repeal of the Public Utility Holding Company Act.

The Bush Report at the time was largely ignored.

The climactic phase of the S & L crisis dubbed as "the greatest scandal in the history of American banking" soon followed. Between 1980 and 1989, a total of 890 S & Ls with $348 billion in assets went out of business. Including mergers, the total number of S & Ls would decline from 3234 in 1986 to 1645 in 1995. The market share of S & Ls for single family mortgage loans would decline from 53 percent in 1975 to 30 percent in 1990. The total direct costs of the S & L debacle would be calculated to be $152.6 billion between 1986 and 1995. Some of the loss could be attributed to a collapse in real estate values and the fall of crude oil prices by 50 percent, which particularly hit Texas hard where 14 of the 20 largest S & L failures would occur.

In all, the Federal Savings and Loan Insurance Corporation between 1986 and 1989 would close or resolve failures of 296 S & Ls with total assets of $125 billion. Between 1989 and 1995, the Resolution Trust Corporation would close or resolve failures of 747 S & Ls with total assets of $394 billion. The combined closings of 1043 S & Ls with total assets of $519 billion would make this the largest industry restructuring since the New Deal.

Some financial regulators estimated that 40 percent of S & L failures were attributable to fraud or insider trading while the 1993 National Commission on Financial Institution Reform, Recovery and Enforcement estimated that fraud accounted for 10 to 15 percent of total losses. By 1992, over 1000 individuals would be charged with crimes in connection with the S & L debacle.

In 1984, the Federal Savings and Loan Insurance Corporation would close the Empire Savings and Loan in Mesquite, Texas, costing taxpayers $284 million. At the time of its closing, Empire had 317 outstanding construction loans, almost all of which were delinquent. It also had 658 loans to investors used to finance the purchase of completed but unoccupied condominium units. Most of these loans also were delinquent. The criminal conviction of Danny Faulkner and others included evidence of a conspiracy to steal $165 million from Empire.

Subsequently, the Federal Home Loan Bank Board under the leadership of Edwin Gray who began as chair in 1983 would reverse its aggressive deregulation of the S & L industry, restricting S & Ls from making investments in corporate stock and raise required capital to 7 percent for new S & Ls with a goal of doubling the industry average to 6 percent.

In March 1985, Home State Savings Bank in Cincinnati, the largest Ohio S & L, a $1.4 billion privately insured state S & L, experienced deposit runs after it lost $144 million in transactions with ESM Government Securities, which the SEC closed as insolvent. Governor Richard Celeste soon ordered all 71 state insured S & Ls closed for three days to stem other deposit runs that had begun when the Ohio Deposit Guarantee Fund disclosed it had insufficient funds to pay off Home State depositors. These were the first Bank Holidays since the Great Depression.

In May 1985, after reports of a criminal investigation at Old Court and Merritt Commercial Savings and Loan in Baltimore, a deposit run caused the closure of the $813 million S & L. Old Court had grown nearly tenfold from deposits of $86 million by offering depositors the highest interest rates in the nation, paying rates as high as 20 percent, which it used to finance investments primarily in commercial construction and unimproved land loans that equaled 70 percent of its deposits. By mid-May, all 102 Maryland S & Ls covered by the state insurance program were experiencing deposit runs. Governor Harry Hughes declared a state of emergency and ordered monthly withdrawals be limited to $1000 per account. In June, the Maryland legislature enacted a law requiring all state S & Ls to become members of the Federal Savings and Loan Insurance Corporation or be liquidated.

Columbia Savings and Loan of Beverly Hills, California had invested $3 billion in junk bonds and grown from $373 million in assets in 1981 to $10 billion by 1986, much from securities trading sales. Columbia's portfolio of junk bonds once worth $4.3 billion was worth less than half that amount or approximately $2.1 billion when it was taken over by the Office of Thrift Supervision in January 1991. In 1989, after junk bond prices plummeted, Columbia recorded a $1.3 billion loss. In September 1991, Columbia's depositors received a payout of $3.25 billion, then the largest in United States history.

In 1988, Sunbelt of Dallas, Texas had expanded from $90 million in assets to $3.2 billion in seven years based on its reckless lending. Its CEO, Edwin McBirney, nicknamed "Fast Eddie," was known for his lavish lifestyle, including seven planes. The failure of Sunbelt in 1988 would cost the government nearly $3.8 billion.

In 1988, Silverado Savings and Loan failed at a cost of $1.3 billion. Neil Bush, the son of Vice President Bush, was on the Silverado Board and was accused of multiple breaches of fiduciary duty such as approving $132 million in loans to business partners without informing the Silverado Board that the loan applicants were his partners. Bush would be banned from the banking industry, pay a $50,000 fine and be one of 11 Silverado officers who in 1991 settled a Resolution Trust Corporation suit for $26.5 million and a further $23 million to the Silverado Indemnity Fund.

The most highly publicized failure was that of Lincoln Savings and Loan and its notorious owner Charles Keating. Lincoln was a large S & L with $4.9 billion by 1989, that had grown from $1 billion in 1984 by investing in hotels, stock, and debt securities, but virtually no home mortgages. In 1987, when a Federal Home Loan Bank Board audit uncovered evidence of fraud and criminal acts, Keating had successfully importuned United States Senators Dennis DeConcini, John McCain, Alan Cranston, John Glenn, and Don Riegel to meet with Federal Home Loan Bank Board Chair Edwin Gray to urge that the Board go easy on Keating. Gray characterized the meeting as "tantamount to an attempt to subvert the regulatory process." Subsequently, the meeting and the total of $1.3 million in direct and indirect campaign contributions to the five senators would be disclosed. Cranston, DeConcini, and Riegel were reprimanded by the Senate Ethics Committee and chose not to seek reelection. McCain and Glenn were criticized by the Senate Ethics Committee for "poor judgment" and John McCain's 2000 Presidential Campaign would be damaged by the scandal. The 1989 bankruptcy of Lincoln Savings and Loan would cost $2.6 billion. Some 23,000 Lincoln bondholders were defrauded. Keating would be convicted of federal and state fraud, racketeering, and conspiracy and spend four and one-half years in prison before his convictions were overturned in 1996. In 1999, he would plead guilty to wire fraud and be sentenced to the time he had earlier served.[39]

None of the S & Ls were directly subject to Fed regulation and the Fed largely stayed on the sidelines during the crisis. In 1985, the Federal Savings and Loan Insurance Corporation was insolvent and had to cease operations briefly. On January 2, 1985, Volcker wrote the Federal Home Loan Bank Board: "[W]e strongly support your efforts to tighten the capital requirements for FSLIC-insured depositories, and our questions concern whether the actions specifically go far enough."

In contrast to the hands-on role of Ben Bernanke in the 2007–2009 financial crisis working with Treasury Secretary Hank Paulson and New York Fed President Tim Geithner to address the risk of systemic collapse, Volcker's 1992 memoir is almost surprisingly blasé: "The debt crisis was on an express train of its own, and by late 1981 or 1982 there was not much anyone could do to head it off."

The 1993 National Commission on Financial Institution Reform, Recovery and Enforcement would reach a brutally different conclusion:

> In 1979 with inflation already accelerating, the Organization of Petroleum Exporting Countries (*OPEC*) engineered a doubling of oil prices. In reaction, inflation in the U.S. moved into double digits for the second time in five years. The Federal Reserve under its new Chairman, Paul Volcker, shifted to a strong and relentless anti-inflationary monetary policy that lasted from October 1979 through October 1982. The unprecedented severity of the policy produced a massive interest rate shock.... The Federal Reserve succeeded in its objective. However, bringing inflation quickly under control proved costly: market interest rates rose to unprecedented levels (the prime rate, for example, was over 20 percent at its peak), the economy experienced its worst recession since the Great Depression of the 1930s — and the S & L industry was destroyed.

The Fed did address several banks subject to its jurisdiction. In 1982, when Penn Square went bankrupt with over $2 billion in loan participations, including a $1 billion loan participation to Continental Illinois National Bank, the Fed lent $20 million to Penn Square to attempt to prevent insolvency. Volcker explained at a FOMC meeting on October 5, 1982: "If it gets bad enough, we can't stay on the side or we'd have a major liquidity crisis. It's a matter of judgment as to when and how strongly to react. We are not here to see the economy destroyed in the interest of not bailing somebody out."

In 1984, the Federal Reserve Bank of Chicago would make an unprecedented loan of $3.6 billion to Continental Illinois, the seventh largest bank in the United States, then the country's largest commercial and industrial lender, in an unsuccessful attempt to keep the bank operating. The loan would popularize the phrase "too big to fail." Sixteen of the nation's largest banks had provided Continental a $4.5 billion line of credit.

After the failure of Penn Square, Continental's nonperforming loans increased by $400 million to $2.3 billion, prompting on May 10, 1984, what a Fed historian called "a massive run by depositors" who would withdraw $10.8 billion of Continental's $28.3 billion in deposits in 1984. Some $20.7 billion of Continental's deposits had been above the $100,000 FDIC insurance limit and were not insured by the FDIC.

Fear of spillover effects led the FDIC on May 17, 1984, to provide a $1.5 billion capital infusion into Continental and make the controversial decision on May 18, 1984, to protect creditors and depositors with greater than $100,000. After an unsuccessful search for a buyer of Continental Illinois, on July 26, 1984, the FDIC purchased $4.5 billion in bad loans from Continental. Continental, in effect, then was nationalized with the FDIC receiving an 80 percent equity stake in Continental that otherwise would have been the largest bank failure in United States history. In 1994, Bank of America purchased Continental.

While the collapse of Penn Square and Continental Illinois were the most conspicuous failures of the period, they were hardly the only ones. The FDIC would report: "Between 1980 and 1994 more than 1600 banks insured by the Federal Deposit Insurance Corporation (*FDIC*) were closed or received FDIC financial assistance . . . far more than in any other period since the advent of federal deposit insurance in the 1930s."

After the 2007–2009 Financial Debacle, what is most striking about the S & L and banking crises of the 1980s was how little was learned from them. Bank regulators largely continued in separate silos. The virtues of deregulation and freeing depository institutions from burdensome activity or capital restrictions again would be touted. During period of surging economic growth when business activity was most likely to be reckless, regulatory supervision would be reduced. Fed historian Allan Meltzer would make a related point about regulatory priorities: "Volcker continued monetary policy forcefully, but he was less forceful and less successful as a bank supervisor." Volcker later recognized that urging Continental to take drastic remedial action when the Penn Square loan participation proved worthless in 1982 was insufficient. He testified at a Senate hearing: "[O]ne could argue . . . that it would have been better to look at the dividends [meaning presumably stopping the payment of dividends] right then. I think, with hindsight, that's an unassailable argument."[40]

International Policy

Volcker, long experienced in international finance, was, to use Meltzer's term, more forceful with respect to international crises. In 1982, Mexico threatened to default on $60 billion in loans to foreign banks, approximately 40 percent of its annual GNP at the time. For nine leading money center banks, loans to Mexico then averaged about 45 percent of their capital. Volcker coordinated with the Treasury, the International Monetary Fund, and International Central Banks to arrange a $1.85 billion package of Central Bank credits that forestalled the crisis. Shortly later, lending banks agreed not to expect payment until Mexico arranged an IMF loan on August 24, 1982, about half from the United States. The Fed increased an earlier $700 million loan to Mexico with another $325 million, the Treasury advanced $600 million, and Europeans some $925 million. Commercial banks provided $3.5 billion in additional loans. Agriculture credit and advance payments for oil added about $2 billion.

With Mexico losing $100 million a day during 1982, the ultimate resolution of the ongoing crisis was not resolved until Mexico devalued its currency and began an austerity program in exchange for the IMF loan.

Volcker at the October 5, 1982, FOMC meeting summarized the debt problems of Mexico, Argentina, Ecuador, Chile, Bolivia, Costa Rica, Peru, Brazil, and Venezuela. A failure by Mexico or any of these nations threatened United States banks and financial institutions with loans to Mexico.

The Fed's efforts were powerfully augmented by Treasury Secretary James Baker who in an October 1985 speech to the IMF in Seoul, Korea proposed a new program for sustained growth, soon popularly called the Baker Plan. The Baker Plan sought a $9 billion increase in lending by the World Bank and $20 billion from commercial banks over three years to support developing countries. However well intentioned, Volcker wrote in retrospect:

> Unfortunately it did not achieve the results that many of us hoped it would. Private banks simply refused to expand their credits to those countries. There was no role for the creditor governments, which was a serious drawback of the Baker Plan. The result of all this was a rather serious deterioration in the psychology of both debtors and creditors.

Work by the Fed, Treasury, IMF, and international banks was largely ineffective during a period intermittently typified by global recession. Debtor nations net capital outflow increased from $16 billion in 1984, to $24 billion in 1986. Between 1984 and 1986, the current account deficit of heavily indebted developing countries increased from $31 to $49 billion.

International economic weaknesses, in part because of a collapse of oil prices from $25–$35 per barrel between 1980–1985 to $14.18 in 1986, compounded by continuing United States annual budget deficits over $150 billion contributed to a strengthened United States dollar relative to other leading currencies and an increasing United States trade deficit, which reached a record $161 billion in 1987.

High interest rates championed by Volcker and the Fed meant that the dollar appreciated by approximately 50 percent against the currency of the next four largest economies (Japan, Germany, France, and Great Britain). A stronger dollar meant foreign goods were less expensive in the United States and United States goods were more expensive abroad.

In 1985, the mounting trade deficits and the prospect that Congress would enact protectionist legislation led the Reagan Administration to support the Plaza Agreement, galvanized by James Baker, the new Treasury Secretary, in an agreement signed at the New York Plaza Hotel on September 22, 1985, by the G-5, the five leading world economies. This was different from the Baker Plan. The Plaza Plan bluntly described "large imbalances in external positions which pose potential problems" and included:

> [t]he deterioration in its external position which the U.S. experienced from its period of very rapid relative growth; the particularly large impact on the U.S. current account of the economic difficulties and the adjustment efforts of some major developing countries; the difficulty of trade access in some markets; and the appreciation of the U.S. dollar. The interaction of these factors . . . has contributed to large, potentially destabilizing external imbalances among major industrial countries. In particular the United States has a large and growing current account deficit, and Japan, and to a lesser extent Germany, large and growing account surpluses.
>
> . . . The U.S. current account deficit, together with other factors, is now contributing to protectionist pressures which, if not resisted, could lead to mutually destructive retaliation with serious damage to the world economy; world trade would shrink, real growth rates could even turn negative, unemployment would rise still higher, and debt-burdened developing countries would be unable to secure the export earnings they vitally need.

Each of the G-5 nations pledged to undertake steps to support noninflationary growth and resist protectionist pressures. In nations where budget deficits were too high, including the United States, there was a specific agreement to reduce government expenditures as a share of GNP in order to reduce the budget deficit.

All five nations agreed that exchange rates, as Volcker put it, "should play a role in adjusting external imbalances." Then came the object of the whole exercise: "Some further orderly appreciation of the now non-dollar currencies against the dollar is desirable. [The signatories stand ready] to cooperate more closely to encourage this when to do so would be helpful." At the Plaza Meeting, Japan's Foreign Minister Noboru Takeshita agreed to allow the Japanese yen to fall more than 10 percent relative to the dollar. By October, aided by $3 billion of intervention in international currency markets, the dollar had fallen 12 percent against the Yen and 9 percent against European currencies. By January, the dollar stood an average 25 percent below the peak it had hit one year earlier. The dollar continued to decline for the next two years.

Subsequently, the Plaza Accord hit a wall. As Baker pressed Germany and Japan to adopt policies that would increase United States exports, two key United States trading partners resisted. As Toyoo Gyohten, a senior official in the Japanese Ministry of Finance, wrote in a joint memoir with Volcker: "The surplus nations were obsessed by a deep suspicion that in introducing policy coordination and exchange rate management, the United States was trying to impose on them a system that would benefit only itself. Our response therefore was defensive and displayed a lack of willingness to contribute positively to the global economic benefit. In other words, regrettably, there was a serious lack of mutual trust among the three major countries."

The other leading global economies were deeply concerned by the 25 percent increase in the dollar against other major currencies.

In 1986, the Democrats regained the Senate, picking up seats to achieve a 55–45 majority. The Democratic majority in the House was increased by 5 seats to 258-183, prompting concerns among the central bankers about protectionism. In 1985, according to one count, 400 bills were introduced to protect American products.

During Volcker's time as chair, there was a follow up effort signed on February 22, 1987, that resulted in the Louvre Accord, which created ranges around exchange rates that would be defended by intervention by the six signatory Nations: France, Germany, Japan, Canada, United States, and United Kingdom.

The Louvre Accord reaffirmed "concerns over continuing pressures for protectionism" and "agreed to intensify their economic policy coordination efforts in order to promote more balanced global growth and to reduce existing imbalances." Each of the signatory nations agreed to a specified undertaking. France, for example, agreed to reduce its budget deficit by 1 percent, the United States to reduce its 1988 deficit to 2.3 of GNP from 3.9 percent in 1987.

Only in the last two sentences of the Accord was the basic point underlined: "Further substantial exchange rate shifts among their currencies could damage growth and adjustment prospects in their countries. In current circumstances, therefore, they agreed to cooperate closely to foster stability of exchange rates around current levels."

The exchange rates ranges were kept secret. Whether this and other efforts at international coordination might have worked became moot after global stock markets dramatically fell in October 1987. The United States Dow Jones lost 22.6 percent on October 19, 1987, prompting James Baker to persuade Reagan to again let the dollar depreciate, which it did between October and December 1987, declining from 1.80 to 1.63 Deutsche marks per dollar.

In 1987, Volcker decided not to seek reappointment as Fed Chair. Alan Greenspan had been interviewed by Treasury Secretary Baker for the Fed Chair in March 1987. Reagan wrote in the spring of 1987: "We're going to see if Alan Greenspan will take the job if Paul will step down gracefully." Volcker and Baker were not in agreement about international currency coordination. Both Baker and former Treasury Secretary Regan were not supportive of Volcker's reappointment. In Bob Woodward's account:

> Baker thought that Reagan should have his own Fed chairman — someone from his party, someone in tune with his values. As Baker frequently remarked, Volcker was a "known Democrat," as if the Fed chairman were a subversive. Baker had no illusions that a Fed chairman could be ordered about or subjected to political control. But he found Volcker needlessly aloof and prickly, unreceptive to the sorts of consensus solutions Baker preferred.

In June 1987, Reagan announced that Alan Greenspan would succeed Volcker in August 1987, when Volcker's second four-year term as chair ended. On February 24, 1986, Volcker had been confronted by a 4–3 majority of the Fed Board, all nominated by Reagan, who sought to cut interest rates when Volcker believed it was unwise to do so. In Woodward's account:

> One of Baker's early picks for the Fed board was Manuel H. Johnson Jr., his 36 year old assistant treasury secretary, a former Green Beret intelligence specialist. Johnson had told his boss that he believed interest rates should be lowered, and that the Fed's interest rate policy should be coordinated with the White House and Treasury.
>
> Soon after Johnson joined the board in 1986, he told Volcker he was expected to vote for an interest rate cut the first chance he got. "I felt compelled to vote for one. It's needed," Johnson said. Volcker was appalled, concluding that Johnson had made a deal.
>
> . . ."Is Baker pressuring you to do this?" Volcker asked, putting his feet on his desk and lighting a cigar.
>
> "I'm sure Jim Baker supports this," Johnson replied. "He knows how I'll vote."
>
> On February 24, 1986, Johnson and three other board members took charge and voted 4 to 3 to lower the discount rate. Volcker found himself in the minority for the first time.
>
> "Good-bye," he announced to the board after the vote was taken. "You're going to have to do it on your own." He got up and walked out, slamming the door. Hard. He didn't type, so when he got back to his office he wrote out his resignation letter by hand. Voting down the chairman was an outright rebellion as far as he was concerned, an un-Federal Reserve thing to do. It was a staggering breach of club etiquette. Federal Reserve tradition virtually compelled the board to deal with disagreements and division by working toward consensus. Meet Tuesday. Meet Wednesday. Meet Thursday. If it was the chairman who disagreed, by God, they should meet endlessly.

Volcker's account in his memoir was more muted: "While only one or two reserve banks were any longer initiating requests to reduce the discount rate, much to my surprise and for motives I still do not fully comprehend, a sudden vote was forced on the board to approve such a reduction by a four-to-three majority. . . . A unilateral cut at that time was entirely unacceptable to me." The vote was reconsidered later with the Board then reflecting a preference for coordinated rate cuts with Germany and Japan.

By the conclusion of Volcker's eight years as chair, the role and powers of the Federal Reserve System were fully developed.

As with William McChesney Martin, Volcker had ably defended the qualified independence of the Fed. Volcker was a realist and well understood that in Washington, all power was bounded. But within the realities of a four-year term and presidential power to appoint Fed governors, Volcker had achieved the near impossible in 1981 and 1982 by shrinking the growth of the money supply with coordinate higher interest rates. Hyperinflation had been tamed. The psychology that high rates of inflation were inevitable had been beaten. This had been Volcker and the Fed's signal achievement during Volcker's time as chair and would have been impossible in the electoral political process alone either under Carter or Reagan. Only an agency with the bounded independence of the Fed and a Fed chair as strong willed and talented as Volcker could have achieved this. The subsequent decades of lower inflation and economic expansion were Volcker's greatest legacy.

But taming hyperinflation, as critical as it was, came with enormous costs. Double digit unemployment, the partial destruction of the S & L industry, and the undermining of international financial practices also were aspects of the sometimes brutal economic realities of the 1980s.

The Fed's focus during Volcker's time as chair largely was on monetary policy. While the Fed in the post-World War II period justifiably could be proud of its talented examination and technical staff, other aspects of the Fed's statutory responsibilities including bank supervision and the Fed's role in administering consumer legislation such as the Truth in Lending or Equal Credit Opportunities Acts received at best second order attention.

Volcker to a greater degree than Bernanke, Paulson and Geithner in 2007–2009 deferred to the jerrybuilt structure of American finance with dual federal and state regulation of the S & L, securities, insurance, and housing industries. Keeping to his lane may have been politically wise but made the Fed's response to the 1980s S & L and banking crises reactive, often laggard. The role that the Fed achieved in 2008 and 2009 was to have a greater responsibility in managing National and international systemic risk.

Could hyperinflation have been tamed with substantially lower costs? This is the ultimate policy question about Volcker's Chairmanship and a fair response to this question must begin by recognizing the political limits of the Fed. In a political administration long backed by substantial majorities of the American electorate that was willing to accept massive deficits rather than raise taxes or cut defense spending, the Fed's powers were limited.

Volcker understood that compromise was necessary to achieve a seat at the table for coordination of the Fed monetary policy with the Executive Branch tax and budget policies. Coordination in every political administration from Franklin Delano Roosevelt on came with tensions and costs. The Fed frequently had to push back against administration and congressional pressures to cut interest rates. Political administrations, both Democrat and Republican, regularly resisted Fed recommendations to cut budgets or raise taxes as politically insensitive.

Volcker built on the Fed role decisively initiated by William McChesney Martin to secure participation in international finance as a critical function for the Fed. This role also was bounded. The Treasury and the president took the lead in devaluation or currency exchange decisions, and always took the lead with respect to tariffs. But Volcker's background in international finance and global network of financial and political leaders who respected his competence and political skill gave Volcker a broad role in international finance.

By the end of Volcker's two terms, the role of the Fed had been fortified as an equal or near equal with the Treasury in United States economic policy making. The Fed was the United States Central Bank and was respected or criticized as such. Much was left incomplete at the end of Volcker's second term, most significantly the cleanup of the S & L and banking debacles and continued efforts to stabilize international finance. But the generally favorable view with which his Chairmanship was regarded was fairly earned. Volcker had used his talent, realism and political skills to fundamentally redirect the trajectory of the United States economy.[41]

The Greenspan Chairmanship

Volcker was succeeded by Alan Greenspan, who would serve nearly 19 years as chair, from 1987 to 2006, the second longest tenure in Fed history, exceeded only by William McChesney Martin. Greenspan served under four presidents: Reagan, George H.W. Bush, Clinton, and George W. Bush. Bob Woodward entitled his 2000 book about Greenspan, *The Maestro.* Greenspan was hailed at the Kansas City Federal Reserve Jackson Hole Conference in 2005 as the greatest Central Banker in history, a man who, along with Secretary of the Treasury Robert Rubin and Deputy Treasury Secretary Larry Summers, was depicted on a *Time* Magazine cover as The Committee to Save the World after their efforts to ameliorate debt crises in Mexico, Thailand, Indonesia, South Korea, and Russia during the 1990s.

Greenspan as Federal Reserve chair would be much praised for his responses to the October 1987 Stock Market Crash and terrorist attacks on September 11, 2001. He would help fortify a booming economy after the Dot-Com crash of 2000, with low interest rates and light touch Fed oversight of mortgages and mortgage debt. His response, as he later wrote to the financial uncertainty of 2000 and 2001, "was to maintain our program of aggressively loosening short-term interest rates."

In retrospect, his support of the easy money policies of the 2000s would be the basis of the most fervent criticism of Greenspan's chairmanship. He would be brutally criticized after the 2007–2009 Crisis for contributing to the housing bubble. Senate Majority Leader Harry Reid in 2005 would call Greenspan "one of the biggest political hacks we have in Washington" for his support of President Bush's plan to privatize Social Security. Economist Paul Krugman would echo Reid's critique of Greenspan's support of privatizing Social Security as well as criticizing Greenspan's support of the Bush 2001 tax cuts in a *New York Times* 2005 opinion excoriating the Three-Card Maestro for "repeatedly shilling for whatever the Bush administration wants, he has betrayed the trust placed in Fed Chairman, and deserves to be treated as just another partisan hack."

Greg Ip, writing in the *Wall Street Journal* in 2008, described Greenspan's reputation as tarnished in the view of his critics on two main grounds:

> First, they say, his Fed lowered rates too much from 2001 to 2003 to cushion the economy from the bursting dotcom bubble. Then it took too long to raise them again. Low rates fueled mortgage borrowing, driving home prices to unsustainable heights.
>
> Second, they say, the Fed was lax in its regulatory role. The central bank failed to press for stiffer rules for underwriting

> mortgages to people who ultimately couldn't afford them, they say. Also, they say, the Fed failed to anticipate banks' exposure to risky home buyers, leaving them with too little capital to absorb the eventual losses on those mortgages.

A balanced view was accorded Greenspan by Benjamin Friedman in a 2008 review of Greenspan's book, *The Age of Turbulence*:

> [I]t is worth recalling that U.S. monetary policy — broadly defined as the management of interest rates in order to control inflation and to maintain stable growth — has had a strikingly good run during the last two decades.
>
> The United States experienced only two recessions during that time, in 1990–1991 and in 2001 (there were four during the prior twenty years, and four during the twenty years before that), with neither lasting longer than eight months and in neither case involving a decline in total production as great as 1 percent. Unemployment averaged just 5.2 percent of the labor force (4.9 percent during the most recent ten years). Already by the mid-1980s price inflation had abated to 4 percent per year, down from near-double digits at the beginning of the decade, but since then it has been lower still and also far more stable. During the last ten years the average annual price increase, apart from food and energy, has been 1.75 percent, with no year's rise either below 1.25 percent or more than 2.25 percent.

Much has been made of Greenspan's early involvement with the libertarian Ayn Rand and the politics of objectivism. A 1966 article, reprinted in Ayn Rand's book, *Capitalism: The Unknown Ideal*, Greenspan wrote entitled *Gold and Economic Freedom* would excoriate statists for their "hysterical antagonism toward the gold standard" and in the heated language of a committed libertarian explain:

> Stripped of its academic jargon, the welfare state is nothing more than a mechanism by which governments confiscate the wealth of the productive members of a society to support a wide variety of welfare schemes. A substantial part of the confiscation is effected by taxation. . . . In the absence of the gold standard, there is no way to protect savings from confiscation through inflation.

Greenspan's politics by the time he began at the Fed two decades later were more nuanced. In his 2007 memoir, Greenspan would criticize Rand's philosophy as naïve:

> According to objectivist precepts, taxation was immoral because it allowed for government appropriation of private property by force. Yet if taxation was wrong, how could you reliably finance the essential functions of government, including the protection of individuals' rights through police power? The Randian answer, that those who rationally saw the need for government would contribute voluntarily, was inadequate. People have free will; suppose they refused?

Greenspan nonetheless was the most deregulatory chair in recent Fed history. Greenspan found "the broader philosophy of unfettered market competition compelling." In 1998, he would oppose federal regulation of derivative securities as "unnecessary." Greenspan viewed specific provisions of the 2002 Sarbanes-Oxley Act as "[decreasing] U.S. competitive flexibility." He long articulated the belief "that the Glass-Steagall Act, which in 1933 separated the business of securities underwriting from commercial banking was based on faulty history."

Greenspan earned a B.A. degree from New York University's Stern School of Management in 1948 and an M.A. in 1950. Greenspan would describe what was then called the NYU School of Commerce, Accounts and Finance as "the largest and possibly the least prestigious part of NYU. It had ten thousand students and people thought of it more as a trade school than a real college. . . . But to my mind, this was unfair. I got a very good education." He later pursued a Ph.D. at Columbia working with faculty adviser Arthur Burns, which he did not complete because he was "just too busy to get it done." In 1977, he would be awarded a Ph.D. in Economics from N.Y.U.

Greenspan's "primary obsession was math." In 1951, at Columbia, Greenspan worked with Professor Jacob Wolfowitz, a mentor who helped him "to see that I might someday attempt to understand and forecast the economy as a whole," through what was then called mathematical statistics and later econometrics. "In later years I developed," Greenspan wrote, "some skill in building quite large econometric models and came to a deeper appreciation of their uses and, especially, their limitations. Modern dynamic economies do not stay still long enough to allow for an accurate reading of their underlying structure."

From 1948 to 1953, he worked at the Conference Board, a private institution underwritten by major corporations, which did "thorough, disciplined research, based on the theory that the availability of objective knowledge might help businessmen and union leaders find common ground." Greenspan recalled:

> Almost from the start, I began publishing articles in *Business Record*, the Conference Board's monthly journal. The first, about trends in small manufacturers' profits, was based on a brand-new statistical series from the Federal Trade Commission and the Securities and Exchange Commission. After wringing every detail from the data, I declared, with all the enthusiasm of youth, "Since small business may act as a barometer of cyclical movements, a survey of both the immediate and long-term trends in small corporate manufacturing is of particular interest."
>
> Over the next few years, my work gained momentum. Somebody picked up on one of my articles and wrote about it in the *New York Times*, and even mentioned my name. I finished my master's degree at NYU and continued publishing in a steady stream — articles on housing starts, the new-car market, consumer credit, and other current subjects. I was gaining confidence in my ability to take in data and make them tell a story. And while I was far from comfortable trying to comprehend the economy as a whole — leave that to the Keynesians — I understood more and more about its parts and how they connected.

Throughout Greenspan's career as Fed Chair, data more than theory would matter. Fed economist Rolen Hetzel would describe Volcker and Greenspan as sharing "an intense dislike of inflation and a concern for inflationary expectations," but criticized Greenspan for leading the Federal Open Market Committee without an articulated Greenspan strategy. "Greenspan's . . . characterization of the Fed was that of crisis manager."

For most of 32 years beginning at the age of 27, Greenspan was chair and president of Townsend-Greenspan, a highly successful New York City economic consulting firm. "The key," Greenspan wrote, "to Townsend-Greenspan's appeal was our ability to translate economic analysis into a form business leaders could apply in making decisions." Greenspan based models on forecasts and empirical data.

By 1968, when Greenspan joined Richard Nixon's campaign for president:

> I had long since decided to engage in efforts to advance free-market capitalism as an insider, not a critical pamphleteer. When I agreed to accept the nomination as chairman of the President's Council of Economic Advisors, I knew I would have to pledge to uphold not only the Constitution but also the laws of the land, many of which I thought were wrong. The existence of a democratic society governed by the rule of law implies a lack of unanimity on almost every aspect of the public agenda. Compromise on public issues is the price of civilization, not an abrogation of principle.

Greenspan worked as interim Budget Director before Nixon's 1969 Inaugural. Between 1974 and 1977, Greenspan served as chair of the Council of Economic Advisers under Presidents Nixon and Ford. Greenspan only agreed to accept the position as chair of the Council of Economic Advisors after he was reassured by Nixon's Chief of Staff Alexander Haig that Nixon would not reimpose wage and price controls.[42]

Philosophically, Greenspan was attracted to Reagan's "clarity of... conservatism." Reagan often used the line on the stump:

> "Government exists to protect us from each other. Where government has gone beyond its limits is in deciding to protect us from ourselves." A man who talks in such terms is clear on what he believes. Very rarely in those days would you find conservatives who didn't fudge on social issues. But Reagan's kind of conservatism was to say that tough love is good for the individual and good for society. That proposition starts with a judgment about human nature. If it's accurate, then it implies much less government support for the downtrodden. Yet mainstream Republicans were conflicted about thinking or talking in such terms, because they seemed contrary to Judeo-Christian values. Not Reagan. Like Milton Friedman and other early libertarians, he never gave the impression he was trying to be on both sides of the issue.

Between 1981 and 1983, Greenspan chaired a bipartisan commission to address the what was estimated to be a $150 to $200 billion Social Security deficit anticipated during the 1980s. Greenspan led what came to be known as the Greenspan Commission with considerable skill. Commission members as disparate as Alexander Trowbridge, who led the National Association of Manufacturers, and Representative Claude Pepper, an 81-year-old Florida Democrat who, Greenspan aptly described as "a senior citizen's icon," accepted

Greenspan's support of Pat Moynihan's aphorism: "You're entitled to your own opinion, but you're not entitled to your own facts."

The 15-member commission, with five members named by Reagan, five by Tip O'Neil, the Speaker of the House and five by Senate Majority Leader Howard Baker in consultation with Senate minority leader agreed to several compromises, what Greenspan termed "pain for everyone." Employers were subject to accelerated increases in payroll taxes. Employers also were subject to higher taxes and the age of eligibility for unreduced benefits was raised in two stages to 67 by the year 2027. Retirees had to accept six-month delays in cost of living increases and beginning in 1984, up to one half of Social Security benefits for benefit recipients above income thresholds were subject to income taxation. Both the Greenspan Commission Report and the Social Security Amendments based on that Report that were enacted in April 1983 were praised for then successfully resolving the Social Security funding crisis.

By 1987, the Reagan presidency was in its twilight. For all Reagan's success with the economy and helping end the Cold War, he had been badly battered by the Iran Contra Scandal. In flat contravention to the 1982 Boland Amendment, which prohibited the Defense Department or CIA from helping fund the Nicaraguan Contras, the Reagan Administration was found to have sold 2000 missiles to Iran and redirected the proceeds to the Contras. Reagan denied direct knowledge of the deal but *Wall Street Journal* and *Washington Post/ABC* Polls reported that 66 and 69 percent of the American people believed that Reagan was lying. After the Democrats won control of the Senate in 1986, two Reagan nominees for the United States Supreme Court, Robert Bork and Douglas Ginsburg, were not confirmed.

In contrast, on August 3, 1987, the Senate confirmed Greenspan as Fed Chair by a near unanimous vote of 91–2. He was sworn in eight days later on August 1, 1987.

Greenspan began in Volcker's shadow. When Greenspan had been nominated, the *Wall Street Journal* had published an article reflecting doubts in the financial community that Greenspan would act sufficiently independently of the Reagan Administration:

> By picking Mr. Greenspan, who headed the Council of Economic Advisers under President Ford, Mr. Reagan signed on a man who comes as close as anyone to enjoying Mr. Volcker's credibility in financial markets. The 61-year-old economist is expected to generally pursue policies on inflation, interest rates

> and economic growth that may appear almost indistinguishable from Mr. Volcker's.
>
> Even so, Mr. Greenspan faces a dauting challenge in proving to the financial markets that he is a worthy replacement for the outgoing Fed chief. The bond market, reacting to the news that Mr. Volcker won't stay on, took its worst pounding in years. The dollar also plunged yesterday against all major currencies.

In early September 1987, at a time when commodity prices, as the Fed Annual Report explained, were "soaring" and "sharp declines in the dollar and bond prices signaled the possibility of greater inflationary dangers," the FOMC voted unanimously to raise the discount rate to 6 percent, a .5 percent increase. In Woodward's account, Volcker called: "Congratulations. Now that you've raised the discount rate, you're a central banker."

Greenspan in the first years of his chairmanship was a determined inflation fighter. In April 1987, the Fed raised the federal funds rate to 6.5 percent when the 30-year bond interest rate had risen from 7.4 percent at the start of 1987 to 8.5 percent. After his August confirmation, 30-year bonds continued to rise. On September 22, 1987, the FOMC increased the federal funds rate to 7 percent. In early October, Greenspan appeared on the television program *This Week with David Brinkley* and warned about "dangerously high interest rates" if financial markets fears of rising inflation "start to mushroom." The 30-year bond rate did continue to soar, reaching 10.25 percent on October 19.

Rising interest rates typically lead to lower stock market prices. On September 22, 1987, the Dow Jones Industrial Average lost 75.23 points (approximately 2.9 percent). From the close of trading on October 13, 1987, to the close of trading on October 19, 1987, the Dow Jones Industrial Average fell 769 points (31 percent), including a one-day drop on October 19, 1987, of 508 points (22.6 percent) on a record volume of 604 million shares. In percentage terms, this was the largest one day decline in history, approximately double the 11.7 percent decline in the stock market on October 29, 1929, the largest fall of the 1929–1933 Stock Market Crash. In the first hour of trading on October 19, the Dow Jones Industrial Average underwent a kind of "free fall," losing 220 points, or 11.2 percent.

Greenspan, working closely with New York Federal Reserve President Gerry Corrigan, responded calmly. On October 20, the Fed put out a one sentence statement before the stock market opened that was reassuring: "The Federal Reserve, consistent with its responsibilities as the Nation's central bank, affirmed today its readiness to support the economic and financial system." Corrigan made dozens of calls to leading banks and securities firms urging them to continue lending and trading — "stay in the game." As Greenspan paraphrased Corrigan's basic message:

> Simply ordering a bank to make a loan, say, would be an abuse of government power and would damage the functioning of the market. Instead, the gist of Gerry's message to the banker had to be: "We're not telling you to lend; all we ask is that you consider the overall interests of your business. Just remember that people have long memories, and if you shut off credit to a customer just because you're a little nervous about him, but with no concrete reason, he's going to remember that." That week Corrigan had dozens of conversations along these lines, and though I never knew the details, some of those phone calls must have been very tough. I'm sure he bit off a few earlobes.
>
> As all this was going on, we were careful to keep supplying liquidity to the system. The FOMC ordered the traders at the New York Fed to buy billions of dollars of treasury securities on the open market. This had the effect of putting more money into circulation and lowering short-term rates. Though we'd been tightening interest rates before the crash, we were now easing them to help keep the economy moving.

In part because of the Fed's measured response to the October 19, 1987 crash, the economy stabilized, growing at 2 percent in the first three months of 1988 and 5 percent in the next three months. By the spring of 1988 as it became clear that the economy still was strong, the focus of the Fed shifted to a "concern about a worsening of inflation" and a "tightening of the reserve market that began in late March [1988] and continued in several steps into 1989." Short term interest rates at the end of 1988 were about 2.5 percent higher than they were in the spring.[43]

The George H.W. Bush Presidency

On November 8, 1988, George H.W. Bush was decisively elected President with 53.4 percent of the popular vote to 45.6 percent to Massachusetts Governor Michael Dukakis. This was the first presidential election since Roosevelt and Truman that an incumbent party had won the presidency for a third consecutive term. Congress was little changed. The Democratic Majority in the Senate increased by one Senator to 55–45; the Democratic majority in the House increased by two seats to 260–175.

Bush's campaign combined two contradictory themes. On the one hand, Bush sought a "kinder, gentler nation" typified by "a brilliant diversity spread like stars, like a thousand points of light in a broad and peaceful sky." He would be a more moderate President than Reagan who would sign the Americans with Disabilities Act of 1990, amendments to the 1990 Clean Air Act, and amendments to enhance Head Start. Unlike Reagan who pointedly insisted: "[G]overnment is not the solution to our problem, government is the problem," Bush more mildly would state: "I do not hate government. A government that remembers that the people are its master is a good and needed thing."

On the other hand, Bush was intensely competitive. He ran highly negative ads designed by conservative stalwarts Roger Ailes and Lee Atwater to defeat Bob Dole in the primaries and against the Democratic Candidate Michael Dukakis in the general election. The Willie Horton ad lambasted Dukakis for the furlough of a convicted African American murderer helped Bush overcome a 13 to 16 point Dukakis lead in polls on Memorial Day. Atwater bragged in June: "If I can make Willie Horton a household name, we'll win the election."

In a similar tough guy spirit, Bush had paraphrased a line from a Clint Eastwood movie in his acceptance speech: "The Congress will push me to raise taxes, and I'll say no, and they'll push, and I'll say no, and they'll push again, and I'll say to them, 'Read my lips: No new taxes.' "

The Bush presidency would best be remembered for foreign policy achievements, so much so that when Bush cowrote his memoir, *A World Transformed*, with National Security Advisor Brent Scowcroft, he ignored domestic policy and the economy. Bush's adroit handling of the end of communism in Russia and the unsuccessful coup attempt against the final Soviet leader Mikhail Gorbachev, the broad international coalition Bush assembled that responded to Iraq and its leader Saddam Hussein with Operation Desert Storm, his negotiation of the North American Free Trade Agreement (*NAFTA*), and two Strategic Arms Reduction Treaties would be highlights of his presidency.

But Bush's presidency would rise and fall on the economy. In his nomination acceptance speech, Bush emphasized his determination to continue Reagan's economic record:

> Eight years ago I stood here with Ronald Reagan and we promised, together, to break with the past and return America to her greatness. Eight years later look at what the American people have produced: the highest level of economic growth in our entire history....
>
> Consider the size of our triumph: A record high percentage of Americans with jobs, a record high rate of new businesses—a record high rate of real personal income....
>
> Inflation was 12 percent when we came in. We got it down to four. Interest rates were more than 21. We cut them in half. Unemployment was up and climbing, now it's the lowest in 14 years....
>
> We've created seventeen million new jobs in the past five years—more than twice as many as Europe and Japan combined.

For Bush, the $152.6 billion deficit he inherited from Reagan would be the albatross that would undermine his presidency. Bush understood that unless he was willing to compromise with Democratic majorities in the House and Senate and raise taxes, there would not be sufficient legislative support for spending caps. In June 1990, Bush, broke his "Read My Lips" pledge not to raise taxes and agreed to support the bipartisan 1990 Omnibus Budget Reconciliation Act. The 1990 Tax Act increased the highest individual income tax rate from 28 to 31 percent, limited itemized deductions, raised the cap on Medicare taxable wages from $53,400 to $125,000, imposed a 30 percent excise tax on luxury automobiles priced at $30,000 or over, boats at $100,000 or more, airplanes above $250,000, and furs more than $10,000, as well as increased gasoline taxes by 5 cents per gallon, and increased taxes on tobacco and alcohol.

These tax increases combined with the simultaneously enacted Budget Enforcement Act that capped discretionary domestic spending and imposed a PAYGO or "pay as you go" system requiring budget cuts or tax increases equal to any new spending would prove inadequate during Bush's term, 1989–1993, to move towards a more balanced budget. The federal deficit would escalate to $221 billion in 1990, $269.2 billion in 1991, $290.3 billion in 1992. Debt as a percentage of GDP would grow from 39.3 to 47.9 percent between 1989 and 1993.

Bush feared as he wrote in his diary on April 2, 1989: "I cannot break my 'Read My Lips' pledge. I would be totally destroyed if I did." Conservative opposition to Bush effectively began after the 1990 tax deal. Republican Minority Leader Newt Gingrich informed Bush on September 30, 1990, that he could not support the tax increases. "It breaks your word, and it is a mistake, and I won't do it." John Meacham explained in his biography of Bush:

> Gingrich represented a conservative worldview in which Ronald Reagan, the rightful king, had been replaced by Bush, a pale usurper who was betraying the tax-cutting principles on which the Republican presidential ascendancy of the 1980s had been built. "Bush was a Connecticut moderate Republican translated to Texas," Gingrich recalled. "He was probably a Ford Republican, really. I was a conservative Reaganite who wanted to take on the welfare state and defeat the Soviet Union. Bush was not viscerally opposed to the welfare state and had been more for managing the Soviet threat in the Cold War than he had been for rolling it back. Those were profound differences."

The nation began a recession in 1990 which lasted until 1991 with a slow recovery. Unemployment grew from 5.9 percent in Bush's first year to 7.8 percent in July 1992. Unemployment only declined to 7.3 percent by December 1992.

During Bush's presidency, Greenspan dealt primarily with Treasury Secretary Nicholas Brady, Office of Management and Budget Director Richard Darman, and Chair of the Council of Economic Advisers Michael Boskin.

Nicholas Brady, a long-time friend of Bush and a fellow Yale graduate, had served more than three decades on Wall Street and risen to become chair of the investment firm of Dillon Read, was named Secretary of Treasury. Brady had briefly been a United States Senator from New Jersey. As a long-time corporate chief executive officer, he was more used to hierarchical command than political give and take.

Richard Darman was Director of the Office of Management and Budget. "Darman," Greenspan would write in his memoir, "was in many ways similar to David Stockman — a major league policy intellectual and a believer in sound fiscal management. Unlike Stockman, though, Darman was often less direct with people and was more driven by political expediency. Over time, I learned to keep my distance."

Brady and Darman were sharply critical of the Fed. Both favored sharper interest rate cuts than Greenspan at times was willing to support. "Darman," in Woodward's account, "went on a binge of criticizing the Fed. He flooded Greenspan with memos and taxes. His core argument was that the Fed was mismanaging the money supply." Darman also believed that a public declaration that rates would be lowered would give the economy a needed boost. Greenspan would be upset when Darman on *Meet the Press* in August 1989, tartly declared: "It's important to not merely support Chairman Greenspan but the other members of the Board and the [Federal Open Market Committee] . . . be more attentive to avoid tipping the economy into recession."

In 1991, Greenspan received a letter from Brady after a White House lunch with Bush and eight prominent economists, each of whom opined a short-term interest rate cut "could do no harm." Brady's letter stated: "Alan, in my travels, you stand alone in your view" and complained bluntly of the "lack of forceful leadership by the Fed."

The impasse on monetary policy led Brady to cancel the weekly luncheon between the Treasury Secretary and the Fed Chair. Greenspan continued: "With the election year nearing, the administration decided to change its approach to the Fed and its pigheaded Chairman. The 'Greenspan account' as they called it in the White House, shifted to [Council of Economic Advisers] Chairman Michael Boskin and the President himself."[44]

Greenspan's relationship with Bush was more genteel. Greenspan would consider Bush's defeat in 1992 "tragic." Bush, who Greenspan believed had done a flawless job on the nation's most important policy issues — the confrontation with, and eventual collapse of the Soviet Union and also the Gulf War — deserved reelection.

Yet the perennial administration pressures to cut rates persisted under Bush. Greenspan had declined to support lowering interest rates before the 1990 Tax and Budget Deal. In his 1991 State of the Union address, Bush argued: "There has been too much pessimism. Sound banks should be making sound loans now, and interest rates should be lower, now." During the 1990–1992 recession and sluggish recovery, the Fed would ease monetary policy in 1991, in ten separate steps lowering the federal funds rate from 7 to

4 percent. At year-end 1991, the discount rate was at its lowest level in nearly 30 years. The federal funds rate was down to 4 percent, its lowest sustained level since the 1960s. Throughout much of 1992, the Federal Reserve System reported: "The discount rate was reduced to 3 percent, and short-term rates generally closed the year at their lowest levels since the early 1960s."

From the point-of-view of Bush, the critical moment for Greenspan and the Fed came later in 1992 after Greenspan had been renominated for a second term as Fed Chair on July 10. On June 23, 1992, Bush informed the *New York Times*: "I'd like to see another lowering of interest rates." The Fed had cut the discount rate and federal funds rate by 0.5 percent on July 2 immediately after Department of Labor had reported that unemployment had risen to 7.8 percent. On September 4, 1992, the Fed lowered the Federal Funds Rate by another 0.25 percent. With the economy exhibiting renewed growth in the second half including a 4 percent gain in GDP, the Fed declined to go further keeping short term interest rates unchanged toward the end of the year.

Years later, Greenspan would be saddened to learn that Bush blamed him for his 1992 election loss. "I reappointed him and he disappointed me," Bush would state in a 1998 television interview. Greenspan assumed that Brady and Darman had convinced Bush that the Fed had sabotaged him.[45]

Despite these tensions, the Fed and the Bush Administration had considerable success cleaning up the S & L and bank crises of the 1980s.

By 1985, the Federal Savings and Loan Insurance Corporation (*FSLIC*) had only $4.6 billion remaining in its S & L insurance fund. In 1986, Federal Home Loan Bank Board Chair Edwin Gray estimated that for the FSLIC to resolve S & Ls needing assistance, it would cost $23.5 billion.

In 1986, the Treasury and Federal Home Loan Bank Board presented a FSLIC recapitalization plan authorizing the FSLIC to borrow up to $15 billion by issuing 30-year bonds through a new financial corporation. The interest on the 30-year bonds would be paid by future S & L deposit insurance premium revenues, including as necessary, special assessments. Repayment of the 30-year bonds would be provided by the commitment of up to $3 billion from the 12 federal home loan bank boards. The full plan anticipated $25 billion to resolve failed or failing S & Ls by also using S & L special assessments and debt sales by the FSLIC.

The Reagan administration under this plan would not add to the already swollen federal deficit and sought during the 1986 election year to avoid the negative publicity that would occur had the administration acknowledged that the FSLIC was insolvent.

Congress also felt little sense of urgency. There had not been widespread depositor runs on the S & Ls and the Federal Home Loan Bank Board through mergers and changes in accounting principles had kept even insolvent S & Ls operating. The degree to which the regulatory accounting principles of the Federal Home Loan Bank Board masked the widespread insolvency of the S & L industry in 1986 was then not generally understood. Moreover, the United States Savings & Loan League, the industry's lobbying organization opposed the Treasury/Federal Home Loan Bank Board recapitalization plan as placing an intolerable burden on solvent S & Ls.

Neither the Senate nor the House moved with alacrity. Only in 1987, did the Senate pass a bill with a $7.5 billion recapitalization. No more than $3.75 billion could be spent in any 12-month period. The subsequently enacted House bill authorized only $5 billion and included a provision modeled on the Federal Home Loan Bank Board's much criticized Capital Forbearance Program, which allowed S & Ls with a net worth as low as 0.5 percent to continue to operate. The House bill would "forebear" requiring compliance with the higher S & L industrial capital requirements when there was compliance with specified good faith provisions.

On March 3, 1987, Frederick Wolf, Director of the General Accounting Office, Accounting and Management Division, testified to a House subcommittee on the accelerating deterioration of the FSLIC's solvency. The FSLIC's insurance fund had $6.3 billion in 1981. The GAO in 1987 had "preliminarily determined that the FSLIC needs to establish a contingent liability in the range of $8 billion to handle cases that will require attention in the near future." The FSLIC, in the GAO's estimate, "would have a deficit of over $3 billion at the end of 1986." And the FSLIC was not addressing its full case load: "In 1986, FSLIC acted on only about half of its serious cases. During the same time, its serious case list doubled in size. At December 31, 1985, FSLIC had 93 cases involving S & Ls that it considered to be in serious financial trouble. One year later, the list virtually doubled to 183."

The GAO believed anything less than the $25 billion proposed in the Treasury/Federal Home Loan Bank Board plan "would be too little." The GAO warned, however, that the $25 billion proposed in the Reagan administration plan would only work:

> without depleting the fund's reserves as long as FSLIC's income is augmented either by continuing special premium assessments, which are phased out over 5 years under the proposal, or by receipts from sales of assets acquired through liquidations. We wish to emphasize that this solution, however, virtually preempts FSLIC's future income stream to deal with current problems. Accordingly, if the industry were to suffer significant further declines — either from imprudent management at individual institutions or from adverse economic conditions — FSLIC would not have funds available to deal with the consequences.

In a separate GAO Report on the Treasury/Federal Home Loan Bank Board for FSLIC recapitalization, the GAO pointedly added:

> Officials at Treasury have said that two primary determinants of the recapitalization plan's structure were (1) the plan had to be financed by the industry and (2) there should be no effect on the federal budget deficit. Elimination of one or both of these two criteria would expand the financing options available to rescue FSLIC. For example, it would be simpler and less expensive if FSLIC were to borrow the needed funds directly from Treasury, and rely on industry financing to repay the loan through a combination of a $3 billion contribution from the FHL Banks and a redirection of a portion of FSLIC's future income stream. Such a plan, however, would increase the budget deficit by $15 billion as the money was spent to resolve FSLIC cases.

In July 1987, Congress enacted a revised version of the Federal Savings and Loan Insurance Corporation Enabling Act raising the FSLIC additional capitalization to $8.5 billion. After the GAO March 1987 Report and Testimony, the White House threatened a veto unless this amount was increased further. This was marginally achieved in the Competitive Equality Bank Act of 1987, which Reagan signed on August 10, 1987.

Similar to the Treasury/Federal Home Loan Bank Board proposal, a new Financing Corporation or *FICO* was authorized to borrow up to $10.825 billion with the *proviso* that no more than $3.75 billion could be borrowed each year. FICO was to be capitalized by a $3 billion investment by the 12 federal home loan banks in nonvoting stock in FICO. FICO would operate under the management of a three member board, two of whom would be selected by the Federal Home Loan Bank Board from among the presidents of the Federal Home Loan Bank Boards, and the third director would be the Director of the Office of Finance of the Federal Home Loan Bank.

There was no direct United States government investment in FICO, which was intended to recapitalize the FSLIC, nor were FICO or FSLIC obligations guaranteed by the full faith and credit of the United States.

The Competitive Equality Banking Act of 1987 prohibited the FSLIC from terminating an FSLIC insured S & L, but the FSLIC could continue to arrange mergers. Accounting principles were tightened to require generally accepted accounting principles, not the more latitudinous regulatory accounting principles, standards and require the Federal Home Loan Bank Board to use an asset classification system consistent with the asset classification system of the federal banking agencies. The Federal Home Loan Bank Board was allowed to continue a forbearance program with S & Ls with a net worth 0.5 percent or less if it determined:

> that the [S & L's] weak capital condition is not the result of imprudent operating practices, such as practices that were speculative at the time the practices were undertaken, insider abuses, excessive operating expenses, dividends paid by the association, or actions taken solely for the purpose of qualifying for capital recovery under this subsection.

Qualified S & Ls and other thrift institutions were required to maintain 60 percent or more of their assets in loans, equity or securities in residential real estate or manufactured housing.[46]

The inadequacies of the Competitive Equality Banking Act of 1987 soon were apparent. By year end 1987, there were 940 S & Ls (33 percent of the industry) whose capital was below the required 3 percent. Of those 940 S & Ls, 505 were considered by the GAO to be insolvent, 435 were denominated by the GAO to be low net worth, meaning capital between 0 and 3 percent. The total 1987 loss of these 940 institutions was $10 billion and "losses continued in 1988."

The FSLIC using a combination of the first $3.75 billion of Competitive Equality Banking Act funds, sales of S & L assets from earlier liquidations and FSLIC notes disposed of 205 S & Ls in 1988, 26 through liquidations and 179 through sales to acquirers. To persuade acquirers to take over insolvent S & Ls, the FSLIC had to absorb the thrift's negative net worth "hole"; the difference between the insolvent S & Ls assets and its deposit liabilities. A subsequent calculation of FSLIC resolution costs for 1988 would be $46.6 billion.

In February 1989, a GAO Report to Congress on the Thrift Industry Problem criticized the FSLIC's projection of resources available to it through 1998 as "[falling] short of what the [FSLIC Insurance] Fund will need to become financially sound:"

- Even if FSLIC's revenue assumptions are realized, we estimate that over the 3 years 1989, 1990, and 1991, FSLIC will need additional funds for insurance losses on presently insolvent or undercapitalized institutions amounting to at least $50 billion.
- In addition, we estimate FSLIC will need $5 billion for future insurance losses related to institutions that are not now severe problem cases, $10 billion to cover financing costs for case resolutions, and $20 billion to establish adequate insurance fund reserves.
- In total, therefore, we estimate that to be restored to sound financial condition FSLIC will need at least $85 billion over the next decade in addition to the amounts included in FSLIC's cash flow projection.

On February 6, 1989, the Bush Administration presented an S & L resolution plan that was responsive to the magnitude of the crisis. Bush proposed a $50 billion fund to liquidate or merge failed S & Ls. Some $20 billion of the $50 billion would be from the United States Treasury; $30 billion would be raised through debt security sales by a version of FICO, now called the Resolution Funding Corporation or REFCORP. The S & L industry largely would be responsible for capitalizing REFCORP and repaying the $30 billion principal to REFCORP. The Federal Home Loan Bank Board would be abolished and replaced by a new oversight agency within the Department of Treasury. The FSLIC also would be abolished and S & L deposit insurance subsequently would be provided by the Federal Deposit Insurance Corporation (*FDIC*) which insured bank deposits. S & L required capital would be doubled to 6 percent.

The S & L lobbyist, the powerful United States Savings & Loan League, tried in vain to object to increased capital requirements. There was anger in Congress at the League's earlier reassurances that the S & L debacle was smaller than feared and on its way to resolution through Federal Home Loan Bank Board and FSLIC efforts. Republican Senator Phil Gramm, long a champion of free markets, articulated a bipartisan fury when he told a League spokesman: "[I]f anyone has been irresponsible here, it has been the League." Then Democratic Senator Richard Shelby was more pointed in telling League Chair William O'Connell: "[Y]ou have already destroyed your own industry." Chuck Schumer, then a member of the House of Representatives, explained how "ticked off at the thrifts" members of the House were: "Laissez-faire is over. Leaving it up to the thrifts and regulators just doesn't work anymore."

On August 9, 1989, Bush signed the Financial Institutions Reform, Recovery and Enforcement Act, popularly known as FIRREA, which enacted virtually each core aspect of his February 1989 proposal.

The most important aspect of FIRREA, economist Lawrence White, a member of the Federal Home Loan Bank Board between 1986 and 1989 would write, was "[p]roviding more money, to continue the disposals of the insolvent thrifts." FIRREA did not attempt to do this on the cheap as had the ineffectual Competitive Equality Banking Act of 1989. This time a minimum of $50 billion was authorized, $20 billion in the form of direct appropriations from the United States Treasury with a new Resolution Funding Corporation (*REFCORP*), successor to FICO, authorized to issue bonds and other debt securities up to $30 billion. If necessary, the Treasury would back up REFCORP to cover interest payments due on the $30 billion.

REFCORP was financed by $1 billion contributed in 1989 and 1990 by the Federal Home Loan Banks and $300 million in assessments each year. FICO also was required to transfer $1.2 billion in funds to the Resolution Trust Corporation (*RTC*), funds which earlier had been contributed by the federal home loan banks.

The initial $50 billion would prove insufficient. On March 23, 1991, Congress would appropriate another $30 billion to cover the cost of resolving the S & L debacle through the Resolution Trust Corporation Funding Act of 1991. Another $25 billion was appropriated on December 21, 1991, when the Resolution Trust Corporation Refinancing, Restructuring and Improvement Act of 1991 was enacted. Some of these monies would be returned to the

United States Treasury. The total loss cost for implementing FIRREA would be $87.9 billion. When combined with the $64.7 billion estimated costs of the FSLIC after January 1, 1986, the total government resolution costs of the S & L debacle would be $152.6 billion. An additional $88 billion would be paid through the life of the REFCORP's $30 billion bonds, $300 million from federal home loan banks, and $2.3 billion from government appropriations. Martin Mayer would encapsulate the collective anger with his book about the collapse of the savings and loan industry, *The Greatest-Ever Bank Robbery*, calling it "the worst public scandal in American history."

REFCORP's purpose was to fund the RTC, whose basic duty was "to manage and resolve all cases involving depository institutions — the accounts of which were issued by the Federal Savings and Loan Insurance Corporation . . . before the enactment of the Financial Institutions Reform, Recovery and Enforcement Act" and for which a conservator or receiver had been appointed after January 1, 1989. Until its closure on December 31, 1995, the RTC would resolve 747 failed thrifts, with book value of $458 billion, recovering $397 billion for taxpayers at a recovery rate of 86 percent. A remaining $7.7 billion of assets was placed under the management of the FDIC when the RTC closed.

At its height in 1991, the RTC employed 8000 with regional offices in Atlanta, Dallas, Denver, and Kansas City and sales offices in 28 cities. Some 2166 defendants would be convicted of financial crimes, approximately $2.5 billion would be recovered by the Department of Justice from fraud and professional liability claims, including $1 billion from junk bond financier Michael Milken and Drexel Burnham Lambert.

A new Office of Thrift Supervision (*OTS*) was established subject to the oversight of the Secretary of the Treasury with a director of the OTS having the powers previously vested in the Federal Home Loan Bank Board. The director was required to apply generally accepted accounting principles comparable to or more stringent than those used by the federal banking agencies. Commercial, corporate, business, or agricultural loans could not exceed 10 percent of the assets of a federal savings association. Investments in tangible personal property including vehicles, manufactured homes, machinery, equipment or furniture similarly could not exceed 10 percent of the assets of a federal savings association. Consumer loans for personal, family, or household purposes could not exceed

30 percent of a federal S & L's assets. Commercial real estate mortgages were required to be reduced from 40 percent of assets to four times an S & L's net worth. The maximum loan that could be made to a single borrower was reduced from 100 percent of net worth to 15 percent. Out-of-state branching was restricted. The director was required to adopt a minimum capital requirement of 3 percent, no more than 1.5 percent of which could be goodwill. After 1994, goodwill no longer could be included in the 3 percent capital requirement. S & Ls engaged in riskier forms of loans could be required to hold risk-based capital up to 8 percent of their total assets.

The 1989 Act required qualifying thrifts to have qualified thrift investments equal to or exceeding 70 percent of the S & L's portfolio assets, a standard more demanding than the 60 percent requirement in the 1987 Competitive Equality Banking Act. Failure to comply with the 70 percent qualified thrift investment standard could lead to restrictions on a qualified thrift's investments, activities, advances, and dividends.

The FSLIC and the Federal Home Loan Bank Board were abolished. The FDIC took over the administration of the FSLIC insurance fund and was empowered to administer two new funds, the savings association insurance fund for S & Ls and a separate bank insurance fund for federal savings banks that were chartered under the Home Owners' Loan Act. S & Ls could now display a sign communicating that, as with banks in the FDIC, their deposits were backed by the full faith and credit of the United States, then up to $100,000 per insured deposit.

Congress intended the FDIC to be more independent "from the institutions the deposit of which it insures by providing an independent board of directors, adequate funding and appropriate powers." The FDIC would now be led by a five person Board consisting of the Comptroller of the Currency, the director of the newly created Office of Thrift Supervision, and three presidential nominees, confirmed by the Senate. After February 28, 1993, no more than three members of the FDIC board could be members of the same political party.

The FDIC was empowered to be appointed a conservator or receiver of a federal S & L, regardless of state law. When the FDIC determined that severe financial conditions threatened the stability of a significant number of S & Ls, or S & Ls possessing significant financial resources, the FDIC could authorize a merger, consolidation, or transfer of assets to another S & L or insured bank. The FDIC could provide assistance to an S & L upon receiving a proposal from the Savings Association Insurance Fund before grounds exist for appointment of a conservator or receiver.

With respect to S & Ls, the FDIC was provided with cease and desist authority, power to remove an institution-affiliated party who violated any law, power to impose industry-wide removal, suspension, or prohibition orders upon a removed person, expanded civil and criminal money penalties, as well as whistleblower and bounty provisions.

The 12 Federal Home Loan Bank Boards continued but now reported to a new Federal Housing Finance Board, an independent agency in the executive branch, with a five-person Board of Directors, the Secretary of Treasury, and four citizens appointed by the president with the advice and consent of the Senate.[47]

The Bush administration also modestly addressed the 1980s Banking Crisis.

The Competitive Equality Banking Act of 1987, adopted during the Reagan presidency, provided only a few consequential provisions about banks. The 1987 Act reaffirmed that deposits up to the statutorily prescribed amounts in federally insured depository institutions "are backed by the Full Faith and Credit of the United States." The Glass-Steagall Act restrictions on the securities activities of national banks were extended to insured nonmember banks. The Act adopted a one-year moratorium on other bank activities such as a prohibition on any Federal Banking agency issuing any rule, regulation, or order that would increase the insurance powers of banks, bank holding companies, foreign banks, or other companies subject to the Bank Holding Company Act.

A bank holding company, after the Competitive Equality Banking Act, that acquired a nonbank bank before the enactment of the Act could retain it if: (1) the non-bank did not engage both in the taking of demand deposits and in commercial lending, and (2) it did not increase the number of locations from which it conducted its business after March 5, 1987.

Emergency interstate acquisition of banks in danger of closing were permitted when the failing bank had assets of more than $500 million or when affiliated banks both had assets of more than $500 million and the $500 million in assets equaled more than 33 percent of the total assets of the affiliated insured banks.

The 1989 Financial Institutions Reform, Recovery and Enforcement Act expanded the definition of *bank* in the Federal Deposit Insurance Act to include:

> (A) . . . any national bank, State bank, and District bank, and any Federal branch and insured branch;
> (B) includes any former savings association that —
> (i) has converted from a savings association charter; and
> (ii) is a Savings Association Insurance Fund member.

Bank holding companies were expressly authorized to acquire S & Ls.

In 1991, Congress enacted the Federal Deposit Insurance Corporation Improvement Act, which recapitalized the bank insurance fund and empowered the FDIC to require annual reports and financial conditions and management from each depository institution and required all depository institutions to have an independent audit committee. Each depository institution "which is engaged in the business of receiving deposits other than trust funds . . . may become an insured depository institution."

Several provisions encouraged each federal banking agency including the FDIC to take prompt corrective actions to resolve the problems of insured depository institutions albeit "at the least possible long-term costs to the deposit insurance fund." Capital distributions after an insured depository institution was found to be undercapitalized were prohibited. Undercapitalized institutions were subject to monitoring by the appropriate Federal banking agency and had to submit an acceptable capital restoration plan. Undercapitalized insured depository institutions also were subject to asset growth restrictions.

Significantly undercapitalized institutions or undercapitalized institutions that failed to implement capital restoration plans would be required to recapitalize, have interest rates that they paid on deposits, asset growth and annuities restricted. The federal banking agency could order the election of new directors, dismiss directors or senior executives or require the employment of qualified senior executives. Deposits from correspondent banks could be prohibited.

Bank holding companies could be required to divest or liquidate any subsidiary in danger of becoming insolvent when it "poses a significant risk to the institution or is likely to cause a significant dissipation of the institution's assets or earnings."

Senior executive compensation in an undercapitalized institution had to be approved by the appropriate federal banking agency when it involved a bonus or at a higher rate than the officer received in the 12 months preceding the institution becoming undercapitalized.

Critically undercapitalized institutions were prohibited from making any payment of principal or interest on subordinated debt within 60 days after becoming critically undercapitalized. Within 90 days after an institution became critically undercapitalized, the appropriate federal banking agency was required to appoint a receiver or conservator and to restrict the activities of the institution.

Each federal banking agency for an insured depository institution and depository institution holding companies was required to prescribe:

> (1) Standards relating to—
> (A) Internal controls, information systems, and internal audit systems . . . ;
> (B) Loan Documentation;
> (C) Credit Underwriting;
> (D) Interest Rate Exposure;
> (E) Asset Growth; and
> (F) Compensation, Fees, and Benefits . . . ; and
> (2) Such other operational and managerial standards as the agency determines to be appropriate.

In addition, each Federal banking agency was required to prescribe:

> (1) Standards specifying—
> (A) A maximum ratio of classified assets to capital;
> (B) Minimum earnings sufficient to absorb losses without impairing capital; and
> (C) To the extent feasible, a minimum ratio of market value to book value for publicly traded shares of the institution or company; and
> (2) Such other standards relating to asset quality, earnings, and valuation as the agency determines to be appropriate.

Greater emergency power was given to the Secretary of Treasury, upon the written recommendation of two-thirds of the FDIC and Federal Reserve Board to take additional actions "with respect to an insured depository institution that would have serious adverse effects on economic conditions or financial stability," or as the subsection put it "Systemic Risk."

Federal Reserve discount window advances were limited so that no Federal Reserve bank could make an advance to an undercapitalized institution when the loan was outstanding for more than 60 days in any 120-day period except when the head of the federal banking agency certifies in writing in advance that the depository institution is viable.

Whistleblower provisions were established by the Federal Deposit Insurance Act.

The FDIC was required to implement a semiannual risk based assessment system to calculate for each depository institution the probability that the deposit insurance fund would incur a loss on that institution.

One year after enactment of the Federal Deposit Insurance Corporation Improvement Act of 1991 no insured state bank could engage as principal in any activity that was not permissible for a national bank unless:

> (1) the Corporation has determined that the activity would pose no significant risk to the appropriate deposit insurance fund; and
>
> (2) the State bank is, and continues to be, in compliance with applicable capital standards prescribed by the appropriate Federal banking agency.

An insured state bank could not engage in insurance underwriting or acquire or retain any equity investment, except to the extent that it was permissible for national banks.

The FDIC was given back-up enforcement powers if a separate appropriate federal agency declined to act upon an FDIC recommendation of an enforcement action.

Each appropriate federal banking agency was required within nine months of the enactment of the Federal Deposit Insurance Corporation Act of 1991 to adopt uniform real estate lending regulations.

New limits were placed on extensions of credit to executive officers, directors, and principal shareholders of member banks.

To reduce the systemic risks posed by large bank failures, the Fed was directed to prescribe standards to limit the risks posed by an insured depository institution's exposure to other depository institutions.

In 2007–2009, none of the laundry list of new enhanced FDIC, Fed, and other appropriate federal banking agency powers would prove effective in preventing or limiting the Financial Meltdown. The 1987, 1989, and 1991 federal S & L and banking acts did not address the structure of the banking industry itself. Long after the halcyon memory of the virtuous thrift institution led by Jimmy Stewart in the 1947 Academy Award Best Picture *It's a Wonderful Life* had been supplanted by a generation of S & L cupidity neither Congress, federal banking regulatory agencies, nor the executive branch effectively addressed such fundamental questions as why do we have so many different types of federal and state banks? What were the risks of the regulators' different standards and policies, enforcement, state quality, and leadership? What were the risks of competition among the regulators?

The closest the Bush Administration came was the Treasury's 1991 Report, *Modernizing the Financial System: Recommendations for Safer, More Competitive Banks* (1991). Similar to the 1984 Task Group on Regulation of Financial Services, *Blueprint for Reform*, which then Vice President Bush had chaired, the Treasury's 1991 Report largely ignored the S & L and bank failures of recent past and instead addressed how to make the nation's banking system more "sound [and] internationally competitive."

The 1991 Treasury Report recommended interstate branching and increasing bank powers to offer insurance and purchase securities. To reduce exposure, the Treasury proposed "[reining] in the overexpanded scope of deposit insurance, [improving] supervision by strengthening the role of capital; and [assessing] risk-based premiums." A new federal banking agency within the Department of Treasury would replace the Comptroller of the Currency and Office of Thrift Supervision. The Fed would lose its existing authority over national banks but would continue to regulate state chartered banks that were members of the Federal Reserve System and insured nonmember state banks then regulated by the FDIC.

During the Bush Administration, none of the Treasury's 1991 recommendations were enacted.

The role of the Fed in bank supervision was muted. In 1989, the Fed amended its Bank Holding Company Act regulation to implement the 1989 Financial Institution Reform, Recovery and Enforcement Act's authorization for bank holding companies to acquire savings associations. In April 1992, the Fed amended its Bank Holding Company Act regulation to permit to expand permissible bank holding company activities to include full service securities brokerage and financial advisory services and mergers, acquisitions, and divestitures, as well as structuring of loan syndications and interest rate swaps. In June and September 1992, further procedural steps were taken "to reduce regulatory burden and simplify the application process" for Bank Holding Company Act activities.[48]

The Clinton Presidency

In November 1992, Bush was defeated for reelection by Bill Clinton in a three person race. Clinton won 43 percent of the popular vote and 370 of the electoral college votes to Bush's 37.4 percent with 168 electoral college votes, and Independent Ross Perot's 18.9 percent. Perot's third party popular vote was the largest in United States history since Teddy Roosevelt's 1912 Bull Moose campaign. Significantly, 27 percent of Republicans and 68 percent of Independents voted for Clinton.

The Senate essentially remained unchanged with the Democratic majority now 56–44, down one seat from 1990. The House also retained a large Democratic Party majority, 258–176, down 9 representatives.

Bush's 1992 reelection campaign was derided by his former Chief of Staff, John Sununu, and others including Tip O'Neil as "the worst run Presidential campaign in history." Bush's support for 1990 tax increases despite his "Read My Lips" pledge at the 1988 Republican Convention had inspired a determined primary challenge by the conservative Patrick Buchanan, former Nixon speechwriter and a cohost of the CNN News program *Crossfire.* Buchanan blasted Bush as "King George" for his mishandling of the economy, and support of the North American Free Trade Agreement, winning a surprising 40.4 percent for a second place finish in the February 18, 1992, New Hampshire primary and overall 22.5 percent of the total vote cast in the Republican primaries. Buchanan would cause further damage to Bush on the first night of the Republican Convention with his strident call for a culture war against the Democrats' support for homosexual rights, gays in the military, and abortion on demand. Buchanan proclaimed: "There is a religious war going on in this country. . . . The war is for the soul of America." Buchanan also attacked the rising tide of immigration: "Our own country is undergoing the greatest invasion in its history, a migration of millions of illegal aliens from Mexico. . . . A country that cannot control its own borders can scarcely call itself a state any longer."

Bush soon after the New Hampshire Primary informed the *Atlanta Constitution* that his support for tax increases in 1990 had been his "biggest mistake," a *mea culpa* he repeated in his 1992 nomination acceptance speech: "[T]wo years ago I made a bad call on the . . . tax increase."

The tax support flip-flop may have saved the Vice Presidential nomination for his unpopular Vice President Dan Quayle, whom Campaign Manager Jim Baker, Bush's two sons, George W. and Jeb, and speechwriter Peggy Noonan, favored replacing. On July 27, 1992, Bush wrote in his diary: "The bottom line on Quayle is, if he is dumped, I'm attacked for not keeping my word, 'Read My Lips,' no loyalty, looking after myself and not the 'other guy.' " Clinton would be more dismissive. After Quayle promised to be the "pit bull terrier" of the Bush campaign, the Democratic Party frontrunner responded, "Quayle's claim would strike terror into the heart of every fire hydrant in America."

Ross Perot, a telegenic billionaire, founder of Electronic Data Systems, by 1968 according to *Fortune* magazine was the richest man in Texas, also would prove a formidable Bush opponent. Bush and Perot detested each other. Bush considered Perot "a weirdo," "crazy," "paranoid," a "strange little egomaniac, nurtured on conspiracy theories." Perot proved adept at striking back. When Bush criticized Perot in the first presidential debate for not having any government experience, Perot responded that Bush "had a point. I don't have any experience in running up a $4 trilling debt." Perot with his folksy manner — "It's just that simple" was a favorite line — and charts relentlessly excoriated Bush on budget deficits and anticipated job loss because of NAFTA, which Perot claimed would be responsible for the "giant sucking sound" of jobs relocating to Mexico. In June 1992, Perot led both Bush and Clinton in a *Time* magazine poll before withdrawing from the campaign on

July 16 during the Democratic Convention, only to reenter on October 1, 1992, in time for the three presidential debates.

Bush was weakened by a perceived lack of passion at least for domestic policy compared to his spirited campaign in 1988. On August 22, 1992, he would write in his diary: "I just wish it were over." A memorable moment during the campaign would occur on October 15, 1992, during the second presidential debate, held in a Town Hall format, when Bush began his response to a question: "How has the national debt personally affected . . . your [life]?" by seeming to be totally out of touch with the young person who posed the question: "Well, I think the national debt affects everyone. Obviously it has a lot to do with interest rates." During the debate, he twice looked at his wristwatch, underlining his discomfort.

Clinton's response to the young woman's question, emphasizing "I feel your pain," emotionally connected him with the television audience:

> I've been governor of a small state for twelve years. . . . I have seen what's happened in this last four years when in my state, when people lose their jobs, there's a good chance I'll know them by their names. . . . When a factory closes, I know the people who ran it. When the businesses go bankrupt, I know them. And I've been out here for thirteen months meeting in meetings just like this ever since October with people like you all over America, people that have lost their jobs, lost their livelihood, lost their health insurance.

The public perception of a failing economy doomed Bush's reelection. Clinton, in retrospect, would write: "How did Americans come to choose their first baby-boom President, the third youngest in history, only the second governor of a small state, carrying more baggage than an ocean liner? Surveys of voters leaving the polls indicated that the economy was by far the biggest issue for them, followed by the deficit and health care, with the character issue trailing." Exit polls reported that 70 to 75 percent of respondents believed the economy was poor or not so good. Unemployment at times in 1992 was 7.8 percent, the highest it had been since 1984. The Center for Media and Public Affairs calculated that 96 percent of evening TV news programs between July and September 1992 "focused on economic weaknesses and shortcomings."

"In the end," Clinton explained: "I . . . won the debate over what the election was about. . . . The basic dynamic of the campaign has been set: Bush claimed to represent family values and trustworthiness, while [Clinton] was for economic and social change."

At Georgetown University on October 23, 1991, Clinton articulated a variety of slogans. At Georgetown University on October 23, 1991, he spoke of a New Covenant:

> [T]o shoulder our common load. When people assume responsibility and shoulder that common load, they acquire a dignity they never knew before. When people go to work, they rediscover a pride that was lost. When fathers pay their child support, they restore a connection they and their children need. When students work harder, they find out they all can learn and do as well as anyone else on Earth. When corporate managers put their workers and their long-term profits ahead of their own paychecks, their companies do well, and so do they. When the privilege of serving is enough of a perk for people in Congress, and the President finally assumes responsibility for America's problems, we'll not only stop doing wrong, we'll begin to do what is right to move America forward. And that is what this election is really all about — forging a New Covenant of change that will honor middle-class values, restore the public trust, create a new sense of community, and make America work again.

Clinton's 1992 campaign brochure, *Fighting for the Forgotten Middle Class*, began: "Bill Clinton will cut taxes for the middle class and make the rich pay their fair share." The brochure emphasized: "Putting people first: It's time to put people first": "That is the core of our national economic strategy for America. And that will be the fundamental idea that guides [us]. . . ." Clinton emphasized populist rhetoric:

> For more than a decade our government has been rigged in favor of the rich and special interests. While the wealthiest get richer, middle-class Americans work harder and earn less while paying higher taxes to a government that fails to provide what we need: good jobs in a growing economy, world-class education, affordable health care, and safe streets and neighborhoods. Economic growth will not come without a national economic strategy to invest in people and meet the competition. Today, we have no economic vision, no economic leadership and no economic strategy.

Clinton's campaign best would be remembered for the middle line of a three-line sign that James Carville, Clinton's campaign manager, put up his first day on the job:

> Change v. More of the Same
> The Economy, Stupid
> Don't Forget Health Care

Clinton was able to overcome accusations of being "Slick Willie" by what Bush termed his alleged draft dodging, claims of womanizing, his acknowledgement that he had smoked marijuana, then illegal, but "had not inhaled" with his vision of "The New Economy."

On April 16, 1992, Clinton delivered a speech on the economy at the University of Pennsylvania's Wharton School of Business, "home to much of America's economic potential" but also where "in the 1980s students nicknamed the Investment Banking Club 'The Unindicted' and the Wharton 'Wall of Fame,' which honors alumni chosen by the students, kept photos of Donald Trump, who glorified the art of the deal, and Michael Milken on display until Trump went bankrupt and Milken was on his way to jail."

In the Wharton speech, Clinton stressed how his new covenant would apply to economic policy. For the forgotten middle class, Clinton stressed "the '80s was an economic disaster":

> People who make over $200,000 saw their incomes rise fifteen times faster than average Americans. The average middle-class person, by contrast, is working 158 hours a year more than in 1969 for about the same income — an extra month of work without extra pay. A new social order is emerging, more unequal, more divided, more impenetrable to those who seek to get ahead. . . .
>
> . . . The single driving idea behind economic policy in the '80s has been to keep taxes low on corporations and upper-income individuals and keep government out of our way. . . .
>
> This policy hasn't worked. The current administration has compiled the worst economic record in 50 years. George Bush's Presidency has produced slower economic growth, slower job growth, and slower income growth than any administration since the Great Depression — and the biggest deficits and highest middle-class tax burden of any administration in history.

Clinton sought:

> * First, we need to grant every American the fundamental right to a good education, lifelong learning and training, in a world where what you can earn depends on what you can learn.
>
> * Second, we need to invest the time, the patience, and the money to rebuild our economy and make it grow again.
>
> * Finally, we need to demand change throughout our society — from business, labor, and government — and work together to forge a new social compact for economic growth....
>
> **In the new economy, infrastructure means information** as well as transportation. More than half the U.S. workforce is employed in information-intensive industries, yet we have no national strategy to create a national information network. Just as the interstate highway system in the 1950s spurred two decades of economic growth, we need a door-to-door fiber optics system by the year 2015 to link every home, every lab, every classroom, and every business in America....
>
> This country doesn't need a new program for every problem, and we won't get change simply by spending more on programs already on the books. We need to reinvent government to deliver new services in different ways, eliminate unnecessary layers of management, and offer people more choices. We also need to show the discipline to put our fiscal house in order.
>
> In a Clinton Administration, government will no longer be able to grow faster than ordinary people's ability to pay for it can grow. I want to lead a government prepared to end spending that doesn't work and reinvent programs to make sure they will. I've proposed a 3 percent across the board cut in the federal bureaucracy. We should give the President a line-item veto, and elect a President with the resolve to use it.

Clinton had built an enviable record as Arkansas governor in economic development, education, and crime. In 1991, the National Governance Association had labelled Clinton the most effective Governor in the Country in an annual *Newsweek* survey. He and his wife, fellow Yale Law graduate Hillary Rodham Clinton, had built a network of friends, FOBs or Friends of Bill, through his role beginning in 1985 in the Democratic Leadership Council, a moderate organization, as Clinton wrote, "dedicated to forging a winning message for the Democrats based on fiscal responsibility, creative new ideas and social policy, and a commitment to a strong national defense."

The Democratic Leadership Council epitomized what Bob Woodward termed:

> a movement of self-styled "New Democrats" who rejected the party's liberal orthodoxy. Mostly Southerners, they were trying to convince the middle class that the Democratic Party could be strong on foreign and defense policy, moderate in social policy, and disciplined in spending tax money and taming runaway government. While retaining the ideals of the New Deal and the Great Society, New Democrats sought more efficient activism.

Clinton became the National Chair of the Democratic Leadership Council in 1990. He warned his fellow Democrats on May 6, 1990: "Too many of the people who used to vote for us, the very burdened middle class we are talking about, have not trusted us in national elections to defend our national interests abroad, to put their values into our social policy at home, or to take their tax money and spend it with discipline. We've got to turn these perceptions around or we can't continue as a national party."

The moderation of the Leadership Council's policies would offend some more progressive Democrats as would Clinton's sharp retort to rap singer Sister Souljah, who after riots in Los Angeles had asked: "If black people kill black people every day, why not have a week and kill white people?" Clinton, addressing Reverend Jesse Jackson's Rainbow Coalition had snapped back: "If you took the words 'white' and 'black' and reversed them, you might think [White Nationalist] David Duke was giving the speech.... We have an obligation, all of us, to call attention to prejudice whenever we see it." Jackson and others in the black community were deeply offended.

Clinton accepted the Democratic Party nomination on July 17, 1992, nine days after the inspired choice of Tennessee Senator Al Gore to be his Vice Presidential nominee. Gore's selection defied, as Clinton write in his memoir, "the conventional wisdom that the Vice-Presidential candidate should provide a political and geographic balance. We were from neighboring states. He was even younger than I was [Clinton then was 45 years old]. And he, too, was identified with the new Democratic wing of the party." "Al,"

Clinton concluded, "would provide balance in a far more important way. He knew things I didn't. . . . Al was an expert on national security, arms control, information technology, energy and the environment." The two energetic Southerners provided a sharp contrast to Bush, who in 1991 had been diagnosed with Graves' disease, which periodically led to listlessness, cardiac arrhythmia, and an overactive thyroid.

Gore on July 15 had been nominated by acclamation, began his acceptance speech by describing dreaming of being the warm-up act for Elvis, the nickname Clinton's staff chose for Clinton given his often stated love for Elvis Presley, all of whose songs Clinton could sing.

Clinton was formally nominated by New York Governor Mario Cuomo the next evening. Cuomo paid homage to Clinton's determination to stay in the race after accusations of a 12-year affair with Gennifer Flowers had nearly derailed Clinton's campaign before the critical New Hampshire primary. Cuomo introduced Clinton as "someone smart enough to know; strong enough to do; sure enough to lead, the Comeback Kid, a new voice for a New America."

Clinton's acceptance speech followed the video, *The Man From Hope*, the name of the Arkansas town where he had been born. Clinton said in part:

> The choice you face is clear.
>
> George Bush talks a good game. But he has no game plan to compete and win in the world economy. I do.
>
> He won't take on the big insurance companies to lower costs and provide health care to all Americans. I will.
>
> He won't streamline the federal government, and change the way it works; cut 100,000 bureaucrats, and put 100,000 more police on your streets. I will
>
> He never balanced a budget. I have. Eleven times.
>
> He won't break the stranglehold special interests have on our elections and lobbyist have on our government. I will.
>
> He won't give mothers and fathers a chance to take some time off from work when a baby's born or a parent is sick. I will.
>
> He doesn't have a commitment to keep family farms in the family. I do.
>
> He hasn't fought a real war on crime and drugs. I will.
>
> He won't crack down on polluters, clean up the environment and take the lead on creating jobs in environmental technologies. I will. . . .

> And he won't guarantee a woman's right to choose. I will.
>
> . . .
>
> But we Democrats have some changing to do too. It is time for us to realize that there is not a government program for every problem. And if we really want to use government to help people, we've got to make it work. . . .
>
> That is why we need a new approach to government. A government that offers more empowerment and less entitlement; more choices for young people in public schools and more choices for older people in long-term care. A government that is leaner, not meaner; that expands opportunity, not bureaucracy; that understands that jobs must come from growth in a vibrant and vital system of free enterprise. I call it a New Covenant — a solemn commitment between the people and their government — based not simply on what each of us can take but on what all of us must give to make America work again.

The Clinton campaign was buoyed by a well-received five-day bus tour beginning the day after the Convention ended that covered 1000 or so miles through New Jersey, Pennsylvania, West Virginia, Ohio, Kentucky, Indiana, and Illinois. Clinton memorably played the saxophone wearing dark sunglasses on a late night television program. His indefatigable campaign style, as he put it in New Hampshire in an appeal to voters: "I'll be there for you 'til the last dog dies," would build a 20-point lead over Bush by the time of the August Republican Convention. Bush relentlessly attacked Clinton's character, as Bush contrasted his service in World War II with Clinton's opposition to Vietnam: "While I bit the bullet, he bit his nails," and Bush's strong performance in the third presidential debate, sharply cutting Clinton's lead to 2 points in an October 29 *CNN/USA Today* poll. Clinton's victory may have been assured by the indictment on the Friday before the election of Reagan Secretary of Defense Casper Weinberger by the Iran-Contra Special Prosecutor Lawrence Walsh with text in the indictment suggesting that then-Vice President Bush had played a greater role in the illegal arms sales to Iran than he previously had acknowledged.[49]

Clinton was a natural politician. As Clinton Senior Advisor George Stephanopoulos wrote: Clinton was "Secretariat, the ultimate political thoroughbred." He was a product of the South, where he had been elected Arkansas Attorney General at 28 and Governor at 30. He was voted out of office after one term, then won the governorship for five additional terms.

Clinton would thrive in high school, Georgetown University, Yale Law School, and as a Rhodes Scholar. His natural gifts, his gregarious nature, his boundless energy, his hunger for success, his need for human contact propelled his career.

Blessed with a prodigious memory, Clinton mastered the details of first state, then federal, programs at a level unmatched by any 20th or 21st century president. "Whatever the subject," wrote historian James Patterson, "Social Security, health care, the minimum wage, taxes, trade, education, obscure social programs — Clinton appeared to have an amazing command of information." Clinton was a gifted storyteller, able to make palatable to general audiences' policy technicalities by relating policy to human experiences.

Clinton would be criticized for compromises, becoming mired in the minutiae of the legislative process, and failing to effectively communicate a compelling vision for his presidency.

Politics, Clinton well knew, was the art of the possible. To succeed after the humiliating congressional losses in the 1994 midterm elections, Clinton hired Dick Morris, a bipartisan practitioner of negative advertising, who as a consultant was hated by Clinton's more progressive supporters as "a sleazy son of a bitch," "the underside" of American politics. Morris helped Clinton "triangulate" a course between a Republican dominated Congress and Clinton's more liberal social ideals that led to his reelection in 1996.

"Clinton was," as historian Sean Wilentz wrote:

> not one thing or another, but many things at the same time, and somehow they all hung together. He was a product of rakish Hot Springs, Arkansas, who was also a Rhodes scholar and a student of history and public policy. He was a white southerner who grew up in the civil rights era, identified closely with blacks, yet also understood the resentments of many southern whites. He was a man temperamentally drawn to reasoned conciliation and compromise who could also be sentimental, impulsive, and stubborn.

Initially Clinton tried to accomplish too much, too soon. To satisfy the progressive wing of his party, he championed ambitious initiatives in health care, jobs, the environment, education, gun control, voting rights, and home ownership, among many other topics. At the same time, Clinton sought to advance the more centrist goals of the New Democrats: deficit reduction, welfare reform, and a crime bill.

To critics of the Clinton presidency, such as Bob Woodward, Clinton was indecisive, chaotic in his leadership, habitually late to meetings, and undisciplined. His temper tantrums were legendary, "purple rages," outbursts as violent as a tropical storm. Historian James Patterson wrote:

> Aides who marveled at Clinton's political skill or who approved of his policies nonetheless resented not only his indecisiveness and sloppiness but also his unpredictability and hot temper. They came to believe that he was unusually self-indulgent, inconsiderate, self-pitying, and narcissistic. If it suited his purposes, he might lie to them. If things went wrong, he might fly into a temper tantrum and blame long-suffering people around him. While he was skilled at "feeling the pain" of voters, he was often a poor listener who dominated conversations. What mattered above all to Clinton, these aides concluded, was advancing his own political standing.

To admirers such as Robert Rubin, his Secretary of the Treasury between 1995 and 1999, Clinton's willingness to listen to a wide variety of opinions reflected a "good process," a determination to hear all relevant opinions including dissenting views, including as Harris wrote "even when there were none."

Rubin viewed Clinton as a misunderstood president, far more serious in purpose and achievements than some journalists reported. Leaders, Rubin urged, should be judged on results. Rubin praised the Clinton administration "as deeply engaged with global integration, the emergence of new technologies, and the spread of market-based economics.... Bill Clinton was the first American president with a deep understanding of how these issues were reshaping our economy, our country, and the world."

Clinton could be exceedingly reckless. His $200 haircuts, holding up traffic on a Los Angeles Airport runway, his Administration's replacement of White House Travel Officers with political supporters, his lack of appreciation of the likely backlash by senior military commanders to gays in the military, his sloppiness in background checks on Cabinet nominees such as Attorney General designee Zoe Baird, his scandalous behavior with women, as well as his lying under oath about his sexual relationship with Monica Lewinsky, weakened his ability to command Congressional majorities early in his presidency and led to his impeachment in December 1998, by the House of Representatives. He was not convicted by the Senate in 1999. By then, the Faustian bargain of the Clinton administration had been accepted by the public. He was a man polls would consistently recognize who "[did] not have high personal or ethical standards," who had transformed the American economy. At the height of the impeachment process in December 1998, Gallup reported that Clinton had a 73 percent approval rating.

In achieving political success, Clinton survived his own early overreaching on issues such as health care, Republican Congresses during the last six years of his presidency, his personal failings because of his ability to embrace the economic revolution wrought by what Clinton called the Information Age, and emphasis especially after 1994 focus on financial discipline and deficit reduction while defending a core liberal social agenda, including Medicare and Social Security.[50]

Clinton assembled a coterie of senior administrators and associates as variegated as his own personality.

At the apex of his advisors was his wife, Hillary, and Vice President Al Gore. Hillary likely saved Clinton's candidacy in New Hampshire by protectively appearing with her husband on the CBS program *60 Minutes* in response to the Gennifer Flowers allegation of a 12-year affair with Bill. Hillary Clinton would lead Clinton's Health Care Task Force with Ira Magaziner, as well as provide broader advice on pivotal issues. Hillary was often characterized as Bill's equal in intelligence and ambition and later would serve as Senator from New York and Secretary of State, as well as be the first woman to run for United States president from a major political party. She would challenge traditional notions of marriage, but lack her husband's natural political gifts.

Al Gore also would be a ubiquitous top advisor, prominent in the Clinton administration for serving as point man on the environment and reinventing government initiatives and consequential in advising Clinton on Cabinet selection and Congressional relations. Gore was a master of technical detail, particularly passionate about the environment, but often wooden in public appearances.

Clinton assembled an administration designed to "look like America," simultaneously giving prominence to political advisers such as James Carville, Paul Begala, Dick Morris, pollsters, notably Stan Greenberg, and media advisers like Mandy Grunwald, along with communications strategists such as George Stephanopoulos and David Gergen who was recruited in 1993, in part because of his service in three earlier Republican administrations when Clinton appeared to be badly stumbling.

As with earlier presidents, Clinton's economic and monetary teams were led by his Secretary of Treasury and Federal Reserve chair. During his eight years in office, Clinton was served by three Secretaries of Treasury, beginning with former Texas Senator Lloyd Bentsen, who at times had been Chair of the Joint Economic Committee and was the 1988 Democratic presidential candidate. Bentsen would serve between 1993 and 1994; Robert Rubin would be Treasury Secretary between 1995 and 1999; Larry Summers between 1999 and 2001.

Bentsen was respected on Wall Street. As with Clinton, Bentsen was committed to economic growth, deficit reduction, and reducing poverty as priorities. He worked effectively with Greenspan in sharp contrast to the rough edges and public and private criticism of monetary policy by George H.W. Bush's Secretary of Treasury Nicholas Brady and Budget Director Richard Darman. Bentsen would perform a notable role in helping enact the North American Free Trade Agreement and on the Uruguay Round on the General Agreement on Tariffs and Trade. Bentsen, 71 years old when he accepted Clinton's offer to be Treasury Secretary, would retire from the Clinton Administration after the 1994 midterm elections.

Robert Rubin succeeded Bentsen in 1995. Rubin was a 26-year veteran of Goldman Sachs who became its co-senior partner, a Democrat, a major fundraiser who had been deeply involved in the earlier campaigns of Mondale and Dukakis, who not only strongly believed in the importance of fiscal discipline, but also American leadership on trade liberalization, poverty, and the environment. His visceral reaction to a speech during the 1980s by liberal Senate leader Ted Kennedy "advocating a whole host of government programs that sounded worthwhile to me" was "How are we going to pay for this?" Intellectually sophisticated, he would title his memoir *In an Uncertain World* and emphasize the need for probabilistic decision making, in which Rubin would write:

> [O]nce you enter the realm of probabilities, nothing is ever simple again. A truly probabilistic view of life quickly leads to the recognition that almost all significant issues are enormously complex and demand that one delve into those complexities to identify the relevant considerations and the

> inevitable trade-offs. Some people I've encountered in various phases of my career seem more certain about everything than I am about anything. That kind of certainty isn't just a personality trait I lack. It's an attitude that seems to me to misunderstand the very nature of reality — its complexity and ambiguity — and thereby to provide a rather poor basis for working through decisions in a way that is likely to lead to the best results.

Rubin would serve as an "honest broker," chairing Clinton's White House National Economic Council, designed by Clinton to operate in the same way that the National Security Council did bringing relevant agencies together to formulate and implement policy. Rubin would be effective because of his low key manner, his firm determination on deficit reduction, and his recognition of the fundamental differences between politics and business. He would be Clinton's most successful Treasury Secretary, credited with particular success in the Clinton period economic turnaround, sometimes called Rubinomics, and his role in a succession of financial meltdowns in Asia, Russia, and Latin America. In his memoir, Clinton called Rubin a "rock of stability" because Rubin spoke up for Clinton at a critical Cabinet Meeting during the darkest days of the Monica Lewinsky scandal.

Clinton's third Treasury Secretary, Larry Summers, had worked closely with Rubin at both the National Economic Council and Treasury as Rubin's key Deputy. Rubin credited Summers with driving the United States policy response to the Asian Crisis. A Harvard Professor of Economics by 28, Summers was brilliant, often acerbic, and later would serve as President of Harvard between 2001 and 2006, before resigning in the wake of a no confidence vote after disparaging remarks about women in science.

Rounding out Clinton Administration initial key economic advisors were Laura Tyson, Economics Professor at the University of California at Berkeley, to chair the Council of Economic Advisors. Tyson later would succeed Rubin and lead the National Economic Council.

Leon Panetta, Chair of the House Budget Committee, was chosen to be Director of the Office of Management and Budget. Panetta from his first meeting in Little Rock declared "I'm a deficit hawk." Panetta had earlier been a Republican in charge of the Civil Rights Enforcement Division of Nixon's Department of Health, Education, and Welfare. When he insisted on rigorous enforcement, he had been fired by H.R. Haldeman, Nixon's Chief of Staff, subsequently a badge of honor. Panetta would be disciplined as Budget Director and in 1994 became Clinton's Chief of Staff succeeding Mack McLarty, a Clinton boyhood friend who rose to become CEO of Arkla Inc., a *Fortune* 500 natural gas concern, whose light touch to the office led to much criticism. He was badly miscast for the role and derided as "Mack the Nice." In 1997, Panetta in turn would be succeeded as Chief of Staff by Erskine Bowles.

Robert Reich, a Rhodes Scholar simultaneous with Clinton, would be Clinton's influential Secretary of Labor between 1993 and 1997, and a fervent voice for investment rather than deficit reduction.[51]

With Greenspan, Clinton formed one of the most successful odd couples of United States politics. Greenspan, a libertarian Republican, and Clinton, a centrist Democrat with a long list of expansive programmatic priorities, bonded over a mutual preference for deficit cuts and later over the fight for free trade in the North American Free Trade Agreement and on joint efforts to stabilize economies in Mexico, Asia, Russia, and Latin America.

For Greenspan, Clinton's most significant decision would be the president's determination in 1993, to work for a comprehensive Omnibus Budget Reconciliation Act, combining close to $500 billion in budget cuts and tax increases. In his memoir, Greenspan praised the budget cuts as "an act of political courage. It would have been very easy to go the other way." Greenspan advised Lloyd Bentsen how deep the cuts should be — "Not less than $130 billion a year by 1997" — and met with the president on January 28 and June 9, 1993, to express support for the president's unpopular budget plan. Critically, Greenspan and the Fed did not undercut in 1993 the favorable impact the Clinton Fiscal Plan would have on the bond markets with a Fed interest rate increase. Their incipient partnership was symbolized when Greenspan sat next to Hillary Clinton on February 17, 1993, when Clinton introduced his economic plan in a nationally televised address to a joint session of Congress. Greenspan would recognize that Clinton had taken "a page from John F. Kennedy's book" with his senior economic team. "All of Clinton's economic-policy appointees were fiscally conservative centrists like Doug Dillon, the Republican banker whom Kennedy picked as Treasury Secretary. Choosing them made Bill Clinton seem about as far from the classic tax-and-spend liberal as you could act and still be a Democrat."

There was no formal deal among Clinton, Bentsen, and Greenspan, but a shared understanding. Deficit cuts and stable interest rates worked hand-in-hand.

On December 3, 1992, at their initial meeting, Greenspan had stressed to Clinton that long-term interest rates were at an unusual 3 to 4 percent higher than short-term rates, the equivalent to an inflation premium. Greenspan explained that the bond market anticipated that the federal deficit would continue to grow in the coming years. Inflation would inevitably soar at some time. Bob Woodward summarized Greenspan's key points:

> The double-digit inflation of the late 1970s had been induced by the budget deficits from the Vietnam War. Investors were now wary and demanding a higher long-term return because of the expectations on the federal deficit.
>
> . . . [I]f the new administration removed or altered that expectation by exerting some control on the deficit, the market expectations would change. Bond traders would have more faith that inflation would stay under control. Long-term rates would drop, galvanizing demand for new mortgages. And since homeowners increasingly used refinancing as a source of consumer credit, they would be able to buy more automobiles, appliances, home furnishings, and a whole variety of consumer goods. This spending would expand the economy — a significant payoff.
>
> In addition, Greenspan said, as inflation expectations dropped, investors would get smaller returns on bonds. As a result, they would shift their money to the stock market. The stock market would climb — another payoff.

For his part, Clinton respected Greenspan's experience and "enormous influence over the economy" and felt he could work with Greenspan because: "I believed in the independence of the Federal Reserve; [and] thought it was essential to cut the deficit." Clinton would express private frustrations with the Fed when it raised interest rates in 1994, but never articulated criticism of the Fed publicly. The president's commitment to deficit reductions at the expense of a middle class tax cut and investments in social programs would be deeply divisive in his administration and with progressive Democrats. James Carville facetiously captured the spirit of many in saying: "I used to think if there was reincarnation, I wanted to come back as the President or the Pope or a .400 baseball hitter.

But now I want to come back as the bond market. You can intimidate everybody." Laura Tyson, Council of Economic Advisers Chair, more gently chided the deficit hawks for treating the bond market as the new God.

In retrospect, the Clinton Economic Program emphasizing deficit reduction and protection of core social programs would be the most successful fiscal and monetary program of the past century.

The deficit declined from $290.3 billion in 1992, to an aggregate $452.7 billion surplus between 1998 and 2001, reducing the total deficit from $3.77 to $3.32 billion, "the fiscal equivalent," the *New York Times* would opine, "of the fall of the Berlin Wall." Debt as a percentage of GDP would decline from 47.8 to 31.4 percent between 1993 and 2001. Had Clinton's economic policy been continued after the 2000 election, the nation was on track to be debt free within a decade.

In his Farewell Address on January 18, 2001, Clinton recognized his economic record as a hallmark achievement:

> Our economy is breaking records with more than 22 million new jobs, the lowest unemployment in 30 years, the highest homeownership ever, the longest expansion in history. Our families and communities are stronger. Thirty-five million Americans have used the family leave law; 8 million have moved off welfare. Crime is at a 25-year low. Over 10 million Americans receive more college aid, and more people than ever are going to college. Our schools are better. Higher standards, greater accountability, and larger investments have brought higher test scores and higher graduation rates. More than 3 million children have health insurance now, and more than 7 million Americans have been lifted out of poverty. Incomes are rising across the board. Our air and water are cleaner. Our food and drinking water are safer. And more of our precious land has been preserved in the continental United States than at any time in 100 years.

During the late 1990s, GDP growth averaged more than 4 percent annually. The typical American family had a real gain in annual income of $8,000 between 1993 and 2000. Inflation averaged 2.6 percent during Clinton's two terms compared to 6.1 percent between 1970 and 1992. By 2000, the unemployment rate had declined from 7.3 percent when Clinton took office to 3.8 percent in April 2000. The poverty rate fell to 11.3 percent, with African American unemployment halved from 14.1 percent in January 1993, to 7 percent in 2000, the lowest rate on record. Homeownership was 67.7 percent near the end of Clinton's presidency.[52]

The path to the Clinton economic turnaround was a rocky one.

On January 6, 1993, Bush's Office of Management Director Richard Darman had announced that the 1997 budget deficit would be $360 billion or $50 billion higher than previously forecast. Regardless of whether Darman and others had known this before the election and delayed the announcement to try to help Bush, this tied the Clinton Administration's hands.

At a meeting with his economics team on January 7, Clinton jettisoned the middle class tax cut he had pledged throughout the presidential campaign and began scaling back programmatic investments. Clinton had promised to cut the annual deficit in half by 1997. The revised budget forecast meant the deficit was likely to be nearly a third higher in 1997.

For Clinton, by January 7 deficit reduction had become the "threshold issue," as Robert Rubin later would write. Greenspan had told a Clinton senior adviser of a Federal Reserve Board Staff Study calculating that for every 1 percent of GDP of deficit reduction (then roughly $70 billion), bond rates would decrease 0.66 percent. This would stimulate the recovery and the reduction in deficits and federal government interest rate costs would free up resources for Clinton's investments. Alan Blinder, then Laura Tyson's Deputy at the Council of Economic Advisers, forcefully had argued on January 7th that without the restoration of fiscal discipline, the recovery would be "choked off" by higher interest rates. Even before the Clinton Omnibus Budget Plan was adopted, public knowledge that Clinton was serious about deficit reduction had led to a fall in 30-year Treasury bonds from 7.4 percent on December 31, 1992, to 6.83 percent on February 23, 1993, six days after Clinton presented his economic plan.

On February 17, 1993, Clinton presented his economic plan to "set our Nation on [a] new course." Clinton now proposed "an immediate package of jobs investments of over $30 billion to put people to work now, to create a half a million jobs: jobs to rebuild our highways and airports, to renovate housing, to bring new life to rural communities, and spread hope and opportunity among our Nation's youth." This was scaled back from as much as $88.8 billion in jobs and training he earlier had anticipated proposing.

To further increase investment and deficit reduction, Clinton emphasized that he was proposing "something no American Government has ever been called upon to do at the same time before, spending must be cut and taxes must be raised."

Clinton said of budget cuts:

> [T]o revolutionize Government we have to ensure that we live within our means, and that should start at the top and with the White House. In the last few days I have announced a cut in the White House staff of 25 percent, saving approximately $10 million. . . . I have cut the Federal bureaucracy, or will over the next 4 years, by approximately 100,000 positions, for a combined savings of $9 billion. . . .
>
> Tonight I call for an across-the-board freeze in Federal Government salaries for one year. And thereafter, during this 4-year period, I recommend that salaries rise at one point lower than the cost of living allowance normally involved in Federal pay increases.
>
> Next, I recommend that we make 150 specific budget cuts [which he calculated would cut federal spending by a total of $246 billion].

In 1997, Clinton estimated that budget cuts would amount to "$140 billion in that year alone from the deficit, a real revenue increase, a real deficit reduction." The cuts included the peace dividend created by lower Defense Department needs after the fall of the Soviet Union, elimination of programs Clinton urged were no longer needed such as nuclear power research and development, and other cuts that were "really tough ones," such as reduced interest subsidies for the Rural Electric Administration.

Combined with the budget cuts were tax increases to be imposed on "those who benefited the most in the past:"

> For the wealthiest, those earning more than $180,000 per year, I ask you all who are listening tonight to support a raise in the top rate for Federal income taxes from 31 to 36 percent. We recommend a 10 percent surtax on incomes over $250,000 a year, and we recommend closing some loopholes that let some people get away without paying any tax at all.
>
> For businesses with taxable incomes in excess of $10 million, we recommend a raise in the corporate tax rate, also to 36 percent, as well as a cut in the deduction for business entertainment expenses.

Clinton emphasized: "98.6 percent of America's families will have no increase in their income tax rates, only 1.2 percent at the top." He stressed there will "be no cuts in benefits for Medicare."

Clinton did propose taxes on Social Security and energy consumption:

> The plan does ask older Americans with higher incomes, who do not rely solely on Social Security to get by, to contribute more. This plan will not affect the 80 percent of Social Security recipients who do not pay taxes on Social Security now. . . .
>
> . . . I recommend that we adopt a BTU tax on the heat content of energy as the best way to provide us with revenue to lower the deficit because it also combats pollution, promotes energy efficiency, promotes the independence, economically, of this country as well as helping to reduce the debt, and because it does not discriminate against any area. . . .
>
> Taken together, these measures will cost an American family with an income of about $40,000 a year less than $17 a month. It will cost American families with incomes under $30,000 nothing because of other programs we propose, principally those raising the earned-income tax credit.

The Earned Income Tax Credit, enacted in 1975 and expanded in 1978, provided a tax credit for wage earners with lower incomes above the standard personal deduction.

In aggregate, the February 17 Clinton economic plan was expected to achieve the president's goal of nearly a $500 billion budget deficit reduction over five years.

In the same February 17 economic policy speech, Clinton introduced an ambitious social agenda, including a future comprehensive plan for health care reform, expansion of Head Start, increased resources for education, national service, a commitment to end welfare "as we know it," a tough crime bill, campaign finance reform, and a motor voter bill.

The Omnibus Budget Plan would be enacted by the skin of its teeth on August 6, after a 218 to 216 vote in the House followed by a 50–50 vote in the Senate, with Vice President Al Gore casting the decisive 51st vote in favor of the plan.

In retrospect, Clinton would blame his failure to relentlessly campaign for his economic plan as a "critical tactical mistake." Rubin explained: "The President told me that in 1993, we had 'left the field.' . . . Clinton should have been out talking about his economic program every day. He told me he would never again attempt a major policy initiative without an integral and forceful communication and political strategy. He also said he should have made an intense effort to frame the debate from the very beginning."

Republicans and the business community depicted the Clinton economic package as a tax increase, so effectively that when California Senator Dianne Feinstein ran for reelection in 1994, 42 percent of Californians believed their taxes had been raised in 1993. The Republicans saw the taxes as a "job killer," "a one way ticket to recession."

Compounding Clinton's early failure to campaign for his economic plan were a series of amateur hour mistakes. During the period before his February 17, 1993 speech, Clinton's support would be weakened by his January 29, 1993, reversal of his earlier commitment to gays in the military in favor of a six-month deferral of a decision and ultimately the awkward "don't ask, don't tell" policy that would lead to the discharge of over 10,000 gay members of the military.

On January 22, 1993, Clinton's first nominee for Attorney General, Zoe Baird, would be withdrawn after it was disclosed she had employed illegal immigrants and failed to pay Social Security taxes for them. In his memoir, Clinton would acknowledge: "Zoe had not misled us in any way.... We had failed to evaluate the matter properly."

In May 1993, there would be controversy over the White House Travel Office, dubbed Travelgate by William Safire. In June, the withdrawal of prominent Law Professor Lani Guinier, Clinton's nominee to lead the Civil Rights Division of the Justice Department after press attacks explained that Guinier had articles favoring race-based proportional representation, rather than conventional voting rights, to remedy voting discrimination. The Clinton administration during its early months sometimes looked like the gang that could not shoot straight. By June 5–6, 1993, Clinton's approval rating, according to Gallup, would reach its nadir, 37 percent. A private poll commissioned by Clinton pollster Stan Greenberg was worse. Only 28 percent rated Clinton's job performance as "excellent" or "good."

The Omnibus Budget Bill suffered a series of cuts during the period of Clinton's perceived weakness. Clinton had proposed a total of $231 billion in investments over five years. On March 18 and 19, 1993, the House by a vote of 243–183 passed a Resolution approving the broad outline of Clinton's five-year plan, but limited 1994 investments to less than $1 billion and 1995 investments to $6 billion.

The House had responded to a Congressional Budget Office estimate that the Clinton budget plan would fall $50 billion short of its five-year deficit reduction target and used budget cuts to social investments to address the shortfall.

The Senate, with 43 Republican votes, filibustered, knowing that 60 votes were needed to end a filibuster.

On April 21, 1993, Congress declined to enact Clinton's proposal for the first $16.3 billion of his $30 billion investment in job creation. This was a small part of a $496 billion budget reduction package. In political terms, the defeat was telling. A sufficient number of Democrats had abandoned Clinton's short-term fix for high levels of minority youth unemployment, prompting Clinton to bitterly declaim: "Where are all the Democrats?" "I hope," he told his advisers, "you're all aware that we're all Eisenhower Republicans and we are fighting Reagan Republicans. We stand for lower deficits and free trade and the bond market. Isn't that great?"

By May, Clinton had seen his short-term stimulus package defeated, several cuts in longer term investments, and delayed the administration's health care reform until after the Omnibus Budget Bill was enacted.

Clinton persuaded David Gergen, a well-respected veteran of three Republican administrations, to join the White House as Counselor and help his administration with organization and communications.

In July, the Clinton administration tapped Roger Altman, the experienced Deputy Treasury Secretary, to lead a War Room. Altman believed that the economic plan was losing public support to Republican accusations that the plan was another tax and spend Democratic Party proposal. By then, the mood of Clinton and many on his team was that nothing mattered except winning. A defeat on the economic plan likely would lead to a one-term presidency.

To secure the enactment of the budget plan, the Senate Finance Committee replaced the environmentally friendly BTU tax with a 4.3 cent-a-gallon increase in the gasoline tax, and more spending cuts. On July 29, 1993, the House and Senate agreed on the 4.3 cent-a-gallon gas tax, a "pathetic" outcome as Treasury Secretary

Bentsen put it, in place of all fuels BTU tax that had been meant to shift fuel use from coal and oil to natural gas and better protect the environment.

As enacted, the Omnibus Budget Reconciliation Act of 1993 did succeed in achieving Clinton's deficit reduction goal. In celebrating his August 10, 1993, signing the Act, Clinton exalted:

> What we heard tonight at the other end of Pennsylvania Avenue was the sound of gridlock breaking. . . . After 12 long years, we can say to the American people tonight we have laid the foundation for the renewal of the American dream. . . . After a long season of denial and drift and decline, we are seizing control of our economic destiny.

Some $241 billion in tax increases were included in the Act. Without a single Republican voting for the Act, Democratic majorities in the House and Senate approved:

- Increasing the two top brackets of individual taxation from 31 percent to 36 percent for taxpayers with annual taxable income over $51,900 to $250,000 and 39.6 percent for taxable income over $250,000.
- The corporate tax rate was increased from 34 percent to 35 percent for corporations earning between $10 to $15 million, 38 percent for income from $15 to $18.33 million, and 35 percent above $18.33 million.
- A gas tax of 4.3 cents per gallon was enacted.
- 85 percent of Social Security benefits were subject to income taxes, increasing from the previous 50 percent.
- The $135,000 cap on the 29 percent Medicare tax was removed.
- The Alternative Minimum Tax was increased from 24 percent to 26 for taxable income below $175,000 and 28 percent for taxable income above $175,000.
- A 10 percent luxury tax was applied to the price of any passenger vehicle whose price exceeded $30,000.
- The Estate Tax for estates between $2.5 and $3 million was set at 53 percent and for tax increased above $3 million at 55 percent.

- Meal and entertainment tax deductions were reduced from 80 to 50 percent.
- Under Internal Revenue Code § 162(m), no corporate tax deduction could be taken for income above $1 million with a critical exception for performance based compensation determined by the Corporate Board's Compensation Committee.

Over the five-year period of the Clinton plan, $255 billion in spending cuts were achieved, most in the military or Medicare.

Military spending had declined in nominal dollars from $427.7 billion in 1984, the first year of Bush's presidency, to $358.6 billion in 1993, the first year of Clinton's presidency. The 1993 budget deal reduced military spending further to $338.6 billion in 1994, on a glide path to a low of $296.7 billion in 1998.

The Medicare federal portion of capital payments and inflation updates were reduced as were payments for skilled nursing facilities, hospice, capital related costs of outpatient hospitals, and ambulatory surgical center services.

Additional savings were achieved through modifications of the Medicaid drug rebate and services for *bona fide* emergency serves for undocumented aliens.

There also were modest social investments.

The Earned Income Tax Credit was expanded with 40 percent credit for two or more qualifying children for years beginning in 1995 in place of earlier phase out percentages of 20 or 21 percent. For each taxable year after 1994, cost of living adjustments were applied.

Some 95 areas could be designated Empowerment, Enterprise Communities and Rural Development Investment Areas, based on poverty rates and were eligible for such incentives as Empowerment Zone Tax Exempt Facility Zones and Employment Tax Credit for qualified wages.

Medical child support was required for children born out of wedlock or not living with a parent in an insurer's service area.

The states were required to establish pediatric vaccine programs.

Several provisions were enacted to strengthen and preserve families such as a provision creating an incentive program for states to develop, establish, expand or operate a program of family preservation services and community based family support and separate provisions creating entitlement funding for state courts to assess and improve proceedings related to foster care and adoption.

Tax deductions were prohibited for corporate lobbying expenditures.

In 1997, the Taxpayer Relief Act would make further changes. A $500 tax credit for each child under 17 was added, interest on qualified education loans could be deducted up to $2500 in 2001, penalty free withdrawals from individual retirement accounts for higher education were authorized, a new education individual retirement account was established, the long-term capital gains rate was reduced from 28 to 20 percent, the first $500,000 in capital gains on home sales for a married couple or $250,000 for an individual taxpayer was exempted from taxation, new Roth individual retirement accounts were established, and estates under $1 million were exempted in 2008 from federal estate taxes.[53]

Both in the runup to the 1993 enactment of the Omnibus Budget Reconciliation Act and in the political roller coaster that occurred in the Clinton Administration after its sharp defeat in the 1994 congressional elections, there was general concord between the fiscal policy of deficit reduction as consistently pursued by Clinton and relatively low interest rates maintained by the Fed.

Throughout 1993, the discount rate was left unchanged at 3 percent, despite what the Federal Reserve Annual Report characterized as "considerable strength in the fourth quarter of 1992" with a real GDP increase of 5.75 percent, which would have justified an interest rate increase early in 1993 and "ambiguous indications" before the May 1993 Federal Open Market Committee Meeting. Greenspan during the pre-enactment period had cautioned the House Banking Committee not to back away from Clinton's $500 billion deficit reduction target. "If you appear to be backing off, I think the markets would react appropriately, negatively."

The enactment of the Omnibus Act had preceded, if not helped cause, a "sharp" increase in real GDP in the second half of 1993, with GDP growth throughout 1993 equal to 3.25 percent, inflation as measured by the Consumer Price Index edged lower in 1993, to 2.75 percent, and nearly 2 million jobs were added in 1993. In his second State of the Union address on January 25, 1994, Clinton could state:

> Led by the Vice President, we launched a campaign to reinvent Government. We cut staff, cut perks, even trimmed the

> fleet of Federal limousines. After years of leaders whose rhetoric attacked bureaucracy but whose action expanded it, we will actually reduce it by 252,000 people over the next 5 years. By the time we have finished, the Federal bureaucracy will be at its lowest point in 30 years.

The favorable economic consequences of the 1993 Omnibus Budget Reconciliation Act were overshadowed by the failure of Clinton's 1993 comprehensive health care program.

Clinton had emphasized health care reform in his 1992 election campaign. Comprehensive health care was the last great plank of the liberal agenda developed by Franklin Delano Roosevelt, amplified by Lyndon Johnson, Clinton's chance for political immortality. Clinton once explained: "If I don't get health care, I'll wish I didn't run for President."

Clinton's conciliatory instincts were cast aside for what Clinton characterized as "our most urgent priority:"

> This health care system of ours is badly broken, and it is time to fix it. Despite the dedication of literally millions of talented health care professionals, our health care is too uncertain and too expensive, too bureaucratic and too wasteful. It has too much fraud and too much greed.

Health care in 1993 involved approximately one-seventh of the United States economy, a $1 trillion system of hospitals, physicians, and other providers, insurance, education, and research.

Clinton sought to achieve several goals simultaneously.

First, he sought universal access to health care. As he explained in his September 22, 1993, Address on Health Care:

> Millions of Americans are just a pink slip away from losing their health insurance and one serious illness away from losing all their savings. Millions more are locked into the jobs they have now just because they or someone in their family has once been sick and they have what is called the pre-existing condition. And on any given day, over 37 million Americans, most of them working people and their little children, have no health insurance at all.

In his memoir, Clinton stressed the significance of his proposal to those with pre-existing conditions: "More than eighty million Americans had 'pre-existing conditions,' health problems that meant they were paying more for insurance, if they could get it, and often couldn't change jobs without losing it."

Second, Clinton sought cost containment: "[Our] medical bills are growing at over twice the rate of inflation, and the United States spends over a third more of its income on health care than any other nation on Earth. And the gap is growing, causing many of our companies in global competition severe disadvantage. There is no excuse for this kind of system." It was calculated that private expenditures for health care had increased from $246 billion in 1980, to $880 billion in 1993. Clinton urged: "Reform must produce savings in this health care system. It has to. We're spending over 14 percent of our income on health care. Canada's at 10. Nobody else is over 9."

Third, Clinton believed he was proposing a system that was politically feasible "without enacting any broad-based taxes." Clinton rejected price controls to address skyrocketing costs. They had not worked under Nixon. There was little reason to assume that they could work now. He rejected a government single payer system such as the existing Canada system or Medicare for All in favor of building on the existing private insurance system. Clinton would explain in his second State of the Union address on January 25, 1994, that his comprehensive health care plan:

> builds on what works today in the private sector, to expand employer-based coverage, to guarantee private insurance for every American. And I might say, employer-based private insurance for every American was proposed 20 years ago by President Richard Nixon to the United States Congress. It was a good idea then, and it's a better idea today.
>
> Why do we want guaranteed private insurance? Because right now 9 out of 10 people who have insurance get it through their employers. And that should continue. And if your employer is providing good benefits at reasonable prices, that should continue, too.

To make the private health care system work "without harming the quality of health care," Clinton proposed a complex system of managed competition:

> First, to give groups of consumers and small businesses the same market bargaining power that large corporations and large groups of public employees now have, we want to let market forces enable plans to compete. We want to force these plans

> to compete on the basis of price and quality, not simply to allow them to continue making money by turning people away who are sick or old or performing mountains of unnecessary procedures. But we also believe we should back this system up with limits on how much plans can raise their premiums.
>
> The second thing I want to say is that unless everybody is covered — and this is a very important thing — unless everybody is covered, we will never be able to fully put the brakes on health care inflation. Why is that? Because when people don't have any health insurance, they still get health care, but they get it when it's too late, when it's too expensive, often from the most expensive place of all, the emergency room. . . .

Clinton understood that this would require an employer mandate: "Every employer should provide coverage, just as three-quarters do now. Those that pay are picking up the tab for those who don't today. I don't think that's right."

Managed care in the Clinton plan required community ratings. To ensure that every person was insured at the same cost, the plan required basing insurance rates not on an individual's risk factors such as age or a pre-existing condition, but on the costs throughout a community. This meant the young and healthiest individuals, in effect, would subsidize the costs of older or sicker individuals.

And the Clinton plan sought to give every American a choice among at least three "high quality plans": "You can stay with your current doctor, join a network of doctors and hospitals, or join a health maintenance organization. If you don't like your plan, every year you'll have a chance to choose a new one. The choice will be left to the American citizen, the worker, not the boss and certainly not some Government bureaucrat."

Clinton emphasized: "Unless we do this, our workers will lose \$655 in income each year by the end of the decade. Small businesses will continue to face skyrocketing premiums. And a full third of small businesses now covering their employees say they will be forced to drop their insurance. Large corporations will bear bigger disadvantages in global competition. And health care costs devour more and more and more of our budget."

In retrospect, virtually every aspect of the substance and process of the Clinton Health Care Proposal would be criticized. The plan would be labelled a "historic misadventure," a political catastrophe.

The appointment of Hillary Clinton to lead the Health Care Task Force became a lightning rod for criticism. Hillary was undoubtedly qualified to do so. As Clinton explained on January 25 when he created the Task Force:

> As many of you know, while I was Governor of Arkansas, Hillary chaired the Arkansas Education Standards Committee, which created public school accreditation standards that have since become a model for national reform. In 1984–85, Hillary served as my designee on the Southern Regional Task Force on Infant Mortality. She was Chair of the Arkansas Rural Health Committee in 1979–80. And she has also served on the Board of the Arkansas Children's Hospital, where she helped establish Arkansas's first neo-natal unit.

The Clinton Task Force would be attacked for the secretiveness of its procedures. Although the purpose of the Task Force was to develop a legislative proposal "by listening to all parties" and "preparing health care reform legislation to be submitted to Congress within 100 days of [Clinton] taking office," the Task Force made a pivotal political mistake in not earlier involving Congress. The Task Force held only one public meeting but met at least 20 times behind closed doors in April and May 1993 to develop its proposal.

While the Task Force included the Secretaries of the Treasury, Defense, Veterans Affairs, Health and Human Services, Labor, and Commerce Departments, as well as the Director of the Office of Management Budget, and was advised by an independent working group Chaired by Ira Magaziner, that included 300 permanent federal government employees, 40 "special government employees" and an unknown number of consultants, it was widely believed that this was Hillary's initiative, aided and abetted by Magaziner.

In 1993, Clinton would defeat a lawsuit brought by the Association of American Physicians and Surgeons challenging whether a presidential spouse could lead an advisory task force. The Federal District of Columbia Court of Appeals concluded that the president's spouse was "the functional equivalent of an assistant to the President" and could do so.

More importantly, Hillary supported a series of unfortunate policy recommendations. Hillary and Magaziner both had wanted to include health care reform legislation in the 1993 Omnibus Budget Reduction Act because it ultimately would achieve significant cost savings and could be passed under Senate rules by a simple 51 vote majority. The Congressional Budget Office declined to give credit for future but uncertain savings in any budget the Clinton

Administration developed. To obviate short-term cost increases, Magaziner's earlier health care transition plan had recommended "short term price controls," one of many concepts anathema to several Clinton senior advisers including Treasury Secretary Bentsen, National Economic Council leader Rubin, and Secretary of Health and Human Services Secretary Donna Shalala.

When introduced on November 20, 1993, the Clinton Health Security Act was 1342 pages in length. In a Congress that routinely enacted lengthy budget and tax legislation, the length itself was not that exceptional. But the Clinton's approach to legislation was counterproductive. At the conclusion of Clinton's second State of the Union address on January 25, 1994, as Clinton recounted: "I held up a pen and said I would use it to veto any bill that didn't guarantee health insurance to all Americans." John Harris aptly characterized the veto threat as "a tactical error; it limited the president's flexibility to negotiate and compromise at the very moment he should have been expanding his room for maneuver." Until August 1994, Clinton rejected recommendations such as that of New York Senator Daniel Patrick Moynihan to seek an incremental approach to universal health care.

A galvanized Republican party opposition supported by lobbyists such as the Health Insurance Associates of America, the United States Chamber of Commerce, and the Conservative Heritage Foundation, skewered the Clinton plan. What Clinton called "a $300 million misinformation campaign" included television commercials featuring an apocryphal middle ages couple, Harry and Louise, were devastatingly effective in communicating their confusion trying to make sense of the Clinton health care plan while poring over details at their kitchen table.

By the end of April 1994, Clinton would acknowledge in his memoir "we had lost the health care communications battle." In March, a majority of respondents to a *Wall Street Journal/ WBC* poll opposed it. A *Wall Street Journal* article highlighted that most Americans did not understand it.

For the Republican party, defeating Clinton's healthcare proposal was a do or die issue. Republican Strategist Bill Kristol in December 1993, warned: "The long-term political effects of a successful... health care bill will be even worse — much worse.... It will revive the reputation of... Democrats as the generous protector of middle-class interests. And it will at the same time strike a punishing blow against Republican claims to defend the middle class by restraining government."

In June 1994, Senate Minority Leader Bob Dole announced he would use his powers of filibuster to block any health care legislation and make Clinton's health care proposal a major issue in the midterm elections.

Senate Majority Leader George Mitchell threw in the towel in September 1994. He was unable to bring in enough Republican votes to break Dole's filibuster. The Clinton plan never reached a Senate floor vote.

The postmortems soon began. James Patterson wrote: "The majority of Americans (those with health insurance) seemed mostly content with fee-for-service arrangements and exerted little pressure for erection of a new and complicated system." Liberals had not enthusiastically endorsed the plan, preferring a Single Payer System. Seasoned politicians such as Treasury Secretary Lloyd Bentsen felt that the Deficit Reduction Plan and Health Care Plan were too much for our political system to process at one time. Senator Moynihan urged Clinton to pursue welfare reform first.

For Clinton, there were smaller victories. In his first two weeks in office, Clinton had signed the Family and Medical Leave Act that guaranteed workers in businesses with more than 50 employees up to 12 weeks in unpaid leave in case of family medical emergencies. Clinton also revoked the gag order that prohibited abortion counseling in federally funded abortion clinics and signed an Executive Order permitting the use of fetal tissue in medical research.

In 1997, Congress would enact the Children's Health Insurance Plan, which by 2010 provided health care to 7.6 million children, the largest expansion of federal health care since Medicaid was enacted in 1965.[54]

But the political consequences of the defeat of Clinton's health care initiative were devastating. Robert Rubin would attribute the 1994 Republican landslide to five factors:

> First, by the time of the election, the economy's strength and the contribution made by Clinton's decisions were not yet clear. The second was the mischaracterization of our deficit reduction as a tax increase on the middle class, which proved extremely hard to shake. Related to that was a third factor: the misimpression, fueled by the healthcare plan, which itself was misleadingly described by opponents, that Clinton was an old-style, big-government liberal. Fourth was the effect in some elections of

> Clinton's advocacy of gun control legislation. A fifth and final factor was a series of issues and episodes [including White Water, gays in the military, Travelgate, poorly vetted nominees], mostly minor but blown out of proportion by the press, manipulated by political adversaries, and, as a contributing factor, sometimes mishandled in some respects by the White House.

Pivotal was the failure of the health care initiative. Historian Sean Wilentz concluded: "Above all, the final collapse of the health care initiative in September 1994 reinforced the impression that the administration, despite its early self-assurance, was inept as well as inexperienced."

Pivotal also was the political prowess of Newt Gingrich, who had nationalized elections to the House of Representatives with a Contract with America he coauthored. At a press conference six weeks before the 1994 election on September 27, 1994, Gingrich presented the Contract. Gingrich, then House Minority Whip, number two in the House hierarchy, was a Republican party firebrand who had sought to "build a much more aggressive, activist party" as he explained in March 1989, when elected Minority Whip. His combative approach would be credited with helping the Republicans gain control of the House in 1994 with a stunning gain of 54 seats and be dubbed The Gingrich Revolution. In 1995, Gingrich would be elected Speaker of the House and named *Time* magazine's "Man of the Year" with an article characterizing Newt Gingrich in sweeping terms: "*How One Man Changed the Way Washington Sees Reality*," describing Gingrich as "ruthlessly, brilliantly obnoxiously hammering together inevitabilities."

The Contract, coauthored by Gingrich and House Republican leader Dick Armey, based in part on President Reagan's 1985 State of the Union address, was signed by all but two of the Republican Members of the House. The Contract promised within the first 100 days of the next Congress, if the Republicans won control, to bring 10 bills to the House for a vote:

> **1. The Fiscal Responsibility Act**
>
> A balanced budget/tax limitation amendment and a legislative line-item veto to restore fiscal responsibility to an out-of-control Congress, requiring them to live under the same budget constraints as families and businesses.

2. The Taking Back Our Streets Act

An anti-crime package including stronger truth-in-sentencing, "good faith" exclusionary rule exemptions, effective death penalty provisions, and cuts in social spending from this summer's "crime" bill to fund prison construction and additional law enforcement to keep people secure in their neighborhoods and kids safe in their schools.

3. The Personal Responsibility Act

Discourage illegitimacy and teen pregnancy by prohibiting welfare to minor mothers and denying increased AFDC for additional children while on welfare, cut spending for welfare programs, and enact a tough two-years-and-out provision with work requirements to promote individual responsibility.

4. The Family Reinforcement Act

Child support enforcement, tax incentives for adoption, strengthening rights of parents in their children's education, strong child pornography laws, and an elderly dependent care tax credit to reinforce the central role of families in American society.

5. The American Dream Restoration Act

A $500 per child tax credit, begin repeal of the marriage tax penalty, and creation of American Dream Savings Accounts to provide middle class tax relief.

6. The National Security Restoration Act

No U.S. troops under U.N. command and restoration of the essential parts of our national security funding to strengthen our national defense and maintain our credibility around the world.

7. The Senior Citizens' Fairness Act

Raise the Social Security earnings limit which currently forces seniors out of the work force, repeal the 1993 tax hikes on Social Security benefits and provide tax incentives for private long-term care insurance to let Older Americans keep more of what they have earned over the years.

8. The Job Creation and Wage Enhancement Act

Small business incentives, capital gains and indexation, neutral cost recovery, risk assessment/cost-benefit analysis strengthening the Regulation Act, and unfunded mandate reform to create jobs and raise worker wages.

9. The Common Sense Legal Reform Act

"Loser Pays" laws, reasonable limits on punitive damages and reform of product liability laws to stem the endless tide of litigation.

10. The Citizen Legislature Act

A first-ever vote on term limits to replace career politicians with citizen legislators.

Clinton later acknowledged:

> Gingrich had proved to be a better politician than I was. He understood that he could nationalize a midterm election with the contract, with incessant attacks on the Democrats, and with the argument that all the conflicts and bitter partisanship in Washington the Republicans had generated must be the Democrats' fault since we controlled both Congress and the White House.

The 1994 midterm elections were hailed as "the end of the New Deal," "the completion of what Ronald Reagan began." Clinton would write: "On November 8, we got the living daylights beat out of us, losing eight Senate seats and sixty-four House seats, the largest defeat for our party since 1946, when the Democrats were routed after President Truman tried to get health insurance for all Americans." No incumbent Republican Senator, Representative, or Governor lost. Nationally known Democrats such as New York Governor Mario Cuomo and House Speaker Tom Foley were defeated. Gingrich for a period became was the dominant figure in national politics.

In an unprecedented nationally televised address to the nation on April 7, 1995, for a Speaker of the House, Gingrich stated in part:

> . . . We outlined 10 major proposals in the Contract that would begin to break the logjam of the past; the House passed nine of them. First, we passed the Shays Act which makes the Congress obey all the laws that other Americans have to obey. The House

passed it, the Senate passed it, and the President signed it. . . . We passed a balanced budget amendment in the House with bipartisan support; it has been temporarily defeated in the Senate by one vote.

. . .

As promised, we introduced a constitutional amendment on term limits, but we failed even though 85% of House Republicans voted for it. . . .

In both the House and the Senate we passed a line item veto.

. . .

Other Contract proposals have passed the House and are being worked on in the Senate. We passed regulatory reform, legal reform and welfare reform. We passed a $500 tax credit per child. We passed an increase in the earning limit for senior citizens, so they won't have their social security checks cut if they earn extra money. We passed a capital gains tax cut and indexed these gains to spur the savings and investments that create jobs.

Even with all these successes and others, the Contract with America is only a beginning. It is the preliminary skirmish to the big battles yet to come.

The big battles will deal with how we remake the Government of the United States. . . .

A truly compassionate government would replace the welfare state with opportunity. The welfare system's greatest cost is the human cost to the poor. In the name of "compassion" we have funded a system that is cruel and destroys families. Its failure is reflected by the violence, brutality, child abuse and drug addiction in every local TV news broadcast. . . .

Everywhere I go, Americans complain about an overly complicated tax code and an arrogant, unpredictable and unfair Internal Revenue Service. . . .

We will improve Medicare by offering a series of new Medicare options that will increase senior citizens control over their own health care and guarantee them access to the best and most modern systems of health research and health innovation.

. . .

. . . I want to reassure all of you who are on Social Security, or will soon retire, that your Social Security is fine. No one will touch your Social Security, period. . . .

Next month we will propose a budget that is balanced over seven years. The budget can be balanced even with the problems of the federal government. It can be balanced without touching a penny of Social Security and without raising taxes. In fact, spending overall can go up every year. We simply must

> limit annual spending increases to about 3% between now and 2002.

A few days later on April 18, 1994, as historian Sean Wilentz wrote:

> President Clinton held a press conference in prime time, but, in sharp contrast to the media coverage being lavished on Gingrich, only one network agreed to broadcast it. Responding to a pointed question about whether he feared he was not even being heard anymore, Clinton was pathetic. "The Constitution gives me relevance," he replied. "The power of our ideas gives me relevance. . . . The President is relevant here.

This was the low point of the Clinton presidency.

Over time, a few of the Contract with America Bills were enacted and others were of consequence in the passage of compromise legislation.

No amendment to the Constitution to require a balance budget was enacted. But Gingrich could rightfully claim the House enactment of this provision and the near Senate enactment were of consequence in the passage of the Balanced Budget Act in 1997.

The Line Item Veto was enacted and signed by Clinton but held to be unconstitutional by the United States Supreme Court in 1998 on the ground that it violated the Constitutionally mandated requirements for repeal of laws. "There is no provision in the Constitution that authorizes the President to enact, to amend or to repeal statutes."

Other Contract with America Bills were passed in the House and not approved in the Senate such as the National Security Restoration Act, limiting United States troops from serving under the United Nations. Some did not emerge from a Congressional Conference Committee after being passed by both Houses, such as a moratorium on federal regulation, or were vetoed by Clinton, such as the Loser Pays and Limits on Punitive Damages provisions of the Common Sense Legal Reform Act. A constitutional amendment to establish 12-year term limits on members of the House and Senate failed to receive the required two-thirds majority in the House.

Clinton was able to reverse his political fortunes and win reelection in 1996, by moving to a more centrist position on several of his policies and working with Dick Morris, by 1994 to practice "triangulation." As Clinton explained triangulation, it "[bridged] the divide between Democrats and Republicans and taking the best ideas of both." He acknowledged "to many liberals and some in the press corps, triangulation was compromise without conviction, a cynical ploy to win reelection." Historian John Harris aptly stated: "As 1995 arrived, the President's back against the wall, the idealism and vainglory of the early years yielded to a determination to survive Gingrich's Republican onslaught. The Clinton presidency had entered its realistic phase, and Dick Morris was the instrument — the living extension — of Bill Clinton's realism."

Morris, backed by sophisticated survey data, urged Clinton to support the most popular aspects of the Contract with America, specifically support a balanced budget, reduce the deficit, shrink government, prune burdensome regulations, and sign a welfare bill. But Morris adamantly counseled Clinton to reject the social aspects of the Republican agenda such as the party's hostility to abortion rights and environmental protection, Federal aid to education, the harshness of the Gingrich revolution. Vehemently oppose cuts in popular entitlement programs such as Medicare. And above all else, don't flip flop. "It is never worth the price. If we've said something before, we are bound by it. . . . Don't ever, ever change your mind."

Throughout 1994 and 1995, Clinton balanced centrism with clear lines in the sand. On December 15, 1994, Clinton proposed a Middle Class Bill of Rights, including a $500 tax credit for families with incomes of $75,000 or less, tax deductibility for college tuition and expanded individual retirement account tax exclusions. On January 24, 1995, in his second State of the Union address, Clinton assimilated several popular Contract with America ideas including the Line Item Veto, welfare reform, the Middle Class Bill of Rights now with a tax cut of $500 for families with children under 13, a tax deduction for all education and training after high school, an expansion of individual retirement accounts to permit "people to . . . withdraw from it, tax free for the cost of education, health care, first-time home buying, or the care of a parent." He reminded the audience: "[L]ast year we passed a very tough crime bill: longer sentences, "three strikes and you're out," almost 60 new capital punishment offenses, more prisons, more prevention, 100,000 more police." On June 13, 1995, in a nationally televised address, Clinton proposed to balance the budget in ten years, not seven as proposed by the Republicans, but without the proposed Republican cuts in education, health care, and the environment and without the massive tax cuts proposed by the Republicans. Most emphatically in his third State of the Union address on January 23, 1996, Clinton announced: "The era of big government is over."

But Clinton articulated limits to his willingness to bend. He would veto bills that included "loser pays" provisions for private lawsuits, repeal the ban on assault weapons, weaken food safety or environmental regulation, or curb the president's power to have the United States military participate in United Nations peacekeeping missions. Emphatically, Clinton opposed Republican tax cuts, describing them as three times larger than what the government could afford.

Clinton's comeback was aided by Gingrich's tendency to overreach. During the 1994 election Campaign, Gingrich had called the Democrats "the enemy of normal Americans." Gingrich claimed without evidence that 25 percent of the Clinton staff had used drugs before joining the White House. Gingrich characterized a psychotic South Carolina woman who drown her children as reflecting the "sick society" that the Democrats had created. Democratic values, Gingrich claimed, were responsible for the large number of out-of-wedlock births to teen mothers. Within a few years of becoming Speaker of the House, Gingrich supported appointment of six independent counsels to investigate the Clinton Administration, including Ken Starr whose four year investigation of Clinton, initially in White Water financial transactions, ultimately to the Monica Lewinsky sex scandal, Clinton's perjury to attempt to cover it up and lead to Clinton's impeachment by the House on a party line vote in December 1998, but also to Congress ending the independent counsel process in 1999. Clinton would be acquitted by the Senate in 1999. The *Washington Post*'s Haynes Johnson would characterize Starr as the "relentless, self-righteous Inspector Javert [the villain in Victor Hugo's novel, *Les Miserables*], a humorless moralist, a puritan in Babylon, out of touch with contemporary attitudes. A zealous ideologue."

Clinton, in contrast, appeared presidential in his dignified but forceful response to the April 1995 explosion of the Federal Murrah Building in Oklahoma City which killed 168 people, including 19 children. At the time, this was the worst incident of domestic terrorism in American history. Clinton vowed to capture the killers and "treat them like killers." The culprits were soon captured and found to be right wing extremists. Clinton's sermon four days later to an audience of 18,000 helped the nation cope, stating: "Let us let our children know that we will stand up against the forces of fear."

Eighty-four percent of respondents to an NBC/*Wall Street Journal* poll approved of Clinton's handling of the attack in Oklahoma City.

Gingrich's tendency to overreach was most significantly manifest in his April 1995 threat not to increase the federal debt limit as a bludgeon to pressure Clinton to accept massive budget cuts.

In the first week of June 1995, Clinton vetoed a $16 billion package of rescissions from the existing budget, including cuts to Americorps, summer jobs for young people, education funds, and environmental protection. On June 29, 1995, the Clinton administration and Republican Congress compromised on the rescissions, restoring $700 million for education, Americorps, and the safe drinking water program.

Gingrich upped the ante. The federal government fiscal year ended on September 30, 1995, without a budget for the new budget year beginning October 1, 1995. Clinton and the Republican Congressional majority were at loggerheads over proposed Republican cuts to Medicare, Medicaid, food stamps, the student loan program, Americorps, environmental regulation, and Clinton's earlier initiative to add 100,000 new police officers. The Republican budget bills would have cut taxes for the wealthiest taxpayers and increased taxes on lower income taxpayers by cutting back the earned income tax credit.

Gingrich's leverage remained the threat not to raise the debt ceiling. The federal government had not defaulted in its 206 year history. Default, Clinton, Treasury Secretary Rubin, and many in the financial community believed would shake confidence in the United States reliability as a borrower, inevitably raising interest rates, and undermine the United States ability to persuade other nations deeply in debt to honor their debt commitments.

On November 10, 1995, the Republican majority in Congress sent Clinton a continuing resolution, popularly called a CR, to keep the government open but only if Clinton accepted a $270 billion increase in Medicare premiums, and a corresponding cut in taxes as well as cuts in education and the environment. Shortly later, Congress sent Clinton an extension of the debt limit, as Clinton wrote in his memoir, "that was worse than the CR." Not only did the Debt Limit Extension include the earlier budget but "also stripped from the Secretary of the Treasury the fund management flexibility he had had since the Reagan years to avoid default under extraordinary circumstances. Even worse, it lowered the debt limit again after thirty days, virtually ensuring a default."

Clinton dug in his heels and refused to accept the Republican budget as he put it at a November 13, 1995, meeting with Republican leaders Gingrich, Dick Armey, Dole, and Democratic leaders Senator Daschle and House Minority Leader Gephardt, "even if I drop to 5 percent in the polls."

Clinton vetoed both the Continuing Resolution and Debt Ceiling Bills At midnight on November 13, 1995, the federal government shut down. Almost 800,000 federal employees were sent home, national parks closed, Social Security, veterans' benefits, and safety inspection were suspended. Clinton approved Treasury Secretary Rubin borrowing $61 billion from the Civil Service Retirement Fund and a federal savings program to avoid default for several months.

Gingrich on November 15th, in what he later termed his "single most avoidable mistake" as Speaker complained to a *Christian Science Monitor* reporter that Clinton had snubbed him on the flights to and from Israeli Prime Minister Yitzhak Rabin's funeral by not discussing the budget with him and that he and Senate Majority Leader Dole had been forced to use Air Force One's rear exit. This, Gingrich explained, was "part of why you ended up with us sending down a tougher continuing resolution." Gingrich was ridiculed for explaining the federal government shutdown in terms of a personal grievance. A *New York Daily News* cartoon depicted him as a "cry baby" in diapers, holding a rattle.

Clinton on November 19, 1995, again publicly stated he would work for a seven-year balanced budget agreement, which he believed with deficits dropping faster than was expected could be achieved without the draconian Republican budget cuts. That day, he also signed two appropriations bills for the legislative branch, Treasury Department, Postal Service, and general government operations, returning 200,000 of the 800,000 federal employees back to work. The initial federal government shutdown soon ended with a short term Congressional Resolution.

On December 6, 1995, the Republicans approved their budget, prompting a second shutdown on December 16th. The second shutdown lasted three weeks with public sentiment decisively swinging against Gingrich as "unfeeling and mean-spirited, willing to disrupt the government's ability to function in order to attack a cornerstone of the American Welfare State," as historian Sean Wilentz later wrote.

By early January 1996, the Republican Congressional leadership sent Clinton continuing resolutions to keep the government open without draconian budget cuts. Gingrich conceded to Clinton: "We made a mistake. We thought you would cave." Elsewhere, Gingrich would admit: "In retrospect, if I were doing it all over again, we would consciously avoid the government shutdown. It was clearly wrong."

Large majorities of the public blamed the Republicans for the federal government shutdown. Moody's and Standard & Poor's, the leading bond rating agencies, warned that the AAA rating of federal government bonds were at risk, meaning that if a lower rating was applied to the federal government, interest rates would rise. The Republican majority subsequently supported raising the federal debt limit, agreed to fund the federal government for the current fiscal year and accepted Clinton's seven-year deficit reduction plan without the full Republican budget cuts.[55]

Robert Dole, Senate Majority Leader, former Vice Presidential nominee, was nominated by the Republicans to challenge Clinton in 1996. Dole, 73 years old, was instinctively more moderate in style and substance than Gingrich. He was a wounded World War II hero who sought to run a campaign that would be "the bridge to a time of tranquility, faith and confidence." He scorned the Clinton administration as containing "a core of the elite who never grew up, never did anything real, never sacrificed, never suffered and never learned."

To secure the nomination, Dole gravitated to the right, choosing supply side enthusiast Jack Kemp as his Vice President. Dole and Kemp supported a 15 percent across-the-board tax cut, flatter taxes, school choice, and a strengthened national defense. Dole ran on a Republican Party platform that also supported:

> elimination of the Departments of Commerce, Housing and Urban Development, Education, and Energy, and the elimination, defunding or privatization of agencies which are obsolete, redundant, of limited value, or too regional in focus. Examples of agencies we seek to defund or to privatize are the National Endowment for the Arts, the National Endowment for the Humanities, the Corporation for Public Broadcasting, and the Legal Services Corporation.

Later in August, the Clinton campaign was "rocked" as Clinton put it by news reports that Dick Morris had been carrying on a year-long relationship with a prostitute while advising Clinton. Morris promptly resigned.

"Where is the outrage?" Dole repeatedly demanded.

Clinton campaigned as the candidate of the "vital American center." On August 22, 1996, Clinton, after earlier vetoing two Republican Welfare Reform Bills, took a decisive step to fortify his support. He signed a controversial Welfare Reform Act that he had negotiated with the Republican leadership, including Gingrich. The Personal Responsibility and Work Opportunity Act barred immigrants from receiving welfare and put a five-year limit on how long a welfare recipient could receive cash assistance.

The Act outraged liberal members of Congress by ending aid to families with dependent children that provided cash assistance to low income families in favor of a program of block grants to states. In aggregate, the number of Americans receiving cash assistance would drop from 12.2 million in 1996 to 5.3 million in 2001. Senator Daniel Patrick Moynihan would label the new Welfare Act "the most brutal act of social policy since Reconstruction."

Several Clinton Cabinet members including Health and Human Services Secretary Shalala, Labor Secretary Reich, and Treasury Secretary Rubin urged a veto. Dick Morris had pleaded with Clinton to sign the bill as a key to reelection. Clinton ultimately agreed after noting the new Act's "serious flaws" signed into law a Welfare Act "to end welfare as we know it."

Clinton won the election because of the economy. By the time of his acceptance speech on August 29, 1996, 10 million new jobs had been created, 4.4 million Americans owned a home of their own for the first time. Clinton campaigned against what he characterized as a Republican "$550 billion tax scheme that will force them to ask for even bigger cuts in Medicare, Medicaid, education and the environment than they passed and I vetoed last year," tarring Dole as part of the Gingrich-Dole Congressional Republican leadership.

For the Democrats, the 1996 election results were mixed. Clinton would be reelected with 49.2 percent of the popular vote and 379 Electoral College votes to 40.7 percent for Dole and 159 electoral college votes and 8.4 percent for Perot. These results were more decisive than the 1992 presidential election when Clinton became president with a 43 percent popular vote. But Congress remained in Republican hands, with their majority in the House marginally reduced from 230–204 to 226–207 and increased in the Senate from 52–48 to 55–45.

Underlying Clinton's economic record was a tacit concord with the Federal Reserve. In February 1994, with the GDP growing at 5.5 percent, the Fed raised the discount rate from 3 to 4.75 percent, a significant increase but not so high that it stultified GDP growth of 3.5 percent in 1994. The Fed further raised the discount rate to 5.25 percent in 1995. The GDP rose more than 3 percent in 1996. By November, Greenspan would write in his memoir, "when President Clinton would win reelection, activity was expanding at a solid 4 percent rate." Unemployment was trending down from 6 percent in 1994 "on its way to 4 percent or lower." The Dow Jones Industrial Average doubled from 3243 the day in 1993 when Clinton took office to 6448 by year end 1996. Nonetheless, the Federal Reserve Open Market Committee declined to raise interest rates at its September 24, 1996, meeting.[56]

Clinton reappointed Greenspan on February 22, 1996. Treasury Secretary Rubin and National Economic Council Chair Tyson strongly urged Greenspan's reappointment. As Woodward wrote: "Tyson's main point was that they had come to view Greenspan almost as a member of their team. They didn't think of him as a Republican. He wasn't running the Fed as a Republican."

The alliance between the Clinton administration and Greenspan was most fully achieved in international finance.

In the fall of 1993, Clinton had impressed Greenspan "by fighting for the ratification of NAFTA," Greenspan wrote:

> The treaty, negotiated under President Bush, was designed primarily to phase out tariffs and other trade barriers between Mexico and the United States, though it also included Canada. Labor unions hated it, and so did most Democrats, as well as some conservatives; few Congress watchers thought it had a prayer. But Clinton argued, in effect, that you cannot stop the world from turning; like it or not, America was increasingly part of the international economy, and NAFTA embodied the belief that trade and competition create prosperity, and you need free markets to do that. He and the White House staff went all out, and after a two-month struggle they got the treaty approved.

NAFTA was an achievement for Clinton rooted in his strong commitment to free trade. But the deal had required working with leading Republicans such as Gingrich and opposing long-time allies such as House Majority Leader Dick Gephardt, who feared that

American corporations would move their operations to Mexico with lower labor costs and weaker environmental laws.

Clinton's basic argument, as historian Sean Wilentz summarized: "Ending trade barriers would force American exporters to be more efficient and competitive, and that this would increase their market share and, in turn, eventually benefit American workers." Clinton promoted NAFTA as part of a "national export strategy." At the December 1993 signing ceremony of the treaty, Clinton emphasized: "NAFTA means jobs, American jobs, and good-paying American jobs. If I didn't believe that, I would not support the agreement." Greenspan subsequently praised Clinton as "a risk taker who was not content with the status quo. Again, he's shown a preference for dealing in facts."

The Clinton Administration would negotiate approximately 300 trade agreements with other nations, including the 1993 General Agreement on Tariffs and Trade, which reduced worldwide tariffs by $740 billion and established the World Trade Organization to move toward uniform trade rules.[57]

The most significant collaboration between the Clinton administration and the Fed was the so-called Committee to Save the World, comprised of Greenspan, Treasury Secretary Rubin, and Deputy Treasury Secretary Larry Summers, who supervised the United States response to the financial crises in Mexico in 1995, Asia in 1997, including Thailand, Malaysia, South Korea, and Indonesia, Russia in 1998, and Brazil in 1999.

The facts in each instance were different, but the involvement of Greenspan in what could have been treated primarily as the province of the president and the Treasury instead evolved into a relationship that was close and one of mutual trust, setting in motion four and one half years of "breakfasts or lunches at least once a week, along with many other meetings and discussions," as Rubin and Greenspan separately recalled.

Mexico throughout the early 1990s had borrowed heavily, building up a large trade deficit using first peso denominated bonds, later tesobonos, short-term debt Mexican bonds, convertible into dollars at a fixed exchange rate. The peso was overvalued by an estimated 50 percent relative to dollars by the end of 1994. When the Mexican economy collapsed in 1994, after a violent insurgency in the Chiapas region and the assassination of a prominent Mexican politician, the outgoing Mexican government spent over $15 billion to prop up the Mexican peso at a fixed rate of three pesos per dollar. Newly installed Mexican President Ernesto Zedillo, in late December 1994, pressured by the deterioration of the peso in foreign exchange markets, allowed the peso to float freely. The peso soon fell to five pesos to the dollar. With only about $6 billion in foreign exchange reserves left, investors sold Mexican bonds and pesos. A further $30 billion of dollar indexed Mexican debt was due for payment in 1995, including $10 billion in the first three months of the year. Rubin explained: "Mexican authorities had lost control of their country's finances." Even with dollar interest rates approaching 20 percent, "the private sector was unlikely to produce loans on the scale needed to prevent default."

Greenspan urged Rubin to respond to the crisis with "a substantial amount of money, significantly more than we thought we needed" to stabilize the Mexican economy. This was the "least-worst" of available policy options. Rubin and Summers on January 10, 1995, recommended to Clinton a United States loan guarantee of $25 billion, knowing that the IMF also would provide "a significant amount of money." Clinton concurred, later explaining:

> If Mexico defaulted on its obligations, the economic "meltdown," as Bob Rubin tried to avoid calling it, could accelerate, with massive unemployment, inflation, and, very likely, a steep and prolonged recession because the international financial institutions, other governments, and private investors would all be unwilling to put more money at risk there.
>
> As Rubin and Summers explained, the economic collapse of Mexico could have severe consequences for the United States. First, Mexico was our third-largest trading partner. If it couldn't buy our products, American companies and employees would be hurt. Second, economic dislocation in Mexico could lead to a 30 percent increase in illegal immigration, or half a million more people each year. Third, an impoverished Mexico would almost certainly become more vulnerable to increased activity by illegal drug cartels, which were already sending large quantities of narcotics across the border into the United States. Finally, a default by Mexico could have a damaging impact on other countries, by shaking investors' confidence in emerging markets in the rest of Latin America, Central Europe, Russia, South Africa, and other countries we were trying to help modernize and prosper. Since about 40 percent of American exports went to developing countries, our economy could be hurt badly.

Clinton convened a meeting with Senate leaders Dole and Daschle and House leaders Gingrich and Gephardt, each of whom soon supported the plan. After further encouragement from Senate Banking Chair Alfonse D'Amato, the Clinton administration request was increased to $40 billion to "overpower" the crisis.

The reaction generally on Capitol Hill and with the public, in sharp contrast, was overwhelmingly negative. Rubin recounted:

> Many Democratic legislators had bucked their supporters in organized labor to vote for NAFTA. Now the opponents of NAFTA were taunting them — *look, we told you so.* On the Republican side, some of the new group of highly energized freshmen were eager to fight the President and skeptical of international engagement. Why help a country that sends us narcotics and illegal immigrants, especially when that help would benefit Wall Street at the same time?

A Poll in the *Los Angeles Times* reported that people in the United States opposed helping Mexico by 79 to 18 percent. Some economists criticized the moral hazard of appearing to bail out Mexico, setting up the expectation that other countries would be bailed out in the future as well.

By the end of January, it was clear that a United States loan guarantee to Mexico of $40 billion as revised to $20 billion with an IMF commitment of $17.8 billion would not be approved by Congress.

The Treasury on January 31, 1995, with Clinton and Greenspan's support authorized $20 billion from its Exchange Stabilization Fund, the Roosevelt era fund established to stabilize currencies when the United States departed from the gold standard, to support Mexico. This $20 billion, combined with $17.8 billion from the IMF and $10 billion from other central banks provided a total of $47.8 billion.

The Clinton Administration did not seek a congressional vote on the Exchange Stabilization Fund intervention, and the Mexican loan guarantee remained highly unpopular. Some in Congress were furious. Democratic Representatives Maxine Waters pointedly asked Rubin whether the bondholders who would be protected by the loan guarantees were Rubin's "Wall Street buddies." When the Mexican economy began to stabilize, *New York Times* columnist Tom Friedman described the Mexican intervention as "the least popular, least understood, but most important foreign policy decision of the Clinton Presidency." Despite anxiety whether Mexico would take other necessary steps to rebuild confidence and attract private capital, the United States role in the Mexico crisis worked. By 1997, Mexico repaid its crisis loans to the United States in full.

The United States subsequently worked to increase IMF resources by 45 percent, providing $17.9 billion to the IMF. The expanded IMF resources would be consequential in subsequent crises in Asia, where South Korea would receive $58.2 billion in IMF Funds, Indonesia, $47.7 billion, and Thailand, $17.2 billion, as well as in Russia, which would receive $22.6 billion in IMF Funds, and Brazil, $41 billion.

The United States role in responding to the Asian contagion, Russia, and Brazil was different. In Russia in 1998, Clinton's relative weakness with Congress blocked efforts to further increase United States support for the IMF. On August 17, 1998, Russia devalued its currencies and defaulted on its loans. With United States stock markets dropping 20 percent from summer peaks, the Fed joined other central banks in easing policy in the fall. The Fed approved a .25 percent interest rate decrease on September 29, 1998, and a further .25 percent cut on November 17, 1998. Greenspan in a September 4, 1998, speech in Berkeley, California characterized the approach of the Fed and the Clinton administration by warning the United States could not remain "an oasis of prosperity" if the rest of the global economy weakened. The Russian economy, after a 10 percent drop in real GDP in 1998, recovered about half that loss in 1999.

In South Korea, Greenspan worked with Rubin to persuade United States banks led by Citicorp's John Reed to agree to a standstill agreement with South Korea that allowed it time to recover.[58]

The highlight of Clinton's second term would be the economy. In 1997, real GDP would increase 3.75 percent, household net worth would grow more than $3.5 trillion, 3 million jobs would be added to nonfarm payrolls, inflation would rise a scant 1.9 percent. In 1998, GDP would increase by more than 4 percent, 2.8 million nonfarm jobs would be added, inflation would decline to 1.5 percent, the federal government would record a $69 billion surplus, the first surplus in nearly three decades, followed by a $125.6 billion surplus in 1999, and a $236.2 billion surplus in 2000. In 1998, the stock market soared with the technology heavy Nasdaq market up nearly 40 percent, the Standard & Poor 500 Composite Index up 25 percent, and the Dow Jones and New York Stock Exchange up more than 15 percent. The market was even better in 1999, during what Greenspan would describe as "the giddiest boom of all." The Nasdaq would rise an astonishing 86 percent, the Dow Jones 25 percent, the Standard & Poor, 20 percent. The Dow Jones would top 4000 on February 23, 1995; 5000 on November 21, 1995; 6000 on December 14, 1996; 7000 on February 13, 1997; 8000 on July 16, 1997; 9000 on April 6, 1998; 10,000 on March 26, 1999; 11,000 on July 1, 1999.

Clinton's economic performance would result in job approval ratings over 70 percent on various dates in 1998 and 1999 and consistently over 60 percent for the balance of his term despite the Monica Lewinsky sex scandal and 1998 impeachment.

During midterm elections, the party not in the White House usually increases its representatives in Congress. In 1998, the Republican majority in the House shrank from 226–207 to a narrower 223–211. Three days after what was viewed as a humiliating defeat, Newt Gingrich announced he would not continue as Speaker at the end of his term in January 1999. Clinton later would write: "Newt Gingrich stunned us all by announcing that he was resigning as Speaker and from the House. Apparently, he had a deeply divided caucus, was facing an assault on his leadership because of the election losses, and didn't want to fight anymore."

Commenter Steve Kornacki described "a backlash against Gingrichism itself, an awakening of the white collar professional class that found itself alienated by this new Republican Party." Gingrich also had been "wounded" as historian Sean Wilentz put it: "[I]n January 1997 by the release of a Report by the House Ethics Committee documenting flagrant abuses by the Speaker of laws governing nonprofit institutions and conducting partisan activities at the taxpayers' expense. Gingrich was officially reprimanded and fined $300,000, the most severe penalty ever assessed against a Speaker of the House. Gingrich tried to shrug off the episode by blaming it on vengeful leftists."[59]

Throughout the climactic years of the Clinton era stock market boom, Greenspan, unlike William McChesney Martin, was reluctant to take the punch bowl away just as the party got going.

On December 5, 1996, Greenspan gave an often quoted speech that warned that "irrational exuberance" could "unduly [escalate] asset values, which then become subject to unexpected and prolonged contractions." But there was little follow through. Throughout 1997, the discount rate was left unchanged at 5 percent. In congressional testimony on July 21, 1998, Greenspan explained that: "[W]e need to be aware that monetary policy tightening actions in the United States could have outsized effects on our sensitive financial markets in Asia."

Economist Robert Hetzel concluded: "In fall 1997, the FOMC suspended its practice of raising the funds rate in response to strength in economic activity. For the next year and a half, it relied on forecasts that economic weakness in Asia would slow unsustainably high domestic growth."

As the stock market surge reached what Greenspan called the "giddy" phase in 1999, with the Dow Jones Industrial Average rising from 7000 in February 1997, to over 11,000 in 27 months, Greenspan and the Fed hesitated. He shared with Clinton a belief that technological innovation and productivity accelerated and had created a new economy. Bob Woodward characterized Greenspan as believing that information technology defined the period:

> Something profoundly different had occurred. Computers and the Internet were at the root of the extraordinary productivity improvement. Computers allowed vastly better inventory management in a way that had been unimaginable only years before. What was truly remarkable, however, was the vast dissemination throughout society of the new technology and the speed of the dissemination. All of this dissemination added productivity growth throughout the economy. There was little question that further major advances lay ahead. They were truly in a capital equipment investment boom.

Clinton would add that Greenspan was "one of the very first in his profession to recognize the power and the impact of new technologies on the new economy, how they changed all the rules and all the possibilities."

There was belief we had begun a "third industrial revolution." Historian James Patterson captured the spirit of the times:

> The Internet, advancing rapidly after 1991, seemed to become an almost irresistible force, at least to investors. When stock in Netscape, which created a popular Web browser, was initially offered to the public in August 1995, its price per share zoomed upward from $14 to $71 in one hour. Within four months its capitalization exceeded that of Apple Computer, Marriott International, United Airlines, and Tyson Foods. A dot-com mania obsessed investors in the next few years, driving the NASDAQ

> index, which featured technology stocks, up by 86 percent in 1999 alone. By 1999, the stock of Microsoft, the leading producer of software, had a listed value of more than $500 billion. Its rapid growth enabled its widely photographed chairman, Bill Gates, with a net worth of more than $50 billion, to become by far the richest person in the United States.

Greenspan testified in Congress in 1999 about his concern that stock prices might be too high but added the Fed would not second guess "hundreds of thousands of informed investors." Moreover, "[w]hile bubbles that burst are scarcely benign, the consequences need not be catastrophic for the economy."

In his memoir, Greenspan added:

> Reflecting on this, the *New York Times* editorialized: "That sounds markedly different from the old Greenspan, who 30 months ago warned investors against " 'irrational exuberance.' " Despite the article's tone — you could almost hear the *harrumph*— the editor's impression was correct. I'd come to realize we'd never be able to identify irrational exuberance with certainty, much less act on it, until after the fact. The politicians to whom I explained this did not mind; on the contrary, they were relieved that the Fed seemed disinclined to try to end the party.

Clinton reappointed Greenspan for a five-year term on January 4, 2000. By then, Greenspan had become a media rock star. *Fortune* titled an article: "In Greenspan We Trust." On March 4, 1999, a *New York Times* editorial asked: "Who Needs Gold When We Have Greenspan?"

The Fed did raise the federal funds rate at which banks borrowed from the Fed from 4.75 to 6.5 percent between mid-1999 and mid-2000, adding the advice to investors that they should take a hard look at whether they had underestimated the risk of trading securities. Economist Paul Krugman would insist in his 2009 critique, *The Return of Depression Economics and the Crisis of 2008*, Greenspan: "didn't raise interest rates to curb the market's enthusiasm; he didn't even seek to impose margin requirements on stock market investors. Instead, he waited until the bubble burst, as it did in 2000, then tried to clean up the mess afterward."

By 2000, it was too late to staunch the speculative surge and bust, popularly known as the Dot.com bubble. The technology heavy

Nasdaq would drop from 5049 to less than 1104, nearly 80 percent, from early 2000 to the fall of 2002. The Dow Jones would decline 38 percent from its high of 11,723 to 7286; the S&P 500 would fall 49 percent from 1527 to 777.

The Fed backpedaled on monetary policy, reducing the federal funds rate from 6.5 percent to 1 percent between January 2001 and June 2003. In 2001, the Fed approved 12 reductions in the discount rate, lowering the basic rate by 4.75 percent from 6 percent at the beginning of 2001, to 1.25 percent in December. During 2002, the Fed approved a further .5 percent reduction in the discount rate to .75 percent.

Greenspan long had a close relationship with the second President Bush. Greenspan had supported Clinton's commitments to deficit reduction and shoring up Social Security before considering further tax cuts. By January 25, 2001, the Congressional Budget Office estimated the budget surplus would equal $281 billion in 2001, $313 billion in 2003, $359 billion in 2003, exceeding $500 billion in 2006, the year reduced debt could be fully paid off, rising to a surplus of $5.6 billion over ten years. If $3.1 billion was treated as untouchable, reserved for Social Security and Medicare, this left, Greenspan believed, "a prospective $2.5 trillion in usable funds."

Greenspan testified in favor of a glide path to a balanced budget, including implicit support for a version of Bush's proposed $1.6 trillion tax cut or the Democrats proposed $700 billion plan. The *New York Times* would report that Greenspan was helping President Bush in much the same way he had supported Clinton's 1993 deficit cut initiative, writing: "Just as [Greenspan's] hedged backing of Mr. Clinton's plan provided invaluable political cover [to the Democrats who] voted to raise taxes, his guarded endorsement of a tax cut... gave impetus to the effort by Republicans to push through the biggest tax cut since the Reagan administration."

On June 7, 2001, Bush signed a $1.35 trillion tax cut. When combined with the broad stock market declines that reduced capital gains tax, this set in motion the rapid deficit growth in the Bush Administration, beginning with a $158 billion deficit in 2002. The second Bush president's deficits would be further aggravated by the September 11, 2001, terrorist attacks, which contributed to the 2001 economy "[turning] in its weakest performance in a decade." Unemployment would increase by 1.8 percent between late 2000, to December 2001, from 4 to 5.8 percent, with "job losses... especially large following the terrorist attacks on September 11." Gross Domestic Product would grow by a mere 1 percent in 2001.[60]

Banking Regulation During the Clinton Administration

During the Clinton presidency, the Clinton administration and Greenspan supported a succession of deregulatory banking laws, rules, and interpretations.

In 1994, Congress enacted the Riegle-Neal Interstate Banking and Branching Efficiency Act. By the mid-1990s, the United States had a crazy quilt system of bank branching. By 1990, 46 states allowed out-of-state bank holding companies to acquire state banks under specified circumstances. But the restrictions frustrated the establishment of nationwide banking systems. The Bank Holding Company Act of 1956 prohibited interstate acquisition of a bank by a bank holding company unless the laws of the state authorized the acquisition in the state of acquisition. Only seven bank holding companies operated in 10 or more states. President Clinton and Treasury Secretary Bentsen supported nationwide banking but under laws and regulations that were not "made for another time in America."

With bipartisan support, the Riegle-Neal Interstate Banking and Efficiency Act of 1994 swept away virtually all restriction on interstate banking, overriding the laws of 36 states that allowed interstate banking only on a reciprocal or regional basis. The purpose of Riegle-Neal, Richard Kovacevich, Chief Executive Officer of Norwest Corporation insisted at the signing ceremony, is to "[allow] banks to serve our customers wherever they are, wherever they want to be, and doing it faster, better and at a lower cost."

Under the Act, the Fed could approve a bank holding company to acquire an adequately capitalized out-of-state bank "without regard to whether each transaction is prohibited under the law of any state" subject to the restriction that no bank holding company could control more than 10 percent of the total amount of deposits of insured United States depository institutions.

Mergers between insured banks from different states were permitted "without regard to whether such transaction is prohibited under the laws of any State" unless a state before June 1, 1997, opted out of this provision. Forty-eight states acceded to this provision with only Texas and Montana opting out. In 1997, the Riegle-Neal Clarification Act applied state community reinvestment, consumer protection, fair lending, and establishment of interstate branching to out-of-state banks to the same extent as state laws applied to out-of-state national banks.[61]

In 1994, the Federal Reserve Board went further and approved an order permitting a bank holding company under the Glass-Steagall Act to engage in underwriting, "provided that the company engaged in the underwriting and dealing activities derives no more than 10 percent of its total gross revenue from underwriting and dealing in bank-ineligible securities over any two-year period." In 1997, the Federal Reserve Board raised the revenue limit for underwriting by bank holding company subsidiaries to 25 percent.

So broad were the Fed 1994 and 1997 orders that they meant, in effect, there were few practical limits on bank holding companies engaging in securities underwriting as well as securities brokerage that had been earlier permitted as long as securities activities proceeded through affiliated corporations.

The 1994 Riegle-Neal Interstate Banking Act and Fed expansion of permissible bank holding company securities activities set in motion a bank merger wave of historic proportions. In 1997 alone, Bankers Trust acquired Alexander Brown for $1.7 billion; U.S. Bancorp purchased Piper Jaffrey, then the 11th largest securities firm in the United States; First Union acquired broker-dealer Wheat First Butcher Savings; Swiss Bank acquired investment firm Dillon, Read for $600 million; NationsBank bought Montgomery Securities for $1.2 billion.

In April 1998, Citicorp announced the largest financial merger of all to that date, a $83 billion merger with Travelers Group, a leading insurance provider that also owned two securities firms, Salomon Brothers and Smith Barney. The Citicorp-Travelers merger was impermissible under then-existing restrictions on bank holding company activities because insurance underwriting was impermissible and the acquisition of Salomon Smith Barney was potentially in excess of the 25 percent securities revenue ceiling established by the Fed. The Fed conditionally approved the merger with a two-to-five year period for Citicorp to divest nonconforming activities to satisfy the Travelers Group Citicorp Order that nonconforming activities be less than 15 percent of the new holding company's combined assets and less than 20 percent of its revenues.

The Fed, which required bank holding companies and state chartered banks subject to Fed regulation, and the Treasury Department, which included the Office of the Comptroller of the Currency that supervised nationally chartered banks, both enthusiastically supported the comprehensive overhaul of commercial bank, investment bank, and insurance laws to permit financial supermarkets with one stop shopping for financial services. They shared the concern of leading United States financial firms that United States firms were at a significant disadvantage when competing against European or Japanese universal banks that were allowed to combine commercial banking, investment banking, and insurance operations. Greenspan believed "liberalization in [United States] markets was long overdue." He had long favored repeal of the Glass-Steagall Act separation of commercial and investment banking.

Clinton supported the Act on conditions. The Act had to protect the safety and soundness of the system, give financial institutions a choice as to how they were organized, strengthen the separation between banking and commerce and protect consumers and urban communities, principally by strengthening consumer safeguards through privacy provisions and provisions requiring financial institutions to share financial data, and preservation of the viability of the Community Reinvestment Act, which was enacted to reduce discrimination against racial minorities.

Financial institutions spent an estimated $300 million to support passage of the Gramm-Leach-Bliley Act in November 1999.

To secure veto proof majorities of 90–8 in the final Senate vote and 362–57 in the House, proponents of the bill, led by Senator Phil Gramm, Chair of the Senate, agreed to several compromises favored by Clinton and the Senate Democrats who initially had voted 44-1 against the new law. These included strengthening the Community Reinvestment Act, new financial privacy provisions, ATM disclosure, and four years of $15 million per year support for microenterprises. At the signing ceremony on November 12, 1999, Clinton began his remarks by congratulating "Chairman Gramm for the accommodation that was reached in the end that could command broad support and gave us this legislation." Clinton would characterize the Gramm-Leach-Bliley Act as a victory as free market advocate Phil Gramm put it "for freedom and free markets" and a victory as consumer advocacy proponent Representative LaFalce said "for consumer protection. And both of them are right. And I always believed that one required the other." Clinton also would thank

"Chairman Greenspan, for your constant advocacy of the modernization of our financial system."[62]

As enacted, the Gramm-Leach-Bliley Act repealed the Glass-Steagall Act separation of commercial and investment banking. Earlier judicial decisions and Fed and Comptroller of the Currency Orders and regulations had gone far toward eviscerating the Glass-Steagall Act, but Gramm-Leach-Bliley was the *coup de grâce.*

In the place of the Glass-Steagall Act "divorcement" of commercial and investment banking as Franklin Delano Roosevelt had characterized it, Gramm-Leach-Bliley authorized a financial institution to choose to be a financial holding company that could engage in or acquire any company that the Fed determined was engaged in activities that were financial in nature or "complementary to a financial activity and does not pose a substantial risk to the safety and soundness of depository institutions or the financial system generally." Alternatively, a financial institution could be or remain a bank holding company. Foreign banks under specified conditions also could operate as financial holding companies within the United States.

Financial holding companies could engage in securities activities, including securities underwriting, without asset or revenue limits as well as life and property insurance, including insurance underwriting or annuity issuance, and all other activities that the Fed had determined satisfied their earlier "closely related to banking" or "proper incidents thereto" standards. Those provisions not only gave *carte blanche* to the Citicorp-Travelers merger but that of virtually all other financial supermarkets operating simultaneously in commercial banking and securities and insurance activities.

A general prohibition of bank, bank holding company or financial holding company operation of nonfinancial or commercial firms was enacted but it was qualified by authority for a firm that became a financial holding company to retain entities engaged in commercial activities for 10 years. If a financial holding company was predominantly engaged in permissible financial activities, the Fed and Treasury were authorized to issue rules permitting merchant banking for financial holding companies. This meant investing in commercial companies. Before Gramm-Leach-Bliley, bank holding companies could only invest up to 5 percent of their assets in commercial companies. The limits on banks entering commerce worked both ways and were intended to prevent commercial firms such as Walmart from buying a savings and loan or operating a bank in its stores.

In 2001, the Fed and Treasury issued a regulation restricting financial holding companies' investments in commercial companies to financial holding company investments for no more than 10 years, that were part of a *bona fide* underwriting, merchant or investment banking activity, and the financial holding company did not routinely manage or operate the commercial company.

The Fed also could authorize financial holding companies to engage in activities that involved financial assets other than money or securities.

There were conditions for engaging in the expanded financial activities, most notably, a financial holding company or any insured depository institution would be barred if its rating under the Community Reinvestment Act of 1977 was less than a "satisfactory record of meeting community credit needs." Each bank holding company also was expressly required to be "well capitalized" and "well managed."

The authority of national nanks was defined to include control of financial subsidiaries that engaged in activities that were "financial in nature" or "incidental" to a permitted activity as determined by the Treasury Secretary. National banks, however, were not directly authorized to provide insurance as a principal, such as insurance underwriting, or engage in real estate development. National banks could continue earlier approved "activities such as insurance agency, but were not permitted to provide title insurance or annuity contracts." The Treasury Secretary could authorize activities that involved financial assets other than money or securities. Financial subsidiaries of national banks after a five-year experience with financial holding companies might also be permitted by the Fed and Treasury to engage in merchant banking.

To regulate depository institutions, securities, and insurance subsidiaries, Gramm-Leach-Bliley built on what the earlier Bush Task Force and Senator Gramm termed functional regulation. The Fed retained its regulation of bank holding companies and state insured banks but added regulation of financial holding companies. The Treasury through the Office of the Comptroller of the Currency continued to regulate national banks. The Federal Depository Insurance Corporation continued to regulate deposit insurance and bank liquidations and reorganizations. State banking regulation was continued.

Securities firms including broker-dealers, mutual funds, and investment advisers remained subject to concurrent SEC and state jurisdiction. The SEC was authorized, but not required, to engage in elective supervision of investment bank holding companies that combined securities activities with an insured bank.

Insurance regulations remained at the state level consistent with the 1945 McCarren-Ferguson Act. A key step toward the enactment of Gramm-Leach-Bliley occurred in 1997 when the Independent Insurance Agents of America announced the organization would support legislation facilitating the affiliation of banks and insurance firms if regulation of insurance activities continued at the state level. Gramm-Leach-Bliley established the National Association of Registered Agents and Brokers subject to the supervision and oversight of the National Association of Insurance Commissioners to provide a mechanism by which uniform licensing, appointment, continuing education, and insurance producer qualifications and requirements could be adopted and applied on a multistate basis. NAIC oversight required a majority of the states representing at least 50 percent of commercial lines insurance satisfy specified uniformity or reciprocity conditions by 2002. By 2002, state regulators certified that a sufficient number of states and territories had satisfied the Gramm-Leach-Bliley requirements.

Savings and loan federal regulation, the Federal Housing Finance Board, and the Resolution Funding Corporation were continued.

There were tensions in the functional regulation enacted by Gramm-Leach-Bliley. At the boundary between banking and securities, for example, banks secured broad exclusions from the definitions of *broker* and *dealer* in the Securities Exchange Act, which were the predicates of SEC banking securities sales practice regulation. A bank would not have to register with the SEC as a broker under the Securities Exchange Act if it: (1) entered into an arrangement with a broker (so-called third party broker arrangements); (2) effected securities transactions as a trustee, typically through a trust department; (3) engaged in statutorily permissible securities transactions in commercial paper, exempted securities, qualified Canadian government obligations, or foreign standardized credit enhanced debt; (4) engaged in specified stock purchase plans such as employee benefit or dividend reinvestment plans; (5) engaged in sweep accounts; (6) engaged in affiliate transactions as earlier defined in the Bank Holding Company Act of 1956; (7) engaged in private securities offerings as defined in the Securities Act of 1933 with specified limitations; (8) engaged in safekeeping and custody activities; (9) sold identified banking products as defined in the Gramm-Leach-Bliley Act as long as they were sold to statutorily defined qualified (meaning institutional) investors; (10) sold municipal securities; or (11) engaged in up to 500 other *de minimis* transactions.

While some of these exclusions from the federal securities laws had long existed, others such as the *de minimis* transactions exclusion were new and seemed particularly designed for community banks least likely to be cognizant of investor protection concerns.

The Act also included provisions Clinton and the Senate Democrats had sought such as a detailed part on privacy that protected customers from disclosure of information provided to financial institutions, more of a priority after the Gramm-Leach-Bliley Act when financial institutions would have new opportunities to cross-market information to affiliates for customers who sought to remain solely bank, insurance, or securities customers. The Act also addressed disclosure of ATM fees and insurance customer protections, as well as the much emphasized Community Reinvestment provisions.

In the wake of the Fed's 1998 determination to approve the Citicorp-Travelers merger and the 1999 enactment of Gramm-Leach-Bliley, the floodgates were open to a *New Financial Order.* In 1998 alone, BankAmerica and NationsBank merged to form the nation's largest bank. In 1999, Fleet Bank created the nation's eighth largest bank by merging with BankBoston. The new firm owned two securities firms, Robertson Stephens and discount broker Quick & Reilly. In 2000, Chase Manhattan, in 1991 the acquirer of the former Manufacturers Hanover and 1996, Chemical Bank, making Chase for a period the country's largest bank holding company, acquired J.P. Morgan for $31 billion.[63]

ENDNOTES:

1. 1 Historical Statistics of the United States: Colonial Times to 1970, 224 (Bureau of the Census 1975); 2 Historical Statistics at 1007, 1019, 1056; SIFMA Fact Book 30 (2018); ACCI 2017 Fact Book, Chapter 7; Ralph Zuljan, Allied and Axis GDP, originally published in World War II, Suite101.com (Feb. 1, 2003); Wikipedia, Economy of the United States 11 (Feb. 2019).

2. 7 Louis Loss, Joel Seligman & Troy Paredes, Securities Regulation 197–262 (5th ed. Wolters Kluwer 2017); H.R. Rep. No. 1383, 73d Cong., 2d Sess. 8 (1934); Eccles, Readjustment of Margin Requirements, 33 Fed. Res. Bull. 149–150 (1947); Milton Friedman & Anna Schwartz, A Monetary History of the United States 1857–1960, 493–517 (Princeton Univ. Press 1965).
3. Allan Meltzer, A History of the Federal Reserve: Volume 1: 1913–1951 415, 490–662, 719 (Univ. of Chicago Press 2003); Friedman & Schwartz, supra n. 2, at 556; Roosevelt -Address to Congress (May 16, 1940); Roosevelt Address at Charlottesville, Va., June 10, 1940; Roosevelt Fireside Chat, Dec. 16, 1940; Fireside Chat, May 27, 1941; Roosevelt Address to Congress Leading to a Declaration of War Against Japan (Dec. 8, 1941); Message to Congress Requesting War Declaration with Germany and Italy (Dec. 11, 1941); The Cost of U.S. Wars Then and Now, Blog (Feb. 21, 2019); Jerry Markham, A Financial History of the United States: Volume 2, 261–265 (Routledge 2015); Executive Orders 8629 (Jan. 7, 1941); 8734 (Apr. 11, 1941); 8875 (Aug. 28, 1941); 9040 (Jan. 24, 1942); Emergency Price Control Act of 1942, Pub. L. No. 77–421, 56 Stat. 23, 77th Cong., 2d Sess. (Jan. 30, 1942); David Ginsburg, The Emergency Price Control Act of 1942: Basic Authority and Sanctions, 9 Law & Contemp. Probs. 22 (1942); Arthur Herman, Freedom's Forge: How American Business Produced Victory in World War II ix (Random House 2012).
4. Emergency Price Control Act of 1942, Pub. L. No. 729, ch. 578, 56 Stat. 765, 77th Cong., 2d Sess. (1942); Hugh Rockoff, Price and Wage Controls in Four Wartime Periods, 41 J. Econ. Hist. 381 (1981); Wage and Price Controls, Int'l Encyclopedia of Soc. Sciences (2008); World War II Rationing on the U.S. Homefront, Ames Historical Society.
5. Sarah Binder & Mark Spindel, The Myth of Independence: How Congress Governs the Federal Reserve 132–138 (Princeton Univ. Press 2017); Friedman & Schwartz, supra n. 2, at 550–555; Meltzer, supra n. 3, at 518–519, 557–558, 583–585, 592, 603, 615–627, 650–651.
6. David McCullough, Truman 469 (Simon & Schuster 1992); Meltzer, supra n. 3, at 610–612, 629–726; Meltzer, Volume 2, at 251; Friedman & Schwartz, supra n. 2, at 574–579, 610–612, 621–625; Rockoff, supra n. 4, at 382; Markham, supra n. 3, at 270, 287, 300–301; Employment Act of 1946, Pub. L. No. 79–304, ch. 33, 79th Cong., 2d Sess. (1946); Binder & Spindel, supra n. 5, at 124–128, 144–150, 150–164; George Shultz & Kenneth Dam, Economic Policy beyond the Headlines 20 (Univ. of Chicago Press 2d ed. 1998); Harry S. Truman, Special Message to Congress Presenting a 21 Point

Program for the Reconversion Period (Sept. 6, 1945); Harry S. Truman, Statement by the President upon Signing Resolution To Aid in Protecting the National Economy against Inflationary Pressures (Aug. 16, 1948); Donald McCoy, The Presidency of Harry S. Truman 41–66, 104, 127–129, 172, 179–180, 230, 263–284 (Univ. of Kansas Press 1984); Federal Reserve Bank of Atlanta, A History of the Federal Reserve Bank of Atlanta 1914–1989; Monetary, Credit and Fiscal Policies, Report of the Joint Comm. on the Economic Report of the Congress, S. 1843, 81st Cong., 2d Sess. 18–19, 22 (1950); Defense Production Act of 1950, Pub. L. No. 81–774, ch. 932, 64 Stat. 798, 81st Cong., 2d Sess. (1950); Dictionary of American History, Office of Price Stabilization (2003); Executive Order No. 10,161 (Sept. 9, 1950); Testimony of Marriner Eccles before Joint Comm. on Econ. Rep. (Jan. 25, 1951); 38 Fed. Res. Bd. Annual Report 96–105 (1951); Marvin Goodfriend, The 1951 Fed-Treasury Accord: Its Historic Significance and Relevance for Current Policy, Fed. Res. Bank of Philadelphia Forum, The History of Central Banking in the U.S. (Dec. 6, 2013); Evan A. Schnidman, Essays on Federal Reserve Bank Evolution, Transparency and Market Interaction (Ph.D. Dissertation Harvard Univ. Dep't of Gov't Aug. 2013); Bremner, Chairman of the Fed: William McChesney Martin Jr. and the Creation of the Modern American Financial System 75–80, 98–99 (Yale Univ. Press 2004); William McChesney Martin, The Transition to Free Markets, Remarks before Econ. Club of Detroit (Apr. 13, 1953).

7. Meltzer, supra n. 3, Vol. 1, at 712, 737; Vol. 2, at 35, 59, 83–86, 89, 92–98, 100–101, 108–111, 117, 121–128, 131–133 136–143, 157–170, 176–186, 193, 253–263; Friedman & Schwartz, supra n. 2, at 632–636, 676–699; Markham, supra n. 3, Vol 3, at 3; Binder & Spindel, supra n. 5, at 169–170; Bremner, supra n. 6, at 89, 104–110, 112–117; Robert Hetzel, The Monetary Policy of the Federal Reserve 49–55 (Cambridge Univ. Press 2008).
8. Historical Statistics of the United States: Colonial Times to 1970, Part 1 at 135, 164, 199, 210, 224, 241; Part 2 at 618, 977, 1006–1007 (1975); Meltzer, supra n. 3, Vol. 2, at 264; Staff Report on Employment, Growth, and Price Levels of the Joint Econ. Comm. of the United States Congress, 86th Cong., 1st Sess. (1959).
9. Meltzer, supra n. 3, Vol. 2, at 87–88, 103–106, 131–133, 156, 196–197, 226–231, 659.
10. Pub. L. No. 511, ch. 240, 70 Stat. 133 (May 9, 1956); S. Doc. No. 173, 75th Cong., 3d Sess. 8–9 (1938); S. Rep. No. 1095, 84th Cong., 1st Sess. (1955); Meltzer, supra n. 3, at 198, 202, 206–207, 225–226, 233–247, 646; Saule Omarova & Tahyar Margaret, That Which We Call a Bank: Revisiting the History of Bank Holding Company

Regulations in the United States, 31 Rev. Banking & Fin. L. 113 (2012); FSOC, 2018 Ann. Rep. 57–92; Carl Sax & Martin Sloan, The Bank Holding Company Act Amendments of 1970, 39 Geo. Wash. L. Rev. 1200, 1201 (1970); Federal Reserve Ann. Rep. 49–50 (2017); Joe Mahon, Bank Holding Company Act of 1956, Federal Reserve History (2013); Note, The Bank Holding Company Act of 1956, 7 Duke L.J. 1 (1957); Markham, supra n. 3, at 15–17.

11. Bremner, supra n. 6, at 91–92; John Wood, William McChesney Martin, Jr., A Revaluation (Fed. Reserve Region Focus Winter 2006); Gavyn Davies, How the Fed Defeated President Truman to Win Its Independence, *Financial Times* (Jan. 20, 2012); William Greider, Secrets of the Temple: How the Federal Reserve Runs the Country 327–329 (Simon & Schuster 1987); Godfrey Hodgron, Obituary: William McChesney Martin, *The Independent* (Aug. 21, 1998); Federal Reserve History, Treasury-Fed Accord March 1951 (Nov. 22, 2013); Federal Reserve History, William McChesney Martin, Jr.; Meltzer, supra n. 3, at 707–713.
12. Dwight D. Eisenhower, Mandate for Change 33, 64, 121–130, 296–297 (Doubleday 1963); Dwight D. Eisenhower, Waging Peace 218 (Doubleday 1965); Sherman Adams, First-Hand Report 154 (Harper & Bros. 1961); Emmet Hughes, The Ordeal of Power (Atheneum 1963); Greider, supra n. 11, at 329; Peter Conti-Brown, The Power and Independence of the Federal Reserve 48 (Princeton Univ. Press 2016); Meltzer, supra n. 3, at 135 n. 140, 150, 153, 161, 301–315; Seymour Harris, The Economics of the Political Parties with Special Attention to Presidents Eisenhower and Kennedy xxvi, 85, 90, 93, 111 (MacMillan Company 1962); Bremner, supra n. 6, at 93–94, 115–117, 121–136; Hetzel, supra n. 7, at 52, 68.
13. John F. Kennedy, The New Frontier, Democratic Nomination Acceptance Speech (July 15, 1960); Democratic Party Platform (July 11, 1960); Republican Party Platform (July 25, 1960); 1962 Economic Report of the President; John F. Kennedy Inaugural Address (Jan. 20, 1961); Robert Dallek, An Unfinished Life: John F. Kennedy 1917–1963, at 332–333 (Little Brown 2003); Meltzer, supra n. 3, at 301, 312, 338, 406; Harris, supra n. 12, at 115, 142–143, 155–162; Nathan Rott, "Ask Not . . ."; JFK's Words Still Inspire 50 Years Later, NPR; Interview with James Tobin, *The Region* (Minneapolis Fed. Res. Bank Dec. 1, 1996); Memorandum to Chairman Martin from James L. Knipe, Paper on Public Criticism of the Federal Reserve System (Feb. 9, 1962); Joseph Thorndike, Paul Samuelson on Tax Policy in the Kennedy Administration (Dec. 29, 2009).
14. Arthur Schlesinger, A Thousand Days: John F. Kennedy in the White House 623–624 (Houghton Mifflin rev. ed. 2002); Bremner, supra n. 6, at 152–157; Harris, supra n. 12, at xxii, 28–31, 113, 119; Meltzer,

supra n. 3, at 269, 315–324, 334–385; Wood, supra n. 11, at 3, 5–6; 1962 Economic Report of the President at 88–89, 98–99; Friedman & Schwartz, supra n. 2, at 633–636; Hetzel, supra n. 7, at 34–35, 51, 60–61.

15. John F. Kennedy Special Message to Congress on Gold and Balance of Payments Deficit (Feb. 6, 1961); John F. Kennedy Special Message to Congress on Balance of Payments (July 18, 1963); Interest Equalization Tax, Pub. L. No. 88–563, 78 Stat. 809 (Sept. 2, 1964); Meltzer, supra n. 3, at 342–365, 388, 393–397, 411–420, 424; 1962 Econ. Report of the President at 5, 145–148, 151–153, 158; Bremner, supra n. 6, at 152–153; Markham, supra n. 3, at 328; Hetzel, supra n. 7, at 103; CD Researcher, Gold Stock and the Balance of Payments (Oct. 17, 1962).
16. Pub. L. No. 87–722, 76 Stat. 668 (Sept. 28, 1962); Comptroller of the Currency: A Year of Reform: A Prelude to Progress, 1963 Ann. Rep; Comptroller of the Currency, 1965–1966 Ann. Rep.; Paul Volcker & Toyoo Gyohten, Changing Fortunes: The World's Money and the Threat to American Leadership 39 (Time Books 1992); Meltzer, supra n. 3, at 399, 404–405, 466; Markham, supra n. 3, at 336–340; James Saxon, Address before the National Bank Division, American Bankers Association, San Francisco, California (Oct. 24, 1966); Saxon letter to Senator A Willis Robertson (Apr. 7, 1986).
17. Bremner, supra n. 6, at 173–180, 184–185; Wood, supra n. 11, at 6; Kennedy Special Message to Congress on the Balance of Payments (July 18, 1963); John F. Kennedy, Remarks to Economic Club of New York (Dec. 14, 1962); Lyndon Johnson, First State of the Union (Jan. 8, 1964); John F. Kennedy, Annual Message to Congress on the State of the Union (Jan. 14, 1963); Meltzer, supra n. 3, at 267, 367–368, 375, 399, 422–437, 498, 540–557; Robert Caro, The Years of Lyndon Johnson: The Passage of Power 346, 393–396, 422–433, 462, 469–483, 498, 540–557 (Albert Kropf 2012); The Mellon and Kennedy Tax Cuts: A Review and Analysis, Staff Study, Subcomm. on Monetary and Fiscal Policy, Joint Econ. Comm, 97th Cong. 2d Sess. (June 18, 1982); Bruce Bartlett, When Tax Cuts Were a Tough Sale, *New York Times*, Jan. 22, 2013; Revenue Act of 1964, Pub. L. No. 88–272, 78 Stat. 19 (Feb. 26, 1964); Lyndon Johnson, Address to Joint Sess. of Congress (Nov. 27, 1963); 2 Historical Statistics of the United States: Colonial Times to 1970 1105 (U.S. Dep't of Commerce 1975).
18. Bremner, supra n. 6, at 148, 186–201, 211–214, 229–232, 258–259; Meltzer, supra n. 3, at 437–444, 491–493; Robert Caro, The Years of Lyndon Johnson: Master of the Senate (Alfred A. Knopf 2002); William McChesney Martin, Monetary Policy and Cost Push Inflation Consent Memo to President Johnson (Jan. 1964); Hetzel, supra n. 7, at 70; Statement on Federal Reserve Bank discount rate and

Regulation Q Changes Issued by the Federal Reserve Board of Governors (Nov. 22, 1964); Wood, supra n. 11, at 6.

19. Economic Report of the President (1965); Increases in Discount Rates of the Federal Reserve Bank of New York and the Federal Reserve Bank of Chicago and Increases in Maximum Interest Rates on Time Deposits under Regulation Q (Dec. 6, 1965); William McChesney Martin, the Federal Reserve's Role in the Economy, Address before Life Ins. Ass'n of Am., New York City (Dec. 8, 1965); Markham, supra n. 3, Vol. 3, at 3; Meltzer, supra n. 3 at 441–460; Bremner, supra n. 6, at 1–2, 209–212; Helen Fessenden, 1965: The Year the Fed and LBJ Clashed, Fed. Reserve Econ. Focus 4 (Third/Fourth Quarter 2016).
20. Lyndon Johnson, Special Message to Congress, The State of the Budget and the Economy (Aug. 3, 1967); The President's News Conference on the Tax Message (Aug. 3, 1967); 54th and 55th Fed Reserve Ann. Rpt. (1967–1968); Federal Open Market Committee Memoranda of Discussion (March 14 & April 19, 1968); Meltzer, supra n. 3, at 271, 274–275, 459–460, 493–494, 532, 536–537; Bremner, supra n. 6, at 220–226, 233–239, 255; Hetzel, supra n. 7, at 70–75; Fessenden, supra n. 19, at 5–7; Wood, supra n. 11, at 6; H. Gardiner Ackley, 82, Dies, Presidential Adviser, *N.Y. Times*, Feb. 21, 1998; David Halberstam, How the Economy Went Haywire, *The Atlantic* (Sept. 1972); John Sloan, President Johnson, The Council of Economic Advisers and the Failure to Raise Taxes in 1966 and 1967 Presidential Stud. 89; William McChesney Martin, "Good Money is Coined Freedom," remarks to Economic Club of Detroit (March 18, 1968); Hobart Rowen, Major Tax Hike Seen if Troop Need Grows, *Washington Post*, Mar. 5, 1967, summarized in Bremner at 233; Tax Increase Debate, 1967 Year in Review (1967).
21. Lyndon Johnson Remarks on Vietnam and Not Seeking Reelection (March 31, 1968); Act to Eliminate the Reserve Requirement for Federal Reserve Notes and for U.S. Notes and Treasury Notes of 1890, Pub. L. No. 90–269, 82 Stat. 50 (March 18, 1969); Special Drawing Rights Act, Pub. L. No. 90–349 (June 19, 1968); Revenue and Expenditure Control Act of 1968, Pub. L. No. 90–364, 82 Stat. 251 (June 28, 1968); Treasury Report to Congress on the Use of Special Drawing Rights by IMF Member Countries (Aug. 2010); Federal Reserve Open Committee Memorandum of Discussion (Mar. 14, 1968); 55th Fed. Reserve Ann. Rep. (1968); Executive Order 11,387 (Jan. 1, 1968); Volcker & Gyohten, supra n. 16, at 45; Bremner, supra n. 6, at 2, 5–6, 239–243, 246–249, 261–263, 272, 277, 280–282; Meltzer, supra n. 3, at 27, 47, 271–280, 382–388, 468–479, 503–511, 536–538, 687, 715–731; Fessenden, supra n. 19, at 5–7; Wood, supra n. 11, at 7; Historical Statistics of the United States:

Colonial Times to 1970, at 1023 (U.S. Dep't of Commerce 1975); Markham, supra n. 3, at 335–340.

22. Richard Nixon, The Memoirs of Richard Nixon (Grosset & Dunlap 1978); Richard Nixon, First State of the Union Address (Jan. 22, 1970); Nixon, Second State of the Union Address (Jan. 22, 1971); Nixon Speech (Aug. 15, 1971); Nixon Address to Nation on the Post-Freeze Economic Stabilization Programs: The Continuing Fight Against Inflation (Oct. 7, 1971); Economic Stabilization Act of 1970, Pub. L. No. 91–379, 84 Stat. 799 (Aug. 15, 1970), and Pub. L. No. 92–210, 85 Stat. 744 (Dec. 22, 1971); Export Expansion Finance Act of 1971, Pub. L. No. 92–126, 85 Stat. 345 (Aug. 17, 1971); Amendment to Gold Reserve Act, Pub. L. No. 92–110 (Sept. 21, 1973); Shultz & Dam, supra n. 6, at 109–131; Volcker & Gyohten, supra n. 16, at 77–90, 119–125, 293–302; Michael Jensen, Severe Economic Problems Are Being Left by Nixon, *New York Times*, Aug. 9, 1974; Burns letter to Mr. President (June 21, 1971); Burns, Handwritten Journal (Aug. 22, 1971, Nov. 6, 1971, Nov. 8, 1971, Nov. 26, 1971, Jan. 8, 1974, Aug. 4, 1974); Paul McCracken, Economic Policy in the Nixon Years, 26 Pres. Stud. Q. 165 (Winter 1996); Meltzer, supra n. 3, at 38, 485–486, 558, 561–563, 575, 586, 599–604, 613–630, 672–676, 756–812, 838, 865–882; William Silber, Volcker: The Triumph of Persistence 76–122 (Bloomsbury Press 2012); Paul Krugman, The Gold Bug Variations (Nov. 22, 1996); Roger Lowenstein, The Nixon Shock, *Bloomberg Business Week* (Aug. 4, 2011); 57th Federal Reserve Ann. Rep 13, 19–20, 77–81, 146–147 (1970); 58th Federal Reserve Ann. Rep. 4, 8, 15–17, 28, 31, 41, 51–53, 62, 67, 76–95, 116, 169 (1971); 59th Federal Reserve Ann. Rep. 3, 38, 59–63, 78–81, 96–103, 178, 184 (1972); 60th Federal Reserve Ann. Rep. 5–9. 31, 34–35, 41, 60–61, 106–108, 113–114, 138, 168, 191, 224 (1973); 61st Federal Reserve Ann. Rep. 3–6, 12–14, 27, 33, 39–41, 46, 65, 67, 74–78, 95–97, 100, 222, 301–307 (1974); 63d Federal Reserve Ann. Rep. 72 (1976); Friedman & Schwartz, supra n. 2, at 688–700; William Geider, Secrets of the Temple: How the Federal Reserve Runs the Country at 61–62, 66–67 (Simon & Schuster 1987); Gene Healy, Remembering Nixon's Wage and Price Controls, *D.C. Examiner* (Aug. 16, 2011); Wage-Price Freeze is Endorsed by 49% in a Gallup Survey, *New York Times* (Mar. 14, 1971); Louis Harris, Public Concern over Wage and Price Commissions (Feb. 14, 1972).

23. Stephen Ambrose, Nixon: Ruin and Recovery 1973–1990, at 154–155 (Simon & Schuster 1991); Volcker & Gyohten, supra n. 16, at 118; 58th Federal Reserve Ann. Rep. 76–95 (1971); 59th Fed. Reserve Ann. Rep. 68–70, 96–97 (1972); 60th Federal Reserve Ann. Rep. 106–108, 113–114 (1973); 61st Federal Reserve Ann. Rep. 75–78 (1974).

24. The Report of the President's Commission on Financial Structure and Regulation (Dec. 1971); Clifton Luttrell, The Hunt Commission Report—An Economic View (Fed. Res. Bank of St. Louis June 1972); James Tobin, Deposit Interest Ceilings on Monetary Control, 2 J. Money, Credit & Banking 4 (1970); George Kaufman, A Proposal for Eliminating Interest Rate Ceilings on Thrift Institutions: Comment, 4 J. Money, Credit & Banking 735 (1972); Meltzer, supra n. 3, at 605–612, 647–653, 835–836; Markham, supra n. 3, at 5–10; Joel Seligman, The Transformation of Wall Street: A History of the Securities and Exchange Commission and Modern Corporate Finance 536–537 (Aspen Pub. 3d ed. 2003); Nixon Memoirs, supra n. 22, at 517–520; Stephen Ambrose, Nixon: The Triumph of a Politician 1962–1972, at 237, 455–458 (Simon & Schuster 1989); Jerry Markham, Banking Regulation: Its History and Future, 4 N.C. Banking Inst. 221 (2000); 57th Federal Reserve Ann. Rep. 17–18, 22, 62–63, 74 (1970); 60th Federal Reserve Ann. Rep. 49–53, 86, 96–97, 105–106, 110–111, 230 (1973); 61st Federal Reserve Ann. Rep. 93, 102 (1974); 63d Federal Reserve Ann. Rep. 49, 133 (1976).
25. Gerald R. Ford's Remarks Upon Taking the Oath of Office as President (Aug. 9, 1974); Gerald Ford, Whip Inflation Now Speech (Oct. 8, 1974); President Gerald R. Ford, State of the Union (Jan. 15, 1975); Tax Reduction Act, Pub. L. No. 94–12, 89 Stat. 26 (May 29, 1975); Executive Order 11,808 (Sept. 30, 1974); Hetzel, supra n. 7, at 108–116; Meltzer, supra n. 3, at 883–896, 970–972, 985–990; Binder & Spindel, supra n. 5, at 171; Andrew Markham, Gerald R. Ford and the 1975 Tax Cut, 26 Pres. Stud. Q. 738 (1996); Markham, supra n. 3, at 69; 62d Federal Reserve Ann. Rep. 5, 7, 13–17, 32, 35, 45, 53–56, 67–84, 87, 94–103, 117–120, 134, 136–141 (1975); 63d Fed. Reserve Ann. Rep. 7, 12, 32, 38, 71, 133, 141, 254–255 (1976).
26. 1976 Democratic Party Platform (July 12, 1976); Jimmy Carter Acceptance Speech (July 15, 1976); Jimmy Carter Inaugural Address (Jan. 20, 1977); Jimmy Carter, Keeping Faith: Memoirs of a President 72–79, 112, 526 (Bantam Books 1983); Meltzer, supra n. 3, at 901–1007; Hetzel, supra n. 7, at 117–128; Greider, supra n. 11, at 66–67; G. William Miller, Former Chairman of the Federal Reserve and Treasury Secretary Dies at 81, *New York Times* (Mar. 19, 2006); Charles Schultze Oral History (Miller Center Jan. 8–9, 1982); Stuart Eizenstat, President Carter: The White House Years, at 20–22, 38–56, 78, 85–86, 278, 281–284, 295–300, 307 (St. Martin's Press 2018); Burton Kauffman & Scott Kaufman, James Earl Carter, at 1–21, 31, 39, 71–72 (Univ. of Kansas Press 2d ed. 2006); 64th Federal Reserve Ann Rep. 6, 141 (1977).
27. Presidential Statement: Carter's January 31, 1977, Message to Congress Outlining His Proposals for Stimulating the Economy; Carter,

State of the Union Address (Jan. 19, 1978); Carter, Anti-Inflation Policy Remarks to American Society of Newspaper Editors (Apr. 11, 1978); Carter, Anti-Inflation Program (Oct. 24, 1978); Tax Reduction and Simplification Act, Pub. L. No. 95–30 (May 23, 1977); 64th Fed. Reserve Ann Rep. 3, 6, 11 (1977); 65th Fed. Reserve Ann. Rep. 3, 5, 7, 11–13 (1978); 66th Fed. Reserve Ann. Rep. 3, 5, 11–12 (1979); Carter, supra n. 26, at 77–78; W. Carl Biven, Jimmy Carter's Economy: Policy in an Age of Limits (Univ. of North Car. Press 2002 reprint); Eizenstat, supra n. 26, at 278, 286–294, 300–302, 308–310, 318–320; Kaufman & Kaufman, supra n. 26, at 33–36, 63, 99–101, 119–121, 126, 172; Schultze, supra n. 26, at 9–10, 33–37, 40–42; Meltzer, supra n. 3, at 938;

28. Ann. Report of Secretary of Treasury and the State of Finances xxv–xxvi, 421–425 (Fiscal Hear 1978); Schultz, supra n. 26, at 42, 45; Eizenstat, supra n. 26, at 321–334; Kaufman & Kaufman, supra n. 26, at 136–137; Meltzer, supra n. 3, at 928–944; Hetzel, supra n. 7, at 125–127; 65th Federal Reserve Ann Rep. 3, 25–30, 34, 90–94 (1978); 66th Federal Reserve Ann. Rep. 16 (1979).
29. Full Employment and Balance Growth Act, Pub. L. No. 95–523, 92 Stat. 1887 (Oct. 27, 1978); Revenue Act of 1978, Pub. L. No. 95–600, 92 Stat. 2763 (Nov. 6, 1978); W. Carl Biven, Jimmy Carter's Economy: Policy in an Age of Limits 31–93, 185–207 (Univ. of N. Carolina 2002); Binder & Speidel, supra n. 5, at 171–180; Eizenstat, supra n. 26, at 305, 314–320; Kaufman & Kaufman, supra n. 26, at 134–140; Hetzel, supra n. 7, at 117–118, 125; Meltzer, supra n. 3, at 925, 944, 985–994; Clyde Haberman, The California Ballot Measure that Inspired a Tax Revolt, *New York Times* (Oct. 16, 2018).
30. Eizenstat, supra n. 26, at 137–239, 375, 661–693; Carter, supra n. 26, at 102–103, 115–120; Bevin, supra n. 29, at 193; Meltzer, supra n. 3, at 938–946; Markham, supra n. 3, at 66; Schultze, supra n. 26, at 56–58, 88; Kaufman & Kaufman, supra n. 26, at 137–183; Carter Budget Message and Some Proposals (Jan. 23, 1979); Energy Security Act of 1980, Pub. L. No. 96–294, 94 Stat. 611 (June 30, 1980); Carter Energy Address to the Nation (April 5, 1979); Jimmy Carter, Energy and National Goals — A Crisis of Confidence (July 15, 1979).
31. Volcker & Gyohten, supra n. 16, at 5, 23; Meltzer, supra n. 3, at 1008–1025; Hetzel, supra n. 7, at 152–153, 172; Eizenstat, supra n. 26, at 335–353; Bevin, supra n. 29, at 142–144, 218–222, 245–246; Greider, supra n. 11, at 34–35, 45–47, 68–70, 76–86; Bender & Spindel, supra n. 5, at 187–192; 66th Federal Reserve Ann. Rep. 108–109.
32. 66th Federal Reserve Ann. Rep. 14, 31, 200–205 (1979); Text of Fed's Announcement of Measures to Curb Inflation, *New York Times* (Oct. 8, 1979); Transcript of Paul Volcker Press Conference (Oct. 6, 1979); Volcker & Gyohten, supra n. 16, at 165–174; David Lindsey,

Athanasios & Rosche, The Reform of October 1979: How It Happened and Why (Fed. Res. Bd. Fin. & Econ. Discussion Series 2005–02); Bill Medley, Volcker's Announcement of Anti-Inflation Measures October 1979 (Fed. Res. Hist.); Meltzer, supra n. 3, at 1030–1049; Eizenstat, supra n. 26, at 346; Greider, supra n. 11, at 117–118, 149; Kaufman & Kaufman, supra n. 26, at 205–207; Hetzel, supra n. 7, at 156.

33. Jimmy Carter State of the Union Address (Jan. 22, 1980); Jimmy Carter, Anti-Inflation Program: Remarks Announcing the Administration's Program (Mar. 14, 1980); Monetary Policy and Open Market Operations in 1980, FRBNY Quarterly Rev. at 56 (Summer 1981); 67th Federal Reserve Ann. Rep. 16–18, 53, 75–80, 120–125, 153, 160, 171–173; Credit Control Act of 1969, Title II of Pub. L. No. 91–151 (1969); Executive Order 12,201 (Mar. 14, 1980); Stacey Shreft, Credit Controls: 1980 Econ. Rev. 25 (Nov./Dec. 1980); Volcker & Gyohten, supra n. 16, at 171–173; Silber, supra n. 22, at 125–234; Meltzer, supra n. 3, at 1047–1064; Kaufman & Kaufman, supra n. 26, at 207–210; Hetzel, supra n. 7, at 155–173; Eizenstat, supra n. 26, at 347–351; Greider, supra n. 11, at 117, 146–151, 188–221; Markham, supra n. 3, at 61–64.

34. Biven, supra n. 29, at 1–3, 11; Kaufman & Kaufman, supra n. 26, at 194–201, 211–217, 235–250; Hetzel, supra n. 7, at 160–166, 177–178; Volcker & Gyohten, supra n. 16, at 174–178; Meltzer, supra n. 3, at 1075–1149; 68th Federal Reserve Ann. Report 4, 28, 76–77 (1981); 69th Federal Reserve Ann. Rep. 5, 11–12, 14, 74 (1982); 70th Federal Reserve Ann. Rep. 3–5, 12, 14 (1982); 71st Federal Reserve Ann. Rep. 3, 5, 10 (1984); 72d Federal Reserve Ann. Rep. 5 (1985); 73d Federal Reserve Ann. Rep. 5 (1986); 75th Federal Reserve Ann. Rep. 5, 10, 12 (1985); H.W. Brands, Reagan: The Life 137 (Doubleday 2015).

35. 1980 Republican Platform (July 15, 1980); Ronald Reagan, First State of the Union Address (Jan. 26, 1982); Ronald Reagan, A Time for Choosing (Oct. 27, 1964); Ronald Reagan, Acceptance of the Republican Nomination for President (July 17, 1980); Ronald Reagan, Inaugural Address (Jan. 20, 1981); Ronald Reagan, An American Life: The Autobiography 138–145, 230–232, 298 (Simon & Schuster 1990); Edwin Cowan, Reagan Delivers his Budget to Congress with a Warning to Remember "Our Mandate," *New York Times* (Mar. 11, 1981); Meltzer, supra n. 3, at 1082–1087, 1142; Volcker & Gyohten, supra n. 16, at 174–184, 240–241; Richard Reeves, President Reagan: The Triumph of Inauguration 14 (Simon & Schuster 2005); Brands, supra n. 34, at 206, 211, 241–248, 317–318; Stephen Hayward, The Age of Reagan: The Conservative Counterrevolution 43, 276 (Three Rivers Press 2009).

36. Ronald Reagan, Address to the Nation on the Economy (Feb. 5, 1981); Ronald Reagan, Address before a Joint Session of Congress on the State of the Union (Jan. 26, 1982); Ronald Reagan, Address before a Joint Session of Congress on the Program for Economic Recovery (April 28, 1981); Ronald Reagan, Address on Federal Tax Reduction Legislation (July 27, 1981); Reagan, An American Life, supra n. 35, at 279–288, 312–339; Bowsher v. Snyar, 478 U.S. 714 (1986); James Baker, Work Hard, Study and Keep Out of Politics 142–150, 156, 161, 186–188, 234 (G.P. Putnam & Sons 2006); William Greider, The Education of Savid Stockman, *Atlantic* (Dec. 1981); Hayward, supra n. 35, at 83–91, 145–150, 187, 192, 232–233, 276–277, 375–380; Reeves, supra n. 35, at 12–13 51–52, 65–78, 81, 232–234; Brands, supra n. 34, at 182–213, 247–248, 272, 321–322; Cowan, supra n. 35; The Budgets of the United States Government Fiscal Years 1981, 1982 and 1983; Congr. Budget Off., An Analysis of President Reagan's Budget Revisions for Fiscal Year 1982 (Staff Working Paper Mar. 1981); 71st Federal Reserve Ann. Rep. 33 (1983); 74th Federal Reserve Ann Rep.; Economic Recovery Tax Act of 1981, Pub. L. No. 97–34, 95 Stat. 172 (Aug. 13, 1981); Office of Tax Analysis, Revenue Effects of Major Tax Bills (OTA Working Paper 81, Rev. Sept. 2006); Greider, supra n. 11, at 395–398, 541–542, 570–574; Garry Wills, Reagan's America 436–437 (Penguin Books 1985); Volcker & Gyohten, supra n. 16, at 177–181; Michael Boskin, Reagan and the Economy: The Successes, Failures and Unfinished Agenda 103 (ICS Press 1987); Meltzer, supra n. 3, at 1087; Tax Equity and Fiscal Responsibility Act of 1982, Pub. L. No. 97–248, 96 Stat. 324 (Sept. 3, 1982).
37. Depository Institutions Deregulation and Monetary Control Act, Pub. L. No. 96–321, 94 Stat. 132 (Mar. 31, 1980); Garn-St. Germain Depository Institutions Act of 1982, Pub. L. No. 97–320, 96 Stat. 1469 (Oct. 15, 1982); American Bankers Ass'n v. Board of Governors, 686 F.2d 953 (D.C. Cir. 1979); 68th Federal Reserve Ann. Rep. 33 (1981); 70th Federal Reserve Ann. Rep. 17 (1983); Markham, supra n. 3, Vol. 3, at 68–75; Greider, supra n. 11, at 154–159, 165–176; Meltzer, supra n. 3, at 1013, 1052–1053, 1059, 1067, 1097; David Mason, From Buildings and Loans to Bail-Outs: A History of the Savings and Loan Industry 1831–1995, at 213–220 (Cambridge Univ. Press 2004); Jerry Markham, Banking Regulation: Its History and Future, 4 N.C. Banking Inst. 221 (2000).
38. Ronald Reagan Remarks on Signing the Garn-St. Germain Depository Institutions Act of 1982 (Oct. 15, 1982); Report of the Task Group on Regulation of Financial Services, Blueprint for Change 83 (July 2, 1984); National Commission on Financial Institution Reform, Recovery and Enforcement, Origins and Causes of the S &

L Crisis: A Blueprint for Reform 1–57 (July 1993); Securities Industry Assn. v. Board of Governors, 486 U.S. 207 (1984); National Bank of N.C. v. Variable Annuity Life Ins. Co. 513 U.S. 251 (1985); Clarke v. Securities Indus. Ass'n, 479 U.S. 388 (1987); Securities Indus. Ass'n v. Board of Governors, 821 F.2d 810 (D.C. Cir. 1987); Securities Indus. Ass'n v. Board of Governors, 839 F.2d 47 (2d Cir. 1988); 70th Federal Reserve Ann. Report 73 (1983); 73d Federal Reserve Ann. Rep. 672 (1985); Seligman, supra n. 24, at 682, 683; David Stockman, The Triumph of Politics: Why the Reagan Revolution Failed (Harper & Row 1986); Mason, supra n. 37, at 220–229; Markham, supra n. 3, at 132–133, 139, 167; Markham, supra n. 3, Vol. 3, at 9; Donald Langevoort, Obsolescence and the Judicial Process: The Revisionist Role of the Court in Federal Banking Regulation, 85 Mich. L. Rev. 672 (1985); Daniel Fischel, Andrew Rosenfeld & Roland Stillman, The Regulation of Banks and Bank Holding Companies, 73 Va. L. Rev. 301 (1987).

39. Report of the Task Group, supra n. 38; FDIC, The S & L Crisis: A Chrono-Bibliography (Dec. 2002); FDIC, The Savings and Loan Crisis and Its Relationship to Banking, In History of the Eighties ch. 4 (2018); Mason, supra n. 37, at 224–240, 276–296; Markham, supra n. 3, at 166–172; Timothy Curry & Lynn Shibut, The Cost of the Savings and Loan Crisis: Truth and Consequences, FDIC Banking Rev. 26 (Dec. 2000); Chip Brown, Leaders of Empire Thrift Scandal Sentenced, *Associated Press* (Jan. 16, 1992); Lawrence White, The S & L Debacle: Public Policy Lessons for Bank and Thrift Regulation (Oxford Univ. Press 1991); 3 Convicted in Failure of Home State, *New York Times* (Mar. 3, 1987); Gary Klott, Old Court: Fast Growth, But High Risk Taking, *New York Times* (May 20, 1985); Running Wild at First Maryland Savings and Loan, *New York Times* (Apr. 17, 1988); Steven Batoff, Maryland's Savings and Loan Crisis of 1985: The Resulting Legislative Reform, 16 U. Balt. L. Rev. 403 (1987); Tom Furlong, How a Texas S & L Ends Up Costing the U.S. So Much, *Los Angeles Times* (Dec. 4, 1988); Michael Lev, U.S. Seizes Columbia Savings, *New York Times* (Jan. 26, 1991); Ronald Ostrow & Robert Rosenblatt, S & L Crisis Puts President's Son on the Hot Seat, *Los Angeles Times* (July 9, 1990); Henry David Russo, Neil Bush, Others Settle Silverado Lawsuit for $49.5 Million, UPI Archives (May 30, 1991); Matt Schudel, Charles H. Keating, Jr., Central Figure of Savings-and-Loan Scandal, Dies at 90, *Washington Post* (Apr. 2, 2014); Philip Shenon, Did Charles Keating Go to Jail for Nothing?, *Politico* (Apr. 4, 2014).

40. Meltzer, supra n. 3, at 1105–1106, 1172–1177, 1199; Volcker & Gyohten, supra n. 16, at 180, 71 Fed. Reserve Ann. Rep. 61 (1984); Greider, supra n. 11, at 624–631; Markham, supra n. 3, at 76–78;

Robert Bennett, Penn Square's Failed Concept, *New York Times* (Aug. 16, 1982); Renee Haltorm, Failure of Continental Illinois, May 1984 (Federal Reserve History); FDIC, The Banking Crises of the 1980s and Early 1990s: Summary and Implications, Chapter 1 in History of the Eighties, supra n. 39.

41. Volcker & Gyohten, supra n. 16, at 187–296; Meltzer, supra n. 3, at 1105–1106, 1113–1119, 1125–1127, 1135, 1142, 1179–1183, 1191–1194; Announcement [of] the Ministers of Finance and Central Bank Governors of France, Germany, Japan, the United Kingdom and the United States (Plaza Accord) (Sept. 22, 1985); Statement of the G-6 Finance Ministers and Central Bank Governors (Louvre Accord) (Feb. 22, 1987); Boskin, supra n. 36, at 80–83; Douglas Hyman & Robert Doane, The International Debt Management Act of 1988: Has the Baker Plan Been Replaced?, 1989 BYU L. Rev. 593; 74th Fed. Annual Rep. 23–26 (1987); Clyde Farnsworth, Bankers at IMF Talks Cautious on Baker Plan, *New York Times* (Oct. 9, 1985); Brands, supra n. 34, at 668–669; Bob Woodward, Maestro: Greenspan's Fed and the American Boom 16–20 (Simon & Schuster 2000).

42. Alan Greenspan, The Age of Turbulence: Adventures in a New World 29–76 (Penguin Press 2007); Alan Greenspan, Gold and Economic Freedom (1968); Woodward, supra n. 41, at 31, 34–35; Hetzel, supra n. 7, at 196–205; Reid Sticks by Greenspan Comments, *Washington Times* (Mar. 4, 2005); Paul Krugman, Three-Card Maestro (Feb. 18, 2005); Greg Ip, His Legacy Tarnished, Greenspan Goes on the Defensive, *Wall Street Journal* (Apr. 8, 2008); Benjamin Friedman, Chairman Greenspan's Legacy, *New York Rev. of Books* (Mar. 20, 2008).

43. Social Security Amendments of 1983, Pub. L. No. 98–21, 98th Cong., 1st Sess. (Apr. 20, 1983); Greenspan, supra n. 42, at 86–96, 103–110; John Svahn & Mary Ross, Social Security Amendments of 1983: Legislative History and Summary of Provisions, Social Security Bull. (July 1983); Seligman, supra n. 24, at 589–590; Woodward, supra n. 41, at 25, 32–33; Hetzel, supra n. 7, at 185–189; Paul Blaustein, Nominee Greenspan Shares Volcker's Goals but Not Yet His Clout, *Wall Street Journal*, June 3, 1987; Brands, supra n. 34, at 437–446, 515–570; Reeves, supra n. 35, at 362–389, 394–398, 402–414; 74th Federal Reserve Ann. Rep. 72–73 (1987); 75th Federal Reserve Ann. Rep. 3–5 (1988).

44. George Bush & Brent Scowcroft, A World Transformed (Vintage Books 1999); John Meacham, Destiny and Power: The American Odyssey of George Herbert Walker Bush chs. 28–46 (Random House 2015); George Bush Acceptance Speech (Aug. 18, 1988); George Bush Inaugural Address (Jan. 20, 1989); Omnibus Budget Reconciliation Act of 1990, Pub. L. No. 101–508, 104 Stat. 1388

(Nov. 5, 1988); Greenspan, supra n. 42, at 118–122; Woodward, supra n. 41 at 61–63, 71–81; 79th Federal Reserve Ann. Report 3, 15 (1992).

45. Greenspan, supra n. 42, at 120–122; 78th Federal Reserve Ann. Rep. 19–22 (1991); 79th Federal Reserve Ann. Rep. 4, 21–26, 106 (1992); Woodward, supra n. 41, at 77–94; Meacham, supra n. 44, at 409–410.
46. Competitive Equality Banking Act of 1987, Pub. L. No. 100–86, 100 Stat. 552 (Aug. 10, 1987); GAO, Testimony of Frederick Wolf, The Federal Savings and Loan Insurance Corporation — Financial Condition and Recapitalization Issues (GAO/T-AFMD-87-4 Mar. 3, 1987); GAO, Thrift Industry: The Treasury/Federal Home Loan Bank Board Plan for FSLIC Recapitalization (GAO/GGD-87-46BR Mar. 3, 1987); National Commission on Financial Institution Reform, Recovery and Enforcement, supra n. 38, at 57–59; Mason, supra n. 37, at 229–234; White, supra n. 39, at 135–140; Martin Mayer, The Greatest Ever Bank Robbery: The Collapse of the Savings and Loan Industry (Collier Books 1990); 74th Federal Reserve Ann. Rep. 173–176 (1987).
47. Financial Institutions Reform, Recovery and Enforcement Act of 1989, Pub. L. No. 101–73, 103 Stat. 183 (Aug. 9, 1989); GAO, Troubled Financial Institutions: Solutions to the Thrift Industry Problem (GAO/GGD-89-47); Resolution Trust Corporation Funding Act of 1991, Pub. L. No. 102–18, 105 Stat 58 (1991); Resolution Trust Corporation Refinancing, Restructuring and Improvement Act of 1991, Pub. L. No. 102–233, 105 Stat. 1761 (1991); Annual Report of the Thrift Depository Protection Oversight Board & Resolution Trust Corporation for Calendar Year 1995; 1995 Ann. Rep. of the Resolution Trust Corporation; Comptroller General Report on the Audit of the Resolution Trust Corporation's 1994 and 1995 Financial Statements; White, supra n. 39, at 147–151, 175–200; National Commission on Financial Institution Reform, Recovery and Enforcement, supra n. 38, at 61; Mason, supra n. 37, at 234–265; Anthony Providenti, Playing with FIRREA, Not Getting Burned: Statutory Overview of the Financial Institutions Reform, Recovery and Enforcement Act of 1989, 59 Fordham L. Rev. 5323 (1991).
48. Competitive Equaling Bank Act of 1987, supra n. 46; Financial Institution Reform, Recovery and Enforcement Act of 1989, supra n. 47; Federal Deposit Insurance Corporation Improvements Act of 1991, Pub. L. No. 102–242, 105 Stat. 2236 (Dec. 19, 1991); Dep't of Treasury, Modernizing the Financial System: Recommendations for Safer, More Competitive Banks (1991); Congressional Budget Office, Options for Reorganizing Federal Banking Agencies (Sept. 1993); 76th Fed. Reserve Ann. Rep. 61–62 (1989); 79th Fed. Reserve Ann. Rep. 101–103 (1992); Meltzer, supra n. 3, at 1201.

49. Bill Clinton, My Life (Alfred A. Knopf 2004); Meacham, supra n. 44, at 501–522; John Robert Greene, The Presidency of George Bush 151–179 (Univ. Press of Kansas 2000); James Patterson, Restless Giant xv–xvi, 292–295 (Oxford Univ. Press 2005); John Harris, The Survivor: Bill Clinton in the White House xxiii (Random House 2006); Sean Wilentz, The Age of Reagan: A History 1974–2008, at 324–327 (Harper Collins 2008); Bob Woodward, The Agenda: Inside the Clinton White House 19, 32–34 (Simon & Schuster 1994); Bill Clinton, The Economy (Wharton School of Business, Apr. 16, 1992); Bill Clinton, I Still Believe in a Place Called Hope, Acceptance Speech, Democratic Convention (July 17, 1992); Bill Clinton, The New Covenant: Responsibility and Rebuilding the American Community (Oct. 23, 1991); Bill Clinton, Fighting for the Forgotten Middle Class (1992 Campaign Brochure).
50. George Stephanopoulos, All Too Human: A Political Education 122, 124, 276, 362–367 (Little Brown 1999); Robert Rubin, In an Uncertain World 114, 121, 135, 163–165 (Random House 2003); Harris, supra n. 49 at xiv–xv, xxi, xxiii, 13, 55–57, 160–164, 300, 384; Patterson, supra n. 49, at 248–249, 318–320; Wilentz, supra n. 49, at 26; Woodward, supra n. 49, at 25, 185–186, 225, 315; Jack Goodwin, Clintonomics 124, 177 (American Management Association 2009); Gallup Presidential Approval Ratings — Gallup Historical Statistics and Trends (2019).
51. Clinton, supra n. 49, at 451–454, 636, 810, 856; Woodward, supra n. 49, at 27, 32–34, 52–53, 59–63, 73–75, 80, 98, 103, 208–211, 216, 225; Patterson, supra n. 49, at 324; Wilentz, supra n. 49, at 332–333; Harris, supra n. 49, at x–xix, xxvii–xxx, 27–29, 63–66, 82–84, 99–101, 149, 155, 220, 259–261, 328–329, 390; Rubin, supra n. 50, at x–xi, 95–98, 109, 163–164, 192, 203–205, 251, 298–299, 383–400.
52. Bill Clinton, Farewell Address (Jan. 18, 2001); CBO, The Budget and Economic Outlook 2016–2026 App. F: Historical Budget Data (Jan. 2016); Greenspan, supra n. 42, at 142–150, 182–183; Clinton, supra n. 49, at 451; Woodward, supra n. 49, at 69–70, 209, 227–229, 269; Wilentz, supra n. 49, at 371; Dow Jones Industrial Average Yearly Returns (2019).
53. Omnibus Budget Reconciliation Act of 1993, Pub. L. No. 103–66, 107 Stat. 312 (Aug. 10, 1993); Taxpayer Relief Act of 1997, Pub. L. No. 105–34, 111 Stat. 787 (Aug. 5, 1997); Clinton, supra n. 49, at 458–497, 520–523, 533–538; Patterson, supra n. 49, at 331–333; Harris, supra n. 49, at xxvii–xxviii, 4–6, 19–24, 60, 78–93; Rubin, supra n. 50, at 119–131, 162; Greenspan, supra n. 42, at 145; Woodward, supra n. 49, at 48–51, 82–98, 120–127, 131, 162, 211–217, 242–253, 269, 280; Wilentz, supra n. 49, at 327–331; Gallup Presidential Approval Ratings — Bill Clinton (2019); James Kuhn & Stanley

Akers, U.S. Military Spending, 37 References & Users Serv. Q. 173 (Winter 1997); Council on Foreign Relations, Trends in U.S. Military Spending (July 15, 2014); U.S. Military Spending, 1946–2009.

54. Statement of President Clinton, The White House (Jan. 25, 1993); Bill Clinton, Address on Health Care Reform (Sept. 22, 1993); Bill Clinton, Second State of the Union Address (Jan. 25, 1994); Association of Am. Physicians & Surgeons v. Hillary Rodham Clinton, 997 F.2d 898 (D.C. Cir. 1993); Children's Health Insurance Providers Services (CHIPS) Act of 1997; Clinton, supra n. 49, at 482–483, 492, 495, 547, 555–557, 576–577, 594–595, 601, 620–621; Rubin, supra n. 50, at 148–151; Patterson, supra n. 49, at 272, 326–330; Harris, supra n. 49, at 25–26, 118–119; Wilentz, supra n. 49, at 332–334, 347, 349; Woodward, supra n. 49, at 119–120, 198–200, 266; Federal Reserve System Ann. Rep. 3, 5, 13, 27, 98 (1993).
55. Balanced Budget Act of 1997, Pub. L. No. 105–33, 111 Stat. 251; William J. Clinton, State of the Union Address (Jan. 24, 1995); William Jefferson Clinton, State of the Union Address (Jan. 23, 1996); Contract with America (Sept. 27, 1994); Newt Gingrich, Address to the Nation (Apr. 7, 1995); Clinton v. City of New York, 524 U.S. 417 (1998); Clinton, supra n. 49, at 631–695, 720, 742, 826, Rubin, supra n. 50, at 153–154, 161–175; Wilentz, supra n. 49, at 347–376; Patterson, supra n. 49, at 324–326, 343–345, 371–378; Harris, supra n. 49, at 149–150, 153–158, 161–185, 215–217, 231–239; Steve Kornacki, The Red and the Blue 351 (Harper Collins 2018); Steven Komarow, House Republicans Elect Gingrich to No. 2 Spot, Chart Battle with Democrats (Associated Press Mar. 22, 1989); Lance Morrow, Newt Gingrich's World: How One Man Changed the Way Washington Sees Reality (Dec. 25, 1995).
56. Clinton Address to the Democratic National Convention (Aug. 29, 1996); Clinton, supra n. 49, at 704, 721–734; Robert Dole Acceptance Speech to the Republican Convention (Aug. 15, 1996); 1996 Republican Party Platform; Personal Responsibility and Work Opportunity Reconciliation Act of 1996, Pub. L. 104–193, 101 Stat. 2105; 81st Federal Reserve Ann. Rep. 110 (1994); 82d Federal Reserve Ann. Rep. 102 (1995); 83d Federal Reserve Ann. Rep. 7 (1996); Greenspan, supra n. 42, at 118–124, 153–155, 170–178; Rubin, supra n. 50, at 358–359; Patterson, supra n. 49, at 372–378; Harris, supra n. 49, at 240–258; Wilentz, supra n. 49, at 364–370.
57. Clinton, supra n. 49, at 432, 540, 546–547, 636, 745–746; William J. Clinton, State of the Union Address 26 (Jan. 24, 1995); 85th Federal Reserve Ann. Report 33 (1998); 86th Federal Reserve Ann. Report 25 (1999); Greenspan, supra n. 42, at 149; Patterson, supra n. 49, at 333–334; Wilentz, supra n. 49, at 334–335; Woodward, supra n. 49, at 55–56, 317–319; Jack Goodwin, Clintonomics

230–240 (American Management Ass'n 2009); Woodward, supra n. 41, at 155–166.

58. Clinton, supra n. 49, at 641–645, 806, 827; Greenspan, supra n. 42, at 156–160, 187–191; Rubin, supra n. 50, at 3–38, 216–222, 228–250, 274–292; Hetzel, supra n. 7, at 206–215; Harris, supra n. 12, at 158–159; Wilentz, supra n. 49, at 356–357; Woodward, supra n. 49, at 138–144, 189–192, 206–214.

59. Clinton, supra n. 49, at 822–826; Kornacki, supra n. 55, at 5–6, 352; Wilentz, supra n. 49, at 372; 84th Federal Reserve Ann. Report 4, 8, 14, 17 (1997); 85th Federal Reserve Ann. Report 9, 19–20, 26 (1998); 86th Federal Reserve Ann. Report 20 (1999); 87th Federal Reserve Ann. Report 13 (2000); Patterson, supra n. 49, at 378, 394–396; Greenspan, supra n. 42, at 197.

60. 85th Federal Reserve Ann. Rep. 3, 89 (1997); 88th Federal Reserve Ann. Rep. 3, 11, 25, 208 (2001); 89th Federal Reserve Ann. Rep. 157 (2002); Greenspan, supra n. 42, at 176–177, 197–202, 213–215, 217, 233, 238–240; Hetzel, supra n. 7, at 218–227, 241–242; Patterson, supra n. 49, at 360–361; Rubin, supra n. 50, at 322–323, 330, 369; Woodward, supra n. 49, at 195, 213–215, 223–224; Markham, supra n. 3, Vol. 3 at 340.

61. Riegle-Neal Interstate Banking and Branching Efficiency Act of 1994, Pub. L. No. 103–328, 108 Stat. 2338 (Sept. 29, 1994); Riegle-Neal Clarification Act of 1997, Pub. L. No. 105–24, 111 Stat. 238 (July 3, 1997); Susan McLaughlin, The Impact of Interstate Banking and Branching Reform: Evidence from the States, 1 Current Issues in Econ. & Fin. (Fed. Res. Bank of N.Y., May 1995); Jonathan Broder, Financial Services Deregulation, 28 CQ Researcher Issue 13 (Apr. 6, 2018); Matthew Sherman, A Short History of Financial Deregulation in the United States (Center for Econ. & Policy Research July 2009); Bill Medley, Riegle-Neal Interstate Banking and Branching Efficiency Act of 1994 (Fed. Res. History Sept. 1994); Markham, supra n. 3, Vol. 3 at 241–242.

62. Statement by President Bill Clinton at the signing of the Financial Modernization Bill (Nov. 12, 1999); Federal Reserve Bd., Travelers Group, Citicorp Order (Sept. 23, 1998); Seligman, supra n. 24, at 683–688; Chase Manhattan Corp., 1994 WL 575, 297 (F.R.B. 1994); Fed Abandons Most Section 20 Firewalls, Sets Operating Standards for Subsidiaries, 29 Sec. Reg. & L. Rep. (BNA) 1171 (1997); Testimony of Greenspan, supra n. 42, at 198–199; Markham, supra n. 24, at 11–12; Markham, supra n. 3, Vol. 3, at 303–304, 341–342; Omarova & Margaret, supra n. 10, at 125–126; Sherman, supra n. 61, at 9–10; Lissa Broome & Jerry Markham, The Gramm-Leach-Bliley Act: An Overview (2001).

63. Seligman, supra n. 24, at 685–689; Gramm-Leach-Bliley Act, Pub. L. No. 106–102, 113 Stat. 1338 (Nov. 12, 1999); 86th Federal Res. Ann. Rep. 175–180 (1999); 88th Federal Res. Ann. Rep. 204 (2001); Michael Barr, Howell Jackson & Margaret Tahyar, Financial Regulation: Law and Policy 353, 673–677 (Foundation Press 2016); Jolina Cuaresma, The Gramm-Leach-Bliley Act, 17 Berkeley Tech. L.J. Jan. 2002); Broome & Markham, supra n. 62; Markham, supra n. 3, Vol. 3, at 303–304; Markham, supra n. 24, at 262–265.

5

The Porousness of Securities and Insurance Regulation and the Consolidation of the New Financial Order

Compounding the evisceration of the Glass-Steagall Act separation of commercial banking and the securities industry was the growing porousness of securities and insurance regulation in the post-World War II period.

In the years after World War II, the relative significance of the Securities and Exchange Commission deteriorated. Roosevelt's favorite independent regulatory agency lost its capacity to fully secure its self-chosen mandate as the investor's advocate, surrendering authority over financial futures to the Commodities Futures Trading Commission, most pensions to the Department of Labor while a growing array of products and financial firms were exempted or excluded from the scope of the Federal securities laws.

The history of the SEC, which I elaborated at greater length in *The Transformation of Wall Street,* is not linear. The Commission achieved considerable success fortifying its role in its core fraud and disclosure missions, modernizing securities market regulation and extending its jurisdiction to options, tender offers, and municipal securities.

Truman's SEC

The SEC began a 15-year post-war decline during the presidency of Harry Truman. President Truman had little interest in the day-to-day administration of the Commission. Truman characterized his attitude in December 1945, when he remarked at a press conference: "I have had so many things to think about that I haven't looked at the stock market, because I have never been interested in the stock market personally." A 1948 Staff Report of the Hoover Commission on Organization of the Executive Branch of the Government observed: "Since the war, President Truman has asked little more than to be kept informed of the activities of the [Securities and Exchange] Commission." Emblematic of Truman's lack of personal interest in the SEC was the delay, until 1948, in return of the Commission's headquarters from Philadelphia, where it had spent World War II as a nonessential federal agency.[1]

Although corporate law reform was never a priority of his administration, Truman was committed to the continuance of the SEC. Following Roosevelt's example, Truman named three former staff members among his first six Commission appointments. When World War II ended, the SEC had a staff of approximately 1150 employees. Until the Korean War began, in June 1950, Truman's Bureau of the Budget regularly approved SEC budgets sufficient to increase modestly the Commission's personnel.[2]

Yet Truman, to some degree, subverted the effective continuance of the SEC by the mediocrity of other Commission appointments. The appointments process, generally, was the Achilles' heel of the Truman administration. Throughout Truman's presidency, he was regularly criticized for appointing "party hacks," "cronies," or "fixers" to leading federal positions while dismissing, demoting, or pressing for the resignation of leading New Dealers, such as Henry Wallace, Harold Ickes, James Landis, and Marriner Eccles. One sympathetic student of Truman's independent regulatory appointments estimated that "over half of Truman's selections involved political considerations."[3]

Truman's SEC appointments were made with the same erratic regard for merit as the appointments made throughout much of the rest of his administration. Illustrative were Truman's choices for SEC chair. After Ganson Purcell resigned, the SEC was led for 18 months by James Caffrey, a Roosevelt appointee who had served for nine years as administrator of the SEC's Boston and New York

Regional Offices.[4] When Caffrey resigned, Truman persuaded the Commission to elect Edmond Hanrahan chair. In 1946, Hanrahan had been appointed by Truman to the Commission as a reward for his prowess as a New York City Democratic Party fundraiser. Hanrahan was, SEC General Counsel Roger Foster recalled, an "honest Tammany politician," with a "back-slapper's temperament." Although an attorney, Hanrahan had no background in securities law. So lacking in qualifications for the job had he been that SEC Commissioner Robert McConnaughey not only voted against Hanrahan, but took the unusual step of recording in the *SEC Minutes* his belief that the SEC's "Chairman should be a person with experience in the Commission's affairs."[5]

Little better qualified was Harry McDonald, whom Truman recommended as SEC chair after Hanrahan retired in 1949. Although McDonald for 14 years had been a member of a Detroit investment bank, his primary business experience was in the dairy industry. Appointed to the Commission in 1946 at the recommendation of Truman's foreign policy ally Senator Arthur Vandenberg, McDonald was the first Republican to serve as SEC chair, and he was named to that position because of his friendship with Harry Truman. As fellow Commissioner Robert Millonzi recalled: "Both men were Shriners, both men were Masons." In the evenings, when Truman would relax with friends and play his piano, McDonald often was called on to sing "Wagon Wheels," a song Truman particularly enjoyed. McDonald must have had a remarkably affecting voice. Three former SEC senior officials separately suggested during interviews that McDonald literally sang his way to the position of SEC chair.

McDonald himself was candid about his lack of qualifications. He began his maiden address as SEC chair with "My election as Chairman . . . was a complete surprise to many, including myself." As chair, McDonald largely followed the advice of senior Commission staff members such as Associate General Counsel Louis Loss or fellow Commissioner and former staff member Donald Cook, who in 1950 was named to be the Commission's first, and only, Vice Chair, because, as Cook explained, "McDonald did not understand the securities statutes."[6]

Cook, Truman's final SEC chair, was an able attorney and business school graduate with seven years' experience in the Commission's Public Utilities Division, where he had risen to become

Assistant Director, before leaving in 1945 to become Attorney General Tom Clark's Executive Assistant. Under the provisions of the Reorganization Act of 1949, the president was given the direct power to select SEC chairs beginning in 1950. Cook was appointed a Commissioner primarily because of political considerations. As Cook explained in an interview, during World War II he had served as Counsel to Senator Lyndon Johnson's Naval Subcommittee and had befriended both Johnson and House Speaker Sam Rayburn. When, in 1949, President Truman had informed Rayburn that he could name the next SEC Commissioner, Rayburn selected Cook. Out of loyalty to his political sponsors, Cook served from 1950 to 1952 as Chief Counsel to Senator Johnson's Committee on Korean War Preparedness while simultaneously directing the SEC, first as vice chair, then, beginning in February 1952, as chair.[7]

By failing to appoint to the SEC a single leading academic or leading figure in the securities field, Truman contributed to an intellectually stagnant Commission. In spite of considerable growth in the securities business during Truman's presidency and a backlog of unfinished projects left by the New Deal, the SEC after Purcell's 1946 departure did not initiate a single major study for the balance of the Truman administration. The only significant legislation recommended by Truman's SEC was the 1950 Frear Bill, which would have enacted William Douglas's 1938 proposal to subject securities traded over the counter to the same level of regulation as securities traded on a national securities exchange. In part, the Commission's inactivity was the result of chairs who lacked the background or the ability to study effectively the SEC's regulatory performance. It was men like Hanrahan and McDonald whom James Landis probably had in mind in 1960 when he reported to President-elect Kennedy that resolution of important SEC regulatory problems had been delayed for years in the post-World War II period because of the "incapacity of the Commissioners themselves to grasp the essence of those problems and the significance of their resolution to the financial community."[8]

Throughout the Truman administration, the Commission largely would be staff driven. The Commission would complete the most comprehensive restructuring of a United States industry with its enforcement of the Public Utility Holding Company Act of 1935 by 1952.[9]

The Lowpoint of the SEC: Eisenhower Years

During the Eisenhower administration, the Securities and Exchange Commission reached its nadir. Although the SEC long retained its reputation as the best of the independent regulatory agencies, its enforcement and policymaking capabilities were less effective than at any other period in its history. This was not because the Eisenhower administration *per se* was hostile to the effective administration of the securities laws. By 1953, the disclosure and antifraud rules of the securities statutes generally commanded bipartisan support. With market volume still ascending from its late New Deal depths, the organized exchanges and corporate issuers regarded the SEC's disclosure program and antifraud enforcement as advantageous to maintain market confidence.

The effective enforcement of the securities laws and the necessary expansion of the SEC's jurisdiction nevertheless were frustrated by the Eisenhower administration's greater commitment to a balanced budget, elimination or prevention of what it termed "excessive" federal regulation, and its general preference for amicable federal government-private business relations.[10]

Eisenhower's parsimony, on top of reductions in the SEC staff made during World War II and the Korean War, severely curtailed the Commission's enforcement programs. At its height, the SEC had 1723 employees in 1941. During the Truman administration, the Commission reached its highest level of employment in 1947, when it employed a staff of 1200. At that level, the bipartisan Hoover Commission found, the SEC had a backlog in its examinations of annual reports filed by corporations under the 1934 Securities Exchange Act and was unable to inspect brokers and dealers annually.

The Korean War resulted in further personnel cuts. By June 30, 1953, the SEC staff had been reduced to 773 employees. Approximately 150 jobs had been eliminated without harm to the Commission's capabilities as the public utilities program largely concluded. The elimination of 300 other employees between 1947 and 1953 "drained much of [the Commission's] vitality," wrote Truman SEC Commissioner J. Howard Rossbach. On March 3, 1953, Commissioner Richard McEntire stated: "Because of the necessity of curtailing our operations to the extent that we have, the Commission is not able to do an adequate job in administering the seven statutes entrusted to it."[11]

Even before Eisenhower's first SEC chair was confirmed, the Budget Bureau recommended cuts in the SEC's 1954, budget that resulted in a 10 percent reduction of the Commission's staff, leaving the SEC 699 employees on June 30, 1954. Donald Cook criticized the impending staff cut in an April 1953 public statement expressing his "firm belief that people will be defrauded by the hundreds in ways that we could check and would be able to stop if we had the staff we need." Ralph Demmler, confirmed as Eisenhower's first SEC chair in June 1953, implicitly agreed. On July 13, 1953, Demmler wrote Senator Leverett Saltonstall, Chair of the Senate Subcommittee on Independent Offices Appropriations, that any further budget reduction "might have the effect of crippling [the Division of Corporation Finance's] ability to clear registration statements within the time schedules imposed by the issuers and underwriters [and] would automatically curtail the enforcement activities of the Commission." On November 17, 1953, Demmler wrote Budget Director Dodge that a proposed 8 percent cut in the SEC's 1955 budget "would be reflected primarily in curtailed enforcement activities and in delayed regulatory proceedings. The Commission considers that to the extent such curtailments and delays occur it will be failing to discharge its statutory responsibilities." Despite Demmler's warnings, the Budget Bureau insisted on a 6 percent cut. By June 30, 1955, the SEC's staff was reduced to 666 persons, the lowest level in the post-World War II period.[12]

As Demmler predicted, the SEC's enforcement program in 1954 and 1955 was curtailed. Memoranda were circulated to SEC regional administrators, encouraging them to rely on state authorities whenever possible to investigate and prosecute securities violations as one means "to save manpower." As Demmler testified on February 10, 1955, the SEC annually could inspect the books of only about 1000 of the nation's 4100 broker-dealers because "it does not have the staff to carry out regular periodic examinations." SEC investigations in 1955 led to the conviction of only seven persons for securities fraud, the lowest figure in the Commission's history.

These beliefs were most visibly evident during the term of Chair Ralph Demmler. Demmler, a securities law practitioner from a leading Pittsburgh corporate law firm, arrived at the SEC affirming that "the principles behind the Acts which the Commission administers are basically sound." He repeatedly underscored his loyalty to the SEC with such statements as: "It goes without saying that the

Commission as presently constituted does not intend to sabotage the statutes it administers. The Federal Securities laws are not in the hands of their enemies."

But Demmler also was loyal to the values of the Eisenhower administration. He began his time as chair by stating his intention to comply with a Bureau of the Budget request for "suggestions for methods of reducing expenditures for Fiscal 1955." This, Demmler philosophically was prepared to do. Although he repeatedly noted that he sought to retain "those things in our procedures which are good and valid," with equal frequency he indicated his intention to eliminate SEC regulations and forms "which are unnecessary or unduly cumbersome." The complementary goals of reducing expenditures and eliminating unnecessary regulation significantly influenced the policies of Demmler's SEC.[13]

After the Democrats won control of Congress in November 1954, the Eisenhower administration's management of the SEC came under sharp attack. Between September 1953 and January 1955, Standard and Poor's index of 480 common stocks rose by 50 percent. Accompanying the market rise was evidence of the most widespread pattern of speculative activity and securities fraud to occur since the late 1920s. Beginning in the spring of 1954, an unparalleled number of "penny" uranium company securities were sold, employing a 1933 Securities Act small issue exemption.[14]

The early 1950s saw a vast increase in boiler rooms, where typically 20 to 30 telephones would be used by former carnival workers, pitchmen, confidence game operators, or bookmakers who would promote fraudulent or highly speculative securities to lists of unsophisticated investors.[15]

Walter Winchell in his weekly radio and television broadcasts fed the speculative climate by offering such "tips" as his April 1953 statement that the "biggest oil strike in North American history . . . may be confirmed tomorrow by Amurex Oil Development Company." Winchell's tips were not illegal, since he was not paid to make them and he usually culled his information from published sources, but they frequently sent corporation stock prices jolting upward. "In January 1955," Wall Street historian Robert Sobel wrote, "Winchell claimed that had a person purchased round lots in all the forty or so stocks he had mentioned in the previous year, he would have a paper profit of around a quarter of a million dollars." Winchell's claim was not true, but the confabulations of a man who had once been the nation's most popular radio commentator, reported Sobel, "drew many thousands of speculators into the markets."

The SEC's response to the 1950s' revival of securities speculation and the Winchell Market convinced *Time* magazine, among others, that, as an article was entitled, in providing "Protection for Investors: The SEC is Unequal to the Job."[16]

After Demmler's departure, the SEC was led for two years by Chair J. Sinclair Armstrong, then for the balance of the Eisenhower administration by Chair Edward Gadsby. With even the New York Stock Exchange lobbying to expand the Commission's staff, the SEC was able to increase its personnel to 1087 during the last six years of the Eisenhower administration. But, as was recognized by Armstrong and Gadsby and by a Booz Allen and Hamilton Study contracted by the Eisenhower Budget Bureau, the SEC's staff increases never kept pace with the booming securities markets. Between 1955 and 1961, the SEC staff grew by 63 percent. During the same period, the number of investors, representatives of New York Stock Exchange firms, and the value of shares traded on the NYSE approximately doubled; the number of registered National Association of Securities Dealers (*NASD*) representatives increased by 130 percent. Stimulating this growth was a soaring Dow Jones Average, which rocketed from a low of 388.2 in 1955, to a high of 734.9 in 1961. In the longer view, between 1945 and 1961, the SEC's staff decreased by 6 percent. Over this 16-year period, the value of mutual funds increased from $1.3 to $22.8 billion; the dollar value of trading of over-the-counter shares increased eightfold; the dollar value of new securities increased fivefold.[17]

The late 1950s bull market was accompanied by the type of speculative climate in which securities fraud thrives. During the late 1950s, not only boiler rooms and marginal brokerage houses, but some New York Stock Exchange firms employed get rich quick advertisements. In one, a New York Stock Exchange firm recommended "six securities which we believe should be able to double over the next few months." Hot issues dominated the new securities markets. The SEC's *Special Study of the Securities Markets* later was to explain:

> From 1959 until the market decline of early 1962, the distribution of securities by companies that had not made a previous public offering reached the highest level in history. . . . The public eagerly sought stocks of companies in certain "glamour"

> industries, especially the electronics industry, in the expectation that they would quickly rise to a substantial premium — an expectation that was often fulfilled. Within a few days or even hours after the initial distribution, these so-called hot issues would be traded at premiums of as much as 300 percent above the original offering price. In many cases the price of a "hot" issue later fell to a fraction of its original offering price.[18]

In a market in which one financial writer claimed, "Almost any issue with a Buck Rogerish tinge to its name was bound to go into orbit," former ballroom dancer Nicholas Darvas's *How I Made $2,000,000 in the Stock Market* sold more than 100,000 copies within five weeks of its publication date. "The problems of the Securities and Exchange Commission are relatively simple," James Landis would write President-elect Kennedy in 1960; "much of the delays that characterize its operation stem from the fact that it, more than any other agency, has been starved for appropriations. Even the recent increases have not restored the amounts formerly available."[19]

The SEC's regulatory efforts deteriorated throughout the Eisenhower administration also because of a shift in the agency's operating assumptions. During the New Deal period, the SEC had focused its enforcement efforts on the New York Stock Exchange and the leading securities broker-dealers on the assumption that sustained scrutiny of the industry's leaders would stimulate the most vigorous industry self-regulation. By contrast, the SEC during the Eisenhower years tended to share with the New York Stock Exchange the assumption that securities fraud was unlikely to be perpetrated on the leading exchanges or by the leading broker-dealers.

Instead, successive Eisenhower Chairs Demmler, Armstrong, and Gadsby emphasized the strengthening of regional offices to combat boiler rooms, fraudulent penny stocks, and exploitative local broker-dealers. Between 1950 and 1960, the proportion of SEC employees in regional offices grew from 31 to 41 percent.[20]

The combination of SEC understaffing and emphasis on regional office antifraud actions left wide gaps in the Commission's enforcement program. The Commission's 1963 *Special Study of Securities Markets* was particularly critical of the SEC's passive role in supervising securities exchange and NASD self-regulation, finding that "responsibilities at the heart of the Commission's role of protecting public investors . . . such as continuous examination of changing market circumstances and regulatory needs, appraisal, and reappraisal of the adequacy of the existing regulatory measures, and in particular, evaluation and oversight of the operation of the self-regulatory agencies" had been largely ignored.[21]

Criticism of SEC regulation of the leading broker-dealers was nearly as severe. During the late 1950s, the securities brokerage industry collectively experienced a rapid expansion, with the result that, as SEC Chair William Cary testified in 1961: "Many securities salesmen work on a part time basis; many have no particular qualifications to sell securities; and most important, many are not subject to the kind of supervision which ensure high ethical standards." With the SEC able to inspect broker-dealers on average only once every three years, and to inspect brokerage houses located in New York City on average only once every five or six years, the SEC's 1963 *Special Study of Securities Markets* identified several instances in which leading brokerage houses had engaged in what Cary delicately termed "questionable merchandising techniques."[22]

Comparable weaknesses occurred in the SEC's supervision of mutual funds and other investment companies. In two addresses in 1962 and 1963, William Cary explained: "From the enactment of the 1940 [Investment Company] Act until 1961, there had been inspection of only 30 investment companies." Given the number of investment companies, this meant each firm would be inspected once every 12 years, a frequency Cary termed "inadequate, indeed absurd."[23]

Ultimately, the gaping weaknesses in the Eisenhower Administration's SEC enforcement program resulted in the near complete collapse of self-regulation on the American Stock Exchange, the most serious stock market scandal since Richard Whitney's defalcations were revealed in the spring of 1938. Unlike the situation in the New York Stock Exchange after the Whitney scandal, the governance of the New York Curb Exchange had not been effectively reorganized. From January 1953, when the New York Curb Exchange was renamed the American Stock Exchange, through May 1961, when the SEC initiated a comprehensive staff investigation of the Exchange, governance of the American Stock Exchange was dominated by four men, Joseph Reilly, Charles Bocklet, James R. Dyer, and John J. Mann. All four were specialists or former specialists. This meant that governance of the American Stock

Exchange was in the hands of floor members, not brokers who dealt with the public. It was exactly the pattern of governance that the SEC had attempted to end on the NYSE after the Whitney scandal.[24]

In 1951, the Curb Exchange had hired Edward McCormick to be its president. McCormick, who for 17 years had worked for the SEC, had become a Commissioner, in part, as a result of writing in 1948 one of the earliest scholarly books on the Commission, *Understanding the Securities Act and the SEC.* McCormick's principal job as Exchange president, however, was not regulating floor transactions; it was obtaining new listings of securities for the exchange. Throughout his 10 years as Exchange president, McCormick made so many trips throughout the country to meet with officials of corporations that potentially could list their securities on the American Stock Exchange, "that McCormick was considered by the membership principally as a salesman rather than as an administrator," reported an SEC Staff Study in 1962.

The salesmanship of the American Stock Exchange (*Amex*) resulted in a number of securities of dubious quality being listed on the exchange. In the early 1950s, the SEC was highly concerned about the sale of Canadian mining and oil securities in the United States. Twelve such Canadian issues were listed on the exchange in 1952 alone. By December 31, 1960, 104 Canadian securities were traded on the Amex, over half of which had lost money in two of the three preceding fiscal years. Relaxation of listing requirements led to the listing of several other securities of marginal companies. In 1955, for example, the exchange had acceded to the request of one of its leading specialists and agreed to list New Pacific Coal and Oils Ltd., despite the fact that the firm had reported no income during any of the previous three years. At the same time, McCormick indicated in his 1953–1954 *Report of the President of the American Stock Exchange* that the exchange was "bending every effort to cultivate a greater interest in securities by persons in the lower and middle income groups." Throughout the 1950s, the Amex was the highly conspicuous hub of a securities speculation revival.[25]

By 1956, the Commission had become aware of serious securities violations committed by two leading American Stock Exchange members in connection with a distribution of Crowell-Collier convertible debentures. Crowell-Collier, then best known as the publisher of the struggling *Collier's* magazine, had sustained such substantial operating losses in 1953 and 1954 that it was advised by investment bankers that a distribution of common stock would be impossible. By May 1955, bank creditors were pressing the company. It was anticipated that large loans due in August 1955, would not be extended unless additional long-term financing was obtained from other sources. The firm's financial circumstances then were so precarious that a House of Representatives subcommittee later found that had Crowell-Collier made the public disclosures required by the 1933 Securities Act, "the disclosures probably would have vitiated efforts to raise additional capital." Instead, Crowell-Collier turned to American Stock Exchange broker-dealer Edward Elliot, who proposed a private placement of $4 million of debt securities called debentures convertible immediately into common stock.

It always had been the law under the Securities Act that if a security was sold to a sufficiently small number of investors "able to fend for themselves" in a nonpublic offering, no registration was required. At the time, it was widely believed that a private placement had to be limited to no more than 25 people, none of whom could act as an underwriter and resell the security to others. In 1955, Elliot sold $3 million of debentures to 27 purchasers, securing from each an investment letter representing that "said debentures are being purchased for investment and the undersigned has no present intention of distributing the same." The investment letters were generally ignored, with the result that the debentures were, in fact, sold to 79 purchasers representing 88 people. Since none of the purchasers was fully informed of the precarious financial condition of Crowell-Collier, the distribution involved patent violations of the 1933 Securities Act. In 1956, the same investment letter procedure was employed to sell another $1 million of debentures.

Among those to whom Elliot sold the debentures was James Gilligan, a general partner of Gilligan, Will & Co., then the leading specialist on the American Stock Exchange. In October 1955, Gilligan succeeded in having Crowell-Collier common stock listed on the Amex with himself as its specialist. Gilligan also helped to distribute $500,000 of the debentures, violating the 1933 Securities Act by reselling the unregistered securities to friends and associates.

Approximately one year later, the SEC commenced an investigation of the Crowell-Collier private placement, tentatively concluding in November 1956, that the firm had illegally claimed a private placement exemption. But the Commission's prosecution of this offense was restrained. No disciplinary action was taken against

Crowell-Collier after it agreed to file a registration statement in June 1957. In August 1957, the Commission commenced an Administrative Proceeding, which in 1958 resulted in a 20-day suspension from the NASD of Elliot and Company, Edward Elliot's brokerage firm, and a five-day NASD suspension of Gilligan, Will.

No effort was made by the SEC to learn whether Elliot and Company or Gilligan, Will had participated in other similar distributions. Nor was an effort made to learn why the American Stock Exchange had not questioned the claimed private placement of the Crowell-Collier securities when the securities were listed, despite the revelation in 1957 that Edward McCormick had purchased $15,000 of the illegally distributed Crowell-Collier debentures. Nor was any effective effort made to discover whether Elliot and Company or Gilligan, Will had violated other securities laws. So passive was the Commission's investigation and prosecution of the *Crowell-Collier* case that in January 1959 the House Special Subcommittee on Legislative Oversight published a detailed report concerning the Commission's performance in the case that concluded:

> The record indicates that from July 1955 to December 21, 1956, a period of 18 months, the Commission failed to take any affirmative action even though it had notice of numerous specific instances where the violations had officially come to its attention. Because of the Commission's failure to take immediate effective action, many subsequent violations by all the participants occurred.

Had the SEC pressed its investigation, it presumably would have learned that in 1955, Gilligan, Will had orchestrated a distribution of 200,000 shares of Guild Films to 172 people employing an equally questionable claim of private placement exemption. James Gilligan later testified that the Commission's five-day suspension of him from NASD "had no effect whatsoever on him financially," since he was primarily a specialist, not dependent on NASD membership for his livelihood. A 1962 SEC Staff Report would find that in the five years after the Commission began its 1956 investigation of the Crowell-Collier distribution, Gilligan, Will participated in the distribution of unregistered securities for at least six other corporations.

In other instances, the Report found, Gilligan, Will had benefited from inside information as a result of a close relationship with a corporate issuer's management or had made off the exchange purchases of securities that as a specialist, then were a violation of an American Stock Exchange rule. The Report also found that questionable floor trading activity systematically had occurred at the Gilligan, Will post on the American Stock Exchange. It was apparent that Amex officials were efficiently aware of "the entire pattern of activities conducted by Gilligan, Will . . . that the exchange might have been expected to act promptly in putting a halt to them." The SEC, in 1962, would find "that Gilligan was immune from disciplinary action by the Exchange. He testified that he has not been the subject of a disciplinary action of the Exchange for at least 20 years." Only in February 1962, after publication of the SEC's Staff Report on the American Stock Exchange, was James Gilligan barred from serving as an Amex specialist for five years.[26]

The same SEC passivity that emboldened James Gilligan and Edward Elliot permitted the more serious securities law violations committed by their fellow Amex specialists, the father-and-son team of Gerard A. (Jerry) and Gerald F. Re. Between 1954 and 1960, the Res illegally distributed over $10 million of securities on the American Stock Exchange. They manipulated the prices of several securities. They illegally touted shares. They bribed brokers to tout shares. They took advantage of inside information. They caused to be published false and misleading prospectuses by at least four firms. They systematically failed to keep required records, and routinely ignored the section of the 1934 Securities Exchange Act that provides that if the Commission permits specialists to act as dealers, the SEC shall "restrict his dealings so far as practicable to those reasonably necessary to maintain a fair and orderly market." The Res may have violated 10 separate provisions of the 1933 and 1934 Securities Acts and an equal number of rules of the American Stock Exchange, well justifying the SEC's subsequent conclusion that the Commission's two leading market manipulation cases to that date, 1930s' actions against Michael Meehan and Charles Wright, "became almost trivial" by comparison.

In 1961, a bristling SEC brief would lead to the expulsion of the Res from the American Stock Exchange for their "prostitution of the specialists' important role [which] resulted in many millions of dollars of harm to thousands of unsuspecting investors." The Re scandal was most shocking because it occurred nearly 30 years after the creation of the SEC. "Almost unnoticed," financial journalist Frank Cormier would write, "Jerry and Gerald Re had turned back the clock to an earlier era, reviving some of the very practices that had led to federal regulation of Wall Street. The two specialists were living proof of the fact that history repeats itself — if men back the wisdom and fortitude to learn from the mistakes of the past."

Revelation of the apparently criminal securities violations committed by the Res persuaded the SEC in May 1961 to authorize a comprehensive staff investigation of the American Stock Exchange. The SEC Staff Study of the American Stock Exchange concluded in January 1962 that the Exchange's "manifold and prolonged abuses by specialists and floor traders . . . make it clear that the problem goes beyond isolated violations and amounts to a general deficiency of standards and a fundamental failure of controls." No one disputed this conclusion. But a candid discussion of how so prolonged "a fundamental failure of controls" could exist after the creation of the SEC did not appear in the Study's Report. There was one frank commentary, however, in a 1962 Memorandum by Philip Loomis, Director of the Division of Trading and Exchanges, written to Chair William Cary. To the SEC of the 1950s, "Exchange regulations was not approached as an enforcement problem, it being assumed, until the contrary became evident, that the American Stock Exchange was basically aware of its responsibilities and honestly conducted." This was an avoidable contributing cause of what Loomis termed the "breakdown" of "self-regulation on the American Stock Exchange."[27]

Variable Annuities

To the Commission's credit, even during its bleakest years, it did defend its core jurisdiction with respect to insurance products and companies that sold variable annuities.

The federal securities laws exempted as the Securities Act of 1933 explained: "Any insurance or endowment policy or annuity contract or optional annuity contract, issues by a corporation subject to the supervision of the insurance commissioner, bank commissioner, or any agency or officer performing like functions, of any State or Territory of the United States or the District of Columbia."

The exemption of insurance regulation was buttressed by Congress's enactment of the McCarran-Ferguson Act in 1944 that declared that: "No Act of Congress shall be construed to invalidate, impair or supersede any law enacted by any State for the purpose of regulating the business of insurance."

The question of categorization as between securities and traditional insurance and annuities arose most acutely with the development of the variable annuity. The distinguishing feature of the variable annuity is that the purchaser or annuitant's payments purchase units in a fund of securities, similar to the purchase of mutual fund shares This marriage of the insurance and mutual fund concepts would not work unless the buyers' funds were invested in common stocks.

The SEC in 1956 sued in the District of Columbia to enjoin a local life insurance company, Variable Annuity Life Insurance Company (known as *VALIC*), from selling variable annuities without registration under the Securities Act and the Investment Company Act. The district court, finding that the contracts had characteristics of both securities and insurance, concluded that both statutes would apply "if it were not for the clear and explicit language of the McCarran Act and the fact that the defendants [a second similar company had intervened] are licensed and regulated by the Insurance Departments of this District and the states where they operate." The Court of Appeals affirmed on the ground that "[t]he definitions in the Securities Act and the Investment Company Act indicate that if the Insurance Commissioner of a state subjects the business to his supervision, it is the business of insurance."

The Supreme Court reversed in a 5-4 opinion written by Justice Douglas that stated in relevant part:

> While all the States regulate "annuities" under their "insurance" laws, traditionally and customarily they have been fixed annuities, offering the annuitant specified and definite amounts beginning with a certain year of his or her life. The standards for investment of funds underlying these annuities have been conservative. The variable annuity introduced two new features. First, premiums collected are invested to a greater degree in common stocks and other equities. Second, benefit payments vary with the success of the investment policy. The first variable annuity apparently appeared in this country about 1952 when New York created the College Retirement Equities Fund to provide annuities for teachers. It came into existence as a result of a search for a device that would avoid paying annuitants in depreciated dollars. . . .
>
> . . . [T]he variable annuity places all the investment risks on the annuitant, none on the company. The holder gets only a *pro rata* share of what the portfolio of equity interests

> reflects — which may be a lot, a little, or nothing. . . . But we conclude that the concept of "insurance" involves some investment risk-taking on the part of the company. The risk of mortality, assumed here, gives these variable annuities an aspect of insurance. Yet it is apparent, not real; superficial, not substantial. In hard reality the issuer of a variable annuity that has no element of a fixed return assumes no true risk in the insurance sense.

Justice Brennan concurred, noting that in 1933 and 1940 when the Securities Act and the Investment Company Act were enacted, "the sort of 'variable annuity' contract with which we are concerned in this case did not exist."

Over time, the SEC regulation of insurance products with variable returns and investment risks was extended by the Supreme Court, in 1967, to flexible fund annuities, which were optional annuity plans with characteristics similar to the variable annuities in *SEC v. Variable Annuity Life Insurance*, variable life insurance and other hybrid products. The Commission adopted exemptive rules and compliance approaches to achieve an uneasy détente with the insurance industry.[28]

The SEC Revitalized under Cary

During a sustained period, beginning with the 1961–1964 SEC chairmanship of William Cary, the SEC was substantially revitalized. But it was a bounded revitalization. The Commission was able to flesh out its core securities mission by strengthening its fraud and disclosure programs, extending its jurisdiction to standardized options and tender offers and modernizing securities markets by ending fixed commission rates, inspiring creation of the electronic Nasdaq Market, and laying the groundwork for a unified National Market System.

Two days after his election as president, John Kennedy signified his determination to revitalize the federal regulatory agencies by announcing that former SEC Chair James Landis had agreed "to undertake a study in an area of long concern to us both, a study of the federal regulatory agencies." Both the Landis Report and private memoranda circulated by Landis within the White House recommended a return to what might be termed the Roosevelt formula for the selection of SEC Commissioners. This involved appointing a combination of leading academics or others with broad policy planning ability and elevating senior SEC staff members. Landis was particularly concerned that qualified staff members regularly be advanced to commissionerships, viewing this as important to the SEC's ability to retain a high caliber staff. The Kennedy Administration first offered the SEC's chair to Harvard Law School Professor Louis Loss, then well known as the author of the multivolume treatise *Securities Regulation*. When Loss declined, the chairmanship was offered to Columbia Law Professor William Cary, the author of the most widely used law school casebook on corporations. Cary accepted.

Landis's description of the SEC's "budget starvation" helped persuade the Bureau of the Budget and Congress to add 250 new employees to the SEC's staff during the Kennedy administration's first fiscal year. Landis also pointed out that many commissions, including the SEC, had neglected their policymaking functions.

Landis, however, recognized that for the SEC and the other independent regulatory agencies to realize a full revitalization would require a White House Office committed to serve as a "protagonist of the agencies" before Congress and the Bureau of the Budget. By 1961, it was obvious that no president regularly could devote as much attention to any of the regulatory agencies as Roosevelt had devoted to the SEC. Without a White House protector, Landis anticipated that the agencies neither would receive adequate support for legislative initiatives from the White House's lobbyists nor be sympathetically treated by the Bureau of the Budget. The Kennedy Administration soon concluded it could not afford Landis's proposed White House agency czar. Kennedy's 1960 election had been accompanied by the loss of 20 liberal Democrats from the House of Representatives, making the House more conservative than the White House. For Kennedy to secure passage of even his less controversial legislative initiatives requiring husbanding "bargaining power for its most effective use," as Arthur Schlesinger, Jr. later wrote.

The SEC received no effective White House support in seeking passage of new enabling legislation between 1961 and 1963. Chair William Cary did not once see President Kennedy on official business, and found that Ralph Dungan, the White House aide expected to oversee the Commission, also "literally had no free time to talk with us." Even when Cary was concerned that the Kennedy administration's Comptroller of the Currency was attempting to sabotage the Commission's 1963 Securities Acts Amendments Bill, the White House did not effectively intervene.[29]

The absence of White House support for new SEC legislation, coupled with the conservative leadership of the House of Representatives, fundamentally affected the SEC during the chairmanship of William Cary. In retrospect, Cary described himself as "convinced that no major step forward can be achieved by an old line regulatory agency in the absence of support from some of the leaders in the industry it regulates. . . . Even as to rulemaking, if none of the industry's spokesmen feel there is a need and complaints mount, congressmen are likely to intervene and commence inquiry, and a Committee may either stall the proposal or kill it."[30] During Cary's chairmanship, only one legislative initiative was advanced, the "noncontroversial" Securities Acts Amendments Bill. More far reaching legislation, such as a bill to reform the mutual fund industry, was deferred.

The Kennedy administration's noninterference with the SEC, its tangible support for the Commission through the budgetary and appointments process, as well as the administration's air of idealism and reform, did contribute to the SEC's revival. Not the least of the Kennedy administration's contributions was the appointment of William Cary as chair. Cary provided a link to the spirit and goals of the New Deal's SEC. At Yale Law School in 1934, he had been a student in one of the last corporate finance courses taught by William Douglas. He had served on the SEC's staff between 1938 and 1940, initially under Chair Douglas. As chair, Cary reflected an intellectual style and outlined policy goals reminiscent of Douglas's SEC chairmanship. Like Douglas, Cary insisted on balancing reform aims with technical rigor. He often quoted Karl Llewellyn's aphorism "Technique without ideals is a menace; ideals without technique are a mess."

During his chairmanship, Cary revived efforts to complete several unfinished projects first attempted during the New Deal, including the enactment of a statute extending the Securities Exchange Act's requirements to all unlisted firms above a minimum size and a highly publicized attempt to abolish floor trading.

The work of the New Deal's SEC has been preceded by a generation of study of the securities markets and corporations law. The Pecora Hearings, the Federal Trade Commission's Study of Public Utilities, the SEC's own reports on Stock Exchange Governance, Segregation of Brokers and Dealers, Protective Committees, and Investment Companies, had provided an informed basis for major SEC policy initiatives. No comparable study had been made of the securities markets for over 20 years when Cary arrived. As the securities industry expanded and qualitatively changed, the pathbreaking studies of the New Deal period were increasingly dated.

Cary began at the SEC with "no overall policy view," but with a determination to restore the Commission's policymaking capability and to increase its attraction to highly competent staff members. The principal vehicle for achieving both aims was the 1961–1963 *Special Study of the Securities Markets.*[31]

The *Special Study* was the single most influential report published in the history of the SEC; it provided a foundation for several reforms that occurred in the securities industry during the ensuing 15 years. In large measure, the *Special Study* was a factual documentation of the limits of self-regulation in the securities industry. Although Cary's transmittal letters and the report itself repeatedly stated a "continued belief in self-regulation as an ingredient in the protection of the investor," the report's findings illustrated that without the "pointed stimuli" of the SEC, securities industry self-regulation frequently had been self-interested and self-protective, often failing to produce standards of conduct superior to those that existed before the enactment of the securities laws. In most of the principal areas covered by the report — entry requirements, selling practices, back office problems, exchange floor members, fixed commission rates, mutual fund selling practices, and exchange disciplinary procedures — similar disadvantages of securities industry self-regulation were found. In several instances, such as floor trading regulation, the SEC's post-war passivity had, in fact, permitted a deterioration of standards.[32]

Illustrative of the *Study's* findings was its discussion of fixed rate commission rates. During the 1946–1961 period, SEC oversight of the securities market structure had been minimal. Characteristic of the SEC's approach during this time was its review of New York Stock Exchange commission rate increases. Under Section 19(b) of the 1934 Securities Exchange Act, the SEC was directed to regulate "the fixing of reasonable rates of commission." Twice during the New Deal period, in 1938 and 1942, the SEC interposed no objection to NYSE's commission rate increases. The SEC's response in both instances primarily was stimulated by declining brokerage income, occasioned by lower trading volume. Before the

1938 increase, average daily volume had declined to 1,492,000 shares, approximately one-third the 1929 level. Before the 1942 increase, volume had undergone a further severe decline to an average daily total of 619,000 shares. During the post-war period, however, with trading volume rising, in 1961, to a level of 4,085,058 shares traded on average daily, there existed no comparable justification for SEC passivity in reviewing New York Stock Exchange commission rates. Nonetheless, in 1947, 1953, and 1958, the SEC had permitted the Exchange to raise its commission rates. In none of these instances did the SEC set forth a standard for determining "reasonable rates of commission," nor, found the *Special Study*, did the Commission ask for sufficient data from broker-dealers about firm and transaction costs to evaluate fully the reasons for the rate increases.[33]

By the time of the *Special Study*, lack of rate competition among New York Stock Exchange members encouraged four major types of anticompetitive practice in the securities industry. First, it had become common for the large brokerage houses to engage in nonrate competition, usually through such ancillary services as investment research, safekeeping of customers' securities, or collection and delivery of investor dividends, rights, and warrants. Since the New York Stock Exchange had used brokerage house cost data to justify its 1947, 1953, and 1958 rate increases, the bundling of brokerage services provided a mechanism for raising brokerage rates and brokerage house income even if the costs of executing transactions had not increased.

Second, institutional and other investors who purchased large blocks of securities formally were prohibited from negotiating volume discounts in spite of the lower per share cost of large volume purchases. In some instances, when securities listed on the New York Stock Exchange also were traded on a regional exchange or over the counter, lower commission rates could be negotiated off the NYSE. When a competitive market maker was not available, the New York Stock Exchange's anti-rebate rule required large volume investors to pay the standard commission rate and receive the equivalent to a price discount in such forms as investment research or installation at the broker's expense of a direct wire.

Third, in the mutual fund field, the absence of volume discounts, resulted in a practice known as give-ups. Although Exchange members were prohibited from rebating commissions to nonmembers, they were permitted to give up portions of their commissions to other Exchange members. A mutual fund could arrange for a broker to give up part of the commission to a second Exchange member, who could benefit the fund by selling the mutual fund's shares. Give-ups were an additional commission paid by mutual funds to retail sales organizations. Give-ups also raised the costs of administering mutual funds by requiring the funds' directors to use research or other services that they might otherwise consider unnecessary, rather than receive volume discounts. In practice, give-ups were running as high as 60 percent of commission rates by the time of the *Special Study*.

Finally, the Exchange's rate structure encouraged Exchange members to raise investors' costs through reciprocal trading and service arrangements. The New York Stock Exchange required that nonmember broker-dealers pay full commissions for executing orders on the Exchange. For nonmember broker-dealers, the combined expense of paying an NYSE member a full commission plus bearing their own overhead costs when executing an order for a customer created a powerful financial incentive to develop alternative markets for the trading of securities listed on the Exchange. To reduce this incentive, the Exchange permitted its members to reduce the nonmember broker-dealers' costs by providing reciprocal commission business. The *Special Study* found, "This reciprocal commission business is generally placed under arrangement involving reciprocal ratios' of 2 to 1, 3 to 1, or similar ratios, that is, the NYSE Member will direct $1 in commissions to the nonmember for each $1.50, $2, or $3 of commissions received." Like nonprice competition, the provision of services to large volume investors, and give-ups, reciprocal commission business was a mechanism by which Exchange members shared some of the profits created by a noncompetitive commission rate structure with nonmembers to preserve the noncompetitive rate structure. Inevitably, reciprocal commission arrangements delayed or decreased the likelihood of competitive market makers evolving and thus raised investor costs.[34]

During William Cary's time as chair, the abolition of fixed New York Stock Exchange commission rates was not a priority. Challenging the NYSE's commission rate structure would have resulted in a direct conflict between the SEC and the Exchange on the issue of greatest dollars and cents significance to the Exchange. Cary's strategy was to achieve as much as he could in cooperation with the Exchange before confronting the Exchange on issues that would produce conflict. Cary made this point publicly, explaining to the Investment Bankers Association in 1962: "At this time our internal job is consolidation and improvement. We are not interested in growth as such." To the extent that "growth as such" meant the SEC would assume its responsibilities under Section 19(b) of the 1934 Securities Exchange Act and regulate the reasonableness of commission rates, this objective was not realized at any time during Cary's time as chair.[35]

American Stock Exchange Reorganization

An early benefit of the Cary SEC's nonconfrontational approach was the rapid reorganization of the American Stock Exchange. By the time Cary was sworn in as SEC Chair on March 27, 1961, Trading and Exchanges Division Director Philip Loomis and Associate Director Ralph Saul had nearly completed the Re investigation. On May 4, 1961, the Commission considered the Division's recommending the revocation of Gerald A. Re's and Gerald F. Re's registrations as brokers and their expulsion from the American Stock Exchange. Cary startled the Trading and Exchanges Division's enforcement attorneys by insisting on expelling both men that day instead of waiting until the publication of a formal opinion. The rapidity of the expulsion, like the scathing language of the opinion that he wrote, was meant, in Cary's words, "to be a dramatic way of announcing shock." Eight days after the expulsion, the SEC approved a Trading and Exchanges Division recommendation to investigate the rules, policies, practices, and procedures of the American Stock Exchange.

By then, evidence already accumulated indicated how deficient was the self-regulatory system of the American Stock Exchange. Neither its president, Edward McCormick, nor the four specialists who long had dominated its management, Joseph Reilly, Charles Bocklet, James Dyer, and John Mann, had taken steps to commence a housecleaning. Carry wrote:

> Under these circumstances, if anyone in government wanted headlines, this was a unique opportunity. Like Galahad, we could have publicly denounced the American Stock Exchange. If the SEC had worried about its "image," we should have sought immediate proceedings and publicly forced through a reorganization plan. Then we might have been hailed as "vigorous and tough" — politically attractive labels.

Instead, Cary employed the technique by which William Douglas had forced through the 1937–1938 reorganization of the New York Stock Exchange and, if anything, utilized it more deftly. Douglas had worked with the brokerage house dominated Conway Committee to wrest control from the floor members who then controlled the New York Stock Exchange's governance. Analogously, Cary recruited the considerably greater relative influence of the New York Stock Exchange's leading brokerage firms to reorganize the Amex.

Although the leading New York Stock Exchange brokerage firms also were members of the American Stock Exchange, they had had almost no involvement in its governance. A fall 1961 meeting with Cary, Loomis, and others of the SEC led to an abrupt change in attitude. Cary emphasized that the problems on the Amex eventually could threaten investor confidence in the NYSE as well. Specifically, the SEC made plain that if the financial community's leaders would not take responsibility for cleaning up the Amex, the SEC would be compelled to hold public hearings, a course of action that might well lessen investor confidence in securities trading generally.

Goldman, Sachs's influential partner Gustave Levy, who, in October 1961, agreed to head a Committee of New York Stock Exchange Leaders to recommend steps necessary to reform the Amex, soon stated: "I think that every house on Wall Street wants to help the Curb at this time."

On January 5, 1962, a copy of the SEC's *American Stock Exchange Report* was delivered to the Amex Board of Governors. The next day it was published. The SEC Report pointedly faulted "a small self-perpetuating group dominated by specialists" for the Amex's "fundamental failure of control." On January 7, Gustave Levy met with the Amex Board of Governors and secured understandings that the four specialists the SEC blamed for mismanagement of the Amex would not stand for reelection. By January 8, the Amex Nominating Committee had named a new Exchange Chair.

The Levy Committee, in its final report of February 15, 1962, detailed the constitutional changes necessary to end the specialist hegemony of the Amex. As the Conway Committee 24 years earlier had recommended to reform the New York Stock Exchange after a similar debacle, the Levy Committee urged that the Board of Governors be the sole policymaking body of the Amex, with specialists limited to a small minority of its membership. Administrative responsibility for the management of the Exchange would repose in a president and professional staff, rather than in specialist dominated standing committees. Indeed, the Levy Committee went beyond the Conway Committee in this aspect of its reform proposal and recommended that the Amex's standing committees be abolished. Other portions of the Levy Committee Reports detailed measures to reform listing requirements, membership structure, and enforcement. Nearly all of these recommendations subsequently were adopted.

"Probably never," concluded John Brooks, "has any stock exchange reformed itself so thoroughly so fast." The SEC at all times controlled the course of the reorganization, though not its precise details or the choice of the Amex's new leadership. By allowing the Levy Committee to design the Exchange's new Constitution and select the Amex's new leadership, the SEC was able to act for the most part through unpublicized conferences and to effect improvements in the caliber of the Amex's enforcement activities without political or financial costs to the Commission.[36]

Legislative and Rule Initiatives Under Cary

The Cary Commission was considerably less bold in its legislative and rule initiatives.

Lacking both a Congressional sponsor to introduce new securities legislation or an understanding that President Kennedy would endorse a securities bill, Cary's SEC early determined that its initial 1963 legislative proposals would be far narrower than the full list recommended by the Special Study. Cary's April 3, 1963, Transmittal Letter accompanying the first part of the *Special Study* indicated that the SEC intended to recommend either five or six legislative proposals: a new law extending the 1934 Securities Exchange Act's regulations to unlisted securities with 300 or more shareholders, a proposal authorizing standards of character, competence, and financial responsibility as requirements for entry into the securities business, an amendment of the 1933 Securities Act increasing from 40 to 90 days the period during which a prospectus had to accompany a new security issue, a statute regulating private firms that published over-the-counter quotations, an act barring fraudulent corporate publicity, and, possibly, legislation concerning securities credit. After discussions with representatives of the securities industry and the Federal Reserve Board, the SEC announced on June 3,

1963, that it had further pared its initial legislative package by deferring submission of proposals to regulate over-the-counter quotations, securities credit, and false and misleading corporate publicity.[37]

The essence of Cary's strategy to secure enactment of the 1963 legislative proposals was to win general securities industry support for a "noncontroversial" bill. Later, one liberal member of Congress was to criticize the SEC's bill precisely because "there isn't a single provision opposed by the industry." Given the lack of White House and Congressional support for the bill, Cary appeared correct in his assessment that passage of any bill in the 88th Congress would have been "impossible" without substantial securities industry support.

After the first part of the *Special Study* was published, on April 3, 1963, the Commission's discussion of its legislative proposals with the financial community was formalized. At the SEC's request, representatives of the New York Stock Exchange, the American Stock Exchange, the Investment Bankers Association, the Association of Stock Exchange Firms, and the Investment Company Institute, among others, formed the Industry Liaison Group to negotiate a mutually acceptable bill. Meetings were held with the Industry Liaison Group and separately with the Investment Bankers Association throughout the latter half of April and May 1963. SEC compromises resulted in virtually the entire leadership of the securities industry testifying in favor of the Commission's 1963 bill.[38]

The SEC's Securities Acts Amendments Bill was introduced in the House and the Senate on June 4, 1963. The most significant provision of the bill proposed to apply the period disclosure, proxy, and insider trading sections of the 1934 Securities Exchange Act to all securities issuers with a class of stock held by 500 or more investors and total assets exceeding $1 million. Popularly known as the Frear-Fulbright Bill, since Senators J. Allen Frear and J. William Fulbright earlier had introduced similar bills, legislation to apply the 1934 Act to unlisted firms above a minimum size first had been seriously considered in 1938, when SEC Chair Douglas privately recommended to President Roosevelt that all corporations with $1 million or more in assets be subject to the periodic disclosure provisions of the 1934 Act, and a New York Stock Exchange Report publicly proposed a comparable initiative.[39]

At Cary's direction, the *Special Study* had addressed the major unresolved substantive questions raised by the earlier efforts to enact the Frear-Fulbright Bill. First, what should be the scope of the bill? The *Study* recommended that all 5500 over-the-counter firms with 300 or more shareholders, irrespective of firm assets, should be subject to the 1934 Securities Exchange Act to the same extent with respect to reporting, shareholder voting, and insider trading as firms listed on an Exchange. To lessen the SEC's administrative burden, the *Study* recommended that the Act be phased in over four years.

Second, should banks, already subject to federal or state banking regulations, be required to comply with the Frear-Fulbright standards? The *Special Study* reported that approximately 1000 banks had 300 or more shareholders. Although the banks were subject to periodic inspection by the Comptroller of the Currency, the Federal Reserve Board, the Federal Deposit Corporation, or state authorities, this regulation primarily was intended to protect depositors. A sample of 358 banks with 300 or more shareholders showed the same deficiencies in shareholder reporting and proxy voting statements found in unlisted firms generally. The *Study* recommended that banks with 300 or more shareholders should be subject to the 1934 Act's disclosure, proxy, and insider trading provisions, with the soon to be controversial caveat that the SEC could exempt banks subject to federal or state regulatory authorities that enforced equivalent requirements. For the same reasons, the *Study* recommended that insurance companies with 300 or more shareholders, although subject to state insurance commission regulation, should be subject to the Frear-Fulbright Bill.

As a result of SEC negotiations with the securities industry's representatives in April and May, the Commission made notable compromises of its initial draft bill before transmitting it to Congress in early June. Approximately 1600 firms were excluded from the coverage of the bill when the ultimate jurisdictional test was raised from at least 300 shareholders to at least 500 shareholders and at least $1 million in assets. This compromise split the difference with the securities industry. The Investment Bankers Association in late June indicated that it preferred that the new bill be applied only to unlisted corporations with at least 1000 shareholders.

The SEC fully acquiesced to industry insistence that investment banks that made a market in over-the-counter securities be exempt from the prohibition of profitable short-term insider trading. The SEC agreed with the *Special Study* that investment banks whose members served both as market makers and as corporate directors in a given security had the opportunity to exploit inside information, but the Commission decided to rely on its general power to prosecute insider trading abuses and new rulemaking authority to deal with the problem. Congressman John Dingell later would term this compromise a "license to steal" and accuse the SEC of having made a "contract" with the securities industry on this issue. Of course, the SEC had. But without its acquiescence on this issue, the Commission might not have been able to retain the support of the Investment Bankers Association and the NASD for the rest of the Frear-Fulbright Bill, which, after enactment, was expected to extend the 1934 Securities Exchange Act's periodic disclosure, proxy, and insider trading provisions to 3900 new firms in what would be the most significant extension of the securities laws since 1940.

Finally, the securities industry convinced the SEC that the bill should at first exempt foreign securities, with the understanding that the SEC could require such securities to be subject to the Act when it found that substantial trading existed in the United States or that it was necessary to protect investors.[40]

The Senate, by voice vote, passed the SEC's 1963 Securities Bill on July 30, 1963, less than two months after its introduction. The only substantial opposition to the bill came from Comptroller of the Currency, James J. Saxon, who was in the process of using his own disclosure provisions for banks subject to his Office's regulation and resented the Commission's argument that the Comptroller's requirements would not be "at least equal in effectiveness to those imposed by the SEC." Since the Comptroller regulated only a portion of the banks that would have been subject to the SEC's bill, the total exemption for banks from the bill that Saxon wanted might have resulted in some banks with more than 500 shareholders and $1 million in assets having no shareholder disclosure requirements and all banks above that size following no effective proxy or insider trading rules. Senators Williams and Javits successfully offered an amendment, endorsed by the American Bankers Association and the SEC, requiring the three federal banking agencies to enforce the applicable standards of the 1934 Securities Exchange Act for all banks subject to their jurisdiction. Although the SEC's June 4 draft bill probably would have led to the same result, the Williams-Javits amendment facilitated swift Senate enactment of the Securities Bill by ending opposition from the American Bankers Association.

Comptroller Saxon remained opposed. The following February, Saxon circulated a letter to the chief executive officers of all national banks, renewing his total opposition to inclusion of banks in the SEC's bill. Although Saxon was requested by the White House to cease his opposition and was criticized by the American Bankers Association for misrepresenting the bank related provisions of the bill, he persisted and later almost single handedly defeated the Commission's bill in the House Rules Committee.[41]

The Securities Acts Amendments Bill received a far less enthusiastic reception in the House, where it was to linger 14 months before final passage. For the first 10 of these months, Cary recalled feeling at the "mercy" of Congressman Oren Harris, the Commerce Committee chair who "so dominated the situation by reason of his knowledge and experience that no action was taken until he saw fit." Harris was a Southern Democrat comfortable with the moderately progressive leadership that House Speaker Sam Rayburn and Senate Majority Leader Lyndon Johnson had exercised in Congress during the late 1950s. Although he confessed unfamiliarity with securities markets, Harris supported the SEC *Special Study* and the philosophy of the 1933 and 1934 Securities Acts because he did not "believe you will find anybody today that has anything to do whatsoever with the securities business that would recommend the repeal of those Acts of 1933 and 1934" and because the late Sam Rayburn had told Harris about the passage of the 1933 and 1934 Acts "time after time."

At the same time, Harris enthusiastically supported Southern business interests, once interrupting Chairman Cary's analysis of why there were so many stock insurance companies in the South issuing promotional securities to insist "What I am trying to find out is why it is that this area is subjected to greater promotional activity than any other? I am trying to find out. If I can help build up the insurance business or any other business in the South or Southwest, I want to do it." Throughout the Commerce Committee's extended consideration of the Securities Acts Amendments Bill, Harris pressured the SEC to negotiate compromises with the insurance industry and state securities and insurance officials in the same manner as it earlier had done with the leaders of the national securities industry and the American Bankers Association.[42]

For several months after Cary testified before the House Commerce Committee on April 3, 1963, Harris refused to schedule hearings on the SEC's Securities Bill "until the entire report is filed." Harris also began a protracted effort to negotiate a compromise between the SEC and the insurance industry. Before the Senate Commerce Committee, several insurance lobbying organizations had made a last minute effort to secure a full exemption for insurance firms from the Frear-Fulbright Bill. By a 9-6 vote, the Senate Commerce Committee rejected an amendment that insurance companies be required to file with the SEC only the financial statements they already filed with state insurance commissioners. The insurance industry lobbyists, joined by the state insurance commissioners, continued their efforts in the House.

At Harris's request, Cary met privately on at least three occasions with Harris and representatives of the insurance industry or the state insurance commissioners, notably including the Insurance Commissioner of Arkansas. At these meetings and in subsequent public colloquy, Harris expressed concern that the SEC's Bill would weaken the authority of the state insurance commissioners, who historically had regulated the insurance industry. An SEC analysis of 1961–1963 price fluctuations of unlisted stock insurance corporations provided a factual basis for Cary to argue that prices of insurance securities were "volatile and exhibited wide price fluctuations," presumably because there were few "data available for a sound evaluation of each company." Congressman Harris publicly acknowledged to Cary that "very frankly, I think you have made a very good case." But Harris disputed the SEC's position that the 50 states' insurance commissioners were incapable of improvements and held up Commerce Committee consideration of the SEC's Bill for six months until "it became apparent," wrote Cary, "that a compromise was a political necessity."

In December 1963, the National Association of Insurance Commissioners (*NAIC*) published a Stockholder Information Supplement to the insurance industry's uniform annual reporting form. The insurance commissioners of all 50 states and the District of Columbia wrote the House Commerce Committee that they would require insurance companies to provide stockholders with the information required by the Supplement. Harris, in turn, required the SEC to accept an exemption in its Frear-Fulbright Bill for all insurance companies subject to state regulation of annual statements and proxies equal to the standard prescribed by NAIC and a state statute substantially the same as the short swing insider trading provision of the 1934 Securities Exchange Act. This compromise subjected unlisted stock insurance companies to roughly the same pattern of regulation as the American Bankers Association earlier had secured for unlisted banks.[43]

In late January, the SEC secured the aid of a more influential lobbyist. President Johnson endorsed the Securities Acts Amendments Bill in his Budget Message. Two weeks later, in his February 5, 1964, Special Message on Consumer Interests, Johnson devoted considerable attention to the bill, concluding: "Legislation . . . has already passed the Senate and is pending before the Interstate and Foreign Commerce Committee in the House. . . . I recommend prompt enactment of this disclosure legislation for over-the-counter securities."[44]

Congressman Harris's enthusiasm for the Securities Acts Amendment Bill was perceptibly greater after President Johnson's endorsement. Nonetheless, Harris held the Securities Bill before the House Commerce Subcommittee and full Commerce Committee another three months, until the SEC accepted a series of additional revisions, including language sought by Harris clarifying the preexisting implied exemption for farmers' cooperatives; language retaining the intrastate exemption for broker-dealers; and a compromise provision determinedly sought by Insurance Securities, Incorporated, a direct seller of mutual funds, and by Harris, allowing broker-dealers who preferred not to belong to an industry self-regulatory organization to subject themselves instead to comparable direct SEC regulation.

There was a final holdup. On June 3, 1964, the SEC was informed by Congressman Harris that "Judge Smith was proving reluctant to let our Bill out of the Rules Committee," because Comptroller of the Currency Saxon had persuaded Smith to insist on an amendment to the Frear-Fulbright portion of the bill to the effect "that the Comptroller of the Currency shall not be under a duty to exercise the powers given him under our bill." This would have meant that the Comptroller had the power to exempt banks subject to his jurisdiction, a power that would have been intolerable to the SEC and Harris, as well as to the insurance industry, which reluctantly had accepted a legislative regimen equal to — but not greater than — that imposed on banks. With the intercession of Senate Commerce Chairman Robertson, Smith's colleague from Virginia, a compromise was engineered that satisfied both Saxon and the SEC: the Comptroller and other banking agencies in carrying out their responsibilities under the SEC's Bill were required to issue regulations "substantially similar" to those issued by the Commission unless they found that "implementation of substantially similar regulations . . . are not necessary or appropriate in the public interest or for the protection of investors, and publish such findings, and the detailed reasons therefor, in the *Federal Register*."

The Securities Act Amendments were signed into law on August 20, 1964, a little over 14-1/2 months after the "noncontroversial" bill was introduced. To Cary, the legislative process demonstrated how limited was the capacity of an independent regulatory agency like the SEC to initiate legislation in the post-New Deal period. "Without the cooperation of both Congress and the Executive," Cary wrote in his memoirs, "little constructive can be achieved. To reemphasize the point, an agency is literally helpless if either branch is uninterested or unwilling to lend support."[45]

Similar political realities caused the SEC to compromise several rule initiatives, most notably with respect to New York and American Stock Exchange floor traders, who traded for their own accounts which some at the Commission derogated as having "a license to steal" because of their presence on the Exchange floor and opportunity to take advantage of information more rapidly than other investors. An SEC release "agree[d] that a rule abolishing floor trading on the New York and American Stock Exchanges should be developed unless these Exchanges demonstrate that its continuance would be consistent with the public interest." The Commission ultimately accepted a compromise that 75 percent of floor trader transactions be "stabilizing" or against the price trend rather than push for abolition.

Similarly, with respect to the New York Stock Exchange's 360 specialists who bought and sold stocks on the Exchange floor to make markets, the Commission's American Stock Exchange Report underlined the specialists' information advantages:

> In his unique capacity, the specialist stands at the heart of the Exchange market mechanism. He has intimate knowledge

> of the past market action of the stocks in which he specializes. He also has sole access to the specialist book, showing outstanding orders both below and above the market, which affords him a great competitive advantage over the public. In addition, he exercises a significant influence on the public appraisal of a security, since he is the one who quotes the market.

Regulation of the New York Stock specialist system was, as *Fortune* magazine put it, "Wall Street's Main Event." Over time, the competitive specialist system established during the New Deal largely had been replaced by a system of noncompetitive specialists, who by 1961 were responsible for 26 percent of the share volume on the New York Stock Exchange.

The *Special Study* concluded that "the Exchange's regulatory and surveillance programs [had] been inadequate . . . in the area of the conflicts of interests which arise from the specialist's unique role as both broker and market maker." Specialist discipline, in large measure, was meted out by fellow floor members.

Cary had discussed with his fellow Commissioners a proposal to eliminate the inherent conflict of interest in the specialists' dual broker and dealer roles. Cary discussed having Exchange employees assume the specialist role. "The New York Stock Exchange had the capital," Cary argued. "It could cover any dealer losses."

This proposal was not given serious consideration. Instead, the Commission negotiated with the New York Stock Exchange a rule requiring specialists to observe a "negative" obligation not to deal excessively and an "affirmative" obligation to trade when necessary to stabilize the market. The Commission agreed to an awkward compromise under which the New York Stock Exchange, not the SEC, issued the rule and the Exchange retained considerable ability to supervise the specialist trading obligations. A 1972 Senate Staff Study critically concluded: "Under the rule, the SEC cannot enforce the specialist's 'affirmative' obligation at all, and it can enforce the 'negative' obligation only indirectly and then only in a limited and time consuming manner."[46]

Enforcement Under Cary

Only with respect to securities litigation did Cary's Commission consider itself unrestricted by the political limitations that bound its legislative and rulemaking program. In broadening the bases for private litigants to bring damages actions against corporate officers and directors who exploited inside information or distributed false and misleading proxy statements, Cary's SEC fundamentally altered securities law enforcement.

Cary had arrived at the SEC with one goal: To use the federal 1934 Securities Exchange Act to reverse state corporate law decisions concerning insider trading, such as the Massachusetts Supreme Judicial Court's 1933 opinion *Goodwin v. Agassiz.* The question in *Goodwin* had been a classical one in securities law: Could a corporate director with nonpublic (or *inside*) knowledge of facts that would increase the share price of a security purchase stock from an uninformed shareholder without informing him or these facts? *Goodwin* had held that the purchase of stock by a director with inside knowledge was permissible if done "impersonally" through a stock market.

Cary did not believe the law could be "coextensive with morality," but he insisted that it was shocking for either courts or business executives to believe that it was permissible conduct for executives to use inside information for their personal benefit.

Within months of assuming the position of chair, Cary wrote an SEC Administrative Opinion, *In the Matter of Cady, Roberts & Co.*, that not only contravened *Goodwin v. Agassiz*, but also expanded the utility of Rule 10b-5 as a basis for private causes of action. This rule was soon to be of such significance in securities law that Harvard Law School's Louis Loss would remark in 1969, "The great Rule 10b-5 seems . . . to be taking over the universe gradually."

Section 10(b) of the 1934 Securities Exchange Act was a catch all or residual antifraud provision meant to outlaw types of manipulation not specifically proscribed by the Act's more precise denunciation of touting, wash sales, and other forms of stock market fraud identified by the Pecora Hearings. By its terms, the section provided that "it shall be unlawful . . . to use or employ, in connection with the purchase or sale of any security . . . any manipulative or deceptive device or contrivance in contravention of such rules and regulations as the Commission may prescribe." Nearly identical language in the 1933 Securities Act prohibited fraud in the offer or sale of securities. Section 10(b) was not employed by the SEC until March 21, 1942, when the Commission adopted Rule 10b-5. The rule provided that it shall be unlawful for any person in connection with the purchase or sale of any security "(1) to employ any device, scheme, or artifice to defraud, (2) to make any untrue statement of a material fact or to omit to state a material fact necessary in order to make the statements made, in the light of the circumstances under which they were made, not misleading, or (3) to engage in any act, practice, or course of business which operated or would operate as a fraud or deceit upon any person."

In 1943, the SEC issued a report concerning the Ward LaFrance Trucking Corporation's purchases of its own stock. In the report, it "called attention" to the existence of Rule 10b-5. The rule, however, was relatively little used during the next 18 years because of uncertainty as to whether it applied to purchases or sales effected through securities exchanges. This was the decisive issue in *Goodwin v. Agassiz* and the decisive issue that *Cady, Robert* resolved with its holding that a person possessing inside information must either disclose it to others from whom he seeks to purchase or sell stock or abstain from trading until the inside information becomes publicly known, regardless of whether the person engages in securities transactions face to face or over a securities exchange.

Cary's SEC also supported private enforcement of the securities law through the SEC's successful appearance as *amicus curiae* in the Supreme Court's 1964 case *J.I. Case v. Borak.* In *Borak,* the Court held that stockholders had an implied statutory right to bring damages actions when they were defrauded by corporate proxy solicitations, agreeing with the SEC's argument that "private enforcement of the proxy rules provides a necessary supplement to Commission action. As in antitrust treble damage litigation, the possibility of civil damages or injunctive relief serves as a most effective weapon in the enforcement of the proxy requirements."

The cumulative effect of the SEC's actions in *Cady, Roberts* and *Borak* was rapidly apparent. The Annual Report of the Director of the Administrative Office of the United States Courts noted that a total of 171 private civil cases filed in United States District Courts were based on the federal securities and commodities statutes in 1961, the year *Cady, Roberts* was decided. By 1963, it had reached 1091.[47]

Cohen's SEC

No president, not even Roosevelt, professed that such elaborate benefits flowed from the securities laws as did Lyndon Johnson during the first year of his presidency. The securities laws "authored [by] my very dear, beloved friend, the late Sam Rayburn . . . has helped make all of us a nation of capitalists," Johnson insisted. The SEC itself was a "dramatic demonstration" of the federal government's leadership and wisdom, responsible, in part, for boosting "the market value of stocks listed on the New York Stock Exchange [to] a new high of $465 billion [on July 31, 1964] as contrasted to a value of $23 billion prior to the enactment of the first Federal securities law in 1933."

Yet it was obvious soon after Kennedy's assassination that Johnson did not want the Commission to play so crusading a role that it prevented the business community from supporting his administration. Johnson's legislative priorities initially were civil rights and poverty legislation, both causes that he believed business could support, especially during the painful aftermath of Kennedy's assassination. Greeting the heads of the independent regulatory agencies on December 3, 1963, Johnson bluntly told the Commission chairs not to rock the boat: "We are challenged . . . to concern ourselves with new areas of cooperation [with industry] before we concern ourselves with new areas of control."

As soon as Cary was convinced that the Securities Acts Amendments Bill was likely to pass, he publicly announced his intention to resign. He officially resigned as chair the day the legislation was signed. Just before Johnson signed the Securities Acts Amendments Bill and the Order designating Cary's fellow Commissioner Manuel Cohen to be the new SEC chair, Johnson publicly announced to "my friend, Manuel Cohen" that Cohen, too, would be expected not to rock the boat: "A new era of regulatory relationship is coming, a relationship sincerely devoted to confidence, to understanding, to a responsible role on the part of government in helping and not harassing our American capitalistic system." Throughout the Johnson presidency, the SEC staff size essentially remained static at the 1390–1400 employee level.[48]

Cohen's appointment as chair beginning in August 1964 was greeted with "jubilation" by the SEC staff. He was the first staff member to rise through the ranks to the position of chair in close to 30 years. Cohen reciprocated the staff's loyalty. He never forgot Chair Demmler's politically motivated dismissal of SEC General Counsel Roger Foster in 1953, and rehired the semiretired Foster to be an SEC Special Counsel.

Cohen began his chairmanship as a demanding and determined taskmaster and was only briefly slowed by a heart attack early in 1965. The son of a milk deliveryman, who had earned his law degree in Brooklyn Law School's night program while driving a taxi by day, Cohen believed in hard work, in promotion solely in merit, and in the federal government and the SEC. These beliefs were reflected in his intense loyalty to the Commission. Meyer Eisenberg, Cohen's third Executive Assistant, recalled, "Manny was impatient with everyone who worked for him, as he was impatient with himself. He wanted the Commission to perform better; he wanted the staff to perform at the highest level of any government agency. He held everyone to his standards. No piece of paper ever left his office unmarked or unedited."

As Cohen had progressed within the SEC, he developed what those closest to him characterized as a "limitless faith in his ability to talk to anybody about anything." To David Ratner, Cohen's second Executive Assistant, this faith was the product both of Cohen's considerable self-confidence and of his understanding that in Washington "the person who argues longest rather than the person with the best arguments often wins legal or political battles." A joke from one of Manny's speeches contains more truth than humor. Someone reportedly asked Manny's wife what her husband actually *did* as SEC chair. She replied: "I can't describe it exactly, but if *I* did it, it would be called nagging."

The policy views of Cohen, particularly during his first years as chair, were deeply influenced by his 19 years as an SEC staff member. Cohen joined the Commission in 1942, roughly at the beginning of the Commission's long post-New Deal decline. By 1952, his legal ability was well recognized, and he was named Chief Counsel of the SEC's Division of Corporate Finance, then considered the elite division of the agency.

When Byron Woodside became an SEC Commissioner in 1960, Cohen succeeded his long-time Chief as Director of the Division of Corporate Finance. James Landis's recommendation led to Cohen's appointment as a Commissioner in 1961. William Cary, in a letter to President Kennedy urging Cohen's 1961 Commission appointment, underlined Cohen's long experience as the Counsel and intellectual leader of the Corporate Finance Division: "He is the lawyer's lawyer *par excellence*, and is so recognized by the corporate bar in this country." In terms of sheer technical ability to employ the antifraud concepts of the securities laws, Manny Cohen, among the

Commission's staff in the 1950s, unquestionably was, as Irving Pollack wrote, "Mr. SEC."

In March 1964, after Cary's plan to leave the SEC were known within the Commission, Cohen publicly articulated a theory of SEC-securities industry relations in an address to the Investment Bankers Association entitled "Cooperative Regulation."

Subsequent events would transform Cohen into one of the most activist SEC chairs of the post-war period, one not reluctant to employ Douglas's metaphoric shotgun. But he began his position as chair, as he explained in the March 1964 address, with this belief:

> A new rule must not have a shotgun effect. Rather, the approach must be affirmative and selective. It will involve, even at this stage, the cooperation of the industry.... Neither the Commission nor the industry can allow a disagreement to lead to a breakdown in the lines of communication or to a failure of cooperation in other tasks.[49]

The securities industry fundamentally changed during the 1960s. Trading and new issue volume reached unprecedented levels. Between 1960 and 1968 the total annual dollar volume of stocks traded on the New York Stock Exchange increased nearly fourfold, from $38 billion to $145 billion, a rate considerably exceeded by the eightfold increase in the dollar volume of trading on the American Stock Exchange from $4.2 to $34.8 billion and the 534 percent increase in trading on the regional exchanges from $3.1 to $16.6 billion. Between 1960 and 1969, the number of new securities annually registered with the SEC increased from 1426 to 3645, with the dollar value of new issues increasing from $14.4 to $86.8 billion. This staggeringly rapid increase in volume led to a tenfold increase in pretax profits of New York Stock Exchange members between 1962 and 1968, but the SEC, in the words of the Commission's 34th Annual Report, was "almost overwhelmed by the sheer volume of activity."

Simultaneous with the enormous 1960s growth in trading volume was a rapid institutionalization of the stock markets. In the post-war period up until the SEC's 1963 Special Study, aggregate stock trading by mutual funds, commercial bank trust departments, insurance companies, pension funds, and other institutional investors ranged, according to various studies and samples, between 17 and 28 percent of total New York Stock Exchange volume. In the next six years, the dramatic rise in aggregate institutional trading "transformed those institutions," reported the SEC in 1971, "into a major, if not the dominant factor in the equity market." By 1969, institutional investors accounted for 52 percent of NYSE volume, with individual and nonmember broker-dealer trading for the first time reduced to a minority of transactions on the Exchange.

The simultaneous surge in aggregate stock exchange volume and in the proportion of institutional trading by the late 1960s threatened to fundamentally alter the structure of the stock exchanges. Between the last quarter of 1964 and the first quarter of 1969, the percentage of total New York Stock Exchange volume transacted through block trades of 10,000 or more shares grew from 2 to 12 percent. The difficulties Exchange specialists experienced in handling large block trades, together with the rigidity of the Exchange's fixed commission rate schedule and related membership rules that afforded institutional traders neither volume discounts nor the right to become Exchange members, created incentives for institutional investors to trade New York Stock Exchange listed securities off the Exchange floor on the over-the-counter third market. Institutional traders often were prevented from securing the price and liquidity advantages of third market trading by New York Stock Exchange interpretations of its Rule 394, which usually forbade an Exchange member from trading Exchange listed securities over-the-counter.

By the end of Cohen's tenure as chair, plans to automate securities trading operations were sufficiently advanced to portend another fundamental pressure to alter the historic structure of the stock markets. The SEC's 1968 Annual Report predicted, "Automation is on the threshold of revolutionizing the system of quotations for unlisted securities." In 1968, the NASD, after four years of consultation with the SEC, hired the Bunko-Ramo Corporation to build and operate Nasdaq, a national electronic data processing and communications system to provide instantaneous over-the-counter price quotations from over-the-counter market makers for each security listed within the Nasdaq system.[50]

The 43-month-long Dow Jones price rise, beginning in June 1962, was instrumental in stimulating the decade's record trading volume. It also stimulated a protracted period of securities speculation immortalized by *The New Yorker*'s financial correspondent, John Brooks, as the Go-Go years. By Brooks's definition, "the term 'go-go' came to designate a method of operating in the stock market . . . characterized by rapid in and out trading of huge blocks of stock, with an eye to large profits taken very quickly, and the term was used specifically to apply to the operation of certain mutual funds, none of which had previously operated in anything like such a free, fast, or lively manner."

The speculation of the Go-Go years created a pressure to reverse the SEC's post-World War II period of narrow interpretation of its statutory responsibilities. Trading volume over the American Stock Exchange and the over-the-counter markets in speculative issues resulted in rapid price run ups in securities ranging from Kentucky Fried Chicken, selling at close to 100 times its last reported earnings in April 1967, to Boothe Computer, a minor computer leasing firm, which rose from 18 to 46 on the first day it was offered to the public. The Amex, foundering after the Res scandal with a mere 6.8 percent of total stock exchange volume in 1962, nearly tripled that percentage in the next six years, primarily as a result of the Go-Go period's fascination with the newer and smaller firms listed there, as contrasted with the New York Stock Exchange's list of older, larger, and less speculative firms. As Brooks emphasized, the most publicized actors during the Go-Go years were mutual fund managers who adopted the strategy of seeking the most profitable short-term performance, typically emphasizing a greater proportion of investment in speculative or growth common stocks than mutual fund managers historically had.[51]

Initially less evident than the rapid 1960s volume surge, the growing institutionalization of the stock markets, or the revival of securities speculation were political changes in the federal government that also placed enormous pressure on the SEC to assume a more activist role. By the late 1960s, the market self-correcting premises of the mainstream economic theory were so widely accepted by both the Democratic and Republican parties that the Justice Department Antitrust Division and the Federal Trade Commission under both President Johnson and President Nixon would adopt nearly identical positions in urging the SEC to use its statutory authority to abolish price fixing in the stock markets and the mutual fund industry.

It was during the time when Manuel Cohen served as chair, 1964 to 1969, that the SEC began the process of redefining its primary functions in light of the fundamental changes then occurring in the structure of the securities markets, the Go-Go years' revival of securities speculation, and the greater political influence of the economic theory of competition. In each of the principal policy issues that Cohen's SEC addressed — mutual fund reform, the restructuring of the securities markets, the 1960s conglomerate merger wave — Cohen came to believe, as he stated during the last months of his time as chair, that "Wall Street must change with the times and it rarely moves toward reform unless it is pushed."

Cohen made the same point more forcefully after he left the SEC, during a 1971 debate with economist George Stigler. "The most prominent current weaknesses of the securities industry," Cohen said, "can be attributed not to excessive regulation but to a failure of regulation." Instead of disclosure, occasional fraud actions, and consultation with industry, Cohen now emphasized "the infusion of competition [as] one of the principal reasons for the success of regulation of the securities industry," a regulatory tool necessary to remove "arbitrary impediments to fair and free markets." Cohen's disposition late in his career to use government power to create "fair and free markets" was conveyed most memorably in his October 1968 response to Presidential Candidate Richard Nixon's criticism that the SEC had been engaged in "heavy handed bureaucratic regulatory schemes." "Regulation," insisted Cohen, "is not a dirty word. We should not be ashamed to regulate."[52]

Cohen's progress from a lawyer's lawyer and advocate of cooperative regulation to a proponent of securities industry competition and regulatory activism paralleled the SEC's institutional redirection during the 1960s. But the SEC as an institution changed less than did its chair. The Commissioners who led the SEC in the 1964–1969 period were unwilling fully to support Cohen's priorities or his attempts to increase competition in the mutual fund industry and securities markets. As a consequence, Cohen's SEC, in general, progressed slowly, occasionally was unable to explain clearly its regulatory proposals, and left Cohen personally at the conclusion of his chairmanship with the conviction that "in so many ways, we have just begun."[53]

Enforcement Under Cohen

Cohen's long experience at the SEC enabled him to rapidly take steps to strengthen the SEC's enforcement program. During the Truman and Eisenhower administrations, the enforcement program of the home office of the SEC's Trading and Exchanges Division had been minimal, generating a total of 50 cases during the 1950s. In large measure, the program was "a paper pushing outfit," recalled future Enforcement Division Director Stanley Sporkin, whose function was to process requests from the regional offices for formal investigations and answer investors' complaint letters.

The 1961 SEC action expelling the Res convinced Chairman Cary, Stanley Sporkin recalled, that "the Commission needed a home office preemptive strike capability." Later in 1961, Cary transferred Assistant General Counsel Irving Pollack, then the SEC's expert in developing securities fraud cases for referral to the Justice Department for criminal prosecution, to the Trading and Exchanges Division to be its Associate Director and rebuild the home office's enforcement programs. During the three years of Cary's chairmanship, the home office of the Trading and Exchanges Division initiated approximately as many cases as it had in the previous 26 years of the SEC's existence, averaging 40 new cases per year as compared with the 1950s annual average of five.

Manuel Cohen promoted the expansion of the home office enforcement program of what was by then renamed the Trading and Markets Division. From the beginning of his chairmanship, Cohen encouraged enforcement actions to expand the potential targets of SEC civil litigation and the interpretive contours of the securities laws. The most significant action, *SEC v. Texas Gulf Sulphur*, was brought against officers and directors of a large mining corporation for fraudulent insider trading on a securities market. The SEC's action against Texas Gulf Sulphur resulted in a landmark 1968 Second Circuit Court of Appeals decision that sustained the SEC's factual allegations that several Texas Gulf Sulphur Company directors, officers, and employees had violated Rule 10b-5 by purchasing stock and stock options without disclosing their knowledge of an extraordinary mineral discovery in Timmins, Ontario. The Second Circuit's decision was doctrinally significant for its definition of when information was "material," its application of the *Cady, Roberts* rule that a corporate insider possessing nonpublic material information about his corporation could not buy or sell corporate securities until the information becomes public, and its comment that "tippees" or outsiders receiving nonpublic material inside information also could be held liable if they purchased a security before the nonpublic information was disseminated.

By the end of the Cohen chairmanship, the enforcement program of the home office of the SEC's Trading and Markets Division had grown to a staff of over 100 people. The program continued to initiate an average of 40 new cases a year during the 1965–1969 period and played a role in developing an increased number of criminal prosecutions under the securities laws. Largely because of Cohen's role in providing the staff and doctrinal support for the SEC's enforcement efforts, Stanley Sporkin would describe Cohen's time as chair as "truly the Golden Age of the Commission." From the point of view of the SEC's Enforcement Division, this was an appropriate characterization.[54]

During Cohen's chairmanship, the Commission also modestly responded to the 1960s conglomerate merger wave.

Between 1962 and 1969, 22 percent of the companies included on the *Fortune 500* list of largest manufacturing corporations were acquired. In 1968 alone, 26 of the largest 500 manufacturing firms were absorbed by other firms; in that one year, nearly 10 percent of all independent manufacturing corporation with $10 million or more in assets ceased to exist independently.

The conglomerate mystique was widely recognized as a stimulus to the feverish common stock speculation of the 1960s Go-Go years, pushing Ling-Temco-Vought (*LTV*) common stock, for one example, from $11 per share in 1964 to $136 in the 1968–1969 period. Inevitably, the high costs of buying "instant earnings" with fixed interest debt securities and cumulative preferred stock caught up with LTV, and its common stock fell to $21 per share in March 1970, a decline of 85 percent during a period when the Dow Jones Industrial Average dropped 23 percent and Standard and Poor's Industrial Average 26 percent. LTV's experience was consistent with that of many other large conglomerates during this period. Between the stock market's 1968–1969 peak and March 1970, when the Dow Jones Average fell 23 percent, Litton common stock dropped 75 percent; Gulf & Western, 74 percent; Textron, 60 percent.

The SEC supported highly compromised accounting professions' steps to improve merger accounting and address information loss caused by conglomerate mergers through limited segment disclosure of the components of a merged firm. Most consequentially, the Commission supported the addition of provisions to the Securities Exchange Act, known as the Williams Act, to subject cash tender offers to buy a target corporation's stock to additional disclosure.

Under the Williams Act and enabling rules, any person who acquired more than 5 percent of a registered security had to send copies of required information within 10 days to the SEC, the issuer, and each Exchange on which the security was traded. Before a person could make a tender offer, that person also had to file with the SEC, as well as the security holder, a separate disclosure document. A similar section applied to issuer purchases of their own stock through a self-tender offer. The Williams Act also made it unlawful for *any* person to make any untrue statement of a material fact, "or to engage in any fraudulent, deceptive, or manipulative acts or practices," in connection with any tender offer or any solicitation in opposition to or in favor of a tender offer.[55]

Mutual Fund Legislation

Inevitably, reform of the mutual fund industry was the SEC's legislative priority during Cohen's chairmanship. Between 1940, when the Investment Company Act was adopted, and 1966, mutual fund net assets had increased from $450 million to $38.2 billion, and the number of mutual fund investors had increased twelvefold, from approximately 300,000 investors in 1940 to more than 3.5 million in 1965. By the mid-1960s, the funds had become a matter of widespread controversy. Discarding historically cautious investment approaches, fund managers, led by Gerald Tsai, emphasized "performance" by concentrating their investment portfolios in growth stocks rather than in "balanced" portfolios. In the early 1960s, Tsai popularized a new style of institutional investment management, emphasizing quick turnover of large blocks of securities. The new performance oriented approach was widely emulated; the Investment Company Institute calculated that an average mutual fund turned over 13 percent of its common stock holdings in 1953 and 17.6 percent in 1960, but turnover reached 46.6 percent in 1968 and 55.6 percent during the second quarter of 1969. The "cult of performance" raised questions about the riskiness of mutual funds and about the impact of their large block transactions on the securities exchanges. Offshore fund holding companies, like Bernard Cornfeld's Fund of Funds, suggested a less profound inquiry: Were foreign based mutual fund holding companies being employed as vehicles for tax evasion? It was difficult to understand why United States citizens would pay double the notoriously high sales loads of domestic mutual funds but for the italicized enticement of the Fund of Funds' prospectus: *"The names and addresses of all investors are held in strictest confidences at all times."*[56]

That the SEC did not develop legislative recommendations concerning mutual funds until December 1966 was a matter of considerable embarrassment at the Commission. In 1958, the SEC had commissioned the University of Pennsylvania's Wharton School of Finance and Commerce to prepare a study of the implications of the mutual funds' growth. This was the only research study of any consequence initiated by the SEC during the Eisenhower period.

SEC concern about mutual fund costs intensified during Cary's chairmanship. In 1961, Chairman Cary requested Joseph Weiner, then acting as a consultant to the Commission, to prepare a study of the administration of the Investment Company Act. Weiner's study, one of a series he made on the securities laws, was not published but was widely circulated within the Commission.

Weiner reported that the marketing of mutual funds presented problems "fully as acute" as the "exaction of monopoly prices" by mutual fund advisers. "Under the present typical method of compensating the investment adviser any increase in the number of outstanding shares automatically increases the advisory fee. This creates a great incentive to secure increased sales." Since mutual funds usually were "sold" by salespeople, not "bought" by unsolicited investors, the sales load paid on mutual fund shares had increased during the 1950s as rival funds had competed to *increase* commission rates "to have the salesmen push their product in preference to the products of others. Weiner was particularly critical of the front-end load on periodic payment mutual funds, the most extreme type of what Manuel Cohen later would call "this perverse" form of competition. Under the Investment Company Act of 1940, up to one half of the payments made in the first year of a periodic payment plan purchase of a mutual fund typically running 10 years could be deducted from the salesman's commission.

In 1962, the SEC published the Wharton School's *Study of Mutual Funds.* Although the Wharton School *Study* made no legislative recommendations, its factual findings suggested the need for fundamental reforms. The most publicized finding of the *Wharton Study* was that for the 1952-1958 period the average performance of mutual funds did not differ appreciably from what would have been achieved by a randomly assembled portfolio of securities with the same division among asset types. The *Wharton Study* found no significant relation between the rates of management fees and performance results nor between the initial sales charges and performance results.[57]

The *Wharton Study*, however, found there usually was no resulting benefit to shareholders. While three fourths of a sample of investment advisers for individual clients scaled their fees according to the amount of money to be managed or by negotiation, 85 percent of a second sample of investment advisers charged mutual funds a flat rate, usually 0.5 percent per annum, regardless of the size of the fund to be managed.

The advisory fee rates of mutual funds also tended substantially to exceed the management costs in the small number of internally managed mutual funds. In 1966, the SEC Report on Investment Company Growth would calculate that the median fee of 57 externally managed funds in 1965 was 0.48 percent, roughly twice the 0.25 percent estimated median management cost of 11 leading internally managed funds.

By 1962, the typical commission or sales load on a mutual fund ran between 8 and 8.5 percent, with retail sales organizations receiving between two-thirds and three-fourths of the load. Of the 30 largest mutual funds in 1950 for which data were available in 1966, 13 increased and none decreased their sales load during that 16-year period; 18 of the funds increased the proportion of the sales load distributed to retail sales organizations. Although the no-load funds generally gave investors 8 to 8.5 percent greater value than load funds and on average performed as well as load funds, as of 1963, the 30 existing no-load funds accounted for a mere 3 percent of the total assets of the investment company industry.[58]

The Cary commission's response to the *Wharton Study* was deliberately low keyed, deferring mutual fund reform until the 1964 Securities Acts Amendments were passed.

The *Special Study* chapter on mutual funds concluded that "serious consideration should be given to the elimination of future front-end load plans. Contracts to buy investment company shares on a periodic payment basis were first offered to the public in 1930. By the time the SEC published its New Deal period report, *Investment Trusts and Investment Companies*, these funds' potential for exploiting unsophisticated investors was recognized. Total commission charges on completed contract plans in some cases amounted to 20 percent of the sum invested. Usually, all of the first year's payments were deducted for sales load and other charges, leaving the investor with little or no investment if shares were redeemed early. These findings prompted Congress to enact a provision of the Investment

Company Act of 1940, limiting sales loads to 9 percent of the total proposed payments on contractual plans and prohibiting the deduction of more than 50 percent of the first year's payments for sales commissions.

In the late 1950s, the widespread employment of contract plans recurred with first year front-end loads equal to the 50 percent statutory limit. The *Special Study* "conservatively estimated" that, though front-end loading had been an infrequent practice as late as 1956, by 1962 "more than one-fourth of the 2.6 million persons investing in mutual funds are doing so through contractual plans." The Study concluded:

> The combined factors of the incentive to high-pressure selling which the front-end load provides to salesmen, the essentially unsupervised nature of home selling of plans, the complexity of the security sold, and the lack of financial sophistication of so many of the purchasers of plans creates a problem of a fundamental nature which cannot be solved through the mere application of the doctrine of disclosure.[59]

By the time Manuel Cohen began as SEC chair in August 1964, the SEC had been studying the mutual fund industry for six years. Cohen concurred in the *Wharton Study's* conclusion that the "conflict of interest between mutual fund managers and shareholders" inherent in the structure of the funds resulted in mutual fund shareholders "incurring excessive costs in the acquisition and management of their investments." As published in December 1966, the *Report of the Securities and Exchange Commission on the Public Policy Implications of Investment Company Growth* represented the Cohen Commission's official view on how the mutual fund industry should be reformed. More than any other Study of the period, it also illustrated the fundamental intellectual conflict between the Commission's legalistic approach to economic regulation and the competition oriented theory of the antitrust laws. As Dr. Sidney Robbins was to write of the Commission's 1966 Mutual Fund Report, the SEC "forgot its economics." The Report's analysis was rejected virtually unanimously by economists, including MIT's Paul Samuelson, later a Nobel laureate, Yale's Henry Wallich, the University of Chicago's George Stigler, Irwin Friend, principal author of the 1962 *Wharton Study*, and Donald Farrar, who was to serve as Director of the SEC's 1968–1971 *Institutional Investor Study*. The Report's analysis also would be rejected by President Johnson's Council of Economic Advisers, the Justice Department's Antitrust Division, and, in 1972, when, as a practical matter, it was too late, a subsequent SEC Staff Report.[60]

The fundamental issue in mutual fund regulation during the postwar period was the persistence of higher sales loads and advisory fees than would have occurred if there had been effective competition. Payment of an 8 to 8.5 percent sales load could be viewed as irrational given the existence of no-load funds with comparable performance records. Similarly, the standard 0.5 percent annual advisory fee then was about twice the median fee that investment advisers charged individual clients or that internally managed mutual funds charged their shareholders. Yet externally managed mutual funds dominated the industry.

In large measure, the persistence of mutual fund extracompetitive costs was the result of federal laws and regulations prohibiting or inhibiting competition. The SEC prevented the no-load funds from paying securities brokers a commission when they recommended no-load securities (this, of course, would have changed no loads into low loads) and strictly limited the newspaper advertisements of all mutual funds. The combination of infrequent recommendations by stock brokers and ineffectual advertising prevented the no-loads from effectively competing with the sales efforts of the load funds that then dominated the mutual fund industry. In a 1967 statement to the United States Senate, Irwin Friend recommended that the SEC employ its historically preferred technique of "full disclosure" to improve the competitive opportunity of the no-load funds. This would have required the publication on the front page of the prospectus of each mutual fund (including any sold with the typical 8 to 8.5 percent commission rate) of information "in a manner prescribed by the SEC," comparing the performance and costs of the fund being offered with the corresponding group averages for load and no-load funds.

Given the *Special Study's* findings about the lack of sophistication of many mutual fund investors, it is difficult to understand how any technique short of that proposed by Friend could ensure that the relatively large proportion of inexperienced investors who purchased mutual funds did so on an informed basis. But the SEC's 1966 *Report on Investment Company Growth* did not make legislative recommendations to enable no-load funds to be more competitive.[61]

The most controversial statutory restraint on mutual fund industry competition was § 22(d) of the 1940 Investment Company Act. Section 22(d) long has been recognized as a "notable exception to the general Congressional policy against price fixing." It prohibited retail securities dealers from selling mutual funds "except at a current offering price described in the prospectus." This prevented price competition among mutual fund retailers and, in the often echoed view of the SEC's 1966 *Report on Investment Company Growth*, was responsible "in part [for] the failure of competition among principal underwriters to bring price benefits to mutual fund investors."

Against this economic and regulatory background, the SEC's 1966 *Report on Investment Company Growth* must be accounted among the most poorly reasoned studies ever prepared by the Commission, striking both for its failure adequately to analyze central policy questions and for the extent to which the Report's legislative recommendations were influenced by political expediency rather than the needs of investors or the theory of competition that elsewhere regulated the economy through the antitrust laws.

The SEC in 1966 did not propose the repeal of § 22(d). The Report offered two explanations of the Commission's decision. First, the abolition of § 22(d) might lead more mutual funds to distribute their securities through directly employed sales personnel rather than independent retail organizations. Unless the SEC intended to subsidize inefficient sales personnel, this was a result the Commission presumably should have favored. Second, retail price competition would permit knowledgeable investors to achieve greater cost savings than those investors most in need of protection. This argument, too, was not persuasive. "Knowledgeable" investors presumably already purchased no-load funds. If abolition of § 22(d) alone was insufficient to lead to greater retail price competition, nothing prevented the SEC from also recommending changes in mutual fund advertising and prospectus requirements to increase the information available to potential mutual fund investors.

The conservatism and lack of economic training of some of Johnson's appointees to the Commission also had some bearing on the SEC's refusal to recommend that § 22(d) be repealed, as did the concern of some Commissioners that repeal would put a large number of small broker-dealers out of business. Lack of study of the economic consequences of repeal of § 22(d) later would discourage the Senate Banking Committee from recommending abolition of the section, although the Committee indicated that it otherwise had been inclined to do so. When the SEC at the Senate Banking Committee's request did make a study of "potential economic impact of a repeal of Section 22(d)" in 1972, it found that repeal would lead to lower sales costs, "most of the savings would go to small investors," the impact on the securities industry and on most retail sellers of mutual fund shares would be "extremely modest" except on part-time sales personnel, who represented the least efficient segment of the industry, and that "the repeal of Section 22(d) is unlikely to lead to protracted net redemptions on an industry-wide basis."

The 1966 SEC Report Group instead proceeded as many trial lawyers would. It assembled data comparing the 8 to 8.5 percent typical mutual fund sales load with the usually lower commission rates paid on securities purchased on an exchange, over the counter, and from a new issue. Apparently because the National Association of Securities Dealers then limited dealer spreads to 5 percent, the SEC's 1966 Report recommended that the Investment Company Act be amended to provide that sales charges for mutual funds be limited to 5 percent.[62]

There were similar analytic shortcomings in the second principal recommendation of the SEC's 1966 *Report on Investment Company Growth*, that investment advisers be limited to a "reasonable" fee when managing mutual funds, taking into account the nature and extent of services, the quality of services, economies of scale, and other factors "as are appropriate and material." In the federal District Courts where it was to be enforced, the SEC's "reasonableness" standard undoubtedly would have been more effective in limiting advisers to fees equal to an arm's-length bargain than the "waste" doctrine then applied by the state courts. This was a traditional lawyer's solution to the problem of compensating a monopolist. As federal Second Circuit of Appeals Judge Henry Friendly testified to the Senate Banking Committee in 1967, "Determining whether charges or other business practices are reasonable is nothing new for courts."

But neither the SEC's 1966 *Report on Investment Company Growth* nor Commission testimony adequately explained why a reasonableness standard should be preferred to the compulsory internalization of mutual fund management. In economic theory, it is assumed that the costs of a single firm efficiently performing a function will be less than the costs for performing a function that includes a transaction between two firms. Savings from the elimination of transaction costs and duplicative overhead had been a clear efficiency achieved by the SEC in its simplification of public utility holding companies. That savings also could be achieved by eliminating external advisers in the mutual fund industry was suggested by both the 1962 Wharton School and the 1966 SEC Investment Company Studies, which found that the expenses of the small number of existing internally managed mutual funds tended to run about half those of the much larger number of externally managed funds. Such savings later led plaintiff's attorney Abe Pomerantz to testify in favor of compulsory internalization of mutual fund management: "Why can't the mutual fund do what every other American corporation does: internalize its management, *i.e.*, hire and pay for its executive talent?"

The SEC never satisfactorily answered this question, instead arguing that its reasonableness standard was less "drastic" than compulsory internalization, more "cautious," and "genuinely conservative." Such arguments hardly were a substitute for an empirical study of the practicality of compelling internalization.[63]

Building on the earlier research of the 1963 *Special Securities Market Study*, the Commission's third principal mutual fund proposal was to abolish front-end loads on contract plans through statutory language prohibiting "the amount of sales load deducted from any one payment [exceeding] proportionately the amount deducted from any other payment."

Long before the SEC's bill was introduced, the mutual fund industry began assembling a lobby to defend existing practices. The lobby was unparalleled in its employment of former SEC commissioners and senior staff officials. James Landis, having left the White House staff in 1961, was employed as the Chair of the Association of Mutual Funds Plan Sponsors in 1962 to draft statements defending the front-end load feature of contract plans. Eisenhower SEC Chair Ralph Demmler served as an attorney to the Investment Company Institute during 1967 legislative hearings. A second Eisenhower SEC chair, Edward Gadsby, in 1960 a critic of investment adviser "monopoly prices," by 1968 would be a registered lobbyist for several funds. By then, also, Sidney Robbins, Chief Economist of the SEC's Special Study, would be an unaffiliated Director of the Oppenheimer Fund and would write, with Oppenheimer Fund President Leon Levy, an adversarial article opposing the Commission's mutual fund legislative proposals.[64]

The most effective mutual fund industry criticisms of the SEC's legislative proposals focused on the analytical deficiencies of the Commission's 1966 Report on Investment Company Growth. Five days after the Report was published, *The New York Times*, long the SEC's most influential journalistic ally, joined the mutual fund industry in arguing that the Report had a "major defect": "The Report fails to . . . provide economic justification for its demand that the initial sales load be limited to 5 percent." This inadequacy, the *Times* reported, was "the result of the SEC's orientation, which is legal, not economic."

Before Senate Banking Committee Hearings began on the SEC's 1967 Mutual Fund Bill, Committee Chair John Sparkman circulated a compromise proposal to the Investment Company Institute, the NASD, and the New York and American Stock Exchanges. In place of the SEC bill's 5 percent limit on sales charges, Sparkman asked: Would the industry support a provision requiring the NASD to set reasonable mutual fund sales loads subject to SEC oversight? The provision was endorsed within a week by the NASD and both Exchanges, with the Investment Company Institute alone insisting that no new legislation was necessary. Sparkman's compromise was the first of a series of substantive alterations made by the Senate before it enacted the SEC's Mutual Fund Bill on July 26, 1968. Although the SEC's original bill had recommended the abolition of the front-end load on mutual funds purchased through a periodic payment plan, the Senate bill limited the load to no more than 20 percent in any one year or more than 64 percent over the first four years. The Senate bill retained the SEC's reasonableness standard for assessing investment adviser fees but added a rebuttable presumption that fees were reasonable if ratified by a majority of shareholders and disinterested directors. These Senate modifications substantially weakened the SEC's bill. Nonetheless, the Commission reluctantly supported the Senate bill, with the agency taking no official position on a fourth Senate alteration, an amendment introduced by Senate McIntyre to authorize banks to enter the mutual fund industry through their management of commingled investment accounts.[65]

In a highly unusual event, a 4–3 majority of the House Commerce Subcommittee on Commerce and Finance refused to report out any version of the Mutual Fund Bill for consideration by the full Commerce Committee, and the bill died in the House in September

1968. Newspaper accounts attributed the surprise vote to the waning influence of the lame duck Johnson administration and the lobbying activities of the mutual funds, noting particularly the prominent role played by J. Edward Day, former Postmaster General, on behalf of the Association of Mutual Fund Sponsors, the trade association of the front-end load contractual plans.[66]

After President Nixon accepted Manuel Cohen's resignation as SEC chair in February 1969, the Mutual Fund Bill passed by the Senate in July 1968 was further compromised before its enactment into law in December 1970. From the mutual fund industry's perspective, three compromises were of paramount importance. The 1968 Senate-passed bill would have authorized banks to operate commingled investment accounts in direct competition with mutual funds. The 1970 Act dropped this provision, leaving the Glass-Steagall Banking Act as controlling law. Early in 1971, the Supreme Court held that the Glass-Steagall Act bars bank managed commingled investment accounts.

The 1970 Act also altered the reasonableness standard for appraising investment adviser fees initially recommended by the SEC and passed, with qualification, by the Senate in 1968. The Senate-passed reasonableness standard went far toward limiting advisory fees to amounts equal to an arm's-length bargain by defining *reasonable* as taking into account fees paid by other clients of an adviser, the nature and extent of services provided, and other relevant and material factors, presumably including economies of scale, the fees charged by rival investment advisers, and the management costs of internally managed funds. By contrast, the 1970 Act, without definition either in the statute or Congressional Reports, provided that "the investment adviser of a registered investment company shall be deemed to have a fiduciary duty with respect to the receipt of compensation for services."

The 1970 Act loosened the 1968 Senate-passed bill's front-end load limitation. The Senate-passed bill, itself a significant compromise of the SEC's effort to abolish front-end loads on mutual fund periodic payment plans, had provided that the sales load on a contract load could be no more than 20 percent of the first year's payments or 64 percent of the first four years. The 1970 Act retained this standard, but provided that the sponsors of the mutual fund alternatively could elect to sell funds with a 50 percent front-end load as long as the funds retained no more than a 15 percent commission if the securities were redeemed within the first 18 months.

This alternative meant that SEC efforts to eliminate the 50 percent front-end load possible under the 1940 Investment Company Act had been defeated in instances when funds chose the alternative load restriction and their shareholders did not formally redeem their shares for a year and a half.

The 1970 Act did retain Senator Sparkman's compromise sales load provision. In place of the SEC's proposed 5 percent limit on mutual fund sales loads, the Act directed the NASD to prohibit its members from charging an "excessive sales load but shall allow for reasonable compensation for sales personnel, broker-dealers, and underwriters and for reasonable sales loads to investors." The rules subsequently adopted by the NASD permitted its members to continue to charge the traditional 8.5 percent fee, except on large volume purchases of $10,000 or more, as long as a mutual fund reinvested dividends without further fee and offered rights of accumulation.[67]

The full significance of the SEC's legalistic approach to mutual fund legislation became clear beginning in 1969. Despite candidate Richard Nixon's attack on the SEC's "heavy handed bureaucratic regulatory schemes," the Nixon Administration's Justice Department consistently testified in favor of the repeal of the Investment Company Act's resale price maintenance provision, a reform potentially more far reaching in its cost savings for investors than the SEC's initial proposed 5 percent sales load limit. The political lesson was plain. SEC reform initiatives that relied on marketplace competition to protect investors were far more likely to command bipartisan support from liberal consumer minded members of Congress and conservative free enterprise proponents than direct agency rate regulation. In the Johnson and Nixon Administrations, this was a lesson the Commission's leadership reluctantly, but inevitably, assimilated.[68]

Commission Rate Regulation

No issue did more to bring into question the historic reputation of the SEC as "an outstanding example of the independent commission at its best" than the Commission's handling of a related cluster of stock exchange commission rate and membership rules in the 1963–1973 period.

To MIT economist Paul Samuelson, the SEC's historic indifference to efficient competition in the securities industry was "sad, if not scandalous." The University of California's Lawrence Shepard in an often cited book, *The Securities Brokerage Industry,* would make the more extreme point that in commission rate regulation, the SEC had performed like a captive agency, "championing [the interest of] the regulated," permitting "noncompetitive pricing and entry practices [to] flourish" under the Commission's regulatory umbrella. So "timid a watchdog" did journalist Louis Kohlmeier believe the SEC in mutual fund and commission rate regulation, that he urged in his 1969 book, *The Regulators,* that the Commission be "abolished as it now exists."[69]

As distinguished from the SEC's lengthy evasion of the fundamental economic issues in the mutual fund field, in the last year of Cohen's time as chair, the SEC did set in motion an investigatory process that eventually led to a fundamental restructuring of the securities exchanges, including the total abolition of fixed commission rates in 1975. This result was, in part, the consequence of pressure brought by Congress, the Department of Justice, and private parties on the SEC to assume the responsibility of creating competition in the securities markets.

The statutory basis for these political pressures was a section of the 1934 Securities Exchange Act, which empowered the SEC "to alter or supplement" registered stock exchange rules when "necessary or appropriate for the protection of investors or to insure fair dealing" with respect to 13 categories of exchange rules, including "the fixing of reasonable rates of compensation." By its plain language, the section did not expressly exempt exchange commission rates from the anti-price fixing rules of the antitrust laws. Nor did congressional debate, Congressional Reports, or testimony in 1934 decisively indicate whether an antitrust exemption was to be implied or how the Securities Exchange Act was to be harmonized with the antitrust laws.

The Supreme Court first faced the issue in 1963, when it decided the case of *Silver v. New York Stock Exchange.* Harold J. Silver was not a member of the New York Stock Exchange. In June 1958, Silver had established Municipal Securities, Incorporated, in Dallas, Texas, to trade municipal and corporate securities. In that year, he was granted "temporary approval" by the NYSE to install direct private telephone wires to 10 member firms of the Exchange, as well as a direct teletype connection to one member firm and a stock ticker service that came directly from the Exchange itself. In February 1959, without any explanation, the New York Stock Exchange ordered the member firms to discontinue all wire and teletype communications with Silver, and simultaneously withdrew its own stock ticker service. As practical matter, these steps put Silver's Municipal Securities, Incorporated, out of business. Since the actions of the Exchange and its member firms were what is called in antitrust law a group boycott or concerted refusal to deal, the Supreme Court held: "It is plain, to begin with, that removal of the wires by collective action of the Exchange and its members would, had it occurred in a context free from other federal regulation, constitute a *per se* violation of § I of the Sherman [Antitrust] Act." Nor, in these circumstances, was the Court willing to grant the New York Stock Exchange immunity from liability by implying an antitrust exemption:

> The Securities Exchange Act contains no express exemption from the antitrust laws or, for that matter, from any other statute. This means that any repealer of the antitrust laws must be discerned as a matter of implication, and "it is a cardinal principle of construction that repeals by implication are not favored." Repeal is to be regarded as implied only if necessary to make the Securities Exchange Act work, and even then only to the minimum extent necessary.

The Supreme Court in *Silver* held that an anticompetitive act of a stock exchange could be implicitly exempt from the antitrust laws only when it both was "within the scope and purposes of the Securities Exchange Act" and either subject to direct SEC review or observed such procedural safeguards as the notice, explanation, and fair hearing the Court held that the Exchange should have afforded Harold Silver before effectively destroying his business.[70]

An even more significant antitrust challenge to the rules of the New York Stock Exchange began in December 1964, when non-Exchange member Morris Schapiro indicated to the SEC his intention to file a lawsuit contesting New York Stock Exchange Rule 394. Rule 394, as then interpreted, prohibited a member of the Exchange from buying or selling nearly all Exchange-listed common stocks in the over-the-counter market even if an over-the-counter dealer could provide a better price or lower transaction costs. Under the *Silver* case's holding that the rules of the New York Stock Exchange were to be considered implicitly exempt from the antitrust laws "only if necessary to make the Securities Exchange Act work, and even then only to the minimum extent necessary," it was doubtful whether Rule 394 could have survived an antitrust challenge before the Warren Supreme Court.

A 1965 SEC Staff Report on Rule 394 generalized: "At the present time the fact that a customer might obtain a better execution in an off board trade is not considered to be an appropriate justification for an off board trade. . . . The early position in the 1940s that the 'customer's interest comes first' is now secondary to the interest of the Exchange in preserving the market as it is now constituted and preserving the minimum commission rate schedule."[71]

The SEC's response to the 1965 Staff Report represented the rock bottom low point of the Cohen Commission. On November 24, 1965, a contingent of New York Stock Exchange officials led by Exchange President Keith Funston, met with the SEC's Commissioners and stated that "they cannot live with [the Staff Report's] proposals." Subsequently, Funston would make the same point more colorfully in public, stating early in 1966: "Rule 394 is one of the pillars of the Exchange and we cannot, and will not, budge on this issue."

Believing that further negotiations with the Exchange would not be fruitful, "unless we advise the Exchange of the intention to release the report," Trading and Markets Division Director Pollack and his staff soon recommended that the SEC "publish the Report in order to invite comments and alternative solutions."

The full SEC refused to publish the Report. Indeed, it was not to be made public for six years, until Morris Schapiro successfully sued the Commission to gain access to it under the Freedom of Information Act.

After more months of discussion, the SEC formally acceded to an Exchange proposal outlined in a letter from Keith Funston to Manuel Cohen, dated September 15, 1966. The proposal, soon to be NYSE Rule 394(b), permitted an Exchange member to solicit an over-the-counter market maker to participate in the execution of an order off the floor of the Exchange only if several conditions were satisfied, including "a diligent effort to explore the feasibility of obtaining a satisfactory execution of the order on the floor," trading being limited to over-the-counter dealers who satisfied specified SEC capital and other requirements; and the filing of a written report concerning the transaction. The rule further required that just before the transaction was executed with the over-the-counter dealer, the Exchange member was to give the specialist and other floor brokers present a second chance to meet the over-the-counter dealer's price. At the Exchange's request, to increase the likelihood of clothing the rule with an antitrust immunity, the SEC formally directed the Exchange to adopt the new rule, officially finding it to be "necessary and in the public interest."

Immediately after Rule 394(b) went into effect, the Exchange interpreted it to prohibit an Exchange member from requesting a quotation from an over-the-counter dealer before checking the Exchange specialist's price and contacting an Exchange Floor Governor. If an Exchange member did request a quotation from an over-the-counter dealer in advance, the Exchange disqualified the member from subsequently executing a transaction under Rule 394(b) because of failure to check the floor first. As a practical matter, this interpretation of Rule 394(b) almost fully subverted whatever effect the rule might have had in increasing securities market competition. In all, the SEC staff estimated in October 1967, less than 1 percent of all third market trading occurred under Rule 394(b).[72]

Other pressures mounted on the SEC to initiate a comprehensive review of the New York Stock Exchange's commission rate schedule. The NYSE long had restricted its membership to persons and firms who actively devoted the major portion of their time to the securities business. Until 1970, the New York Stock Exchange denied membership to any publicly held corporation. These rules were meant to prevent institutional investors and other "customers" from joining the Exchange and reducing their costs by eliminating the need to pay brokerage fees. As the percentage of securities transactions initiated by institutional investors soared during the 1960s, the Exchange's prohibition of institutional membership became another "pillar of the Exchange," nearly as important as Rule 394 in maintaining a commission rate schedule at a higher-than-competitive level.

Beginning in 1965, the New York Stock Exchange ban on institutional membership was challenged. Early that year, a brokerage subsidiary of Waddell and Reed, the investment manager for United Funds, then the nation's fourth largest mutual fund organization was formed for the express purpose of joining the Pacific Stock Exchange to reduce brokerage costs when purchasing or selling New York Stock Exchange listed securities dually listed on that Exchange. At the time the Pacific Coast Exchange did not prohibit institutional members. Under the threat of an antitrust suit, the Exchange reluctantly permitted Waddell and Reed's brokerage subsidiary to join, but it hurriedly adopted an exclusionary rule denying membership to any firm or its affiliates whose shares were publicly held. The Pacific Coast Exchange's new ban on institutional members almost immediately was challenged by Investors Diversified Services, the nation's largest mutual fund organization, which succeeded in securing Pacific Coast Exchange membership for its own securities brokerage subsidiary, as did two other mutual fund organizations. They managed to do this before the Pacific Coast Exchange succeeded in barring additional institutional investors with a new rule barring members who were controlled by persons or firms outside the securities business.

The institutional membership controversy was renewed in 1967, when the faltering Philadelphia-Baltimore-Washington Stock Exchange determined actively to recruit institutional members to increase its trading volume. Within a relatively short period, 50 institutional members were generating approximately 40 percent of this minor exchange's business. The trading in New York Stock Exchange listed securities diverted either to the Pacific Coast Exchange or to the Philadelphia-Baltimore-Washington Stock Exchange did not measurably reduce New York Stock Exchange volume. But the existence of institutional members on these two regional exchanges was a visible reminder that the NYSE's own prohibition of institutional members might not survive an antitrust suit under the *Silver* case's rule permitting anticompetitive practices "only if necessary to make the Securities Exchange Act work, and even then only to the minimum extent necessary."[73]

Only with respect to give-ups was the Cohen Commission able to assemble a majority in favor of a significant reform. The mutual funds' desire to use give-ups also created an incentive to trade NYSE listed securities on a regional exchange, where give-ups could be directed to non-NYSE members who sold mutual fund shares. Between 1964 and 1968, the amount of investment company directed give-ups effected through NYSE member firms increased more than 700 percent, from $11.4 million to $91.7 million, meaning that in 1968, Exchange members gave up 38 percent of the $243 million in commissions they received from investment companies. During those same four years, give-ups effected on regional exchanges increased 1900 percent, to approximately $19 million in

1968. "Give-ups and reciprocal business practices in connection with institutional trading," the SEC would report early in 1968, "have become so widespread that it may plausibly be argued that, in the case of large institutional orders, there is in economic substance no fixed commission rate" but rather an anomaly: "Competition in the securities industry between institutional managers and brokers and between Exchanges has operated to reduce very substantially the amount of commissions actually *retained* by executing brokers — but with relatively little impact or effect as yet on the commissions actually *paid* by the public investors who invest through institutional media."[74]

By 1968, the strategy of Chair Cohen and Eugene Rotberg, his closest adviser on commission rate issues, had undergone a profound transformation. Throughout most of his time as chair, Cohen had attempted to persuade the NYSE to reform its fixed rate schedule in a manner that could survive an antitrust challenge. He suggested that the Exchange institute a significant volume discount and voluntarily abolish give-ups. Leonard Leiman, Cohen's executive assistant in the 1964–1966 period, recalled: "While trying to persuade the Exchange leadership to make the necessary changes, he was almost single handedly restraining the Antitrust Division of the Department of Justice and some members of Congress, pleading for time to allow the industry to correct itself without judicial or legislative interference." There were several reasons for the Cohen-Rotberg jawboning strategy, including doubts that the courts or Congress could reform the Exchange's commission rate structure as quickly or as expertly as the SEC; a belief that no reform as momentous as the abolition of fixed rates could be effected until at least some securities industry leaders favored it; uncertainty about the impact of the abolition of fixed rates on small broker-dealers, regional exchanges, and the third market; a recognition that it would be strategically easier for the SEC to control the self-regulatory efforts of the exchanges if it had power to approve rate increases than if they were determined by negotiation; and anxiety that unfixed rates might lead to lower rates for institutional investors but higher rates for small individual investors.

Had the Exchange been less stubborn in its response to Chair Cohen's arguments, much of the momentum for unfixing commission rates might have been slowed. But the Exchange confounded Cohen by not rationally pursuing its self-interest, and Cohen, increasingly alarmed by the size and prevalence of mutual fund give-ups, which mocked every argument the Exchange offered to justify its fixed rate schedule, began to pursue an alternative strategy, that of building securities industry and Congressional support for the ultimate abolition of fixed commission rates. The publication of the SEC's Rule 10b-10 release in January 1968 was the first public notice of Cohen's new strategy. Cohen did not then or at any time in the remaining 13 months of his time as chair, directly demand the abolition of all fixed rates. He continued to believe it was wiser for the SEC to encourage securities industry initiatives for negotiated rates rather than have the SEC assume the political risks of so controversial a reform. Moreover, Cohen was far out in front of most or all of the other four SEC Commissioners, who did not yet agree that all fixed rates should be abolished.[75]

Thus, paradoxically, while Cohen's Rule 10b-10 strategy eventually did help facilitate the abolition of fixed commission rates, the purpose of the proposal was little understood at the time. As Paul Samuelson subsequently was to say of the SEC's "very small progress" toward effective competition in the securities industry during this period: "Where was the SEC in all those years? . . . [T]he Securities and Exchange Commission should long ago have acted to promote equitable and efficient competition and to control private monopoly." Four and a half years had passed since the Special Study recommended that the SEC make a comprehensive study of the NYSE's commission rate structure. During those years, the SEC had discussed with the Exchange volume discounts, nonmember access to the Exchange floor, Rule 394, and banning give-ups. But the SEC had never articulated an economic analysis that justified why fixed commission rates should exist in the first place nor gathered sufficient empirical data to prepare such an analysis. On the single most significant dollars and cents issue subject to the SEC's authority, the Commission, quite simply, was unable to act effectively.

At this point, the Justice Department intervened. Aware of the divisions among the SEC's Commissioners that had for a long time limited the SEC's ability to address the commission rate issues, the Justice Department's Antitrust Division on April 1, 1968, filed a 67-page comment on the SEC's proposed Rule 10b-10. The comment was based on the premise, second nature to any economist or practicing antitrust attorney, but rarely set forth in official SEC documents during the postwar period, that "the most obvious interest of the investing public" in regulation of stock exchanges was "to be protected from excessive commission charges.

Given the Justice Department's ability under the *Silver* case to initiate an antitrust action and attempt to show that fixed commission rates and the NYSE's restrictive membership rules were "not necessary to make the Securities Exchange Act work," Ratner reported, "the intervention of the Antitrust Division was in itself sufficient to trigger the calling of a public hearing on stock exchange commission rates" by the SEC.

Even before the Commission Rate Hearings began on July 1, 1968, Cohen was able to employ the Justice Department's antitrust threat to persuade an SEC majority to demand on May 28, 1968, that the New York Stock Exchange abolish fixed commission rates for transactions in excess of $50,000 or put into effect a schedule of volume discounts specified by the SEC, and, in either event, reduce or eliminate charges for nonmember transactions on the NYSE.

Three days before the SEC's Commission Rate Hearings began, the NYSE's Board of Governors agreed to a series of interim reforms as its response to Cohen's May 28 letter. The Exchange agreed "in principle" to put into effect volume discounts of unspecified size, phase out give-ups over a one-year period if the SEC used its power to prohibit give-ups on all other registered exchanges, and adopt a one-third discount for nonmembers. The Exchange's interim reforms of its commission rate schedule were, in fact, quite modest. Nonetheless, the SEC was able to report, soon after the Commission Rate Hearings began, both that give-ups would be abolished by the end of the year and that the Exchange's interim volume discount, if in effect in 1967, would have reduced total commissions paid to NYSE members by 7 percent, or approximately $150 million.[76]

The NYSE's interim commission rate reforms had the practical effect of focusing the SEC's Hearings on the most fundamental issue: whether the Exchange should be permitted to fix rates through a minimum commission schedule or whether all rates should be negotiated and rate levels determined by competition. In mid-August 1968, essentially for the first time in its history, the New York Stock Exchange attempted publicly to justify price fixing in the securities brokerage industry with the publication of a 137-page analysis of "economic effects of negotiated commission rates on the brokerage industry, the market for corporate securities, and the investing public."

The Exchange's economic analysis presented a worst case scenario of the possible consequences of abolishing fixed commission rates. The analysis emphasized the "possible chaos" that would occur if the abolition of minimum fixed rates led to a further fragmentation of the market in trading exchange listed securities.

Without fixed rates, the Exchange's economic analysis predicted, few large commission brokerage firms would remain members of NYSE. According to the Exchange's analysis, this could only harm investors, particularly small investors:

> The decline of the specialist system would thus be the first step in the weakening of the overall central securities market to the detriment of all investors. Stock price swings would tend to become more pronounced than at present. A weakening of specialist support could at times lead to sudden collapses (or undue rises" of stock prices on announcement of unexpected news.

Fragmented trading in Exchange-listed securities also would produce, the Exchange predicted, "wider spreads in quotations," since trading on the NYSE would be "thinner."

The Exchange predicted that with a plethora of market makers in Exchange-listed securities, each with thin volume, and no reliable record of price and volume, whatever savings investors might achieve from lower commission rates probably would be more than offset by poorer executions.

The Exchange also argued that small investors would be harmed through the unbundling of securities broker services. Without minimum commission rates, the Exchange urged, brokerage firms would sharply curtail investment research and information services. Discount brokers "would probably become dominant in the securities business," for "negotiated rates would force most firms to discontinue or reduce all services other than the execution of orders."

The New York Stock Exchange's economic analysis concluded: "All of the benefits of a competitive system, without the serious drawbacks of negotiated rates, can be achieved by designing an appropriate schedule of minimum commission rates. A new schedule of regulated commission rates has been proposed with better potential benefits and without the drawbacks of the Justice Department's proposal." Presenting the NYSE economic analysis at the

SEC Commission Rate Hearings, President Haack added one final argument designed to appeal to the SEC's cautious majority:

> One does not remove the keystone to an industry which is responsible for billions of dollars of public money, which operates the largest securities market in the world, and which facilitates the raising of the bulk of new capital for this country without presenting irrefutable evidence. We are dealing with a delicate mechanism. This is not an area where one experiments, tries a new system, and returns to the old if the results are unsatisfactory. Destruction of the minimum commission rate would produce irreversible consequences. An erroneous decision will have far reaching effects. I am sure the Commission shares our view that, in this area, one must proceed with extreme caution.

The New York Stock Exchange's economic defense of fixed commission rates was subjected to a two-pronged response. Consistent with the strategy of the SEC's January 1968 Rule 10b-10 Release, the SEC's staff did not call directly for the abolition of fixed commission rates during the initial months of the Commission Rate Hearings, but instead presented several weeks of testimony, Eugene Rotberg explained, "designed to discredit fixed rates by showing that fixed rates neither, in fact, existed nor were essential to the Exchanges' viability." The character of the SEC staff's indirect challenge to the NYSE's fixed commission rate structure was illustrated by Rotberg's interrogation of Exchange Vice President Robert Bishop on July 1, 1968, the first day of the hearings. Throughout the course of the day-long examination, Rotberg made obvious that the NYSE could not satisfactorily answer such questions as why the commission on 100 shares of \$10 stock was \$17 while the commission on 100 shares of \$80 stock was \$47, in spite of the fact that no greater work was involved for a broker to execute one order than the other; why there was no volume discount; or how the Exchange's antirebate rule could be harmonized with give-ups or such reciprocal business practices as an insurance firm placing orders with a brokerage house only if the brokerage house agreed to purchase insurance from it.

Four months later, the Justice Department's Antitrust Division began a second attack on the New York Stock Exchange's defense of fixed commission rates, directly calling for the abolition of fixed rates. For several days, beginning October 30, 1968, the Department presented testimony of four of the country's leading economists,

MIT's Paul Samuelson, Princeton's William Baumol, the University of Chicago's Harold Demsetz, and Yale's Henry Wallich, as well as the testimony of Boston College economist Michael Mann, then serving on the Department of Justice staff. All agreed that fixed commission rates could not be justified and that a competitive commission rate system was both preferable and workable.

To the economists, there were two principal defects of the NYSE fixed commission rate system and related exclusionary practices, such as Rule 394 and the prohibition on institutional membership. First, the failure of the commission rate schedule to reflect actual brokerage costs had resulted in excessive or monopolistic profits.

In dollars and cents terms, fixed commission rates had resulted in a greater than six-fold increase in brokerage income in the 1961–1968 period, with aggregate securities commission income of NYSE members increasing from $613 million to $3.245 billion, making Wall Street, *Forbes* magazine stated in June 1968, "perhaps the greatest growth industry in the U.S." By shielding Exchange members from the rigors of competition, fixed rates had the further consequence of sheltering inefficiency.

The economists agreed that the incentive of high commission rates was not necessary to maintain a centralized trading market. "On the contrary," argued Harold Demsetz, noting that the Exchange had misconstrued the results of his research, "there is good economic evidence that a central market will always draw the preponderance of trading activity in a given security because of its inherent efficiencies, unless external costs, such as high commissions, impede the natural growth of the market." Lower competitive commission rates were likely to increase the volume of trading on the New York Stock Exchange and improve its liquidity.[77]

The Justice Department predicted that the elimination of fixed rates generally would lower commissions charged to investors and would unbundle the securities industry. This would enable investors to pay only for research and advisory services that they, in fact, used, and would reward cost efficient brokerage houses and the investment advisers whom the investors chose in a competitive market.[78]

The momentum for unfixing brokerage commission rates and structuring the securities markets accelerated in the next six years, culminating in the 1975 Securities Act Amendments that facilitated the establishment of a National Market System and ended fixed commission rates. But the 1969–1975 period began with the erratic character of President Nixon's SEC appointments. Richard Nixon's clearest interest in the SEC during his first years of his presidency was to use his appointment powers for political purposes unrelated to the securities industry. Just as his October 1968 campaign letter criticizing the SEC for proposing "heavy handed bureaucratic regulatory schemes" was an obvious appeal for Wall Street financial contributions, approximately half of Nixon's 10 SEC appointments were made for predominantly political reasons. Embarrassment over the performance of Nixon's first SEC chair, Hamer Budge, coupled with Nixon's determination after his third chair, G. Bradford Cook, was implicated in the Watergate scandal to make SEC Commissioner appointments strictly on merit, led to the appointment of several highly qualified persons to be SEC Commissioners. At no time in SEC history, including the New Deal, was the Commission simultaneously served by five more able Commissioners than it was during the 1973–1975 period, when Chair Ray Garrett and Commissioners Philip Loomis, John Evans, A.A. Sommer, and Irving Pollack led the SEC.

When Nixon began his presidency in January 1969, he had the statutory power to name the SEC's chair, but there were no vacancies on the Commission. This meant, as a practical matter, that Nixon could have retained Manuel Cohen as chair until the next vacancy on the Commission occurred or named one of the two Republican members of the Commission, Hamer Budge and Richard Smith, to be chair. Not knowing Smith, Nixon in February 1969 abruptly dismissed Cohen as chair and named Budge, a former colleague from the House of Representatives, to be chair of the SEC.

In 1964, Budge had been a controversial Johnson political appointee to the Commission. A five-term Congressman from Idaho until he was defeated for reelection in 1960, Budge had served as judge in Idaho until House Republican leader Charles Halleck persuaded Johnson to nominate Budge to the SEC. Lacking any experience in the securities industry, Budge, innately conservative, in June 1969 characterized his general approach to federal regulation with the observation: "Just as an across the board statement, I feel the government should not tell people how to conduct their affairs." Largely because of Budge's hostility to the use of federal regulatory power, Senator Lee Metcalf termed him "the worst possible choice" for the SEC when Budge was confirmed by the Senate in June 1964.

As chair, Budge attempted to reverse the activism of the later Cohen years. Budge viewed the SEC as quasijudicial in nature; he preferred that fundamental decisions concerning the securities industry be made by Congress, the federal courts, or the industry itself, and limiting the Commissioners' functions largely to a review of staff initiatives. To Budge's credit, he did rely on highly competent senior staff officials, notably General Counsel Philip Loomis, Trading and Markets Division Director Irving Pollack, and Alan Levenson, whom Budge appointed to direct the Division of Corporate Finance.

President Nixon's Administrative Council on Executive Organization in 1971 would complain: "The SEC as a collegial body at times finds itself debating what is to be done while problems in the investment community continue to mount. Protracted proceedings and deliberations prevent it from keeping pace with change in the investment community." Other critics were more blunt. *Business Week*, in September 1969, reported concern on Wall Street "that [the] SEC may be grinding to a halt" because of "the men the President has chosen."

The most serious criticism of the Budge SEC was that its approach to the Commission's budget was self-defeating. During 1969, Budge's first year as chair, 4706 securities registration statements were filed, nearly double the 1968 total. Simultaneously, the broker-dealer firms' back office problems reached crisis proportions. The SEC's *35th Annual Report* emphasized: "In fiscal year 1969 . . . the Commission was so inundated with complaints [against broker-dealers] that at times it was unable to make a prompt reply to a complainant, much less an investigation of his charges." Despite the recommendations of some in Congress and fellow SEC Commissioners Richard Smith and James Needham, Budge did not seek an adequate appropriation for 1970 or 1971 fiscal years.

Before Budge left the SEC in January 1971, the Commission made considerable progress toward alleviating the broker-dealer back office crisis, and secured enactment of three new securities laws, the Securities Investors Protection Act, the 1970 Investment Company Act Amendments, and the 1970 Williams Act Amendments. None of these accomplishments lessened congressional frustration with Budge's leadership of the SEC.[79]

William Casey, Nixon's second SEC Chair, like Hamer Budge, was chosen primarily for political reasons. An attorney with little experience in the securities field, Casey was a law partner of former

Republican Party National Chair Leonard Hall. In 1966, Casey had been an unsuccessful candidate for a Republican congressional nomination and in 1968 a major financial contributor to Republican candidates. Casey was a man of diverse parts. During World War II, he had assisted David K.E. Bruce in coordinating the activities of the French Resistance and later was Chief of OSS intelligence operations in the European theater. After the war, Casey amassed a fortune, principally as a tax attorney and venture capitalist investor and promoter of new enterprises. Author of several books, Casey served as Chair of the Board of Editors of the Institute for Business Planning, a subsidiary of Prentice-Hall, and lectured on tax law at New York University.

Casey proved to be a decisive and able administrator. Rapidly concluding that neither the SEC nor industry self-regulation was working "as well as it should," Casey repaired several of the Commission's obvious defects. With the aid of Commissioner Herlong, who until 1969 had been a member of the influential House Ways and Means Committee, Casey extracted from the White House Office of Management and Budget and Congress budget increases sufficient to expand the SEC staff from 1356 to 1814 between December 1971 and the 1974 fiscal year. At Casey's insistence, General Counsel Philip Loomis was elevated to a Commissionership in 1971.[80]

Casey's chairmanship was dominated by two issues: the future of fixed commission rates and the development of a central securities market system. In the period between Budge's resignation in January 1971 and the beginning of Casey's time as chair in mid-April, the SEC ordered the New York Stock Exchange to require competitive rates on all securities transactions in excess of $500,000. The SEC also recommended in its Letter of Transmittal accompanying the *Institutional Investor Study* as "a major goal and ideal of the securities markets . . . the creation of a strong central market system for securities of national importance, in which all buying and selling interest in these securities could participate and be represented under a competitive regime."

Subject to conflicting Congressional and industry pressures concerning commission rates, the Casey SEC moved gingerly forward on this issue, eliminating fixed rates on orders about $300,000 in February 1972, and subsequently stating its intention to reduce the fixed rate breakpoint to $100,000 by 1974.

In sharp contrast, with the publication of the SEC's *Statement on the Future Structure of the Securities Markets* in February 1972, Casey became the first SEC chair to address the mechanics of an electronically linked national securities market system. The *Future Structure Statement* represented a turning point in SEC history. The Commission assumed what Ray Garrett later as chair termed "a new role in relation to our market system." Instead of being content to police a system developed and operated by the private sector, the Commission has undertaken a leading role in developing a new system."[81]

After Casey resigned his chairmanship in February 1973, to become Undersecretary of State, President Nixon nominated G. Bradford Cook to be the SEC chair. At 35, Cook was the youngest man ever nominated to the position. As with Budge and Casey, Cook's nomination was more a reward for political services than a judgment on the merits. Cook's father, an influential Midwestern Republican fundraiser, had been a senior official in Nixon's 1968 and 1972 presidential campaigns. Cook had considerable paper qualifications for the job. A 1962 graduate of the University Nebraska Law School, Cook had been a partner in the Chicago law firm of Winston and Strawn, specializing in corporate and securities law, when, in 1971, Chair Casey hired him to be the SEC's General Counsel. As General Counsel, Cook worked with Casey on the development of the SEC's 1972 *Future Structure Statement.* When the SEC was reorganized in August 1972, Cook was named Director of the Division of Market Regulation, becoming the senior staff official responsible for the SEC's two most important projects at the time, commission rate regulation and the central securities market. During Cook's brief time as chair, the SEC continued the Casey Commission's policies, notably publishing the March 1973 *Policy Statement on the Structure of a Central Market System,* amplifying the Casey SEC's February 1972 *Future Structure Statement.*

Seventy-four days after beginning as SEC chair, Cook resigned, the first SEC Commissioner to be implicated in a scandal. During his confirmation hearings, Cook had testified that "I have had very few calls from the White House" and that these contacts with the White House had "all been innocuous, to say the least." Flatly contradicting this testimony, a mid-May 1973 criminal indictment, charging former Attorney General John Mitchell, former Secretary of Commerce Maurice Stans, and Robert Vesco with obstruction of justice, alleged that Stans "did cause" G. Bradford Cook to delete all references from a separate SEC injunction action alleging that Vesco had made a secret $200,000 cash contribution to the

Committee to Re-Elect the President. The indictment also alleged that Stans caused Cook to request the SEC staff not to file publicly certain transcripts of testimony relating to the Vesco contribution.[82]

Subsequently Ray Garrett, Jr. became the new chair. Garrett, a partner in the Chicago law firm of Gardner, Carton, Douglas, Children and Waud, a conservative but essentially apolitical man, had been a member of the SEC staff between 1954 and 1958, for most of that period as Director of the Division of Corporate Regulation. During his ensuing law firm career, Garrett had been a recognized leader of the national corporate and securities bar. In 1965, he had been selected Chair of the American Bar Association's Section on Corporation, Banking, and Business Law. Subsequently, Garrett chaired the Advisory Committee for the Corporate Department Financing Project of the American Bar Foundation and served as a consultant to Harvard Law School Professor Louis Loss's American Law Institute Federal Securities Law Codification project. For personal reasons, Garrett initially declined the SEC chairmanship and recommended instead a fellow leader of the corporate and securities bar, A.A. Sommer, Jr. Sommer, a partner in the Cleveland law firm of Calfee, Halter, Calfee, Griswold and Sommer, was a member of the Board of Governors of the NASD and a frequent lecturer and writer on securities, corporate, and accounting law. But he was not acceptable to the Nixon administration as SEC chair because he was a Democrat. After Sydney Herlong's term as commissioner expired in June 1973, Alexander Haig, Nixon's Chief of Staff, persuaded Garrett to accept the SEC chairmanship, and Sommer agreed to be a commissioner.

Senator Harrison Williams reflected the sentiments of many when he termed the nominations of Garrett and Sommer "a most refreshing breath of fresh air." The two new commissioners were sworn in together early in August 1973. Six months later, Nixon made his final SEC appointment. After Garrett, in the words of SEC Commissioner John Evans, "laid his own position on the line," Nixon nominated Irving Pollack to be a commissioner. Like his close friend Manuel Cohen, Pollack was a graduate of Brooklyn Law School and a career Commission Staff Attorney. Pollack was aptly described by *Time* as the "Maigret of the SEC" for his role in building up the SEC's headquarters enforcement staff while associate, and then full, Director of the Commission's Division of Trading and Markets.

The cumulative effect of Nixon's declining political influence during the Watergate scandal and his appointment of five highly competent but apolitical Commissioners to serve during Garrett's 1973–1975 time as chair was that the SEC gained an unusual degree of independence from the White House. Under Garrett, the style of the New Deal and Cohen SEC was revived. Discussion at the SEC table was uninhibited. Garrett, even when his initial policy preferences on such pivotal issues as commission rates did not prevail, vigorously defended Commission decisions in public.[83]

Roderick Hills, Gerald Ford's choice for SEC chair after Garrett resigned in October 1975, was a less influential chair than Garrett or Casey. Hills was an honors graduate of Stanford Law School, Law Clerk to Supreme Court Justice Stanley Reed, and a founding partner of a Los Angeles law firm. Subsequently, Hills had been a visiting Professor at Harvard Law School during the 1969–1970 academic year and Chair of the Board of the Republic Corporation between 1971 and 1975. Nonetheless, Hills began with the fundamental disadvantage of possessing little actual experience in the securities field. He was a labor law specialist whose appointments, first as Counsel to President Ford in April 1975, then as SEC chair six months later, were inspired by Ford's desire to give Hills meaningful assignments while Hills's wife served as Ford's Secretary of Housing and Urban Development. Hills's chief contributions as SEC chair would be the defense of the Commission's questionable payments disclosure program and supporting the initiation of an SEC Advisory Committee Study of its corporate disclosure program.[84]

The Back Office Crisis

The 1967–1970 broker-dealer firm back office crisis was the most serious failure of securities industry self-regulation in the Commission's history, a collapse of industry regulatory controls so complete that it permitted, in the SEC's retrospective view, "the most prolonged and severe crisis in the securities industry in 40 years."

The back office crisis occurred in two phases. During the period from 1967 to early 1969, as SEC Chair Budge testified, "brokerage firms [found] themselves in the paradox of being forced out of business by having too much business." Average daily reported volume on the New York Stock Exchange grew by 265 percent between 1964 and 1969, from 4.89 million shares per average day in 1964 to 12.97 million shares in 1968, reaching a high of 14.9 million shares per average day during the month of December 1968.

Back office inefficiency in processing the increasing number of securities transactions increased concurrently:

> The operational crisis in the securities industry first reached major dimensions in August of 1967 [the SEC subsequently reported]. Newspaper reports of that period recall the feverish efforts of the Wall Street community to keep up with each day's business: Stock certificates and related documents were piled "halfway to the ceiling" in some offices; clerical personnel were working overtime, six and seven days a week, with some firms using a second or even a third shift to process each day's transactions.

To alleviate the back office paper crunch, the exchanges and the NASD shortened the trading day for a brief period in August 1967 and for about six weeks beginning in January 1968.[85]

These palliatives had little effect. Total complaints to the SEC concerning broker-dealers skyrocketed from 3991 in the 1968 fiscal year to 12,494 in 1969, with nine out of ten complaints describing back office problems, "particularly the failure to deliver customer funds and securities" in a timely manner. In April 1968, the first months during which the New York Stock Exchange gathered relevant statistics, member firms' fails (that is, failure to deliver securities by the settlement day) came to $2.67 billion, subsequently rising to $4.12 billion in December 1968. Throughout 1969 and 1970 the dollar value of fails declined, but as late as July 1969, SEC Chair Budge reported, "One out of every 8.4 transactions was a fail."

The rising number of securities customer complaints and fails was symptomatic of an industry wide loss of control of recordkeeping. In the four year period 1967–1970, the New York Stock Exchange would find it necessary to intervene directly in the affairs of nearly 200 member organizations, over half of the Exchange member firms that dealt with the public, because of firms' operational deficiencies.[86]

The first broker-dealer firm liquidation related to the crisis occurred in May 1968, with the failure of the small NYSE firm of Pickard & Company, which had 3500 customers. In consenting to an SEC Administration Order in October 1968, Pickard admitted egregious violations of the securities laws, including misrepresenting its financial condition to lenders, who lost over $2 million as a result of the firm's liquidation, illegally selling unregistered stock, and manipulating the price of Rowland Products common stock.[87]

Between May 14, 1969 and May 26, 1970, the Dow Jones Industrial Average fell 35 percent, from a high of 968.85 to a low of 631.16, precipitating a decline in New York Stock Exchange volume from a 1968 daily average of nearly 13 million shares to a 1969–1970 daily average of approximately 11 million shares. The volume decline resulted in industrywide losses. For example, the average NYSE member firm reported a loss of 2.9 percent from securities business in 1969, compared with a profit of 9.9 percent in 1968. To cushion securities firm unprofitability, the SEC in April 1970 approved an emergency $15 surcharge on all brokerage transactions of fewer than 1000 shares. Even with the surcharge, an SEC survey of 72 leading securities firms in May 1970 found that month's aggregate expenses exceeded aggregate income by nearly 11 percent.

The securities industry's prolonged unprofitability, coupled with the financial losses created by the 1967–1968 back office operations breakdown set in motion the greatest rash of broker-dealer firm failures in Wall Street's history. Approximately 160 New York Stock Exchange member organizations went out of business in 1969 and 1970, about 80 merging with other firms, and the other 80, found a 1972 House of Representatives report, "quietly dissolved, self-liquidated, or retired from the securities business." It was a period of "perpetual crisis" in New York Stock Exchange President Haack's view, a period during which, subsequent SEC Chair William Casey opined, "firms and self-regulatory authorities were thrashing about in all directions fighting to avoid catastrophe," their problem comparable to that of Kutuzov, the Russian Commander-in-Chief in Tolstoy's *War and Peace*, who was "always in the midst of a series of shifting events and so he never can at any moment consider the whole import of an event that is occurring."[88]

In March 1970, the first major brokerage house failure occurred when McDonnell & Company collapsed. McDonnell & Company, journalist Chris Welles wrote was:

> one of the largest and most respected houses on Wall Street, which only two years before had had $33 million in annual revenues, a net worth of $15 million, 26 branch offices throughout the United States and in France, membership on eight stock exchanges including three (seats) on the Big Board, 1500 employees including 350 salesmen, and close to 100,000 customers who made some 3500 trades daily.

The firm's subsequent liquidation cost nearly $19 million, with the New York Stock Exchange Special Trust Fund expending about $9 million, and the McDonnell family absorbing losses believed to be close to $10 million.[89]

After McDonnell & Company's collapse, the frequency of Exchange member firm failures accelerated. Less than two weeks later, Baerwald & De Boer was placed in liquidation; in April, Kleiner, Bell & Company; by June, four other firms: Meyerson & Company, Fusz-Schmelzle, Orvis Brothers, and Blair & Company. Of these failures, the most serious was that of Blair & Company, which, as recently as February 1969, had attempted to rescue the foundering Schwabacher & Company through a merger. The New York Stock Exchange set aside $26 million from the Special Trust Fund for Blair & Company, the most the Exchange was to expend directly on a liquidation. The following month, July 1970, the Exchange began its third major liquidation, allocating $21.8 million to protect the 70,000 customers of Dempsey-Tegeler & Company. With its Special Trust Fund depleted, the Exchange refused to protect the customers of three small firms that also failed in August 1970: First Devonshire Corporation, Charles Plohn & Company, and Robinson & Company.[90]

It was then that the two most serious events of the back office crisis occurred. In October 1970, Goodbody and Company, the nation's fifth largest brokerage house, with nearly 250,000 customers, neared collapse and was hurriedly merged with Merrill Lynch, the nation's largest brokerage firm, after the Exchange arranged a $21 million bail out of Goodbody's subordinated loans and guaranteed up to $30 million indemnification for lawsuits that might be filed against Goodbody. Simultaneous with Goodbody's near bankruptcy, F.I. duPont, Glore Forgan, the second largest member firm of the New York Stock Exchange, neared the precipice, surviving only after $79 million, according to one newspaper account, was advanced to the firm, principally by Electronics Data Systems' H. Ross Perot.[91]

The primary cause of the back office crisis was incompetent broker-dealer firm management during the 1964–1968 securities volume surge. Securities firm managers almost invariably were sales oriented, often less concerned with the drearier task of administering back offices. There was no mystery about this. "The industry's problem," Exchange President Haack told *Business Week* in June 1968, "is its failure to gear total capacity of doing business to its capacity to produce business. Produce, produce, produce — and keep down the overhead — that has always been the rule."

Between 1965 and 1968, NYSE member firms increased their total number of offices by 21 percent from 3521 to 4278. The total number of registered sales representatives grew even more dramatically, increasing 55 percent, from 33,805 in 1965 to 52,466 in 1969. Many broker-dealer firms did not adequately take into account the difficulties of a similar rapid expansion of back office personnel. At the height of the stock market's volume surge, 1967-1968, Exchange member firms added a total of 25,000 employees to back offices, an increase of 20 percent in one year. The number of money errors in 1968 was five times the 1964 rate. Non-money errors increased at least three times as much.

This increased error rate was the primary cause of the seven and a half fold increase in NYSE member firm losses from errors and bad debts between 1964 and 1969. During that period, losses increased from 2.46 percent of net income before partners' compensation and taxes to 18.77 percent.[92]

Several firms attempted to end back office operational losses by abrupt conversion to computerized facilities, on some occasions with catastrophic results. "One of the main reasons for the failure of Goodbody & Company. . . was its overambitious efforts to automate," explained Donald Regan of Merrill Lynch, the firm called in to rescue Goodbody through an 11th hour merger. "That ill-fated effort only succeeded in getting Goodbody in deeper trouble. It was trapped in the midst of change: efforts to automate failed, while manual procedure was deserted in anticipation of automation's success." Similar "instant computerization" problems plagued several other NYSE firm members forced to liquidate during the 1968–1970 period, including McDonnell & Company, Amott, Baker & Company, Schwabacher & Company, and Fusz-Schmelzle & Company, as well as Lehman Brothers, which narrowly survived collapse.[93]

The way in which securities firms financed their operations was another cause of the failure of many broker-dealers. The principal mechanism for ensuring adequate capital structures in the securities industry were the net capital rules issued by most stock exchanges and elsewhere enforced by the SEC.

There were substantial differences between the net capital rules of the NYSE and the SEC. The Exchange rule proved particularly ineffective in ensuring that Exchange members would have on hand sufficient liquid assets to meet their obligations during the back office crisis. Exchange Rule 325 counted as capital subordinated loans or secured demand notes from customers or partners, which, as of 1970, made up 40 percent of the capital of all Exchange member partnerships and 34 percent of the capital of Exchange member corporations. Subordinated loans from customers or partners were an evanescent form of capital, which, under Exchange Rule 325, could be withdrawn on as little as 90 days' notice, even if withdrawal would result in the financial collapse of a firm or a violation of the net capital rule.

As the 1969–1970 period's financial difficulties mounted, precisely this occurred at firms such as F.E. duPont, which had $12.7 million in excess net capital at the end of December 1970 but projected capital withdrawals of $24.8 million by August 1971.[94]

With "brokerage firm . . . operations backed up like the Long Island expressway in rush hour traffic," as one Exchange member firm officer informed the *Wall Street Journal* in August 1967, the SEC repeatedly met with Exchange and NASD officials during the next 15 months. But it was not until the collapse of Pickard & Company in the spring of 1968 that the SEC made its first significant direct response to the back office crisis. In April 1968, the SEC approved a NYSE rule to begin collecting monthly fails data from member firms. In May, the SEC and Exchange initiated a campaign to inspect every major firm in the United States. According to the *National Journal*: "The investigations disclosed that back office problems were worse than the SEC had suspected, and the agency invoked a seldom used provision of the 1934 Act, threatening 40 to 50 firms with suspension of their registrations unless they cleaned up their paper backlogs." Various restrictions were placed on the operations of 47 Exchange member firms, including, a Senate Subcommittee Staff Study explained, "no new sales offices, no increase in the number of registered representatives, no firm trading (that is, for member accounts), no solicitation of margin accounts, no underwriting, special [weekly] reporting, and restriction to a certain number of trades per day or week." In June, the SEC persuaded the Exchange to limit trading to a four day week.[95]

These restrictions failed to avert the subsequent wave of insolvencies at Exchange member firms, because they were put into effect too late to prevent substantial error losses. On July 19, 1968, Chair

Cohen informed Exchange representatives at a meeting recorded in the Commission's minutes that the NYSE's own statistics indicated that the situation was worsening.

With NYSE members enjoying record volume and profits, its representatives resisted these and most other SEC proposals that might limit exchange volume. President Haack repeatedly insisted that "he would . . . advocate singling out O-T-C business for restriction." The SEC did not then insist on imposition of industry-wide restrictions to reduce share volume, in part because of fear that they would precipitate an investor panic.

The extent to which the SEC continued to defer to Exchange regulation of member firms' operations and finances after the Commission became aware of the crisis was not defensible. As was obvious in SEC oversight of NYSE self-regulation, at least since the time of the Whitney scandal, Exchange regulators often are reluctant to take steps that would put member firms out of business or would generally reduce member firms' income. It was exactly these kinds of steps that were necessary throughout the crisis. In retrospect, it is obvious that investors would have been better protected had the SEC, earlier in the crisis, conducted investigations of broker-dealer firms' operations and imposed firm or industry wide enforcement restrictions. The Commission's back office enforcement program began too late to prevent the wave of broker-dealer firm failures during the 1969–1970 period.

In the aftermath of the back office crisis, several reforms were adopted. Most significantly, in December 1970, Congress enacted the Securities Investor Protection Act, creating a Securities Investor Protection Corporation (*SIPC*) to administer a fund providing $50,000 of insurance protection to each customer of virtually all broker-dealers registered with the SEC. Although SIPC was to be financed by assessments from its broker-dealer membership, the Corporation, if given SEC approval, could borrow up to $1 billion from the United States Treasury, making SIPC a more reliable guarantor than the New York Stock Exchange Special Trust Fund, which was a discretionary fund that had run out of money during the summer of 1970. Besides creating the equivalent to a Federal Deposit Insurance Corporation for the securities industry, the Securities Investor Protection Act also sweepingly defined the SEC's powers to: "Require any self-regulatory organization to adopt any specified alteration of or supplement to its rules, practices, and procedures with respect to the frequency and scope of inspections and examinations relating to the financial condition of members of such self-regulatory organization and the selection and qualification of examiners.[96]

Believing that "early warning signals were inadequate to foretell financial and operational difficulties in a reliable and timely manner," the SEC in July 1971, employed its rulemaking authority to require almost all registered broker-dealers to give immediate notice, by telegram, whenever their net capital was insufficient or their books and records were not current. After four years of negotiations with the securities industry and interim reforms, the Commission in July 1975 adopted a Uniform Net Capital Rule, ending the power of the NYSE and other exchanges to promulgate or create by interpretation less stringent net capital rules than those of the SEC.[97]

Combined, these statutory and rule revisions lessened the likelihood of another back office crisis. But they did not succeed in stemming a substantial reduction in individual trading on the securities exchanges. Between 1970 and 1975, the total number of individual owners of corporate stock and mutual funds sharply declined, from 30.85 million investors in 1970 to 25.27 million in 1975, the only reduction in the number of investors to occur during the 1952–1980 period. Individual investor aggregate trading volume also plummeted. In 1973, private investors bought and sold 20 percent less listed stock than they had in 1968. While individual investors in 1961 had accounted for 61 percent of the dollar value of nonmember trading volume on the New York Stock Exchange, by 1974, their share volume was less than 30 percent.

There were several causes of the small investors' flight, including discouragement after losses in the 1969–1970 market break, high bond interest rates, and the widespread belief that institutional investors received preferential treatment from brokers or inside information or had the power to manipulate stock prices. But virtually everyone agreed that the back office crisis also was a contributing cause of the individual investors' exodus. A 1973 Report for the New York Stock Exchange based on 1234 interviews with small or potential investors found that three in ten small investors personally had experienced such back office problems as lost or late delivered securities; 57 percent agreed "if trading volume continue to increase, many brokerage firms will have the same bad paperwork foul-ups they had several years ago."[98]

The End of Fixed Commission Rates

The back office crisis significantly influenced the ongoing policy debates on fixed commission rates and the structure of the securities markets. First affected were the commission rate issues. Unexpectedly, in May 1969, New York Stock Exchange member firm Donaldson, Lufkin & Jenrette filed a registration statement with the SEC preliminary to a sale of common stock to the public, abruptly bringing to a head a nearly decade-long debate within the Exchange on whether member firms could be publicly owned. The Exchange's opposition to public ownership of member firms was bound up with the Exchange's opposition to institutional membership. Mutual funds, insurance companies, and other institutional investors were barred from Exchange membership primarily by two provisions of the Exchange's Constitution: The first prohibited public ownership of member firms; the second required the "primary purpose" of every member firm to be "the transaction of business as a broker or dealer in securities." For eight years, the Exchange had hesitated to repeal the prohibition of member firm public ownership because of its concern that repeal would prompt the Justice Department or an institutional investor to bring an antitrust suit challenging the "primary purpose" requirement. Such a suit, if successful, might have permitted institutions directly to own seats on the Exchange. The Exchange's concern was a realistic one. But when Donaldson, Lufkin announced that it had had to decline institutional business for lack of capital and argued that the public sale of common stock was the least expensive way an Exchange member could secure permanent capital to deal in large block transactions and expand or computerize facilities, the Exchange had little choice but to remove its total prohibition of member firm public ownership.

On July 17, 1969, the New York Stock Exchange voted in principle "to support the concept of public ownership of equity securities issued by member corporations," subsequently reaffirming the proviso that any publicly owned member firm and any parent firm must be primarily engaged in business as brokers or dealers in securities. The New York Stock Exchange Constitution officially was amended in March 1970. Within four years, Donaldson, Lufkin and 15 other securities firms, including Merrill Lynch, E.F. Hutton, Bache & Company, Paine, Webber, Jackson & Curtis, Reynolds Securities, and Dean Witter were being publicly traded.[99]

The anticipated challenge to the New York Stock Exchange's prohibition of institutional members began four months before the new Public Ownership Rule went into effect, continued to be intensely debated for close to six years, only to be resolved by the 1975 Securities Acts Amendments. In 1973, a lengthy SEC Release on the subject was able to state, with little risk of exaggeration, "We doubt whether any topic, and all of its concomitant ramifications, has been studied as intensively as this one, by so many different governmental bodies and individuals." Complex though the institutional membership debate was, much of its intensity could be traced to two core issues. First, how much profit should broker-dealers be allowed to earn from the execution of institutional investor securities transactions? By the early 1970s, mutual funds, insurance companies, pension funds, and other institutional investors were generating 60 to 70 percent of nonmember trading volume on the New York Stock Exchange. Their primary motivation in seeking Exchange membership was to reduce the costs of securities transactions.

Second, what should be the boundaries between stock exchange membership and other financial industries? Under the rules of the New York Stock Exchange and most other exchanges, an exchange member whose predominant business was securities brokerage or dealing could manage a mutual fund, pension fund, or generally otherwise engage in the business of institutional investors, but an insurance company, mutual fund, or pension fund whose predominant business was money management could not be a member of the exchange. So self-serving a rule appeared unfair, as was recognized by several leaders of the NYSE itself, including Gustave Levy, who in January 1971 acknowledged, "Our Achilles' heel has always been that we have been in the money management business and the money managers could not get into ours."[100]

The climactic institutional membership debate effectively began in November 1969, when the Justice Department filed comments with the SEC suggesting that the requirement in the NYSE's proposed Public Ownership Rule that a member firm's primary purpose "be the transaction of business as a broker or dealer in securities" was a violation of the antitrust laws. It was unlikely, claimed the Department, that the primary purpose provision was exempted by the *Silver* decision, since it probably was not necessary "to achieve a legitimate goal of the Exchange Act."

The SEC soon agreed with the Justice Department that two other restrictions in the NYSE's Public Ownership Rule proposal were not "supported by a showing of self-regulatory purpose sufficient to outweigh their anticompetitive impact." The Commission asked the Exchange to remove from its rule proposal conditions barring an Exchange member from having as a customer any nonmember who acquired a 5 percent or greater participation in the member firm's profits and requiring that no more than 49 percent of a member corporation's voting stock be held by the public. But the SEC did not judge the permissibility of the Primary Purpose Test before the Exchange Public Ownership Rule became effective on March 26, 1970. Instead, it agreed with the Exchange to review the appropriateness of the requirement after it had had the benefit of an exchange study of institutional membership, which, the SEC requested, "be completed no later than July 1, 1970."[101]

The New York Stock Exchange Institutional Membership Study was never delivered to the SEC. But the broker-dealer subsidiaries of the Investors Diversified Services (*IDS*), then the nation's largest mutual fund complex, and of the Dreyfus Corporation applied for NYSE membership in January 1971, with IDS threatening to file an antitrust suit challenging the Exchange's primary purpose test if its application was rejected.

The Martin Report, *Report on the Securities Markets,* published early in August 1971, became the basis for renewed NYSE opposition to institutional membership. William McChesney Martin, former president of the New York Stock Exchange and later chair of the Federal Reserve System, was among the best respected figures in financial regulation. With one significant exception, Martin endorsed the Exchange's one-sided "primary purpose" rule. Citing "the concentration of economic power which might result from institutional membership," the risk "that institutional membership could lead to a market dominated by dealers dealing for their account," and the need "to facilitate regulation," Martin recommended that banks, trust companies, insurance companies, and other institutions be barred from Exchange membership, although Martin noted "that the purchase of 25 percent or less of the voting securities of a member corporation by an institution is not prohibited" by the Exchange's Primary Purpose Rule. Since member firms had handled "reasonably well" the "unavoidable conflicts of interest [that] arise when money management and brokerage functions are combined within a single profit making firm," Martin also endorsed allowing Exchange members to engage in all forms of money management, with the significant, but unexplained, exception of managing or advising mutual funds.[102]

The SEC, in its February 1972 *Statement on the Future Structure of the Securities Markets* and its April 1972 *White Paper on Institutional Membership*, adopted a position on institutional membership similar to that of the Martin Report. But the bases for the Commission's position were different from those in the Martin Report. The SEC's *White Paper* recognized that the institutional membership issue "first came to the fore" because of the Exchange's "rigid, fixed commission" schedule. By April 1972, however, the SEC had unfixed commission rates on transactions above $500,000, scheduled the breakpoint to drop to $300,000 with "further significant reductions in the breakpoint... highly probable in the not too distant future." The Commission concluded, "as a general rule... membership [in the securities markets]... should be open to those... who have the primary purpose of serving the public as brokers or market-makers." Adopting a recommendation of the New York Stock Exchange, the SEC defined *primary purpose* with the soon to be controversial *80-20* Rule, which required a firm to do at least 80 percent of its commission business with unaffiliated customers in order to be eligible for membership on any exchange. The SEC concurred with the Martin Report that an exchange member should be allowed to engage in money management including managing of advising mutual funds as long as no more than 20 percent of its trading volume was executed on behalf of such affiliates, primarily because the Commission thought "it important that a portion of broker-dealer income be based on a more stable source than commission business." With a similar regard for lessening the securities industry's capital crisis, the SEC recommended abolition of the New York Stock Exchange Parent Test, which prohibited a nonsecurities firm from establishing or acquiring a securities broker-dealer firm. As long as the parent corporation provided no more than 20 percent of the trading volume of the subsidiary securities firm, the SEC saw "no reason either of law or policy why this should not be permitted. The establishment of such a subsidiary doing a brokerage business for the public provides a useful source of permanent capital for the securities industry." On May 26, 1972, the SEC formally requested each national securities exchange to adopt a rule incorporating these restrictions on institutional membership no later than July 31, 1972.[103]

Substantial opposition to the SEC's recommended exchange rule regulating institutional membership began soon after the Commission's February 1972 *Future Structure Statement.* More than any other exchange, the minuscule Philadelphia-Baltimore-Washington Stock Exchange, 43 percent of whose trading volume derived from institutional members was not in compliance with the SEC's recommended rule, and would be affected by the Commission's proposal. Facing the possibility of extinction, the Philadelphia Exchange refused to issue the SEC recommended rule. On August 3, 1972, after it became apparent that several other exchanges also had not adopted the proposed rule, the SEC formally circulated for public comments its own institutional membership regulation, Rule 19b-2. Most New York Stock Exchange members and the Securities Industry Association (the successor to the Investment Bankers Association and the Association of Stock Exchange Firms) "wholeheartedly" favored the SEC rule. The SEC officially promulgated Rule 19b-2, incorporating a three-year grace period. The rule was scheduled to become effective on March 15, 1973.

More effective opposition to the SEC's Rule 19b-2 emerged in Congress. Although both the Senate Securities and House Commerce and Finance Subcommittees accepted the Commission's arguments in favor of barring institutions from exchange membership, neither Subcommittee supported the SEC's 80-20 Primary Purpose Test. One Senate Banking Committee Report excoriated Rule 19b-2 as "a regretful chapter in the Commission's generally distinguished history." In 1975, as part of the Securities Acts Amendments, Congress directed the SEC to adopt a near total ban on securities brokerage firms transacting business on behalf of affiliated institutional accounts, to become effective on May 1, 1978.[104]

The practical effect of the Commission decision not to permit institutional memberships on the securities exchanges was to add to the already considerable pressure to unfix commission rates totally.

On April 5, 1971, fixed rates on orders above $500,000 were eliminated. This meant that 5 percent of securities commission income was initially subject to competition.

A similar gradualism was pursued by the Casey Commission. Its February 1972 *Statement on the Future Structure of the Securities Markets* characterized as "a powerful argument against any precipitous movement to competitive commissions" the possibility of a "severe decline in the revenue of the securities industry if competitive rates were suddenly introduced on all institutional business," aggravating the injury wrought by "the industry's recent financial crisis." "Nevertheless," the Statement announced, "we have determined that a reduction in the breakpoint at $300,000 should take effect in April 1972." The following month Casey testified that the SEC anticipated reaching the $100,000 level for negotiated rates by the spring of 1974, with successive reductions in the breakpoint tentatively scheduled for April 1973 and April 1974. This remained the SEC's policy until late March 1973, when Chair Cook announced that, in light of the "serious financial situation in the brokerage community at this time," the Commission would not require an interim reduction in the negotiated rate level in April 1973, although it remained committed to lowering the breakpoint for negotiated rates to $100,000 by April 1974.[105]

It soon became obvious that the SEC's *ad hoc* approach to the commission rate issues was no longer viable. With the SEC's January 1973 promulgation of Rule 19b-2, barring institutions from exchange membership, and Congressional support for the ban on institutional membership, negotiated commission rates remained the single practical means for institutional investors to obtain reductions in the cost of securities transactions.

Securities industry support for fixed rates eroded. NYSE President Robert Haack became the first major figure in the industry to state publicly his personal opposition to fixed commission rates, in a remarkable address entitled *Competition and the Future of the New York Stock Exchange*, delivered on November 17, 1970. In Haack's view, the New York Stock Exchange could no longer afford fixed rates. Haack had come to believe that fixed rates were responsible for the rapidly increasing diversion of business in NYSE-listed securities to the regional exchanges and the over-the-counter third market. Not only did fixed rates jeopardize the role of the NYSE as a central securities market; they also threatened the profitability of Exchange members. Regulatory lag, implied Haack, had been responsible, in part, for the large number of securities firms that sustained losses in 1969 and 1970. Similar losses were likely to recur as long as the industry remained subject to a commission schedule requiring SEC approval. "Better would it be," urged Haack, "for the industry to make its own competitive adjustments as economic conditions warrant, rather than to work on a new schedule as it has for almost eight years with still no end in sight."

Haack appreciated, long before the issue was decided by the SEC or Congress, that the introduction of negotiated rates would blunt much of the momentum for institutional membership. In the long run, the financial self-interest of Exchange members would be better served, Haack argued, if NYSE members accepted rate competition but held on to all commission business executed on the Exchange, rather than preserving fixed rates and allowing institutional members to execute 60 to 70 percent of nonmembers' transactions without employing an Exchange member as a broker or dealer.

Within one year of Haack's celebrated address, several other securities industry leaders publicly endorsed competitive rates, including Merrill Lynch's Donald Regan; Investment Bankers Association President Wheelock Whitney; Weeden and Company's Donald Weeden; Paine, Webber, Jackson & Curtis's James Davant; Salomon Brothers' William Salomon; Lehman Brothers' Andrew Sage; and reversing his earlier position, Goldman, Sachs's Gustave Levy.[106]

The abolition of all fixed commission rates was announced in an SEC Release exactly five weeks and one day after the August 6, 1973, swearing in of SEC Chair Ray Garrett and Commissioner A.A. Sommer. With roughly half of its member firms losing money during the first seven months of 1973, and aggregate pretax losses of $195 million on total securities activities sustained during that period, the NYSE earlier had proposed an increase of 10 percent in commission charges on transactions up to $5000 and of 15 percent in commission charges on transactions above $5000 up to $300,000. Hearings on the Exchange rate proposal were held in July 1973. Chair Garrett "entered the subject with the rather strong feeling that a practice that had lasted almost 200 years must be sound and should not be declared improper." It soon became apparent to Garrett that all four of the SEC's other Commissioners disagreed with him. Within a month after his swearing in, Garrett, too, became convinced "that fixed commission rates are doomed. The question is who will kill them and when and under what conditions."[107]

On September 11, 1973, the SEC approved the NYSE's requested commission rate increase, but announced, "The Commission will act promptly to terminate the fixing of commission rates by national stock exchanges after April 30, 1975, if the stock exchanges do not, on their own initiative, adopt rule changes achieving that result in advance of that date." There were no dissenting votes. From that date until the actual abolition of all fixed rates on May 1, 1975, Garrett, "the reluctant dragon," led the SEC in resisting lobbying efforts of the New York Stock Exchange and the Securities Industry Association (*SIA*) to pressure the Commission to reverse or defer its decision totally to unfix commission rates.

After voluntarily lifting fixed rates on orders of $2000 or less in April 1974, the NYSE steadfastly opposed the SEC's decision to abolish all fixed rates. Since a March 1, 1973, resolution of the Exchange's Board of Governors, the Exchange nominally had favored competitive commission rates, but only if the SEC or Congress simultaneously took steps "to maintain the flow of orders to the nation's auction markets" by eliminating third market trading in securities listed on the NYSE.

The vehemence of the securities industry's opposition to rate competition was characterized by Commissioner John Evans in an address delivered two weeks before the May 1, 1975, date for the abolition of fixed rates:

> It has been predicted that competitive rates will destroy the New York Stock Exchange as well as the other Exchanges in the country, create confusion and chaos in the markets for securities, destroy the greatest financial communications system the world has ever known, reduce the participation of small investors in our securities markets, bring about destructive competition and thus cause a high rate of failure among broker-dealers and concentrate the securities business in a handful of firms, lower the standards in the industry, weaken desirable surveillance mechanisms that protect public investors, reduce the depth and liquidity of our markets, eliminate public markets for many securities, destroy our capital raising mechanism, and bring about the downfall of our free enterprise system.
>
> May 1, the day by which barriers to competitive rates must be removed, is sometimes referred to as "Mayday," a term used as an international distress signal. One witness at our recent 19b-3 hearings concerning whether to adopt a rule prohibiting exchanges from fixing minimum public commission rates repeated the Mayday reference and added, "I would like to carry this one step further. Mayday is a great holiday in Russia. And Russia has said there is no need to fight democracy. It will burn itself out. Well, Commissioners, you have the candle and the matches, and it will be a short fuse."[108]

On January 23, 1975, the SEC formally adopted Rule 19b-3, ending on May 1, 1975, all fixed commission rates charged nonmembers. Days later, NYSE announced that it would not bring a suit contesting the rule. By then it was obvious the suit would have been pointless. Congress soon also adopted legislation abolishing all fixed rates.[109]

May Day initially proved almost as beneficial for NYSE as it did for investors. Exactly as Haack anticipated in his November 1970 address, the unfixing of commission rates reversed the fragmentation in the trading of exchange listed securities. Third market volume shrank from 7.87 percent of total volume in Exchange listed securities in 1972 to less than 3 percent in 1978, when Weeden and Company, then the largest third market dealer, announced its decision to end third market operations. By September 1980, NYSE was responsible for 88 percent of the transactions in Exchange listed securities. The regional markets maintained approximately 10 percent of the volume in Exchange listed securities both before and after May Day; the third market, with a share of 2 percent, had virtually disappeared.

Simultaneously, commission rate levels were substantially reduced. Between May 1, 197, and the end of 1980, a study conducted by the SEC's Directorate of Economic and Policy Analysis calculated that commission charges computed as a percentage of the principal value of securities transactions declined 57 percent for institutional investors and 20 percent for individual investors.

The profitability of the securities industry was enhanced. As the Justice Department's economic witnesses had predicted at the SEC's 1968 Commission Rate Hearings, a reduction in securities transaction costs contributed to increased securities volume. Between 1974 and 1980, aggregate share volume on national securities exchanges more than tripled. While NYSE member firms doing a public business in aggregate lost money in 1973 and barely broke even in 1974, the same firms earned average profits of 13.7, 14.2, 6.2, 7.7, 9.8, and 14.2 percent during the first six years that they were subject to negotiated rates.[110]

The Central Market System

With the total unfixing of brokerage commission rates in 1975, the restructuring of the securities markets by means of an electronically linked central market system became the SEC's regulatory priority.

During the late 1960s and early 1970s, four primary considerations led the SEC and Congress to conclude that the NYSE specialist system was no longer capable of providing the best execution of all Exchange listed securities transactions.

First, NYSE specialists alone often were unable to perform adequately as a dealer offsetting large institutional buy and sell orders, popularly called block orders. Between the fourth quarter of 1964 and the third quarter of 1970, block trades of 10,000 or more shares grew from 2.1 to 14.8 percent of total NYSE volume. By the time the Institutional Investor Study was published in 1971, 35 percent of the volume in block trades of 10,000 or more shares in NYSE listed shares was executed off the Exchange floor, either in the regional markets or the over-the-counter market.[111]

Second, faith waned that the NYSE specialists alone could provide the best execution in Exchange listed securities grew within the SEC that market maker competition was likely to provide better executions for investors than SEC and Exchange regulation of exchange specialists.

The back office crisis provided a third basis for doubting that the specialist system was capable of providing the best execution for all NYSE listed securities transactions. In the aftermath of the crisis, several private industry and Congressional studies concurred with the SEC's *Study of Unsafe and Unsound Practices of Brokers and Dealers* that "the methods of handling securities certificates in effecting deliveries and transfers are positively archaic." A typical individual investor buy order during the 1960s required a brokerage firm to use approximately 33 different documents to execute and record the transaction. Virtually all of the steps in executing an order were manual.

The automation and linkage of securities clearance and settlement facilities suggested a more effective system. By automating securities ordering via a nationwide computer network linking brokers to market makers to clearance and settlement facilities, error costs could be reduced and savings could be achieved by the elimination of floor brokers and the integration of transaction reporting, quotation, recordkeeping, and regulatory organizations. In 1977, SRI International estimated that the cost savings from the creation of an electronically linked central securities market would be more than $130 million a year.[112]

The fourth primary reason for doubting that the New York Stock Exchange specialist system could provide the best execution of all NYSE listed securities transactions was the design and successful implementation of the Nasdaq over-the-counter quotation system in February 1971.

Before Nasdaq began operations, quotations in the over-the-counter securities had been reported in daily "pink sheets" published by the National Quotation Bureau, listing bid and asked prices of each dealer in each stock for the previous trading day. To obtain up to the minute competitive quotations, a stockbroker or dealer had to telephone one or more dealers in an over-the-counter security; the time and difficulty involved in telephoning over-the-counter dealers frequently discouraged brokers or dealers placing orders from engaging in rigorous comparative shopping.

Nasdaq dramatically improved the quality of the over-the-counter securities market. In the Nasdaq Level 1 service, brokers or dealers could view a representative quotation for any Nasdaq security. On Level 2, brokers or dealers could view the current bid and ask prices of each market maker for any Nasdaq security available. Level 3 service allowed Nasdaq market makers to enter new quotations into the system.

Nasdaq Levels 2 and 3 service revolutionized the over-the-counter (*OTC*) market. At the touch of a few buttons, a broker or dealer could instantly see the competitive quotations of all market makers in a given security. Newspapers could be supplied with volume data concerning each over-the-counter security for the first time. Investors could obtain current quotations. The simultaneous availability of rival market makers' quotations narrowed price spreads. Several economic studies corroborated this result. One calculated that between 1970 and 1972, the mean market spread for a sample of over-the-market securities was reduced from 0.4871 to 0.4028.[113]

Taking into account each of the four primary considerations that inspired the movement to create an electronically linked central securities market, it was possible by the early 1970s to envision the contours of a new National Securities Market System. Employing computer technology, all securities market makers — the exchange specialists, the over-the-counter dealers, the exchange block positioners — could be linked by a composite transaction and quotation reporting system. Removal of Rule 394 and other barriers to market maker competition would give the market greater "depth," since the capital of more market makers would be available to handle temporary imbalances in supply and demand. If each exchange specialist's limit order book was replaced with a system wide limit order book, investor would have a more effective guarantee of best order execution. The fragmentation of the securities market into numerous unconnected market centers could be prevented either by technology that automatically matched and executed best bids and offers or by a best execution rule that prevented any broker from executing a transaction when a better price was available elsewhere in the system. Price spreads would be kept close by competing market makers and by centralizing volume within the electronic market. Market orders would be executed by brokers or dealers through Nasdaq type desk consoles. The brokers or dealers would match buy or sell orders against the system wide limit order book or against the entries of other brokers and dealers. Simultaneously, the central computer facility could record the transaction on a system wide transaction tape and arrange securities clearance and settlement. Eventually, a central computer could replace entirely the exchange's floor brokers and back office personnel and reduce reliance on exchange specialists. Hardwood exchange floors could be superseded by brokerage firm desk consoles and a central computer facility in a nationwide "exchange without walls."[114]

There were difficult technical problems and policy decisions involved in converting a system of unaffiliated securities exchanges and over-the-counter markets into a nationwide electronic securities system. The major obstacles, however, were political. There was virtually no incentive for the NYSE and the specialists and other floor members who dominated its governance to help create a central market system that could reduce NYSE floor members' profits by removing their monopoly in listed securities trading and increasing the effectiveness of market maker competition. Similarly, there was no incentive for *any* securities exchange to support a central market system that would increase the proportion of listed security orders that could be executed upstairs by broker-dealer firms that were exchange members. To the regional exchanges in particular, the threat posed by an efficient central market system was acute. Much or all of their order flow might be more efficiently handled by market makers in major broker-dealer firms such as Merrill Lynch.

The SEC's role in facilitating the creation of the central electronic market was pivotal. Only the SEC had the authority and expertise to prod or compel the NYSE and the other exchanges to accept change, referee alternative proposals, and prevent industry initiatives from excluding competition or unnecessarily raising transaction costs. From the outset, it was predictable that progress toward creation of a central market system would turn on how effectively the SEC moved the securities industry to implement technology that would reduce investor costs.

The SEC's first formal statement concerning the need to create a national securities market system appeared in the Transmittal Letter accompanying the publication of its *Institutional Investor Study* in March 1971. Disclaiming any intent to mandate or describe in detail the future structure of the securities markets, the SEC stated that its "objective" would be "to see a strong central market system created to which all investors have access, in which all qualified broker-dealers and existing market institutions may participate in accordance with their respective capabilities, and which is controlled not only by appropriate regulation but also by the forces of competition."

Five months later, the NYSE joined the issue, with the publication of William McChesney Martin's eagerly awaited *Report on the Securities Markets.* Martin, writing as an independent unpaid adviser of the New York Stock Exchange Board of Governors, began with the assertion that "competition between markets has not been beneficial because it has depended upon unequal regulation which, among other things, has not required full disclosure and equal responsibility of participants." Without considering whether market maker competition ever could be beneficial, Martin proceeded to outline a national market system almost entirely opposite to that proposed by the SEC, one in which the NYSE's monopolistic position in trading listed securities largely would be preserved. Martin recommended that the NYSE, the Amex, and the regional exchanges be integrated to provide a single, national auction market for each security qualified for listing. All over-the-counter trading in exchange listed securities would be prohibited, because, wrote Martin, "there is no doubt that the growth of the third market presents a danger to the maintenance of fair and disclosed pricing and to the regulatory system." Martin asserted: "The New York Stock Exchange has, to some extent, all of the characteristics prescribed above for the proposed national exchange system."[115]

The NYSE and a committee of 52 broker-dealer firms soon endorsed the basic conclusions of the Martin Report. Among others in the securities industry, reported the *New York Post*'s Carol Mathews, "the 26-page report was met with hoots of laughter and private expression of disbelief." Nineteen economists, ranging from the University of Chicago's Milton Friedman to MIT's Paul Samuelson, signed a petition endorsing the recommendations of the SEC in its *Institutional Investor Study* Transmittal Letter, stating: "Acceptance of the recommendations of the Martin report would help to reestablish the eroding monopoly power of the New York Stock Exchange and to subject that power primarily to regulation by the monopolist." *Business Week* accurately concluded: "The Martin Report has lost Wall Street a chance to bring about reform on its own."[116]

Three weeks after the publication of the Report, Chairman William Casey announced that the Commission would hold Hearings on the Future Structure of the Securities Markets. These Hearings culminated in the SEC's February 1972 *Statement on the Future Structure of the Securities Markets*, which was most significant for its rejection of the Martin Report's proposal to abolish the third market and its reaffirmation of the SEC's commitment to market maker competition.[117]

Cook's SEC subsequently outlined some of the concrete steps necessary to create a nationwide electronic market system in its March 1973 *Policy Statement on the Structure of a Central Market System.* Three broad projects were envisioned. First, creation of a system-wide communications system. Second, since "the most important objective of the system is to foster the development of strong competition among its participants," the 1973 Statement called for the elimination of unjustifiable impediments to market maker competition. Specifically, it noted that "restrictions such as Rule 394, regardless of their past appropriateness, are incompatible with a central market system and will have to be rescinded by the time the quotation system is in operation." Finally, the 1973 Statement anticipated creation of a system-wide specialist limit order book and, apparently also an electronic execution system.[118]

The Commission subsequently waffled. Shortly before the 1973 *Central Market Policy Statement* was published, SEC chair designate Cook predicted: "In my judgment, all of the major elements of this system . . . can and should be in operation no later than two years from now." But the SEC during the 1977–1981 chairmanship of Harold Williams ceased to treat as "the most important objective of the system . . . the development of strong competition among its participants." The goal of maximum market maker competition was subordinated to the objective of avoiding disruptions in securities trading while implementing a central market system. Williams memorably defended the SEC's slow progress in 1979 by stating, "I am not about to be the person to come back to Congress and say I am sorry I implemented your program and it blew [up]. The capital markets of this country are too important."[119]

The SEC's efforts to facilitate creation of a central electronic market initially focused on implementation of a system-wide communications network. Before the SEC's effort to create a composite transaction reporting system, the only transaction or last sale price reporting of exchange listed securities was provided by NYSE and Amex ticker tapes and electronic displays, which gave a continuous report of transactions executed on the floor of the two New York City exchanges. Offboard trading in New York Stock Exchange listed securities effected by regional exchange or third market market makers was not reported on NYSE tape. The SEC's attempt to create a composite transaction tape essentially was a proposal to increase the visibility of regional exchange specialists and over-the-counter dealers who made markets in NYSE listed securities by including reports of their transactions on the same tape that reported transactions executed on the NTSE.

For four years, NYSE "foot dragging" as SEC Commissioner Sommers put it, delayed implementation of a composite tape. In an effort to break the deadlock, the SEC in March 1972 proposed for comment Rule 17a-15, which required each exchange and the NASD to file on or before June 15, 1972, a plan with the Commission for the dissemination of transaction reports in listed securities. Significantly, the proposed rule stated that "vendors," not the exchanges, would provide consolidated transaction reporting.

In their comments on proposed Rule 17a-15, the New York and American Stock Exchanges sharply questioned the SEC's authority to issue the rule or deprive them of their right to derive income from the dissemination of last sale data. The two exchanges proposed an alternative to a rule requiring vendor administration of the consolidated tape; they suggested that the system be administered by their jointly owned subsidiary, the Securities Industry Automation Corporation (*SIAC*). This would permit the NYSE and Amex to retain income from last sale data while making feasible retransmission by commercial vendors on a fee basis. The SEC agreed, both because of Commission uncertainty about its statutory authority and because, as subsequent SEC Chair Ray Garrett explained, an SIAC system "will be compatible with ticker and cathode ray tube equipment presently found in most brokerage officers [and] is not expected to increase the costs of broker-dealers who now subscribe to either of the present New York or Amex tapes." In August 1972, the SEC revised the rule consistent with the NYSE and Amex SIAC proposal, and in November 1972 adopted Rule 17a-15.[120]

The more significant component of the central market communications network was the composite quotation system. "Such a system," wrote the SEC's Advisory Committee on Market Disclosure in November 1972, is "the cornerstone on which a central market system will be built." Unlike the composite last sale reporting tape, the composite quotations system provided the basis for a significant potential diversion of securities trading from the New York and American Stock Exchanges to the regional exchanges and the third market.

In March 1972, simultaneous with the circulation of the first draft of its proposed composite transaction Rule 17a-15, the SEC circulated for comment proposed Rule 17a-14, requiring every exchange and the NASD to make available to vendors specialist and over-the-counter dealer quotations in exchange listed securities "on a current and continuing basis."

Until the month before enactment of the 1975 Securities Acts Amendments, the NYSE refused to participate in any composite quotations system that included over-the-counter dealer quotations in exchange listed securities or to recognize the SEC's power to adopt Rule 17a-14. The principal concern of the NYSE was that a composite quotations system would enable Exchange member firms to act as upstairs market makers rather than routing their orders to the Exchange floor, and might lead to the "demise" of the New York Stock Exchange.

In August 1974, the SEC published a revised version of Rule 17a-14, permitting the exchanges and the NASD to file a plan to implement a composite quotations system. The revised proposal specified, however, that independent vendors would be permitted to disseminate composite quotations. Both the New York and American Stock Exchanges indicated that they would refuse to file a plan to implement a composite quotations system. The NYSE's Comment Letter on the proposed rule stated that "proposed Rule 17a-14 is beyond the authority of the Commission under the existing provisions of the Securities Act of 1934," it "would deprive the Exchange of property in violation of the due process provisions of the Constitution of the United States," and was "premature [since] the proposed rule appears designed to require the creation of an entity that would be an integral component of an as yet undefined central market system."[121]

Only when passage of the 1975 Securities Acts Amendments seemed inevitable did the New York and American Stock Exchanges agree in principle to the dissemination of its quotations.

Employing the authority granted by the 1975 Amendments, the SEC laboriously fashioned, over the next two and a half years, Rule 11Ac1-1, to ensure that the exchanges and over-the-counter dealers provided reliable quotations to independent vendors. As adopted in January 1978, the rule required each registered exchange and the NASD during trading hours continuously to make available to quotation vendors the highest bid and lowest offer communicated on an exchange floor or by a third market dealer, including the number of shares covered by the bid or offer. The rule facilitated efforts by composite quotation services like GTE Information Systems, Instinet, and Nasdaq to provide broker-dealers with desktop cathode ray displays of competitive quotations in listed securities similar to the quotations in over-the-counter securities that Nasdaq had begun disseminating in 1971.

The most significant restraint on market maker competition, New York Stock Exchange Rule 394, effectively barred an Exchange member from executing a trade off the floor through an over-the-counter dealer. The anticompetitive nature of Rule 394(b) had been repeatedly criticized by the SEC. Implicitly in its 1971 *Institutional Investor Study* Transmittal Letter and its 1972 *Statement on the Future Structure of the Securities Markets,* and explicitly in its 1973 *Policy Statement on the Structure of a Central Market System,* the SEC indicated its intention to eliminate Rule 394 as part of its program to implement a competitive central market system.[122]

As enacted in April 1975, the Senate Securities Acts Amendments Bill contained provisions charging the SEC with an affirmative obligation to eliminate anticompetitive restraints, such as Rule 394, if they could not be justified by the purposes of the 1934 Securities

Exchange Act, and granting it the fail safe power to confine trading in listed securities to exchange floors, but only if lesser steps failed to correct any adverse effect on the fairness and orderliness of the market for listed securities caused by third market trading.[123]

Given the plain language of the 1975 Securities Acts Amendments, the legislative history, and the SEC's statements of intent in 1971, 1972, and 1973, the Congress that enacted the 1975 Securities Law must have assumed that the SEC soon would require the NYSE to rescind Rule 394 and permit Exchange members to trade with third market dealers unless the Commission identified new and significant events that neither it nor the Congress earlier had considered.

That the SEC under these circumstances did not proceed to abolish Rule 394 was one of the most significant policy reversals in the Agency's history.[124]

The SEC's December 1975 *Report on Rule 394* deferred full repeal of Rule 394 and permitted Exchange members to act as over-the-counter market makers until the exchanges and NASD had an opportunity to develop more of a central securities market system.

The approach of the SEC during Harold Williams's time as chair was frustratingly halting. In June 1977, the SEC proposed its long anticipated Rule 19c-2 to rescind fully the NYSE's off board trading restrictions. The enduring restrictions in Rule 394, by then, had been renumbered Exchange Rule 390. The SEC's June 1977 Release dismissed as unlikely the possibility that removal of Rule 390 would lead to "a significant increase in fragmentation" of the securities markets. But even if it did, the SEC did not perceive why "the adverse effects of any such increase would not be prevented or ameliorated as a natural consequence of competitive forces in the marketplace. Finally, if competitive forces alone . . . are insufficient to combat those effects," the SEC was confident that new regulations "would presumably be adequate to address that problem.[125]

In the next four years, the SEC's faith in either marketplace competition or its own rulemaking initiatives to ameliorate the risks associated with full rescission of the NYSE's off board trading rules waned perceptibly. The policy shift was so poorly explained that it can be understood only as a consequence of divisions within the SEC.

The policy change was announced officially in January 1978, when a Commission Release stated that further consideration of its proposed Rule 19c-2 to abolish all NYSE off board trading restrictions would be deferred until the agency could evaluate securities industry and stock exchanges responses to several other central market initiatives.[126]

The impression conveyed by the January 1978 Release — that the SEC subsequently would adopt Rule 19c-2 — turned out to be an erroneous one. Late in 1978, the SEC approved changes in the Amex's domestic and foreign listing requirements that increased the number of issuers eligible to list securities on the Amex. The practical effect of the Commission's action was to permit the extension of the Amex's off board trading restrictions to a new group of securities that previously had been traded in the competitive over-the-counter market. Commissioners Evans and Pollack sharply dissented, because they believed the SEC's approval of the new Amex listing requirement would result in "the curtailment or elimination of intense interdealer competition in the OTC market with little possibility of intermarket competition between the Amex and the OTC markets."

The Evans and Pollack dissent inspired the SEC, in April 1979, to propose and later adopt Rule 19c-3, prohibiting all off board restrictions on securities listed on an exchange after April 26, 1979. Only in 2000 was Rule 390 fully rescinded.[127]

The caution and vacillation of the SEC during the 1975–1981 period influenced the character and time of implementation of the central computer and electronic technology necessary to complete the National Securities Market System. By the mid-1970s, the SEC had a clear choice. On the one hand, the Commission could facilitate development of an electronic securities market in which brokers and dealers could view all available quotations including limit orders in a given security on a desktop screen and directly execute orders or make offers and bids by pressing keys on a computer console. Limit orders were not immediate orders to buy or sell a security, but rather to buy when a designated price was reached. This model of the National Market System popularly known as a Hard CLOB, that is, a Composite Limit Order Book, which could automatically execute orders approach, and throughout the late 1970s was most nearly approximated by the Cincinnati Stock Exchange.

Politically, acceptance of a hard CLOB was difficult. A hard CLOB system inevitably would lead to more effective market maker competition at the expense of the existing securities exchanges. At the very least, a hard CLOB system would make floor brokers and physical exchange floors unnecessary. In place of floor brokers congregating at specialists' posts to shout orders in an "auditory crowd," there would be brokers and dealers in their offices throughout the country, creating a "visual crowd" as they communicated bids and offers via computer consoles and visual displays.

As an alternative to a hard CLOB system, most exchanges favored, the National Market System that preserved the exchange floors' central role. Beginning in April 1978, the American, Boston, Midwest, New York, Pacific, and Philadelphia Stock Exchanges began operating the Intermarket Trading System (*ITS*). ITS was a communications system allowing specialists and floor brokers on one exchange floor to transmit buy and sell orders to market makers on another exchange floor. If a specialist or floor broker saw a better price on the composite quotations system available on another exchange, the ITS system allowed her or him to transmit a commitment to trade to the appropriate market maker on that exchange. The market maker there would either accept the commitment or he or she could decline.

There were important differences between a hard CLOB system and ITS. Brokers and dealers could utilize a hard CLOB system from their offices. The ITS system required orders first to be routed to an exchange and then allowed only specialists and floor brokers to have access to the ITS computer consoles. A hard CLOB system permitted automatic execution of orders. ITS allowed market makers to reject orders even when they earlier had published quotations indicating that they would transact business at the order price. Alternatively, specialists could increase their bid to match better offers in the system. This discouraged competitive quotations, because the NYSE specialist could match the off the floor quotation. A hard CLOB system automatically matched highest bids and lowest offers. As originally designed, ITS was a discretionary system, and could not guarantee that investors would receive best order execution. A hard CLOB system would have one system wide limit order book against which all brokers and dealers could execute orders. As originally envisioned, the ITS system would permit separate specialists' limit order books on each exchange.[128]

In January 1978, the Williams SEC issued the first of two significant statements on the development of the National Market System.

Responding to Congressional criticism of the SEC's lack of leadership, the January 1978 Statement began by stressing that implementation of the National Market System must be "accelerated . . . if the idea of a national market system is to progress beyond the theoretical stage and become a functioning reality."

The January 1978 Release's discussion of limit order protection, however, amounted to a terse, contradictory statement that left in doubt the Commission's objectives in facilitating the National Market System. On the one hand, the SEC urged the securities exchanges and the NASD to submit a plan, no later than September 30, 1978, for the design, construction, and operation of a Composite Limit Order Book (which the SEC now called a Central Limit Order File). The SEC reaffirmed its intention to require strict price and time priority and seemed to go further than its earlier CLOB releases in suggesting that brokers, as well as specialists and other market makers, should be allowed to enter directly, alter, or withdraw limit orders. The SEC's January 1978 Release threatened that if the securities exchanges or the NASD was unable to submit an appropriate plan, "[t]he Commission intend[ed] to commence rulemaking to consider the manner and timing of compulsory development of a central file [including the question of whether that task should be assigned principally to a single self-regulatory organization]."

Only in the aftermath of its January 1978 Release did the Williams SEC fully make clear that it would not compel the securities exchanges to participate in a Composite Limit Order Book employing price and time priority. In March 1979, the Williams SEC, in its second significant release on the development of the National Market System, agreed to give the New York and regional exchanges an opportunity to modify the ITS system to provide limit order protection. After extensive citation of the arguments made by the New York and Midwest Stock Exchanges, the Williams SEC abandoned its commitment to price and time priority because "the Commission recognizes the possibility that introduction of a system based upon the absolute time priority concept could have a radical and potentially disruptive impact on the trading process as it exists today."[129]

The Williams SEC, which had not required a hard CLOB system in its January 1979 Release, announced that it would "encourage and, if necessary, mandate the prompt development of comprehensive market linkage and order routing systems to permit the efficient transmission of orders (i) among the various markets for qualified securities . . . and (ii) from brokers and dealers to all qualified markets."

Automated routing of orders from brokers directly to specialists' posts predated the Commission's 1978 Release. In 1976, the NYSE had begun operating its Designated Order Turnabout (*DOT*) system to permit member firms to reduce their costs by avoiding the expense of floor brokerage and improve their efficiency in handling small orders (that is, market orders up to 299 shares; limit orders up to 500 shares). By 1979, DOT orders accounted for 10 percent of all reported NYSE share volume. In 1981, the NASD commenced pilot operations of an enhanced Nasdaq System, known as Computer Assisted Execution System (*CAES*). CAES enabled broker-dealer firms to route buy and sell orders for automatic execution by any authorized OTC market maker disseminating quotations through the Nasdaq system. Broker-dealer firms could route market orders or limit orders and could designate a particular market maker to which the order would be routed or enter an undesignated order, which would be routed to the market maker with the best quotation, determined by price and time priorities.

The most significant National Market System initiative of the Williams SEC culminated in an April 1981 Order requiring the securities exchanges participating in the ITS System and the NASD to implement, by March 1, 1982, an automated interface between the ITS and Nasdaq systems, including a broker to market maker order routing system and automatic execution capability.

It soon was clear that if NYSE Rule 390 remained in effect, the ITS system could hardly be considered a national securities market system. Data published in the SEC's February 1981 Monitoring Report on the Operation of the Intermarket Trading System underlined how trivial was the impact of regional exchange specialists trading through the ITS system. The Report found: "In terms of share volume, the ITS accounted for 3.1% of total NYSE volume in [871] ITS stocks during November 1980." The New York Stock Exchange dominated ITS trading participating in about 90 percent of all ITS trades.[130]

The initial steps towards development of the National Market System were patently inadequate. To an unwarranted degree the SEC seems to have been concerned with preserving existing institutions and jobs. Electronic technology was approved, but as with the ITS, it often was superimposed on exchange floor operations rather than used to replace them. Delays in implementing the system were granted frequently. SEC decisions often were not adequately explained. What made the Commission's performance so troublesome was that the SEC clearly had the responsibility to be "the investor's representative." No investors' organization that effectively existed could countervail the efforts of the Securities Industry Association and the New York Stock Exchange. Given this reality, an SEC more firmly in control of implementing the National Securities Market System would have served investors far better.

Enforcement and Disclosure

During the same period that the Commission began its development of the National Market System, the SEC substantially strengthened its core enforcement and disclosure programs.

The Commission's approach to corporate bribery was pivotal to the expansion of its enforcement program. The Commission's corporate bribery program indirectly was inspired by a 1972 Common Cause lawsuit against the Financial Committee of President Nixon's Committee to Reelect the President. Before April 7, 1972, when the Federal Election Campaign Act of 1971 went into effect, individual contributions to political candidates to finance primary campaigns did not have to be disclosed. Common Cause, aware that Nixon's Finance Committee had raised over $22 million by that date, brought a suit in a federal District Court to require disclosure of the names of the contributors, arguing that most of the money actually would be used to finance Nixon's general election and therefore did have to be disclosed under the law in effect. Five days before the 1972 election, the Committee agreed to make available the origins of $6 million in contributions that it had received before March 10, 1972. In September 1973, as part of a final settlement of the Common Cause lawsuit, the Committee made public information about another $11.4 million in contributions it had received between March 10 and April 7, 1982. Among the latter disclosures was a list of 29 contributors, kept by Nixon's personal secretary, Rosemary Woods. Two of the contributors were firms that had made illegal campaign contributions.

Soon after its formation in late May 1973, the Watergate Special Prosecution Force began an investigation into illegal corporate campaign contributions made during the 1972 presidential election. In July 1973, Special Prosecutor Archibald Cox announced an amnesty program. Corporate officers who came forward voluntarily and admitted illegal political contributions, stated Cox, would find "their voluntary acknowledgement . . . considered as a mitigating circumstance in deciding what charges to bring." American Airlines confessed to a one count violation in October 1973 and received a $5000 fine. During the next two months, Minnesota Mining and Manufacturing, Goodyear, Braniff, Gulf Oil, Ashland Oil, Phillips Petroleum, and Carnation also made voluntary disclosures. Twelve other firms later were indicted by the Watergate Special Prosecutor. Subsequently, the Special Prosecutor brought additional charges against Gulf Oil and Ashland Oil as a result of their failure to make full disclosure during initial investigations.

The use of slush funds created by fictitious or unrecorded transactions to finance illegal corporate campaign contributions early attracted the interest of the SEC's Enforcement Division, then led by Director Stanley Sporkin. By their nature, slush funds require falsification both of corporate internal financial records and the financial statements filed with the SEC. The moving of funds outside the normal recordkeeping process presented the opportunity for outright theft of corporate assets. Arrangements were made for the SEC to have access to the information gathered by the Watergate Special Prosecution Force and initiate its own corporate fraud program.[131]

The Commission's first action was brought in April 1974, against American Ship Building Company and its Chief Executive Officer, George Steinbrenner. The complaint alleged that both the Company and Steinbrenner had violated the 1934 Securities Exchange Act by failing to record or disclose illegal contributions made since 1970. On October 4, 1974, American Ship Building and Steinbrenner agreed to settle the SEC's action by a Consent Decree. The chief consequence of the Consent Decree was the appointment of a Special Review Committee, composed of three independent outside directors.

A similar enforcement approach was employed by the SEC in 12 other cases filed through May 1976. After identifying evidence of falsification of corporate books and records, the Commission in each case agreed to a Consent Decree requiring the corporate defendant to establish an independent Special Review Committee to conduct a full investigation of the irregularities alleged in the SEC's complaint.

This Special Committee procedure was the key to the SEC's program on questionable payments. Enforcement Division Director Stanley Sporkin knew that if he frequently went to trial in questionable payment cases, it would drain the resources of his Division, minimizing the number of questionable payments cases the SEC could pursue. But he also knew how much a guilty corporate executive would prefer a single Special Committee Report to a protracted trial, and a summary voluntary disclosure of his firm's illegal payoffs to a Special Committee Report. By insisting that the Special Committee Reports be painstakingly assembled and highly detailed, Sporkin created a powerful incentive for firms to voluntarily disclose to the SEC.

By mid-1975, the number of SEC questionable payments investigations had increased so rapidly that the full Commission concluded it could no longer afford to deal on a case-by-case basis with determining what specific disclosure each firm publicly would be required to make. In 1975 testimony before the House Subcommittee on International Economic Policy, Commissioner Philip Loomis outlined an SEC Voluntary Disclosure Program. As refined over the following six months, the program allowed a firm that had made questionable or illegal payments to avoid an SEC enforcement action by conducting its own investigation of the payments. Such an investigation was typically supervised by the company's nonemployee directors, with the assistance of the firm's accounting firm and, if necessary, independent outside counsel. At the conclusion of the investigation, a complete report had to be submitted to the full Board of Directors. Material information compiled during the investigation had to be publicly disclosed in a filing with the SEC.

In September 1975, Cities Service Company became the first firm to file with the SEC a voluntary disclosure of its overseas bribery and record falsification. Ultimately close to 400 firms voluntarily admitted having bribed foreign or American political or commercial officials or making illegal American campaign contributions. Another 62 firms' questionable payments would be proven in SEC enforcement actions.

As a result of the Commission's Questionable Payment Program, in 1977 Congress enacted the Federal Corrupt Practices Act, which required every corporation subject to the Securities Exchange Act to "make and keep books, records and accounts, which, in reasonable detail, accurately and fairly reflect the transactions and dispositions of the assets of the issuers," and "devise and maintain a system of internal accounting controls" that "provided reasonable assurance that transactions are executed in accordance with management's general or specific authorization."[132]

In May 1976, SEC Chair Roderick Hills also requested that the NYSE consider amending its listing requirements so that each listed company had to "maintain an audit committee composed of independent directors with full access to all information and regular private meetings with outside auditors." In 1977, the NYSE made the change.[133]

In 1977, the Commission substantially modernized its corporate disclosure requirements with the adoption of Regulation S-K and the integrated disclosure system. There were multiple bases for Regulation S-K.

In 1966, Milton Cohen, previously Director of the Commission's 1963 *Special Study of Securities Markets,* had written an influential Harvard Law Review article, *Truth in Securities Revisited,* that began:

> [T]he combined disclosure requirement of these statutes would have been quite different if the 1933 and 1934 Acts (the latter as extended in 1964) had been enacted in opposite order, or had been enacted as a single, integrated statute — that is, if the starting point had been a statutory scheme of continuous disclosure covering issues of actively traded securities and the question of special disclosures in connection with public offerings had been faced in this setting. Accordingly, it is my plea that there now be created a new coordinated disclosure system having as its basis the continuous disclosure system of the 1934 Act and treating *1933 Act* disclosure needs on this foundation.

In 1969, the Commission's Disclosure Policy Study concurred with Cohen's proposal for a coordinated disclosure system. In *Disclosure to Investors: A Reappraisal of Administrative Policies Under the '33 and '34 Securities Acts,* popularly known as the Wheat Report after the Study Director, Commissioner Francis M. Wheat, provided rationales to justify placing greater emphasis on 1934 Act filings and streamlining registration statements filed by companies subject to a continuous disclosure system. The Wheat Report stressed that the fact that the aggregate volume of new equity securities had traditionally been a small percentage of aggregate exchange trading volume was one justification for placing greater emphasis on 1934 Act filings. The Report argued that information in SEC filings would be rapidly disseminated because of intermediaries in the investment process, such as professional money managers, brokerage firm research staffs, and investment advisers, who would study these filings and filter out key new information to a wider public, and also because of advances in the technology of data dissemination.

Subsequently, the Commission's 1977 *Advisory Committee Report* carried these points further, asserting that "competition among analysts results in securities prices that reflect a broad set of information." This competition, in part, is dependent on "a uniquely active and responsive financial press which facilitates the broad dissemination of highly timely and material company oriented information to a vast readership."[134]

The 1977 Advisory Committee, popularly known as the Sommer Committee, after its chair, Commissioner A.A. or Al Sommer, persuasively restated the case for the Commission corporate disclosure program and provided the intellectual basis for the extension of the SEC's disclosure requirements from historical information to forecast or soft information, which was particularly of value to outside investors trying to buy and sell securities on a level playing field with inside corporate officers and directors.

During the post-war period, the SEC's mandatory disclosure program had been justified on three bases. First, several SEC and academic studies demonstrated that at least during the early decades of the Commission's existence, the mandatory disclosure provisions of the 1933 Securities Act had led to a reduction in underwriter costs, a savings to investors that typically exceeded the direct costs of registering a security with the SEC. Second, the securities laws had reduced, though not eliminated, securities fraud. Finally, it was widely believed by those who participated in the securities markets that the SEC's disclosure programs had increased investor confidence in the securities markets, especially during the first two decades after World War II, which had contributed to more investors and higher securities prices.[135]

In the post-World War II period, no aspect of the SEC's work was more strongly supported by the securities industry than corporate disclosure. The administrative technique, popularized by the SEC, of regulating by mandated disclosure rather than by more direct government controls indeed had a profound influence on post-World War II legislation. The 1957 Civil Rights Act, air, water, and toxic substances pollution statutes, the Occupational Safety and Health Act, the Equal Employment Opportunity Act, the Truth in Lending Act, the Employee Retirement Income Security Act, and innumerable other federal statutes employed the concept of mandatory disclosure.[136]

Nevertheless, beginning in the 1960s, economic research raised fundamental questions about the usefulness of the SEC's corporate disclosure program. Several studies appeared to corroborate the efficient market hypotheses, which, in its semistrong form, posited that securities prices rapidly reflected all public information about the underlying security. Thus, efforts to acquire and analyze public data concerning firms could not be expected to yield superior investment results. A dramatic corroboration of this theory appeared in several studies which documented that the professional investors who managed mutual funds did not outperform randomly selected investment portfolios. For securities law, the crucial implication of the efficient market hypothesis was that securities prices theoretically would be the same regardless of whether most investors received or read mandatory corporate prospectuses and reports. All that was necessary was that a sufficient number of investors act on available public data.

Similar fundamental questions were raised by the portfolio theory, which posited that since investment risk could be substantially reduced by diversification of an investment portfolio, the value of data concerning any individual security's risks or potential rewards was substantially lessened.[137]

Two libertarian economists, the University of Chicago's George Stigler and the University of Rochester's George Benston, attempted to corroborate a more sweeping hypothesis: that there was no value to the mandatory disclosure required by the 1933 and 1934 Securities Acts. In 1964, Stigler published a study comparing the performance of a sample of new issue stock prices during the years 1923–1928 before the enactment of the 1933 Securities Act, and 1949–1955, after enactment. Finding no significant differences in new issue prices relative to market prices in the two periods, Stigler concluded that "the SEC registration requirements had no important effect on the quality of new securities sold to the public." Data errors in Stigler's research and some highly debatable inferences he drew from his Study "substantially invalidated" Stigler's conclusion, in the words of Wharton School professor Morris Mendelson and the opinion of others.[138]

Professor Benston's articles concerning the SEC's mandatory disclosure program presented a more detailed critique. Of most significance was a 1973 Benston article entitled *Required Disclosure and the Stock Market: An Evaluation of the Securities Exchange Act of 1934.* In this article, Benston combined historical and empirical research to attempt to demonstrate "that the disclosure requirements of the Securities Exchange Act of 1934 had no measurable positive effect on the securities traded on the NYSE. There appears to have been little basis for the legislation and no evidence that it was needed or desirable.

Benston argued that the 1934 Securities Exchange Act did not deter much securities fraud. His argument was that little fraud existed before the law was enacted. He wrote:

> A search of the available literature, including the Senate and House hearings on the proposed securities legislation, fails to reveal much evidence of fraud in the preparation or dissemination of financial statements prior to 1934. For example, Wiley Rich, the author of a comprehensive survey of the legal responsibilities of accountants, states that "an extensive search has revealed not a single American case in which a public accountant has been held liable in a crime for fraud."

Echoing the efficient market hypothesis, Benston then published the results of a study to illustrate that the financial data published in the disclosure documents required by the 1934 Act "on average" were not "timely or relevant" when published. A second Benston Study purported to demonstrate that the mandated disclosure of corporate sales figures "were of no apparent value to investors."

Several economists criticized the appropriateness of Benston's studies, the quality of his research designs, and his analysis of his empirical findings. There also were glaring deficiencies of Benston's historical research. Benston's suggestion that there was little securities fraud before 1934 was ludicrous. His "search of the available literature" apparently did not lead him to read of a single enforcement action brought by any of the 47 states that enacted Blue Sky securities regulation laws between 1911 and 1933. Yet in the year 1932 alone, the State of New York alone secured injunctions against 1522 persons and firms and instituted 146 criminal prosecutions.[139]

The cumulative significance of economic theories such as the efficient market hypothesis, portfolio theory and the Stigler and Benston critiques prompted the SEC, during the chairmanship of Roderick Hills, to appoint A.A. Sommer to chair an Advisory Committee on Corporate Disclosure.

A principal achievement of the Sommer Committee was to publish a rationale for a mandatory corporate disclosure system that took into account the recent economic literature. The Sommer Committee's majority began with the premise that "reliable and timely information sufficient to the needs of those who have the responsibility for the allocation of investment [capital] resources is essential to the efficient allocation of resources in any economy."

The Report offered four grounds for doubting that market forces alone would result in the publication of sufficient, reliable, and timely data. First, "very often there are significant motives for at least temporary concealment of adverse information on the part of corporate executives. Often a sizable part of management's total compensation, such as benefits from stock options or stock bonus plans, depends upon the price levels of the company's securities." Second, the actual experiences of many financial analysts led them to believe that in the absence of requirements imposed by federal law they would be seriously handicapped in securing corporate data. Third, even if analyst interest could prompt disclosure of adequate firm data, the vast majority of publicly traded securities were not followed by analysts. Finally, securities analysts sought information for themselves and their customers: "They do not regard themselves as surrogates for the universe of investors and hence do not feel under obligation to disseminate widely information which they secure."

Nor did the Sommer Committee Report believe that the efficient market hypothesis, even if valid, remedied these market imperfections:

> The efficient market hypothesis, as commonly articulated, is indifferent to the quantity and quality of information that is available to investors. The market price of a security reflects true information and false information with equal efficiency.... Thus, a fraudulent income statement, not known to be false, will be reflected in the market price of the security to the same extent as a true one.[140]

The Sommer Report championed a soft information revolution notably to improve the quality of information outside investors did receive. For over three decades, the SEC had generally prohibited the publication of predictions of a firm's future economic performance on the grounds that such projections were not facts, were inherently unreliable, would be given undue credence by investors, and thus would be susceptible to improper manipulation by unscrupulous corporate managers. An often quoted explanation of the SEC's traditional policy barring earnings forecasts was published by Harry Heller, long a senior SEC Staff Attorney, in a 1961 law review article:

> As early as 1904 Veblen expressed the view that the value of an investment basically is a function of future earning power. . . .
>
> The question will be raised, if the determination of future earnings is the prime task confronting the investor, why not require or permit a direct prediction of such earnings? The answer to this is that the Securities Act, like the hero of [the television program] "Dragnet," is interested exclusively in facts. Conjectures and speculations as to the future are left by the Act to the investor on the theory that he is as competent as anyone to predict the future from the given facts.[141]

By the early 1970s, the SEC's policy on earnings forecasts was being severely criticized. The most influential critic was Professor Homer Kripke. In a 1970 law review article entitled *The SEC, the Accountants, Some Myths and Some Realities,* he dismissed the SEC's traditional policy as nonsense. Noting that virtually all corporations used:

> projections of future sales and revenues and capital needs as the basis for making very important decisions as to borrowing, building new plants, establishing new branches, ordering materials, hiring and training labor, etc. . . . Management . . . certainly is in a better position than the public to forecast where the company is going.

By prohibiting disclosure of earnings projections in SEC filings, the Commission had perpetrated an inequitable form of differential disclosure:

> The professionals get management projects informally through press conferences, speeches to analysts' societies, or

press releases, and these projections form the basis for professional judgments. Under its present system the SEC precludes the giving of this information equally to all investors through the documents filed with it. . . .

The importance of this point on projections cannot be overestimated. If there is any hope that the public or even the professionals can make an informed investment judgment, it must start from a crystallization of all of the plethora of information into a projection for the future. The management is in the best position to make the initial estimate; on the basis of it the professional or investor could then make his own modifications. No other single change could add as much meaning to the unmanageable and unfocused flood of facts in present Commission documents.[142]

Soon after beginning as chair, William Casey initiated a review of the SEC's policy barring the publication of earnings projections. In 1973, the Commission issued a *Statement on the Disclosure of Projections of Future Economic Performance*, which permitted earnings projections to be published in SEC documents:

> Information gathered at the hearings reinforced the Commission's own observation that management's assessment of a company's future performance is information of significant importance to the investor, that such assessment should be able to be understood in light of the assumptions made, and that such information should be available, if at all, on an equitable basis to all investors.[143]

The Sommer *Advisory Committee on Corporate Disclosure* in 1977 concluded that a voluntary projection disclosure program was more appropriate than a mandatory program for disclosure of most forward looking information. But the Sommer Committee supported broadening what Regulation S-K's Management, Discussion and Analysis of Financial Condition and Results of Operations from numerical tests to increase management analysis of capital budget plans, setting in motion the later adoption by the Commission of the requirement that management identify and disclose "known trends or any known demands, commitments, events or uncertainties" that likely would result in the company's "liquidity increasing or decreasing in any material way." Similar forward-looking information was required for capital resources, results of operations and risk factors.[144]

Standardized Options and The CFTC

In 1973, the Commission built on its existing authority to regulate standardized options. Trading in individual stock options predates the SEC. Initially, options were called puts and calls. A put is an option to sell at a certain price within a certain period; a call is an option to buy. The economic *raison d'être* of these options was to serve as a hedge (a form of insurance) against future market movements. For example, a person who owned stock might buy a put as insurance that he or she would be able to sell if the market fell below a specified price.

Until 1973, these options were generally traded by professional investors, endorsed by stock exchange firms, and then bought and sold in the over-the-counter market.

Trading in securities options underwent a radical change after the creation of the Chicago Board Options Exchange (*CBOE*) in 1973, which was soon followed by options trading on the American, Philadelphia, and Pacific Stock Exchanges, with the NYSE joining the field in 1982. The CBOE pioneered two concepts: (1) contract standardization, making options fungible by fixing the exercise months and exercise or strike prices; and (2) establishment and joint ownership by all the options exchanges of the Options Clearing Corporation (*OCC*), which became the issuer as well as the guarantor of the traded options. Soon there were four types of listed options traded by options exchanges: stock options, stock index options, debt options, and foreign currency options.[145]

In 1974, Congress created the Commodities Futures Trading Commission (*CFTC*) and extended earlier enacted federal legislation dating back to the Grain Futures Act of 1922 and the Commodity Exchange Act of 1936, which solely regulated future contracts for agricultural commodities to the CFTC's exclusive jurisdiction on futures on financial instruments including stock and stock indices, government securities, such as Ginnie Mae certificates or 90-day Treasury Bills, and foreign currency.

The SEC's acquiescence to CFTC jurisdiction over financial futures was a fundamental mistake. Stock options and stock futures are similar in economic function. Both can be used to hedge the risk of owning underlying securities or can be used to speculate in a security's future performance. Most significantly, both are derivatives of securities that are a core responsibility of the SEC.

On several occasions after the creation of the CFTC, the SEC sought to consolidate regulation of financial futures jurisdiction into the SEC, rather than have two financial products that act as substitutes for each other subject to two agencies. In 1978, while the CFTC was undergoing a reauthorization proceeding, the SEC attempted to secure jurisdiction from the CFTC over futures, options, and leverage contracts derived from securities. The House Agriculture and the Senate Agriculture, Nutrition, and Forestry Committees rejected the SEC's attempt, emphasizing a preference that jurisdiction over all future trading should remain in a single agency. This was less a judgment on the merits than the inevitable consequence of vesting congressional oversight of the SEC and the CFTC in separate committees in both the House and the Senate. The parochial politics of congressional oversight would prove particularly dysfunctional during the 1987 Stock Market Crash and the 2007–2009 Financial Meltdown.[146]

Employee Benefit Plans

The SEC's resolution of its relationship with employee benefit plans also was ragged. In a broad sense, all employee benefit plans can be reduced to two basic categories: defined benefit plans and defined contribution plans.

A defined benefit plan pays fixed or determinable benefits, for example, 50 percent of an employee's final year's compensation. A defined contribution plan, in contrast, does not guarantee a fixed amount of benefits. Benefits vary depending on the investment success of the plan. This is roughly analogous to annuities with traditional insurance and annuities providing a specified dollar payout and variable annuities providing payments based on the investment success of the variable annuity. As earlier discussed, traditional insurance and annuities are exempt from the federal securities laws; variable annuities are considered securities and subject to the federal securities laws.

Employee benefit plans have further complexity. Both defined benefit and defined contribution plans can provide for employee contributions and can be contributory or rely solely on employer contributions and be noncontributory. Both defined benefit and defined contribution plans may be voluntary (the employee decides whether to contribute) or mandatory (the employee has no choice whether to contribute).

Initially, there was no specific reference in the Securities Act to employee pension or profit sharing plans of any kind. The 1970 Amendments to § 3(a)(2) of the Securities Act for the first time gave statutory reference to certain "stock bonus, pension or profit-sharing plan[s]. . . ."

In 1974, Congress enacted the Employment Retirement Security Act, popularly known as ERISA, vesting the Department of Labor with powers to require information about plans to be filed with the Department and participants upon request and overseeing employers' and investment manager fiduciary duties under employee benefit plans. While ERISA preserved a role for the Department of Treasury largely acting through the Internal Revenue Service, the SEC was provided no direct role in development of fiduciary duties or supervision of pension plan investment managers.

In 1979, the Supreme Court limited the ability of the SEC to address pension plans. In *International Brotherhood of Teamsters v. Daniel*, the Court held that a noncontributory, mandatory pension plan did not constitute a security within the meaning of the Securities Act of 1933 or the Securities Exchange Act of 1934.

The Court rejected the argument that an employee's participation in a noncontributory, compulsory pension plan was an investment contract, in part because there was no investment of money or expectation of profit from investment performance. The Court also rejected arguments by the SEC in its *amicus curiae* brief that past actions of Congress evidenced an understanding that pension plans are securities. In 1934, Congress had not adopted an amendment to the Securities Act that would have exempted employee stock investment and stock option plans from the Act's registration requirements. The Court explained: "At no time, however, did Congress indicate that pension benefits in and of themselves gave a transaction the characteristics of a security."

The Court similarly rejected an argument from the 1970 Amendment that extended the § 3(a)(2) exemption to participations in certain tax exempt plans, reading that amendment as recognizing "only that a pension plan had 'an interest or participation' in the fund in which its assets were held, not that prospective beneficiaries of a plan had any interest in either the plan's bank maintained assets or the plan itself." And the Court was unpersuaded by the SEC's longstanding administrative construction: "In 1941, the SEC first articulated the position that voluntary, contributory plans had investment characteristics that rendered them securities under the Acts. At the same time, however, the SEC recognized that noncontributory plans were not covered by the Securities Acts because such plans did not involve a sale within the meaning of the statutes."

Finally, the Court observed: "If any further evidence were needed to demonstrate that pension plans of the type involved are not subject to the Securities Acts, the enactment of ERISA in 1974 . . . would put the matter to rest."

The SEC subsequently issued interpretations in 1980 and 1981 concluding that the Court's decision in *Daniel* precluded an SEC determination that any pension plan that either was noncontributory or compulsory could be characterized as a security.

The SEC, however, did continue to view a contributory voluntary plan as capable of being a security because, in contrast to the plan in *Daniel*, such plans involved a separate investment of money and an expectation of profits from investment performance. While several courts disagreed with the SEC that even a contributory voluntary defined benefit plan could be a security, the Commission Releases provided a basis for urging that contributory voluntary defined contributions were securities. But the Commission never sought congressional resolution of the issue and unlike variable annuities that state law generally requires to be administered in separate accounts, all employee benefit plans today are subject to the Department of Labor. As with the SEC-CFTC frictions, the separate administration of employee benefit plans by the Labor Department created tensions, most notably in the Department of Labor's ill-fated initiative beginning in 2016 to develop fiduciary duty rules applicable to investment advice different from the SEC's approach. In 2018, the Fifth Circuit Court of Appeals vacated the Labor Department's rule.[147]

Expansion of Securities Trading, 1977–2000

Between 1977 and 2000, there were dramatic expansions in virtually every aspect of securities trading. Total annual share volume on national securities exchanges, for example, increased from

7.125 billion shares in 1977 to 155 billion shares in 2000. The total value of effective registrations under the Securities Act increased from approximately $93 billion in 1977, to $2.4 trillion in 2001. Where there had been a total of 4347 registered broker-dealers in 1976, earning an aggregate total revenue of $8.9 billion, by 2001 the Commission supervised over 7900 broker-dealers, with total revenues of over $186 billion.

Underlying this almost unimaginable growth was the longest sustained bull market in United States history. The Dow Jones Industrial Average rose from 875 at year end 1981 to 11,497 in 1999, paralleling similar surges in other leading composite indexes. Between 1981 and 2000, the NYSE stock market capitalization increased nearly 11 fold from $1.1 to $12.4 trillion.[148]

As significant as the general expansion in the size of the SEC's mandate were differences in its nature. During the 1980s, the hostile tender offer became the dominant method of seeking control over publicly traded corporations, eclipsing virtually all other questions in corporate governance. At approximately the same time, securities trading, long dominated by a small number of financial instruments, specifically stocks, bonds, and debentures, rapidly diversified with the maturing of such derivative securities as options, futures and swaps, the proliferation of new techniques to securitize assets such as collateralized mortgage obligations, and the growth of previously little used forms such as commercial paper.

Securities trading became increasingly international. In 1975, United States investors purchased and sold $3.3 billion of foreign stocks, and foreign investors purchased and sold $26 billion of United States stocks. By 1987, United States investors purchased and sold $187 billion of foreign stock. International investors purchased and sold $481.5 billion of United States stocks.[149]

Underlying the expansion of the securities markets and the growth of derivative trading was a technological revolution. By the mid-1980s, the computer was performing an increasingly significant role in order origination. Computers could print order tickets, submit orders, clear transactions, and maintain records virtually simultaneously. Federal Reserve Chair Alan Greenspan was hardly alone in observing: "The speed of information flow together with institutionalization of equity holdings imply that new information can very promptly induce a heavy imbalance of orders on one side or the other of the market."[150]

Of the four SEC chairs between 1977 and 1992, John Shad, President Reagan's first chair, served longest and was the most significant. Shad had had a role in Republican party fundraising in the 1980 elections. In this he was hardly unique. Joseph Kennedy, the first SEC chair, had also had a role in fundraising. Shad had worked at the E.F. Hutton brokerage firm since 1963 and had risen to be vice chair of its Board before being named SEC chair.

The Shad SEC was weakest in its reluctance to seek new legislation to resolve the emerging issues of the period. During Shad's six years as chair, the Commission's most significant legislative enactment was the noncontroversial Insider Trading Sanctions Act of 1984, which authorized the Commission to seek civil penalties not to exceed three times the profit gained or loss avoided as a result of insider trading.

The Shad SEC shied away from the type of factually intensive staff or special studies that had long been employed to support the Commission's legislative initiatives. The Commission published 10 studies of tender offers between 1983 and 1986. One was the *Report of the Advisory Committee on Tender Offers*, which had few factual findings. The balance were economic studies of the Office of the Chief Economist on narrow topics such as the impact of defensive stock repurchases on a corporation's stock performance. There was never a broad factual investigation of tender offers during Shad's time as chair. Subsequently, SEC Chairs Ruder and Breeden would preside over broader factual inquiries concerning the October 1987 Stock Market Crash and would pursue farther reaching legislative agendas, albeit with mixed results.

The effective result was a competent but cautious Commission, successful in achieving incremental change and avoiding significant missteps but less successful in formulating broad policy responses to major contextual developments.[151]

Tender Offers

No issue better illustrated the strengths and weaknesses of the Commission during Shad's time as chair than its response to the rise of the hostile tender offer. In 1968, when Congress enacted the limited disclosure approach to tender offers in the Williams Act Amendments to the Securities Exchange Act, W.T. Grimm & Co. estimated that approximately $43 billion value of consideration had been exchanged in total merger and acquisition activity. By 1988, merger and acquisition activity had experienced a staggering increase to over $226 billion, with hostile or unsolicited tender offers to buy the stock of target corporations emerging as the most controversial aspect of the 1980s merger wave.[152]

Throughout the 1980s, the states responded with alacrity to the increase in hostile tender offer activity by adopting pro incumbent management tender offer statutes to frustrate hostile bids. The Supreme Court's 1982 decision in *Edgar v. MITE Corp.* seemed to mark a death knell for this type of statute. *MITE* reviewed the Illinois Business Takeover Act. Under the Act, any takeover offer had to be registered with the Illinois Secretary of State if the target company was a corporation or other issuer of securities of which shareholders located in Illinois owned at least 10 percent of the class of equity securities subject to the offer, or for which any two of the following three conditions were met: (1) the corporation had its principal executive officer in Illinois, (2) it was organized under the laws of Illinois, or (3) at least 10 percent of its stated capital and paid in surplus were within Illinois.

Justice White wrote for a five justice majority an opinion that the Illinois statute violated the United States Constitution's Commerce Clause because the burden it imposed on interstate commerce through its incidental regulation was "excessive in light of the local interests the Act purports to further."[153]

In 1987, the Supreme Court dramatically shifted direction when it sustained the Indiana Control Share Acquisitions Act in *CTS Corp. v. Dynamics Corp. of America.* Unless a corporation opted out by amending its articles of incorporation or bylaws, the Indiana law applied to any corporation incorporated in Indiana that had (1) at least 100 shareholders, (2) its principal place of business, its principal office, or substantial assets in Indiana, *and* (3) either more than 10 percent of its shareholders resident in Indiana, *or* more than 10 percent of its shares owned by Indiana residents, *or* 10,000 resident shareholders.

The Act focused on the acquisition of control shares, which occurred whenever an entity acquired shares that, but for the operation of the Act, would bring it voting power equal to any of three thresholds: 20, 33 1/3, or 50 percent. An entity that acquired control shares did not acquire voting rights unless a majority vote of all disinterested shareholders holding each class of stock approved a resolution.

Justice Powell, for a six justice majority, held that the Indiana Act did not violate the Constitution's Supremacy or Commerce Clauses:

> The principal objects of dormant Commerce Clause scrutiny are statutes that discriminate against interstate commerce.... The Indiana Act is not such a statute. It has the same effects on tender offers whether or not the offeror is a domiciliary or resident of Indiana. Thus, it "visits with effects equally upon both interstate and local businesses...."[154]

The state law response to *CTS* was to popularize enactment of moratorium statutes that went considerably beyond the Indiana statute. In 1985, before *CTS*, New York had adopted legislation to regulate tender offers for New York corporations by prohibiting any person who bought 20 percent or more of a corporation's stock from "engaging in any business combination" with the corporation for five years without the Board's approval *before* the acquisition of the 20 percent, and permitting 20 percent purchase after that only with the consent of a majority of disinterested stockholders or payment of the same amount to all stockholders in accordance with a statutory formula.

Few state tender offer statutes more clearly intended to frustrate hostile takeovers than did the New York law. The Ad Hoc Committee on Corporate Legislation of the Association of the Bar of the City of New York stated in a November 1985 Interim Report:

> The Committee believes that the provisions of the bill represent a major transfer of rights and power from stockholders to the Board of Directors in place at the time of an unfriendly takeover bid. Proposed Section 912 would in effect give the incumbent Board significant power to discourage unfriendly tender offers. This could curtail the opportunity for stockholders to realize a premium over current market, as generally happens in a hostile takeover bid.

After *CTS*, Delaware and other jurisdictions adopted their own versions of moratorium statutes.

At approximately the same time, state corporate law judicial decisions authorized other takeover defenses. Most notably, in 1985, the Delaware Supreme Court in *Moran v. Household International, Inc.* permitted corporations to adopt poison pills or rights plans. Under the plan challenged in *Moran*, if a hostile bid was made for Householder International, its stockholders held rights allowing them to purchase the common stock of the bidder at one half its market value. This poison pill would raise the cost of a bidder's attempt to acquire control of a target and, if enforceable, might be a showstopper that totally deterred the hostile bid.

Poison pills were widely adopted. As of August 1990, according to the Investor Responsibility Research Center, 759 of 1487, or 51 percent, of large public companies had adopted poison pills.

The Commission largely responded to the hostile tender offers of the 1980s by deferring to the marketplace, state corporate law, or the stock markets, which cumulatively strengthened the defenses available to target corporation's incumbent management. The Commission never sought to preempt even the farthest reaching state tender offer statutes. Similarly, although the Commission was willing to file an *amicus* brief in opposition to the poison pill in the *Moran* case, it was unwilling to campaign for federal legislation to prohibit or discourage the use of this type of defense.[155]

Few takeover defenses were more likely to be successful than dual class capitalization. In one typical dual class capitalization, insiders receive common stock with multiple votes per share; public stockholders receive shares with one vote per share. Dual class capitalization permitted the insiders to control a majority of the votes of a corporation while owning a minority of its stock.

Since 1926, the NYSE had refused to list nonvoting common stock. In July 1986, the NYSE approved a proposal permitting dual class capitalization for corporations whose stock was listed on the Exchange.

The SEC in 1987 proposed Rule 19c-4, which was intended to add to the rules of most of the exchanges and NASD, a prohibition against listing on an exchange or including in Nasdaq the equity securities of an issuer that issued securities or took other corporation action having "the effect of nullifying, restricting or disparately reducing the per share voting rights" of holders of one or more classes of outstanding registered common stock of the issuer. The proposed rule permitted initial public offerings of stock with disparate voting rights or subsequent public offerings of lesser voting stock, as well as the issuance of stock with lesser voting rights in an acquisition. The result would have been that any firm could have a dual class common structure by issuing additional common stock with lesser voting rights or could convert all of its existing common stock into a dual class common structure by first repurchasing stock and then issuing new stock.

Rule 19c-4 was adopted in July 1988. In adopting the rule, the Commission broadened the list of permissible exceptions to the "one common share, one vote" principle. The Commission permitted disparate voting schemes to be established by, among other means:

(1) An initial public offering;
(2) A subsequent issuance of common stock with a *lower* (but not higher) number of votes per share;
(3) Any scheme adopted before the grandfather date of July 7, 1988;
(4) Corporate action taken pursuant to state statute, such as the Indiana statute held constitutional by the Supreme Court in *CTS Corp. v. Dynamics Corp. of America*, that requires a state's domestic corporations to condition the voting rights of a beneficial or record holder of a specified threshold percentage of the corporation's voting stock on approval of the corporation's independent shareholders;
(5) Poison pills.

Rule 19c-4 was promptly vacated by the District of Columbia Court of Appeals as having been issued in excess of the Commission's mandate. The Court of Appeals decision did not, however, prohibit the securities exchanges or the NASD from adopting the equivalent to former Rule 19c-4 as part of their own rules. In 1990, before the District of Columbia Court of Appeals decision, the NYSE effectively did so. Later, with respect to its top tier of securities, the Nasdaq did so as well.[156]

The alternative approach available to the Commission would have been to deny the NYSE's proposed weakening of rule amendments and to seek new legislation to raise the standards of other exchanges and the Nasdaq to a "one common share, one vote" standard. This approach would have been more consistent with the neutrality principle of the Williams Act provisions in the Securities Exchange Act. The most significant result of the Commission's policies in the tender offer area was to weaken the "one common share, one vote" principle.[157]

Market Structure

Securities market structure issues continued to dominate the Commission's agenda. In the period preceding the October 1987

Stock Market Crash, the focus of the Commission was on reducing episodic volatility caused by "triple witching Fridays," when stock options, stock index options, and stock index futures simultaneously expired. The SEC Division of Market Regulation worked with the CFTC and relevant stock, options, and futures markets to encourage development of such remedial measures as: (1) The publication during trading sessions of substantial order imbalances on NYSE stocks to stimulate counterbalancing orders, and (2) the shifting of the expiration of *some* options or futures to the opening rather than the closing of the market, taking advantage of stock opening procedures designed to handle order imbalances and providing the stock market with an entire trading session in which to minimize the impact of any order imbalance.

Although these steps may have reduced volatility on "triple witching Fridays," they were irrelevant to the 508 point or 22.6 percent Stock Market Crash on Black Monday, October 19, 1987. A number of fundamental factors such as rising interest rates, persistent United States trade and budget deficits, and declines in the value of the United States dollar relative to other currencies were in part responsible for the broad stock market price decline between August and October 1987. But the extraordinarily sharp stock price break between October 13 and 20, 1987, also implicated several market mechanisms collectively responsible for extraordinary periods of order imbalances. These included the following: (1) Trading strategies involving stock index futures such as index arbitrage and portfolio insurance that were responsible at various times on October 19 and 20 for significant percentages of NYSE trading volume; (2) the breakdown of linkages among stock, options, and futures markets; (3) the overwhelming of the capacities of stock exchange specialists and over-the-counter dealers to absorb the huge influx of sell orders and provide price continuity, causing many market participants to generate sell orders out of fear or panic because of uncertainty about the accuracy and timeliness of quotation and last sale information, counterparty solvency, credit availability, and concern that entire markets would be closed or substantially disrupted.[158]

The October 19–20, 1987, Market Crash revealed particularly significant operational problems with the DOT system. On those two days, DOT processed 471,513 and 584,992 orders respectively, compared to the September 1987 daily average of 138,600 orders.

The 1987 Presidential Task Force on Market Mechanisms led by Nicholas Brady, soon to be Secretary of Treasury, characterized this situation as a "breakdown of the computerized DOT system because of inadequate capacity," explaining:

> A total of 396 million shares were routed through DOT, but 112 million shares were not executed, of which 92 million were limit orders. Because timely information was scarce, investors did not know if their limit orders had been executed and therefore did not know to set new limits.

According to the Brady Report's analysis, the Dow Jones Industrial Average decline of 300 points in the last hour and 15 minutes on October 19 was in part caused by this market "disconnection."[159]

The October 19, 1987, Stock Market Crash prompted a number of far-reaching regulatory proposals, including:

1. Appointment of a single regulatory agency to coordinate intermarket activities;
2. Transfer of jurisdiction over financial futures from the CFTC to the SEC;
3. Empowerment of the Federal Reserve Board to set margin levels on financial futures as it did on stocks;
4. Abolition of such derivative instruments as financial index futures or index options;
5. Adoption of circuit breakers such as price or volume trading halts, or investor position limits;
6. Creation of a single stock market trading post for trading of baskets of stock underlying index futures or options;
7. Improvements in stock, options, and futures operational systems — including improved program trading reporting;
8. Changes in stock exchange specialist capital and stock allocation rules.
9. Changes in stock exchange short sales rules;
10. Improvements in stock market and futures exchange enforcement of rules against such forms of manipulation as front running; and

11. Further automation of stock, options, and futures exchanges with the ultimate object of creating a national computerized trading system.

Throughout the balance of the 1980s and into the 1990s, the SEC played a significant role in the study and resolution of several of these proposals.

Of particular consequence were the jurisdictional proposals regarding who should regulate stock index futures. Building in part on the premise that "the markets are stocks, stock index futures, and stock options — are in fact one market," the Brady Report, in its most controversial proposal, urged "that one agency must have the authority to coordinate a few but critical intermarket regulatory issues, monitor intermarket activities and mediate intermarket concerns." In making this proposal, the Brady Report distinguished intramarket (within one market) regulatory issues, which it believed should be left to the SEC and CFTC, from intermarket (across markets) issues. "The few important intermarket issues which need to be harmonized by a single body include clearing and credit mechanisms, margin requirements, circuit breaker mechanisms such as price limits and trading halts, and information systems for monitoring intermarket activities." The Report concluded that "the weight of the evidence suggests that the Federal Reserve is well qualified to fill the role of the intermarket agency."

The Brady Report intermarket agency proposal proved short lived. Less than one month after its publication, Federal Reserve Board Chair Alan Greenspan "seriously [questioned] this recommendation:"

> To be effective, an oversight authority must have considerable expertise in the markets subject to regulation, something that the CFTC and SEC have developed over time. Moreover, were the Federal Reserve to be given a dominant role in securities market regulation there could be a presumption by many that the federal safety net applicable to depository institutions was being extended to these markets and the Federal Reserve stood ready to jump in whenever a securities firm or clearing corporation was in difficulty.[160]

The issue of whether the CFTC's jurisdiction over stock index futures should be transferred to the SEC separately occasioned one of the most significant legislative defeats in the SEC's history.

In 1981, the SEC approved proposed rule changes by the Chicago Board Options Exchange (*CBOE*) designed to accommodate trading in options on the Government National Mortgage Association (*GNMA*) or GNMA securities. On petition of the Chicago Board of Trade (*CBOT*), which had traded GNMA *futures* since 1975, the Seventh Circuit Court obviated this rule. The majority held that the SEC was without jurisdiction because of the CFTC statute gratuitously added that GNMA options were not even *securities*, despite the "right to . . . purchase" language of the securities laws' definition.

Against this background, the SEC Chair Shad and CFTC Chair Johnson entered into an agreement to clarify the respective jurisdictional responsibilities of the two agencies pending the enactment of clarifying amendments to the securities and commodities laws.

The agreement left untouched the CFTC's exclusive jurisdiction over commodity futures trading on Boards of Trade in Futures Contracts or Options on Futures Contracts, on securities issued or guaranteed by the United States government, or on other SEC exempted securities.

On the other hand, the agreement recognized the SEC as the sole federal regulator of the securities options market apart from options on futures contracts. In recognition of the SEC's unique responsibilities over the markets for corporate and municipal securities, the two agencies specified certain criteria that were to govern CFTC approval of futures trading in a group or index of such securities, in addition to affording the SEC an opportunity for an oral hearing before the CFTC and judicial review in which to object.

In the Futures Trading Act of 1982, Congress enacted the Shad-Johnson Accord into law, with the refinement that after December 9, 1982, any futures contract on a group or index of securities or options on such contract could be vetoed by the SEC if the SEC found that the contract (1) could not be settled in cash, (2) was readily susceptible to manipulation, or (3) was not reflective of the market or a substantial segment of the market for all publicly traded equity or debt securities. The Seventh Circuit decision concerning CBOE Options in GNMA securities was in effect overruled by this 1982 legislation.[161]

Through the time of the October 1987 Crash, the controversy between the SEC and the CFTC had been largely a legalistic one occasioned by the one sidedness of the exclusive rather than concurrent jurisdiction formula in the 1974 Commodities Futures

Trading Commission Act. The main significance of this formula concerned the question of which agency would regulate new financial instruments.

The October 1987 Crash raised more profound questions about the extent to which trading in financial futures could have an impact on stock market trading.

The essence of this overlap involved program trading strategies. *Program trading* was the term used to describe the acquisition or sale, typically by an institutional investor, of a portfolio of stocks. When this occurred on the NYSE, it usually involved trading through the DOT system, often through the execution of a previously identified list of securities.

Alternatively, an institutional investor might buy an index of stocks to ensure that it did as well as the market as a whole. Index portfolios were less expensive to administer than portfolios that required turnover of individual stocks, since they were assembled by replicating an index such as the Standard & Poor's (*S&P*) 500 and did not require investment advisory fees comparable to that of a portfolio with discretionary turnover. As of May 31, 1987, the value of indexed assets for United States pension funds equaled $187.96 billion, of which $124.07 billion tracked United States equity indexes.

In February 1988, the SEC staff reported that an estimated 25 percent of all institutional trading was accomplished by use of program trades, with list order processing through the DOT system averaging 16.6 million shares in August 1987.[162]

At the time of the October 1987 Crash, the two most common program trading strategies were index arbitrage and portfolio insurance.

Index arbitrage exploited the price differences between a stock index future, such as the S&P 500, and the composite value of the underlying stock. There was usually a differential. For example, on January 27, 1989, the S&P 500 closed at 293.82; the S&P stock index futures for March expiration closed at 296.30. This differential reflected such factors as: (1) The higher transaction costs for the individual stocks than for the S&P stock index futures, (2) the time remaining until expiration of the index, (3) the institution's carrying cost, and (4) the dividends to be paid on the stocks in the index through expiration. An institution could sell a futures contract and buy the underlying stock if the differential exceeded the risk free interest rate to expiration and the transaction costs in the futures minus the dividend yield on the index to expiration.

Portfolio insurance was the term that referred to a number of dynamic hedging strategies to limit losses during a stock market decline. A typical program might insure 95 percent of a current portfolio's value. When a market index such as the S&P 500 declined to a trigger point, a computer would generate an order to sell S&P 500 stock index futures as a technique to insure against further declines. If the market declined further, additional short positions in the S&P 500 future might be taken. Portfolio insurance was not free. The SEC staff reported that the cost of maintaining a minimum of 95 percent of a current portfolio's value "was estimated to be potentially underperforming a rising market by two to four percent." But if an institution was willing to pay that price, it could participate in any market advance net of the cost of the stock index futures and insure a portfolio against broad market declines. Through October 1987, portfolio insurance was one of the fastest growing products among institutional investors; various sources estimated that $60 to $90 billion of equity assets were then under portfolio insurance administration, an estimated fourfold increase during 1987.

The October 1987 Crash revealed problems caused by the popularity of portfolio insurance. Because these programs were meant to insure against market declines by selling futures, they added to sales pressure in the stock market when the price of the stock index futures was being driven down. There was an irony here. Futures stock indexes were then generally preferred to stock transactions because of the greater liquidity of the futures markets. But sales pressure in the stock index futures market rapidly led to dramatic price declines in the futures markets, which in turn led to sales pressure in the stock market because of index arbitrage and direct portfolio insurance stock sales. According to the Brady Report:

> By reasonable estimates, the formulas used by portfolio insurers dictated the sale of $20 to $30 billion of equities over this short time span [October 19-23, 1987]. Under such pressures, prices must fall dramatically. Transaction systems, such as DOT, or market stabilizing mechanisms, such as the NYSE specialists, are bound to be crushed by such selling pressure, however they are designed or capitalized.[163]

From the SEC's point of view, there were significant problems in coordinating with the CFTC to respond to the October 1987 Crash. This belief was not merely parochial. The CFTC acknowledged in its Final Report on the October 1987 Market Break that "interindustry coordination could have been better" on October 19 and 20 concerning whether trading in individual stocks would be halted and whether, as rumored, the entire NYSE would be closed at midday on October 20. These coordination problems were aggravated by what were then stark differences in the regulatory approaches of the two agencies. The CFTC was then perceived as being more free market in nature, while the SEC was seen as more regulatory. This faith inspired the belief of one former United States Senator and many at the SEC that "the Commodity Futures Trading Commission is about as sluggish a regulatory agency as you can find."[164]

In July 1988, the SEC proposed, by a 3-2 vote, amending the federal securities laws and the Commodity Exchange Act to transfer to the SEC the CFTC's jurisdiction over stock index futures and options on stock index futures.

In 1990, the Bush Administration formally proposed legislation to give the SEC jurisdiction over "any and all stock index products." With the CFTC and the oversight Committees in Congress adamantly opposed, this proposal ultimately failed in its original and various compromise forms. Whatever the merits of consolidating all securities and securities derivative trading in a single agency, Congress again was the roadblock. The nation again paid a price for Congressional Committee protectionism in 2007–2009.[165]

In October 1988, the NYSE, the other major stock exchanges, the CBOE, and the two leading financial futures exchanges did adopt a system of coordinated trading halts. "In general," the Commission stated of the trading halts, "the circuit breaker rules provide that trading in all of these markets would halt for one hour if the Dow Jones Industrial Average (*DJIA*) declines 250 points or more from its previous day's closing level and, thereafter, trading would halt for an additional two hours if the DJIA declined 400 points from the previous day's close."[166]

On other issues, the SEC achieved some minor victories. In 1990, Congress enacted the Market Reform Act. This Act enhanced the Commission's ability to suspend trading in emergencies such as that of October 1987 and authorized the Commission to require large traders to report information as a device to give the SEC better warning of the type of rapid intermarket trades that characterized the trading of financial futures index and stock trading.[167]

SEC Enforcement

Ultimately, the effectiveness of the SEC's mandatory disclosure system turns on its enforcement. Enforcement gives the program teeth in the vernacular of the 1930s, by compelling compliance with what otherwise might be viewed as hortatory standards. In the 1980s, the best publicized series of enforcement claims involved a wide variety of fraudulent practices, including insider trading and manipulation alleged against Drexel Burnham Lambert executive Dennis Levine; arbitrageur Ivan Boesky; Michael Milken, Drexel Burnham's most significant trader and the king of junk bonds; and Drexel Burnham itself. In takeover related cases, the SEC Enforcement Division displayed a perseverance and resourcefulness that the Commission as a whole lacked in addressing the policy questions generated by tender offers.

In May 1986, the SEC filed an action against Levine, which alleged that he had illegally earned $12.6 million by trading securities in at least 54 corporations while in possession of material nonpublic information about actual or proposed tender offers or mergers. Levine consented to a permanent injunction against future violations of the federal securities laws and disgorged $11.6 million in illegal profits. He was sentenced to two years in prison.

Levine agreed to testify against Ivan Boesky, who agreed to pay the equivalent of $100 million in cash and assets and was also sentenced to prison. Boesky in turn agreed to testify against Michael Milken, arguably the most influential investment banker of the 1980s. Milken and the firm he helped lead, Drexel Burnham Lambert, ultimately agreed to pay a total of $1.3 billion, part into a fund to settle civil lawsuits and for civil and criminal penalties. Of this amount, Milken personally paid $900 million and served two years in prison. Drexel was obligated to pay the balance and was forced into bankruptcy reorganization.

This series of cases, along with several related actions, went far to create the impression that Wall Street had become a *Den of Thieves*, as a best selling book was entitled.[168] The Levine-Boesky-Milken cases also provided the backdrop for the most enduring consequence of the 1980s enforcement effort, a significant expansion of the Commission's remedial authority.

After the Levine-Boesky-Milken cases persuaded Congress that "[d]espite the stiffer penalties enacted by Congress in 1984, the last few years have seen a dramatic increase in insider trading cases," Congress enacted the Insider Trading and Securities Fraud Enforcement Act of 1988.

The 1988 Act preserved the Commission's ability to seek a civil penalty of up to three times an insider trader's profit gained or loss avoided. The Act also permitted a penalty to be imposed upon a person who controls an insider trader; that penalty was not to exceed the greater of $1 million or three times the insider's profit gained or loss avoided. The Act included a bounty provision authorizing a payment to informers, not to exceed 10 percent of amounts imposed as a civil penalty.

This Enforcement Act added three types of judicial and administrative remedies to the Commission's statutory arsenal: (1) Both the federal courts and the Commission were empowered to award civil monetary penalties for a broad variety of federal securities law violations in addition to insider trading; (2) the Commission was authorized to issue cease and desist orders; and (3) the legislation affirmed the authority of a federal court to bar an individual from serving as an officer or director of a reporting company.[169]

By pushing to expand the boundaries of governmental and private securities law enforcement, the Commission had long risked, and sometimes experienced, a judicial backlash. Rule 10b-5, which once had threatened "to take over the universe gradually," was limited by a series of Supreme Court decisions, beginning in the mid-1970s.

In 1975, the Court held that private standing (the right to bring suit) under Rule 10b-5 was limited to actual buyers or sellers of securities.[170]

The following year the Court held that a private claim for damages under Rule 10b-5 could not be pled in the absence of an allegation of intent to deceive, manipulate, or defraud on the part of the defendant. An allegation of negligence would not suffice.[171]

In 1977, the Court held that a breach of fiduciary duty would not violate Rule 10b-5. There must be proof of fraud.[172]

In 1991, the Supreme Court adopted a one year after discovery of a wrong and a three years after violation statute of limitations for Rule 10b-5 private litigation that, in many instances, shortened the earlier applicable limitations period.[173]

Chairman Arthur Levitt

Between 1993 and 2001, the boom years of the great bull market, Arthur Levitt served as SEC hair. It was a period of near boundless ebullience. Early in his time as chair, Levitt began a speech: "Just before the SEC's creation in 1934, the Dow Jones Industrial Average hit an all time low of 41 points. In 1994, it hit an all-time high of 3978.36." By 1997, he would observe, "[i]n the past 12 months alone, . . . The Dow Jones Industrial Average has broken the 5000, 6000 and 7000 point levels." In 1999, the Dow would reach 11,497.

Arthur Levitt, Jr. brought a strikingly protean background to the Commission. He often stressed the significance of his father, Arthur Levitt, Sr., who served between 1955 and 1978 as New York State Comptroller. One newspaper characterized Levitt's father as "Mr. Integrity." Levitt himself would recognize in an address in New York City: "For some New Yorkers, however, there will always be only ONE Arthur Levitt. No matter what I may achieve in my own life, no matter what esteem I may earn, it will never approach the esteem with which my late father is still remembered in this town — long after his 24 years as New York State Comptroller."

Levitt's own career was more variegated than his father's. He grew up in Crown Heights, a Brooklyn neighborhood across the river from Wall Street, graduating from private Poly Prep High School and in 1952 from Williams College, where he majored in English. After service in the Air Force, he worked from 1954 to 1959 as Assistant Promotion Director for Time, Inc., essentially as a salesman. His career in finance began in 1959 with Kansas City based Oppenheimer Industries selling cattle as tax shelters. "My life changed dramatically," Levitt would recall decades later, "when one of the prospects I called upon, M. Peter Schweitzer, then a top official at Kimberly-Clark, said to me, 'Arthur, if you can sell cows, chances are you'd be good at selling stock.' He told me his son-in-law, Arthur Carter, was starting up a brokerage firm with a group of friends and that they were looking for suitable partners."

In 1963, Levitt joined Carter, Berlind & Weill, initially working as a broker; by 1978, he was president of the successor firm, Shearson Hayden Stone, after mergers with Hayden Stone in 1970, and Shearson Hammill in 1974.

While Sandy Weill achieved greater influence within Shearson, Levitt achieved conspicuous success outside. In 1975, he became a governor of the American Stock Exchange and from 1978–1989, he served as its president. Soft spoken, a consensus builder, Levitt appeared nonideological enough that Republican Ronald Reagan considered him for the position of SEC chair before Democrat Bill Clinton later appointed him.

Levitt was a gifted public speaker, who could be thoughtful and witty, and take a broad view of major public topics, but whose views did not easily fit into a predictable pattern. In his SEC memoir, Levitt would recall a 1972 speech, Profits and Professionalism, which he delivered "over my partners' protests" calling on the securities industry to pay brokers "on the returns their clients received" rather than on the basis of commissions. More typical of his pre-SEC addresses would be remarks he delivered as SEC chair in 1995:

> I came to the Commission after a long career in business, most of it in the industry I now regulate. That experience has inevitably shaped my views and priorities. . . .
>
> Regulation can be a blunt instrument, with unintended consequences. Wall Street is a free market, and we prefer to use market forces.
>
> We'll regulate where warranted — but it's my strong belief that a call for legislation or rulemaking should be only a last resort to the kinds of consensus actions that have characterized our approach to the industry.

At his most extreme, Levitt would observe: "Every time we create a regulation, somewhere deep inside of me, I feel diminished."

Levitt during this period also strongly disagreed that "there is nothing inherently wrong with insider trading. . . . [I]nsider trading undermines the faith investors have in the fairness of our capital markets. Without that faith, they will hesitate to participate and the entire system will weaken."

At Levitt's most eloquent, he would inform the NASD: "Yours is an honorable profession. At his best, a broker is much more than a salesman — he's a trained and talented professional who performs a vital service." This was surely Levitt's self-image.

During his years as chair, Levitt changed. He arrived at the SEC not viewing himself as a reformer. Levitt spent much time reaching out to corporate and securities leaders, in part to avoid being captured by the SEC's career staff, which he initially viewed as too responsive to congressional overseers lead by Democrats John Dingell and Ed Markey. In Levitt's office was a palace guard of talented associates hired partly from outside the SEC and partly retaining key members of his predecessor Chairman Breeden's staff. But Levitt, the establishmentarian who wore a Patek-Philippe watch and owned a yacht, who, on occasion would quote Thucydides complaining about the "deterioration of character throughout the Greek world" hardened, became more driven, more confrontational. In part, the change was a reaction to the 1994 Republican congressional election victories. Levitt, by nature was a centrist, a balancer, a man with an innate sense that reasonable people could find reasonable solutions to difficult problems. But he also was a man who loved a fight and was highly competitive. When the Republican Party secured control of both Houses of Congress in 1994 for the first time in 48 years, Levitt's SEC confronted the most hostile legislative majority that the Commission had faced since the early 1950s. The 1994 Republican campaign "Contract with America" targeted burdensome securities laws in one of its 10 planks.

Before the 1994 election, Levitt often asserted that "[t]he first priority of the SEC is to protect the individual investor." After 1994, putting the investors first resonated differently in a more shrilly partisan political climate. Levitt would quote SEC Chair William O. Douglas, by then a liberal icon, on the cover of the SEC 1999 Annual Report, "We are the investor's advocate," and dedicate the Commission's Public Meeting Room to Douglas, where these words would be embossed in glass. Levitt toughened on defense.[174]

A core issue during the Levitt chairmanship was resources. During the first Bush administration, 1989–1993, the Commission budget grew from $142.6 million to $253.2 million, an average of 19 percent per year; its staff from 2604 positions to 3083, or an average of 4.6 percent per year.

Growth during the Levitt chairmanship was considerably slower. Between 1993 and 2000 the SEC budget grew from $253.2 million to $382.4 million or an average of 6 percent per year. Staff positions grew from 2940 to 3235 or an average of 1.4 percent per year. During the 1990s bull market, virtually every significant measure of securities activity grew far faster. Between 1993 and 2000, the dollar value of securities filed for registration grew from $868 billion to $2.3 trillion, an average increase of 24 percent per year; the number of underwritten securities offerings more than doubled in the shorter period of 1993 to 1999, increasing from 6443 to 13,923. Similarly, the dollar value of investment companies grew from $2.4 trillion in 1993 to $7 trillion in 2001, an average annual increase of 24 percent per year; the number of investment company portfolios grew from 21,200 to 34,312 during the same period, an annual average increase of 7.8 percent per year. In the 1992 calendar year, the SEC supervised 8200 broker-dealers with 34,000 branch offices and 427,000 registered representatives. By 2001, the number of registered broker-dealers had declined to 7900, but the number of branch offices had increased to 87,765, an average annual increase of 17.6 percent, and the number of registered representatives grew to 683,230, an average annual increase of 6.7 percent. The value of stock listed on all exchanges approximately tripled between 1992 and 2000, increasing from $3.97 to $11.73 trillion.

Throughout this period fees collected by the SEC far exceeded its annual appropriations. In 1993, total fee collections of $517 million represented 204 percent of the SEC's appropriated spending authority of $253 million. By 2001, the SEC deposited $2.06 billion in the United States Treasury or 539 percent of the Commission's $382.4 million budget.[175]

Neither the Clinton administration nor Congress gave the SEC adequate new budgetary or staff support during Levitt's time as chair.

As a general matter, the Clinton White House was little concerned with the SEC. With the exception of the Gramm-Leach-Bliley Act of 1999, which primarily addressed banks, the Clinton White House exhibited little interest in securities legislation. To be sure, the Clinton White House rarely questioned an SEC decision during Levitt's time as chair. But what the Clinton administration appeared most to want was an SEC sufficiently well run that it would not require White House attention. Only once, near the end of Clinton's term, did Levitt meet privately with Clinton. Levitt did not meet Clinton alone before being nominated and had relatively few contacts with White House staff during his years at the SEC. Significantly, he possessed a veto over the SEC commissioner appointments or reappointments, but Levitt had no demonstrated ability to initiate a nomination.

Before Levitt was confirmed, President Clinton's 1994 budget called for a reduction of 42 positions in the Commission budget. With a few exceptions, Clinton's appointments to the SEC, other than Levitt, were undistinguished, often appointed for transparently political reasons, rather than qualification to be a Commissioner. For sustained periods during the Clinton administration only two or three Commissioners in fact were in office. In 1995, the Commission took the unprecedented step of adopting a Quorum Rule to provide that if the number of Commissioners in office was as few as two or one, that number would be sufficient for a quorum.

In November 1993, Levitt testified in favor of self-funding as a means to resolve the problem of insufficient staff: "To ensure that the Commission has adequate resources it must be self-funded. Under a self-funding arrangement known as full cost recovery, the Commission would be authorized to use filing and transaction fee collections to fund all agency operations instead of using annual appropriated funds." Congress was unwilling to give up the purse strings.

After the 1994 congressional elections, budget appropriations for the Commission became more difficult. Soon after the new Congress was convened an effort was led by the Senate Congressional Affairs Committee to halt the effectiveness of all new federal rules, including SEC rules, adopted between November 9, 1994, and June 30, 1995.

Levitt attempted to defuse the deregulatory enthusiasm by appointing Phillip K. Howard, author of a book critical of federal regulation entitled *The Death of Common Sense* and a lawyer with securities law experience, to chair a Commission Task Force on Disclosure Simplification. In 1996, this Task Force recommended the elimination of a total of 81 Commission rules and 22 forms, as well as the modification of dozens of others.

In 1996 and 1997, the Commission adopted several Task Force recommendations. Cumulatively the changes that the Commission made eliminated or modified a number of marginal aspects of the integrated disclosure system. The basic system remained largely intact. But the political implication of this Task Force was clear. The Commission would have to backpedal by administrative action to reduce the likelihood of more deregulatory legislation. Levitt's business background made the backpedaling appear less contrived to those favoring deregulation.[176]

This type of initiative may have strengthened Levitt's hand in what was a particularly difficult budget cycle. In September 1995, the Senate Appropriations Committee approved a bill cutting the

Commission's budget by 20 percent to $237 million for FY 1996, after the full House had adopted a bill to freeze the Commission budget at $297 million.

The Commission did receive an FY 1996 budget of $301 million, including $4 million in prior year carryover funds, with no increase in staff positions. For FY 1997, Levitt began his budget testimony by wistfully noting that when the Commission had last submitted an authorization request in June 1994 covering FY 1995–1997, the Agency had sought $382.7 million for FY 1997. In February 1996, Levitt sought an authorization of $317 million for FY 1997, which, in May 1996, Levitt testified that the president requested be reduced to $308.2 million as part of a no growth budget. Congress approved $305.4 million for FY 1997, which, when combined with prior year carryover funds of $5.7 million, equaled $311.1 million, and again meant no increase in staff.

To achieve this funding level, Levitt characterized the SEC as "reinvent[ing] itself," continually [searching] out new ways of regulating more effectively but less intrusively, and at a lower cost to industry and investors." Among other steps, the Commission raised the total asset threshold for registrants to be subject to the Securities Exchange Act from $5 million to $10 million, reducing the number of companies subject to the registration requirements of that Act.

For 1998 fiscal year, President Clinton again directed the SEC to seek a no growth budget with respect to staffing levels and a $12 million larger appropriation overall, most of which "would go to mandatory increases in pay and related personnel benefits." For the fourth consecutive year, Congress froze staff positions.

The Clinton FY 1999 budget request sought an increase of $26.1 million and 30 new staff positions above the SEC's 1998 appropriation. Congress ultimately approved a budget that added 62 positions and $36 million to the 1999 appropriation.[177]

In retrospect, it is clear that the 1999 fiscal year increase was too little, too late. As early as 1998, newspapers were publishing articles with headlines such as "SEC Turnover Rate Leaves Agency Scrambling in Fight against Fraud." Or as a May 1998, article put it: "Ten Things the SEC Won't Tell You: Number 1: 'We're Overwhelmed.' " In 1998, in a move unprecedented at the Commission, a growing number of staff began to explore unionization as a response to increase uncompensated extra hours, known as donated time and low pay. By a greater than two to one votes cast, unionization was approved in 2000 for 1800 non-management SEC lawyers, accountants, and support workers.

President Clinton and Congress supported a staff increase in the 2000 FY of 134 positions (4.2 percent) and a budget increase of $26.3 million. In 2001, Clinton and Congress supported a staff increase of 50 positions (1.5 percent) and a budget increase of $44.9 million.

Levitt repeatedly testified to the urgency of a considerably broader effort to staunch the growing inability of the Commission to effectively perform its core functions. In February 2000, Levitt asserted: "The SEC is in the midst of a serious staffing crisis. In the last two years, the Commission has lost 25% of its attorneys, accountants and examiners." After detailing threats to "our ability to oversee the nation's securities markets and to respond in a timely manner to the changing events . . . in our markets," Levitt urged that SEC salary levels should be at the same levels as those in the banking regulatory agencies such as the Federal Reserve, the Office of the Comptroller of the Currency, and the Federal Deposit Insurance Corporation, popularly known as pay parity, a salary increase of roughly 29 to 34 percent. In Levitt's view, pay parity would improve staff morale and lengthen the service time of the most talented entry level staff to "a minimum of three to five years."[178]

What was most significant about the growing imbalance in staff relative to its workload was that it undermined some core functions of the Commission, such as review of corporate issuer annual reports by the Division of Corporation Finance more severely than it reduced the effectiveness of the Commission to pursue new initiatives.

Throughout Levitt's time as Chair, the number of enforcement actions rose, averaging 489 enforcement actions initiated per year between 1994 and 2001, compared with 359 per year averaged between 1990 and 1993. Particular attention was devoted to microcap or penny stock fraud and day trading abuses as well as traditional areas such as unregistered securities, financial fraud, and insider trading. To Levitt a vigorous enforcement program "was more interesting as an emotional and intellectual challenge than a complex rule."

With approximately 3000 staff throughout the Levitt chairmanship, the Commission had the capacity to address effectively many of the burgeoning securities industry's regulatory challenges. But it was spread thin and increasingly so in the last years of the Levitt chairmanship. In October 2002, a Staff Report of the Senate Governmental Affairs Committee found that in FY 2001 the Division of Corporation Finance was able to complete a full review of only 2280 of 14,600 Form 10-K Annual Reports filed by public companies, roughly 16 percent, far short of the Division's stated goal to review every company's annual report at least once every three years. "Of more than 17,300 public companies, approximately 9200, or 53%, have not had their Form 10-Ks reviewed in the past three years." Enron, the most notorious example of staff neglect, had last received a partial review of its Form 10-K Annual Report in 1997 and had been last subject to a full review in 1991.[179]

The Pay-to-Play Rules

Soon after confirmation, Levitt supported a campaign to end pay-to-play practices involving the municipal bond dealers and bond counsel who were the attorneys who provided legal opinions in municipal bond offerings. Levitt's efforts had a long historical background. In 1933, Congressman Rayburn had supported an exemption for municipal securities from the Securities Bill to preserve political support for what became the Securities Act of 1933. After the New York City bond crisis nearly led to that City's default in 1974–1975, Congress amended the Securities Exchange Act to create the Municipal Securities Rulemaking Board (*MSRB*), as a self-regulatory organization to oversee municipal securities dealers. The subsequent default by the Washington Public Power Supply System after expending $2.25 billion to construct two nuclear power plants led to the SEC approving an MSRB rule to require the mandatory filing of Municipal Offering Statements and to adopt Rule 15c2-12, which required specified municipal securities underwriters to obtain and evaluate municipal offerings statements.

By the time Levitt began his chairmanship, the municipal securities market had substantially grown. A 1994 SEC Release reported: "There are approximately 1.3 million municipal securities issues outstanding, representing over $1.2 trillion in securities. In 1993, 17,000 new issues took place with a record value of $335 billion." It was also increasingly a market tarnished by questionable payments. The Commission explained:

> There have been numerous reported instances where registered municipal securities dealers, their employees, and related parties, allegedly have made payments, political contributions, or entered into business ventures with political figures apparently to obtain the underwriting business of municipal securities issuers. Specific abuses have been alleged in several state and local governments, including Alabama, California, Colorado, the District of Columbia, Florida, Illinois, Kentucky, Massachusetts, Michigan, New Jersey, New York, Ohio, Oklahoma, and Wisconsin.[180]

An SEC Staff Report on the Municipal Securities Market stressed as its first "significant [area] where improvements can be made": "[I]nappropriate political contributions and other forms of influence peddling practices by municipal broker-dealers to obtain underwriting business."

After revision in December, MSRB Rule G-37 was adopted in April 1994. Rule G-37 prohibited brokers, dealers, and municipal dealers from engaging in municipal securities business with an issuer within two years after a contribution to an official of the issuer made by (i) the dealer, (ii) any associated municipal finance professional, or (iii) any political action committee controlled by a dealer or any municipal finance professional. A constitutional law challenge to Rule G-37, primarily on First Amendment grounds, failed in 1995.[181]

In March 1995, Levitt publicly announced "the next stage of [the] initiative: How to prevent lawyers and lobbyists from acting as surrogates for firms and making contributions on their behalf."

As the SEC moved its focus to the American Bar Association (*ABA*) which adopted the profession's Model Rules of Professional Responsibility, the intensity of opposition mounted.

In 1999, the ABA Standing Committee on Ethics and Professional Responsibility proposed a Model Rule to prohibit a lawyer or law firm from accepting a government legal engagement or judicial appointment "if the lawyer or law firm makes a political contribution or solicits political contributions for the purpose of obtaining or being considered for that type of legal engagement or appointment."

Then, stunningly, at its 1999 House of Delegates Meeting the ABA declined by a vote of 164–146 to adopt the Model Rule, only to reverse course a few months later and in February 2000 adopt the rule by a vote of 266–157. This culminated a four-year roller coaster ride, ultimately won in part because of Levitt's perseverance and his ability to work with some leaders of the legal profession to build a coalition. Victory was not without cost. Levitt believed that the ABA Rule was "symbolic" — "this was the least they could do, what they did was to get the votes." The length of time necessary to adopt the Lawyer's Pay-to-Play Rule extended so late into the Levitt chairmanship that the Commission was not able to extend pay-to-play restrictions to investment advisers.[182]

Regulation FD

Late in his chairmanship, Levitt took on what became known as Regulation FD, an important new disclosure requirement. Enforcement actions against insider trading had been emphasized in the Commission since the Cary Commission decided the *Cady, Roberts* matter in 1961. In 1980, the Supreme Court had rejected a "parity of information" approach in *Chiarella v. United States.* Instead the Court held that there must be a breach of fiduciary or other relationship of trust and confidence before § 10(b) and Rule 10b-5 of the Securities Exchange Act would hold an insider liable for illegal trading.

Three years later, in *Dirks v. SEC,* the Supreme Court focused on the "tipping" or providing of material nonpublic information by an insider to an outsider. Following *Chiarella* the Court held in *Dirks* that an outsider such as an investment analyst is only prohibited from trading when information has been provided improperly in breach of a fiduciary duty. The Supreme Court delineated as criteria to determine whether a breach of fiduciary duty had occurred: "[w]hether the insider receives a direct or indirect personal benefit from the disclosure, such as a pecuniary gain or a reputational benefit that will translate into future earnings."

While the *Dirks* decision had the virtue of leaving room for investment analysts to "ferret out and analyze information," it had two fundamental flaws. First, a violation of its tipper-tippee breach of fiduciary duty theory often was impossible to prove, as the Supreme Court recognized in 1997 in *United States v. O'Hagan.*

O'Hagan adopted an alternative misappropriation liability theory under which a person could be held liable for misappropriating confidential information for securities trading in breach of a fiduciary duty owed to the source of information. "In lieu of premising liability on a fiduciary relationship between company insider and purchaser or seller of the company's stock, the misappropriation theory premises liability on a fiduciary-turned-trader's deception of those who entrusted him with access to confidential information."

O'Hagan made it easier to prove a breach of fiduciary duty, but it left unaddressed a second result of *Chiarella* and *Dirks*. In the absence of a breach of a fiduciary duty, insiders and privileged outsiders were permitted to trade earlier on the basis of disclosed information than other investors. The most common way that unequal disclosure could occur was popularly known as selective disclosure. A corporation with good or bad news could provide it to brokerage firm or institutional investor investment analysts, who could trade or recommend trades before the information was generally disclosed to the public.

To Levitt, " '[s]elective disclosure' had gotten out of hand in the 1990s and put small investors at a disadvantage to the analysts, brokers, and institutional investors who were routinely getting advance information on corporate earnings ahead of the rest of the market. That was wrong, plain and simple."

An internal review led by General Counsel Harvey Goldschmid concluded with skepticism that the Supreme Court would be willing to stretch the *Dirks* tipper-tippee theory to cover selective disclosure when it was uncertain that corporate insiders personally had received a "pecuniary gain or reputational benefit."

Goldschmid proposed a new regulation be based on federal securities laws that authorize the Commission to regulate communications between public companies and the marketplace. "If the SEC can require companies to reveal material information in SEC filings or a prospectus prior to a stock offering, or to observe a 'quiet period' for 25 days after an offering, then why not require them to disclose important information to all shareholders simultaneously?"[183]

In 1998, the Commission proposed Regulation FD (for *Fair Disclosure*). The Proposal Release emphasized the inequity of selective disclosure: "As a recent academic study indicated, selective disclosure has the immediate effect of enabling those privy to the information to make a quick profit (or quickly minimize losses) by trading before the information is disseminated to the public."

Proposed Regulation FD sought "to the maximum extent practicable" to require an issuer or any person acting on its behalf that intentionally disclosed material nonpublic information to do so to the public through such means as a press release.

The Regulation FD Proposal Release prompted intense criticism. The Commission received 6000 comment letters, the largest number in its history. Comments from the securities industry were almost uniformly negative. The securities industry stressed the chill factor: Fear of liability would cause corporate issuers to stifle the free flow of information.

The August 2000 Adoption Release narrowed Regulation FD to avoid a chilling effect on issuer disclosure:

> First, we have narrowed the scope of the regulation so that it does not apply to *all* communications with persons outside the issuer. The regulation will apply only to communications to securities market professionals and to any holder of the issuer's securities under circumstances in which it is reasonably foreseeable that the security holder will trade on the basis of the information.
>
> Second, we have narrowed the types of issuer personnel covered by the regulation to senior officials and those persons who regularly communicate with securities market professionals or with security holders. The effect of these first two changes is that Regulation FD will not apply to a variety of legitimate, ordinary course business communications or to disclosures to the media.
>
> Third, to remove any doubt that private liability will not result from a Regulation FD violation, we have revised Regulation FD to make absolutely clear that it does not establish a duty for purposes of [the basic fraud] Rule 10b-5 under the Securities Exchange Act of 1934. The regulation now includes an express provision in the text stating that a failure to make a disclosure required solely by Regulation FD will not result in a violation of Rule 10b-5.

Regulation FD required the issuer or any person acting on its behalf who privately disclosed material nonpublic information simultaneously to publicly disclose the information in the case of an intentional disclosure and promptly to do so in the case of a nonintentional disclosure. Regulation FD exempted disclosures to attorneys, investment banks, and accountants when they "owe a duty of trust or confidence to the issuer," to any other person "who expressly agrees to maintain the discussed information in private," to credit rating agencies, and in connection with most securities offerings under the Securities Act of 1933.

To Levitt, Regulation FD was a successful "experience in democracy" achieved because of information technology advances: "Thanks to a combination of Reg FD and technology, investors are benefitting from an information bonanza. The Internet makes it easy for companies to offer live broadcasts of analyst conference calls and quarterly earnings announcements. The beauty of such webcasting is that it's convenient and inexpensive."[184]

Legislation Under Chairman Levitt

Much of Levitt's chairmanship was spent attempting to defuse far reaching proposals for new legislation that were ultimately enacted by Congress in 1995, 1996, and 1999.

The Private Securities Litigation Reform Act of 1995 was the first of this series of generally hostile laws. Levitt's own approach to litigation reform attempted to find a middle ground, both in the public debate and within the Commission. At times, Levitt and the SEC as an institution would appear indecisive or as if they were sending mixed signals. The self-confidence and leadership that Levitt provided on many other issues was often absent on the 1995 Act. The enactment of the 1995 Act would mark a low point in Levitt's relationship with Congress.

The class action was the key to private securities litigation. Beginning with a $5.3 million settlement in a 1963 Securities Act case, the device had grown dramatically in frequency of use and size of settlement or award, reaching an apogee late in the 1980s. Indeed, per an iron law of unintended consequences, the single decision that inspired the most significant threat to private enforcement of the federal securities laws was a 1988 decision that a private plaintiff won. In *Basic, Inc. v. Levinson*, a divided United States Supreme Court held that plaintiffs in a class action did not individually have to prove that they relied on a false statement. Instead, reliance would normally be presumed by dint of the fraud on the market theory. As one court explained: "The fraud on the market theory is based on the hypothesis that, in an open and developed securities market, the price of a company's stock is determined by the available material information regarding the company and its business.... Misleading statements will therefore defraud purchasers of stock even if the purchasers do not directly rely on the misstatements." A credible false favorable statement normally will cause a stock's price to rise. An investor may not have read the statement but will rely on it by paying the higher price for the shares.

By eliminating the need to prove that each member of a class of federal securities plaintiffs individually had relied on a false statement, the *Basic* decision facilitated the formation of larger plaintiff classes and larger damages assessments against defendants, notably the more than $700 million recovered in the Washington Public Power Supply Service litigation late in the 1980s.[185]

In January 1994, Levitt delivered a major address in San Diego, entitled Private Litigation under the Federal Securities Laws. While he sought to find a middle ground on a contentious issue, his remarks struck some odd themes for a chair who asserted that he valued investor protection above all else:

> A litigation system imposes tremendous unnecessary costs when it is abused by investors or their attorneys. Our challenge is to find ways to minimize its costs while preserving the rights of defrauded investors.

Levitt specifically endorsed limited legislative reforms to permit shifting the cost of a defendant's attorneys' fees when a case was brought without any substantial basis in fact or law and to prevent law firms from using professional plaintiffs or otherwise maintaining an inventory of shareholders to serve as nominal plaintiffs in class action filings. In April 1994, he subsequently pared down his fee shifting proposal and urged that it should be consistent with the already existing mechanism for such assessments in the Federal Rules of Civil Procedure.

At this point, the United States Supreme Court implicitly weighted in on the side of those who sought to limit the securities class action and held on a 5-4 vote in *Central Bank of Denver, N.A. v. First Interstate Bank of Denver, N.A.* that a private plaintiff could not maintain an aiding and abetting lawsuit under Rule 10b-5 against parties who knowingly provided substantial assistance to a securities fraud such as an accountant or an attorney, reversing several Court of Appeals decisions.[186]

After the Republican party gained control of both houses of Congress in the 1994 elections, the movement for private securities litigation reform rapidly accelerated. An earlier debate about empirical evidence was succeeded by the triumphant certitude of an ideological majority.

On January 4, 1995, the Common Sense Legal Reforms Act of 1995, was introduced in the House, with five sponsors and 115 co-sponsors. Had this bill been enacted in its original form, the securities class action would have all but ended. The bill:

- Adopted the English Rule for private securities actions, requiring a losing party to pay the prevailing party's reasonable attorneys' fees and other expenses.
- Required a plaintiff to plead and prove actual knowledge of a wrong and intent to deceive to prevail under Section 10(b), rather than various forms of recklessness, as was then enforced in virtually all federal circuits.
- Established new pleading requirements for scienter or fault which, in most cases, would be difficult if not impossible to meet ("allege specific facts demonstrating the state of mind of each defendant at the time the alleged violation occurred").
- Required that a plaintiff allege and prove actual reliance to establish either a material misrepresentation or material omission. Not only would this reverse *Basic, Inc. v. Levinson* for material misrepresentations where reliance normally was presumed by dint of the fraud on the market doctrine, but it would have created the extraordinary burden for a plaintiff to prove that he or she actually relied on an omission.

Levitt on February 10, 1995 testified against the initial H.R. 10, stating in part:

> The Commission opposes a move to the more drastic measures that have been proposed, however, such as imposing automatic fee shifting under a strict "English Rule," eliminating antifraud liability based on reckless conduct, and eliminating the fraud on the market theory of liability. Proposals such as these, by severely limiting the private remedy against fraud and undermining the incentives for market participants to comply with the disclosure laws, could fundamentally damage the integrity and discipline of our capital markets, which are now the strongest and safest in the world.[187]

On February 10, 1995, Representative Jack Fields, Chair of the House Subcommittee on Telecommunications and Finance, announced a bipartisan agreement, initially engineered with then Democratic Representative W.J. "Billy" Tauzin, which resulted in modification of the losers pay, culpability, and fraud on the market proposals in the original bill.

After markup in the House Subcommittee on Telecommunications and Finance and the Committee on Commerce, the Securities Litigation Reform Act was reported to the full House on February 24, 1995. In this form, the bill would have amended the Securities Exchange Act to:

- Authorize fees and expenses by the prevailing party, if the court determined that: "(A) the position of the losing party was not substantially justified, (B) imposing fees and expenses on the losing party or the losing party's attorney would be just, and (C) the cost of such fees and expenses to the prevailing party is substantially burdensome or unjust."
- Require explicit pleading of fault ("It shall not be sufficient for this purpose to plead the mere presence of facts inconsistent with a statement or omission alleged to have been misleading").
- Require proof of reliance and causation for any misstatement or omission, but also allow reliance to be proven by the fraud on the market presumption if "the issuer of the security has a class of securities listed and registered on a national securities exchange or quoted on the automated quotation system of a national securities association."
- Create a safe harbor for the publication of forward-looking statements.
- Stay discovery during consideration of a motion to dismiss a complaint that may include statements within the safe harbor for forward-looking statements.

The House Committee on Commerce urged the case for these far reaching proposals:

> Today, our litigation system allows, indeed encourages, abusive "strike suits".... Strike lawsuits are lawsuits filed by class

> action attorneys on behalf of shareholders whose once attractive stock purchases have failed to live up to their expectations. Volatile stock prices, rapid product development, and technological changes make growing companies a target. As a result, high technology, biotechnology, and other growth companies are hardest hit.[188]

After debate on the House floor and modest amendments, the bill was enacted by the full House by a vote of 325-99 on March 8, 1995.[189]

In June 1995, the Senate enacted a counterpart Securities Bill by a vote of 70-29. The Senate bill was most significantly different than the House adopted bill because the Senate bill would:

- Add new procedures for the appointment as lead plaintiff of the member or members most capable of adequately representing the plaintiff class. This statute would include a presumption that the most adequate plaintiff is the one who has the largest financial interest in the relief sought by the class.
- Require imposition of mandatory sanctions under the Federal Rules of Civil Procedure when the court makes a finding that that rule had been violated.
- Add less demanding pleading requirements under the 1934 Act for claims alleging material misrepresentations or omissions.
- Add a statutory basis for aiding and abetting liability for Commission — but not private — actions under the 1934 Act.[190]

The lead plaintiff procedure in the Senate bill was inspired by a law review article by Elliot Weiss and John Beckerman, *Let the Money Do the Monitoring: How Institutional Investors Can Reduce Agency Costs in Securities Class Actions*. To deter the problems associated with the then common practice of usually appointing as lead counsel the lawyer who filed the first complaint, Weiss and Beckerman proposed that the investors (normally institutional investors) with the largest stakes should serve as lead plaintiffs.

The lead plaintiff provision was far less draconian than the losers' pay approach to attorneys' fees.[191]

Only in December 1995, six months after the Senate had adopted S. 240, was a Conference Committee appointed to reconcile the two versions of the Private Securities Litigation Reform Act. The Conference Report was somewhat unique, in that much of the statutory language was negotiated with the SEC, but the accompanying Statement of the Managers was not. The ultimate Act involved a considerable improvement over the original version of the bill introduced in January 1995. The Managers' Statement, in contrast, reflected the same fire breathing mood as the Report accompanying the earlier House bill.

Frustration with the Managers' Statement may have contributed to the odd denouement of the legislative process. After the House enacted the Conference Committee Bill by a vote of 320-102, and the Senate by a 65-30 vote, President Clinton vetoed the Act, principally because he found that "the pleading requirements of the Conference Report with regard to a defendant's state of mind impose an unacceptable procedural hurdle to meritorious claims," only to have the veto overridden by both Houses of Congress, and H.R. 1058 became law. This was the first time a Clinton veto had been overridden.[192]

Be that as it may, the Private Securities Litigation Reform Act of 1995 enacted amendments to the Securities Act of 1933 and to the Securities Exchange Act of 1934 that required the procedure for appointment of lead plaintiffs in class actions originated by the Weiss and Beckerman article.

The 1995 Act included a novel version of attorney fee shifting that included a presumption in favor of shifting of attorneys' fees and costs when a party or attorney violated any requirement of the relevant Federal Rule of Civil Procedure.

Congress adopted far reaching pleading requirements that reached each private complaint that alleged a defendant had "omitted to state a material fact necessary in order to make the statements made, in the light of the circumstances in which they were made, not misleading; the complaint shall specify each statement alleged to have been misleading, the reason or reasons why the statement is misleading, and, if an allegation regarding the statement or omission is made on information and belief, the complaint shall state with particularity all facts on which that belief is formed."

A great achievement of the earlier adopted Federal Rules of Civil Procedure had been to establish simplified notice pleading as the norm for initiating a lawsuit. The Private Securities Litigation Reform Act enshrined new more prolix pleading standards that had the practical effect of further reducing securities trials on the merits, which already were scarce, and substituting a dispute resolution system almost entirely comprised of pretrial motions and settlements.

The defendant was given a safe harbor in the Securities Act and Securities Exchange Act even when he or she could not offer and prove sufficient meaningful cautionary statements because the plaintiff was still required to prove a higher fault standard of actual knowledge rather than the lower recklessness or negligence standards available earlier under the federal securities laws' antifraud provisions.

This was not so much a safe harbor as a safe ocean. Before, a plaintiff who could prove that a defendant had been reckless in preparing an earnings projection or other forward looking statement could bring a case and initiate discovery. After the 1995 Act, the plaintiff had to establish that the defendant had actual knowledge of a false projection before filing a lawsuit.

The Commission won a victory when its power to prosecute persons for aiding and abetting was restored in the Securities Exchange Act.

What was most troublesome about the 1995 Reform Act was that the complexity and unevenness of the evidence of these abuses was neither acknowledged nor fully examined. The tone, particularly of the Managers Statement, was regrettable for its one sidedness.

The performance by Levitt and the Clinton White House was also uneven. Levitt's early statements, especially his January 1994, address in San Diego, were supportive of restrictive litigation legislation. While the restrictions that Levitt supported were limited and accompanied by pro-plaintiff provisions such as a restoration of aiding and abetting and an extension of the statute of limitations, Levitt had broken with a long tradition of SEC support for private litigation to augment the Commission's own enforcement efforts.

There was poor coordination with the White House. More effective lobbying by the White House before or long after the June 1995 Senate vote might have resulted in a bill whose veto could have been sustained or a less far reaching new law. The White House was divided.

Levitt did meet on several occasions with General Counsel Abner Mikva, who was sympathetic to Levitt's position. Others in the White House were less sympathetic. When Levitt made a deal, in November 1995, to accept a safe harbor for forward-looking statements, the White House remained mute. Only at the last moment did Clinton veto the bill on thoroughly plausible grounds, but there was little or no follow through in terms of White House lobbying and the veto was overridden. Clinton did not speak to Levitt before the veto.[193]

Further evidence of the limited ability of the Levitt SEC or President Clinton to resist pressure for limitations on shareholder litigation occurred in 1998. When an increased number of class actions were brought in state court after the 1995 Act, both Clinton and Levitt supported the Securities Litigation Uniform Standards Act of 1998, whose purpose was to prevent state private securities class actions "from being used to frustrate the operation and goals of the [Private Securities Litigation Reform Act of 1995]."

The 1998 Act was a narrowly focused law that retained traditional state law rights and remedies but prohibited specified state securities class actions. In contrast to the 1995 Act, the 1998 Act reflected more disciplined legislative advocacy by the SEC. The Commission succeeded in securing a joint letter from Senators Dodd [D-CT] and D'Amato [R-NY] that the 1995 Act had not been intended to eliminate recklessness as a basis of liability under Rule 10b-5 or to change the Second Circuit pleading standard. The managers of the House version of the 1998 Act agreed: "It is the clear understanding of the managers that Congress did not, in adopting the [1995] Reform Act intend[] to alter the standards of liability under the [1934 Securities] Exchange Act."[194]

Levitt exhibited greater success in domesticating Congressman Jack Fields' [R-TX] July 1995 proposal for a Capital Market Deregulation and Liberalization Act. Fields, the Chair of the House Telecommunications and Finance Subcommittee, sought "the most sweeping reform of securities laws in the past 40 years." Among its many provisions, the initial Fields Bill would have preempted most state requirements with respect to securities registration, broker-dealer registration and regulation, and investment company and investment adviser regulation. In the Fields Bill, as introduced, the states generally would have been limited to receiving notice of federal filings and collecting fees for certain securities registrations, enforcing state antifraud provisions, and registering broker-dealers, their agents, investment advisers, and their representatives through a centralized registration system. This would have significantly reduced the concurrent securities regulatory system that had existed in the United States since 1933.[195]

Levitt responded to the initial Fields Bill, which he considered "outrageous," with dexterity. Rather than categorically reject the Fields Bill, he urged in an October 1995 speech to the state securities administrators' organization, North American Securities Administration Association or *NASAA*, a "middle ground," with "coordination and cooperation" in six areas: investment advisers; investment companies; registration of brokers; examination of broker-dealers; registration of corporate securities; and enforcement authority.[196]

A less contentious Securities Investor Protection Act of 1996 subsequently moved through the Senate. The bill from the start had bipartisan sponsors, notably Republican Senators D'Amato and Gramm [R-TX], and Democratic Senator Dodd. The bill included detailed revisions of the Investment Company Act, "[m]any," Levitt testified, "of these changes were proposed in the Commission Staff Study on the Investment Company Act." Most significantly, the Senate bill built on a Senator Gramm proposal that called for division of investment advisor regulation, generally with all investment advisers with $25 million or less under management exclusively subject to state law and those with more exclusively subject to federal law.

With a few other bells and whistles, most notably a reduction in SEC fees, the law, ultimately grandly styled, the National Securities Markets Improvement Act of 1996 (*NSMIA*), was enacted late in September 1996.

NSMIA was most significant for its partial preemption of state law in the securities offering and shareholder report areas. Under the amended federal Securities Act of 1933, no state statute, rule, order, or other administrative action could require the registration of a covered security or impose merit standards, prospectus requirements, or proxy reporting requirements for covered securities.

The Act preserved state authority "to investigate and bring enforcement actions with respect to fraud or deceit, or unlawful conduct by a broker or dealer, in connection with securities or securities transactions." NSMIA preempted aspects of the securities registration and reporting processes for specified covered securities.

The Act did not diminish state authority to investigate and bring enforcement actions generally with respect to securities transactions.

The states were authorized to require filings of any document filed with the SEC for notice purposes "together with annual or periodic reports of the value of securities sold or offered to be sold to a person located in the State (if such sales data is not included in documents filed with the Commission), solely for notice purposes and the assessment of any fee, together with a consent to service of process and any required fee."

NSMIA preempted state law from "[establishing] capital, custody, margin, financial responsibility, making and keeping records, bonding, or financial or operational reporting requirements for brokers, dealers, municipal securities dealers, government securities brokers, or government securities dealers that differ from, or are in addition to the requirements in those areas established under [the Securities Exchange Act]." In one fell swoop, NSMIA banned all state broker-dealer capital, custody, financial responsibility, recordkeeping, and reporting requirements that went beyond those of the federal Securities Exchange Act.

NSMIA subjected to state regulation advisers with assets under management of $25 million or less or who were solely advisers to federally registered investment companies. Any adviser with assets under management of $25 million or more was required to register solely under the Investment Advisers Act and not state law.

Both Levitt and Fields could take some pride in an improved harmonization of state and federal securities laws. Federal covered securities were not preempted in their securities registration requirements. Broker-dealers registered with the SEC could not be subject to inconsistent and more demanding state regulatory provisions. Investment adviser regulation effectively was divided between federal and state regulators. At the same time, there remained state regulation of more local securities, continued registration of broker-dealers, their agents, investment advisers, and investment adviser representatives and largely untouched enforcement and antifraud powers. Given the SEC's enduring budget and staff weaknesses, this preservation of state enforcement powers was particularly critical.[197]

Market Regulation Under Levitt

The Levitt SEC exhibited considerable success addressing other market structure and market regulation issues. The Levitt SEC changed the period for securities transactions to be settled from five days to three, modestly reducing failures to deliver securities and error costs.[198]

Over a five-year period, the Levitt SEC instituted decimalization of securities trading, replacing stock price quotes in 1/8th points with 1/10th points or decimals. The phase-in to decimalization began on the NYSE in August 2000 and was fully completed by April 9, 2001. This proved to be one of the best planned initiatives of the Levitt SEC. A 2002 Commission Release would summarize the first two months experience of decimal pricing with the new uniform minimum price variation for most stocks of a penny. Initial quoted spreads on the NYSE narrowed an average of 37 to 43 percent and on the Nasdaq an average of 50 percent.[199]

In 2000, Levitt jawboned the New York Stock Exchange into fully rescinding Rule 390, which in a limited form had continued after Rule 19c-3 was adopted in April 1979, allowing Rule 390 to continue for stocks listed on the Exchange before April 26, 1979, but not those listed afterwards.[200]

The most significant market structure issues the Levitt SEC addressed concerned the Nasdaq electronic over-the-counter stock market.

In 1994, the Justice Department's Antitrust Division announced it was investigating "the possibility of anticompetitive practices in the over-the-counter stock market," in part because of a March 1994 study by Professors William Christie and Paul Schultz entitled, *Why Do Nasdaq Market Makers Avoid Odd Eighths Quotes?*

The Christie and Schultz Study concluded in part:

> ... [W]e [have] examine[d] ... an extensive sample of inside bid and inside ask quotes for 100 of the most active Nasdaq stocks in 1991. We find that spreads of one eighth are virtually non-existent for a majority of this sample.... We believe that this surprising result reflects an implicit agreement among market makers to avoid using odd eighths in quoting bid and ask prices and that a large number of market makers per stock is not necessarily synonymous with competition.

The SEC later began its own investigation of Nasdaq trading practices. Levitt reported in his SEC memoir:

> What we found was shameful and shocking. We were able to document that some Nasdaq market makers were secretly agreeing to keep spreads wide. They were fixing prices in violation of antitrust laws — to the detriment of investors. Market makers who tried to narrow the spread by quoting prices in between the acceptable even eighths gap were verbally harassed or ostracized. Some market makers conspired with other dealers against their own customers.

In 1996, the SEC and the NASD agreed to a Consent Settlement, under which the NASD was censured. As part of the settlement the Board of Directors of NASD authorized $25 million and committed to expend an additional $75 million over five years, to enhance its systems for market surveillance, including the development and implementation of an enhanced audit trail, surveillance, enforcement, and internal audit.[201]

There was considerable SEC follow through. Before the Consent Settlement, in 1994, the NASD had appointed former Senator Warren Rudman to head a Select Committee to review Nasdaq structure and governance.

In 1995, the Rudman Select Committee on Structure and Governance concluded: "Fundamental change is needed." The Rudman Committee recommended reconstituting the NASD into the parent company with two subsidiaries: the Nasdaq Stock Market and NASD Regulation Inc., responsible for regulating the broker-dealer profession. The NASD Board of Governors and later the SEC adopted these recommendations.

Levitt insisted on new management at NASD and the Nasdaq. Levitt recruited Frank Zarb for the job, later recalling: "Zarb and I had worked together at Shearson Hayden Stone in the 1960s, and I knew I could trust him."

Underlying the Nasdaq debacle, Levitt believed was a basic flaw:

> Today, . . . Nasdaq market makers often quote prices in private, "hidden" markets that are better than the prices they quote on Nasdaq. Retail customers don't have access to those other markets, which go by such names as Instinet and SelectNet, and have to trade at the prices on the Nasdaq screen. This is exactly the situation that Congress wanted to avoid. In order to

> make the prices in these hidden markets public, our Rules would require market makers who quote their best prices in these hidden markets to quote the same prices on Nasdaq.

The effect, Levitt later observed, was to transfer billions of dollars from investors to brokers.[202]

The Commission in 1996 adopted a new Quote Rule. As amended, the Quote Rule required a specialist or OTC market maker to make publicly available the price of any order it placed in an electronic communications network (*ECN*) *if* the ECN price was better than the specialist's or OTC market maker's public quotation. The Commission also adopted a Display Rule, to require OTC market makers and specialists to display any customer limit order when the order was placed at a price superior to the market maker's or specialist's quotation.

The two Order Handling Rules had a surprising impact. Within a few years, Nasdaq spreads had narrowed by approximately one third "saving investors," Levitt later would report, "$25 billion in the first year."

The Levitt SEC supported the selection of CFTC Chair Mary Schapiro, earlier an SEC Commissioner, to succeed Zarb to lead NASD Regulation. Schapiro in 2006 would become the NASD CEO. In 1999–2000, the NASD Board would sell 75 percent of its stock in Nasdaq. In 2007, NASD and the New York Stock Exchange would combine NASD and New York Stock Exchange regulatory functions into the Financial Industry Regulatory Authority, popularly known as FINRA, and consolidate the two self-regulatory organization's rule books.[203]

Swap Agreements

The most egregious blunder of the Clinton administration, Greenspan and the Fed, and the SEC would concern swap agreements. In 1974, two types of derivative securities had been standardized and traded on exchanges: options and financial futures. In an awkward compromise, options were subject to SEC jurisdiction, financial futures to the CFTC.

Swaps were a third type of derivative instrument. A swap agreement was negotiated between two parties and would allow the parties to trade in the 1990s typically based on changes in the interest rates or foreign currency of two different underlying debt instruments or currencies. For example, if a United States corporation sold its goods abroad to be paid in a foreign currency, it could use swaps to lock in payments in United States dollars. The counterparty could use the swap to speculate in future movements in exchange rates. The value of swaps was calculated in notional amounts based on the size of the underlying debt instrument or currency swapped. Since swaps were not traded on an exchange, they were OTC derivatives.

In 1998, the total estimated notional amount of swaps was $80 trillion, six times the $13.5 trillion total for exchange-traded options and futures combined. Seventy-two percent of swaps were to hedge for or speculate in interest rates, 26 percent for foreign currency, with approximately 2 percent for a potpourri of securities and commodities.

To Fed Chair Alan Greenspan, speaking to a 1999 Financial Industry Association Conference: "By far the most significant event in finance during the past decade has been the extraordinary development and expansion of financial derivatives." The CFTC in a 1989 Policy Statement had declined to regulate swaps as futures or futures options. In 1992, the Futures Trading Practices Act had granted the CFTC authority to exempt OTC Derivatives from most provisions of the Commodities Exchange Act. In 1993, the CFTC had exempted specified swaps and OTC energy contracts.

The 1993 CFTC Swap Exemption was limited to eligible swap participants defined to include regulated financial institutions such as banks or securities broker-dealers, business enterprises with defined levels of total assets or net worth, specified pension funds, state and local governments and individuals with more than $10 million in total assets. The swap agreement could not be a standardized agreement such as an exchange-traded option or future or traded through an exchange.

Greenspan, who advocated deregulation, was effusive in his 1999 remarks and asserted: "The fact that the OTC markets function quite effectively without the benefits of [CFTC regulation] provides a strong argument for development of a less burdensome regime for exchange-traded financial derivatives."

After the CFTC's 1993 Exemption, the market in swaps dramatically grew, accompanied by what the 2011 Financial Crisis Inquiry

Report would characterize as "a wave of significant losses and scandals:"

> In 1994, Procter & Gamble, a leading consumer products company, reported a pretax loss of $157 million, the largest derivatives loss by a nonfinancial firm, stemming from OTC interest and foreign exchange rate derivatives sold to it by Bankers Trust. Procter & Gamble sued Bankers Trust for fraud — a suit settled when Bankers Trust forgave most of the money that Procter & Gamble owed it. That year, the CFTC and the Securities Exchange Commission (*SEC*) fined Bankers Trust $10 million for misleading Gibson Greeting Cards on interest rate swaps resulting in a mark-to-market loss of $23 million, larger than Gibson's prior year profits. In late 1994, Orange County, California, announced it had lost $1.5 billion speculating in OTC derivatives. The county filed for bankruptcy — the largest by a municipality in U.S. history. Its derivatives dealer, Merrill Lynch, paid $400 million to settle claims.

Significantly, in September 1998, the Fed, acting through the Federal Reserve Bank of New York, worked with leading private investment banks to recapitalize the hedge fund, Long Term Capital Management, after its computer model for trading more than $1 trillion in notional amounts of OTC derivatives using $4.8 billion of capital threatened to bankrupt Long Term Capital, initially without knowledge of its major derivatives counterparties or federal regulators.

In May 1998, before Long Term Capital's meltdown, Commodities Futures Trading Commission Chair Brooksley Born announced the CFTC would reexamine the way it regulated the OTC derivatives market, given the market's rapid growth and major losses since 1993.

Treasury Secretary Robert Rubin, Greenspan, and SEC Chair Arthur Levitt issued a joint statement criticizing the CFTC on the day the CFTC issued a Concept Release formally announcing the Commodities Future Trading Commission's reexamination: "We have grave concerns about this action and its possible consequences. . . . We are very concerned about reports that the CFTC's actions may increase the legal uncertainty concerning certain types of OTC derivatives." They proposed and Congress in October 1998 voted a moratorium on the CFTC's ability to regulate OTC derivatives. Alan Greenspan explained: "Aside from safety and soundness regulation of derivatives dealers under the banking and securities laws, regulation of derivatives transactions that are privately negotiated by professionals is unnecessary."

In November 1999, the President's Working Group on Financial Markets, which comprised Larry Summers, Rubin's successor as Treasury Secretary, Arthur Levitt, and William Rainer, who succeeded Brooksley Born as CFTC Chair, published *Over-the-Counter Derivatives Markets and the Commodity Exchange Act.* The President's Working Group echoed Greenspan's deregulatory view:

> The members of the Working Group agree that there is no compelling evidence of problems involving bilateral swap agreements that would warrant regulation under the CEA; accordingly, many types of swap agreements should be excluded from the CEA. The sophisticated counterparties that use OTC derivatives simply do not require the same protections under the CEA as those required by retail investors. In addition, most of the dealers in the swaps market are either affiliated with broker-dealers or [Futures Commodities Merchants] that are regulated by the SEC or the CFTC or are financial institutions that are subject to supervision by bank regulatory agencies.

The President's Working Group unanimously recommended that swap agreements entered into by eligible swap participants, such as those specified in the CFTC's 1993 Swap Agreement, should be excluded from the Commodities Exchange Act. The Presidential Working Group recommended that such swap agreements could have standardized forms "[b]ecause the material economic terms of many swap agreements are similar."

The 1999 President's Working Group proposed a broad exclusion from the Commodities Exchange Act for electronic trading systems in which eligible swap participants trade for their own accounts.

The Working Group recommended repeal of the prohibition on single stock futures and recommended that the SEC and CFTC in the future determine whether single stock futures should be permitted and if so under what conditions.

In 2000, Congress enacted each of these recommendations in the Commodities Futures Modernization Act to provide legal certainty for swap agreements. The Act covered individually negotiated swap agreements between eligible contract participants not executed or traded on a trading facility in any commodity other than an agricultural commodity expressly including agreements based on interest rates, currencies, or other financial or economic interests or property of any kind.

The 2000 Act repealed the 18-year-old Shad-Johnson Agreement's ban on single stock futures in favor of a system of coordinated regulation for such products and other hybrid instruments that are primarily securities or bank deposits that have some characteristics of financial futures.

The 2000 Act excluded individually negotiated transactions in a nonagricultural commodity, which necessarily included oil and energy products, not executed on a trading facility. This exclusion was unusually broad in that it excluded these transactions from the fraud and manipulation provisions of the Commodity Exchange Act. When Enron collapsed in 2001, this exclusion would be criticized as the Enron loophole.

In the aftermath of the enactment of the Commodities Futures Modernization Act, the OTC market dramatically expanded. The 2011 Financial Crisis Inquiry Report would explain: "At year end 2000, when the CFMA was passed, the notional amount of OTC derivatives outstanding globally was $95.2 trillion, and the gross market value was $3.2 trillion. In the seven and a half years from then until June 2008, when the market peaked, outstanding OTC derivatives increased more than sevenfold to a notional amount of $672.6 trillion; their gross market value was $20.3 trillion."

The Commodities Futures Modernization Act would provide the basis for unregulated credit default swaps, which were a factor in the 2007–2009 Meltdown. In 2000, the New York Insurance Department also concluded that naked credit defaults — those with a participant not having an insurable interest — were not subject to state insurance regulation. This meant that firms providing credit default swaps neither were subject to CFTC regulation nor state insurance reserve requirements.

Rarely is there so instantaneous an example of regulation shaping a market. In 2008, 97 percent of the notional amount of OTC derivatives would be traded by five large financial institutions, four of which would require subsidy during the Meltdown — JP Morgan Chase, Citicorp, Bank of America, and Wachovia. The country's five largest investment banks led by Goldman Sachs would be among the world's largest OTC derivatives dealers. AIG, which provided credit default swaps as a form of insurance to OTC dealers, would receive the largest total of federal support in 2008–2009: $182.3 billion in loans.[204]

Accounting and Auditing Standards

Levitt would prove more effective late in his term, focusing on accountant conflicts of interest and corporate governance. In September 1998, Levitt memorably took up the issue of accountant passivity in an address entitled *The Numbers Game*. Levitt would characterize the role of the outside auditor as part of a system of corporate governance. Levitt especially stressed the role of accounting standards and the outside auditor. In *The Numbers Game*, he excoriated "big bath" restructuring charges by which companies would exaggerate expenses to "clean up" their balance sheets so that they could report income later if projected expenses turned out to be smaller; pooling for mergers; cookie jar reserves, which were unrealistically high estimates of future expenses, generating subsequent period profits; abuse of materiality to fail to report small losses; and premature revenue recognition.

Levitt's skepticism of the integrity of the accounting profession prompted a significantly increased number of accounting enforcement actions; new SEC derivative risk disclosure requirements; Staff Accounting Bulletins discouraging exclusive reliance on quantitative measures of materiality, as well as premature revenue recognition; and SEC support for new FASB Rules to address derivatives disclosure. When the Court of Appeals in the District of Columbia twice expressed skepticism that the SEC had authority to adopt a Rule of Practice to discipline accountants based on negligence, rather than an intentional or knowing conduct fault standard, the Levitt Commission persisted and, in 1998, amended its Rules of Practice to adopt a heightened form of negligence as the fault standard for accountants.

But these were collateral to the more significant Levitt concern. The willingness of the outside auditor to act independently of senior corporate executives, in Levitt's view, had deteriorated. In 1998, after acknowledging that questions concerning accounting independence "have become more complex as auditors have entered into new service areas for their clients, auditing firms have merged and restructured their operations, and business practices and technology have become more sophisticated and, increasingly, more global in scope," the Commission announced that "without abdicating its statutory responsibilities," it intended to look to a new standard setting body designated by the AICPA, the Independence Standards

Board (*ISB*), "to provide leadership not only in improving current auditor independence requirements, but also in establishing and maintaining a body of independence standards applicable to the auditors of all Commission registrants."[205]

Soon, the SEC would be involved in a three-year investigation of Waste Management, which would subsequently acknowledge overstating its earnings by $1.4 billion from 1992 to 1997, and its auditor, Arthur Andersen, without admitting or denying fault, would pay a $7 million fine and agree to an injunction prohibiting it from further specified misconduct. Beginning in the winter of 1997, with an anonymous letter, the SEC would begin an investigation of Coopers & Lybrand, which after a merger was part of PricewaterhouseCoopers (*PwC*). Ultimately the SEC would determine that PwC and half of its partners had violated the auditing independent rule "an incredible 8000" times.

The subsequent revision of the SEC auditor independence rules focused on the extent to which an auditor would be banned from providing nonaudit services to audit clients. By 1999, audit firm management consulting and other services dominated the major audit firms. In 1981, only 13 percent of the five largest public accounting firms' total revenues had been generated by management consulting. By 1999, management consulting had grown to 51 percent, with tax services equal to 19 percent, and accounting and auditing services reduced to 30 percent.

In 2000, Ernst & Young agreed to sell its management consulting business to Cap Gemini, a French computer services company. KPMG spun off its consulting business into a separate business, KPMG Consulting, Inc. John Biggs, then chair of TIAA-CREF, in July 2000 flatly proposed: "Independent public accounting firms should not be auditing any company for which they simultaneously provide other services."

In June 2000, the Commission proposed a rule to prohibit a registered public accounting firm (and any associated person of that firm, to the extent determined appropriate by the Commission) that performs for any issuer any audit required: (A) bookkeeping or other services related to the audit client's accounting records or financial statements; (B) financial information systems design and implementation; (C) appraisal or evaluation services; (D) actuarial services; (E) internal audit outsourcing; (F) management functions; (G) human resources; (H) broker-dealer, investment adviser, or investment banking services; (I) legal services; and (J) expert services.

Leading accounting firms "mounted a no-holds barred public relations and lobbying campaign to stop us." Levitt wrote in his SEC memoir: "Within a month of issuing the proposed rule, I received negative letters from 46 members of Congress, including two-thirds of the Senate Banking Committee's Securities Subcommittee. Even normally pro-consumer Democratic Senators, such as Evan Bayh of Indiana and Oregon's Ron Wyden, opposed the rule."

After holding four days of hearings with almost 100 witnesses and receiving nearly 3000 comment letters, in September 2000 Levitt testified before the Senate Banking Committee's Subcommittee on Securities. He unsuccessfully attempted to stress the modesty of the SEC proposal: "[M]ost of the non-audit services addressed in our proposal are already proscribed by the AICPA or the Commission, or are the subject of restrictions proposed by the ISB. Only two of the ten services identified in the proposal — internal audit services and information technology services — are not already the subject of restrictions."

Shortly after the 2000 election, Levitt compromised. In November 2000, the Commission adopted a revised Accounting Independence Rule. The rule was compromised in two respects. First, an audit firm performing audit services also could design or implement financial information statements when it had the audit client's written acknowledgement that the client was responsible to establish and maintain the client's system of internal accounting controls. The SEC also agreed to permit an auditor to provide up to 40 percent of the hours expended on the audit client's internal audit activities in any one fiscal year. The latter was not so much a compromise as capitulation. The new rule did not prohibit any accountant from providing expert opinion services for audit clients.[206]

The Enron Scandal

Within one year after Levitt stepped down as SEC chair, his efforts to address chronic SEC underfunding and understaffing and auditor lack of independence would be addressed by a series of mammoth financial scandals beginning with Enron. Enron was an extraordinarily fast growing provider, primarily of natural gas, electricity, and communication products and services, whose total assets quadrupled between 1996 and 2000 from $16.137 to $65.503 billion. In 2001, Enron was seventh on the Fortune 500 list, with revenues in 2000 of $100.8 billion.

Then, abruptly, essentially without warning, Enron collapsed. A November 8, 2001 Form 8-K stunningly revealed: "Enron intends to restate its financial statements for the years ended December 31, 1997 through 2000 and the quarters ended March 31 and June 30, 2001. As a result, the previously issued financial statements for these periods and the audit reports covering the year-end financial statements for 1997 to 2000 should not be relied upon."

An Enron Special Committee, chaired by University of Texas Law School Dean William Powers was soon appointed.

In April 2002, Enron filed a report with the SEC indicating that its then current management estimated that a write-down of approximately $14 billion will be required.

The Committee's report, known as the Powers Report, subsequently made a series of significant findings with respect to the debacle.

First, Enron employees involved in partnerships created by Enron were enriched "by tens of millions of dollars they should never have received — Fastow by at least $30 million, Kopper by at least $10 million, two others by $1 million each, and two more by amounts we believe were at least in the hundreds of thousands of dollars."

Second, the partnerships, Chewco, LJM[1], and LJM[2], "were designed to accomplish favorable financial statement results, not to achieve *bona fide* economic objectives or to transfer risk." These transactions often did not follow applicable accounting rules that would have permitted keeping assets and liabilities off of Enron's balance sheet:

> They allowed Enron to conceal from the market very large losses resulting from Enron's merchant investments by creating an appearance that those investments were hedged — that is, that a third party was obligated to pay Enron the amount of those losses — when in fact that third party was simply an entity in which only Enron had a substantial economic stake. We believe these transactions resulted in Enron reporting earnings from the third quarter of 2000 through the third quarter of 2001 that were almost $1 billion higher than should have been reported.

The Powers Report found: "The evidence available to us suggests that [outside auditor Arthur] Andersen did not fulfill its professional responsibilities in connection with its audits of Enron's financial statements, or its obligation to bring to the attention of Enron's Board (or the Audit and Compliance Committee) concerns about Enron's internal controls over the related party transactions." Specifically, the Powers Report characterized each of the more than 20 asset sales and hedging transactions between Enron and an Enron created partnership as flawed.

The Powers Report was sharply critical of Enron's Board of Directors:

> With respect to the issues that are the subject of this investigation, the Board of Directors failed, in our judgment, in its oversight duties. . . .
>
> The Board of Directors approved the arrangements that allowed the Company's CFO to serve as general partner in partnerships that participated in significant financial transactions with Enron. . . . The Board substantially underestimated the severity of the conflict and overestimated the degree which management controls and procedures could contain the problem.

A different type of check and balance is provided by outside legal counsel. Shortly after Enron CEO Jeffrey Skilling's resignation in August 2001, Enron Chair Kenneth Lay received an anonymous one-page letter, later described as being sent by an Enron employee, Sherron Watkins, raising questions about Enron's "aggressive" accounting and concluding: "I am incredibly nervous that we will implode in a wave of accounting scandals." Lay, according to the Powers Report, found that the letter was "thoughtfully written and alarming." Enron asked Vinson & Elkins, the same outside counsel who had helped design some of the questionable transactions, to perform a preliminary investigation to determine whether a full investigation should be performed. Vinson & Elkins concluded that a full investigation was not warranted.

The Powers Report was critical of the Vinson & Elkins (*V&E*) investigation: "The result of the V&E review was largely predetermined by the scope and nature of the investigation and the process employed. We identified the most serious problems in the Raptor transactions only after a detailed examination of the relevant transactions and, most importantly, discussions with our accounting advisors — both steps that Enron determined (and V&E accepted) would not be part of V&E's investigation."

In addition, Enron's required public disclosure was, according to the Report, systematically inadequate: "[T]hese disclosures were obtuse, did not communicate the essence of the transactions completely or clearly, and failed to convey the substance of what was going on between Enron and the partnerships."[207]

By early 2002, it was evident that there was broad support for a new approach to auditing regulation. The need for significant reform of the accounting profession was particularly stressed in congressional hearings early in 2002.

Paul Volcker, then chair of the International Accounting Standards Committee Foundation, testified:

> ... [P]roblems, building over a period of years, have now exploded into a sense of crisis. That crisis is exemplified by the Enron collapse. But Enron is not the only symptom. We have had too many restatements of earnings, too many doubts about *pro forma* earnings, too many sudden charges of billions of dollars to *good will*, too many perceived auditing failures accompanying bankruptcies to make us at all comfortable.

Former SEC Chair David Ruder went further and urged creation of a new accounting oversight organization that would be separate from the American Institute of Certified Public Accountants and whose Board would be composed entirely of public members with no connection to the accounting profession.[208]

The push for legislative reform intensified in July 2002 when WorldCom announced a $3.85 billion restatement of its financial reports that subsequently was increased to $7.18 billion. The Senate, on July 15, 2002, adopted the Public Company Accounting Reform and Investor Protection Act, the Sarbanes Bill, by a vote of 97–0. Within 10 days, a House-Senate Conference Committee largely acceded to the substance of the Senate Bill, and in late July, Congress enacted what was styled the Sarbanes-Oxley Act. The vote was overwhelming — 99–0 in the Senate, 423 to 3 in the House.

In July 2002, Congress enacted the Sarbanes-Oxley Act. The most consequential provisions of the Act addressed auditing. The Act created a new Public Company Accounting Oversight Board, soon reduced to the acronym, PCAOB. The PCAOB was to have five full time members, no more than two of whom "shall be or have been certified public accountants." Selection would be made by the SEC, after consultation with the chair of the Board of Governors and the Secretary of the Treasury. Board members would serve staggered five-year terms with a two term limit.

The PCAOB was empowered to receive registration forms from each covered public accounting firm; establish directly or through existing groups or advisory groups, auditing standards; conduct annual inspections with respect to each registered public accounting firm that provides reports for more than 100 issuers and inspections not less frequently than once every three years for other registered public accounting firms; and conduct investigations and disciplinary proceedings of any act or practice, or omission to act by a registered public accounting firm or any associated person of the firm.

The PCAOB could refer any investigation to the SEC, other federal financial regulator, or at the direction of the SEC, to the United States Attorney General, a state Attorney General, or other appropriate state regulatory authority.

All PCAOB rules and disciplinary actions, other than initial or transitional standards, were subject to SEC oversight.

The Sarbanes-Oxley Act required rotation of specified audit firm partners every five years.

The battle that Arthur Levitt had partially lost in November 2000, to ban certain audit firm conflicts of interest was largely won in the Sarbanes-Oxley Act, which provided in relevant part:

> ... [I]t shall be unlawful for a registered public accounting firm ... that performs for any issuer any audit required by this title ... to provide to that issuer, contemporaneously with the audit, any non-audit service, including —
>
> 1) Bookkeeping or other services related to the accounting records or financial statements of the audit client;
> 2) Financial information systems design and implementation;
> 3) Appraisal or evaluation services, fairness opinions, or contribution-in-kind reports;
> 4) Actuarial services;
> 5) Internal audit outsourcing services;
> 6) Management functions or human resources;
> 7) Broker or dealer, investment adviser, or investment banking services;
> 8) Legal services and expert services unrelated to the audit; and
> 9) Any other service that the Board determines, by regulation, is impermissible.

The Sarbanes-Oxley Act further provided: "A registered public accounting firm may engage in any non-audit service, including tax services, that is not described in any of paragraphs (1) through (2) of subsection (g) for an audit client, only if the activity is approved in advance by the Audit Committee of the issuer. . . ."

The Sarbanes-Oxley Act provided that the Board of Director Audit Committees be required to be comprised entirely of independent directors and be authorized to engage independent counsel and other advisors.

In a salute to the frustrations of the Levitt chairmanship, the Sarbanes-Oxley Act authorized — but did not appropriate — a 77 percent increase in the SEC budget to $776 million for fiscal year 2003 with new funds for pay parity, technology, and at least 200 new professionals.

There was much else in the Act. But its essence was indelible. Crisis had caused Congress shortly after Levitt's chairmanship to effectively respond to several of his most fundamental concerns.[209]

The Sarbanes-Oxley Act epitomized the regulatory challenge for the SEC in the post-World War II period. With overwhelming facts, the Commission could secure congressional legislation or support for far reaching legislation. But too often, lack of interest from the White House, hostile or indifferent majorities in Congress, and effective industry lobbying resulted in the SEC becoming a more insular regulator, often quite effective at core functions such as its disclosure system or fraud enforcement, but less able with respect to controversial or emerging issues such as consolidation with the Commodities Futures Trading Commission, regulation of swaps, corporate governance or market structure.

The Post-War Insurance Industry

During the post-World War II period, the United States insurance industry also experienced tremendous growth. By year-end 2017, total insurance held a total of $9 trillion in assets with $7.2 trillion or 78 percent held by the life and health sector, and $2 trillion held by the property and casualty sector.

By 2017, the life insurance industry was dominated by its largest firms, led by Prudential with $596 billion in total assets, MetLife with $427 billion, New York Life with $321 billion, TIAA-CREF with $307 billion, and American International Group (*AIG*) with $290 billion.

The post-World War II period expansion of the industry had been buoyed by new products, notably insurance annuities, variable annuities, and variable life insurance, as well as group life and annuity, credit life insurance, Veteran life insurance, retirement initiatives such as accelerated guaranteed living benefits, disability and long-term care insurance, and alternative risk transfer products, such as catastrophic bonds.

The industry was highly reactive to consumer preferences. By 2011, 68 percent of life insurance premium income was provided by annuities that provided benefits to the annuitant during her or his lifetime, only 26 percent by life insurance, which provided benefits to the insured's beneficiaries.

The insurance industry also was highly reactive to federal legislation.

The Gramm-Leach-Bliley Act of 1999 eliminated barriers separating banking, securities, and insurance companies and authorized the conglomeration of insurers into financial holding companies, led by the legitimation of the 1998 Travelers Insurance Group-Citicorp merger.

The Commodities Futures Modernization Act of 2000 authorized financial services companies to invest in unregulated derivatives, led most notoriously in the insurance industry by American International Group (*AIG*), which became an industry leader in credit default swaps. This level of risk was unusual for the insurance industry. As late as 2017, 49 percent of the life insurance industry's $7.2 trillion assets were in bonds, 32 percent in stocks, 7 percent in mortgages.

By 2017, 13.7 percent of United States life insurance companies were foreign owned. Globally, the United States was responsible for 28 percent of the $4.9 trillion in insurance premiums written in 2017, far eclipsing China with 11 percent, Japan with 9 percent, and the United Kingdom with 6 percent.

To secure greater access to capital markets promoted a widespread movement to demutualize life insurance. Mutual life insurers, owned by their insureds, could not raise money in the stock market or participate in bank or insurance consolidations. Between 1997 and 2003, 15 major life insurers led by industry leader, Metropolitan Life, demutualized. By 2017, 584 of the United States 781 life insurers were stock firms, only 112 mutual. In 2017, 64.7 percent of the $20.4 trillion life insurance in force was written by stock life insurers, 33 percent by mutual life insurers.

Life insurance companies increasingly ceased to be stand-alone companies. By 2011, there were 186 stand-alone companies, 250 groups with an average of 2.48 companies. In 2017 alone there were 93 mergers involving United States insurers with a total value of $87.1 billion.

Insurance industry regulation, unlike that of banks, securities, housing, commodities, or pensions, remained at the state level. State insurance was administered by insurance commissioners in 50 states, the District of Columbia and five territories, each of whom is a member of a private organization, the National Association of Insurance Commissioners (*NAIC*), which has been characterized as "[b]y far the most important single player in state insurance regulation." NAIC serves as the chief lobbyist for the industry and has worked to promote uniformity in state insurance law and regulation and facilitate cooperation among the states.

State insurance regulation focuses on solvency protection of the $4 trillion in policy reserves as of 2017. By 1992, all states augmented their Commissioners' efforts with state guarantee funds, along the lines of the Federal Deposit Insurance Corporation (*FDIC*) or Securities Investor Protection Corporation (*SIPC*). Forty-three states in 2008 had some form of rate regulation for property and casualty insurance.

The most striking aspect of the post-World War II insurance industry has been the degree to which its core products have been subject to competition from nonindustry firms or nonindustry regulators. First, during the 1950s, the SEC subjected variable annuities to securities regulation and were supported by Supreme Court decisions in 1959 and 1967. Then, in 1974, the Employer Retirement Income Security Act was one of many steps at the federal level authorizing employers to become major actors in the pension plan industry, a key competitor to insurance annuities.[210] And ultimately, in 1995, the Supreme Court held in *NationsBank v. Variable Annuity Life Insurance Company* that national banks may serve as agents in the sale of annuities, since they are "incidental" to "the business of banking."

The New Financial Order

By the time of the 2007–2009 Financial Meltdown, financial *regulation* remained atomized into banking, securities, pension plans, insurance, and housing, but finance had become increasingly dominated by financial supermarkets, which could operate in two or more of these industries, both domestically and internationally.

Banks and other depository institutions can charter at the national or state level in the form of banks, savings and loans, or credit unions. Most banks and savings and loans were insured by the FDIC. As of mid-2018, there were 5542 insured commercial banks and savings institutions with total assets of $17.5 trillion. There also were 5480 federally insured credit unions with aggregate assets of $1.4 trillion.

Banking is highly concentrated with the vast majority of banks owned by bank holding companies or by financial holding companies.

The largest bank or financial holding companies are designated global systemically important financial institutions. In 2018, Prudential, the last nonbank global systemically important financial institution, was removed from this list. In 2018, there were eight United States bank or financial holding companies that were global systemically important financial institutions: JP Morgan Chase, Citigroup, Morgan Stanley, Bank of America, Goldman Sachs, Wells Fargo, Mellon, and State Street. These eight accounted for 65 percent of all bank and financial holding companies' $19 trillion in total assets, with the top five responsible for 55 percent of the combined $19 trillion in total assets.

Global Systemically Important Financial Institutions (2018)

	Assets
JP Morgan	$2.6 trillion
Citigroup	$1.9 trillion
Morgan Stanley	$.85 trillion
Bank of America	$2.3 trillion
Goldman Sachs	$.93 trillion
Wells Fargo	$1.9 trillion
Bank of New York Melon	$1.7 trillion
State Street Corporation	$.24 trillion
Total	**$12.43 trillion**

The industries in which each of these bank or financial holding companies operated largely was shaped by federal law or by gaps and omissions in federal or state law.

JP Morgan, for example, the leading private commercial and investment bank in the United States before the New Deal, was required by the Glass-Steagall Act of 1933 to divorce its commercial banking operations that remained in JP Morgan from its securities operations, which in 1935 were separated into Morgan Stanley.

In 1959, JP Morgan Company merged with Guaranty Trust to form a subsidiary, Morgan Guaranty Trust. Ten years later, under the 1956 Bank Holding Company Act, JP Morgan formed a bank holding company to own Morgan Guaranty Trust.

In 1996, JP Morgan substantially expanded its commercial banking activities by merging with Chase Manhattan Bank. The combined company was renamed JP Morgan Chase.

In 2004, JP Morgan Chase merged with Bank One Corporation, a large Chicago-based commercial bank and brought to the combined company Jamie Dimon, who would serve as president and chair from 2004 to 2018.

In March 2008, JP Morgan Chase at Federal Reserve Bank instigation rescued Bear Stearns, then the fifth largest investment bank holding company, which was on the verge of bankruptcy.

This shotgun merger dramatically expanded JP Morgan's presence in the securities industry, later under the name JP Morgan Securities.

In September 2008, JP Morgan bought most of the banking operations of Washington Mutual from the receivership of the FDIC. Washington Mutual at the time represented the largest bank failure in United States history.

Each of these mergers required Federal Reserve Board approval. Congressional or Fed support was necessary for JP Morgan Chase's internal expansion through interstate branching, Automatic Teller Machines (*ATMs*), money market funds, credit cards, and derivatives trading.

Citigroup helped inspire the Gramm-Leach-Bliley Act in 1999, which repealed the Glass-Steagall Act, and subsequently made possible Citigroup's merger with Traveler's Insurance.

Morgan Stanley had expanded by 2018 into mortgage and retail securities-based lending primarily through its retail broker-dealer Morgan Stanley Smith Barney.

Goldman Sachs has remained an industry leader in the securities industry with substantial roles in investment banking with institutional and government clients, financial advisory services, including those for merger and acquisition activities, restructuring and derivative transactions, underwriting, and proprietary trading.

Wells Fargo was a full-service financial holding company with bank, insurance, securities, and commodities operations.

Before the 2007–2009 Financial Meltdown, the top ten largest bank holding companies, which then also included Wachovia, then the fourth-largest bank behind Chase, Bank of America, and JP Morgan, had expanded their dominance of the banking industry from 25 percent in 1990, to 55 percent in 2005. Between 2003 and 2006, Chase, Citigroup, and Bank of America were the top three banks globally in syndicated loans. By the end of 2007, approximately 60 percent of residential mortgages and about 50 percent of credit card loans were securitized. In 2006 and 2007, the top six mortgage lenders, Chase, Wells Fargo, Bank of America, Washington Mutual, and Countrywide controlled a majority of mortgage origination and mortgage servicing. In 2008, three financial holding companies controlled more than one-half of the credit card market.

There were 3800 broker-dealer firms as of June 2018 registered with the SEC with total assets of $4.4 trillion.

Mutual funds, which largely hold stock or debt securities, held $16.6 trillion in September 2018. Exchange-traded funds, created by securities exchanges, compete with mutual funds, and in 2018 held $3.7 trillion in assets.

Money market mutual funds compete with banks for passbook accounts and long have been formed by mutual fund complexes. As of October 2018, money market assets totaled $3.2 trillion.

In 2005, just before the 2007–2009 Financial Meltdown, institutional investors ranked the world's top 10 securities firms in terms of capital:

Rank	Firm	Total capital ($ billion)
1	Morgan Stanley	110.793
2	Goldman Sachs & Co.	105.780
3	Merrill Lynch & Co.	102.582
4	Credit Suisse First Boston	83.521
5	Citigroup Global Market Holdings	76.464
6	Lehman Brothers Holdings	71.406
7	Bear, Stearns & Co.	46.067
8	UBS	16.122
9	Deutsche Bank Securities	7.783
10	Bank of America Securities	7.235

Strikingly, six of the top ten firms were affiliated with bank or financial holding companies (Morgan Stanley, Credit Suisse First Boston, Citigroup, UBS, Deutsche Bank, and Bank of America). After the 2007–2009 Meltdown, Morgan Stanley and Goldman Sachs became bank or financial holding companies, Merrill Lynch merged into Bank of America, Bear Stearns merged into JP Morgan, Lehman Brothers ceased to exist.

Between 2000–2007, the top ten global debt and equity underwriters included three United States banks, Citigroup, Chase, and Bank of America, which in 2004, was replaced by Barclay's, a British bank, three other banks chartered abroad, Credit Suisse, Deutsche Bank, and UBS, and the four leading United States securities firms (Merrill Lynch, Morgan Stanley, Goldman Sachs, and Lehman Brothers). The top ten global underwriters accounted for 60 percent of the proceeds from debt and equity securities between 2005 and 2007, and also became dominant in asset-backed securities, over-the-counter derivatives, and collateralized debt obligations.

In response to the competitive threat posed by commercial banks, lending securities firms merged with financial holding companies such as Shearson in 1993 and Salomon Brothers in 1997 that became part of Citigroup in 1998, and Dean Witter, which was acquired by Morgan Stanley in 1997.

To increase capital or access before the 2007–2009 Financial Meltdown, Morgan Stanley, Lehman Brothers, and Goldman Sachs acquired savings and loans or industrial loan companies.

Hedge funds provide many of the same services that SEC registered mutual funds or registered investment advisers provide, but with less regulation and engage in transactions forbidden to mutual funds, such as short selling. In 2017, there were 9000 hedge funds whose customers typically are wealthy individuals or institutional investors. The net asset value of hedge funds in 2017 was $3.9 trillion. Hedge funds largely operated outside of federal or state regulation. In 2003, SEC Chair Arthur Levitt testified that only about 60 of the nation's then 5700 hedge funds were registered with the SEC. While hedge funds employed a wide array of strategies, their investments often were invisible to federal or state regulators as illustrated by Long Term Capital Management. In 2006, the District of Columbia Circuit Court vacated an SEC rule to require hedge fund managers to register with the Commission as investment advisers.

Pension plans provide retirement income, often by investing in stocks or debt. Pension plans can be public or private and are in addition to Social Security. As of the second quarter of 2018, the combined total assets of pension funds were $23 trillion. Individual pension plans, such as individual retirement accounts, accounted for approximately 28 percent of the retirement services market.

Financial deregulation stimulated greater consolidation in the insurance industry. In 2001, 40 percent of life insurance premiums were concentrated in the top 10 life insurers. By 2017, 51 percent of all life and health insurance was written by the top ten insurers, 34 percent by the top five:

Life & Health Insurance Groups By 2017 U.S. Life Insurance Lines Direct Premiums Written

2016 Rank	2017 Rank	Insurance Group	2017 Direct Premiums Written ($000)	Share of Total (%)
1	1	MetLife Inc.	$86,821,636	13.57
2	2	Prudential Financial Inc.	47,465,693	7.44
3	3	New York Life Insurance Co.	31,852,412	4.99
4	4	Principal Financial Group Inc.	28,142,265	4.41
5	5	Massachusetts Mutual Life Insurance Co.	24,735,091	3.88
7	6	Jackson National Life Insurance Co.	22,439,071	3.52
6	7	American International Group	21,465,665	3.36
9	8	Transamerica Corp.	21,317,714	3.34
8	9	AXA Equitable Life Insurance Co.	21,290,299	3.34
10	10	Lincoln National Corp.	20,397,394	3.20

As of May 2019, there was $33.9 trillion in residential real estate and $18.4 trillion in commercial real estate, of which $10.3 trillion in mortgage debt was provided for residential real estate and $2.4 trillion in mortgage debt was provided for commercial real estate. Mortgages long had been arranged through banks and nonbank mortgage originators for both residences and commercial real estate. Since the 2007–2009 debacle, the nonbank mortgage original market was dominated by a new generation of Internet firms such as Quicken Loans. Mortgage loans often are sold in groups of loans or tranches through a process called securitization, which converts them into securities that can be resold to investors, rather than the traditional mortgage loans, which are held by the bank or savings and loan.

The dominance of the United States economy by a New Financial Order in the years before 2007–2009 was accompanied by risk taking that caused enormous damage to virtually all of these firms and, as documented in Chapter 1, to the United States economy.

Five leaders of the New Financial Order easily would have failed but for rescue mergers or were in essence nationalized: Bear Stearns, Lehman Brothers, Wachovia, Merrill Lynch, and AIG. A similar fate was suffered by Washington Mutual, which failed and whose assets were acquired by Chase, as well as Countrywide, which failed and whose assets were acquired by Bank of America. Goldman Sachs, Morgan Stanley, Citigroup, and Bank of America survived only because of federal government rescue packages.

If there is one indelible lesson from the 2007–2009 Financial Meltdown, it is this. The New Financial Order could not effectively be regulated by the outdated New Deal Model of Financial Regulation.[211]

ENDNOTES:

1. Gale Peterson, President Harry S. Truman and the Independent Regulatory Commissions 221, 226–229 (Ph.D. Univ. of Md. 1973); Staff Report on the Securities and Exchange Commission, Comm. on Independent Regulatory Commissions III-3 (Sept. 1948); Bernard Schwartz, The Professor and the Commissions 42 (Knopf 1959); Louis Kohlmeier, The Regulators 34, 237 (Harper & Row 1969).

   This section of Chapter 5 abridges Chapters 8–14 of Joel Seligman, The Transformation of Wall Street: A History of the Securities and Exchange Commission and Modern Corporate Finance (3d ed. Aspen Pub. 2003).
2. Peterson, supra n. 1, at 229–232, 371–372; Staff Report, supra n. 1, at III-5, IV-11; 12th SEC Ann. Rep. 126–127; 13th SEC Ann. Rep. 138; 14th SEC Ann. Rep. 124; 15th SEC Ann. Rep. 193–195; 16th SEC Ann. Rep. 167–168.

3. Alonzo Hamby, Beyond the New Deal: Harry S. Truman and American Liberalism 55–59, 71–72, 79, 82, 90, 133–134, 161, 213, 335–338, 344 (Columbia Univ. Press 1973); Alfred Steinberg, The Man from Missouri 301 (Putnam's 1962); Peterson supra n. 1, at 17–18, 48, 257.
4. Peterson, supra n. 1, at 231–232; *Time,* Aug. 5, 1946, at 79; *Commercial & Fin. Chron.,* July 25, 1946, at 484.
5. *SEC Minutes,* July 23, 1946; Peterson, supra n. 1, at 231; Robert Sobel, Inside Wall Street 171 (W.W. Norton 1977); *New York Times,* July 3, 1946, at 33; Interview with Roger Foster, July 24, 1980.
6. Interview with Donald Cook, Sept. 16, 1980; Peterson, supra n. 1, at 370; *Forbes,* Feb. 15, 1950, at 14–16; *New York Times,* May 25, 1950, at 1, July 29, 1950 at 18; McDonald biography in Caffrey SEC Commissioner Files, Container No. 53; Address of Harry S. McDonald to the Investment Bankers Association, Dec. 4–9, 1949, on file with the SEC.
7. Interview with Donald Cook, Sept. 16, 1980; Peterson, supra n. 1, at 554–555, 557; *Time,* March 10, 1952 at 89; *Business Week,* Jan. 19, 1952 at 27–28.
8. James Landis, Report on Regulatory Agencies to the President-Elect 47 (Dec. 1960).
9. See supra Chapter 3.
10. Arthur Dean, Book Review, 50 Mich. L. Rev. 1396 (1952).
11. 18th SEC Ann. Rep. at 194–196; 15th SEC Ann. Rep. at xiv; Rossbach letter, *New York Times,* Apr. 22, 1954, at 28; Testimony of Richard McEntire, Independent Offices Appropriation Bill Hearing, House Comm. on Appropriations, 83d Cong., 1st Sess. 515 (1953); Study of the Securities and Exchange Commission, Report of House Commerce Comm., House Rep. 2508, 82d Cong., 2d Sess. 1–4 (1952).
12. *New York Times,* Apr. 17, 1953, at 21; Demmler Letter to Leverett Saltonstall, July 13, 1953, Demmler SEC Commissioner Files, Container No. 109; Demmler Letter to Joseph Dodge, Nov. 17, 1953, Demmler SEC Commissioner Files, Container No. 109; 22d SEC Ann. Rep. at 223; 21st SEC Ann. Rep. at 121.
13. *New York Times,* Feb. 11, 1955, p. 32; SEC 35th Ann. Rep. at 199; Philip Loomis, Enforcement Problems Under the Federal Securities Laws, 14 Bus. Law. 680 n. 29 (1959); Interview with Philip Loomis, Sept. 19, 1980; *SEC Minutes,* Sept. 23, 1953, Feb. 16, 1954; Interview with Ralph Demmler, Aug. 24, 1980; Interview with Irving Pollack, July 25, 1980; Interview with Roger Foster, July 24, 1980; Interviews with Byron Woodside, July 22, 1980; Ralph Demmler Confirmation Hearings, Senate Banking Comm., 83d Cong., 1st Sess. (June 11, 1953); Addresses of Ralph Demmler, Sept. 24, 1953, Dec. 2, 1953, Jan. 13, 1954, on file with the SEC; Ralph Demmler

Press Release, July 16, 1953, Demmler SEC Commissioner Files, Container No. 114.

14. Stock Market Study Report, Senate Banking Com., S. Rep. No. 376, 84th Cong., 1st Sess. 1–7 (1955).
15. *Business Week*, Nov. 10, 1956, at 145–150; Stock Market Study Report, supra n. 14, at 10–11; 17th SEC Ann. Rep. at 159–160; William Timbers & Irving Pollack, Extradition from Canada to the United States for Securities Fraud: Frustration of the National Policies of Both Countries, 24 Fordham L. Rev. 301 (1955).
16. Stock Market Hearings, Senate Banking Comm., 84th Cong., 1st Sess. 132–153 (1955); Robert Sobel, NYSE 223 (Weybright & Talley 1975); John Brooks, The Seven Fat Years 193–203 (Harper & Brothers 1958); *Time*, Mar. 15, 1954 at 95–96, July 16, 1956 at 82.
17. Independent Regulatory Commissions, Report of Special Subcomm. on Legislative Oversight, H.R. No. 2711, 85th Cong., 2d Sess. 1–3, 41–50 (1959); Schwartz, supra n. 1, at 6–7, 228–234; Dwight Eisenhower, Waging Peace 311–316 (Doubleday 1965); Sherman Adams, First-Hand Report (Harper Brothers 1961); Letter to Congressman Klein from G. Keith Funston, June 4, 1956, Armstrong SEC Commissioner Files, Container No. 132; Gadsby quoted in *Fortune*, Nov. 1958 at 226; Booz Allen & Hamilton, Survey of Organization and Operations, Securities and Exchange Commission, at 5–6, 27, 197, 201, on file with SEC; 27th SEC Ann. Rep. at 5–6; 11th SEC Ann. Rep. at 94; Robert Sobel, Amex 231 (Weybright & Talley 1972); Report of Special Study of Securities Markets of the Securities and Exchange Commission, House Doc. No. 95, 88th Cong., 1st Sess. I at 21–23, 36 (1963).
18. SEC, Special Study, supra n. 17, I at 245, 487, 550–551.
19. *Time*, Aug. 1, 1960 at 60; Landis, supra n. 8. at 45.
20. Edward Gadsby, Historical Development of the SEC — The Government View, 28 George Wash. L. Rev. 16–17 (1959); Interview with Ralph Demmler, Aug. 24, 1980; Sinclair Armstrong, The Role of the Securities and Exchange Commission in Proxy Contests of Listed Companies, 11 Bus. Law. 122 (1955); Booz Allen & Hamilton, supra n. 17 at Exhibit I; *New York Times*, July 10, 1955 at 22; Address of J. Sinclair Armstrong, Nov. 13, 1956, on file with the SEC.
21. SEC, Special Study, supra n. 17, IV at 711–722.
22. William Cary, Testimony, Securities Markets Investigation Hearings, House Commerce Comm., 87th Cong., 1st Sess. 5 (1961); Booz Allen & Hamilton, supra n. 17, at 128–129.
23. Addresses of William Cary, Nov. 28, 1962, Dec. 2, 1963, on file with the SEC.

24. SEC, Staff Report on Organization, Management, and Regulation of Conduct of Members of the American Stock Exchange at 8–10 (Jan. 3, 1962).
25. Id. at 11–13, 15, 17–18, 55.
26. The Crowell-Collier distribution and Gilligan, Will are described in Independent Regulatory Commissions, Report of the Special House Subcomm. on Legislative Oversight, House Rep. No. 2711, 85th Cong., 2d Sess. 50–53 (1959); SEC, Staff Report, supra n. 24, at 23–46; Gilligan, Will & Co. v. SEC, 267 F.2d 461 (2d Cir. 1959); Sec. Ex. Act Rels. 5562 (1957), 5686 (1958), 5689 (1958); *New York Times*, Feb. 22, 1957 at 30; SEC Special Study, supra n. 17, IV at 582.
27. Frank Cormier, Wall Street's Shady Side 37–38 (Washington, D.C.; Public Affairs Press 1962); Robert Sobel, Amex (Weybright & Talley 1972); Brief of the Division of Trading and Exchanges before the SEC, In the Matter of Re, Re and Sagarese (Apr. 28, 1961); SEC Orders, In the Matter of Re, Re and Sagarese (May 12, 1960 and Aug. 24, 1960); U.S. v. Re, 336 F.2d 306 (2d Cir. 1964); Sec. Ex. Act Rel. 6551 (1961); SEC Litig. Rels. No. 2689 (1963), No. 2741 (1963); SEC Staff Report on the American Stock Exchange at 52–53; Memorandum to Cary from Loomis, Jan. 30, 1962, Cary SEC Commissioner Files, Container No. 202; Re, Re and Sagarese, 41 SEC 230 (1962); SEC Special Study, supra at 17, IV at 577–579, 583; Securities Markets Investigation Hearings, House Commerce Subcomm., 87th Cong., 1st Sess. 123–133 (1961); Memorandum to William Cary from Philip Loomis, Jan. 30, 1962, Cary SEC Commissioner Files, Container No. 202.
28. 2 Louis Loss, Joel Seligman & Troy Paredes, Securities Regulation 1258–1320 (6th ed. 2019); SEC v. Variable Annuity Life Ins. Co., 359 U.S. 65 (1959); SEC v. United Benefit Life Ins. Co., 387 U.S. 202 (1967).
29. Landis, supra n. 8, at 1–7, 11–13, 18, 35–36, 45–48, 66–72, 81–83; Regulatory Agencies of Our Government, Presidential Message, Apr. 13, 1961, Doc. No. 135, 87th Cong., 1st Sess. (1961); Donald Ritchie, James M. Landis 176–185 (Harvard Univ. Press 1980); William Cary, Politics and the Regulatory Agencies 7–26, 36–37 (McGraw-Hill 1967); *New York Times*, Nov. 11, 1960 at 1; Memorandum for Ralph Dungan from James Landis, Aug. 10, 1961, Kennedy Library, White House Staff Papers, James Landis, Box 14, Folder SEC Memoranda; 28th SEC Ann. Rep. at 166; Special Message to Congress: Transmitting Reorganization Plan 1 of 1961, Public Papers of John F. Kennedy 234 (1961); Pub. L. No. 592, 76 Stat. 394–395, 87th Cong., 2d Sess. (1962); Arthur Schlesinger, A Thousand Days 707–713 (Houghton Mifflin 1965); Theodore Sorenson,

Kennedy 339–353 (Harper & Row 1965); Interview with William Cary, Oct. 28–29, 1980.

30. Cary, Politics and the Regulatory Agencies, supra n. 29, at 69.
31. Interview with William Cary, Oct. 28–29, 1980; Memorandum to the Commission from William Cary, re: Lunch with G. Keith Funston, Oct. 15, 1962, Cary SEC Commissioner Files, Container No. 197; Cary, Politics and the Regulatory Agencies, supra n. 29; William Cary, Self-Regulation in the Securities Industry, 49 ABA J. 244 (1963); William Cary, Corporate Standards and Legal Rules, 50 Cal. L. Rev. 408 (1962); *Newsweek*, Dec. 10, 1962, at 69; John Brooks, The Go-Go Years 82–87 (Weybright & Talley 1973).
32. Interview with Cohen, Mar. 11, 1981; Interview with David Silver, Mar. 9, 1981; SEC Special Study, supra n. 17, IV at 693–728.
33. SEC, Special Study, supra n. 17, II at 329–346, 349, 428.
34. Ibid, II at 296, 302–323, 953–955.
35. Cary, Politics and the Regulatory Agencies, supra n. 29, at 245; SEC, Special Study, supra n. 17, II at 323, 349–351; Interview with Milton Cohen, Mar. 11, 1981.
36. Cary, Politics and the Regulatory Agencies, supra n. 29, at 72–73; Sec. Ex. Act Rel. 6551 (1961); Re, Re and Sagarese, 41 SEC 230 (1962); *SEC Minutes*, May 9, 1961, May 12, 1961, May 19, 1961, Dec. 19–21, 1961, Jan. 4, 8, 10, 16, 22, 1962; SEC, Staff Report on Organization, Management and Regulation of Conduct of Members of the American Stock Exchange 1 n. 1, 53–54 (Jan. 3, 1962); Interview with William Cary, October 28–29, 1980; Interview with Philip Loomis, Sept. 9, 1980; SEC, Special Study, IV at 577–583; Address of Edwin Etherington, A Report on the American Stock Exchange: What Out to Be Done, Can Be Done, March 26, 1963, Cary SEC Commissioner Files, Container No. 197; Gustave Levy remark at 15 of transcript of SEC Conference Relating to American Stock Exchange, Feb. 5, 1962, Cary SEC Commissioner Files, Container No. 198; Investor Protection Hearings, House Commerce Comm., 88th Cong., 1st Sess. 417–436, 597–598 (1963); Special Committee for Study of American Stock Exchange (the Levy Committee) Reports, Dec. 31, 1961, Jan. 30, 1962, Feb. 15, 1962; Brooks, supra n. 31, at 51–53; *Newsweek*, Jan. 22, 1962 at 66; Special Committee for Study of American Stock exchange's three Reports dated Dec. 21, 1961, Jan. 30, 1962, Feb. 15, 1962.
37. Cary, Politics and the Regulatory Agencies, supra n. 29, at 99, 111–112; *New York Times*, Feb. 9, 1964, III at 1; Memoranda of the Chairman of the Commission from Arthur Fleischer, Sept. 10, 1962, Jan. 24, 1963, Jan. 31, 1963, Apr. 1, 1963, Cary SEC Commissioner Files, Container No. 179; Memorandum to the Commission from Walter North, May 14, 1963, Cohen SEC Papers, Vol. 32, Item

10; Special Market Study Rels. 25 (Apr. 30, 1963), 33 (July 23, 1963); Letter to the President of the Senate and Speaker of the House of Representatives from William Cary, June 3, 1963, Cary SEC Commissioner Files, Container 204.

38. Cary, Politics and the Regulatory Agencies, supra n. 29, at 69, 95–98; Memorandum to the Commission from Milton Cohen, Dec. 12, 1962, Cohen SEC Papers, Vol. 40, Item 31E; *SEC Minutes*, Apr. 24, 1963, May 14, 1963, May 22, 1963; Memorandum to the Chairman from Douglas North, Changes Made As a Result of Discussions with Industry, Nov. 27, 1963, Cary SEC Commissioner Files, Container No. 200.
39. The history of earlier efforts to enact the Frear-Fulbright Bill appears in Louis Loss, *Securities Regulation* 1149–1164 (Little Brown 1961); SEC, Proposal to Safeguard Investors in Unregistered Securities, House Doc. No. 672, 79th Cong., 2d Sess. (1946); Report of the SEC on S. 2054, 84th Cong., 2d Sess. (1956); SEC, Special Study, supra n. 17, III at 1–17.
40. *SEC Minutes*, Mar. 9, 1962; Memorandum to the Chair from Arthur Fleischer, Mar. 7, 1963, Cohen SEC Papers, Vol. 40, Item 31m; Cary, Politics and the Regulatory Agencies, supra n. 29, at 96–98; House Investor Protection Hearings, supra n. 36, at 78, 90–95; SEC Legislation 1963 Hearings, Senate Banking Comm., 88th Cong., 1st Sess. 14–17, 313–351 (1963); Memorandum to the Chair from Douglas North, Nov. 27, 1963, Cary, SEC Commissioner Files, Container No. 200; SEC Memorandum with Respect to Modification of S. 1642 Proposed by the IBA, June 25, 1963, Cary SEC Commissioner Files, Container No. 183; Proposed IBA Position on the Legislative Proposals of the SEC, June 6, 1963, Cary SEC Commissioner Files, Container No. 202; *Wall Street Journal*, Mar. 26, 1964, at 2.
41. S. 1642, as enacted by the Senate, appears at 54–64 in House Investor Protection Hearings, supra n. 36. The legislative process is described in Senate Legislative 1963, supra n. 40, at 1–4, 171–179, 248–251; House Investor Protection at 1356–1371; *Congressional Record*, 88th Cong., 1st Sess., July 30, 1963, at 13,722; Comptroller of the Currency Press Release, June 5, 1963, Cohen SEC Papers, Vol. 41, Item 20; *New York Times*, July 10, 1963 at 43, July 17, 1963 at 37, July 31, 1963 at 33. Cary's account appears in Politics and the Regulatory Agencies, supra n. 29, at 99–104.
42. Cary, Politics and the Regulatory Agencies, supra n. 29, at 106; House Investor Protection Hearings, supra n. 36, at 268–269, 274, 740–742, 791–792, 890, 917, 1132, 1293; *New York Times*, Nov. 31, 1963, at 55; Schwartz, supra n. 1, at 8–15, 96, 215.
43. Interview with William Cary, Oct. 28–29, 1980; House Investor Protection Hearings, supra n. 36, at 21–27, 82–95, 119–122, 175–178,

291–293, 304–311, 741, 785–789, 893–916, 1001, 1057–1059, 1203–1213, 1271–1283, 1293; Memorandum to the Commission from Cary, June 19, 1963, Cohen SEC Papers, Vol. 33, Item 32; *New York Times,* July 17, 1963 at 37, Feb. 20, 1964, Mar. 20, 1964; Senate Hearings on S. 1642, at 228–241, 267–271, 275–277; *New York Times,* July 17, 1963, at 42; Cary, Politics and the Regulatory Agencies, supra n. 29, at 113–117; *SEC Minutes,* Aug. 25, 1963; Letter to Harvey Combs, Commissioner, Insurance Department, Arkansas, from William Cary, Sept. 18, 1963, Cohen SEC Papers, Vol. 43, Item 12. The ultimate compromise is found in § 12(g)(2)(G) of the 1964 Act. See also House Report No. 1418, 88th Cong., 2d Sess. 9–11 (1964).

44. Public Papers of Lyndon B. Johnson 263, 267 (1963–1964); Cary, Politics and the Regulatory Process, supra n. 29, at 106–110; House Investor Protection Hearings, supra n. 36, at 265, 289, 733–742, 783–784, 822; Memorandum to the Commission from Cary, Oct. 14, 1963, Cohen SEC Papers, Vol. 35, Item 7; *SEC Minutes,* Jan. 8, 1964; *New York Times,* Oct. 9, 1963 at 42, Nov. 17, 1963, III at 1, Nov. 29, 1963 at 36, Jan. 19. 1964, IV at 12, Jan. 22, 1964 at 50, Feb. 9, 1964, III at 1.
45. House Report No. 1418, 88th Cong., 2d Sess. 8–13 (1964); *New York Times,* Feb. 20, 1964 at 39, Apr. 30, 1964 at 47, May 8, 1964 at 43; House Investor Protection Hearings, supra n. 36, at 274; *SEC Minutes,* March 20, 1964, Apr. 28, 1964, Apr. 30, 1964; Cary, Politics and the Regulatory Agencies, supra n. 29, at 4, 109–110, 118–120; Memorandum to the files re: meeting with Congressman Oren Harris on H.R. 6789, June 3, 1964, Cary SEC Commissioner Files, Container No. 201; Interview with William Cary, Oct. 28–29, 1980.
46. See Seligman, supra n. 1, at 323–344.
47. Goodwin v. Agassiz, 283 Mass. 358 (1933); Cady, Roberts & Co., 40 SEC 907 (1961); Ward LaFrance Trucking Corp., Sec. Ex. Act Rel. 3445 (1943); J.I. Case v. Borak, 377 U.S. 426 (1964); Loss, supra n. 39, at 1448–1474; Milton Friedman Remarks, 22 Bus. Law. 921 (1967); William Cary, Corporate Standards and Legal Rules, Walter Perry Johnson Lecture, Mar. 24, 1962, Cary SEC Commissioner Files, Container No. 186; Louis Loss, The American Law Institute's Federal Securities Code Project, 25 Bus. Law. 34 (1960); Cary, Politics and the Regulatory Agencies, supra n. 29, at 84; Interview with William Cary, Oct. 28–29, 1980; Annual Reports of the Director of the Administrative Office of the United States Courts 239 (1961), 199 (1963), 232–233 (1970).
48. Public Papers of Lyndon Johnson 993, 1132, 1150–1151 (1963–1964); Interview with William Cary, Oct. 28–29, 1980; Cary, Politics and the Regulatory Agencies, supra n. 29, at 19, 63; *Wall Street Journal,* May 14, 1964, at 1; Lyndon Johnson, The Vantage Point 27–30,

69–81 (Holt, Rinehart & Winston 1971); *New York Times,* June 6, 1964 at 27, June 9, 1964 at 34, June 21, 1964 at 48, June 22, 1964 at 38; *Nation,* June 22, 1964, at 613.

49. Manuel Cohen, The SEC and Proxy Contests, 20 Fed. Bar J. 91 (1960); Broker-Dealer Selling Practice Standards: The Importance of Administrative Adjudication in Their Development, 29 Law & Contemp. Prob. 691 (1964); Cary's Politics and the Regulatory Agencies, 35 U. Chicago L. Rev. 399 (1968); Addresses dated March 10, 1964, Aug. 11, 1964, Dec. 1, 1964 on file with the SEC; Arthur Mathews & Michael Klein, Manuel F. Cohen in Perspective: Manny — We Miss Your Sparkle!, 46 Geo. Wash. L. Rev. 719 (1978); *Business Week,* July 18, 1964, at 26–27; Leonard Leiman, David Ratner & Meyer Eisenberg, Manuel F. Cohen: In Memoriam, 46 Geo. Wash. L. Rev. 711 (1978); Interviews with Leonard Leiman, March 20, 1981; David Ratner, Feb. 12, 1981; Meyer Eisenberg, March 2, 1981; Philip Loomis, March 4, 1981; Arthur Mathews, March 4, 1981; *Washington Post,* June 18, 1977, at D3; *New York Times,* July 11, 1964, at 1; William Cary Memorandum to the White House, Appointment of SEC Commissioner, July 6, 1961, White House Central Subject File, Box 179, File FG 281, John Fitzgerald Kennedy Library.

50. SEC 34th Ann. Rep. at xvii, xix, 11–12, 15–16; SEC 35th Ann. Rep. at 32, 76, 187; 37th SEC Ann. Rep. at 8–10; *SEC Minutes,* Jan. 31, 1964, Sept. 10, 1964; SEC, Institutional Investor Study, House Doc. No. 92–64, 92d Cong., 1st Sess. 58–62, 119, 1389, 1537–1541, 1622–1633, 1819–1824, 1959–1961, 2160–2161, 2167 (1971); SEC, Special Study, supra n. 17, II at 6, 837–870; Raymond Goldsmith, Institutional Investors and Corporate Stock: A Background Study (Columbia Univ. Press 1973); Robert Soldofsky, Institutional Holdings of Common Stock: 1900–2000 (Univ. of Mich. Bur. of Bus. Research 1971); Lawrence Shepard, The Securities Brokerage Industry 27 (Lexington Books 1975); Chris Welles, The Last Days of the Club 53–60 (Dutton 1975); Sobel, supra n. 16, at 330–354.

51. SEC, 35th Ann. Rep. at 18, 193; Address of SEC Commissioner Hugh Owens, Oct. 20, 1967, reprinted in Investment Company Act Amendments of 1967 Hearings, House Commerce Subcomm., 90th Cong., 1st Sess. 740–744 (1967); John Brooks, supra n. 31, at 127–149, 266–285; Robert Sobel, The Last Bull Market 107, 188–192, 204–205 (W.W. Norton 1980); Peter Wyckoff, Wall Street and the Stock Markets 115, 124, 127–128 (Chilton Book 1972); *Business Week,* Jan. 18, 1969, at 108–114.

52. Cohen quoted in *Institutional Investor,* Feb. 1969 at 75, 149; Manuel F. Cohen & George Stigler, Can Regulatory Agencies Protect

Consumers 39–40 (American Enterprise Institute 1971); Cohen response to Nixon quoted in *Washington Post*, Oct. 9, 1968, at D7.

53. *Institutional Investor*, Feb. 1969, at 149.
54. For a succinct summary of the leading cases of this period, see Mathews & Klein, supra n. 49, at 724–732; see also Interviews with Stanley Sporkin, March 2, 1971, Ralph Saul, March 5, 1981, Ira Pearce, March 20, 1981, Philip Loomis, March 4, 1981, Meyer Eisenberg, March 2, 1981, Arthur Mathews, March 4, 1981; Hillel Black, The Watchdogs of Wall Street (William Morrow 1962).
55. Seligman, supra n. 1, at 417–436; 5 Louis Loss, Joel Seligman & Troy Paredes, Securities Regulation 45–58 (5th ed. 2016).
56. Report of the Securities and Exchange Commission on the Public Policy Implications of Investment Company Growth, House of Representatives Rep. No. 2337, 89th Cong., 2d Sess. 11–16, 156–159 (1966); Irwin Friend, Marshall Blume & Jean Crockett, Mutual Funds and Other Institutional Investors (McGraw-Hill 1970); Brooks, supra n. 31, at 128–149; Sobel, supra n. 51, at 150–159; Sec. Ex. Act Rels. 7816 (1966), 8083 (1967).
57. Carol J. Loomis, The SEC Has a Little List, *Fortune*, Jan. 1967, at 154; *New York Times*, May 16, 1966 at 1, May 17, 1966 at 1, May 18, 1966 at 1; SEC 27th Ann. Rep. at 3–4; SEC 1966 Investment Company Report, supra n. 56, at 132–137, 201–209; Wharton School, A Study of Mutual Funds, House Rep. No. 2274, 87th Cong., 2d Sess. (1962); Friend, Blume & Crockett, supra n. 56, at 17–18.
58. Wharton, supra n. 57, at 3, 6–9, 28–32, 469–471, 480–525, 803–805; House, SEC Investment Company Report, supra n. 56, at 94–104, 121–123, 208–209; SEC Special Study, supra n. 17, IV at 96, 109–100; Mutual Fund Legislation of 1967, Hearings, Senate Banking Comm., 90th Cong. 1st Sess. 177–184 (1967).
59. Interview with William Cary, Oct. 28–29, 1980; SEC, Special Study, supra n. 17, IV at 169–212. See also SEC, Investment Company Report, supra n. 56, at 57–58, 223–247.
60. SEC, Investment Company Report, supra n. 56, at VII; Walter Werner, Protecting the Mutual Fund Investor: The SEC Reports on the SEC, 68 Colum. L. Rev. 2 (1968); Testimony of Paul Samuelson at 1967 Senate Mutual Fund Hearings, supra n. 58, at 347–355; Investment Company Act Amendments of 1967 Hearings, House Commerce Subcomm., 90th Cong., 1st Sess. 20–22 (1967); Investment Company Amendments Act of 1969 Hearings, Senate Banking Comm., 91st Cong., 1st Sess. 55 (1969); Cohen & Stigler, supra n. 52, at 8; Department of Justice, Summary of Statements of Department of Justice, Henry Wallich, and Donald Farrar, SEC Staff Report, Mutual Fund Distribution and Section 22(d) of the Investment Company Act of 1940 69–73 (Aug. 1974); Statement of Irwin

Friend, 1967 Senate Mutual Fund Hearings at 685; Letter from Gardner Ackley, Chairman of the Council of Economic Advisers, Aug. 1, 1967, Senate Mutual Fund Hearings at 957; SEC Staff Report, The Potential Economic Impact of a Repeal of Section 22(d) of the Investment Company Act of 1940 (1972), excerpted in Securities Report (BNA), Nov. 15, 1972.

61. SEC, Investment Company Report, supra n. 58, at 59; SEC, Potential Economic Impact, supra n. 60; Tamar Frankel, The Regulation of Money Managers I at 58, 66, IV at 105–108; Senate 1967 Mutual Fund Hearings, supra n. 58, at 685; Friend, Blume & Crockett, supra n. 56, at 105–108.

62. SEC 1966 Investment Company Report, supra n. 56, at 218–223; SEC Potential Economic Impact, supra n. 60, at 25, 209–223; Senate Mutual Fund Hearings, supra n. 58, at 8, 18–19, 151–155; Frankel, The Regulation of Money Managers, supra n. 61, IV at 41–105; Memorandum of Chair Cohen from Philip Loomis, July 8, 1966, Cohen SEC Papers, Vol. 103c-VI, Item 56; Memorandum to Chair from Richard Phillips, July 27, 1966, Cohen SEC Papers, Vol. 103c-VI, Item 58; Memorandum to Manuel Cohen from Richard Phillips, Oct. 20, 1965, Cohen SEC Papers, Vol 103c-V, Item 37; Address of Manuel Cohen, May 1, 1967, on file with SEC, at 12; *Wall Street Journal*, Dec. 26, 1968 at 6; Interviews with Philip Loomis, March 4, 1981, David Ratner, Feb. 12, 1981; David Ratner, Regulation of the Compensation of Securities Dealers, 55 Cornell L. Rev. 376–377 (1969).

63. SEC, Investment Company Report, supra n. 56, at 143–149; Richard Posner & Kenneth Scott, eds., Economics of Corporation Law and Securities Regulation 2–6 (Little, Brown 1980); Wharton Study, supra n. 57, at 494–495; 1967 Senate Mutual Fund Hearings, supra n. 58, at 704–709.

64. Landis, SEC Special Study, supra n. 17, IV at 179–185; Demmler, 1967 Senate Mutual Fund Hearings, supra n. 58, at 186, 221–232; William O. Douglas, Go East, Young Man 315 (Dell 1974); Robbins, Has the SEC Forgotten Its Economics?, Colum. J. of World Bus. 7 (May-June 1967).

65. The text of the Bill as introduced, S. 1659, appears in 1967 Senate Mutual Fund Hearings, supra n. 58, at 897–956; Letters to Sparkman from the New York Stock Exchange, June 15, 1967, the American Stock Exchange, June 15, 1967, NASD, June 16, 1967, ICI, June 15, 1967, Cohen SEC Papers, Vol. III, Items 5, 12–14. The text of the bill as passed appears in Investment Company Amendments Act of 1969 Hearings, Senate Banking Comm., 91st Cong., 1st Sess. 215–287 (1969); 33d SEC Ann. Rep., at 2; 34th SEC Ann. Rep., at 4–6; 36th SEC Ann. Rep., at 16.

66. *Washington Post*, Sept. 11, 1968 at D7, Sept. 15, 1968 at F1; *Congressional Record*, 90th Cong., 2d Sess., Oct. 3, 1968; at S11,934–11,924, *Congressional Record*, 90th Cong., 2d Sess., Oct. 11, 1968, at S12,582; *Business Week*, Feb. 15, 1969, at 110.
67. Pub. L. No. 91–547, 84 Stat. 1413 (1970); Investment Company Institute v. Camp, 401 U.S. 617 (1971); 27th SEC Ann. Rep. at 14–15; Frankel, supra n. 61, IV at 101–105; Gerard Manges, The Investment Company Amendments Act of 1970: An Analysis and Appraisal After Two Years, 14 Boston College Indus. & Comm. L. Rev. 387 (1973).
68. SEC Staff Report, Mutual Fund Distribution and Section 22(d), supra n. 60, at 69–71.
69. Testimony of Paul Samuelson, Stock Exchange Commission Rates Hearings, Senate Banking Subcomm., 92d Cong., 2d Sess. 142 (1972); Lawrence Shepard, The Securities Brokerage Industry 38 (Lexington Books 1975); Kohlmeier, supra n. 1, at 240–241, 305.
70. Silver v. New York Stock Exch., 373 U.S. 341 (1963); Gordon v. New York Stock Exch. 422 U.S. 664 (1975); Justice Department Brief In the Matter of Commission Rate Structure of Registered National Securities Exchanges, Hearings Before the SEC 24 (1969); Abe Fortas, The Frontier Between the Antitrust Law and the Securities Markets, 61 Ill. B. J. 25 (1972); Louis Loss, Securities Regulation 3156–3157 (Little, Brown 1969); Thomas Linden, A Reconciliation of Antitrust Law with Securities Regulation: The Judicial Approach, 45 Geo. Wash. L. Rev. 179 (1977).
71. The single most useful document concerning Rule 394 was a 211-page SEC Staff Study prepared in 1965. The Study was made public as a result of a Freedom of Information Suit, M.A. Schapiro v. SEC, 339 F. Supp. 467 (D.D.C. 1972), and published with certain omissions in *Securities Reporter* (BNA) No. 132, Dec. 22, 1971, at D1–D49.
72. SEC Staff Report, supra n. 71; Loomis, supra n. 54, at 113; Memorandum to the Commission from Irving Pollack, Rate Structure and Rule 394, Dec. 8, 1965, Cohen SEC Papers; Note, Informal Bargaining Process: An Analysis of the SEC's Regulation of the New York Stock Exchange, 80 Yale L.J. 822 (1971); M.A. Schapiro v. SEC, 339 F. Supp. 467 (D.D.C. 1972); *SEC Minutes*, March 10, 1966, March 24, 1966, May 11, 1966, June 23, 1966, July 13, 1966, July 19, 1966, Apr. 3, 1967; Letter to Manuel Cohen from Keith Funston, Sept. 15, 1966, Cohen SEC Papers; Sec. Ex. Act Rels. 7954, 7981 (1966); Loss, supra n. 70, at 3168–3170; Memorandum to Irving Pollack from Normal Poser, Rule 394(b), Nov. 29, 1966; Memorandum to the Commission from Irving Pollack, Rule 394, Dec. 2, 1966; Memorandum to the Commission from Irving Pollack, Rule 394(b), March 29, 1967; Letter to Keith Funston from Manuel Cohen, Aug. 23,

1967; Letter to Manuel Cohen from Robert Haack, Oct. 3, 1967; Memorandum to the Commission from the Division of Trading and Markets, Rule 394(b), Oct. 26, 1967, Cohen SEC Papers.

73. *SEC Minutes,* June 25, 1965, Aug. 30, 1965; SEC, Institutional Investor Study, supra n. 50, at 2298–2311; Securities Industry Study Report, Senate Banking Subcomm., S. Doc. No. 93–13, 93d Cong., 1st Sess. 71–73 (1973); Wells, supra n. 50, at 81–83; Robbins, supra n. 52, at 276–277.
74. SEC, Institutional Investor Study, supra n. 50, at 2183–2184, 2192; SEC, Investment Company Report, supra n. 56, at 169–187; *Business Week,* Jan. 14, 1967, at 125–128; Welles, supra n. 50, at 74–79; Sec. Ex. Act Rel. 8239 (1968).
75. Memorandum to the Commission from Eugene Rotberg re: New York Stock Exchange Rate Structure Proposals Meeting with Robert Haack and Bob Bishop, Jan. 11, 1968, Cohen SEC papers; *SEC Minutes,* Jan. 12, 1968; Sec. Ex. Act Rel. 8239 (1968); David Ratner, The SEC: Portrait of the Agency as a Thirty-Seven Year Old, 45 St. John's L. Rev. 592 (1971); Lehman, Ratner & Eisenberg, supra n. 49, at 713, 715; Eugene Rotberg, unpublished article, Competition and the Securities Markets, and transcript of remarks of 1969 Institutional Investors public forum both on file with Eugene Rotberg, Washington, D.C.; Interviews with Eugene Rotberg, Feb. 26, 1981, Meyer Eisenberg, March 2, 1981, David Ratner, Feb. 12, 1981, Richard Smith, March 20, 1981;
76. Paul Samuelson, Testimony, Stock Exchange Commission Rates Hearings, Senate Banking Subcomm., 92d Cong., 2d Sess. 142 (1972); Sec. Ex. Act Rels. 8239 (1968), 8324 (1968); Welles, supra n. 50, at 88–89; Comments of the United States Department of Justice on SEC Rel. No. 8239, Apr. 1, 1968, Cohen SEC Papers; Ratner, supra n. 75, at 593.
77. Letter to Manuel Cohen from Robert Haack, Aug. 8, 1968, Fed. Sec. L. Rep. (CCH) ¶ 77,585; Sec. Ex. Act Rel. 8399 (1968); Memorandum to the Commission from Eugene Rotberg, June 6, 1968, Cohen SEC Papers; SEC, Institutional Investor Study, supra n. 50, at 2199–2208. The $150 million saving was frequently noted, see, e.g., 34th SEC Ann. Rep. at 2.
78. A full transcript of the hearings and the Exchange and Just Department comments, analyses, and briefs are available at the SEC library; Exchange Testimony summarized in Memorandum to the Commission from Division of Trading and Markets Office of Policy Research, New York Stock Exchange Commission Rate Proposal, Oct. 1, 1970.
79. Study on Federal Regulation, Senate Committee on Government Operations, 95th Cong., 1st Sess. (1977), Committee Print,

The Regulatory Appointments Process at 7–10; *New York Times*, June 1, 1969 at 1; June 6, 1964 at 27, June 21, 1964 at 48, June 22, 1964 at 38, June 27, 1964 at 28; *Institutional Investor*, June 1969, at 33; *National Journal*, Feb. 20, 1971, at 373–388; *Time*, Aug. 8, 1969, at 69–70; *National Journal*, Feb. 20, 1971, at 377, 380, 387–388; *Business Week*, Sept. 6, 1969, at 28; *Securities Reporter* (BNA), March 4, 1970, at A12; Securities Industry Study, House Rep. No. 92–1519, House Commerce Subcomm., 92d Cong., 2d Sess. at 169–170 (1972); 35th SEC Ann. Rep. at 214; 36th SEC Ann. Rep. at 29, 209.

80. Nomination of William J. Casey, Senate Rep. No. 92–4, 92d Cong., 1st Sess. (1971); 37th SEC Ann. Rep., at vii; 38th SEC Ann. Rep. at 133, 135–136; 40th SEC Ann. Rep. at 138; *National Journal*, Feb. 20, 1971, at 379; *Business Week*, Feb. 6, 1971 at 18, Oct. 16, 1971 at 71; Study of the Securities Industry Hearings, House Commerce Subcomm., 92d Cong., 1st Sess. 169–170, 1714–1715 (1971); *Securities Reporter* (BNA) Aug. 2, 1972 at A11–A13, Aug. 9, 1972 at A10–A11.
81. Sec. Ex. Act Rel. 9079; SEC, Institutional Investor Study, supra n. 50, I at xxiii–xxv; SEC, Statement on the Future Structure of the Securities Markets, at 14–17, 24; Testimony of William Casey, Stock Exchange Commission Rate Hearings, Senate Securities Subcomm., 92d Cong., 2d Sess. 19 (1972); Address of Ray Garrett, The State of the SEC, erroneously dated Mar. 1, 1973, on file with the SEC, at 17.
82. Testimony of G. Bradford Cook, Legislative Oversight of SEC: Agency Independence and the ITT Case Hearings, House Interstate Commerce Special Subcomm., 93d Cong., 1st Sess. 1–41 (1973); *New York Times*, May 17, 1973 at 1, May 26, 1973 at 10; *Juris Doctor*, June-July 1973 at 18–20; *Securities Reporter* (BNA), Feb. 21, 1973 at A9–A10, May 16, 1973 at AA1–AA2.
83. Interview with A.A. Sommer, March 2, 1981; *Securities Reporter* (BNA), Aug. 1, 1973, at A14–A15; Ray Garrett, Jr., Memorial Service, March 7, 1980; *Fortune*, Nov. 1974 at 139–141, 242–253; *Newsweek*, July 16, 1973, at 65–66; *Business Week*, July 14, 1973, at 28–29; 39th SEC Ann. Rep. at ix–xi; 40th SEC Ann. Rep. at x; *Time*, Feb. 11, 1974, at 103; Remarks of John Evans, Ray Garrett, Jr., Memorial Service, Mar. 7, 1980; Interview with Theodore Levine, March 3, 1981; Interview with Ed Herlihy, Feb. 25, 1981.
84. 41st SEC Ann. Rep. at ix; *Securities Reporter* (BNA), Oct. 8, 1975 at AA1–AA6, Feb. 4, 1976 at A1–A2, F1–F5, Apr. 14, 1976 at A14, June 16, 1976 at AA1–AA9.
85. SEC, Study of Unsafe and Unsound Practices of Brokers and Dealers, House Doc. No. 92–231, 92d Cong., 1st Sess. 1, 219, 222 (Dec. 1971); Securities Markets Agencies Hearings, House Commerce Subcomm., 91st Cong., 1st Sess. 8 (1969); House Securities Industry

Study, supra n. 80, at 3; Hurd Baruch, Wall Street: Security Risk 86 (Acropolis Books 1971); 35th SEC Ann. Rep. at 1.

86. 35th SEC Ann. Rep. at 2; Baruch, supra n. 85, at 101–103; SEC, Study of Unsafe and Unsound Practices, supra n. 85, at 53, 95–107; Address of Hamer Budge, Sept. 4, 1969, on file with the SEC; Testimony of Lee Arning, Vice President, New York Stock Exchange, House Securities Industry Hearings, supra n. 87, I at 8.

87. Sec. Ex. Act Rel. 8433 (1968); Securities Industry Study Hearings, Senate Subcomm. on Securities, 92d Cong., 2d Sess., IV at 223–224 (1972); Review of SEC Records of the Demise of Selected Broker-Dealers, Staff Study for the Special Subcomm. on Investigations, House Commerce Comm., 92d Cong., 1st Sess. 136–140 (1971); Brauch, supra n. 85, at 190–191; Welles, supra n. 50, at 165–167.

88. Peter Wyckoff, Wall Street and The Stock Market 130, 134 (Chilton Book 1972); House Securities Industry Study, supra n. 87, at 9–10, 89; House Demise Review, supra n. 87, at 3; Securities Industry Study Report of the Senate Banking Comm., 92d Cong., 2d Sess. 7–8 (1972); Federal Broker-Dealer Insurance Corporation Hearings, Senate Banking Subcomm. on Sec. 1, 91st Cong., 2d Sess. (1970); Baruch, supra n. 85, at 147–149; 2d Securities Investor Protection Corp. Ann. Rep. at 2; *Newsweek*, Oct. 12, 1970, at 87; SEC Study of Unsafe and Unsound Practices, supra n. 85, at 1–2.

89. Welles, supra n. 50, at 172–209; House Demise Review, supra n. 87, at 50–51, 101–102, 122–127; Baruch, supra n. 85, at 193–196.

90. Baruch, supra n. 85, at 196–227; Welles, supra n. 50, at 209–241; House Demise Review, supra n. 87, at 103–110; *Fortune*, Dec. 1970 at 63, Jan. 1971 at 114–116, 154–159.

91. Baruch, supra n. 85, at 231–248; House Demise Review, supra n. 87, at 76–82; Senate Securities Industry, supra n. 88, IV at 263–265.

92. *Business Week*, June 29, 1968, at 4; Donald Regan, A View from the Street 94 (New Am. Libr. 1972); SEC, Study of Unsafe and Unsound Practices, supra n. 85, at 98–105, 117, 145–150; Welles, supra n. 50, at 170.

93. Regan, supra n. 92, at 105; Baruch, supra n. 85, at 106–110, 112, 192, 199; Welles, supra n. 50, at 172–209; SEC, Study of Unsafe and Unsound Practices, supra n. 85, at 120–121.

94. House Demise Review, supra n. 87, at 26–29; SEC, Study of Unsafe and Unsound Practices, supra n. 87, at 49–94; Baruch, supra n. 85, at 154–170, 177–188; Hugh Sowards & James Mofsky, The Securities Investor Protection Act of 1970, 26 Bus. Law. 1272–1273 (1971).

95. *Wall Street Journal*, Aug. 4, 1967 article reprinted in House Securities Markets Agencies Hearings, supra n. 85, at 87–89; SEC, Study of Unsafe and Unsound Practices, supra n. 85, at 251–252, 226–227;

Senate Securities Industry Study Hearings, supra n. 88, IV at 225; *National Journal*, Feb. 20, 1971, at 381; Wyckoff, supra n. 88, at 130.

96. Pub. L. No. 91–598, 84 Stat. 1636–1657. See also Senate Report 91-1218; House Reports 91-1613, 91-1788; Baruch, supra n. 85, at 64–80; David Greenberg, An Analysis of the Securities Investor Protection Act of 1970, 16 Howard L.J. 907 (1971); Soward & Mofsky, supra n. 94, at 1271.

97. SEC, Study of Unsafe and Unsound Practices, supra n. 85, at 2; House Study of the Securities Industry, supra n. 80, at 1080–1081, 1091–1108; Welles, supra n. 50, at 161–162; Sec. Ex. Act Rels. 9268 (1971), 11,497 (1975).

98. James Lorie, Public Policy for American Capital Markets, Secretary and Deputy Secretary of the United States Treasury Department 5 (1974); Address of G. Bradford Cook, Apr. 25, 1973, on file with the SEC; Address of Ray Garrett, March 22, 1974, on file with the SEC; James Sargent, The SEC and the Individual Investor: Restoring His Confidence in the Market, 60 Va. L. Rev. 553 (1974); Charles Rolo, The Case of the Vanishing Investor, *New York Times* Magazine, June 9, 1974, at 14–15, 47–48, 52–53, 58–60; *Dun's*, March 1970 at 124; Securities Exchange Act Amendment of 1973 Hearings, House Commerce Subcomm., 93d Cong., 1st Sess. 678–685 (1973); New York Stock Exchange, Shareownership 1980 (1981); New York Stock Exchange, Marketing Securities to the Small Investor 40, 47 (June 1973).

99. Regan, supra n. 92, at 130–133; 37th SEC Ann. Rep. at 6–8; SEC, Study of Unsafe and Unsound Practices, supra n. 85, at 80; Sec. Ex. Act Rel. 8717 (1969); James Sargent, The SEC and the Institutional Investor, 60 Va. L. Rev. 566–567 (1974); *Fortune*, Aug. 1, 1969 at 88–90, 137–138, 157–159; *Securities Reporter* (BNA), June 4, 1969 at A1–A2, X12–X13, July 23, 1969 at X6, Feb. 18, 1970 at X1–X2, Apr. 1, 1970 at A11–A12.

100. Sec. Ex. Act Rel. 9950 at 36 (1973); Justice Department Statement in House Securities Industry Study Hearings, supra n. 80, VII at 3142; Testimony of American Bankers Association Officials before Fixed Rates and Institutional Membership Hearings, Senate Subcomm. on Sec., 93d Cong., 1st Sess. 284 (1973); 1973 Senate Securities Industry Study, supra n. 73, at 68, 84 (quoting Gustave Levy); 1972 Senate Securities Industry Study, supra n. 87, at 69; Regan, supra n. 92, at 183–184.

101. Submission to SEC, reprinted in *Securities Reporter* (BNA), Nov. 19, 1969, at X37–X42; 1972 Senate Securities Industry Study, supra n. 87, at 61–64; *Securities Reporter* (BNA), Mar. 4, 1970 at A5–A8, A15, Mar. 18, 1970 at A1.

102. *Securities Reporter* (BNA), Nov. 19, 1969 at A3, Jan. 20, 1971 at A1–A3, Jan. 27, 1971 at A1–A2; Welles, supra n. 50, at 94; The Martin Report reprinted in *Securities Reporter*, Aug. 11, 1971, at E1–E7.
103. SEC Statement of the Future Structure of the Securities Markets 20–24 (Feb. 2, 1972); White Paper on Institutional Membership (Apr. 20, 1972), was presented by Chair Casey in testimony to the Senate Subcommittee on Securities and *reprinted* in *Securities Reporter* (BNA), Apr. 26, 1972, at I1–I7; Sec. Ex. Act Rel. 9950 at 34; 39th SEC Ann. Rep. at 8–9.
104. House Securities Industry Study, supra n. 87, at 148–149; 1973 Senate Securities Industry Study, supra n. 73, at 8–9, 64–87; House Rep. 94–123, 94th Cong., 1st Sess. 57 (1975); Senate Rep. 94-75, 94th Cong., 1st Sess. 65–67 (1975). The SEC's 80-20 test also was criticized by Nixon-Ford Justice Department, *Securities Reporter* (BNA), Oct. 4, 1972 at I1–I7, A2–A3, as well as by representatives of the insurance industry, *Securities Reporter* (BNA), Oct. 4, 1972, at A19 and Banking Industry Fixed Rates and Institutional Membership Hearings, Senate Subcomm. on Sec., 93d Cong., 1st Sess. 283–285 (1973). In February and March 1973, the New York Stock Exchange ceased to support the 80–20 Test; see Senate Fixed Rates and Institutional Membership Hearings at 437–438, 465. The relevant Section of the 1975 Securities Acts Amendments appears in 89 Stat. at 110–111.
105. House Securities Industry Study, supra n. 87, at 134; Senate Securities Industry Study, supra n. 87, at 55; Testimony of Richard Howland, Securities Industry Study Hearings, Senate Sec. Subcomm., 92d Cong., 1st Sess. 121–122 (1971); SEC Institutional Investor Study, supra n. 50, I at vii; SEC Future Structure Statement, supra n. 103, at 14–18; Testimony of William Casey, Stock Exchange Commission Rates Hearings, Senate Sec. Subcomm., 92d Cong., 2d Sess. 19 (1972); *Securities Reporter* (BNA) 95, Mar. 28, 1973 at A15–A16.
106. Haack, November 1970 Address; 1972 Senate Securities Industry Study, supra n. 88, at 56, reprinted in *Securities Reporter* (BNA), Nov. 18, 1970, at J1–J3.
107. Sec. Ex. Act Rel. 10,383 (1973); Letter to James Needham from Ray Garrett, Dec. 14, 1973, reprinted in *Securities Reporter* (BNA), Dec. 14, 1973, at M1–M3; Addresses of Ray Garrett, Feb. 12, 1974, Dec. 4, 1974, on file at the SEC; Interview with John Evans, March 3, 1981; Interview with A.A. Sommer, March 2, 1981.
108. *Securities Reporter* (BNA), Feb. 13, 1974 at A4–A5, March 13, 1974, at A7, Oct. 23, 1974 at A2, Dec. 11, 1974 at E1–E3; Testimony of James Needham, Fixed Rates and Institutional Membership Hearings, Senate Subcomm. on Sec., 93d Cong., 1st Sess. 436–437, 464–465 (1973); John Evans Address, Apr. 15, 1975, on file with the SEC.

109. *Securities Reporter* (BNA), Dec. 11, 1974 at AA1–AA2, Dec. 18, 1974 at AA1–AA3; Address of Ray Garrett, Dec. 4, 1974, on file with the SEC; Sec. Ex. Act Rel. 11,203 (1975); *Securities Reporter* (BNA), Feb. 12, 1975 at A1; Pub. L. No. 94–29, 89 Stat. at 107–108.
110. Leroy Verschuur, The Securities Acts Amendments of 1975: A Move Toward Competition 22, 24 (Ph.D., Univ. of Nebraska 1978); Lawrence Goldberg & Lawrence White, eds., The Deregulation of the Banking and Securities Industries 159 (Lexington Books 1979); SEC Monthly Statistical Review, Oct. 1980 at 13; New York Stock Exchange Fact Book 15 (1980); SEC Staff Report, The Securities Industry in 1980 at 83–86, 92–94, App. F1, F2; SEC Fifth Report to Congress on the Effect of the Absence of Fixed Rates of Commissions iii, 48 (May 26, 1977); *New York Times*, March 4, 1979, III at 2, June 1, 1980, III at 1.
111. SEC Institutional Investor Study, supra n. 50, at Chaps. 11 & 12, esp. at 1541, 1587–1607, 1842–1843, 1936, Part VIII at 87–90, 98; 1973 Senate Securities Industry Study, supra n. 73, at 107–109; 1980 block trading data from SEC, The Securities Industry in 1980, supra n. 110, at 4–5 & App. A3.
112. SEC Study of Unsafe and Unsound Practices, supra n. 85, at 35–39, 165–209; House Securities Industry Study, supra n. 87, at 59–77; 1972 Senate Securities Industry Study, supra n. 88, at 2–3, 11–27; SRI cost estimate described in *Securities Week*, July 25, 1977, at 1–2 and Testimony of Junius Peake, Progress Toward the Development of a National Market System Hearings, House Commerce Subcomm., 96th Cong., 1st Sess. 107 (1979). On cost savings, see these hearings, generally at 76–77, 102, 128–129.
113. NASD, Three Issues in the Development of a Central Securities Market System 20–23 (1976); Sec. Ex. Act Rel. 8440 (1968); James Hamilton, Marketplace Organization and Marketability: Nasdaq, the Stock Exchange and the National Market System, 33 Journal of Fin. 487 (1978).
114. Baruch, supra n. 85, at 289; *Securities Reporter* (BNA), Nov. 11, 1970 at A4–A5, Dec. 16, 1970 at A18–A19; House Securities Industry Study, supra n. 79, at 117–130; 1972 Senate Securities Industry Study, supra n. 87, at 33–51; Morris Mendelson, Nostalgia vs. the Computer, 4 Sec. L. Rev. at 503 (1972).
115. SEC, Institutional Investor Study, supra n. 50, at xxii–xxv; The Martin Report, reprinted in *Securities Reporter* (BNA), Aug. 11, 1971, at E1–E7.
116. Statements by Mathews, 90 economists, Lorie, and Samuelson reprinted in House Securities Industry Hearings, supra n. 85, at 2892–2893, 3246, 3249; Donald Farrar, Wall Street's Proposed "Great Leap Backward," Financial Analyst J. (Sept.-Oct. 1971) at

14–16, 59–62; *Business Week*, Aug. 14, 1971 *reprinted* in House Securities Industry Study Hearings, supra n. 87, I at 93. See generally id. at 4005–4010.

117. Sec. Ex. Act Rel. 9315 (1971); SEC Future Structure Statement, supra n. 103, at 7–9; *Securities Reporter* (BNA), Oct. 13, 1971 at A1–A3, Oct. 20, 1971 at A1–A8.

118. SEC Policy Statement on the Structure of a Central Market System, at 8, 18, 21–25, 48, 57–58, 63–64.

119. Address of G. Bradford Cook, Feb. 23, 1973, on file with SEC; Interview with Harold Williams, Nov. 7, 1981; Williams 1979 Testimony quoted in House Committee Print 96-IFC 56, 96th Cong., 2d Sess. (1980). Milton Cohen, whose views were similar to those of Harold Williams, published a detailed explanation of the reasons for a "modest" evolutionary approach, The National Market System — A Modest Proposal, 46 Geo. Wash. L. Rev. 743 (1978).

120. 1973 Senate Securities Industry Study, supra n. 73, at 5–8; Welles, supra n. 50, at 303–309; Interview with A.A. Sommer, March 2, 1981; Lloyd Feller & George Simon, The National Market System in Perspective: A Selective Outline of Significant Events, May 15, 1978, unpublished, on file with the SEC's Division of Market Regulation; Sec. Ex. Act Rels. 9530 (1972), 9731 (1972), 9850 (1972); Advisory Committee Report reprinted in *Securities Reporter* (BNA), July 19, 1972, at E1–E2; Address of Ray Garrett, Jan. 15, 1974, on file with the SEC.

121. Advisory Comm. Report, supra n. 120, at 171–173; SEC, Policy Statement on the Structure of a Central Market System 48 (1973); Sec. Ex. Act Rels. 9529 (1972), 10,909 (1974), 11,406 (1975), 11,288 (1975); *Securities Reporter* (BNA), May 9, 1973 at A10, June 26, 1974 at 10, Sept. 25, 1974 at A5–A6, Jan. 1, 1975 at A14–A16; Wall Street Letter, May 27, 1974, at 1; Welles, supra n. 50, at 309–313.

122. SEC Institutional Investor Study, supra n. 50, I at xxiv–xxv; SEC Statement on the Future Structure of the Securities Market, supra n. 103, at 7–12; SEC Policy Statements on the Structure of a Central Market System, supra n. 118, at 48.

123. House Report 94-229, 94th Cong., 1st Sess. 94–96 (1975); House Report 94-123, 94th Cong., 1st Sess. 94 (1975); Interview with John Evans, March 3, 1981; *Securities Week*, May 12, 1975 at 2, May 19, 1975 at 2–3, June 30, 1975 at 1–2.

124. Address of A.A. Sommer, Oct. 10, 1975, on file with the SEC.

125. Sec. Ex. Act Rels. 11,942 (1975), 13,663 (1977).

126. Sec. Ex. Act Rel. 14,416 (1978).

127. Sec. Ex. Act Rel. 15,769 (1979); Loss, Seligman & Paredes, supra n. 55, at 651–652.

128. Cincinnati hard CLOB system described in House Progress Toward the Development of a National Market System Hearings, House Commerce Subcomm., 96th Cong., 1st Sess. 6–7 85, 93, 132–150, 250–251, 277–285, 475 (1979); House Committee Print 96-IFC 56, 96th Cong., 2d Sess. 28 (1980); SEC, A Monitoring Report on the Operation of the Cincinnati Stock Exchange National Securities Trading System (1981); *Securities Reporter* (BNA), June 21, 1978 at A10–A14, July 12, 1978 at A2–A3, Oct. 4, 1978 at A4; The Intermarket Trading System (*ITS*) described in House Progress Toward the Development of a National Market System Hearings at 6–7, 70–88, 132–150, 250–251; House Committee Print 96-IFC 56, 96th Cong., 2d Sess. 21 (1980); SEC, A Monitoring Report on the Operation of the Intermarket Trading System 5–9 (1981).
129. Sec. Ex. Act Rels. 14,416 (1978), 15,671 (1979. See also House Progress Toward the Development of a National Securities Market, supra n. 128, at 419–421; Letter to George Fitzsimmons, Secretary, Securities and Exchange Commission, from James E. Buck, Secretary, New York Stock Exchange, May 31, 1978, on file with the New York Stock Exchange.
130. House Progress Toward the Development of a National Market System Hearings, supra n. 128, at 143, 191–193; SEC, Monitoring Report on the Operations and Effects of Rule 19c-3, 38–41 (1981); Sec. Ex. Act Rel. 17,744 (1981); SEC, A Monitoring Report on the Operation of the Intermarket Trading System, at 5–6, 10–12, 15, 38, 45 (1981); *Wall Street Journal*, May 5, 1980, at 1, 30.
131. Watergate Special Prosecution Force Reports 71–77 (1975); John Coffee, Beyond the Shut-Eyed Sentry: Toward a Theoretical View of Corporate Misconduct and an Effective Legal Response, 63 Va. L. Rev. 1099 (1977); Address of Ray Garrett, June 27, 1975, on file with the SEC; Ronald Kane & Samuel Butler, Improper Corporate Payments: The Second Half of Watergate, 8 Loyola Univ. (Chicago) L. Rev. 6 (1976); Edward Herlihy & Theodore Levine, Corporate Crisis: The Overseas Payment Program, 8 Law and Policy in Int'l Bus. 554–558, 573–576 (1976).
132. SEC, Report on Questionable and Illegal Corporate Payments and Practices, submitted to the Senate Banking Comm., 94th Cong., 2d Sess. (1976); Kane & Butler, supra n. 131, at 9–11; Loss, Seligman & Paredes, supra n. 28, at 531–546; Testimony of Philip Loomis, The Activities of American Multinational Corporations Abroad Hearings, House Subcomm. on Int'l Econ. Policy, 84th Cong., 1st Sess. 63–64, 180–185 (1975); Interview with A.A. Sommer, March 2, 1981; Interview with Stanley Sporkin, March 2, 1981; 44th SEC Ann. Rep. at 27.

133. Addresses of Roderick Hills, June 21, 1976, June 30, 1976, on file with the SEC; Sec. Ex. Act Rel. 13,346 (1977); SEC, Staff Report on Corporate Accountability 478, 486–506, 607–608, 618, 635–637, printed by Senate Banking Comm., 96th Cong., 2d Sess. (1980); Michael Riley Marget, The Audit Committee, J. of Corp. L. 400 (1978); Edward Greene & Bernard Falk, The Audit Committee: A Measured Contribution to Corporate Governance, 34 Bus. Law. 1229 (1979).
134. Loss, Seligman & Paredes, supra n. 28, Ch. 2.D.1–2; Milton Cohen, Truth in Securities Revisited, 79 Harv. L. Rev. 1340 (1966); SEC, Disclosure to Investors: A Reappraisal of Administrative Policies under the '33 and '34 Securities Acts (1969); Report of the Advisory Comm. on Corporate Disclosure to the SEC, House Comm. on Interstate & Foreign Commerce, 95th Cong., 1st Sess. (Comm. Print. 95–29 1977).
135. Joel Seligman, The Historical Need for a Mandatory Corporate Disclosure System, 9 J. Corp. L. 1 (1983); 1 Louis Loss, Joel Seligman & Troy Paredes, Securities Regulation Ch. 1.G. (6th ed. 2019).
136. See, e.g., Russell Stevenson, The SEC and the New Disclosure, 62 Cornell L. Rev. 50 (1976).
137. Loss, Seligman & Paredes, supra n. 135, at 321–332.
138. Stigler, Public Regulation of the Securities Markets, 37 J. Bus. 120–122 (1964); Irwin Friend & Edward Herman, The SEC Through a Glass Darkly, 37 J. Bus. 382 (1964).
139. George Benston, Required Disclosure and the Stock Market: An Evaluation of the Securities Exchange Act of 1934, 63 Am. Econ. Rev. 132 (1973); Irwin Friend & Randolph Westerfield, Required Disclosure and the Stock Market, 65 Am. Econ. Rev. 467 (1975); Sommer Advisory Comm. Rep., supra n. 134, at 103, I-XLIX.
140. Joel Seligman, The SEC's Unfinished Soft Information Revolution, 63 Fordham L. Rev. 1053 (1995); Advisory Comm. Report, supra n. 134, I at 1–3, I-XLIX.
141. Harry Heller, Disclosure Requirements under Federal Securities Regulation, 16 Bus. Law. 304, 307 (1961); Advisory Comm. Report, supra n. 134, at A266–A273.
142. Homer Kripke, The SEC, the Accountants, Some Myths, and Some Realities, 45 NYU L. Rev. 1151, 1198–1199 (1970).
143. Sec. Act Rels. 5362 (1973), 6084 (1979).
144. Loss, Seligman & Paredes, supra n. 28, at 294–341, 490; Reg. S-K Items 303, 503(c).
145. Loss, Seligman & Paredes, supra n. 28, at 470–478, 764–789, 1369–1381.
146. Commodities Futures Trading Commission Act of 1974, Pub. L. No. 93–463, 88 Stat. 1389 (1974); Grain Futures Act, 42 Stat. 998 (1922);

Loss, Seligman & Paredes, supra n. 28, at 1382–1393; Jerry Markham, The History of Commodity Futures Trading and Its Regulation (Praeger 1987); Jerry Markham, A Financial History of the United States, Vol. 2 at 93–106, 214–225, Vol. 3 at 43–46, 54–64, 81–94.

147. Loss, Seligman & Paredes, supra n. 28, at 1331–1352; Employee Retirement Income Security Act, Pub. L. No. 93–406, 88 Stat. 829 (1974); International Bhd. of Teamsters v. Daniel, 439 U.S. 551 (1981); Sec. Act Rels. 6188 (1980), 6281 (1981; Dep't of Labor, Fiduciary Rule, 81 Fed. Reg. 20,946 (2016); Chamber of Commerce v. Dep't of Labor, 885 F.3d 360 (5th Cir. 2018).

148. Sec. Ann. Rep. 38, 233, 281, 286, 317 (1977); SEC Ann. Rep. 28, 70 (2000); Securities Indus. Ass'n Securities Industry Fact Book 48 (2001).

149. SEC Staff Report on Internationalization of the Securities Markets II-12, II-73 (1987).

150. The Conclusions and Recommendations of the President's Working Group on Financial Markets, Hearing before Senate Comm. on Banking, Hous. & Urban Affairs, 100th Cong., 2d Sess. 37 (1988); SEC, Div. of Mkt. Reg., The Role of Index Related Trading in the Market Decline of September 11 & 12, 1986 20 (Mar. 1987).

151. Former Sec. Ex. Act § 21(d)(2)(A); SEC, Office of Chief Econ., The Impact of Targeted Share Repurchases (Greenmail) on Stock Prices, 1984–1985 Fed. Sec. L. Rep. (CCH) ¶ 83,713 (1984).

152. Economic Report of the President, Transmitted to Congress Feb. 1985, at 193; 23 Mergers & Acquisitions 74 (Mar.-Apr. 1989).

153. Edgar v. Mite, 457 U.S. 624, 640 (1982).

154. CTS Corp. v. Dynamics Corp. of Am., 481 U.S. 69 (1987).

155. Act approved Dec. 16, 1985, ch. 915, 1985 N.Y. Laws 3454, 3458; Interim Report of Ad Hoc Comm. on Corp. Takeover Legis. of Ass'n of Bar of City of N.Y. 5 (Nov. 12, 1985); 5 Loss & Seligman, supra n. 151, at 2283–2292; Moran v. Household Int'l Inc., 500 A.2d 1346 (Del. 1985); Majority of Large U.S. Corporations Have Adopted Poison Pills, LLRC Finds, 22 Sec. Reg. & L. Rep. (BNA) 1659 (1990).

156. Joel Seligman, Equal Protection in Shareholder Voting Rights: The One Common Share, One Vote Controversy, 54 Geo. Wash. L. Rev. 687 (1987); 4 Louis Loss, Joel Seligman & Troy Paredes, Securities Regulation 274–291 (Wolters Kluwer 5th ed. 2015); N.Y. Stock Exch. Subcomm. on Shareholder Participation and Qualitative Listing Standards, Dual Class Capitalization 2–5 (1985); N.Y. Stock Exch. Press Release, New York Stock Exchange Directors Approve Amendment to Allow Dual Classes of Common Stock for Listed Companies 2 (July 3, 1986); Sec. Ex. Act Rels. 23,803 (1986), 24,623 (1987), 25,891 (1988), 25,891 (1988), 27,554 (1989), 28,517 (1990); Issuers Urge SEC Not to Adopt Voting Rights

Standard for Exchanges, 19 Sec. Reg. & L. Rep. (BNA) 1076 (1987); Former Rule 19c-4; Business Roundtable v. SEC, 905 F.2d 406 (D.C. Cir. 1990).

157. Letter to the Author from Robert W. Hamilton (Oct. 6, 1994).

158. Triple-Witching Friday Experiment, 42 Bus. Law. 865 (1987); Stoll & Whaley Program Trading and Expiration Day Effects, Fin. Analysis J., Mar.-Apr. 1987, at 16; Sec. Ex. Act Rels. 24,367 (1987), 25,202 (1987), 25,466 (1988), 25,476 (1988), 25,479 (1988), 26,293 (1988); Ruder, The Impact of Derivative Index Trading on the Securities Markets 7–12 (remarks before Bond Club of Chicago, Oct. 6, 1987, on file with SEC); SEC, Div. of Mkt. Reg., The October 1987 Market Break 3–9 to 3–12, chs. 4–5 (1988); Report of the Presidential Task Force on Market Mechanisms chs. 3–4, 41–42, 49–57 (1988); SEC, Office of Econ. Analysis, Triggering the 1987 Stock Market Crash: Antitakeover Provisions in the Proposed House Ways and Means Tax Bill? (1989); SEC, Office of Econ. Analysis, Program Trading and Price Movement Around the October 1987 Market Break (1989); "Black Monday," The Stock Market Crash of October 19, 1987, Hearings before Senate Comm. on Banking, Hous. & Urban Affairs, 100th Cong., 2d Sess. 387 (1988) (testimony of John Phelan, Chair, NYSE); GAO, Preliminary Observations on the October 1987 Crash 45–47, 50–52 (1988); N. Katzenbach, An Overview of Program Trading and its Impact on Current Market Practices 10–11 (Dec. 21, 1987); Miller, Hawke, Malkiel & Scholes, Preliminary Report of the Commission of Inquiry Appointed by the Chicago Mercantile Exchange to Examine the Events Surrounding October 19, 1987 21 (Dec. 22, 1987).

159. Interim Report of the Working Group on Financial Markets, Submitted to the President of the United States 1–2 (1988); Report of Presidential Task Force, supra n. 158, at 34–36, 40–56, II-21, III-16, 21; SEC, Div. of Mkt. Reg., supra n. 158, at 7–21 to 7–26; GAO, Preliminary Observations, supra n. 158, at 97.

160. Report of the Presidential Task Force on Market Mechanisms, supra n. 158, at 55, 59, 63, 69; "Black Monday" Hearings, supra n. 158, at 98–99;

161. Commodities Futures Trading Commission Act of 1974, 88 Stat. 1389 (1974); Futures Trading Act of 1982, 96 Stat. 2294 (1983); Sec. Ex. Act Rel. 17,577 (1981); Board of Trade of City of Chicago v. SEC, 677 F.2d 1137, 1142 n. 8, 1156–1158 (7th Cir. 1982), *vacated as moot,* 459 U.S. 1026 (1982); SEC and CFTC Press Release (CFTC Rel. 853-881), Dec. 7, 1981, 1981–1982 Fed. Sec. L. Rep. (CCH) ¶83,062

162. Report of the Presidential Task Force, supra n. 158, at III-II n. 3; Langbein & Posner, Market Funds and Trust Investment Law, 1976

Am. Bar Found. Res. J. 1; Langbein & Posner, Market Funds and Trust Investment Law: II, 1977 Am. B. Found. Res. J. 1; SEC, Div. of Mkt. Reg., The October 1987 Market Break 3–3 (1988); Katzenbach, supra n. 158, at 13.

163. *Barron's*, Jan. 30, 1989, at 78, 146; Report of the Presidential Task Force, supra n. 158, at 29 n. 4, 41, 43–44, 55–56.

164. CFTC, Final Report on Stock Index Futures and Cash Market Activity During October 1987 189–190 (1988); Eagleton, Chicago's Markets, Corrupt to the Core, *N.Y. Times*, Nov. 14, 1989, at 27; Sirico, Agencies in Conflict: Overlapping Agencies and the Legitimacy of the Administrative Process, 33 Vand. L. Rev. 101 (1980).

165. Proposed Legislation Prepared in Response to Concerns Raised by the October 1987 Market Break, 1988–1989 Fed. Sec. L. Rep. (CCH) ¶84,306 at 89,353 (July 7, 1988); Rudder, October Recollections: The Future of the U.S. Securities Market, Econ. Club of Chicago 30 (Oct. 20, 1988); Capital Markets Competition, Stability, and Fairness Act of 1990, 1990 Fed. Sec. L. Rep. (CCH) ¶84,608 (1990); Treasury Submits Bill to Give SEC Jurisdiction over Stock Index Futures, 22 Sec. Reg. & L. Rep. (BNA) 859 (1990); Robb, Futures Traders Win in Regulatory Battle, *N.Y. Times*, Oct. 24, 1990, at C9; Senators Fail to Attach Compromise on SEC-CFTC Jurisdiction to Farm Bill, 22 Sec. Reg. & L. Rep. (BNA) 1125 (1990); Senators Fail in Last Minute Effort to Resolve SEC-CFTC Jurisdiction Dispute, 22 id. at 1476.

166. Sec. Ex. Act Rels. 25,198 (1988), 29,868 (1991).

167. Market Reform Act of 1990, 104 Stat. 963 (1990).

168. H.R. Rep. No. 100–910, 100th Cong., 2d Sess. 12 (1988); SEC v. Levine, 881 F.2d 1165 (2d Cir. 1989); SEC v. Levin, Litig. Rel. 11,117 (1986); SEC v. Boesky, Litig. Rel. 11,288 (S.D.N.Y. 1986); Ivan F. Boesky, Sec. Ex. Act Rel. 23,802 (1986); Drexel Burnham Lambert Group, Inc., 995 F.2d 1138 (2d Cir. 1993); SEC v. Milken, 1989–1990 Fed. Sec. L. Rep. (CCH) ¶95,200 (S.D.N.Y. 1990); Lowell J. Milken, Sec. Ex. Act Rel. 28,950 (1991); Michael R. Milken, Sec. Ex. Act Rel. 28,951 (1991); Milken's Prison Term Sliced to Two Years Plus Probation, 24 Sec. Reg. & L. Rep. (BNA) 1175 (1992); Judge Approved $1.3 Billion Drexel Burnham Milden Settlement Pact, 24 Sec. Reg. & L. Rep. (BNA) 332 (1992); James Stewart, Den of Thieves (1991).

169. Insider Trading Sanctions Act of 1984, 98 Stat. 1264 (1984); H.R. Rep. No. 100–910, 110th Cong., 2d Sess. 11 (1988); Insider Trading and Securities Fraud Enforcement Act of 1988, 102 Stat. 4677 (1988).

170. Blue Chip Stamps v. Manor Drug Stores, 421 U.S. 723 (1975).

171. Ernst & Ernst v. Hochfelder, 425 U.S. 185 (1976).

172. Santa Fe Indus., Inc. v. Green, 430 U.S. 462 (1977).

173. Lampf, Pleva, Lipkind, Purpis & Petigrow v. Gilbertson, 501 U.S. 350 (1991).
174. Remarks by Arthur Levitt, Pub. Sec. Ass'n Ann. Meeting, Orlando, Florida, Mar. 4, 1994 at 1; Vise, Roll Call's Owner Answers Clinton's Call, *Washington Post,* Apr. 29, 1993 at B12; Arthur Levitt, Take on the Street 1 (2002); Remarks by Arthur Levitt, Trinity Church Tercentenary, N.Y., N.Y., Mar. 18, 1997 at 1. Maher, Wall Street's Top Cop, *Barron's,* Nov. 27, 1993 at 10; Remarks by Arthur Levitt, The SEC at 60, Nat'l Legal Center for Pub. Int. Mar. 29, 1995, at 2; Address by Arthur Levitt, Growth Industries in the 1980s — Does America Need an Industrial Policy?, Fed. Reserve Bank, Atlanta Conf., Mar. 17, 1983, at 1; Address by Arthur Levitt, 1984 and Beyond: The Future for Growth Capital, Hofstra Univ. Jan. 18, 1984, at 4–5; Remarks by Arthur Levitt, SIA Luncheon, American Stock Exch., Oct. 12, 1987, at 3.
175. Hawthorne, Memo to Arthur Levitt, Rose Petals Today, Inst. Inv., Avg., 1993 at 55, 56; SEC Ann. Rep. 24, 35, 51, 80, 150 (1977); SEC Ann. Rep. 71, 159 (2000); Securities Indus. Assoc., 2001 Securities Industry Fact Book, at 12; SEC Ann. Rep. 34, 169 (2001); SEC Ann. Rep. 53 (2002).
176. Doyle, Clinton Budget Plan Calls for SEC to Cut 42 Posts, *Boston Globe,* Apr. 10, 1993, at 18; Sec. Ex. Act Rel. 35,548 (1995); Testimony of Arthur Levitt, Concerning the Investment Company Institute, before Subcomm. on Sec., Senate Comm. on Banking, Hous. & Urban Affairs 24 (Nov. 10, 1993); Anderson, SEC Task Force is Seeking Ways to Ease Regulations on Business, *Wall St. J.,* Sept. 17, 1995, at A3; SEC Task Force Report on Disclosure Simplification, 1995–1996 Fed. Sec. L. Rep. (CCH) ¶ 85,738 (Mar. 3, 1996).
177. Hume, Democrats Blast Senate Panel's Proposed SEC Funding Cuts, *Bond Buyer,* Sept. 27, 1995, at 3; Cutting the Securities Cops, *Wash. Post,* Oct. 15, 1995, at C6; Testimony of Arthur Levitt, Concerning Fee Collections before Subcomm. on Sec., Senate Banking, Hous. & Urban Affairs Comm., Mar. 24, 1999, at 3–5, 8; Testimony of Arthur Levitt, Concerning the Commission's Authorization Request for Fiscal Year 1997, before Subcomm. on Telecommunications & Fin., House Comm. on Commerce, Feb. 28, 1996, at 1 n. 1; Testimony of Arthur Levitt, Concerning Appropriations for Fiscal Year 1997, before Subcomm. on Commerce, Justice, and State, the Judiciary, and Related Agencies, House Comm. on Appropriations, May 9, 1996, at 1; Testimony of Arthur Levitt, Concerning the Commission's Authorization Request for Fiscal Year 1997, before Subcomm. on Telecommunications & Fin., House Comm. on Commerce, Feb. 28, 1996, at 7; Sec. Ex. Act Rel. 37,156 (1996); Testimony of Arthur Levitt, Concerning Appropriations for Fiscal

Year 1999, before Subcomm. on Commerce, Justice, State, and Judiciary, Senate Comm. on Appropriations 10 (Mar. 19, 1998); Testimony of Arthur Levitt Concerning Appropriations for Fiscal Year 1998, before Subcomm. on Commerce, Justice and State, the Judiciary and Related Agencies, Senate Comm. on Appropriations, Mar. 19, 1997, at 1; SEC Ann. Rep. 213 (1996), 208 (1997), 176 (1998), 197 (1999); Arthur Levitt, An Address on Ethics and Insider Trading, Apr. 14, 1989, at 2; Republican Contract with America: Point Nine: The Common Sense Legal Reform Act, *www.house.gov/house*; Remarks by Arthur Levitt, NASD, May 19, 1994, at 2; Remarks by Arthur Levitt, the SEC Today: Putting Investors First, Practicing Law Inst., N.Y., N.Y., Nov. 3, 1994, at 2.

178. Schroeder, SEC Turnover Rate Leaves Agency Scrambling in Fight against Fraud, *Wall St. J.*, Oct. 23, 1998, at B6; Clark, Ten Things the SEC Won't Tell You, *Smart Money*, May 1999, at 147; Skrzycki, Unionization Vote Grows Out of SEC's Culture, *Wash. Post*, June 4, 1999, at E1; Schroeder, SEC Immersed in Testy Effort by Employees to Unionize, *Wall St. J.*, Aug. 16, 1999, at C1; Skrzycki, At SEC Skies are Suddenly Sunnier, *Wall St. J.*, Jan. 21, 2000, at E1; SEC Workers Vote for Unions, *N.Y. Times*, July 18, 2000, at C7; Testimony of Arthur Levitt, Concerning the Competitive Market Supervision Act, before Senate Comm. on Banking, Hous. & Urban Affairs, Feb. 28, 2000, at 8; SEC Ann. Rep. 159 (2000), 171 (2001).

179. SEC, Ann. Rep. 1 (1997); SEC, Ann. Rep. 1 (2001); Testimony of Arthur Levitt, Concerning Fraud in the Micro Cap Market, Permanent Subcomm. on Investigations, Senate Comm. on Gov't Affairs, Dec. 1, 2000; Testimony of Arthur Levitt, Concerning Day Trading, Permanent Subcomm. on Investigations, Senate Comm. on Gov't Affairs, Sept. 16, 1999; Staff Rep. to Senate Comm. on Gov't Affairs, Financial Oversight of Enron: The SEC and Private Sector Watchdogs 11 (Oct. 8, 2002), at 13.

180. Sec. Ex. Act Rel. 33,868, 56 SEC Dock. 1045, 1046, 1048 (1994); Testimony of Arthur Levitt, Concerning Municipal Bonds and Government Securities Markets, Senate Comm. on Banking, Hous. & Urban Affairs, Jan. 5, 1995, at 22.

181. Statement of Initiative Regarding Political Contributions to State and Local Officials/Candidates, Oct. 18, 1993; SEC, Staff Report on the Municipal Securities Market, 1993 Fed. Sec. L. Rep. (CCH) ¶ 85,217 (Sept. 3, 1993); Sec. Ex. Act Rel. 33,868 (1994) (adoption).

182. Remarks by Arthur Levitt, the SEC at 60, Nat'l Legal Center for Pub. Int., Gen. Counsel Briefing, Washington, D.C., May 29, 1995, at 2–3; Hume, ABA Ethics Panel Chairman Lambasts Pay-to-Play Rule, *Bond Buyer*, Apr. 8, 1997, at 1; Remarks by Arthur Levitt, Lawyers and Ethics: The Problem of Pay-to-Play, Fixed Income Daily Conf. on

Mun. Fin., Philadelphia, Pa., June 26, 1997, at 5; ABA Ethics Committee Proposes New Model Rule on Pay-to-Play, 31 Sec. Reg. & L. Rep. (BNA) 788, 789 (1999); ABA Bounces Pay-to-Play Model Rule, Backs Limitations in Judicial Elections, 31 Sec. Reg. & L. Rep. (BNA) 1071 (1999); ABA Reverses Itself, Adopts New Rule Banning Lawyers' Pay-to-Play Practices, 32 id. 215 (2000); Buescher, ABA Model Rule 7.6: The ABA Pleases the SEC, But Does Not Solve Pay to Play, 14 Geo. J. Legal Ethics 139 (2000).

183. Matter of Cady, Roberts & Co., 40 SEC 907 (1961); Chiarella v. SEC, 445 U.S. 222 (1980); Dirks v. SEC, 463 U.S. 646 (1983); United States v. O'Hagan, 521 U.S. 642 (1997); Levitt, supra n. 174, at 87, 91–92.

184. Sec. Ex. Act Rels. 42,259 (1999); 43,154 (2000); Levitt, supra n. 174, at 88–104; Norris, Wall St. Snarls at SEC Proposal on Disclosure, *N.Y. Times*, 224, Dec. 16, 1999 at C1; Schroeder & Smith, Disclosure Rule Cleared by the SEC, *Wall St. J.*, Aug. 11, 2000, at C1.

185. Loss, Seligman & Paredes, supra n. 135, at 240–353; Basic v. Levinson, 485 U.S. 224 (1988); id. at 241–242; Washington Pub. Power Supply Sys. Sec. Litig., 720 F. Supp. 1379, 1386 (D. Ariz. 1989), *aff'd sub nom.* Class Plaintiffs v. City of Seattle, 955 F.2d 1268 (9th Cir. 1992), *cert. denied sub nom.* Hoffer v. City of Seattle, 506 U.S. 953.

186. Remarks by Arthur Levitt, Private Litigation under the Federal Securities Laws, U. Cal. San Diego, Sec. Reg. Inst., Jan. 26, 1994; Central Bank of Denver, N.A. v. First Interstate Bank of Denver, N.A., 511 U.S. 164 (1994).

187. Testimony of Arthur Levitt, Concerning Litigation Reform Proposals before Subcomm. on Telecommunications & Fin., House Comm. on Commerce 3 (Feb. 10, 1995).

188. Statement of Jack Fields, Subcomm. on Telecommunications & Fin., Hearing on H.R. 10, the Common Sense Legal Reforms Act (Feb. 10, 1995); Hamilton, Shareholder Litigation Bill Modified, *Wash. Post*, Feb. 10, 1995, at D1; Common Sense Legal Reform Act of 1995, H.R. Rep. 104–50, Part I, 104th Cong., 1st Sess. (1995), 1995 Fed. Sec. L. Rep. (CCH) ¶ 85,605 (Feb. 24, 1995).

189. Securities Litigation Reform Act, 1995 Fed. Sec. L. Rep. (CCH) ¶ 85,608 (Mar. 8, 1995); House Passes Bill That Would Limit Suits of Investors, *N.Y. Times*, Mar. 9, 1995, at A1.

190. Taylor, Senate Clears Securities Suit Curb, *Wall St. J.*, June 29, 1995, at A3.

191. Elliot Weiss & John Beckerman, Let the Money Do the Monitoring: How Institutional Investors Can Reduce Agency Costs in Securities Class Actions, 104 Yale L.J. 2053 (1995).

192. H.R. 1058, Conf. Rep. 104–369, 104th Cong., 1st Sess., 1995–1996 Fed. Sec. L. Rep. (CCH) ¶ 85,710 (Dec. 1995); Congress

Overwhelmingly Passes Bill to Reform Private Securities Litigation, 27 Sec. Reg. & L. Rep. (BNA) 1899 (1985); Presidential Veto Message on Private Securities Litigation Reform Act, 1995–1996 Fed. Sec. L. Rep. (CCH) ¶85,714 (Dec. 20, 1995); Walsh, House Overrides Veto of Securities Bill, *N.Y. Times*, Dec. 21, 1995, at A20.

193. 10 Louis Loss, Joel Seligman & Troy Paredes, Securities Regulation 295–354 (Wolters Kluwer 5th ed. 2018).

194. Testimony of Arthur Levitt, Concerning the Impact of the Private Securities Litigation Reform Act of 1995, before Subcomm. on Sec., Senate Comm. on Banking, Hous. & Urban Affairs, July 24, 1997, at 2; Clinton to Offer Plan on Securities Lawsuits, *Wash. Times*, July 25, 1997, at B7; Testimony of Arthur Levitt Concerning H.R. 1689, the Securities Litigation Uniform Standards Act of 1997, before Subcomm. on Fin. & Hazardous Materials, House Comm. on Commerce, May 19, 1998; Conf. Rep. No. 105–803, 105th Cong., 2d Sess., S. Rep. No. 105–182, 105th Cong., 2d Sess., H.R. Rep. 105–640, 105th Cong., 2d Sess.

195. Testimony of Arthur Levitt, Concerning H.R. 2131, the Capital Markets Deregulation and Liberalization Act of 1995, before Subcomm. on Telecommunications & Fin., House Comm. on Commerce, Nov. 30, 1995; Knight, House GOP Pares Goals on Securities Law Reform, *Wash. Post*, Nov. 15, 1995, at F2.

196. Address by Arthur Levitt, The SEC and the States: Toward a More Perfect Union, NASAA, Vancouver, British Columbia, Oct. 12, 1995.

197. Loss, Seligman & Paredes, supra n. 135, at 184–201.

198. Sec. Ex. Act Rel. 33,023 (1993); Remarks by Arthur Levitt, Speeding Up Settlement: The Next Frontier, Symposium on Risk Reduction in Payments, Clearance and Settlement Sys., Pierre Hotel, N.Y., Jan. 26, 1996, at 3.

199. Sec. Ex. Act Rels. 43,230 (2000), 43,232 (2000), 46,280 (2007).

200. Remarks by Arthur Levitt, Dynamic Markets, Timeless Principles, Columbia L. Sch., N.Y., N.Y., Sept. 23, 1999, at 6; Sec. Ex. Act Rel. 42,758 (2002).

201. Justice Investigating Possible Anticompetitive Practices in OTC Market, 26 Sec. Reg. & L. Rep. (BNA) 1389 (1994); Nasdaq: An Embarrassment of Embarrassments, *Business Week*, Nov. 7, 1994, at 122; Christie & Scholtz, Why Nasdaq Market Makers Avoid Odd Eighth Quotes?, 49 J. Fin. 1813–1814 (1994); Levitt, supra n. 174, at 182–184; Sec. Ex. Act Rels. 37,538 (1996), 37,542 (1996).

202. Rep. of NASD Select Comm. on Structure and Governance to NASD Bd. of Gov. (Sept. 15, 1995); NASD Board Agrees to Split Oversight, Regulatory Functions, 27 Sec. Reg. & L. Rep. (BNA) 1842 (1995); Sec. Ex. Act Rels. 37,107 (1996), 37,423 (1996), 37,425 (1996); Levitt, supra n. 174, at 185–189; Fromson, Make Over for a

Tarnished Stock Market, *Wash. Post*, Mar. 17, 1997, at 12; Remarks by Arthur Levitt, Investor Interests as the Common Interest: The SEC's Campaign for Fair Trading Practices, Econ. Club of Chicago, Apr. 24, 1996, at 4; Sec. Ex. Act Rel. 37,619A (1996).

203. Schapiro Head New NASD Regulatory Arm, 27 Sec. Reg. & L. Rep. (BNA) 1915 (1995); Loss, Seligman & Paredes, supra n. 55, at 549–555; Sec. Ex. Act Rel. 44,396 (2001); NASD Board Approves Combination with NASD Regulation, Glauber Announces, 34 Sec. Reg. & L. Rep. (BNA) 966 (2002).

204. Loss, Seligman & Paredes, supra n. 55, at 800–805; Commodities Futures Modernization Act of 2000, Pub. L. No. 106–443, 114 Stat. 276 (2000); GAO Financial Derivatives: Actions Needed to Protect the Financial System (1994); President's Working Group, Over-the-Counter Derivatives Market and the Commodity Exchange Act (Nov. 1999); Hu, Swaps, the Modern Process of Financial Innovation and the Vulnerability of a Regulatory Paradigm, 138 U. Pa. L. Rev. 333 (1989); The Department of Treasury, Blueprint for a Modernized Financial Regulatory Structure 46–48 (2008); Final Report of the National Commission on the Causes of the Financial and Economic Crisis in the United States 45–51 (2011); Michael Barr, Howell Jackson & Margaret Tahyar, Financial Regulation: Law and Policy 1060–1065, 1068–1075 (Foundation Press 2016).

205. Seligman, supra n. 1, at 714–744; Remarks by Arthur Levitt, The Numbers Game, NYU Ctr. for L. & Bus., N.Y., N.Y., Sept. 28, 1998, at 2; Levitt, supra n. 174, at 115–117, 167–172; Testimony of Arthur Levitt Concerning Loan Loss Allowances, before Subcomm. on Sec., Senate Comm. on Banking, Hous. & Urban Affairs, July 29, 1999; Norris, SEC Charges 68 Companies and Individuals with Accounting Fraud, *N.Y. Times*, Sept. 29, 1999, at C2; SAB 99 (1999); SAB 101 (1999); Testimony of Arthur Levitt, Concerning FASB's Proposed Accounting Rules for Derivative Financial Contracts, Subcomm. on Capital Markets, Sec. & Gov't Sponsored Enterprises, House Comm. on Banking & Fin. Serv., Oct. 1, 1997; Sec. Act Rels. 7507 (1998), 7593 (1998).

206. Levitt, supra n. 174, at 122–128; AAER 1405 (2001); Litig. Rel. 17,039 (2001); Sec. Ex. Act Rels. 42,994 (2000), 43,602 (2001); Ernst & Young LLP, 2000 Fed. Sec. L. Rep. (CCH) ¶ 77,863 (avail. May 25, 2000); KPMG, LLP, 2000–2001 Fed. Sec. L. Rep. (CCH) ¶ 78,014 (avail. Oct. 16, 2000); John Biggs, Auditors and Consultants Shouldn't be Too Close, *Wall St. J.*, July 13, 2000, at A26; Testimony of Arthur Levitt, Concerning the Commission's Auditor Independence Proposal, before Subcomm. on Sec., Senate Comm. on Banking, Hous. & Urban Affairs, Sept. 28, 2000.

207. Enron Form 10-K (2000); *Fortune*, Apr. 16, 2001, at F-1; Enron Special Inv. Committee Report (2002); Enron Form 8-K at 2 (Apr. 22, 2002).
208. Senate Comm. on Banking, Housing & Urban Affairs, Hearing on Accounting and Investor Protection Issues Raised in Enron and Other Public Companies, Feb. 12, 2002 (Testimony of Roderick M. Hills) at 1–2; Testimony of David S. Ruder, Feb. 12, 2002, at 4–6; Testimony of Paul A. Volcker, Feb. 14, 2002, at 1.
209. Seligman, supra n. 1, at 624; Loss, Seligman & Paredes, supra n. 28, at 695–842.
210. NationsBank of N.C. v. Variable Annuity Life Ins. Co., 513 U.S. 251 (1995); Federal Ins. Off., Dep't of Treasury, Ann. Report on the Insurance Industry 65–103 (Sept. 2018); American Council of Life Insurers, 2018 Fact Book; NAIC, State of the Life Insurance Industry (Aug. 2013); Markham, Financial History, supra n. 146, Vol. 3, at 31–35, 107–108; Department of Treasury, Blueprint, supra n. 204, at 63–72; Kenneth Abraham & Daniel Schwarcz, Insurance Law and Regulation 111–151 (Foundation Press 2015); Barr, Jackson & Tahyar, supra n. 204, at 336–3511
211. Loss, Seligman & Paredes, supra n. 135, at 51–79 479–482, 501–511; Financial Stability Oversight Council Ann. Rep. (2018); Barr, Jackson & Tahyer, supra n. 204, at 691–712, 966–974, 1027–1038; JP Morgan Chase & Co., Form 10-K for Fiscal Year Ended December 31, 2018; Citigroup, Inc., Form 10-K for Fiscal Year Ended December 31, 2018; Morgan Stanley, Form 10-K for Year Ended December 31, 2018; Bank of America Corporation, Form 10-K for Fiscal Year Ended December 31, 2018; Goldman Sachs Group, Inc., Form 10-K for Year Ended December 31, 2018; Wells Fargo & Co., Form 10-K for Year Ended December 31, 2018; Bank of New York Mellon Corporation, Form 10-K for Year Ended December 31, 2018; State Street Corporation, Form 10-K for Year Ended December 31, 2018; Arthur Wilmarth, The Dark Side of Universal Banking: Financial Conglomerates and the Origins of the Subprime Crisis, 41 Conn. L. Rev. 963 (2009); Goldstein v. SEC, 451 F.3d 873 (D.C. Cir. 2006).

6

A New Financial Regulatory Model for the 21st Century

The 2007–2009 Financial Meltdown was the greatest crisis in United States history after the 1929–1937 Stock Market Crash, Banking Crisis, and Great Depression. Unlike the New Deal financial regulatory model, the legislative response to the 2007–2009 Meltdown, while effective in areas such as requiring banks to hold more capital, was inadequate in terms of restructuring the regulatory model, and weakened the emergency arsenal that existed before the 2010 Dodd-Frank Act. These results were not foreordained.

Before and after the 2010 enactment of the Dodd-Frank Act, there was a virtual cottage industry in proposals to reform financial regulation. Three proposals deserve special notice.

Blueprint, Department of Treasury 2008

In March 2008, the Department of Treasury published *Blueprint for a Modernized Financial Regulatory Structure* (the *Blueprint*), which proposed a three phased restructuring of financial regulation, culminating in an optimal regulatory structure that recognized "the convergence of the financial services industry" and recommended reducing the needless complexity of the pre-2008 regulatory structure to five regulators.

A "market stability regulator" would be responsible for the overall economy. The *Blueprint* recommended that the Federal Reserve System assume this role, continuing its responsibilities with respect to monetary policy, providing liquidity and supervising federally insured depository institutions, federal insurance institutions, and federal financial services providers. The Treasury characterized the enhanced authority as necessary "to deal with systemic risk." The Regulator would have access to or be empowered to require detailed information about covered financial firms, and when necessary, "to require financial institutions to undertake corrective actions to address financial stability problems." The Market Stability Regulator would have authority to use the discount window for nonbank institutions when there was an overall threat to the financial system's stability.[1]

The *Blueprint* next proposed a Prudential Financial Regulatory Agency to provide explicit government guarantees, including federal deposit insurance and state insurance guarantee funds. The *Blueprint* made this recommendation warily:

> Although protecting consumers and helping to maintain confidence in the financial system, explicit government guarantees often erode market discipline, creating the potential for moral hazard and a clear need for prudential regulation. Prudential regulation in this context should be applied to individual firms, and it should operate like the current regulation of insured depository institutions, with capital adequacy requirements, investment limits, activity limits, and direct on-site risk management supervision.

The Prudential Financial Regulatory Agency would assume the roles of the Office of the Comptroller of the Currency with respect to national banks and the Office of Thrift Supervision with respect to savings and loans. There would be one federal charter for all depository institutions, including banks, savings and loans, and federal credit unions. Activity limits would "serve the traditional prudential function of limiting risk to the deposit insurance funds."

The Prudential Financial Regulatory Agency expressly would be empowered to address "the inefficiencies in the state-based insurance regulatory system" through a federal insurance regulatory system applicable to insurers offering retail products when there was a government guarantee. The state guarantee system would remain in place.

To address the inefficiencies of state-based insurance regulation, which made "developing national products cumbersome and more costly, directly impacting the competitiveness of U.S. Insurers" and "create[d] increasing tensions in [the] global [insurance] marketplace," the *Blueprint* proposed an optional federal charter for insurers within the state-based system that would address licensing, regulation and supervision of insurers, reinsurers, and insurance brokers and agents. Only insurance products sold under a federal charter would receive the benefits of federal guarantee insurance. There would be an Office of National Insurance within Treasury to regulate insurance firms with a national charter. "[T]he current state-based regulation of insurance would continue for those not electing to be regulated at the national level."

The Federal Deposit Insurance Corporation would be reconstituted as the Federal Insurance Guarantee Corporation with authority over depository institutions and insurance firm depository insurance.

The *Blueprint* recommended consideration of a separate regulatory authority to conduct prudential oversight of government sponsored enterprises, including Fannie Mae and Freddie Mac.[2]

The new Conduct of Business Regulatory Agency was to be the primary regulatory agency for business conduct, and would focus on the interactions between financial institutions and retail financial services consumers. The Business Regulatory Agency would have oversight responsibilities for depository institutions, insurance and securities firm sales and marketing practices, consumer laws such as the Truth in Lending Act and Real Estate Settlement Act, and the Federal Trade Commission power to address "unfair or deceptive acts in or alleging commerce" as well as anti-discriminatory laws. For securities and futures firms, the Authority would address operational ability, professional conduct and trading, fraud and manipulation, and duties to customers such as investor suitability standards. With respect to insurance, however, the Business Regulatory Authority would not have price controls.

The Business Regulatory Agency would supplant banking regulation at the Federal Reserve, most aspects of the SEC and CFTC, and some aspects of the Federal Trade Commission with respect to retail customers. The Authority would have broad responsibilities in the *Blueprint's* optimal structure including chartering, rulemaking, compliance, and enforcement for firms covered by federal charters, and generally would preempt state regulatory authority. The states would retain clear authority to enact laws against state chartered financial services providers when there was no conflict with federal law. Other state laws applicable to business practices generally such as contract, torts, taxation, and zoning would continue to apply regardless of whether an institution was subject to a state or federal charter.

The *Blueprint* proposed that "the CFTC and SEC should be merged to provide unified oversight and regulation of the futures and securities industries." The *Blueprint* delineated several steps that the SEC should take to modernize its regulatory approach and "preserve the market benefits achieved in the futures area" through the CFTC's principles-based regulatory authority. The SEC would continue in the *Blueprint's* optimal regulatory structure.

The *Blueprint* also recommended the convergence of broker-dealer and investment adviser regulation that offered similar products to retail investors.

The *Blueprint* not only recommended that self-regulatory organizations such as Financial Industry Regulation Authority (*FINRA*) be retained, but that investment advisers should be subject to a self-regulatory organization similar to that of FINRA's oversight of broker-dealers.

State regulation would be preempted with respect to financial firms when engaged in a national market, whether federal or state chartered. States would retain authority with respect to state-chartered financial service firms not in a national market.[3]

The Treasury *Blueprint* proposed a Corporate Finance Regulator to continue the SEC's responsibilities over corporate disclosures, corporate governance, accounting oversight and similar functions.[4]

In its short-term recommendations, the *Blueprint* proposed designating the President's Working Group on Financial Markets as the coordinator of financial policy including systemic risk, market integrity, investor and consumer protection, and capital markets competitiveness. The Presidential Working Group since formation in 1988 had been dominated by the Department of Treasury. While the *Blueprint* explained: A new Executive Order amplifying the President's Working Group "should in no way alter, limit or in any way change" any of the Working Group's existing statutory roles and responsibilities, the combination of the continuation of the Presidential Working Group and the Federal Reserve becoming the Market Stability Regulator meant that fiscal and monetary policy firmly would remain in the hands of the president, Treasury, and Fed.[5]

The *Blueprint* recommended a Mortgage Origination Commission to address gaps in mortgage origination oversight. The authority to draft national mortgage lending standards would remain with the Federal Reserve. To reduce confusion in the enforcement of federal mortgage lending standards, the *Blueprint* recommended that mortgage originators that are affiliates of depository institutions would be jointly subject to federal holding company and state supervision. For independent mortgage originators, "the industry responsible for the majority of subprime loan originators in recent years," the states would enforce federal mortgage lending standards.

The *Blueprint* sought to move United States financial regulation from a functional model based on the underlying financial industries to an objectives-based regulatory structure that sought to improve regulatory effectiveness "by more closely linking the regulatory objectives of market stability regulation, prudential financial regulation and business conduct regulation to regulatory structure."[6]

The March 2008 publication of the Department of Treasury *Blueprint* was ill-timed. The Bear Stearns and subsequent crises overwhelmed the possibility of a meaningful debate over this far-reaching proposal. There was much to debate. In the *Blueprint*, the CFTC would be merged into the SEC. Insurance regulation was subject to a federal charter. Consumer and investor protection received little emphasis.

Nonetheless the *Blueprint* represented a determined attempt to address the structural inefficiencies of the pre-2008 financial regulatory model in the age of financial supermarkets.

The Bipartisan Policy Center Road Map

In 2014, after the 2010 enactment of the Dodd-Frank Act, the Bipartisan Policy Center, established by former Senate Majority Leaders Howard Baker, Tom Daschle, Bob Dole, and George Mitchell published *Dodd-Frank's Missed Opportunity: A Road Map for a More Effective Regulatory Architecture*, which similarly proposed a Prudential Regulatory Authority to consolidate the supervisory and examination authority of the Comptroller of the Currency, FDIC, and Federal Reserve into a unified prudential regulator for all banks and savings and loans and their holding companies. The Fed would become the primary macro-prudential supervisor for overseeing financial market trends, activities, products and practices that might pose a systemic risk to financial stability and the unified financial stability regulator for all systemically important institutions, including nonbank noninsured financial institutions. A single federal charter would be phased in for savings and loans and continued for national banks.

The FDIC role would continue as a depository insurance and resolution agency with a backup role to supervise all banks and savings and loans for which it guarantees deposits.

A new Federal Insurance Regulator would be created to regulate insurance companies with a national insurance charter. The national insurance charter would be mandatory for systemically important financial institutions and optional for other insurance companies.

The Financial Stability Oversight Council created by the 2010 Dodd-Frank Act would be continued but with authority to set heightened standards and safeguards for systemically risky activities. The FSOC would be empowered to adjudicate rulemaking disputes among members.

An Office of Financial Research would be established as an independent agency, removing it from within the Treasury Department.

The SEC and CFTC would be merged into a Capital Markets Authority. The Bipartisan Policy Center Report quoted Barney Frank, chair of the House Financial Services Committee: "The existence of a separate SEC and CFTC is the single largest structural defect in our regulatory system."

All regulatory agencies would be funded outside of annual congressional appropriations. The SEC would be funded through its existing fee and assessment structure.

The Volcker Alliance Proposed Restructuring

The third study of our financial regulatory system, *Reshaping the Financial Regulatory System: Long Delayed, Now Crucial,* was published in 2015 by the Volcker Alliance. The Alliance had been formed in 2013 by former Fed Chair Paul Volcker.[7]

The Volcker Alliance analysis began with the premise that the current financial regulatory system was incapable of regulating the financial system:

> The system for regulating financial institutions in the United States is highly fragmented, outdated, and ineffective. A multitude of federal agencies, self-regulatory organizations (SROs), and state authorities share oversight of the financial system under a framework riddled with regulatory gaps, loopholes, and inefficiencies. Never coherently designed, the regulatory framework developed in a piecemeal fashion over the past 150 years, as Congress established a plethora of new agencies and eliminated others primarily in response to financial panics and periods of economic instability. Notably, while the regulatory structure has seen some modification in recent decades, its foundational elements have been in place since the 1930s.
>
> Unlike the regulatory system, however, the financial system has experienced significant transformation in the past few decades:
>
> - Banking system assets have become concentrated in a handful of extremely large, exceedingly complex, globally active, and highly diversified institutions, with huge trading books and even, in some cases, ownership of industrial assets such as coal mines, oil tankers, and power plants;
> - The less regulated market outside the traditional banking system, or shadow banking, has emerged as a bigger part of the whole financial system, with increased reliance on potentially unstable forms of short-term funding that create the risk of contagion and fire sales (notably, nonbank financial institutions hold two-thirds of all credit market assets);
> - Financial products have rapidly and fundamentally changed, becoming exceedingly complex and substantially increasing the opacity of the financial system;
> - Alternative investment funds, such as hedge funds and private equity funds, have become highly leveraged, including through the use of derivatives transactions;
> - Assets under management have grown dramatically and become concentrated in the largest fund complexes; and
> - Equities markets have become fragmented, more complex, and less transparent, in part as a result of technological advances, with increasing participation from unregulated entities, such as high frequency trading firms.

The misalignment of financial regulation of finance in the period before 2008 was painfully evident:

> [G]aps in the regulation of the markets for mortgages, short-term funding, and over-the-counter (*OTC*) derivatives allowed significant risks to build in the financial system and ultimately contributed substantially to its collapse. . . . [I]nteragency jurisdictional conflicts often resulted in delays or inaction on critical matters, including the promulgation of rules and interagency guidance on subprime lending. . . . [N]o single agency had a comprehensive understanding of the risks in the financial system, as each agency remained focused only on its area of supervision. Finally, increased opportunities for regulatory arbitrage—particularly in the supervision of large thrift institutions such as American International Group (*AIG*) and Countrywide Financial, and in the now-extinct large, stand-alone investment banks including Lehman Brothers and Bear Stearns—allowed systemic risks to multiply.

As with the Department of Treasury 2008 *Blueprint* and Bipartisan Policy Center, as well as the 1984 Bush Task Force on Regulation of Financial Services, and 1991 Treasury Report *Modernizing the Financial System*, the Volcker Alliance proposed a fundamental restructuring of financial regulation.

The Alliance proposed retaining a Financial Stability Oversight Council (*FSOC*), with the Secretary of Treasury as chair but not as a voting member of FSOC because the Secretary's disproportionate influence could have "a significant adverse influence on regulation and infringe on the independence of regulatory agencies."

The FSOC's Systemic Issues Committee would be shrunk to seven members, specifically the chair of the Fed, the chair of the FDIC, the director of the Federal Housing Finance Agency, the chair of the combined SEC-CFTC, the director of the Consumer Financial Protection Bureau, the director of the Office of Financial Research, and a state insurance commissioner designated by the state insurance commissioners. The Systemic Issues Committee would designate systemically important financial institutions and require new and enhanced prudential standards and safeguards on all activities that could pose a threat to systemic stability, including those conducted outside the sphere of prudential supervision. The Systemic Issues Committee would be authorized to require changes in the rules of member agencies to help maintain financial stability.

The National Credit Union Administration would remain a member of the FSOC, but not a member of the Systemic Issues Committee.

The Office of Financial Regulation would no longer be part of the Department of Treasury, but would become an independent agency, independently financed, with its director a voting member of the Systemic Issues Committee. The independence of the Office of Financial Regulation was intended to "allow for an effective and independent check on the regulatory entities involved in systemic-risk regulation and serve as a powerful safeguards against the groupthink... witnessed in the run-up to the financial crisis."

The Federal Reserve System characterized "as the nation's central bank, must retain primary responsibility for... and have the tools to enforce financial stability." The Fed would remain the lender of last resort and maintain its core function of promoting systemic stability and continue to play a central role in identifying and addressing risks to systemic stability, but surrender its supervisory functions to a new Prudential Supervisory Authority.

The Prudential Supervisory Authority would be an independent regulatory agency that would consolidate the regulatory functions of the Federal Reserve System and the Office of the Comptroller of the Currency. The Office of the Comptroller would cease to exist. The Prudential Authority would supervise bank and savings and loan holding companies, federal and state chartered depository institutions, branches of foreign banks, and other systemically important financial institutions, as well as the SEC and CFTC prudential supervisory functions with respect to broker-dealers, mutual funds, money market funds, swap dealers, futures dealers, and derivatives clearing agencies.

The Prudential Supervisory Authority would include the chairs of the FDIC and the combined SEC-CFTC as well as two presidentially appointed independent members with staggered seven-year terms. The Prudential Supervisory Authority would have a special division for the supervision of community banks to appropriately tailor treatment of these institutions. The Authority would be independently funded through industry assessments or the Federal Reserve.

The FDIC would retain its deposit insurance functions and authority for receivership and resolution of all insured banks and significant financial institutions.

The SEC and CFTC would be merged into a new Investor Protection Capital Market Conduct Agency with authority over investor protection and the structure of securities and derivatives markets. The new Investor Protection and Capital Market Conduct Agency would be funded through fees and assessments and no longer require annual congressional appropriations:

> Merging the SEC and the CFTC to create a new investor protection and capital market conduct agency would (1) eliminate the unnecessary and artificial bifurcation of the securities and derivatives markets; (2) permit the regulators to better understand financial firms' activities and practices by enabling improved market oversight and surveillance of linked markets; (3) reduce the regulatory burden on regulated entities; and (4) eliminate the asymmetrical regulatory treatment of like products, activities, practices, and financial instruments.

The Volcker Alliance proposal was not comprehensive and did not address insurance, housing finance, or pensions.

The urgent need for structural reform of the financial regulatory system was the key point of the *Blueprint*, the Bipartisan Policy Center proposal, the Volcker Alliance plans, and earlier proposals.

If the Department of Treasury *Blueprint* was the financial regulatory system as the Department of Treasury sought to recreate it, the Volcker Alliance represented the view of the independent regulatory agencies, particularly the Fed. Both Reports sought to simplify federal financial regulation by reducing the number of agencies, empowering a dominant regulator to require the adoption of specific rules or specific actions to broadly regulate all federal depository institutions and shadow banks that long largely were outside any federal regulation scheme.

The *Blueprint* emphasized executive branch control through a revitalized Presidential Working Group. The Volcker Alliance emphasized independence from the executive branch through the Systemic Issues Committee.

The 2009 Obama Administration Initiative

In 2009, the Obama administration Department of Treasury made a less ambitious proposal, *Financial Regulatory Reform: A New Foundation: Rebuilding Financial Supervision and Regulation.*

At the apex of the Obama Administration proposal was a Financial Services Oversight Council, whose membership included:

- The Secretary of the Treasury, who would be the Chair;
- The Chair of the Board of Governors of the Federal Reserve System;
- The Director of the National Bank Supervisor;
- The Director of the Consumer Financial Protection Agency;
- The Chair of the SEC;
- The Chair of the CFTC;
- The Chair of the FDIC; and
- The Director of the Federal Housing Finance Agency.

The functions of the Council were more limited than those in the 2008 Treasury *Blueprint*, Bipartisan Center Policy, or Volcker Alliance:

> [T]o facilitate information sharing and coordination, identify emerging risks, advise the Federal Reserve on the identification of firms whose failure could pose a threat to financial stability due to their combination of size, leverage, and interconnectedness . . . and provide a forum for resolving jurisdictional disputes between regulators.

For the largest financial holding companies' capital, liquidity, and risk management standards were intended to be stricter and more conservative than those applicable to other financial firms "to account for the greater risks that their potential failure would impose on the financial system."

Federal regulators were to be directed to issue standards and guidelines to better align financial firm executive compensation practices with long term shareholder value and prevent compensation practices from providing incentives that threatened the safety and soundness of supervised financial institutions.

With AIG in mind, the 2009 Obama Treasury proposal recommended: "Firewalls between banks and their affiliates should be strengthened to protect the federal safety net that supports banks and to better prevent spread of the subsidy inherent in the federal safety net to bank affiliates."

The 2009 Treasury proposal did recommend a single National Bank Supervisor "to conduct prudential supervision and regulation of all federally chartered depository institutions, and all federal branches and agencies of foreign banks." The separate federal savings and loan and thrift charters would be eliminated.

The Federal Reserve would be the sole regulator responsible for consolidated supervision and regulation of the largest bank and financial holding companies. Loopholes for thrift holding companies, industrial loan companies, credit card banks, trust companies, and grandfathered *non*banks would be ended.

OTC derivatives would be subject to new regulation: "To contain systemic risks, the Commodities Exchange Act . . . and the securities laws should be amended to require clearing of all standardized OTC derivatives through regulated central counterparties."

The 2009 Obama Treasury Proposal recommended an independent agency, the Consumer Financial Protection Agency (*CFPA*) to be "a single primary federal consumer protection supervisor to protect consumers of credit, savings, payment, and other consumer financial products and services, and to regulate providers of such products and services." The CFPA would have broad jurisdiction over consumer financial products and services, including credit, savings and payment products. The CFPA would not have authority for investment products and services already regulated by the SEC or CFTC.[8]

All investment advisers to hedge funds, private equity funds, and venture capital funds above a designated minimum threshold would be required to register with the SEC.

The Treasury Proposal did not propose combining the SEC and the CFTC, creation of Federal Insurance Regulator other than supporting an Office of National Insurance within Treasury largely to gather information. The Proposal anticipated future proposals with respect to Fannie Mae, Freddie Mac, and the Federal Home Loan Bank System.

The Federal Reserve Act was proposed to be amended to permit the Treasury Secretary to authorize the Federal Reserve to extend credit to nonbank individuals, partnerships, or corporations in "unusual or exigent circumstances."

The 2009 Treasury Proposal focused on the regulation of derivatives markets:

> The financial crisis was triggered by a breakdown in credit underwriting standards in subprime and other residential mortgage markets. That breakdown was enabled by lax or nonexistent regulation of nonbank mortgage originators and brokers. But the breakdown also reflected a broad relaxation in market discipline on the credit quality of loans that originators intended to distribute to investors through securitizations rather than hold in their own loan portfolios.
>
> We propose several initiatives to address this breakdown in market discipline: Changing the incentive structure of market participants; increasing transparency to allow for better due diligence; strengthening credit rating agency performance; and reducing the incentives for over-reliance on credit ratings. . . .
>
> The federal banking agencies should promulgate regulations that require loan originators or sponsors to retain five percent of the credit risk of securitized exposures.

OTC derivatives would be subject to new regulation:

> To contain systemic risks, the Commodities Exchange Act (*CEA*) and the securities laws should be amended to require clearing of all standardized OTC derivatives through regulated central counterparties (*CCPs*). To make these measures effective, regulators will need to require that CCPs impose robust margin requirements as well as other necessary risk controls and that customized OTC derivatives are not used solely as a means to avoid using a CCP.

On January 21, 2010, President Obama went further and proposed adoption of what came to be known as the Volcker Rule, to prohibit commercial banks from owning, investing, or sponsoring hedge funds, private equity funds, or proprietary trading operations for bank profits, unrelated to serving customers. This was a successor to the Glass-Steagall Act that had more fully divorced commercial and investment banks. Obama's case for the Volcker Rule was quite specific:

> Never again will the American taxpayer be held hostage by a bank that is *too big to fail*. . . .
>
> Our government provides deposit insurance and other safeguards and guarantees to firms that operate banks. We do so because a stable and reliable banking system promotes sustained growth, and because we learned how dangerous the failure of that system can be during the Great Depression.
>
> But these privileges were not created to bestow banks operating hedge funds or private equity funds with an unfair advantage. When banks benefit from the safety net that taxpayers provide—which includes lower-cost capital—it is not appropriate for them to turn around and use that cheap money to trade for profit. And that is especially true when this kind of trading often puts banks in direct conflict with their customers' interests.[9]

The Dodd-Frank Wall Street Reform and Consumer Protection Act

After a fiercely contested legislative battle, Congress enacted the Dodd-Frank Wall Street Reform and Consumer Protection Act on nearly party line votes, in the House with a 237–192 vote, with three Republicans in the majority, and the Senate by a 60–39 vote, with three Republicans, joining the majority. President Obama signed the Act on July 21, 2010, observing with considerable understatement: "Passing this law was no easy task."

The enactment of the Dodd-Frank Act ushered in a new period in United States financial regulation in which the regulatory departments and agencies were less independent of each other, the White House, and Congress. By emphasizing financial stability and systemic risk reduction as paramount goals, the Dodd-Frank Act stressed the need for regulatory coordination, elimination of gaps and omissions, and regulatory tools to optimize early warning and prompt responses to a burgeoning crisis.

The new approach to financial regulation built on the structure of the old financial regulatory agencies. Only one agency—the late unlamented Office of Thrift Supervision—was abolished. Only one new agency, the Bureau of Consumer Financial Protection—was established.

The purpose of Dodd-Frank was stated succinctly:

> To promote the financial stability of the United States by improving accountability and transparency in the financial system, to end "too big to fail," to protect the American taxpayer by ending bailouts, to protect consumers from abusive financial services practices, and for other purposes.

The Dodd-Frank Act established the Financial Stability Oversight Council, essentially the 2009 Treasury's proposal for a Financial Services Oversight Council, with the same abbreviation (*FSOC*), but with a broader list of voting members:

- The Secretary of the Treasury, to serve as Chair of the Council;
- The Chair of the Federal Reserve Board of Governors;
- The Comptroller of the Currency;
- The Director of the Bureau of Consumer Financial Protection;
- The Chair of the Securities and Exchange Commission;
- The Chair of the Federal Deposit Insurance Corporation;
- The Chair of the Commodity Futures Trading Commission;
- The Director of the Federal Housing Finance Agency;
- The Chair of the National Credit Union Administration Board; and
- An independent member appointed by the President, by and with the advice and consent of the Senate having insurance expertise.

There also were nonvoting advisory members on the FSOC:

- The Director of the Office of Financial Research;
- The Director of the Federal Insurance Office;
- A state Insurance Commissioner selected by the State Insurance Commissioners;
- A state Banking Supervisor; and
- A state Securities Commissioner, selected by their peers.

The functions of the Office of Thrift Supervision were transferred to the Fed.

An Office of Financial Research was established within the Treasury, not an independent agency as the Volcker Alliance proposed, to "[collect] data on behalf of the Council, and [provide] such data to the [FSOC] and member agencies." A Financial Research Fund was established in Treasury that after an initial two years of Fed funding, would be funded by assessments on bank holding companies and nonbank financial companies supervised by the Fed. The director of the Office would be approved by the president with the advice and consent of the Senate for a six-year term.

The FSOC's purposes were not to command and control United States financial regulatory departments and agencies, but:

> (A) to identify risks to the financial stability of the United States that could arise from the material financial distress or failure, or ongoing activities, of large, interconnected bank holding companies or nonbank financial companies, or that could arise outside the financial services marketplace;
>
> (B) to promote market discipline, by eliminating expectations on the part of shareholders, creditors, and counterparties of such companies that the Government will shield them from losses in the event of failure; and
>
> (C) to respond to emerging threats to the stability of the United States financial system.

The emphasis of the FSOC's duties was monitoring and deterrence, rather than crisis management, which largely was delegated to the Federal Reserve Board and Federal Deposit Insurance Corporation. As Geithner put it: "Treasury chairs the [FSOC], but it has little power to compel independent regulators to take coordinated actions for the good of the broader system."

The FSOC was authorized on a vote of two-thirds of its voting members, including an affirmative vote of the chair, to require that a United States or foreign nonbank financial company be supervised by the Federal Reserve Board of Governors and subject to prudential standards if "the Council determines that material financial distress at the U.S. nonbank financial company, or the nature, scope, size, scale, concentration, interconnectedness, or mix of the activities of the U.S. nonbank financial company, could pose a threat to the financial stability of the United States."

The FSOC also was authorized "in order to prevent or mitigate risks to the financial stability of the United States that could arise from the material financial distress, failure, or ongoing activities of large, interconnected financial institutions," to make recommendations to the Federal Reserve "concerning the establishment and refinement of prudential standards and reporting and disclosure requirements applicable to nonbank financial companies by the [Fed] and large, interconnected bank holding companies."

The Dodd-Frank Act provided that the FSOC could recommend enhanced prudential standards concerning:

> (A) Risk-based capital requirements;
> (B) Leverage limits;
> (C) Liquidity requirements;
> (D) Resolution plan and credit exposure report requirements;
> (E) Concentration limits;
> (F) A contingent capital requirement;
> (G) Enhanced public disclosures;
> (H) Short-term debt limits; and
> (I) Overall risk management requirements.

If the Federal Reserve determined that a bank holding company with $50 billion or more in total assets posed a threat to United States financial stability, the Fed "shall":

> (1) Limit the ability of the company to merge with, acquire, consolidate with, or otherwise become affiliated with another company;
>
> (2) Restrict the ability of the company to offer a financial product or products;
>
> (3) Require the company to terminate one or more activities;
>
> (4) Impose conditions on the manner in which the company conducts one or more activities; or
>
> (5) If the Board of Governors determines that the actions described in paragraphs (1) through (4) are inadequate to mitigate a threat to the financial stability of the United States in its recommendation, require the company to sell or otherwise transfer assets or off-balance sheet items to unaffiliated entities.

In order to prevent or mitigate risks to United States financial stability that could arise from material financial distress or failure, the Fed on its own could recommend to the FSOC more stringent prudential standards for bank holding companies with $50 billion or more in assets for covered nonbank financial companies.

The Fed was directed to require each covered financial company to develop a resolution plan "for rapid and orderly resolution in the event of material financial distress or failure," including:

> (A) information regarding the manner and extent to which any insured depository institution affiliated with the company is adequately protected from risks arising from the activities of any nonbank subsidiaries of the company;
> (B) full descriptions of the ownership structure, assets, liabilities, and contractual obligations of the company;
> (C) identification of the cross-guarantee tied to different securities, identification of major counterparties, and a process for determining to whom the collateral of the company is pledged; and
> (D) any other information that the Board of Governors and the Corporation jointly require by rule or order.

The Fed was directed to require each covered bank holding company or each supervised nonbank financial company to maintain a debt to equity ratio of no more than 15 to 1, "upon a determination by the Council that such company poses a grave threat to the financial stability of the United States and that the imposition of such requirement is necessary to mitigate the risk that such company poses to the financial stability of the United States."

The Dodd-Frank Act awkwardly addressed disputes among two or more agencies by empowering the FSOC to make recommendations to resolve the dispute. These recommendations required the affirmative vote of two-thirds of the voting members of the Council but were not binding "on the Federal agencies that are parties to the dispute." The FSOC, in other words, was a mediator, not an arbitrator.

Dodd-Frank sought to end subsidizing firms too big to fail.

The Treasury secretary, in consultation with the president, was empowered to appoint the FDIC as receiver in a covered financial institution, meaning a bank holding company, a company the Fed has determined is predominantly financial in nature, or any subsidiary of these institutions if the company acquires or consents to receivership. If the company did not consent or acquiesce to the receivership, the Treasury secretary could petition the United States District Court for the District of Columbia for an Order authorizing the FDIC's appointment. The Fed, FDIC, SEC, or Director of the Federal Insurance Office could recommend to the Treasury secretary such an appointment upon a vote of not less than two-thirds of the Fed and FDIC for covered financial companies, the Fed and SEC for broker-dealers, and the Fed with the affirmative approval of the Director of the Office of Federal Insurance for a covered insurance company.

All financial companies put into receivership "shall be liquidated. No taxpayer funds shall be used to prevent the liquidation of any financial company" under Dodd-Frank.

The FDIC and SIPC were vested with powers with respect to covered financial companies, securities broker-dealers, with orderly liquidation authority. Orderly liquidation authority was triggered by a vote of the FDIC or SIPC that a covered financial company should be liquidated. The purpose of orderly liquidation was "to provide the necessary authority to liquidate failing financial companies that pose a significant risk to the financial stability of the United States in a manner that mitigates such risk and minimizes moral hazard." The FDIC was directed to exercise its authority "in the manner that best fulfills such purpose," so that:

> (1) Creditors and shareholders will bear the losses of the financial company;
> (2) Management responsible for the condition of the financial company will not be retained; and
> (3) The Corporation and other appropriate agencies will take all steps necessary and appropriate to assure that all parties, including management, directors, and third parties, having responsibility for the condition of the financial company bear losses consistent with their responsibility, including actions for damages, restitution, and recoupment of compensation and other gains not compatible with such responsibility.

An Orderly Liquidation Fund would be funded by obligations issued by the FDIC to the secretary of the Treasury, who, in turn, could sell them. For each covered financial company, maximum obligations limitations could not exceed:

> (A) An amount that is equal to 10 percent of the total consolidated assets of the covered financial company, based on the most recent financial statement available . . . ; and

> (B) The amount that is equal to 90 percent of the fair value of the total consolidated assets of each covered financial company that are available for repayment.

To access the Orderly Liquidation Fund, the FDIC was required to develop its own Orderly Liquidation Plan acceptable to the secretary, and a mandatory repayment plan.

Orderly liquidation was meant to help ensure that no firm would be too big to fail and senior executives and directors would be held responsible for misconduct.

FDIC powers to impose a receivership, in contrast, were cut back and required a recommendation by no fewer than two-thirds of the Fed to the Treasury secretary, who, after consultation with the president could appoint the FDIC as a receiver when:

> (1) the financial company is in default or in danger of default;
> (2) the failure of the financial company and its resolution under otherwise applicable Federal or State law would have serious adverse effects on financial stability in the United States; [and]
> (3) no viable private sector alternative is available to prevent the default of the financial company.

The Dodd-Frank Act included a clawback provision to empower the FDIC, as receiver of a covered financial company, to recover from any current or former senior executive or director "substantially responsible for the failed condition of the covered financial company any compensation received during the 2-year period preceding the date on which the Corporation was appointed as the receiver of the covered financial company, except that, in the case of fraud, no time limit shall apply."

The Dodd-Frank Act authorized the Federal Reserve Board to engage emergency lending programs "for the purpose of providing liquidity to the financial system." The Fed was barred from providing aid to a failing company and was required, as before, to ensure sufficient collateral for an emergency loan. Unlike before the Dodd-Frank Act, the Fed could not establish any emergency lending program or facility without the prior approval of the Treasury secretary. Dodd-Frank directed the Treasury secretary, upon request of the Fed and FDIC, to determine that a liquidity event exists and direct the FDIC to create a program to guarantee obligations of solvent insured depository institutions "during times of severe economic distress, except that guarantee of obligations . . . may not include the provision of equity in any form." The maximum of any guarantee was to be determined by the Treasury secretary in consultation with the president. The FDIC was only permitted to exercise the authority to create and fund an Emergency Stabilization Fund upon approval by Congress in a Joint Resolution.

To former Treasury Secretaries Tim Geithner and Hank Paulson and former Fed Chair Ben Bernanke, the weakening of the federal regulatory emergency arsenal was a critical shortcoming of the Dodd-Frank Act:

> In general, the crisis managers of tomorrow will have less authority and less flexibility to take action to support the financial system than we had. Congress took away the Treasury's power to use the Exchange Stabilization Fund to issue guarantees, even though that power protected the savings of ordinary Americans and vital short term funding for much of corporate America when money market funds were melting down after the Reserve Primary Fund broke the buck. Congress also curtailed the executive branch's ability to take credit risk alongside the Fed, as it had done to backstop consumer credit markets through the Term Asset-Backed Securities Loan Facility. Dodd-Frank even weakened the Fed's traditional lender-of-last-resort programs, adding disclosure rules that, whatever their benefits in terms of transparency, will increase the potential stigma of taking loans from the Fed, making it harder for the Fed to inject liquidity into the system in future crises.

The Dodd-Frank Act did establish a modified version of the Volcker Rule:

> Unless otherwise provided in this section, a banking entity shall not—
>
> (A) Engage in proprietary trading; or
>
> (B) Acquire or retain any equity, partnership or other ownership interest in or sponsor a hedge fund or a private equity fund.

Several activities were permitted to bank entities including proprietary trades on behalf of customers; organizing and offering a private equity or hedge fund, including service as a general partner or managing member or selection of a majority of its directors when the bank provides *bona fide* trust, fiduciary, or advisory services.

The bank investment was limited to no more than 3 percent of its Tier 1 Capital.

These and other exceptions to the Volcker Rule reduced the effectiveness of the Rule's prohibition and occasioned several years of banking agency, SEC, and CFTC rulemaking.

Nonbank financial companies supervised by the Federal Reserve Board were subject to a different standard:

> Any nonbank financial company supervised by the Board that engages in proprietary trading or takes or retains any equity, partnership, or other ownership interest in or sponsors a hedge fund or a private equity fund shall be subject, by rule, . . . to additional capital requirements for and additional quantitative limits with regards to such proprietary trading and taking or retaining any equity, partnership, or other ownership interest in or sponsorship of a hedge fund or a private equity fund.

For nonbank financial companies, this was not the Volcker Rule, but a specification of potential additional capital requirements.[10]

The Fed was authorized to develop uniform standards to reduce the risks of systemically important financial market utilities payment, clearing, and settlement activities. The FSOC by a vote of no less than two-thirds of its members could determine which firms were or were likely to be systemically important.

The Dodd-Frank Act did establish a new Bureau of Consumer Financial Protection. Then Harvard Law Professor Elizabeth Warren in 2007 championed the idea of a Financial Product Safety Commission, writing in a much cited article:

> It is impossible to buy a toaster that has a one-in-five chance of bursting into flames and burning down your house. But it is possible to refinance an existing home with a mortgage that has the same one-in-five chance of putting the family out on the street—and the mortgage won't even carry a disclosure of that fact to the homeowner. . . .
>
> The difference between the two markets is regulation.

Warren in her 2007 and subsequent articles described consumer financial problems in a wide variety of financial products, including credit cards, payday loans, and subprime mortgages. These markets had in common consumers who often were underinformed or did not understand key terms and a failure of third-party information providers such as *Consumer Reports* or federal regulatory agencies to effectively remedy the imbalance between consumers with imperfect information and the complexity for many consumers of many financial products.

Warren emphasized the need for new legislation:

> Americans are drowning in debt. One in four families say they are worried about how they will pay their credit card bills this month. Nearly half of all credit card holders have missed payments in the past year, and an additional 2.1 million families missed at least one mortgage payment. Last year, 1.2 million families lost their homes in foreclosure, and another 1.5 million families are likely headed into mortgage foreclosure this year.
>
> Families' troubles are compounded by substantial changes in the credit market that have made debt instruments far riskier for consumers than they were a generation ago. The effective deregulation of interest rates, coupled with innovations in credit charges (e.g., teaser rates, negative amortization, increased use of fees, cross-default clauses, penalty interest rates, and two-cycle billing), have turned ordinary credit transactions into devilishly complex financial undertakings.

A 2007 study commissioned by the Federal Reserve identified several terms and credit concepts that consumers often did not understand, including:

- When issuers disclose a range of annual percentage rates (*APRs*), that their specific APR will be determined by their creditworthiness;
- That the APR on a "fixed rate" credit card product can change;
- What event might trigger a default APR;
- Which balances the default APR will apply to;
- How long the default APR will apply;
- What fees are associated with the credit card product;
- How the balance is calculated (e.g., two-cycle billing);
- How payments are allocated among different rate balances;
- The meaning and terms of grace period and effective APR;
- The time, or the due date, that payment is due;

- When the introductory rate expires;
- How large the post-introductory rate is; and
- The cost of convenience checks.

The Fed, the Comptroller, and the Office of Thrift Supervision had the power to control specified forms of predatory lending. "But their main mission is to protect the financial stability of banks and other financial institutions, not to protect consumers." As Warren and a co-author wrote in a 2008 article, the federal regulators had "authority without motivation."

Warren highlighted a further problem:

> Consumer financial products are regulated based, principally, on the identity of the issuer, rather than the nature of the product. The subprime mortgage market provides a stunning example of the resulting fractured oversight. In 2005, for example, 23 percent of subprime mortgages were issued by regulated thrifts and banks. Another 25 percent were issued by bank holding companies, which were subject to different regulatory oversight through the federal system. But more than half—52 percent, to be exact—of all subprime mortgages originated with companies with no federal supervision at all, largely stand-alone mortgage brokers and finance companies. This division not only creates enormous loopholes, it also triggers a kind of regulatory arbitrage. Regulators are acutely aware that if they push financial institutions too hard, those institutions will simply reincorporate in another form under the umbrella of a different regulatory agency—or no regulatory agency at all.

Law Professor Adam Levitin criticized consumer protection before the Dodd-Frank Act: "[C]onsumer financial protection regulation was divided among multiple federal and state agencies. This fractured authority created a number of regulatory problems. First, it made consumer protection an orphan mission that tended to 'fall between the cracks' because no agency had an exclusive role of consumer protection in financial services. Only the Federal Trade Commission (the *FTC*) had consumer protection as its primary role, but the FTC had very limited jurisdiction in financial services. The FTC lacked authority over federally chartered or insured banks, thrifts, or credit unions, so only bit players in financial services were within its regulatory ken. Because consumer protection was everyone's responsibility, it became no one's responsibility, and regulatory accountability and performance suffered."

Warren proposed a Financial Product Safety Commission to "review mortgages, credit cards, car loans, and a number of other financial products, such as life insurance and annuity contracts. In effect, the FPSC would evaluate these products to eliminate the hidden tricks and traps that make some of them far more dangerous than others."

In the Dodd-Frank Act, the Bureau of Consumer Financial Protection was given a hybrid status. Proponents of the new Bureau had sought an independent regulatory commission, whose director would be in the president's Cabinet. The Consumer Financial Protection Agency became a Bureau of the Federal Reserve, without Cabinet level status, but with some independence within the Fed. As with the Fed, the Bureau of Consumer Financial Protection was not subject to the annual appropriations process, but subject to a statutory funding cap equal to 12 percent of Fed expenses. The Director of the Bureau could specify the amount that the Fed needed to provide to carry out necessary Bureau activities.

The Bureau was empowered to exercise authority under 18 consumer laws including the Equal Credit Opportunity Act, the Fair Credit Billing Act, the Home Owners Protection Act, the Truth in Lending Act, and Omnibus Land Sales Full Disclosure Act.

The Bureau also was empowered to issue rules, orders and guidance concerning covered persons in insured depository institutions and credit unions with more than $10 billion in total assets. For other depository institutions, the Bureau could require reports.

The Bureau was vested with enforcement powers including investigation and litigation authority.

The Bureau was subject to Congressional oversight and as its advocates painfully learned in the failure to appoint Professor Warren as its initial Director and subsequent revision of its initial rules during the Trump administration, the Bureau is subject to control by presidential appointments, legislative enactments, and rule revisions.

The Dodd-Frank Act excluded the Bureau from regulating merchants, retailers, sellers of nonfinancial goods generally, real estate brokers and agents, firms regulated by the SEC and CFTC, and under most circumstances, automobile dealers.[11]

The Dodd-Frank Act amended the 2006 Credit Rating Reform Act to require each credit rating agency or nationally recognized statistical rating organization (*NRSRO*) to maintain tighter internal controls, empower the SEC to adopt rules barring sales and marketing considerations from influencing the production of credit ratings, and adopt rules requiring NRSROs to secure board of director approval of credit rating methodologies and procedures, including qualitative and quantitative data that were the basis of NRSRO assumptions. At least half of each NRSRO board was required to be independent. SEC and private causes of action of credit rating agencies were facilitated when there was:

> a strong inference that the credit rating agency knowingly or recklessly failed—
> (i) to conduct a reasonable investigation of the rated security with respect to factual elements relied upon by [the NRSRO's] own methodology for evolving risk; or
> (ii) to obtain reasonable verification of such factual elements . . . from other sources that the credit rating agency considered to be competent and that were independent of the issuer.

Significantly, the Dodd-Frank Act directed the SEC and FDIC to remove statutory references to credit ratings. The SEC subsequently removed exemptions or reliance on credit ratings from all relevant SEC rules and forms.[12]

Issuers and any person who issued or initiated an asset-backed security, including securitized mortgages by sale or transfer of asset-backed assets, directly or through an affiliate, were required by Dodd-Frank to retain at least 5 percent of the credit risk for covered assets as "skin in the game." Other Dodd-Frank provisions addressed material conflicts of interest by an underwriter, placement agent, initial purchaser, or any affiliate or subsidiary of an asset-backed security including asset-backed securities such as the collateralized mortgage obligations notorious in the 2007–2009 Meltdown.[13]

The Dodd-Frank Act, building on TARP and subsequent legislation, adopted several sections that regulated executive compensation. One provision required disclosure to the appropriate financial regulator by covered financial institutions of "the structures of all incentive-based compensation paid to the officers, directors" and compensation "that could lead to material loss to the covered financial institution." This provision and SEC rulemaking was excoriated by Columbia Law Professor John Coffee for delegating decisions about which financial compensation structures could cause substantial loss to the covered institutions and requiring little specific data.

Other provisions of Dodd-Frank required nonbinding shareholder votes on the compensation of specified senior executives and on golden parachutes, that is, additional compensation paid when a corporate merger or acquisition occurs. The Dodd-Frank Act required Board Compensation Committees to have members independent of corporate operating management.[14]

Dodd-Frank addressed several gaps in the earlier porous regulatory framework.

Hedge funds before the Dodd-Frank Act often could be organized without disclosure to federal financial regulators. Investment advisers to hedge funds usually were exempt from the federal securities laws when they had fewer than 15 clients within a 12 month period. In 2004, the District of Columbia Court of Appeals in *Goldstein v. SEC* had invalidated an SEC rule that required hedge fund advisers to register as investment advisers under the Investment Adviser Act.

The Dodd-Frank Act reversed *Goldstein* and extended the Investor Advisers Act registration, disclosure, and other substantive provisions to domestic hedge funds, in the Act denominated private funds. The SEC was authorized to share all reports, documents, records, and information it received with the Financial Stability Oversight Council when necessary to address systemic risk posed by a private fund. The Dodd-Frank Act exempted venture capital fund advisers that solely advised one or more venture capital funds and family offices from the Investment Adviser Act registration and disclosure provisions.[15]

The Dodd-Frank Act repealed the Gramm-Leach-Bliley Act prohibition on regulation of security-based swaps and awkwardly divided regulation of the swaps markets between the SEC for security-based swaps and the CFTC for other swaps.

The Dodd-Frank and subsequent rulemaking by the SEC and CFTC addressed security and nonsecurity based swaps, swap dealers, major swap participants, swap dealer registration, clearing agencies, and cross-border swap transactions for a broad panoply of interest, currency, foreign currency, and other swaps. The intent of the Dodd-Frank swap reforms was to centralize trading through clearinghouses and exchanges or if neither would accept the swap transactions, the SEC or CFTC were required to supervise swap transactions to ensure real time public reporting of trade data. Swap dealers and major swap participants were subjected to capital, margin, loan disclosure, and supervision requirements. In exchange-traded and centrally cleared swaps, Dodd-Frank sought to standardize transactions and have the central counterparty guarantee trades.[16]

Critical gaps in the Dodd-Frank approach to financial regulation remained.

The structure of housing finance was lightly addressed. With Fannie Mae and Freddie Mac in conservatorship, there was, as former Treasury Secretary Geithner put it, "no immediate rush." Given the catalytic role housing finance had played in the 2007–2009 Financial Meltdown and the enduring role, even in conservatorship, that government-sponsored enterprises played in the outstanding mortgage market, increasing from 43.8 percent in 2003 of mortgages to 45.7 percent in 2013, this was surprising.

The Dodd-Frank Act did adopt several reforms concerning mortgage lending, with Congress finding that "economic stabilization would be enhanced by the protection, limitation and regulation of the terms of residential mortgage credit and the practices related to such credit, while ensuring that responsible, affordable mortgage credit remains available to consumers." Mortgage originators were prohibited from steering to any consumer a residential mortgage loan that the consumer lacked a reasonable ability to repay or had predatory characteristics or effects such as excessive fees or abusive terms. A mortgage originator could not engage in mortgage practices that promoted disparities among consumers of equal credit worthiness but of different race, ethnicity, gender, or age. Specified prepayment penalties were prohibited and a six-month notice was required to reset hybrid adjustable rate mortgages. Within the Department of Housing and Urban Development, an Office of Housing Counseling was established. Congress acknowledged "that efforts to enhance by the protection limitation, and regulation of the terms of residential mortgage credit and the practices related to such credit would be incomplete without enactment of meaningful structural reforms of Fannie Mae and Freddie Mac."

A 2011 Treasury Department and Department of Housing and Urban Development Report to Congress highlighted that fundamental problems in Fannie Mae and Freddie Mac endured, including a profit maximizing private structure, a complex securitization chain that lacked transparency, lack of standardized mortgage practices or accountability, an implicit government-backed guarantee, inadequate capital requirements, and an inadequate or outdated regulatory regime. Both the Obama administration and the Trump administration proposed plans to withdraw Fannie Mae and Freddie Mac from conservatorship, but neither plan to date has been adopted by Congress.[17]

Insurance similarly was lightly addressed. No federal insurance regulatory agency was created by Dodd-Frank. Instead, Dodd-Frank created a Federal Insurance Office with the Treasury Department to monitor the insurance industry with the exception of health and long-term care insurance and make recommendations to the Financial Stability Oversight Council about insurers that pose a systemic risk. Insurance regulation, including regulation of insurance holding companies, remained at the state level.[18]

The Dodd-Frank Act ignored pension finance altogether.

The most serious deficiencies of the Dodd-Frank Act were structural. In contrast to the Department of Treasury 2008 *Blueprint,* the Bipartisan Policy Center, the Volcker Alliance proposals, and repeated GAO critiques of the byzantine and fragmented structure of United States financial regulation, the Dodd-Frank Act did not address the financial regulatory structure.

The Government Accountability Office summarized the deficiencies of the post Dodd-Frank model of financial regulation in 2016, citing repeated examples in which fragmented United States regulatory structures complicated securities and derivatives oversight split between the SEC and the CFTC, limited insurance oversight, providing inconsistent safety and soundness and consumer protection oversight, delayed regulatory action, complicated the United States position in international negotiations such as those concerning the Basel Accords, and limited the capacity to achieve fully effective systemic risk monitoring.

For former Treasury Secretaries Tim Geithner and Hank Paulson and former Fed Chair Ben Bernanke, Dodd-Frank failed to simplify "the ludicrously byzantine mess" of United States financial regulation.

Why? In countless instances the Obama administration faced the realities of congressional politics. As House Financial Services Chair

Barney Frank explained: "Sure, you can merge the SEC and CFTC. You just can't do it in the United States." Before retiring from Congress in 2012, Frank, however, did introduce legislation to merge the SEC and CFTC.

Nor was parochialism limited to congressional committees. Regulatory agencies, as Geithner and other proponents of Dodd-Frank painfully learned, could be ferocious in defending their turf.

There were high costs to the inability to restructure financial regulation. Geithner emphasized delays in rulemaking, explaining:

> Our reforms largely left in place our stunningly fragmented regulatory structure, with three federal bank supervisors, two market regulators, five agencies responsible for the Volcker Rule, and ten voting members on the council monitoring systemic risks. This level of bureaucratic balkanization is better than what we had in 2007, but it is not good enough. It is the largest source of complexity and delay in the rulemaking for Dodd-Frank. It limits accountability for outcomes. It will slow the regulatory system's ability to evolve in response to future market innovations. [President Obama] and I considered coming back to this in 2011 and 2012, launching a new fight for a much simpler, more consolidated system, but the politics seemed insurmountable.

Serious issues that could be more directly addressed through a simplified regulatory structure were not addressed in Dodd-Frank. How should, for example, the command and control structure of executive departments, such as the Department of Treasury, be harmonized with independent regulatory agencies such as the Federal Reserve or SEC? How do you harmonize the president's power to propose taxes and budgets with the monetary, investor, and consumer protection objectives of the regulatory agencies? Should all independent regulatory agencies be self-funding?[19]

Legislation After the Dodd-Frank Act

After Dodd-Frank, subsequent legislation and rulemaking cut back on some of the more stringent provisions of the 2010 Act.

In April 2012, after minimal hearings, over the opposition of the SEC, Congress enacted the Jumpstart Our Business Startups Act, popularly known as the JOBS Act. The JOBS Act was supported by the oddest of election year coalitions, including President Obama and House Speaker John Boehner, who had agreed on little else during the 112th Congress. The JOBS Act added astonishingly broad exemptions for emerging growth companies (defined to reach, among others, companies with total annual gross revenues of $1 billion) from specified executive compensation and financial data requirements, required only two years of audited financial statements, and permitted emerging growth companies to confidentially submit draft registration statements. A new crowdfunding provision permitted sales up to $1 million during a 12-month period. The Commission was directed to add a new $50 million small issue exemption for securities that were offered and sold publicly.

The Volcker provision of Dodd-Frank required the SEC, Comptroller, the FDIC, and Federal Reserve to adopt rules to implement the provision, which the agencies initially did in 2013. Rules adopted in 2013 gave banks and bank holding companies latitude not to be subject to the Volcker Rule when they created a separate nonbank affiliate. This approached begged a fundamental question: If the Volcker Rule was enacted to reduce systemic risk, why have a different standard for nonbank subsidiaries?

More far reaching regulatory relief was provided to large banks and large bank holding companies in 2018. Dodd-Frank created an enhanced regulatory regime for banks with $50 billion or more in assets. There were estimated to be 38 United States banks or bank holding companies before 2018, subject to Dodd-Frank regulatory regime that were required to comply with:

- Leverage Limits
- Liquidity Coverage Ratio
- Stress Tests
- Living Wills or Resolution Planning
- Counterparty Limits
- Required Chief Risk Officers
- Financial Stability Requirements, when a bank poses a threat to financial stability.

The Economic Growth, Regulatory Relief and Consumer Protection Act of 2018 reduced prudential standards for all but 15 banks with $250 billion or more in assets or $10 billion or more in foreign exposure.

The Economic Growth Act categorically exempted banks and bank holding companies with $50 billion to $100 billion in assets and conditionally exempted banks with $100 billion to $250 billion in assets unless the Federal Reserve determined that the application of the prudential standard was appropriate: "(I) to prevent or mitigate risks to the financial stability of the United States; . . . or (II) to promote the safety and soundness of the bank holding company or bank holding companies."

All banks above $100 billion in total consolidated assets would be subject to supervisory stress tests on a periodic basis, but the requirements of stress tests were lightened. The number of scenarios required, for example, were reduced from 3 to 2 (eliminating the adverse scenario, but retaining the baseline and severely adverse scenarios).

Foreign banks earlier subjected to enhanced regulation under Dodd-Frank when they had $50 billion in global assets and operate in the United States were now subject to enhanced regulation only when they met a $100 billion threshold.

Federal Reserve prior approval of voting interests in nonbank companies with over $10 billion in assets was raised to banks with $250 billion or more in assets.

The new Act created an exemption from the Volcker Rule. A community bank was defined to mean a depository institution or depository institution holding company with total consolidated assets of less than $10 billion. The appropriate federal banking agencies were directed to develop a community bank leverage ratio of not less than 8 percent and not more than 10 percent for qualifying community banks. This was more demanding than the earlier 5 percent leverage ratio. Under the Dodd-Frank Act, when a community bank equaled the community bank leverage ratio, the bank was excepted from all other leverage and risk-based capital requirements.

The community bank exception applied to the Volcker Rule, which now excepted all banks and companies controlling a bank or bank holding company with not more than $10 billion in total consolidated assets and total trading assets and trading liability of not more than 5 percent of total consolidated assets from the Volcker Act prohibition proprietary trading provision.[20]

A New Financial Regulatory Model

Given the inadequacies of Dodd-Frank and long historical experience, what should be the financial regulatory model for the 21st century?

The purpose of the Dodd-Frank Act needs to be fundamentally rewritten. Dodd-Frank, enacted in the aftermath of the 2007–2009 Financial Meltdown more than anything else, sought to promote financial stability, end too big to fail, end bailouts, and protect consumers from abusive financial services practices.

This purpose is flawed and too limited. After the 2008 election and bruising legislative battle to enact Dodd-Frank, it is understandable why Congress would seek to end bailouts and too big to fail. But an absolutionist approach to ending bailouts is fundamentally wrong. Had President Roosevelt not had the power to engage in bailouts and save firms too big to fail in the Great Depression or Presidents Bush and Obama during the 2007–2009 Meltdown, these crises would have been catastrophically worse.

The enemy of financial stability is rigidity. The shackles placed on central bank formation after President Jackson's 1832 veto of the Charter of the Second Bank of United States contributed to the financial crises of 1837, 1857, 1873, 1893, 1907, and 1929–1932. The incapacity of the Weimer Republic to address a currency crisis because of the punitive terms of German post-World War I reparations contributed to the rise of Hitler. The slowness and begrudging initial European Central Bank response to the 2007–2009 Crisis prolonged and amplified crises in several European nations.

In a financial crisis, the president and financial regulators need access to the full array of emergency measures, including deficit spending and, when required, bailouts. Think of the alternative experience in 2007–2009 without the power to bail out failing firms. Several leading United States investment banks including JP Morgan, Citicorp, and Morgan Stanley likely would have failed; the United States auto industry would have lost at least General Motors and Chrysler; housing finance would have been decimated by the bankruptcy of Fannie Mae and Freddie Mac; the insurance industry would have lost AIG, its leading life and health and second leading property and casualty insurer. Given the interconnectedness of our economy through loans, investments and counterparties, the contagion would have had broader impacts on employment, productivity and tax revenues throughout the economy than in fact so painfully occurred.

In a financial crisis, the first thing every nation must do is save its economy from financial catastrophe. The Dodd-Frank Act in its purpose and related regulatory provisions is wrong in making financial stability more difficult, however politically appealing a bumper sticker slogan such as "Too Big to Fail" may be.

The statutory aspiration should be to end bailouts to the extent feasible given relevant economic circumstances. Legislation should never be so lacking in flexibility that it obviates the more serious purpose of a law such as Dodd-Frank, which was financial stability.

Nor was this the only deficiency in Dodd-Frank's purpose. New legislation should expressly add what Dodd-Frank lacked: adding the purpose of protecting investors and capital formation, the insurance, housing, and pension systems, and the independent regulatory agencies, in addition to protecting consumers.

The failure of Dodd-Frank to restructure financial regulation was the Act's most serious error.

During a financial emergency, the nation would be best served not by a weak Financial Stability Oversight Council, but a Financial Regulatory Authority that, along with the president and her or his administration, would be empowered to anticipate and rapidly respond to crisis.

An approach preferable to the Dodd-Frank Act's relatively toothless Financial Stability Oversight Council would be to create a Financial Regulatory Authority that would retain considerable independence from the administration to best ensure that it is not influenced by political considerations such as obscuring a deepening financial crisis before an election or seeking to cut interest rates and increase money supply to create the most vibrant short-term economy at the cost of long-term inflation.

The decisions by the Federal Reserve during Paul Volcker's chairmanship to substantially raise interest rates at the expense of higher unemployment highlight the imperative need for financial regulatory independence. These painful interest rate increases were credited with contributing to sustained economic progress for over two decades, but would have been impossible for a political administration to have achieved. History indelibly teaches one lesson about financial regulation in the United States. An independent regulatory agency is more likely to pursue the long-term interest of the

United States than a political administration, more influenced by the two-year election cycle.

The Financial Regulatory Authority should be empowered to adopt generic standards applicable to all businesses subject to its supervision and in emergencies to coordinate rapid response calling on the resources of each of its members, including the Treasury and Federal Reserve.

Compared to Dodd-Frank, voting membership on the Federal Regulatory Administration should be reduced only to include:

- The Chair of the Federal Regulatory Authority;
- The Secretary of Treasury;
- The Chair of the Federal Reserve Board of Governors;
- The Chair of the National Banking Commission;
- The Chair of the Investment Commission;
- The Chair of the Consumer Financial Protection Commission; and
- The Chair of the National Insurance Commission.

Underlying regulatory agency consolidation is a trade-off. An ideal of the New Deal Financial Regulatory Model was to maximize agency expertise in the industries that were regulated. This meant development of numerous small agencies, sometimes scoffed at as "alphabet agencies." Regulatory expertise often was achieved but at the price of frequent political ineffectuality in the post-World War II period.

SEC Chair Douglas's rejection of Roosevelt's offer to add to the Securities and Exchange Commission's jurisdiction during the New Deal was naïve. To say, as Douglas did, that he did not want to expand the Commission's oversight mission because he personally could not continue to master all aspects of the SEC's jurisdiction historically contributed to the Commission's diminished post-World War II effectiveness. Administration of far larger government or business institutions long has occurred through such familiar techniques as delegation within the institution to divisions with senior internal leaders and regular internal reporting to a leadership group. Douglas did not anticipate how diminished the political effectiveness of the SEC would be in the post-World War II period when the SEC Chair no longer had a strong personal bond with the president and as later SEC Chair William Cary put it, the Commission became a "stepchild" of the executive and Congress, incapable of protecting its budget or achieving needed legislative or fundamental regulatory change without the support of both of these branches of government.

This Financial Regulatory Model begins with a quite different premise. By reducing the number of leading agencies to a manageable number, political effectiveness is stressed. In a seven-person Financial Regulatory Authority, all critical aspects of the economy will be at the table.

The Federal Regulation Authority should be advised by an Office of Economic Research and such other offices as the Federal Regulatory Authority establishes. These could include offices that focus on housing, international coordination of finance, coordination with state regulators, and innovation including new products such as cryptocurrency, new market trading platforms, and new communications media, as well as a critical office focused on risk assessment to facilitate the Federal Regulatory Authority's capacity to remain "ahead of the curve" in anticipating future crises.

Each of the areas addressed by offices is critical in its own right. Deficiencies in housing finance, for example, was the catalyst for the 2007–2009 Financial Meltdown. A strong Housing Finance Regulatory Commission urgently needs to be created, independent of the Department of Housing and Urban Development when Fannie Mae and Freddie Mac emerge from conservatorship. But the need for effective oversight of the housing industry, as important as it is, is just one of a plethora of industry-specific challenges that will confront the Financial Regulatory Authority. A well-funded office to monitor the housing industry and its regulation and communicate to the Financial Regulatory Authority early warnings of incipient crisis is proposed here because of the overarching need to keep the fundamental decisionmaking at the Financial Regulatory Authority with the smallest possible number of decision makers, who can collectively assume responsibility for the overall functioning of the financial regulatory system and supervision of a vast economy.

The new Financial Regulatory Model is intended to completely or nearly completely eliminate at the federal level overlaps, redundancies, and regulatory competition. Salutary aspects of earlier regulation including Dodd-Frank would be retained such as minimum capital and leverage ratios and orderly liquidation planning.

Unlike Dodd-Frank's Financial Stability Oversight Council, the Federal Regulatory Authority by a two-thirds vote would be empowered to adopt prudential standards applicable to all business or regulatory agencies subject to its administration concerning capital requirements, leverage levels, liquidity, resolution plans, concentration, debt limits, and risk management.

Generic rules of the Federal Regulatory Authority should be applicable to all major financial institutions whether banks, investment, insurance, or in housing finance. Major financial institutions should be a broader category than that established by the 2018 Economic Growth, Regulatory Research and Consumer Protection Act and cover banks, investment, insurance, and housing finance firms above a designated dollar threshold such as the $50 billion in total consolidated assets in the original provision in the Dodd-Frank Act, adjusted over time for inflation.

Enhanced powers of the Federal Regulatory Authority during emergencies are inevitable. Whether in war time or in financial panics, the United States has survived by responding with different standards during crisis. We have one written Constitution of the United States but operate under United States Supreme Court decisions as if we have two. As Justice Holmes memorably wrote in *Schenck v. United States*: "When a nation is at war many things that might be said in time of peace are such a hindrance to its effort that their utterance will not be endured so long as men fight and no Court would regard them as protected by any constitutional right."

In crisis or to prevent crisis, the Financial Regulatory Authority should have command and control powers over systemic risk functions in coordination with the White House and Department of Treasury. We have learned from long experience that whatever the law provides when the economy is melting down, there must be a clear equivalent to a war council to provide leadership.

The United States historically has followed a similar approach during financial emergencies. If a financial emergency is dire enough, the White House, the Department of Treasury, and the Federal Reserve lead the response. If appropriations are necessary, Congress is involved, often through an accelerated process such as was clumsily illustrated in 2008 in funding the Troubled Asset Relief Program.

The Federal Regulatory Authority on a two-thirds vote would be empowered to resolve jurisdictional or other disputes between its members. The likelihood of future disputes will be reduced by the reduction of overlapping member agencies in the Financial Regulatory Authority. In any dispute, the disputing member agencies would not be entitled to vote or participate in decisional meetings beyond having the opportunity to present their case. This is a significant enhancement of the FSOC's inability to direct agency dispute resolution.

In the new Financial Regulatory Model, the role of each of the member agencies would be revised to avoid redundancy, regulatory arbitrage, and to simplify administrative efficiency.

The Treasury Department would retain its historical fiscal responsibilities and serve as chief spokesperson for the president, but the Treasury would transfer its oversight role of the Office of the Comptroller to the National Banking Commission and its role in consumer protection to the Consumer Financial Protection Commission.

The Federal Reserve would retain its leadership role in monetary policy and oversee bank and financial holding companies as well as other financial firms above the major financial institution category established in the new Act. This will allow the Fed to have a regulatory role with those banks and other financial firms most likely to pose a systemic risk to the economy. The Fed would no longer oversee state members of the Federal Deposit Insurance Corporation. Oversight of these and other Federal Reserve regulatory functions would be transferred to the National Banking Commission.

The National Banking Commission would oversee all depository institutions and Federal Deposit Insurance. In the National Banking Commission, the former oversight of all national banks, state member banks in the Federal Deposit Insurance Corporation, savings and loans and other thrift institutions, credit unions, and deposit insurance would be consolidated. The functions of the Office of the Comptroller, the Federal Deposit Insurance Corporation, and the National Credit Union Administration would be merged into the National Banking Commission.

This would simplify regulation and oversight. The National Banking Commission would be directed to reduce all covered banking, savings and loan, and credit union regulation to two categories: For-Profit Depository Institutions and Not-for-Profit Depository

Institutions. Parallel to the administration of for-profit and not-for-profit corporations at state Secretary of State offices, the National Bank Commission would oversee both types of institutions, likely through separate divisions or offices.

For-profit depository institutions would have one registration procedure, one rulebook, one team of examiners, one enforcement system. The new regulatory regime would regulate all financial holding companies and stand-alone depository institutions. For covered depository institutions, requirements could be scaled by the size of the firm and include different standards for international operations. State depository regulation could continue for purely interstate firms.

A similar consolidation would occur in the Investment Commission, which would combine the current Securities and Exchange Commission, Commodities Futures Trading Commission, sales practice regulation of pension investment and financial advice to pension plan beneficiaries from the Department of Labor and oversight of all other investment vehicles, including those currently not required to register such as hedge funds. The criteria for registration, rule application, examination, and enforcement would be based on size criteria, not form. The abuses of private banks, such as JP Morgan before 1933 or more recently Long Term Capital Management and post-Gramm-Leach-Bliley swaps, underline that abuse sometimes painfully does occur precisely when institutions are unregulated.

The regulation of pension plan sales practice would be modelled on the Supreme Court's dichotomy of annuity sales, which authorized the SEC to require sales documents for variable annuities where beneficiaries have investment risk, but not traditional annuities, which solely remained subject to state insurance regulation. The Investment Commission would be authorized by Congress to regulate all pension plan offering documents and investment advice where employees make investment decisions such as voluntary plans or where the value of the pension plan is in the form of a defined contribution plan with ultimate value determined by the investments that the pension plan makes. Department of Labor regulation of all labor-related issues would be untouched.

Consolidating investment regulation would vastly simplify rulemaking. Today, for example, we have separate regimes for swaps in the SEC and the CFTC, and historically have long delayed rule or

Order implementation with litigation over whether a given investment is covered by the enabling legislation.

State regulation for investment firms would continue for purely intrastate corporations but would be preempted for financial institutions engaged in interstate operations subject to federal regulation.

The National Insurance Commission also would operate in a system of concurrent state regulation. All insurance firms, whether life and health, property or casualty, or other category above a specified size or engaged in interstate commerce, would be required to register with the National Insurance Commission and be subject to a unified system of registration, rulebook, examination, and enforcement.

The Consumer Financial Protection Commission would no longer be a bureau of the Federal Reserve Board, where it was housed in Dodd-Frank in an effort to ensure the independence of its budget. Instead the Consumer Financial Protection Commission would now be a full-fledged independent regulatory Commission and would have full membership on the Federal Regulatory Authority.

Consolidation of registration, rulebooks, examination, and enforcement would be critical in the new Financial Regulatory Model. By consolidating registration under one system, regulatory arbitrage would be eliminated or largely eliminated. Our economy long was weakened by interest rate differentials between banks and savings and loans or other differences in the powers of rival forms of depository institutions.

A unified registration system should also occur concomitant with a revision of categories of financial institutions. In the investment industry in 2019, there were brokers, dealers, investment advisers, and futures commission merchants, commodity pool operations, and swap dealers. Many have overlapping businesses. It has long been recognized that the differences between securities broker-dealers and investment advisers have narrowed; securities broker-dealers and counterpart financial futures traders offer substitute products. The Investment Commission would be authorized to create new categories such as investment professionals that would subsume areas for registration and regulation and clarify to investors and the industries involved the role of the investment trader.

The 2007 merger of the former National Association of Securities Dealers and New York Stock Exchange regulation into the self-regulatory organization popularly known as FINRA (Financial

Industry Regulatory Authority) illustrates that consolidation of rulebooks, examination and enforcement can be highly advantageous. By reducing rival systems of investor protection into a single system, compliance costs are reduced and investor protection standards clarified.

Consolidation of federal financial regulators' examination and enforcement involves other issues. The Federal Reserve has higher compensation levels than the SEC and other regulatory agencies. This creates a needless competition for qualified staff. To achieve the most effective regulatory system, it is essential to unify costs and benefits for the staff across the federal financial regulatory system.

As with current law, the regulatory agencies would retain a wide panoply of enforcement systems including civil litigation, orders for injunctions, cease and desist, bars from industry, and civil fines. Decisions to initiate civil litigation should solely be made within the relevant independent regulatory commission to minimize the possibility of external political pressures. As with current law, criminal proceedings, however, should be referred to the Department of Justice.

Unification of regulation in a new Financial Regulatory Model would provide Congress an appropriate occasion to revisit three other aspects of the existing laws concerning financial regulation which, on a disquieting number of occasions, have proven dysfunctional.

First, congressional oversight of financial regulation is ineffectively organized. One congressional committee should oversee the Financial Regulatory Authority and its constituent agencies. Until Congress reduces the number of committees involved in oversight of banking, securities, and futures, progress towards an effective system of financial oversight may continue to be frustrated.

Second, rulemaking has increasingly been hampered in recent years by more demanding standards of judicial review. The nation risks returning to the horse and buggy courts of the era of *Lochner v. New York*, in which the New Deal was imperiled by United States Supreme Court decisions holding 12 major pieces of legislation unconstitutional before 1937 and the Court's new and more restrained approach to judicial review of economic regulation. Today, rulemaking at regulatory agencies is imperiled by increasingly demanding judicial review of concepts such as cost-benefit analysis. The increasing time to rule adoption and length of adoption documents often accomplishes little other than to delay administrative agency action and add to the compliance cost of covered firms.

Third, Congress should also revisit the Volcker Rule, now a section of the Dodd-Frank Act. Implicit in the Volcker Rule was acceptance of the underlying structure of financial institutions. Commercial banks could continue to engage in proprietary trading or own a hedge fund or private equity fund, but subject to the Volcker investment limits. The Volcker provision has proven less effective in achieving a modern version of the Glass-Steagall Act to reduce systemic risk in measurable part because Congress in 2018 directed the Financial Stability Oversight Council to reduce the scope of the Dodd-Frank Act, most demanding provisions from the 38 most consequential banks and bank holding companies to a total of 15 and created a broad new exception for community banks with not more than $10 billion in assets. As history illustrates in the housing industry or with cases such as Long Term Capital Management, systemic crisis can originate with firms far smaller than these 2018 exclusions. In an interdependent world of lending and counterparties, the enthusiasm of those who favor deregulation or local business too often has backfired. The Volcker provision of the Dodd-Frank Act needs to be revisited to better match its applicability to risk and to simplify its application by reducing, where appropriate, the number of exemptions and exclusions.

The Financial Regulatory Authority and each member Commission, other than the Department of Treasury, should be an independent regulatory commission, led by a five-person, presidentially appointed Commission, each commissioner or governor being subject to reappointment and having a specified five-year term or, as in the case of the Fed, a 14-year term. Commission appointments should be sequential so that, for example, in a Commission with five-year terms, one appointment is made each year. No more than three members of a Commission should be made from a single political party.

No issue has so long bedeviled financial regulation than that of the independence of regulators. Jackson's 1832 veto of the extension of the Charter of the Second Bank was in part a reaction to the independence of the Second Bank and its sometimes imperious president, Nicholas Biddle. The history of the Federal Reserve since its formation in 1913 has involved ongoing tension between presidents of both political parties and their administrations seeking to pressure the Fed to lower interest rates and increase money supply and the Fed seeking to focus on limiting inflation and supporting long-term economic stability and growth. Supposedly independent regulatory agencies such as the Securities and Exchange Commission or more recently the Bureau of Consumer Financial Protection have seen their ability to perform their statutory missions undermined by budget starvation or hostile leadership appointments.

It is not inevitable that regulatory agencies be independent. "Unitary" theorists have argued that all regulatory agencies should be consolidated into the executive branch. If the president is directly responsible for the performance of an agency, the president might have a greater sense of responsibility for its budget, appointments, legislation, and rules than the president would for an independent agency. Majoritarian theory also favors presidential control. Not only is this idea consistent with the democratic norm of congressional and presidential elections, but it is also the case that a single presidential decision maker, in theory, could prioritize budgetary and legislative preferences more effectively than unconsolidated independent commissions could.

But these considerations, as cogent as they may seem, are less consequential than those that support independent regulatory commissions.

Only with independence can regulatory agencies be largely depoliticized and achieve resolution of specific problems on the basis of standards other than election results. The Fed makes monetary policy decisions less dominated by the imminence of an election than the president. A Fed, in contrast, that was part of the executive branch would find it difficult to ignore the short-term benefits of lower interest rates or greater money supply even when they posed a long-term inflation risk. The unfortunate experience in 1971–1972, when Richard Nixon bullied the Fed into an excessive easing of interest rates and money supply is a pivotal lesson. The nation paid a high price in terms of subsequent hyperinflation.

The depoliticization of independent regulatory agencies is particularly important for agency adjudication and rulemaking. Professor Richard J. Pierce, Jr., of George Washington University, for example, has written: "Insulation from political pressure seems most desirable in the context of adjudicatory decision making by agencies. No one wants the president, or anyone else, to control the outcome of adjudicatory disputes based on the political beliefs or affiliations of the individual whose rights are at stake."

The independence of an agency also strengthens commitment to applicable legislation. Given the press of legislative business, only periodically will Congress consider significant new regulatory legislation. The ultimate loyalty of an independent agency should be to standards in its existing legislation. Quite frequently, this legislation predates the current executive administration.

A depoliticized independent regulatory agency also usually will be more effective at addressing problems requiring technical expertise. This was the emphasis of Frankfurter and Landis during the New Deal. Frankfurter envisioned that a basic challenge of the New Deal period was to create the equivalent of a British Civil Service to better enhance the likelihood of attracting the most talented administrators to the New Deal's plethora of independent regulatory agencies.

This has been imperfectly achieved, but even with all of the pressures of high competitive private salaries, political assaults on "pointy headed bureaucrats," episodic budget and staffing starvation, the regulatory commissions have maintained a higher standard of expertise and professionalism than occurred in earlier periods when regulation was more overtly partisan.

The solution of a substantial number of largely technical problems is likely to continue to be administered by independent government agencies, because Congress, the judiciary, and the states lack sufficient time, expertise, or jurisdiction to perform these functions equally well.

No regulatory agency effectively can be independent without control over its budget. Financial regulatory agency funding today is achieved differently in agencies such as the Federal Reserve, Office of the Comptroller of the Currency, Federal Deposit Insurance Corporation and National Credit Union Administration, which are self-funded largely through member assessments, and agencies such as the Securities and Exchange Commission and Commodities Futures Trading Commission, which are subject to a congressional appropriations process.

The Congressional appropriations process has resulted in the SEC, for example, being on a binge-purge diet. After a legendary start in the New Deal era, when the Commission was considered a model independent regulatory agency, its staff declined from 1678 in 1941 to 667 in 1955.

The SEC's capacity to review corporate filings and market activity deteriorated, and predictably, the late 1950s were marked by a resurgence of fraud. In response, Congress added 250 staff in 1961 and broadened the Commission's jurisdiction, which led to a significant rebound in the Commission's performance.

The SEC, like many other independent regulatory agencies, submits its budget to the White House Office of Management and Budget, which consolidates several agency budgets into a single request. Congress ultimately authorizes and appropriates agency expenditures. The pre-Dodd-Frank Act budget model was fairly criticized for underfunding the SEC, particularly during periods of surges in market activity. It is an erratic model. After periods of crisis, such as that which eventuated in the 2002 Sarbanes-Oxley Act, Congress and the president have been willing to make dramatic adjustments to the SEC's budget. In July 2002, for example, Congress authorized, but did not subsequently appropriate, a 66 percent increase in the Commission's budget.

A movement to self-funding does not raise questions of feasibility. The SEC already had a fee collection mechanism which in 2000 and 2001 collected over $2 billion each year. Each of those year's collections exceeded even the most ambitious SEC budget proposals for 2003 and 2004. If they did not, fee levels can be adjusted. SEC self-funding would reduce the extremes that occur in the appreciable OMB-Congressional process and to depoliticize regulatory agency budgeting.

A practical question is not feasibility, but accountability. Who will watch the watchmen? At the Federal Reserve Board, a straightforward accountability system is in place. Congress has two accountability mechanisms. First, there is an annual independent audit of the financial statement of the Board of the Federal Reserve, as well as each Federal Reserve Bank. Second, Congress retains its general oversight and legislative powers with respect to the Board.

The Federal Reserve Board's self-funding has been a key to its historic high level of performance, its professionalism, and its ability to withstand political pressure. The alternative approach would require the Fed to seek annual budget approval from Congress. At that point, its ability to maintain independence would be undermined.

The Senate initially was persuaded by this type of argument and would have enacted a form of self-funding for the SEC in the Senate bill that became the Dodd-Frank Wall Street Reform and Consumer Protection Act. The Commission would have been authorized to prepare and deliver its own budget to Congress, which would not have been "a request for appropriations."

In the final Dodd-Frank Act, Congress rejected self-funding for the SEC. Congress did authorize significant increases to the SEC's budget for fiscal year 2011, $1.3 billion; growing in steps to $2.25 billion in fiscal year 2015. The Commission also was granted up to $100 million in a reserve fund to be established in the Department of the Treasury. The frailty of the post-Dodd-Frank Act SEC budget process was soon evident. Congress did not appropriate the amounts authorized in the Dodd-Frank Act during the 112th Congress or subsequently.

A significant practical advantage of the Fed approach to budgeting would be to avoid periodic atrophy of SEC staff during boom economies. Just as it has historically been regarded as essential to insulate the Federal Reserve Board from political pressures to protect its judgment on monetary policy, it is wise to insulate the SEC from staff size declines during market surges. History has taught us that one fundamental threat to support for an independent SEC is a successful stock market. Both Congress and the president are most likely to be supportive during periods when investor protection and fraud enforcement are necessary such as during the Enron scandal. An independent budgetary process would be more effective in adjusting the size of the SEC staff to the Commission's regulatory needs during the good times, which ironically are when the SEC is more vulnerable to a lack of budgetary support.[21]

The 2020 coronavirus pandemic (COVID-19) highlights the profound advantages of the New Financial Regulatory Model.

An Office of Risk Assessment would have identified the major financial risks of the COVID-19 Pandemic at the earlier possible point and helped the Federal Regulatory Authority to put in place monitoring systems to measure not only federal, but also potential and actual devastation wrought by the crisis. Each crisis is different. The slowness with which the federal government responded to the COVID-19 Pandemic and the lack of coordination with the states were painful consequences of a delayed and unfocused response.

The new Federal Regulatory Authority in all probability would have stimulated a faster and better coordinated response. An independent Federal Regulatory Authority chair would have had a greater capacity to earlier ring alarm bells than a Secretary of Treasury, who was a leading member of a political administration. The command and control powers of the Federal Regulatory Authority combined with self-funding for all independent regulatory agencies would have strengthened and accelerated the federal government response by reducing political fetters. Most importantly, the explicit recognition in the New Financial Regulatory Model that emergency powers must expand to address each actual crisis and the emphasis on the expertise of independent agency leadership are two critical advantages of the New Model. Facts matter. The New Model would reduce the probability that factual reality would be trampled by political expediency.

No one should have any delusion that this restructuring of financial regulation alone will solve all economic problems in this nation. Restructuring is a part, indeed a vital part, of how a well-functioning government should operate. But without a coordinate fiscal policy to set budgets and taxation at levels that, at a minimum, cap our greatest now known economic challenge, an ever growing budget deficit, no financial regulatory restructuring alone will be decisive. The fiscal objective of capping or rolling back debt will be one of the most profound challenges of the 21st century. This is not a simple matter of accounting. Our national political objectives — how great an investment do we seek to make in social programs, how much sacrifice are we willing to make for the environment, how large a commitment to our national defense will we make — are subsumed in this overarching fiscal question. These issues ultimately will be resolved in our constitutional democracy at the ballot box and ultimately through Congress and the executive.

But under any resolution, a restructured model of financial regulation will have the positive benefits of more effective financial crisis response and prevention, less confused and ineffectual regulation, and greater ultimate accountability to Congress and the White House for supervision of underlying financial industries.

The most obvious objection to this proposed Financial Regulatory Model is that it is infeasible. Congress, it will be urged, would never agree to changes that would reduce the number of agencies and strip existing House and Senate Committees of oversight responsibility.

This is exactly the wrong response. Few in 1926 believed that the New Deal Revolution would occur within a decade. Few in 1858 would have believed that the ensuing decade would conclude with the abolition of slavery and the enactment of a constitutional amendment requiring equal protection for all citizens.

Political reformation in our country must begin with vision, not a calculus of necessary political compromises. At critical moments in our financial history—1789–1791, with the assumption of the national debt and creation of the First National Bank, the 1832 Jacksonian veto of the extension of the Charter of the Second National Bank, the Panic of 1907 and the creation of the Federal Reserve, the New Deal Revolution, the retrenchment wrought under Ronald Reagan—it was a vision of a system fundamentally different than what existed before that led to a new financial regulatory system.

Whether fundamental political change occurs because of financial crisis, war or substantial changes in Electoral results, our historical experience is one of wide pendulum swings, occasions when the previously inconceivable is achieved.

This book is a road map for the future. I do not know when this path will be taken. I do know there will be future moments in our history when a fundamental restructuring of our financial system will be urgently needed.

With the COVID-19 Pandemic, we already have begun a health and financial crisis where the need for a fundamental restructuring of our financial regulatory model, if not other pivotal aspects of the federal government, is readily apparent.

ENDNOTES:

1. The Department of Treasury, Blueprint for a Modernized Financial Regulatory Structure 15–17, 146–156 (March 2008).
2. Id. at 17–19, 157–170.
3. Id. at 19–21, 170–180.
4. Id. at 21.
5. Id. at 75–77.
6. Id. at 143.
7. Volcker Alliance, Reshaping the Financial Regulatory System: Long Delayed, Now Crucial (2015); John Crawford, Tim Karpoft, Angela Allen, Nicole Allen & Michael Margolis, Memorandum Concerning

the Securities and Exchange Commission and the Commodity Futures Trading Commission; Elizabeth Brown, Prior Proposals to Consolidate Federal Regulators; Elizabeth Brown, Consolidated Financial Regulators: Six National Case Studies and the Experience of the European Union. See also Bipartisan Policy Center, Dodd-Frank's Missed Opportunity: A Road Map for a More Effective Regulatory Architecture (Apr. 2011).

8. Department of Treasury, Financial Regulatory Reform: A New Foundation: Rebuilding Financial Supervision and Regulation (2009). See summary in 6 Louis Loss, Joel Seligman & Troy Paredes, Securities Regulation 483–503 (5th ed. Wolters Kluwer 2016).
9. Obama quoted in Loss, Seligman & Paredes, supra n. 8, at 503–505.
10. Dodd-Frank Wall Street Reform and Consumer Protection Act, Pub. L. No. 111–203, 123 Stat. 1376, 111th Cong. (2010); Timothy Geithner, Stress Test: Reflecting on the Financial Crisis 400–405, 413–418, 424–427, 433–434 (Crown Publishers 2014); Michael Barr, Howell Jackson & Margaret Tahyar, Financial Regulation: Law and Policy 681–688, 917–940 (Foundation Press 2016); Ben Bernanke, Timothy Geithner & Henry Paulson, Firefighting: The Financial Crisis and Its Lessons 112–129 (Penguin Books 2019); Loss, Seligman & Paredes, supra n. 8, at 545–583.
11. Elizabeth Warren, Unsafe at Any Rate, Democracy Journal (2007); Oren Barr-Gill & Elizabeth Warren, Making Credit Safer, 157 U. Penn. L. Rev. 101 (2008); John Campbell, Howell Jackson, Bridgette Madrian & Peter Tufano, Consumer Financial Protection, 25 J. Econ. Perspectives 91 (2011); Barr, Jackson & Tahyer, supra n. 10, at 18, 556–577, 605–629; Adam Livitin, The Consumer Protection Bureau: An Introduction, 32 Rev. Banking & Fin. L. 321 (2013); David Carpenter, The Consumer Financial Protection Bureau: A Legal Analysis, Cong. Research Serv. (Jan. 14, 2014).
12. Dodd-Frank Act §§ 931–946; 2 Louis Loss, Joel Seligman & Troy Paredes, Securities Regulation ch. 2.D.2.b (6th ed. Wolters Kluwer 2019).
13. Dodd-Frank Act §§ 941–946; Loss, Seligman & Paredes, supra n. 12, at ch. 3.A.1.l.
14. John Coffee, The Political Economy of Dodd-Frank: Why Financial Reform Trends Tend To Be Frustrated and Systemic Risk Perpetuated, 97 Cornell L. Rev. 1019, 1065–1072; Loss, Seligman & Paredes, supra n. 12, at 467–489; Barr, Jackson & Tahyar, supra n. 10, at 823–827.
15. Goldstein v. SEC, 451 F.3d 873 (D.C. Cir. 2006); 7 Louis Loss, Joel Seligman & Troy Paredes, Securities Regulation 372–384 (5th ed. Wolters Kluwer 2017).

16. 5 Louis Loss, Joel Seligman & Troy Paredes, Securities Regulation 805–935 (5th ed. Wolters Kluwer 2016); Geithner, supra n. 10, at 427; GAO, Financial Crisis: Losses and Potential Impacts of the Dodd-Frank Act 48–53 (GAO 13-180 Jan. 2013).
17. Dodd-Frank Act §§ 1400–1498; Department of Treasury & Department of Housing & Urban Development, Reforming America's Housing Finance Market: A Report to Congress (2011); Geithner, supra n. 10, at 433; Laurie Goodman & E. Seidman, Comment in Land and the City, Proceedings of the 2014 Land Policy Conference (ed. by George McCarthy, Gregory Ingram & Samuel Moody); Trump Seeks to End U.S. Control of Mortgage Giants, *New York Times* (Sept. 6, 2019); Department of Treasury Housing Reform Plan (Sept. 5, 2019).
18. GAO, Financial Regulation: Complex and Fragmented Structure Could Be Streamlined To Improve Effectiveness 53–57 (GAO 16-175 Feb. 2016); GAO, Insurance Markets: Impacts and Regulatory Response to the 2007–2009 Financial Crisis (GAO 13-583 June 2013).
19. See Department of Treasury, supra n. 1; Volcker Alliance, supra n. 7; Bipartisan Policy Center, supra n. 7; GAO, Complex and Fragmented Structure Could Be Streamlined, supra n. 18; Bernanke, Geithner & Paulson, supra n. 10; Geithner, supra n. 10, esp. at 400–405, 434.
20. 1 Louis Loss, Joel Seligman & Troy Paredes, Securities Regulation 66–70 (6th ed. Wolters Kluwer 2019).
21. Joel Seligman, Key Implications of the Dodd-Frank Act for Independent Regulatory Agencies, 89 Wash. U. L. Rev. 1 (2001); Joel Seligman, The New Financial Order: An Essay for Alan Bromberg, 68 SMU L. Rev. 871 (2015); Loss, Seligman & Paredes, supra n. 20, at 525; 3 Louis Loss, Joel Seligman & Troy Paredes, Securities Regulation 489–500 (5th ed. Wolters Kluwer 2018); 1 Richard Pierce, Administrative Law Treatise 65 (4th ed. Wolters Kluwer 2002); Geoff Miller, Symposium: The Independence of Independent Agencies, 1988 Duke L.J. 215.

Index